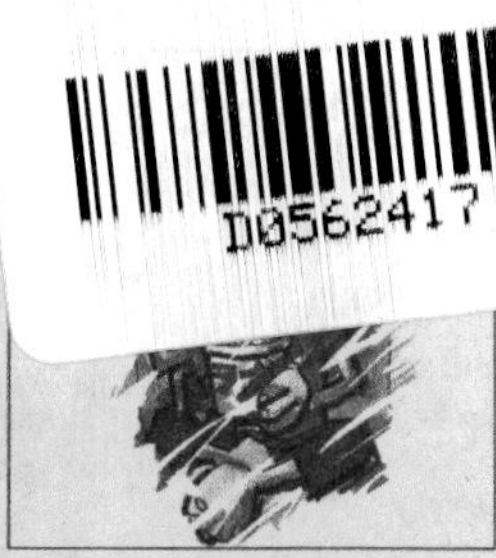

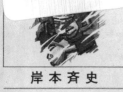

岸本斉史

...gs. With everyone's support, ... comic has been published. ...atic. Speaking of ecstatic, ... time I won an award for one of my manga, I was so happy I was flying high. But this time is 10 times better than that. I don't know how to say it, but this is the happiest moment of my life. But I guess I'm happiest knowing that this comic will be read and enjoyed. Yup, that's it!

—Masashi Kishimoto, 2000

Author/artist Masashi Kishimoto was born in 1974 in rural Okayama Prefecture, Japan. After spending time in art college, he won the Hop Step Award for new manga artists with his manga **Karakuri** ("mechanism"). Kishimoto decided to base his next story on traditional Japanese culture. His first version of **Naruto**, drawn in 1997, was a one-shot story about fox spirits; his final version, which debuted in **Weekly Shonen Jump** in 1999, quickly became the most popular ninja manga in Japan.

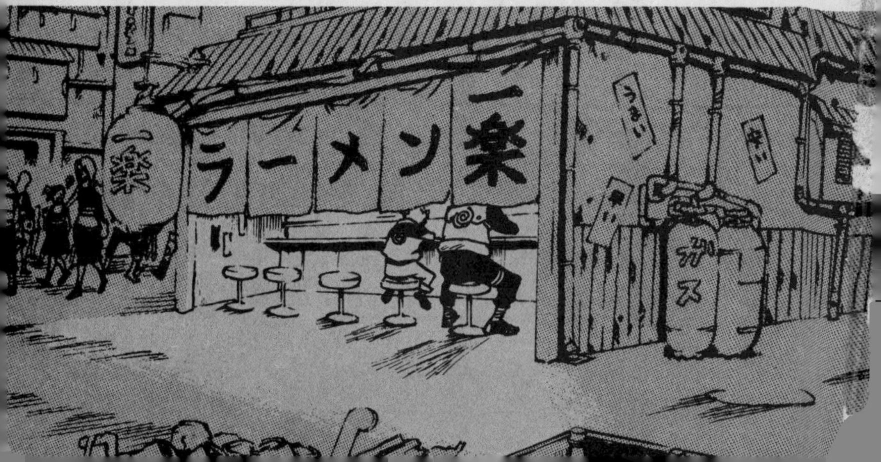
一楽
ラーメン一楽

NARUTO

3-in-1 Edition

Volume 1

SHONEN JUMP Manga Omnibus Edition

A compilation of the graphic novel volumes 1–3

STORY AND ART BY MASASHI KISHIMOTO

Translation/Katy Bridges, Mari Morimoto
English Adaptation/Jo Duffy
Touch-up Art & Lettering/Heidi Szykowny, Inori Fukuda Trant
Design/Sean Lee (Manga Edition)
Design/Sam Elzway (Omnibus Edition)
Senior Editor/Jason Thompson (Manga Edition)
Senior Editor/Joel Enos (Omnibus Edition)

Printed in the U.S.A.

Published by VIZ Media, LLC
P.O. Box 77010
San Francisco, CA 94107

13
Omnibus edition first printing, May 2011
Thirteenth printing, March 2021

VIZ MEDIA
viz.com

PARENTAL ADVISORY
NARUTO is rated T for Teen and is recommended for ages 13 and up. This volume contains realistic and fantasy violence.

ratings.viz.com RATED T TEEN

SHONEN JUMP

VOL. 1
UZUMAKI NARUTO

STORY AND ART BY
MASASHI KISHIMOTO

NARUTO

VOL. 1
UZUMAKI NARUTO

CONTENTS

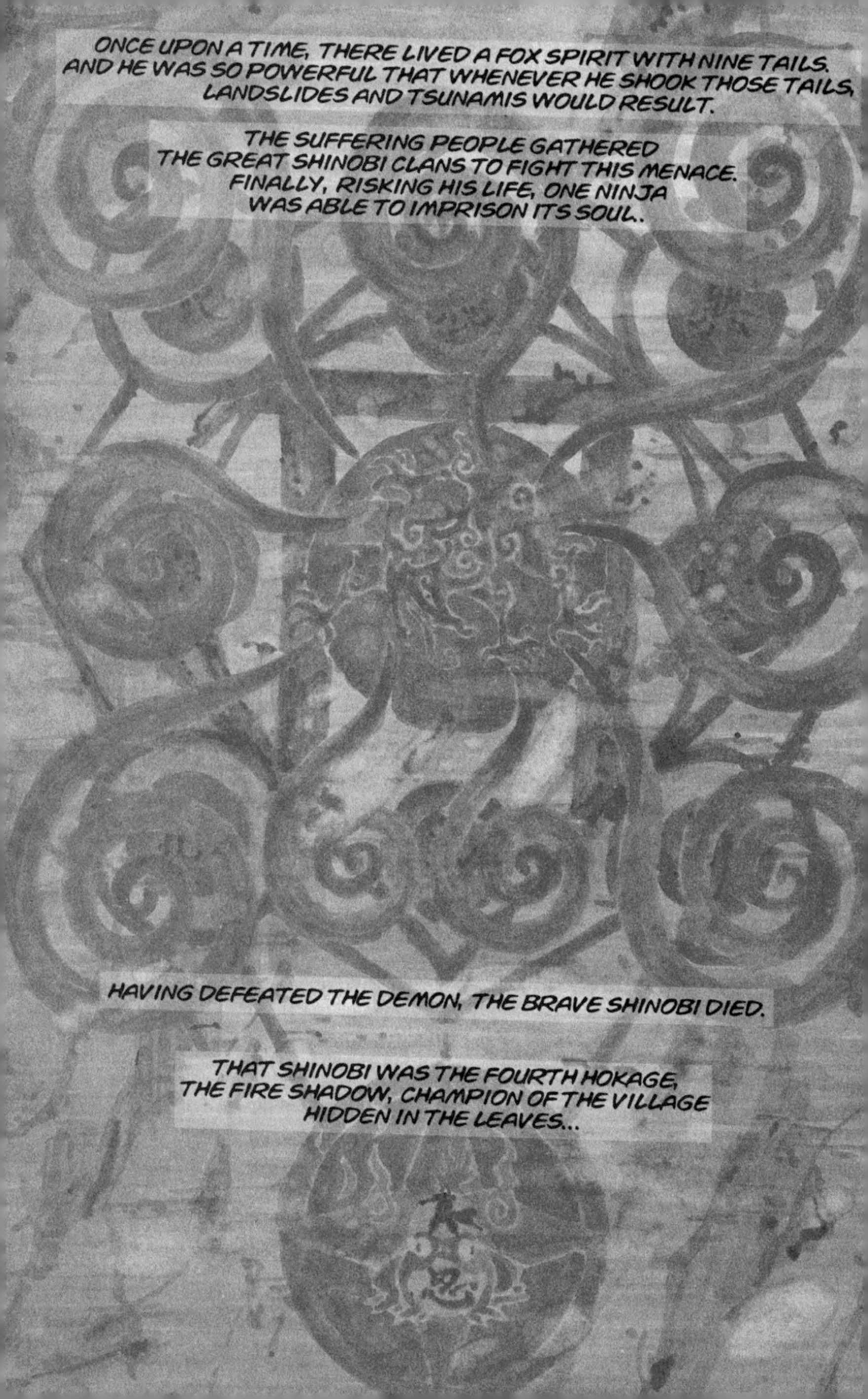
ONCE UPON A TIME, THERE LIVED A FOX SPIRIT WITH NINE TAILS. AND HE WAS SO POWERFUL THAT WHENEVER HE SHOOK THOSE TAILS, LANDSLIDES AND TSUNAMIS WOULD RESULT.
THE SUFFERING PEOPLE GATHERED THE GREAT SHINOBI CLANS TO FIGHT THIS MENACE. FINALLY, RISKING HIS LIFE, ONE NINJA WAS ABLE TO IMPRISON ITS SOUL..
HAVING DEFEATED THE DEMON, THE BRAVE SHINOBI DIED.
THAT SHINOBI WAS THE FOURTH HOKAGE, THE FIRE SHADOW, CHAMPION OF THE VILLAGE HIDDEN IN THE LEAVES...

1: Uzumaki Naruto!

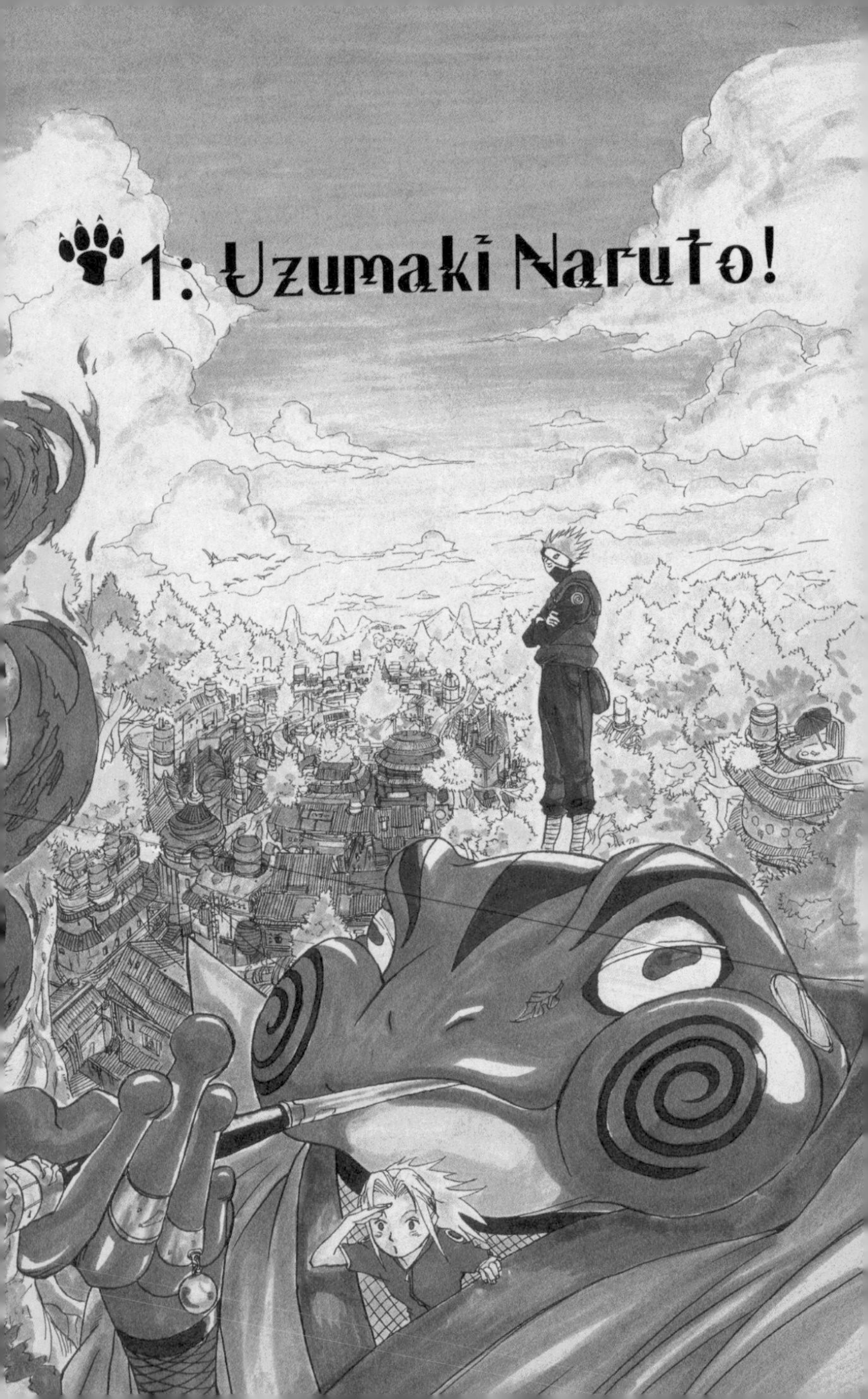

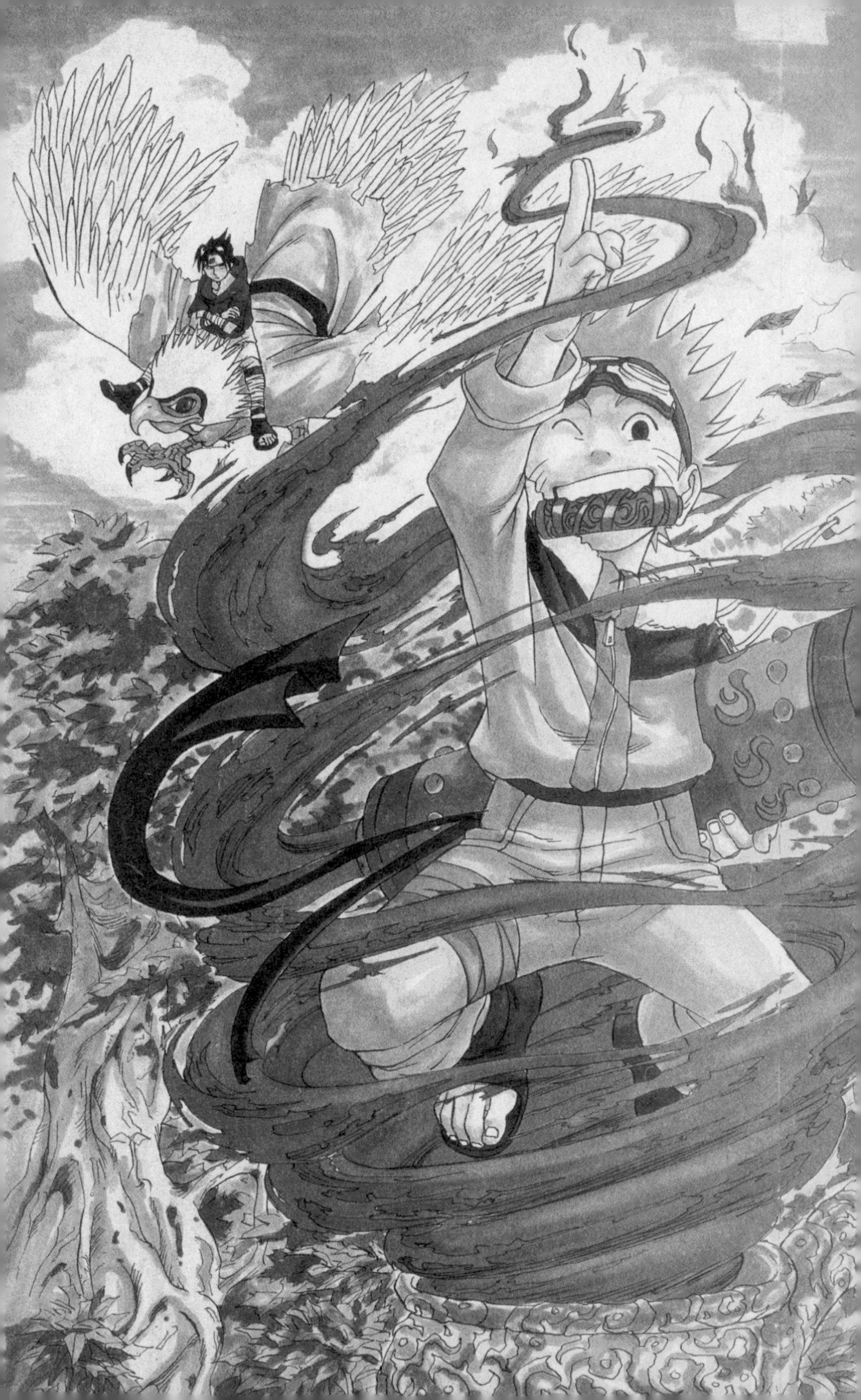

NARUTO

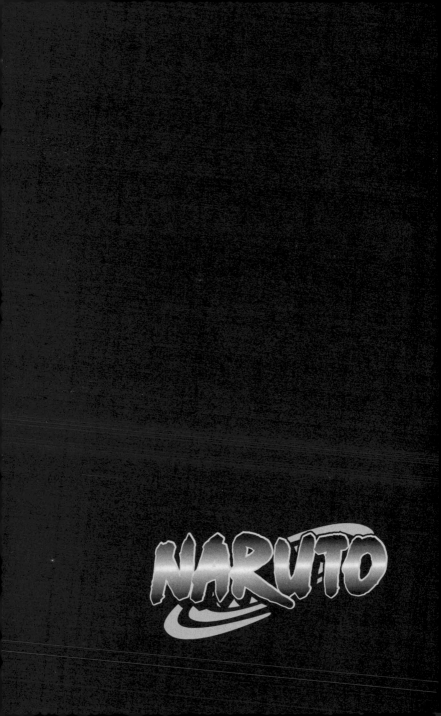

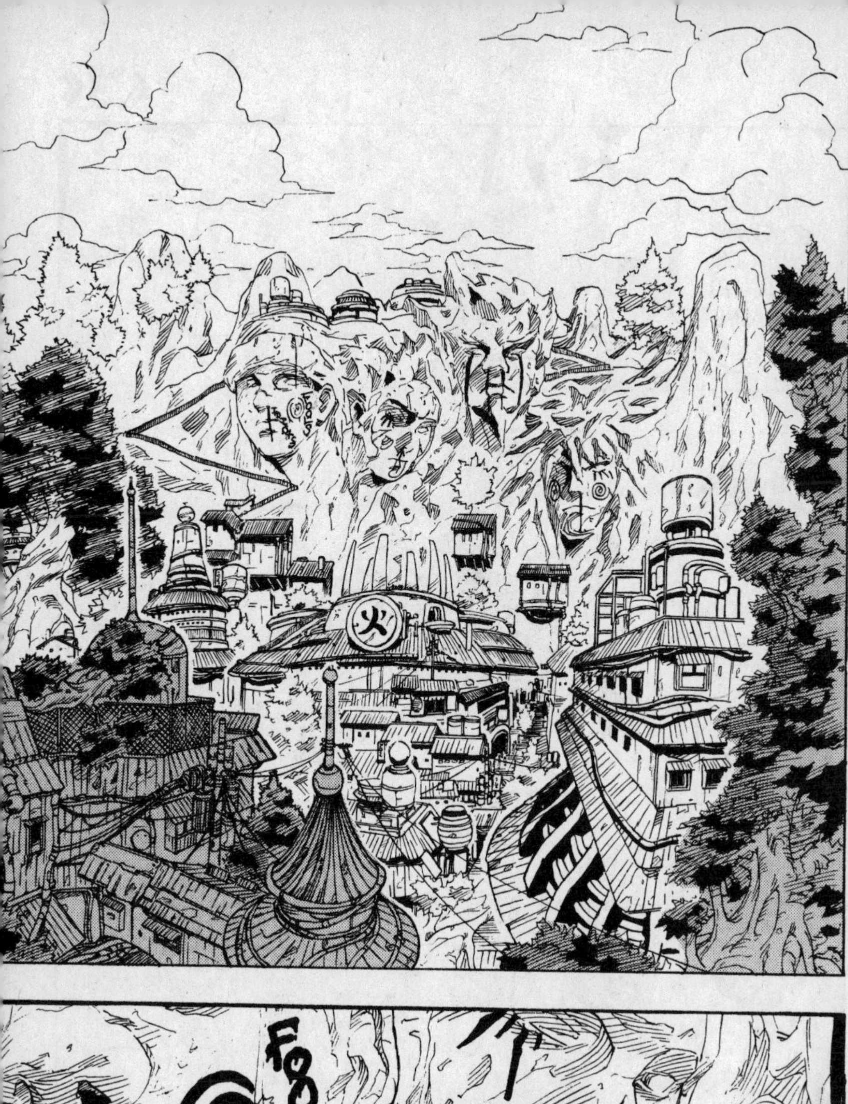

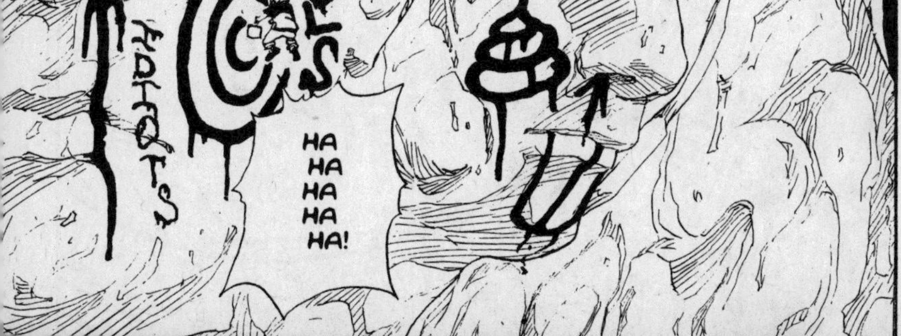
FOOLS
HA HA HA HA HA!
IDIOTS

READ THIS WAY

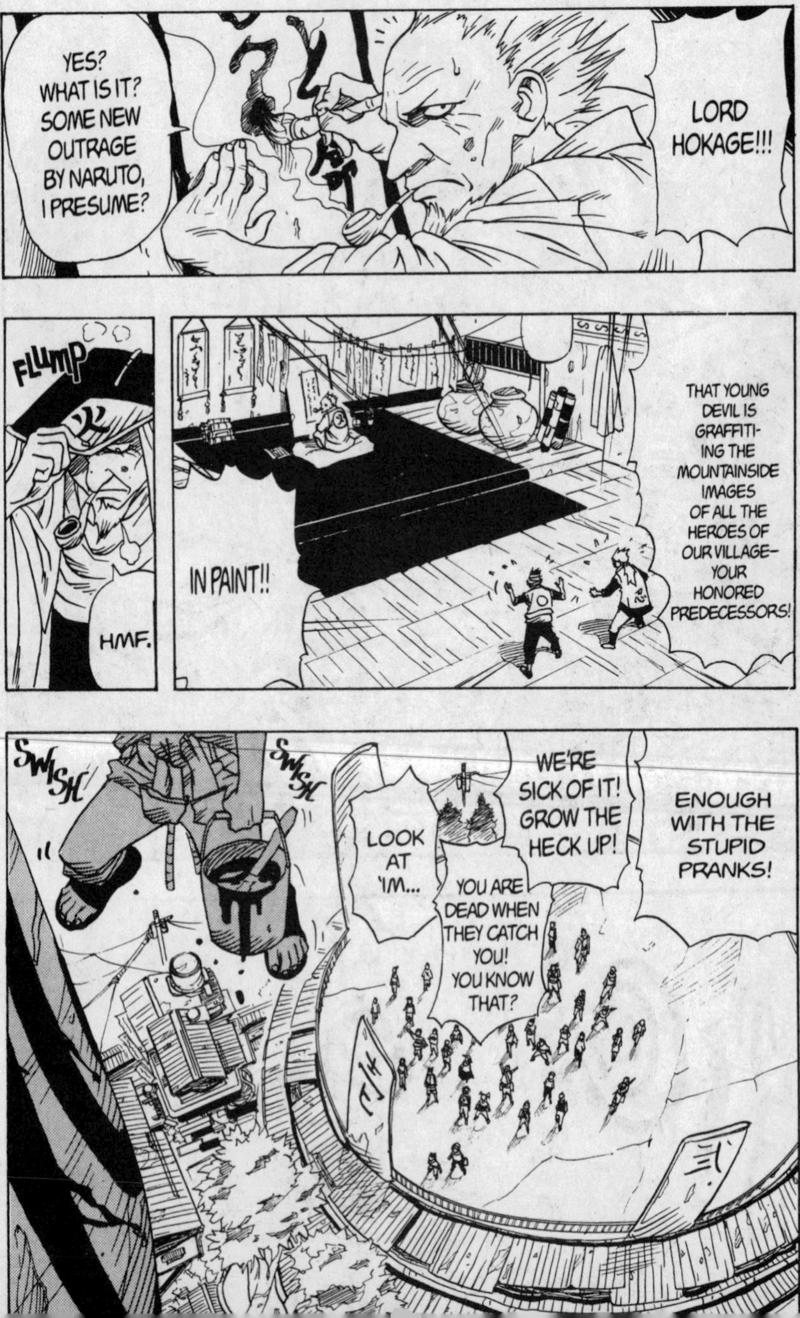

LORD HOKAGE!!!
YES? WHAT IS IT? SOME NEW OUTRAGE BY NARUTO, I PRESUME?
THAT YOUNG DEVIL IS GRAFFITI-ING THE MOUNTAINSIDE IMAGES OF ALL THE HEROES OF OUR VILLAGE–YOUR HONORED PREDECESSORS!
IN PAINT!!
FLUMP
HMF.
ENOUGH WITH THE STUPID PRANKS!
WE'RE SICK OF IT! GROW THE HECK UP!
LOOK AT 'IM...
YOU ARE DEAD WHEN THEY CATCH YOU! YOU KNOW THAT?
SWISH
SWISH

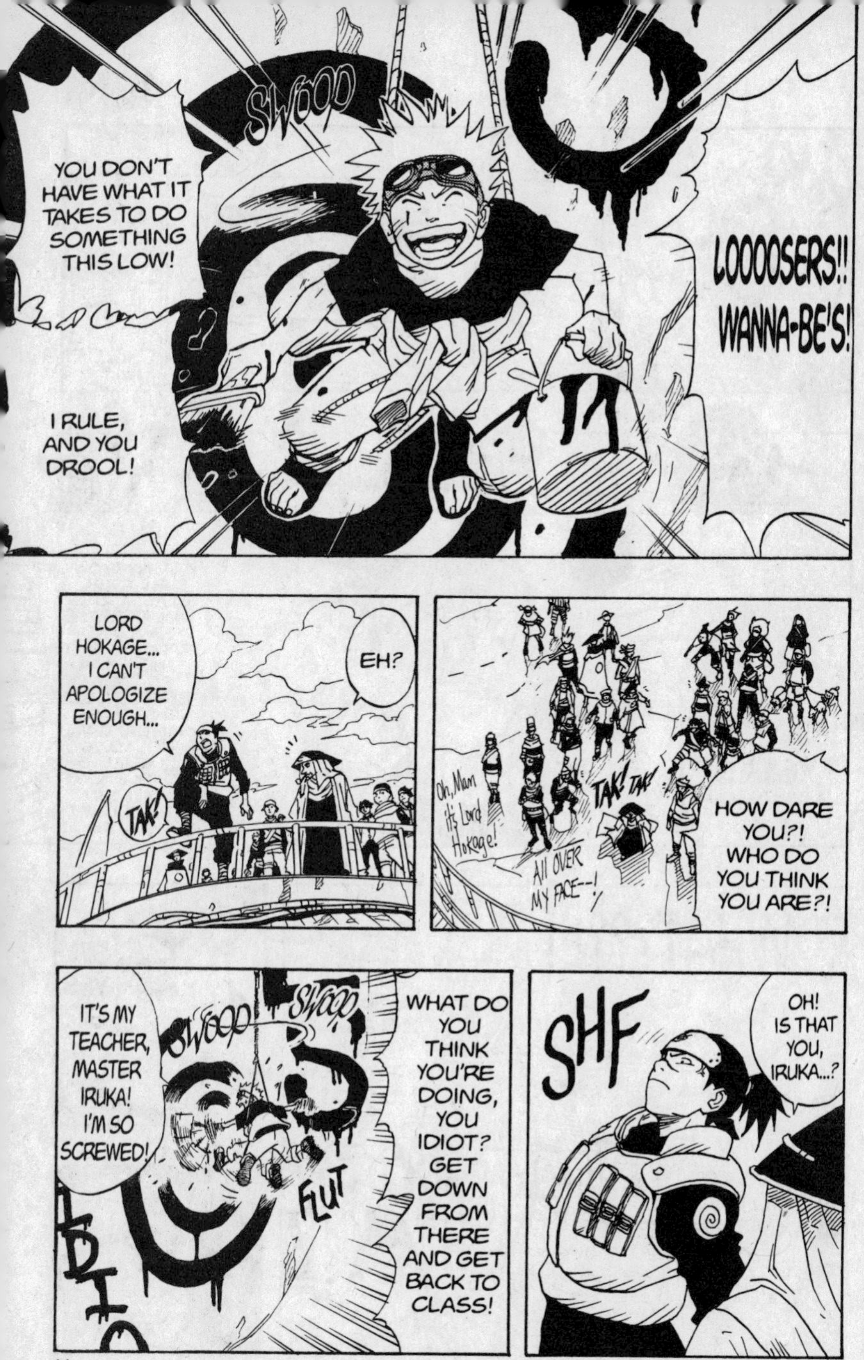
LOOOOSERS!! WANNA-BE'S!
SWOOD
YOU DON'T HAVE WHAT IT TAKES TO DO SOMETHING THIS LOW!
I RULE, AND YOU DROOL!
HOW DARE YOU?! WHO DO YOU THINK YOU ARE?!
TAK! TAK!
Oh, Man it's Lord Hokage!
All OVER MY FACE--!
EH?
LORD HOKAGE... I CAN'T APOLOGIZE ENOUGH...
TAK!
OH! IS THAT YOU, IRUKA...?
SHF
WHAT DO YOU THINK YOU'RE DOING, YOU IDIOT? GET DOWN FROM THERE AND GET BACK TO CLASS!
SWOOP
SWOOP
IT'S MY TEACHER, MASTER IRUKA! I'M SO SCREWED!
FLUT

READ THIS WAY

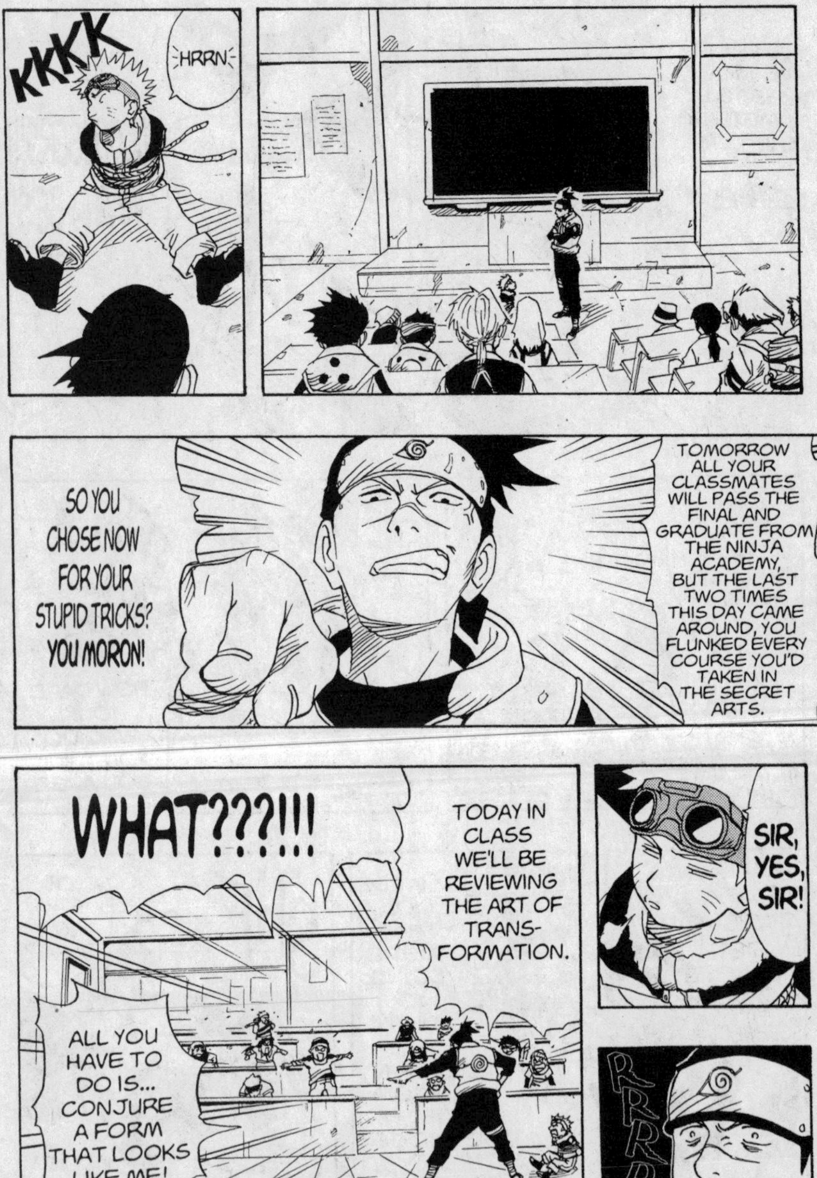
KKKK
HRRN
TOMORROW ALL YOUR CLASSMATES WILL PASS THE FINAL AND GRADUATE FROM THE NINJA ACADEMY, BUT THE LAST TWO TIMES THIS DAY CAME AROUND, YOU FLUNKED EVERY COURSE YOU'D TAKEN IN THE SECRET ARTS.
SO YOU CHOSE NOW FOR YOUR STUPID TRICKS? YOU MORON!
SIR, YES, SIR!
RRRR
TODAY IN CLASS WE'LL BE REVIEWING THE ART OF TRANS-FORMATION.
WHAT???!!!
ALL YOU HAVE TO DO IS... CONJURE A FORM THAT LOOKS LIKE ME!

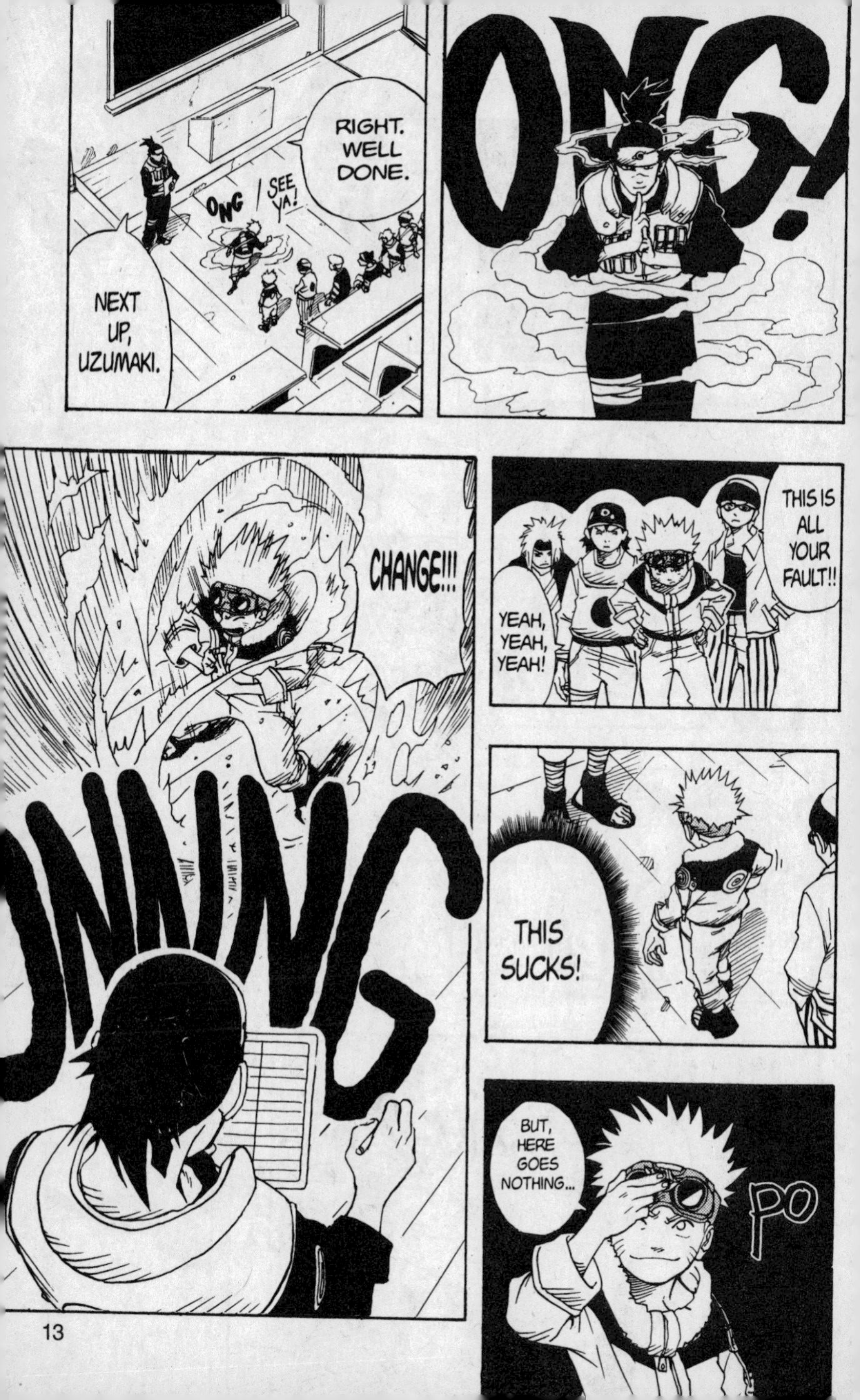
ONG!
RIGHT. WELL DONE.
ONG
SEE YA!
NEXT UP, UZUMAKI.
THIS IS ALL YOUR FAULT!!
YEAH, YEAH, YEAH!
THIS SUCKS!
BUT, HERE GOES NOTHING...
PO
CHANGE!!!

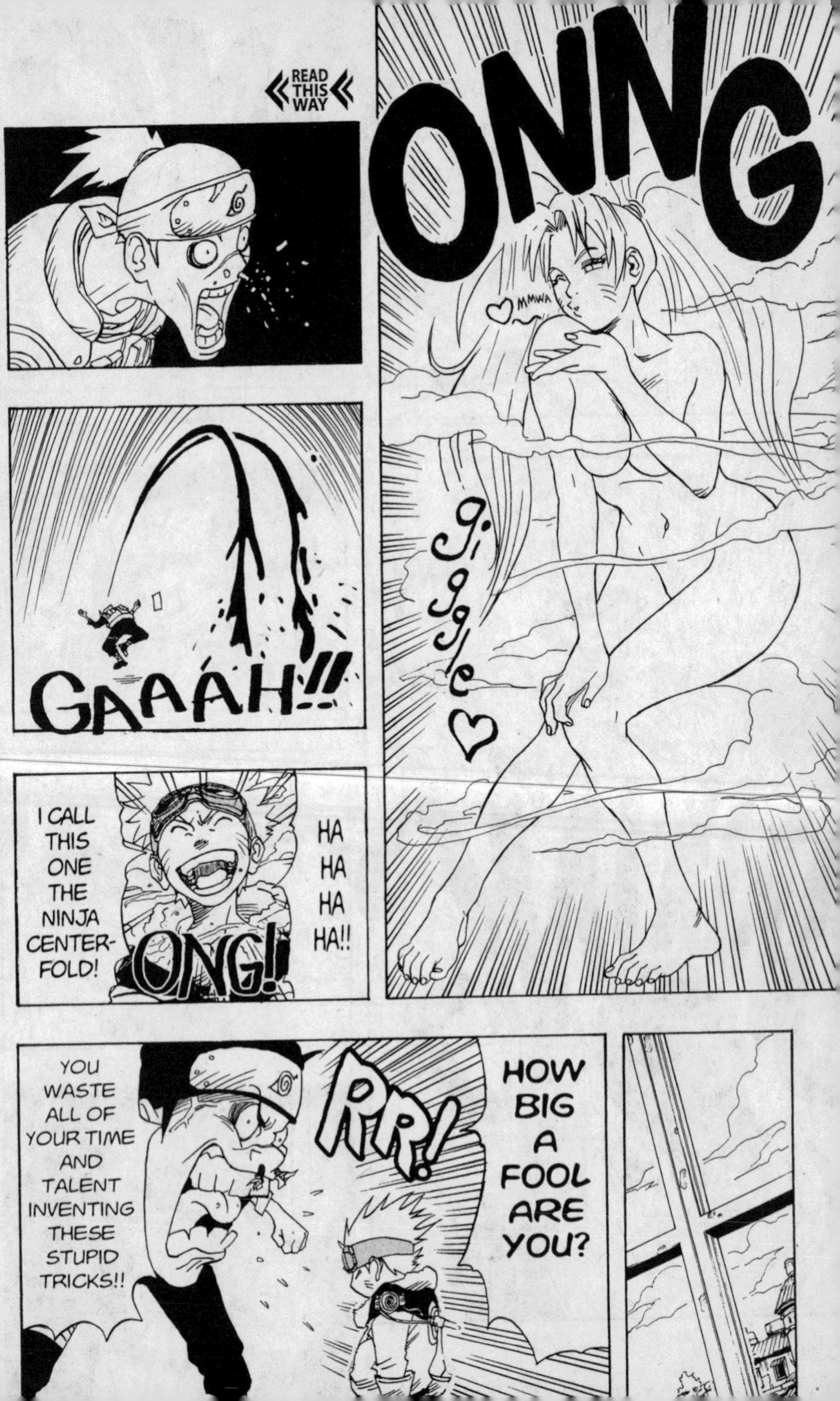
READ THIS WAY
ONNG
MMWA
giggle
GAAAH!!
HA HA HA HA!!
ONG!
I CALL THIS ONE THE NINJA CENTERFOLD!
HOW BIG A FOOL ARE YOU?
RR!
YOU WASTE ALL OF YOUR TIME AND TALENT INVENTING THESE STUPID TRICKS!!

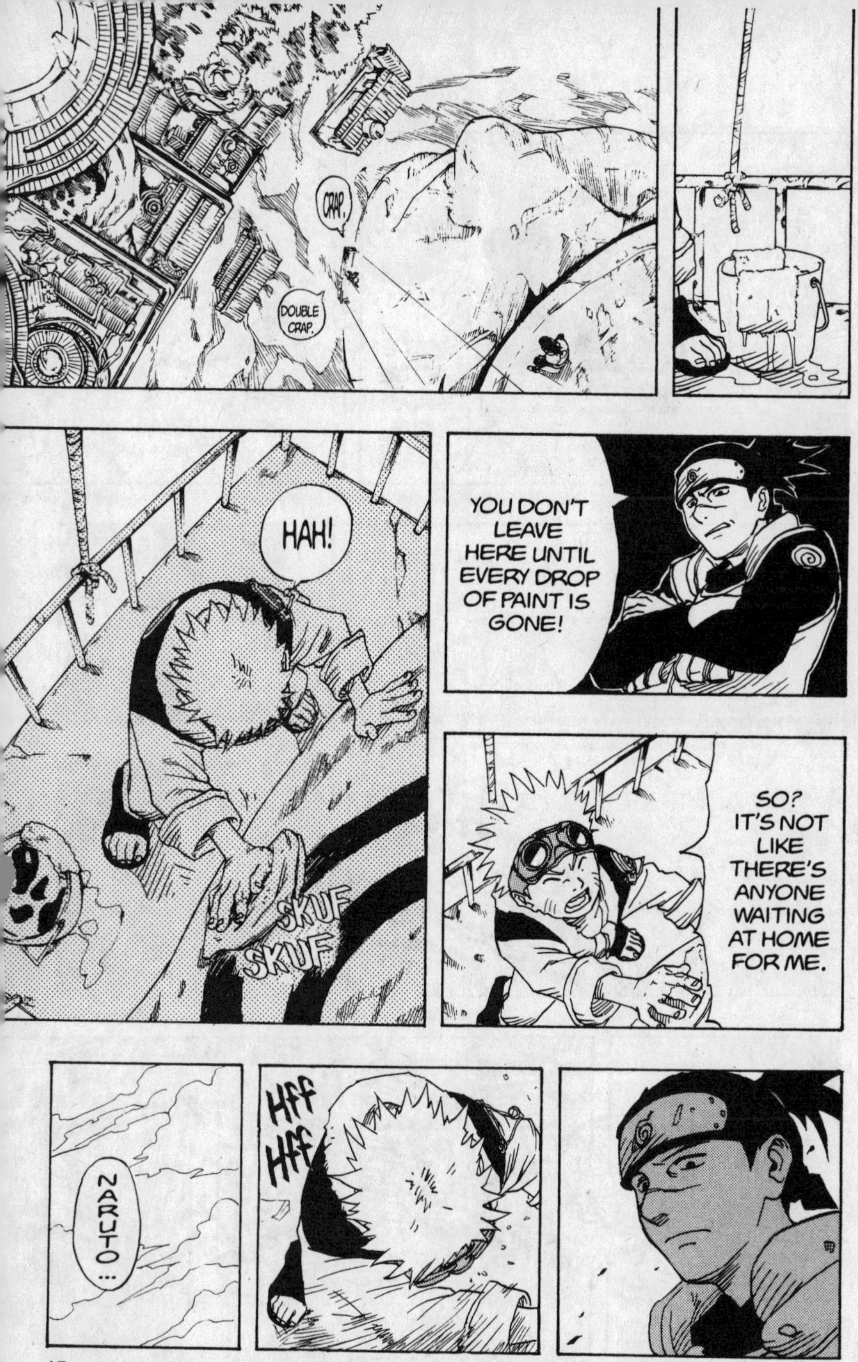
CRAP.
DOUBLE CRAP.
YOU DON'T LEAVE HERE UNTIL EVERY DROP OF PAINT IS GONE!
SO? IT'S NOT LIKE THERE'S ANYONE WAITING AT HOME FOR ME.
HAH!
SKUF SKUF
Hff Hff
NARUTO...

READ THIS WAY

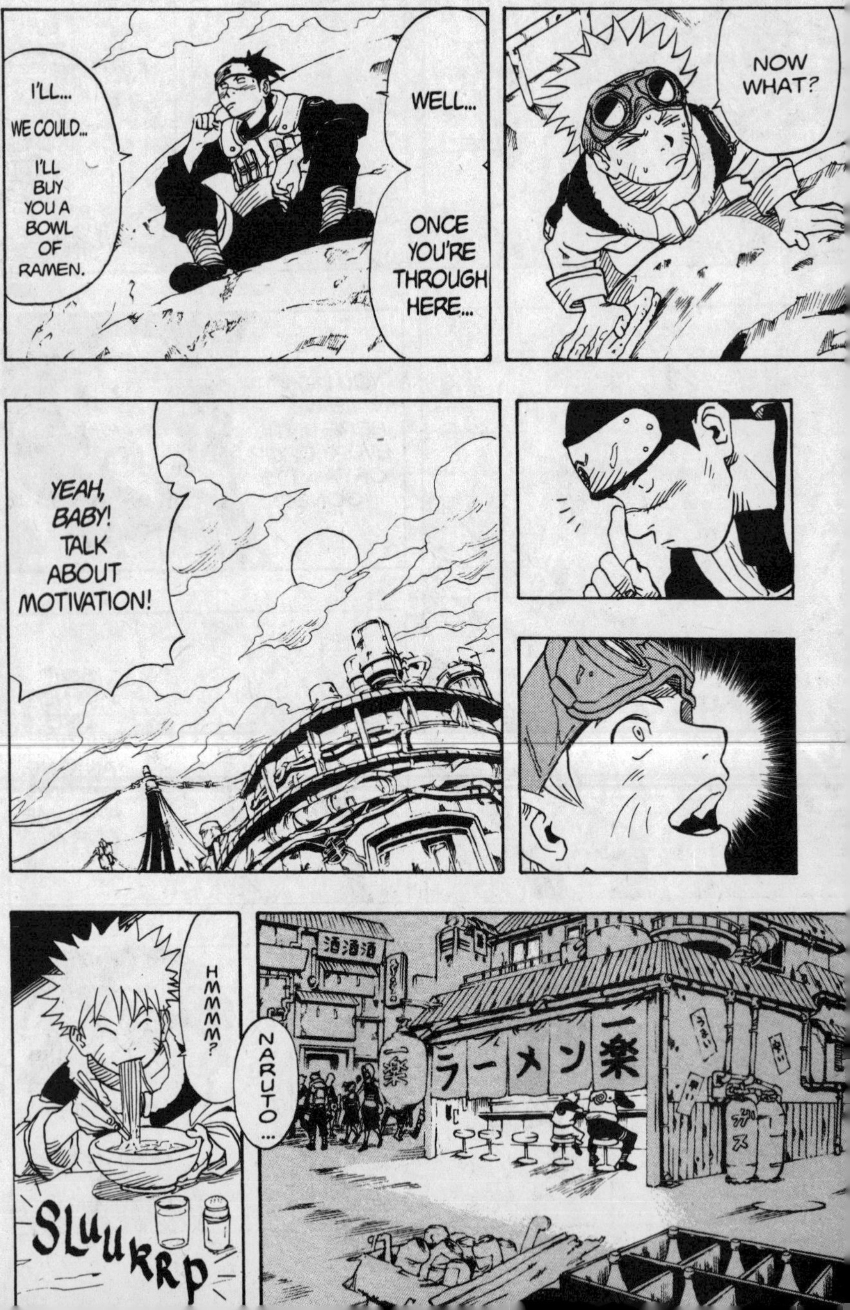
NOW WHAT?
WELL... ONCE YOU'RE THROUGH HERE...
I'LL... WE COULD... I'LL BUY YOU A BOWL OF RAMEN.
YEAH, BABY! TALK ABOUT MOTIVATION!
NARUTO...
HMMMM?
SLUUKRRP
酒酒酒
ラーメン 一楽

READ THIS WAY

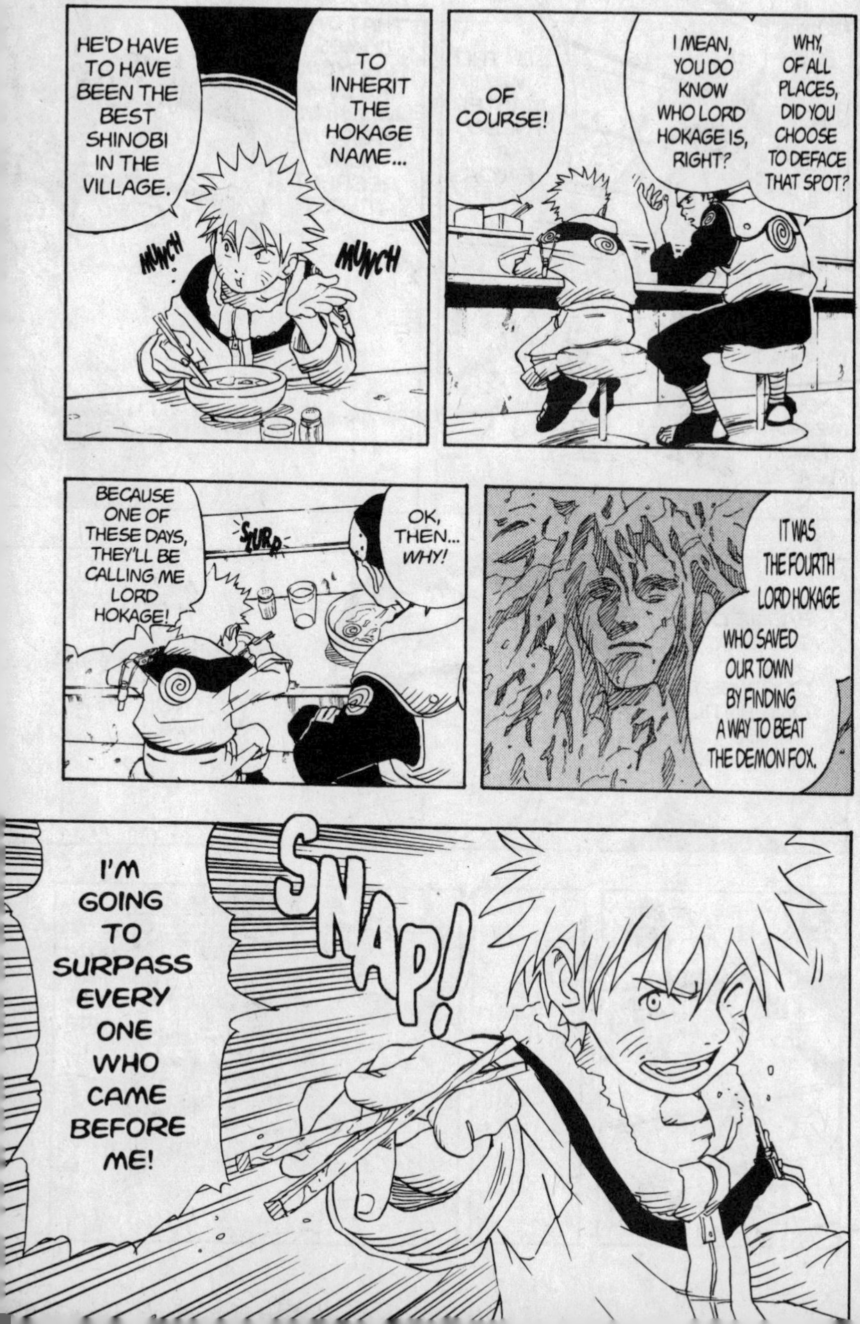

WHY, OF ALL PLACES, DID YOU CHOOSE TO DEFACE THAT SPOT?
I MEAN, YOU DO KNOW WHO LORD HOKAGE IS, RIGHT?
OF COURSE!
TO INHERIT THE HOKAGE NAME...
HE'D HAVE TO HAVE BEEN THE BEST SHINOBI IN THE VILLAGE.
MUNCH
MUNCH
IT WAS THE FOURTH LORD HOKAGE
WHO SAVED OUR TOWN BY FINDING A WAY TO BEAT THE DEMON FOX.
OK, THEN... WHY!
SLURP
BECAUSE ONE OF THESE DAYS, THEY'LL BE CALLING ME LORD HOKAGE!
SNAP!
I'M GOING TO SURPASS EVERY ONE WHO CAME BEFORE ME!

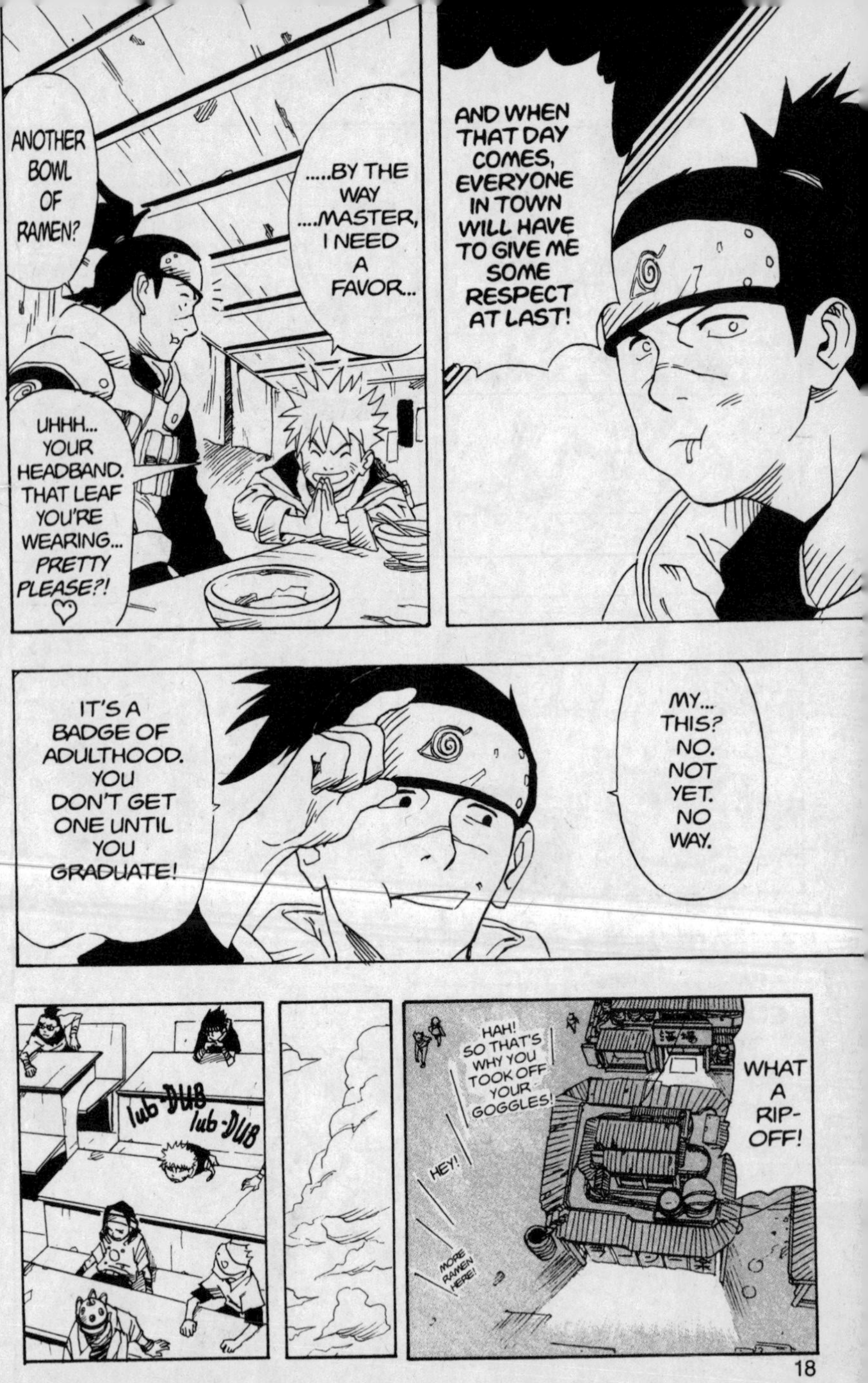
AND WHEN THAT DAY COMES, EVERYONE IN TOWN WILL HAVE TO GIVE ME SOME RESPECT AT LAST!
ANOTHER BOWL OF RAMEN?
.....BY THE WAY ....MASTER, I NEED A FAVOR...
UHHH... YOUR HEADBAND. THAT LEAF YOU'RE WEARING... PRETTY PLEASE?! ♡
MY... THIS? NO. NOT YET. NO WAY.
IT'S A BADGE OF ADULTHOOD. YOU DON'T GET ONE UNTIL YOU GRADUATE!
WHAT A RIP-OFF!
HAH! SO THAT'S WHY YOU TOOK OFF YOUR GOGGLES!
HEY!
MORE RAMEN HERE!
lub-DUB lub-DUB

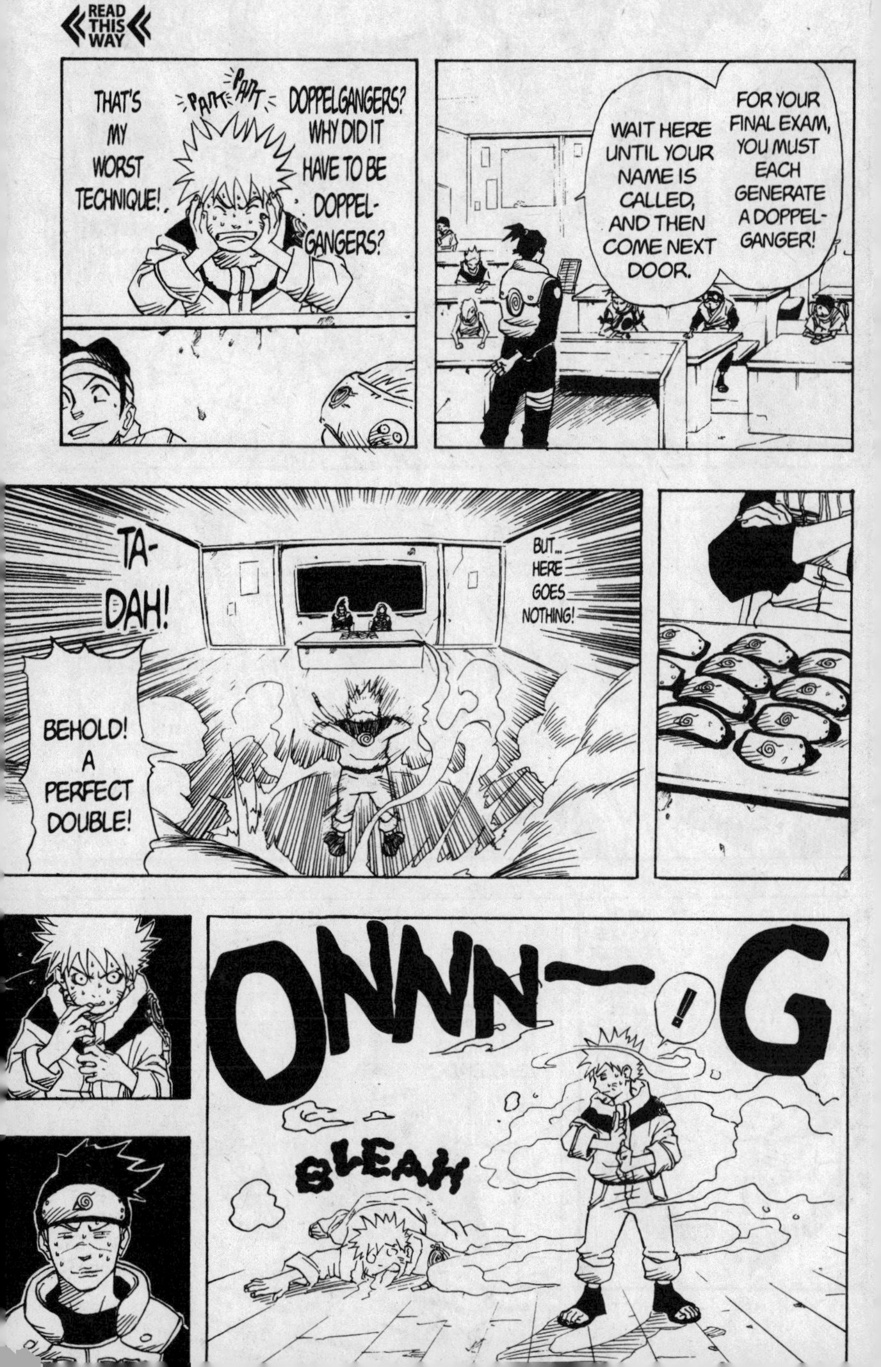
READ THIS WAY
FOR YOUR FINAL EXAM, YOU MUST EACH GENERATE A DOPPELGANGER!
WAIT HERE UNTIL YOUR NAME IS CALLED, AND THEN COME NEXT DOOR.
PANT PANT
DOPPELGANGERS? WHY DID IT HAVE TO BE DOPPEL-GANGERS?
THAT'S MY WORST TECHNIQUE!
BUT... HERE GOES NOTHING!
TA-DAH!
BEHOLD! A PERFECT DOUBLE!
ONNN—G
!
BLEAH

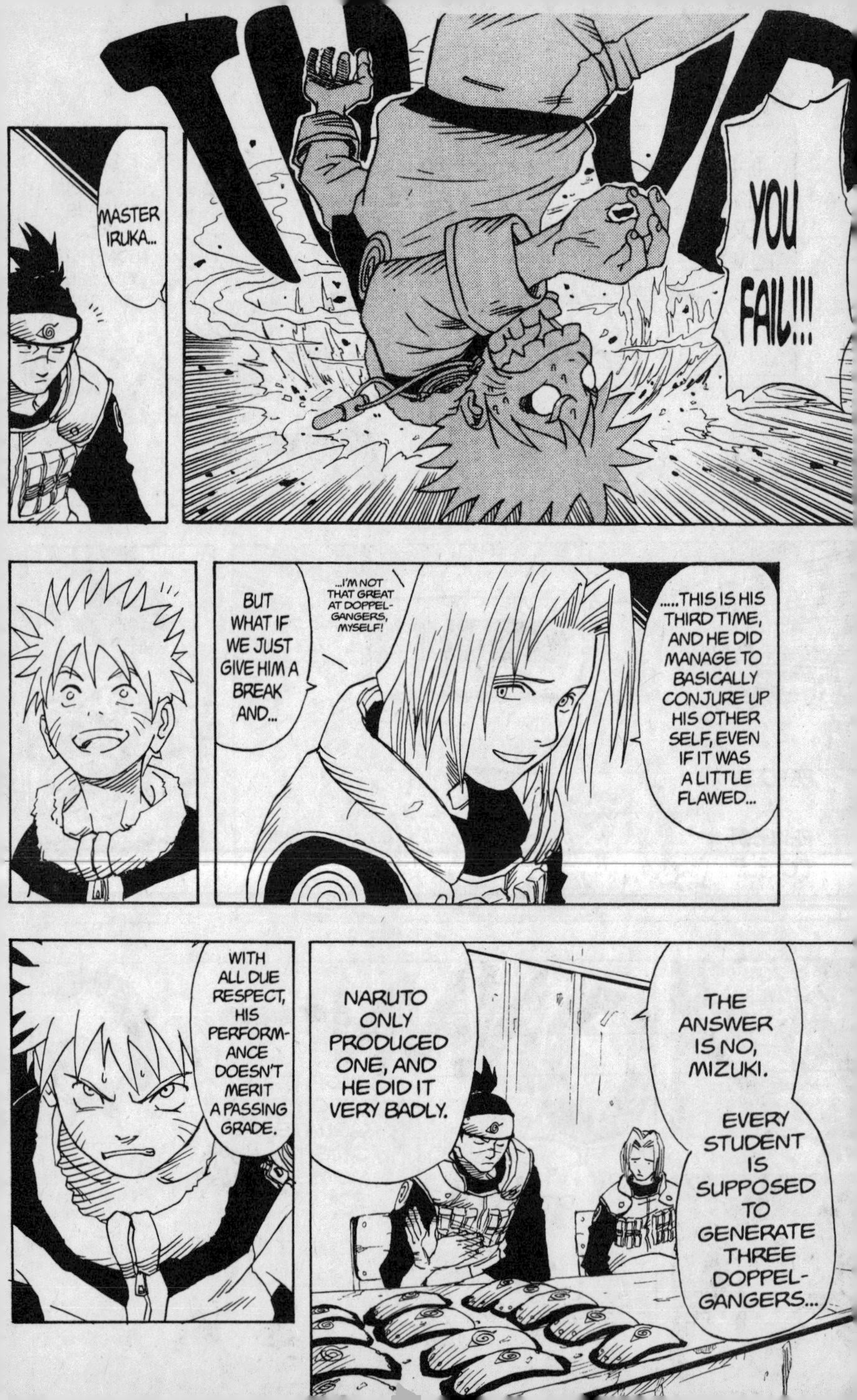

YOU FAIL!!!
MASTER IRUKA...
.....THIS IS HIS THIRD TIME, AND HE DID MANAGE TO BASICALLY CONJURE UP HIS OTHER SELF, EVEN IF IT WAS A LITTLE FLAWED...
...I'M NOT THAT GREAT AT DOPPEL-GANGERS, MYSELF!
BUT WHAT IF WE JUST GIVE HIM A BREAK AND...
THE ANSWER IS NO, MIZUKI.
EVERY STUDENT IS SUPPOSED TO GENERATE THREE DOPPEL-GANGERS...
NARUTO ONLY PRODUCED ONE, AND HE DID IT VERY BADLY.
WITH ALL DUE RESPECT, HIS PERFORM-ANCE DOESN'T MERIT A PASSING GRADE.

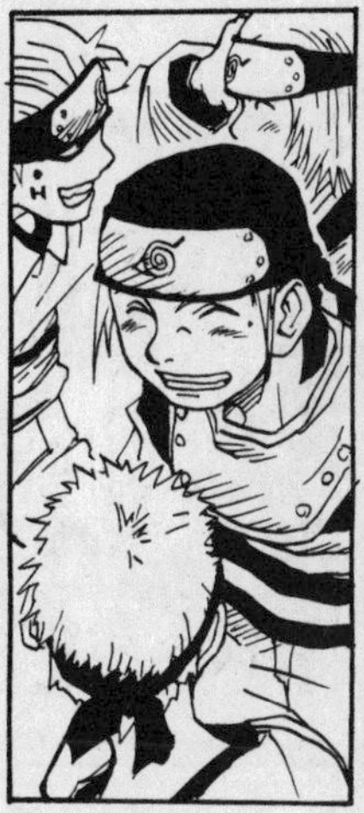

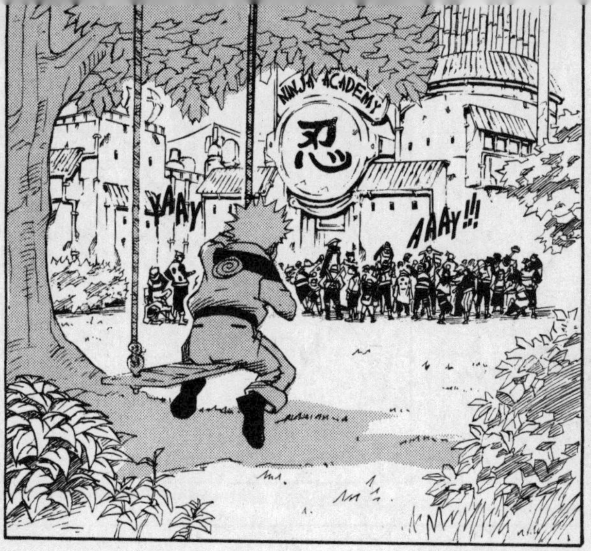
NINJA ACADEMY
忍
AAAY!!!
YAAY

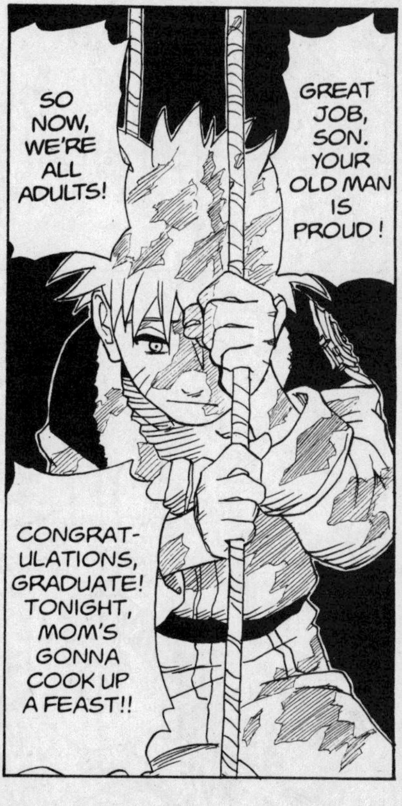
GREAT JOB, SON. YOUR OLD MAN IS PROUD!
SO NOW, WE'RE ALL ADULTS!
CONGRAT-ULATIONS, GRADUATE! TONIGHT, MOM'S GONNA COOK UP A FEAST!!

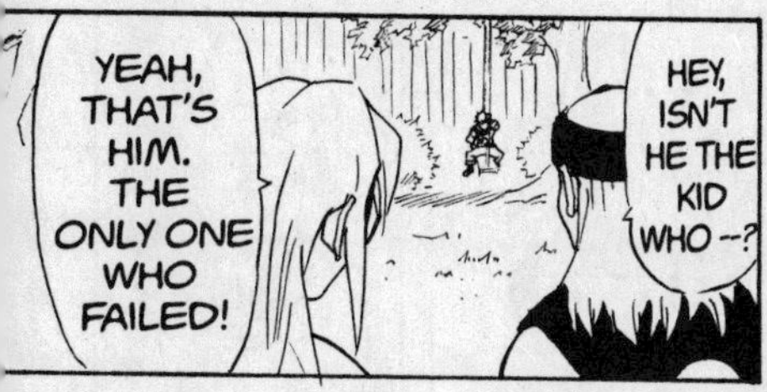
HEY, ISN'T HE THE KID WHO --?
YEAH, THAT'S HIM. THE ONLY ONE WHO FAILED!

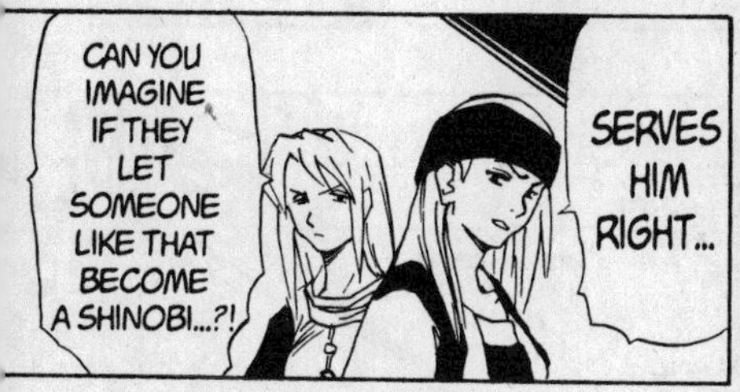
SERVES HIM RIGHT...
CAN YOU IMAGINE IF THEY LET SOMEONE LIKE THAT BECOME A SHINOBI...?!

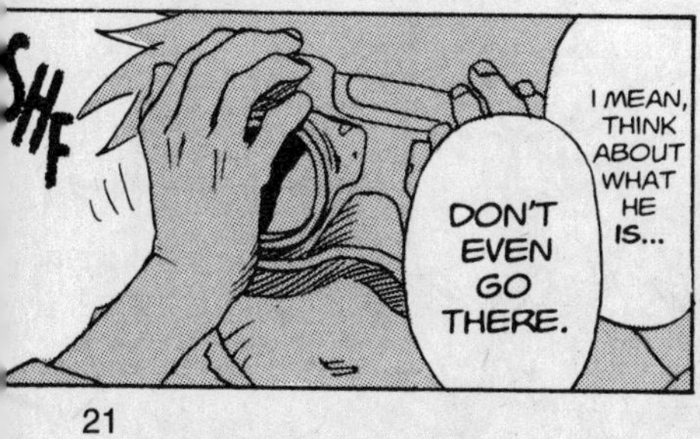
I MEAN, THINK ABOUT WHAT HE IS...
DON'T EVEN GO THERE.
SHF

READ THIS WAY

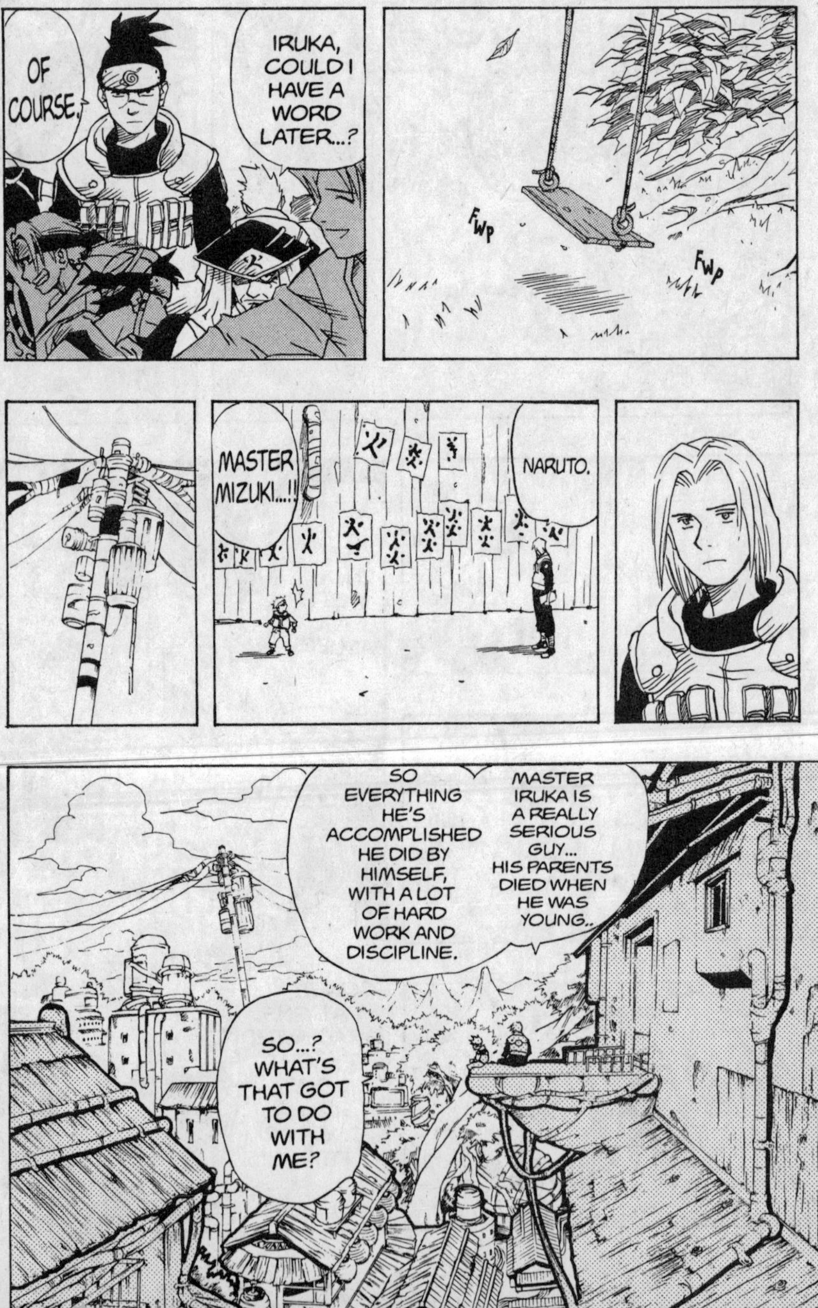
FWP
FWP
IRUKA, COULD I HAVE A WORD LATER...?
OF COURSE.
NARUTO.
MASTER MIZUKI...!!
MASTER IRUKA IS A REALLY SERIOUS GUY... HIS PARENTS DIED WHEN HE WAS YOUNG..
SO EVERYTHING HE'S ACCOMPLISHED HE DID BY HIMSELF, WITH A LOT OF HARD WORK AND DISCIPLINE.
SO...? WHAT'S THAT GOT TO DO WITH ME?

READ THIS WAY

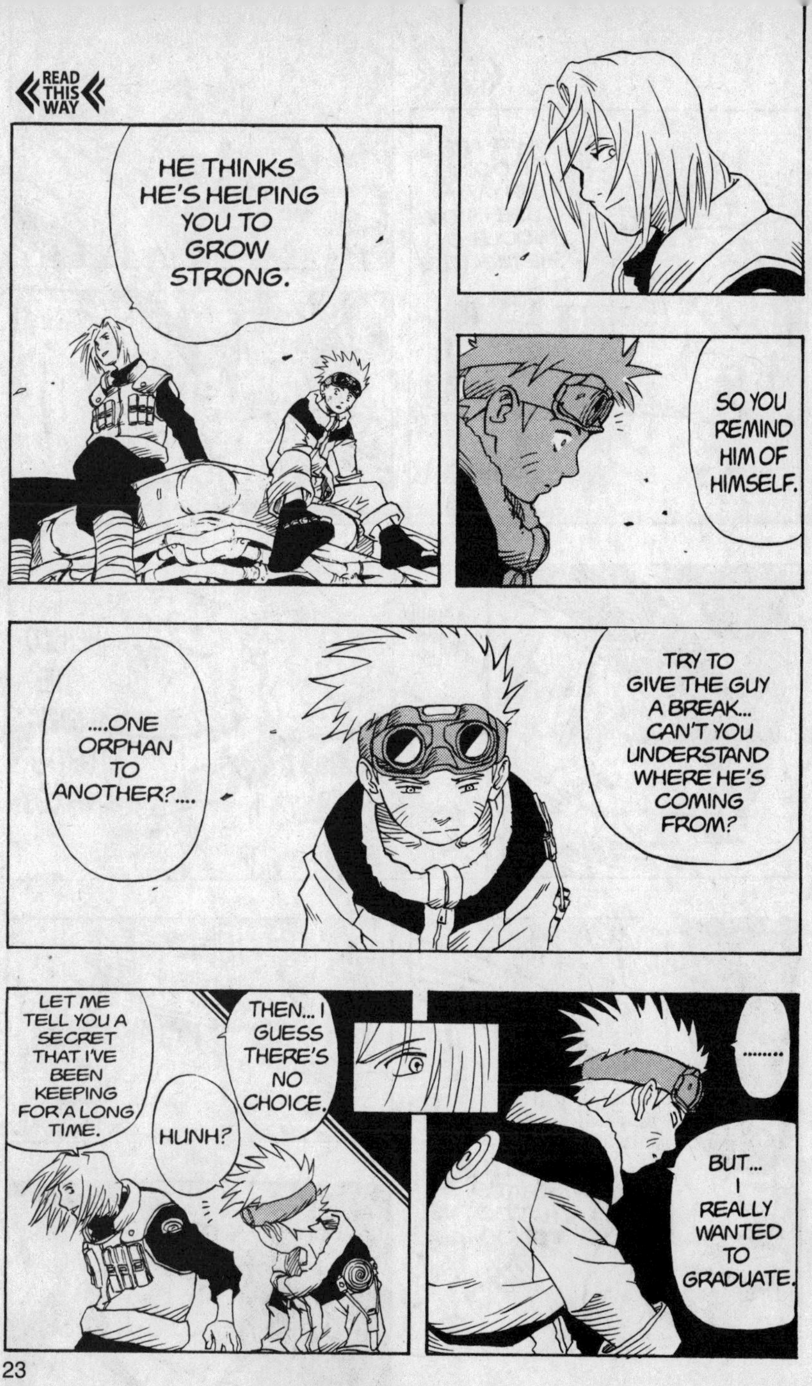
SO YOU REMIND HIM OF HIMSELF.
HE THINKS HE'S HELPING YOU TO GROW STRONG.
TRY TO GIVE THE GUY A BREAK... CAN'T YOU UNDERSTAND WHERE HE'S COMING FROM?
....ONE ORPHAN TO ANOTHER?....
....
BUT... I REALLY WANTED TO GRADUATE.
THEN... I GUESS THERE'S NO CHOICE.
LET ME TELL YOU A SECRET THAT I'VE BEEN KEEPING FOR A LONG TIME.
HUNH?

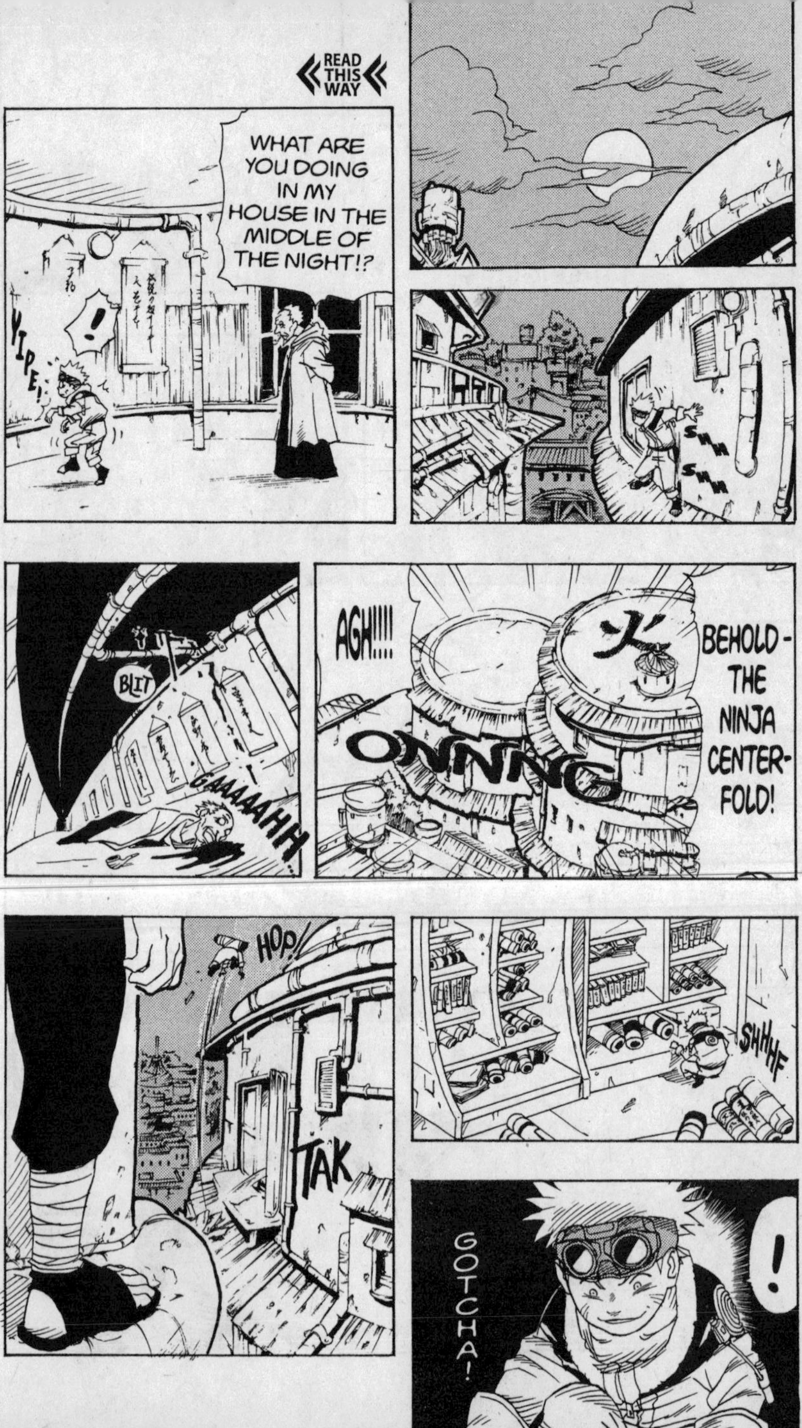
READ THIS WAY
WHAT ARE YOU DOING IN MY HOUSE IN THE MIDDLE OF THE NIGHT!?
!
YIPE!
AGH!!!!
BEHOLD- THE NINJA CENTER-FOLD!
ONNNG
BLIT
GAAAAAAHH
SHHHF
!
GOTCHA!
HOP!
TAK

READ THIS WAY

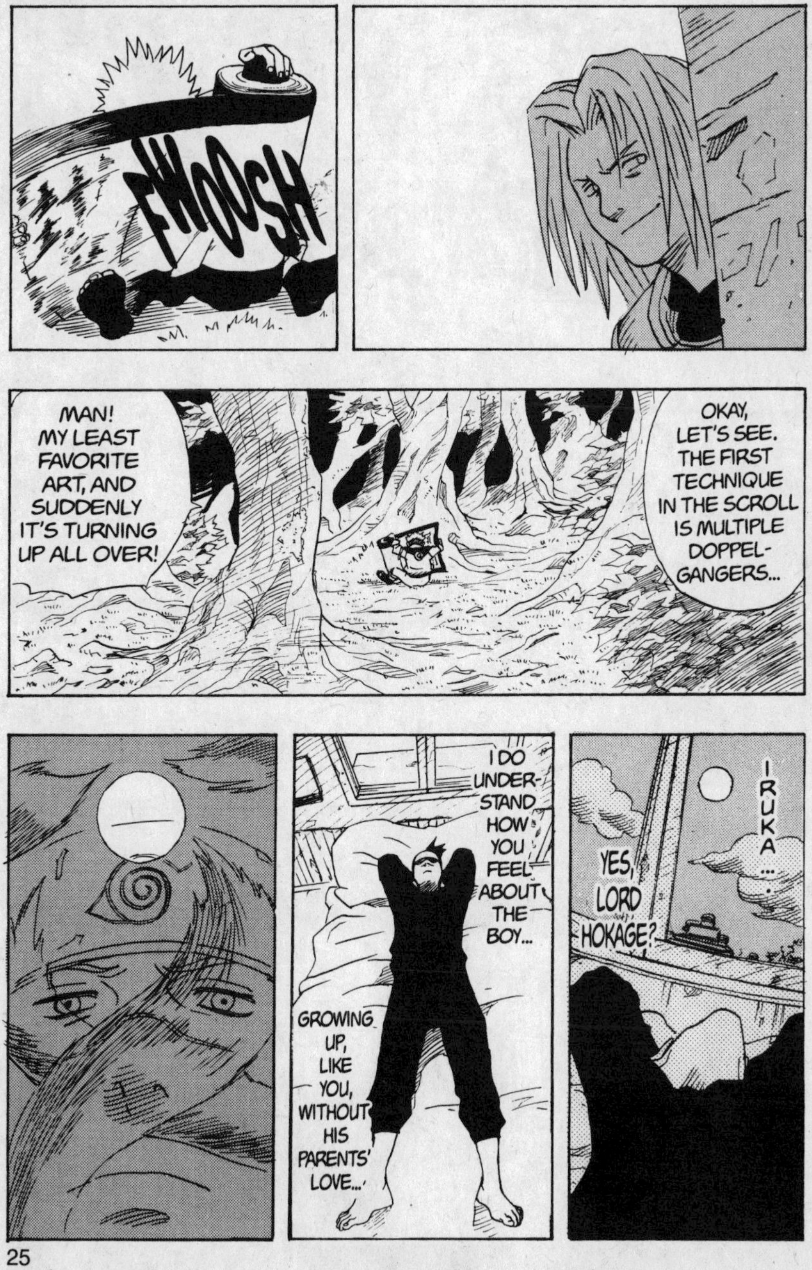

FWOOSH
OKAY, LET'S SEE. THE FIRST TECHNIQUE IN THE SCROLL IS MULTIPLE DOPPEL-GANGERS...
MAN! MY LEAST FAVORITE ART, AND SUDDENLY IT'S TURNING UP ALL OVER!
IRUKA...
YES, LORD HOKAGE?
I DO UNDER-STAND HOW YOU FEEL ABOUT THE BOY...
GROWING UP, LIKE YOU, WITHOUT HIS PARENTS' LOVE...

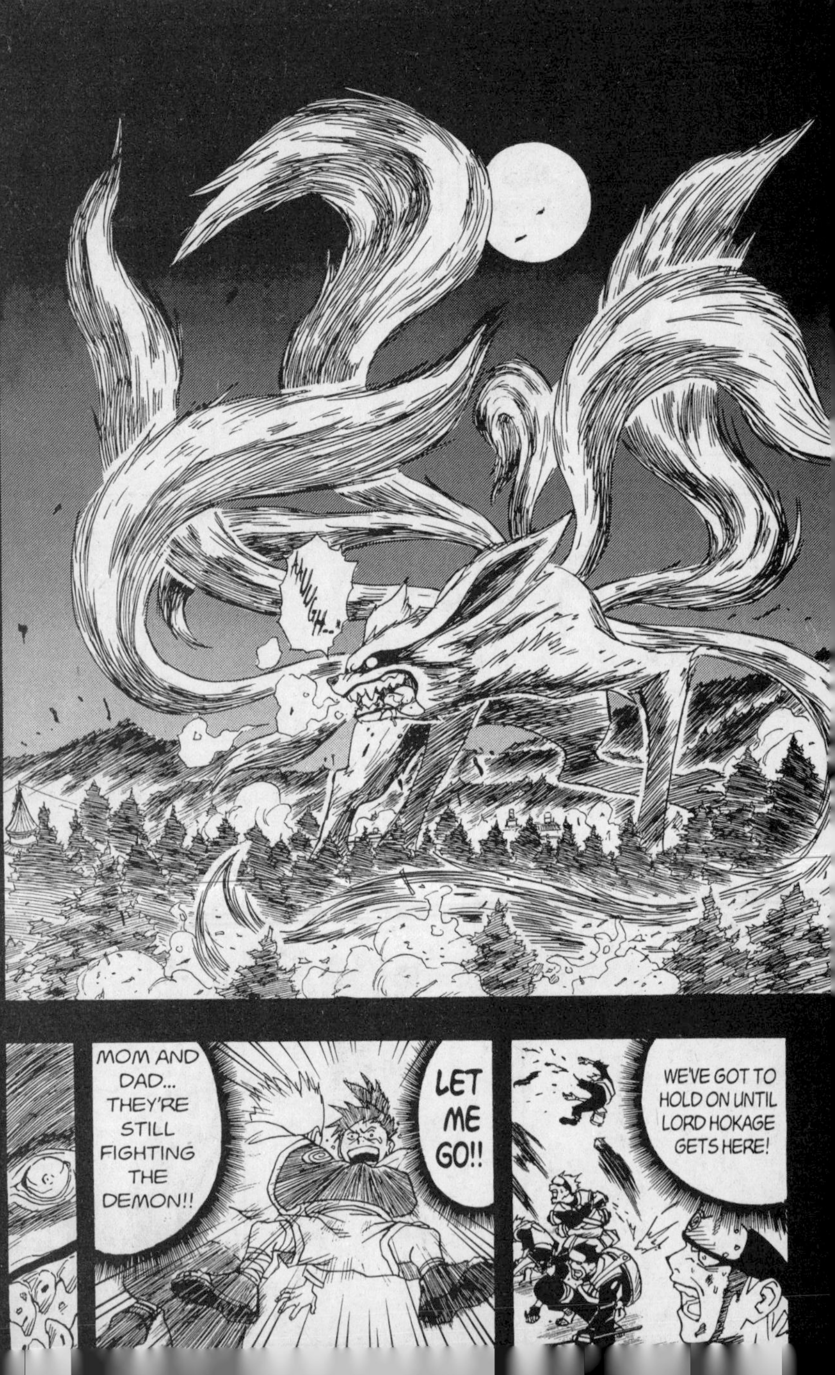
AAUUGH..!
WE'VE GOT TO HOLD ON UNTIL LORD HOKAGE GETS HERE!
LET ME GO!!
MOM AND DAD... THEY'RE STILL FIGHTING THE DEMON!!

READ THIS WAY

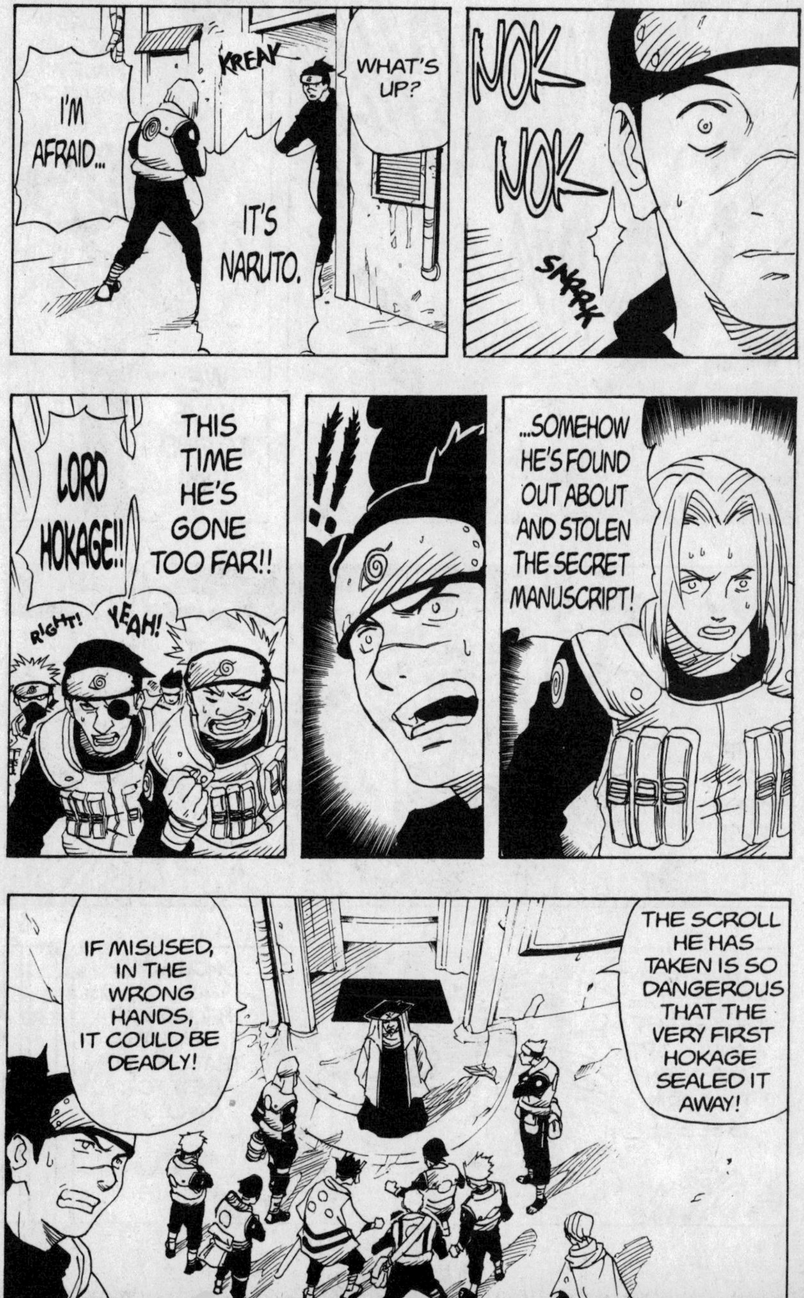
NOK
NOK
SNARK
WHAT'S UP?
KREAK
IT'S NARUTO.
I'M AFRAID...
...SOMEHOW HE'S FOUND OUT ABOUT AND STOLEN THE SECRET MANUSCRIPT!
!!
THIS TIME HE'S GONE TOO FAR!!
LORD HOKAGE!!
YEAH!
RIGHT!
THE SCROLL HE HAS TAKEN IS SO DANGEROUS THAT THE VERY FIRST HOKAGE SEALED IT AWAY!
IF MISUSED, IN THE WRONG HANDS, IT COULD BE DEADLY!

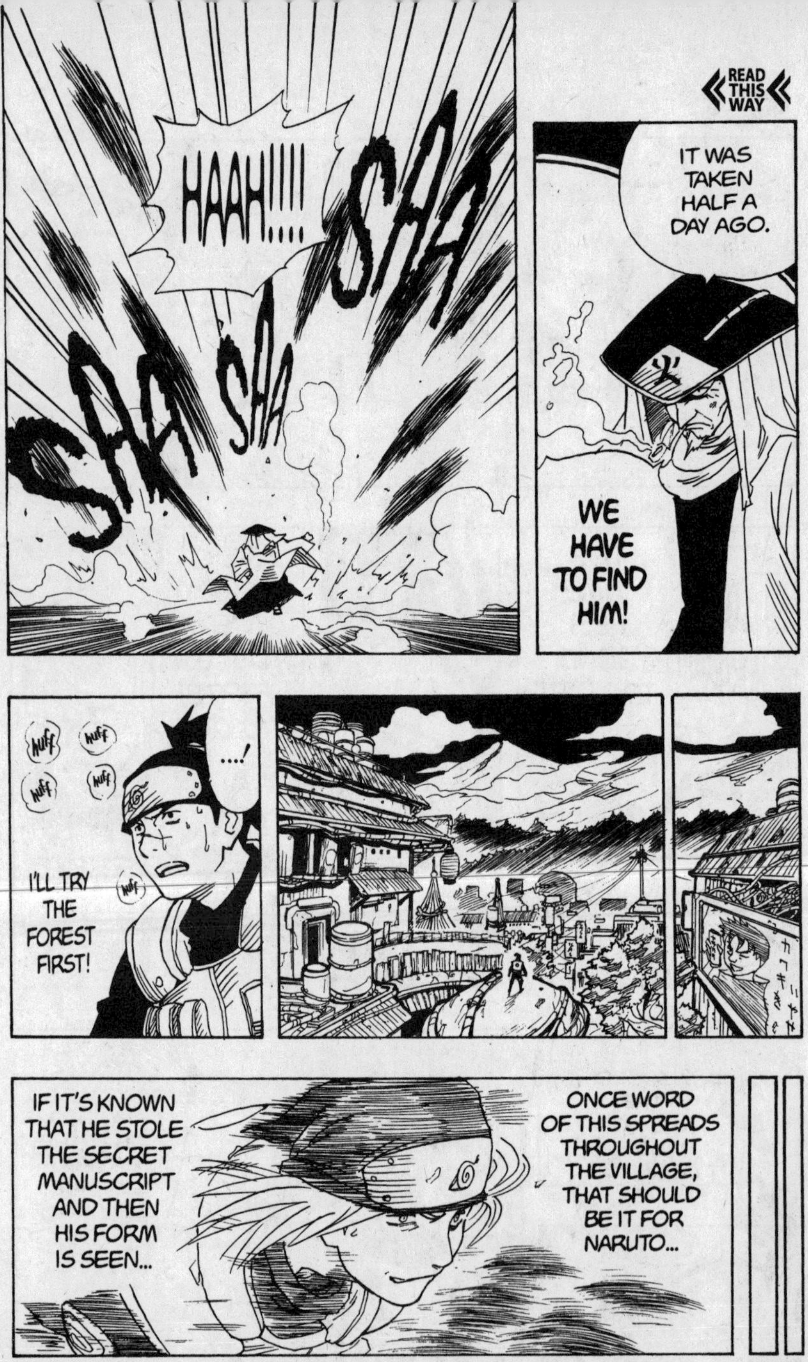
READ THIS WAY
IT WAS TAKEN HALF A DAY AGO.
WE HAVE TO FIND HIM!
HAAH!!!!!
SAA
SAA
SAA
....!
HUFF
HUFF
HUFF
HUFF
HUFF
I'LL TRY THE FOREST FIRST!
ONCE WORD OF THIS SPREADS THROUGHOUT THE VILLAGE, THAT SHOULD BE IT FOR NARUTO...
IF IT'S KNOWN THAT HE STOLE THE SECRET MANUSCRIPT AND THEN HIS FORM IS SEEN...

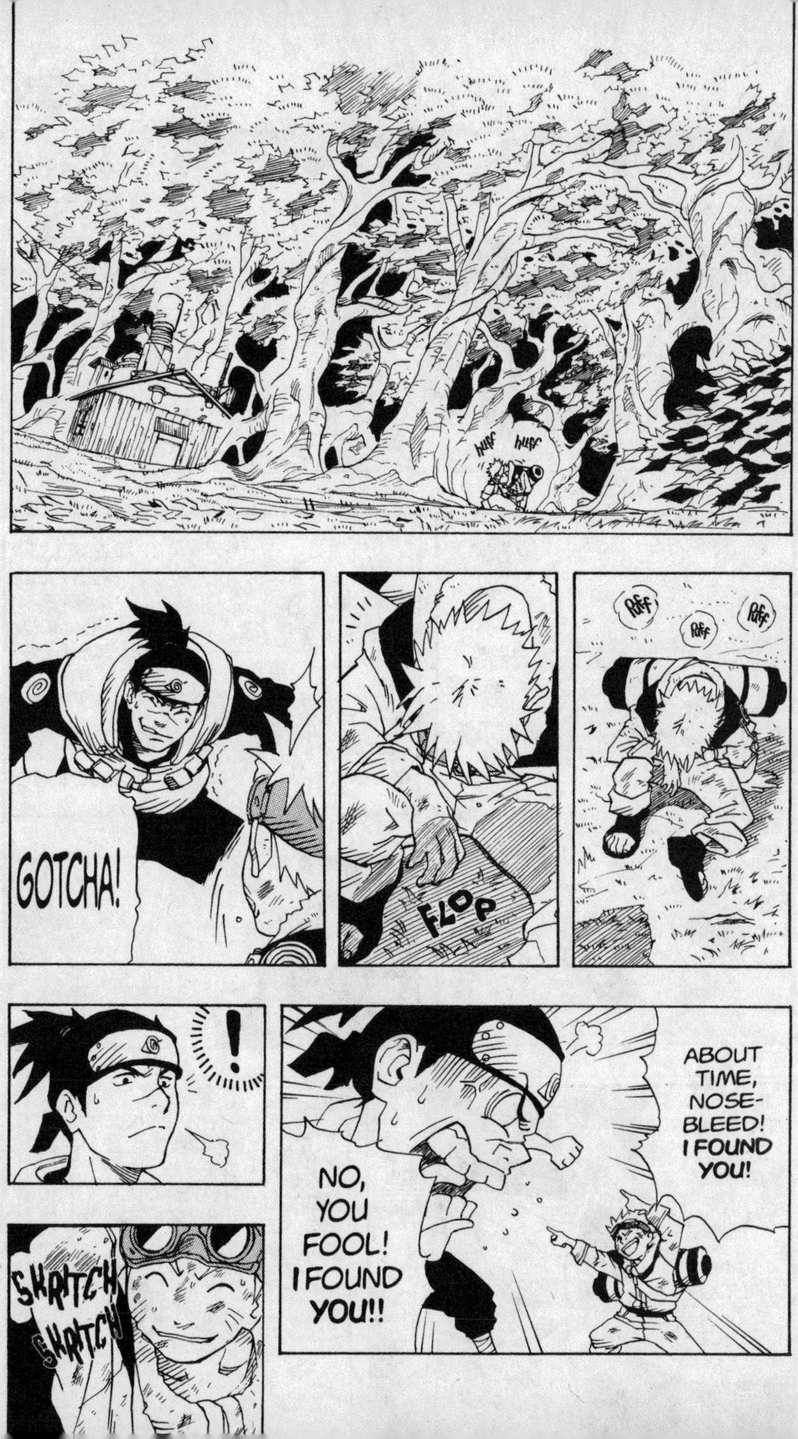
huff
huff
Puff
Puff
Puff
FLOP
GOTCHA!
ABOUT TIME, NOSE-BLEED! I FOUND YOU!
NO, YOU FOOL! I FOUND YOU!!
!
SKRITCH
SKRITCH

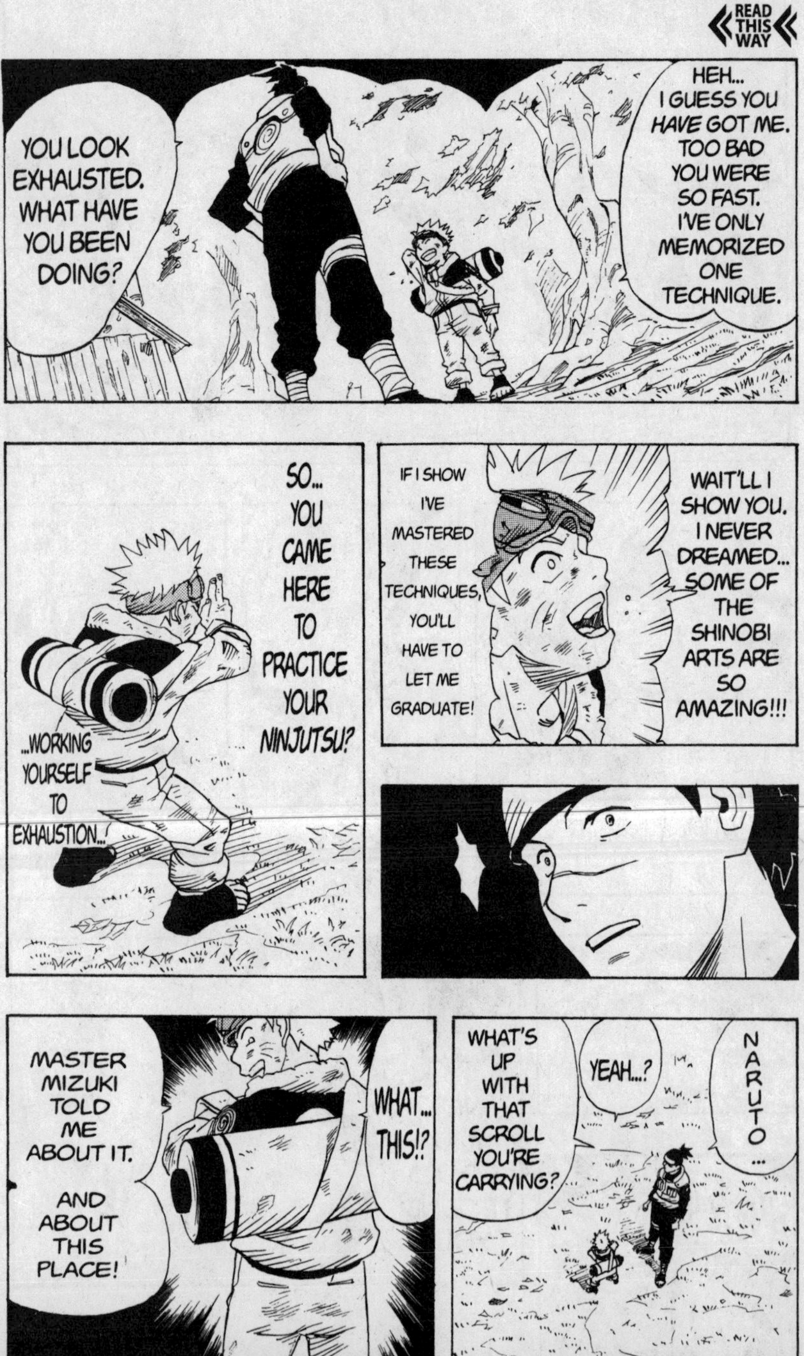
READ THIS WAY
HEH... I GUESS YOU HAVE GOT ME. TOO BAD YOU WERE SO FAST. I'VE ONLY MEMORIZED ONE TECHNIQUE.
YOU LOOK EXHAUSTED. WHAT HAVE YOU BEEN DOING?
WAIT'LL I SHOW YOU. I NEVER DREAMED... SOME OF THE SHINOBI ARTS ARE SO AMAZING!!!
IF I SHOW I'VE MASTERED THESE TECHNIQUES, YOU'LL HAVE TO LET ME GRADUATE!
SO... YOU CAME HERE TO PRACTICE YOUR NINJUTSU?
...WORKING YOURSELF TO EXHAUSTION...!
NARUTO...
YEAH...?
WHAT'S UP WITH THAT SCROLL YOU'RE CARRYING?
WHAT... THIS!?
MASTER MIZUKI TOLD ME ABOUT IT.
AND ABOUT THIS PLACE!

READ THIS WAY

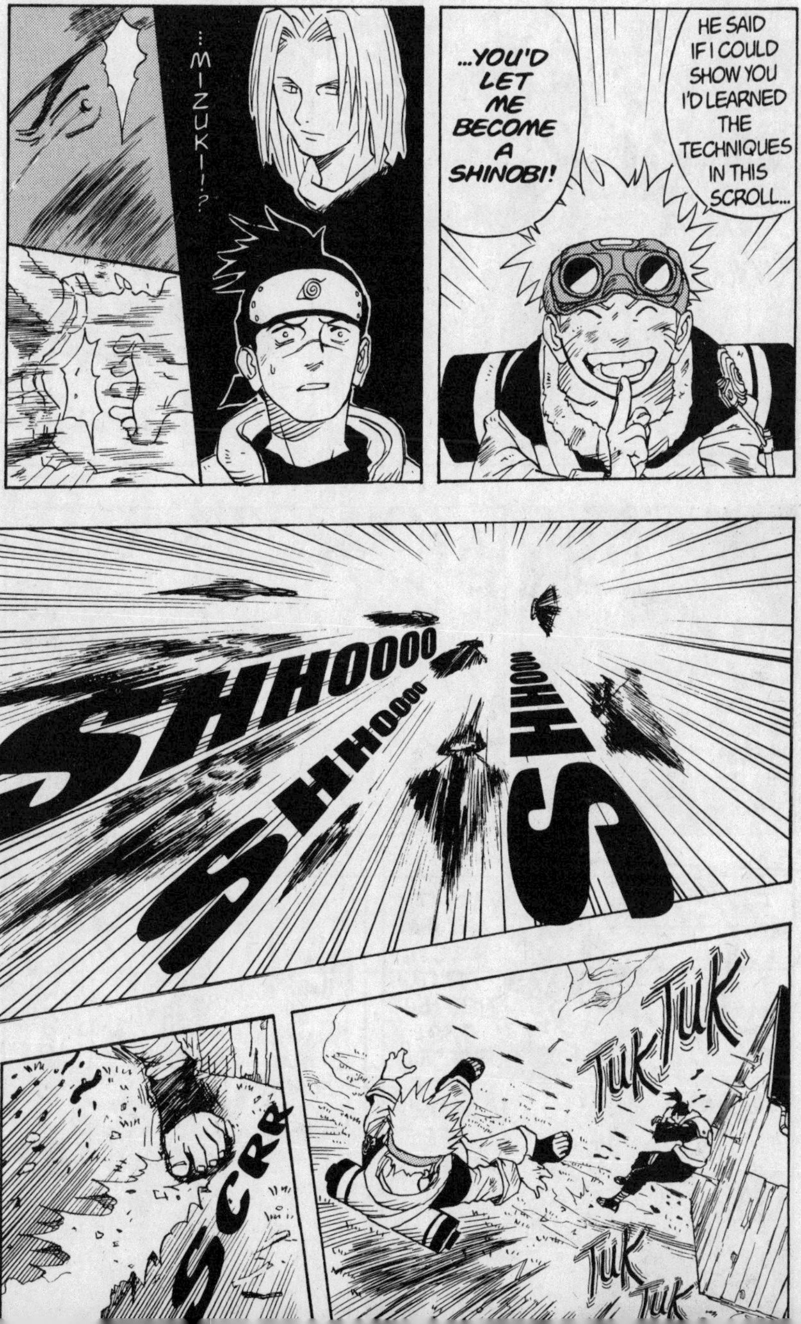
HE SAID IF I COULD SHOW YOU I'D LEARNED THE TECHNIQUES IN THIS SCROLL...
...YOU'D LET ME BECOME A SHINOBI!
...MIZUKI!?
SHHOOOO
SHHOOOO
SHHOOOO
TUK TUK
TUK TUK
SCRR

READ THIS WAY

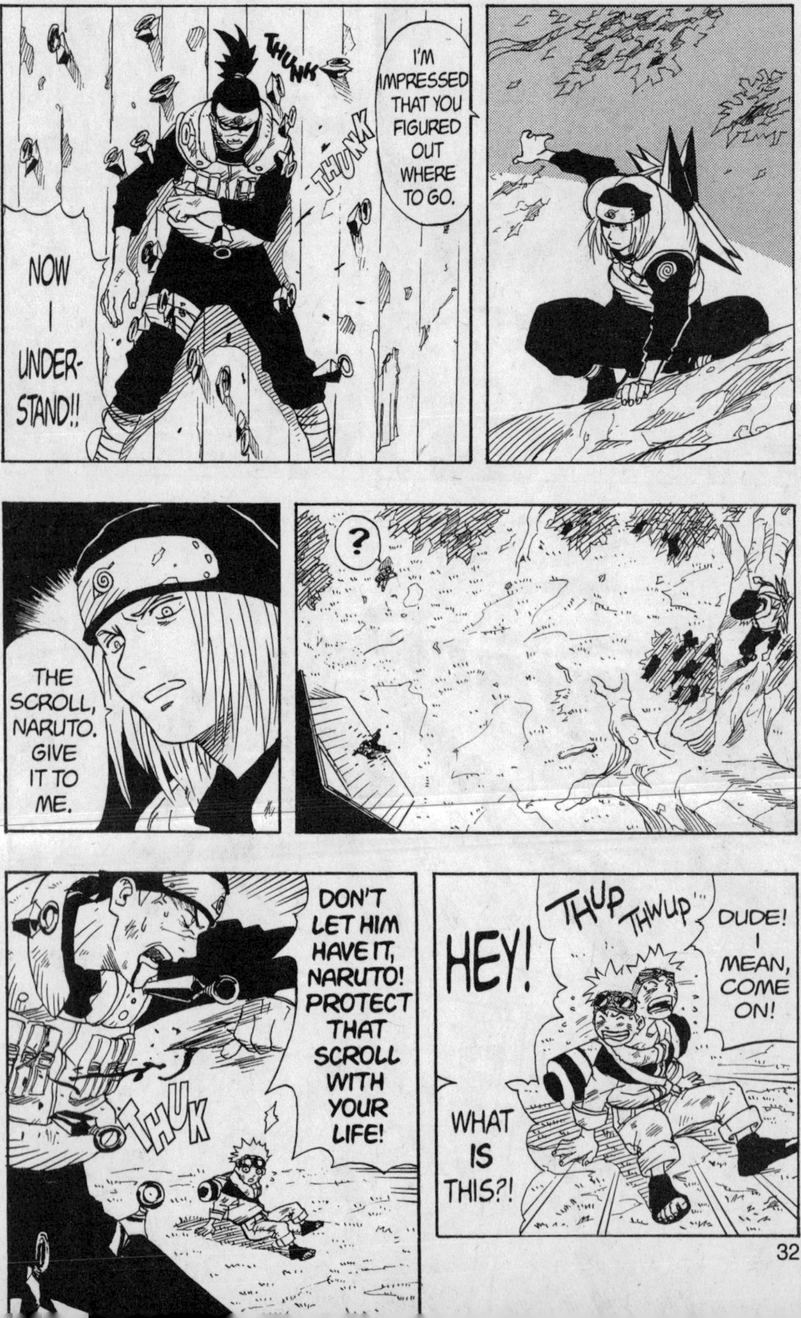
I'M IMPRESSED THAT YOU FIGURED OUT WHERE TO GO.
THUNK
THUNK
NOW I UNDERSTAND!!
?
THE SCROLL, NARUTO. GIVE IT TO ME.
DUDE! I MEAN, COME ON!
THUP THWUP
HEY!
WHAT IS THIS?!
DON'T LET HIM HAVE IT, NARUTO! PROTECT THAT SCROLL WITH YOUR LIFE!
THUK

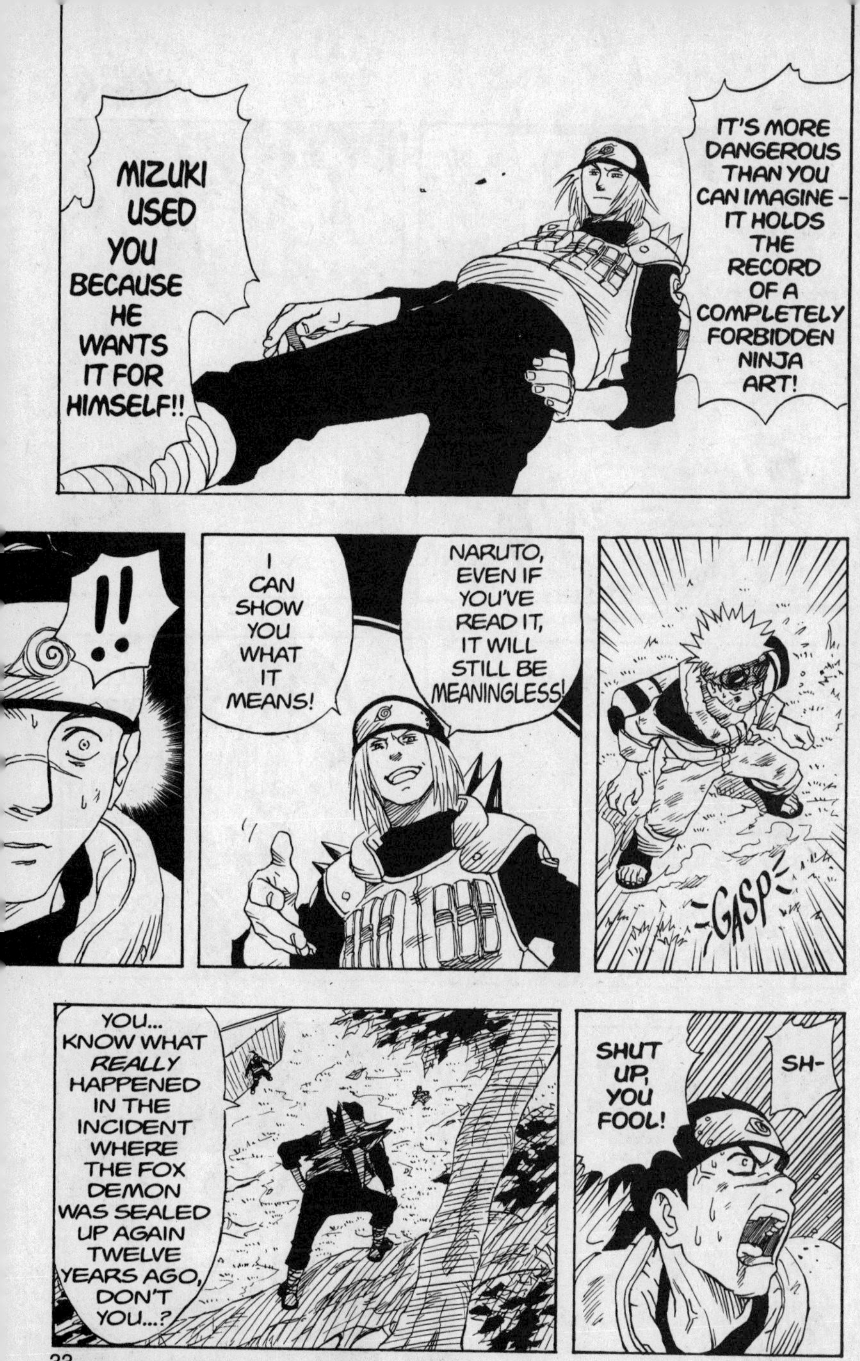
IT'S MORE DANGEROUS THAN YOU CAN IMAGINE - IT HOLDS THE RECORD OF A COMPLETELY FORBIDDEN NINJA ART!
MIZUKI USED YOU BECAUSE HE WANTS IT FOR HIMSELF!!
GASP
NARUTO, EVEN IF YOU'VE READ IT, IT WILL STILL BE MEANINGLESS!
I CAN SHOW YOU WHAT IT MEANS!
!!
SH-
SHUT UP, YOU FOOL!
YOU... KNOW WHAT *REALLY* HAPPENED IN THE INCIDENT WHERE THE FOX DEMON WAS SEALED UP AGAIN TWELVE YEARS AGO, DON'T YOU...?

READ THIS WAY

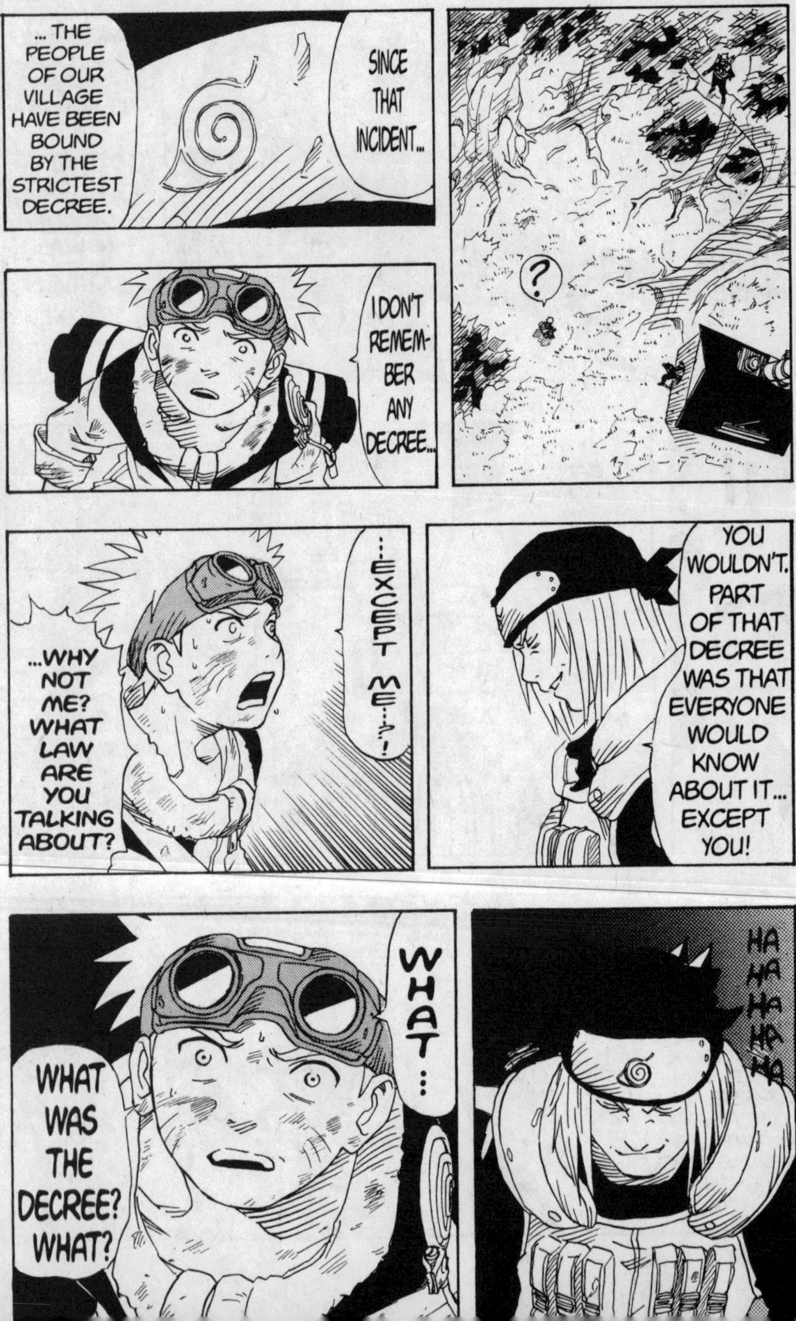
?
SINCE THAT INCIDENT...
... THE PEOPLE OF OUR VILLAGE HAVE BEEN BOUND BY THE STRICTEST DECREE.
I DON'T REMEMBER ANY DECREE...
YOU WOULDN'T. PART OF THAT DECREE WAS THAT EVERYONE WOULD KNOW ABOUT IT... EXCEPT YOU!
...EXCEPT ME...?!
...WHY NOT ME? WHAT LAW ARE YOU TALKING ABOUT?
HA HA HA HA HA
WHAT...
WHAT WAS THE DECREE? WHAT?

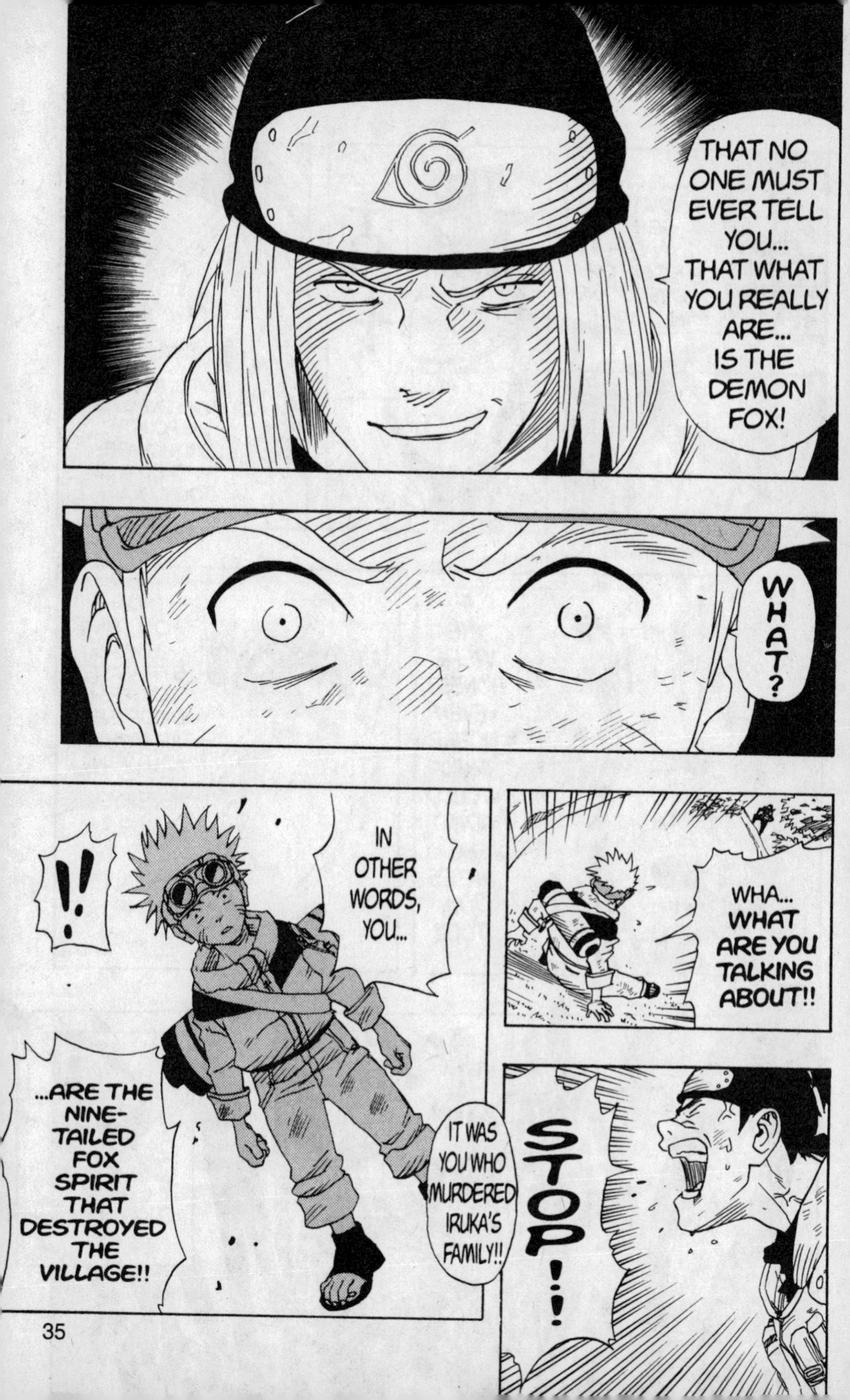
THAT NO ONE MUST EVER TELL YOU... THAT WHAT YOU REALLY ARE... IS THE DEMON FOX!
WHAT?
WHA... WHAT ARE YOU TALKING ABOUT!!
STOP!!
IN OTHER WORDS, YOU...
!!
...ARE THE NINE-TAILED FOX SPIRIT THAT DESTROYED THE VILLAGE!!
IT WAS YOU WHO MURDERED IRUKA'S FAMILY!!

READ THIS WAY

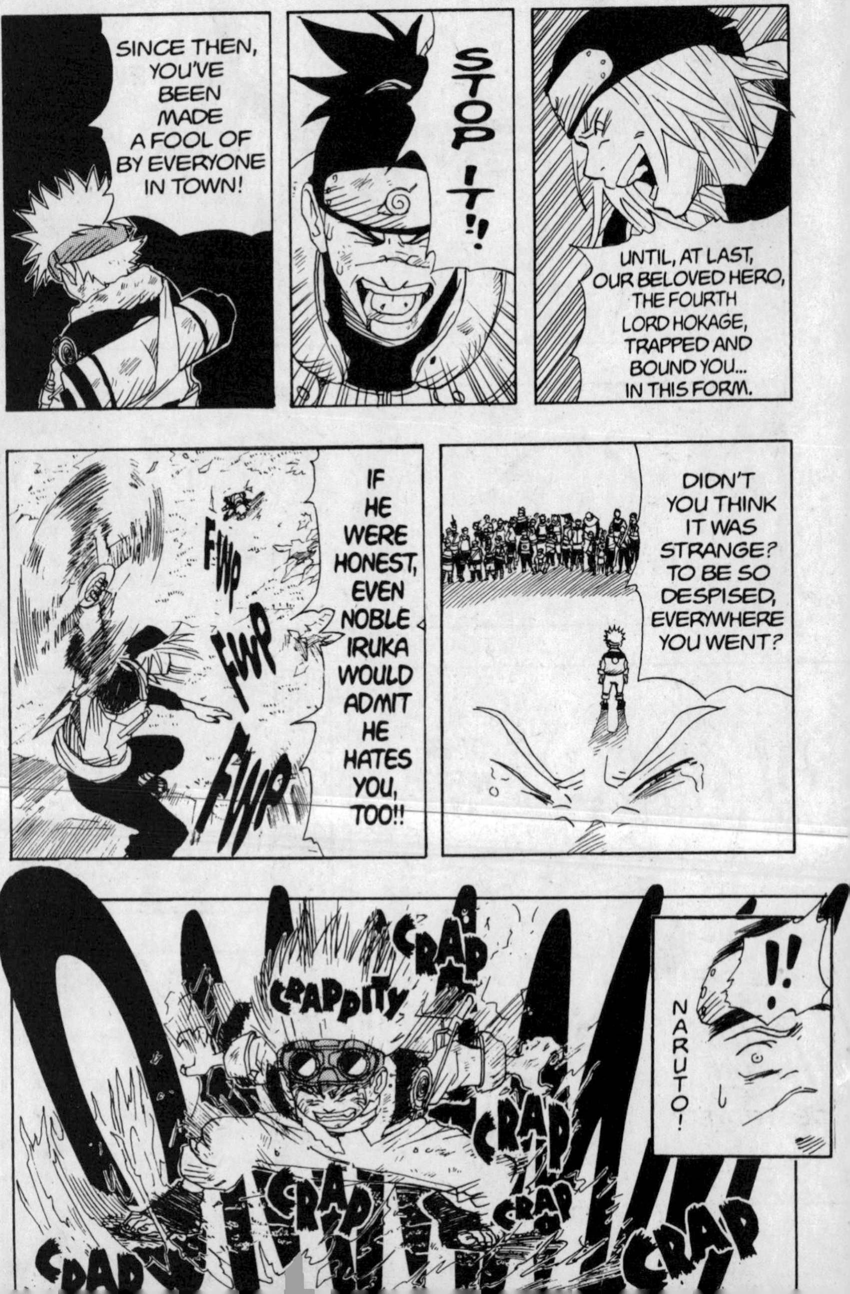
UNTIL, AT LAST, OUR BELOVED HERO, THE FOURTH LORD HOKAGE, TRAPPED AND BOUND YOU... IN THIS FORM.
STOP IT!!
SINCE THEN, YOU'VE BEEN MADE A FOOL OF BY EVERYONE IN TOWN!
DIDN'T YOU THINK IT WAS STRANGE? TO BE SO DESPISED, EVERYWHERE YOU WENT?
IF HE WERE HONEST, EVEN NOBLE IRUKA WOULD ADMIT HE HATES YOU, TOO!!
FWP
FWP
FWP
!!
NARUTO!
CRAP
CRAPPITY
CRAP
CRAP
CRAP
CRAP
CRAP

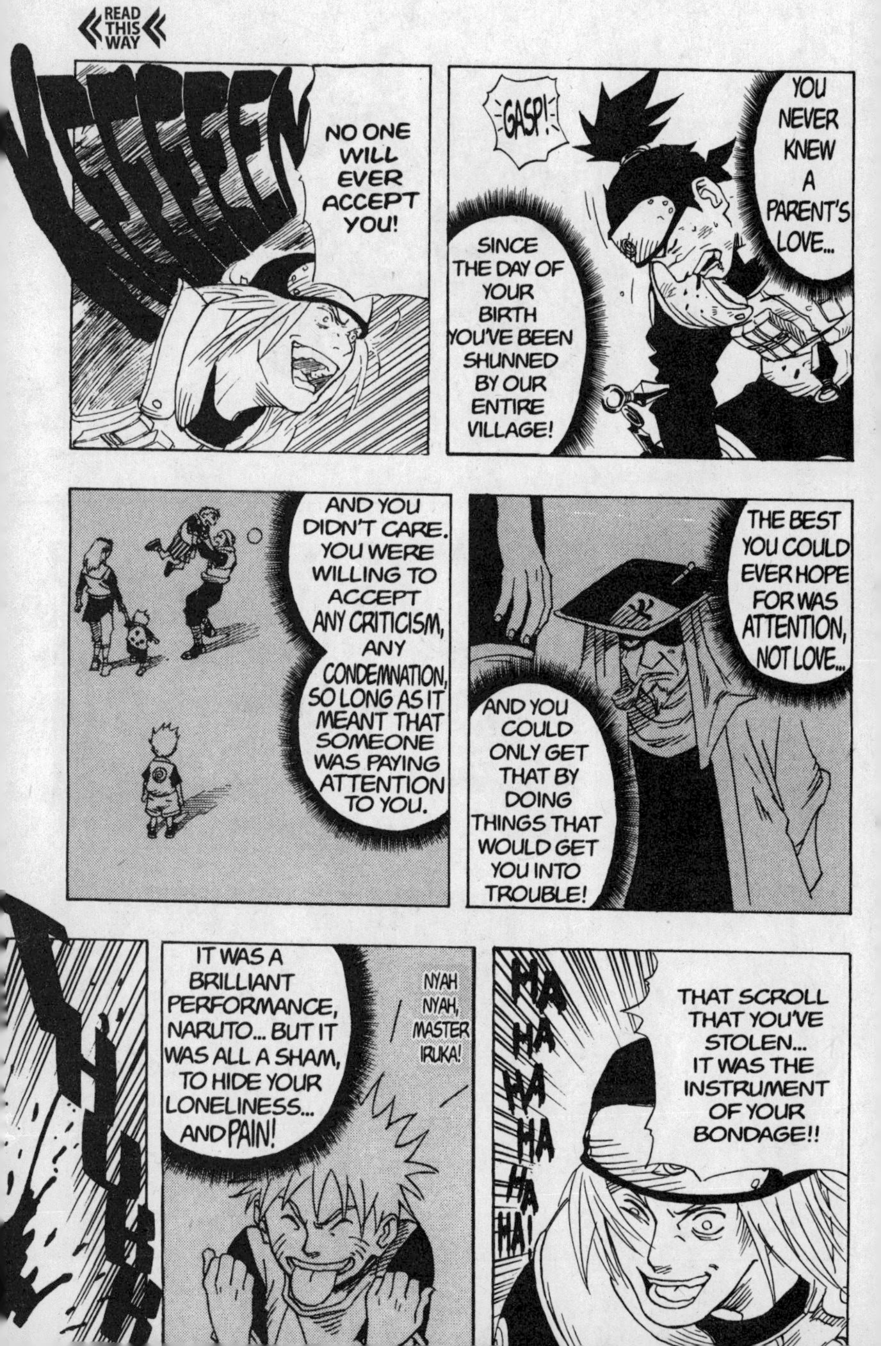
READ THIS WAY
YOU NEVER KNEW A PARENT'S LOVE...
GASP!
SINCE THE DAY OF YOUR BIRTH YOU'VE BEEN SHUNNED BY OUR ENTIRE VILLAGE!
NO ONE WILL EVER ACCEPT YOU!
THE BEST YOU COULD EVER HOPE FOR WAS ATTENTION, NOT LOVE...
AND YOU COULD ONLY GET THAT BY DOING THINGS THAT WOULD GET YOU INTO TROUBLE!
AND YOU DIDN'T CARE. YOU WERE WILLING TO ACCEPT ANY CRITICISM, ANY CONDEMNATION, SO LONG AS IT MEANT THAT SOMEONE WAS PAYING ATTENTION TO YOU.
HA HA HA HA HA HA HA!
THAT SCROLL THAT YOU'VE STOLEN... IT WAS THE INSTRUMENT OF YOUR BONDAGE!!
NYAH NYAH, MASTER IRUKA!
IT WAS A BRILLIANT PERFORMANCE, NARUTO... BUT IT WAS ALL A SHAM, TO HIDE YOUR LONELINESS... AND PAIN!

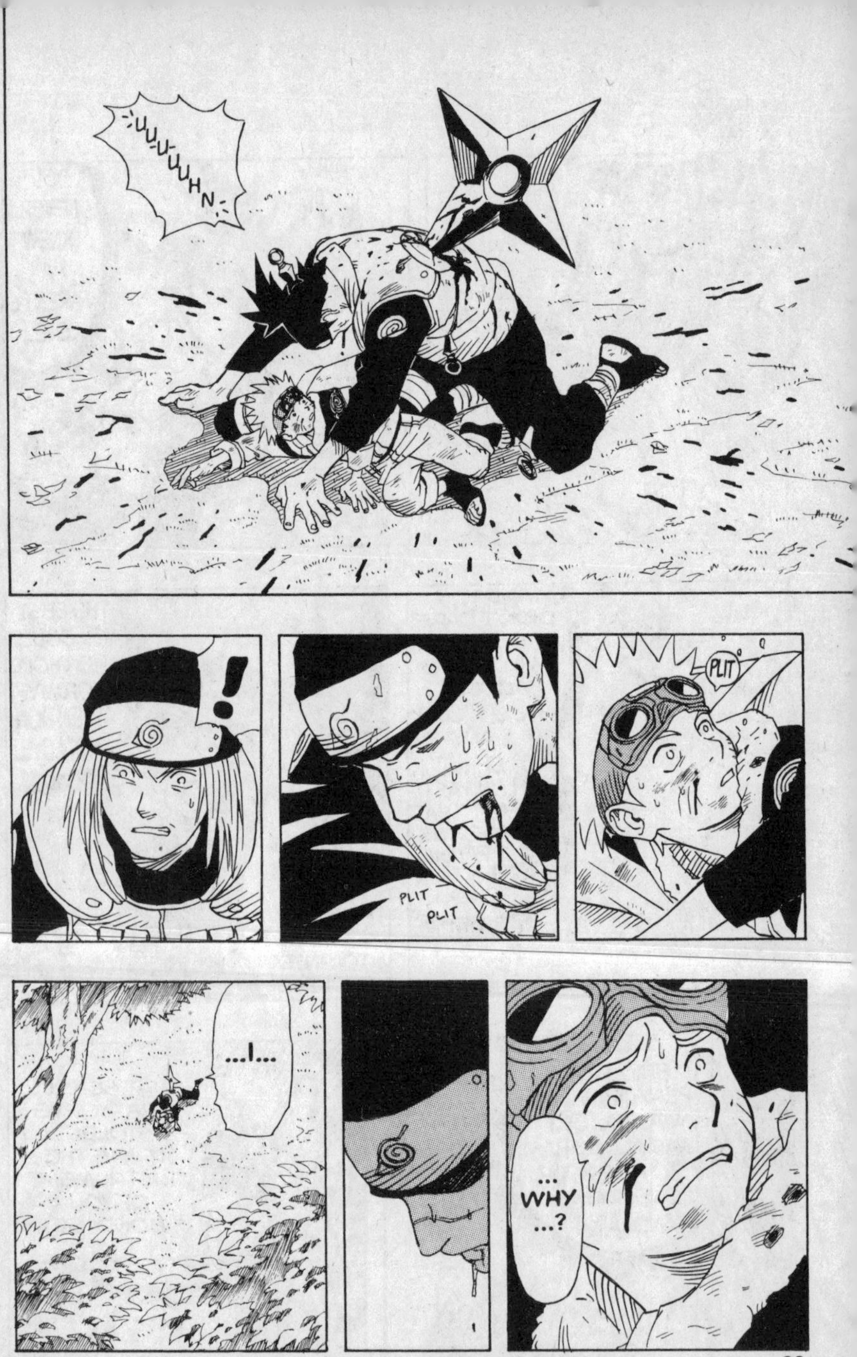
UUU-UUUHN
!
PLIT PLIT
PLIT
...I...
...WHY ...?

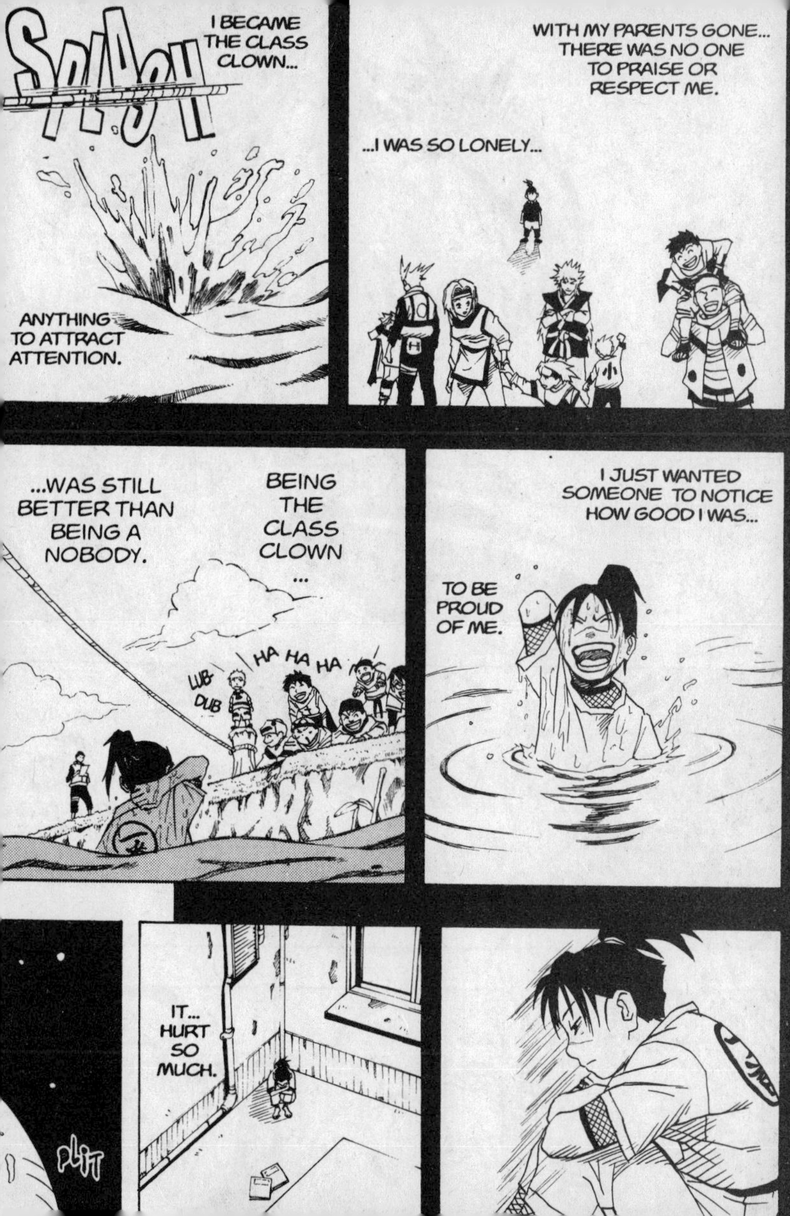
WITH MY PARENTS GONE... THERE WAS NO ONE TO PRAISE OR RESPECT ME.
...I WAS SO LONELY...
I BECAME THE CLASS CLOWN...
SPLASH
ANYTHING TO ATTRACT ATTENTION.
I JUST WANTED SOMEONE TO NOTICE HOW GOOD I WAS...
TO BE PROUD OF ME.
BEING THE CLASS CLOWN...
...WAS STILL BETTER THAN BEING A NOBODY.
HA HA HA
LUB DUB
IT... HURT SO MUCH.
PLIT

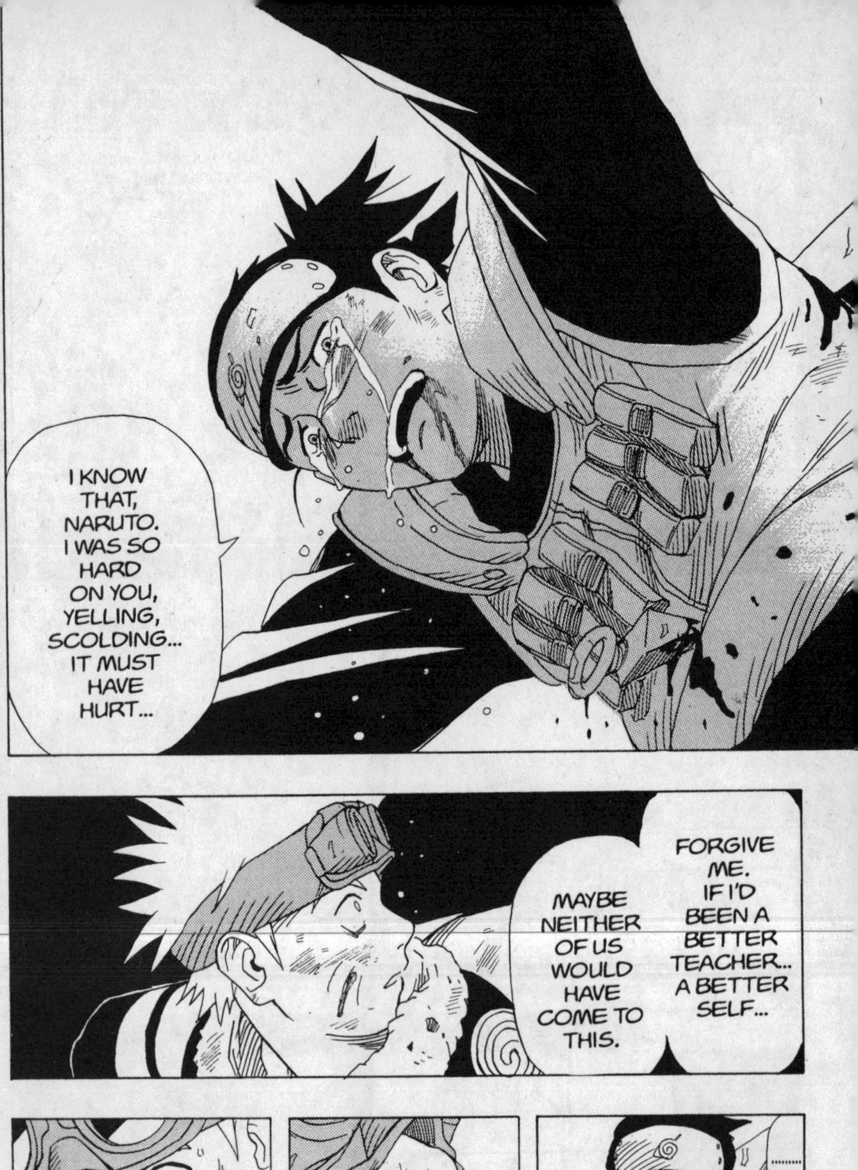
I KNOW THAT, NARUTO. I WAS SO HARD ON YOU, YELLING, SCOLDING... IT MUST HAVE HURT...
FORGIVE ME. IF I'D BEEN A BETTER TEACHER... A BETTER SELF...
MAYBE NEITHER OF US WOULD HAVE COME TO THIS.
......

READ THIS WAY

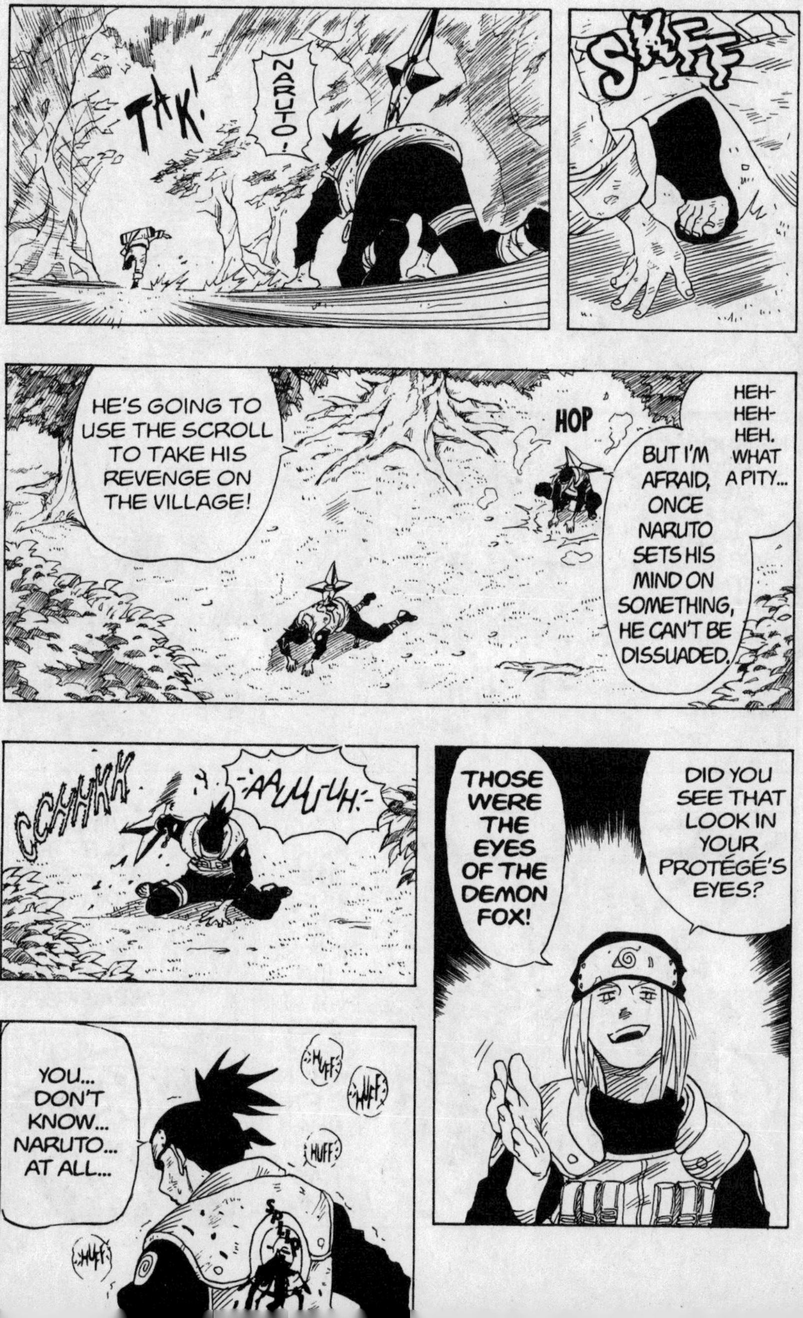
SKFF
NARUTO!
TAK!
HEH-HEH-HEH. WHAT A PITY...
BUT I'M AFRAID, ONCE NARUTO SETS HIS MIND ON SOMETHING, HE CAN'T BE DISSUADED.
HOP
HE'S GOING TO USE THE SCROLL TO TAKE HIS REVENGE ON THE VILLAGE!
DID YOU SEE THAT LOOK IN YOUR PROTÉGÉ'S EYES?
THOSE WERE THE EYES OF THE DEMON FOX!
AAUUU-UH
CCHHKK
HUFF
HUFF
HUFF
YOU... DON'T KNOW... NARUTO... AT ALL...
HUFF

READ THIS WAY

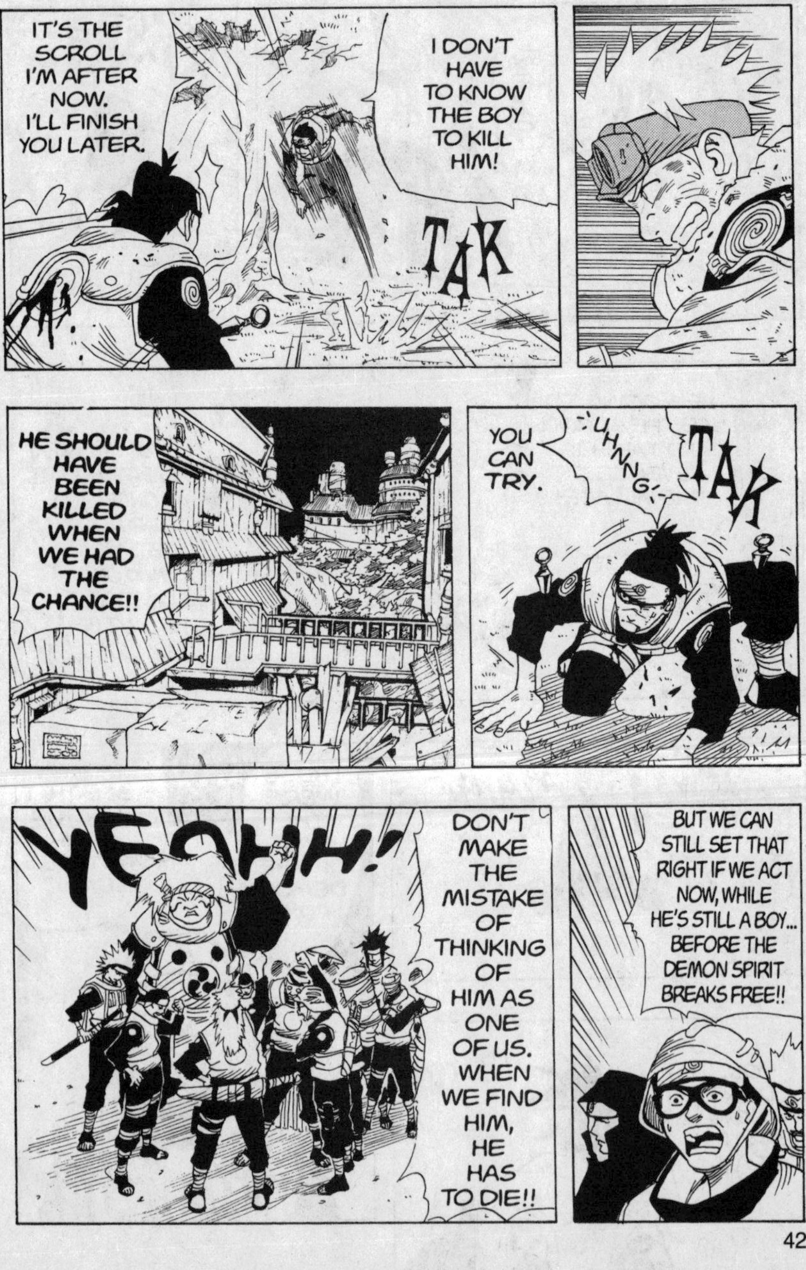
I DON'T HAVE TO KNOW THE BOY TO KILL HIM!
IT'S THE SCROLL I'M AFTER NOW. I'LL FINISH YOU LATER.
TAK
TAK
UHNNG
YOU CAN TRY.
HE SHOULD HAVE BEEN KILLED WHEN WE HAD THE CHANCE!!
BUT WE CAN STILL SET THAT RIGHT IF WE ACT NOW, WHILE HE'S STILL A BOY... BEFORE THE DEMON SPIRIT BREAKS FREE!!
DON'T MAKE THE MISTAKE OF THINKING OF HIM AS ONE OF US. WHEN WE FIND HIM, HE HAS TO DIE!!
YEAHH!

READ THIS WAY

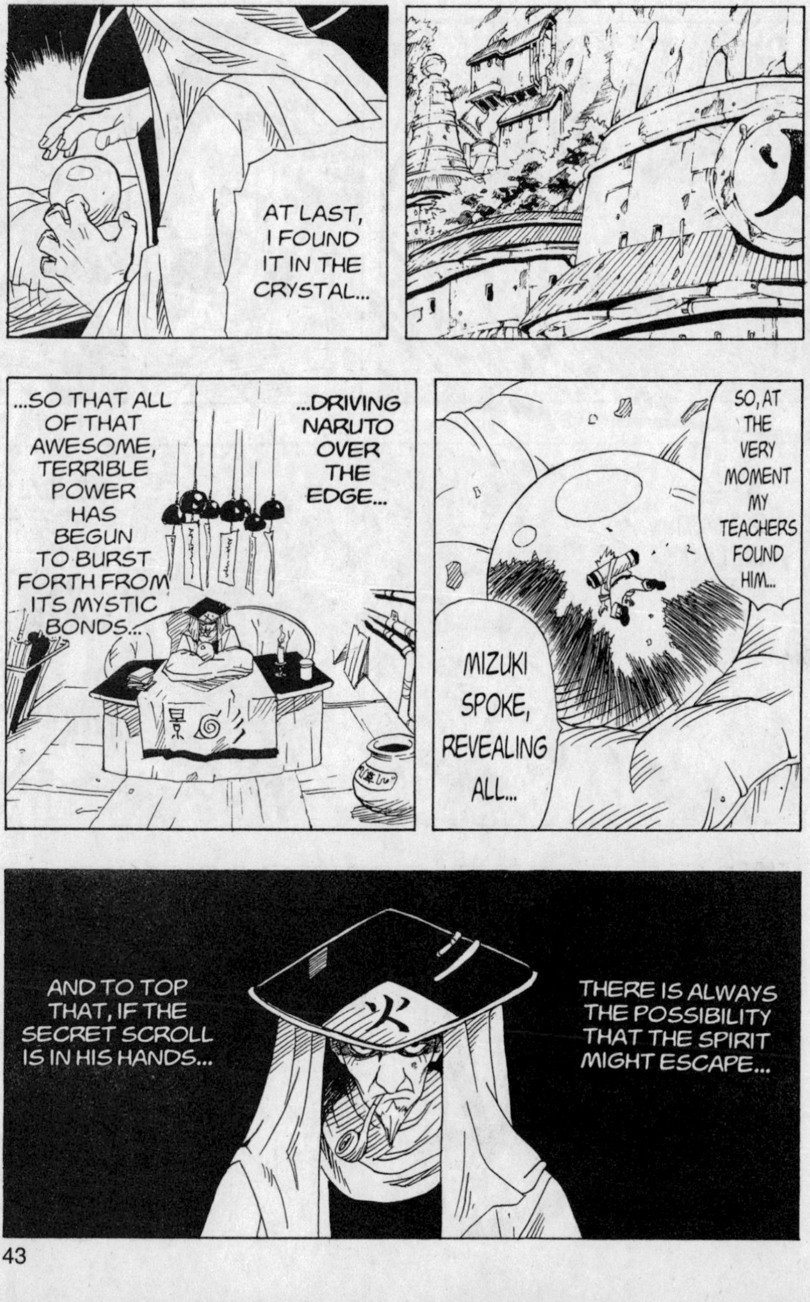
AT LAST, I FOUND IT IN THE CRYSTAL...
SO, AT THE VERY MOMENT MY TEACHERS FOUND HIM...
MIZUKI SPOKE, REVEALING ALL...
...DRIVING NARUTO OVER THE EDGE...
...SO THAT ALL OF THAT AWESOME, TERRIBLE POWER HAS BEGUN TO BURST FORTH FROM ITS MYSTIC BONDS...
THERE IS ALWAYS THE POSSIBILITY THAT THE SPIRIT MIGHT ESCAPE...
AND TO TOP THAT, IF THE SECRET SCROLL IS IN HIS HANDS...

READ THIS WAY

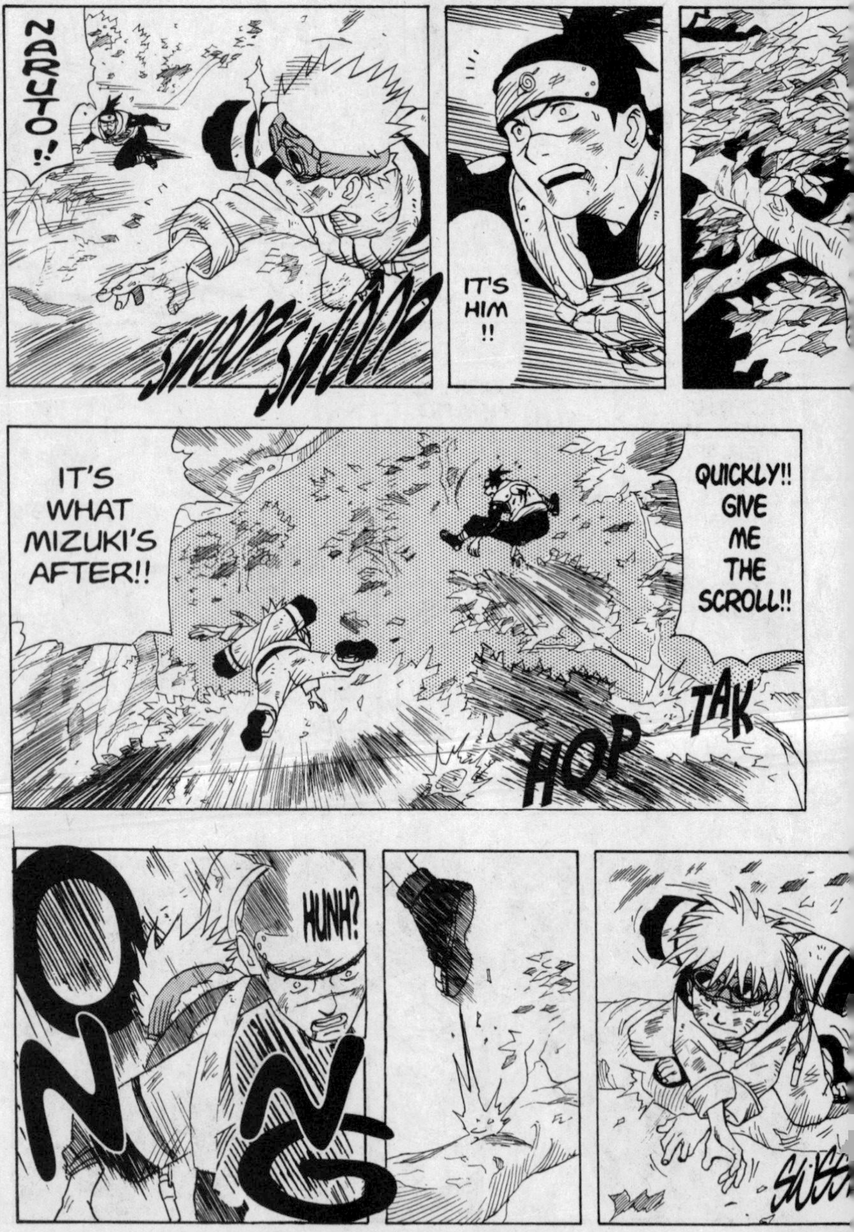

IT'S HIM !!
NARUTO!!
SWOOP SWOOP
QUICKLY!! GIVE ME THE SCROLL!!
IT'S WHAT MIZUKI'S AFTER!!
HOP
TAK
HUNH?
ONG

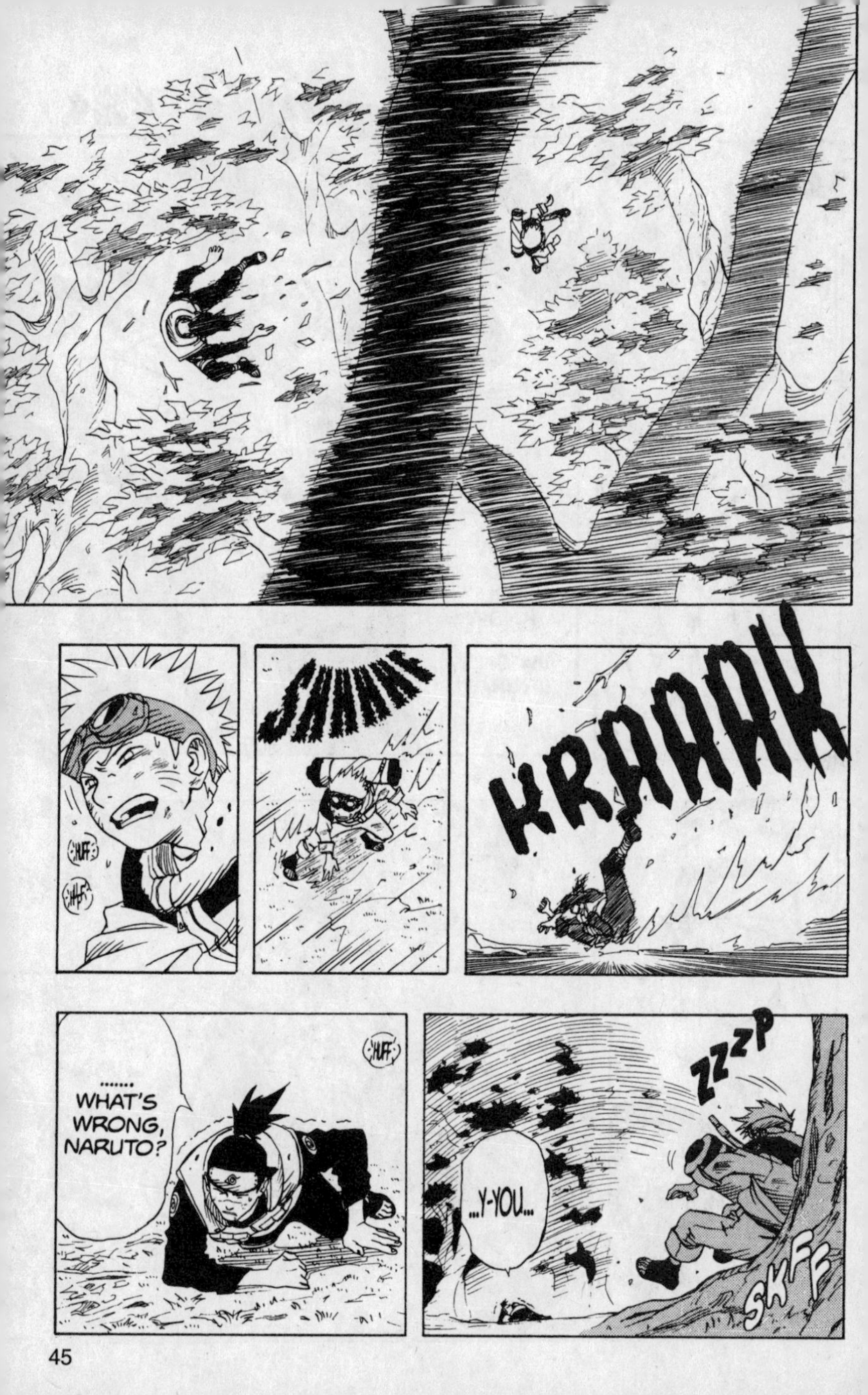
KRAAAK
SHHHHK
HUFF
HUFF
ZZZZP
...Y-YOU...
SKFF
HUFF
...... WHAT'S WRONG, NARUTO?

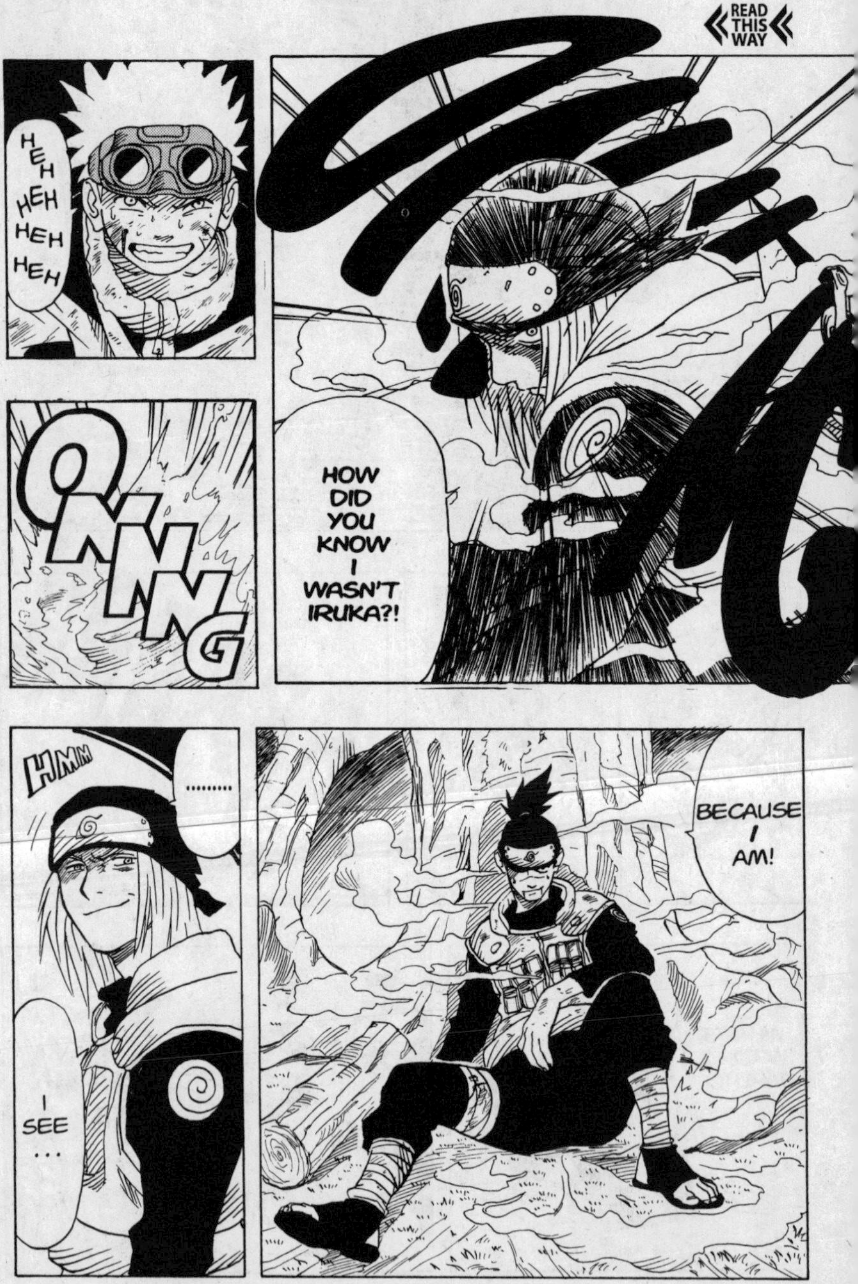
HOW DID YOU KNOW I WASN'T IRUKA?!
HEH HEH HEH HEH
ONNNG
BECAUSE I AM!
....
HMM
I SEE ...

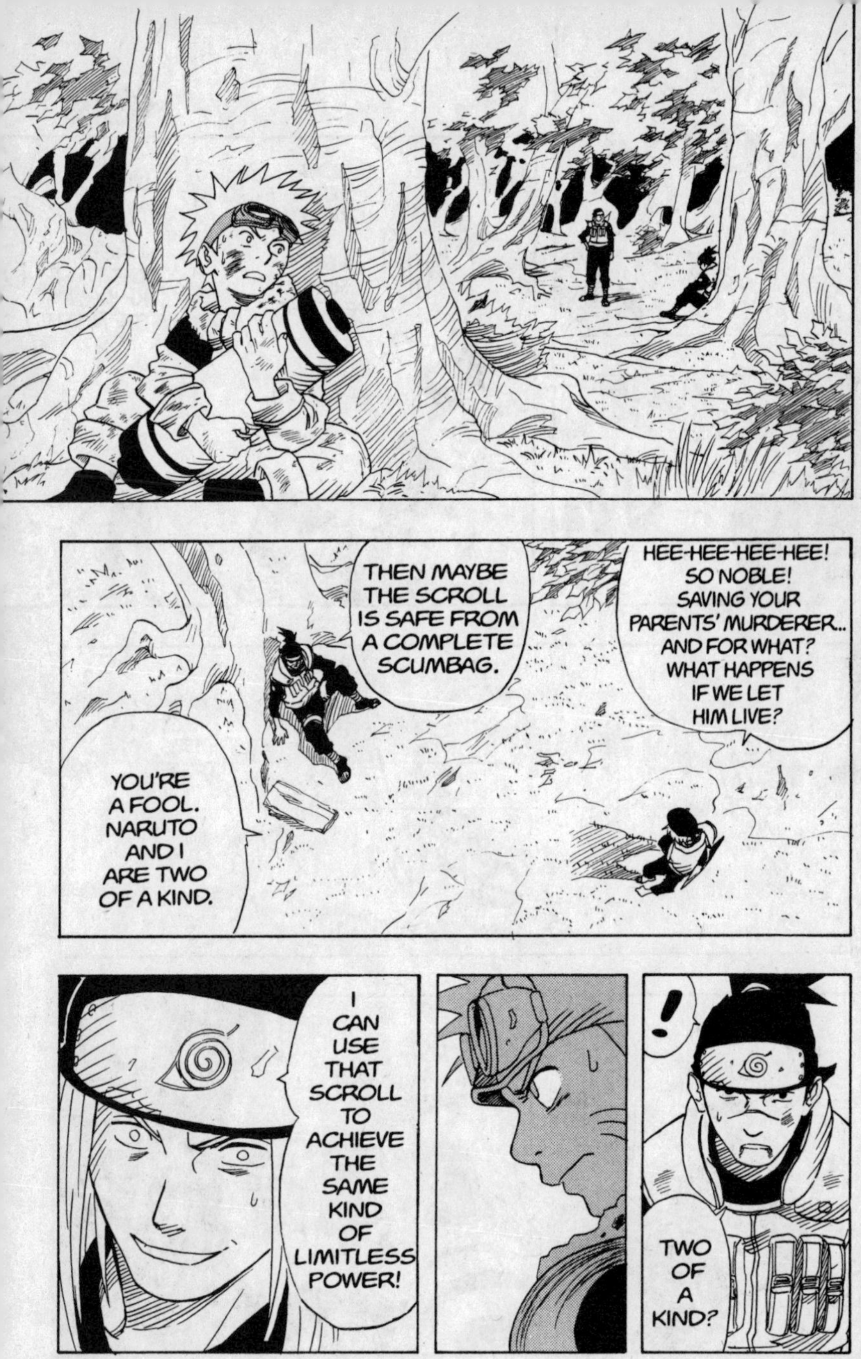
HEE-HEE-HEE-HEE! SO NOBLE! SAVING YOUR PARENTS' MURDERER... AND FOR WHAT? WHAT HAPPENS IF WE LET HIM LIVE?
THEN MAYBE THE SCROLL IS SAFE FROM A COMPLETE SCUMBAG.
YOU'RE A FOOL. NARUTO AND I ARE TWO OF A KIND.
!
TWO OF A KIND?
I CAN USE THAT SCROLL TO ACHIEVE THE SAME KIND OF LIMITLESS POWER!

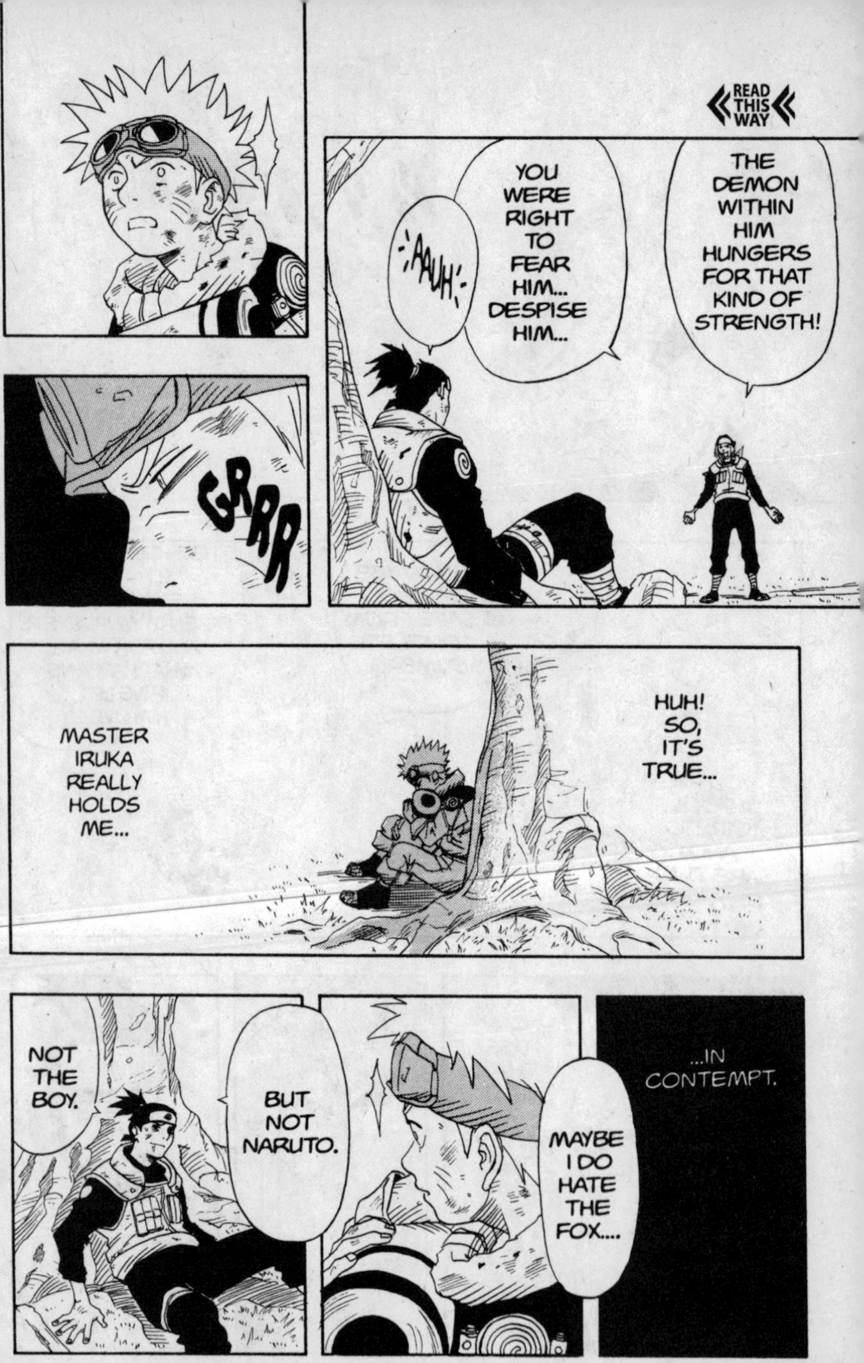
READ THIS WAY
THE DEMON WITHIN HIM HUNGERS FOR THAT KIND OF STRENGTH!
YOU WERE RIGHT TO FEAR HIM... DESPISE HIM...
AAUH
GRRR
HUH! SO, IT'S TRUE...
MASTER IRUKA REALLY HOLDS ME...
...IN CONTEMPT.
MAYBE I DO HATE THE FOX....
BUT NOT NARUTO.
NOT THE BOY.

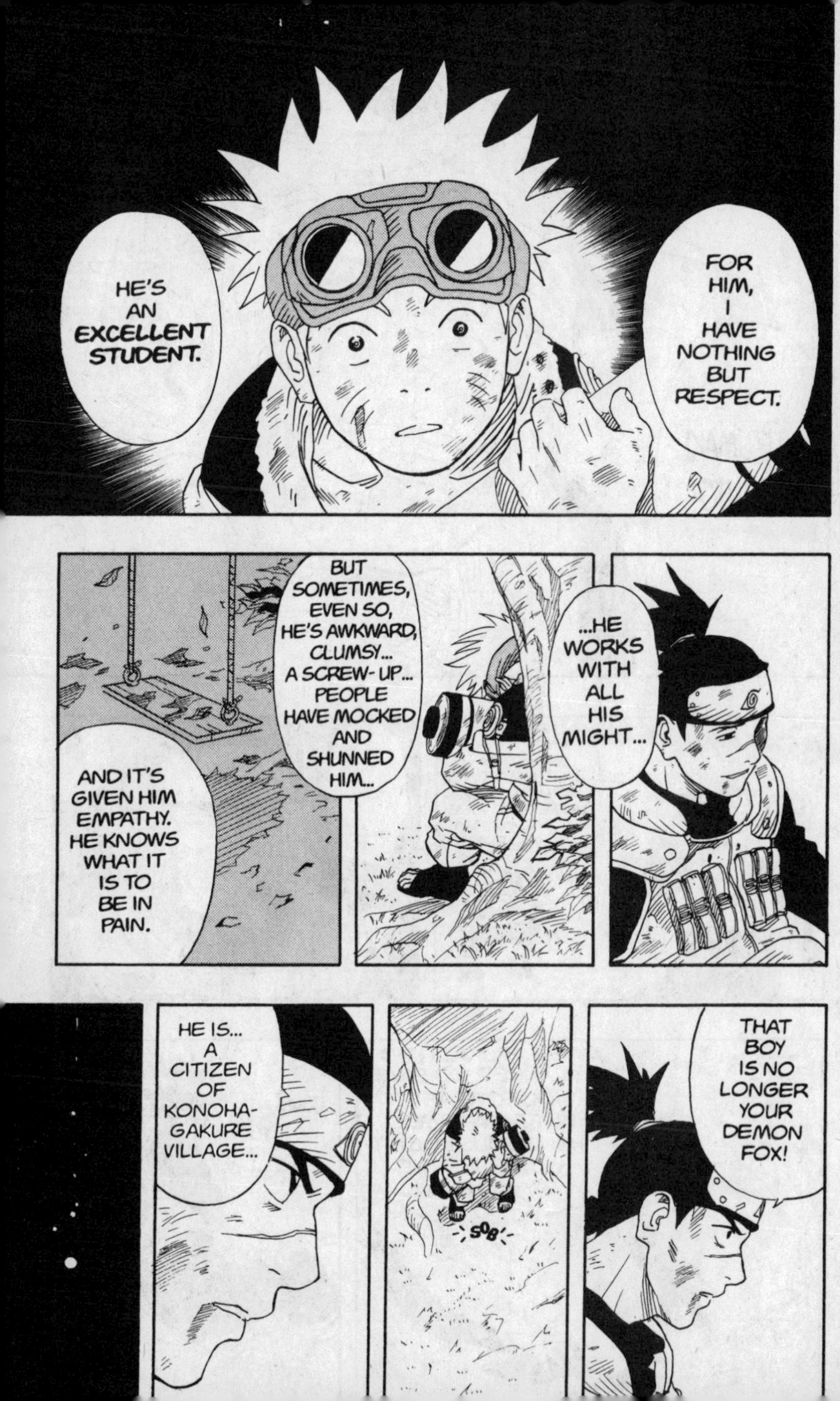
FOR HIM, I HAVE NOTHING BUT RESPECT.
HE'S AN EXCELLENT STUDENT.
...HE WORKS WITH ALL HIS MIGHT...
BUT SOMETIMES, EVEN SO, HE'S AWKWARD, CLUMSY... A SCREW-UP... PEOPLE HAVE MOCKED AND SHUNNED HIM...
AND IT'S GIVEN HIM EMPATHY. HE KNOWS WHAT IT IS TO BE IN PAIN.
THAT BOY IS NO LONGER YOUR DEMON FOX!
SOB
HE IS... A CITIZEN OF KONOHA-GAKURE VILLAGE...

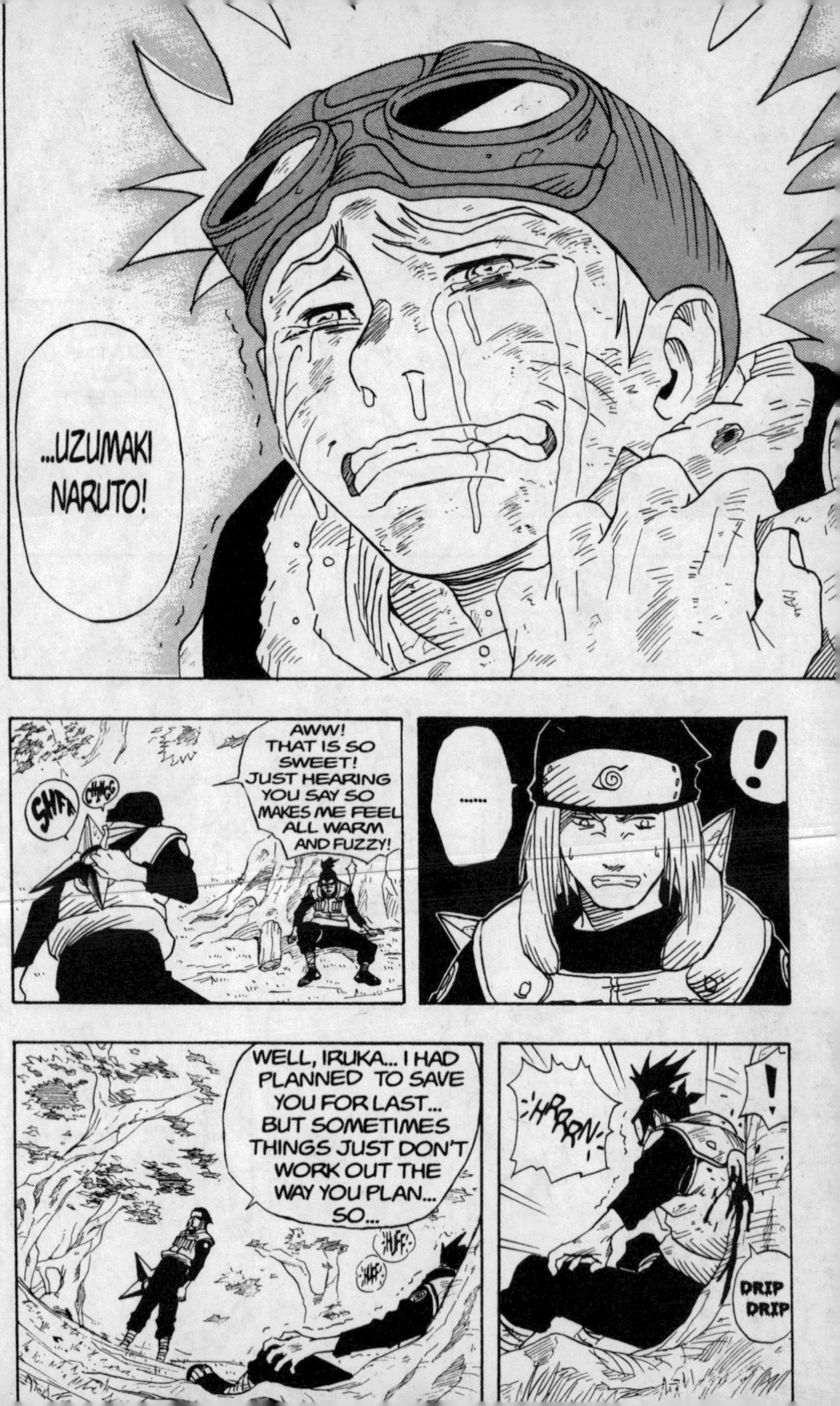

...UZUMAKI NARUTO!
......
!
AWW! THAT IS SO SWEET! JUST HEARING YOU SAY SO MAKES ME FEEL ALL WARM AND FUZZY!
SHFA
HRRRN
!
DRIP DRIP
WELL, IRUKA... I HAD PLANNED TO SAVE YOU FOR LAST... BUT SOMETIMES THINGS JUST DON'T WORK OUT THE WAY YOU PLAN... SO...
HUFF
HUFF

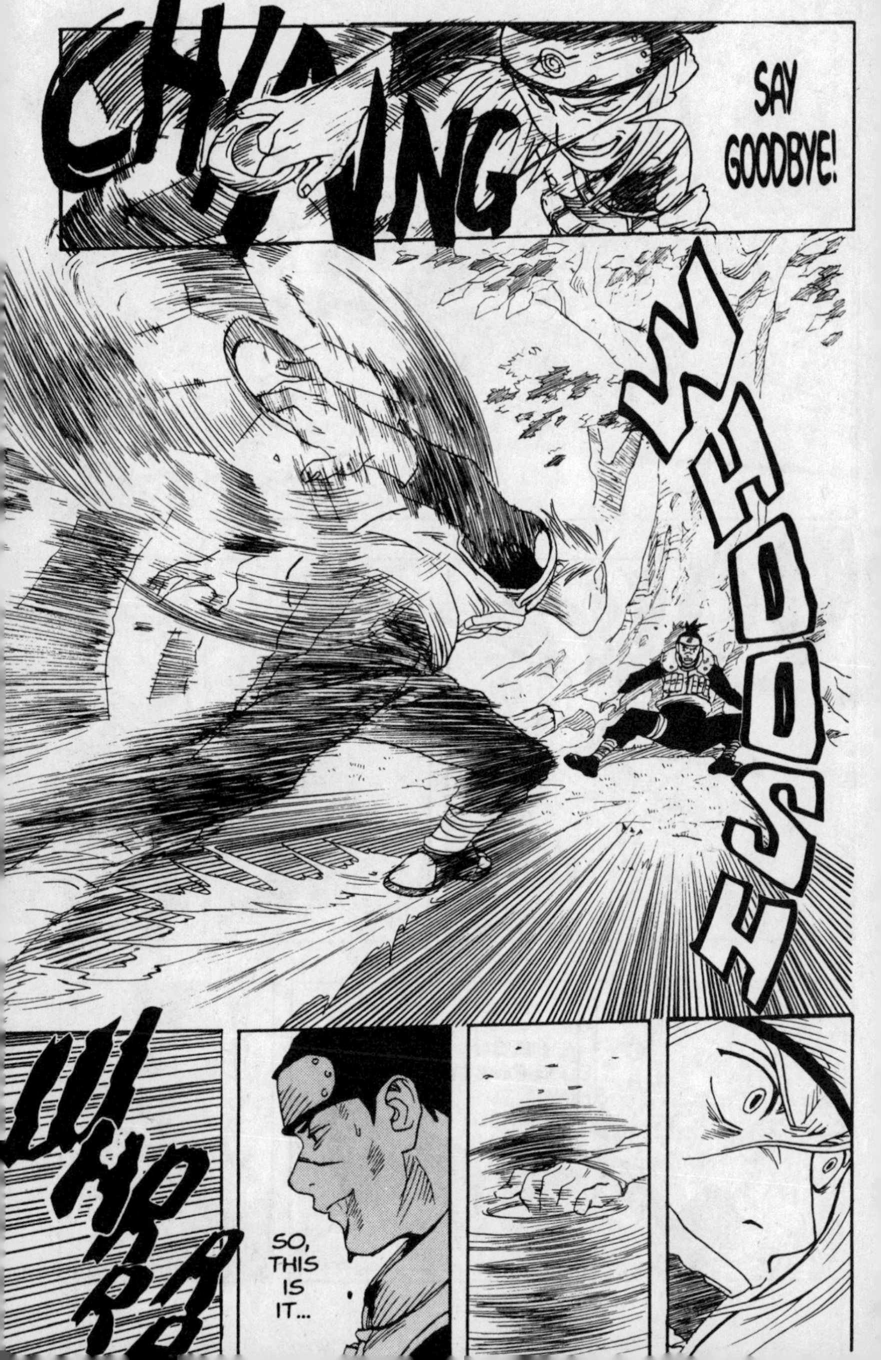
SAY GOODBYE!
CHING
WHOOSH
SO, THIS IS IT...

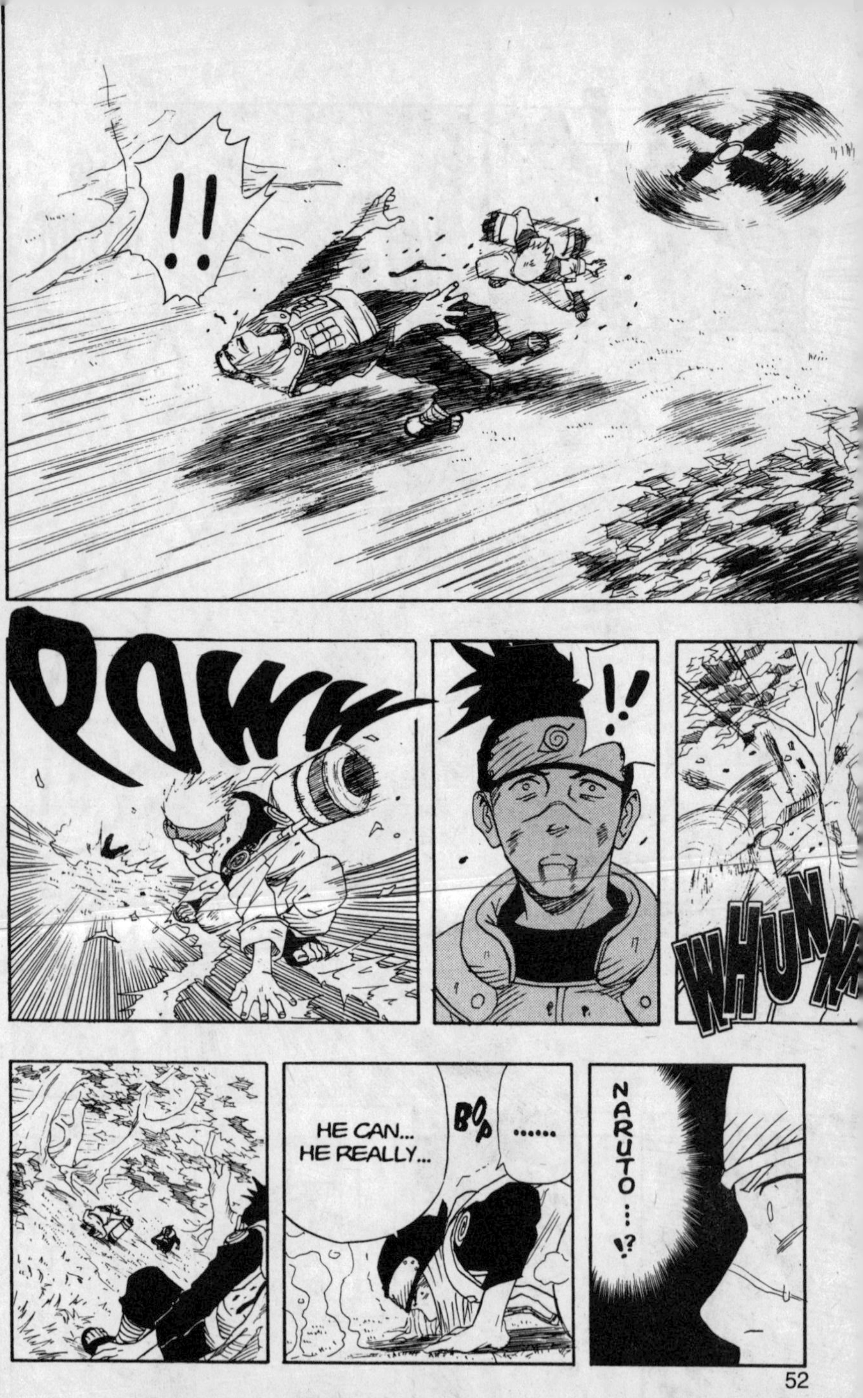
!!
WHUNK
!!
POWW
NARUTO...!?
......
BOP
HE CAN... HE REALLY...

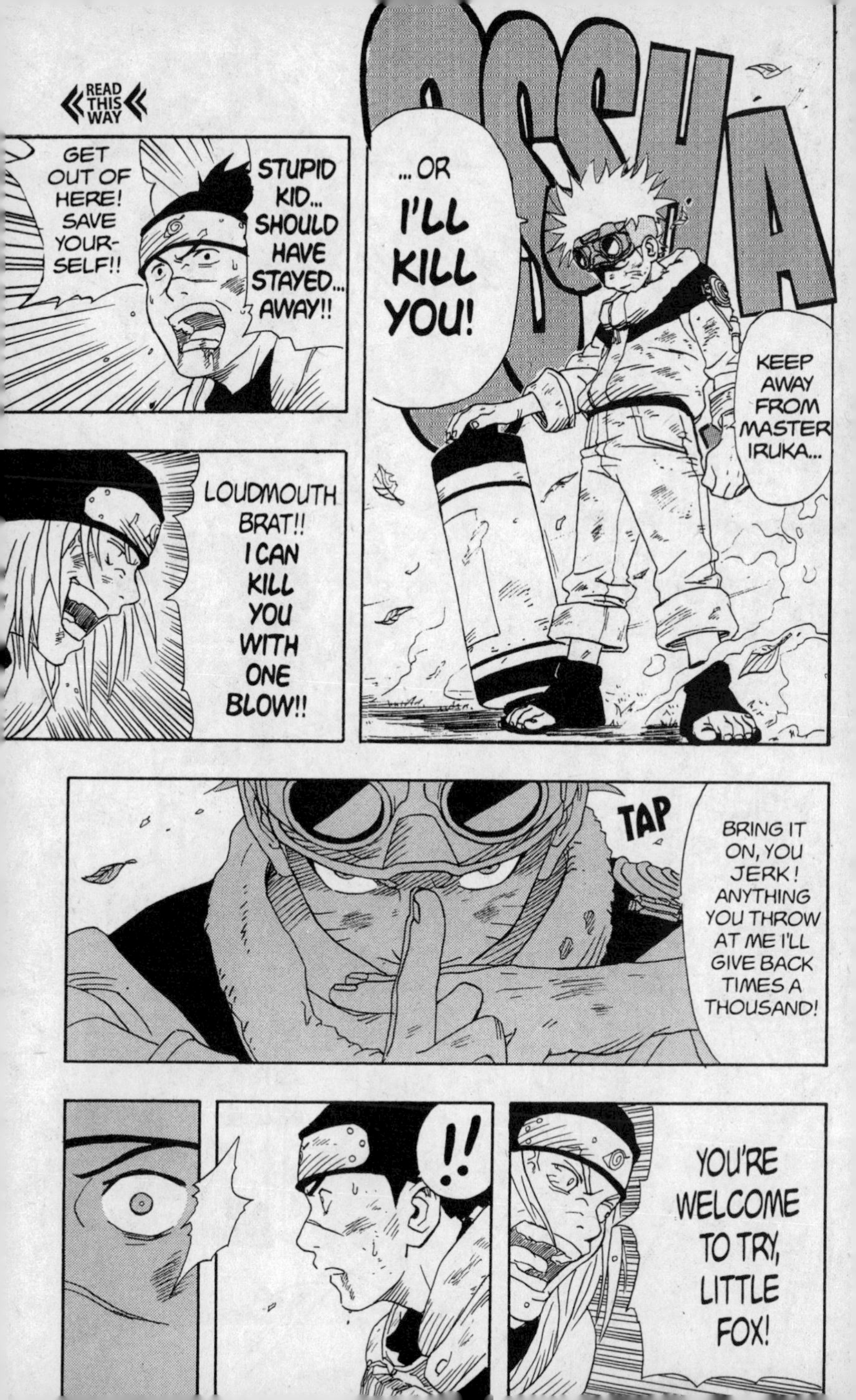
READ THIS WAY
KEEP AWAY FROM MASTER IRUKA...
...OR I'LL KILL YOU!
STUPID KID... SHOULD HAVE STAYED... AWAY!!
GET OUT OF HERE! SAVE YOURSELF!!
LOUDMOUTH BRAT!! I CAN KILL YOU WITH ONE BLOW!!
BRING IT ON, YOU JERK! ANYTHING YOU THROW AT ME I'LL GIVE BACK TIMES A THOUSAND!
TAP
YOU'RE WELCOME TO TRY, LITTLE FOX!
!!

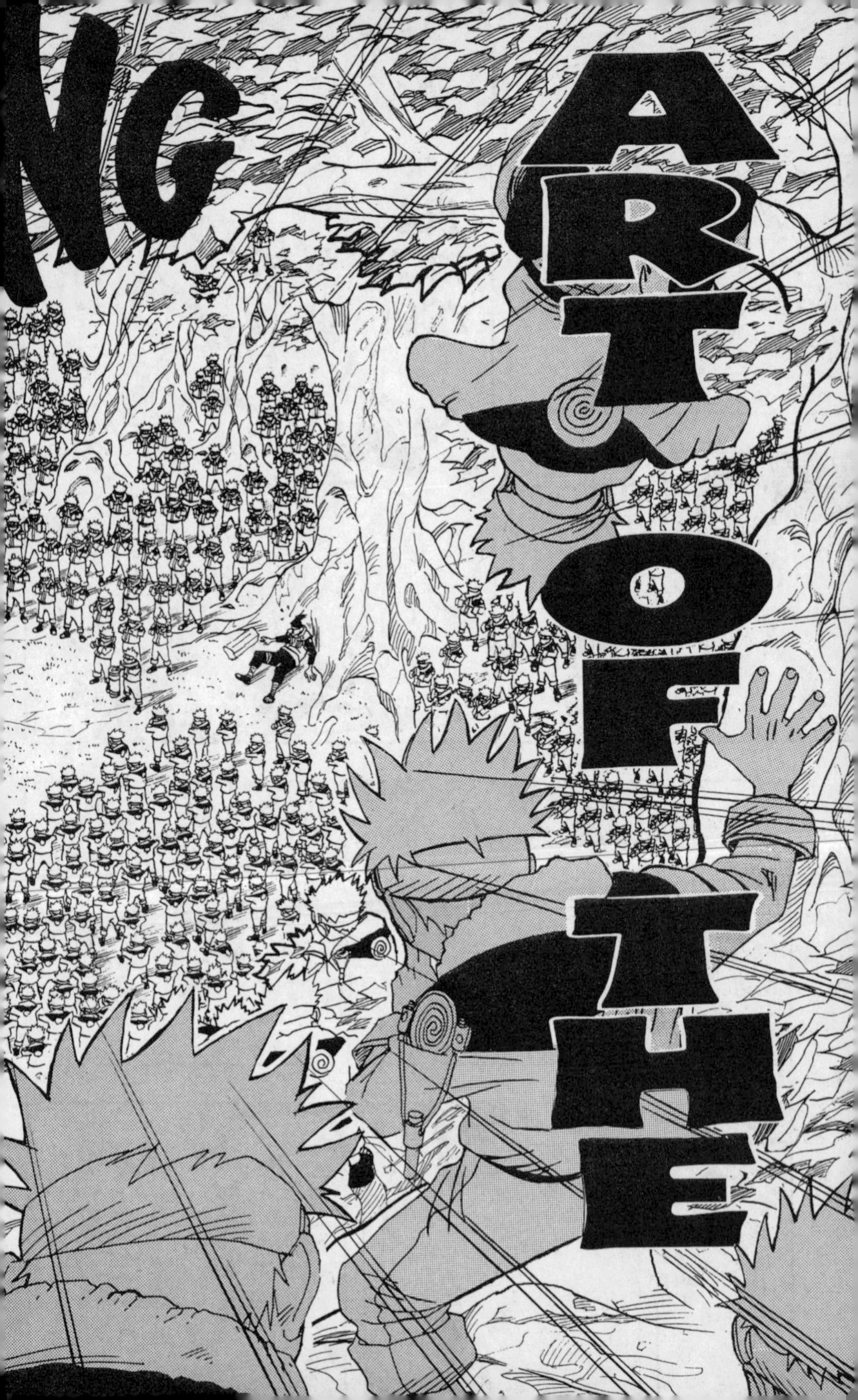
NG
ARTOFTHE

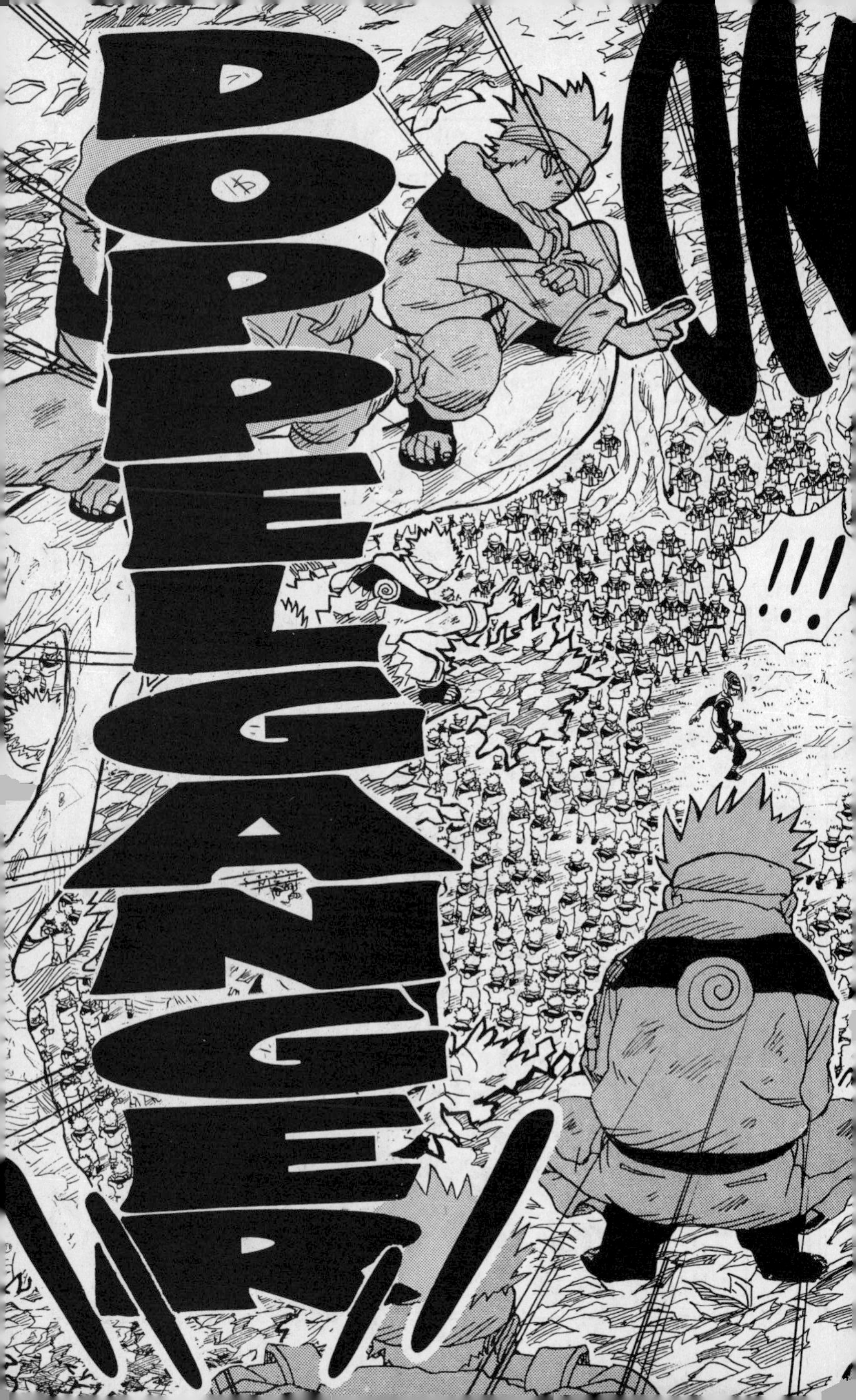
!!!
DOPPELGANGER!!

READ THIS WAY

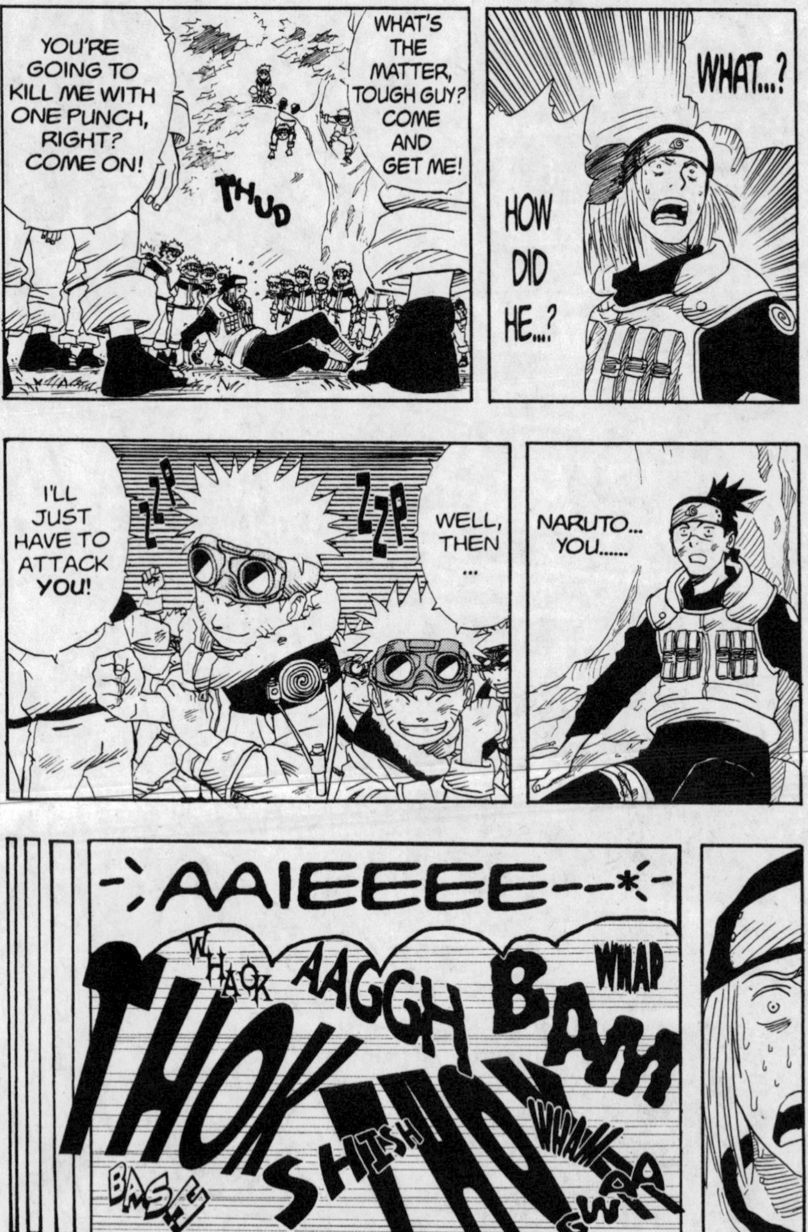
WHAT...?
HOW DID HE...?
WHAT'S THE MATTER, TOUGH GUY? COME AND GET ME!
YOU'RE GOING TO KILL ME WITH ONE PUNCH, RIGHT? COME ON!
THUD
NARUTO... YOU......
ZZP
WELL, THEN ...
ZZP
I'LL JUST HAVE TO ATTACK YOU!
AAIEEEE---*
WHAP
BAM
AAGGH
WHACK
THOK
SHISH
BASH

READ THIS WAY

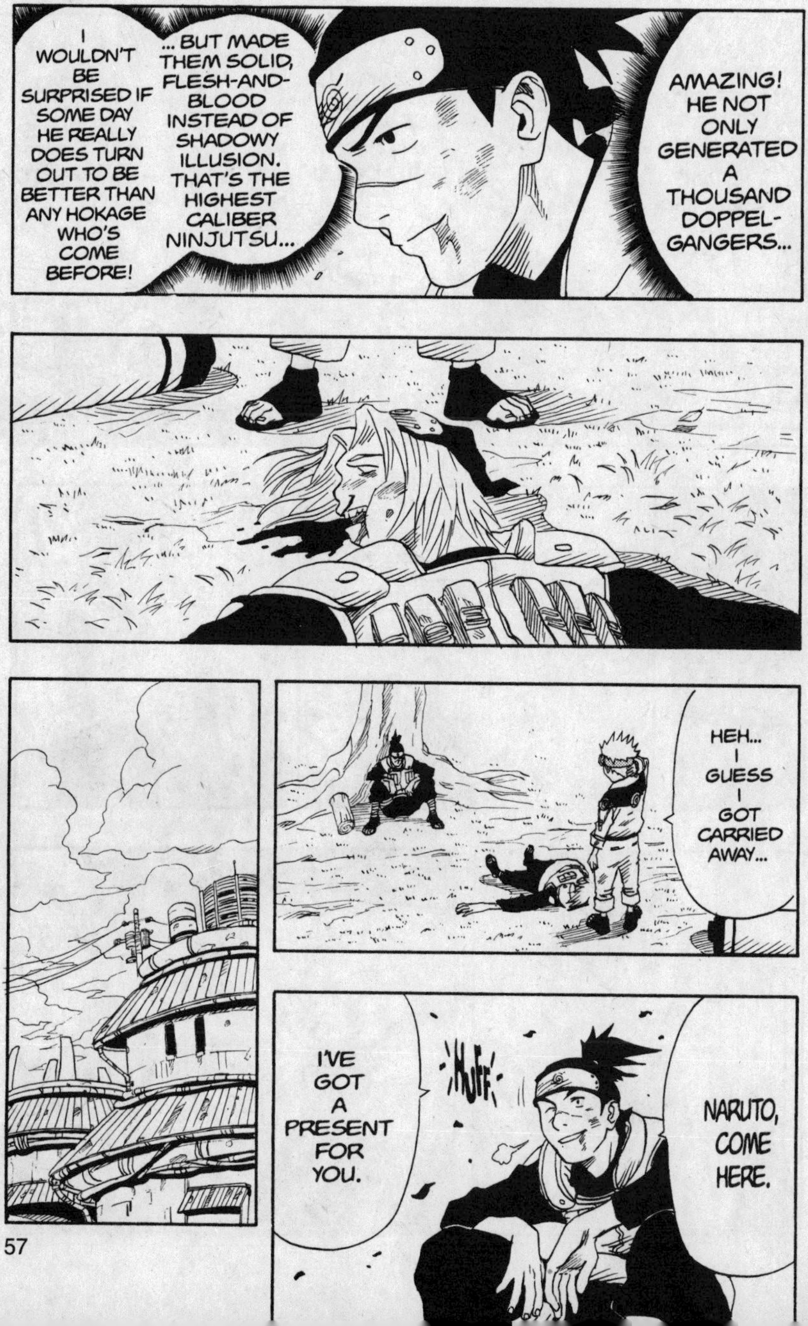
AMAZING! HE NOT ONLY GENERATED A THOUSAND DOPPEL-GANGERS...
... BUT MADE THEM SOLID, FLESH-AND-BLOOD INSTEAD OF SHADOWY ILLUSION. THAT'S THE HIGHEST CALIBER NINJUTSU...
I WOULDN'T BE SURPRISED IF SOME DAY HE REALLY DOES TURN OUT TO BE BETTER THAN ANY HOKAGE WHO'S COME BEFORE!
HEH... I GUESS I GOT CARRIED AWAY...
NARUTO, COME HERE.
HUFF
I'VE GOT A PRESENT FOR YOU.

READ THIS WAY

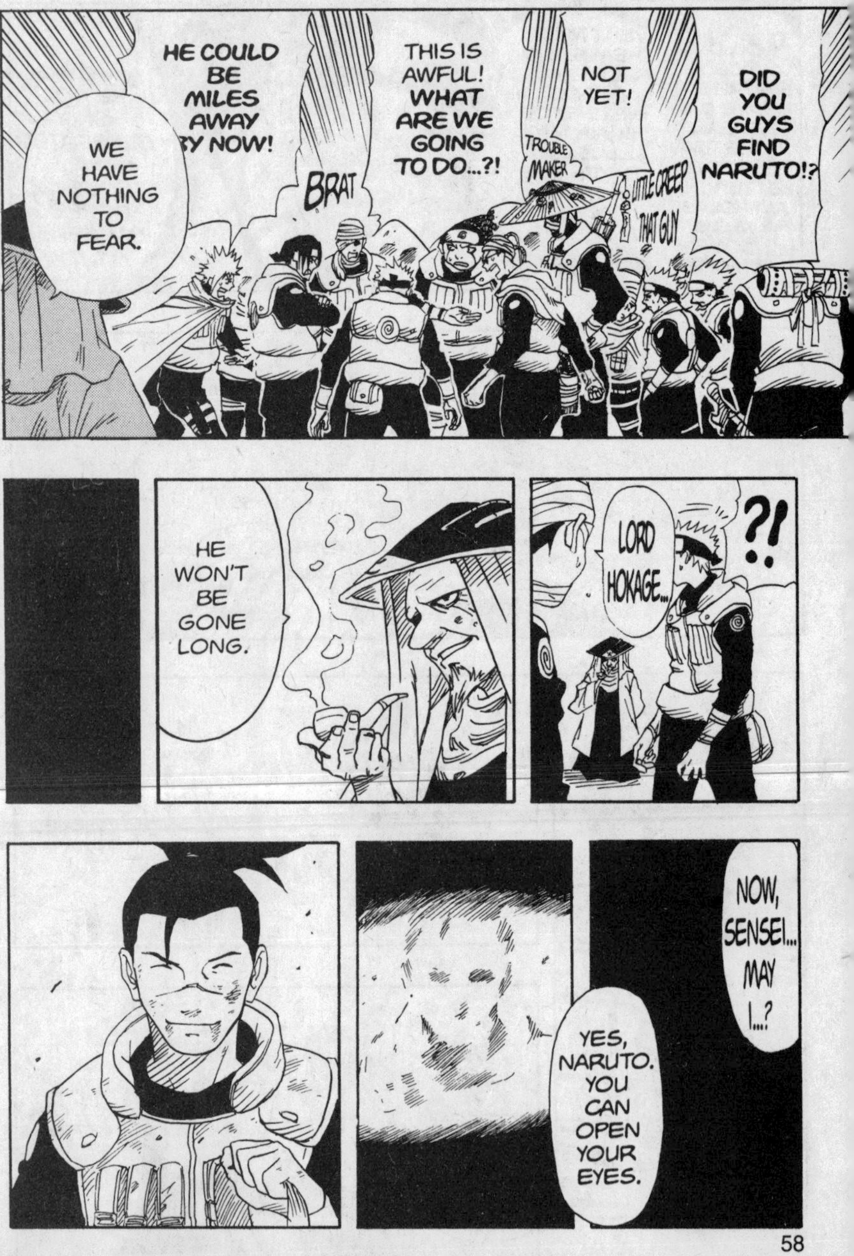
DID YOU GUYS FIND NARUTO!?
LITTLE CREEP
THAT GUY
NOT YET!
TROUBLE MAKER
THIS IS AWFUL! WHAT ARE WE GOING TO DO...?!
BRAT
HE COULD BE MILES AWAY BY NOW!
WE HAVE NOTHING TO FEAR.
?!
LORD HOKAGE...
HE WON'T BE GONE LONG.
NOW, SENSEI... MAY I...?
YES, NARUTO. YOU CAN OPEN YOUR EYES.

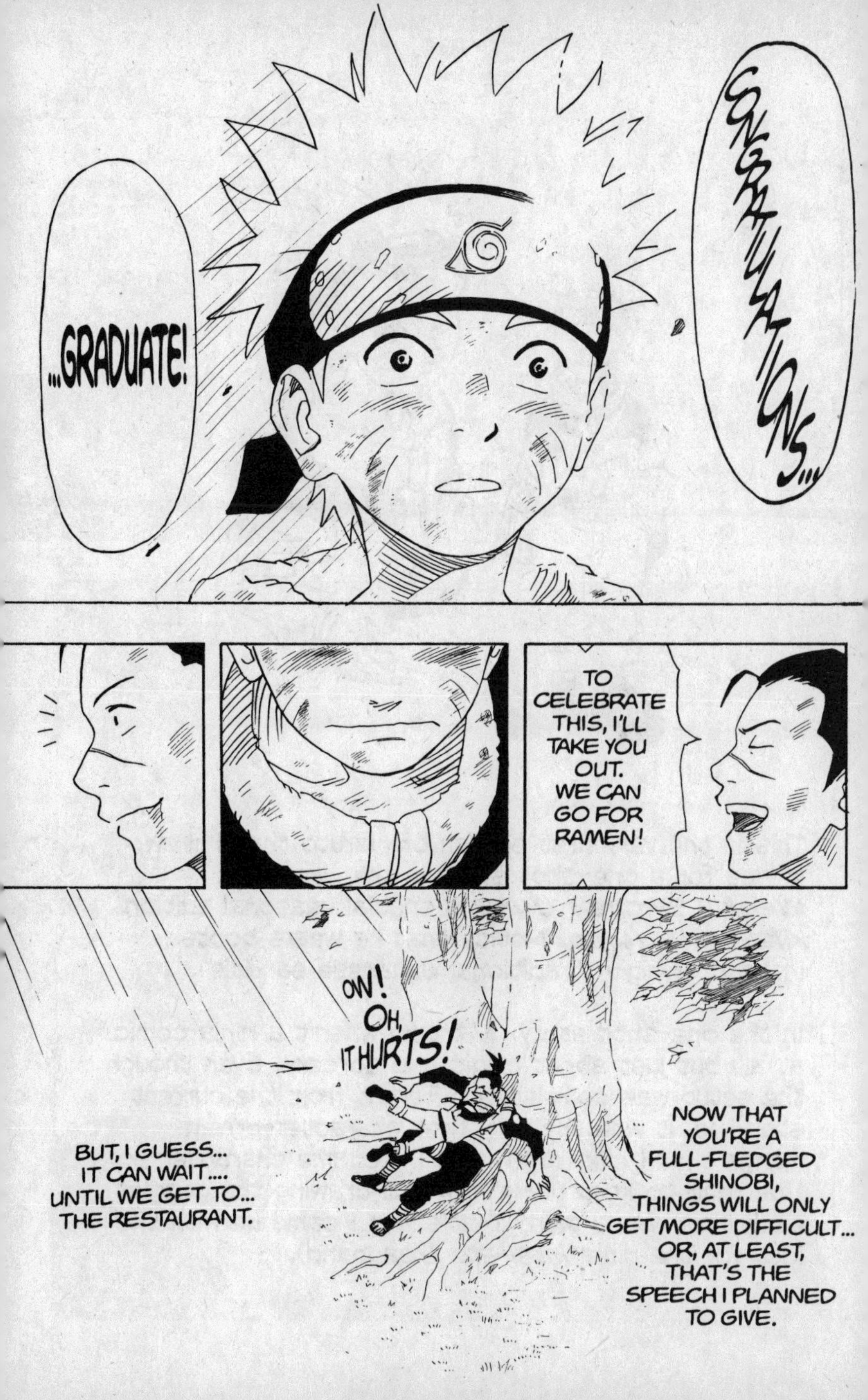
CONGRATULATIONS...
...GRADUATE!
TO CELEBRATE THIS, I'LL TAKE YOU OUT. WE CAN GO FOR RAMEN!
NOW THAT YOU'RE A FULL-FLEDGED SHINOBI, THINGS WILL ONLY GET MORE DIFFICULT... OR, AT LEAST, THAT'S THE SPEECH I PLANNED TO GIVE.
OW! OH, IT HURTS!
BUT, I GUESS... IT CAN WAIT.... UNTIL WE GET TO... THE RESTAURANT.

This is the very first sketch of Naruto that I drew.
It was for a one-shot story in the Japanese
Weekly Shonen Jump's special seasonal edition,
Akamaru Jump. Notice that he wears boots
instead of *zori* (traditional Japanese sandals).

In the one-shot story, *Naruto* wasn't a ninja comic
at all, but just about magic and sorcery. Even though
the setup was completely different from the current
storyline, it was the very first character-driven
manga that I ever drew, and I liked the character so
I decided to keep using him. But drawing the goggles
each time was a pain! That's why I came up with the
idea for the ninja *hitai-ate* (headband).

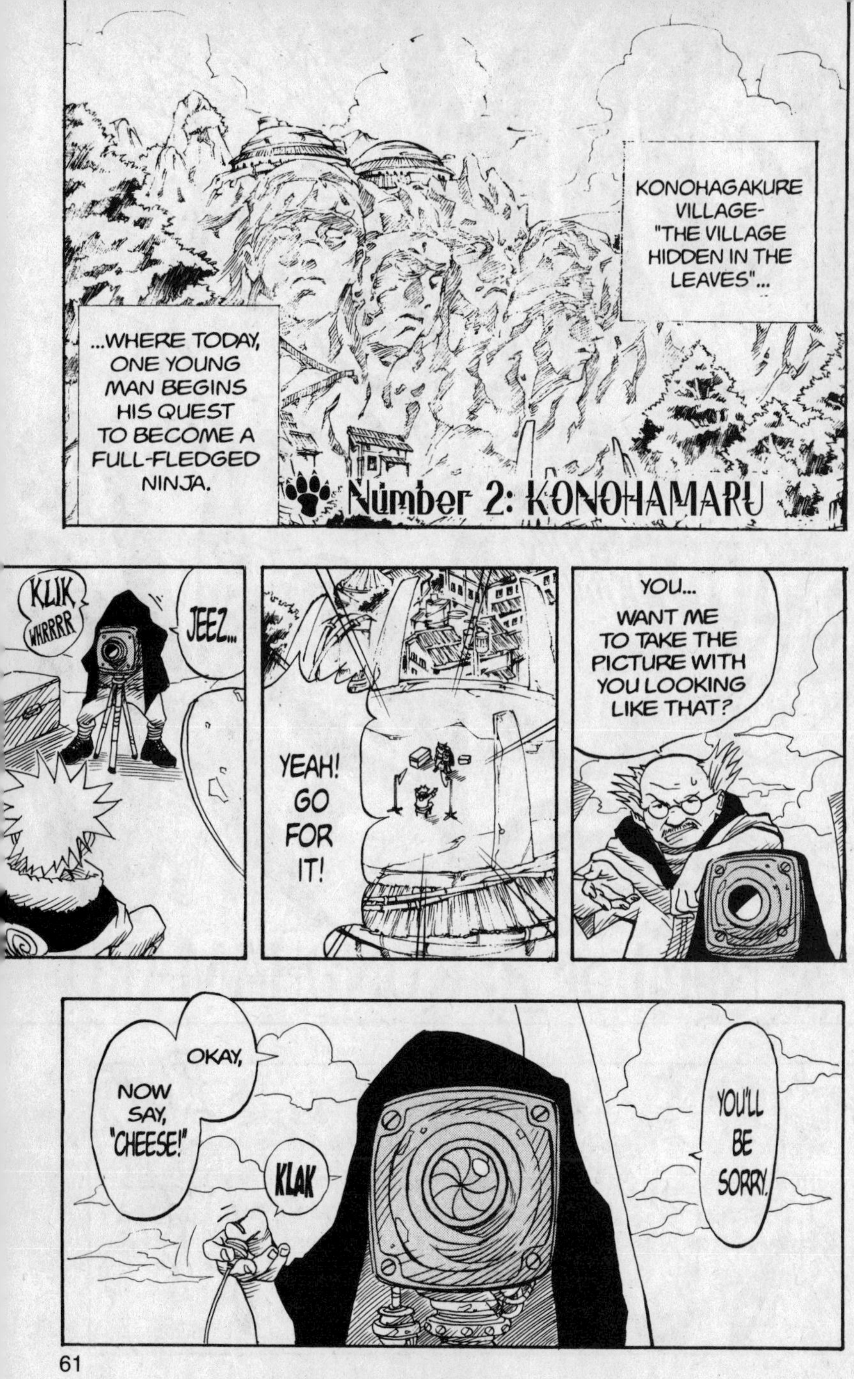

KONOHAGAKURE VILLAGE- "THE VILLAGE HIDDEN IN THE LEAVES"...
...WHERE TODAY, ONE YOUNG MAN BEGINS HIS QUEST TO BECOME A FULL-FLEDGED NINJA.
Number 2: KONOHAMARU
YOU... WANT ME TO TAKE THE PICTURE WITH YOU LOOKING LIKE THAT?
YEAH! GO FOR IT!
JEEZ...
KLIK WHRRRR
YOU'LL BE SORRY.
OKAY, NOW SAY, "CHEESE!"
KLAK

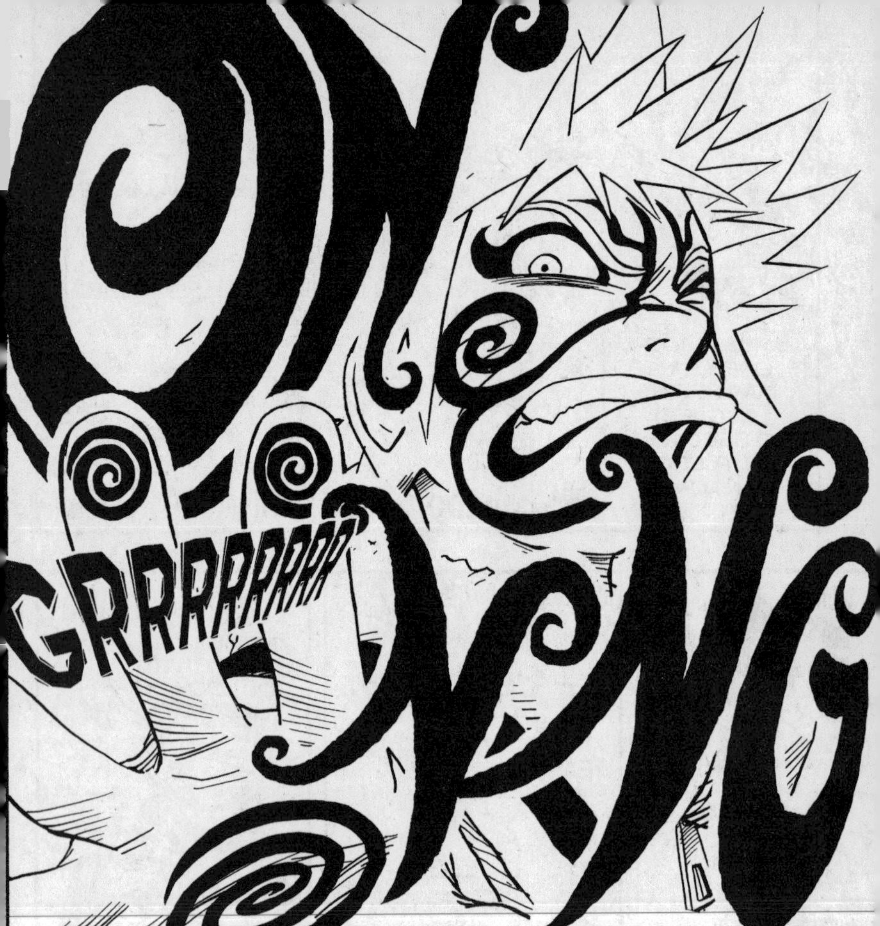
GRRRRRRRR

Number 2: KONOHAMARU

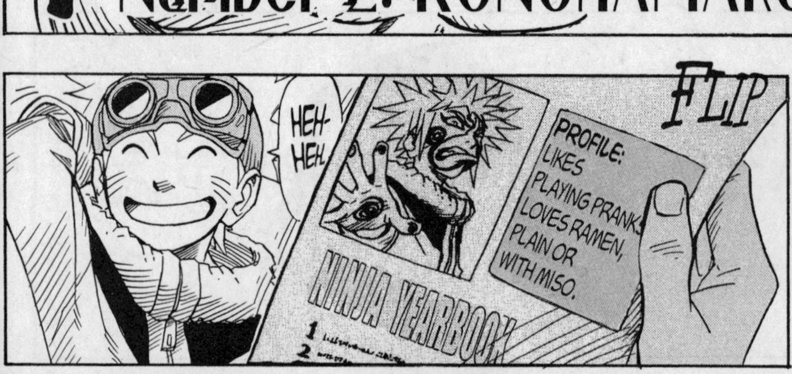
FLIP
PROFILE: LIKES PLAYING PRANKS LOVES RAMEN, PLAIN OR WITH MISO.
NINJA YEARBOOK
HEH-HEH

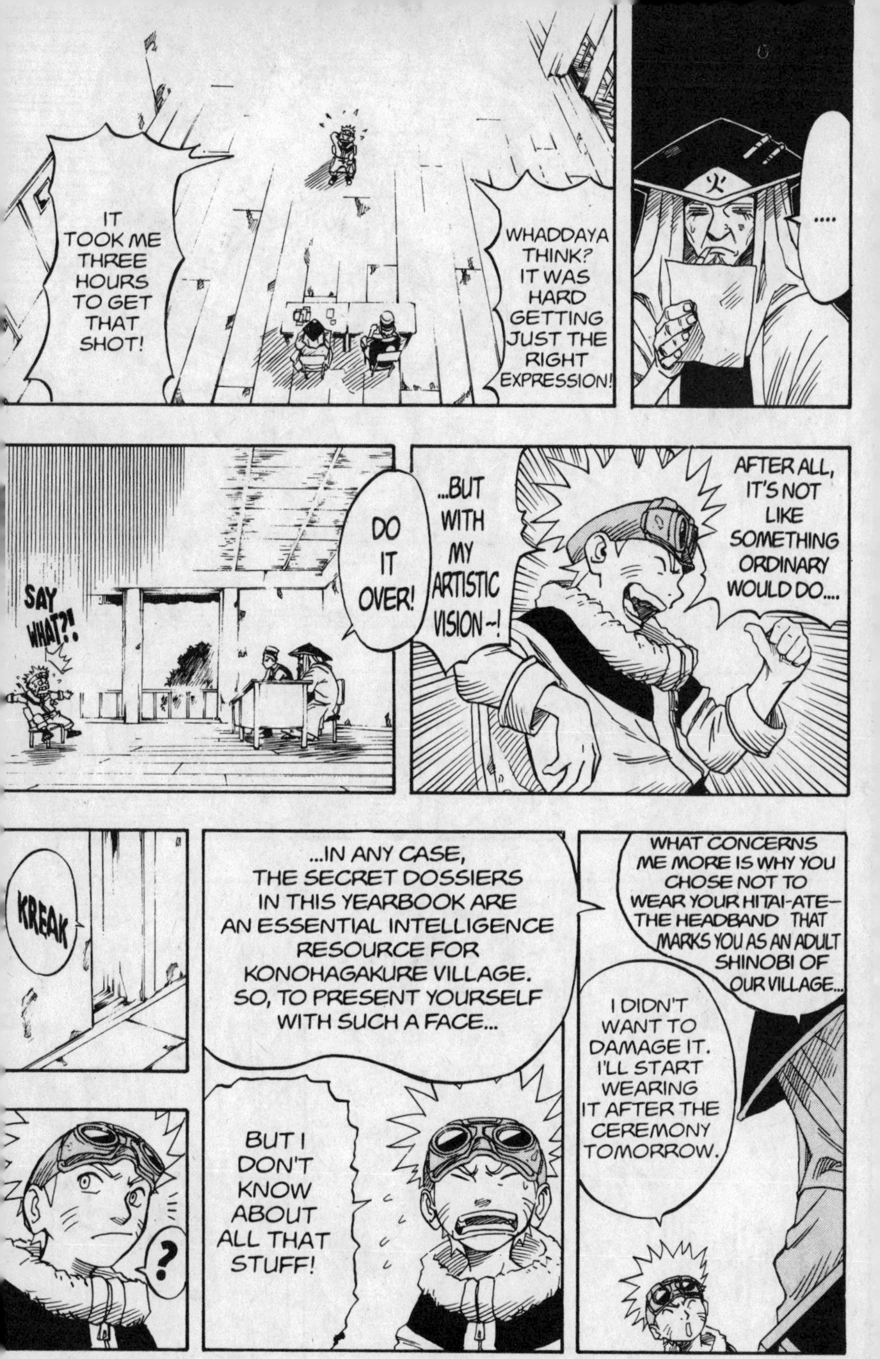
....
WHADDAYA THINK? IT WAS HARD GETTING JUST THE RIGHT EXPRESSION!
IT TOOK ME THREE HOURS TO GET THAT SHOT!
AFTER ALL, IT'S NOT LIKE SOMETHING ORDINARY WOULD DO....
...BUT WITH MY ARTISTIC VISION~!
DO IT OVER!
SAY WHAT?!
WHAT CONCERNS ME MORE IS WHY YOU CHOSE NOT TO WEAR YOUR HITAI-ATE— THE HEADBAND THAT MARKS YOU AS AN ADULT SHINOBI OF OUR VILLAGE...
I DIDN'T WANT TO DAMAGE IT. I'LL START WEARING IT AFTER THE CEREMONY TOMORROW.
...IN ANY CASE, THE SECRET DOSSIERS IN THIS YEARBOOK ARE AN ESSENTIAL INTELLIGENCE RESOURCE FOR KONOHAGAKURE VILLAGE. SO, TO PRESENT YOURSELF WITH SUCH A FACE...
BUT I DON'T KNOW ABOUT ALL THAT STUFF!
KREAK
?

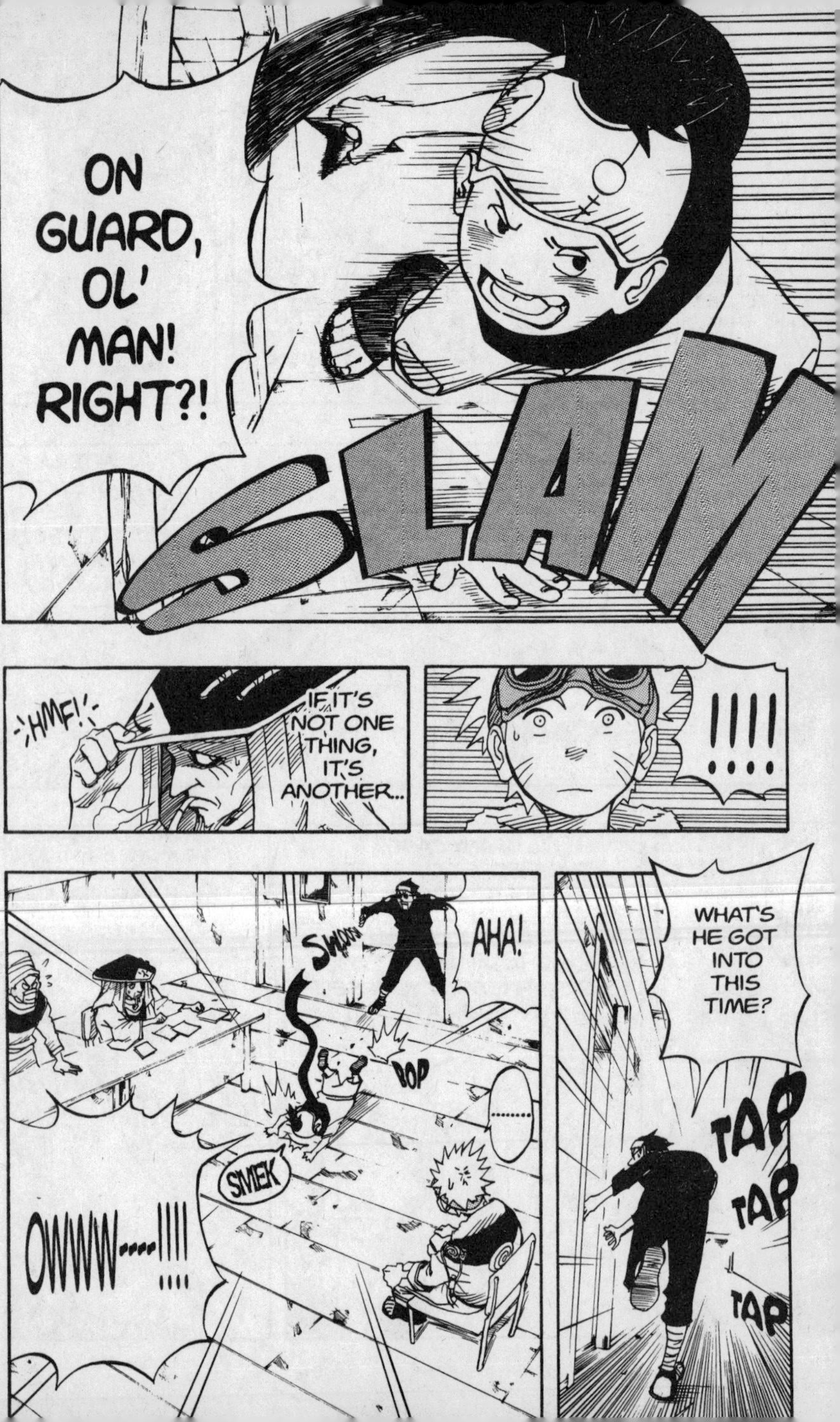
ON GUARD, OL' MAN! RIGHT?!
SLAM
!!!!
HMF!
IF IT'S NOT ONE THING, IT'S ANOTHER...
WHAT'S HE GOT INTO THIS TIME?
TAP
TAP
TAP
AHA!
BOP
......
SMEK
OWWW----!!!!

READ THIS WAY

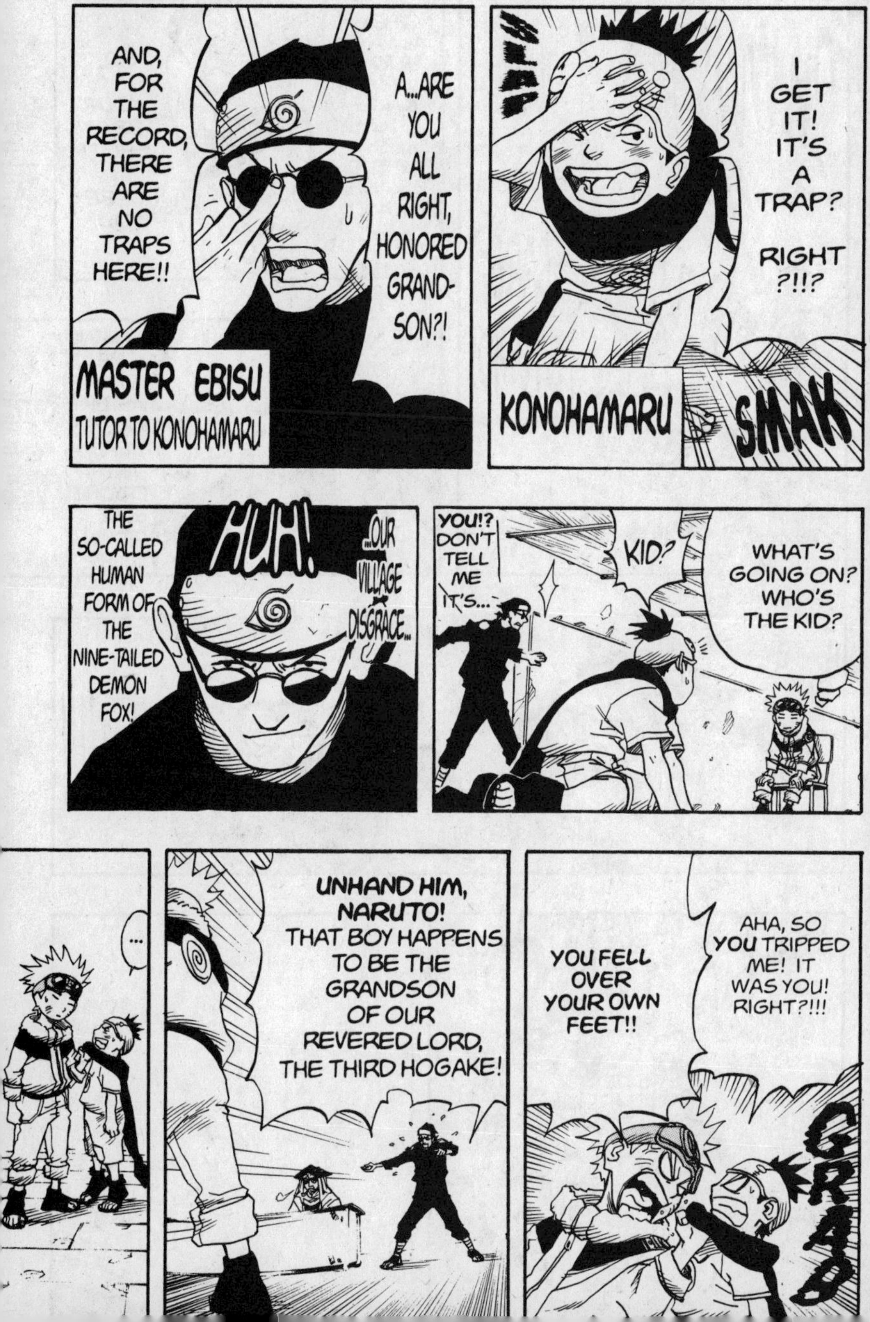
SLAP
I GET IT! IT'S A TRAP? RIGHT?!!?
KONOHAMARU
SMAK
A...ARE YOU ALL RIGHT, HONORED GRANDSON?!
AND, FOR THE RECORD, THERE ARE NO TRAPS HERE!!
MASTER EBISU TUTOR TO KONOHAMARU
WHAT'S GOING ON? WHO'S THE KID?
KID?
YOU!? DON'T TELL ME IT'S...
HUH!
...OUR VILLAGE DISGRACE...
THE SO-CALLED HUMAN FORM OF THE NINE-TAILED DEMON FOX!
AHA, SO YOU TRIPPED ME! IT WAS YOU! RIGHT?!!!
YOU FELL OVER YOUR OWN FEET!!
GRAB
UNHAND HIM, NARUTO! THAT BOY HAPPENS TO BE THE GRANDSON OF OUR REVERED LORD, THE THIRD HOGAKE!
...

READ THIS WAY

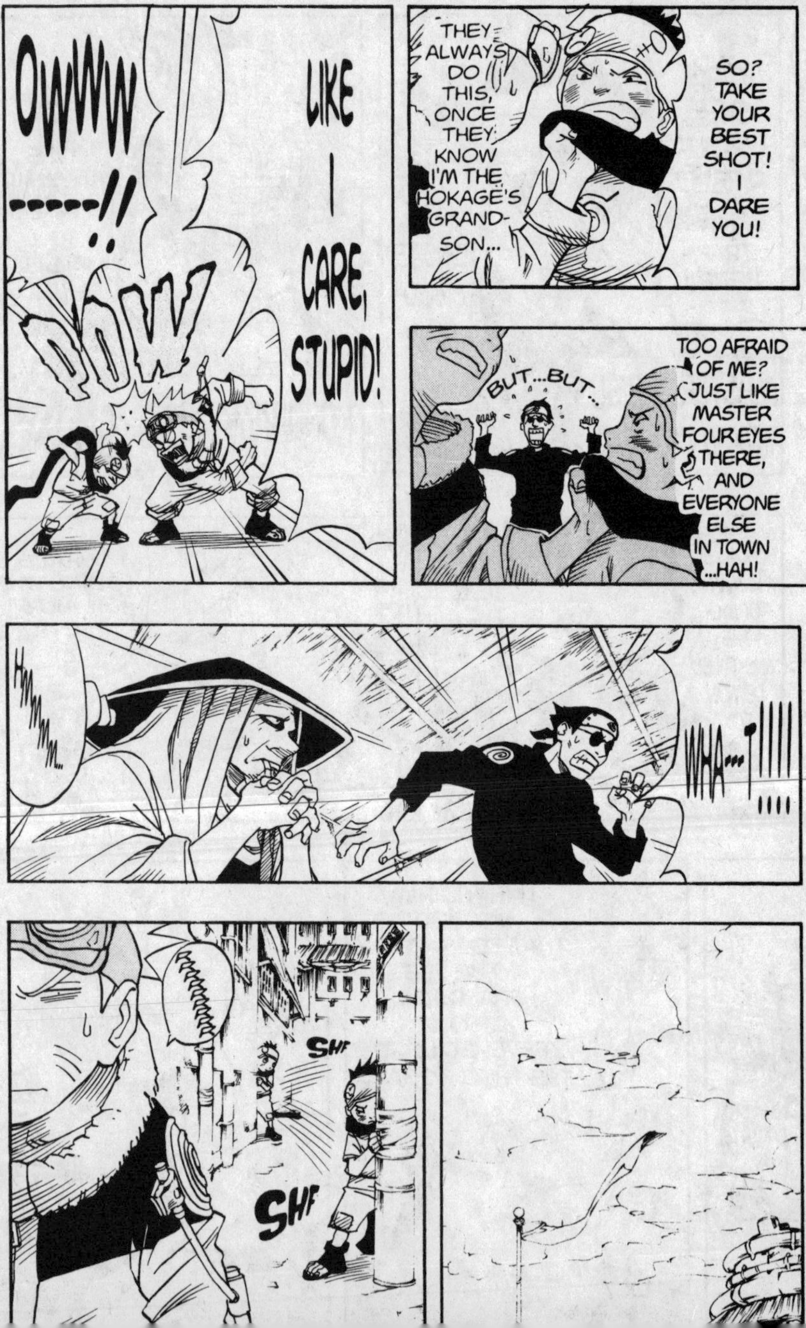
SO? TAKE YOUR BEST SHOT! I DARE YOU!
THEY ALWAYS DO THIS, ONCE THEY KNOW I'M THE HOKAGE'S GRANDSON...
TOO AFRAID OF ME? JUST LIKE MASTER FOUR EYES THERE, AND EVERYONE ELSE IN TOWN ...HAH!
BUT...BUT...
LIKE I CARE, STUPID!
OWWW------!!
POW
WHA...T!!!!!
HMMM...
SHF
SHF

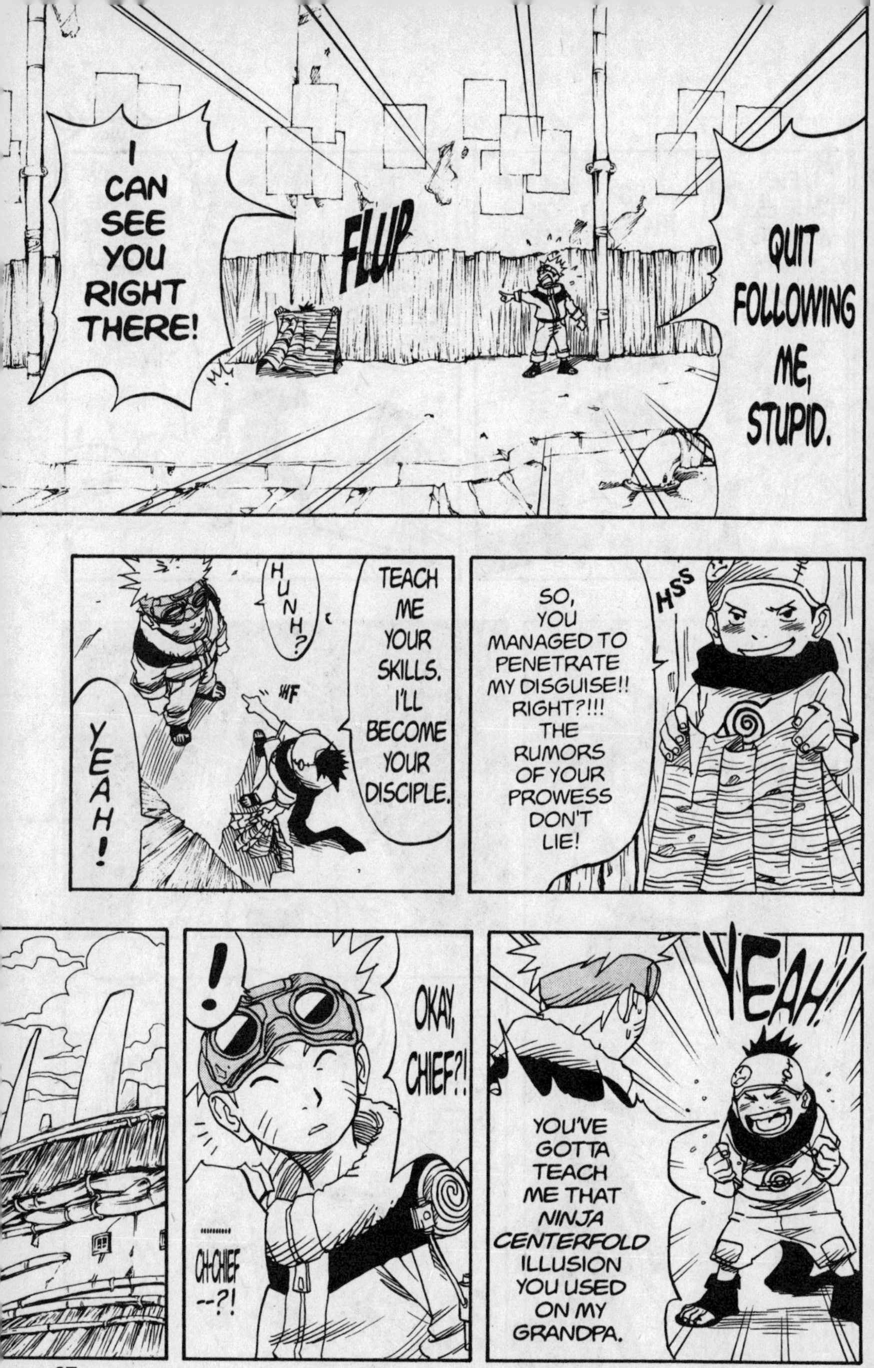
QUIT FOLLOWING ME, STUPID.
FLUP
I CAN SEE YOU RIGHT THERE!
HSS
SO, YOU MANAGED TO PENETRATE MY DISGUISE!! RIGHT?!!! THE RUMORS OF YOUR PROWESS DON'T LIE!
TEACH ME YOUR SKILLS. I'LL BECOME YOUR DISCIPLE.
HUNH?
SHF
YEAH!
YEAH!
YOU'VE GOTTA TEACH ME THAT *NINJA CENTERFOLD* ILLUSION YOU USED ON MY GRANDPA.
OKAY, CHIEF?!
!
....
CH-CHIEF --?!

READ THIS WAY

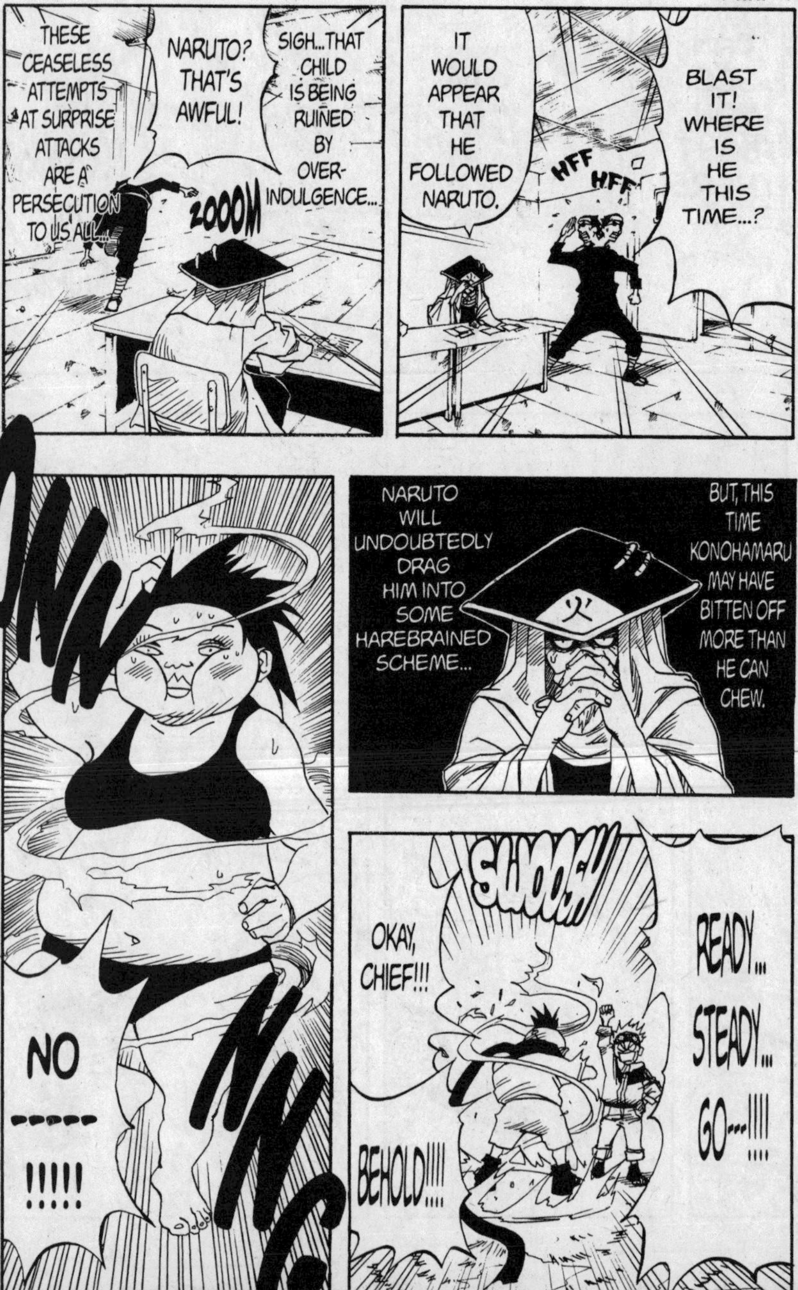

BLAST IT! WHERE IS HE THIS TIME...?
HFF HFF
IT WOULD APPEAR THAT HE FOLLOWED NARUTO.
SIGH...THAT CHILD IS BEING RUINED BY OVER-INDULGENCE...
NARUTO? THAT'S AWFUL!
THESE CEASELESS ATTEMPTS AT SURPRISE ATTACKS ARE A PERSECUTION TO US ALL...
ZOOOM
NARUTO WILL UNDOUBTEDLY DRAG HIM INTO SOME HAREBRAINED SCHEME...
BUT, THIS TIME KONOHAMARU MAY HAVE BITTEN OFF MORE THAN HE CAN CHEW.
SWOOSH
READY... STEADY... GO---!!!!
OKAY, CHIEF!!!
BEHOLD!!!!
NO -----!!!!!!

READ THIS WAY

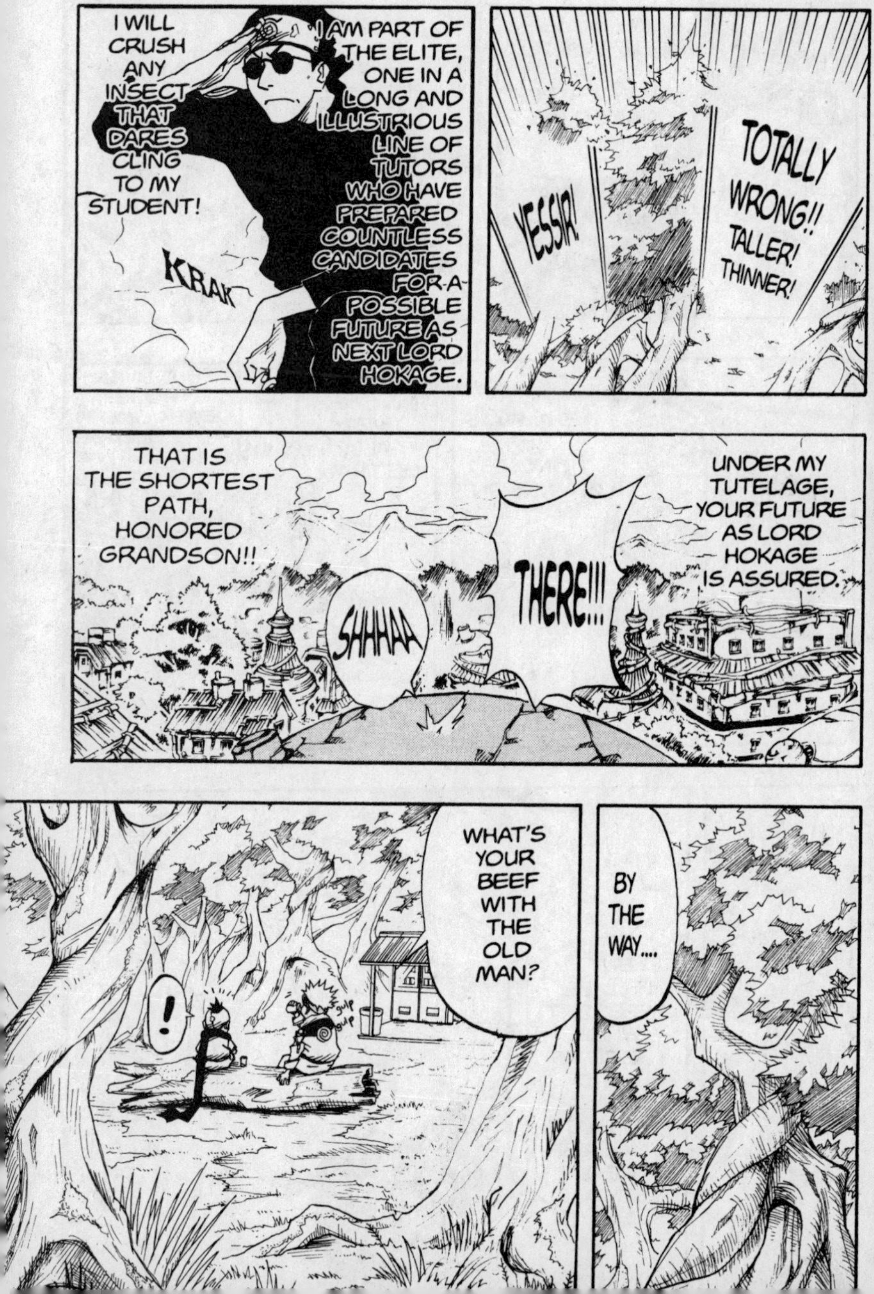
TOTALLY WRONG!! TALLER! THINNER!
YESSIR!
I AM PART OF THE ELITE, ONE IN A LONG AND ILLUSTRIOUS LINE OF TUTORS WHO HAVE PREPARED COUNTLESS CANDIDATES FOR A POSSIBLE FUTURE AS NEXT LORD HOKAGE.
I WILL CRUSH ANY INSECT THAT DARES CLING TO MY STUDENT!
KRAK
UNDER MY TUTELAGE, YOUR FUTURE AS LORD HOKAGE IS ASSURED.
THERE!!!
SHHHAA
THAT IS THE SHORTEST PATH, HONORED GRANDSON!!
BY THE WAY....
WHAT'S YOUR BEEF WITH THE OLD MAN?
!
gulp gulp

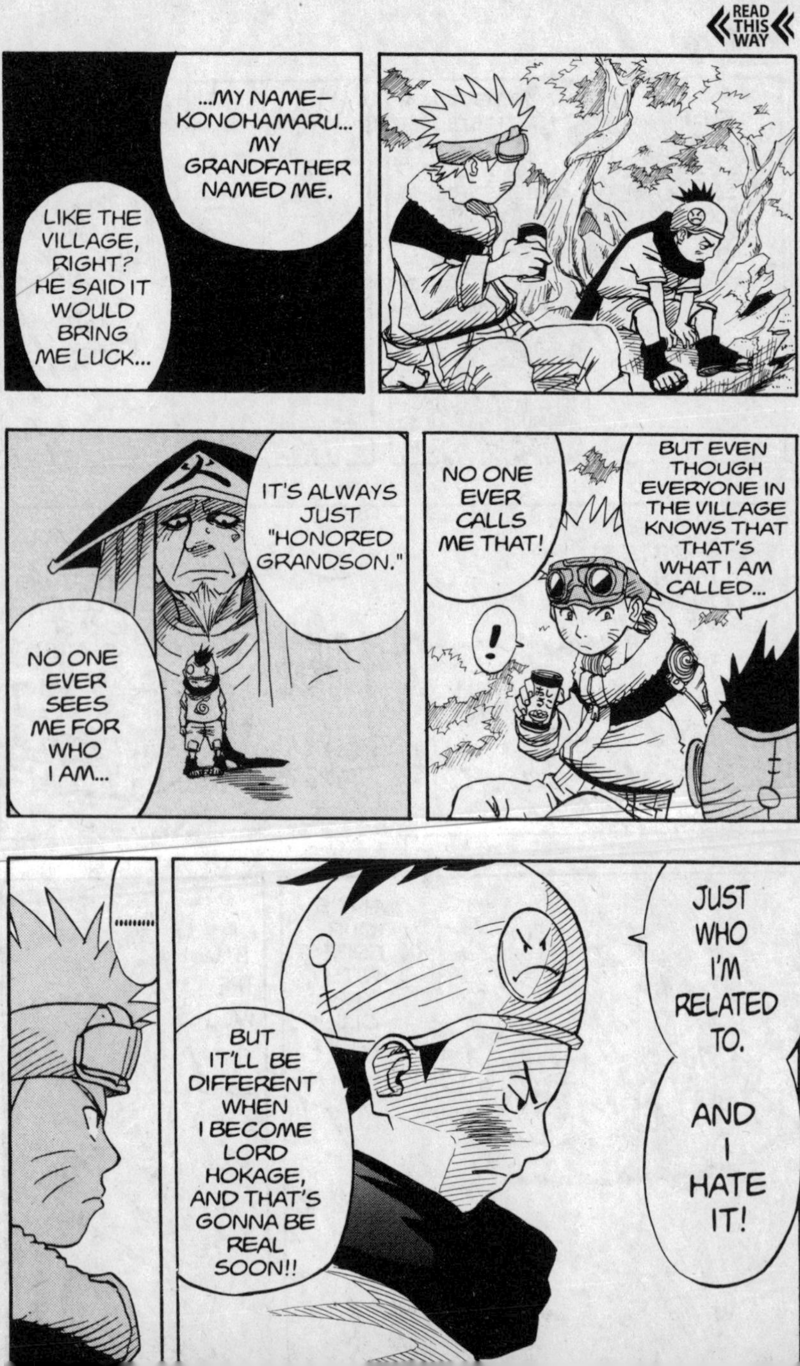
READ THIS WAY
...MY NAME—KONOHAMARU... MY GRANDFATHER NAMED ME.
LIKE THE VILLAGE, RIGHT? HE SAID IT WOULD BRING ME LUCK...
BUT EVEN THOUGH EVERYONE IN THE VILLAGE KNOWS THAT THAT'S WHAT I AM CALLED...
NO ONE EVER CALLS ME THAT!
!
IT'S ALWAYS JUST "HONORED GRANDSON."
NO ONE EVER SEES ME FOR WHO I AM...
JUST WHO I'M RELATED TO.
AND I HATE IT!
BUT IT'LL BE DIFFERENT WHEN I BECOME LORD HOKAGE, AND THAT'S GONNA BE REAL SOON!!
....

READ THIS WAY

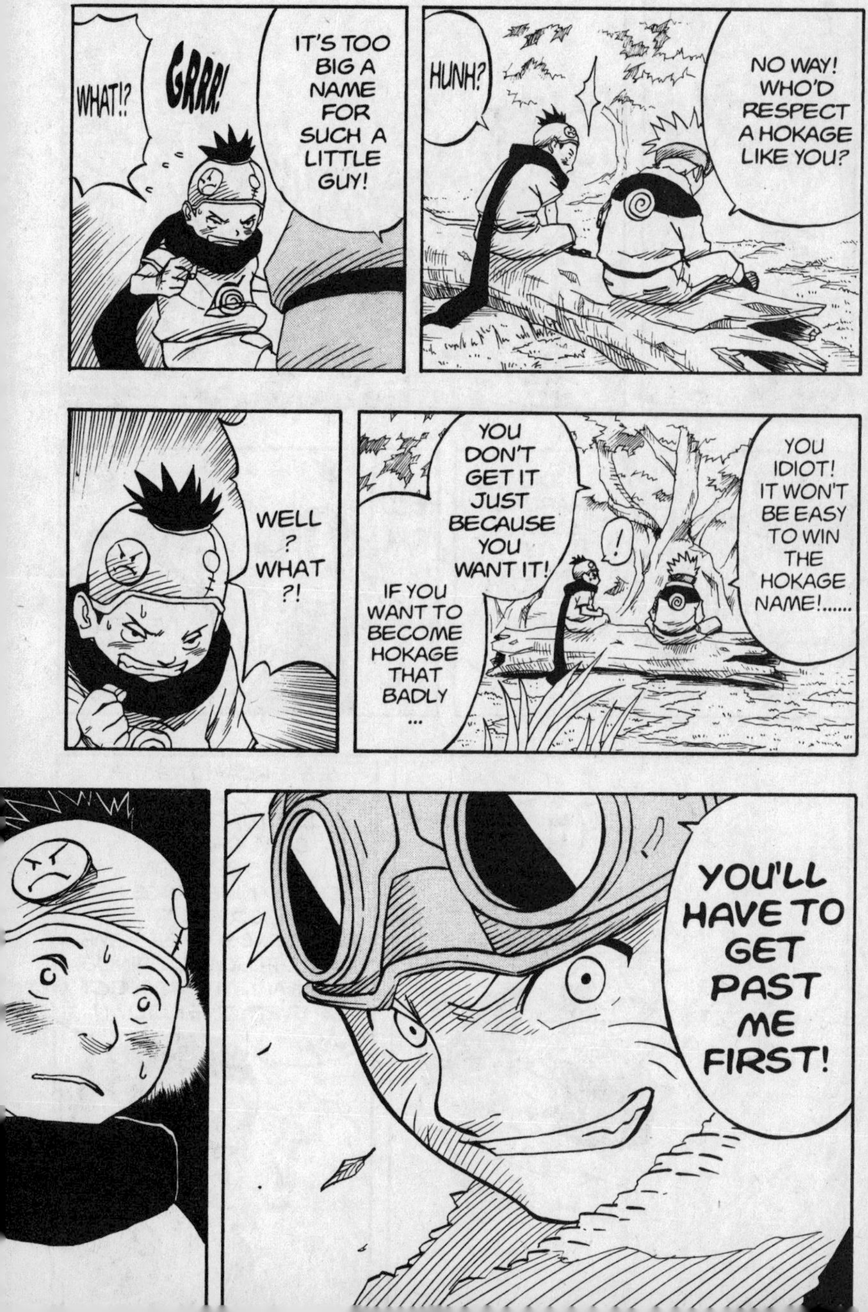
NO WAY! WHO'D RESPECT A HOKAGE LIKE YOU?
HUNH?
IT'S TOO BIG A NAME FOR SUCH A LITTLE GUY!
GRRR!
WHAT!?
YOU IDIOT! IT WON'T BE EASY TO WIN THE HOKAGE NAME!......
!
YOU DON'T GET IT JUST BECAUSE YOU WANT IT!
IF YOU WANT TO BECOME HOKAGE THAT BADLY ...
WELL? WHAT?!
YOU'LL HAVE TO GET PAST ME FIRST!

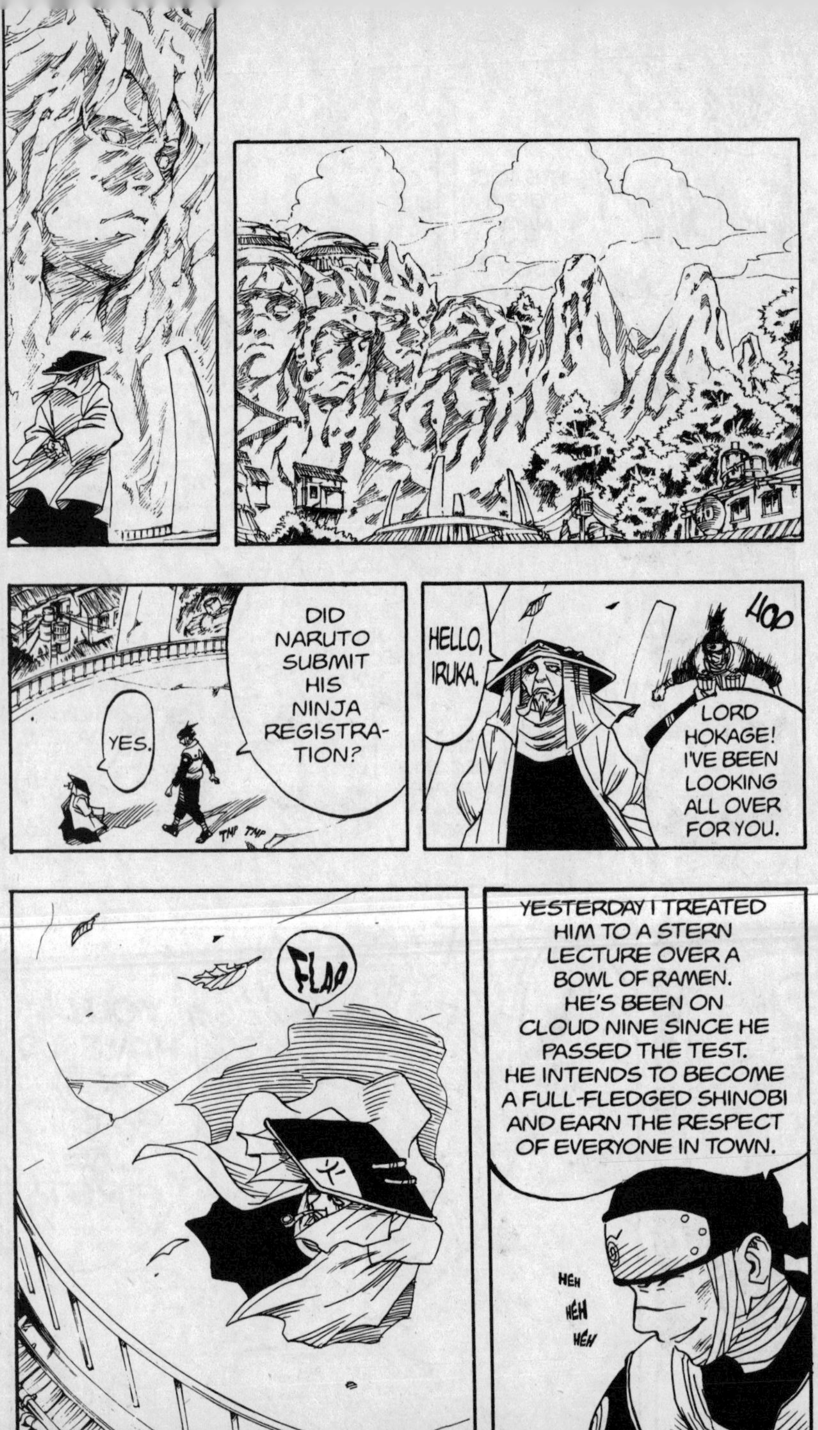
HOP
LORD HOKAGE! I'VE BEEN LOOKING ALL OVER FOR YOU.
HELLO, IRUKA.
DID NARUTO SUBMIT HIS NINJA REGISTRATION?
YES.
TMP TMP
YESTERDAY I TREATED HIM TO A STERN LECTURE OVER A BOWL OF RAMEN. HE'S BEEN ON CLOUD NINE SINCE HE PASSED THE TEST. HE INTENDS TO BECOME A FULL-FLEDGED SHINOBI AND EARN THE RESPECT OF EVERYONE IN TOWN.
HEH HEH HEH
FLAP

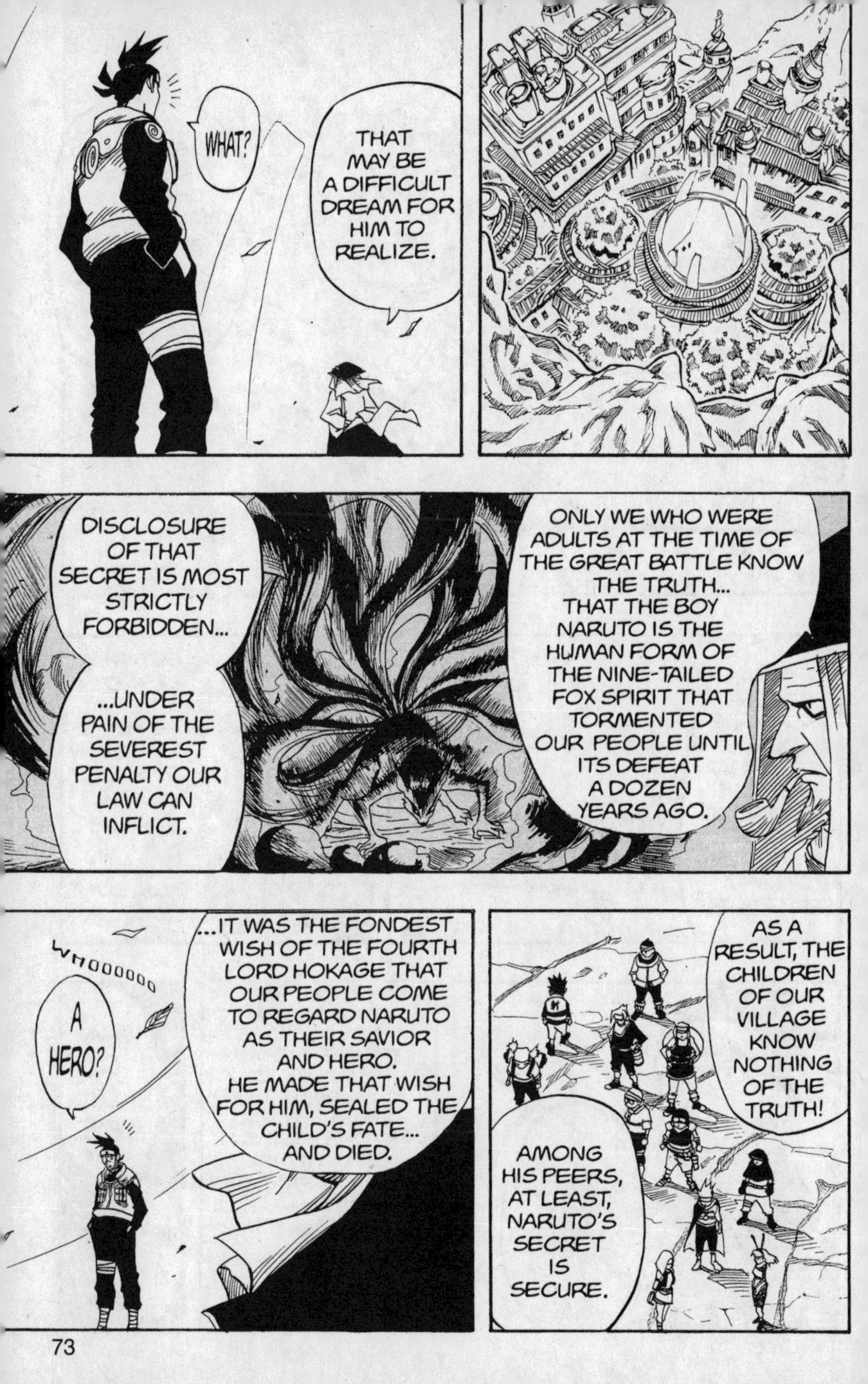
THAT MAY BE A DIFFICULT DREAM FOR HIM TO REALIZE.
WHAT?
ONLY WE WHO WERE ADULTS AT THE TIME OF THE GREAT BATTLE KNOW THE TRUTH... THAT THE BOY NARUTO IS THE HUMAN FORM OF THE NINE-TAILED FOX SPIRIT THAT TORMENTED OUR PEOPLE UNTIL ITS DEFEAT A DOZEN YEARS AGO.
DISCLOSURE OF THAT SECRET IS MOST STRICTLY FORBIDDEN...
...UNDER PAIN OF THE SEVEREST PENALTY OUR LAW CAN INFLICT.
AS A RESULT, THE CHILDREN OF OUR VILLAGE KNOW NOTHING OF THE TRUTH!
AMONG HIS PEERS, AT LEAST, NARUTO'S SECRET IS SECURE.
...IT WAS THE FONDEST WISH OF THE FOURTH LORD HOKAGE THAT OUR PEOPLE COME TO REGARD NARUTO AS THEIR SAVIOR AND HERO. HE MADE THAT WISH FOR HIM, SEALED THE CHILD'S FATE... AND DIED.
WHOOOOOOO
A HERO?

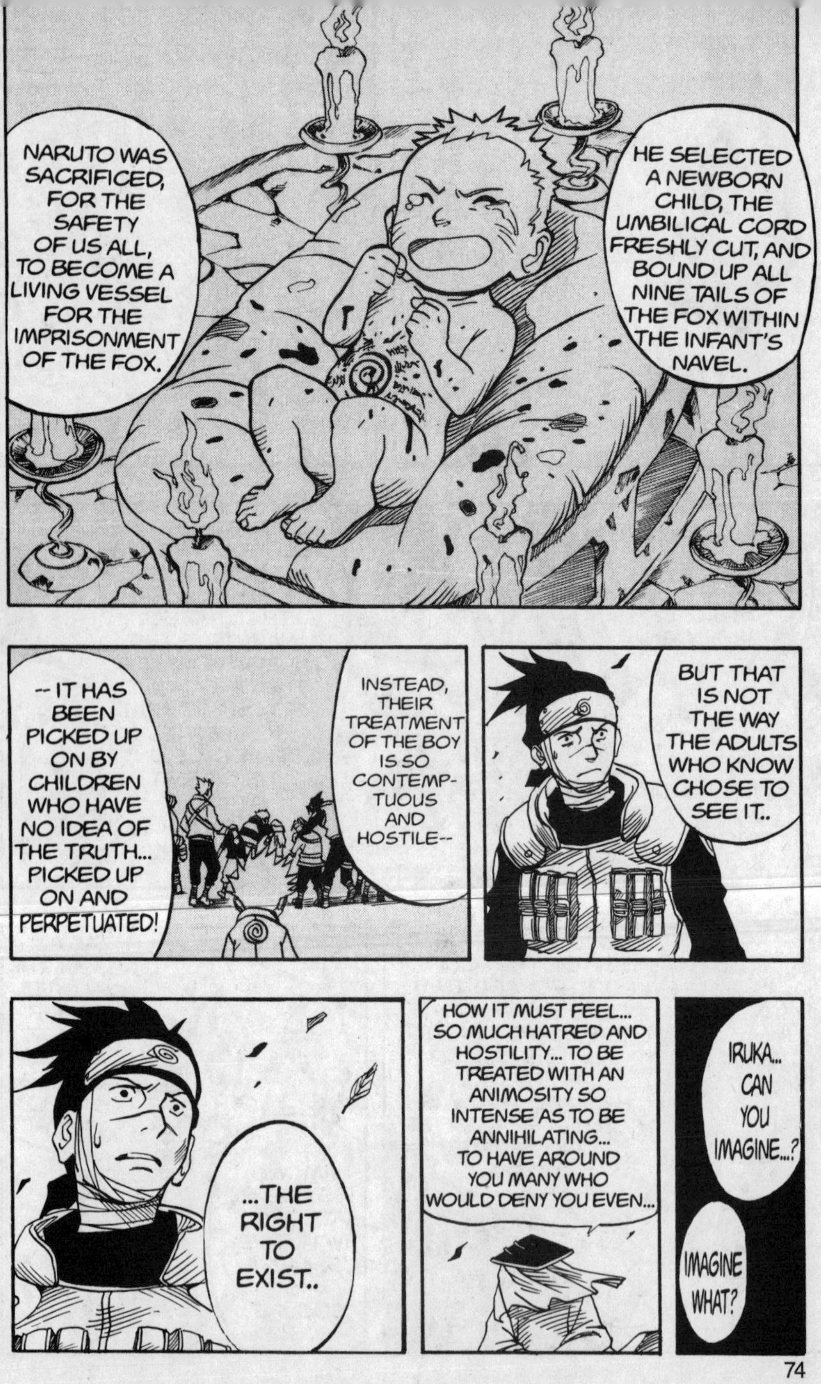
HE SELECTED A NEWBORN CHILD, THE UMBILICAL CORD FRESHLY CUT, AND BOUND UP ALL NINE TAILS OF THE FOX WITHIN THE INFANT'S NAVEL.
NARUTO WAS SACRIFICED, FOR THE SAFETY OF US ALL, TO BECOME A LIVING VESSEL FOR THE IMPRISONMENT OF THE FOX.
BUT THAT IS NOT THE WAY THE ADULTS WHO KNOW CHOSE TO SEE IT..
INSTEAD, THEIR TREATMENT OF THE BOY IS SO CONTEMP-TUOUS AND HOSTILE--
--IT HAS BEEN PICKED UP ON BY CHILDREN WHO HAVE NO IDEA OF THE TRUTH... PICKED UP ON AND PERPETUATED!
IRUKA... CAN YOU IMAGINE...?
IMAGINE WHAT?
HOW IT MUST FEEL... SO MUCH HATRED AND HOSTILITY... TO BE TREATED WITH AN ANIMOSITY SO INTENSE AS TO BE ANNIHILATING... TO HAVE AROUND YOU MANY WHO WOULD DENY YOU EVEN...
...THE RIGHT TO EXIST..

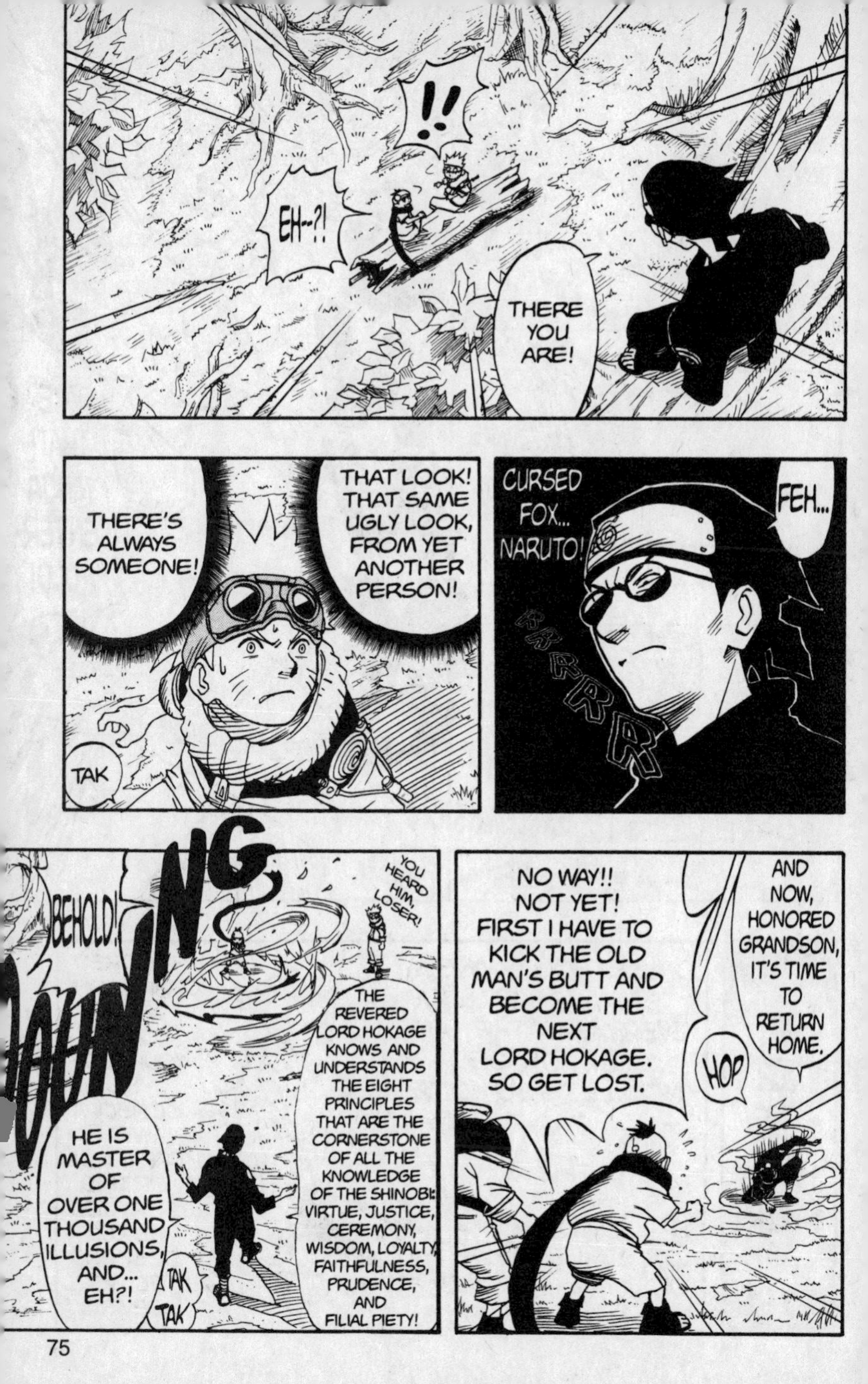
THERE YOU ARE!
!!
EH--?!
FEH...
CURSED FOX... NARUTO!
RRRRR
THAT LOOK! THAT SAME UGLY LOOK, FROM YET ANOTHER PERSON!
THERE'S ALWAYS SOMEONE!
TAK
AND NOW, HONORED GRANDSON, IT'S TIME TO RETURN HOME.
NO WAY!! NOT YET! FIRST I HAVE TO KICK THE OLD MAN'S BUTT AND BECOME THE NEXT LORD HOKAGE. SO GET LOST.
HOP
YOU HEARD HIM, LOSER!
BEHOLD!
THE REVERED LORD HOKAGE KNOWS AND UNDERSTANDS THE EIGHT PRINCIPLES THAT ARE THE CORNERSTONE OF ALL THE KNOWLEDGE OF THE SHINOBI: VIRTUE, JUSTICE, CEREMONY, WISDOM, LOYALTY, FAITHFULNESS, PRUDENCE, AND FILIAL PIETY!
HE IS MASTER OF OVER ONE THOUSAND ILLUSIONS, AND... EH?!
TAK TAK

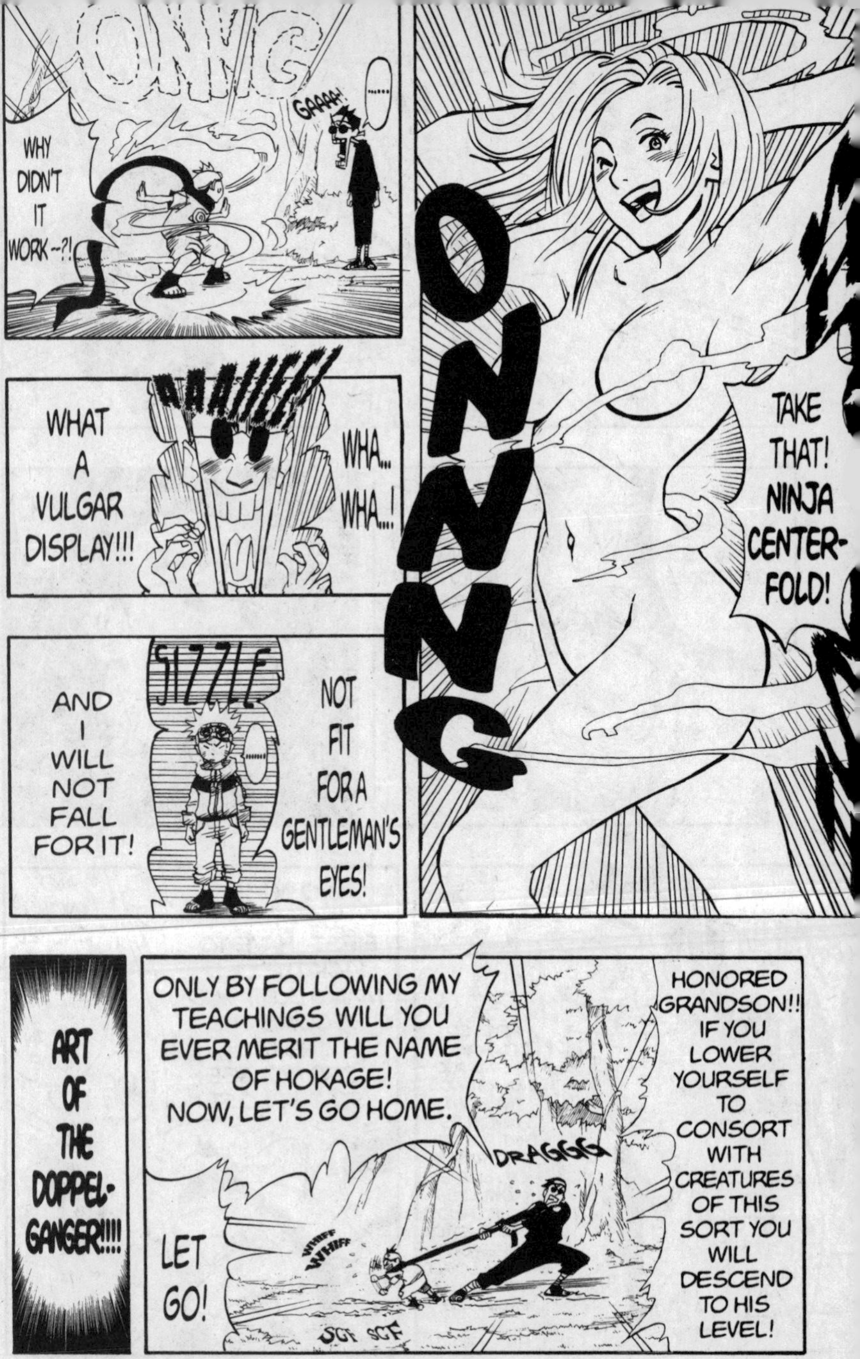
TAKE THAT! NINJA CENTERFOLD!
ONNNG
ONNG
......
GAAAH!
WHY DIDN'T IT WORK--?!
AAAIIEE!
WHA... WHA...!
WHAT A VULGAR DISPLAY!!!
NOT FIT FOR A GENTLEMAN'S EYES!
SIZZLE
......
AND I WILL NOT FALL FOR IT!
HONORED GRANDSON!! IF YOU LOWER YOURSELF TO CONSORT WITH CREATURES OF THIS SORT YOU WILL DESCEND TO HIS LEVEL!
ONLY BY FOLLOWING MY TEACHINGS WILL YOU EVER MERIT THE NAME OF HOKAGE! NOW, LET'S GO HOME.
DRAGGG
LET GO!
WHIFF WHIFF
SCF SCF
ART OF THE DOPPEL-GANGER!!!!

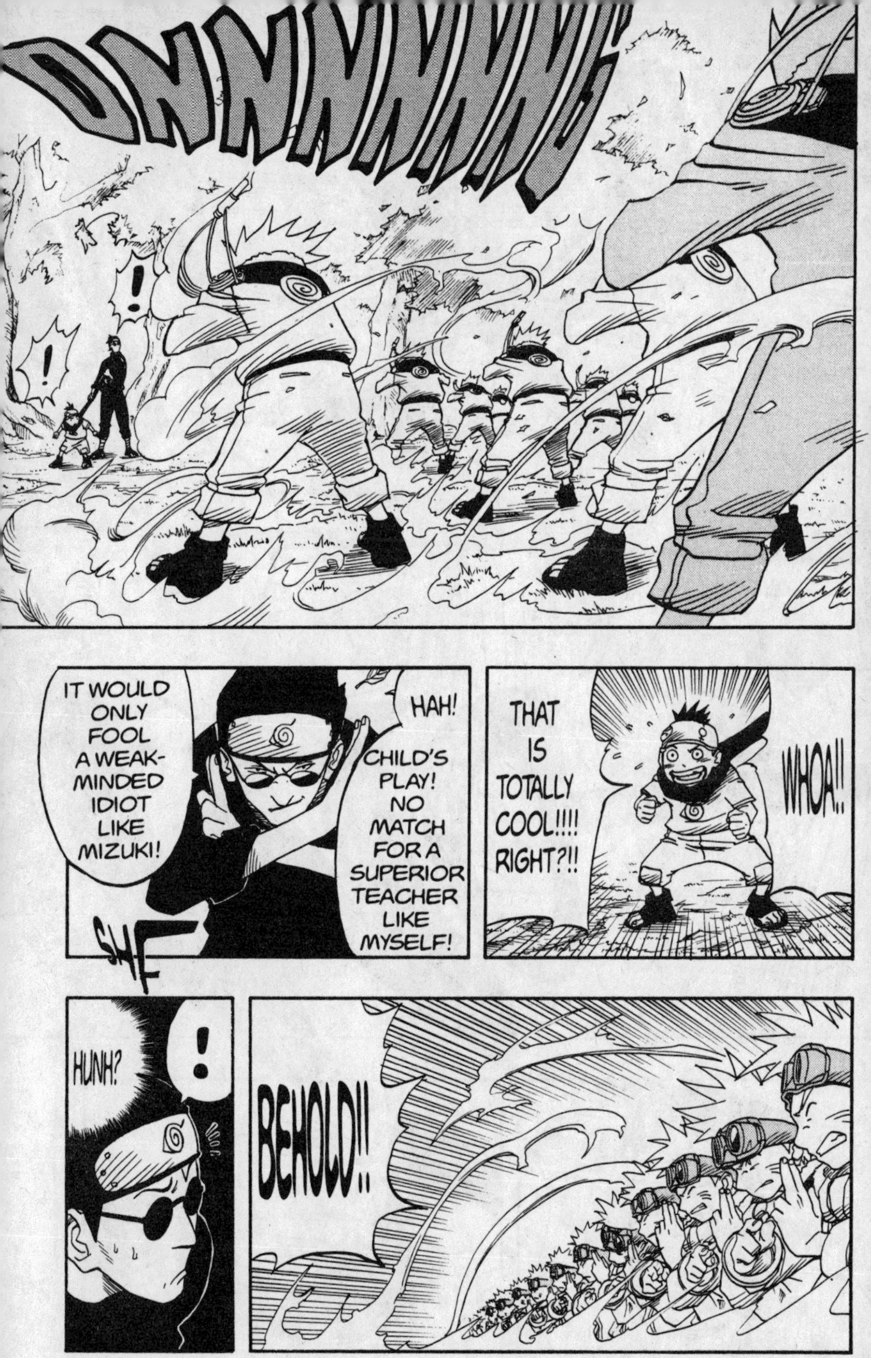
!
!
WHOA!!
THAT IS TOTALLY COOL!!!! RIGHT?!!
HAH!
CHILD'S PLAY! NO MATCH FOR A SUPERIOR TEACHER LIKE MYSELF!
IT WOULD ONLY FOOL A WEAK-MINDED IDIOT LIKE MIZUKI!
SHF
BEHOLD!!
HUNH?
!

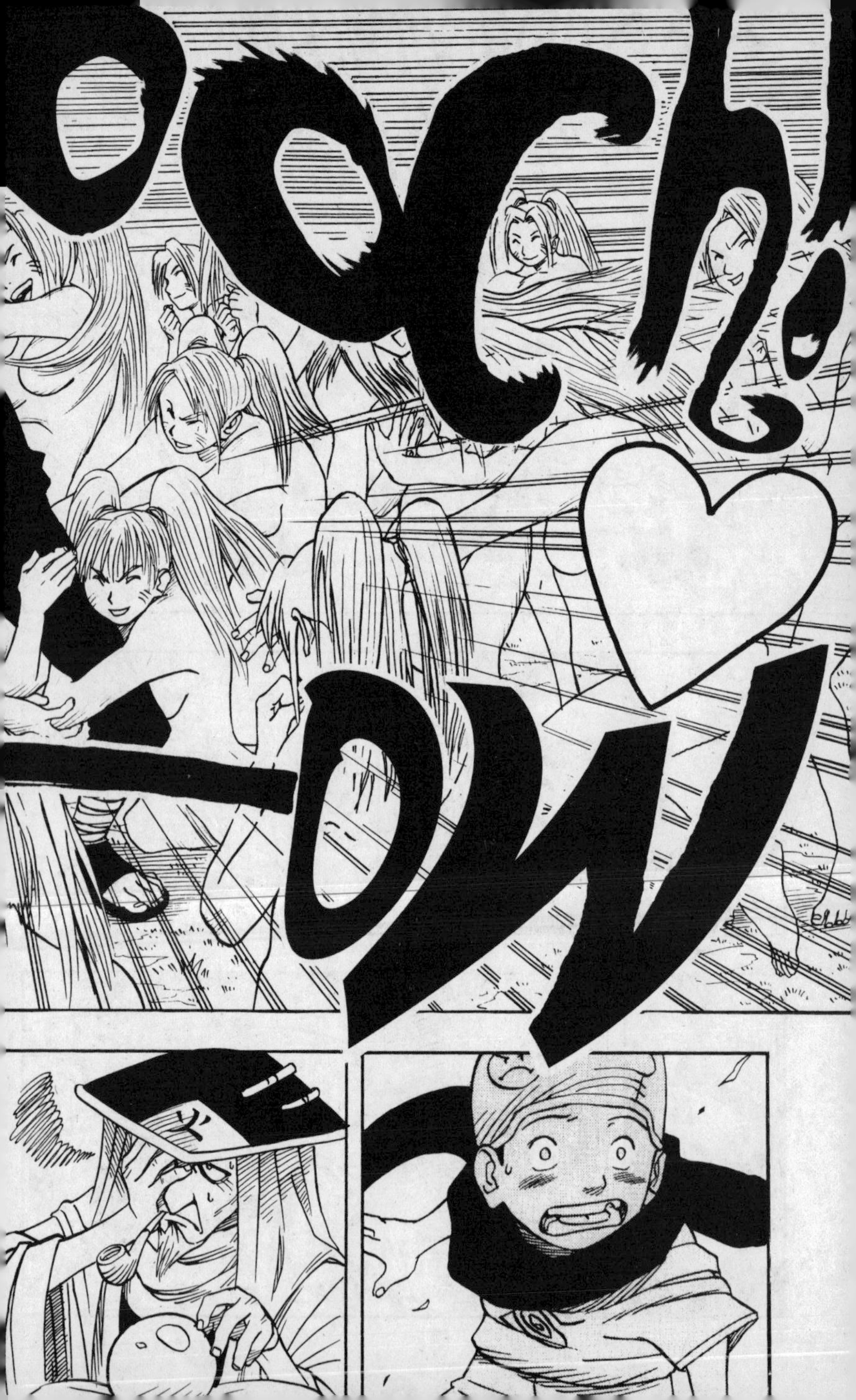
OOCH!
OW♥

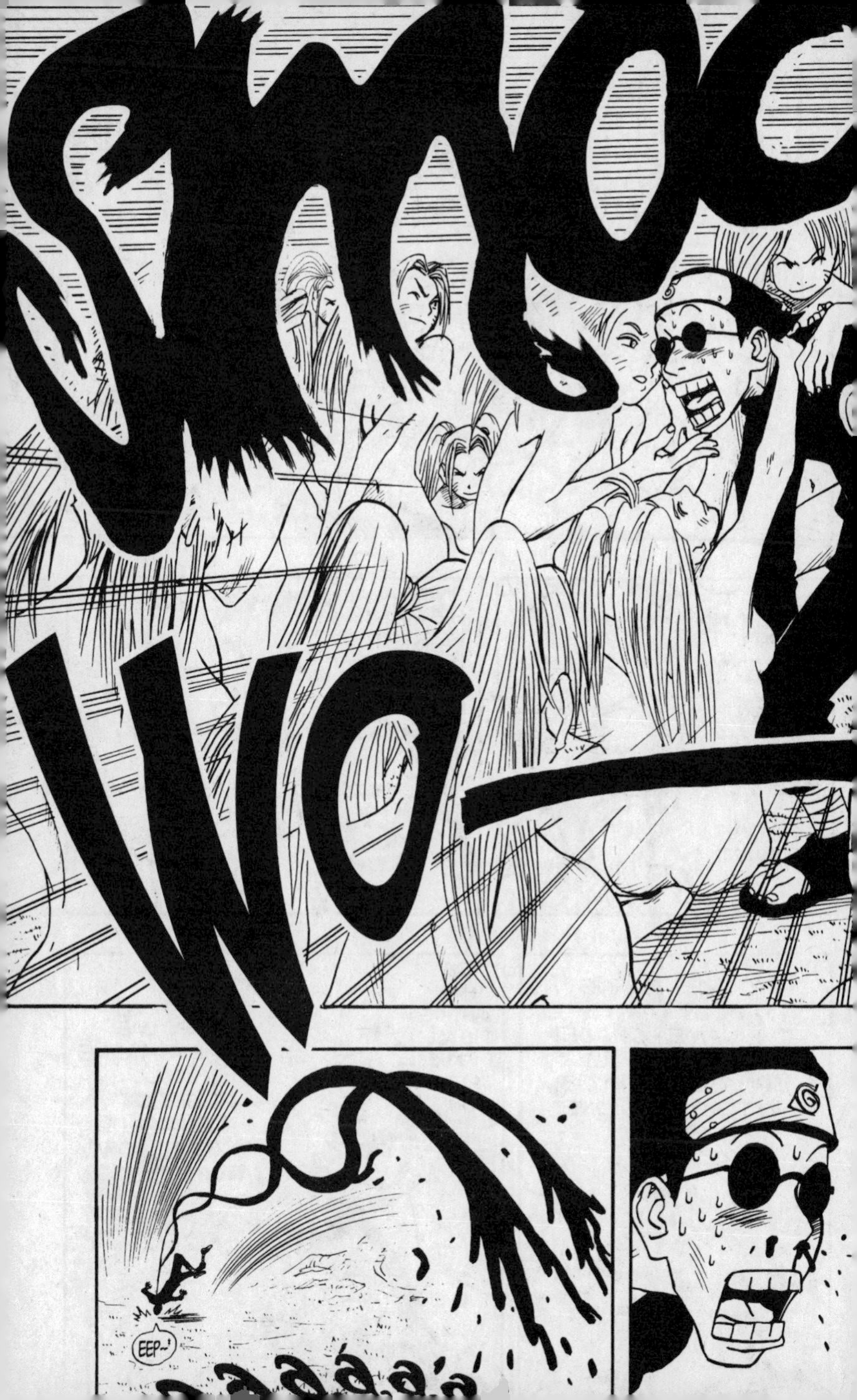
EEP~!

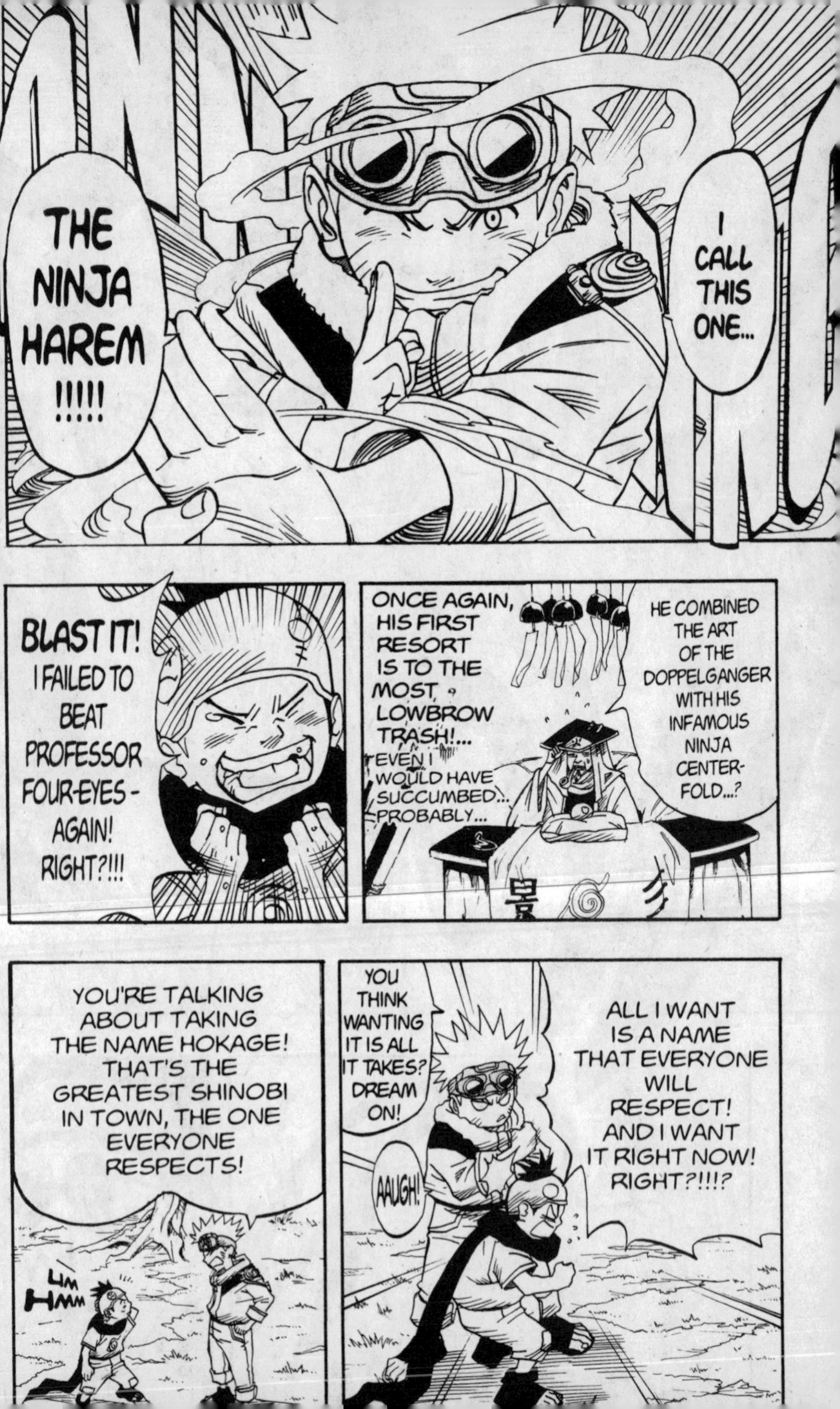
I CALL THIS ONE...
THE NINJA HAREM!!!!!
HE COMBINED THE ART OF THE DOPPELGANGER WITH HIS INFAMOUS NINJA CENTER-FOLD...?
ONCE AGAIN, HIS FIRST RESORT IS TO THE MOST, LOWBROW TRASH!...
EVEN I WOULD HAVE SUCCUMBED... PROBABLY...
BLAST IT! I FAILED TO BEAT PROFESSOR FOUR-EYES - AGAIN! RIGHT?!!!
ALL I WANT IS A NAME THAT EVERYONE WILL RESPECT! AND I WANT IT RIGHT NOW! RIGHT?!!!?
YOU THINK WANTING IT IS ALL IT TAKES? DREAM ON!
AAUGH!
YOU'RE TALKING ABOUT TAKING THE NAME HOKAGE! THAT'S THE GREATEST SHINOBI IN TOWN, THE ONE EVERYONE RESPECTS!
UM HMM

READ THIS WAY

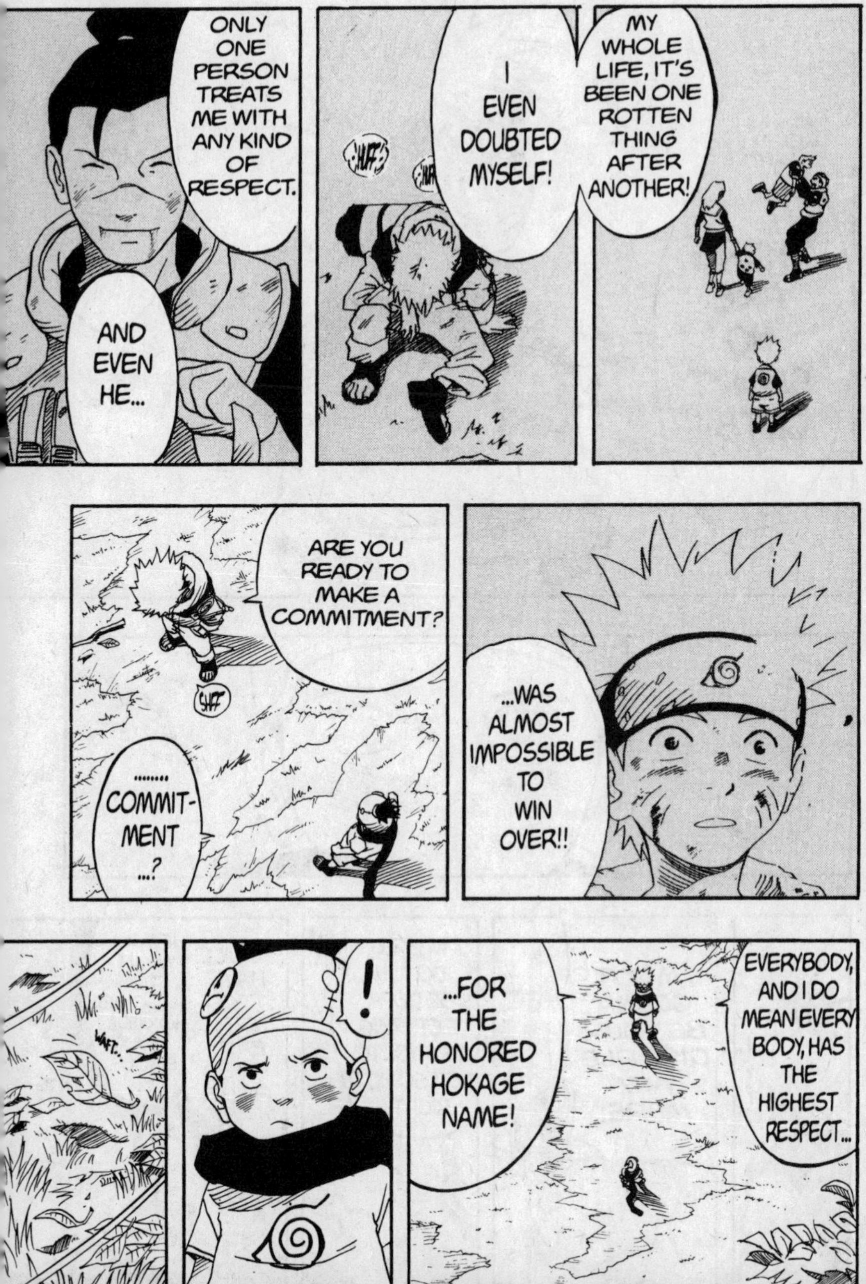
MY WHOLE LIFE, IT'S BEEN ONE ROTTEN THING AFTER ANOTHER!
I EVEN DOUBTED MYSELF!
HUFF
ONLY ONE PERSON TREATS ME WITH ANY KIND OF RESPECT.
AND EVEN HE...
...WAS ALMOST IMPOSSIBLE TO WIN OVER!!
ARE YOU READY TO MAKE A COMMITMENT?
SHFF
.... COMMIT-MENT ...?
EVERYBODY, AND I DO MEAN EVERY BODY, HAS THE HIGHEST RESPECT...
...FOR THE HONORED HOKAGE NAME!
!
WAFT...

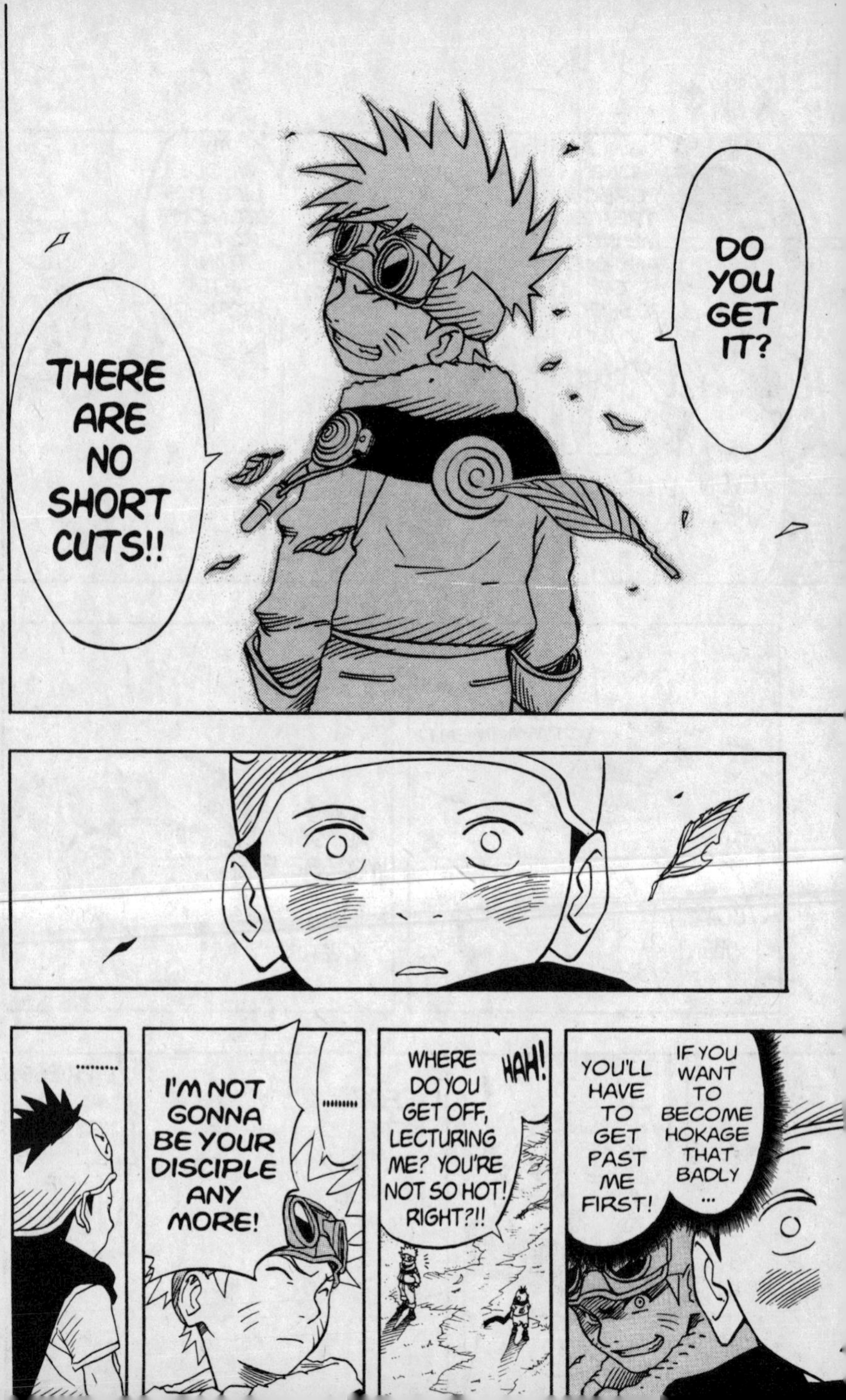
DO YOU GET IT?
THERE ARE NO SHORT CUTS!!
IF YOU WANT TO BECOME HOKAGE THAT BADLY...
YOU'LL HAVE TO GET PAST ME FIRST!
HAH!
WHERE DO YOU GET OFF, LECTURING ME? YOU'RE NOT SO HOT! RIGHT?!!
....
I'M NOT GONNA BE YOUR DISCIPLE ANY MORE!
....

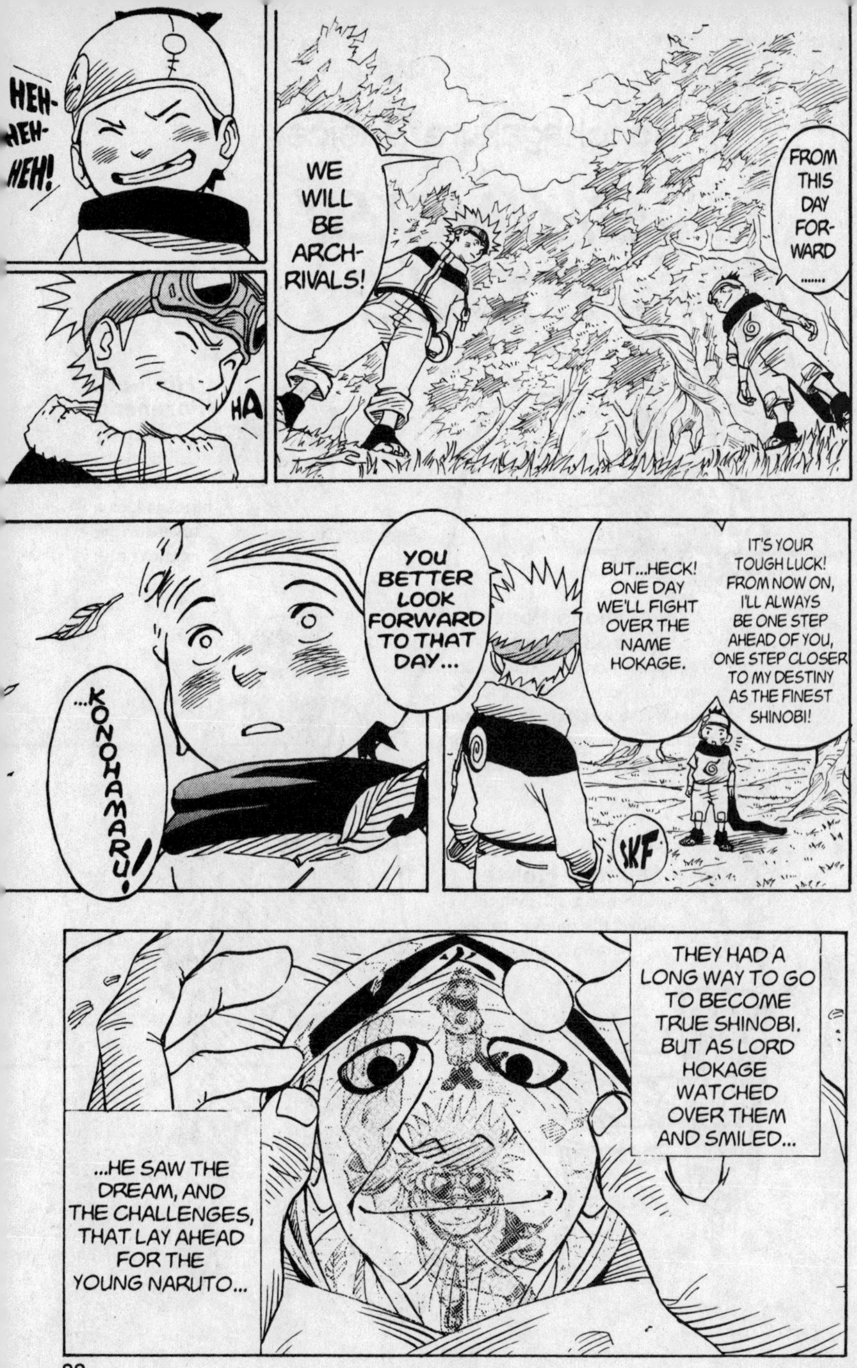
FROM THIS DAY FOR-WARD ......
WE WILL BE ARCH-RIVALS!
HEH-HEH-HEH!
HA
IT'S YOUR TOUGH LUCK! FROM NOW ON, I'LL ALWAYS BE ONE STEP AHEAD OF YOU, ONE STEP CLOSER TO MY DESTINY AS THE FINEST SHINOBI!
BUT...HECK! ONE DAY WE'LL FIGHT OVER THE NAME HOKAGE.
YOU BETTER LOOK FORWARD TO THAT DAY...
SKF
...KONOHAMARU!
THEY HAD A LONG WAY TO GO TO BECOME TRUE SHINOBI. BUT AS LORD HOKAGE WATCHED OVER THEM AND SMILED...
...HE SAW THE DREAM, AND THE CHALLENGES, THAT LAY AHEAD FOR THE YOUNG NARUTO...

Konohagakure Basics:

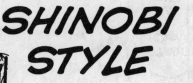

SHINOBI STYLE

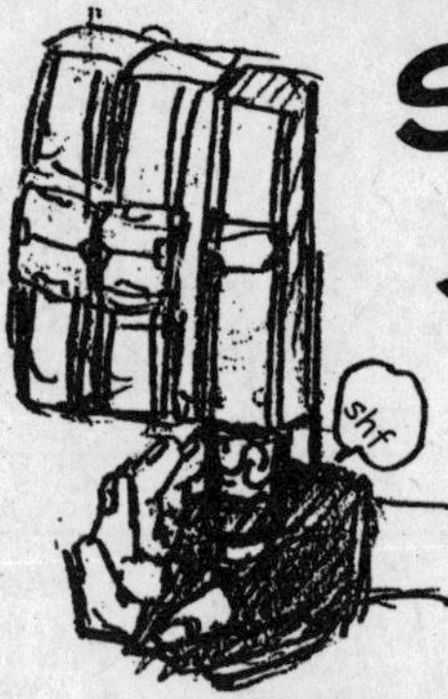
shf

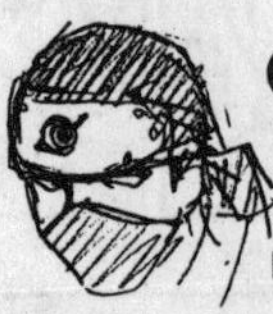

Hitai-ate (Forehead Band)

Can be worn either as a headband, or a cover for the entire head.

Makimono Pouch (Scroll Pouch)

The classic Konohagakure pouch, worn on both the right and left sides of the vest. Scrolls, medicine and ninja tools are extracted from the bottom of the pouches.

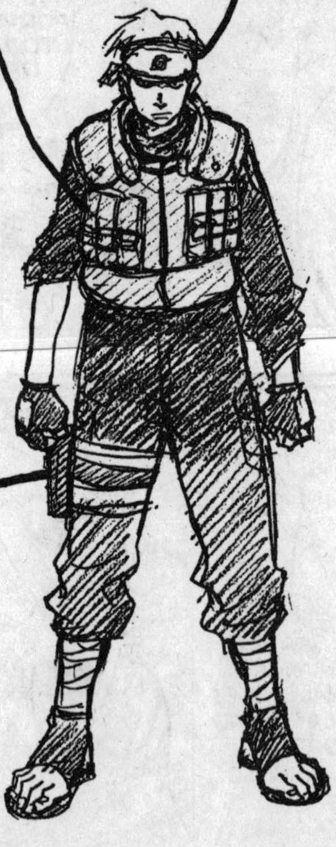

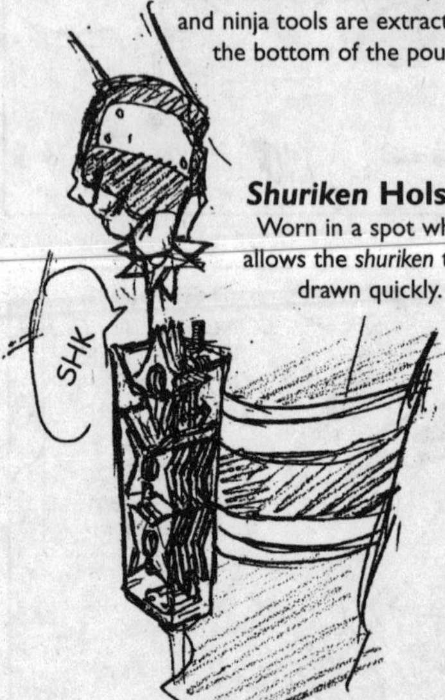
SHK

Shuriken Holster

Worn in a spot which allows the *shuriken* to be drawn quickly.

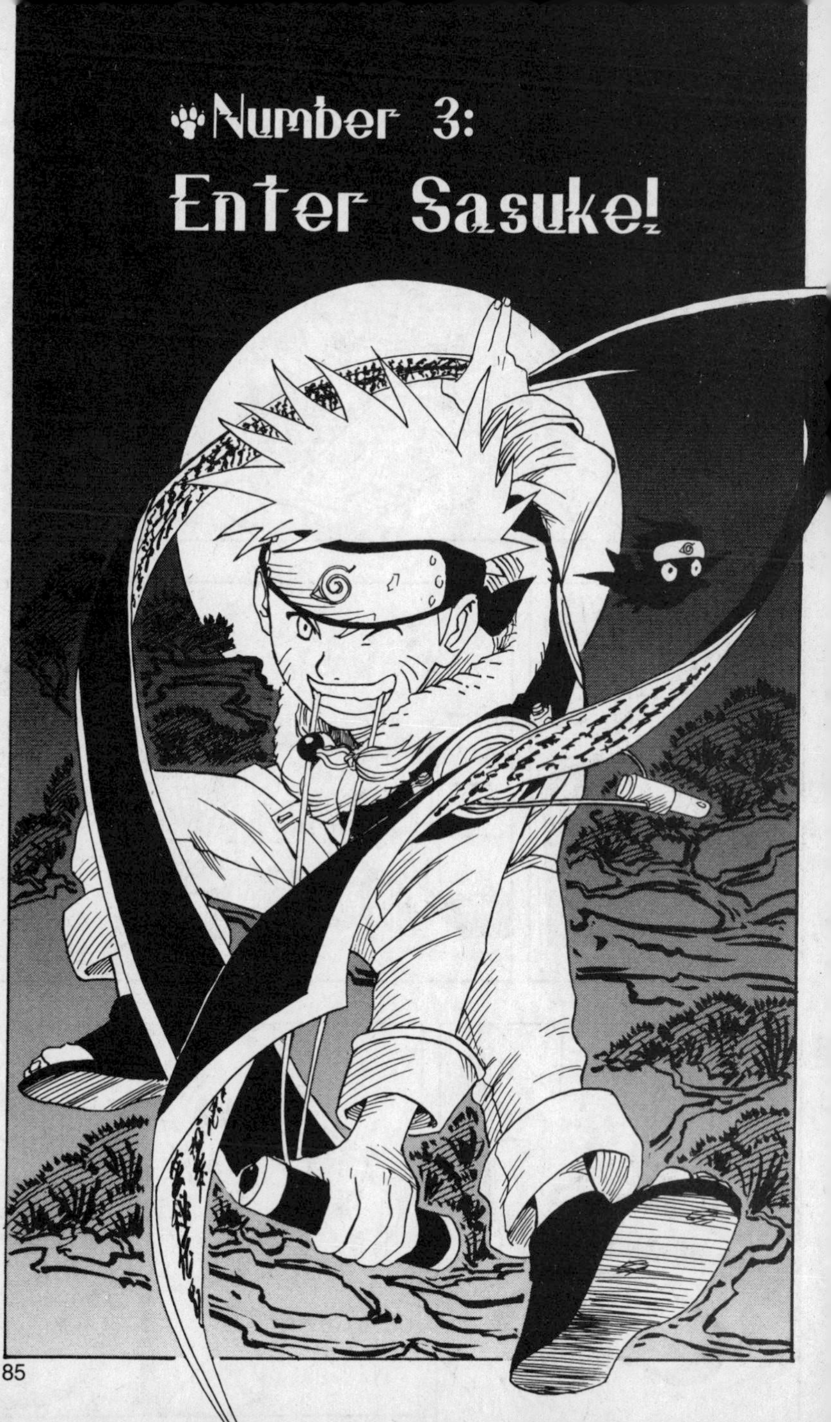
Number 3:
Enter Sasuke!

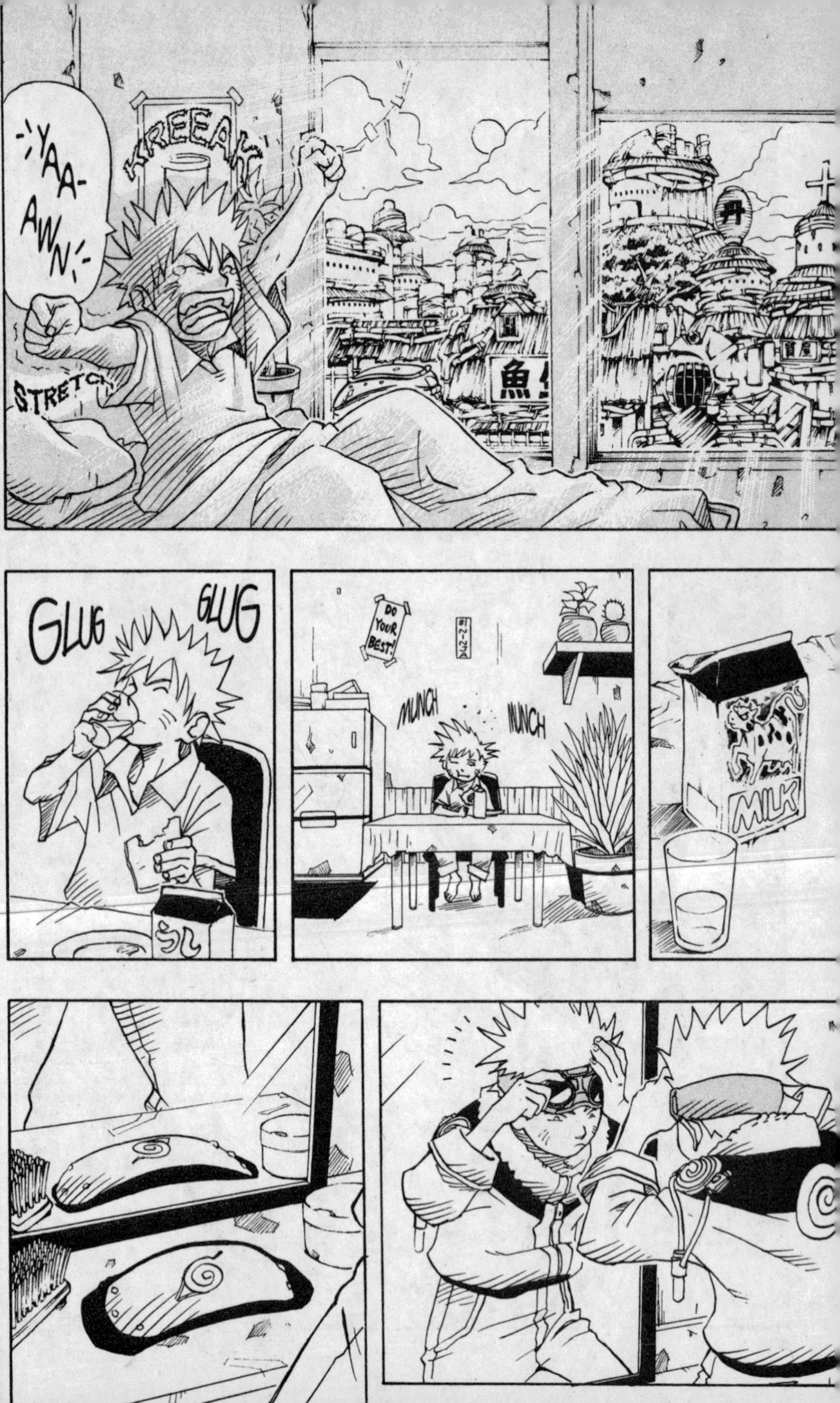
KREEAK
YAA-AAWN
STRETCH
魚
MILK
DO YOUR BEST!
#1 NINJA
MUNCH
MUNCH
GLUG
GLUG
うし

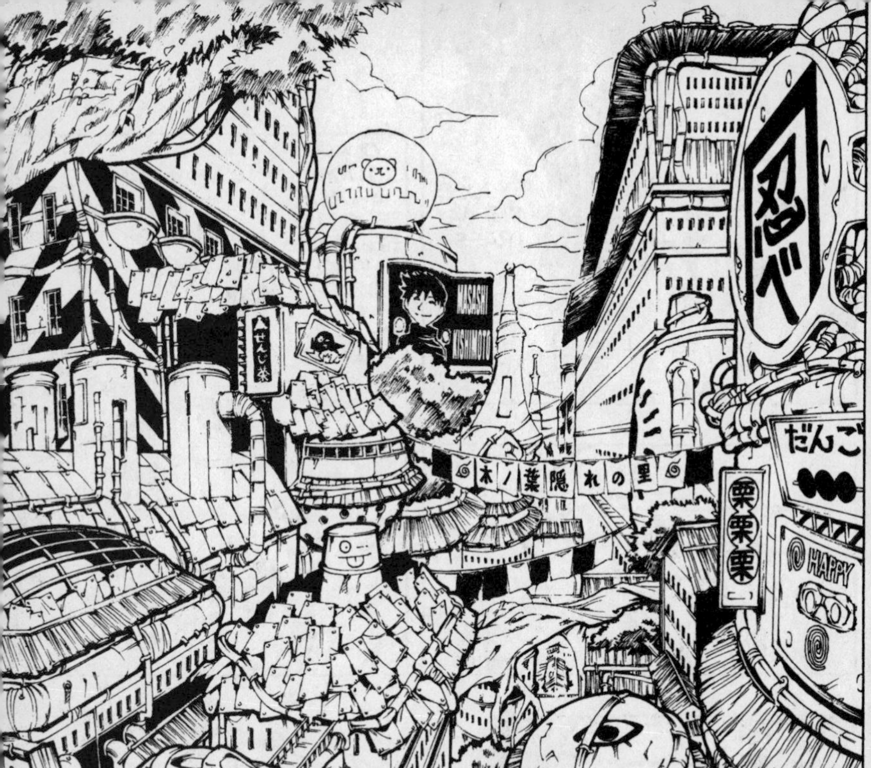
MASASHI KISHIMOTO
木ノ葉隠れの里
だんご
栗栗栗
HAPPY
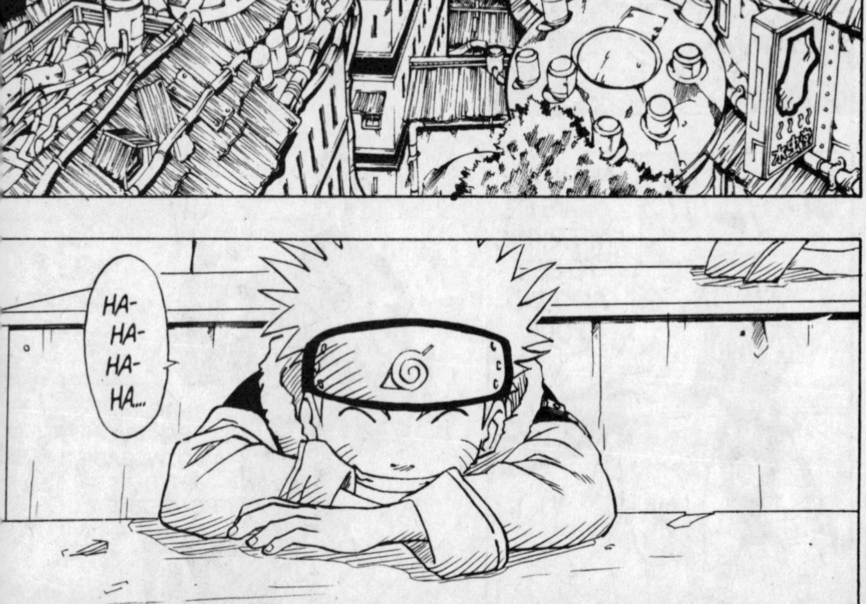
HA-
HA-
HA-
HA...

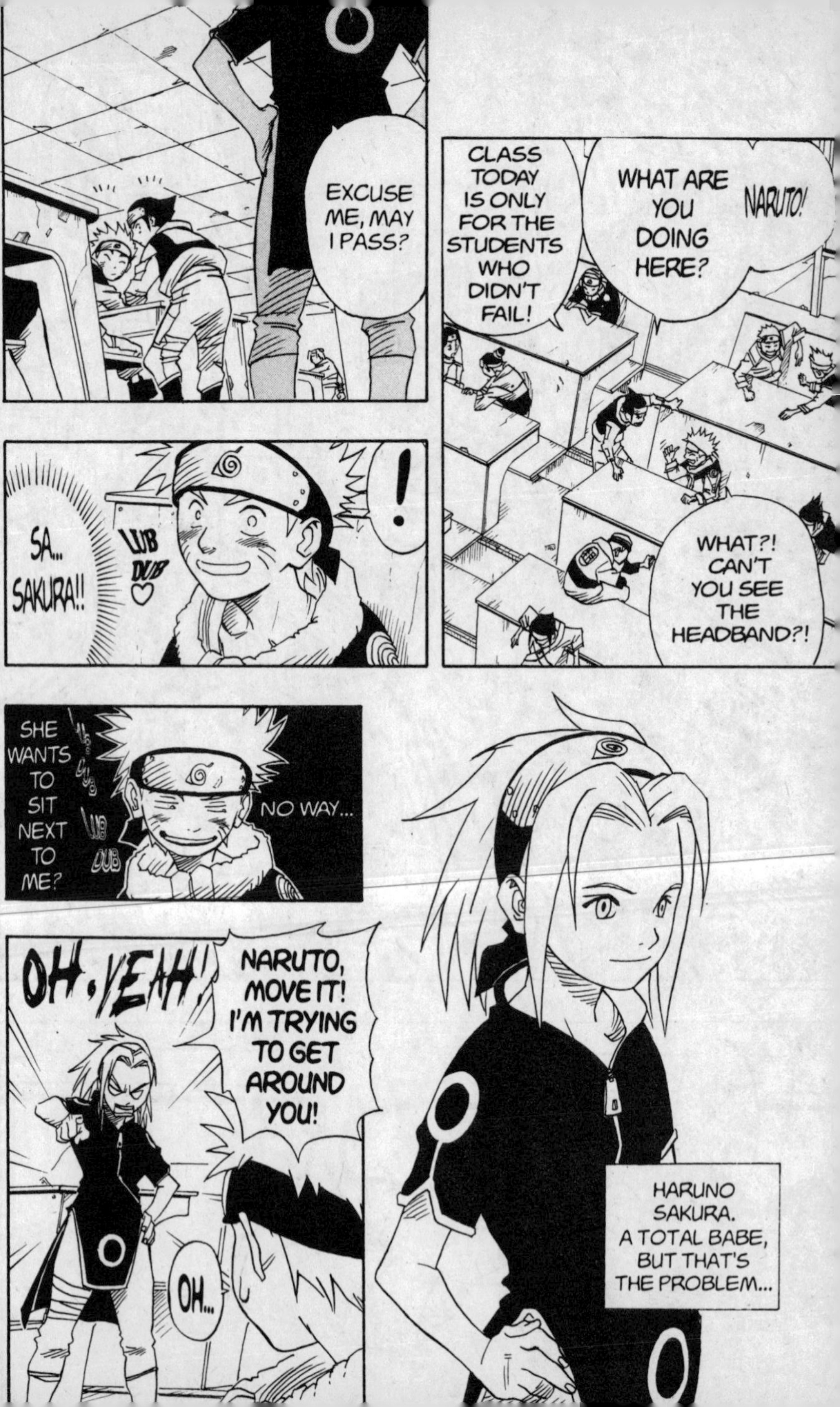
NARUTO!
WHAT ARE YOU DOING HERE?
CLASS TODAY IS ONLY FOR THE STUDENTS WHO DIDN'T FAIL!
WHAT?! CAN'T YOU SEE THE HEADBAND?!
EXCUSE ME, MAY I PASS?
!
LUB DUB
SA... SAKURA!!
NO WAY...
LUB DUB LUB DUB
SHE WANTS TO SIT NEXT TO ME?
HARUNO SAKURA. A TOTAL BABE, BUT THAT'S THE PROBLEM...
NARUTO, MOVE IT! I'M TRYING TO GET AROUND YOU!
OH, YEAH!
OH...

READ THIS WAY

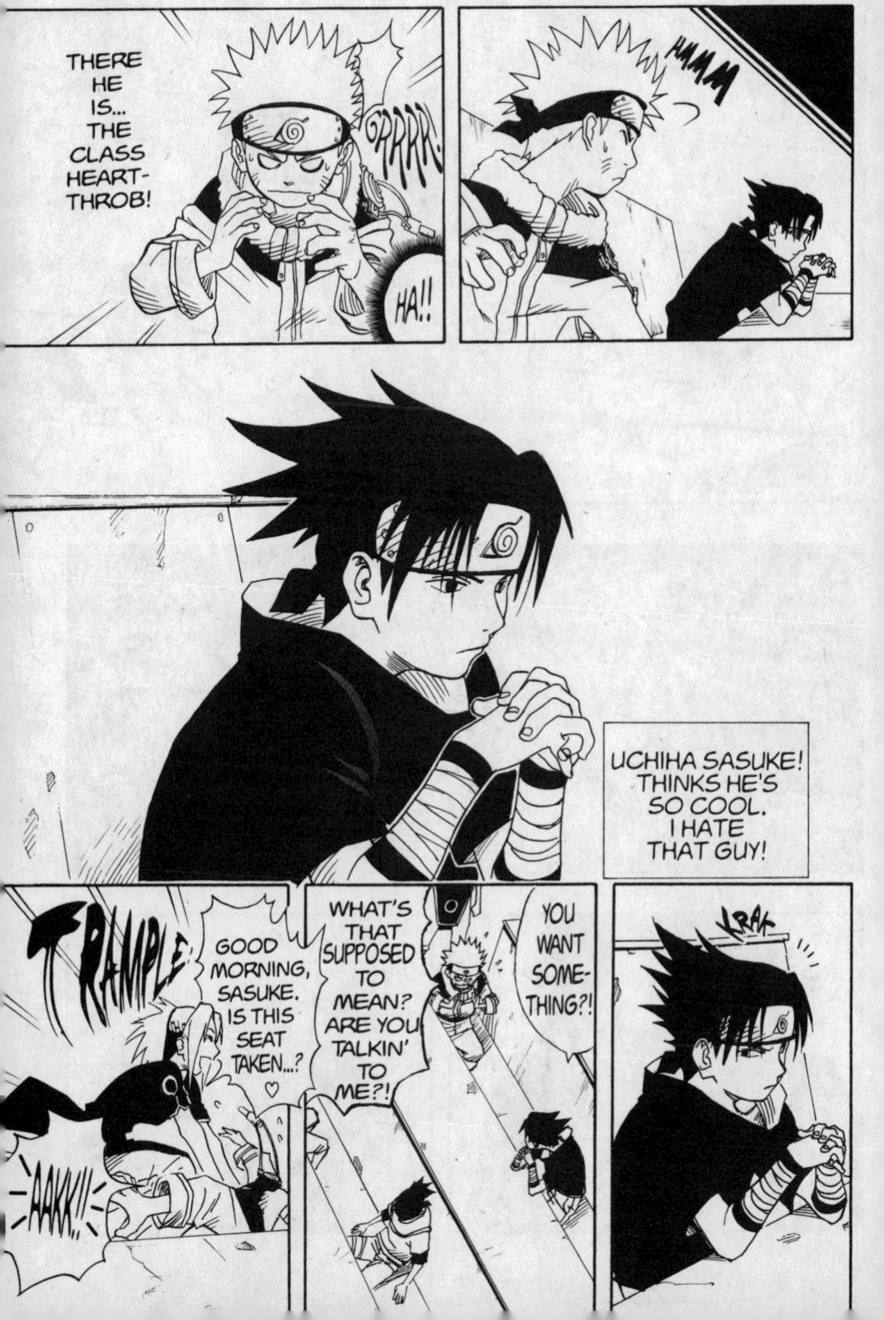
HMMM
THERE HE IS... THE CLASS HEART-THROB!
GRRRR
HA!!
UCHIHA SASUKE! THINKS HE'S SO COOL. I HATE THAT GUY!
KRAK
YOU WANT SOME-THING?!
WHAT'S THAT SUPPOSED TO MEAN? ARE YOU TALKIN' TO ME?!
TRAMPLE
GOOD MORNING, SASUKE. IS THIS SEAT TAKEN...? ♡
AAKK!!

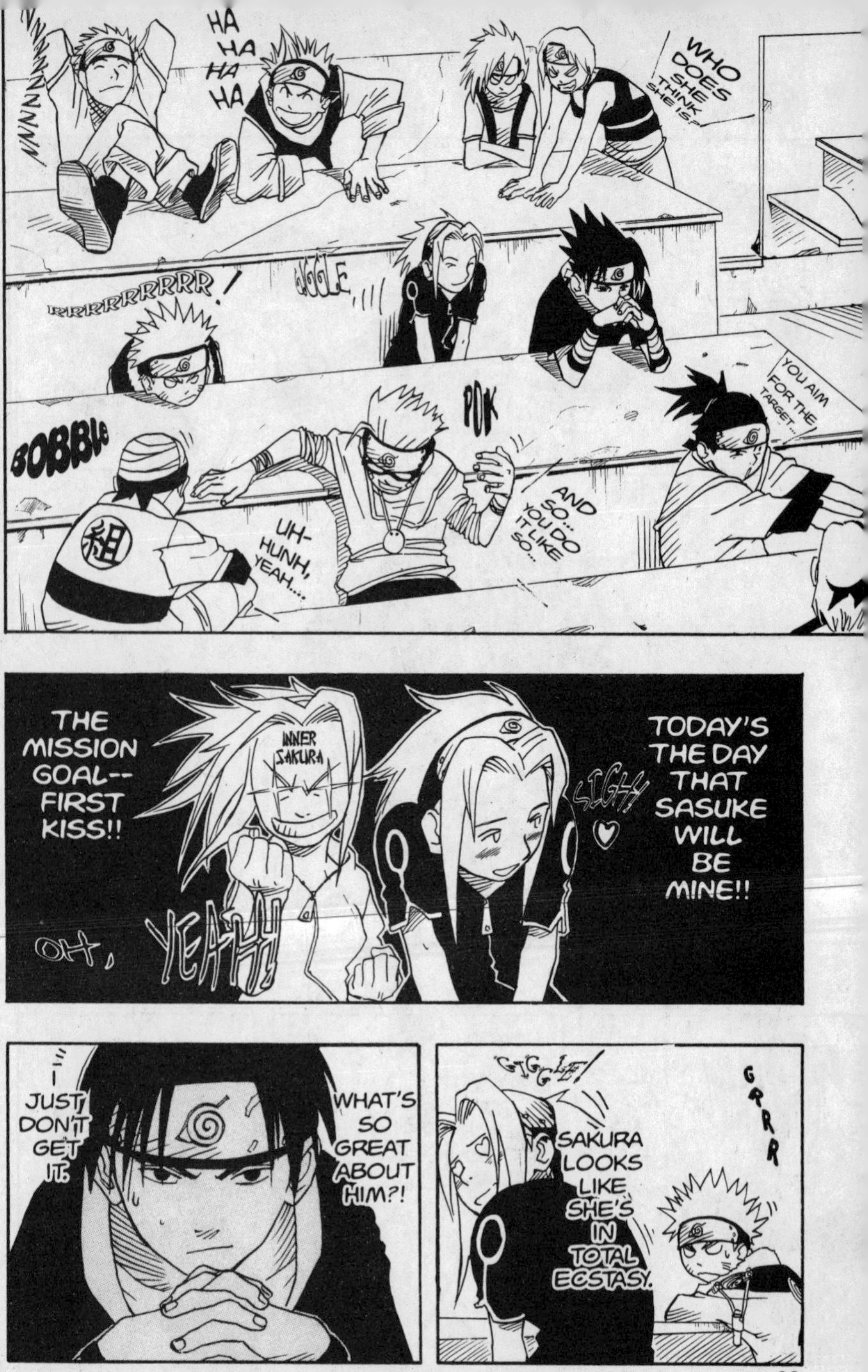
WHO DOES SHE THINK SHE IS?!
HA HA HA HA
YOU AIM FOR THE TARGET...
POK
AND SO... YOU DO IT LIKE SO...
UH-HUNH, YEAH...
BOBBLE
TODAY'S THE DAY THAT SASUKE WILL BE MINE!!
SIGH
INNER SAKURA
THE MISSION GOAL-- FIRST KISS!!
OH, YEAHH
GIGGLE!
GRRR
SAKURA LOOKS LIKE SHE'S IN TOTAL ECSTASY.
WHAT'S SO GREAT ABOUT HIM?!
I JUST DON'T GET IT.

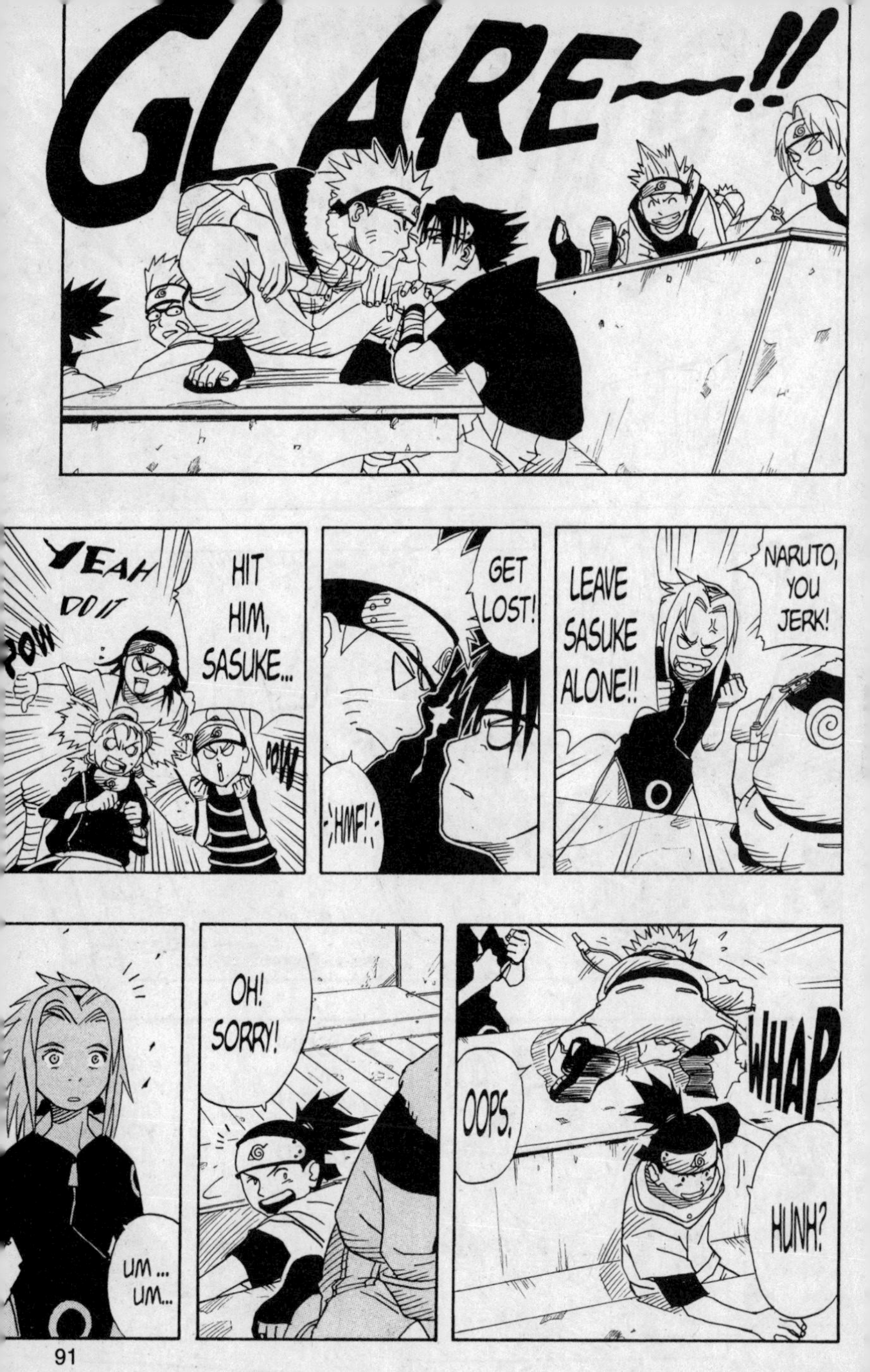
GLARE—!!
NARUTO, YOU JERK!
LEAVE SASUKE ALONE!!
GET LOST!
HMF!
HIT HIM, SASUKE...
YEAH
DO IT
POW
POW
WHAP
HUNH?
OOPS.
OH! SORRY!
UM... UM...

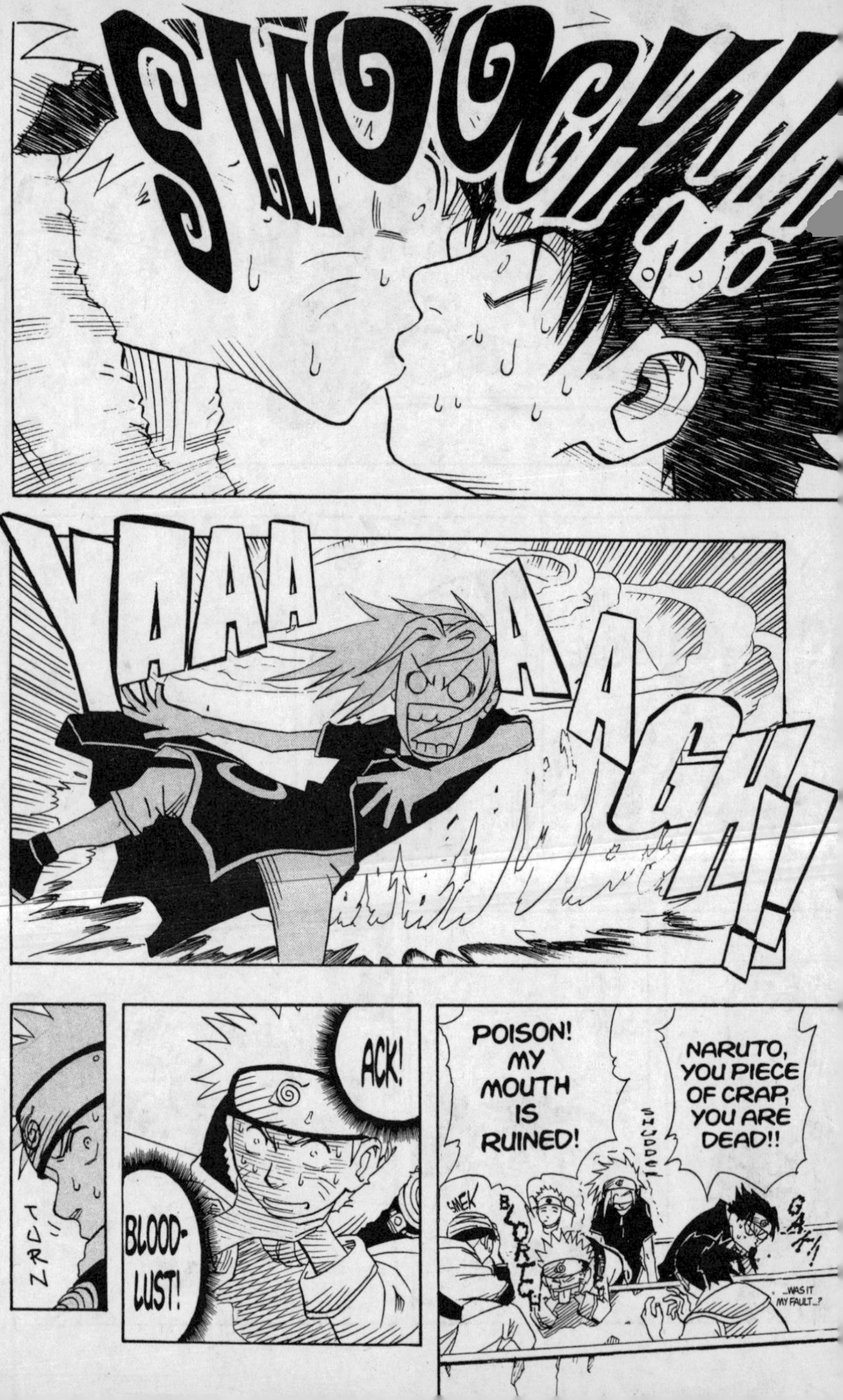
SMOOCH!!
YAAAAACH!!
NARUTO, YOU PIECE OF CRAP, YOU ARE DEAD!!
POISON! MY MOUTH IS RUINED!
SHUDDER
GAK!!
SMEK
BLORTCH
...WAS IT MY FAULT...?
ACK!
BLOOD-LUST!
TURN

READ THIS WAY

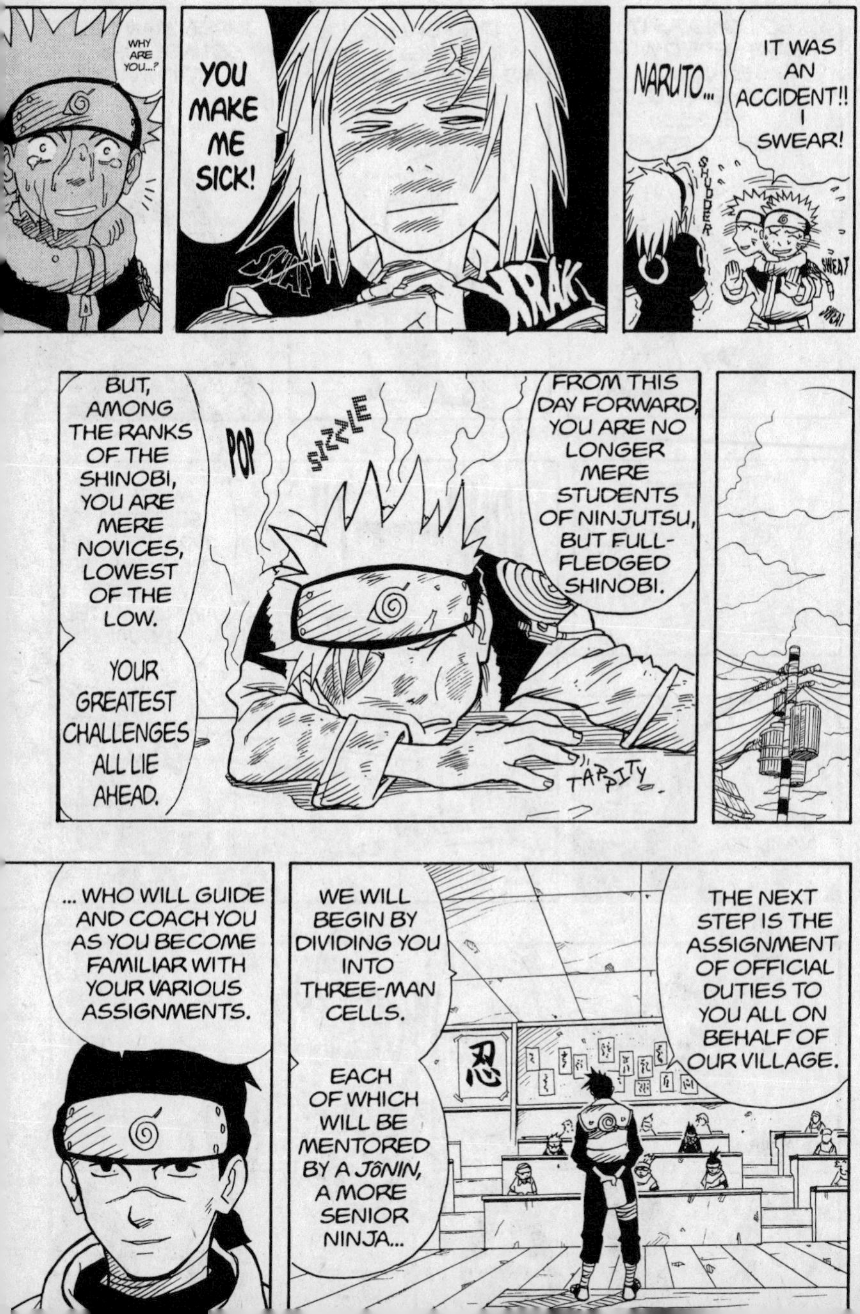
NARUTO...
IT WAS AN ACCIDENT!! I SWEAR!
SHUDDER
SWEAT
SWEAT
YOU MAKE ME SICK!
SNAP
KRAK
WHY ARE YOU...?
FROM THIS DAY FORWARD, YOU ARE NO LONGER MERE STUDENTS OF NINJUTSU, BUT FULL-FLEDGED SHINOBI.
SIZZLE
POP
BUT, AMONG THE RANKS OF THE SHINOBI, YOU ARE MERE NOVICES, LOWEST OF THE LOW.
YOUR GREATEST CHALLENGES ALL LIE AHEAD.
TAPPITY
THE NEXT STEP IS THE ASSIGNMENT OF OFFICIAL DUTIES TO YOU ALL ON BEHALF OF OUR VILLAGE.
WE WILL BEGIN BY DIVIDING YOU INTO THREE-MAN CELLS.
EACH OF WHICH WILL BE MENTORED BY A JÔNIN, A MORE SENIOR NINJA...
... WHO WILL GUIDE AND COACH YOU AS YOU BECOME FAMILIAR WITH YOUR VARIOUS ASSIGNMENTS.

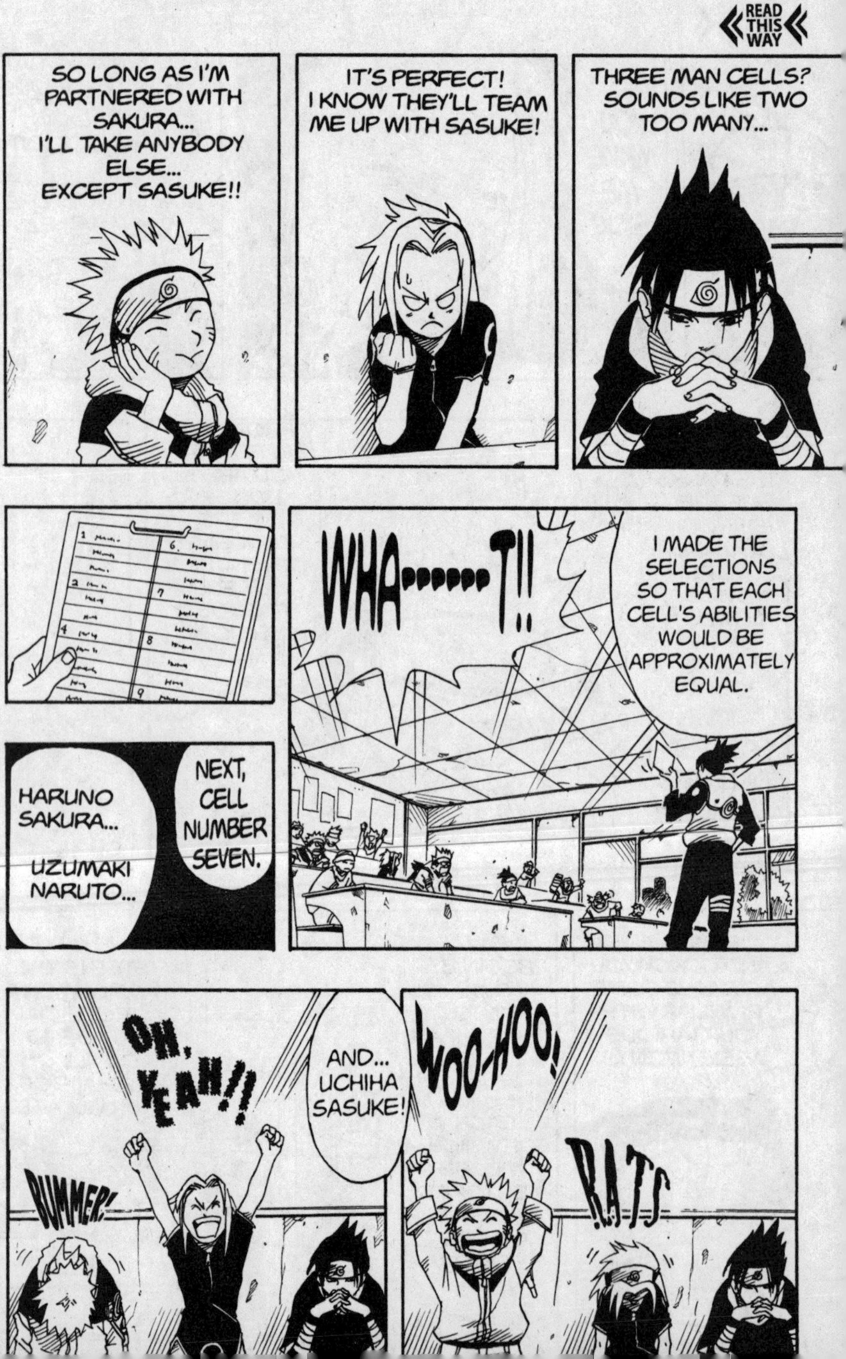
READ THIS WAY
THREE MAN CELLS? SOUNDS LIKE TWO TOO MANY...
IT'S PERFECT! I KNOW THEY'LL TEAM ME UP WITH SASUKE!
SO LONG AS I'M PARTNERED WITH SAKURA... I'LL TAKE ANYBODY ELSE... EXCEPT SASUKE!!
I MADE THE SELECTIONS SO THAT EACH CELL'S ABILITIES WOULD BE APPROXIMATELY EQUAL.
WHAAAAAAAT!!
NEXT, CELL NUMBER SEVEN.
HARUNO SAKURA...
UZUMAKI NARUTO...
AND... UCHIHA SASUKE!
WOO-HOO!
RATS
OH, YEAH!!
BUMMER!

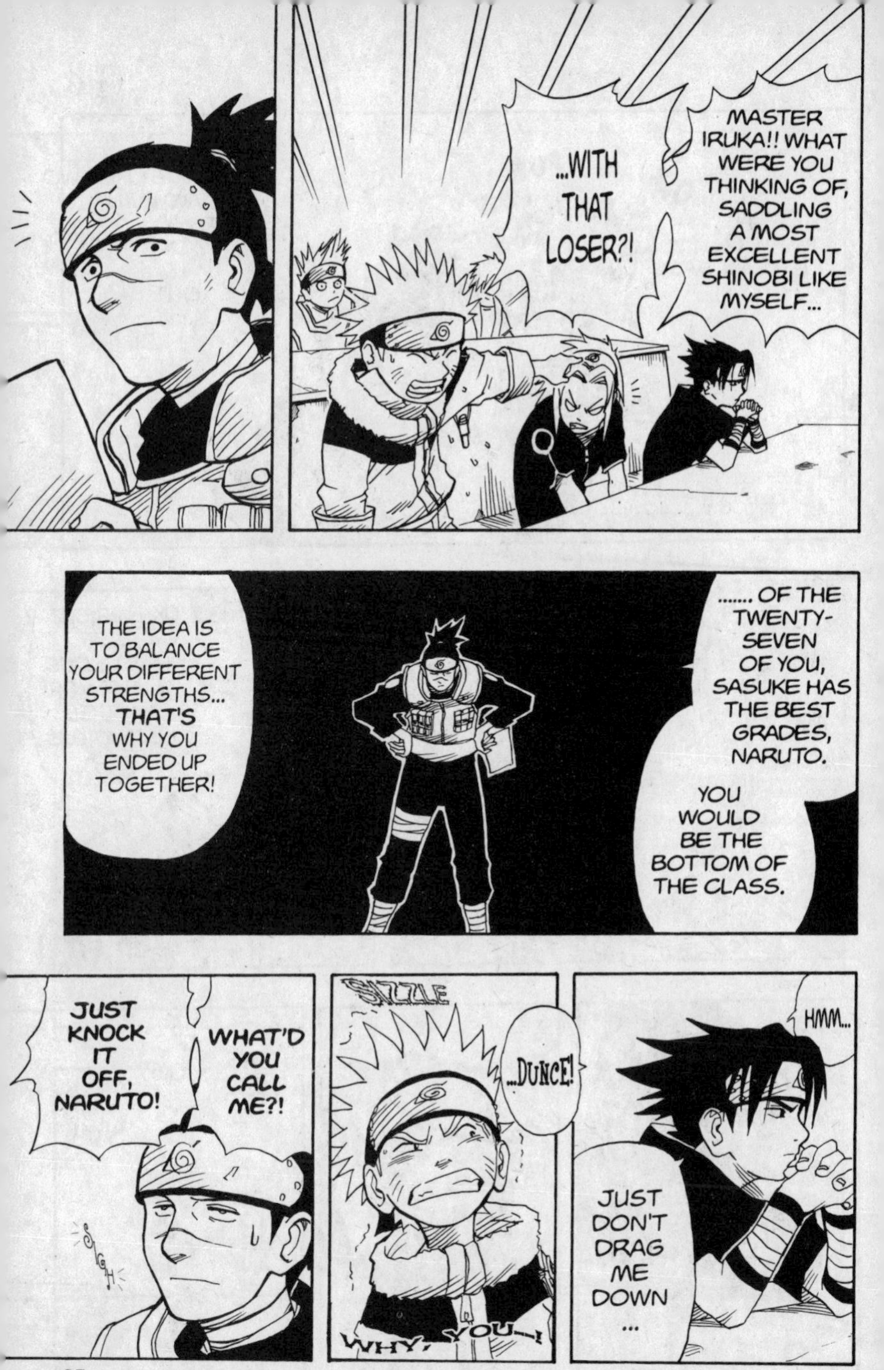
MASTER IRUKA!! WHAT WERE YOU THINKING OF, SADDLING A MOST EXCELLENT SHINOBI LIKE MYSELF...
...WITH THAT LOSER?!
...... OF THE TWENTY-SEVEN OF YOU, SASUKE HAS THE BEST GRADES, NARUTO.
YOU WOULD BE THE BOTTOM OF THE CLASS.
THE IDEA IS TO BALANCE YOUR DIFFERENT STRENGTHS... THAT'S WHY YOU ENDED UP TOGETHER!
HMM...
JUST DON'T DRAG ME DOWN ...
...DUNCE!
SIZZLE
WHY, YOU--!
WHAT'D YOU CALL ME?!
JUST KNOCK IT OFF, NARUTO!
SIGH

READ THIS WAY

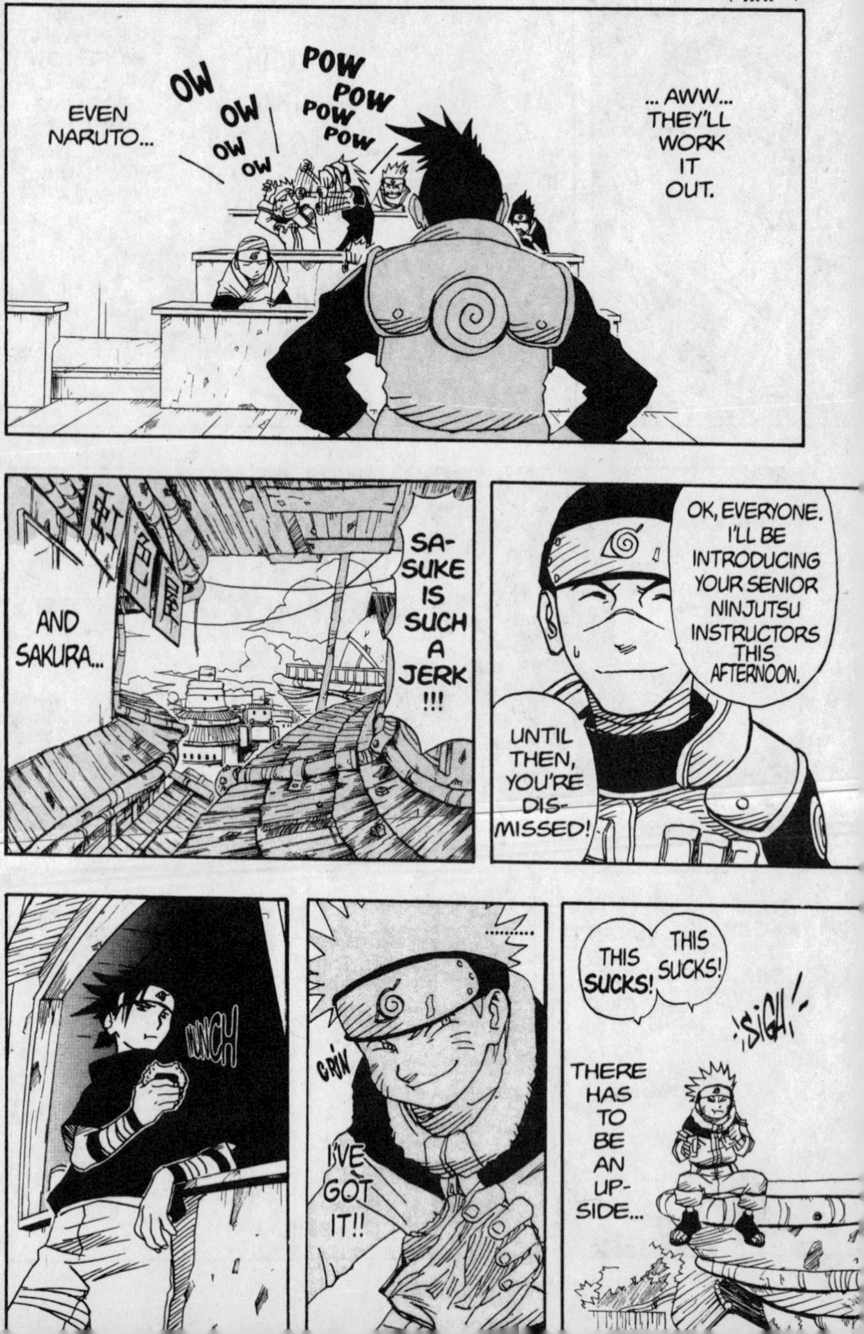
... AWW... THEY'LL WORK IT OUT.
POW POW POW POW
OW OW OW OW
EVEN NARUTO...
OK, EVERYONE. I'LL BE INTRODUCING YOUR SENIOR NINJUTSU INSTRUCTORS THIS AFTERNOON.
UNTIL THEN, YOU'RE DIS-MISSED!
SA-SUKE IS SUCH A JERK!!!
AND SAKURA...
THIS SUCKS!
THIS SUCKS!
SIGH
THERE HAS TO BE AN UP-SIDE...
....
GRIN
I'VE GOT IT!!
MUNCH

READ THIS WAY

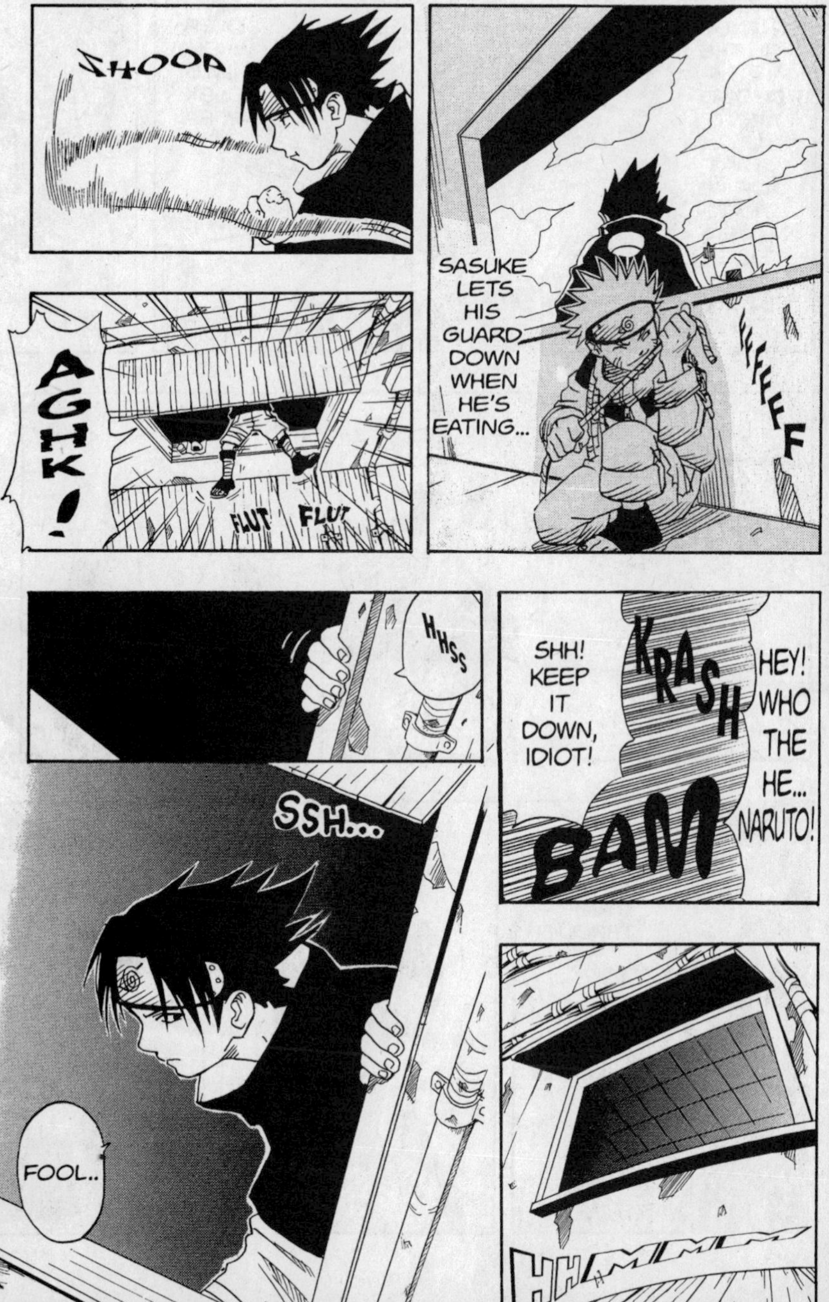
SASUKE LETS HIS GUARD DOWN WHEN HE'S EATING...
FFFFF
SHOOP
AGHK!
FLUT FLUT
HEY! WHO THE HE... NARUTO!
SHH! KEEP IT DOWN, IDIOT!
KRASH
BAM
HHMMMM
HHSS
SSH...
FOOL..

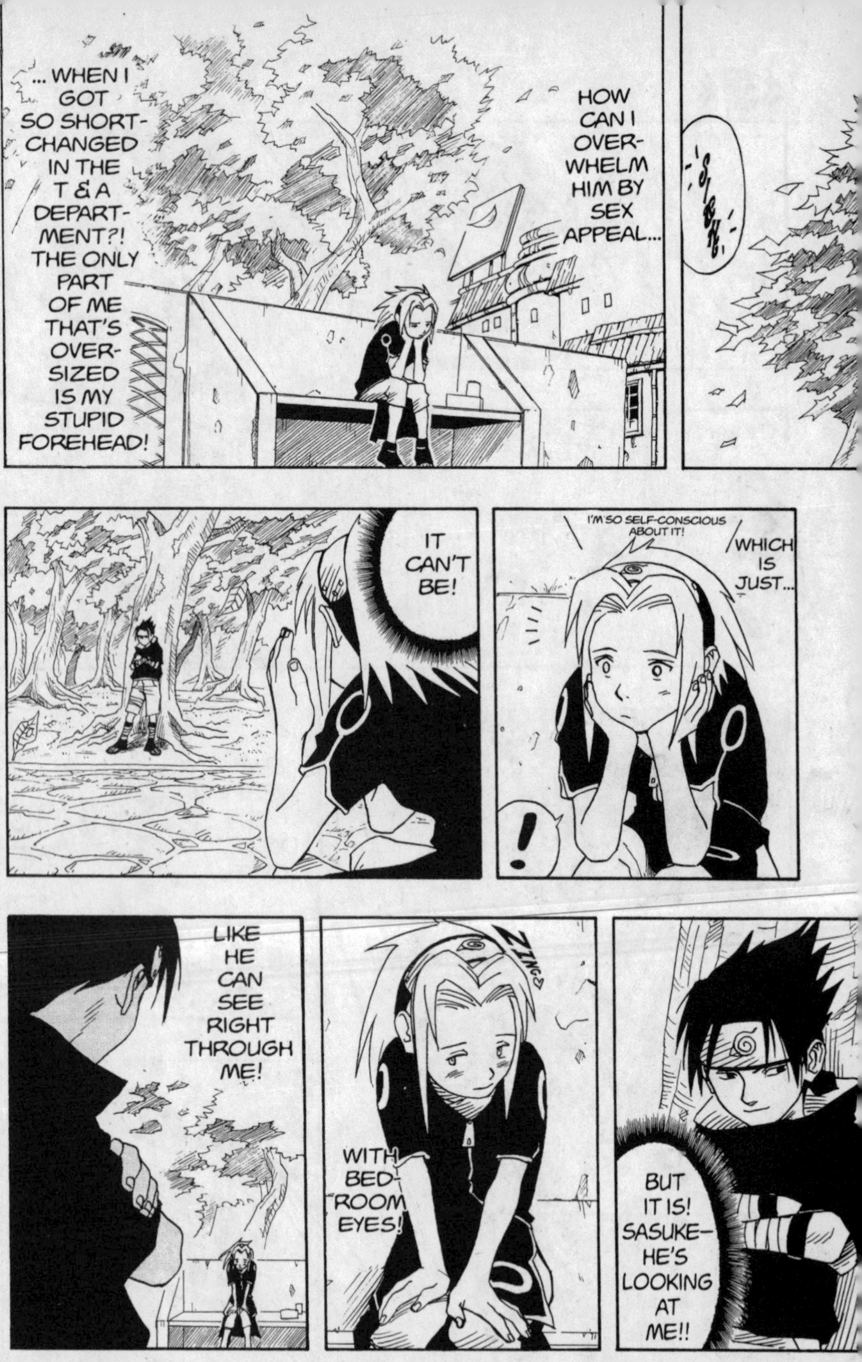
SIGH
HOW CAN I OVERWHELM HIM BY SEX APPEAL...
... WHEN I GOT SO SHORT-CHANGED IN THE T & A DEPARTMENT?! THE ONLY PART OF ME THAT'S OVERSIZED IS MY STUPID FOREHEAD!
I'M SO SELF-CONSCIOUS ABOUT IT!
WHICH IS JUST...
!
IT CAN'T BE!
BUT IT IS! SASUKE— HE'S LOOKING AT ME!!
ZING♡
WITH BED-ROOM EYES!
LIKE HE CAN SEE RIGHT THROUGH ME!

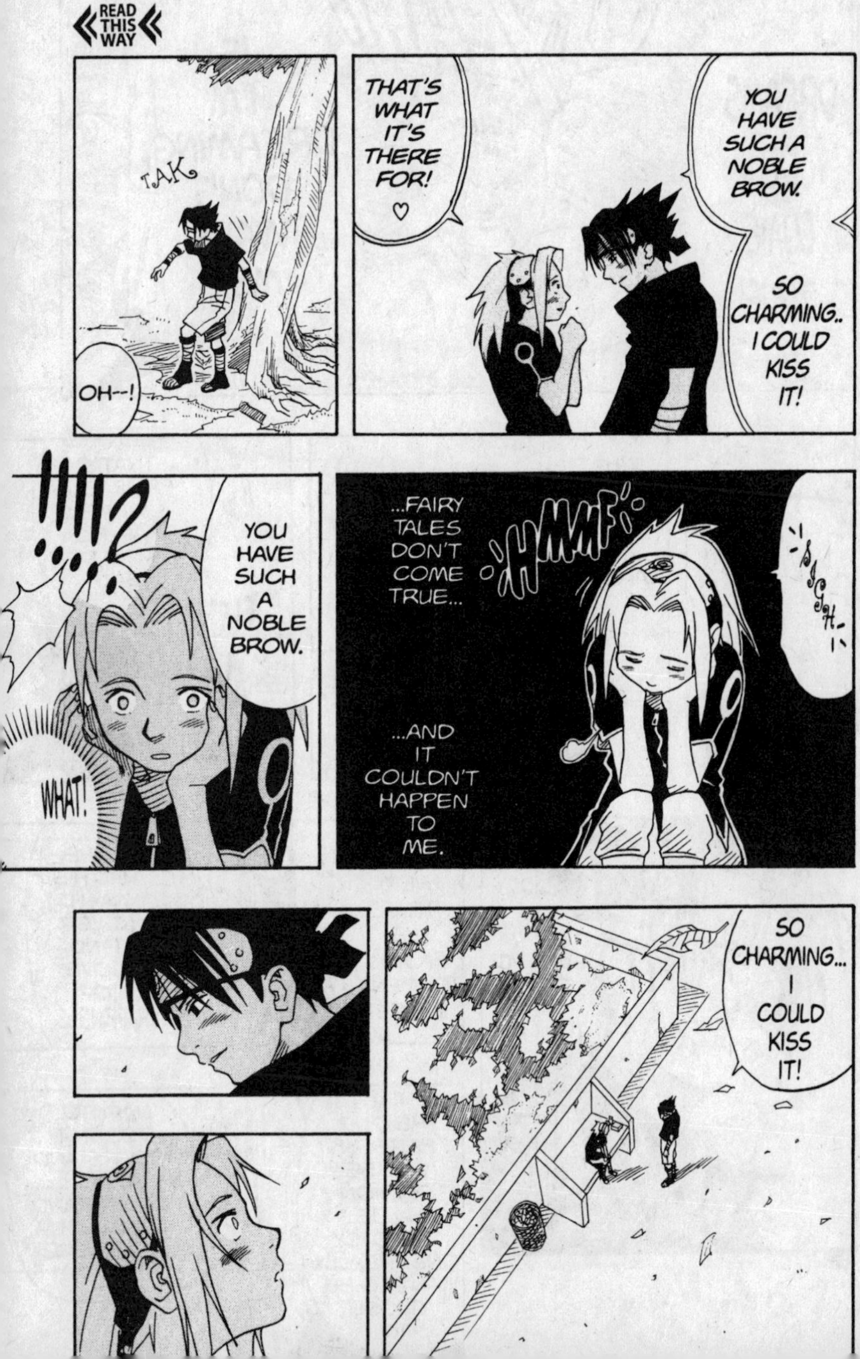
READ THIS WAY
YOU HAVE SUCH A NOBLE BROW.
SO CHARMING.. I COULD KISS IT!
THAT'S WHAT IT'S THERE FOR! ♡
TAK
OH--!
SIGH
...FAIRY TALES DON'T COME TRUE...
HMMF
...AND IT COULDN'T HAPPEN TO ME.
!!!!?
YOU HAVE SUCH A NOBLE BROW.
WHAT!
SO CHARMING... I COULD KISS IT!

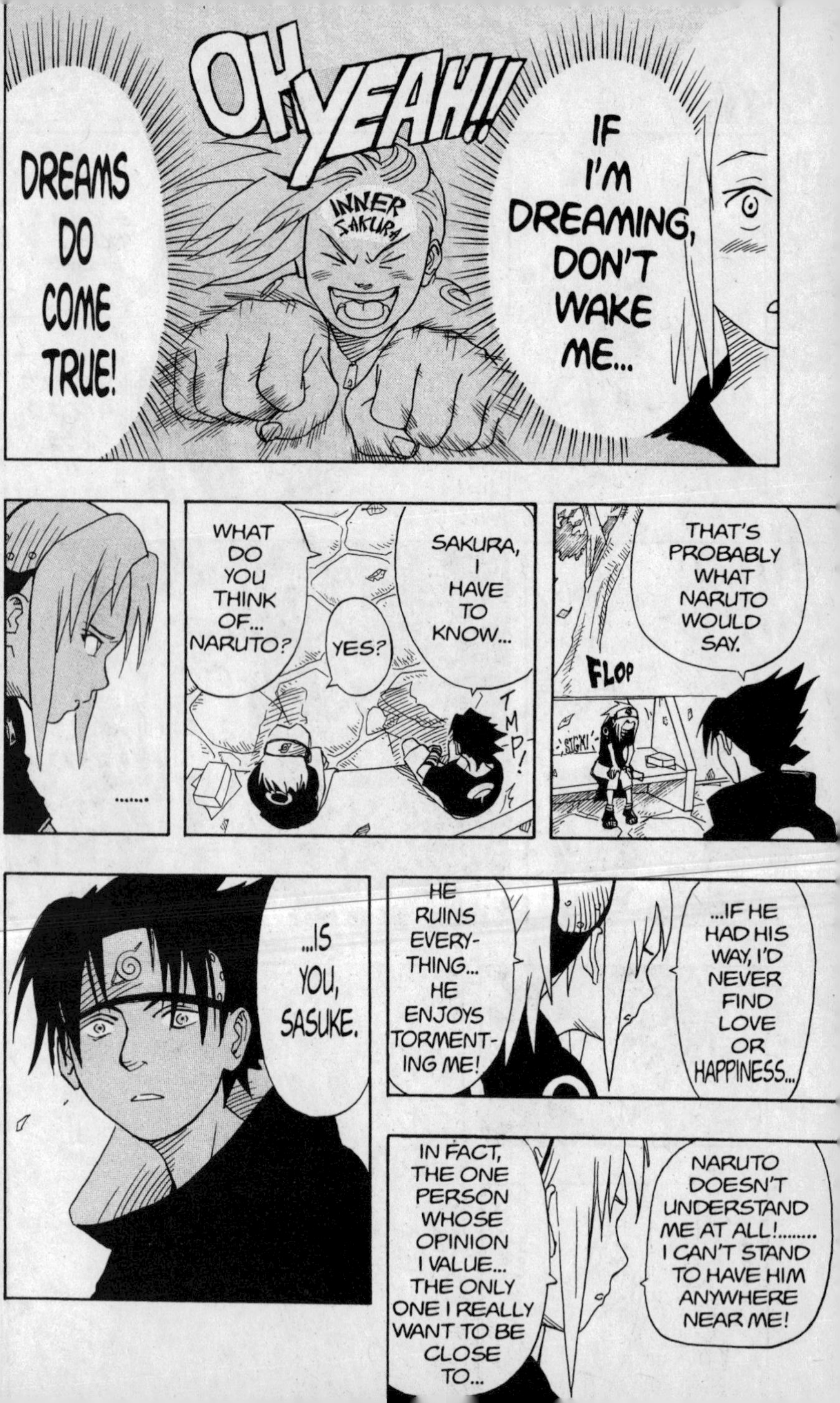
IF I'M DREAMING, DON'T WAKE ME...
OH YEAH!!
INNER SAKURA
DREAMS DO COME TRUE!
THAT'S PROBABLY WHAT NARUTO WOULD SAY.
FLOP
SAKURA, I HAVE TO KNOW...
TMP!
YES?
WHAT DO YOU THINK OF... NARUTO?
....
...IF HE HAD HIS WAY, I'D NEVER FIND LOVE OR HAPPINESS...
HE RUINS EVERYTHING... HE ENJOYS TORMENTING ME!
NARUTO DOESN'T UNDERSTAND ME AT ALL!........ I CAN'T STAND TO HAVE HIM ANYWHERE NEAR ME!
IN FACT, THE ONE PERSON WHOSE OPINION I VALUE... THE ONLY ONE I REALLY WANT TO BE CLOSE TO...
...IS YOU, SASUKE.

READ THIS WAY

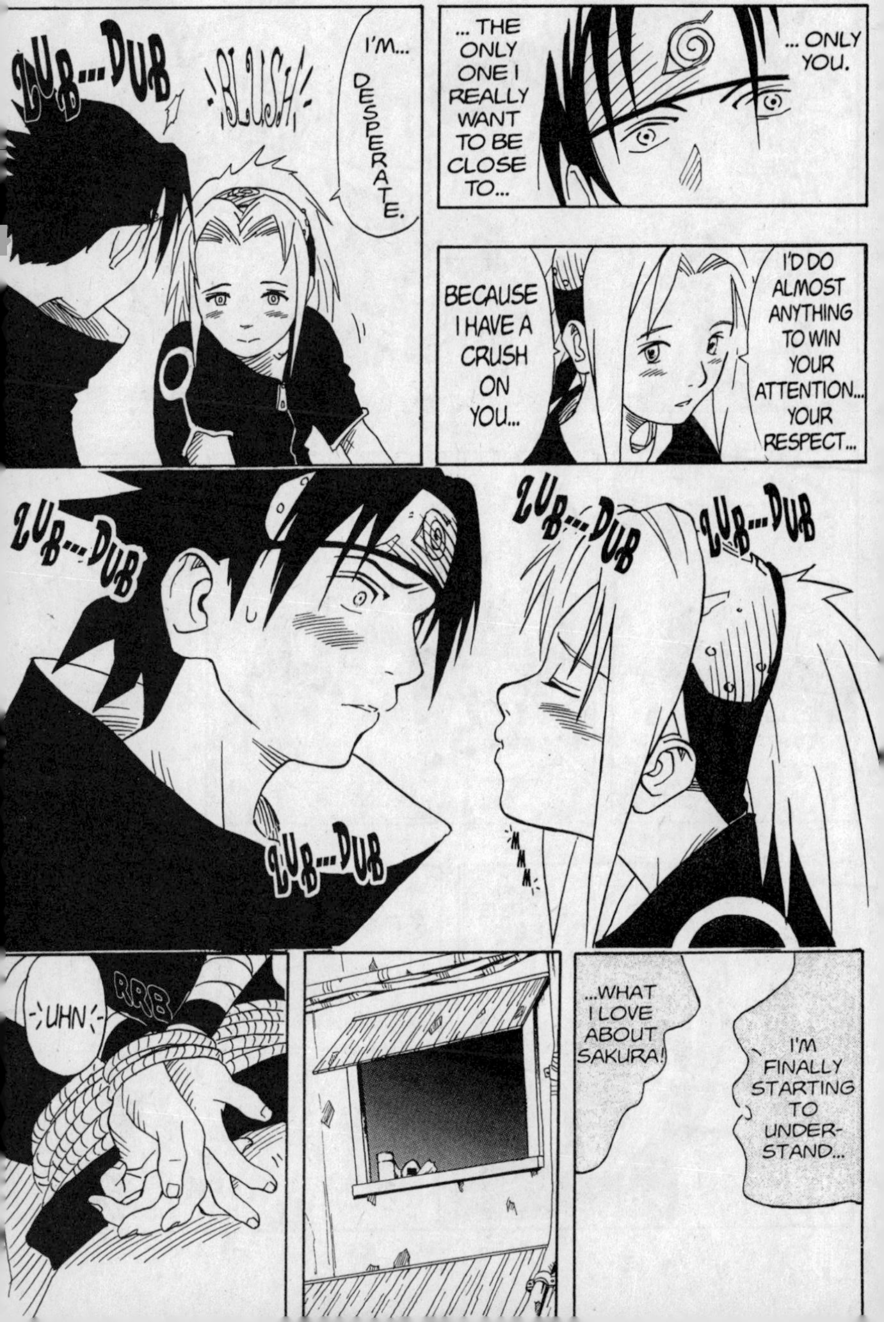

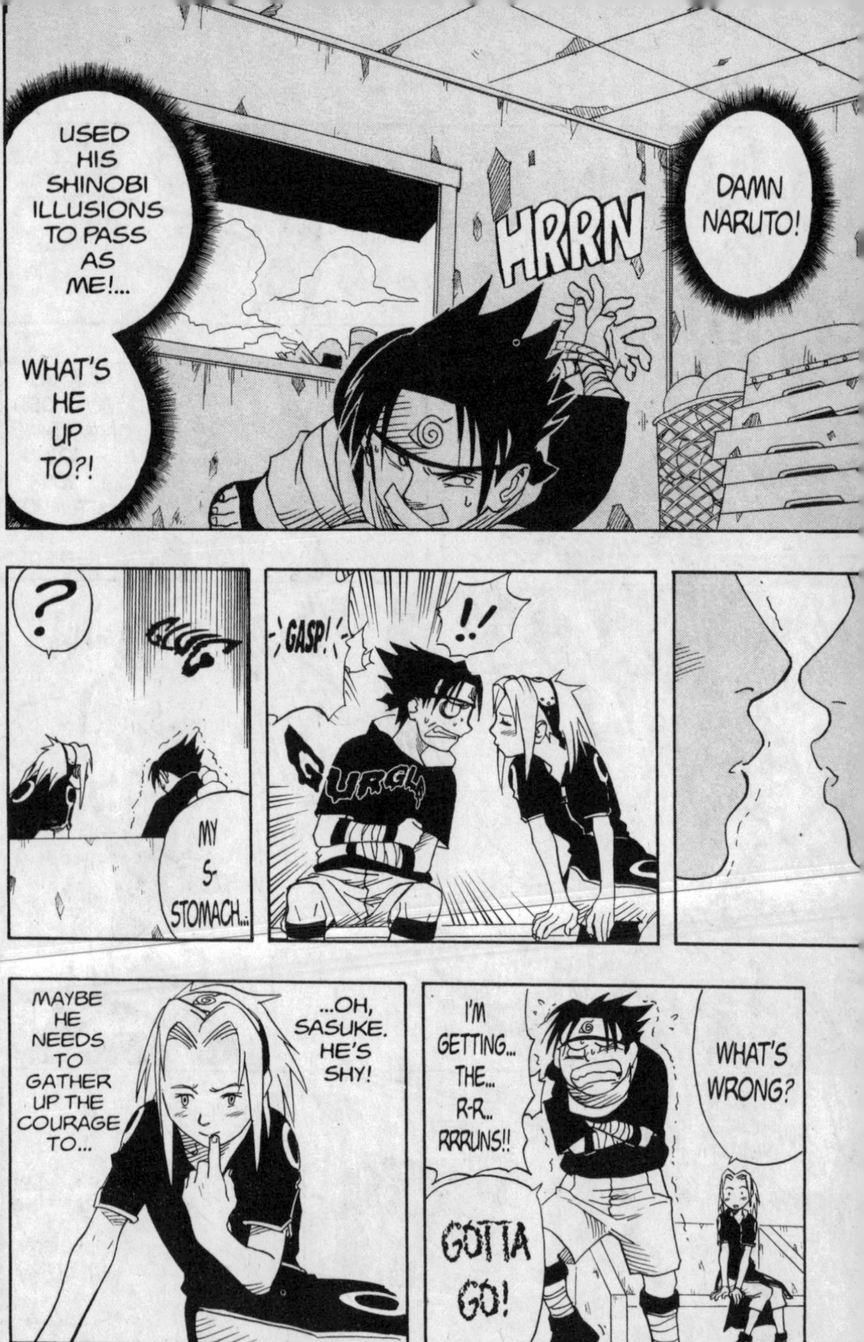
DAMN NARUTO!
HRRN
USED HIS SHINOBI ILLUSIONS TO PASS AS ME!...
WHAT'S HE UP TO?!
!!
GASP!
GURGL
?
GLUG
MY S-STOMACH...
WHAT'S WRONG?
I'M GETTING... THE... R-R.. RRRUNS!!
GOTTA GO!
...OH, SASUKE. HE'S SHY!
MAYBE HE NEEDS TO GATHER UP THE COURAGE TO...

READ THIS WAY

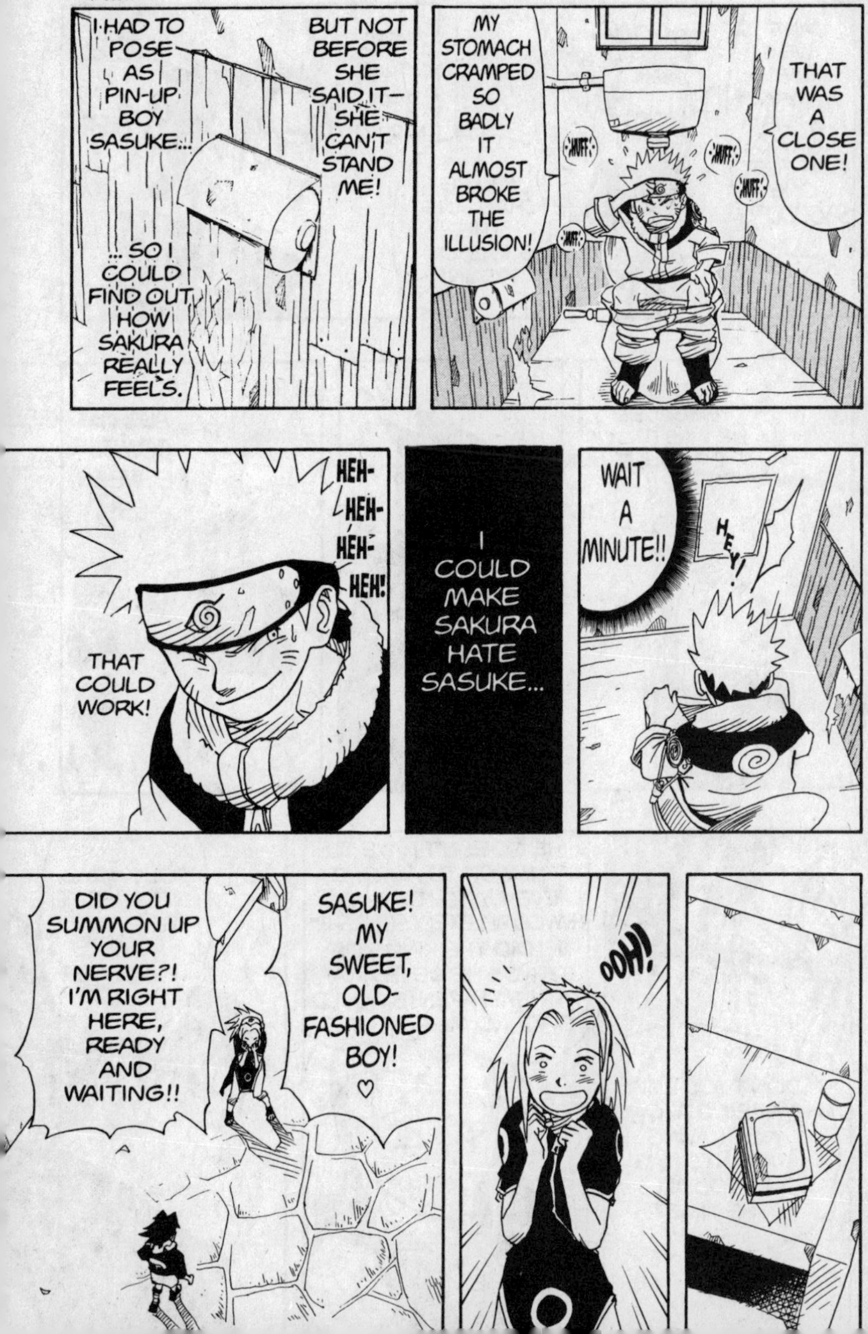
THAT WAS A CLOSE ONE!
MY STOMACH CRAMPED SO BADLY IT ALMOST BROKE THE ILLUSION!
HUFF
HUFF
HUFF
HUFF
I HAD TO POSE AS PIN-UP BOY SASUKE...
...SO I COULD FIND OUT HOW SAKURA REALLY FEELS.
BUT NOT BEFORE SHE SAID IT—SHE CAN'T STAND ME!
WAIT A MINUTE!!
HEY!
I COULD MAKE SAKURA HATE SASUKE...
HEH-HEH-HEH-HEH!
THAT COULD WORK!
OOH!
SASUKE! MY SWEET, OLD-FASHIONED BOY! ♡
DID YOU SUMMON UP YOUR NERVE?! I'M RIGHT HERE, READY AND WAITING!!

READ THIS WAY

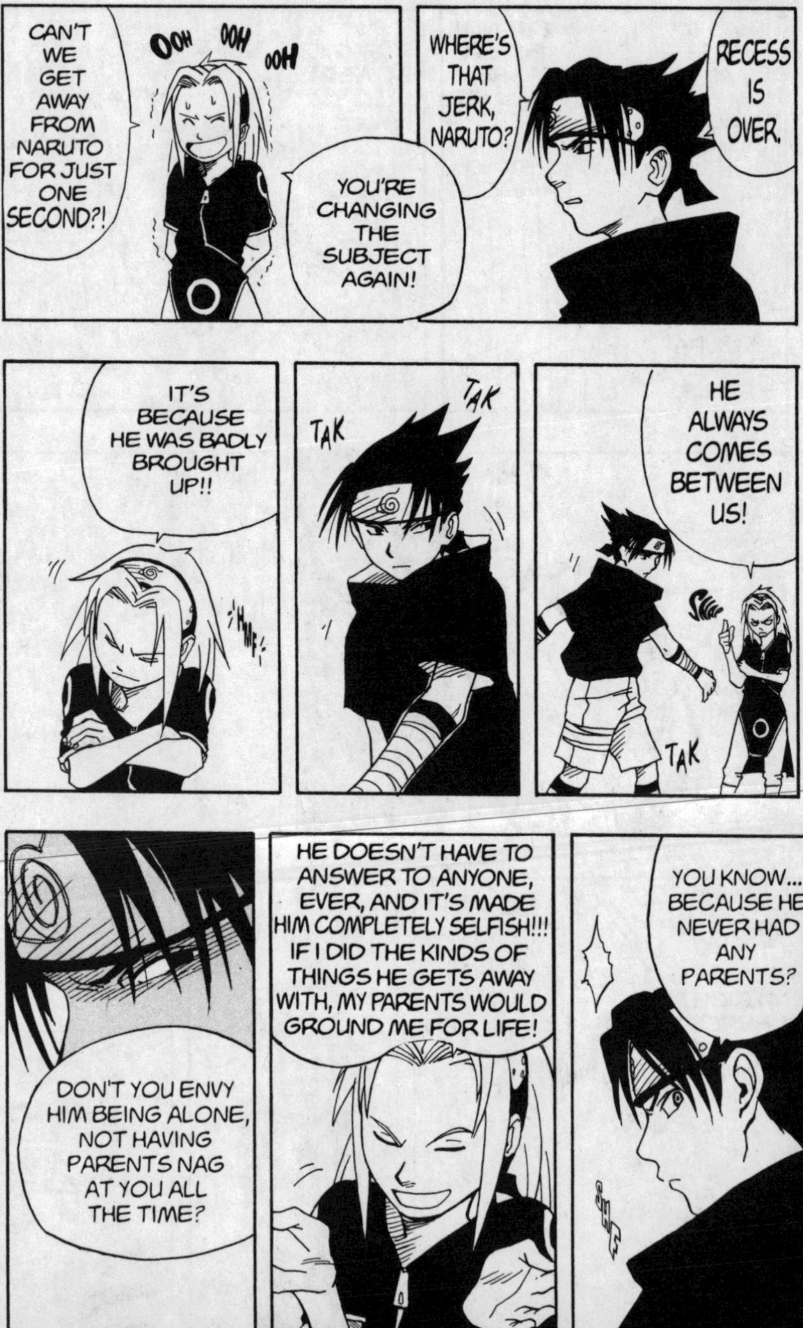
RECESS IS OVER.
WHERE'S THAT JERK, NARUTO?
YOU'RE CHANGING THE SUBJECT AGAIN!
OOH OOH OOH
CAN'T WE GET AWAY FROM NARUTO FOR JUST ONE SECOND?!
HE ALWAYS COMES BETWEEN US!
TAK
TAK
TAK
IT'S BECAUSE HE WAS BADLY BROUGHT UP!!
HMF
YOU KNOW... BECAUSE HE NEVER HAD ANY PARENTS?
HE DOESN'T HAVE TO ANSWER TO ANYONE, EVER, AND IT'S MADE HIM COMPLETELY SELFISH!!! IF I DID THE KINDS OF THINGS HE GETS AWAY WITH, MY PARENTS WOULD GROUND ME FOR LIFE!
DON'T YOU ENVY HIM BEING ALONE, NOT HAVING PARENTS NAG AT YOU ALL THE TIME?

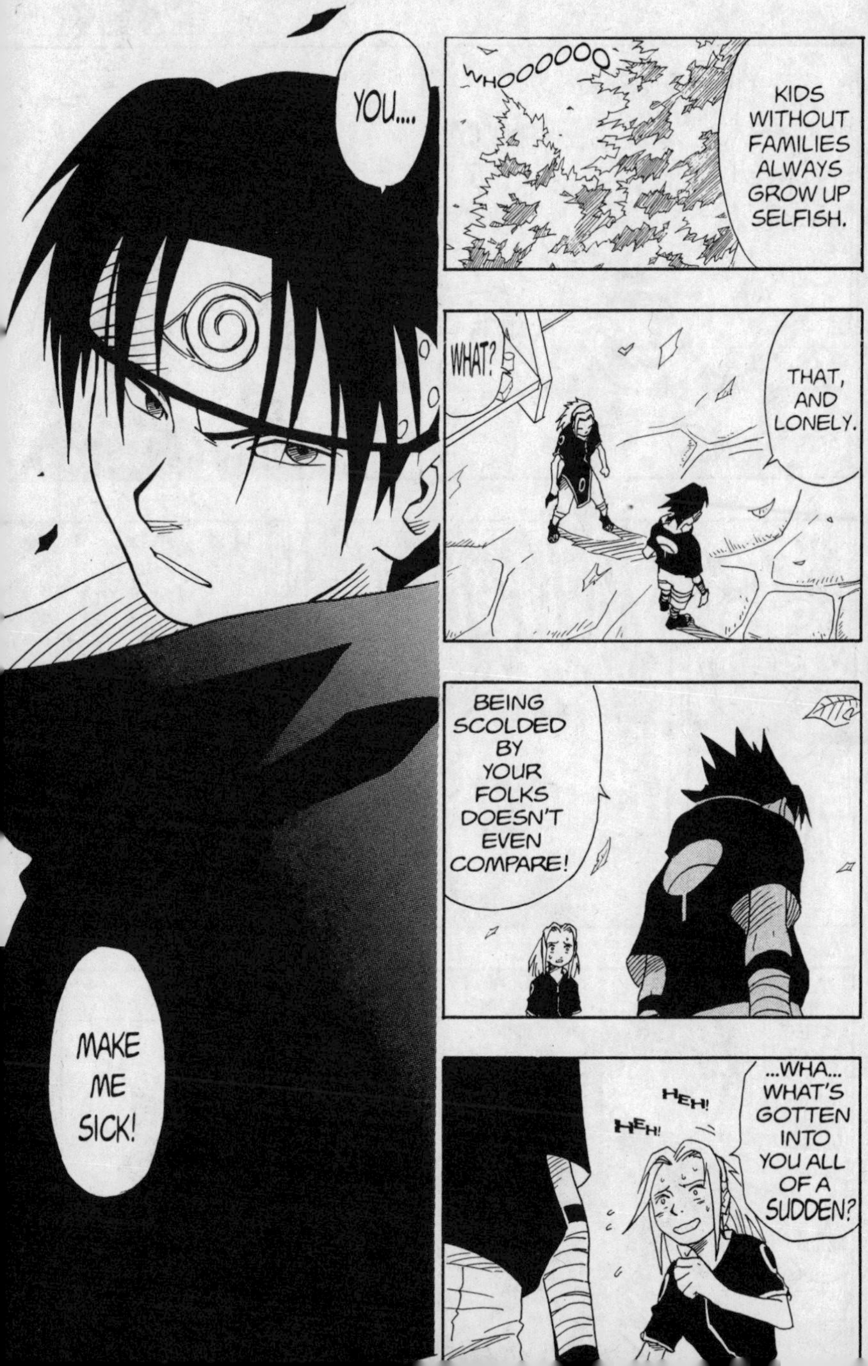
WHOOOOOOO
KIDS WITHOUT FAMILIES ALWAYS GROW UP SELFISH.
THAT, AND LONELY.
WHAT?
BEING SCOLDED BY YOUR FOLKS DOESN'T EVEN COMPARE!
...WHA... WHAT'S GOTTEN INTO YOU ALL OF A SUDDEN?
HEH!
HEH!
YOU....
MAKE ME SICK!

READ THIS WAY

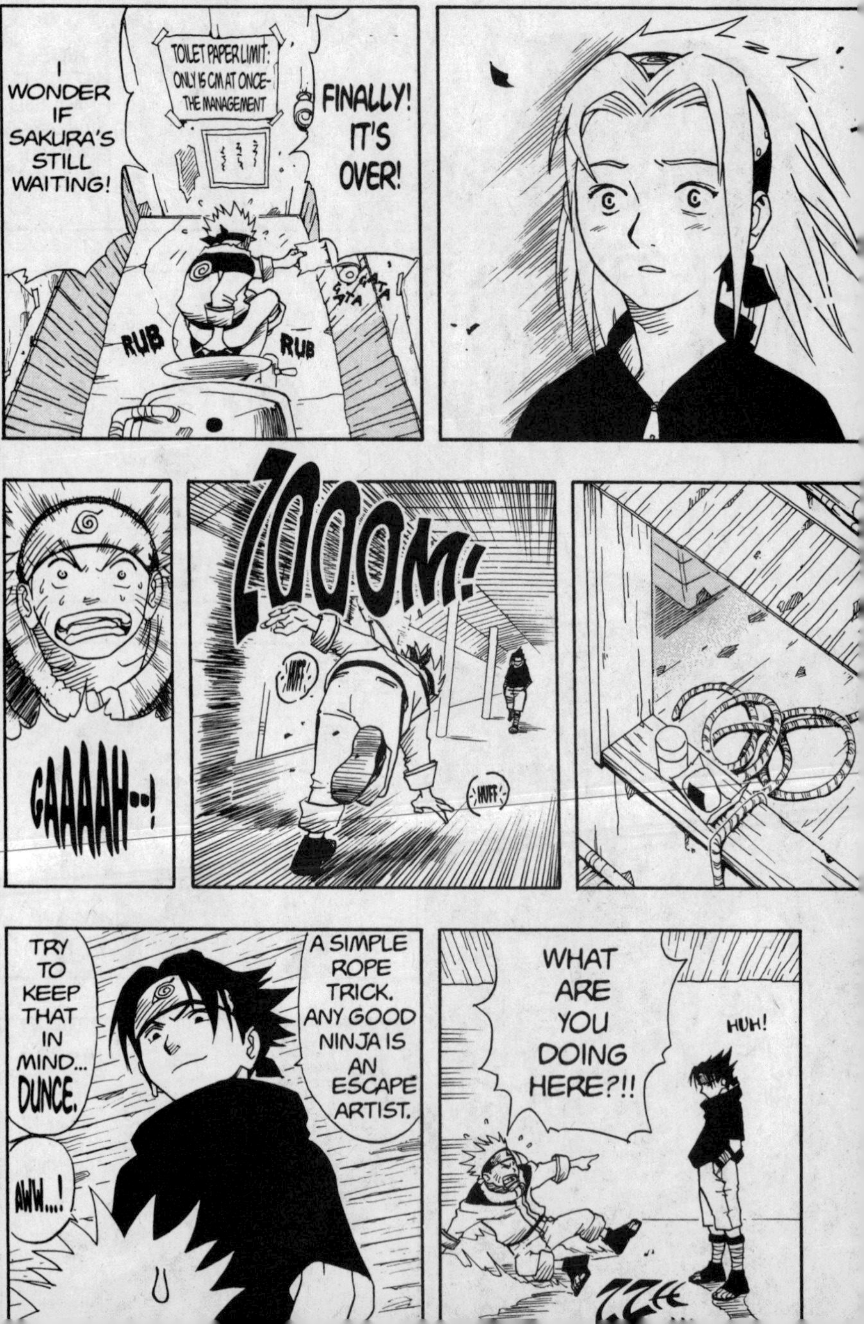
TOILET PAPER LIMIT: ONLY 15 CM AT ONCE- THE MANAGEMENT
FINALLY! IT'S OVER!
I WONDER IF SAKURA'S STILL WAITING!
GATA GATA
RUB
RUB
ZOOOM!
HUFF!
HUFF
GAAAAH--!
HUH!
WHAT ARE YOU DOING HERE?!!
A SIMPLE ROPE TRICK. ANY GOOD NINJA IS AN ESCAPE ARTIST.
TRY TO KEEP THAT IN MIND... DUNCE.
AWW...!

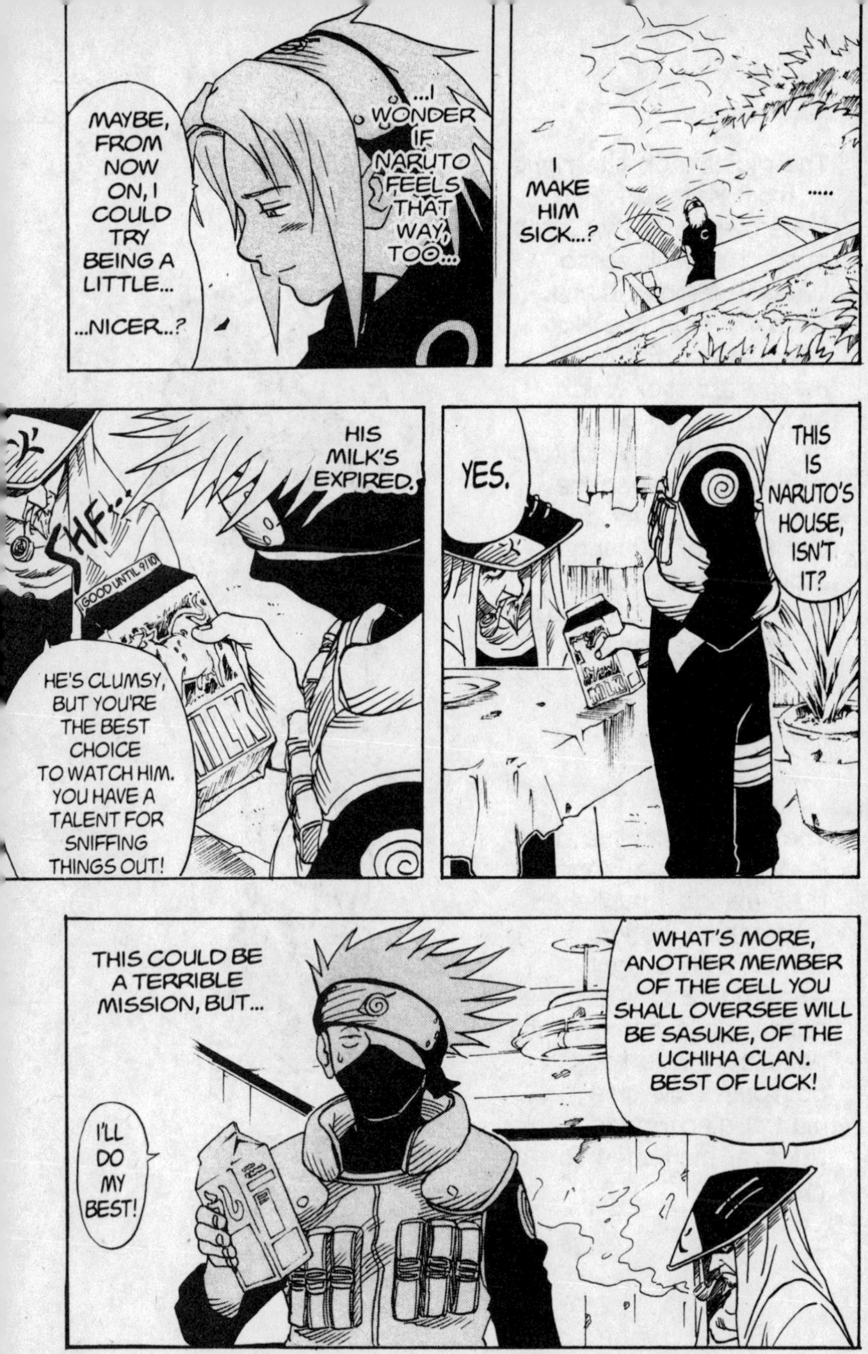
.....
I MAKE HIM SICK...?
...I WONDER IF NARUTO FEELS THAT WAY, TOO...
MAYBE, FROM NOW ON, I COULD TRY BEING A LITTLE...
...NICER...?
THIS IS NARUTO'S HOUSE, ISN'T IT?
YES.
HIS MILK'S EXPIRED.
SHF...
GOOD UNTIL 9/10
MILK
HE'S CLUMSY, BUT YOU'RE THE BEST CHOICE TO WATCH HIM. YOU HAVE A TALENT FOR SNIFFING THINGS OUT!
WHAT'S MORE, ANOTHER MEMBER OF THE CELL YOU SHALL OVERSEE WILL BE SASUKE, OF THE UCHIHA CLAN. BEST OF LUCK!
THIS COULD BE A TERRIBLE MISSION, BUT...
I'LL DO MY BEST!

The picture on the right is from Karakuri ("mechanism"), the first story I submitted to Weekly Shonen Jump. Karakuri won the Hop Step Award for new manga artists, which allowed me to get picked up by my current editor and helped me begin my journey down the road of a manga artist. It's a manga that brings back a lot of memories for me. But, man, the hero sure does have intensely terrifying eyes.

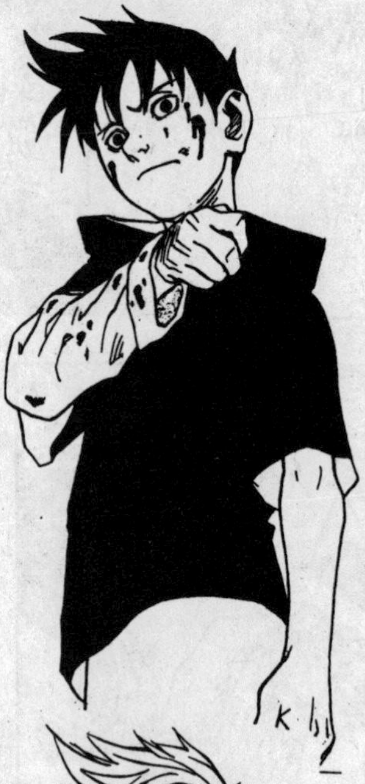

The picture on the right is another one from the first manga I published in Weekly Shonen Jump...that's right, Karakuri! But when the reader polls came in, its popularity was rock bottom! Still, this manga also brings back a lot of memories for me.

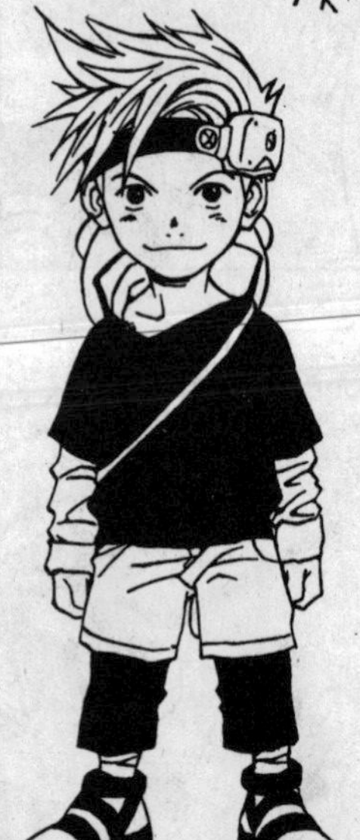

Number 4: Hatake Kakashi!

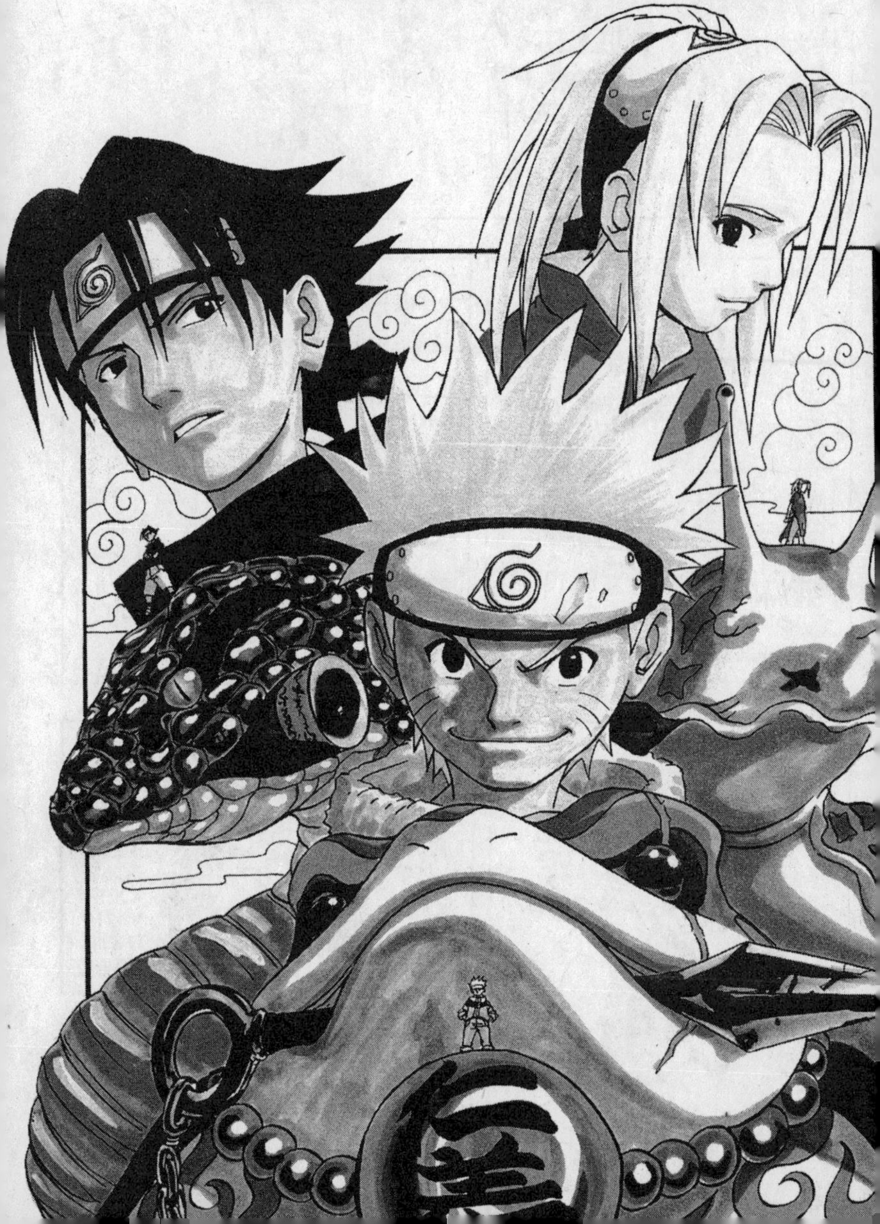

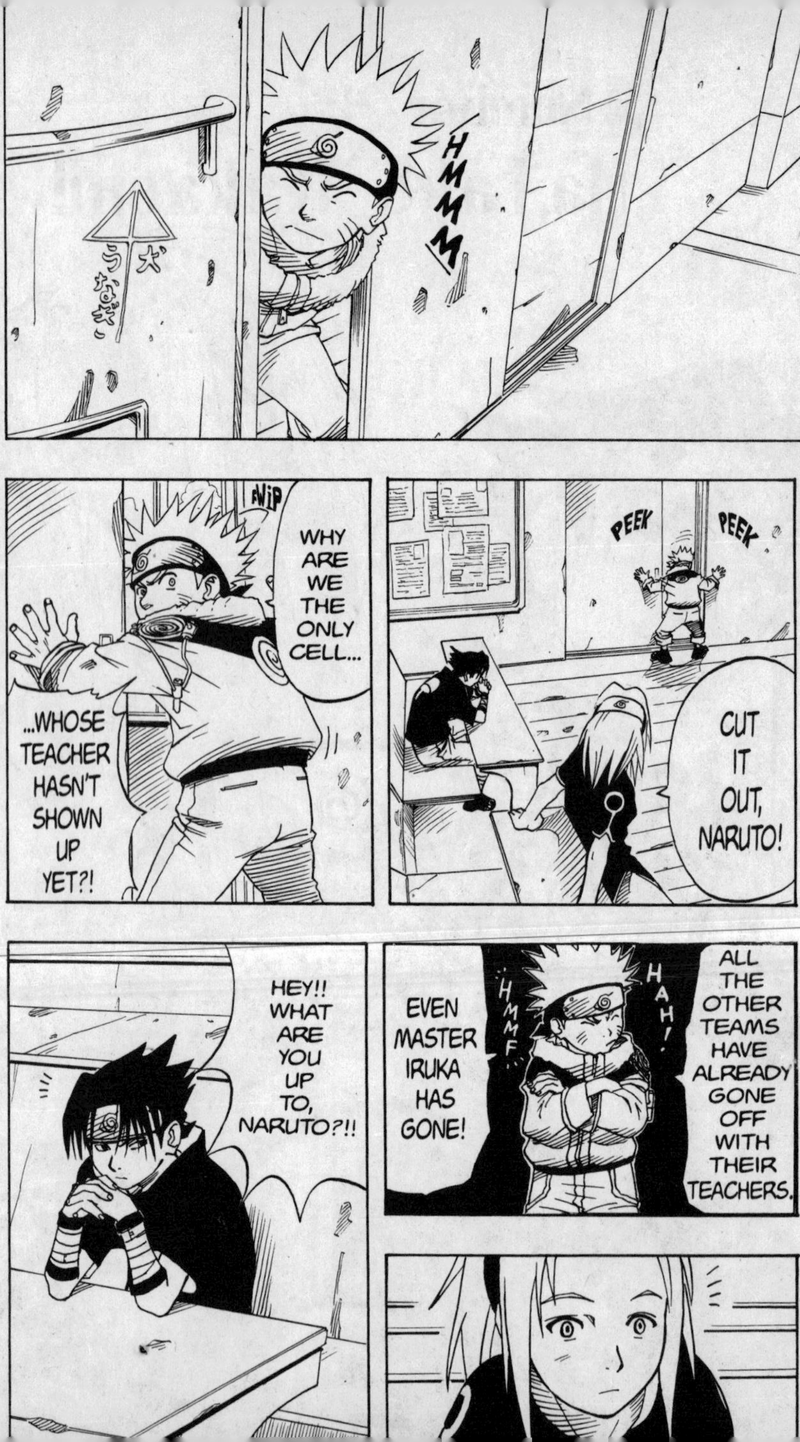
HMMMM
PEEK
PEEK
CUT IT OUT, NARUTO!
FWIP
WHY ARE WE THE ONLY CELL...
...WHOSE TEACHER HASN'T SHOWN UP YET?!
ALL THE OTHER TEAMS HAVE ALREADY GONE OFF WITH THEIR TEACHERS.
HAH!
HMMF
EVEN MASTER IRUKA HAS GONE!
HEY!! WHAT ARE YOU UP TO, NARUTO?!!

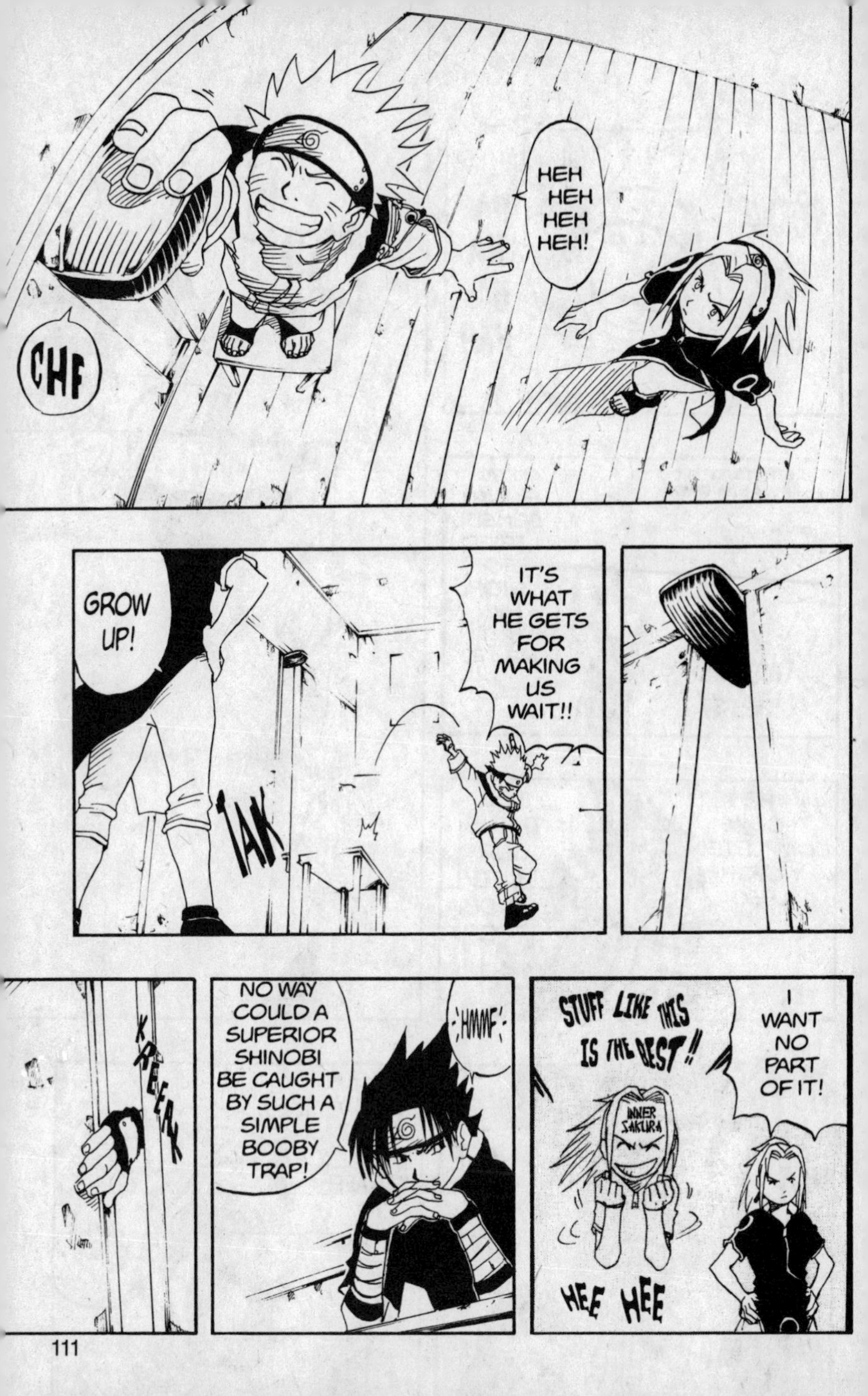
HEH HEH HEH HEH!
CHF
IT'S WHAT HE GETS FOR MAKING US WAIT!!
GROW UP!
TAK
I WANT NO PART OF IT!
STUFF LIKE THIS IS THE BEST!!
INNER SAKURA
HEE HEE
HMMF
NO WAY COULD A SUPERIOR SHINOBI BE CAUGHT BY SUCH A SIMPLE BOOBY TRAP!
KREEAK

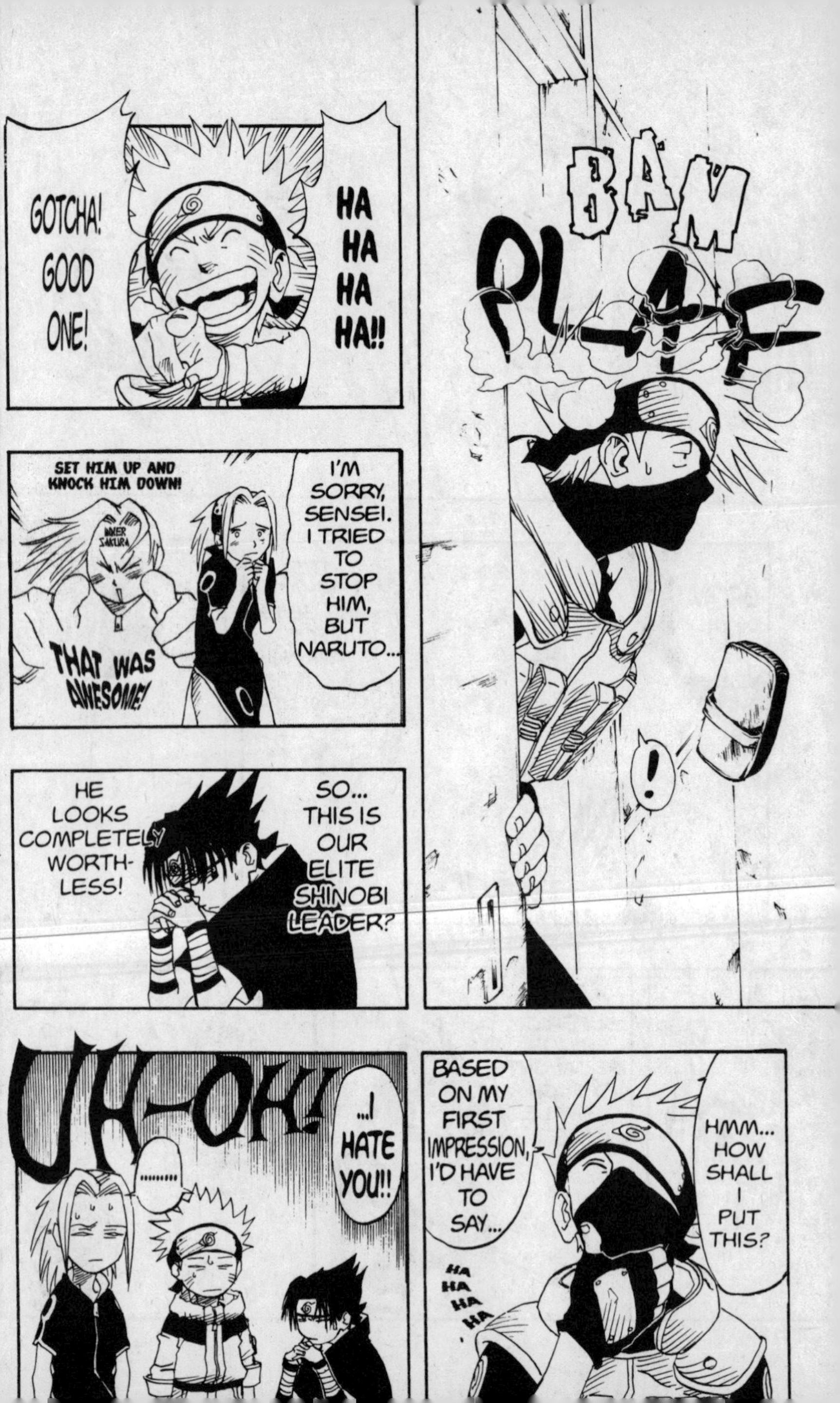
BAM
PLAFF
!
GOTCHA! GOOD ONE!
HA HA HA HA!!
I'M SORRY, SENSEI. I TRIED TO STOP HIM, BUT NARUTO...
SET HIM UP AND KNOCK HIM DOWN!
INNER SAKURA
THAT WAS AWESOME!
SO... THIS IS OUR ELITE SHINOBI LEADER?
HE LOOKS COMPLETELY WORTHLESS!
HMM... HOW SHALL I PUT THIS?
BASED ON MY FIRST IMPRESSION, I'D HAVE TO SAY...
HA HA HA HA
...I HATE YOU!!
UH-OH!
....

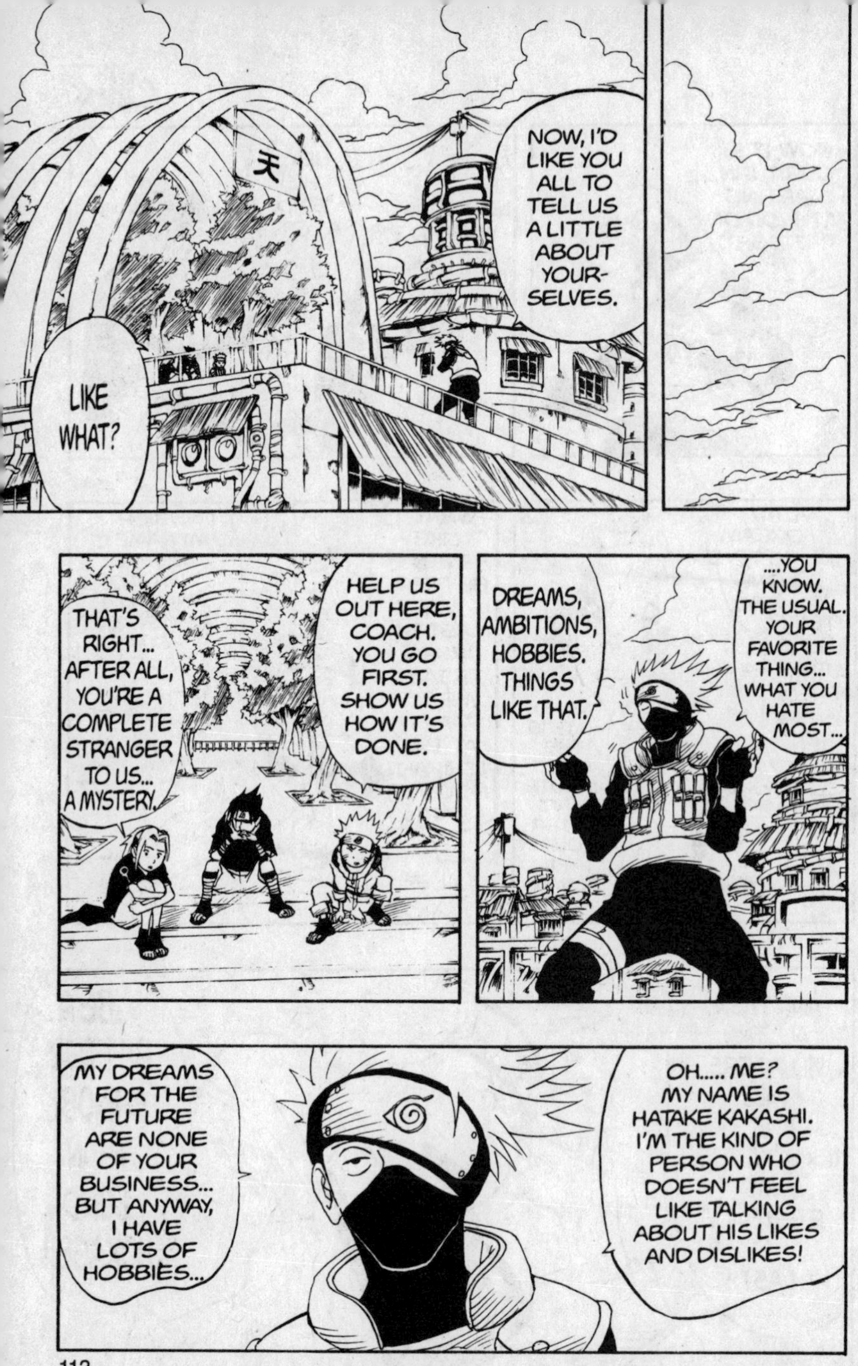
NOW, I'D LIKE YOU ALL TO TELL US A LITTLE ABOUT YOUR-SELVES.
LIKE WHAT?
....YOU KNOW. THE USUAL. YOUR FAVORITE THING... WHAT YOU HATE MOST...
DREAMS, AMBITIONS, HOBBIES. THINGS LIKE THAT.
HELP US OUT HERE, COACH. YOU GO FIRST. SHOW US HOW IT'S DONE.
THAT'S RIGHT... AFTER ALL, YOU'RE A COMPLETE STRANGER TO US... A MYSTERY.
OH..... ME? MY NAME IS HATAKE KAKASHI. I'M THE KIND OF PERSON WHO DOESN'T FEEL LIKE TALKING ABOUT HIS LIKES AND DISLIKES!
MY DREAMS FOR THE FUTURE ARE NONE OF YOUR BUSINESS... BUT ANYWAY, I HAVE LOTS OF HOBBIES...

READ THIS WAY

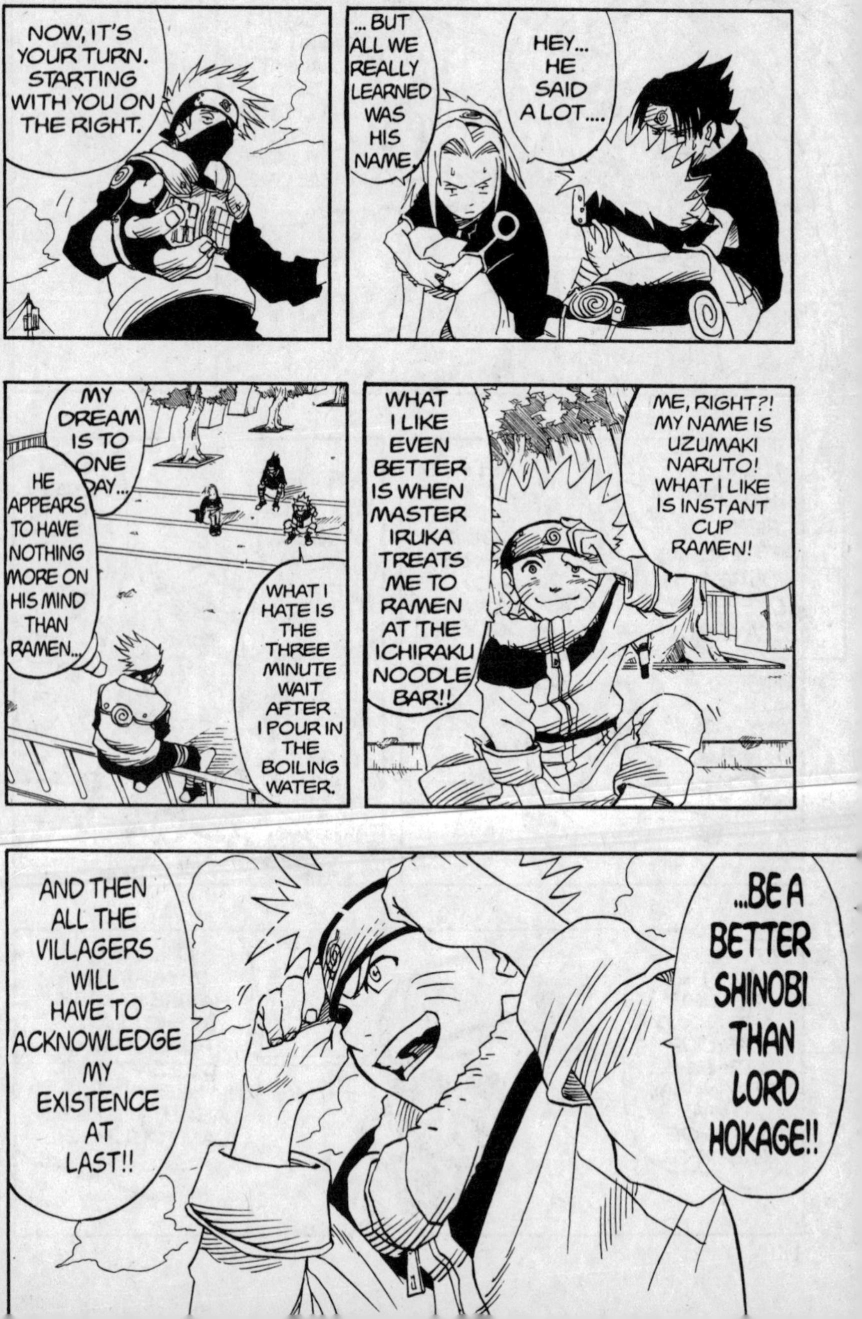
HEY... HE SAID A LOT....
... BUT ALL WE REALLY LEARNED WAS HIS NAME.
NOW, IT'S YOUR TURN. STARTING WITH YOU ON THE RIGHT.
ME, RIGHT?! MY NAME IS UZUMAKI NARUTO! WHAT I LIKE IS INSTANT CUP RAMEN!
WHAT I LIKE EVEN BETTER IS WHEN MASTER IRUKA TREATS ME TO RAMEN AT THE ICHIRAKU NOODLE BAR!!
WHAT I HATE IS THE THREE MINUTE WAIT AFTER I POUR IN THE BOILING WATER.
HE APPEARS TO HAVE NOTHING MORE ON HIS MIND THAN RAMEN...
MY DREAM IS TO ONE DAY...
...BE A BETTER SHINOBI THAN LORD HOKAGE!!
AND THEN ALL THE VILLAGERS WILL HAVE TO ACKNOWLEDGE MY EXISTENCE AT LAST!!

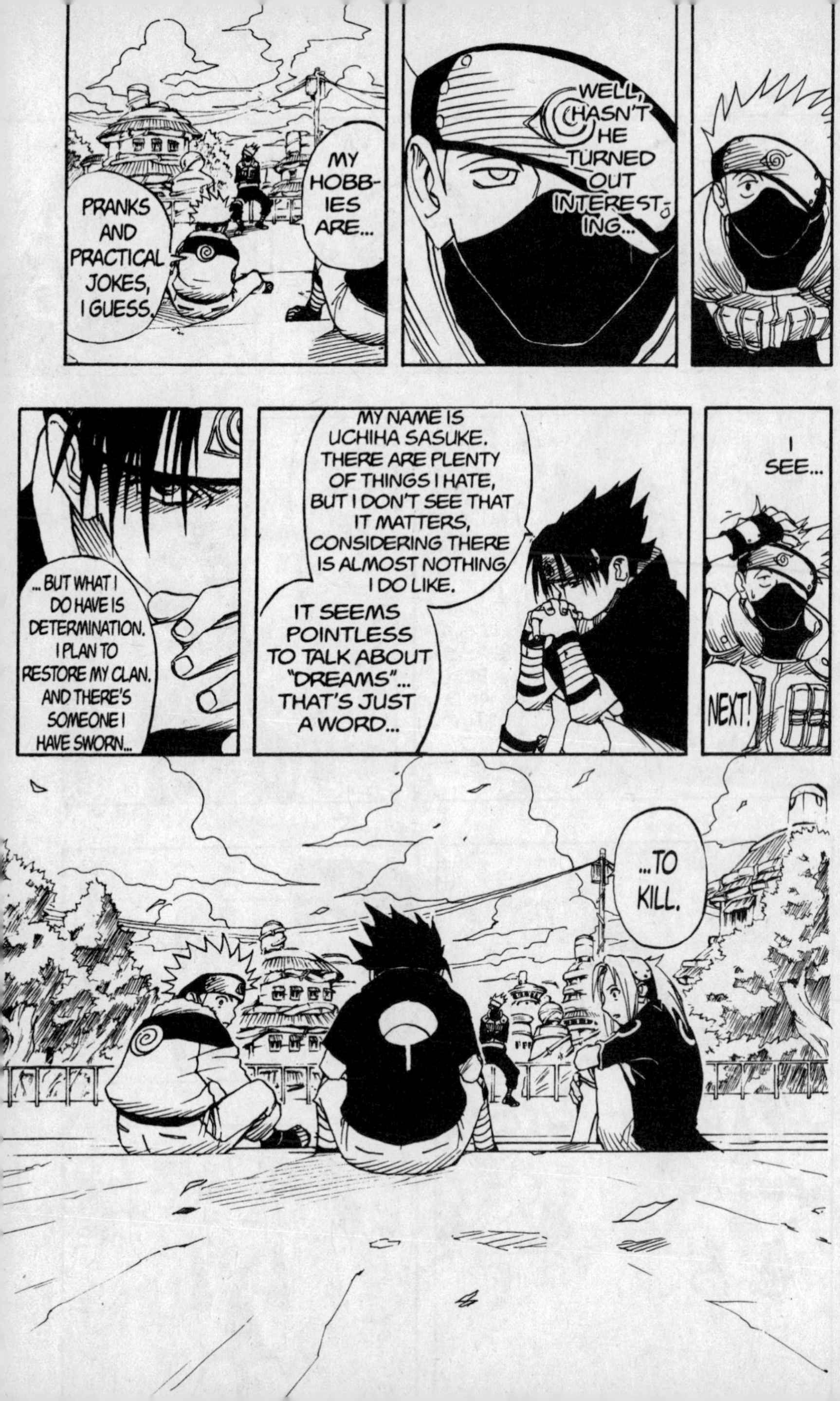
WELL, HASN'T HE TURNED OUT INTERESTING...
MY HOBB-IES ARE...
PRANKS AND PRACTICAL JOKES, I GUESS.
I SEE...
NEXT!
MY NAME IS UCHIHA SASUKE. THERE ARE PLENTY OF THINGS I HATE, BUT I DON'T SEE THAT IT MATTERS, CONSIDERING THERE IS ALMOST NOTHING I DO LIKE.
IT SEEMS POINTLESS TO TALK ABOUT "DREAMS"... THAT'S JUST A WORD...
...BUT WHAT I DO HAVE IS DETERMINATION. I PLAN TO RESTORE MY CLAN. AND THERE'S SOMEONE I HAVE SWORN...
...TO KILL.

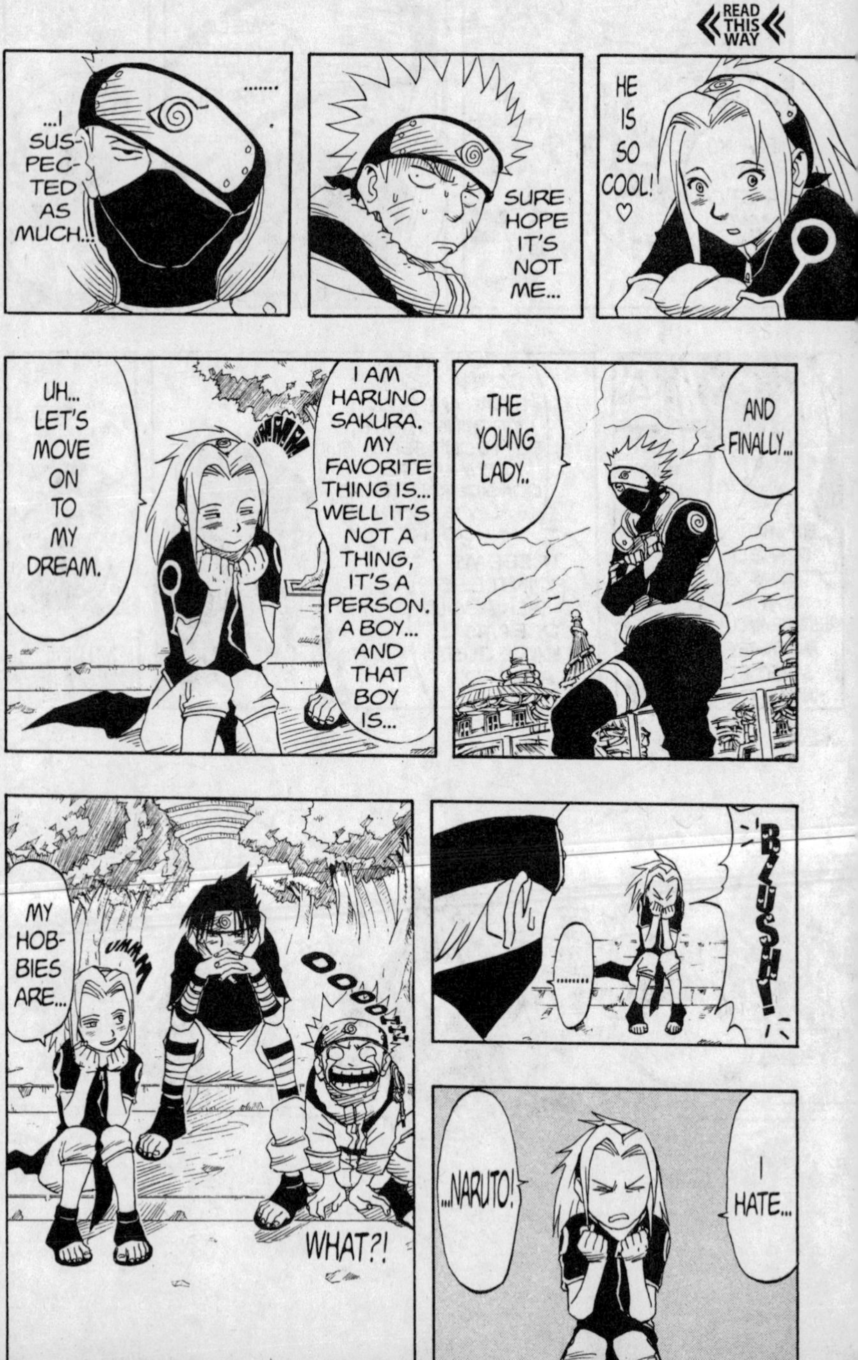
READ THIS WAY
HE IS SO COOL! ♡
SURE HOPE IT'S NOT ME...
......
...I SUSPECTED AS MUCH...
AND FINALLY...
THE YOUNG LADY..
I AM HARUNO SAKURA. MY FAVORITE THING IS... WELL IT'S NOT A THING, IT'S A PERSON. A BOY... AND THAT BOY IS...
UMMM
UH... LET'S MOVE ON TO MY DREAM.
BZUSH!
......
I HATE...
...NARUTO!
MY HOBBIES ARE...
UMMM
OOOOOH
WHAT?!

READ THIS WAY

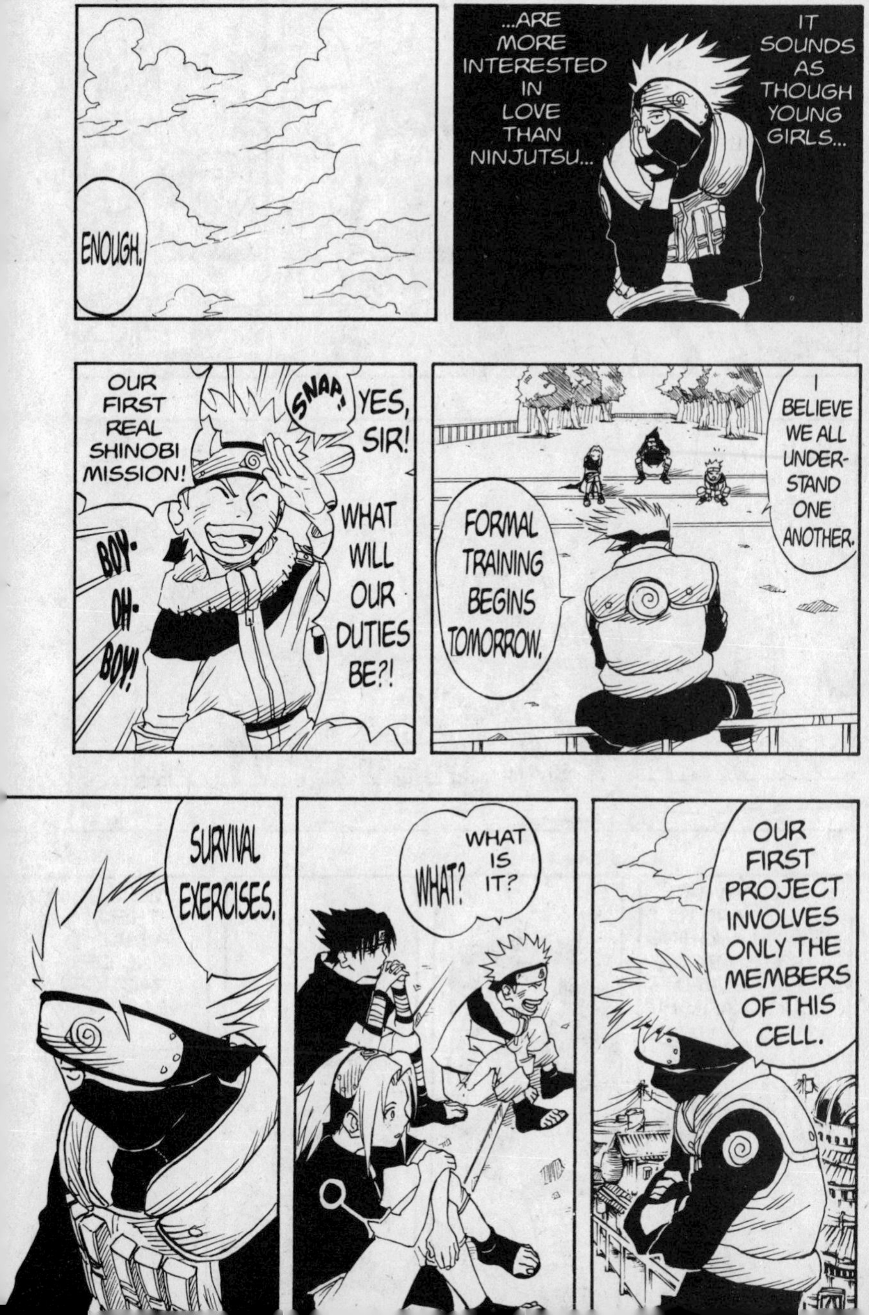
IT SOUNDS AS THOUGH YOUNG GIRLS...
...ARE MORE INTERESTED IN LOVE THAN NINJUTSU...
ENOUGH.
I BELIEVE WE ALL UNDERSTAND ONE ANOTHER.
FORMAL TRAINING BEGINS TOMORROW.
YES, SIR!
SNAP
OUR FIRST REAL SHINOBI MISSION!
WHAT WILL OUR DUTIES BE?!
BOY-OH-BOY!
OUR FIRST PROJECT INVOLVES ONLY THE MEMBERS OF THIS CELL.
WHAT IS IT?
WHAT?
SURVIVAL EXERCISES.

READ THIS WAY

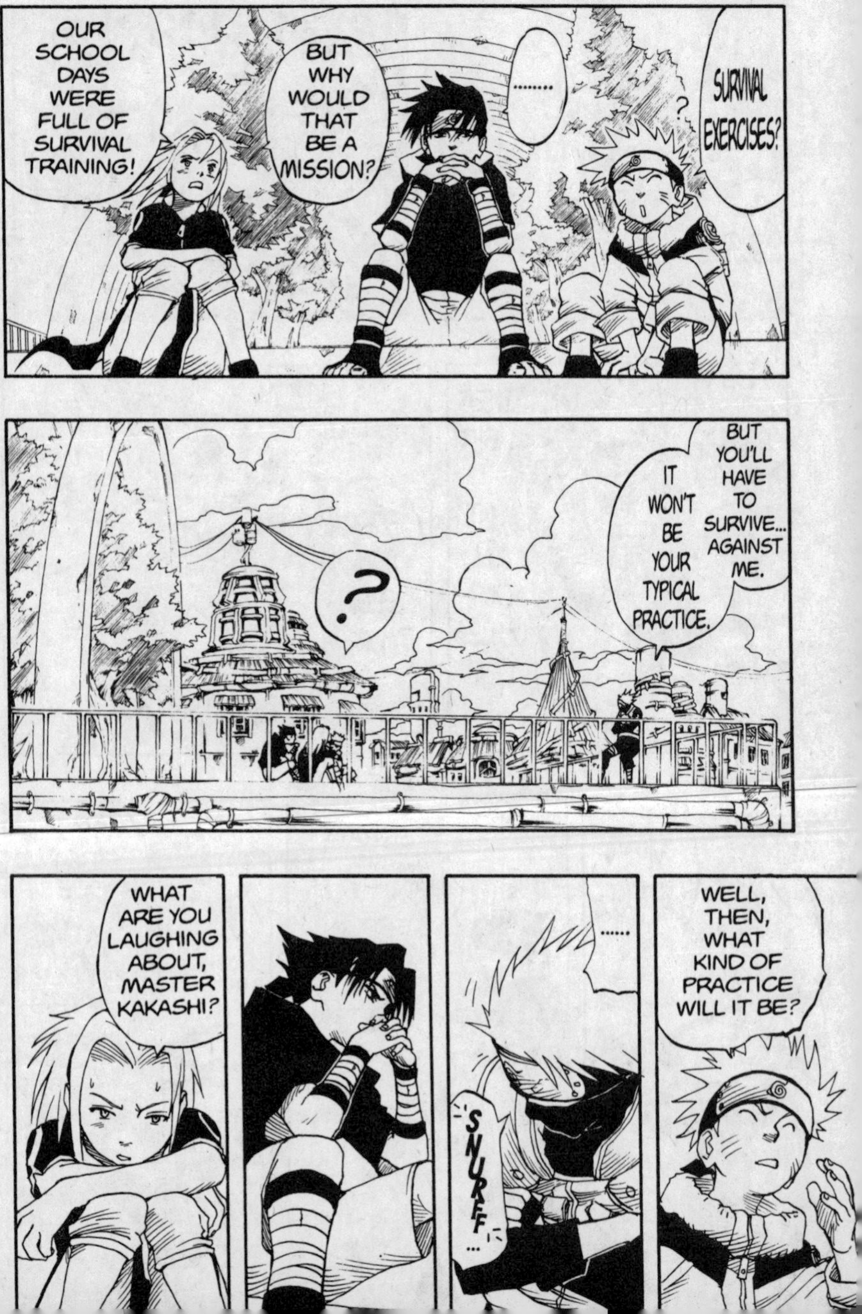
SURVIVAL EXERCISES?
?
....
BUT WHY WOULD THAT BE A MISSION?
OUR SCHOOL DAYS WERE FULL OF SURVIVAL TRAINING!
IT WON'T BE YOUR TYPICAL PRACTICE. BUT YOU'LL HAVE TO SURVIVE... AGAINST ME.
?
WELL, THEN, WHAT KIND OF PRACTICE WILL IT BE?
......
SNURFF...
WHAT ARE YOU LAUGHING ABOUT, MASTER KAKASHI?

READ THIS WAY

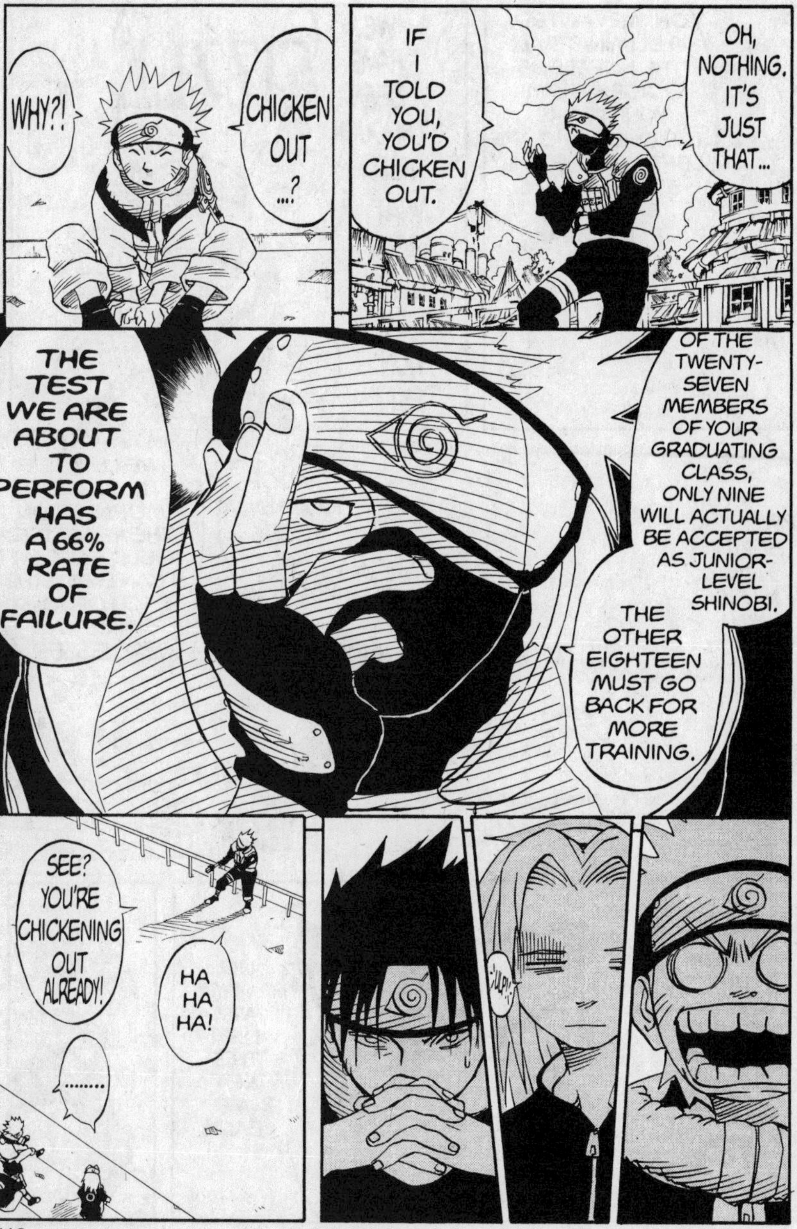
OH, NOTHING. IT'S JUST THAT...
IF I TOLD YOU, YOU'D CHICKEN OUT.
CHICKEN OUT ...?
WHY?!
OF THE TWENTY-SEVEN MEMBERS OF YOUR GRADUATING CLASS, ONLY NINE WILL ACTUALLY BE ACCEPTED AS JUNIOR-LEVEL SHINOBI.
THE OTHER EIGHTEEN MUST GO BACK FOR MORE TRAINING.
THE TEST WE ARE ABOUT TO PERFORM HAS A 66% RATE OF FAILURE.
GULP!!
SEE? YOU'RE CHICKENING OUT ALREADY!
HA HA HA!
....

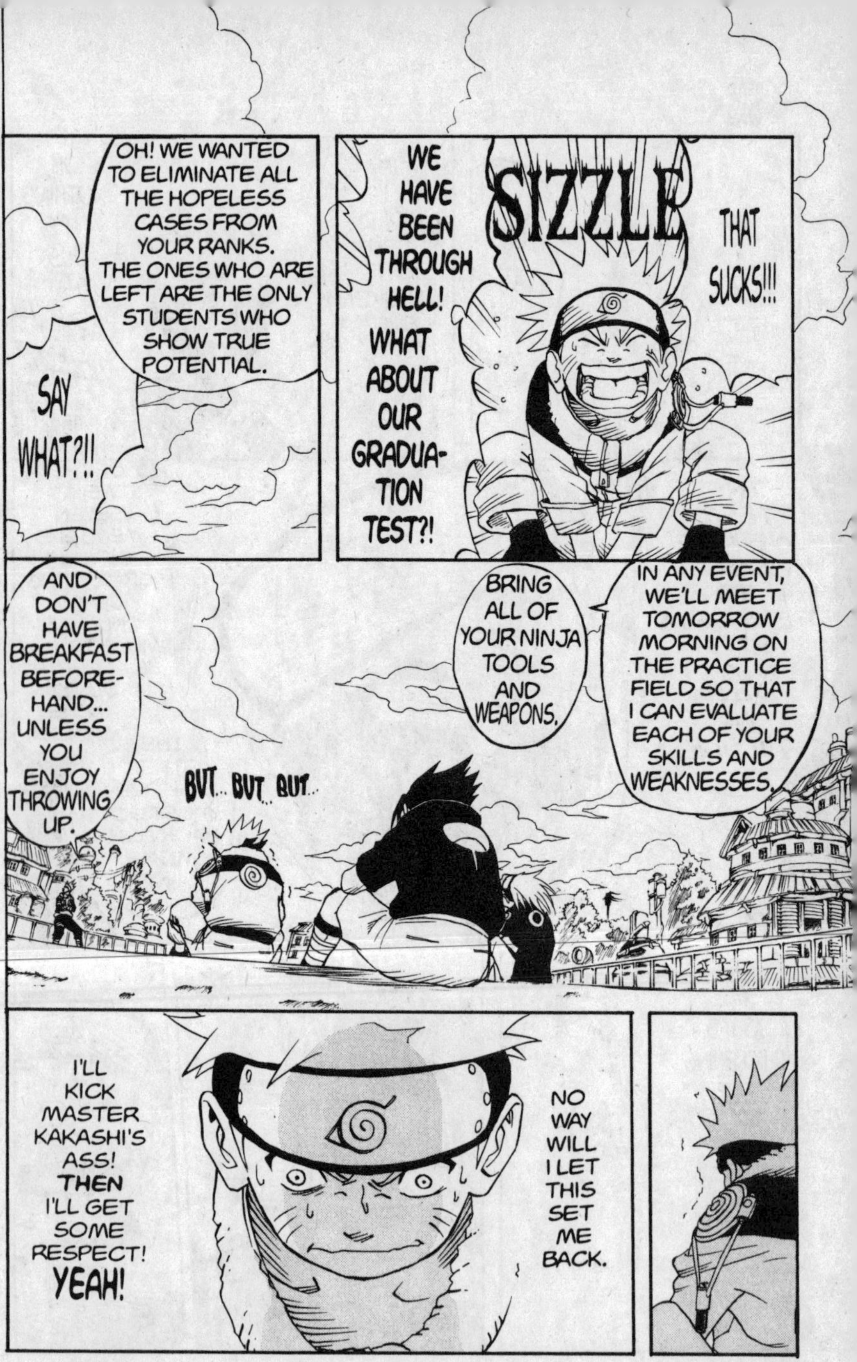
WE HAVE BEEN THROUGH HELL! WHAT ABOUT OUR GRADUATION TEST?!
SIZZLE
THAT SUCKS!!!
OH! WE WANTED TO ELIMINATE ALL THE HOPELESS CASES FROM YOUR RANKS. THE ONES WHO ARE LEFT ARE THE ONLY STUDENTS WHO SHOW TRUE POTENTIAL.
SAY WHAT?!!
IN ANY EVENT, WE'LL MEET TOMORROW MORNING ON THE PRACTICE FIELD SO THAT I CAN EVALUATE EACH OF YOUR SKILLS AND WEAKNESSES.
BRING ALL OF YOUR NINJA TOOLS AND WEAPONS.
AND DON'T HAVE BREAKFAST BEFOREHAND... UNLESS YOU ENJOY THROWING UP.
BUT... BUT QUT...
NO WAY WILL I LET THIS SET ME BACK.
I'LL KICK MASTER KAKASHI'S ASS! THEN I'LL GET SOME RESPECT! YEAH!

READ THIS WAY

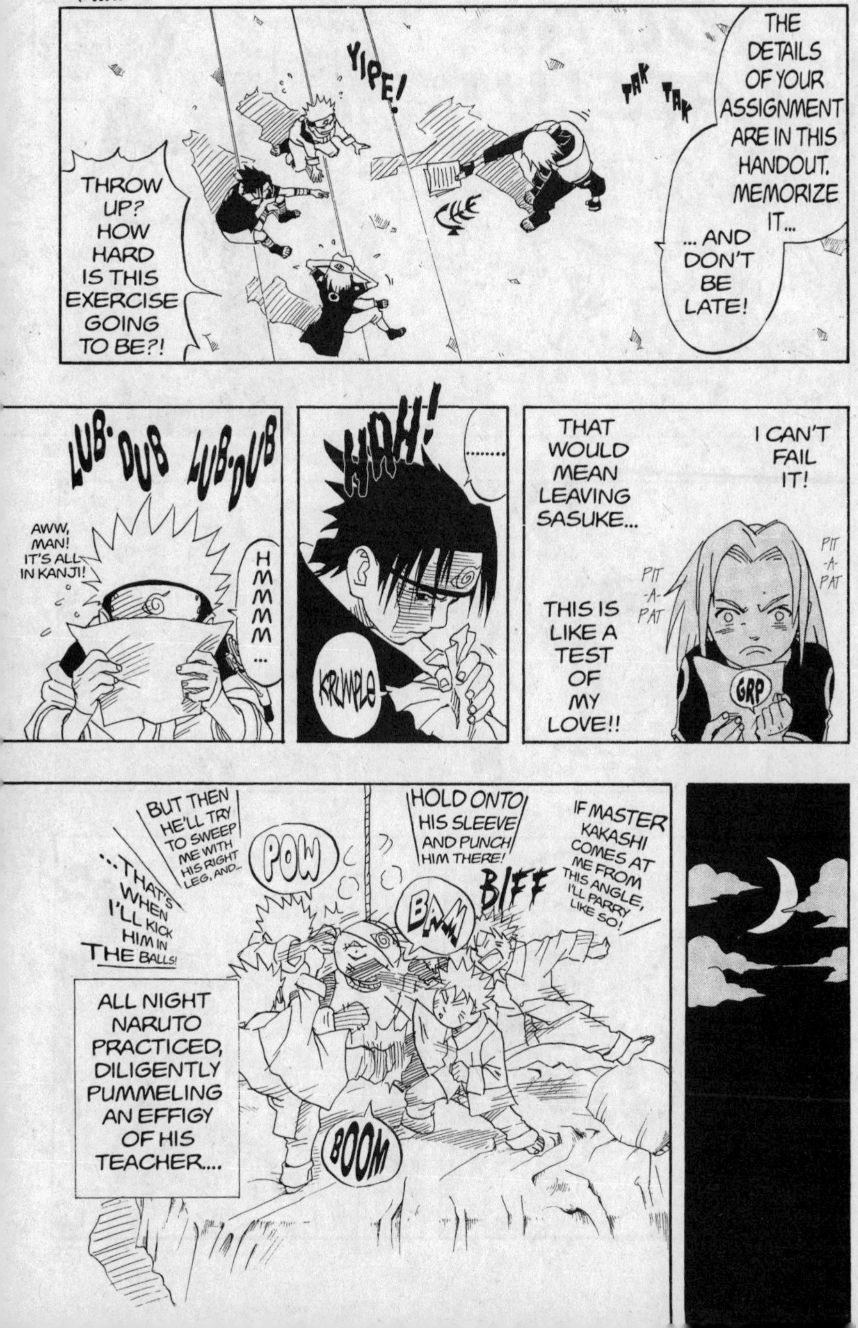
THE DETAILS OF YOUR ASSIGNMENT ARE IN THIS HANDOUT. MEMORIZE IT...
... AND DON'T BE LATE!
TAK TAK
YIPE!
THROW UP? HOW HARD IS THIS EXERCISE GOING TO BE?!
I CAN'T FAIL IT!
THAT WOULD MEAN LEAVING SASUKE...
THIS IS LIKE A TEST OF MY LOVE!!
PIT-A-PAT
PIT-A-PAT
GRP
....
KRUMPLE
LUB-DUB LUB-DUB
AWW, MAN! IT'S ALL IN KANJI!
HMMMM...
IF MASTER KAKASHI COMES AT ME FROM THIS ANGLE, I'LL PARRY LIKE SO!
HOLD ONTO HIS SLEEVE AND PUNCH HIM THERE!
BIFF
BAM
POW
BUT THEN HE'LL TRY TO SWEEP ME WITH HIS RIGHT LEG, AND...
...THAT'S WHEN I'LL KICK HIM IN THE BALLS!
ALL NIGHT NARUTO PRACTICED, DILIGENTLY PUMMELING AN EFFIGY OF HIS TEACHER....
BOOM

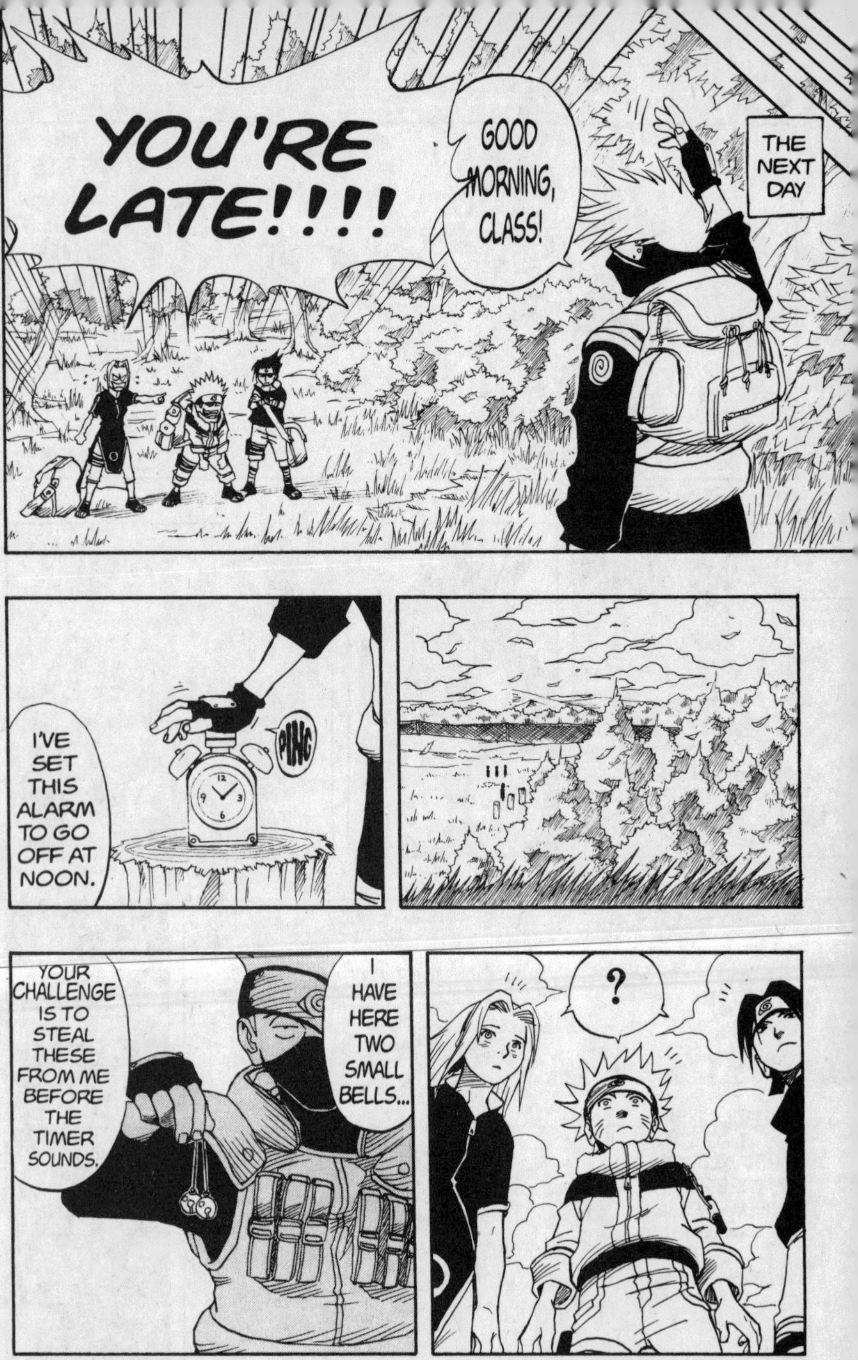
THE NEXT DAY
GOOD MORNING, CLASS!
YOU'RE LATE!!!!
PING
I'VE SET THIS ALARM TO GO OFF AT NOON.
?
I HAVE HERE TWO SMALL BELLS...
YOUR CHALLENGE IS TO STEAL THESE FROM ME BEFORE THE TIMER SOUNDS.

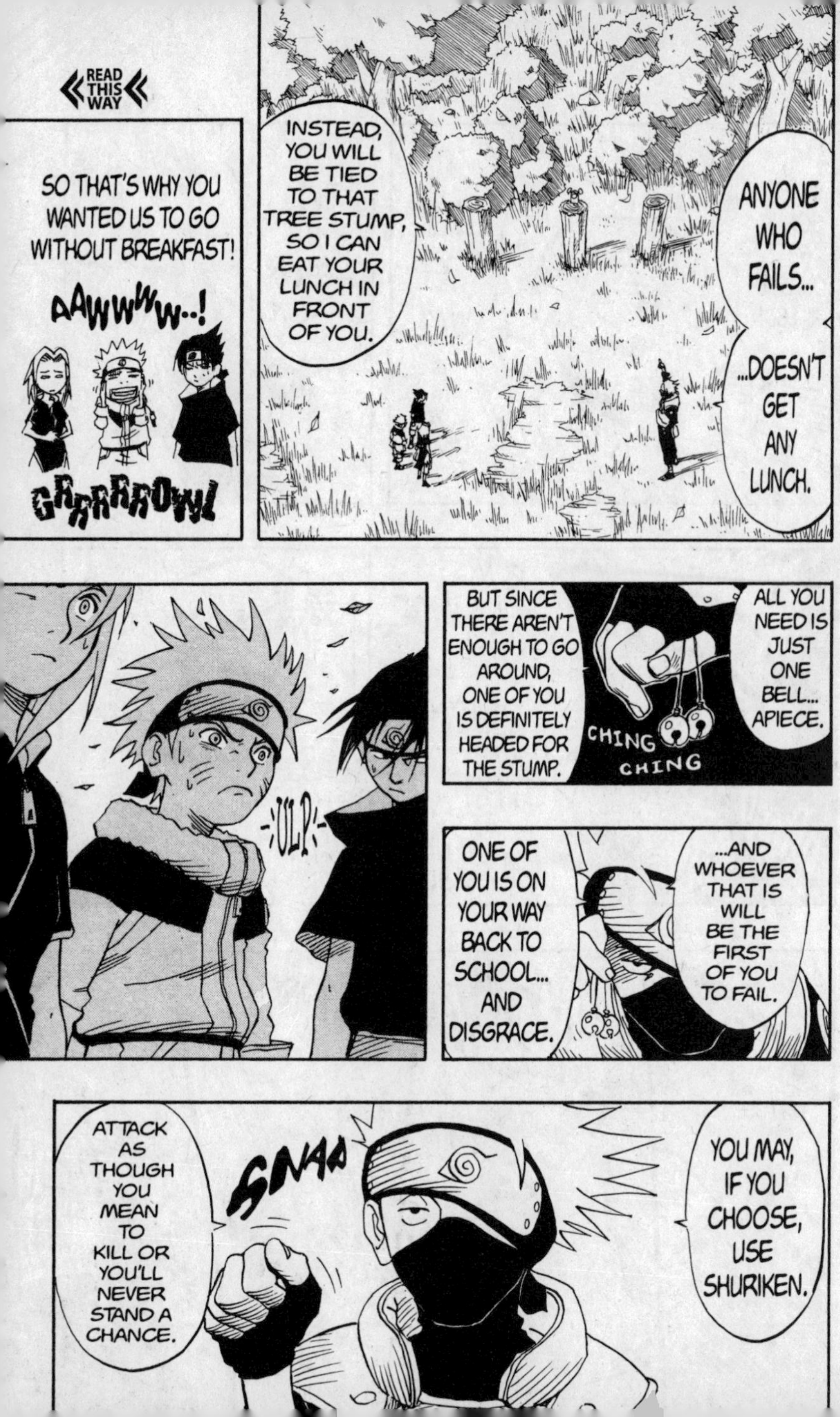
READ THIS WAY
ANYONE WHO FAILS...
...DOESN'T GET ANY LUNCH.
INSTEAD, YOU WILL BE TIED TO THAT TREE STUMP, SO I CAN EAT YOUR LUNCH IN FRONT OF YOU.
SO THAT'S WHY YOU WANTED US TO GO WITHOUT BREAKFAST!
AAWWWW..!
GRRRRROWL!
ALL YOU NEED IS JUST ONE BELL... APIECE.
BUT SINCE THERE AREN'T ENOUGH TO GO AROUND, ONE OF YOU IS DEFINITELY HEADED FOR THE STUMP.
CHING
CHING
...AND WHOEVER THAT IS WILL BE THE FIRST OF YOU TO FAIL.
ONE OF YOU IS ON YOUR WAY BACK TO SCHOOL... AND DISGRACE.
ULP
YOU MAY, IF YOU CHOOSE, USE SHURIKEN.
SNAA
ATTACK AS THOUGH YOU MEAN TO KILL OR YOU'LL NEVER STAND A CHANCE.

READ THIS WAY

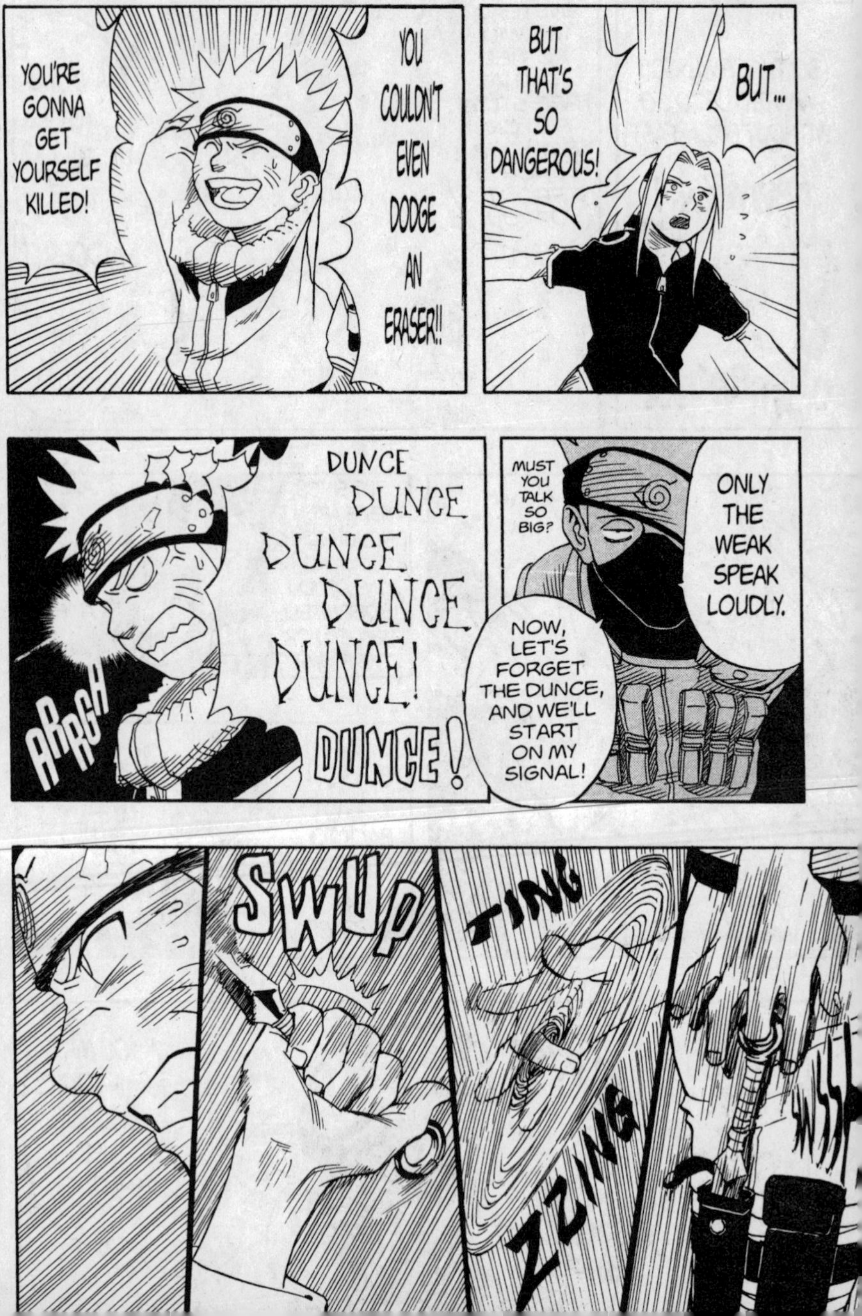
BUT...
BUT THAT'S SO DANGEROUS!
YOU COULDN'T EVEN DODGE AN ERASER!!
YOU'RE GONNA GET YOURSELF KILLED!
ONLY THE WEAK SPEAK LOUDLY.
MUST YOU TALK SO BIG?
NOW, LET'S FORGET THE DUNCE, AND WE'LL START ON MY SIGNAL!
DUNCE DUNCE DUNCE DUNCE DUNCE! DUNCE!
ARRGH
WSSH
TING
ZZING
SWUP

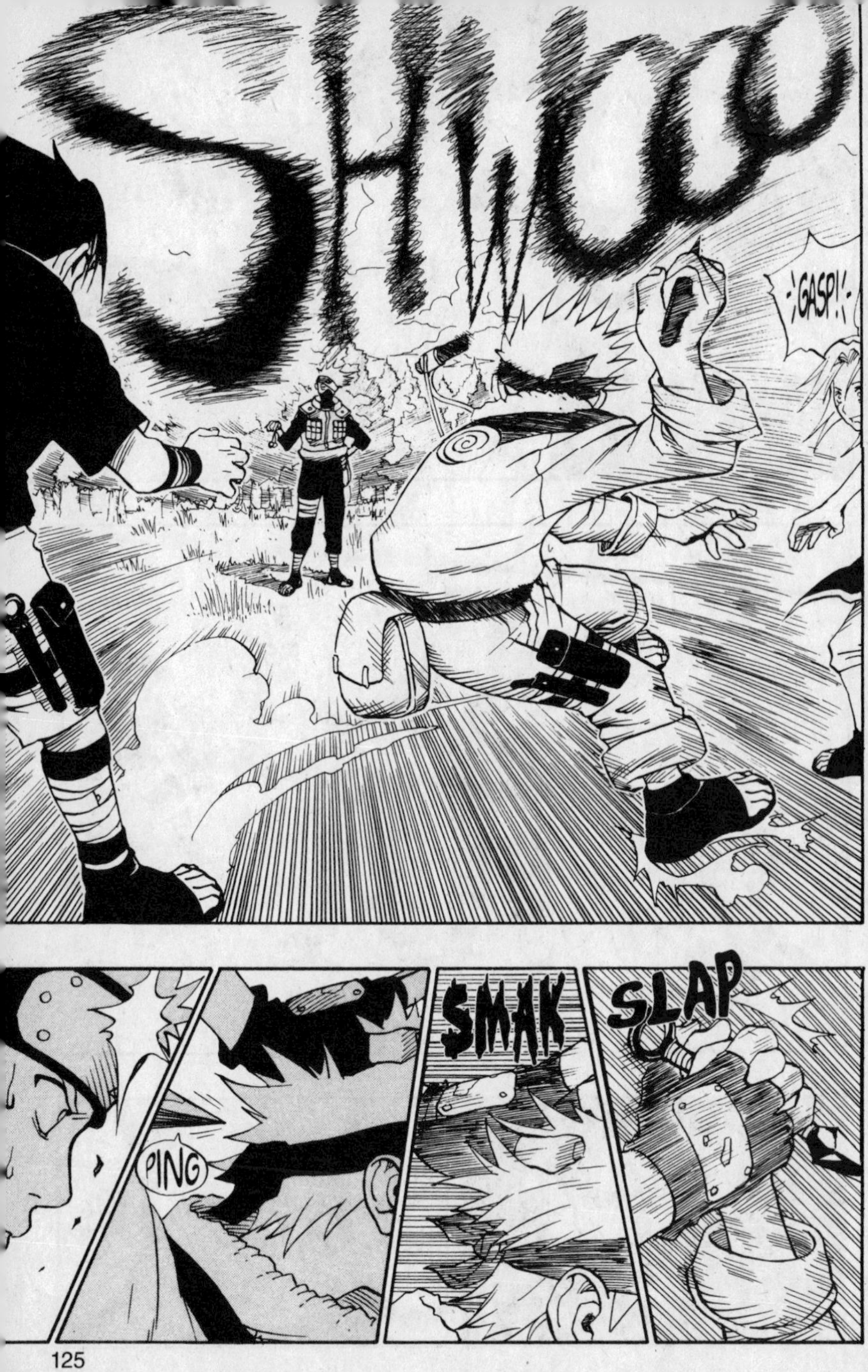
SHWOOO
GASP!
SLAP
SMAK
PING

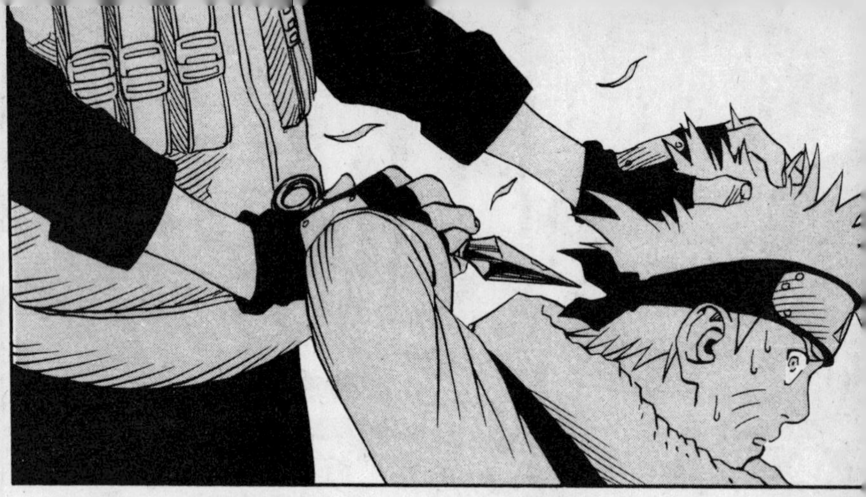

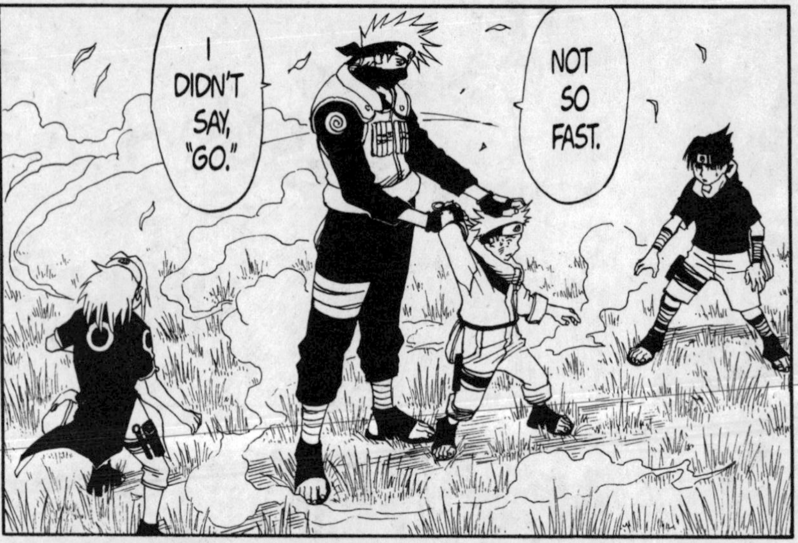
NOT SO FAST.
I DIDN'T SAY, "GO."

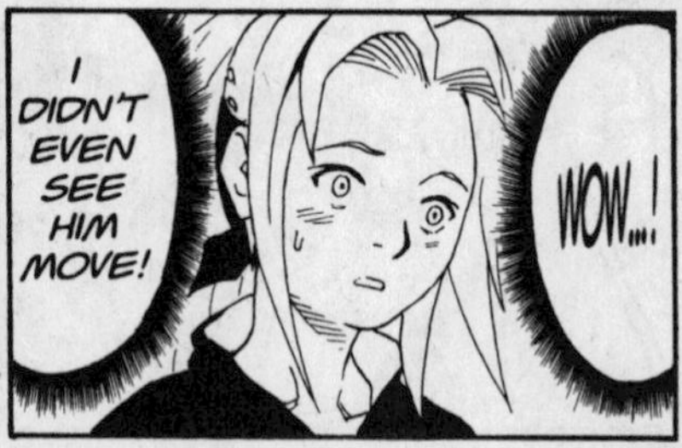
WOW...!
I DIDN'T EVEN SEE HIM MOVE!

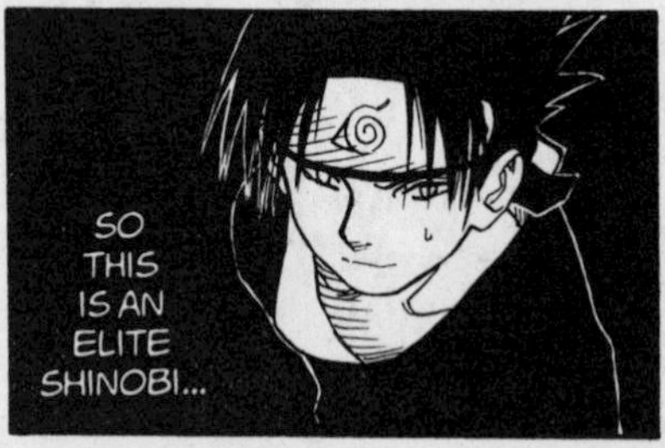
SO THIS IS AN ELITE SHINOBI...

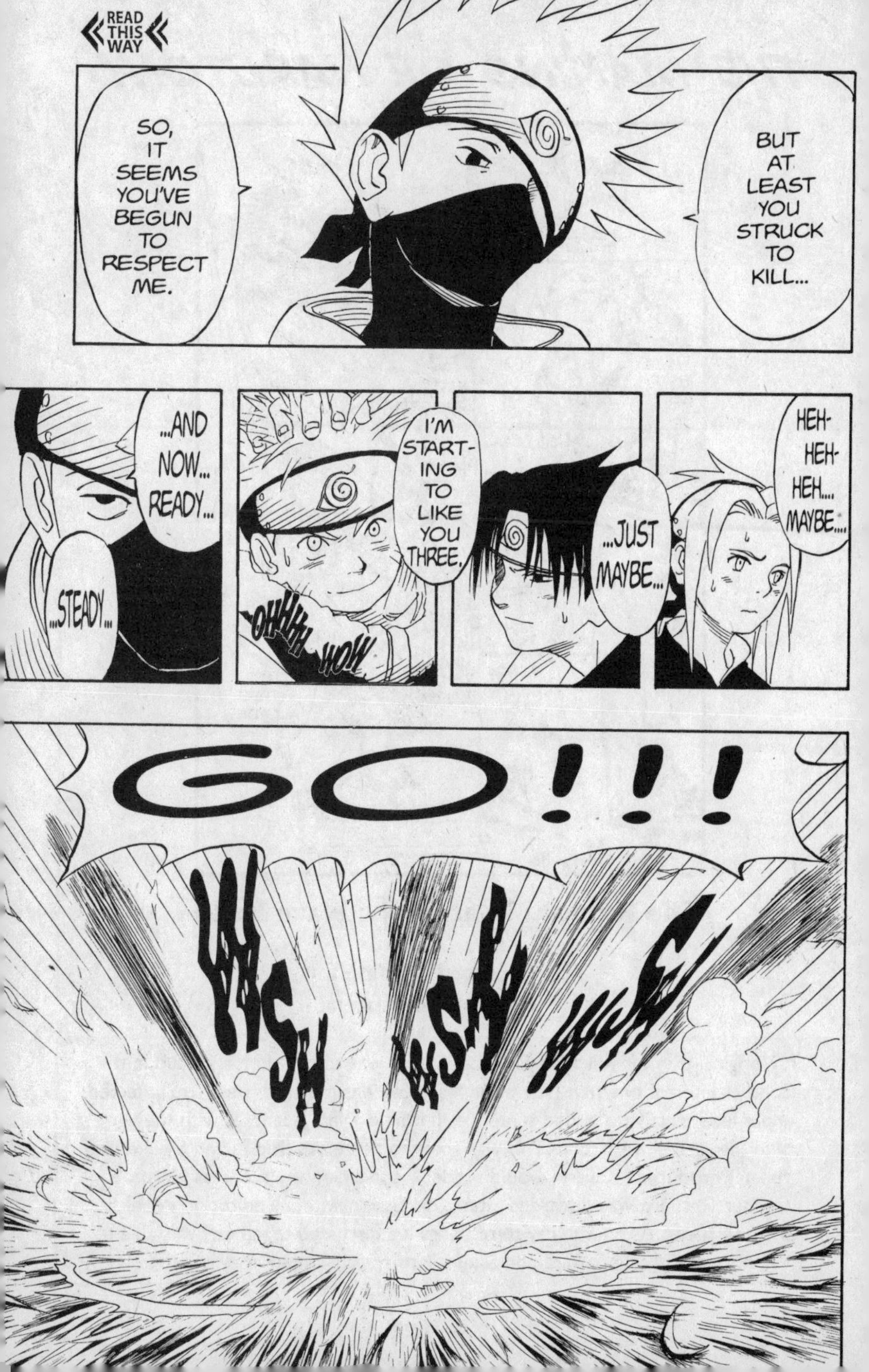
READ THIS WAY
BUT AT LEAST YOU STRUCK TO KILL...
SO, IT SEEMS YOU'VE BEGUN TO RESPECT ME.
HEH-HEH-HEH.... MAYBE....
...JUST MAYBE...
I'M STARTING TO LIKE YOU THREE,
OHHHH WOW
...AND NOW... READY...
...STEADY...
GO!!!
WSH
WSH

THE MAKING OF NARUTO!!!

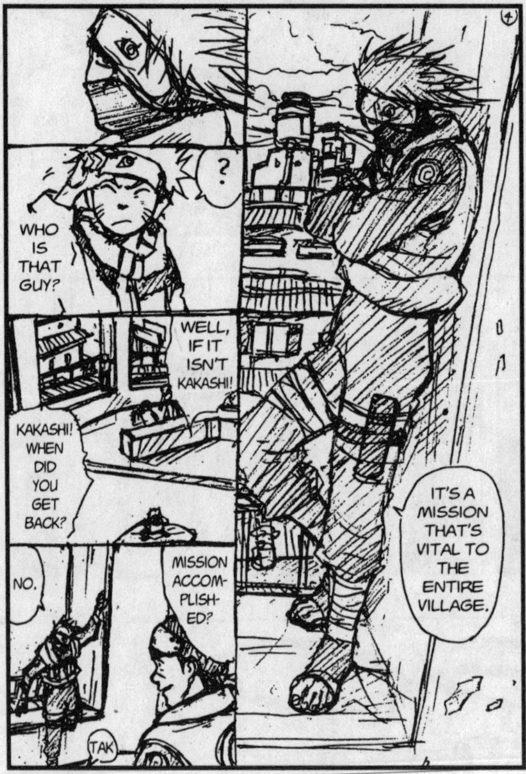
?
WHO IS THAT GUY?
WELL, IF IT ISN'T KAKASHI!
KAKASHI! WHEN DID YOU GET BACK?
MISSION ACCOMPLISHED?
NO.
TAK
IT'S A MISSION THAT'S VITAL TO THE ENTIRE VILLAGE.

The Kakashi That Might Have Been

The Rejected Outline for the Second Chapter

My original plan for Kakashi's first appearance was to have him show up in the second chapter of **Naruto** (see **page #61**). He was meant to be a cool, affected, upper-level ninja who ended sentences (in the original Japanese) with the very polite "*de gozaru*" verb form. This was going to be before Sakura and Sasuke had been introduced. Kakashi would suddenly appear on the scene as Naruto's teacher. This idea was discarded after a discussion with my editor at **Weekly Shonen Jump**. As an outgrowth of things we discussed together, I was able to flesh out Kakashi, Sasuke, and Sakura into the characters they are today.

Number 5: Pride Goeth Before a Fall

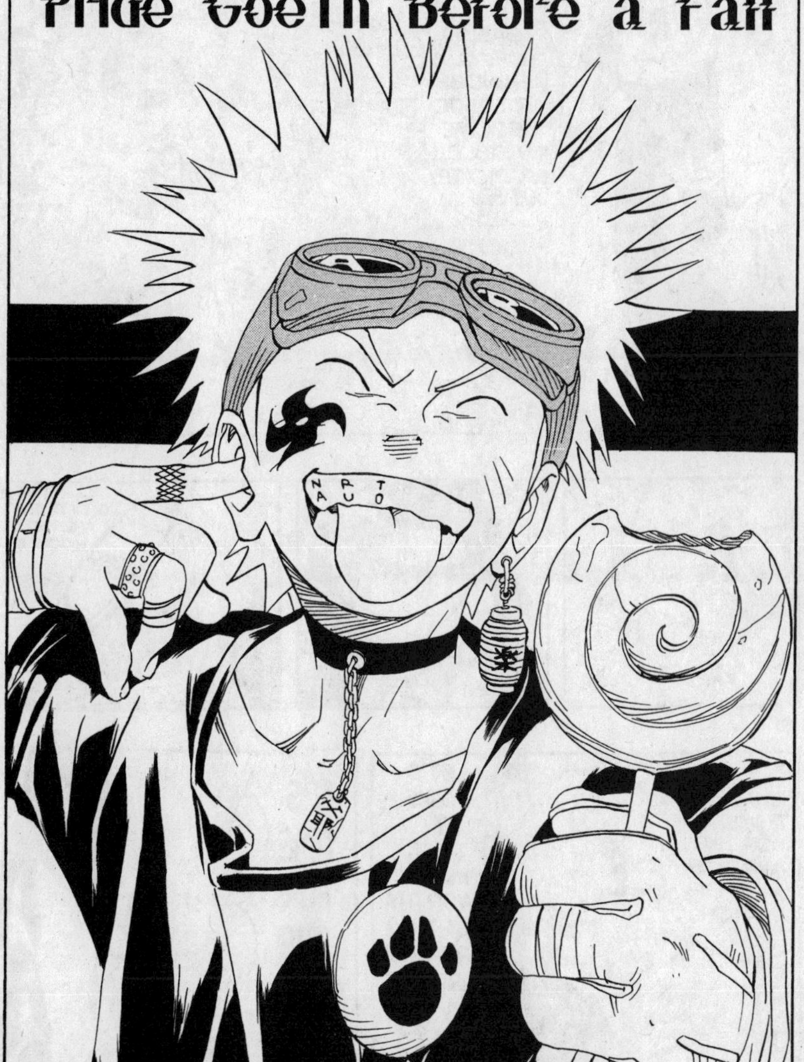

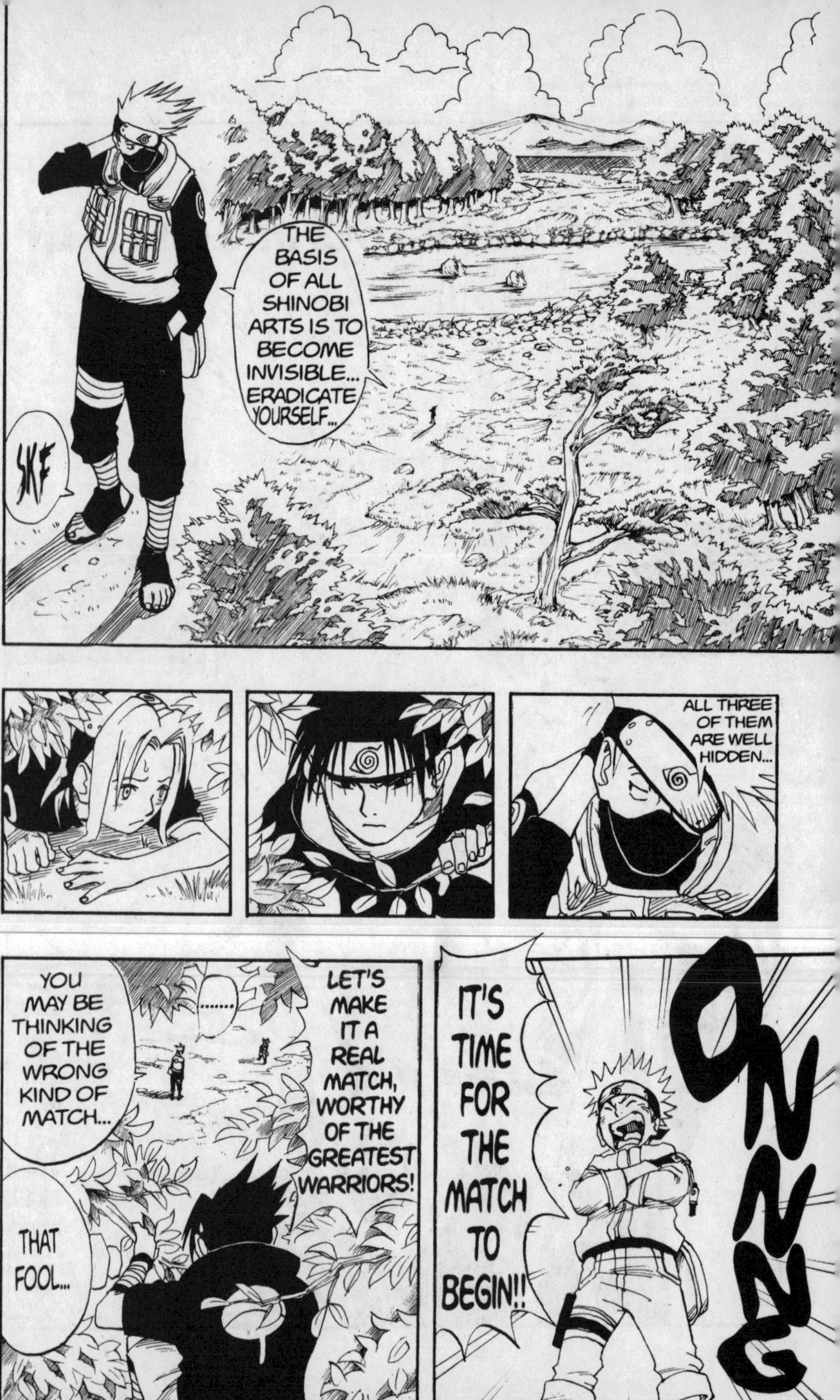
THE BASIS OF ALL SHINOBI ARTS IS TO BECOME INVISIBLE... ERADICATE YOURSELF...
SKF
ALL THREE OF THEM ARE WELL HIDDEN...
IT'S TIME FOR THE MATCH TO BEGIN!!
LET'S MAKE IT A REAL MATCH, WORTHY OF THE GREATEST WARRIORS!
....
YOU MAY BE THINKING OF THE WRONG KIND OF MATCH...
THAT FOOL...

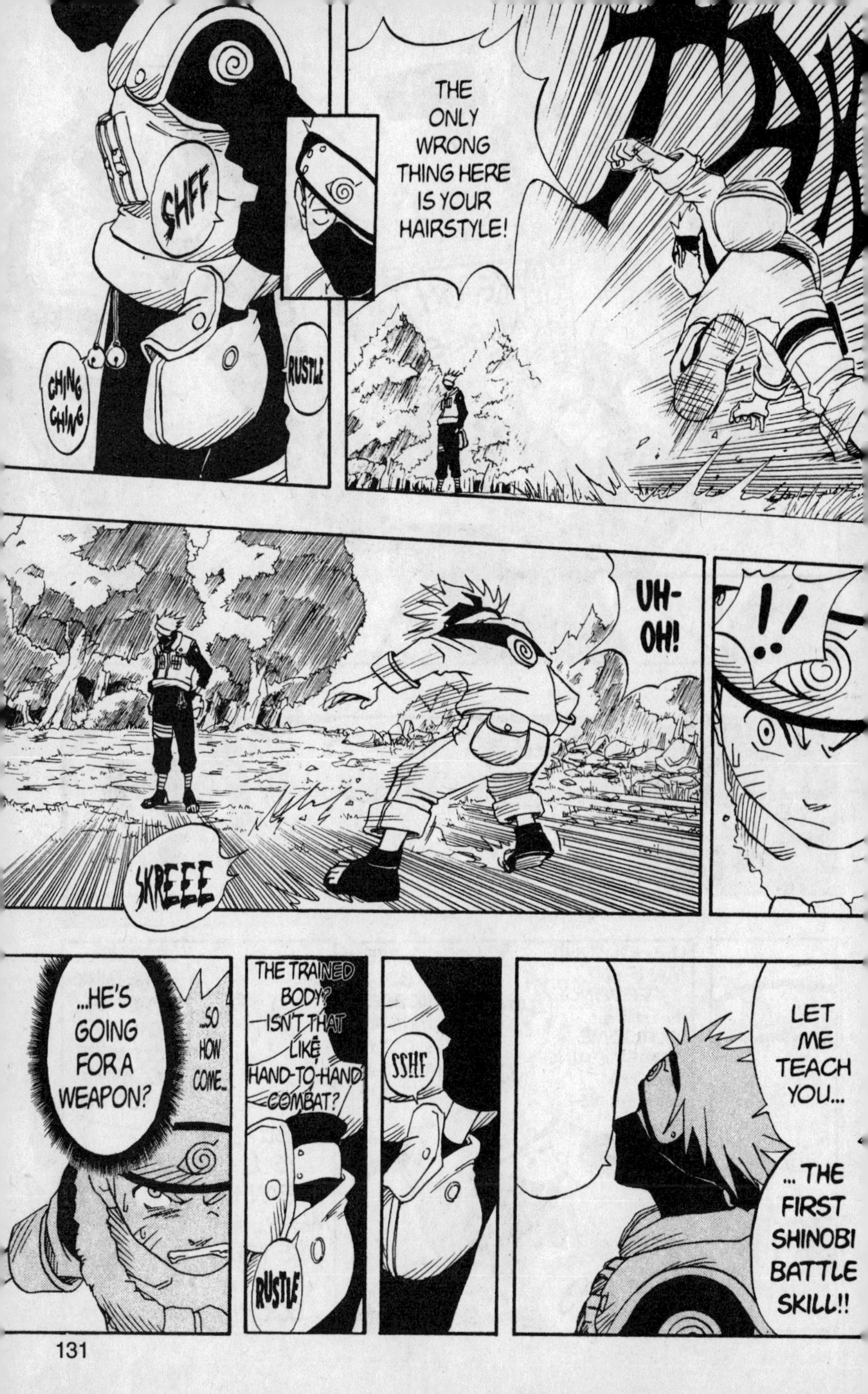
THE ONLY WRONG THING HERE IS YOUR HAIRSTYLE!
RUSTLE
SHFF
CHING CHING
!!
UH-OH!
SKREEE
LET ME TEACH YOU...
... THE FIRST SHINOBI BATTLE SKILL!!
SSHF
THE TRAINED BODY? ISN'T THAT LIKE HAND-TO-HAND COMBAT?
RUSTLE
...SO HOW COME...
...HE'S GOING FOR A WEAPON?

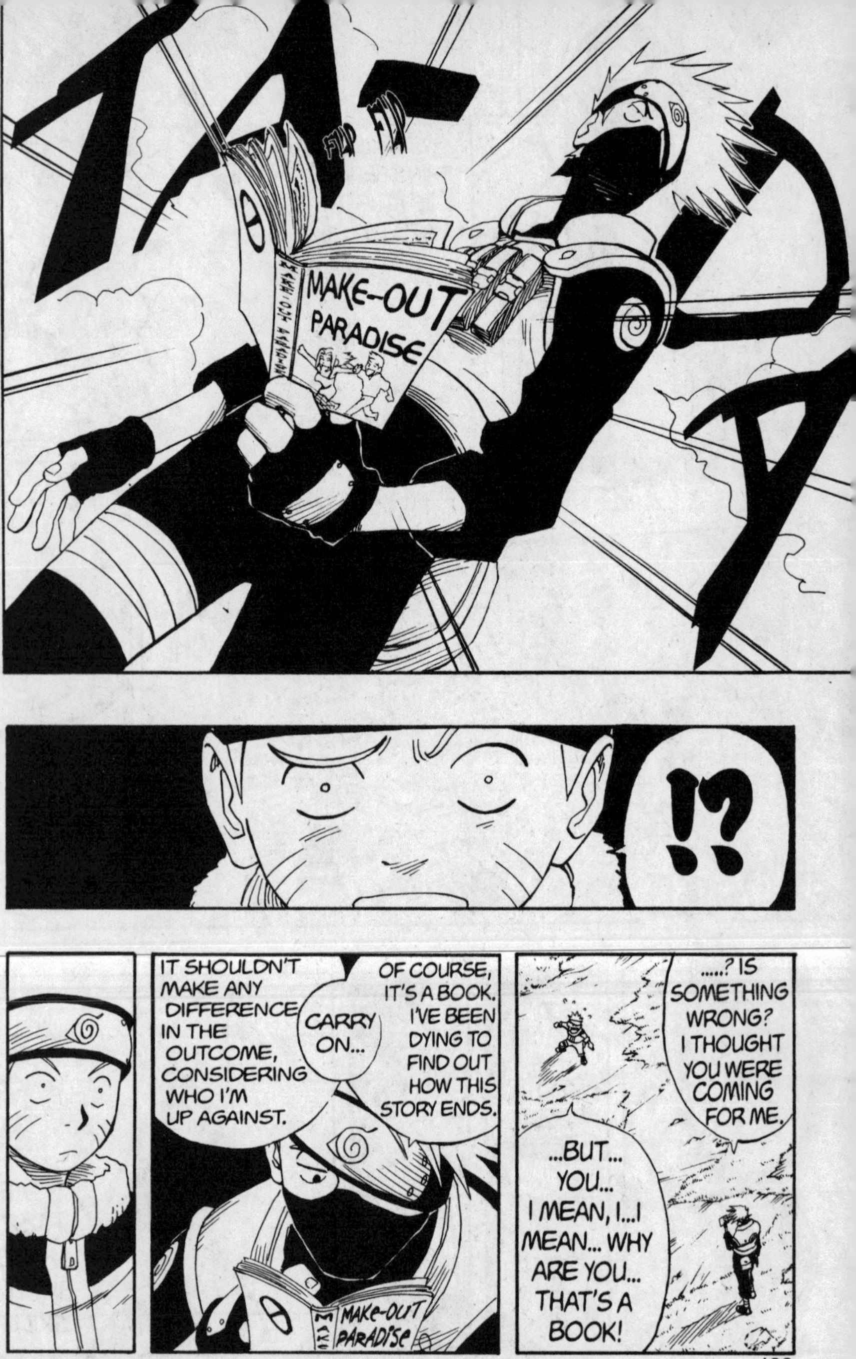
FLIP FLIP
MAKE-OUT PARADISE
!?
.....? IS SOMETHING WRONG? I THOUGHT YOU WERE COMING FOR ME.
...BUT... YOU... I MEAN, I...I MEAN... WHY ARE YOU... THAT'S A BOOK!
OF COURSE, IT'S A BOOK. I'VE BEEN DYING TO FIND OUT HOW THIS STORY ENDS.
CARRY ON...
IT SHOULDN'T MAKE ANY DIFFERENCE IN THE OUTCOME, CONSIDERING WHO I'M UP AGAINST.
MAKE-OUT PARADISE

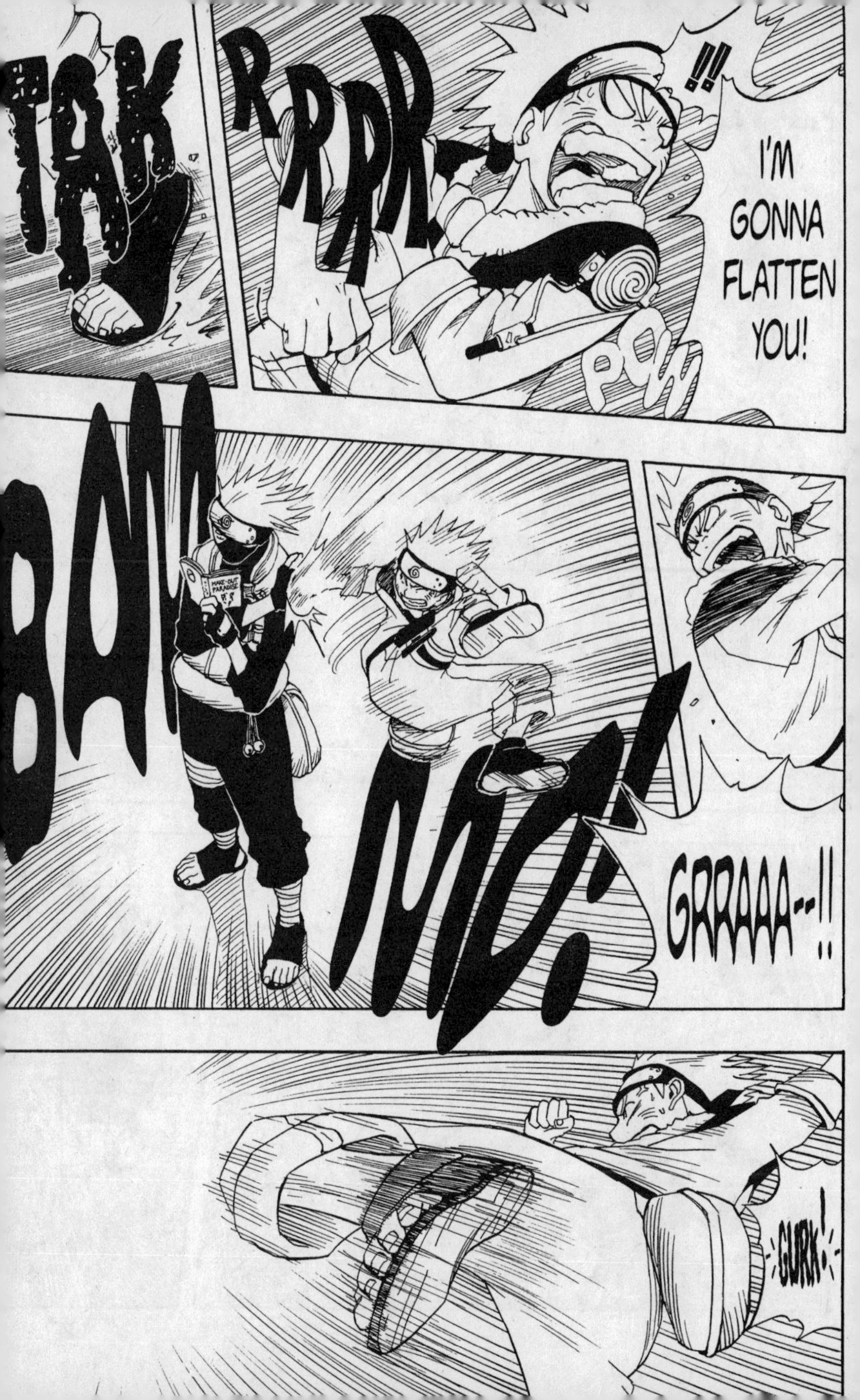
!!
I'M GONNA FLATTEN YOU!
RRRRR
POW
TAK
GRRAAA--!!
MAKE-OUT PARADISE
BAM
GURK!

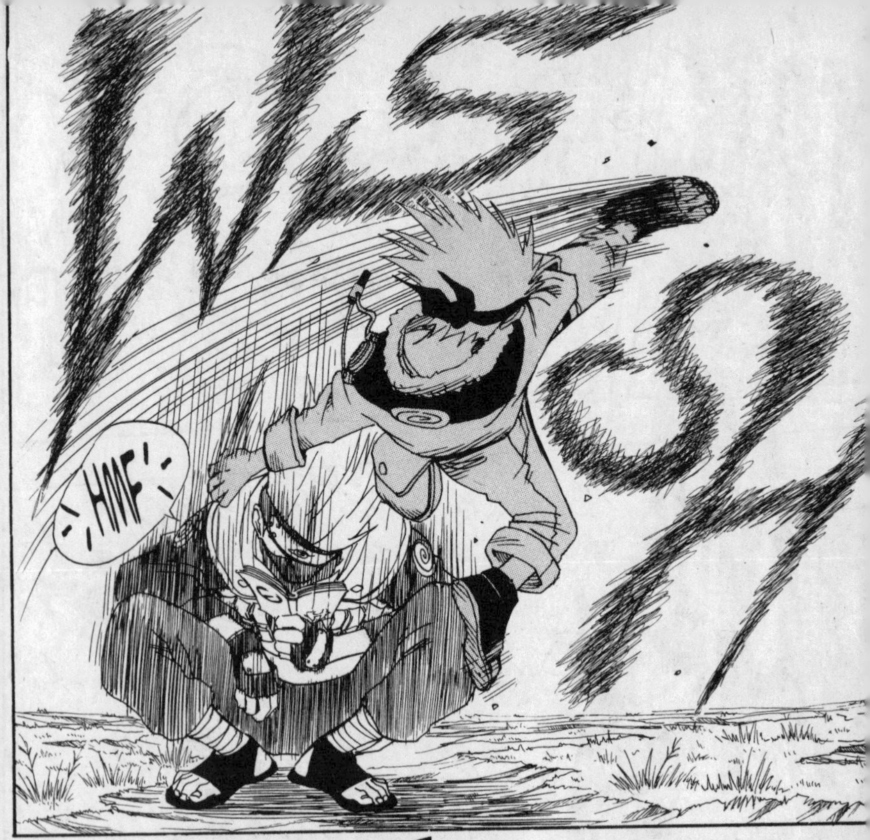
HMF

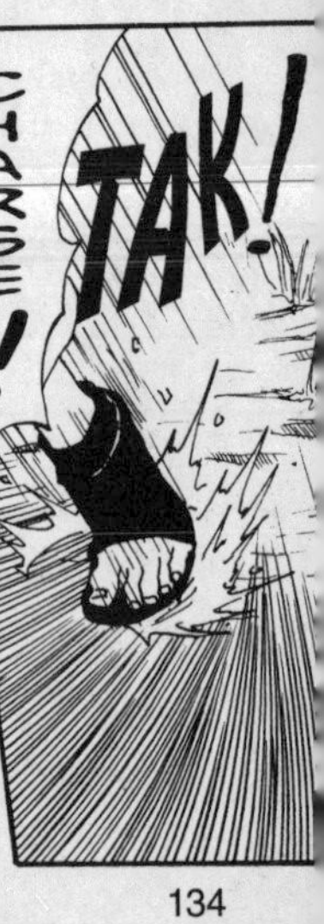
TAK!

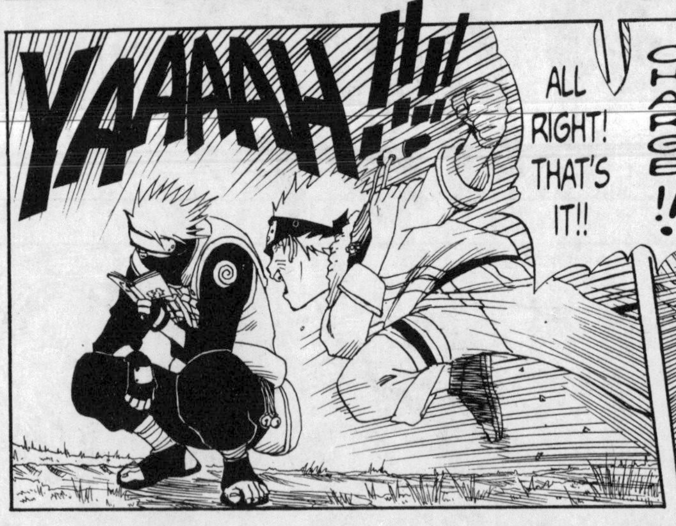
CHARGE!!
ALL RIGHT! THAT'S IT!!
YAAAH!!!

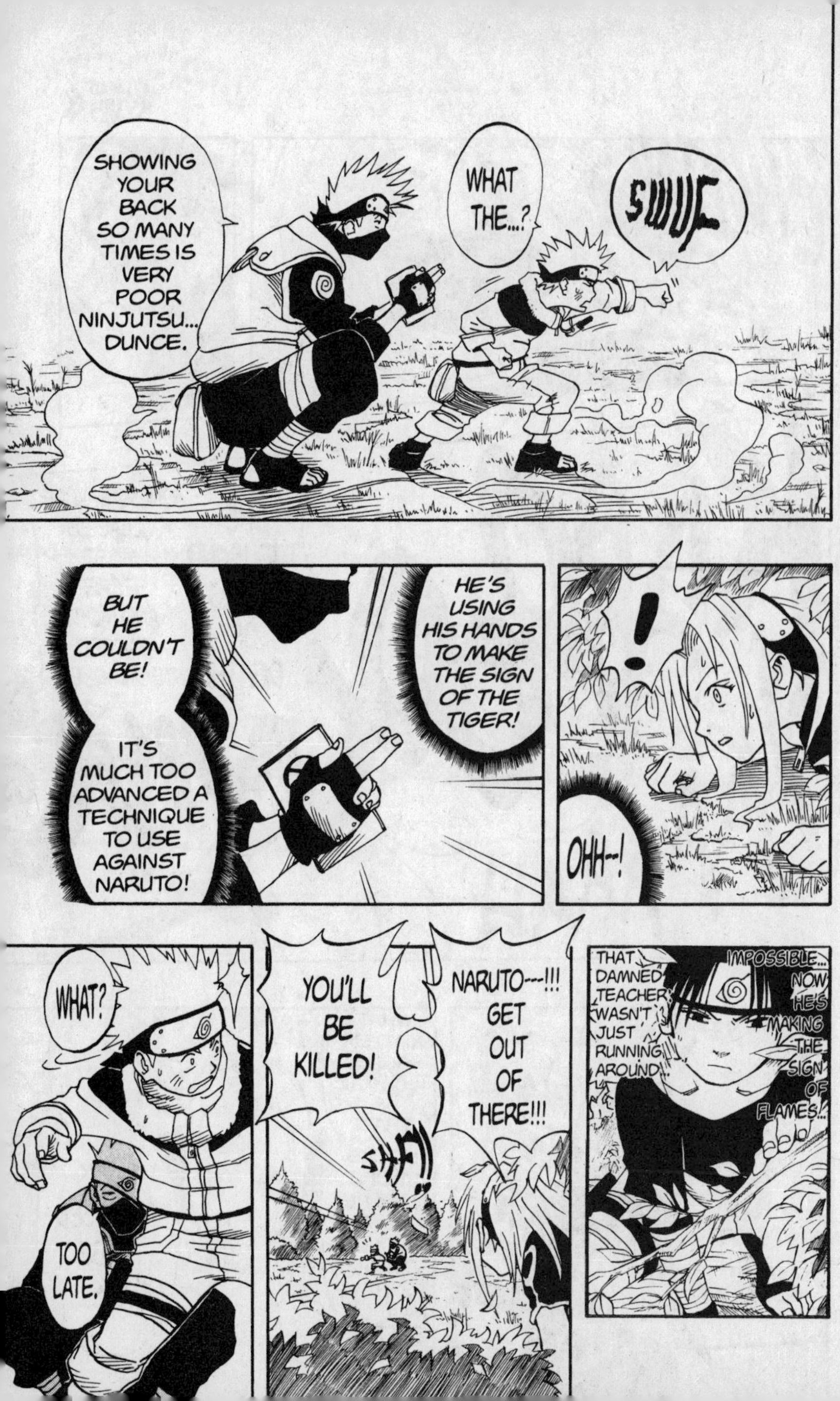
SWUF
WHAT THE...?
SHOWING YOUR BACK SO MANY TIMES IS VERY POOR NINJUTSU... DUNCE.
!
OHH--!
HE'S USING HIS HANDS TO MAKE THE SIGN OF THE TIGER!
BUT HE COULDN'T BE!
IT'S MUCH TOO ADVANCED A TECHNIQUE TO USE AGAINST NARUTO!
IMPOSSIBLE... NOW HE'S MAKING THE SIGN OF FLAMES!...
THAT DAMNED TEACHER WASN'T JUST RUNNING AROUND...
NARUTO---!!! GET OUT OF THERE!!!
YOU'LL BE KILLED!
SHF!
WHAT?
TOO LATE.

READ THIS WAY

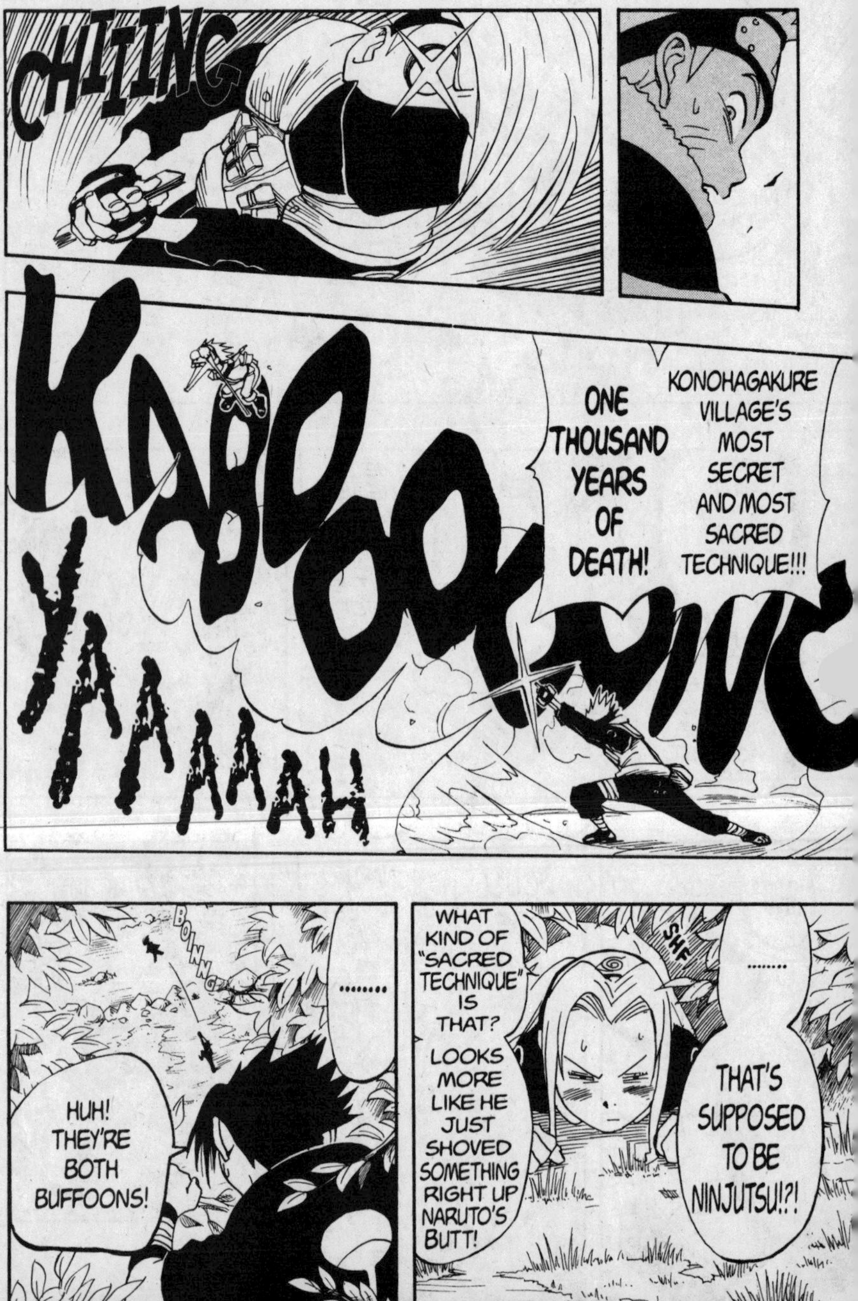
CHIIING
KONOHAGAKURE VILLAGE'S MOST SECRET AND MOST SACRED TECHNIQUE!!!
ONE THOUSAND YEARS OF DEATH!
YAAAAH
SHF
....
WHAT KIND OF "SACRED TECHNIQUE" IS THAT?
LOOKS MORE LIKE HE JUST SHOVED SOMETHING RIGHT UP NARUTO'S BUTT!
THAT'S SUPPOSED TO BE NINJUTSU!?!
BOING
....
HUH! THEY'RE BOTH BUFFOONS!

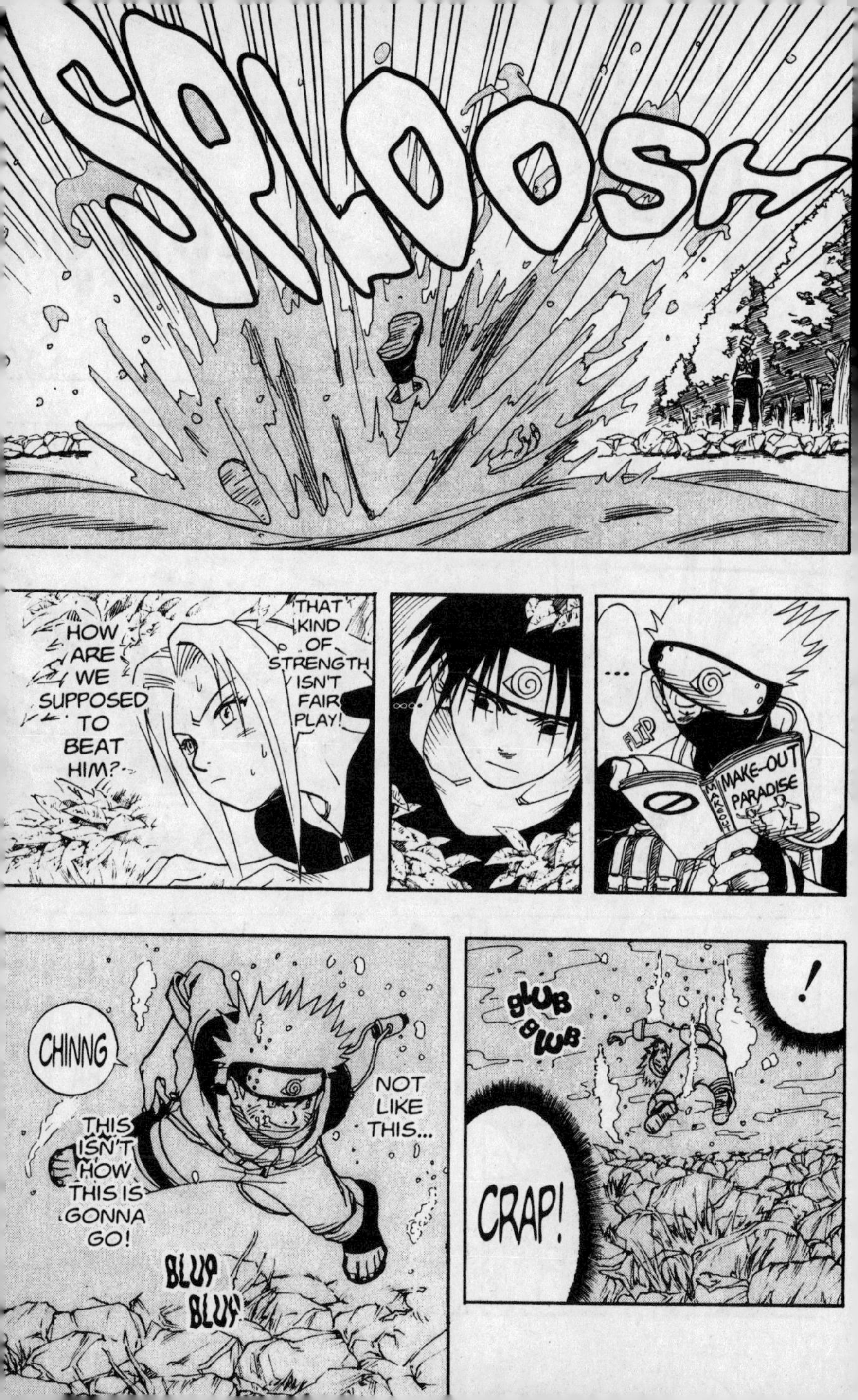
SPLOOSH
...
FLIP
MAKE-OUT PARADISE
MAKE OUT
THAT KIND OF STRENGTH ISN'T FAIR PLAY!
HOW ARE WE SUPPOSED TO BEAT HIM?
!
GLUB GLUB
CRAP!
NOT LIKE THIS...
CHINNG
THIS ISN'T HOW THIS IS GONNA GO!
BLUP BLUP

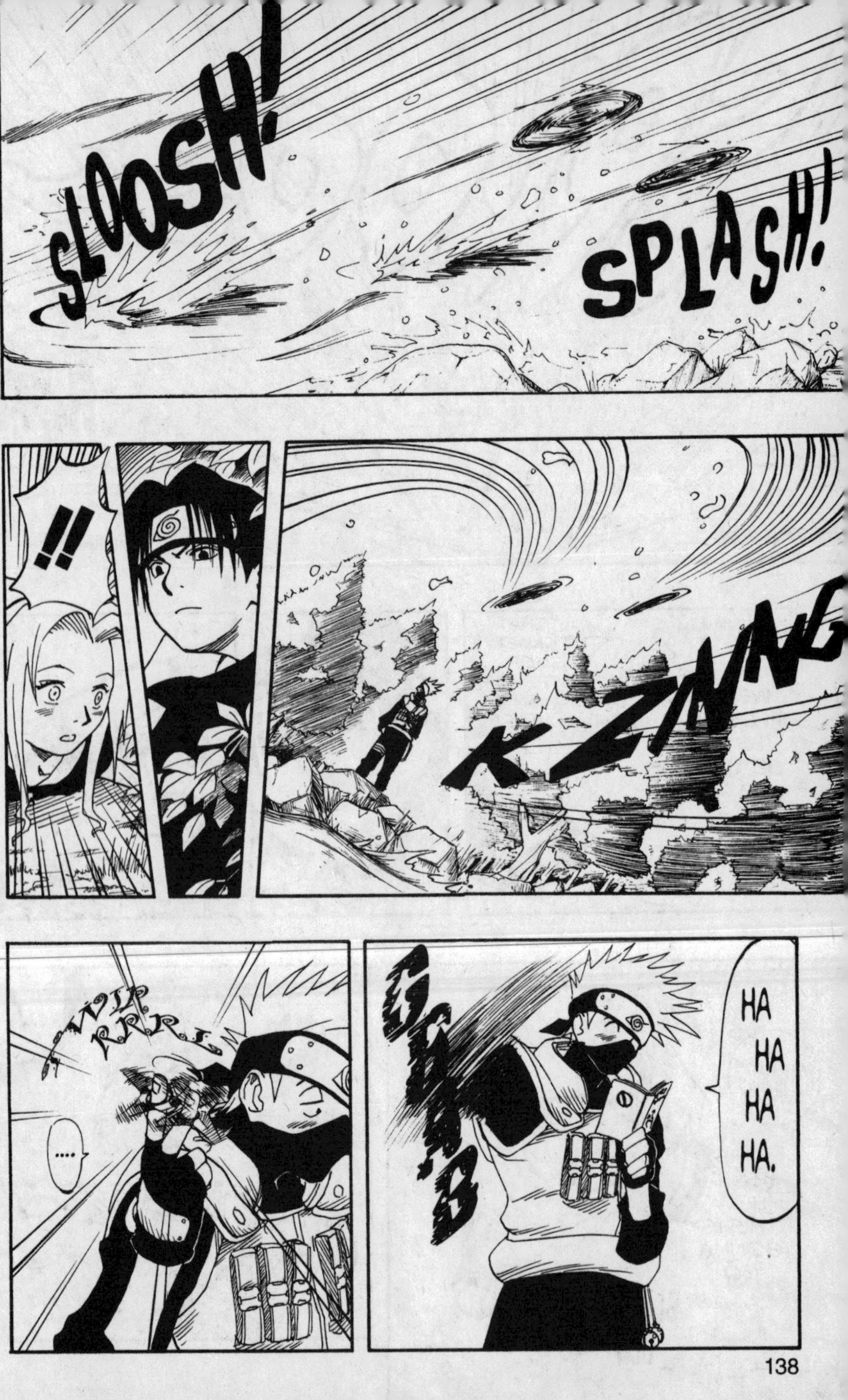
SPLASH!
SLOOSH!
KZWNG
!!
HA HA HA HA.
.....

READ THIS WAY

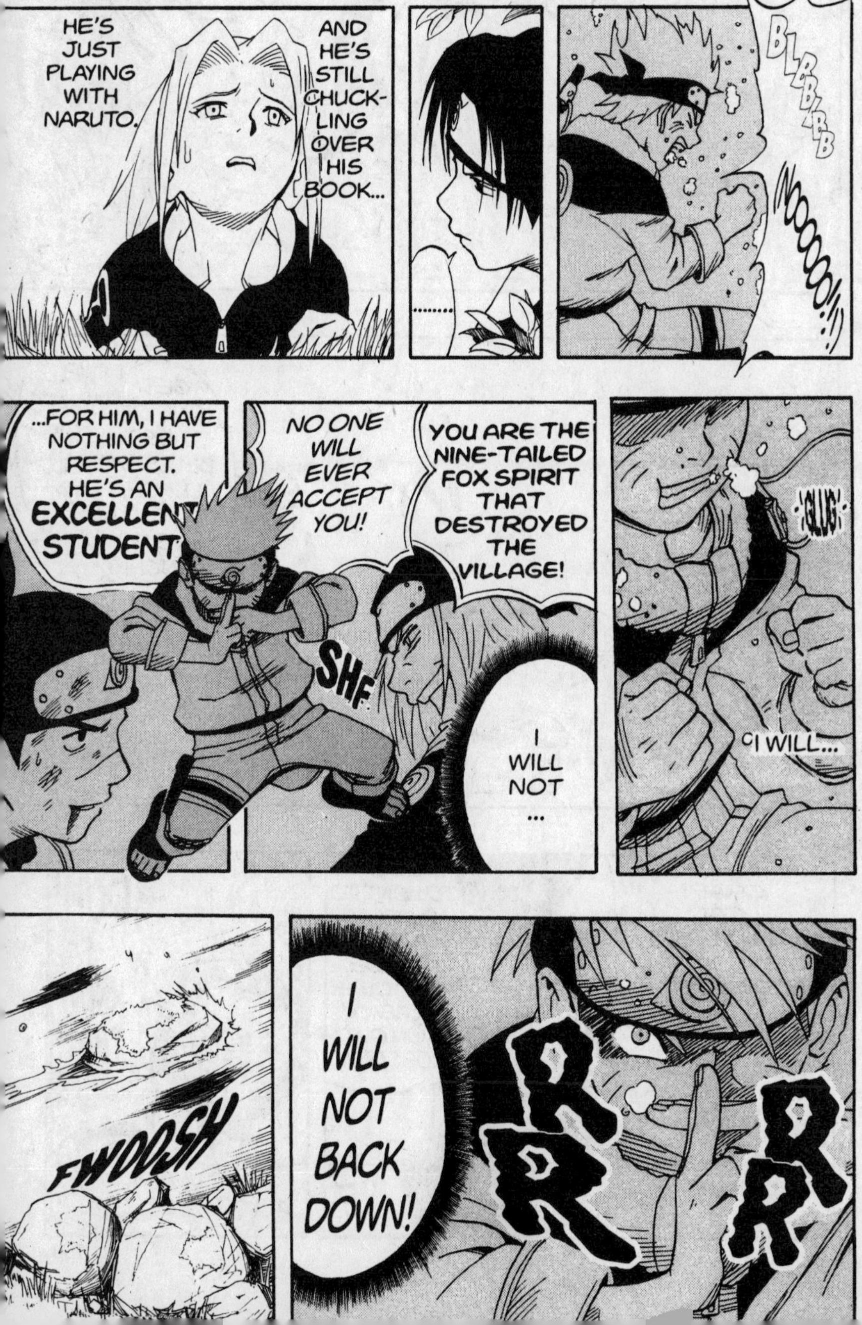
BLBBBB
NOOOOO!!
....
AND HE'S STILL CHUCKLING OVER HIS BOOK...
HE'S JUST PLAYING WITH NARUTO.
GLUG
I WILL...
YOU ARE THE NINE-TAILED FOX SPIRIT THAT DESTROYED THE VILLAGE!
NO ONE WILL EVER ACCEPT YOU!
SHF
I WILL NOT ...
...FOR HIM, I HAVE NOTHING BUT RESPECT. HE'S AN EXCELLENT STUDENT
I WILL NOT BACK DOWN!
RR
RR
FWOOSH

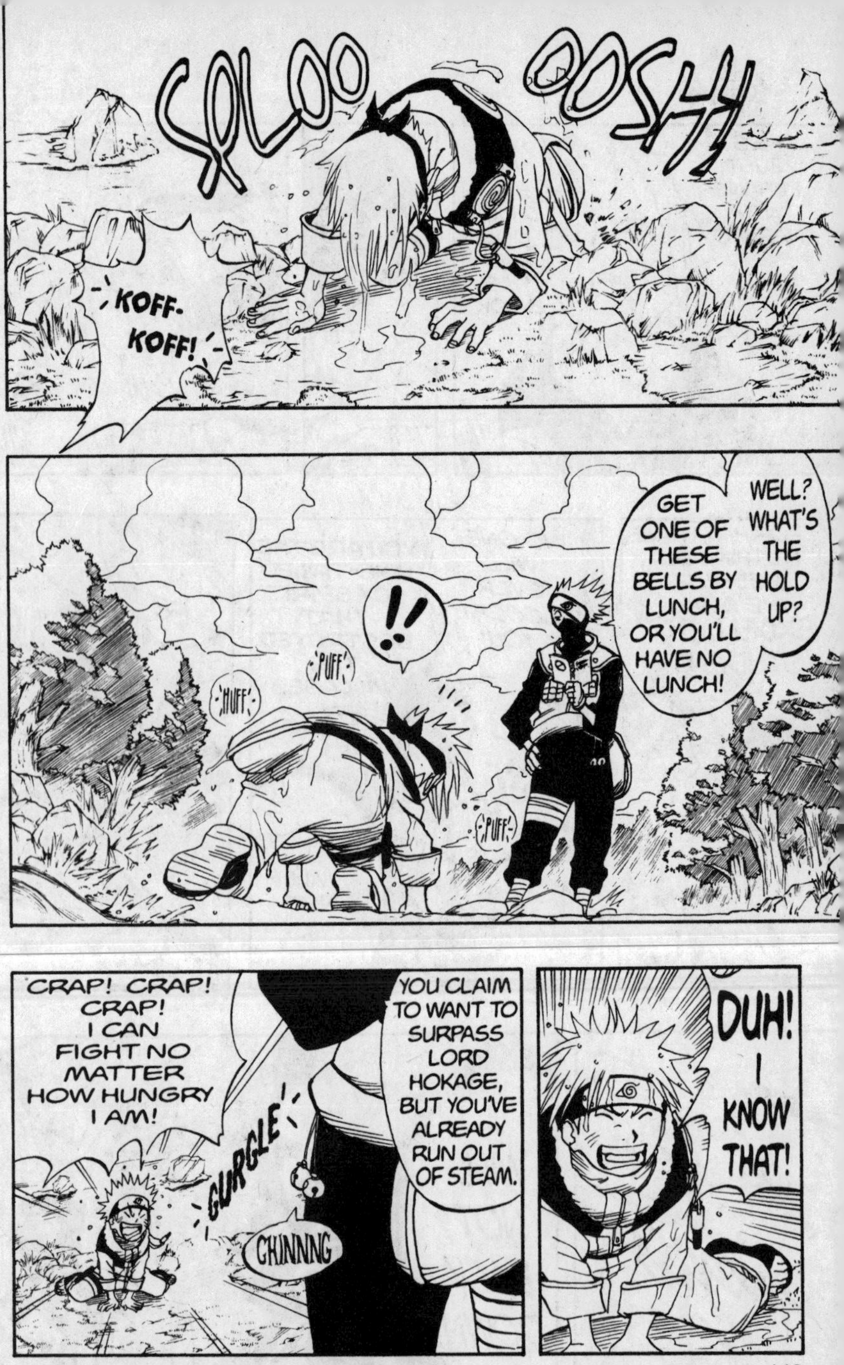
SPLOO OOSH
KOFF-KOFF!
WELL? WHAT'S THE HOLD UP?
GET ONE OF THESE BELLS BY LUNCH, OR YOU'LL HAVE NO LUNCH!
!!
PUFF
HUFF
PUFF
DUH! I KNOW THAT!
YOU CLAIM TO WANT TO SURPASS LORD HOKAGE, BUT YOU'VE ALREADY RUN OUT OF STEAM.
CRAP! CRAP! CRAP! I CAN FIGHT NO MATTER HOW HUNGRY I AM!
GURGLE
CHINNNG

READ THIS WAY

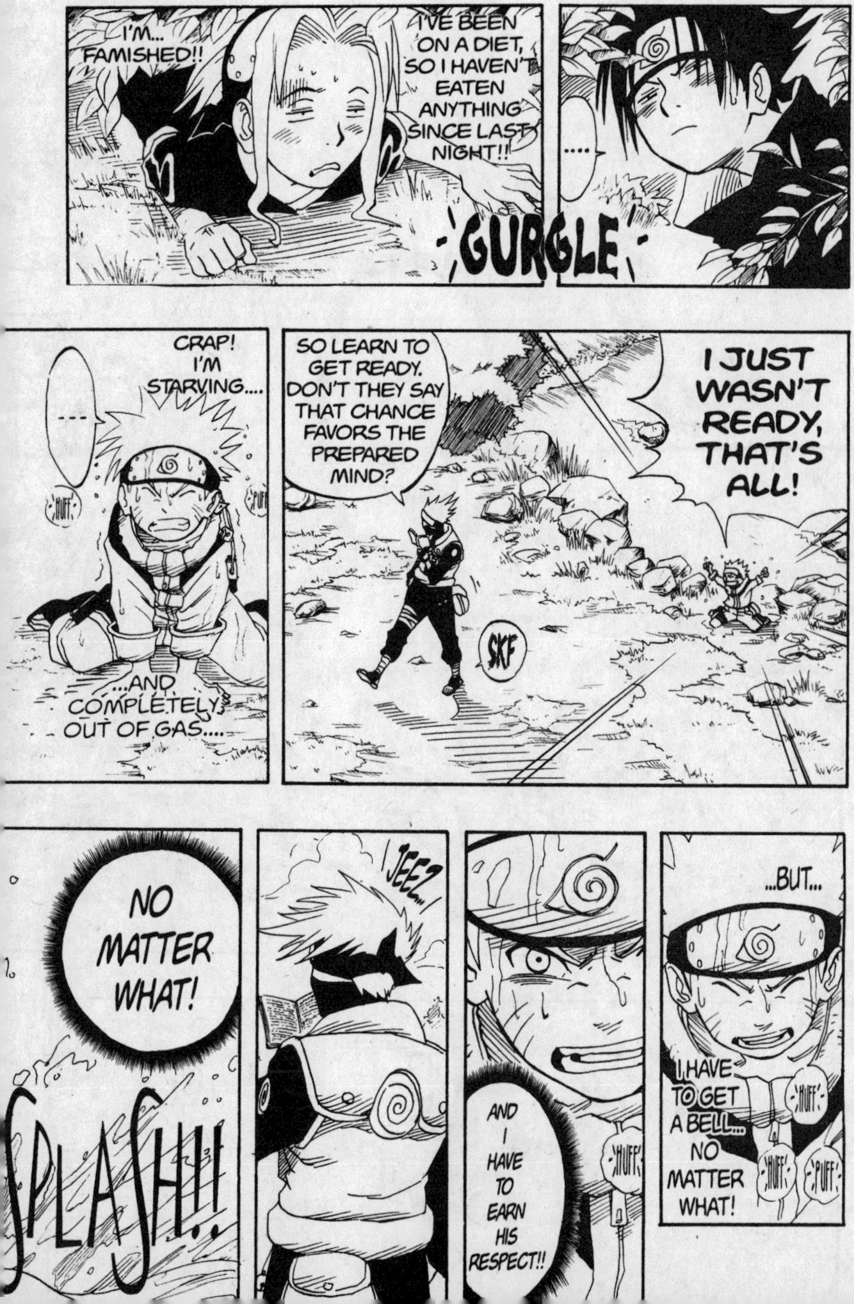
....
I'M... FAMISHED!!
I'VE BEEN ON A DIET, SO I HAVEN'T EATEN ANYTHING SINCE LAST NIGHT!!
GURGLE
I JUST WASN'T READY, THAT'S ALL!
SO LEARN TO GET READY. DON'T THEY SAY THAT CHANCE FAVORS THE PREPARED MIND?
SKF
CRAP! I'M STARVING....

HUFF
PUFF
...AND COMPLETELY OUT OF GAS....
...BUT...
I HAVE TO GET A BELL... NO MATTER WHAT!
HUFF
HUFF
PUFF
AND I HAVE TO EARN HIS RESPECT!!
HUFF
JEEZ...
NO MATTER WHAT!
SPLASH!!

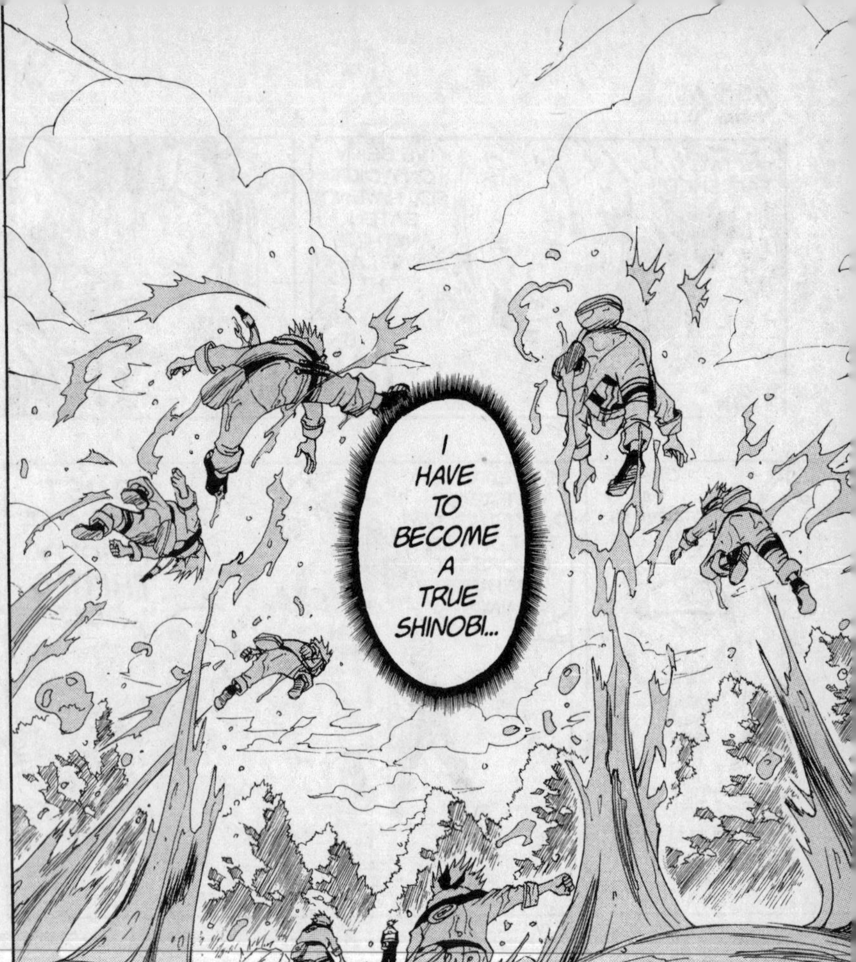
I HAVE TO BECOME A TRUE SHINOBI...

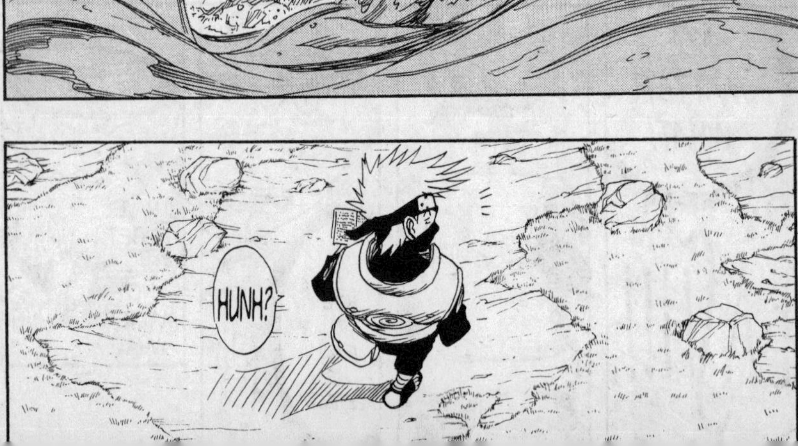
HUNH?

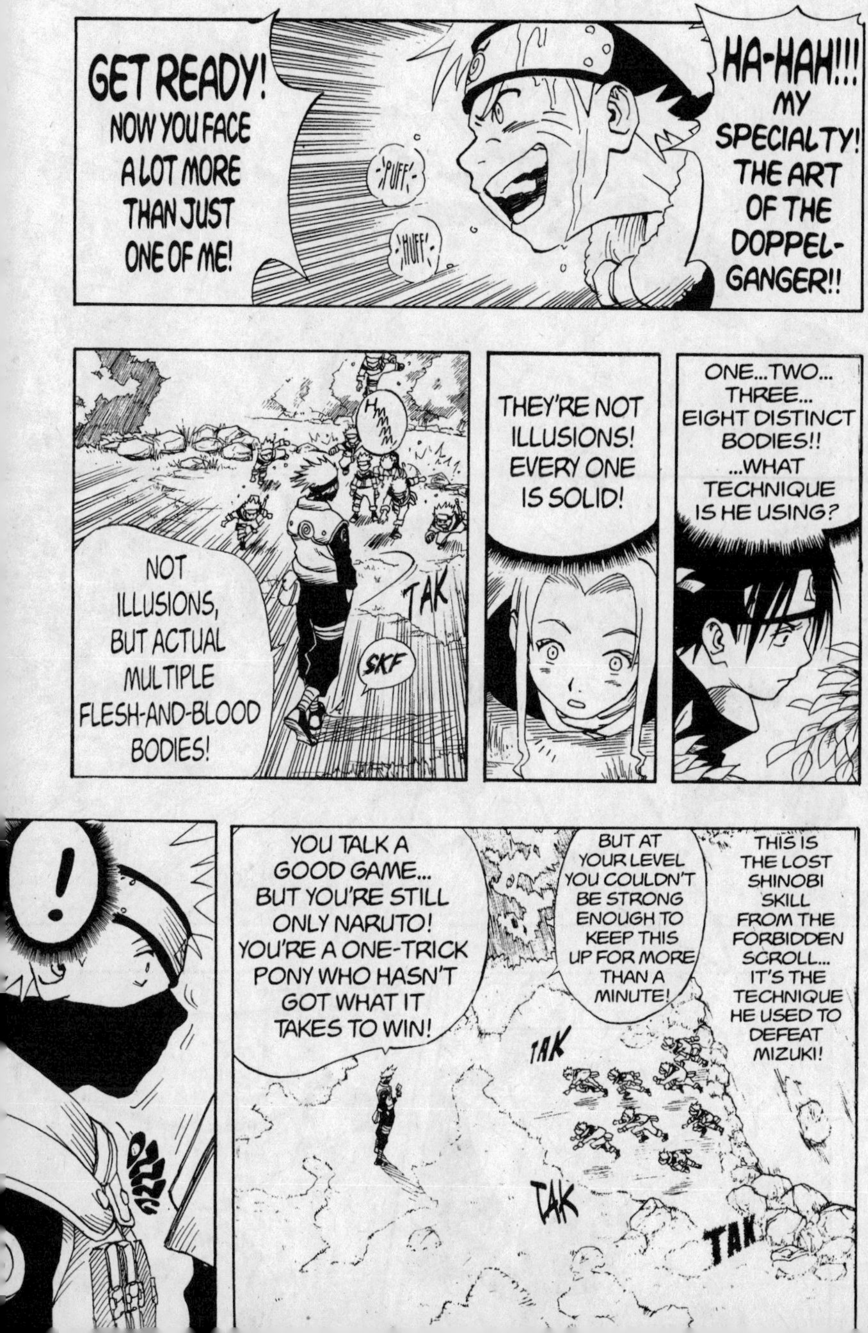
HA-HAH!!! MY SPECIALTY! THE ART OF THE DOPPEL-GANGER!!
PUFF
HUFF
GET READY! NOW YOU FACE A LOT MORE THAN JUST ONE OF ME!
ONE...TWO... THREE... EIGHT DISTINCT BODIES!! ...WHAT TECHNIQUE IS HE USING?
THEY'RE NOT ILLUSIONS! EVERY ONE IS SOLID!
HMMM
NOT ILLUSIONS, BUT ACTUAL MULTIPLE FLESH-AND-BLOOD BODIES!
TAK
SKF
THIS IS THE LOST SHINOBI SKILL FROM THE FORBIDDEN SCROLL... IT'S THE TECHNIQUE HE USED TO DEFEAT MIZUKI!
BUT AT YOUR LEVEL YOU COULDN'T BE STRONG ENOUGH TO KEEP THIS UP FOR MORE THAN A MINUTE!
YOU TALK A GOOD GAME... BUT YOU'RE STILL ONLY NARUTO! YOU'RE A ONE-TRICK PONY WHO HASN'T GOT WHAT IT TAKES TO WIN!
TAK
TAK
TAK
!

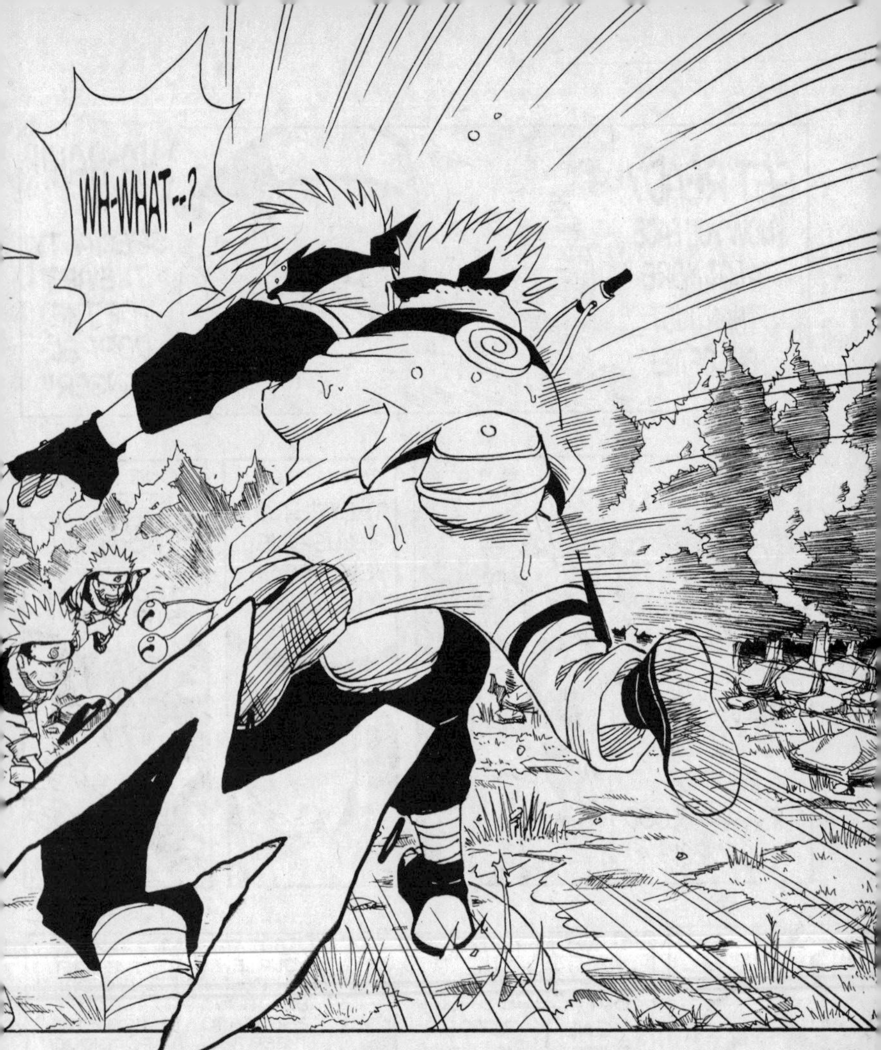
WH-WHAT--?
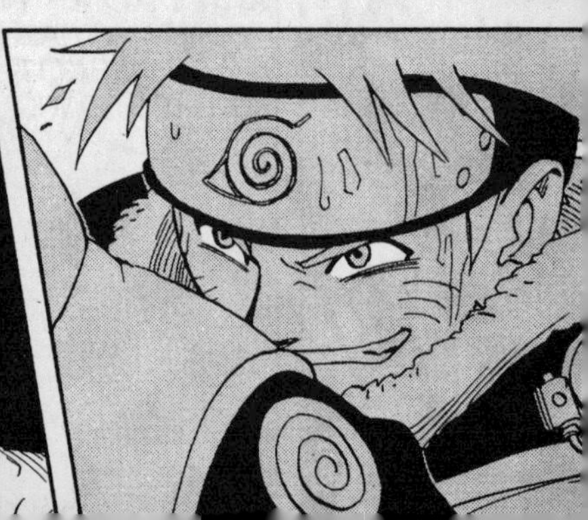
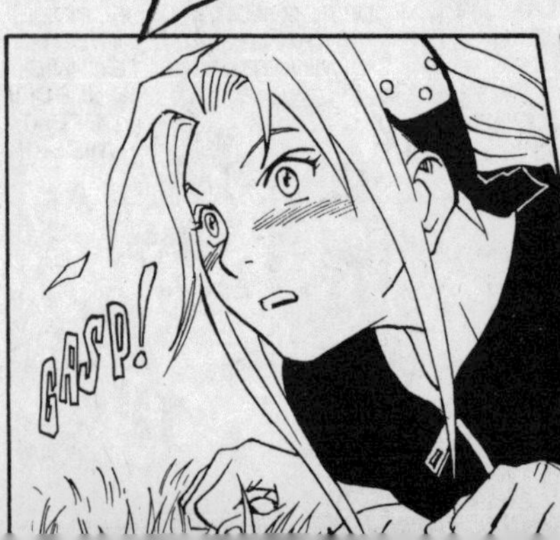
GASP!

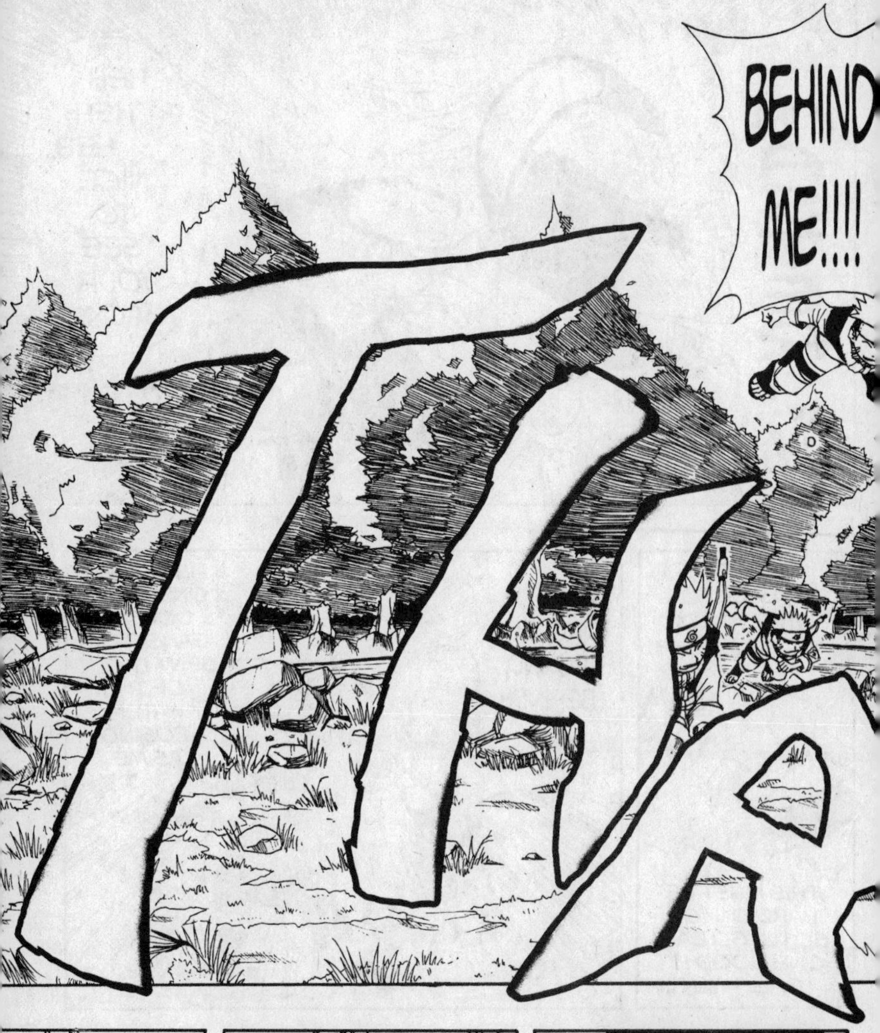
BEHIND ME!!!!
TA
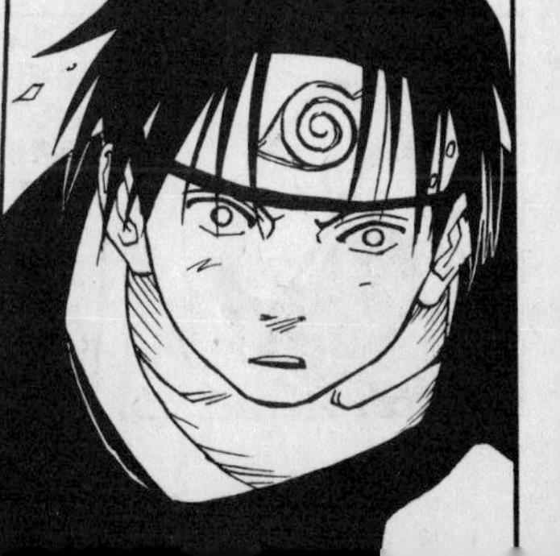
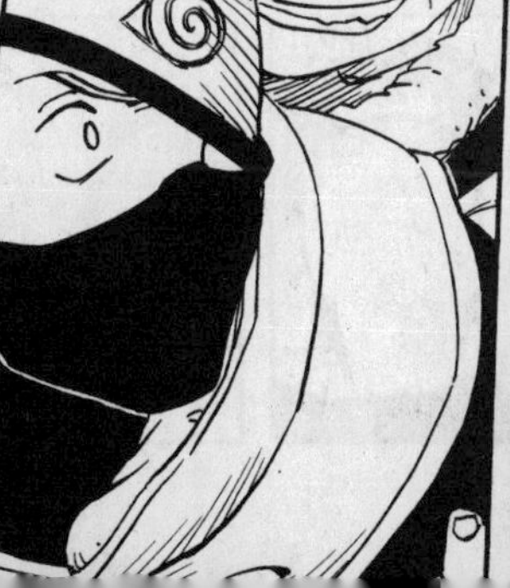
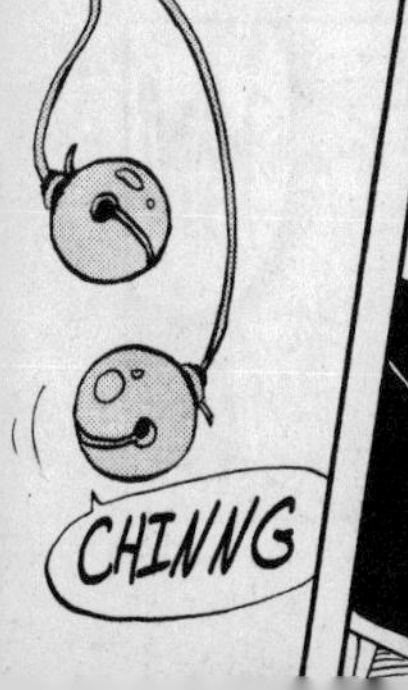
CHINNG

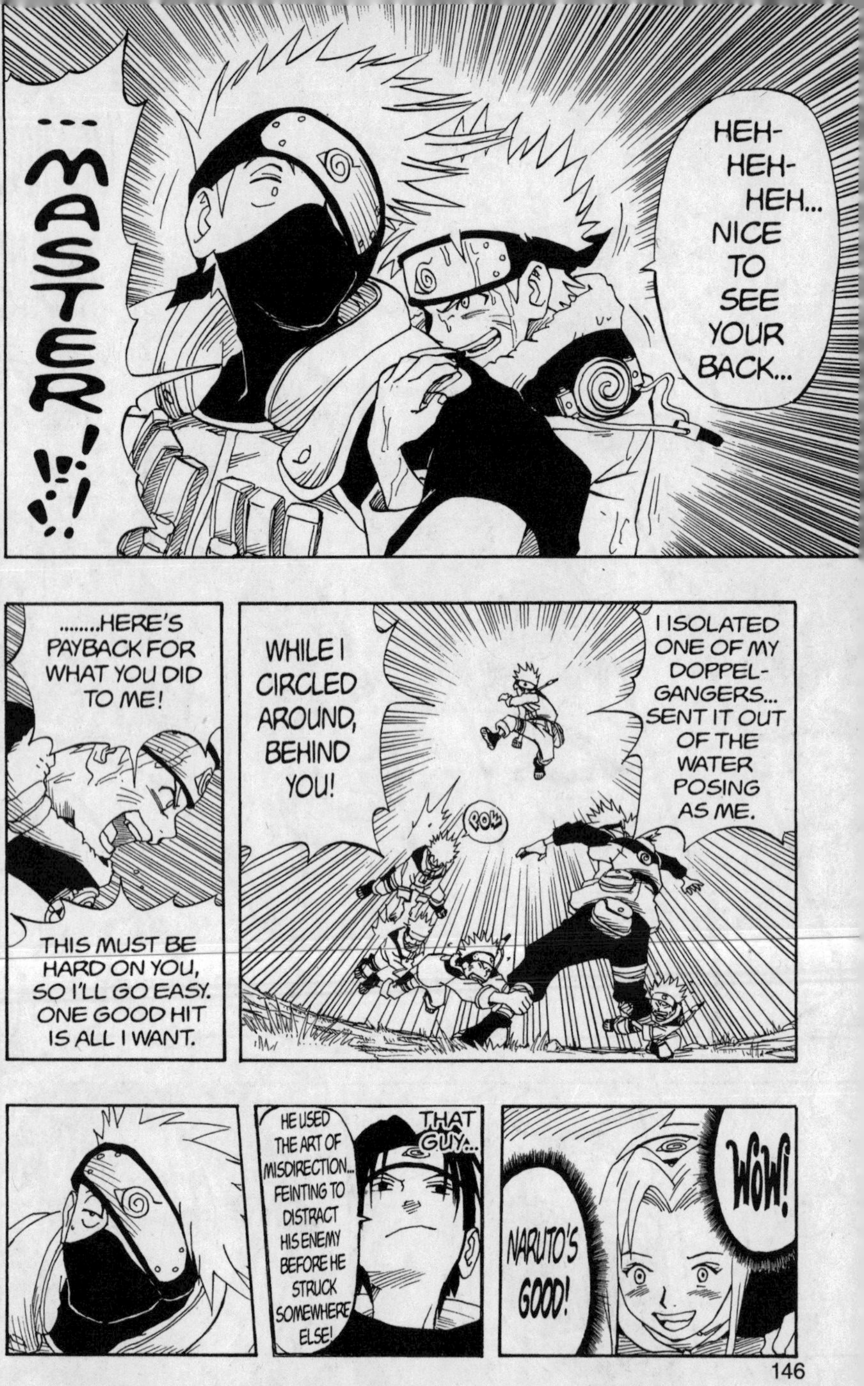
HEH-HEH-HEH... NICE TO SEE YOUR BACK...
...MASTER!!!
I ISOLATED ONE OF MY DOPPEL-GANGERS... SENT IT OUT OF THE WATER POSING AS ME.
WHILE I CIRCLED AROUND, BEHIND YOU!
POW
........HERE'S PAYBACK FOR WHAT YOU DID TO ME!
THIS MUST BE HARD ON YOU, SO I'LL GO EASY. ONE GOOD HIT IS ALL I WANT.
WOW!
NARUTO'S GOOD!
THAT GUY...
HE USED THE ART OF MISDIRECTION... FEINTING TO DISTRACT HIS ENEMY BEFORE HE STRUCK SOMEWHERE ELSE!

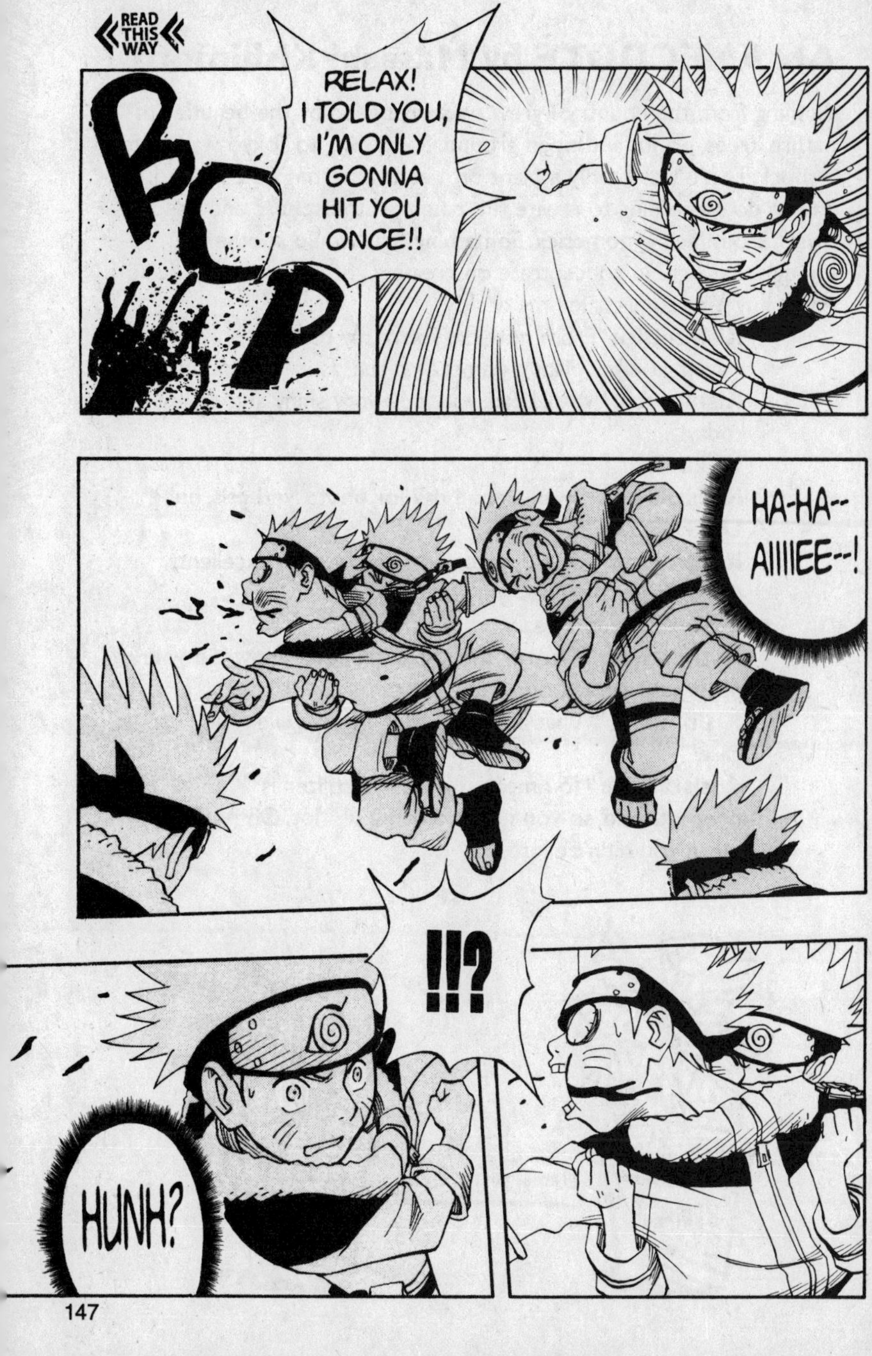
READ THIS WAY
RELAX! I TOLD YOU, I'M ONLY GONNA HIT YOU ONCE!!
BOP
HA-HA-- AIIIIEE--!
!!?
HUNH?

AN ANECDOTE by Masashi Kishimoto

Coming from the country, I grew up surrounded by the beauties of nature, trees, plants, and open ground. So moving to Tokyo was quite a shock. There was hardly a plant or a natural setting to be found. I had to do something to create the country atmosphere and keep myself from feeling homesick. Something that would soothe me enough that I could concentrate on creating good manga. So I decided to buy a houseplant for my desk.

Kishimoto: "From now on, you're my partner!"

I even gave my plant a name: *Ukki-kun*, as in "Mr. Ukki."

Kishimoto: "Well, Ukki, you look very shiny and green today!"

Ukki: "........."

Kishimoto: "It was a good day for photosynthesis, huh?"

Ukki: "........."

Kishimoto: "Today I'm going to give you an excellent fertilizer for vigorous growth!"

We were a super-team.

Assistant A: "What is this, Mr. Kishimoto? How did your plant get all dried out?"

Kishimoto: "What are you saying?! I gave Ukki the best care!"

Assistant A: "You mean this? This fertilizer is concentrated, so you need to dilute it a lot. Oh no! You mean you didn't dilute it?!"

Sigh...

Ukki-kun   (Three months later)   Ukki-kun

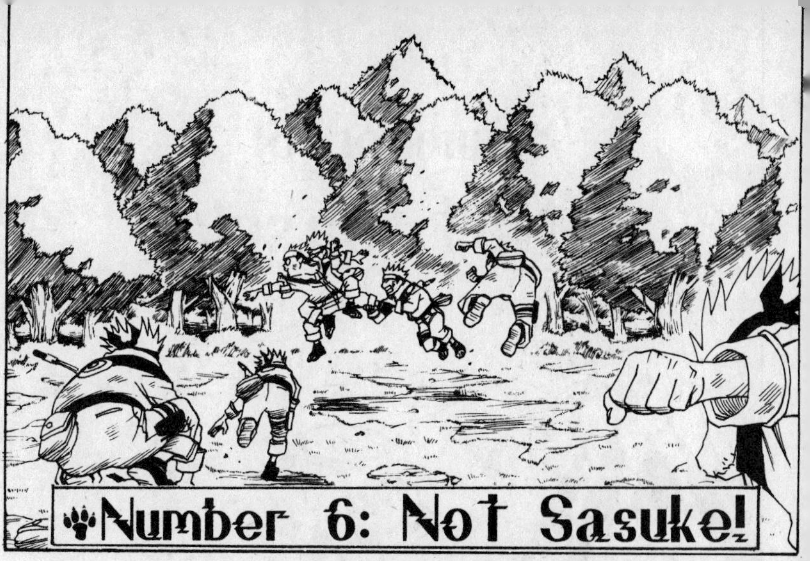

Number 6: Not Sasuke!

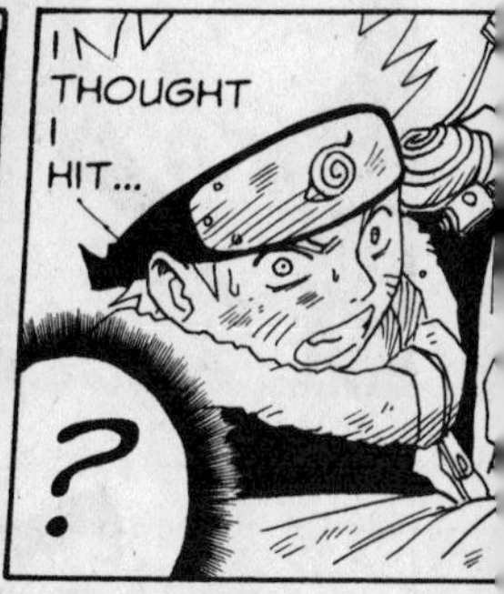
I
THOUGHT
I
HIT...
?

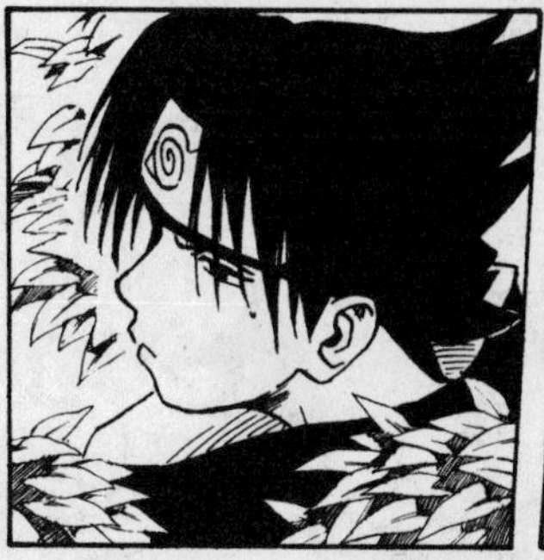

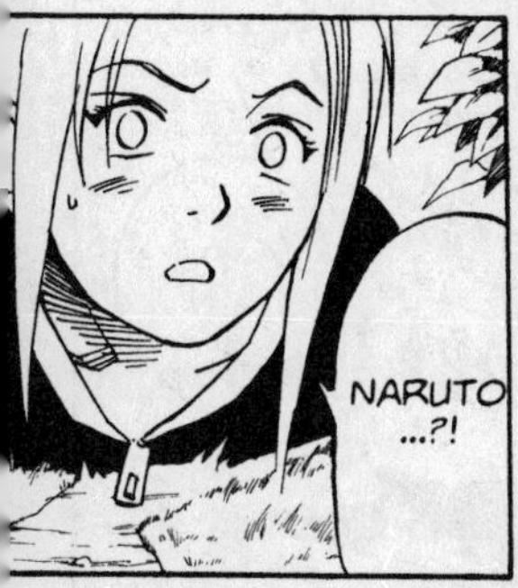
NARUTO
...?!

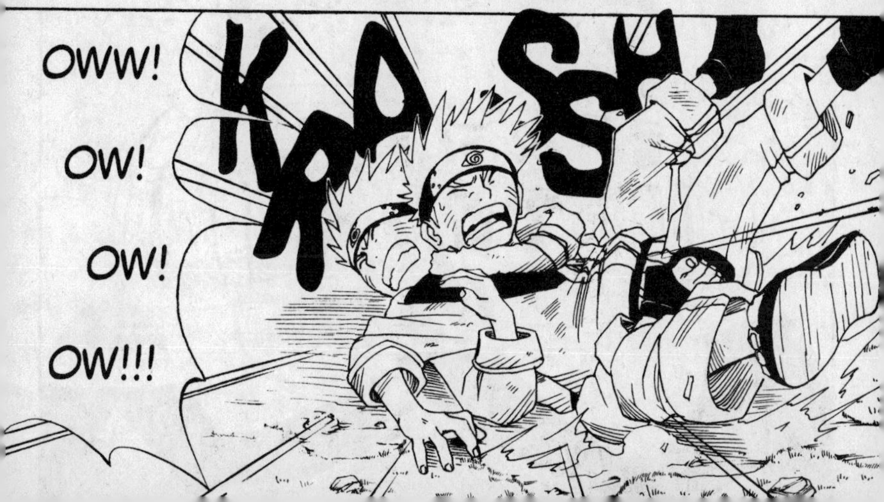
OWW!
OW!
OW!
OW!!!

Number 6:
Not Sasuke!

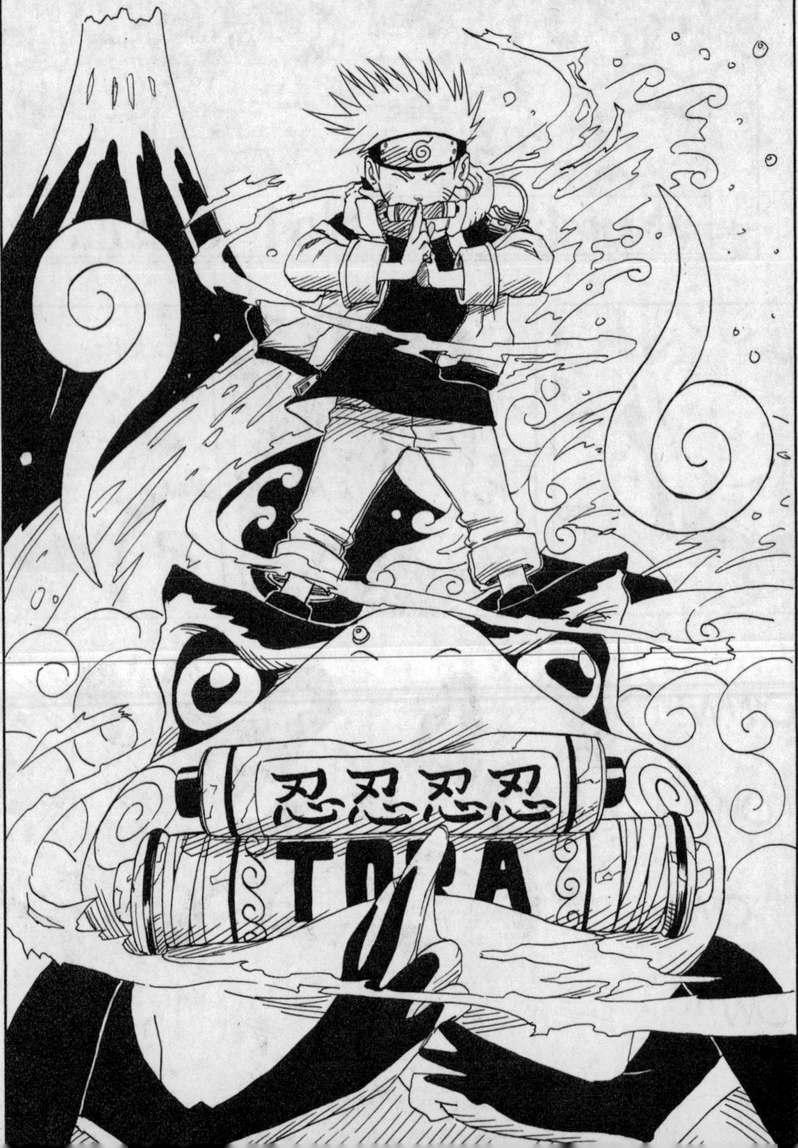
忍忍忍忍

READ THIS WAY

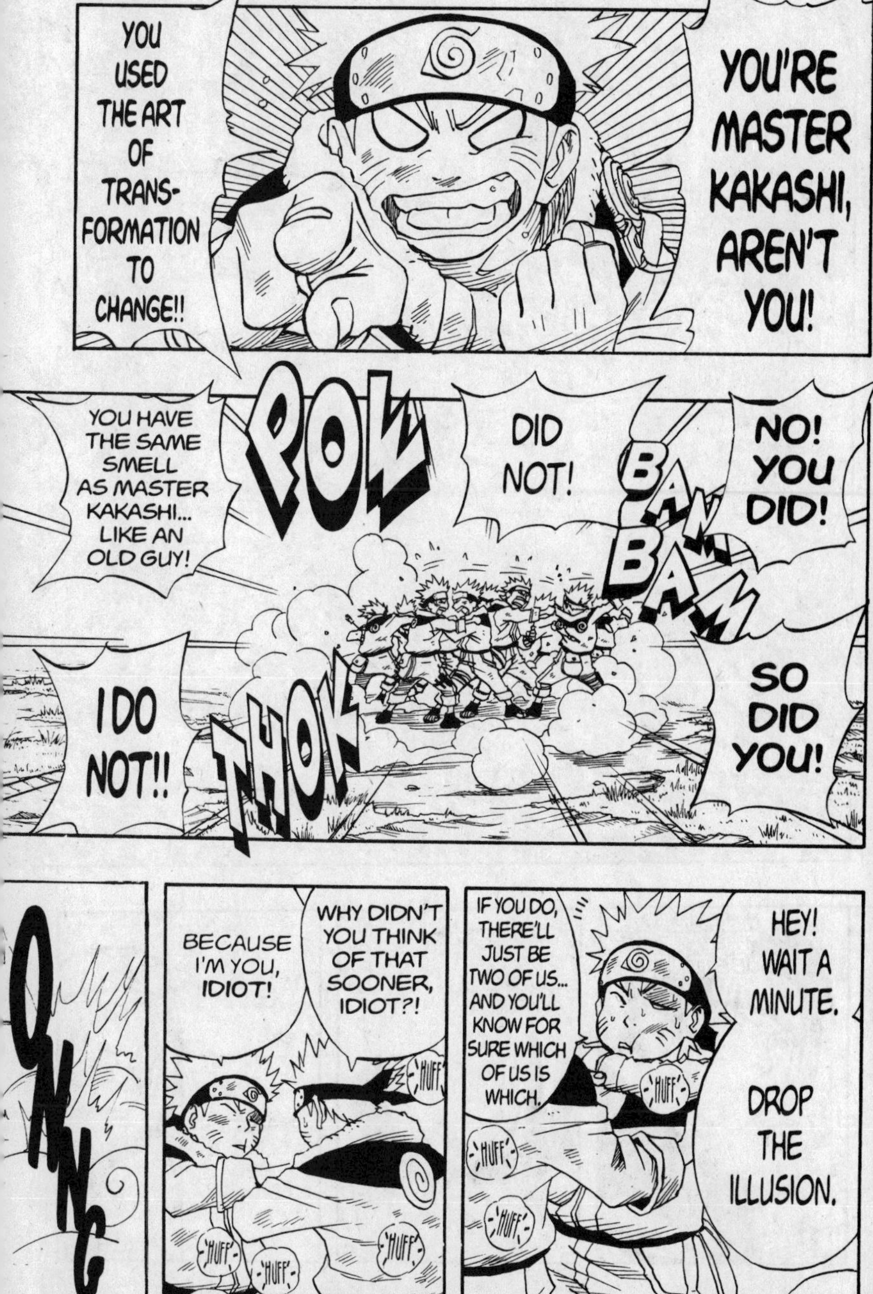
YOU'RE MASTER KAKASHI, AREN'T YOU!
YOU USED THE ART OF TRANS-FORMATION TO CHANGE!!
NO! YOU DID!
BAM BAM
DID NOT!
POW
YOU HAVE THE SAME SMELL AS MASTER KAKASHI... LIKE AN OLD GUY!
SO DID YOU!
THOK
I DO NOT!!
HEY! WAIT A MINUTE.
DROP THE ILLUSION.
IF YOU DO, THERE'LL JUST BE TWO OF US... AND YOU'LL KNOW FOR SURE WHICH OF US IS WHICH.
HUFF
HUFF
HUFF
HUFF
WHY DIDN'T YOU THINK OF THAT SOONER, IDIOT?!
BECAUSE I'M YOU, IDIOT!
HUFF
HUFF
HUFF

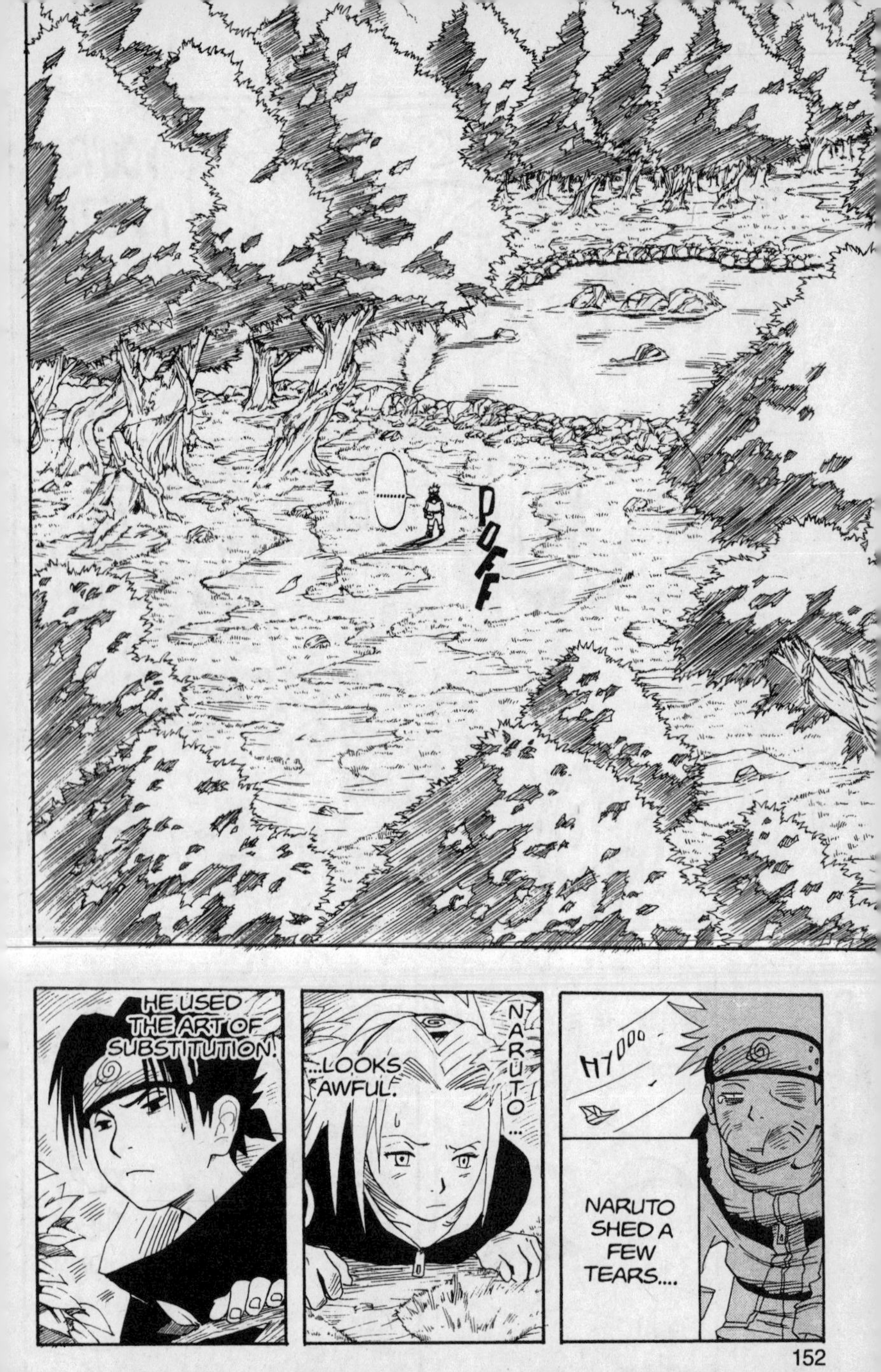
......
POFF
HYOOO
NARUTO SHED A FEW TEARS....
NARUTO...
...LOOKS AWFUL.
HE USED THE ART OF SUBSTITUTION!

READ THIS WAY

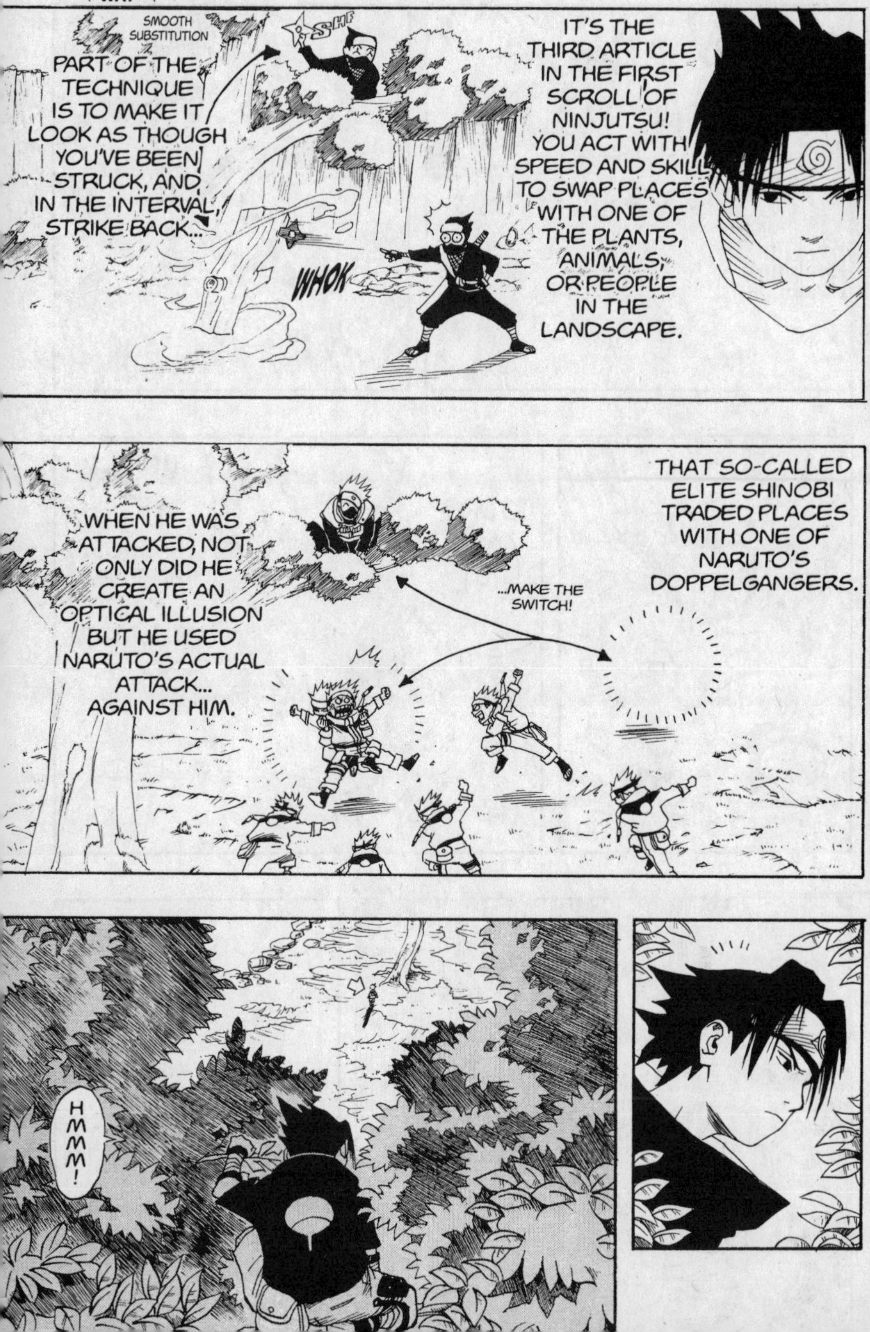
IT'S THE THIRD ARTICLE IN THE FIRST SCROLL OF NINJUTSU! YOU ACT WITH SPEED AND SKILL TO SWAP PLACES WITH ONE OF THE PLANTS, ANIMALS, OR PEOPLE IN THE LANDSCAPE.
SHF
SMOOTH SUBSTITUTION
PART OF THE TECHNIQUE IS TO MAKE IT LOOK AS THOUGH YOU'VE BEEN STRUCK, AND IN THE INTERVAL, STRIKE BACK...
WHOK
THAT SO-CALLED ELITE SHINOBI TRADED PLACES WITH ONE OF NARUTO'S DOPPELGANGERS.
WHEN HE WAS ATTACKED, NOT ONLY DID HE CREATE AN OPTICAL ILLUSION BUT HE USED NARUTO'S ACTUAL ATTACK... AGAINST HIM.
...MAKE THE SWITCH!
HMMM!

READ THIS WAY

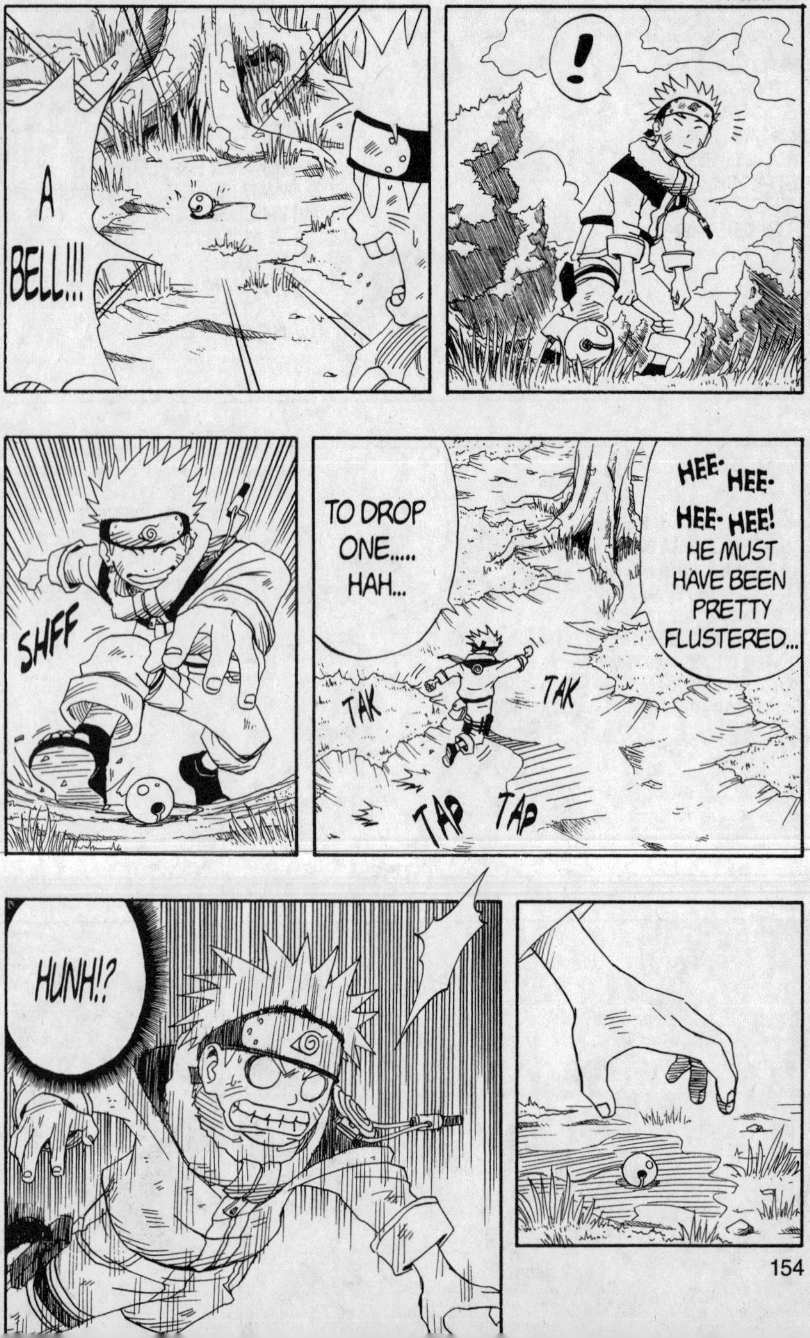
!
A BELL!!!
HEE-HEE-HEE-HEE! HE MUST HAVE BEEN PRETTY FLUSTERED...
TO DROP ONE..... HAH...
TAK
TAK
TAP
TAP
SHFF
HUNH!?

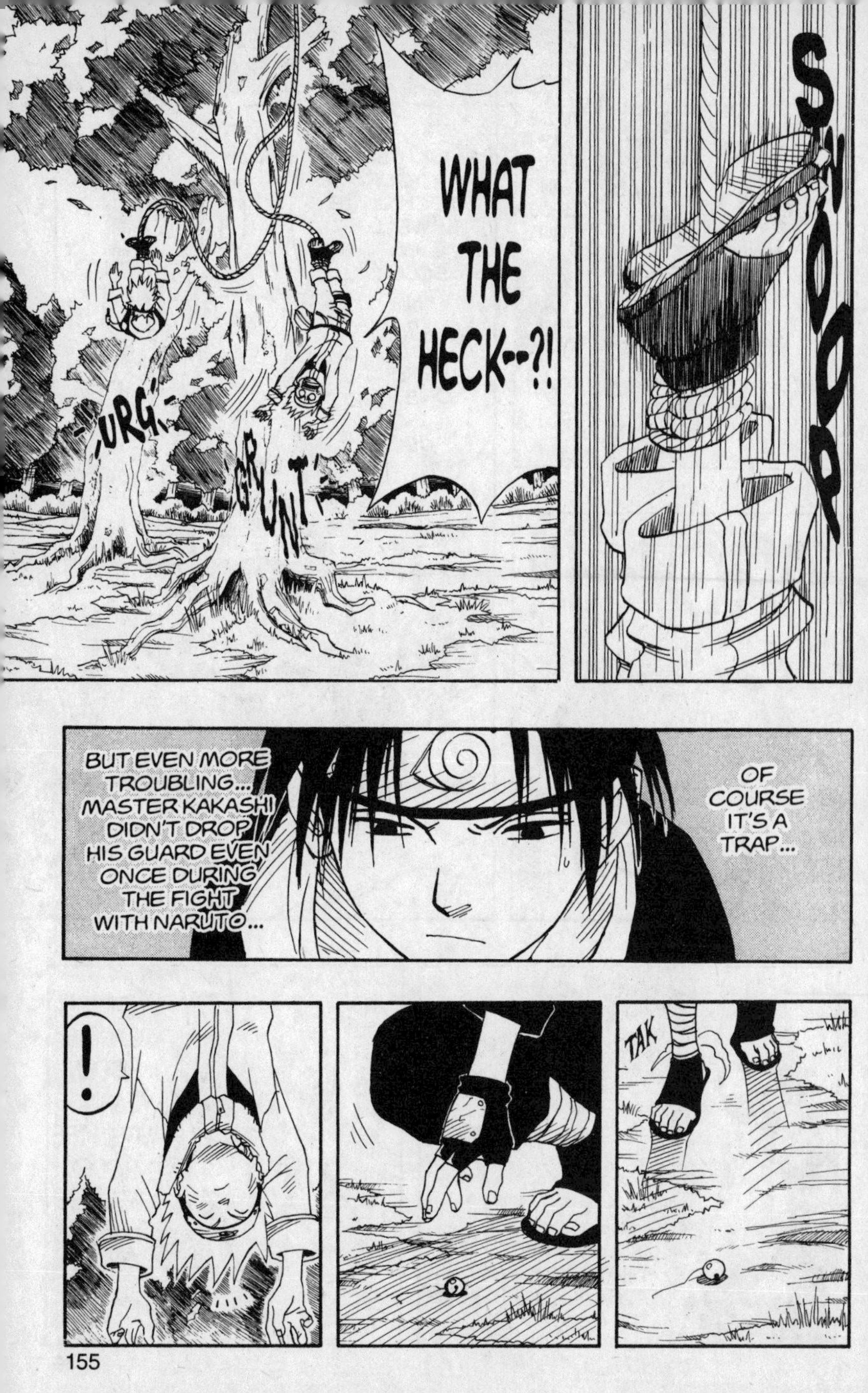
SNOOP
WHAT THE HECK--?!
-URG-
GRUNT
OF COURSE IT'S A TRAP...
BUT EVEN MORE TROUBLING... MASTER KAKASHI DIDN'T DROP HIS GUARD EVEN ONCE DURING THE FIGHT WITH NARUTO...
TAK
!

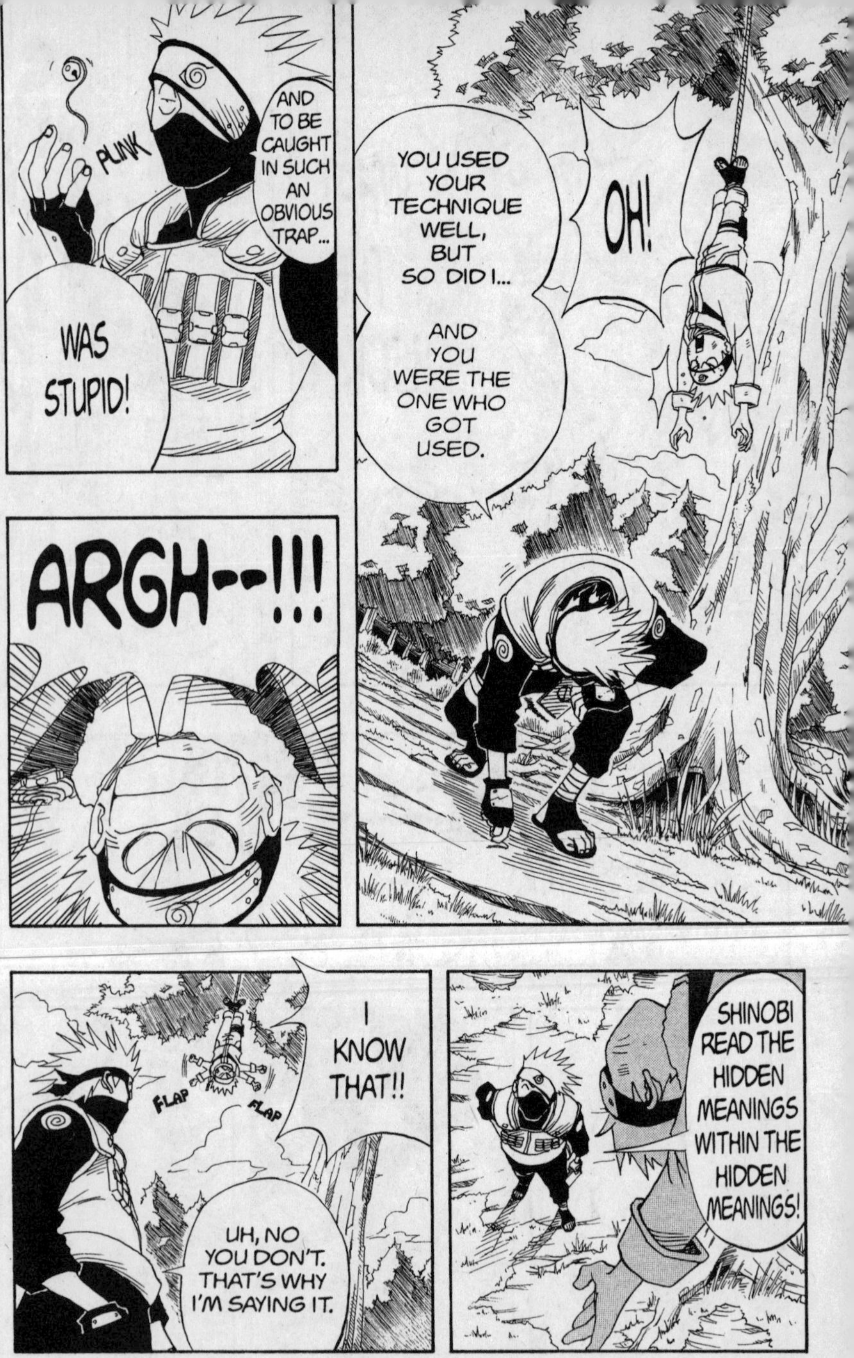
OH!
YOU USED YOUR TECHNIQUE WELL, BUT SO DID I...
AND YOU WERE THE ONE WHO GOT USED.
PLINK
AND TO BE CAUGHT IN SUCH AN OBVIOUS TRAP...
WAS STUPID!
ARGH--!!!
SHINOBI READ THE HIDDEN MEANINGS WITHIN THE HIDDEN MEANINGS!
I KNOW THAT!!
FLAP
FLAP
UH, NO YOU DON'T. THAT'S WHY I'M SAYING IT.

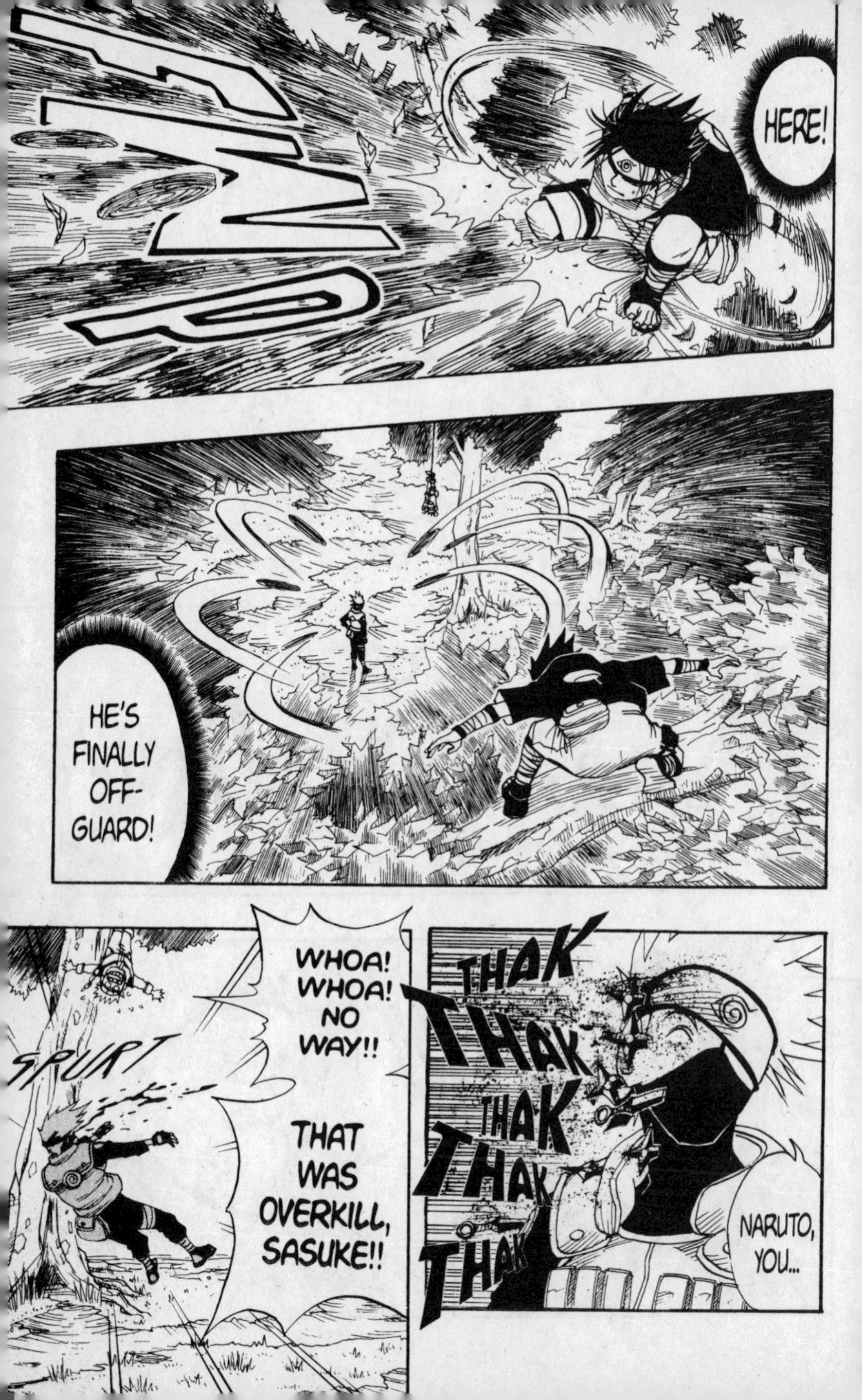
HERE!
HE'S FINALLY OFF-GUARD!
THAK THAK THAK THAK THAK
NARUTO, YOU...
WHOA! WHOA! NO WAY!!
THAT WAS OVERKILL, SASUKE!!
SPURT

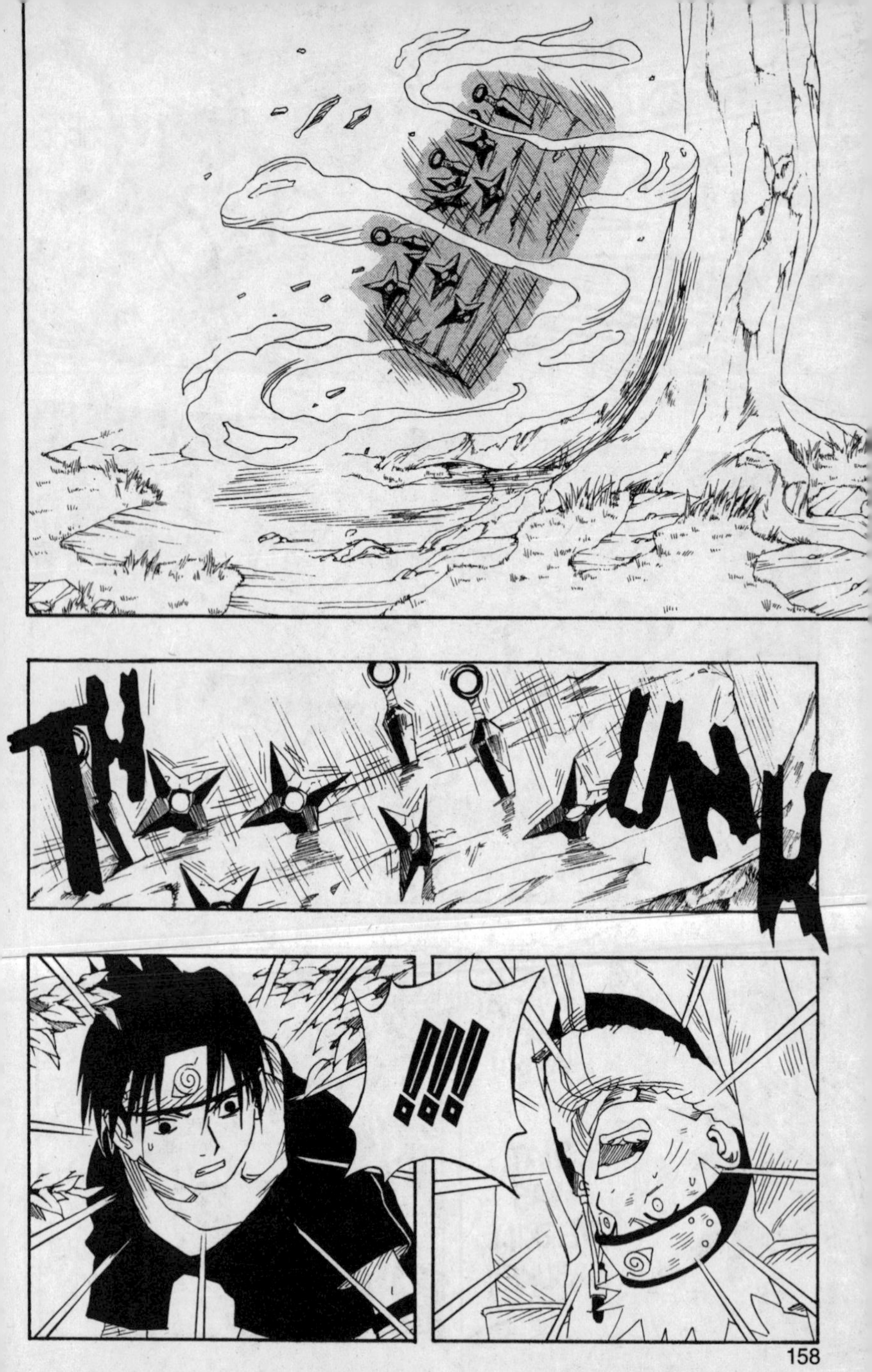
THUNK
!!!

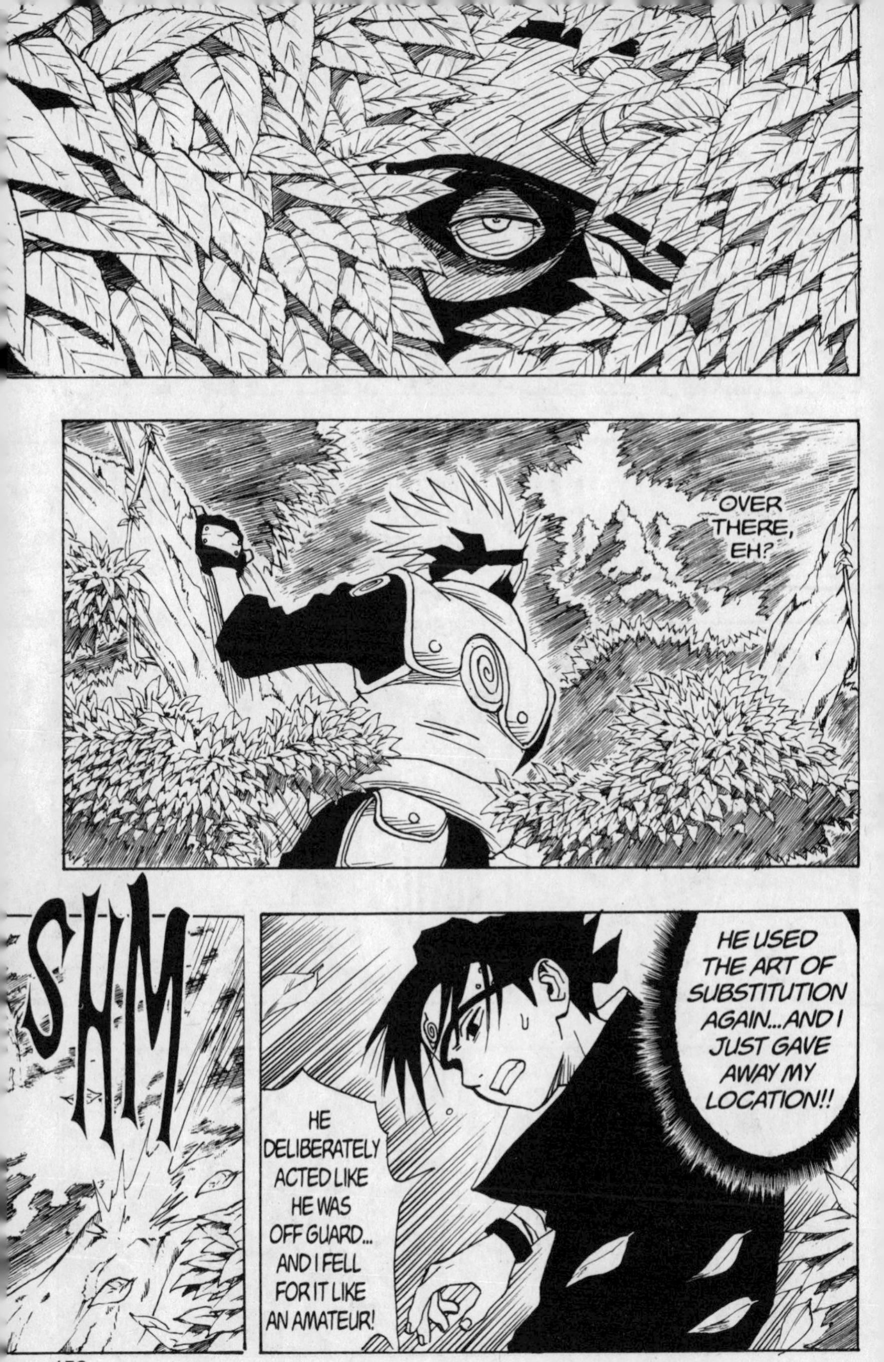
OVER THERE, EH?
HE USED THE ART OF SUBSTITUTION AGAIN...AND I JUST GAVE AWAY MY LOCATION!!
HE DELIBERATELY ACTED LIKE HE WAS OFF GUARD... AND I FELL FOR IT LIKE AN AMATEUR!
SHM

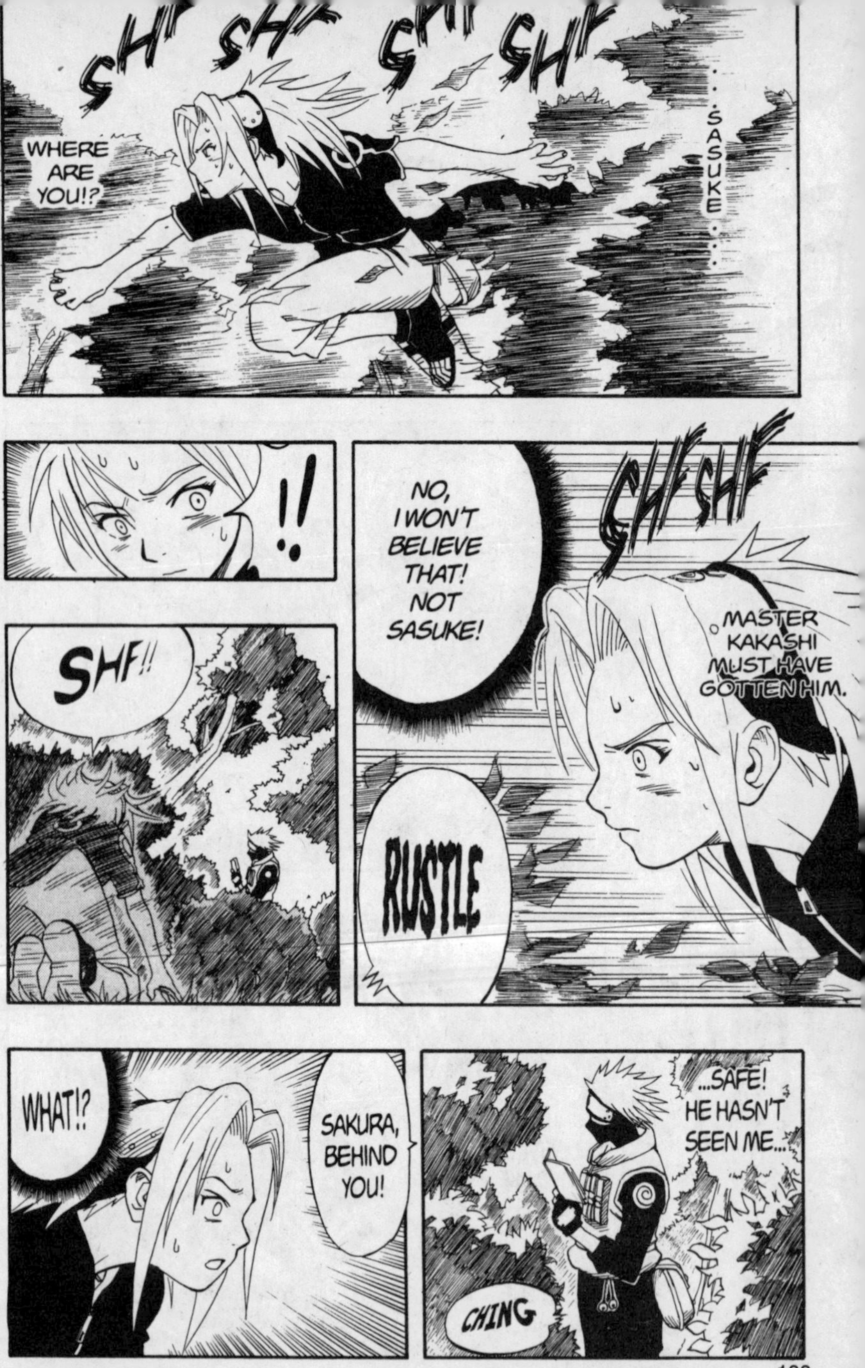
SHF SHF SHF SHF
...SASUKE...
WHERE ARE YOU!?
SHF SHF
MASTER KAKASHI MUST HAVE GOTTEN HIM.
NO, I WON'T BELIEVE THAT! NOT SASUKE!
RUSTLE
!!
SHF!!
...SAFE! HE HASN'T SEEN ME...
CHING
SAKURA, BEHIND YOU!
WHAT!?

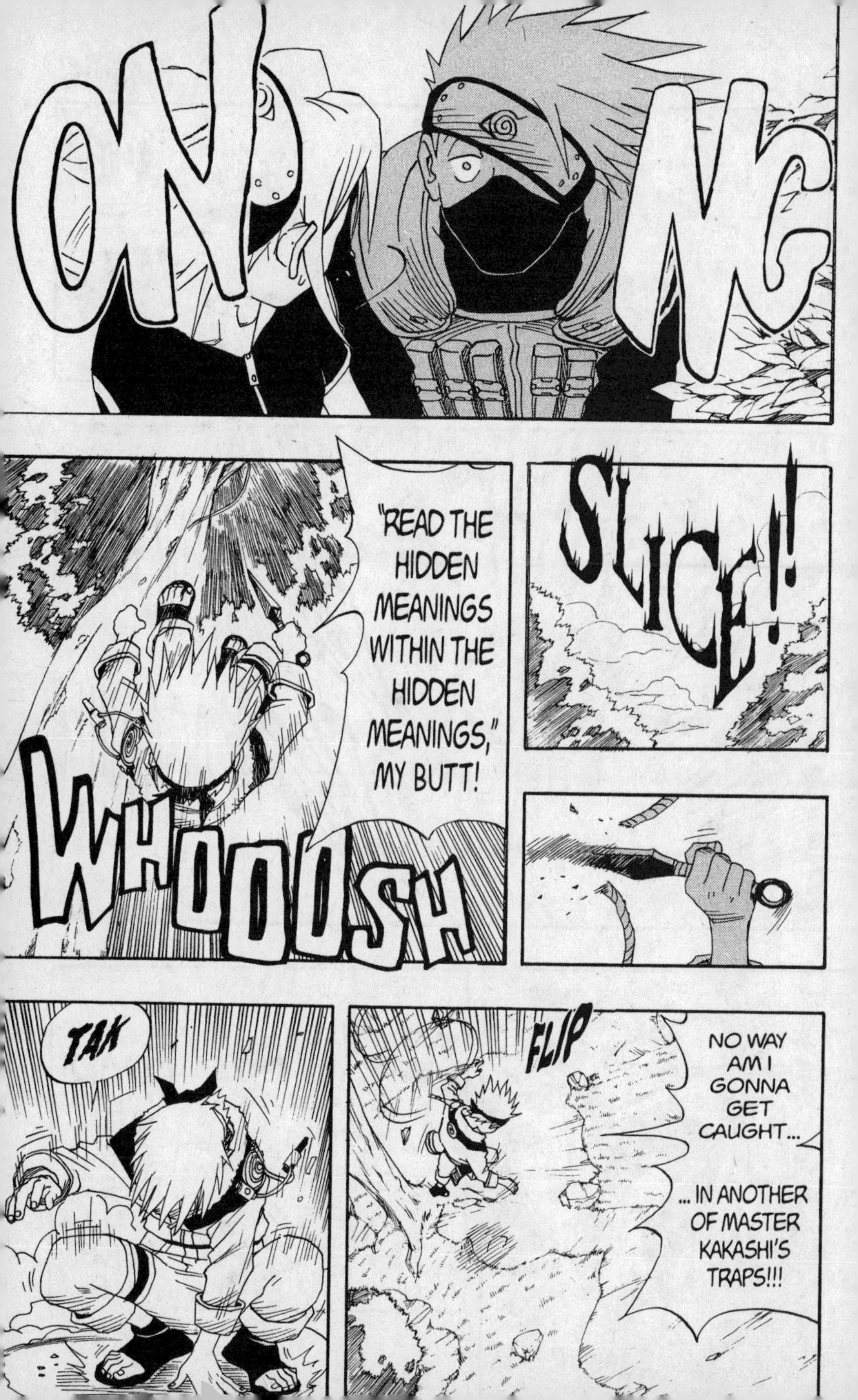
SLICE!!
"READ THE HIDDEN MEANINGS WITHIN THE HIDDEN MEANINGS," MY BUTT!
WHOOOSH
FLIP
NO WAY AM I GONNA GET CAUGHT...
...IN ANOTHER OF MASTER KAKASHI'S TRAPS!!!
TAK

READ THIS WAY

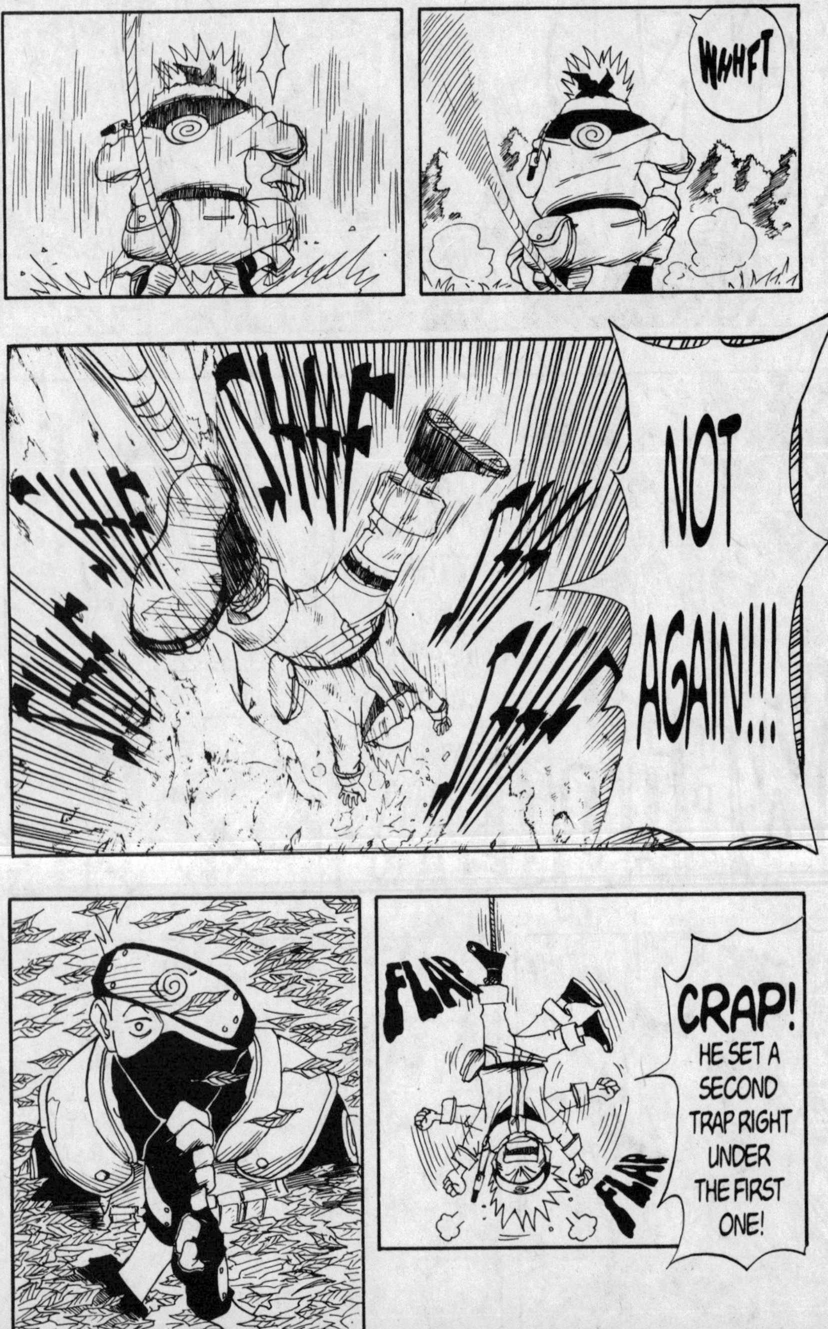
WHHFT
SHFF
NOT AGAIN!!!
FLAP
FLAP
CRAP!
HE SET A SECOND TRAP RIGHT UNDER THE FIRST ONE!

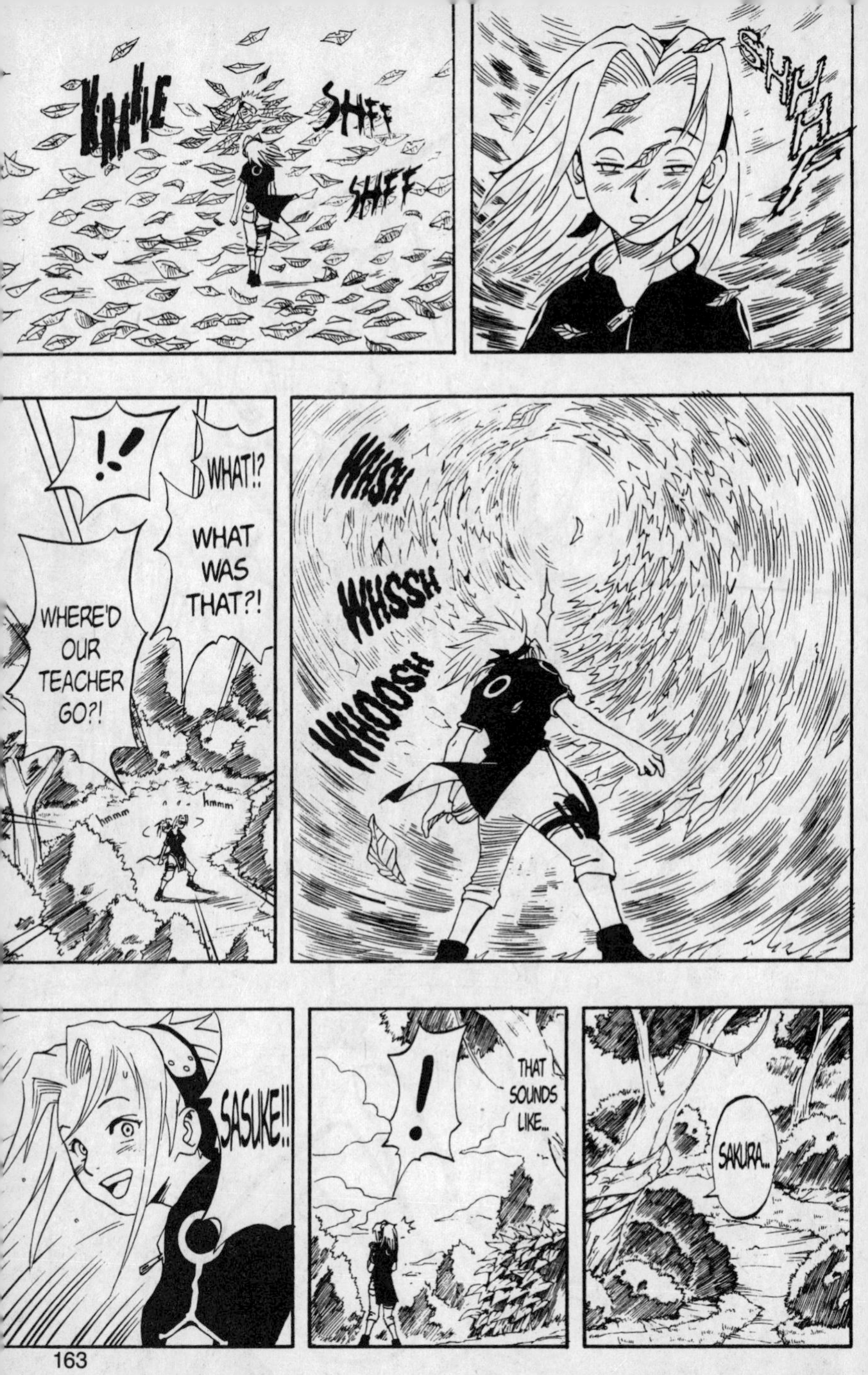
SHHHF
KRAKLE
SHFF
SHFF
WHSH
WHSSH
WHOOSH
!!
WHAT!?
WHAT WAS THAT?!
WHERE'D OUR TEACHER GO?!
hmmm
hmmm
SAKURA...
!
THAT SOUNDS LIKE...
SASUKE!!

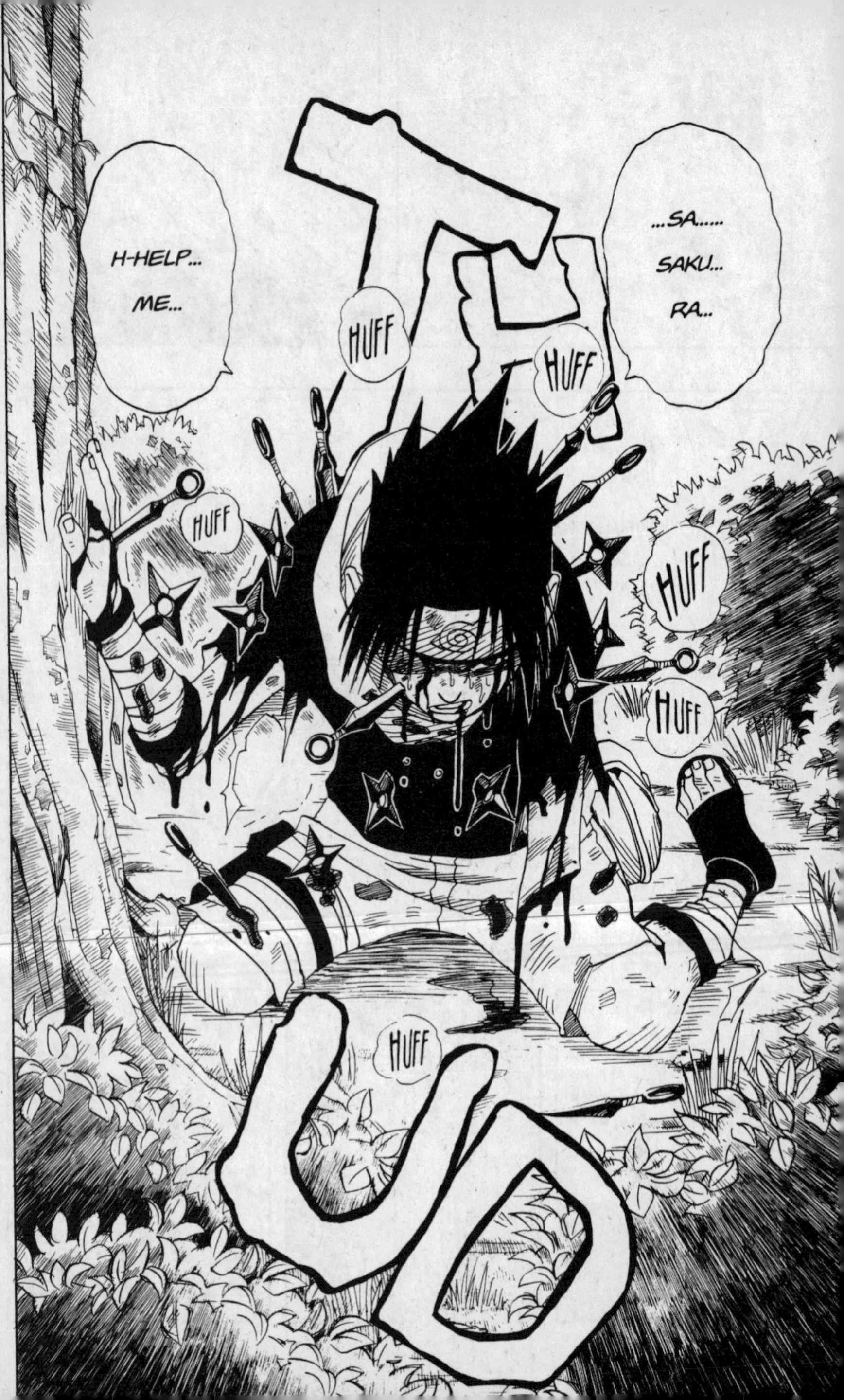
...SA..... SAKU... RA...
H-HELP... ME...
HUFF
HUFF
HUFF
HUFF
HUFF
HUFF

READ THIS WAY

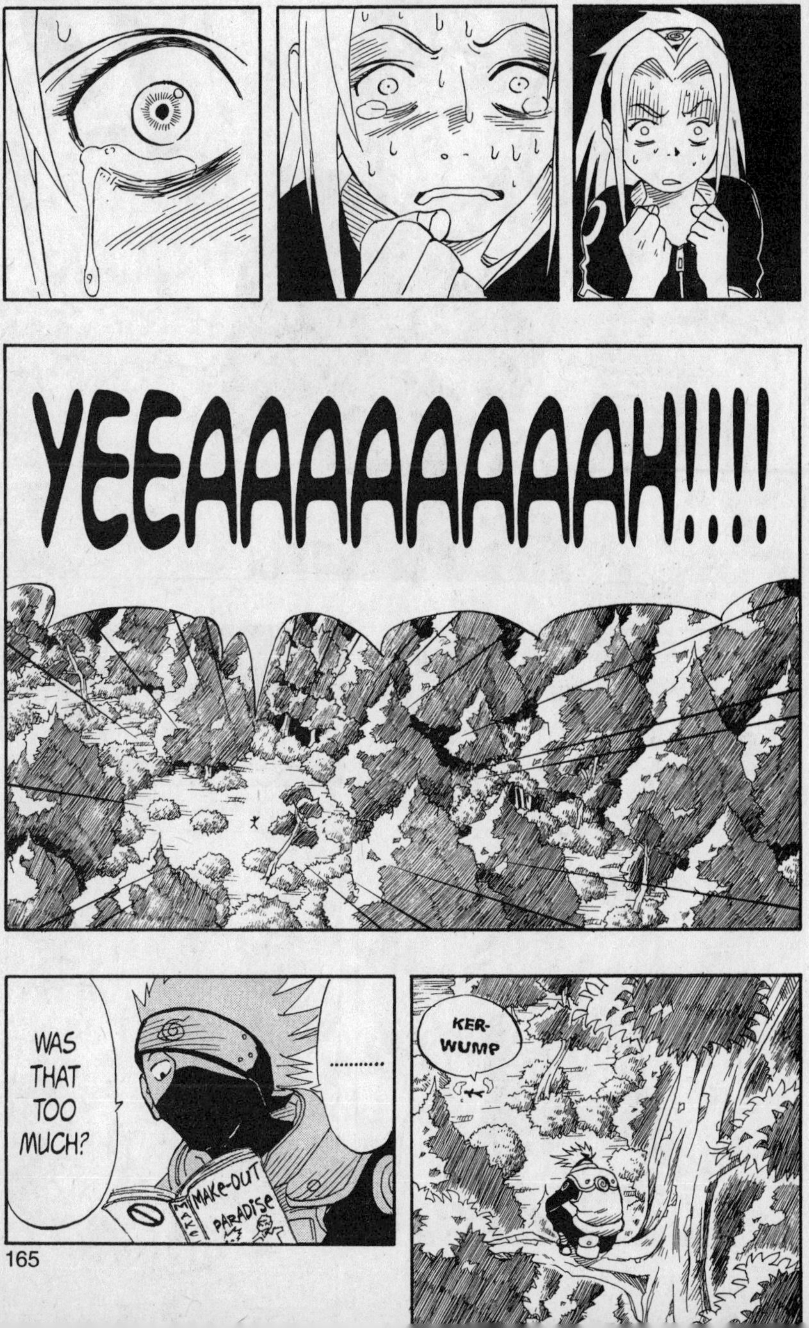
YEEAAAAAAAAH!!!!
KER-WUMP
WAS THAT TOO MUCH?
....
MAKE-OUT PARADISE

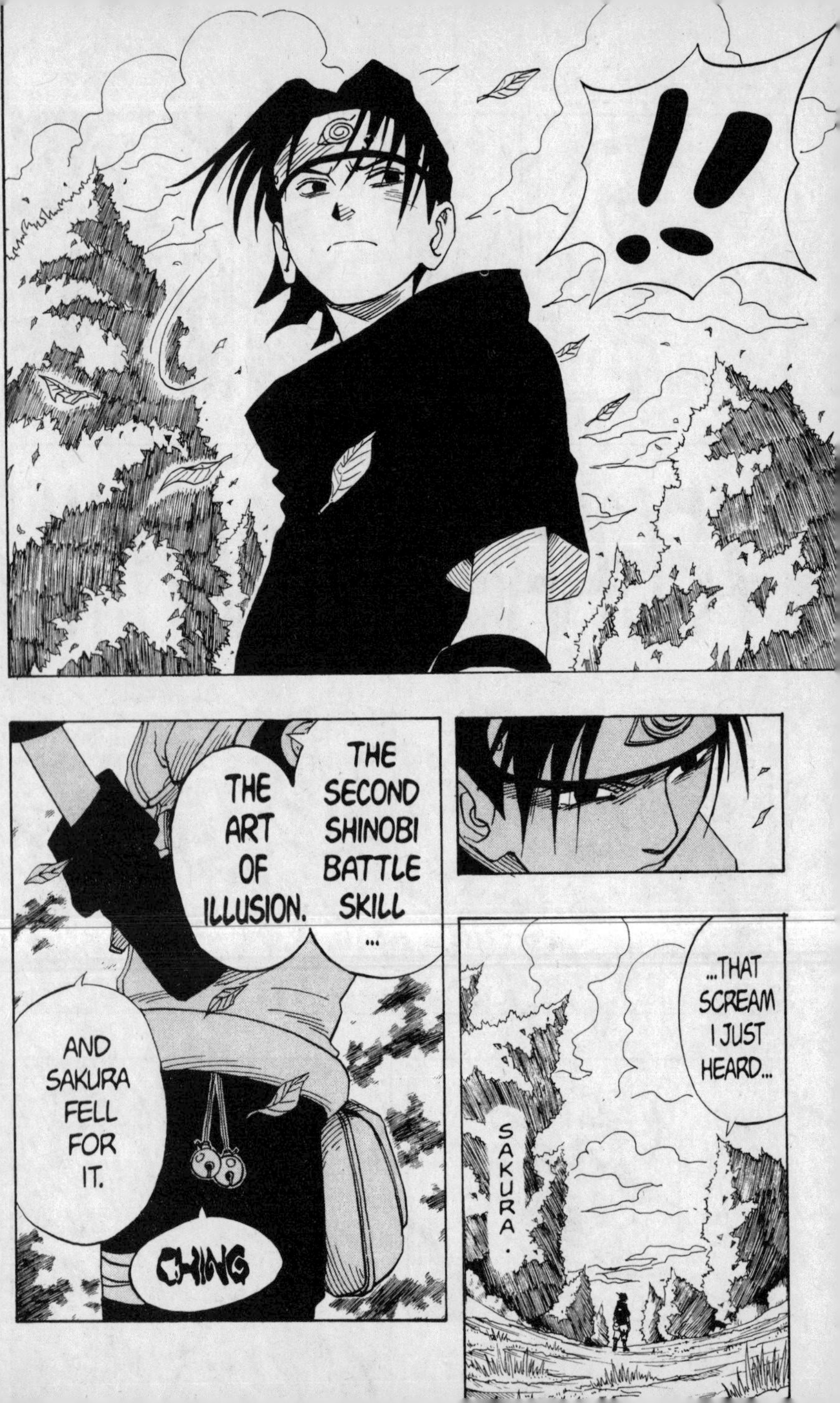
!!
...THAT SCREAM I JUST HEARD...
SAKURA.
THE SECOND SHINOBI BATTLE SKILL...
THE ART OF ILLUSION.
AND SAKURA FELL FOR IT.
CHING

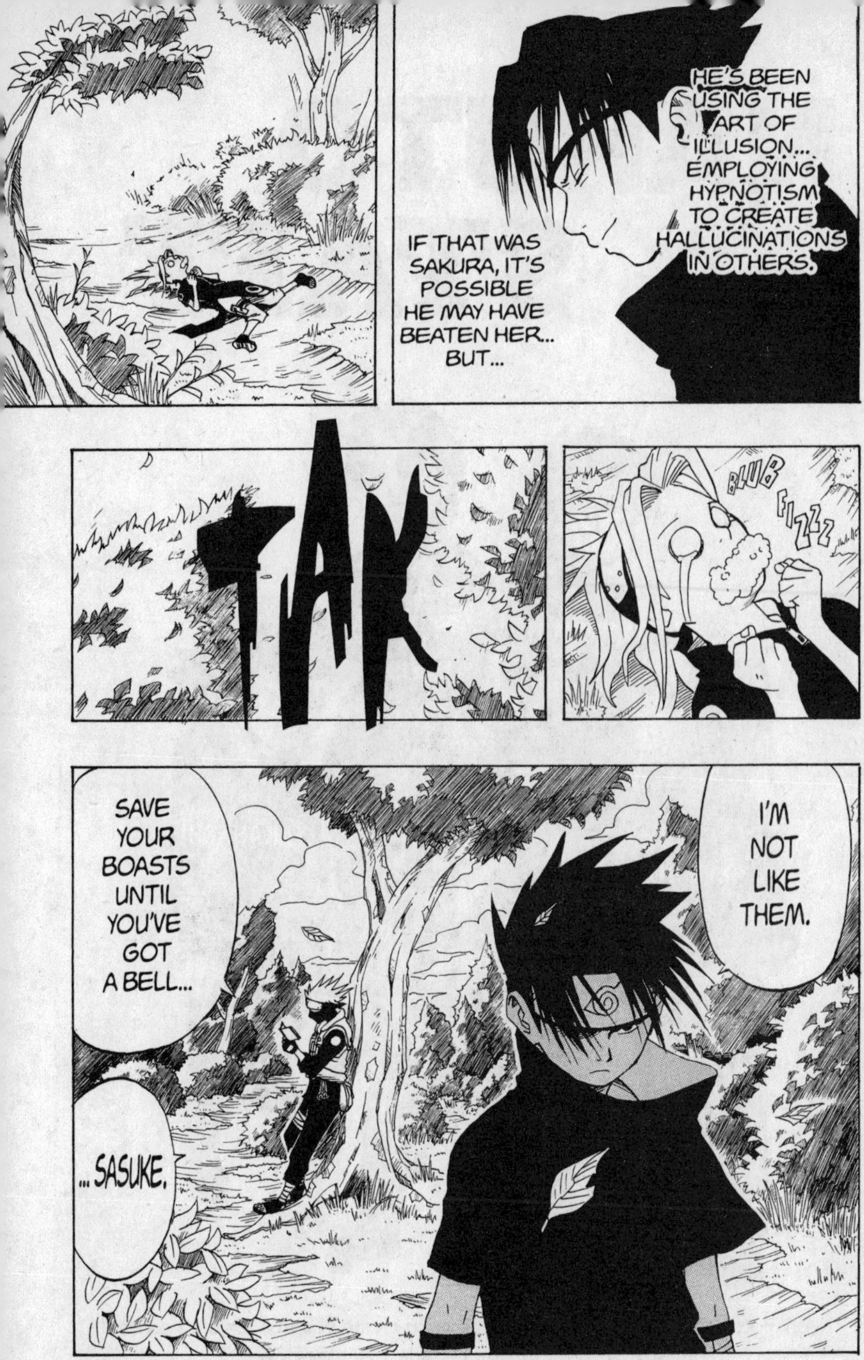
HE'S BEEN USING THE ART OF ILLUSION... EMPLOYING HYPNOTISM TO CREATE HALLUCINATIONS IN OTHERS.
IF THAT WAS SAKURA, IT'S POSSIBLE HE MAY HAVE BEATEN HER... BUT...
BLUB
FIZZZ
TAK
I'M NOT LIKE THEM.
SAVE YOUR BOASTS UNTIL YOU'VE GOT A BELL...
...SASUKE.

NARUTO STAFF

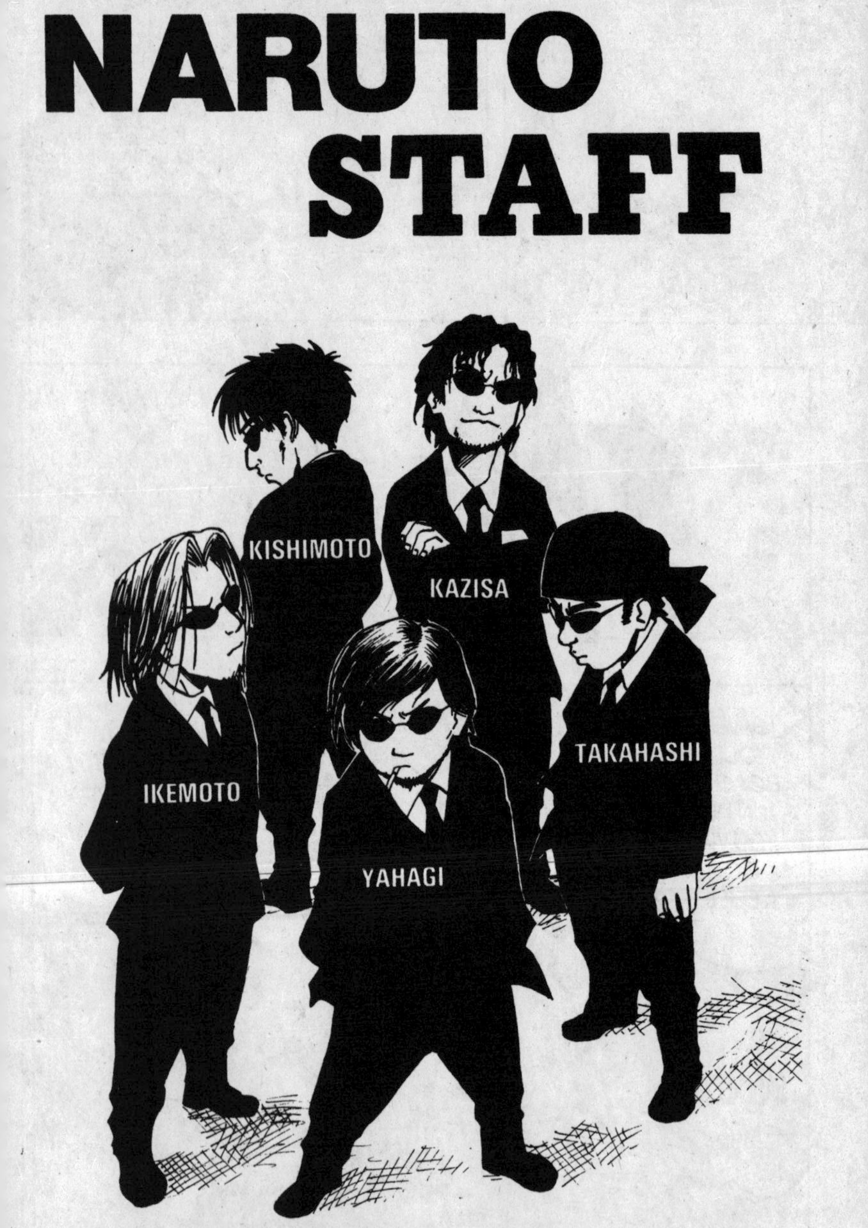
KISHIMOTO
KAZISA
IKEMOTO
TAKAHASHI
YAHAGI

Kishimoto and his assistants work together to create **Naruto** for the Japanese **Weekly Shonen Jump** magazine…20 pages a week!

Number 7: Kakashi's Decision

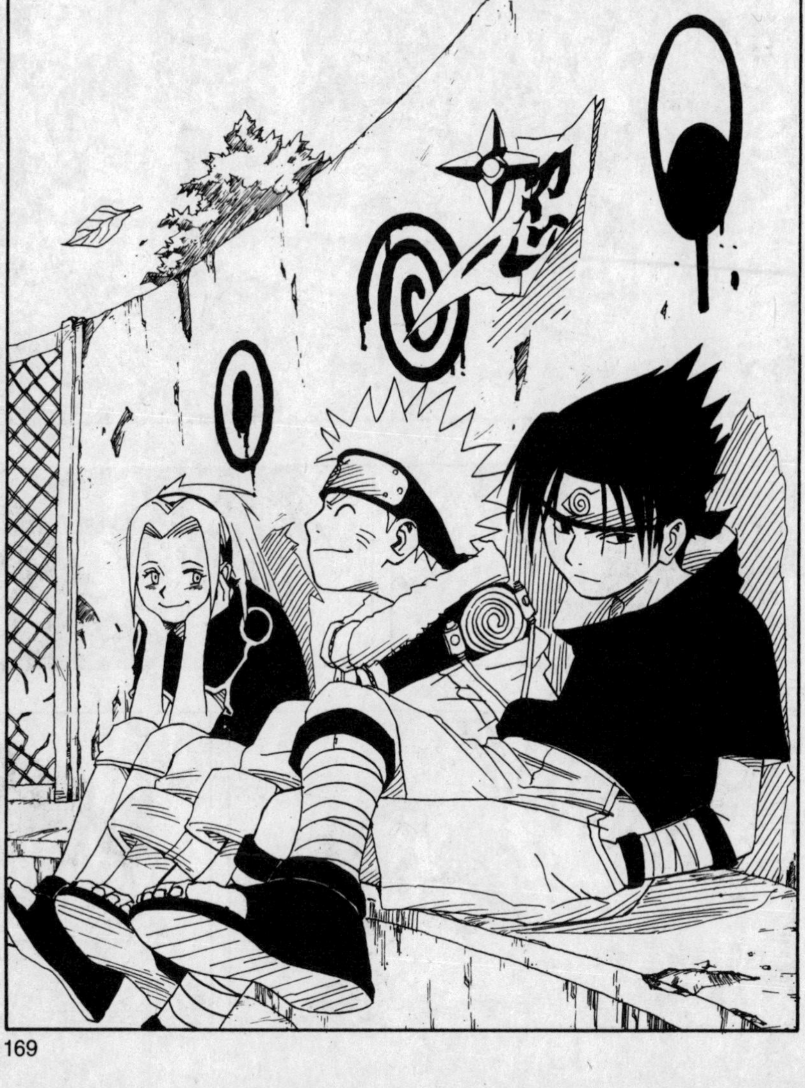

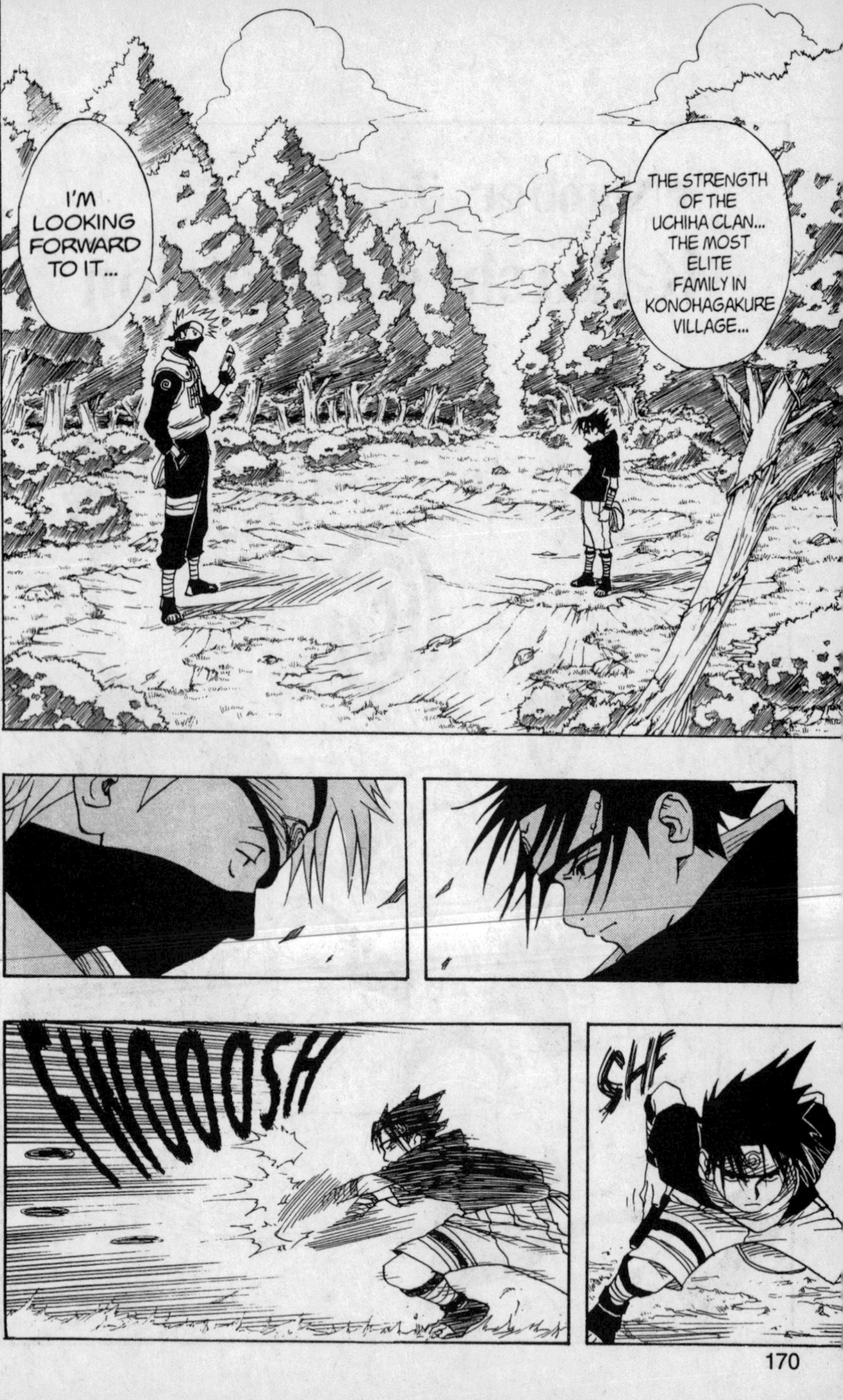
THE STRENGTH OF THE UCHIHA CLAN... THE MOST ELITE FAMILY IN KONOHAGAKURE VILLAGE...
I'M LOOKING FORWARD TO IT...
SH
FWOOOSH

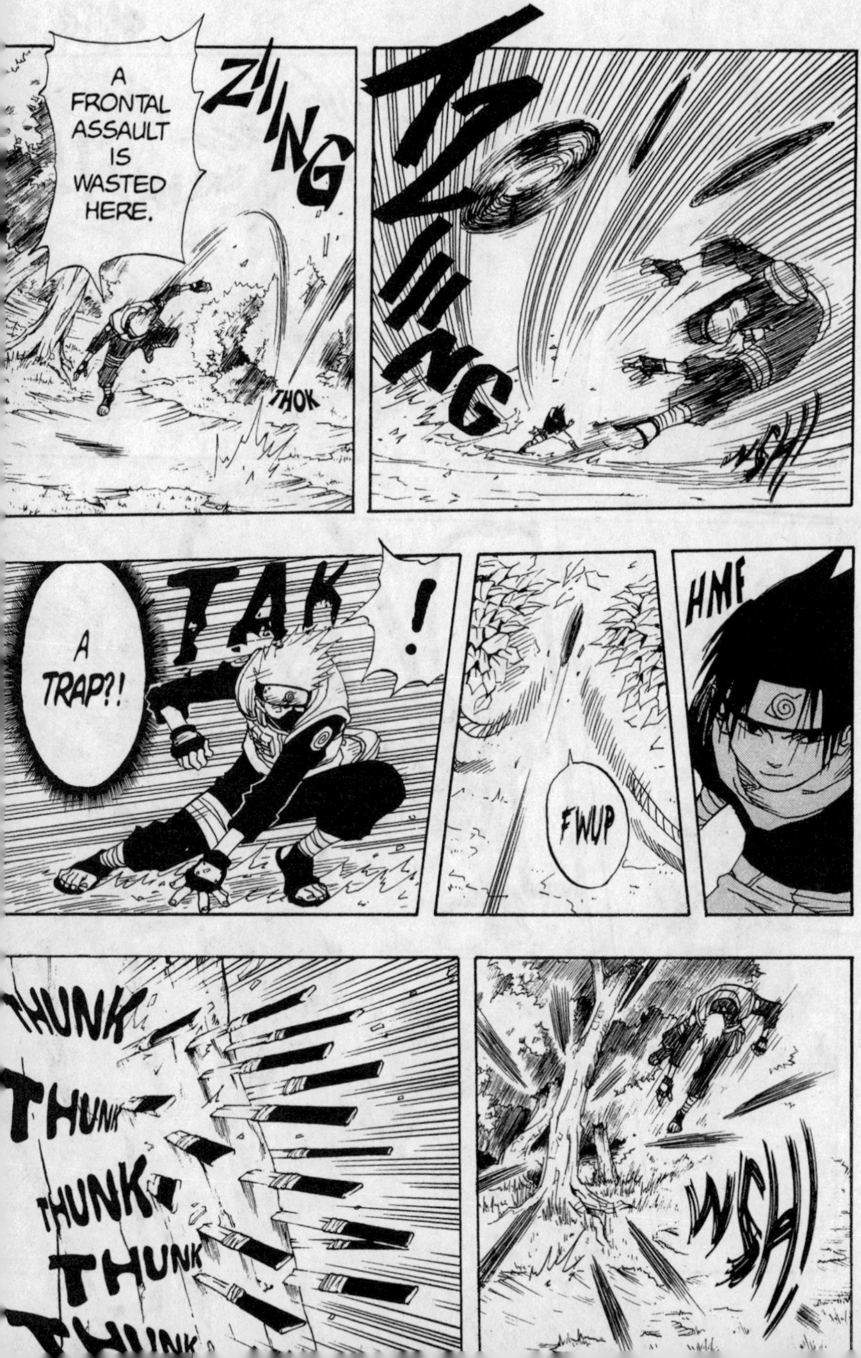

ZIIIING
WSH
ZIING
A FRONTAL ASSAULT IS WASTED HERE.
THOK
HMF
FWUP
TAK
!
A TRAP?!
WSH
THUNK
THUNK
THUNK
THUNK

READ THIS WAY

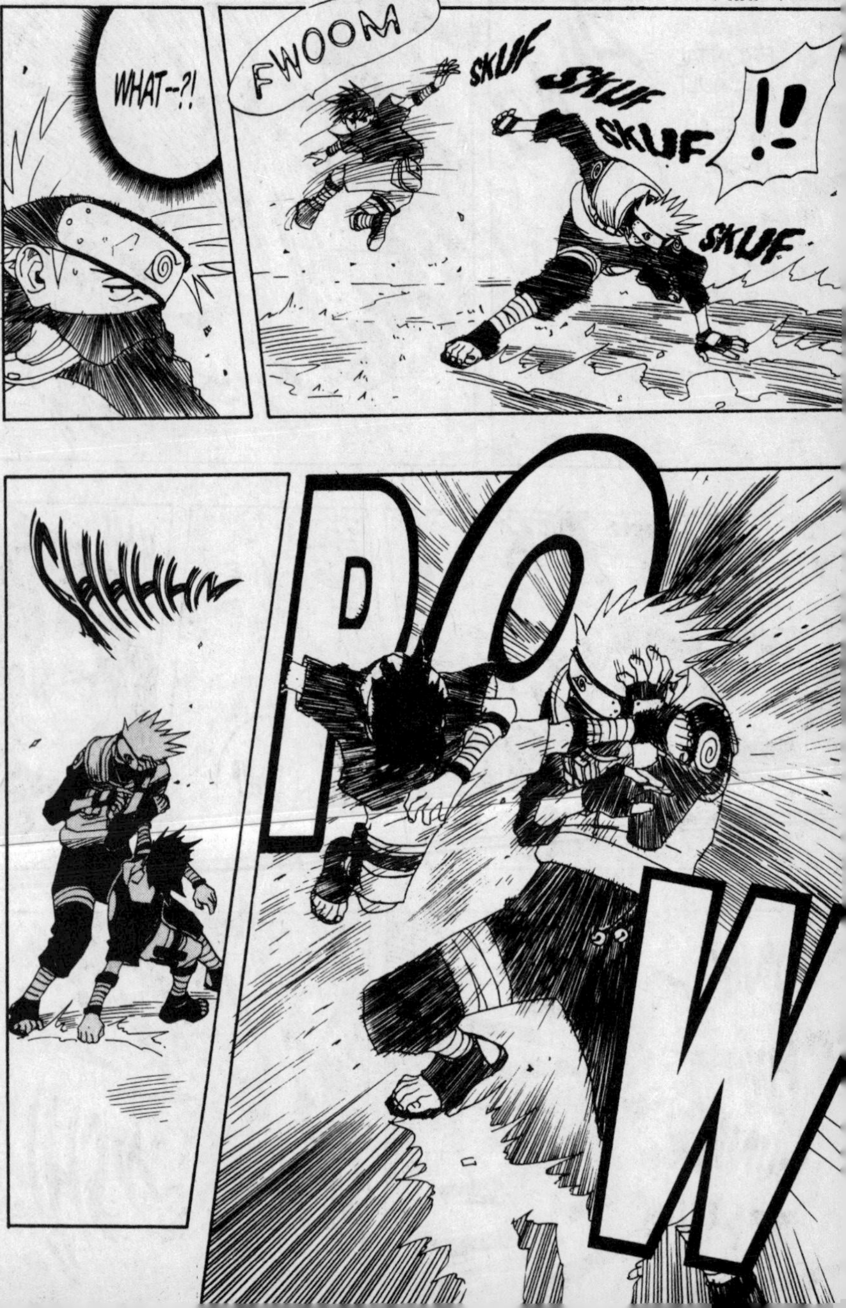
FWOOM
SKUF
SKUF
SKUF
SKUF
!!
WHAT--?!
POW

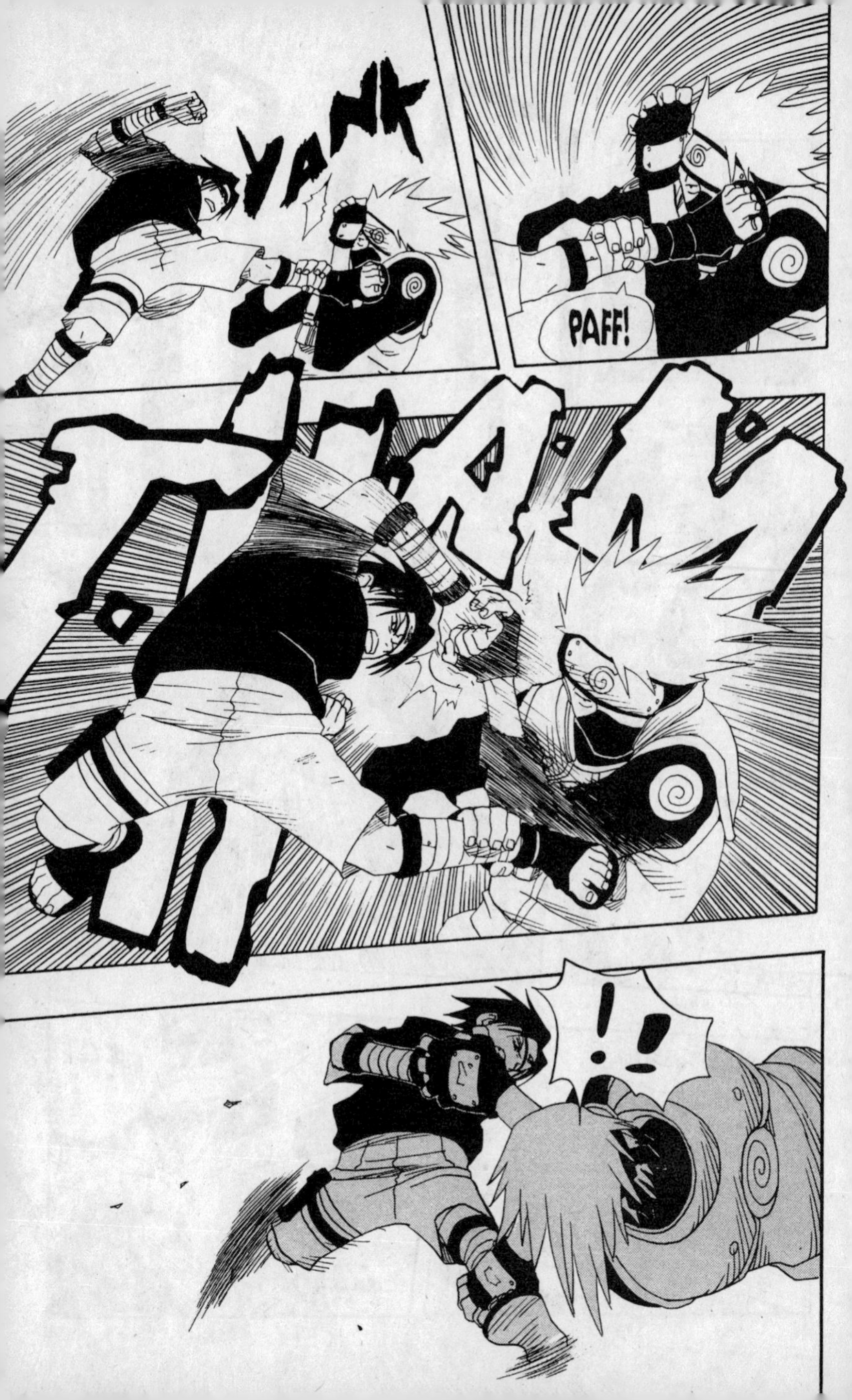
PAFF!
YANK
!!

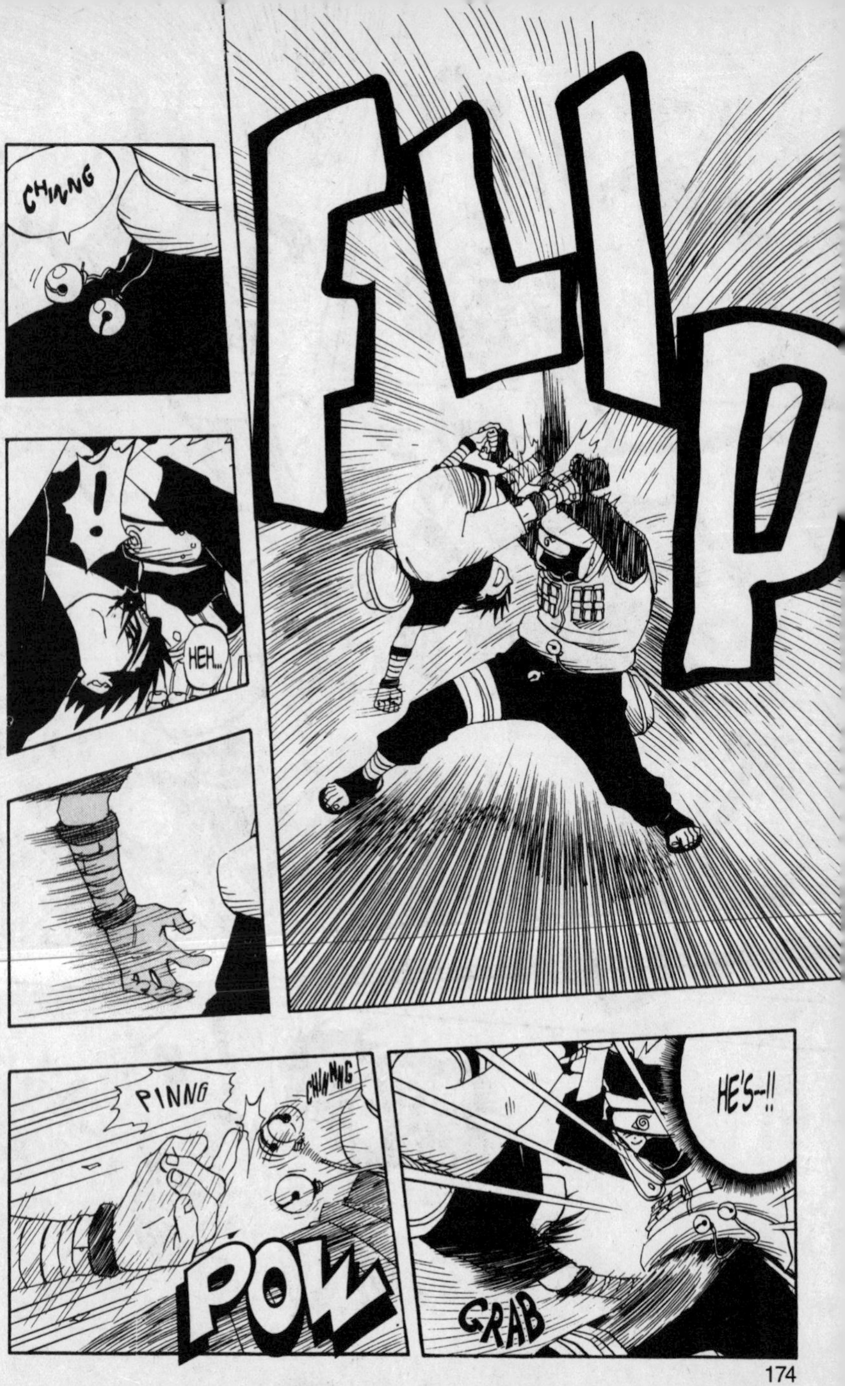
FLIP
CHINNG
!
HEH...
HE'S--!!
GRAB
PINNG
CHINNNG
POW

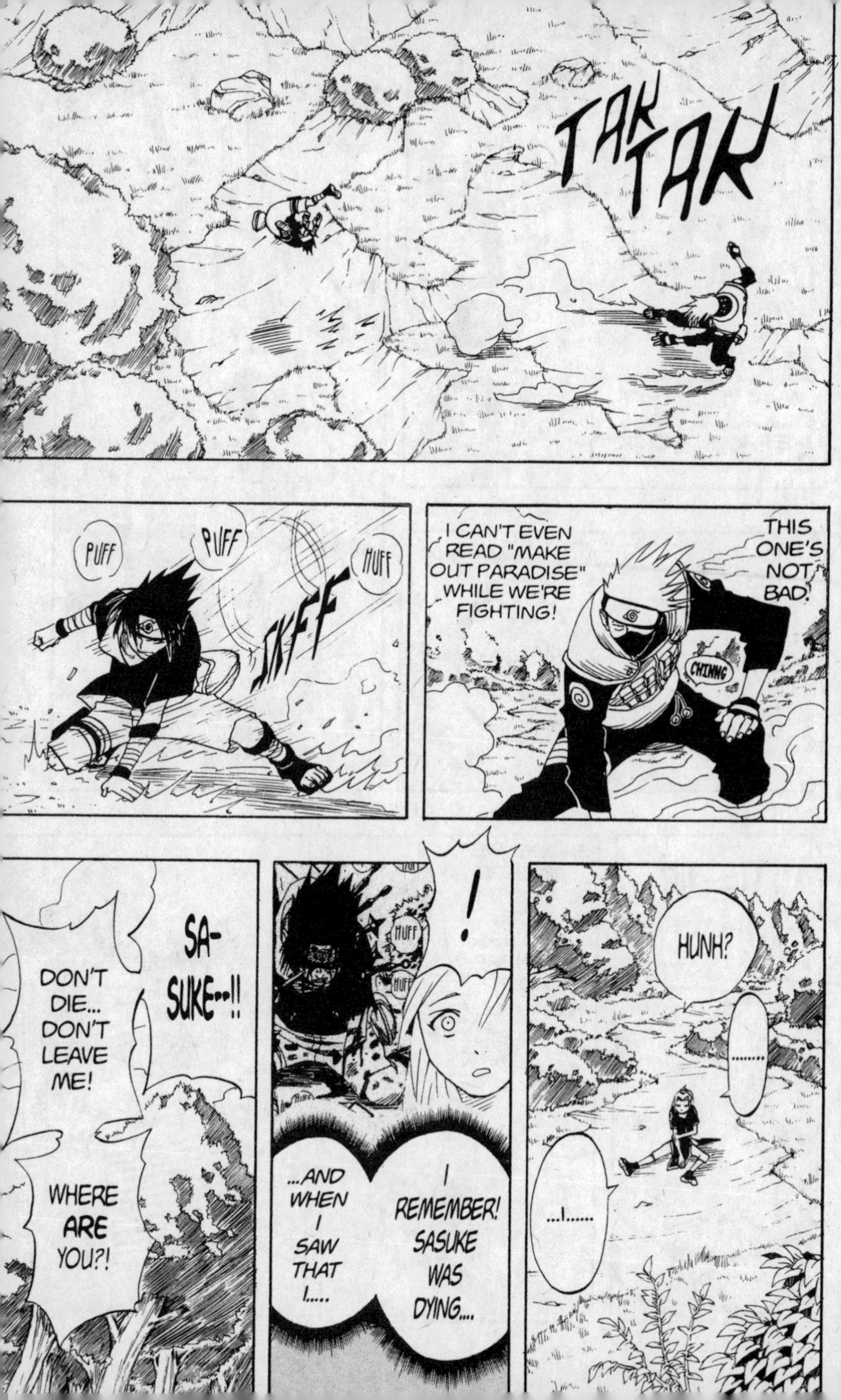
TAK TAK
THIS ONE'S NOT BAD.
I CAN'T EVEN READ "MAKE OUT PARADISE" WHILE WE'RE FIGHTING!
CHINNG
HUFF
SKFF
PUFF
PUFF
HUNH?
....
...I......
!
HUFF
HUFF
I REMEMBER! SASUKE WAS DYING....
...AND WHEN I SAW THAT I.....
SA-SUKE..!!
DON'T DIE... DON'T LEAVE ME!
WHERE ARE YOU?!

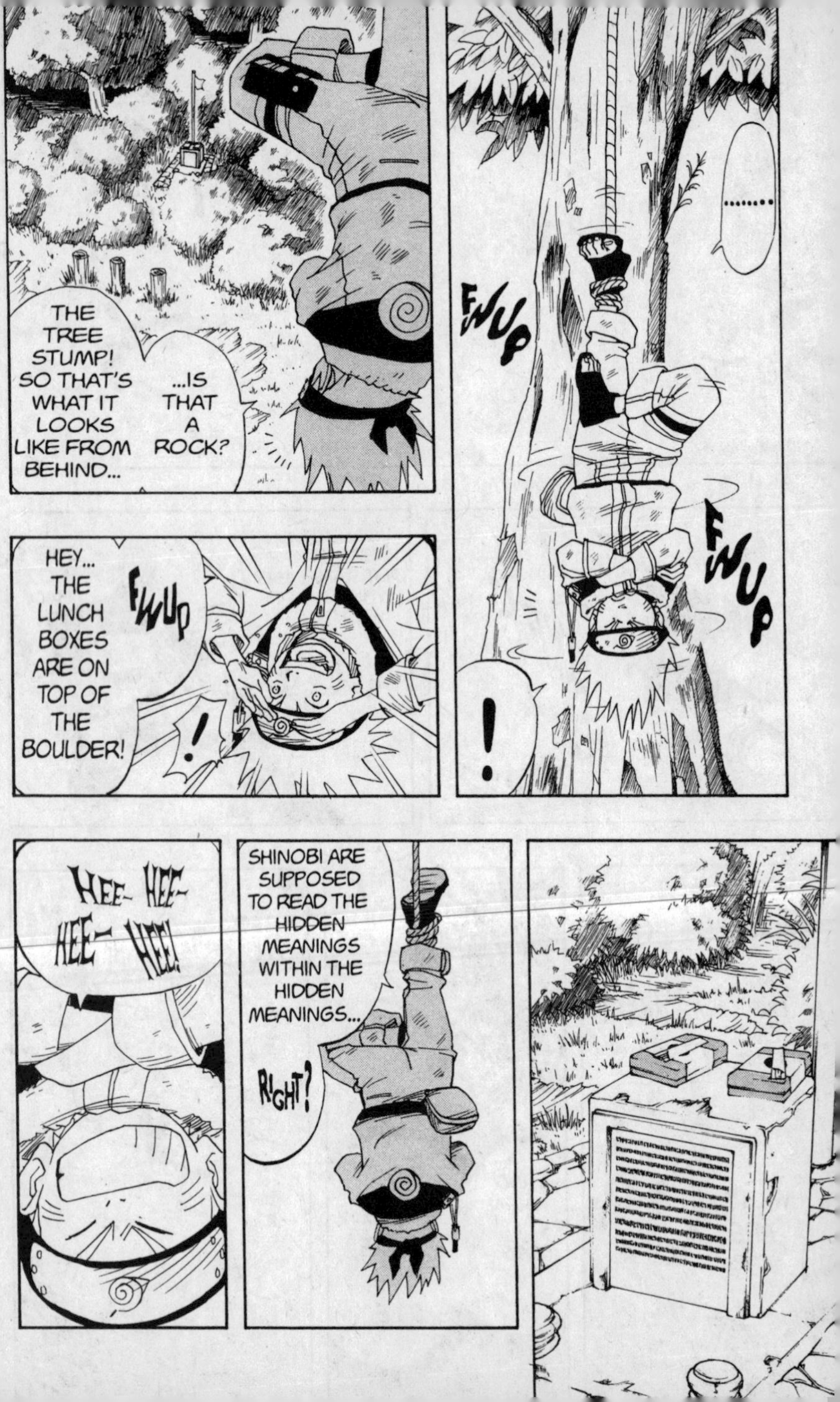
....
FWUP
FWUP
!
THE TREE STUMP! SO THAT'S WHAT IT LOOKS LIKE FROM BEHIND...
...IS THAT A ROCK?
HEY... THE LUNCH BOXES ARE ON TOP OF THE BOULDER!
FWUP
!
SHINOBI ARE SUPPOSED TO READ THE HIDDEN MEANINGS WITHIN THE HIDDEN MEANINGS...
RIGHT?
HEE- HEE- HEE- HEE!

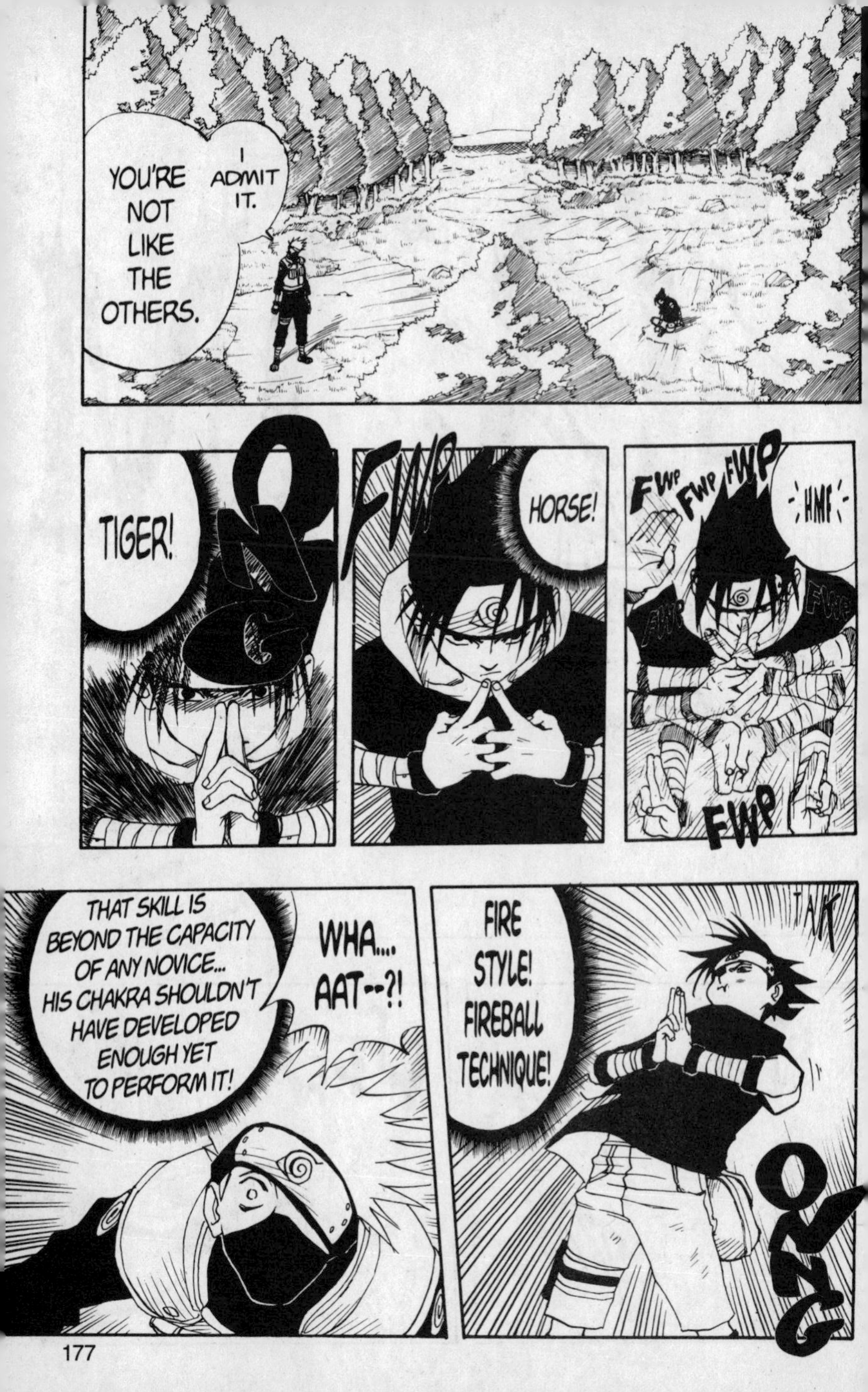
I ADMIT IT.
YOU'RE NOT LIKE THE OTHERS.
FWP FWP FWP
HMF
FWP
FWP
FWP
HORSE!
ONG
TIGER!
TAK
FIRE STYLE! FIREBALL TECHNIQUE!
ONG
WHA.... AAT--?!
THAT SKILL IS BEYOND THE CAPACITY OF ANY NOVICE... HIS CHAKRA SHOULDN'T HAVE DEVELOPED ENOUGH YET TO PERFORM IT!

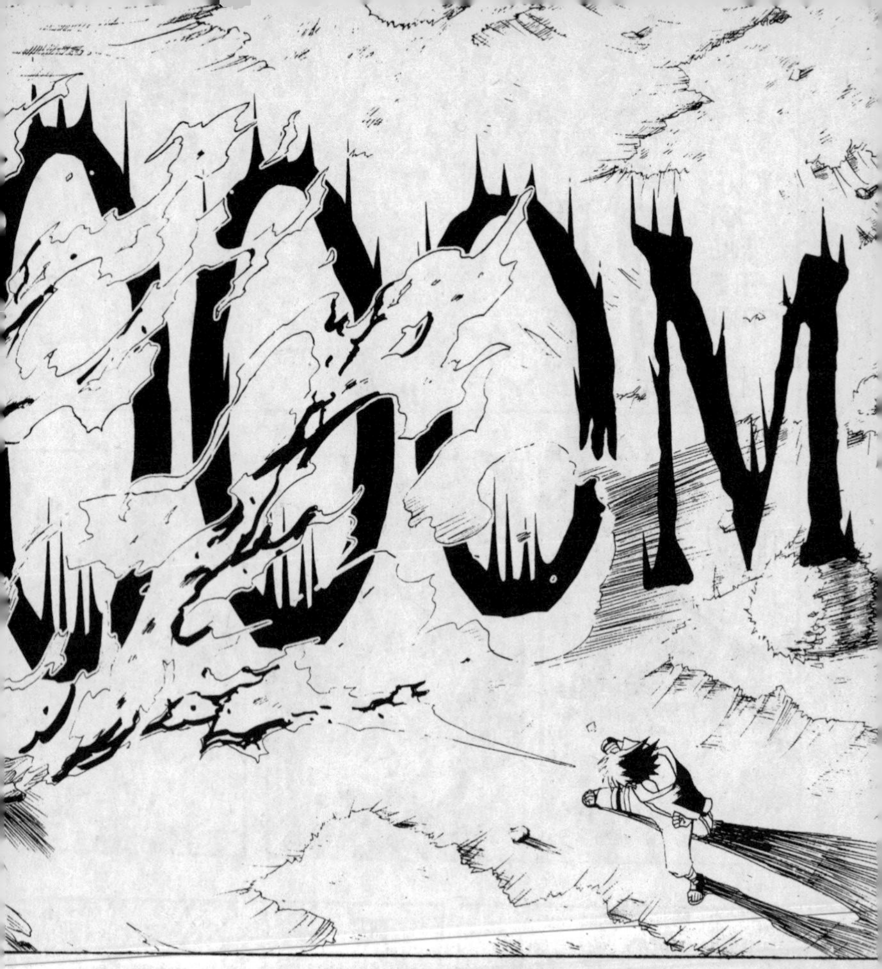

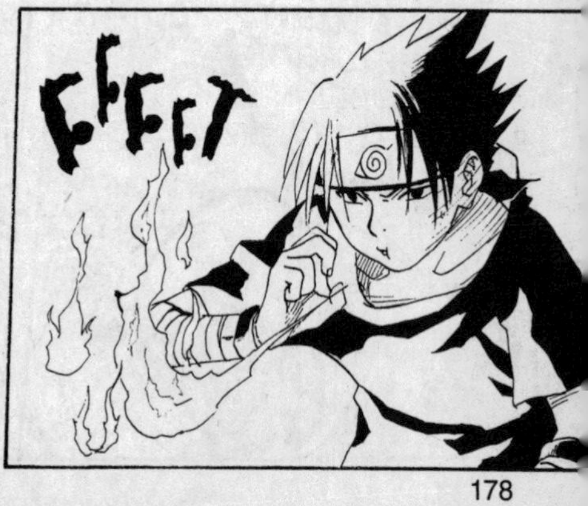
FFFFT

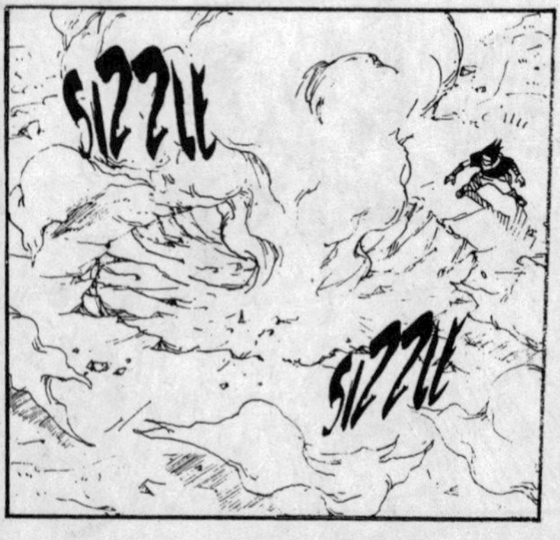
SIZZLE
SIZZLE

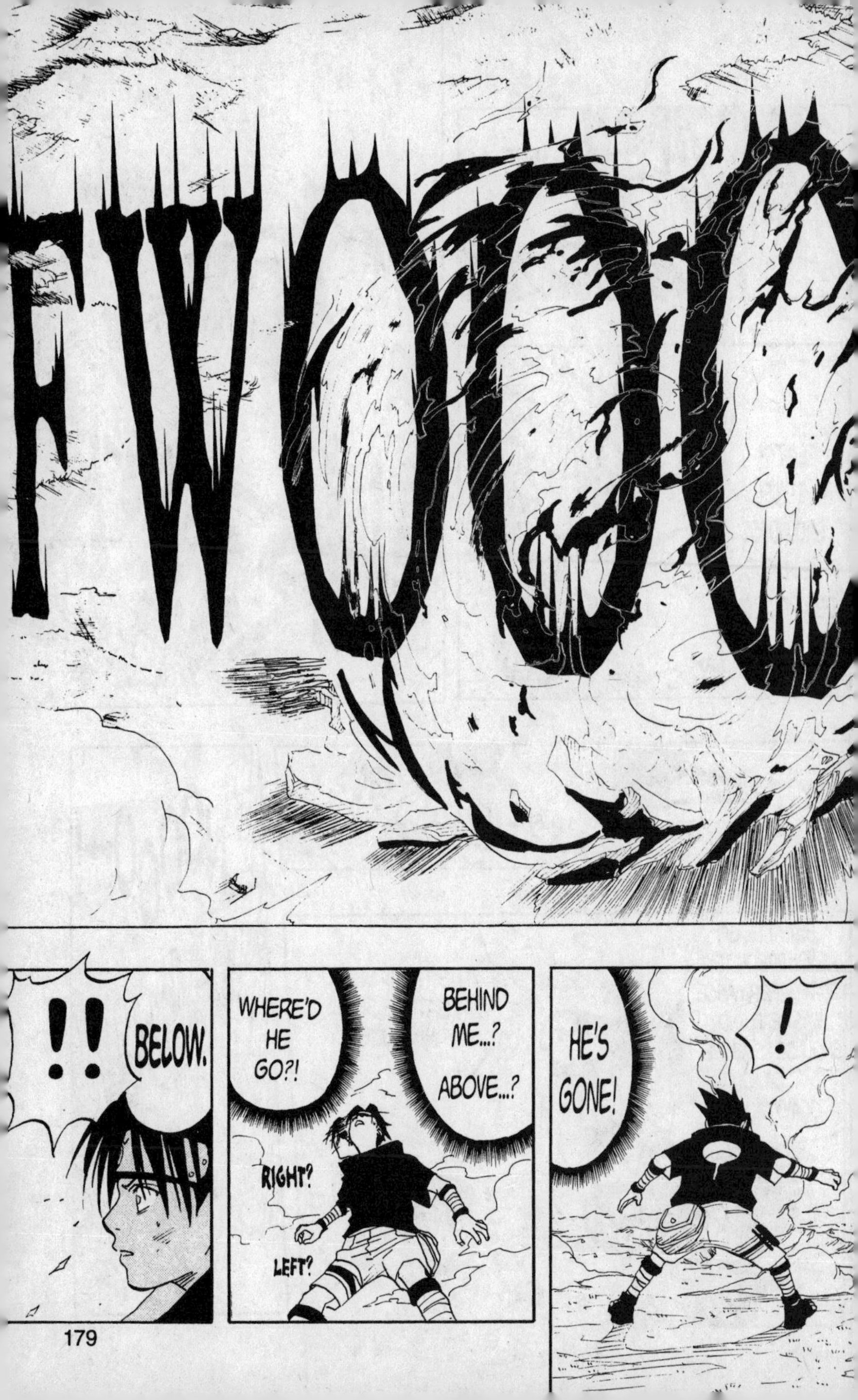
FWOOO
!
HE'S GONE!
BEHIND ME...? ABOVE...?
WHERE'D HE GO?!
RIGHT?
LEFT?
BELOW.
!!

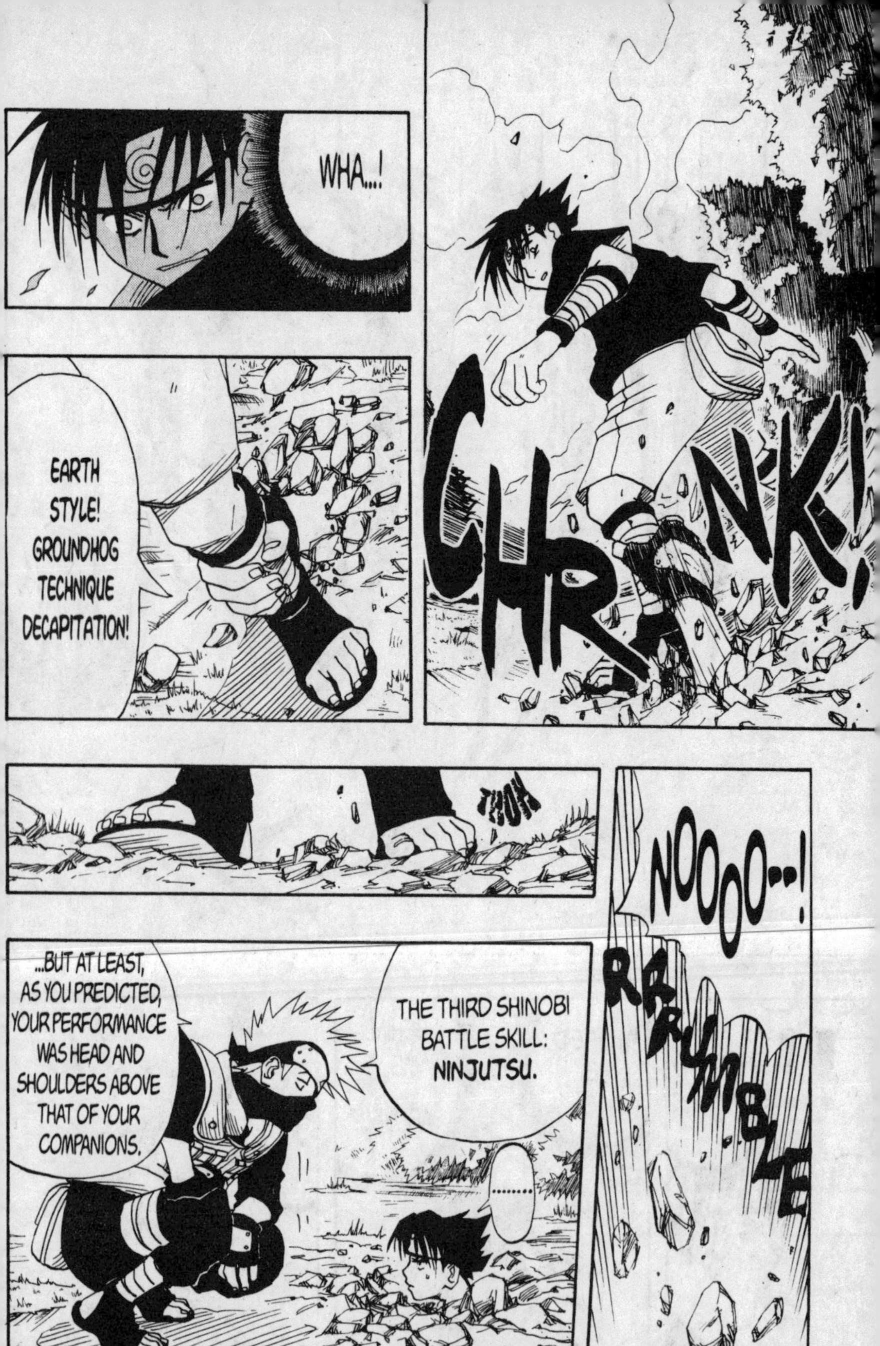
CHRNK!
WHA...!
EARTH STYLE! GROUNDHOG TECHNIQUE DECAPITATION!
NOOOO--!
RRRUMBLE
THE THIRD SHINOBI BATTLE SKILL: NINJUTSU.
....
...BUT AT LEAST, AS YOU PREDICTED, YOUR PERFORMANCE WAS HEAD AND SHOULDERS ABOVE THAT OF YOUR COMPANIONS.

READ THIS WAY

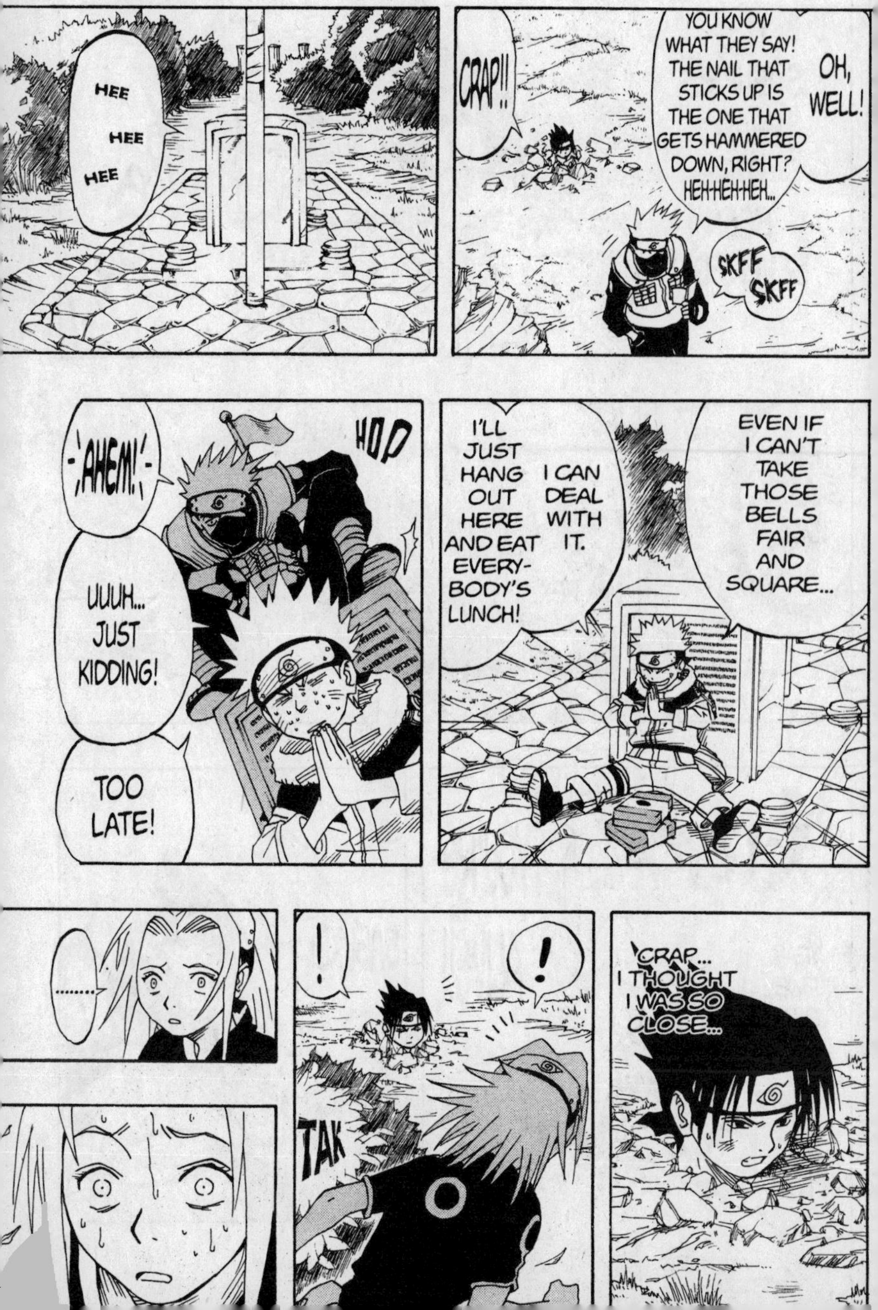
OH, WELL!
YOU KNOW WHAT THEY SAY! THE NAIL THAT STICKS UP IS THE ONE THAT GETS HAMMERED DOWN, RIGHT? HEH-HEH-HEH...
CRAP!!
SKFF SKFF
HEE HEE HEE
EVEN IF I CAN'T TAKE THOSE BELLS FAIR AND SQUARE...
I CAN DEAL WITH IT.
I'LL JUST HANG OUT HERE AND EAT EVERY-BODY'S LUNCH!
HOP
-;AHEM!;-
UUUH... JUST KIDDING!
TOO LATE!
CRAP... I THOUGHT I WAS SO CLOSE...
!
!
TAK
......

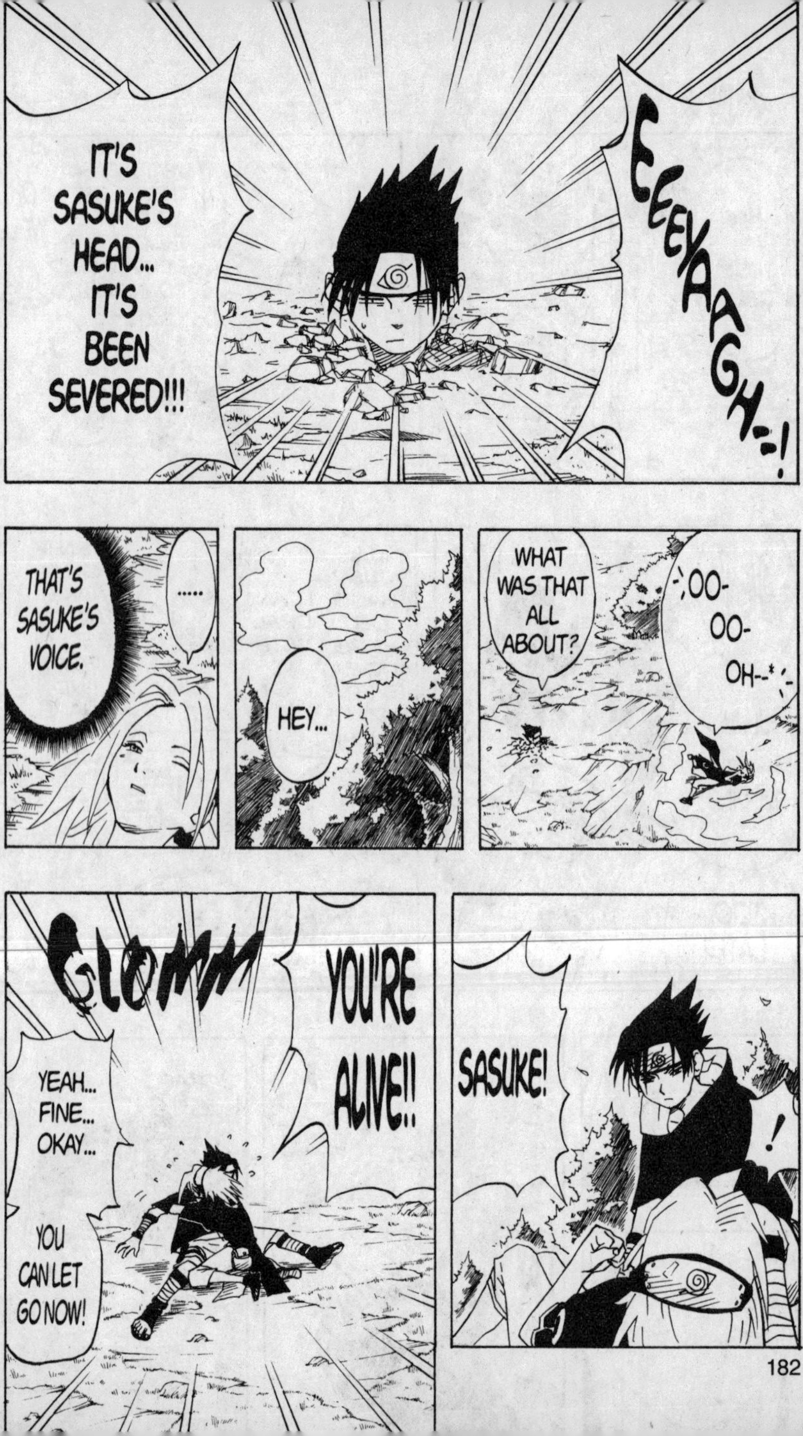
EEEYAAGH--!
IT'S SASUKE'S HEAD... IT'S BEEN SEVERED!!!
OO- OO- OH--*
WHAT WAS THAT ALL ABOUT?
HEY...
.....
THAT'S SASUKE'S VOICE.
!
SASUKE!
YOU'RE ALIVE!!
GLOMM
YEAH... FINE... OKAY...
YOU CAN LET GO NOW!

READ THIS WAY

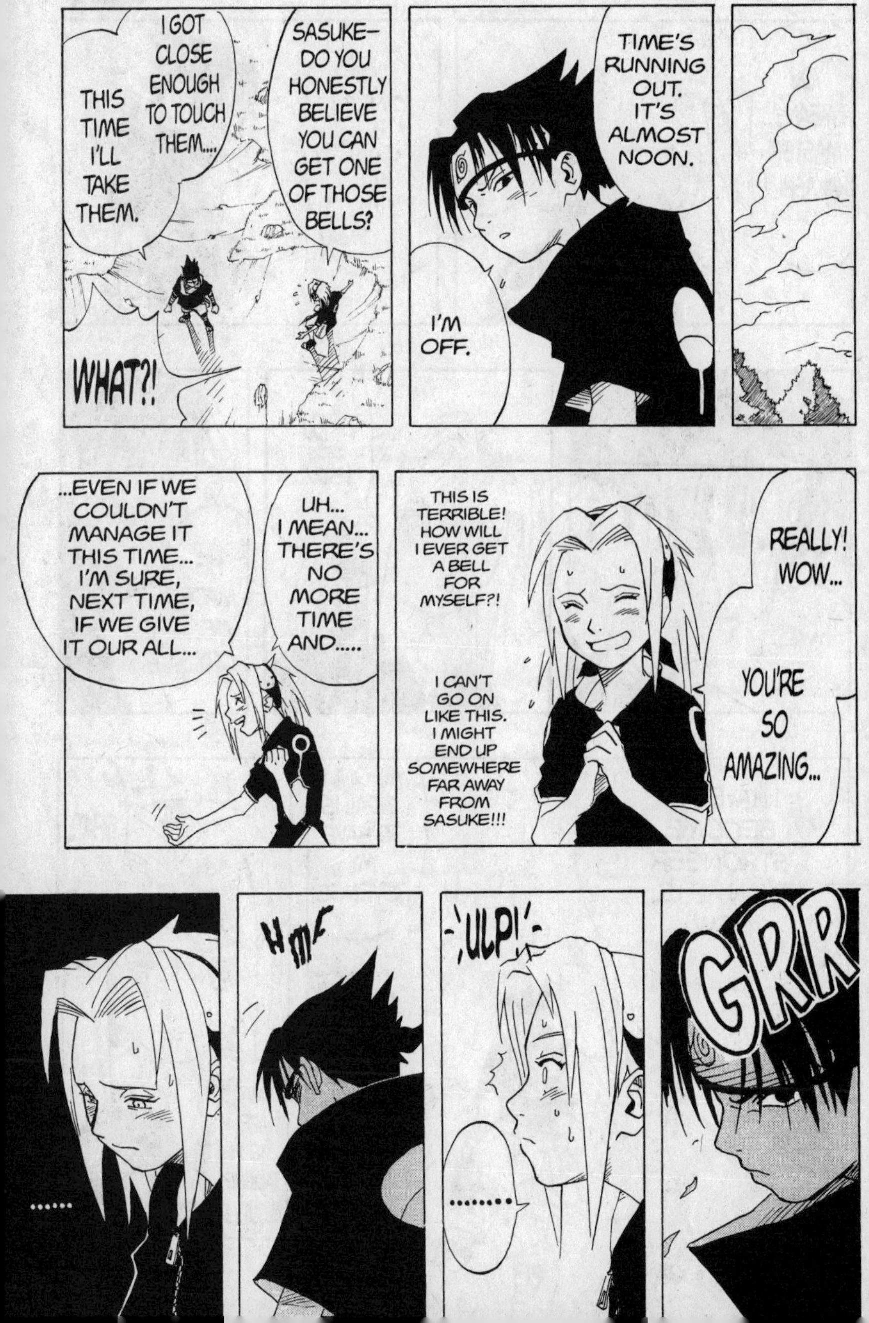
TIME'S RUNNING OUT. IT'S ALMOST NOON.
I'M OFF.
SASUKE— DO YOU HONESTLY BELIEVE YOU CAN GET ONE OF THOSE BELLS?
I GOT CLOSE ENOUGH TO TOUCH THEM....
THIS TIME I'LL TAKE THEM.
WHAT?!
REALLY! WOW...
YOU'RE SO AMAZING...
THIS IS TERRIBLE! HOW WILL I EVER GET A BELL FOR MYSELF?!
I CAN'T GO ON LIKE THIS. I MIGHT END UP SOMEWHERE FAR AWAY FROM SASUKE!!!
UH... I MEAN... THERE'S NO MORE TIME AND.....
...EVEN IF WE COULDN'T MANAGE IT THIS TIME... I'M SURE, NEXT TIME, IF WE GIVE IT OUR ALL...
GRR
ULP!
....
HMF
......

READ THIS WAY

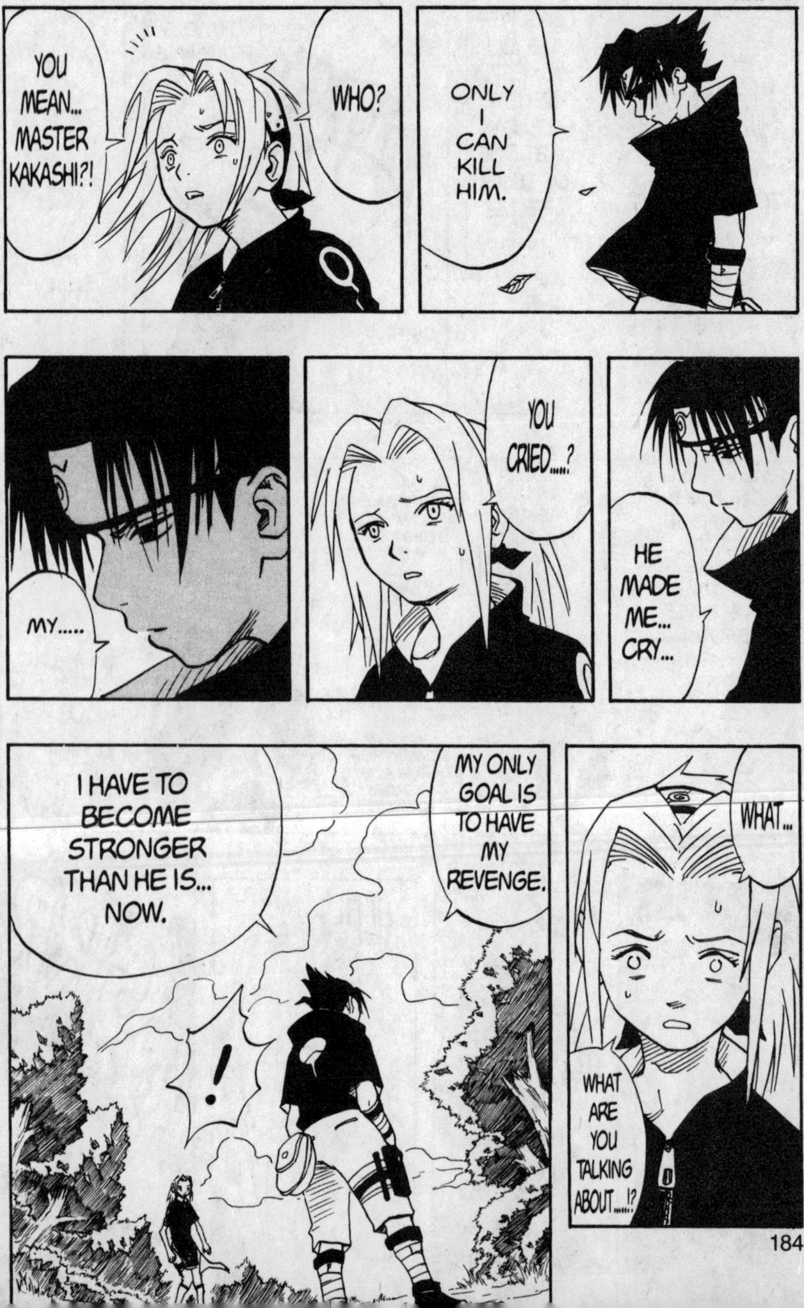
ONLY I CAN KILL HIM.
WHO?
YOU MEAN... MASTER KAKASHI?!
HE MADE ME... CRY...
YOU CRIED.....?
MY.....
WHAT...
WHAT ARE YOU TALKING ABOUT.....!?
MY ONLY GOAL IS TO HAVE MY REVENGE.
I HAVE TO BECOME STRONGER THAN HE IS... NOW.
!

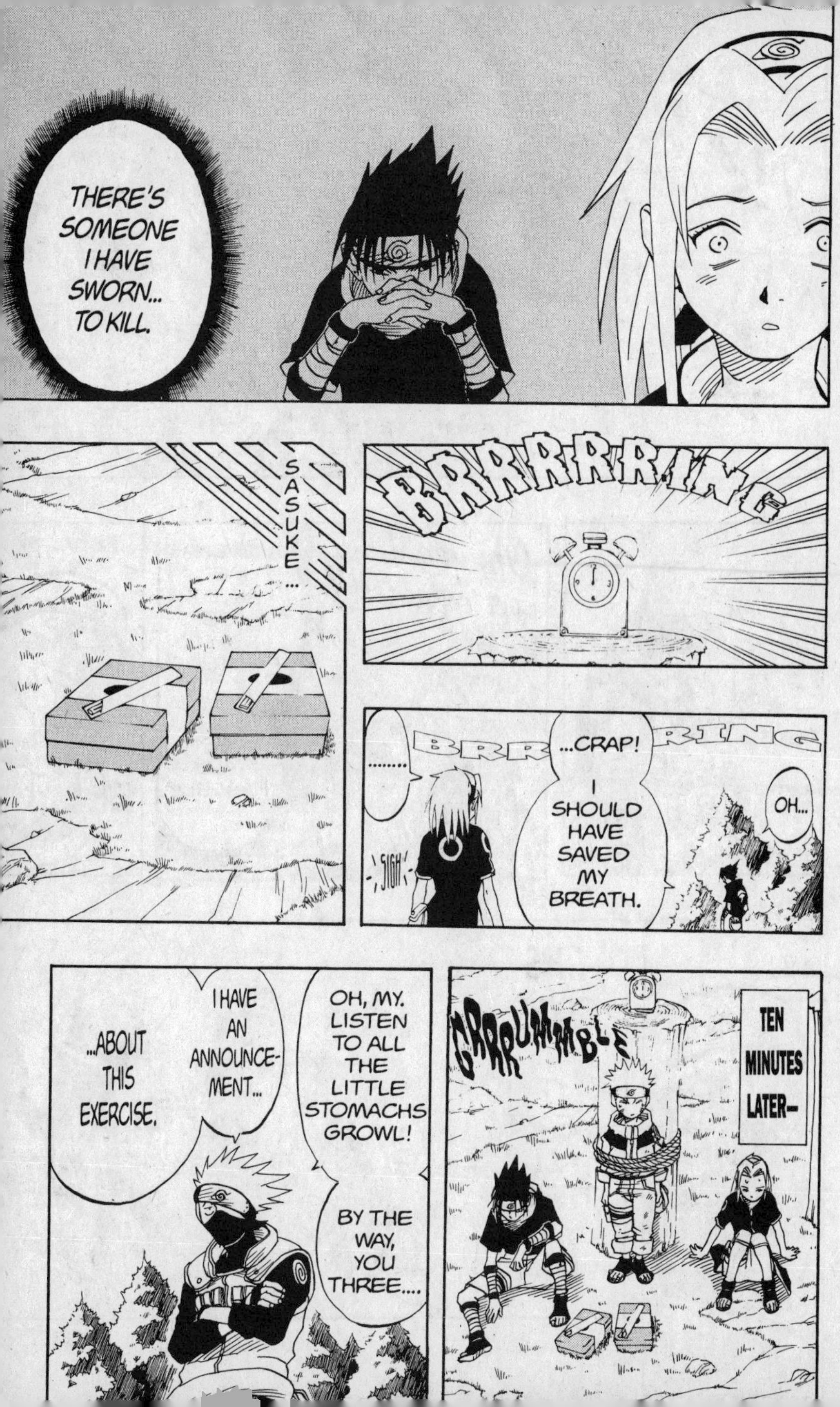
THERE'S SOMEONE I HAVE SWORN... TO KILL.
BRRRRRRING
BRR RING
OH...
...CRAP! I SHOULD HAVE SAVED MY BREATH.
....
SIGH
SASUKE...
TEN MINUTES LATER—
GRRRUMMMBLE
OH, MY. LISTEN TO ALL THE LITTLE STOMACHS GROWL!
BY THE WAY, YOU THREE....
I HAVE AN ANNOUNCEMENT...
...ABOUT THIS EXERCISE.

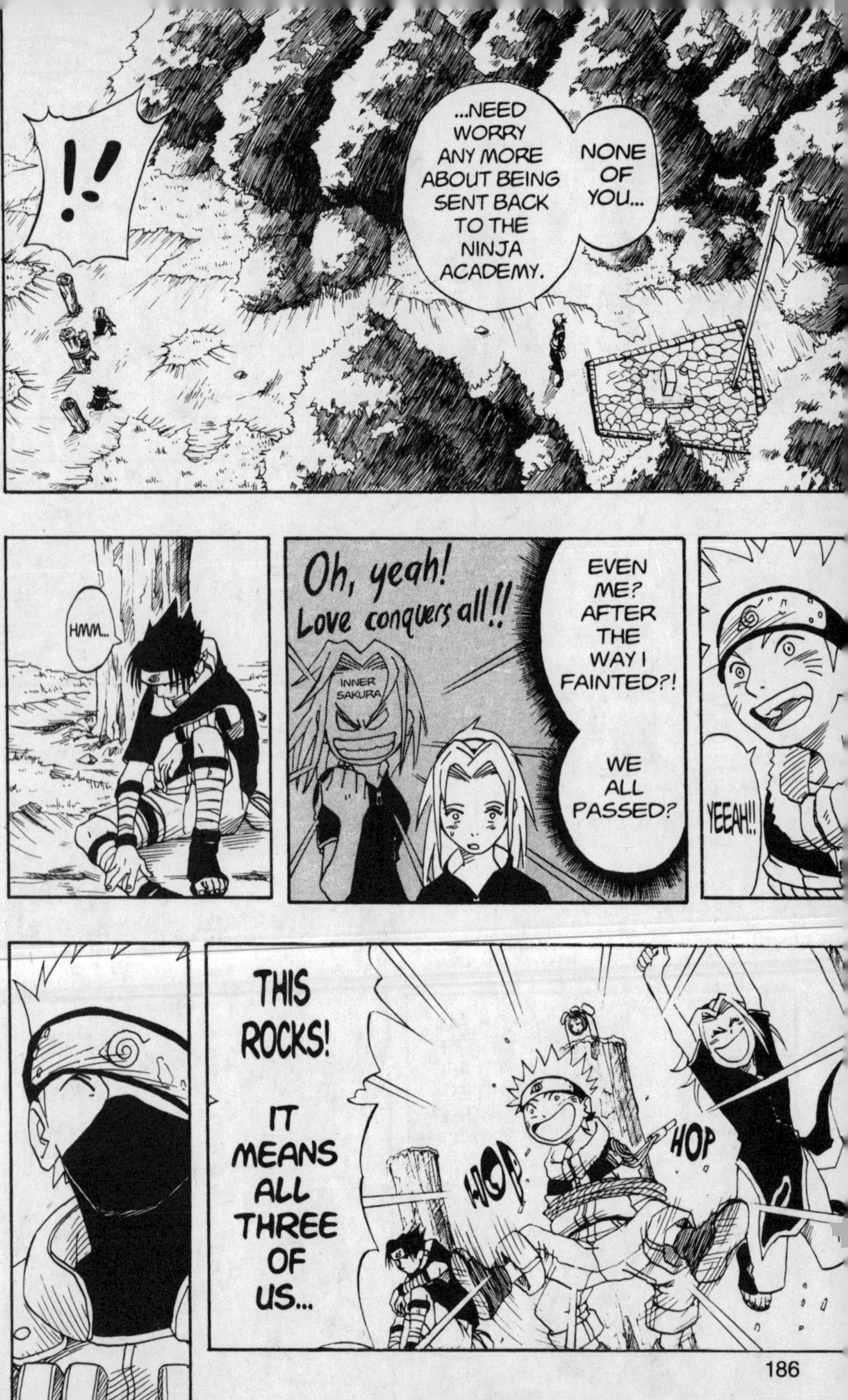
NONE OF YOU...
...NEED WORRY ANY MORE ABOUT BEING SENT BACK TO THE NINJA ACADEMY.
!!
YEEAH!!
EVEN ME? AFTER THE WAY I FAINTED?!
WE ALL PASSED?
Oh, yeah! Love conquers all!!
INNER SAKURA
HMM...
THIS ROCKS!
IT MEANS ALL THREE OF US...
HOP

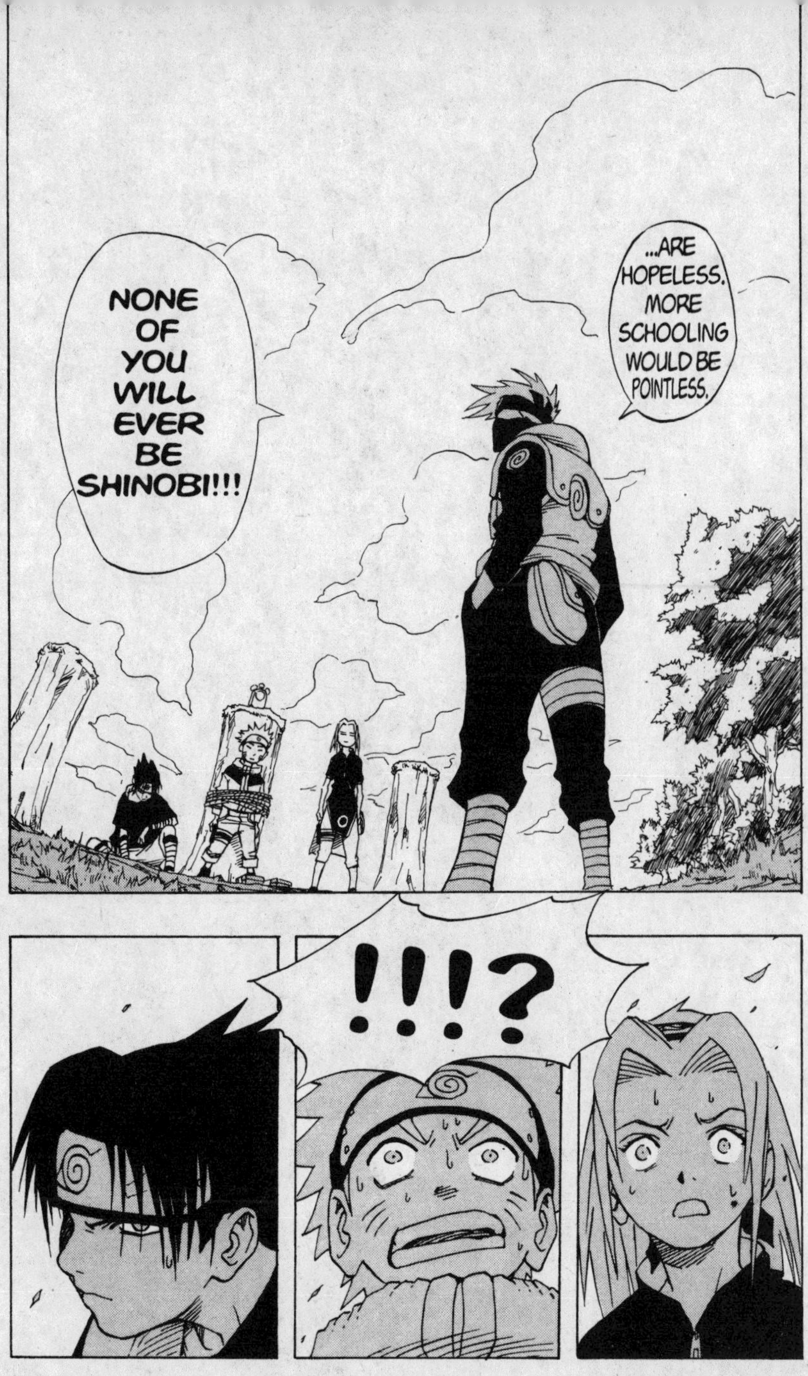
...ARE HOPELESS. MORE SCHOOLING WOULD BE POINTLESS.
NONE OF YOU WILL EVER BE SHINOBI!!!
!!!?

NARUTO

岸本斉史

One day I got a phone call from a relative of mine and got seriously chewed out. Why? The reason was the art I drew of myself in volume one. My aunt saw the picture of me eating ramen and said "Is he only eating ramen *again?!* Every time you came over to my house, you demanded instant noodles instead of the home-cooked meal I had ready for you! You'd better be getting your vegetables!" Don't worry, Auntie—I *am* eating my vegetables. (P.S. They just came out with instant noodles in "Cheese Curry Flavor." It's really tasty.)

—*Masashi Kishimoto, 2000*

NARUTO

NARUTO

VOL. 2

THE WORST CLIENT

STORY AND ART BY
MASASHI KISHIMOTO

SAKURA サクラ
Naruto and Sasuke's classmate. She has a crush on Sasuke, who ignores her. In return, she picks on Naruto, who has a crush on *her*.

NARUTO ナルト
Shunned by the older villagers because of the fox spirit dwelling inside him, Naruto grew up to be an attention-seeking troublemaker. His goal is to become the best ninja ever, and be recognized as the next *Hokage*.

SASUKE サスケ
The top student in Naruto's class, and a member of the prestigious Uchiha clan. His goal is to get revenge against a mysterious person who wronged him in the past.

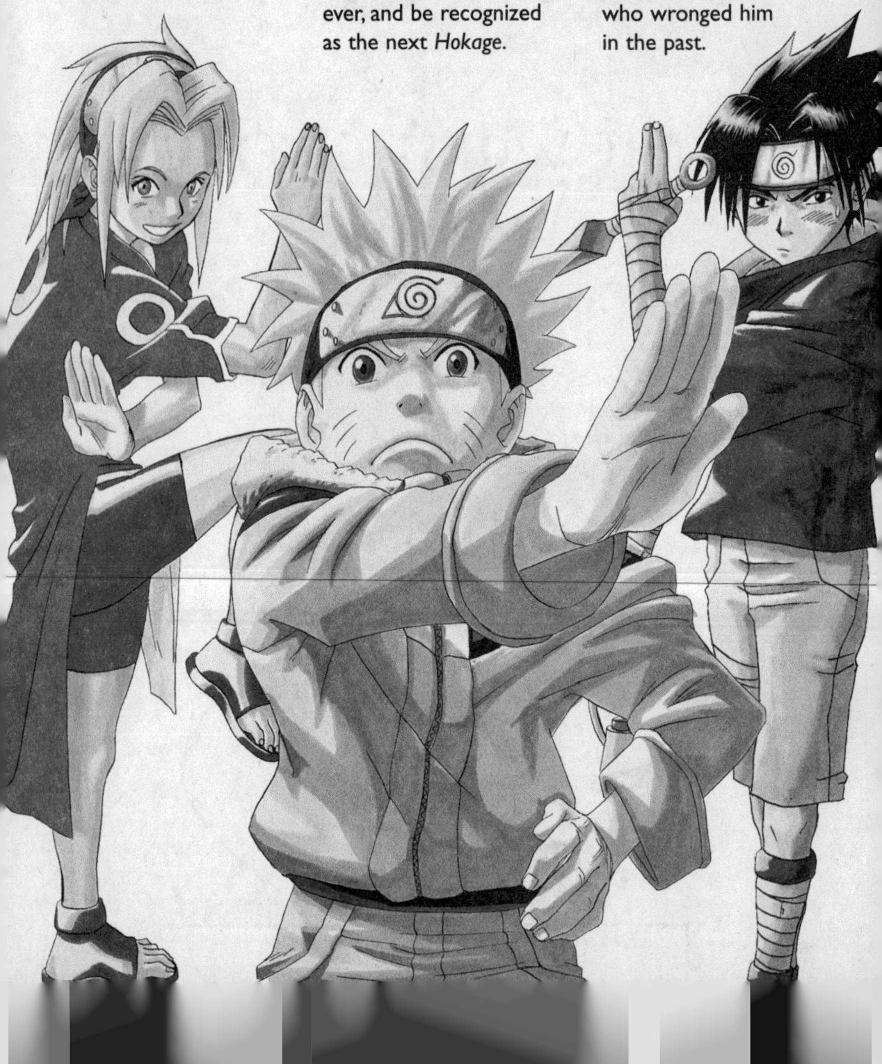

KAKASHI カカシ

An upper-level ninja assigned to train our heroes. Although he seems easy-going, he is a master of *ninjutsu*.

THE THIRD HOKAGE 三代目火影

The most respected person in the village, ever since the fourth *Hokage* died fighting the demon fox. His name means "Fire Shadow."

イルカ IRUKA

Naruto's old teacher at the Ninja Academy. His parents were killed by the demon fox, but he doesn't blame Naruto for it.

THE STORY SO FAR...

Twelve years ago, a giant fox demon attacked the ninja village of Konohagakure, until the *Hokage*, the village champion, managed to defeat it by sealing its soul into the body of a baby boy. Now that boy, Uzumaki Naruto, has grown up and become a ninja-in-training, like his classmates Sasuke and Sakura. Forced to work as a team, the three ninjas received a strange assignment: steal a bell from the belt of their teacher Kakashi. But they failed...and now Kakashi has told them *to give up their hopes of ever being ninja!*

NARUTO

VOL. 2
THE WORST CLIENT

CONTENTS

Number 8: You Failed!

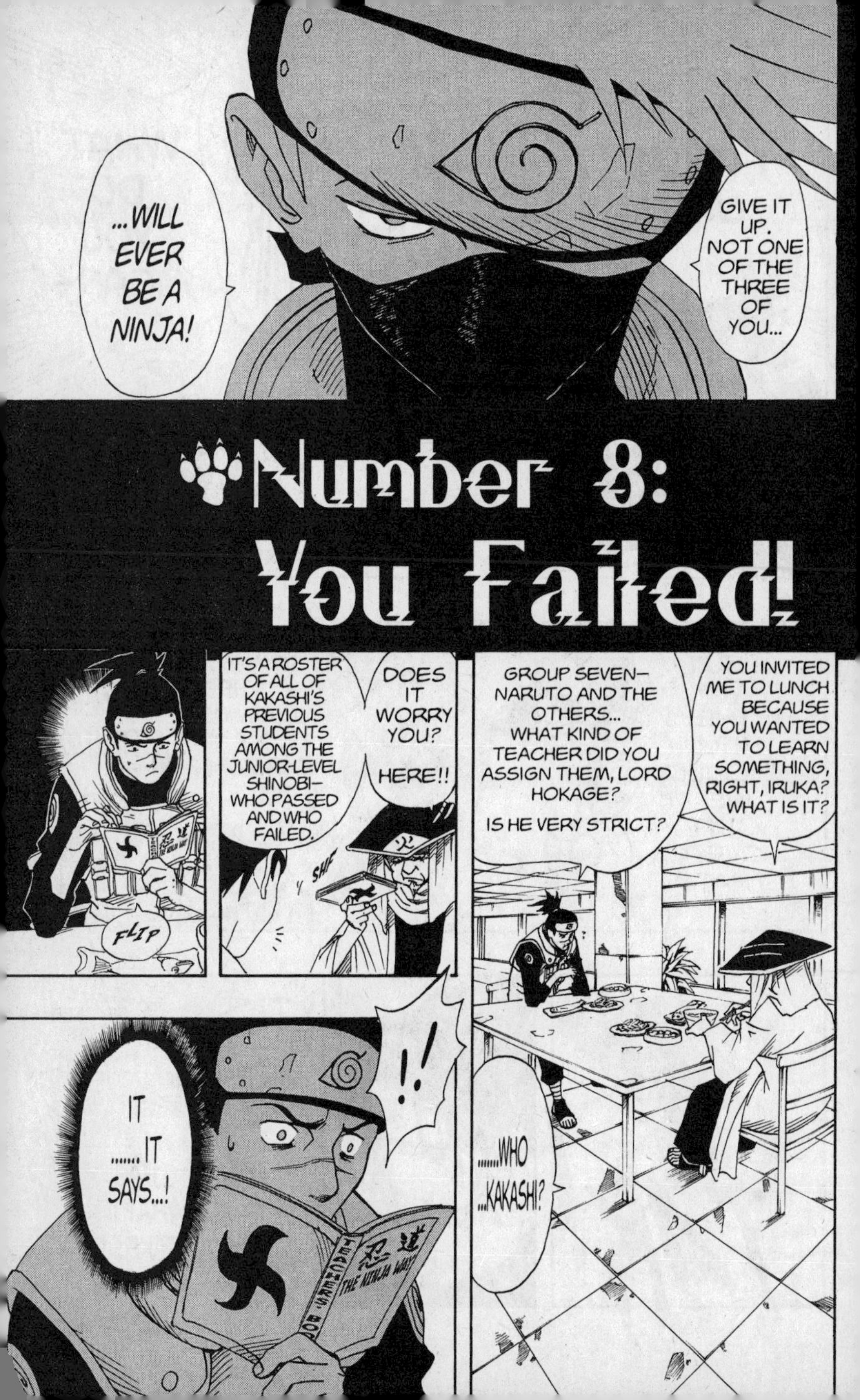

GIVE IT UP. NOT ONE OF THE THREE OF YOU...
...WILL EVER BE A NINJA!
Number 8: You Failed!
YOU INVITED ME TO LUNCH BECAUSE YOU WANTED TO LEARN SOMETHING, RIGHT, IRUKA? WHAT IS IT?
GROUP SEVEN— NARUTO AND THE OTHERS... WHAT KIND OF TEACHER DID YOU ASSIGN THEM, LORD HOKAGE?
IS HE VERY STRICT?
......WHO ...KAKASHI?
DOES IT WORRY YOU?
HERE!!
IT'S A ROSTER OF ALL OF KAKASHI'S PREVIOUS STUDENTS AMONG THE JUNIOR-LEVEL SHINOBI— WHO PASSED AND WHO FAILED.
SHF
FLIP
!!
IT ......IT SAYS...!

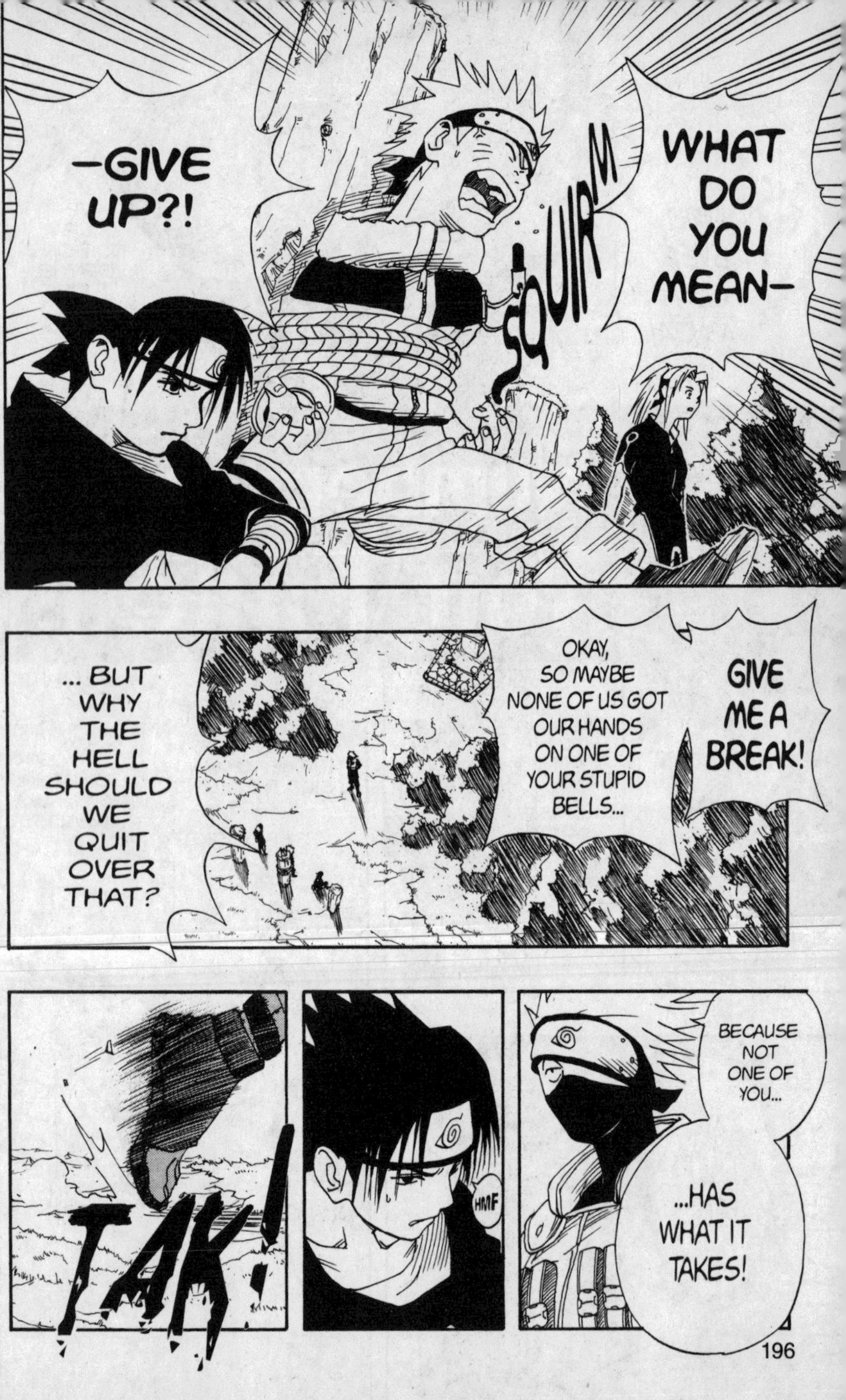
WHAT DO YOU MEAN–
SQUIRM
–GIVE UP?!
GIVE ME A BREAK!
OKAY, SO MAYBE NONE OF US GOT OUR HANDS ON ONE OF YOUR STUPID BELLS...
... BUT WHY THE HELL SHOULD WE QUIT OVER THAT?
BECAUSE NOT ONE OF YOU...
...HAS WHAT IT TAKES!
HMF
TAK!

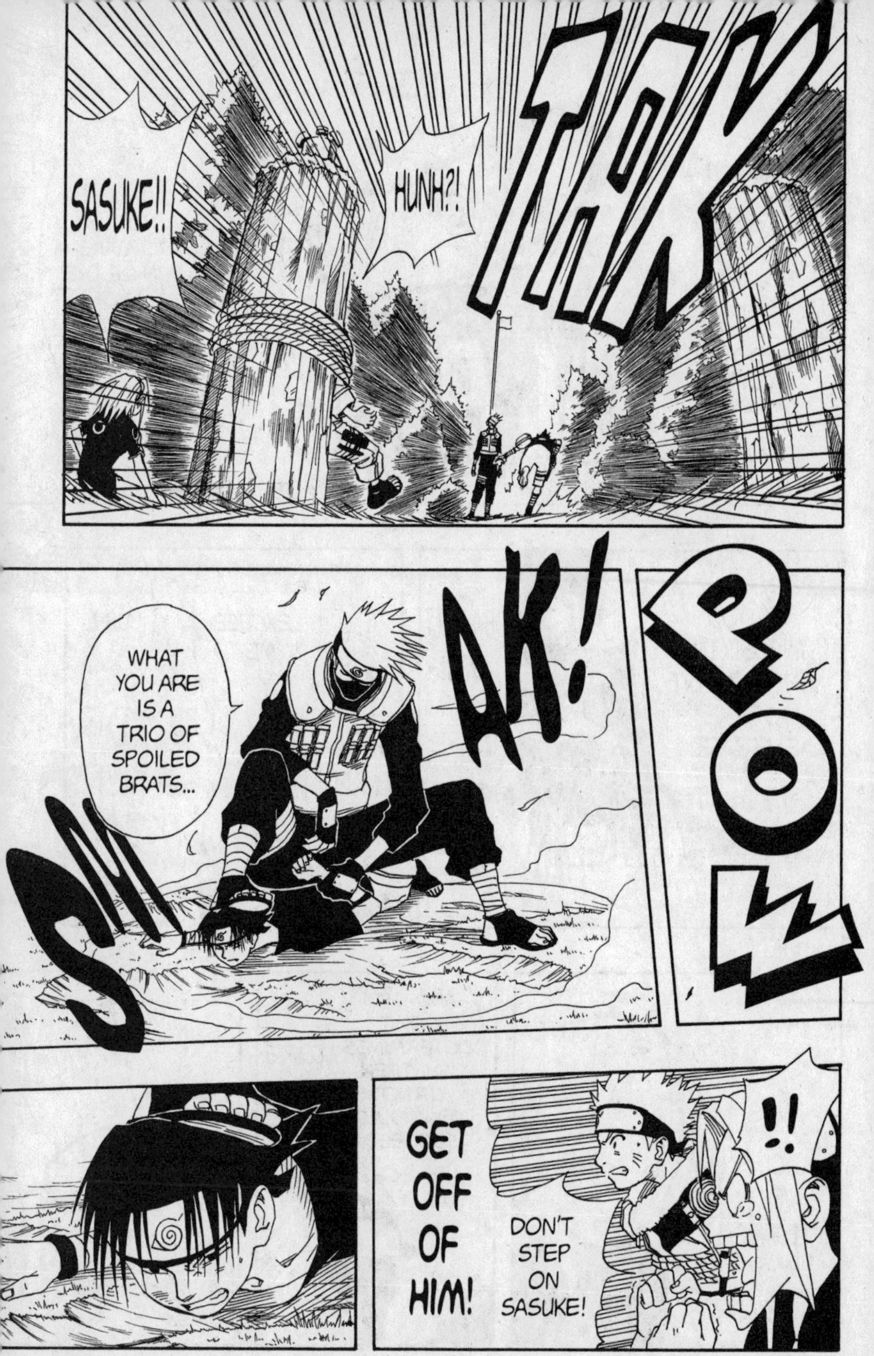
HUNH?!
SASUKE!!
POW
WHAT YOU ARE IS A TRIO OF SPOILED BRATS...
!!
DON'T STEP ON SASUKE!
GET OFF OF HIM!

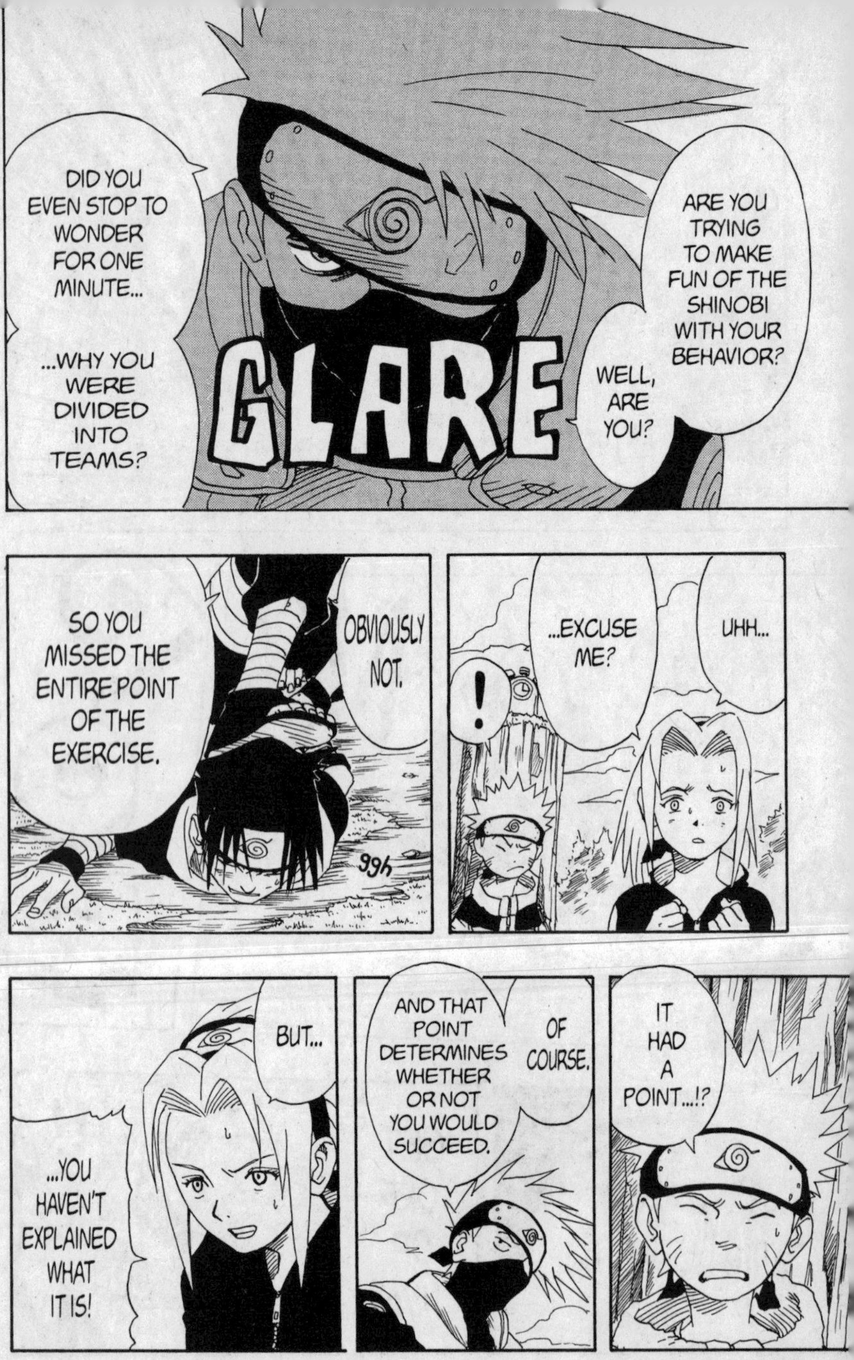
ARE YOU TRYING TO MAKE FUN OF THE SHINOBI WITH YOUR BEHAVIOR?
WELL, ARE YOU?
GLARE
DID YOU EVEN STOP TO WONDER FOR ONE MINUTE...
...WHY YOU WERE DIVIDED INTO TEAMS?
UHH...
...EXCUSE ME?
!
OBVIOUSLY NOT.
SO YOU MISSED THE ENTIRE POINT OF THE EXERCISE.
ggh
IT HAD A POINT...!?
OF COURSE.
AND THAT POINT DETERMINES WHETHER OR NOT YOU WOULD SUCCEED.
BUT...
...YOU HAVEN'T EXPLAINED WHAT IT IS!

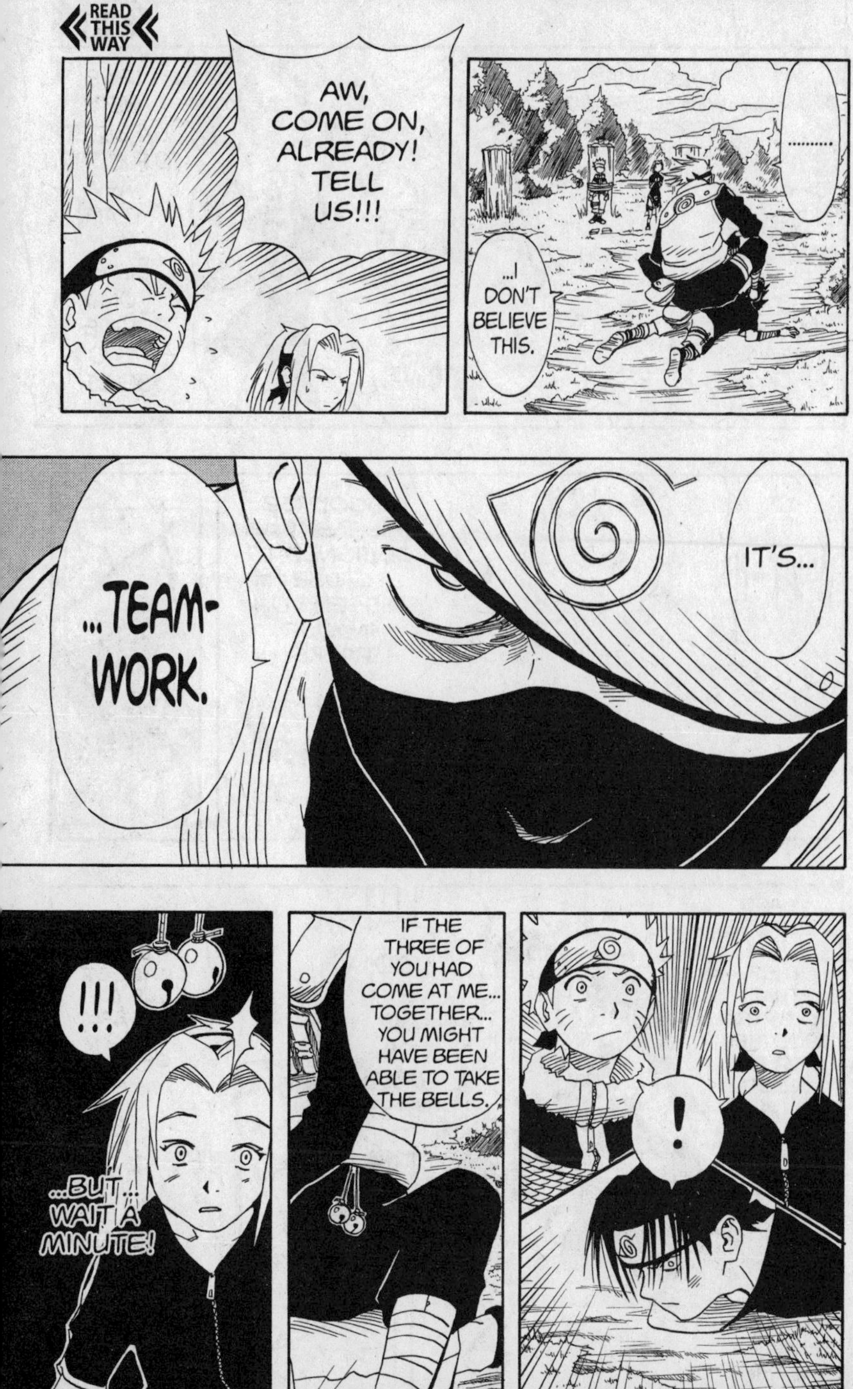
READ THIS WAY
....
...I DON'T BELIEVE THIS.
AW, COME ON, ALREADY! TELL US!!!
IT'S...
...TEAM-WORK.
!
IF THE THREE OF YOU HAD COME AT ME... TOGETHER... YOU MIGHT HAVE BEEN ABLE TO TAKE THE BELLS.
!!!
...BUT... WAIT A MINUTE!

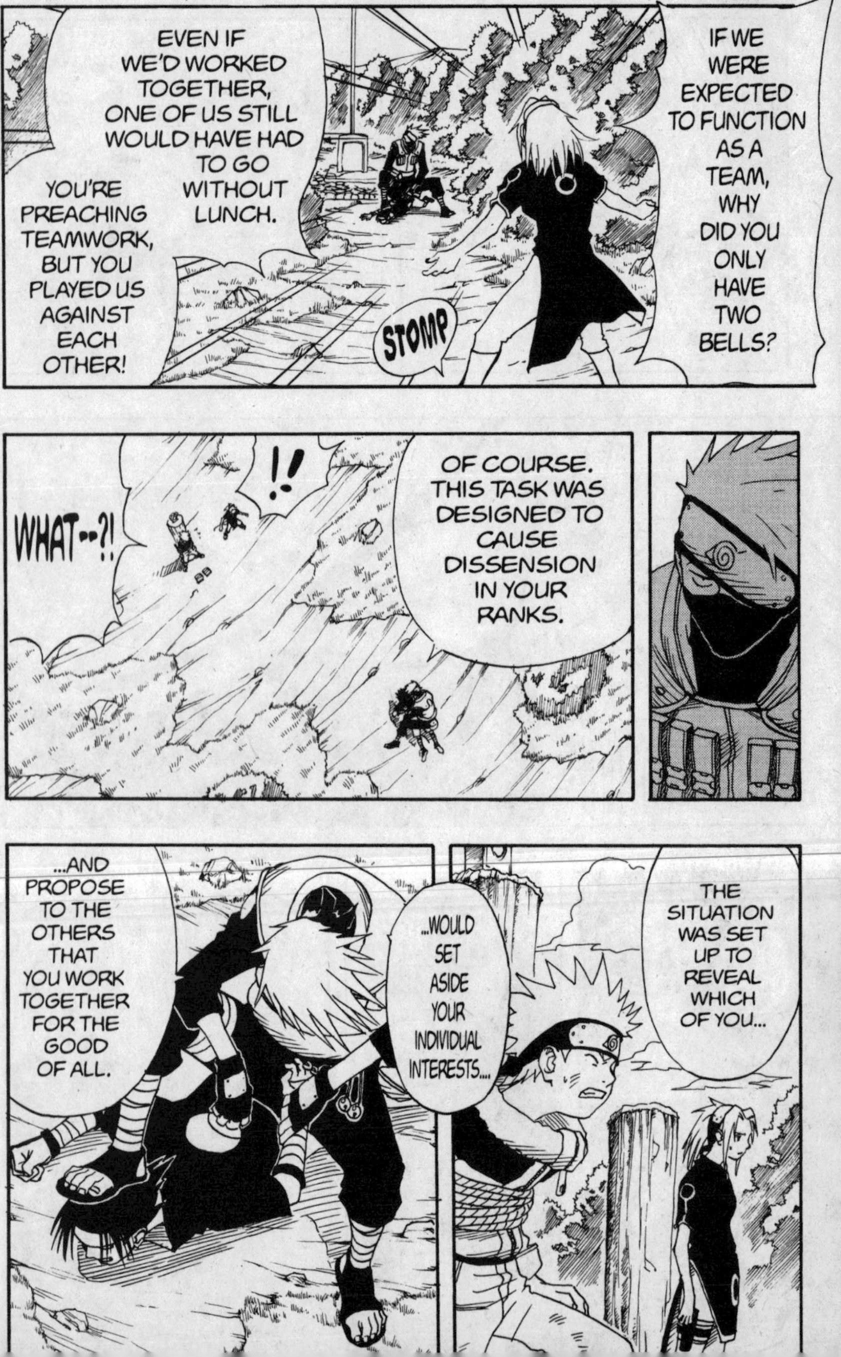
READ THIS WAY
IF WE WERE EXPECTED TO FUNCTION AS A TEAM, WHY DID YOU ONLY HAVE TWO BELLS?
STOMP
EVEN IF WE'D WORKED TOGETHER, ONE OF US STILL WOULD HAVE HAD TO GO WITHOUT LUNCH.
YOU'RE PREACHING TEAMWORK, BUT YOU PLAYED US AGAINST EACH OTHER!
OF COURSE. THIS TASK WAS DESIGNED TO CAUSE DISSENSION IN YOUR RANKS.
!!
WHAT--?!
THE SITUATION WAS SET UP TO REVEAL WHICH OF YOU...
...WOULD SET ASIDE YOUR INDIVIDUAL INTERESTS...
...AND PROPOSE TO THE OTHERS THAT YOU WORK TOGETHER FOR THE GOOD OF ALL.

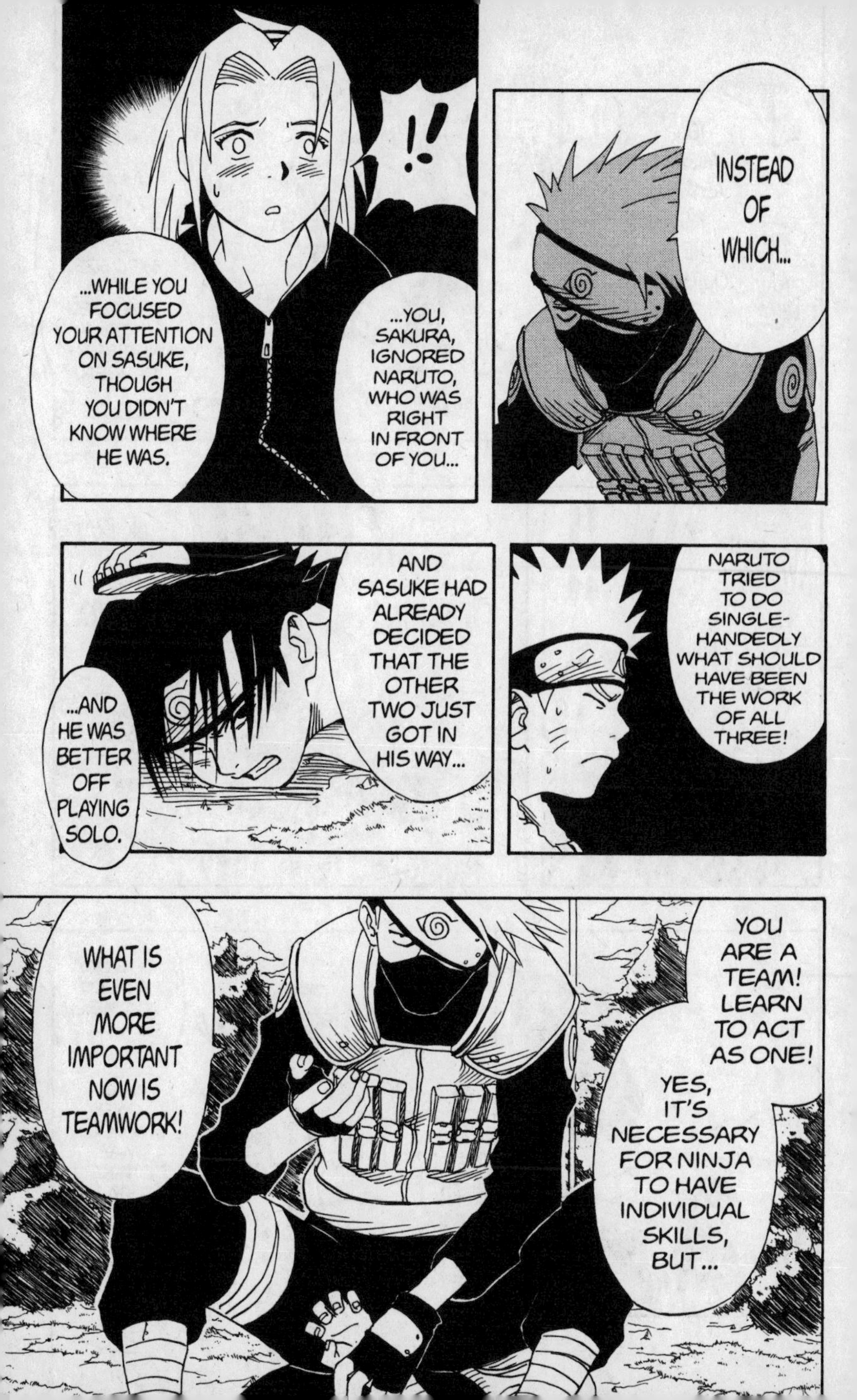
INSTEAD OF WHICH...
!!
...YOU, SAKURA, IGNORED NARUTO, WHO WAS RIGHT IN FRONT OF YOU...
...WHILE YOU FOCUSED YOUR ATTENTION ON SASUKE, THOUGH YOU DIDN'T KNOW WHERE HE WAS.
NARUTO TRIED TO DO SINGLE-HANDEDLY WHAT SHOULD HAVE BEEN THE WORK OF ALL THREE!
AND SASUKE HAD ALREADY DECIDED THAT THE OTHER TWO JUST GOT IN HIS WAY...
...AND HE WAS BETTER OFF PLAYING SOLO.
YES, IT'S NECESSARY FOR NINJA TO HAVE INDIVIDUAL SKILLS, BUT...
WHAT IS EVEN MORE IMPORTANT NOW IS TEAMWORK!
YOU ARE A TEAM! LEARN TO ACT AS ONE!

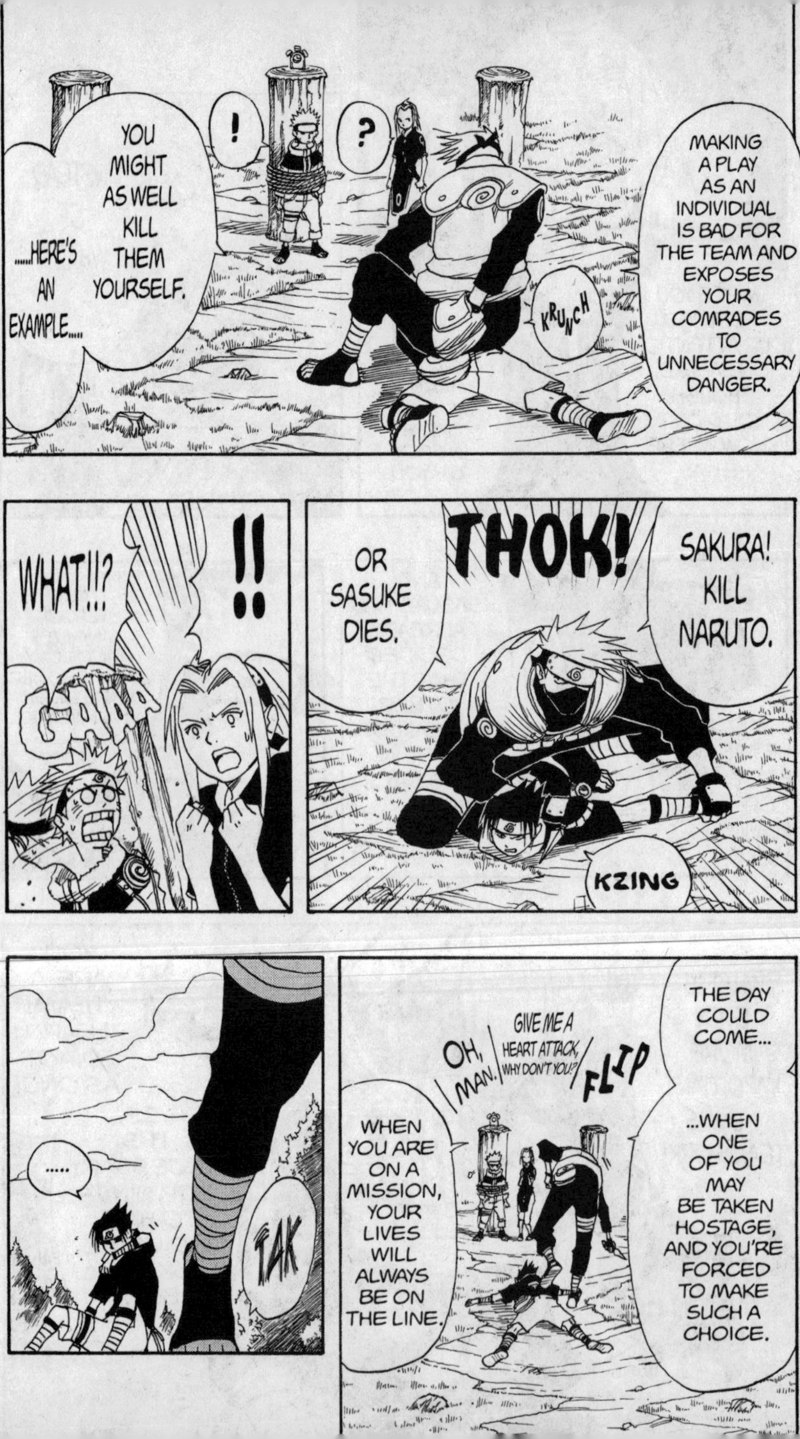
MAKING A PLAY AS AN INDIVIDUAL IS BAD FOR THE TEAM AND EXPOSES YOUR COMRADES TO UNNECESSARY DANGER.
KRUNCH
?
!
YOU MIGHT AS WELL KILL THEM YOURSELF.
......HERE'S AN EXAMPLE......
SAKURA! KILL NARUTO.
THOK!
OR SASUKE DIES.
KZING
!!
WHAT!!?
GAAA
THE DAY COULD COME...
FLIP
GIVE ME A HEART ATTACK, WHY DON'T YOU?
OH, MAN.
...WHEN ONE OF YOU MAY BE TAKEN HOSTAGE, AND YOU'RE FORCED TO MAKE SUCH A CHOICE.
WHEN YOU ARE ON A MISSION, YOUR LIVES WILL ALWAYS BE ON THE LINE.
TAK
......

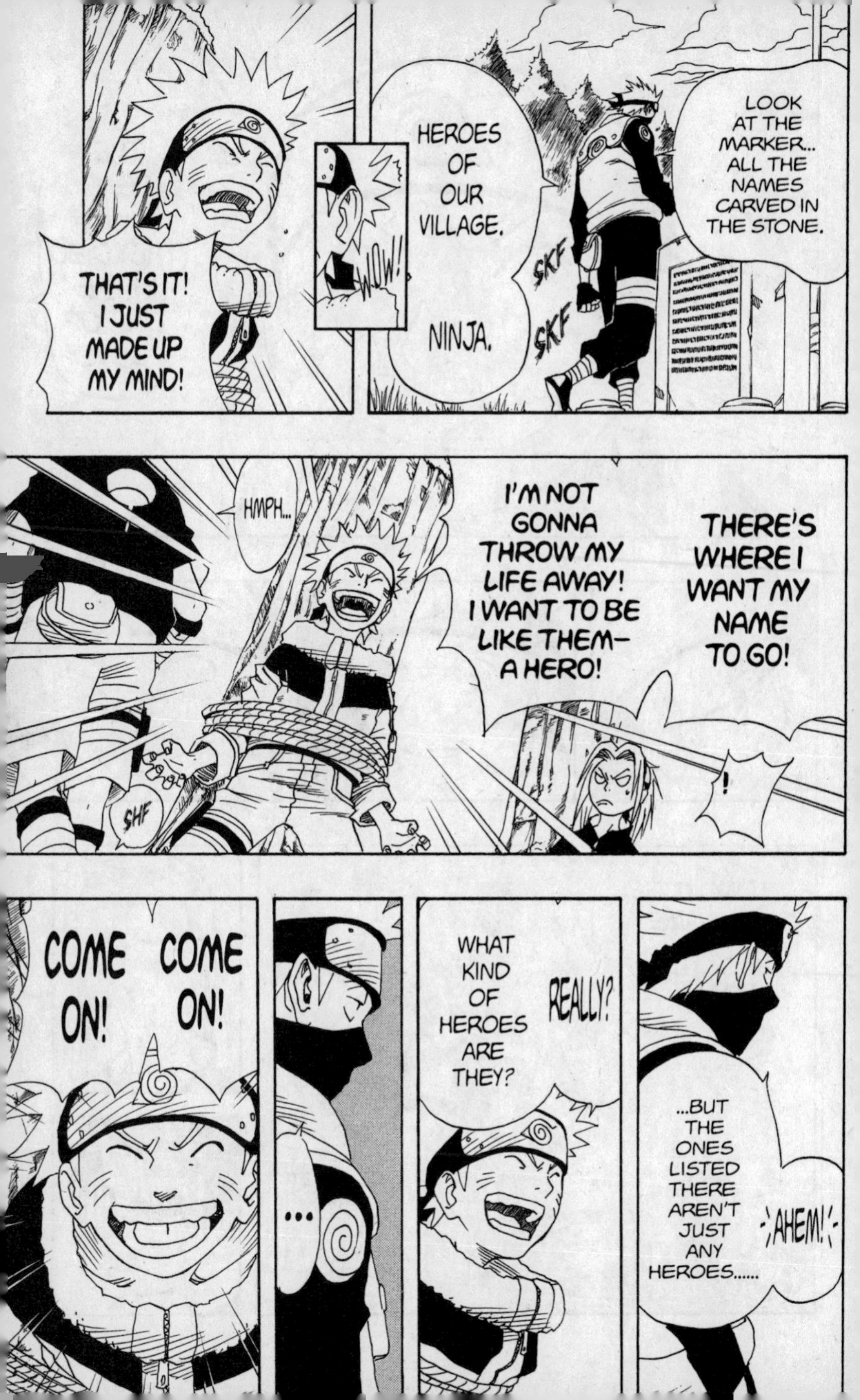
LOOK AT THE MARKER... ALL THE NAMES CARVED IN THE STONE.
SKF
SKF
HEROES OF OUR VILLAGE.
NINJA.
WOW!
THAT'S IT! I JUST MADE UP MY MIND!
!
THERE'S WHERE I WANT MY NAME TO GO!
I'M NOT GONNA THROW MY LIFE AWAY! I WANT TO BE LIKE THEM— A HERO!
HMPH...
SHF
...BUT THE ONES LISTED THERE AREN'T JUST ANY HEROES......
AHEM!
REALLY?
WHAT KIND OF HEROES ARE THEY?
...
COME ON!
COME ON!

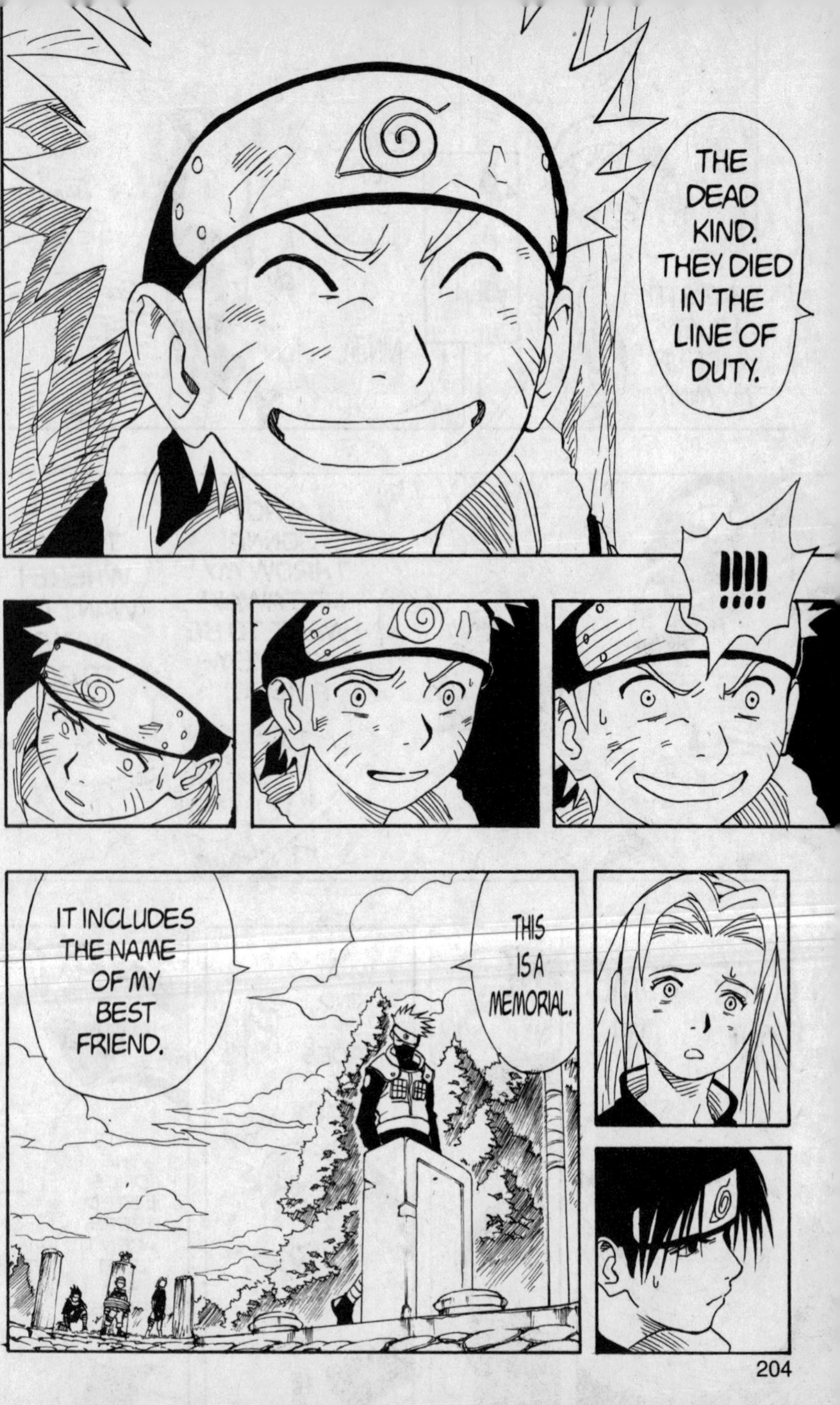
THE DEAD KIND. THEY DIED IN THE LINE OF DUTY.
!!!!
THIS IS A MEMORIAL.
IT INCLUDES THE NAME OF MY BEST FRIEND.

READ THIS WAY

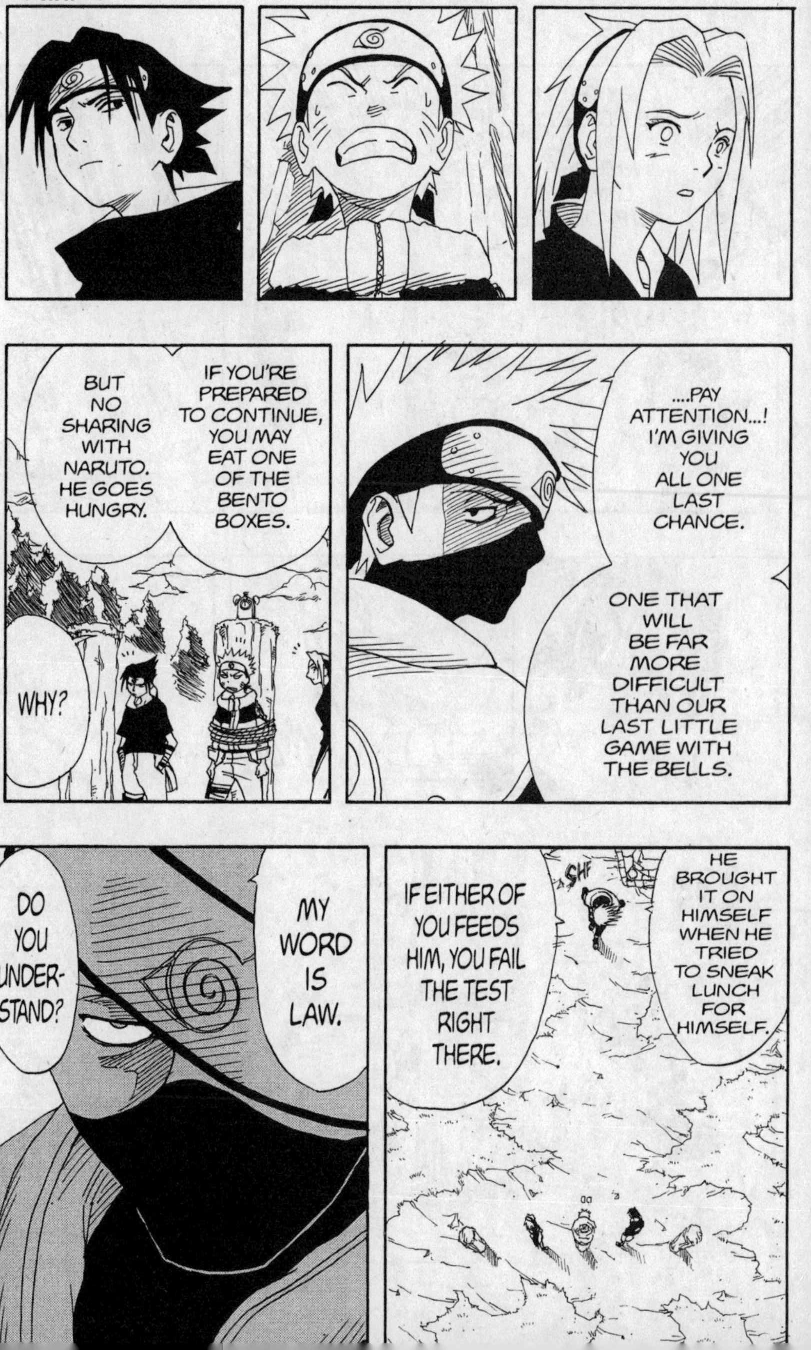
....PAY ATTENTION...! I'M GIVING YOU ALL ONE LAST CHANCE.
ONE THAT WILL BE FAR MORE DIFFICULT THAN OUR LAST LITTLE GAME WITH THE BELLS.
IF YOU'RE PREPARED TO CONTINUE, YOU MAY EAT ONE OF THE BENTO BOXES.
BUT NO SHARING WITH NARUTO. HE GOES HUNGRY.
WHY?
HE BROUGHT IT ON HIMSELF WHEN HE TRIED TO SNEAK LUNCH FOR HIMSELF.
SHF
IF EITHER OF YOU FEEDS HIM, YOU FAIL THE TEST RIGHT THERE.
MY WORD IS LAW.
DO YOU UNDER-STAND?

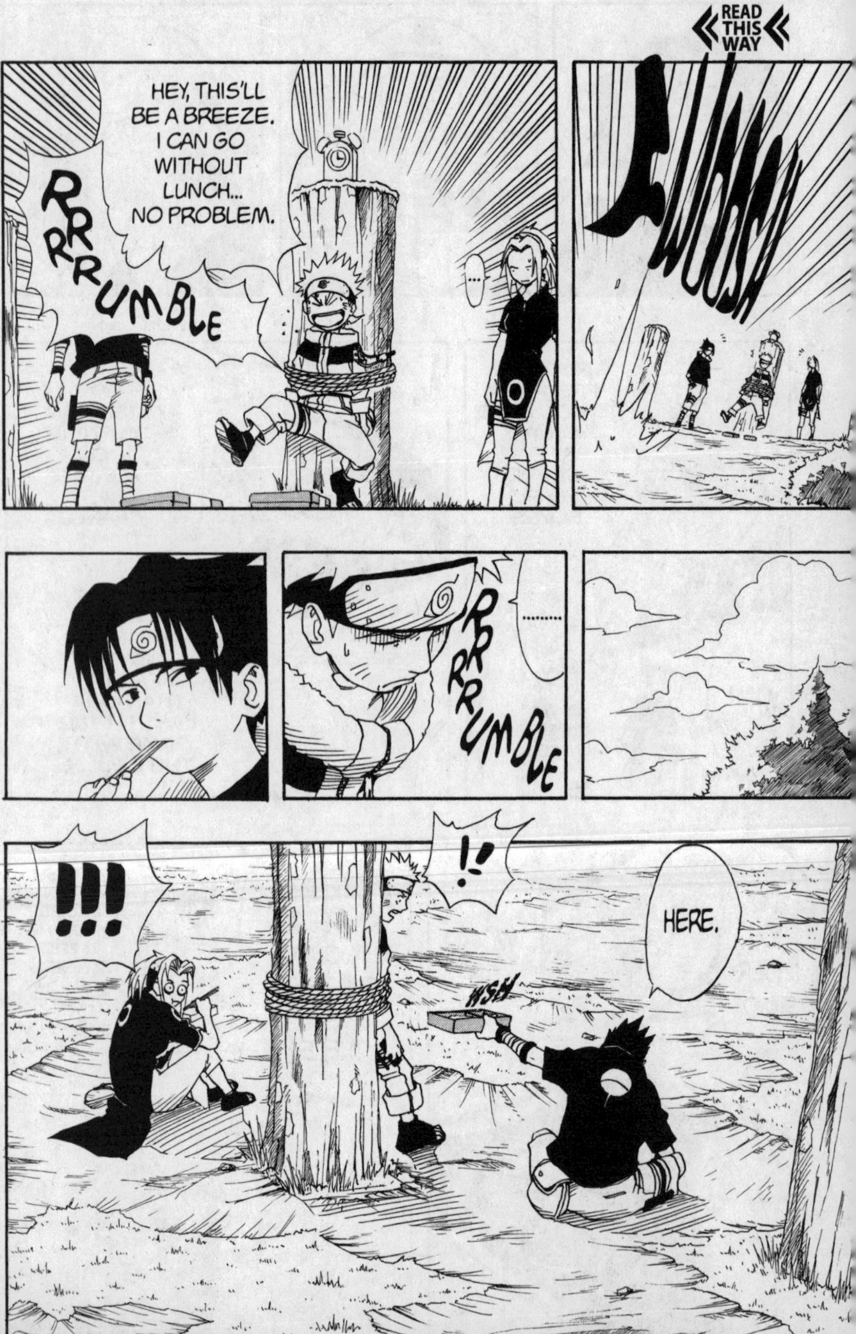
READ THIS WAY
WHOOSH
...
HEY, THIS'LL BE A BREEZE. I CAN GO WITHOUT LUNCH... NO PROBLEM.
RRRRUMBLE
....
RRRRUMBLE
HERE.
WSH
!!
!!!

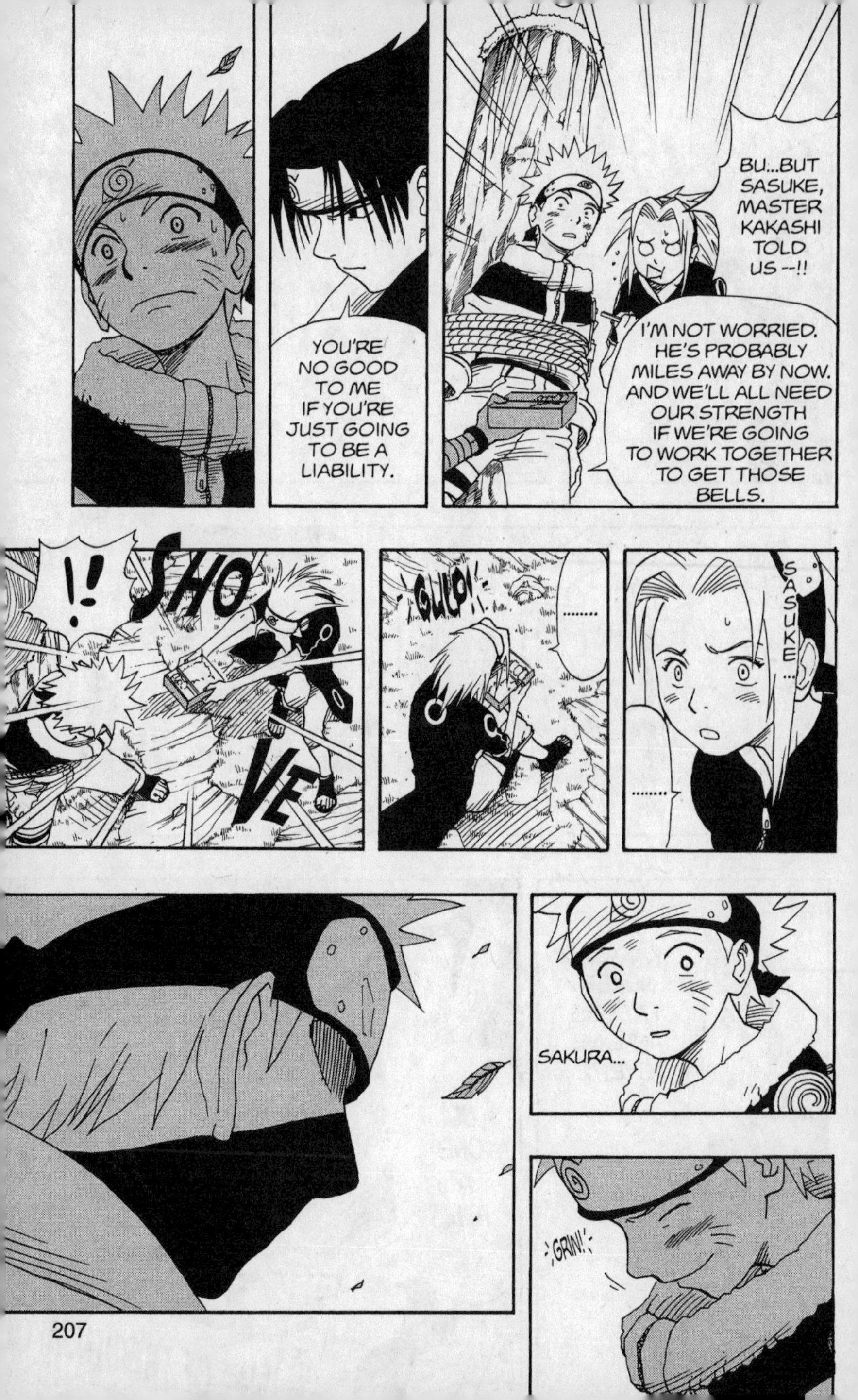
BU...BUT SASUKE, MASTER KAKASHI TOLD US --!!
I'M NOT WORRIED. HE'S PROBABLY MILES AWAY BY NOW. AND WE'LL ALL NEED OUR STRENGTH IF WE'RE GOING TO WORK TOGETHER TO GET THOSE BELLS.
YOU'RE NO GOOD TO ME IF YOU'RE JUST GOING TO BE A LIABILITY.
SASUKE...
....
GULP!
....
!!
SHOVE
SAKURA...
GRIN!

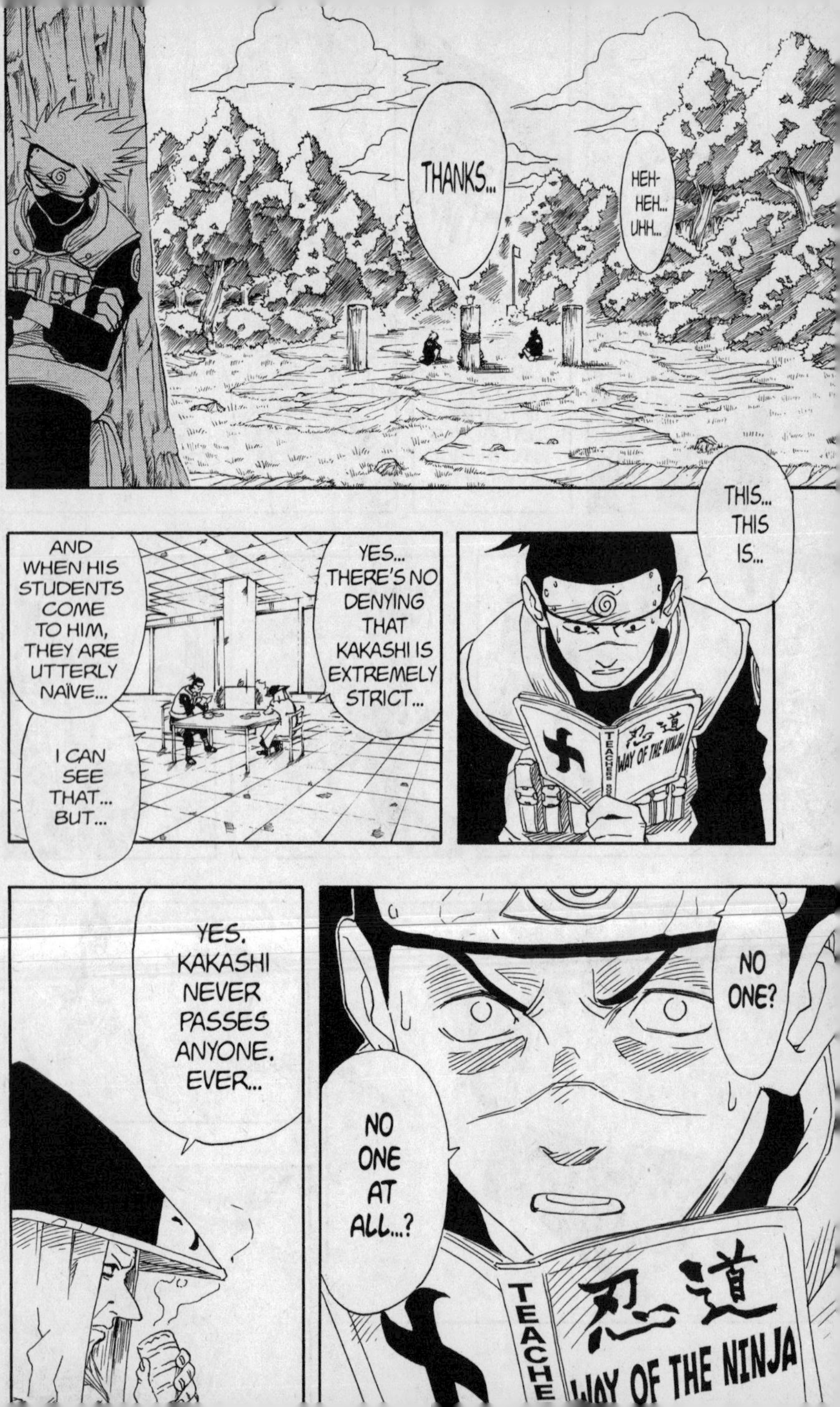
HEH-HEH... UHH...
THANKS...
THIS... THIS IS...
YES... THERE'S NO DENYING THAT KAKASHI IS EXTREMELY STRICT...
AND WHEN HIS STUDENTS COME TO HIM, THEY ARE UTTERLY NAÏVE...
I CAN SEE THAT... BUT...
NO ONE?
NO ONE AT ALL...?
YES. KAKASHI NEVER PASSES ANYONE. EVER...
忍道
WAY OF THE NINJA

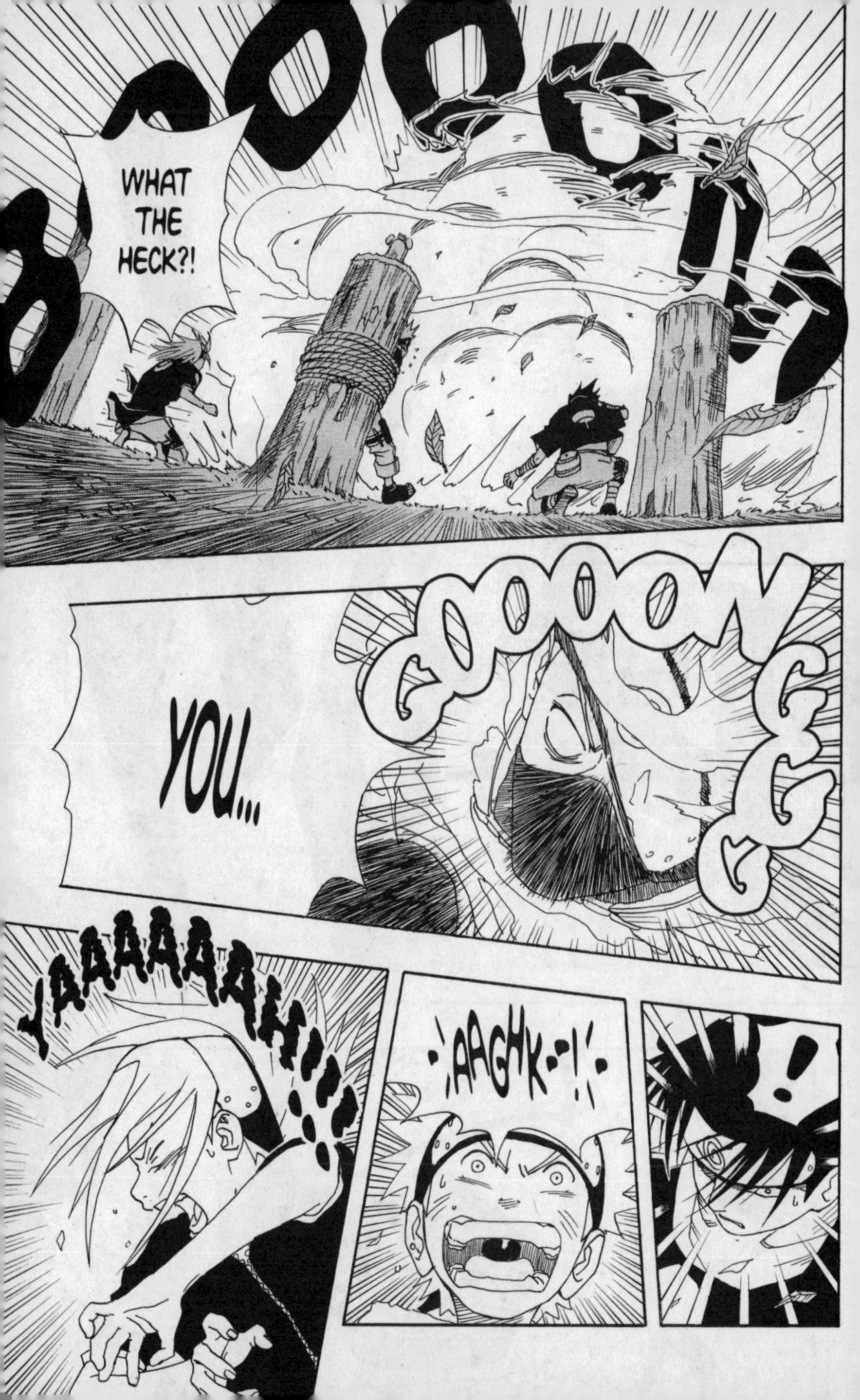
WHAT THE HECK?!
YOU...
GOOOONGG
YAAAAAAH!!
AAGHK-!
!

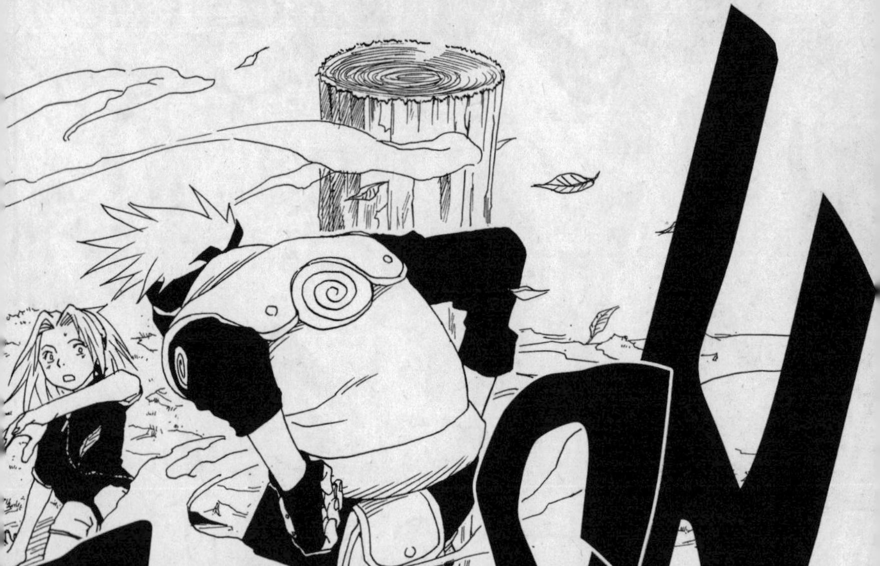

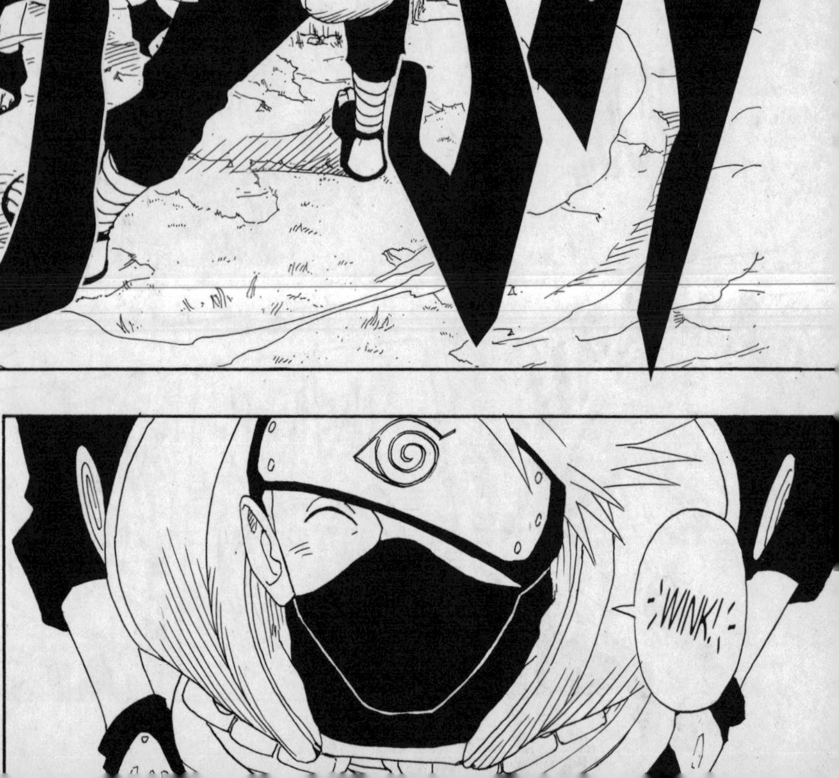
WINK!

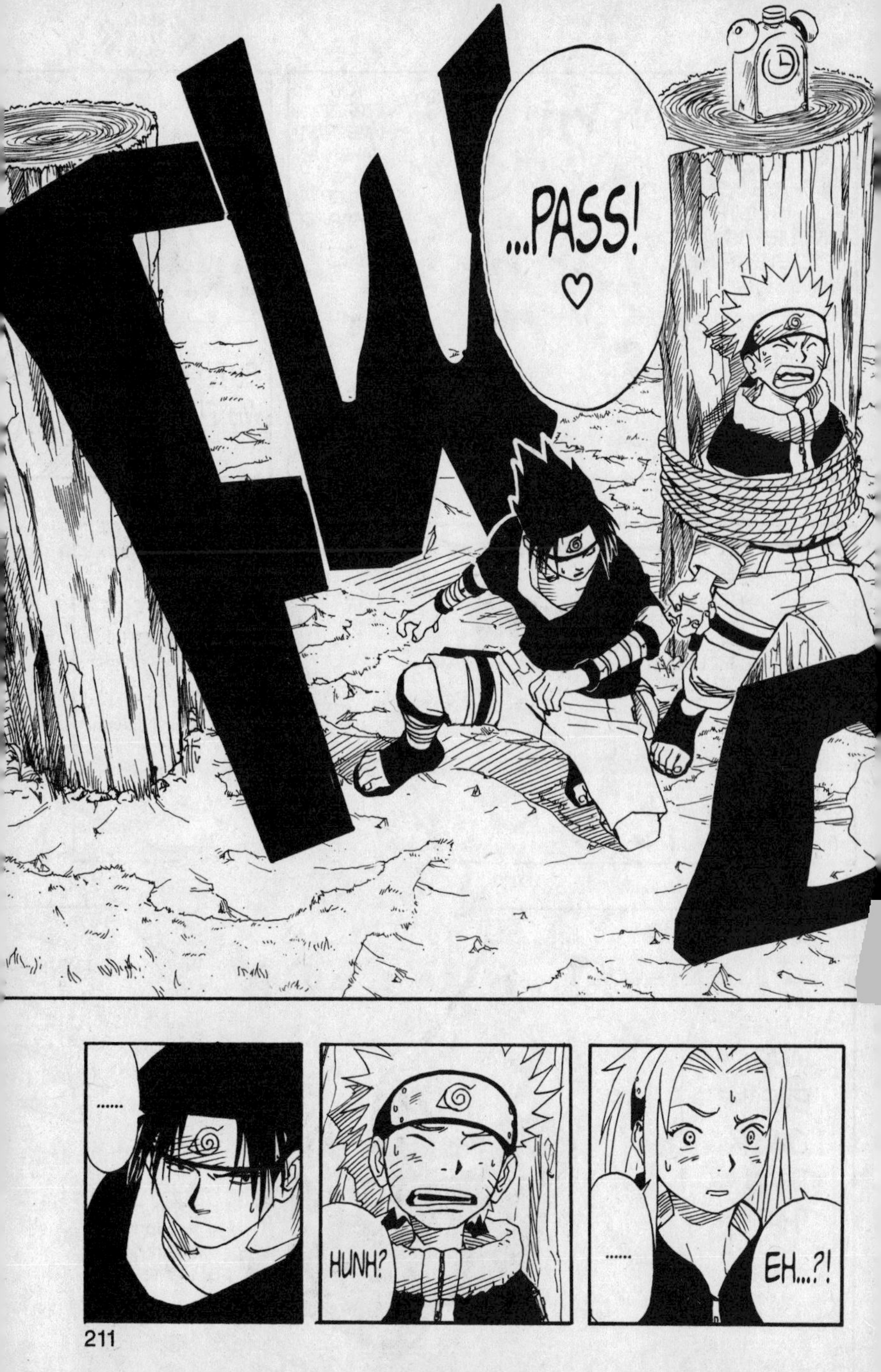
...PASS! ♡
EH...?!
......
HUNH?
......

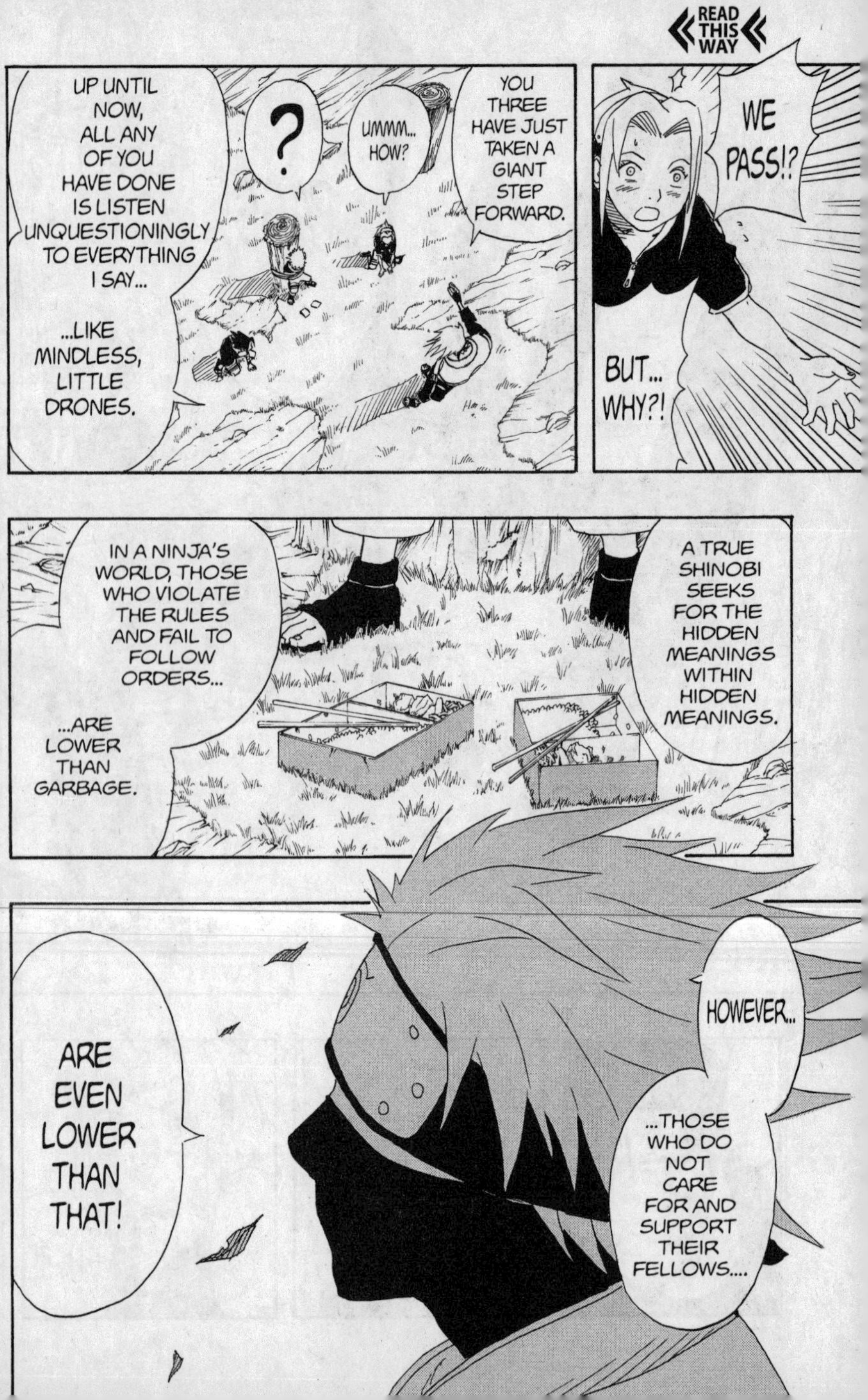
READ THIS WAY
WE PASS!?
BUT... WHY?!
YOU THREE HAVE JUST TAKEN A GIANT STEP FORWARD.
UMMM... HOW?
?
UP UNTIL NOW, ALL ANY OF YOU HAVE DONE IS LISTEN UNQUESTIONINGLY TO EVERYTHING I SAY...
...LIKE MINDLESS, LITTLE DRONES.
A TRUE SHINOBI SEEKS FOR THE HIDDEN MEANINGS WITHIN HIDDEN MEANINGS.
IN A NINJA'S WORLD, THOSE WHO VIOLATE THE RULES AND FAIL TO FOLLOW ORDERS...
...ARE LOWER THAN GARBAGE.
HOWEVER...
...THOSE WHO DO NOT CARE FOR AND SUPPORT THEIR FELLOWS....
ARE EVEN LOWER THAN THAT!

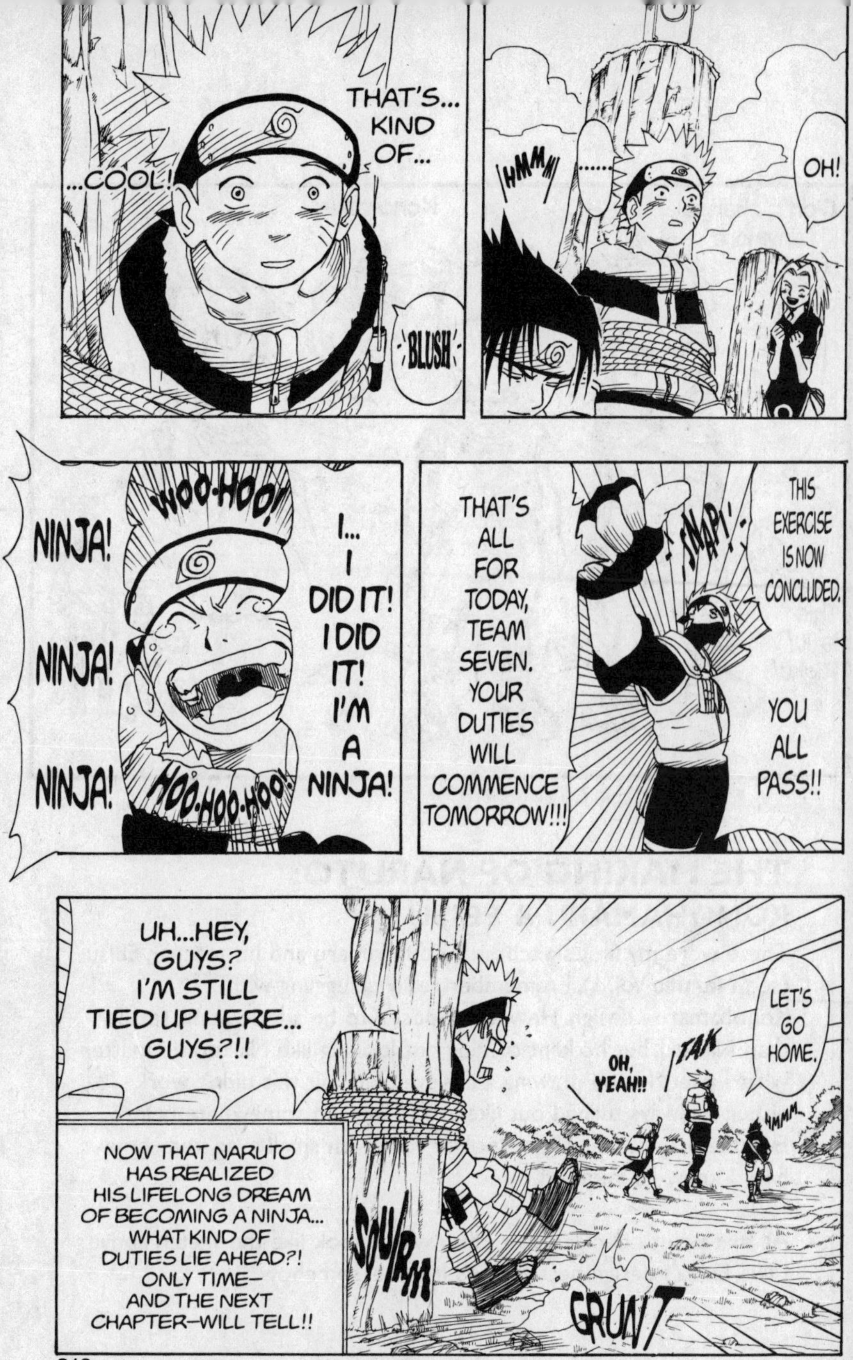
OH!
......
HMMM
THAT'S... KIND OF...
...COOL!
BLUSH
THIS EXERCISE IS NOW CONCLUDED.
YOU ALL PASS!!
SNAP!
THAT'S ALL FOR TODAY, TEAM SEVEN. YOUR DUTIES WILL COMMENCE TOMORROW!!!
I... I DID IT! I DID IT! I'M A NINJA!
WOO-HOO!
HOO-HOO-HOO!
NINJA!
NINJA!
NINJA!
LET'S GO HOME.
TAK
HMMM...
OH, YEAH!!
UH...HEY, GUYS? I'M STILL TIED UP HERE... GUYS?!!
SQUIRM
GRUNT
NOW THAT NARUTO HAS REALIZED HIS LIFELONG DREAM OF BECOMING A NINJA... WHAT KIND OF DUTIES LIE AHEAD?! ONLY TIME—AND THE NEXT CHAPTER—WILL TELL!!

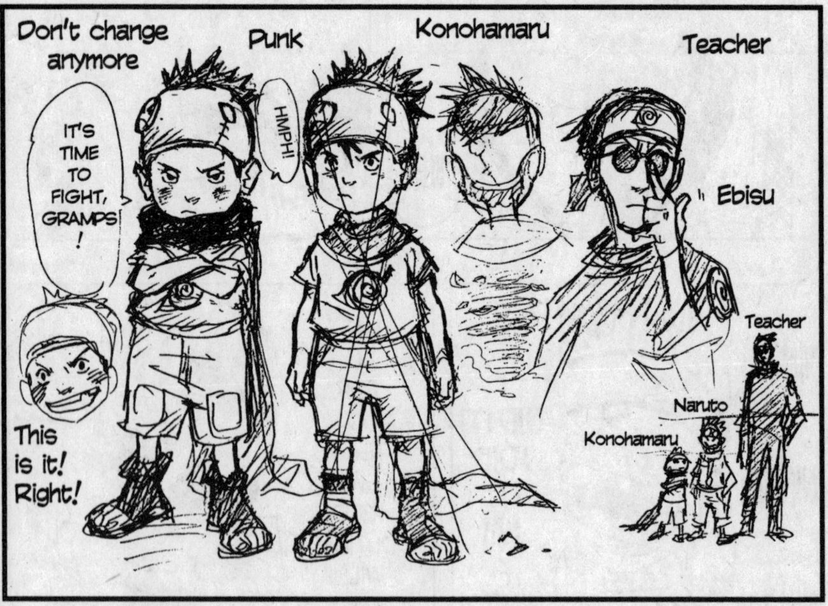
Don't change anymore
Punk
Konohamaru
Teacher
HMPH!
IT'S TIME TO FIGHT, GRAMPS!
Ebisu
Teacher
Naruto
Konohamaru
This is it! Right!

THE MAKING OF NARUTO:
KONOHAMARU & EBISU

These were my first sketches of Konohamaru and his teacher, Ebisu (see **Naruto** Vol. 1). I remember really struggling with Konohamaru's design. He was supposed to be a little punk, smaller than Naruto, but he kept coming out looking like Naruto no matter what I tried. I tried drawing a big-eyed kid, but this didn't work either. It always turned out like a face I'd seen somewhere before. Eventually, I drew an angry-looking face with small eyes, and somehow I knew I'd found it!

At that point I decided that Ebisu would look like the sketch above. I like Ebisu's design because he's like me, somehow...

Number 9: The Worst Client

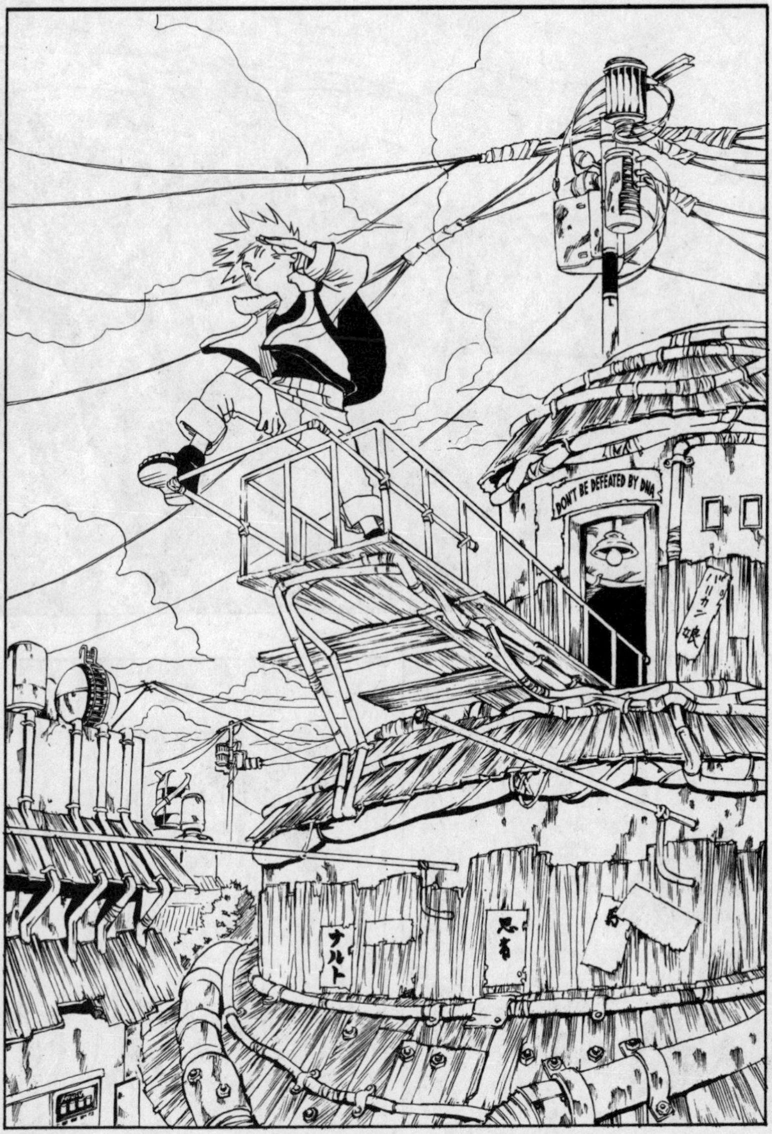
DON'T BE DEFEATED BY DNA
バリカン娘
忍者
ナルト

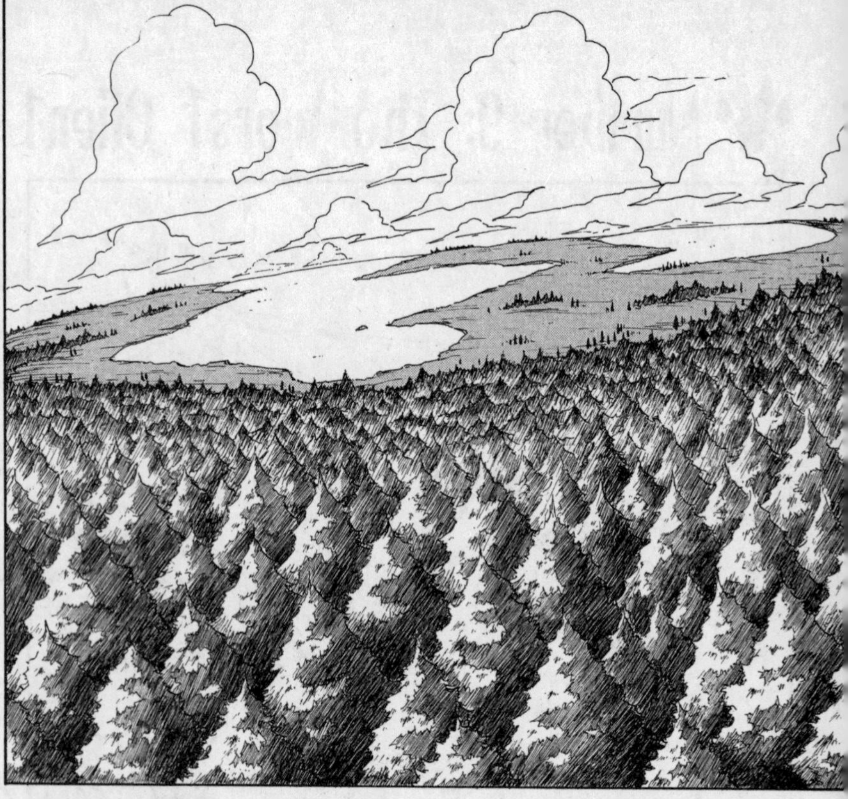

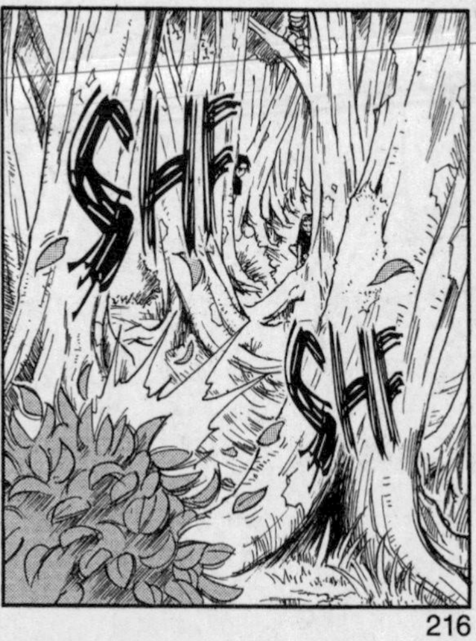
SHF
SHF

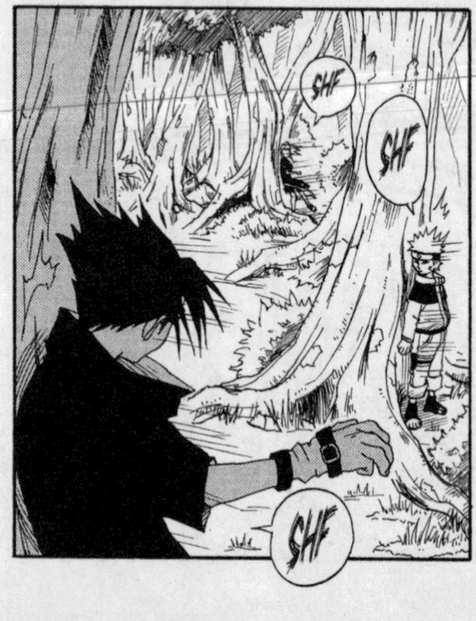
SHF
SHF
SHF

READ THIS WAY

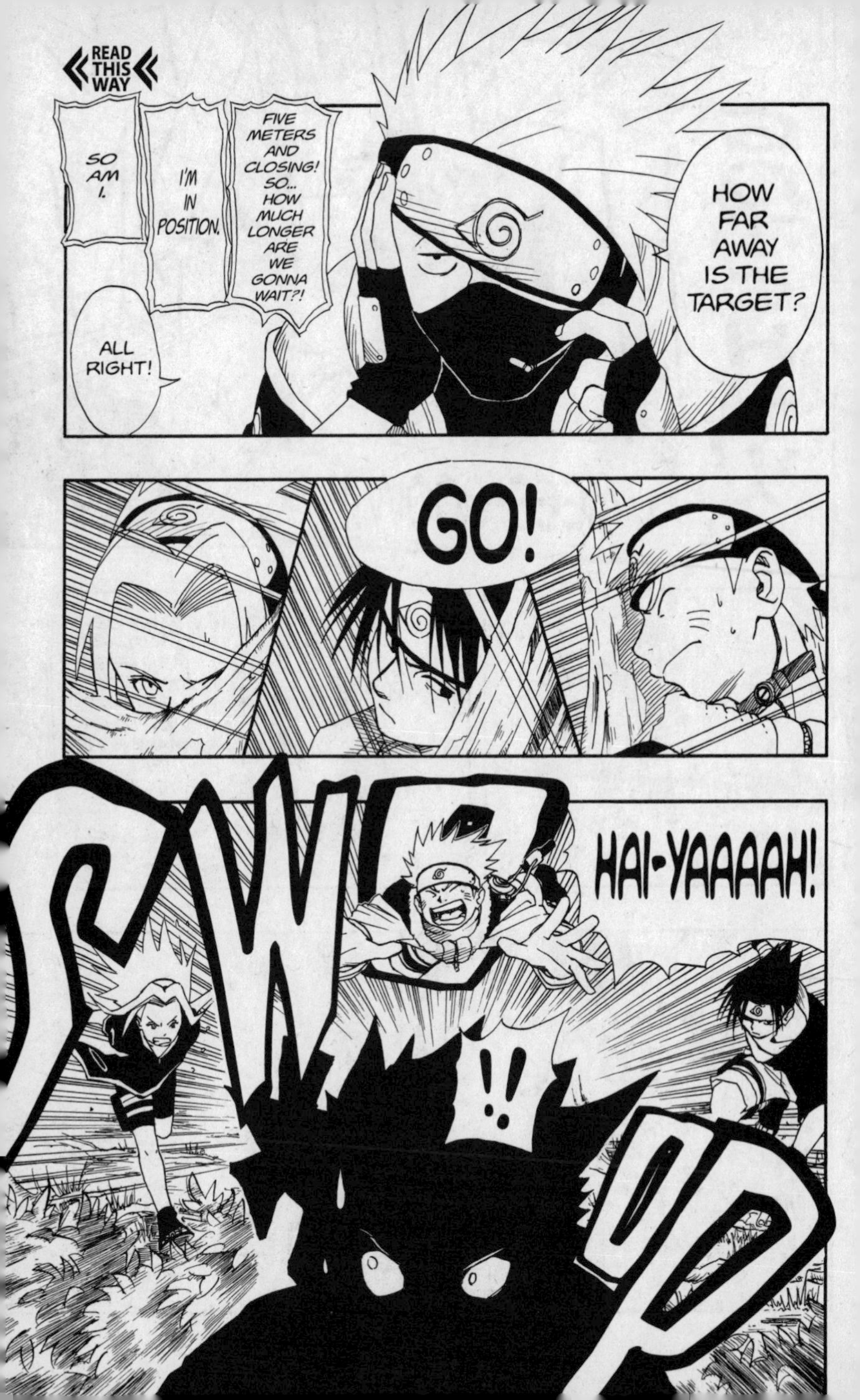
HOW FAR AWAY IS THE TARGET?
FIVE METERS AND CLOSING! SO... HOW MUCH LONGER ARE WE GONNA WAIT?!
I'M IN POSITION.
SO AM I.
ALL RIGHT!
GO!
HAI-YAAAAH!
!!

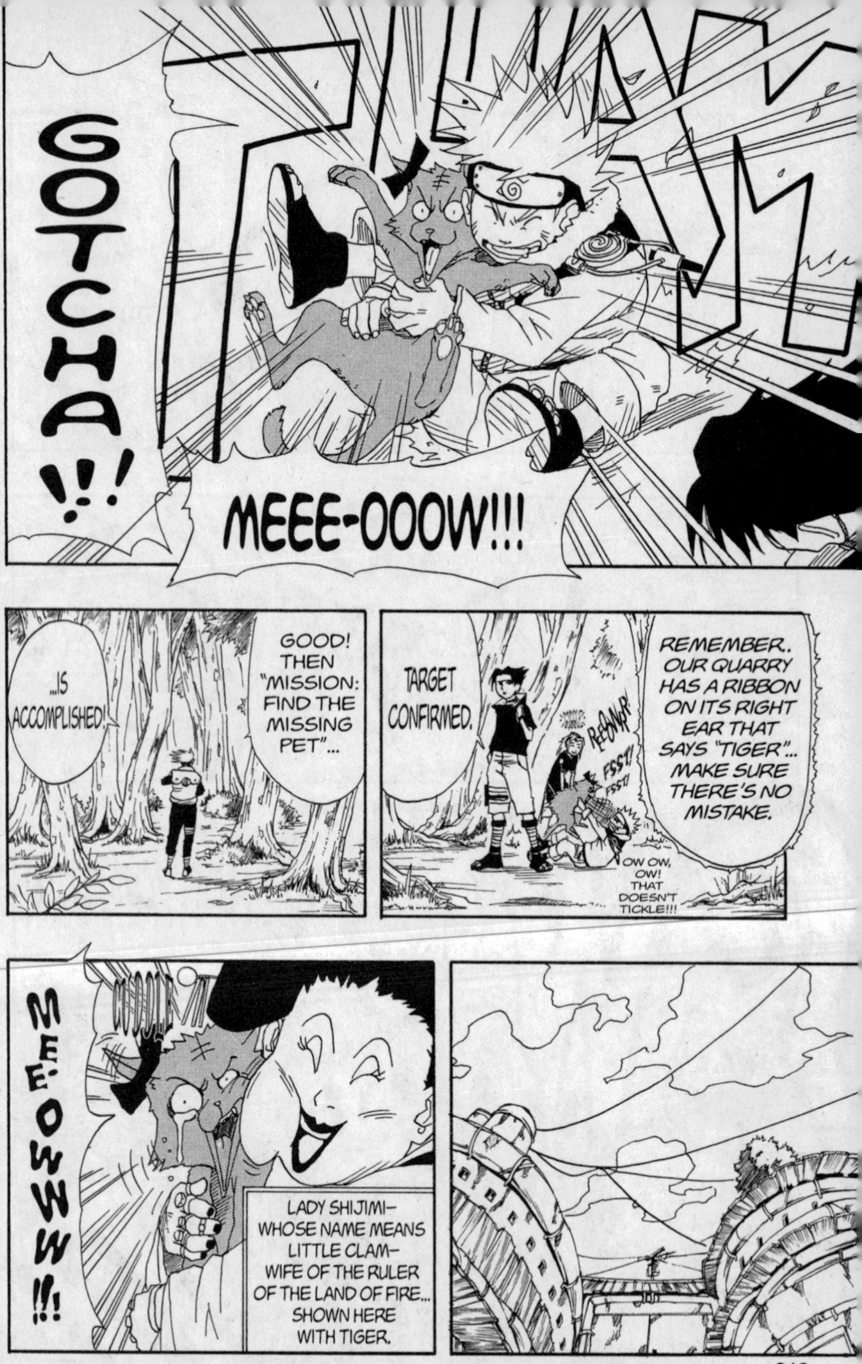
GOTCHA!!!
MEEE-OOOW!!!
REMEMBER.. OUR QUARRY HAS A RIBBON ON ITS RIGHT EAR THAT SAYS "TIGER"... MAKE SURE THERE'S NO MISTAKE.
FSST! FSST!
OW OW, OW! THAT DOESN'T TICKLE!!!
TARGET CONFIRMED.
GOOD! THEN "MISSION: FIND THE MISSING PET"...
...IS ACCOMPLISHED!
LADY SHIJIMI—WHOSE NAME MEANS LITTLE CLAM—WIFE OF THE RULER OF THE LAND OF FIRE... SHOWN HERE WITH TIGER.
MEEOWWW!!!

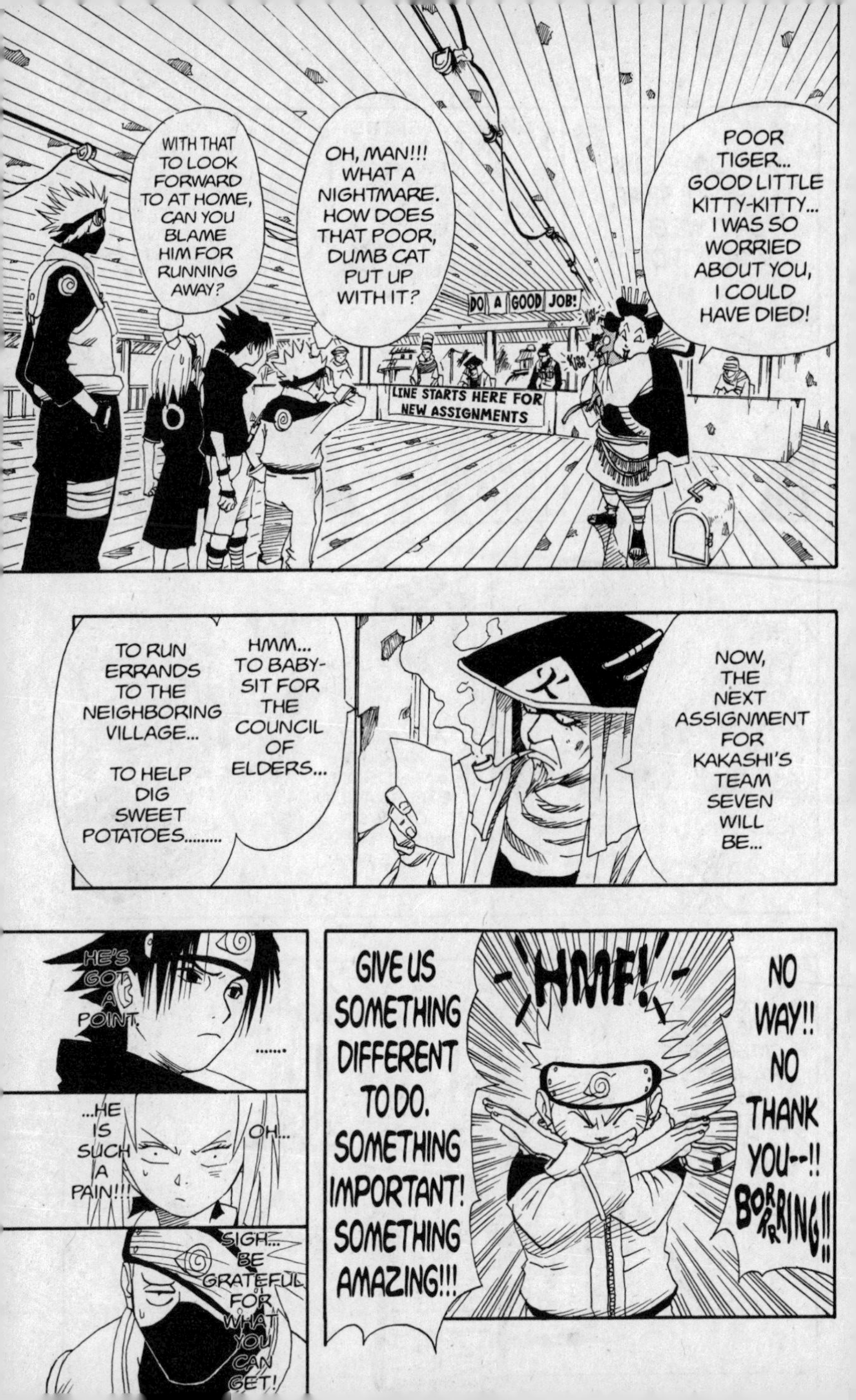
POOR TIGER... GOOD LITTLE KITTY-KITTY... I WAS SO WORRIED ABOUT YOU, I COULD HAVE DIED!
KISS
KISS
DO A GOOD JOB!
LINE STARTS HERE FOR NEW ASSIGNMENTS
OH, MAN!!! WHAT A NIGHTMARE. HOW DOES THAT POOR, DUMB CAT PUT UP WITH IT?
WITH THAT TO LOOK FORWARD TO AT HOME, CAN YOU BLAME HIM FOR RUNNING AWAY?
NOW, THE NEXT ASSIGNMENT FOR KAKASHI'S TEAM SEVEN WILL BE...
HMM... TO BABY-SIT FOR THE COUNCIL OF ELDERS...
TO RUN ERRANDS TO THE NEIGHBORING VILLAGE...
TO HELP DIG SWEET POTATOES.........
NO WAY!! NO THANK YOU--!!
BORRRING!!
HMF!
GIVE US SOMETHING DIFFERENT TO DO. SOMETHING IMPORTANT! SOMETHING AMAZING!!!
HE'S GOT A POINT.
....
OH...
...HE IS SUCH A PAIN!!!
SIGH... BE GRATEFUL FOR WHAT YOU CAN GET!

READ THIS WAY

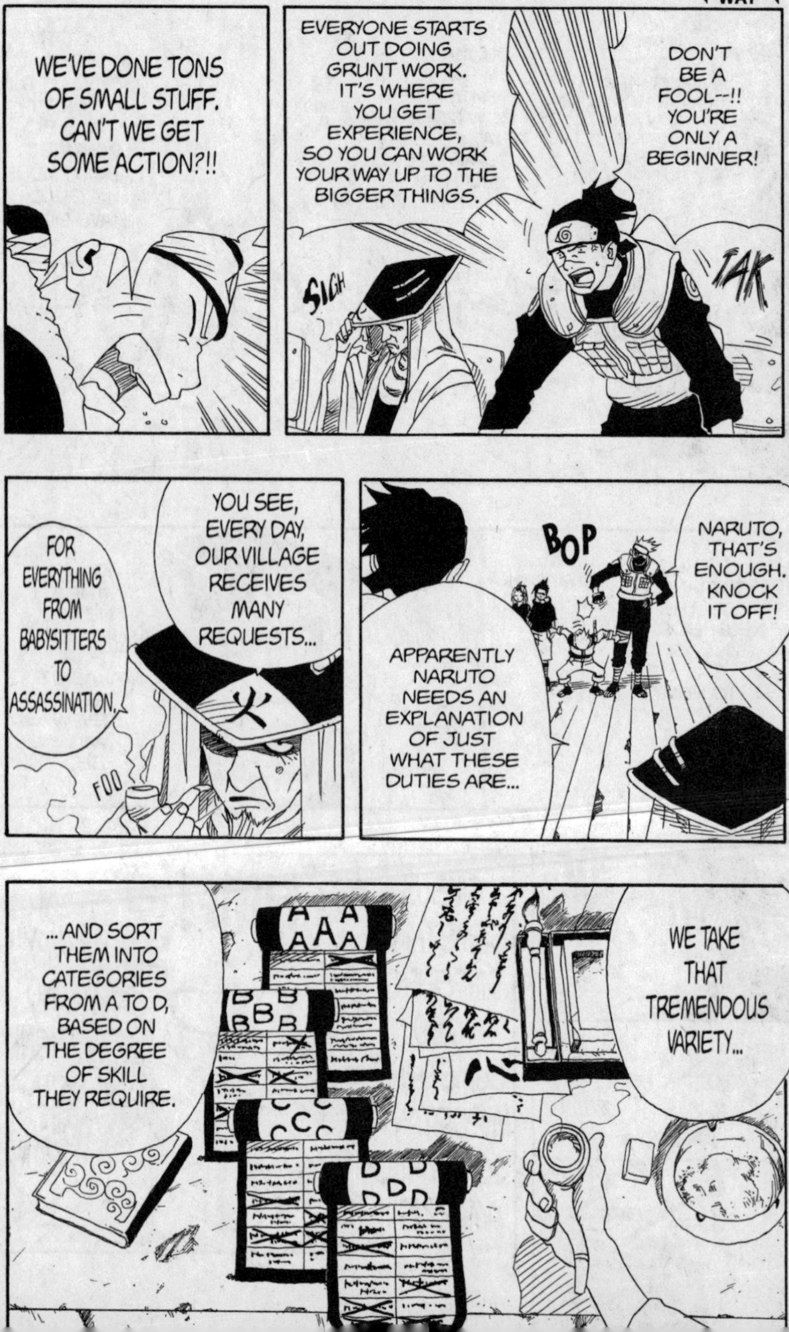
DON'T BE A FOOL--!! YOU'RE ONLY A BEGINNER!
TAK
EVERYONE STARTS OUT DOING GRUNT WORK. IT'S WHERE YOU GET EXPERIENCE, SO YOU CAN WORK YOUR WAY UP TO THE BIGGER THINGS.
SIGH
WE'VE DONE TONS OF SMALL STUFF. CAN'T WE GET SOME ACTION?!!
NARUTO, THAT'S ENOUGH. KNOCK IT OFF!
BOP
APPARENTLY NARUTO NEEDS AN EXPLANATION OF JUST WHAT THESE DUTIES ARE...
YOU SEE, EVERY DAY, OUR VILLAGE RECEIVES MANY REQUESTS...
FOR EVERYTHING FROM BABYSITTERS TO ASSASSINATION.
FOO
WE TAKE THAT TREMENDOUS VARIETY...
...AND SORT THEM INTO CATEGORIES FROM A TO D, BASED ON THE DEGREE OF SKILL THEY REQUIRE.

READ THIS WAY

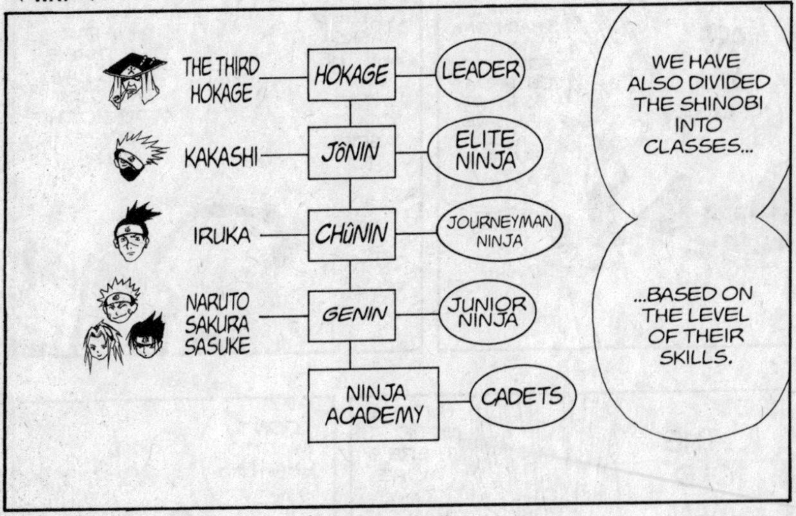
WE HAVE ALSO DIVIDED THE SHINOBI INTO CLASSES...
...BASED ON THE LEVEL OF THEIR SKILLS.
THE THIRD HOKAGE
HOKAGE
LEADER
KAKASHI
JÔNIN
ELITE NINJA
IRUKA
CHÛNIN
JOURNEYMAN NINJA
NARUTO SAKURA SASUKE
GENIN
JUNIOR NINJA
NINJA ACADEMY
CADETS

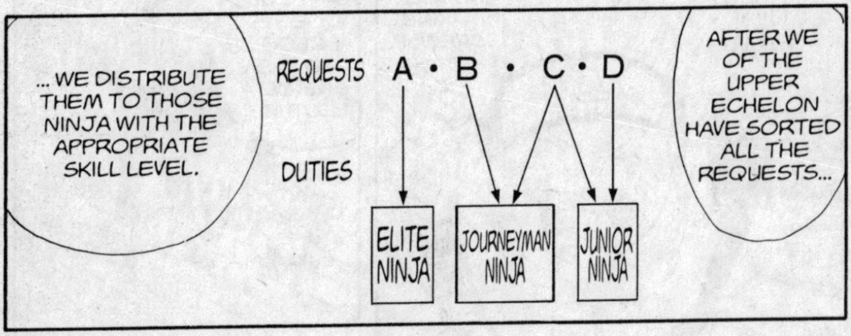
AFTER WE OF THE UPPER ECHELON HAVE SORTED ALL THE REQUESTS...
REQUESTS
A · B · C · D
DUTIES
ELITE NINJA
JOURNEYMAN NINJA
JUNIOR NINJA
... WE DISTRIBUTE THEM TO THOSE NINJA WITH THE APPROPRIATE SKILL LEVEL.

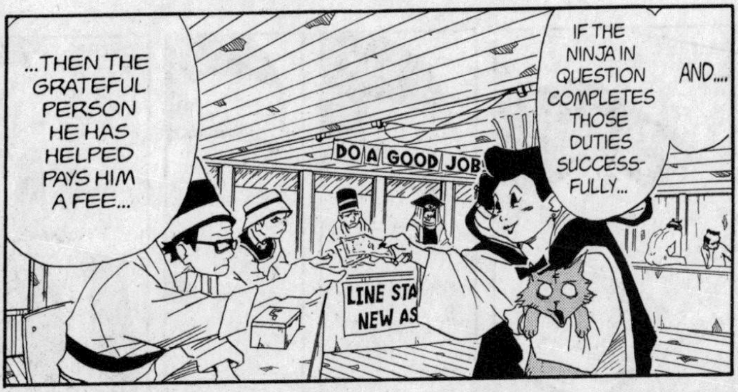
AND....
IF THE NINJA IN QUESTION COMPLETES THOSE DUTIES SUCCESS-FULLY...
DO A GOOD JOB!
LINE STA
NEW AS
...THEN THE GRATEFUL PERSON HE HAS HELPED PAYS HIM A FEE...

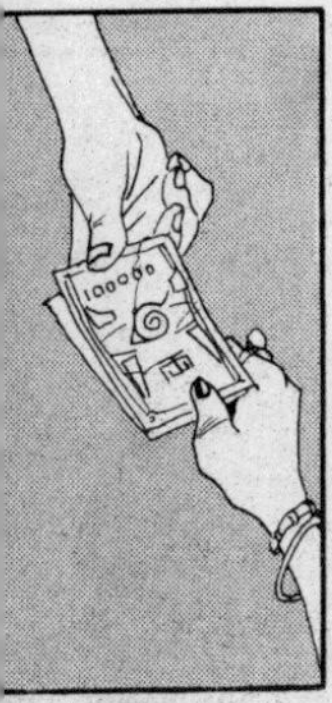

READ THIS WAY

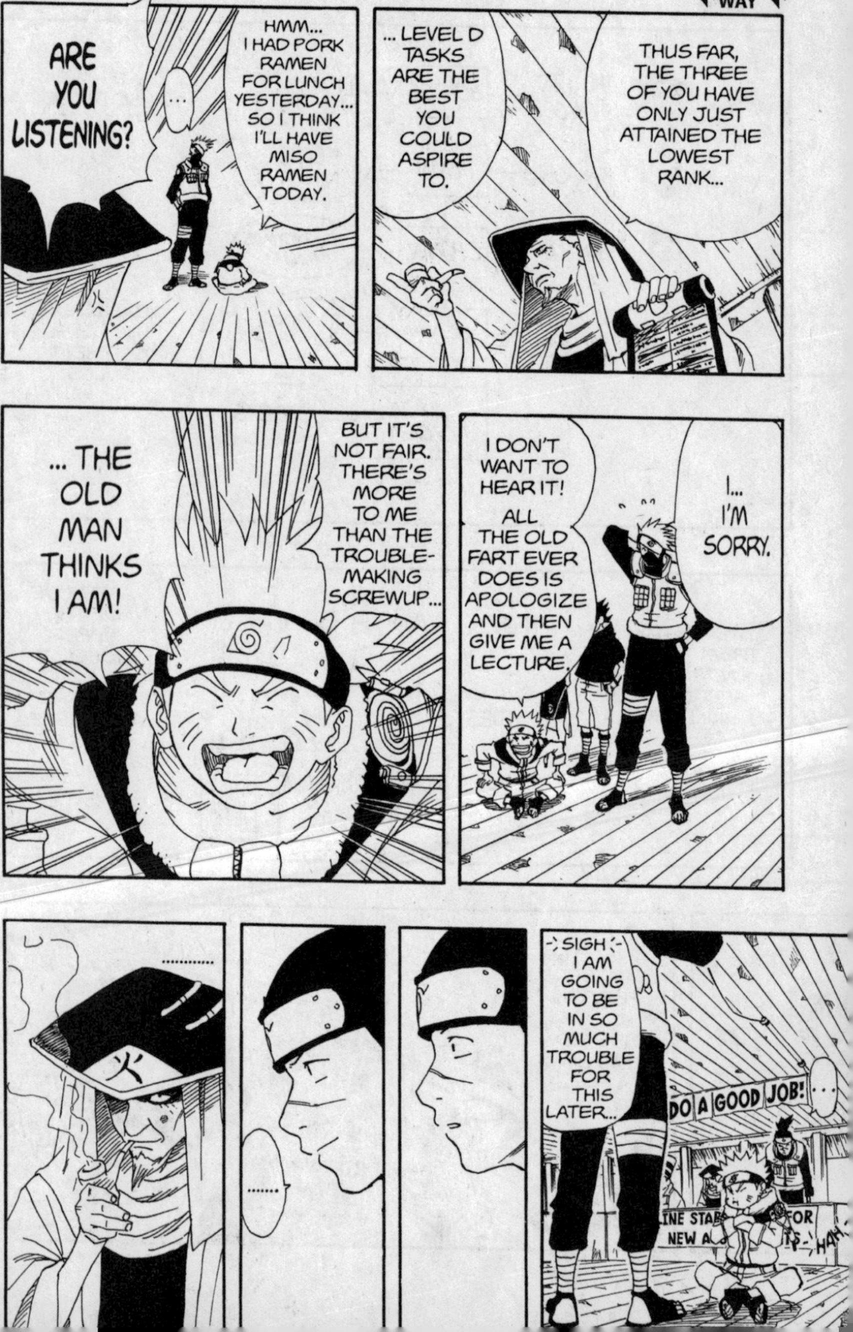
THUS FAR, THE THREE OF YOU HAVE ONLY JUST ATTAINED THE LOWEST RANK...
... LEVEL D TASKS ARE THE BEST YOU COULD ASPIRE TO.
HMM... I HAD PORK RAMEN FOR LUNCH YESTERDAY... SO I THINK I'LL HAVE MISO RAMEN TODAY.
...
ARE YOU LISTENING?
I... I'M SORRY.
I DON'T WANT TO HEAR IT!
ALL THE OLD FART EVER DOES IS APOLOGIZE AND THEN GIVE ME A LECTURE.
BUT IT'S NOT FAIR. THERE'S MORE TO ME THAN THE TROUBLE-MAKING SCREWUP...
... THE OLD MAN THINKS I AM!
-SIGH- I AM GOING TO BE IN SO MUCH TROUBLE FOR THIS LATER...
DO A GOOD JOB!
...
HAH
......
....

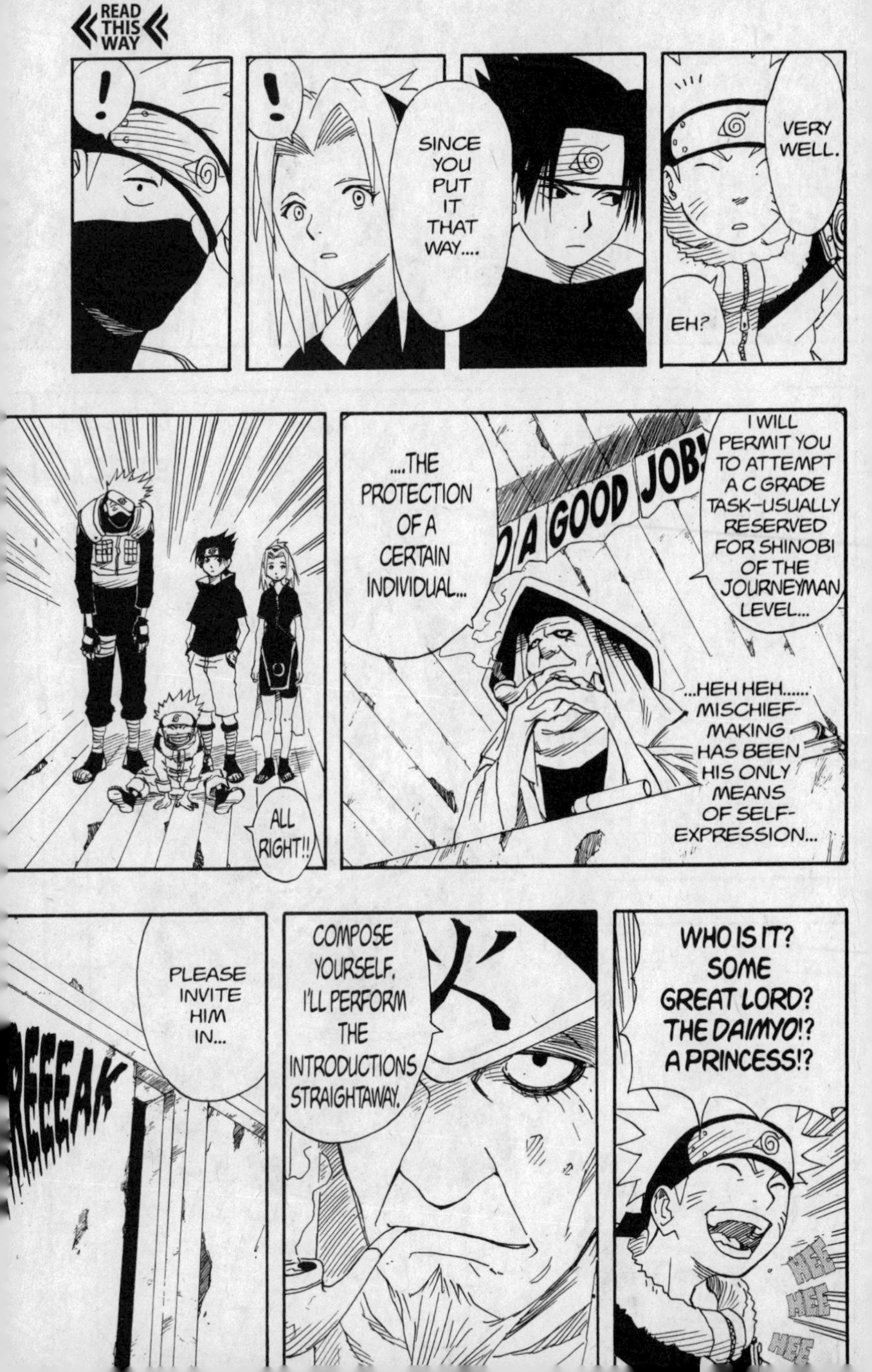
READ THIS WAY
VERY WELL.
EH?
SINCE YOU PUT IT THAT WAY....
!
!
I WILL PERMIT YOU TO ATTEMPT A C GRADE TASK—USUALLY RESERVED FOR SHINOBI OF THE JOURNEYMAN LEVEL...
A GOOD JOB!
....THE PROTECTION OF A CERTAIN INDIVIDUAL...
...HEH HEH...... MISCHIEF-MAKING HAS BEEN HIS ONLY MEANS OF SELF-EXPRESSION...
ALL RIGHT!!
WHO IS IT? SOME GREAT LORD? THE *DAIMYO*!? A PRINCESS!?
HEE HEE HEE
COMPOSE YOURSELF. I'LL PERFORM THE INTRODUCTIONS STRAIGHTAWAY.
PLEASE INVITE HIM IN...

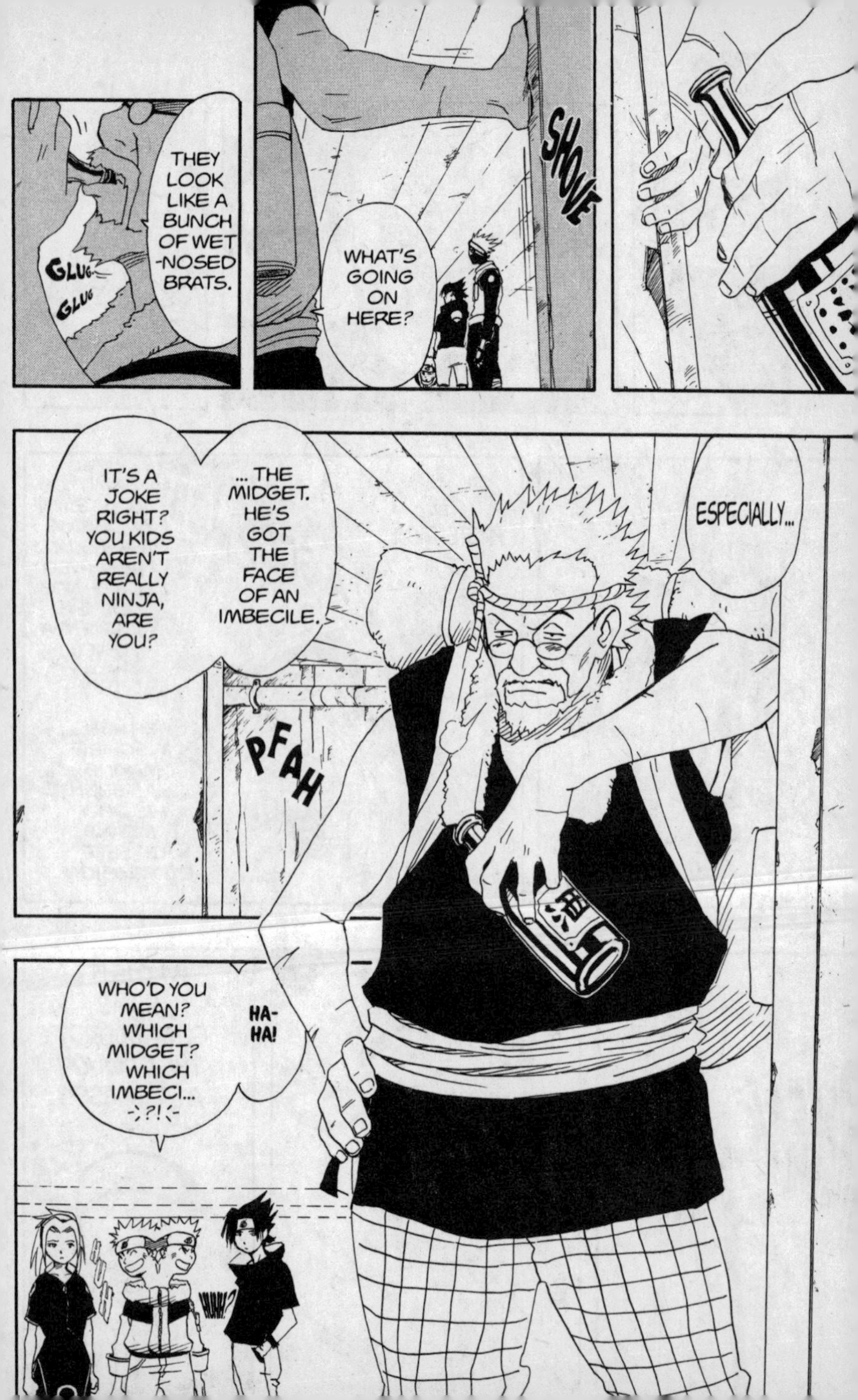
SHOVE
WHAT'S GOING ON HERE?
THEY LOOK LIKE A BUNCH OF WET-NOSED BRATS.
GLUG GLUG
ESPECIALLY...
... THE MIDGET. HE'S GOT THE FACE OF AN IMBECILE.
IT'S A JOKE RIGHT? YOU KIDS AREN'T REALLY NINJA, ARE YOU?
PFAH
HA-HA!
WHO'D YOU MEAN? WHICH MIDGET? WHICH IMBECI... -?!-

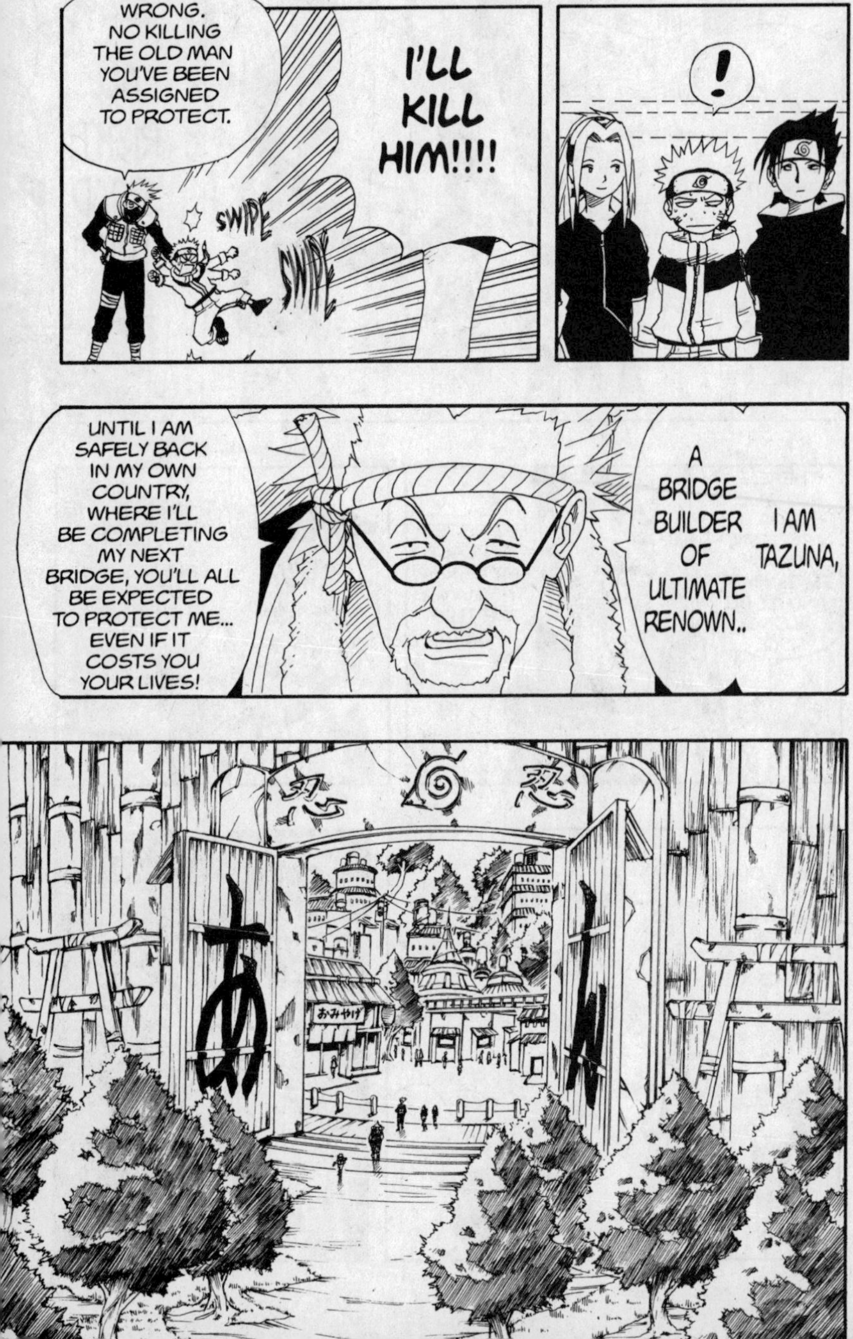
!
I'LL KILL HIM!!!!
SWIPE
SWIPE
WRONG. NO KILLING THE OLD MAN YOU'VE BEEN ASSIGNED TO PROTECT.
I AM TAZUNA, A BRIDGE BUILDER OF ULTIMATE RENOWN..
UNTIL I AM SAFELY BACK IN MY OWN COUNTRY, WHERE I'LL BE COMPLETING MY NEXT BRIDGE, YOU'LL ALL BE EXPECTED TO PROTECT ME... EVEN IF IT COSTS YOU YOUR LIVES!
おみやげ

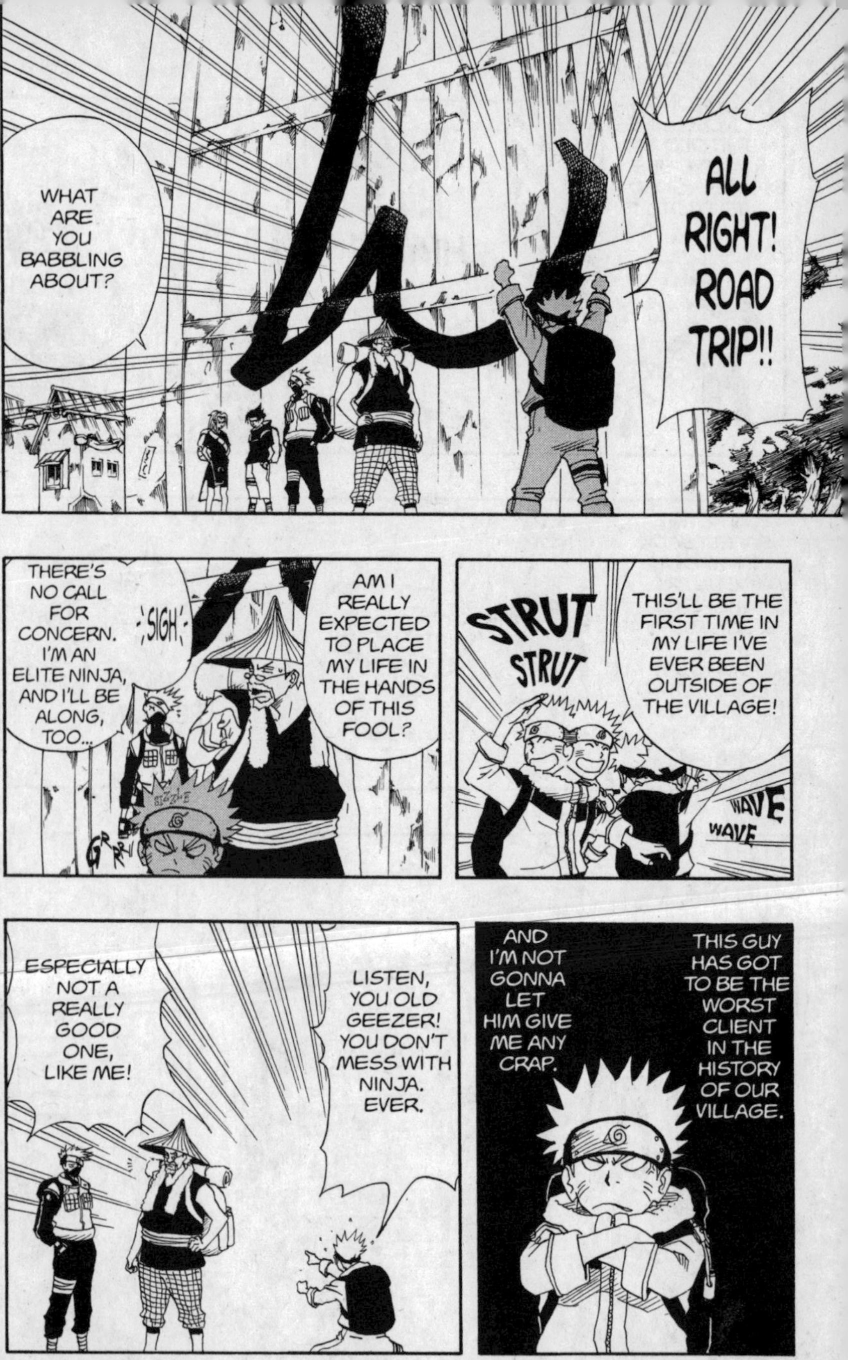

ALL RIGHT! ROAD TRIP!!
WHAT ARE YOU BABBLING ABOUT?
STRUT
STRUT
THIS'LL BE THE FIRST TIME IN MY LIFE I'VE EVER BEEN OUTSIDE OF THE VILLAGE!
WAVE
WAVE
AM I REALLY EXPECTED TO PLACE MY LIFE IN THE HANDS OF THIS FOOL?
SIGH
THERE'S NO CALL FOR CONCERN. I'M AN ELITE NINJA, AND I'LL BE ALONG, TOO...
THIS GUY HAS GOT TO BE THE WORST CLIENT IN THE HISTORY OF OUR VILLAGE.
AND I'M NOT GONNA LET HIM GIVE ME ANY CRAP.
LISTEN, YOU OLD GEEZER! YOU DON'T MESS WITH NINJA. EVER.
ESPECIALLY NOT A REALLY GOOD ONE, LIKE ME!

READ THIS WAY

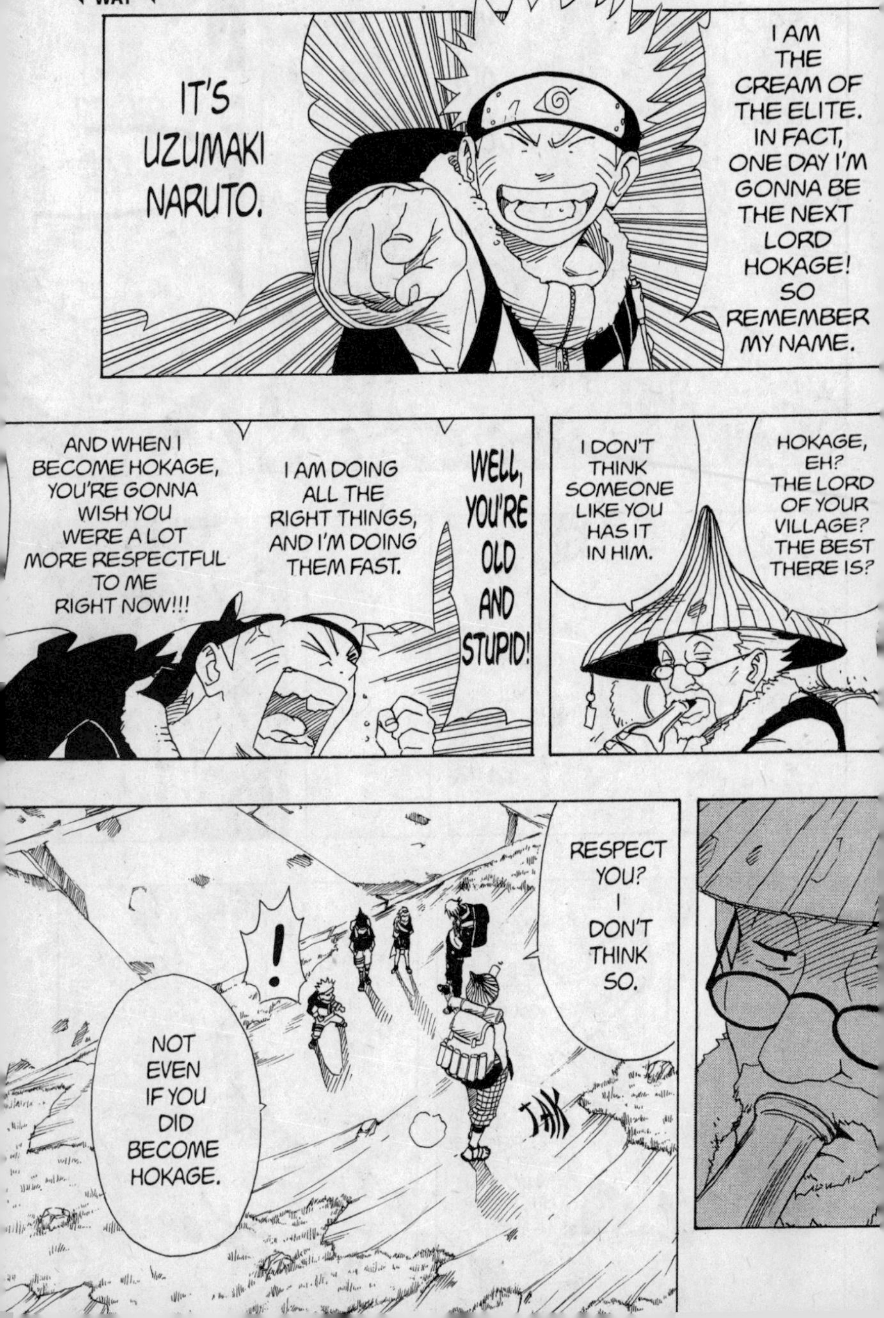

I AM THE CREAM OF THE ELITE. IN FACT, ONE DAY I'M GONNA BE THE NEXT LORD HOKAGE! SO REMEMBER MY NAME.
IT'S UZUMAKI NARUTO.
HOKAGE, EH? THE LORD OF YOUR VILLAGE? THE BEST THERE IS?
I DON'T THINK SOMEONE LIKE YOU HAS IT IN HIM.
WELL, YOU'RE OLD AND STUPID!
I AM DOING ALL THE RIGHT THINGS, AND I'M DOING THEM FAST.
AND WHEN I BECOME HOKAGE, YOU'RE GONNA WISH YOU WERE A LOT MORE RESPECTFUL TO ME RIGHT NOW!!!
RESPECT YOU? I DON'T THINK SO.
!
TAK
NOT EVEN IF YOU DID BECOME HOKAGE.

READ THIS WAY

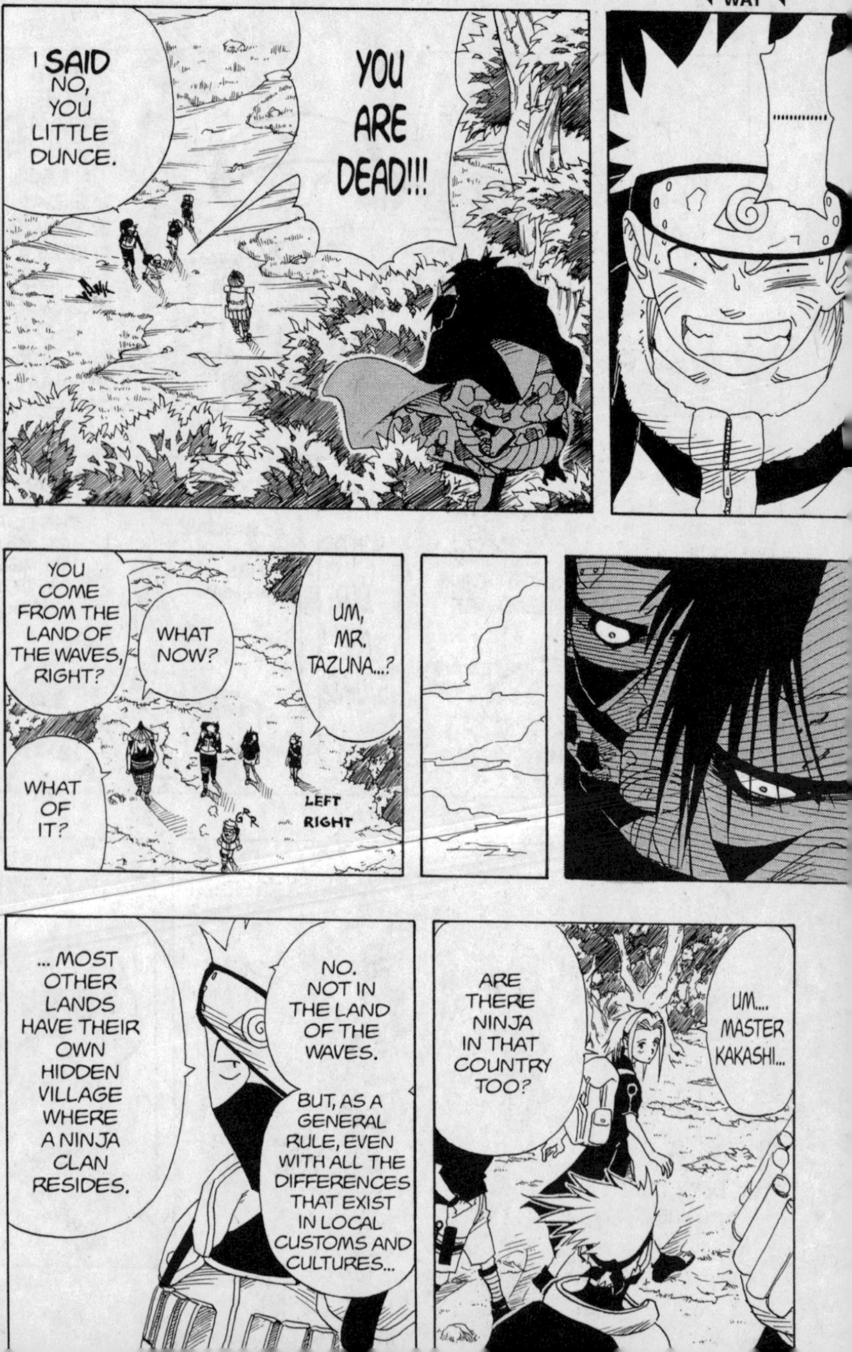
....
YOU ARE DEAD!!!
I SAID NO, YOU LITTLE DUNCE.
UM, MR. TAZUNA...?
WHAT NOW?
YOU COME FROM THE LAND OF THE WAVES, RIGHT?
WHAT OF IT?
LEFT
RIGHT
UM.... MASTER KAKASHI...
ARE THERE NINJA IN THAT COUNTRY TOO?
NO. NOT IN THE LAND OF THE WAVES.
BUT, AS A GENERAL RULE, EVEN WITH ALL THE DIFFERENCES THAT EXIST IN LOCAL CUSTOMS AND CULTURES...
... MOST OTHER LANDS HAVE THEIR OWN HIDDEN VILLAGE WHERE A NINJA CLAN RESIDES.

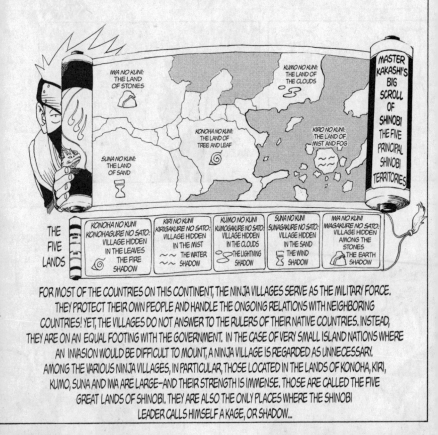

IWA NO KUNI: THE LAND OF STONES

KUMO NO KUNI: THE LAND OF THE CLOUDS

KONOHA NO KUNI: THE LAND OF TREE AND LEAF

KIRO NO KUNI: THE LAND OF MIST AND FOG

SUNA NO KUNI: THE LAND OF SAND

MASTER KAKASHI'S BIG SCROLL OF SHINOBI THE FIVE PRINCIPAL SHINOBI TERRITORIES

THE FIVE LANDS

KONOHA NO KUNI KONOHAGURE NO SATO: VILLAGE HIDDEN IN THE LEAVES THE FIRE SHADOW	KIRI NO KUNI KIRIGAKURE NO SATO: VILLAGE HIDDEN IN THE MIST ~~ ~~ THE WATER SHADOW	KUMO NO KUNI KUMOGAKURE NO SATO: VILLAGE HIDDEN IN THE CLOUDS THE LIGHTNING SHADOW	SUNA NO KUNI SUNAGAKURE NO SATO: VILLAGE HIDDEN IN THE SAND THE WIND SHADOW	IWA NO KUNI IWAGAKURE NO SATO: VILLAGE HIDDEN AMONG THE STONES THE EARTH SHADOW

FOR MOST OF THE COUNTRIES ON THIS CONTINENT, THE NINJA VILLAGES SERVE AS THE MILITARY FORCE. THEY PROTECT THEIR OWN PEOPLE AND HANDLE THE ONGOING RELATIONS WITH NEIGHBORING COUNTRIES! YET, THE VILLAGES DO NOT ANSWER TO THE RULERS OF THEIR NATIVE COUNTRIES. INSTEAD, THEY ARE ON AN EQUAL FOOTING WITH THE GOVERNMENT. IN THE CASE OF VERY SMALL ISLAND NATIONS WHERE AN INVASION WOULD BE DIFFICULT TO MOUNT, A NINJA VILLAGE IS REGARDED AS UNNECESSARY. AMONG THE VARIOUS NINJA VILLAGES, IN PARTICULAR, THOSE LOCATED IN THE LANDS OF KONOHA, KIRI, KUMO, SUNA AND IWA ARE LARGE—AND THEIR STRENGTH IS IMMENSE. THOSE ARE CALLED THE FIVE GREAT LANDS OF SHINOBI. THEY ARE ALSO THE ONLY PLACES WHERE THE SHINOBI LEADER CALLS HIMSELF A KAGE, OR SHADOW...

...THE ULTIMATE COMMANDERS OF ALL OF THE TENS OF THOUSANDS OF SHINOBI THROUGHOUT THE WORLD.

THOSE LEGENDARY LEADERS, HOKAGE—OR FIRE SHADOW—AND MIZUKAGE—OR WATER SHADOW—FOR EXAMPLE... PLUS RAIKAGE, KAZEKAGE, AND TSUCHIKAGE ARE KNOWN TO NINJA EVERYWHERE AS THE FIVE SHADOWS...

READ THIS WAY

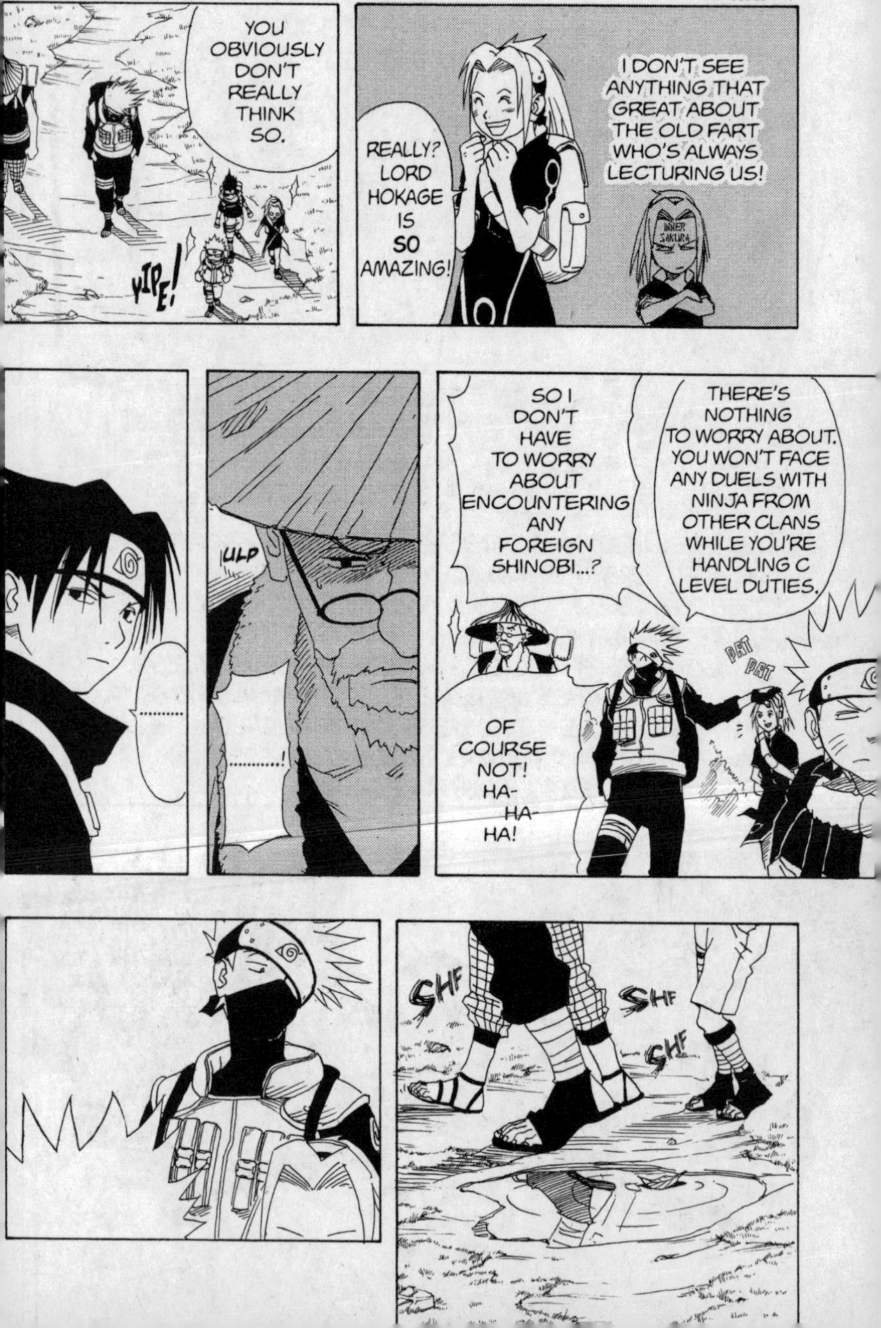
REALLY? LORD HOKAGE IS SO AMAZING!
I DON'T SEE ANYTHING THAT GREAT ABOUT THE OLD FART WHO'S ALWAYS LECTURING US!
INNER SAKURA
YOU OBVIOUSLY DON'T REALLY THINK SO.
YIPE!
THERE'S NOTHING TO WORRY ABOUT. YOU WON'T FACE ANY DUELS WITH NINJA FROM OTHER CLANS WHILE YOU'RE HANDLING C LEVEL DUTIES.
SO I DON'T HAVE TO WORRY ABOUT ENCOUNTERING ANY FOREIGN SHINOBI...?
PAT PAT
OF COURSE NOT! HA-HA-HA!
ULP
..........!
....
SHF
SHF
SHF

READ THIS WAY

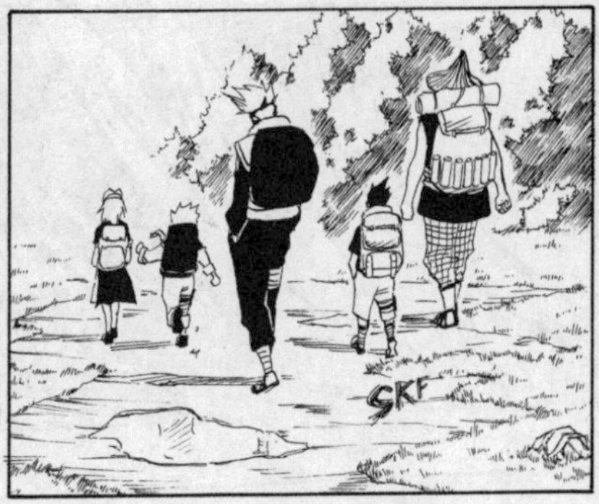
SKF

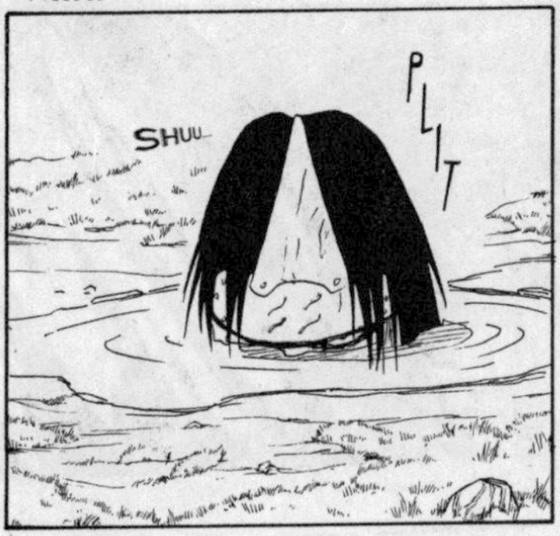
PLIT
SHUU...

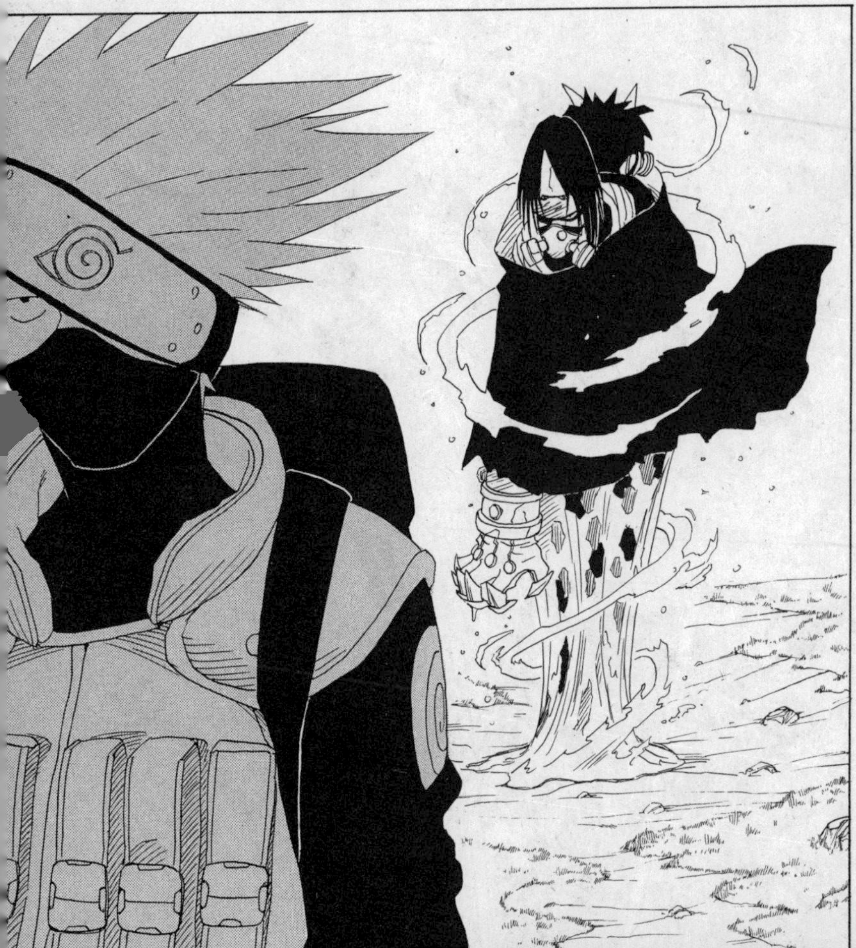

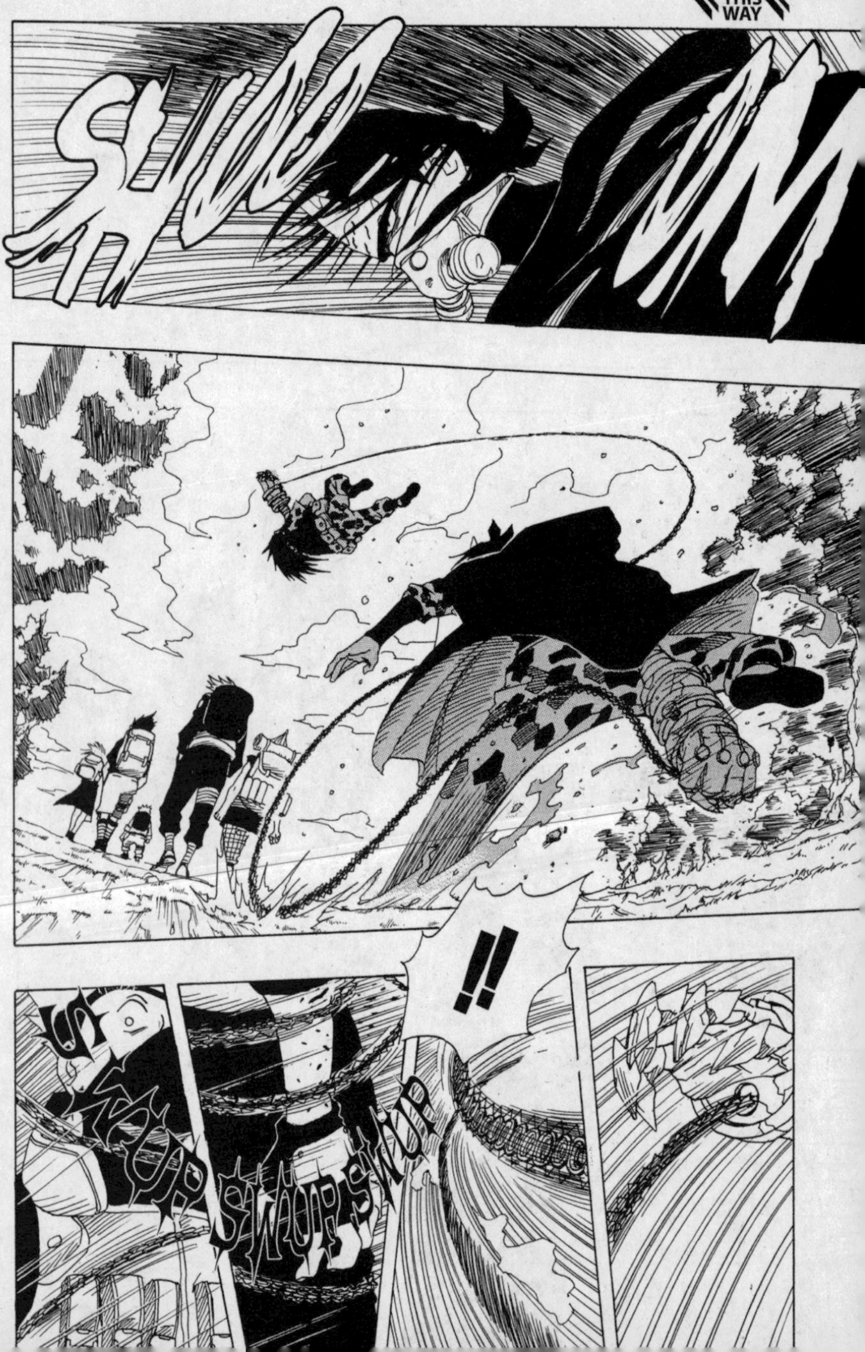
READ THIS WAY
SHUNG
SHUNG
!!
SWOOP SWOOP SWOOP

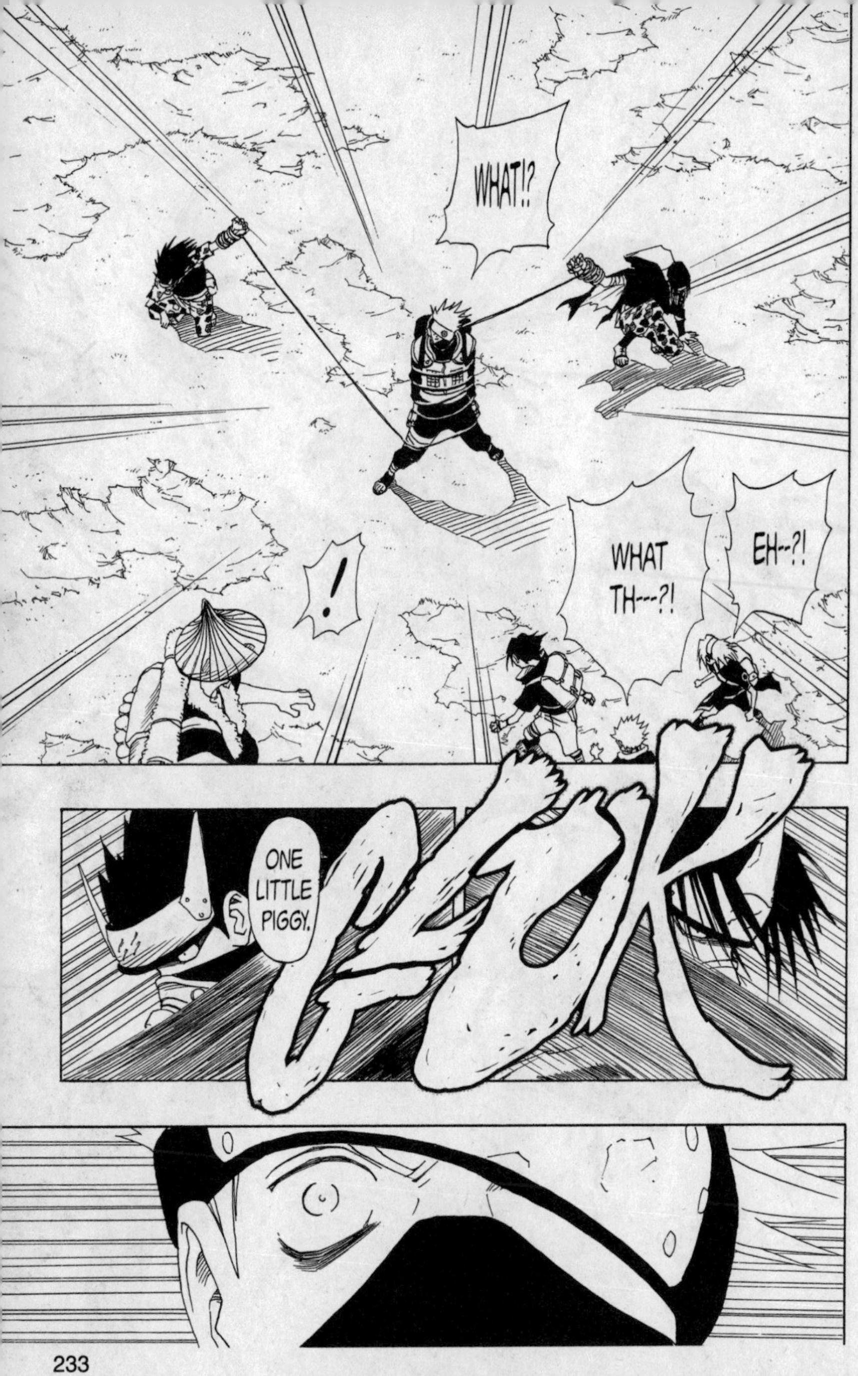
WHAT!?
EH--?!
WHAT TH---?!
!
ONE LITTLE PIGGY.

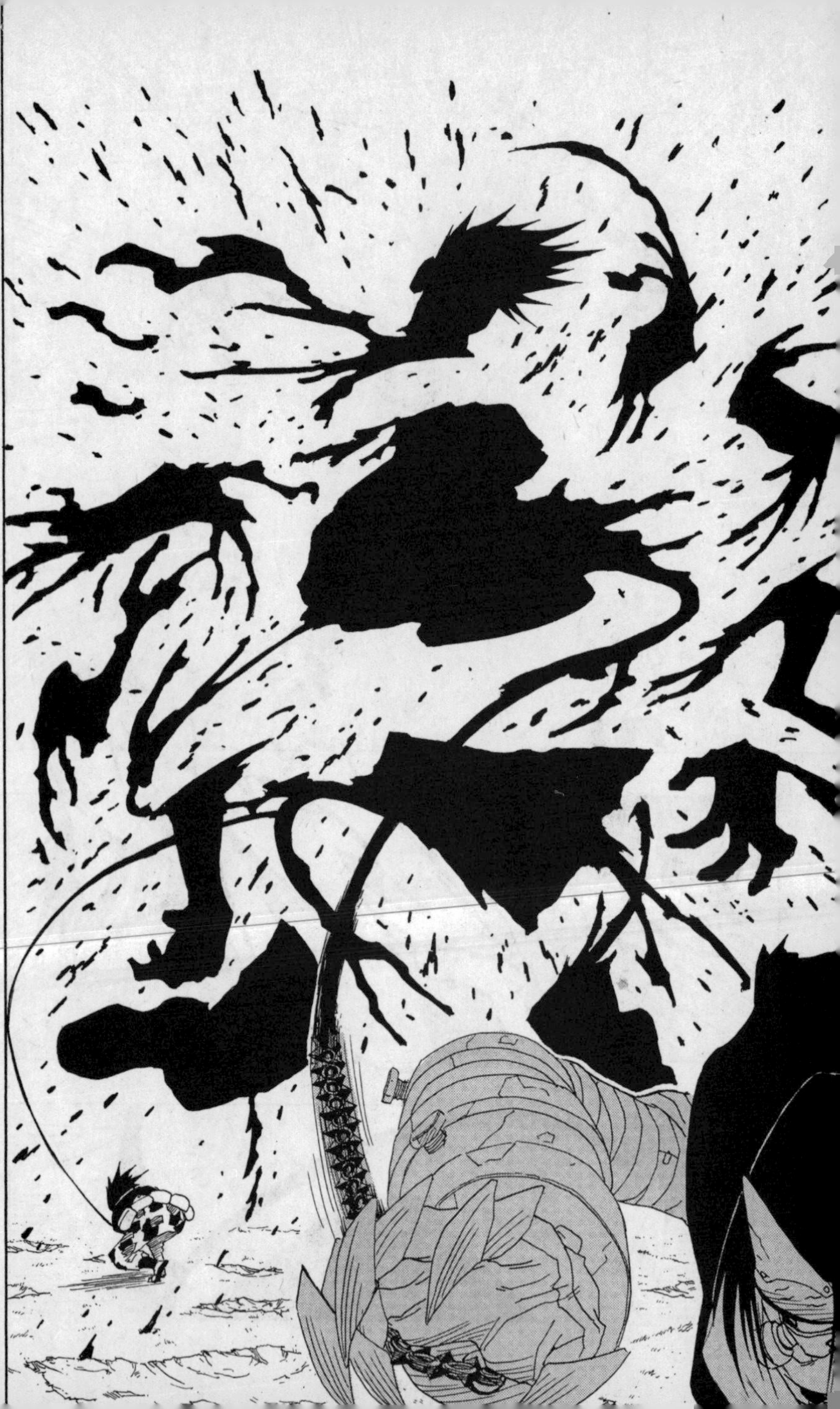

READ THIS WAY

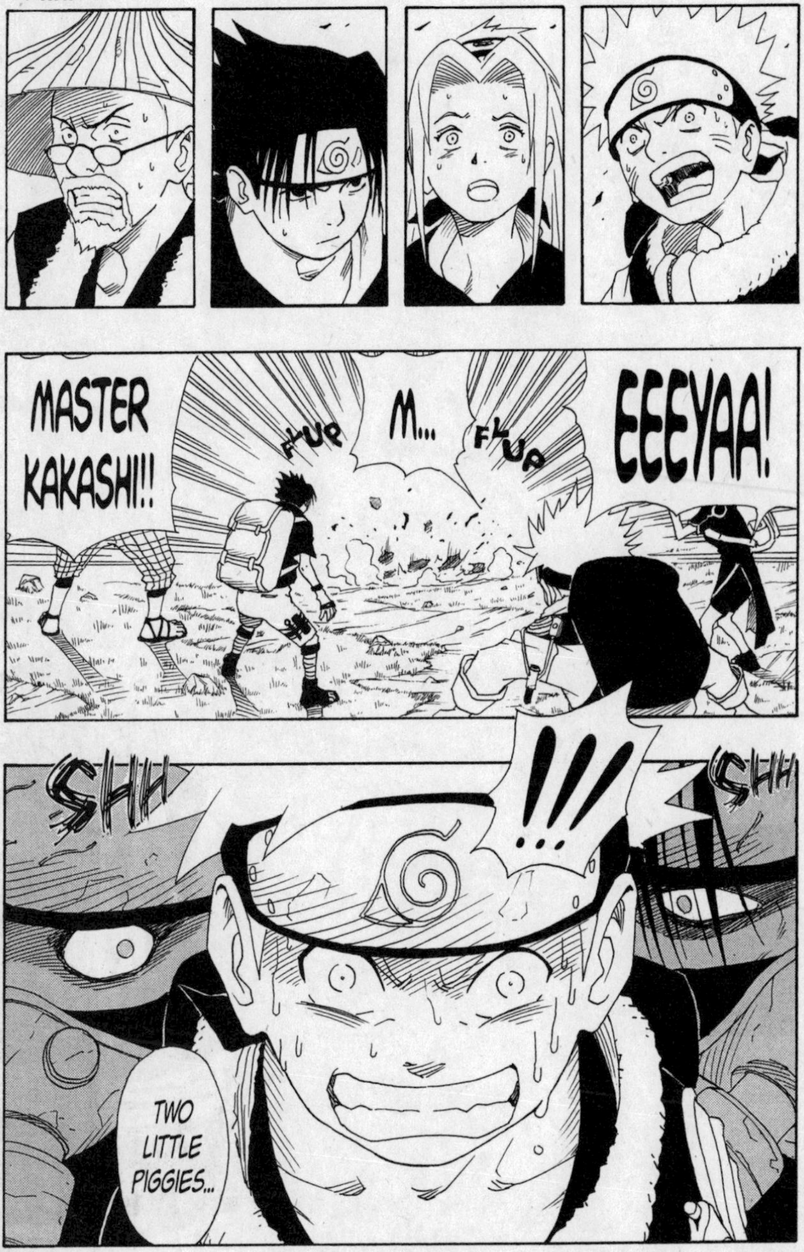
EEEYAA!
FLUP
M...
FLUP
MASTER KAKASHI!!
SHH
!!...
SHH
TWO LITTLE PIGGIES...

Number 10: Target #2

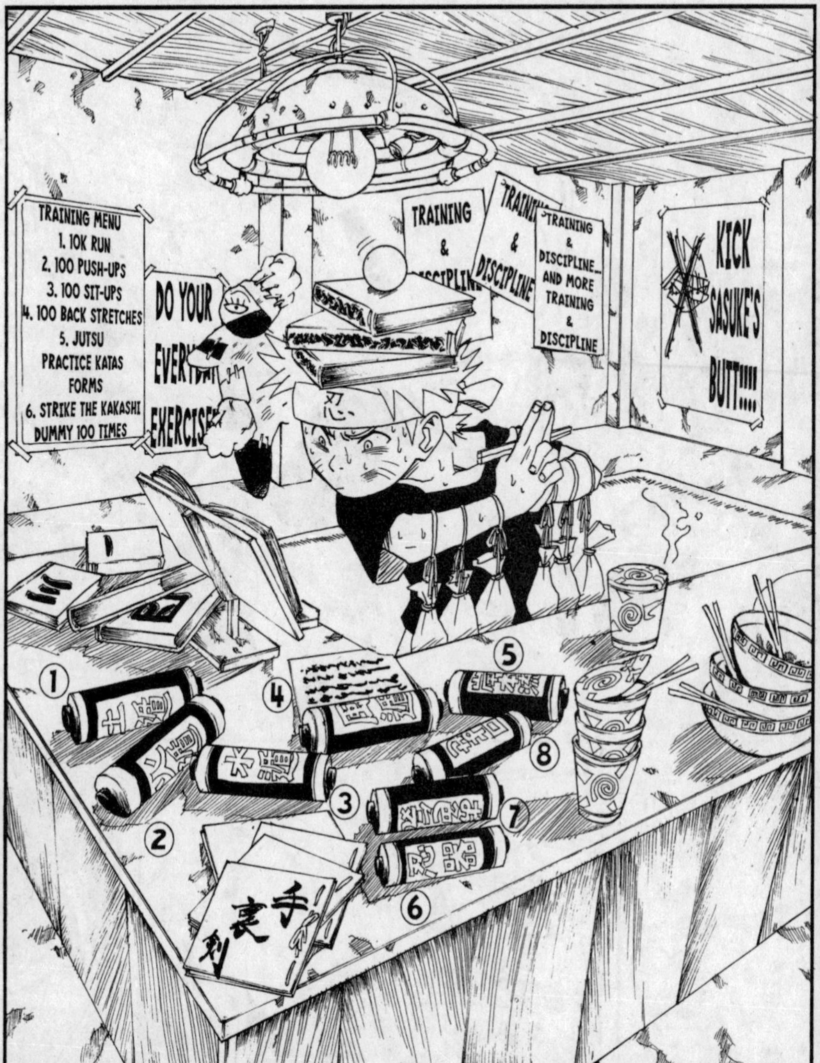
TRAINING MENU
1. 10K RUN
2. 100 PUSH-UPS
3. 100 SIT-UPS
4. 100 BACK STRETCHES
5. JUTSU PRACTICE KATAS FORMS
6. STRIKE THE KAKASHI DUMMY 100 TIMES
DO YOUR EVERYDAY EXERCISES
TRAINING & DISCIPLINE
TRAINING & DISCIPLINE
TRAINING & DISCIPLINE... AND MORE TRAINING & DISCIPLINE
KICK SASUKE'S BUTT!!!!
1
2
3
4
5
6
7
8

SCROLLS: (1) EARTH STYLE (2) FIRE STYLE (3) WATER STYLE (4) WIND STYLE (5) KISHIMOTO TECHNIQUE (6) NINJA WEAPONRY (7) NINJA CENTERFOLD (8) SUMMONING

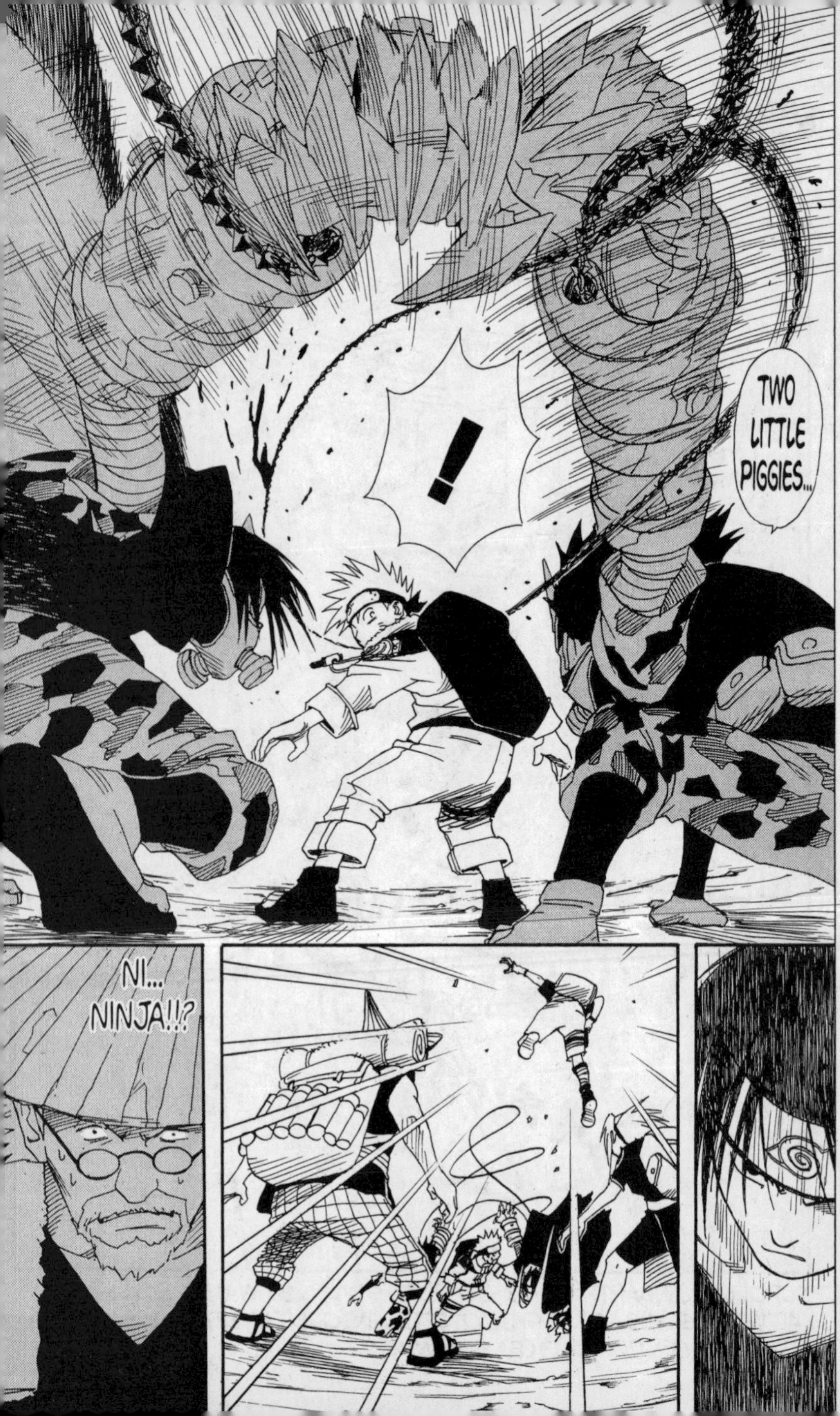
TWO LITTLE PIGGIES...
!
NI... NINJA!!?

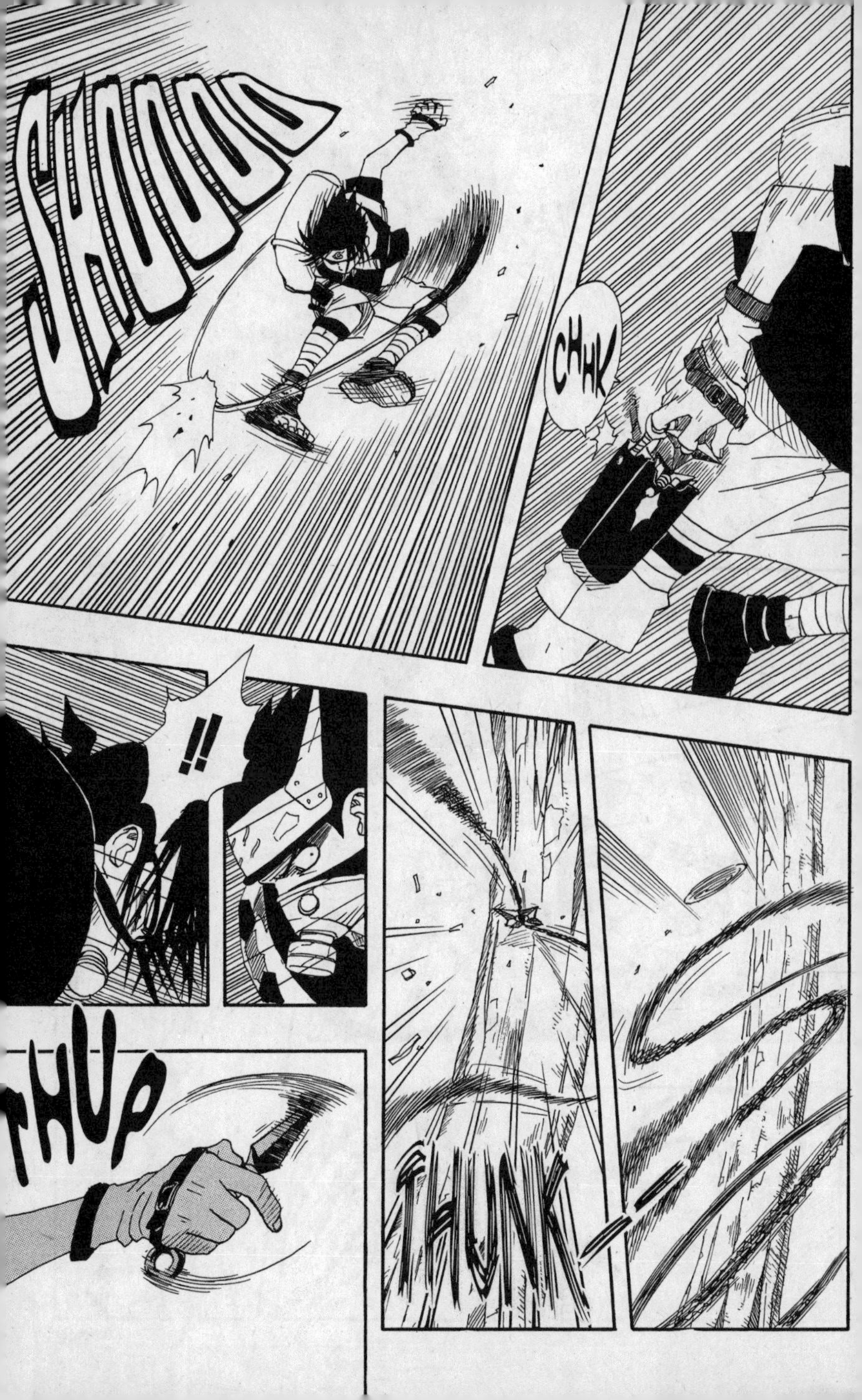
CHHK
SHOOOO
THUNK
!!
THUP

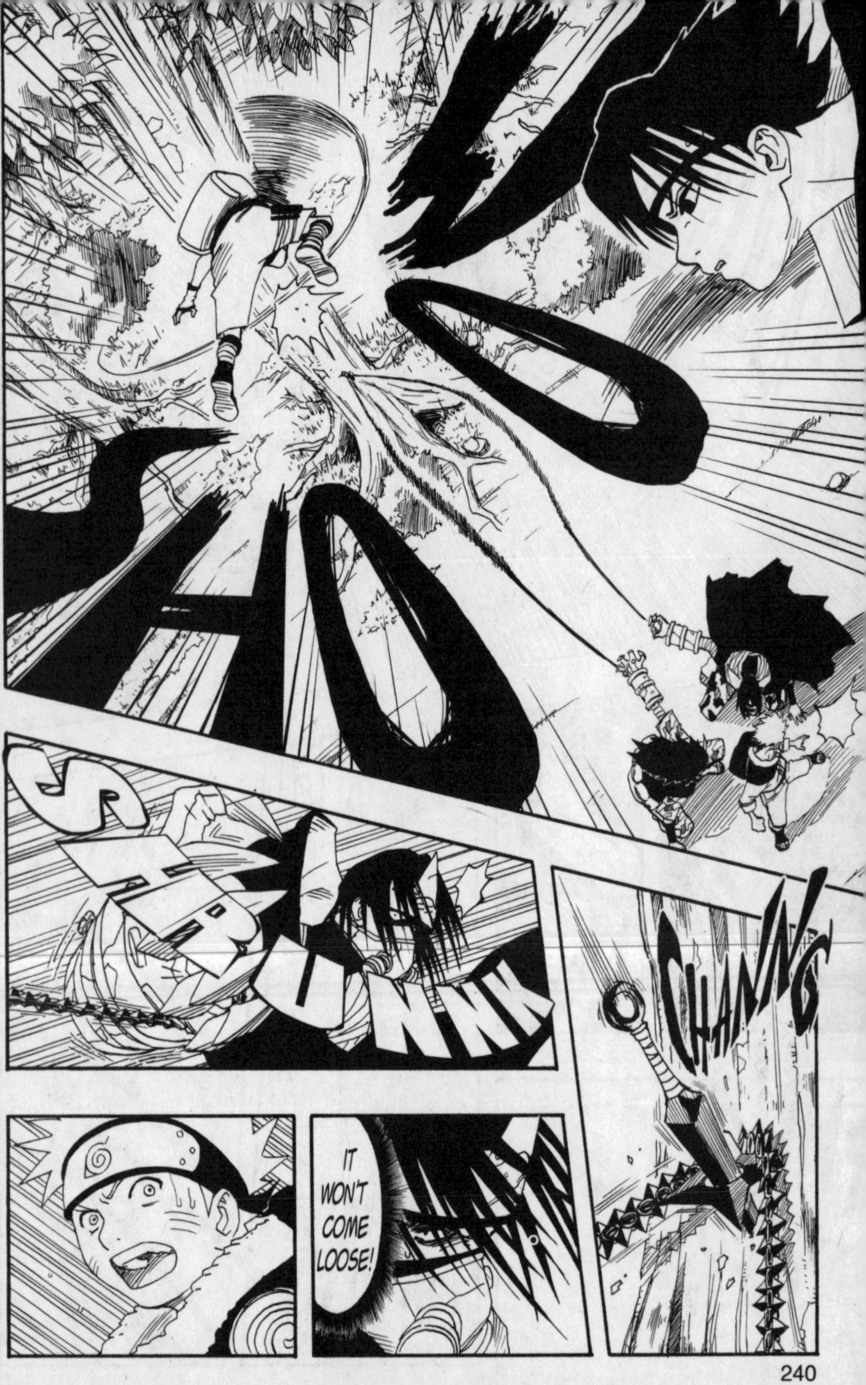

SHOO
SHUNK
CHANG
IT WON'T COME LOOSE!

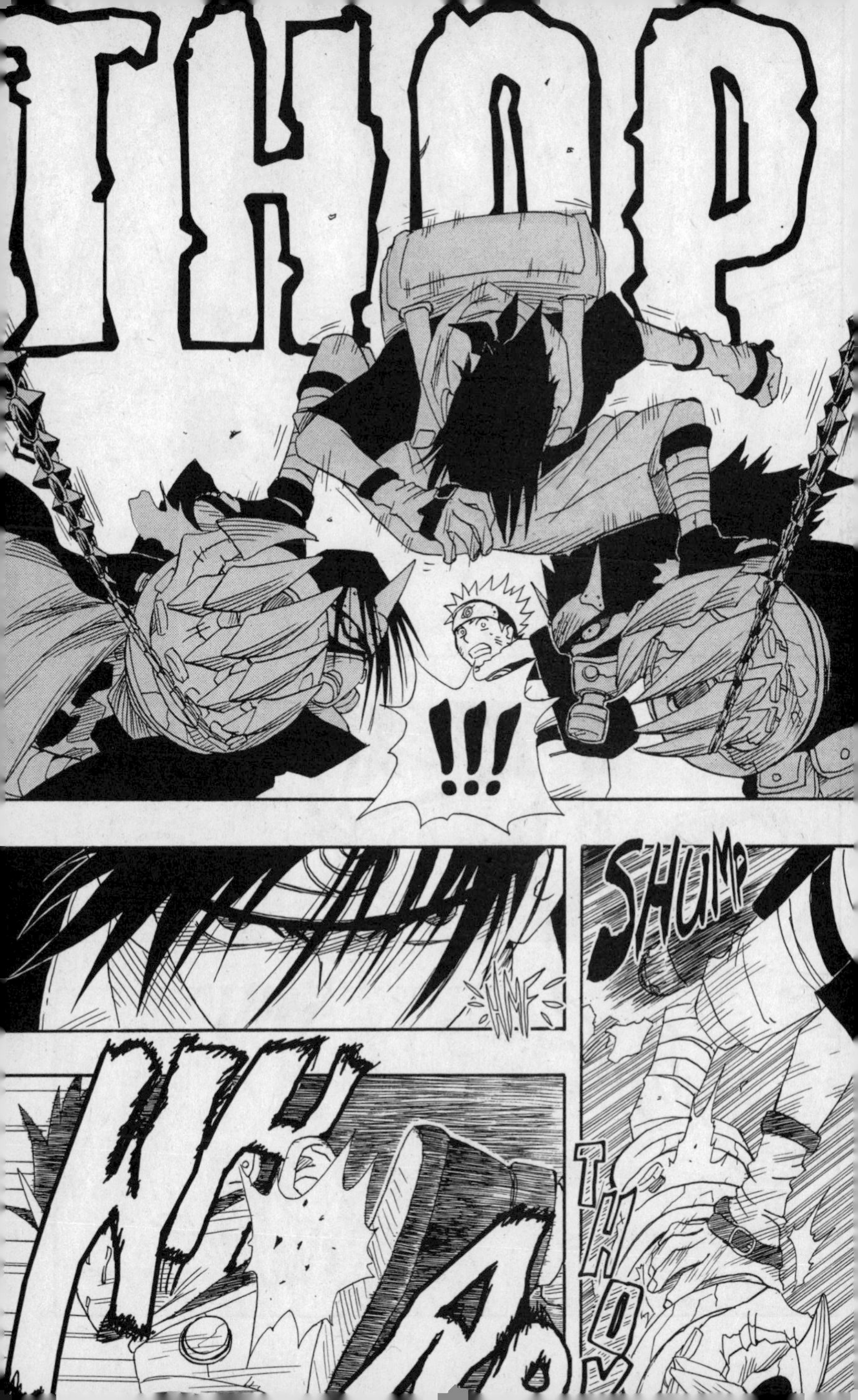
THOP
!!!
SHUMP
HMF
THOK
THWAK

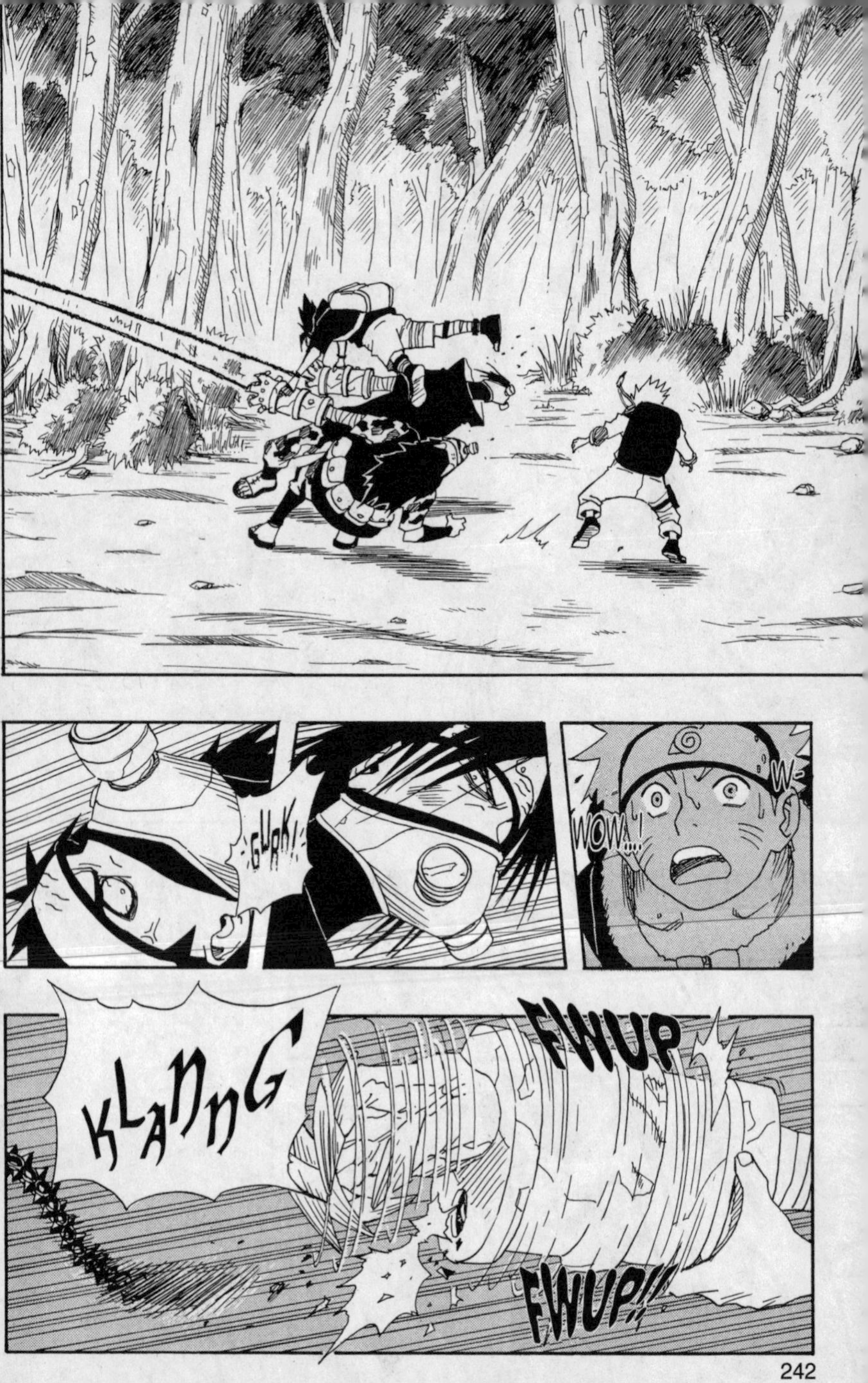
W-
WOW...!
GURK!
FWUP
KLANNG
FWUP!!

READ THIS WAY

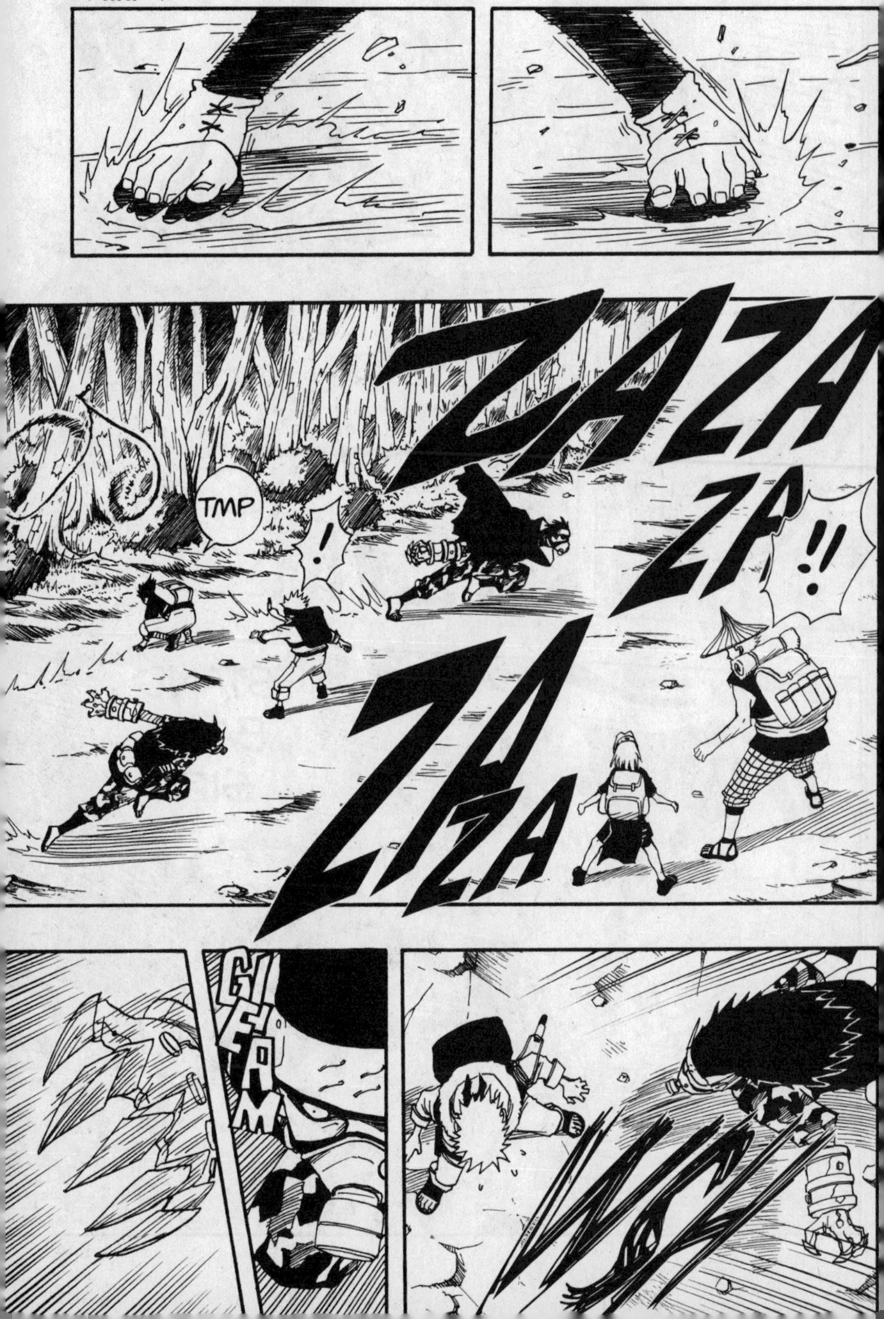
ZAZA
ZA
!!
TMP
!
ZA ZA ZA
GLEAM

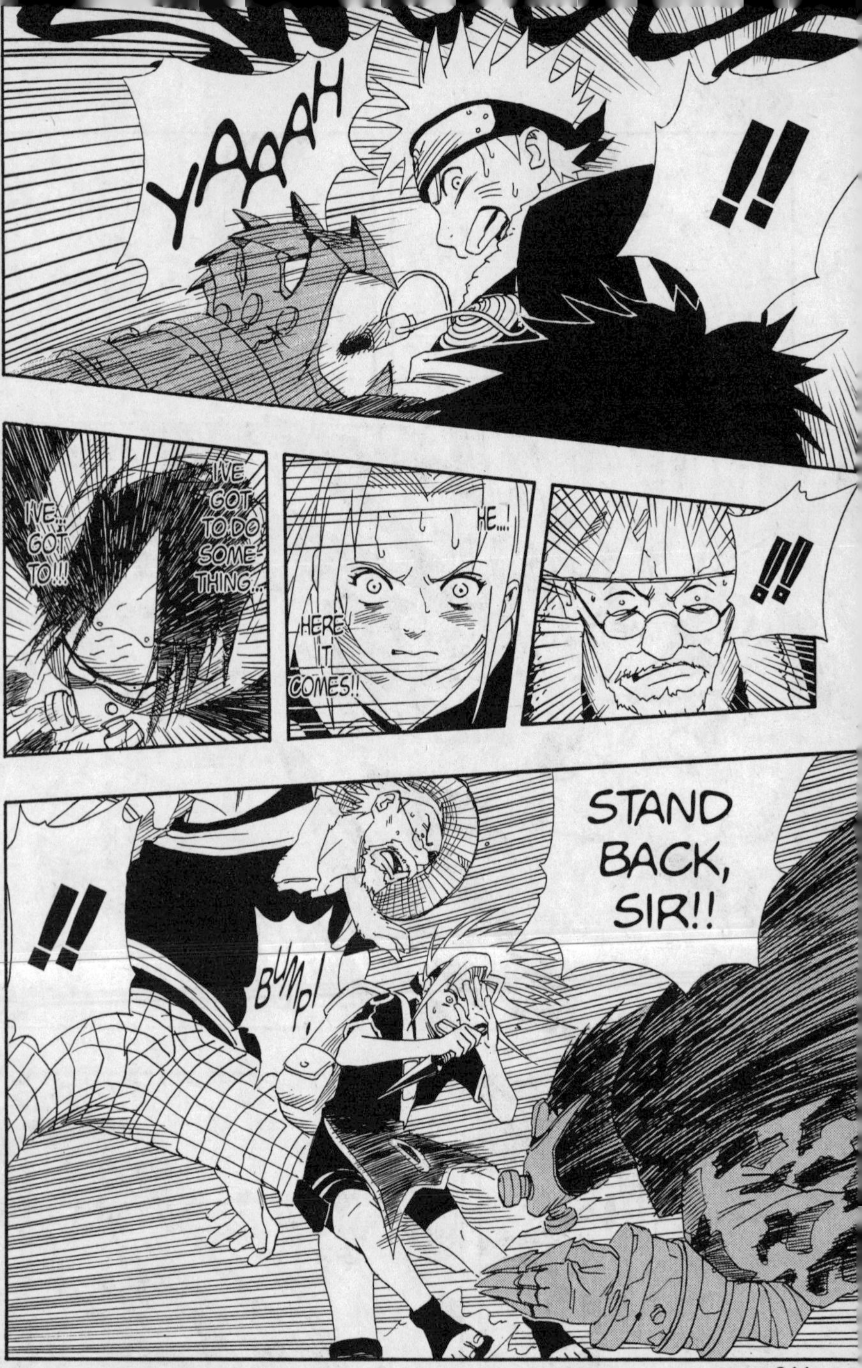
YAAAH
!!
!!!
HE...!
HERE IT COMES!!
I'VE GOT TO DO SOMETHING...
I'VE... GOT TO!!!
STAND BACK, SIR!!
!!
BUMP!

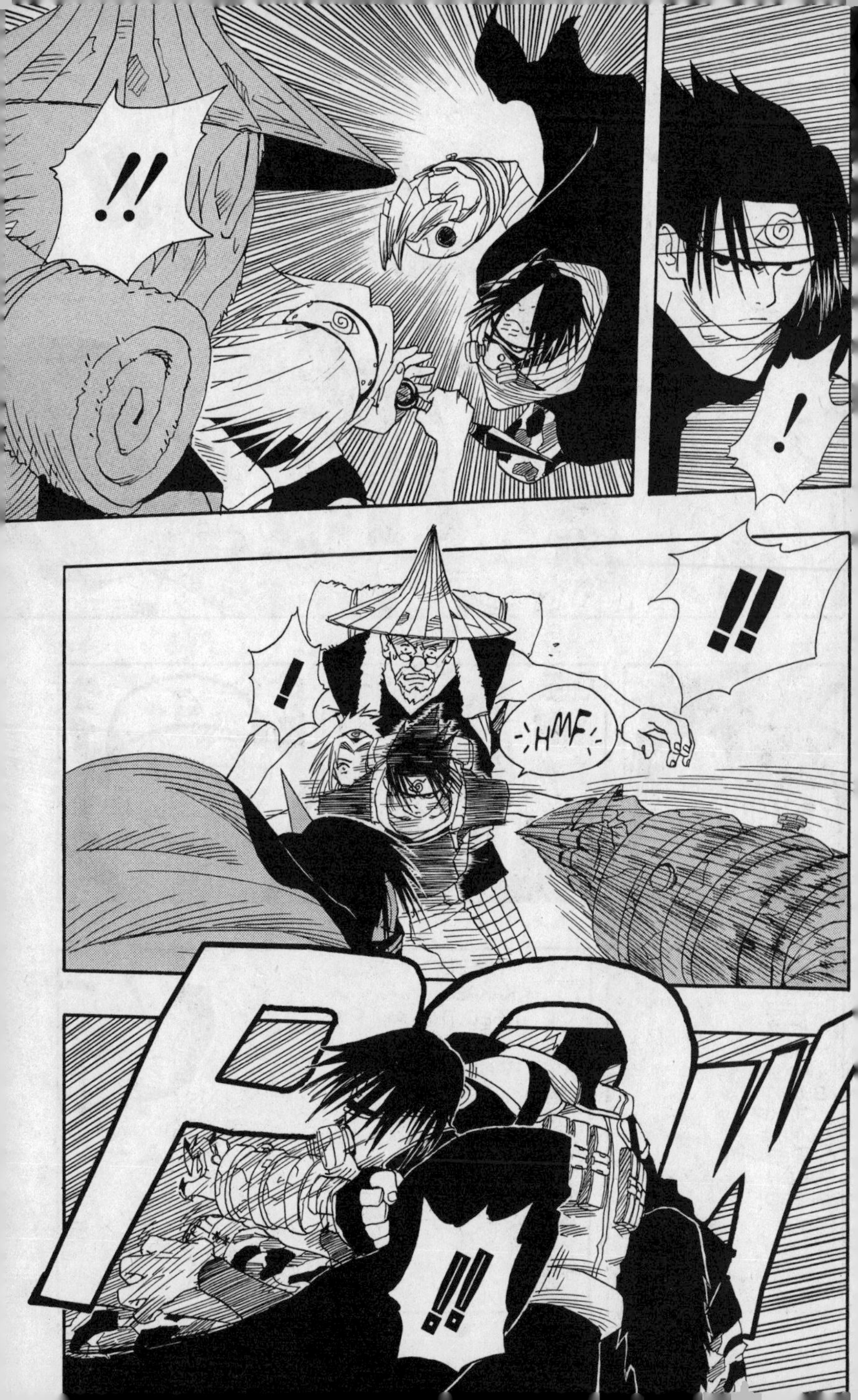
!
!!
!!
HMF
!
POW
!!

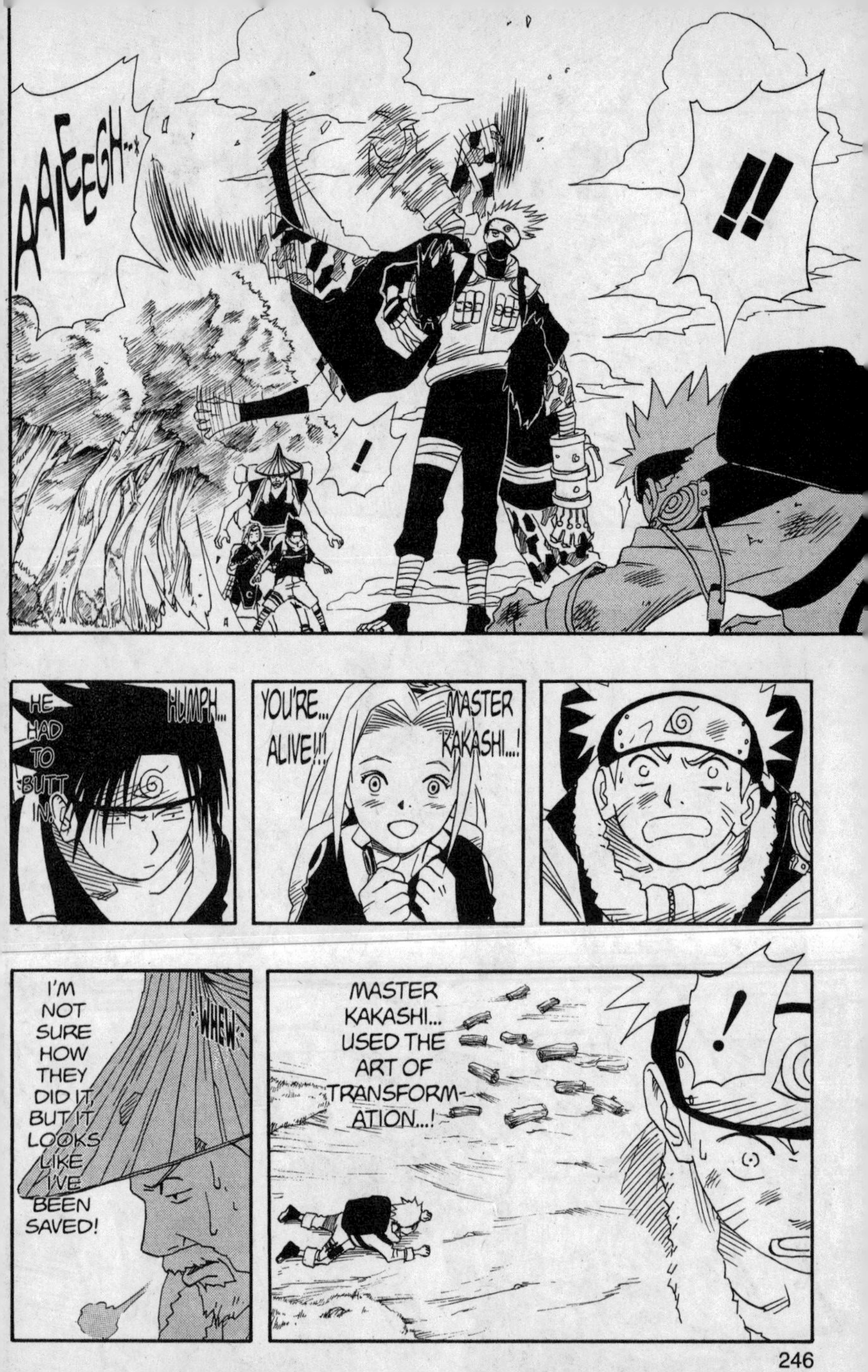
!!
AAIEEGH...
!
MASTER KAKASHI...!
YOU'RE... ALIVE!!!
HUMPH...
HE HAD TO BUTT IN.
!
MASTER KAKASHI... USED THE ART OF TRANSFORM-ATION...!
WHEW
I'M NOT SURE HOW THEY DID IT, BUT IT LOOKS LIKE I'VE BEEN SAVED!

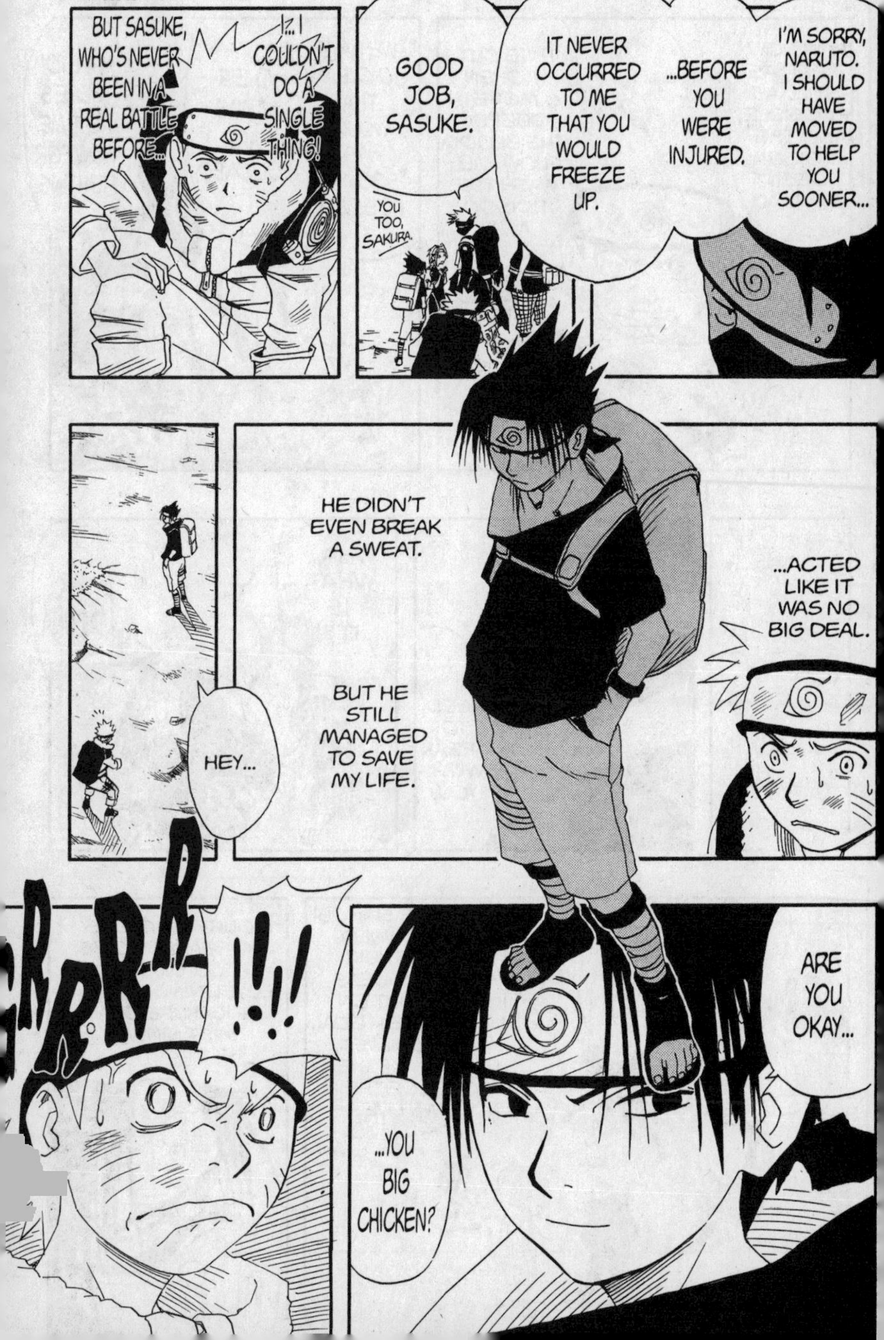
READ THIS WAY
I'M SORRY, NARUTO. I SHOULD HAVE MOVED TO HELP YOU SOONER...
...BEFORE YOU WERE INJURED.
IT NEVER OCCURRED TO ME THAT YOU WOULD FREEZE UP.
GOOD JOB, SASUKE.
YOU TOO, SAKURA.
I...I COULDN'T DO A SINGLE THING!
BUT SASUKE, WHO'S NEVER BEEN IN A REAL BATTLE BEFORE...
...ACTED LIKE IT WAS NO BIG DEAL.
HE DIDN'T EVEN BREAK A SWEAT.
BUT HE STILL MANAGED TO SAVE MY LIFE.
HEY...
ARE YOU OKAY...
...YOU BIG CHICKEN?
!!!
GRRRR

READ THIS WAY

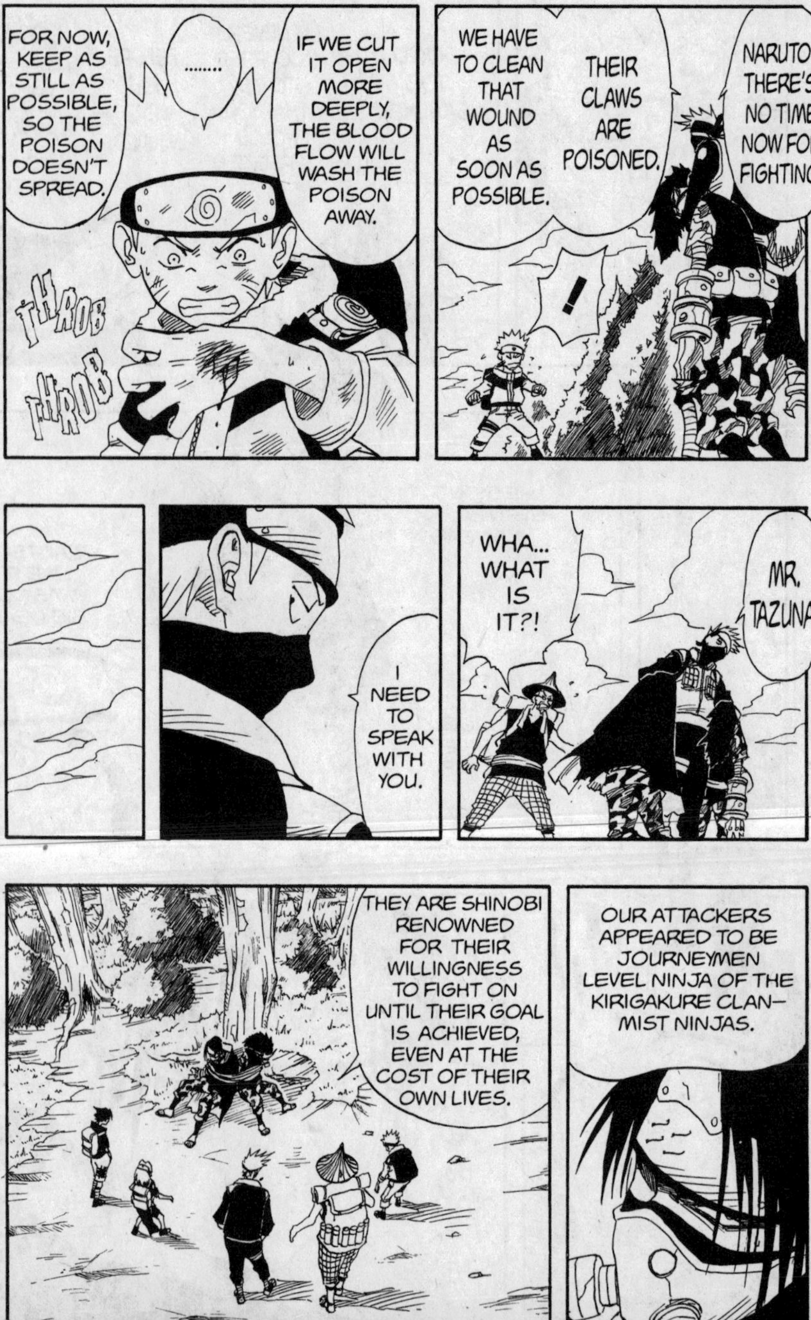
NARUTO! THERE'S NO TIME NOW FOR FIGHTING.
THEIR CLAWS ARE POISONED.
WE HAVE TO CLEAN THAT WOUND AS SOON AS POSSIBLE.
!
IF WE CUT IT OPEN MORE DEEPLY, THE BLOOD FLOW WILL WASH THE POISON AWAY.
....
FOR NOW, KEEP AS STILL AS POSSIBLE, SO THE POISON DOESN'T SPREAD.
THROB
THROB
MR. TAZUNA.
WHA... WHAT IS IT?!
I NEED TO SPEAK WITH YOU.
OUR ATTACKERS APPEARED TO BE JOURNEYMEN LEVEL NINJA OF THE KIRIGAKURE CLAN— MIST NINJAS.
THEY ARE SHINOBI RENOWNED FOR THEIR WILLINGNESS TO FIGHT ON UNTIL THEIR GOAL IS ACHIEVED, EVEN AT THE COST OF THEIR OWN LIVES.

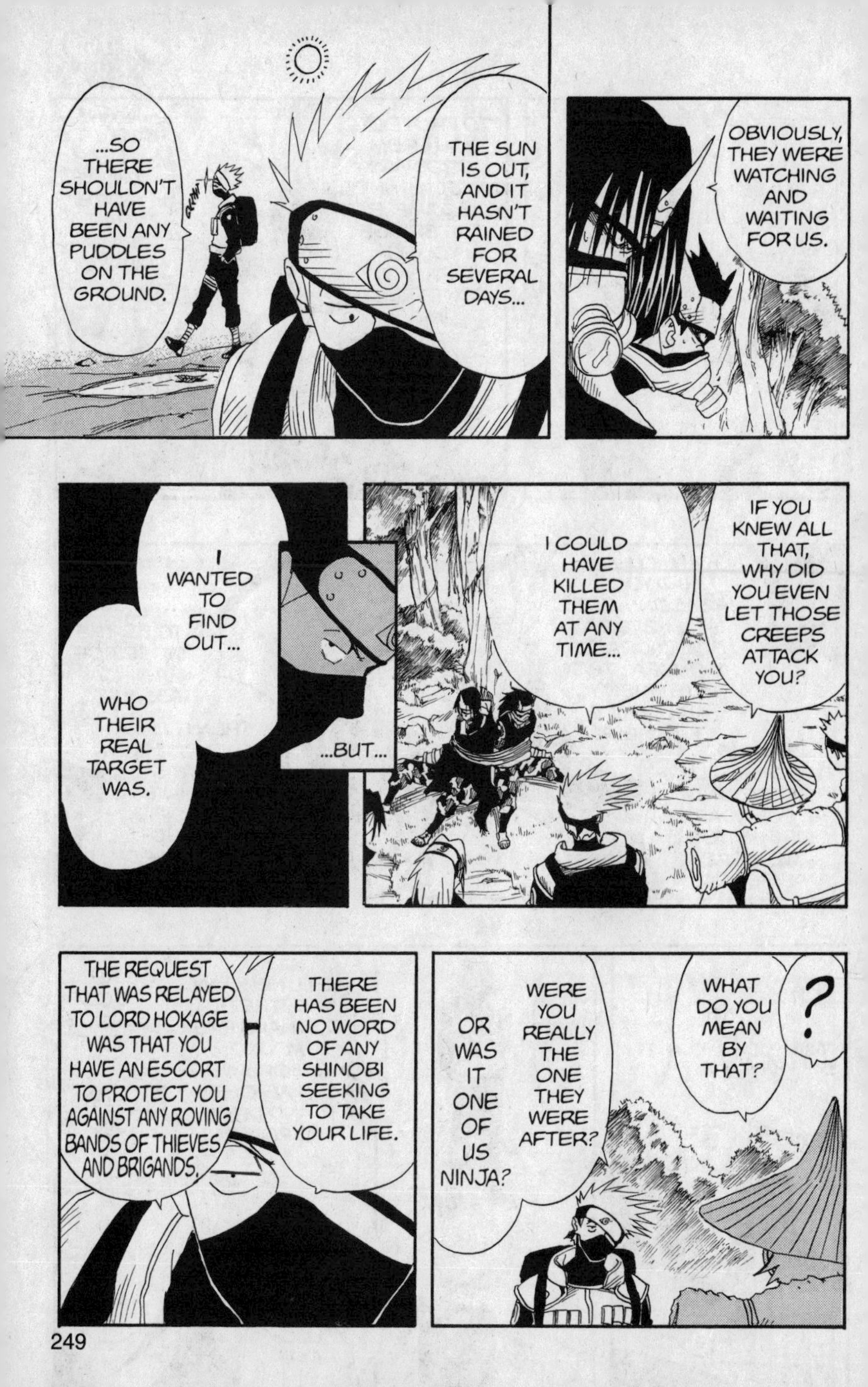
OBVIOUSLY, THEY WERE WATCHING AND WAITING FOR US.
THE SUN IS OUT, AND IT HASN'T RAINED FOR SEVERAL DAYS...
...SO THERE SHOULDN'T HAVE BEEN ANY PUDDLES ON THE GROUND.
IF YOU KNEW ALL THAT, WHY DID YOU EVEN LET THOSE CREEPS ATTACK YOU?
I COULD HAVE KILLED THEM AT ANY TIME...
...BUT...
I WANTED TO FIND OUT...
WHO THEIR REAL TARGET WAS.
?
WHAT DO YOU MEAN BY THAT?
WERE YOU REALLY THE ONE THEY WERE AFTER?
OR WAS IT ONE OF US NINJA?
THE REQUEST THAT WAS RELAYED TO LORD HOKAGE WAS THAT YOU HAVE AN ESCORT TO PROTECT YOU AGAINST ANY ROVING BANDS OF THIEVES AND BRIGANDS.
THERE HAS BEEN NO WORD OF ANY SHINOBI SEEKING TO TAKE YOUR LIFE.

READ THIS WAY

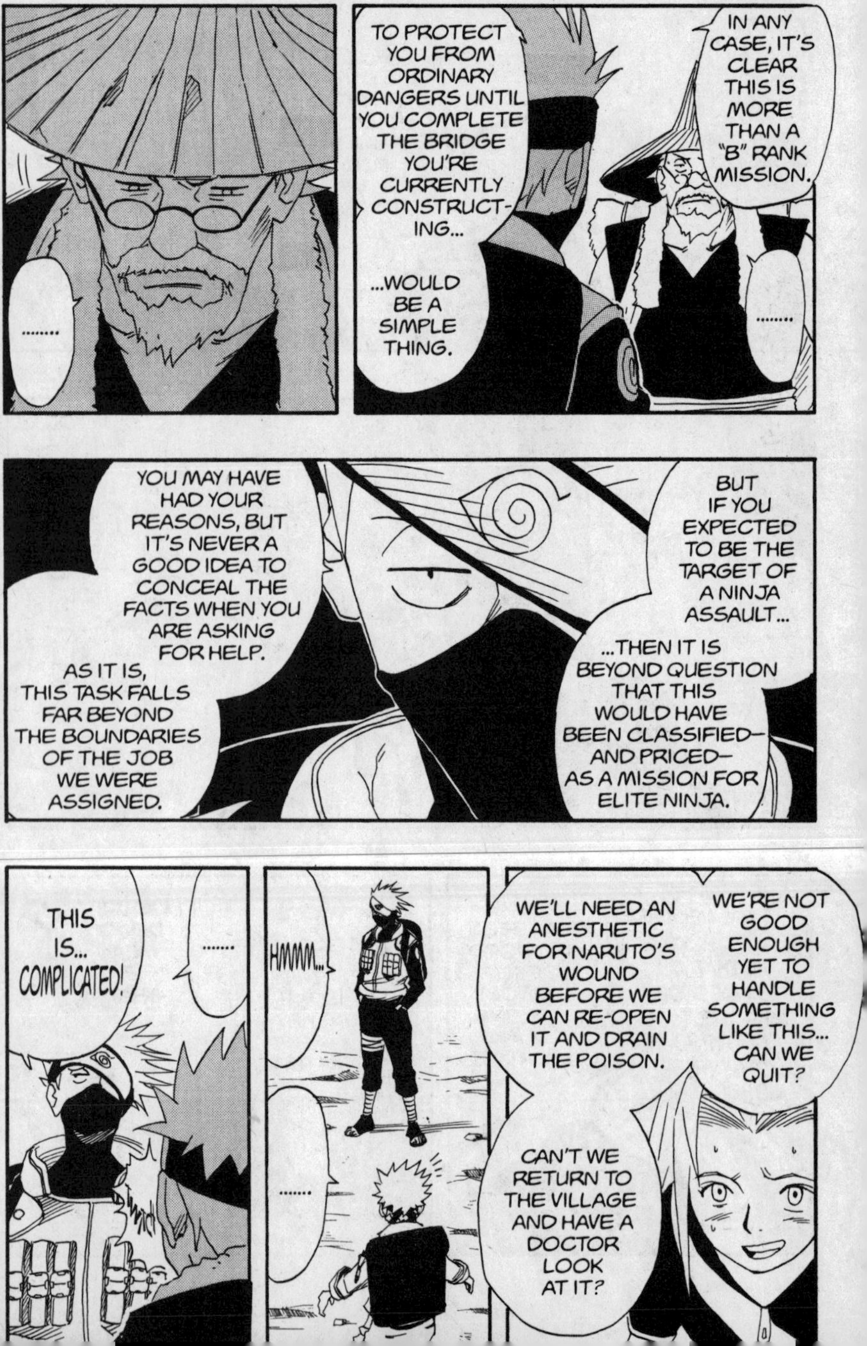
IN ANY CASE, IT'S CLEAR THIS IS MORE THAN A "B" RANK MISSION.
....
TO PROTECT YOU FROM ORDINARY DANGERS UNTIL YOU COMPLETE THE BRIDGE YOU'RE CURRENTLY CONSTRUCT-ING...
...WOULD BE A SIMPLE THING.
....
BUT IF YOU EXPECTED TO BE THE TARGET OF A NINJA ASSAULT...
...THEN IT IS BEYOND QUESTION THAT THIS WOULD HAVE BEEN CLASSIFIED— AND PRICED— AS A MISSION FOR ELITE NINJA.
YOU MAY HAVE HAD YOUR REASONS, BUT IT'S NEVER A GOOD IDEA TO CONCEAL THE FACTS WHEN YOU ARE ASKING FOR HELP.
AS IT IS, THIS TASK FALLS FAR BEYOND THE BOUNDARIES OF THE JOB WE WERE ASSIGNED.
WE'RE NOT GOOD ENOUGH YET TO HANDLE SOMETHING LIKE THIS... CAN WE QUIT?
WE'LL NEED AN ANESTHETIC FOR NARUTO'S WOUND BEFORE WE CAN RE-OPEN IT AND DRAIN THE POISON.
CAN'T WE RETURN TO THE VILLAGE AND HAVE A DOCTOR LOOK AT IT?
HMMM...
....
....
THIS IS... COMPLICATED!

READ THIS WAY

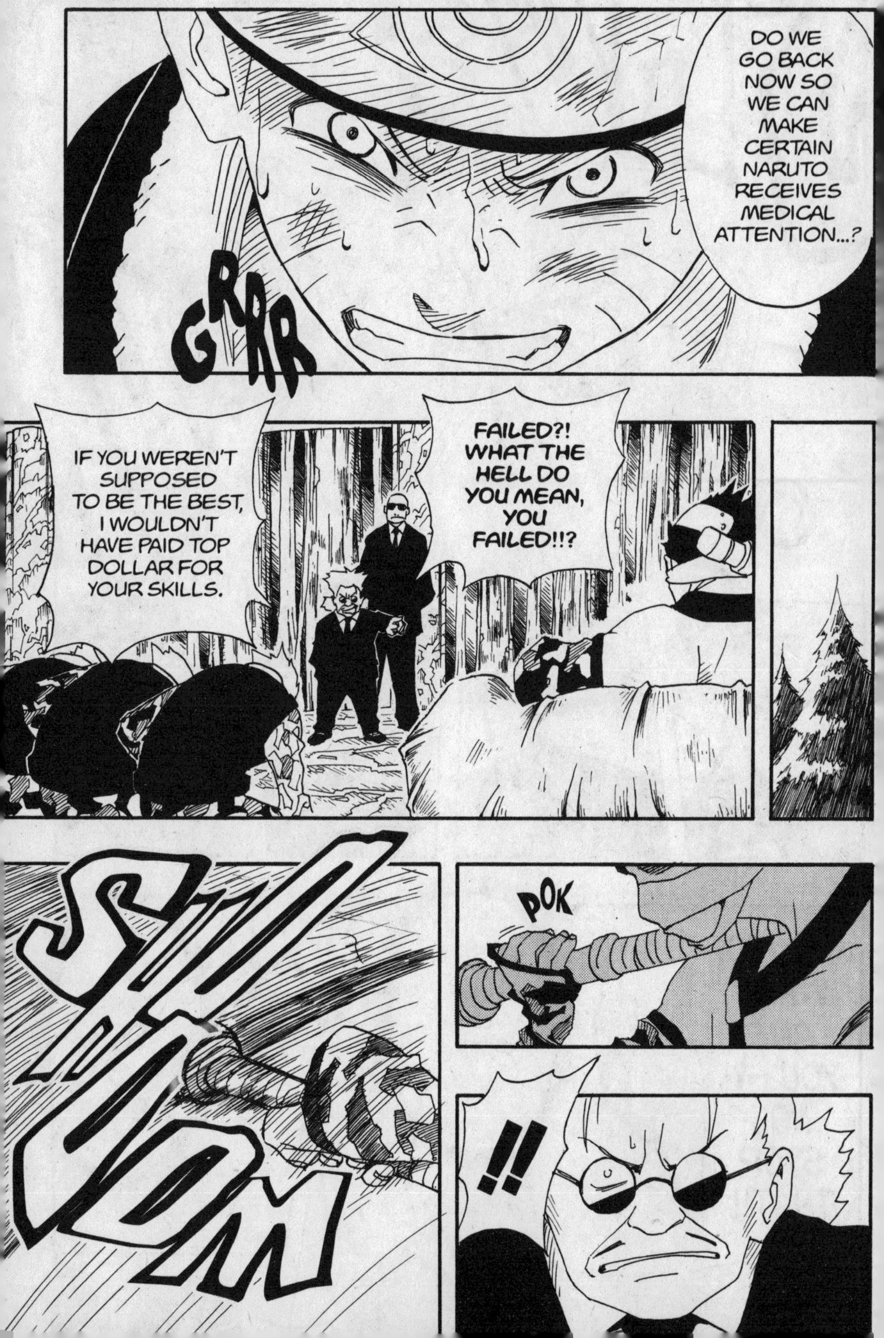
DO WE GO BACK NOW SO WE CAN MAKE CERTAIN NARUTO RECEIVES MEDICAL ATTENTION...?
GRRR
FAILED?! WHAT THE HELL DO YOU MEAN, YOU FAILED!!?
IF YOU WEREN'T SUPPOSED TO BE THE BEST, I WOULDN'T HAVE PAID TOP DOLLAR FOR YOUR SKILLS.
POK
!!
SHOOM

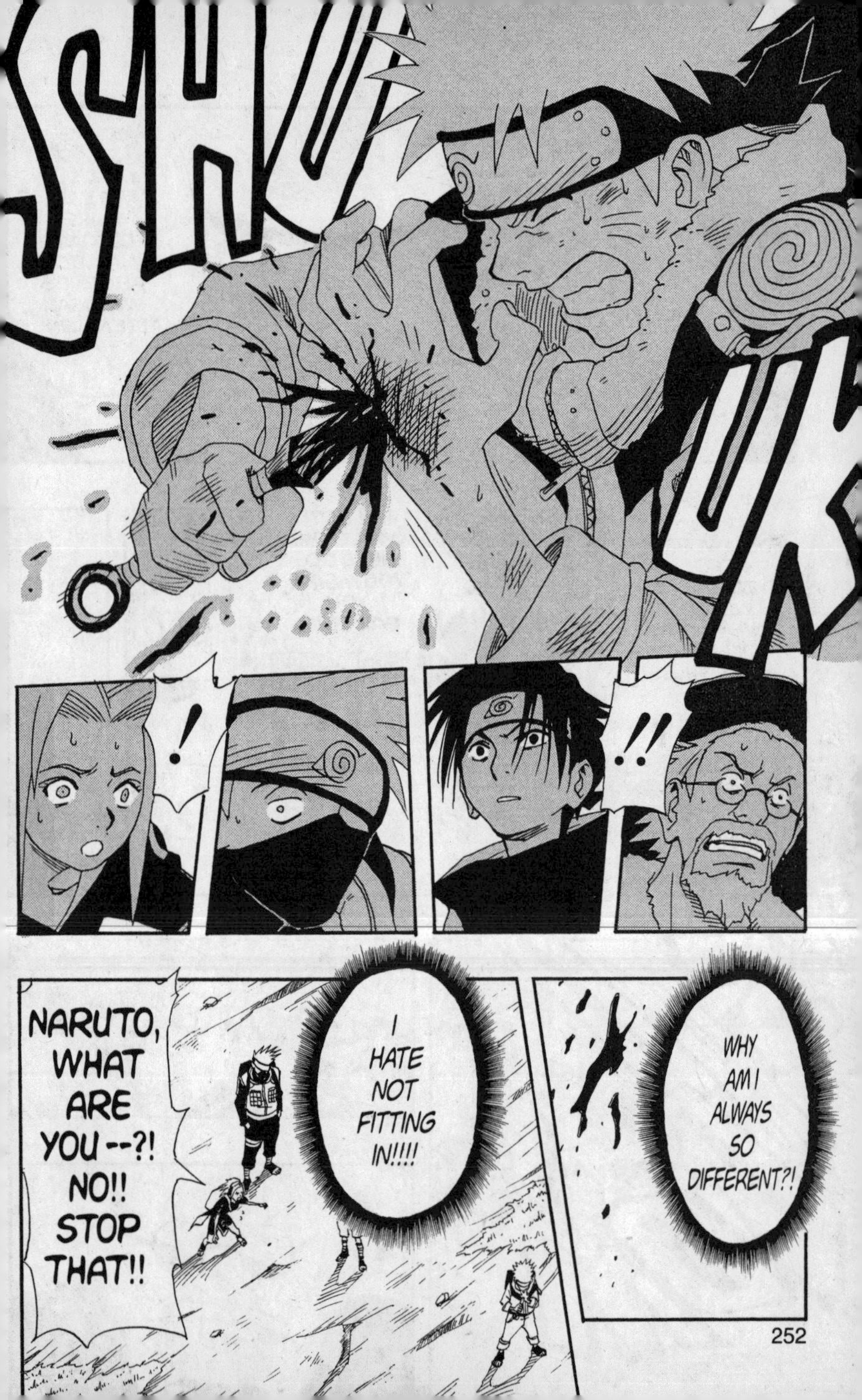
SHUUNK
!!
!
WHY AM I ALWAYS SO DIFFERENT?!
I HATE NOT FITTING IN!!!!
NARUTO, WHAT ARE YOU --?! NO!! STOP THAT!!

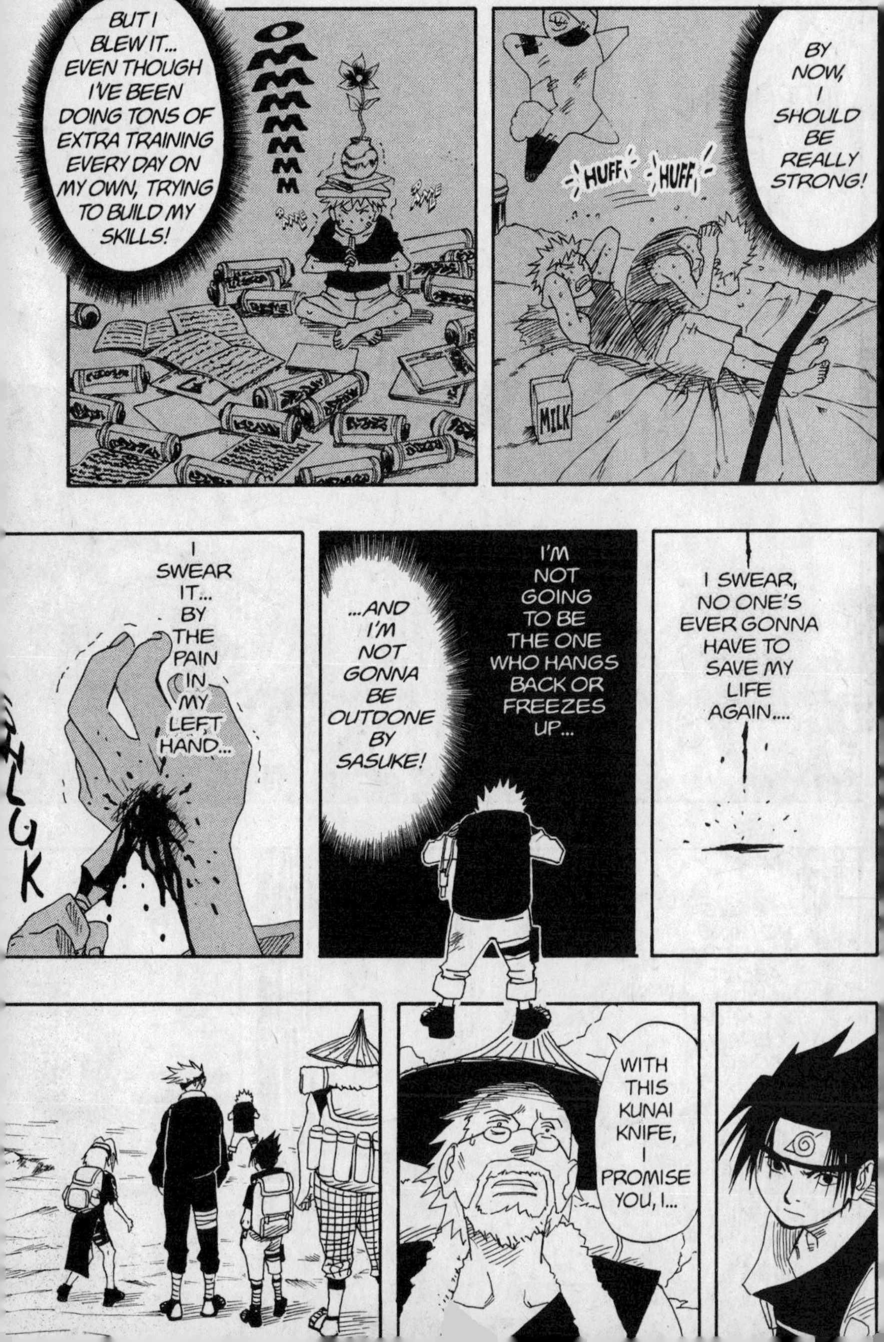
BY NOW, I SHOULD BE REALLY STRONG!
HUFF HUFF
BUT I BLEW IT... EVEN THOUGH I'VE BEEN DOING TONS OF EXTRA TRAINING EVERY DAY ON MY OWN, TRYING TO BUILD MY SKILLS!
OMMMMMMM
I SWEAR, NO ONE'S EVER GONNA HAVE TO SAVE MY LIFE AGAIN....
I'M NOT GOING TO BE THE ONE WHO HANGS BACK OR FREEZES UP...
...AND I'M NOT GONNA BE OUTDONE BY SASUKE!
I SWEAR IT... BY THE PAIN IN MY LEFT HAND...
WITH THIS KUNAI KNIFE, I PROMISE YOU, I...

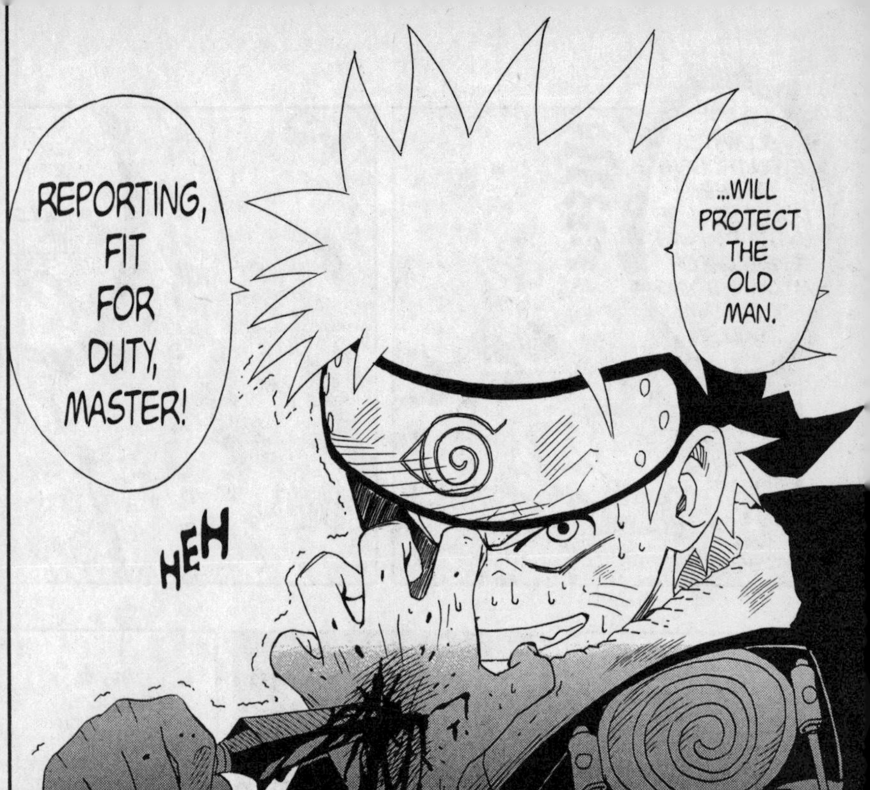
...WILL PROTECT THE OLD MAN.
REPORTING, FIT FOR DUTY, MASTER!
HEH

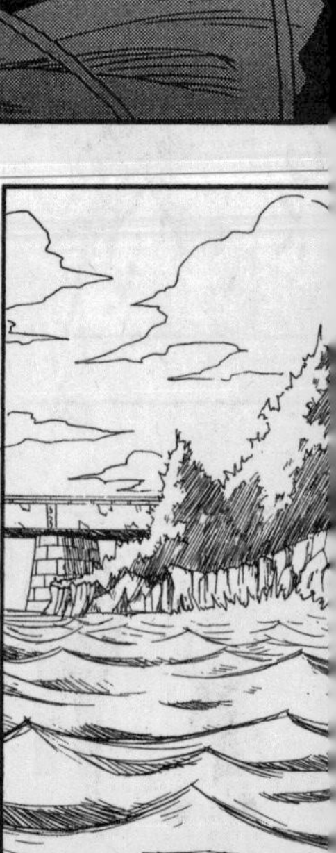

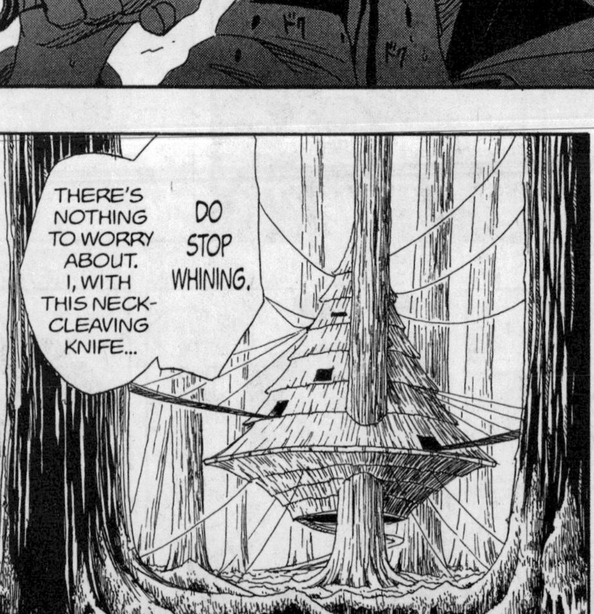
DO STOP WHINING.
THERE'S NOTHING TO WORRY ABOUT. I, WITH THIS NECK-CLEAVING KNIFE...

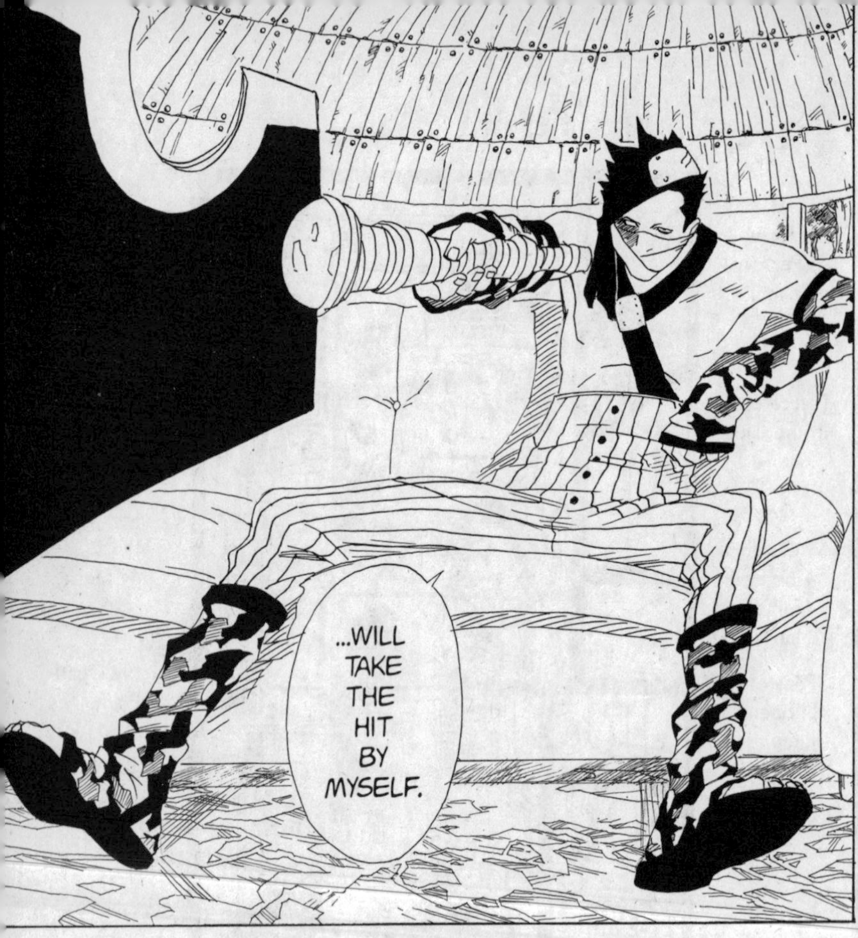
...WILL TAKE THE HIT BY MYSELF.

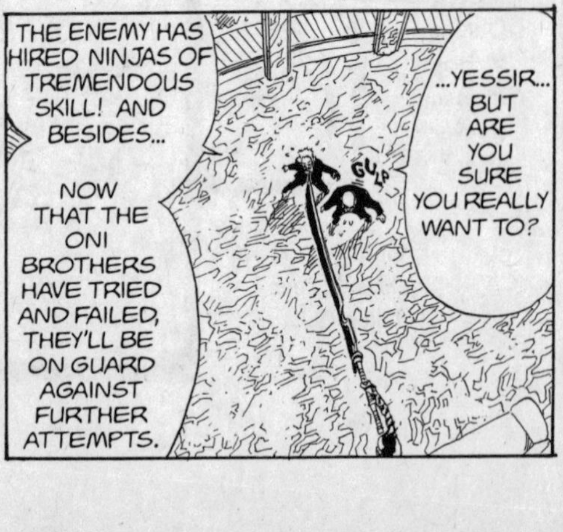
...YESSIR... BUT ARE YOU SURE YOU REALLY WANT TO?
GULP
THE ENEMY HAS HIRED NINJAS OF TREMENDOUS SKILL! AND BESIDES...
NOW THAT THE ONI BROTHERS HAVE TRIED AND FAILED, THEY'LL BE ON GUARD AGAINST FURTHER ATTEMPTS.

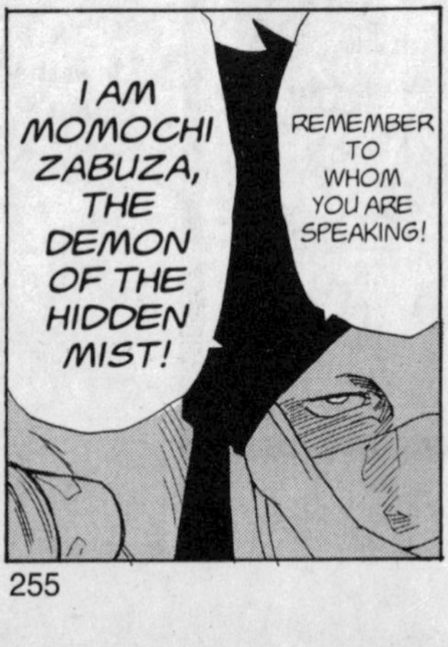
REMEMBER TO WHOM YOU ARE SPEAKING!
I AM MOMOCHI ZABUZA, THE DEMON OF THE HIDDEN MIST!

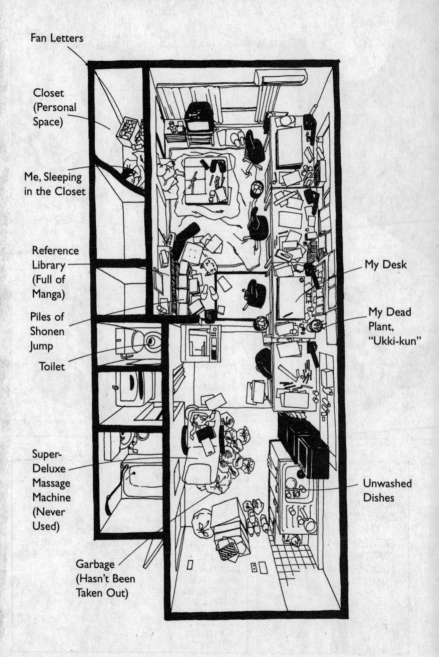

Fan Letters

Closet (Personal Space)

Me, Sleeping in the Closet

Reference Library (Full of Manga)

Piles of Shonen Jump

Toilet

Super-Deluxe Massage Machine (Never Used)

Garbage (Hasn't Been Taken Out)

My Desk

My Dead Plant, "Ukki-kun"

Unwashed Dishes

Number 11: GOING ASHORE

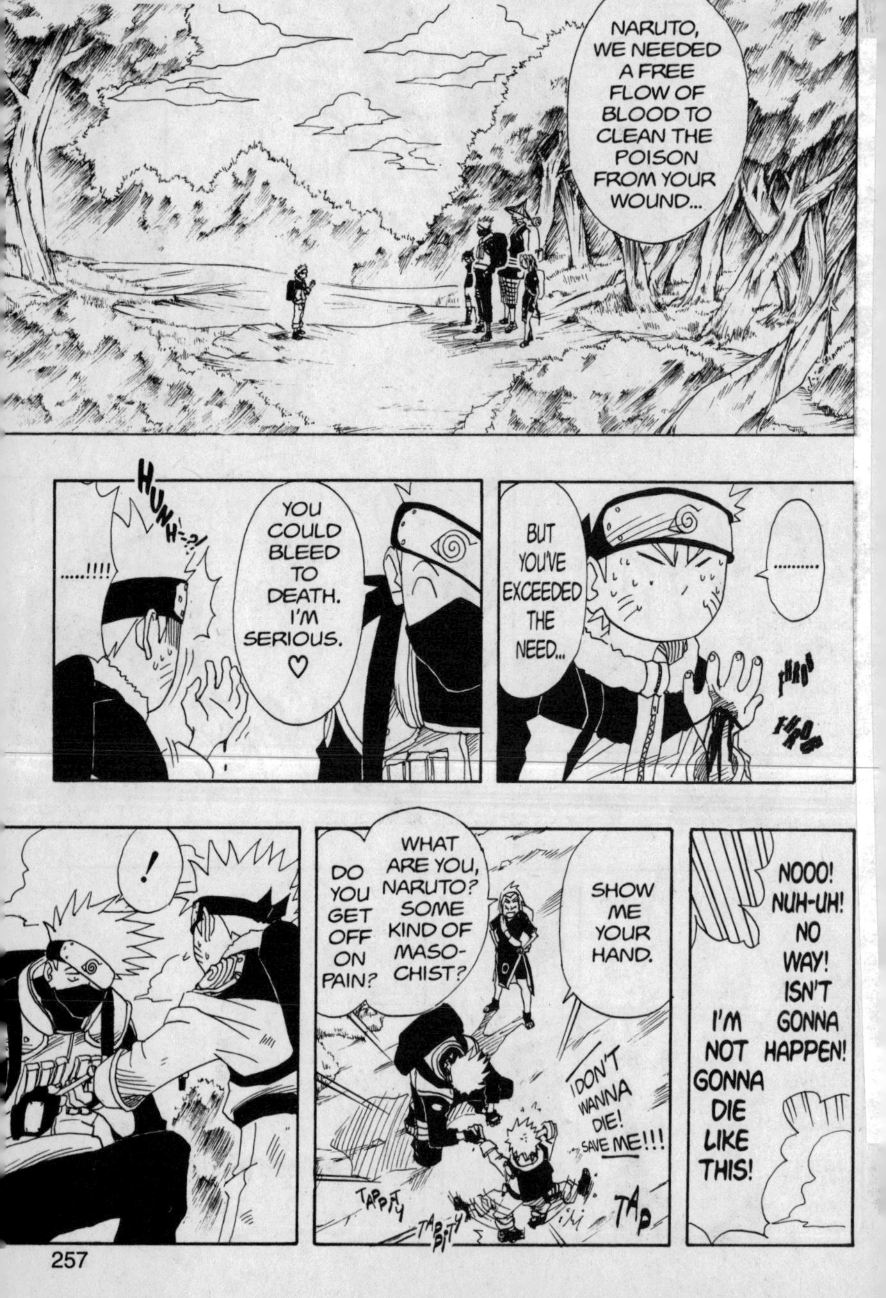
NARUTO, WE NEEDED A FREE FLOW OF BLOOD TO CLEAN THE POISON FROM YOUR WOUND...
....
BUT YOU'VE EXCEEDED THE NEED...
THROB THROB
YOU COULD BLEED TO DEATH. I'M SERIOUS. ♡
HUNH--?!
.....!!!!
NOOO! NUH-UH! NO WAY! ISN'T GONNA HAPPEN!
I'M NOT GONNA DIE LIKE THIS!
SHOW ME YOUR HAND.
I DON'T WANNA DIE! SAVE ME!!!
TAP
WHAT ARE YOU, NARUTO? SOME KIND OF MASO-CHIST?
DO YOU GET OFF ON PAIN?
TAPPITY TAPPITY
!

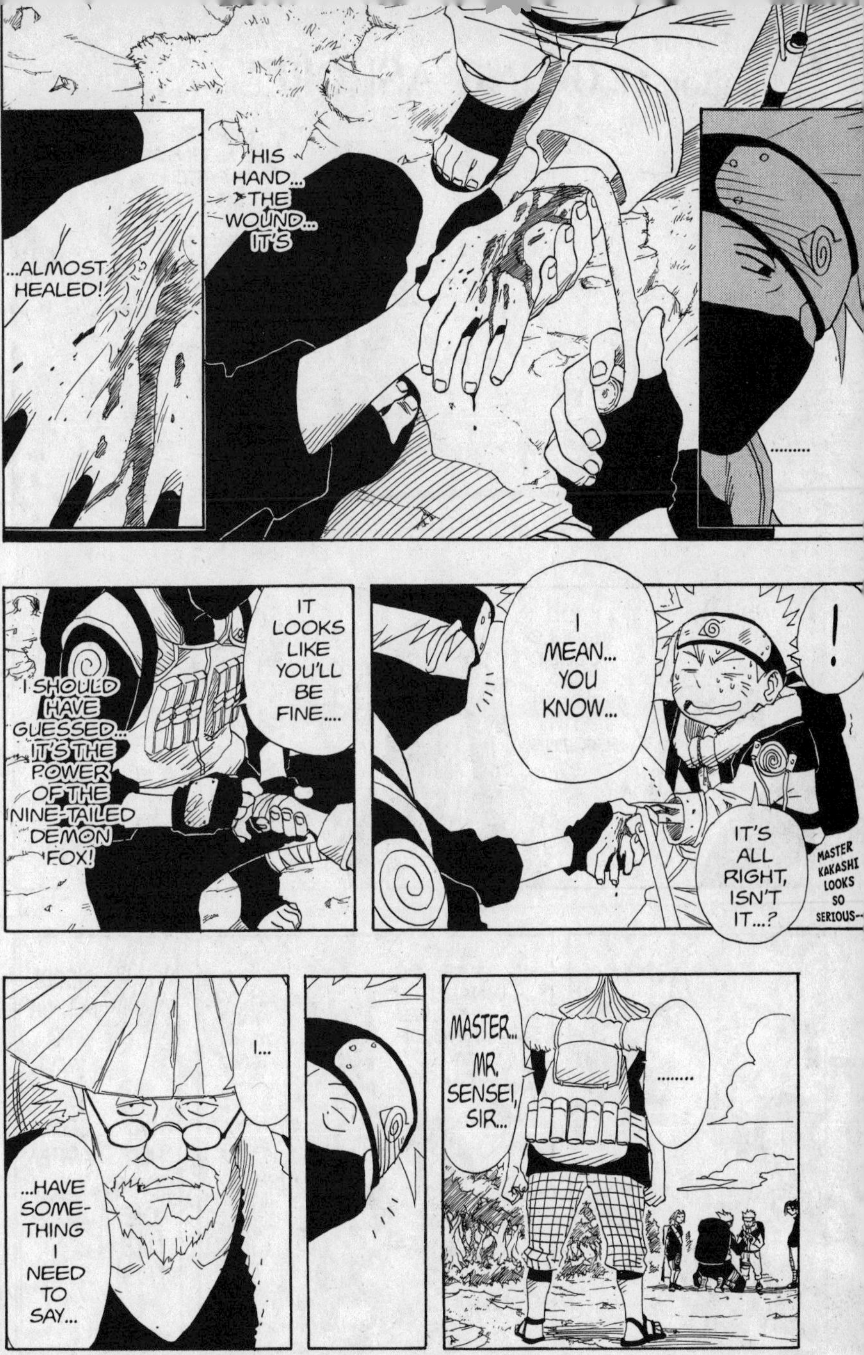
....
HIS HAND... THE WOUND... IT'S
...ALMOST HEALED!
!
I MEAN... YOU KNOW...
IT'S ALL RIGHT, ISN'T IT...?
MASTER KAKASHI LOOKS SO SERIOUS--
IT LOOKS LIKE YOU'LL BE FINE....
I SHOULD HAVE GUESSED... IT'S THE POWER OF THE NINE-TAILED DEMON FOX!
....
MASTER... MR. SENSEI, SIR...
I...
...HAVE SOMETHING I NEED TO SAY...

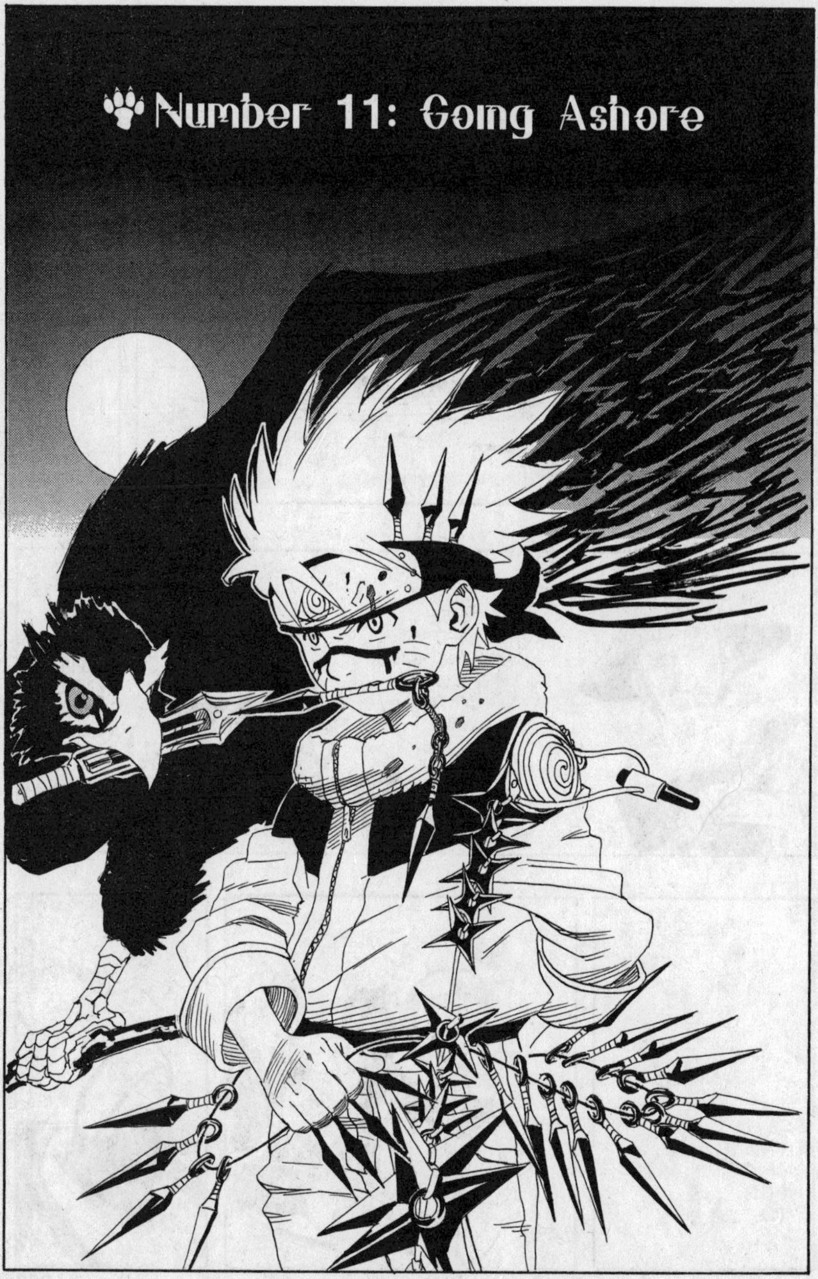
Number 11: Going Ashore

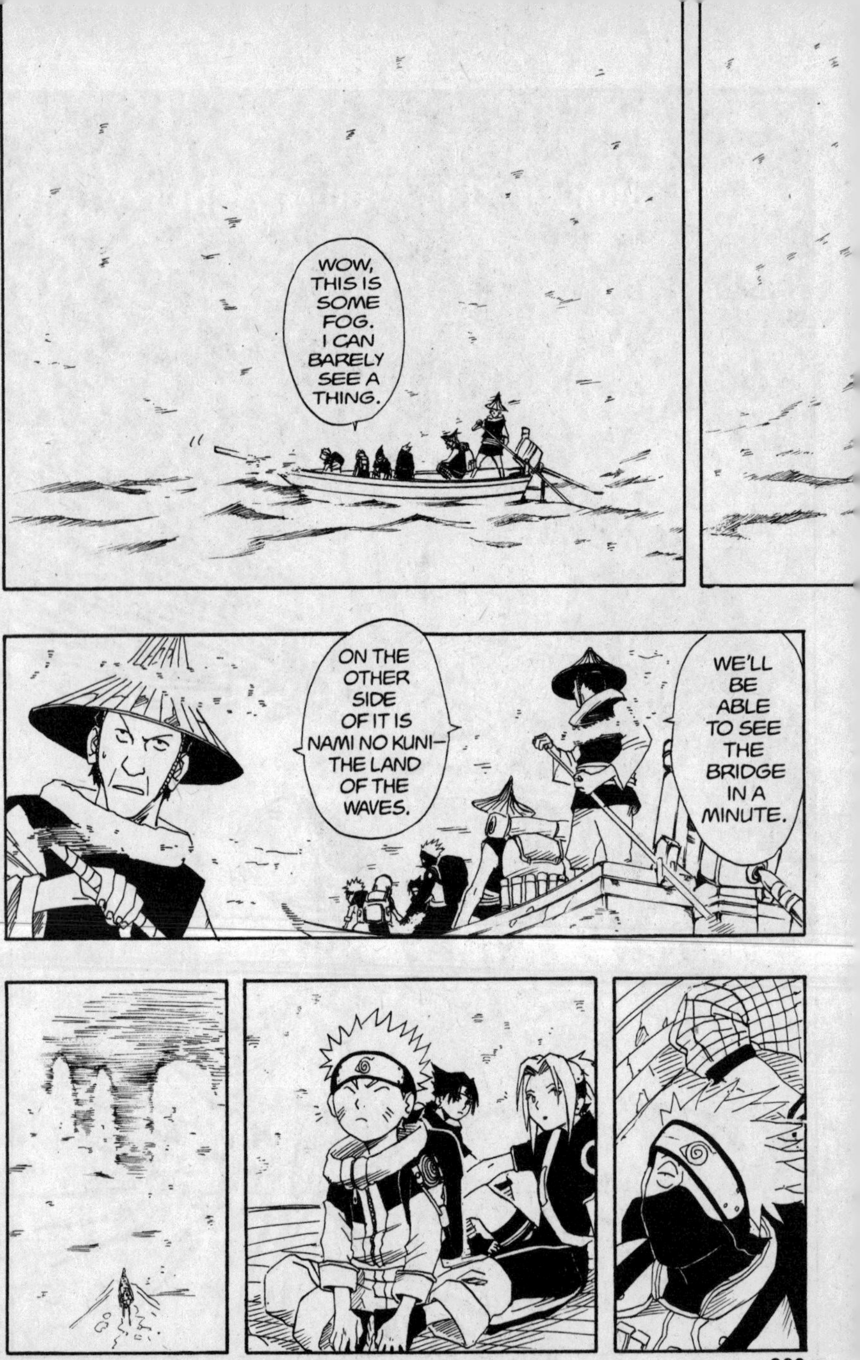
WOW, THIS IS SOME FOG. I CAN BARELY SEE A THING.
WE'LL BE ABLE TO SEE THE BRIDGE IN A MINUTE.
ON THE OTHER SIDE OF IT IS NAMI NO KUNI— THE LAND OF THE WAVES.

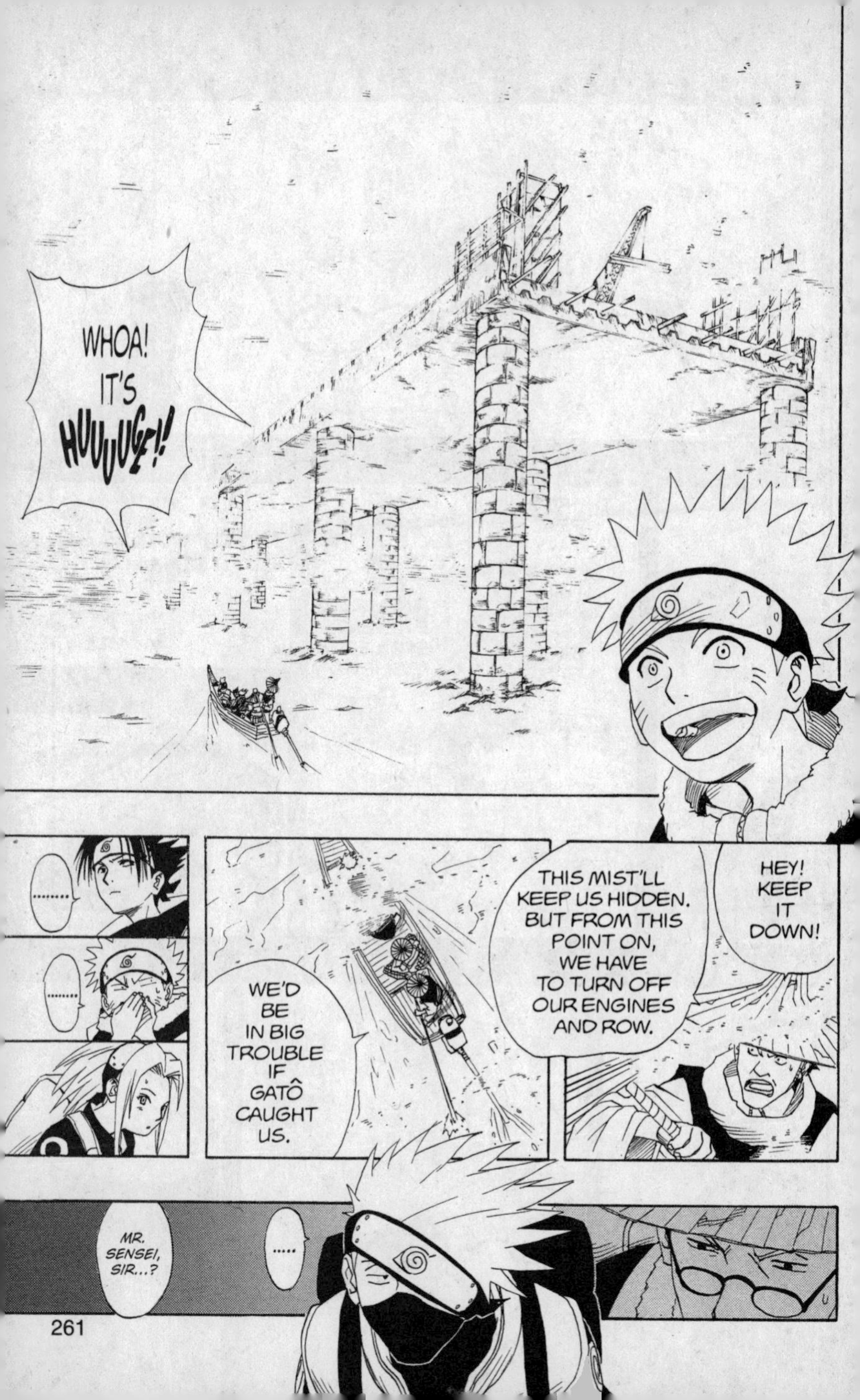
WHOA! IT'S HUUUUGE!!
HEY! KEEP IT DOWN!
THIS MIST'LL KEEP US HIDDEN. BUT FROM THIS POINT ON, WE HAVE TO TURN OFF OUR ENGINES AND ROW.
WE'D BE IN BIG TROUBLE IF GATÔ CAUGHT US.
....
....
.....
MR. SENSEI, SIR...?

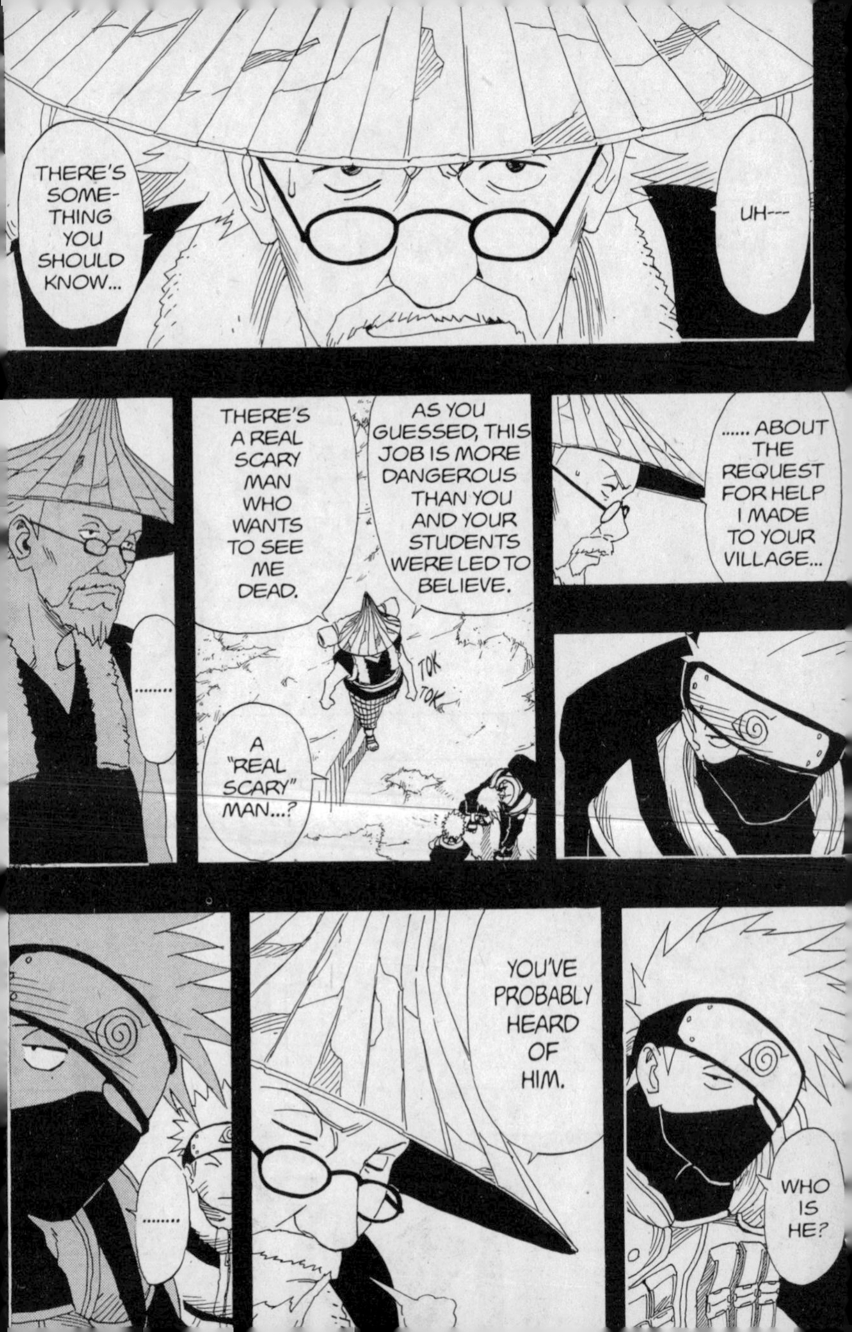
UH---
THERE'S SOMETHING YOU SHOULD KNOW...
...... ABOUT THE REQUEST FOR HELP I MADE TO YOUR VILLAGE...
AS YOU GUESSED, THIS JOB IS MORE DANGEROUS THAN YOU AND YOUR STUDENTS WERE LED TO BELIEVE.
THERE'S A REAL SCARY MAN WHO WANTS TO SEE ME DEAD.
TOK TOK
A "REAL SCARY" MAN...?
....
WHO IS HE?
YOU'VE PROBABLY HEARD OF HIM.
....

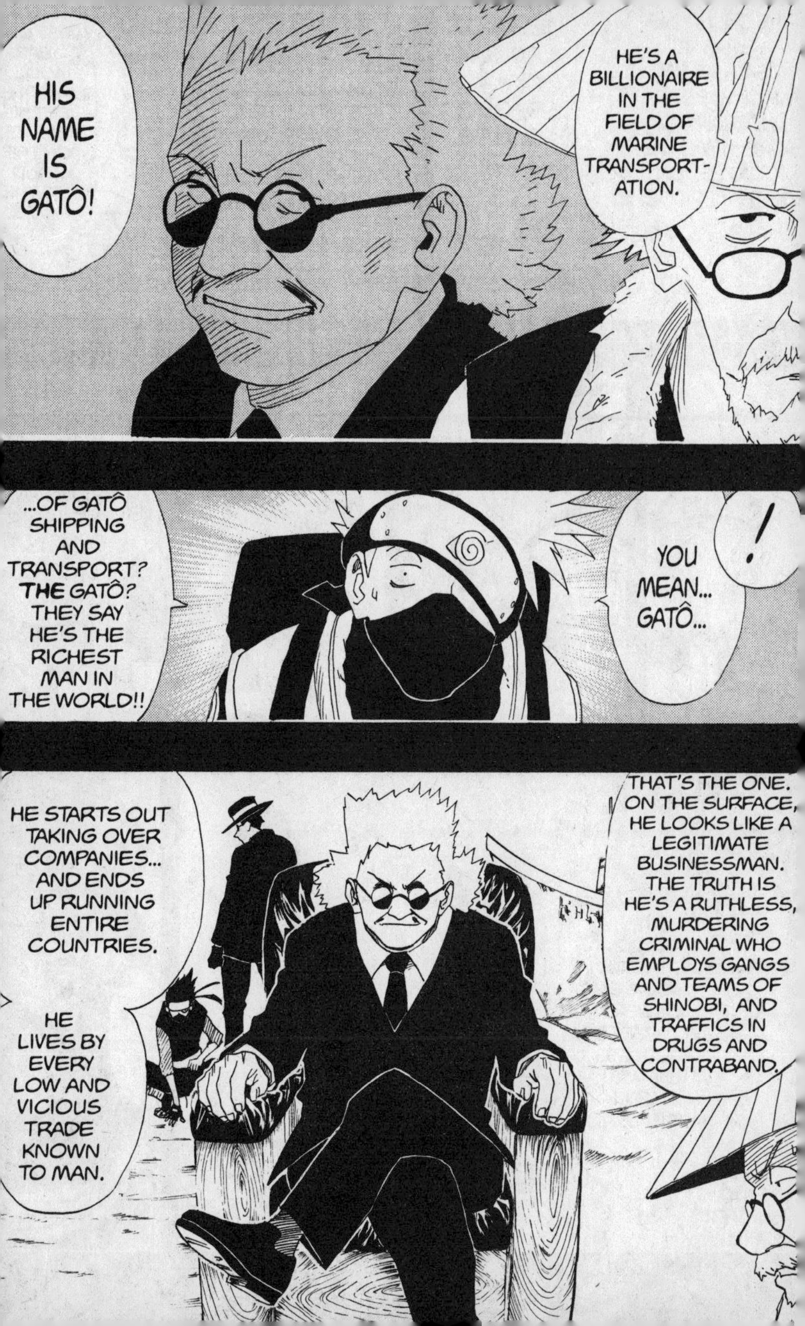
HE'S A BILLIONAIRE IN THE FIELD OF MARINE TRANSPORT-ATION.
HIS NAME IS GATÔ!
!
YOU MEAN... GATÔ...
...OF GATÔ SHIPPING AND TRANSPORT? **THE** GATÔ? THEY SAY HE'S THE RICHEST MAN IN THE WORLD!!
THAT'S THE ONE. ON THE SURFACE, HE LOOKS LIKE A LEGITIMATE BUSINESSMAN. THE TRUTH IS HE'S A RUTHLESS, MURDERING CRIMINAL WHO EMPLOYS GANGS AND TEAMS OF SHINOBI, AND TRAFFICS IN DRUGS AND CONTRABAND.
HE STARTS OUT TAKING OVER COMPANIES... AND ENDS UP RUNNING ENTIRE COUNTRIES.
HE LIVES BY EVERY LOW AND VICIOUS TRADE KNOWN TO MAN.

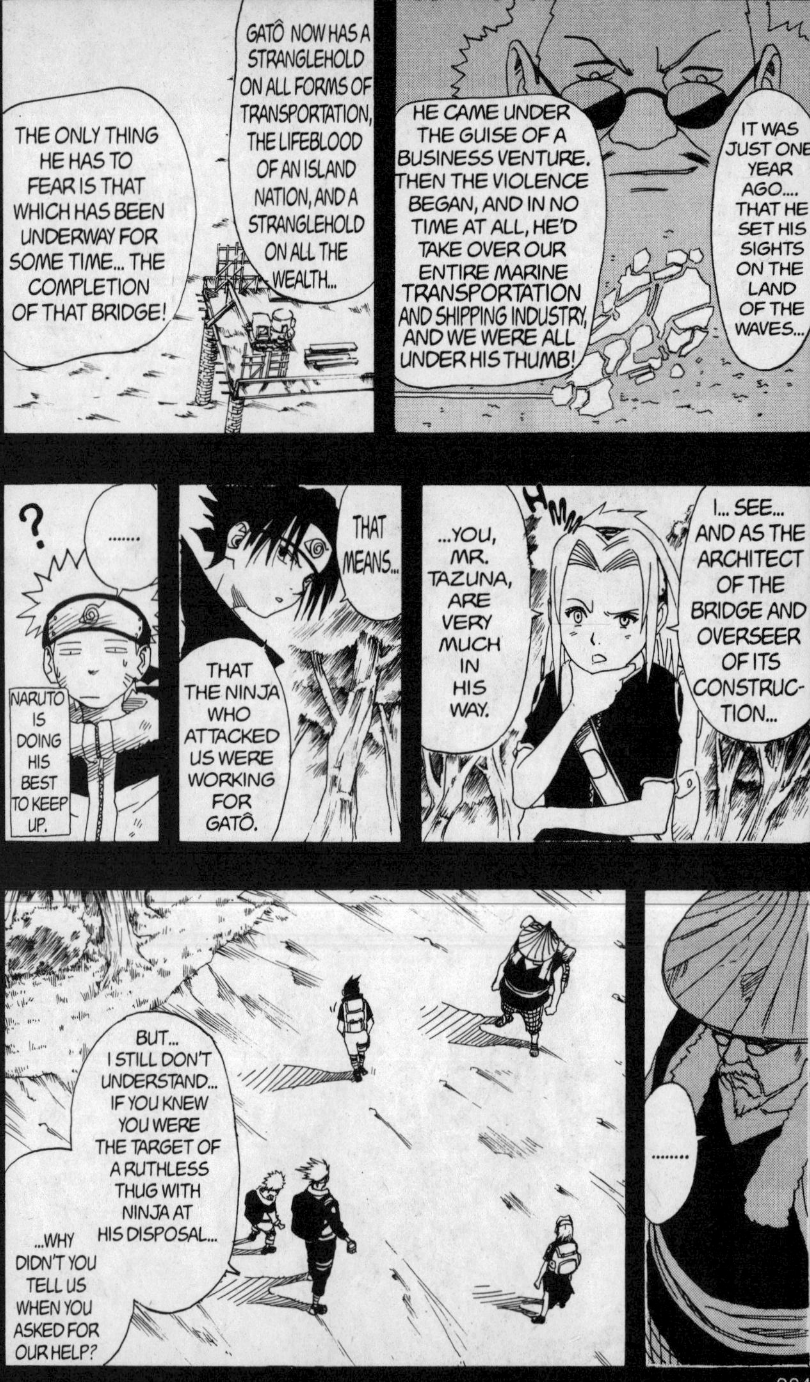

IT WAS JUST ONE YEAR AGO.... THAT HE SET HIS SIGHTS ON THE LAND OF THE WAVES...
HE CAME UNDER THE GUISE OF A BUSINESS VENTURE. THEN THE VIOLENCE BEGAN, AND IN NO TIME AT ALL, HE'D TAKE OVER OUR ENTIRE MARINE TRANSPORTATION AND SHIPPING INDUSTRY, AND WE WERE ALL UNDER HIS THUMB!
GATÔ NOW HAS A STRANGLEHOLD ON ALL FORMS OF TRANSPORTATION, THE LIFEBLOOD OF AN ISLAND NATION, AND A STRANGLEHOLD ON ALL THE WEALTH...
THE ONLY THING HE HAS TO FEAR IS THAT WHICH HAS BEEN UNDERWAY FOR SOME TIME... THE COMPLETION OF THAT BRIDGE!
I... SEE... AND AS THE ARCHITECT OF THE BRIDGE AND OVERSEER OF ITS CONSTRUCTION...
...YOU, MR. TAZUNA, ARE VERY MUCH IN HIS WAY.
HMM
THAT MEANS...
THAT THE NINJA WHO ATTACKED US WERE WORKING FOR GATÔ.
?
....
NARUTO IS DOING HIS BEST TO KEEP UP.
....
BUT... I STILL DON'T UNDERSTAND... IF YOU KNEW YOU WERE THE TARGET OF A RUTHLESS THUG WITH NINJA AT HIS DISPOSAL...
...WHY DIDN'T YOU TELL US WHEN YOU ASKED FOR OUR HELP?

READ THIS WAY

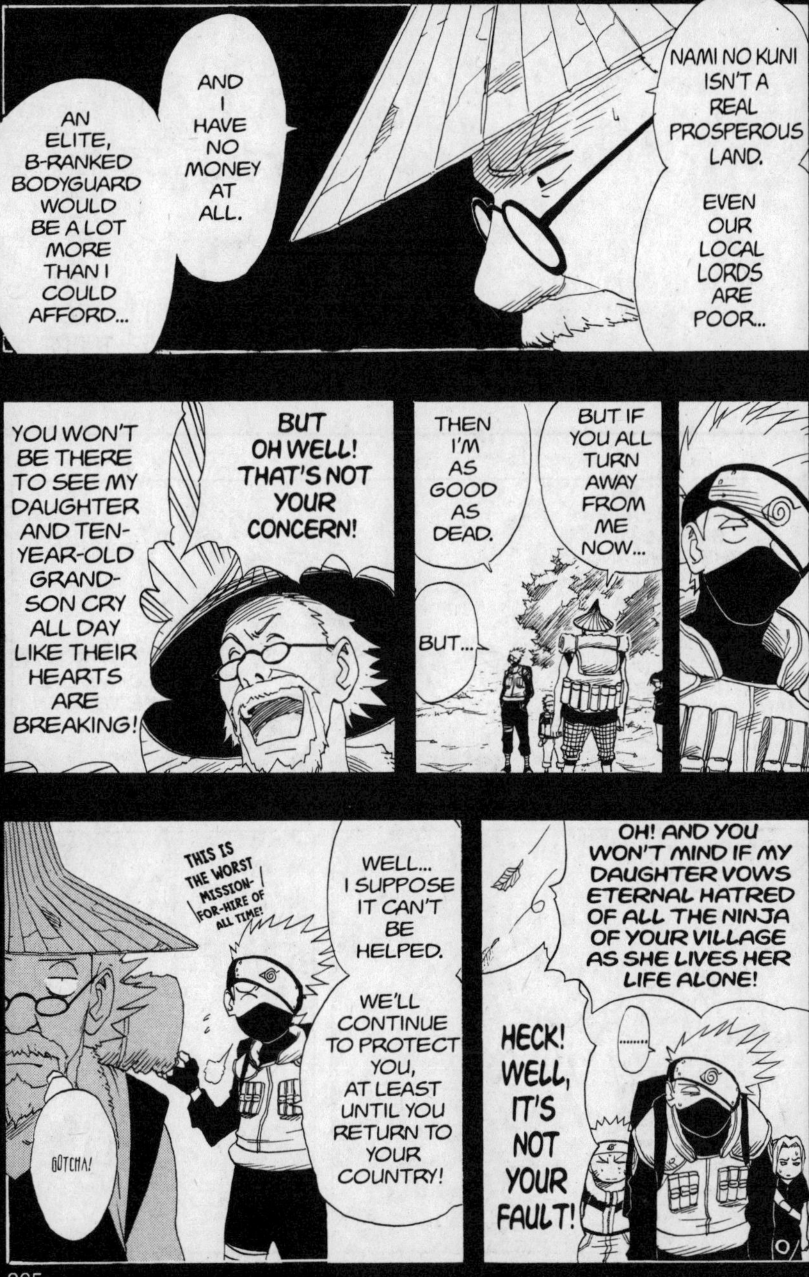

NAMI NO KUNI ISN'T A REAL PROSPEROUS LAND. EVEN OUR LOCAL LORDS ARE POOR...
AND I HAVE NO MONEY AT ALL.
AN ELITE, B-RANKED BODYGUARD WOULD BE A LOT MORE THAN I COULD AFFORD...
BUT IF YOU ALL TURN AWAY FROM ME NOW...
THEN I'M AS GOOD AS DEAD.
BUT...
BUT OH WELL! THAT'S NOT YOUR CONCERN!
YOU WON'T BE THERE TO SEE MY DAUGHTER AND TEN-YEAR-OLD GRANDSON CRY ALL DAY LIKE THEIR HEARTS ARE BREAKING!
OH! AND YOU WON'T MIND IF MY DAUGHTER VOWS ETERNAL HATRED OF ALL THE NINJA OF YOUR VILLAGE AS SHE LIVES HER LIFE ALONE!
HECK! WELL, IT'S NOT YOUR FAULT!
....
WELL... I SUPPOSE IT CAN'T BE HELPED. WE'LL CONTINUE TO PROTECT YOU, AT LEAST UNTIL YOU RETURN TO YOUR COUNTRY!
THIS IS THE WORST MISSION-FOR-HIRE OF ALL TIME!
GOTCHA!

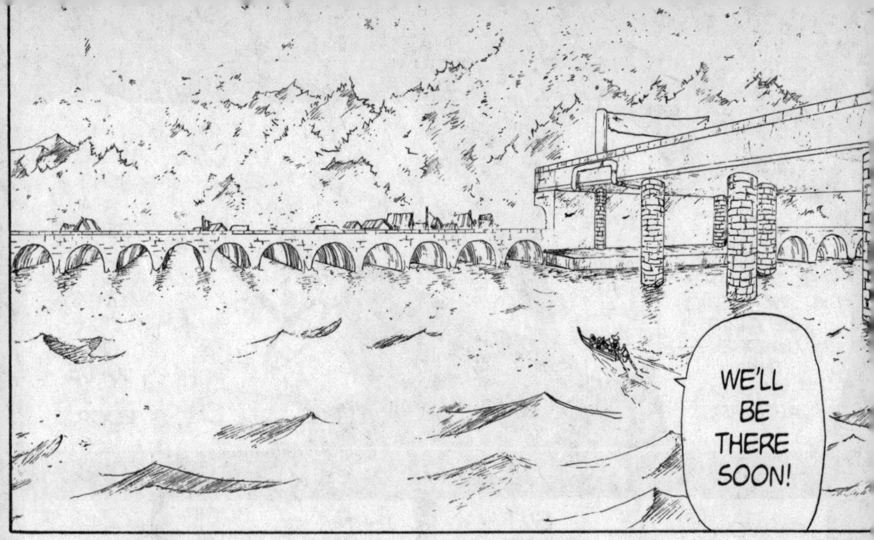
WE'LL BE THERE SOON!

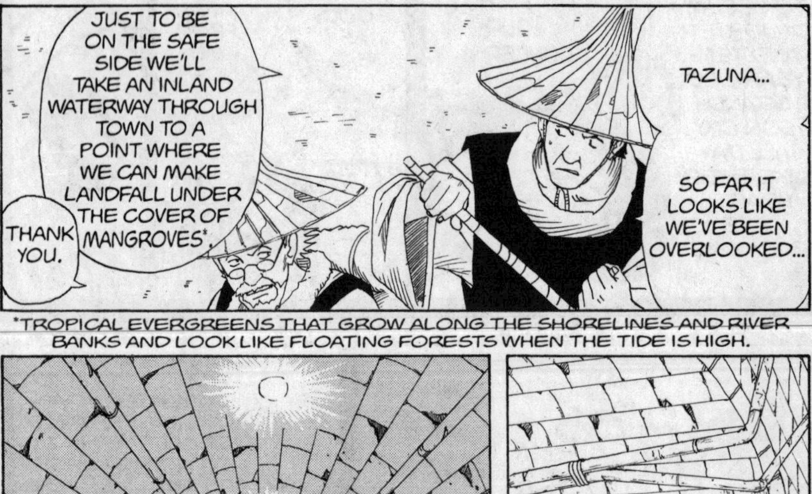
TAZUNA... SO FAR IT LOOKS LIKE WE'VE BEEN OVERLOOKED...
JUST TO BE ON THE SAFE SIDE WE'LL TAKE AN INLAND WATERWAY THROUGH TOWN TO A POINT WHERE WE CAN MAKE LANDFALL UNDER THE COVER OF MANGROVES*.
THANK YOU.

*TROPICAL EVERGREENS THAT GROW ALONG THE SHORELINES AND RIVER BANKS AND LOOK LIKE FLOATING FORESTS WHEN THE TIDE IS HIGH.

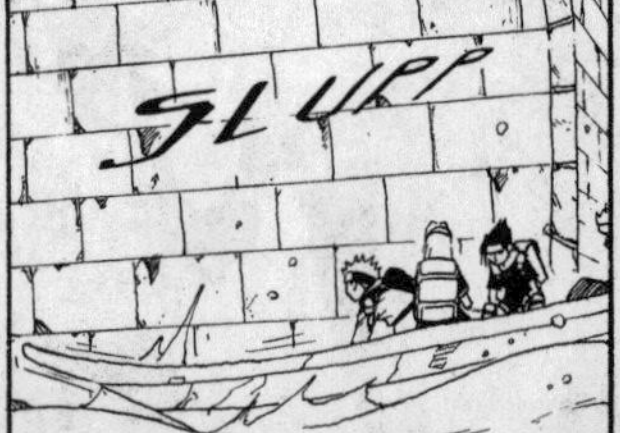
SLUPP

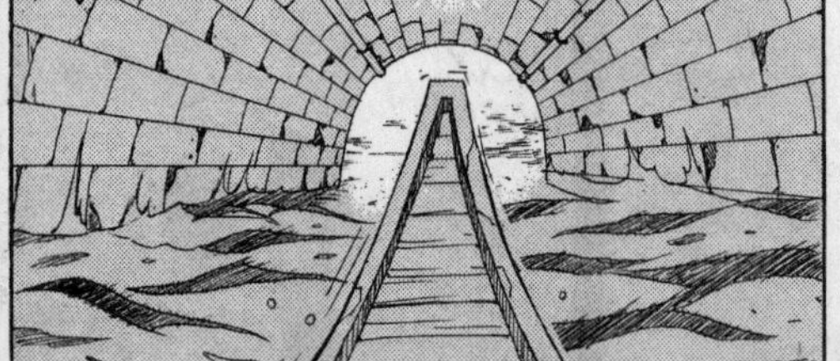

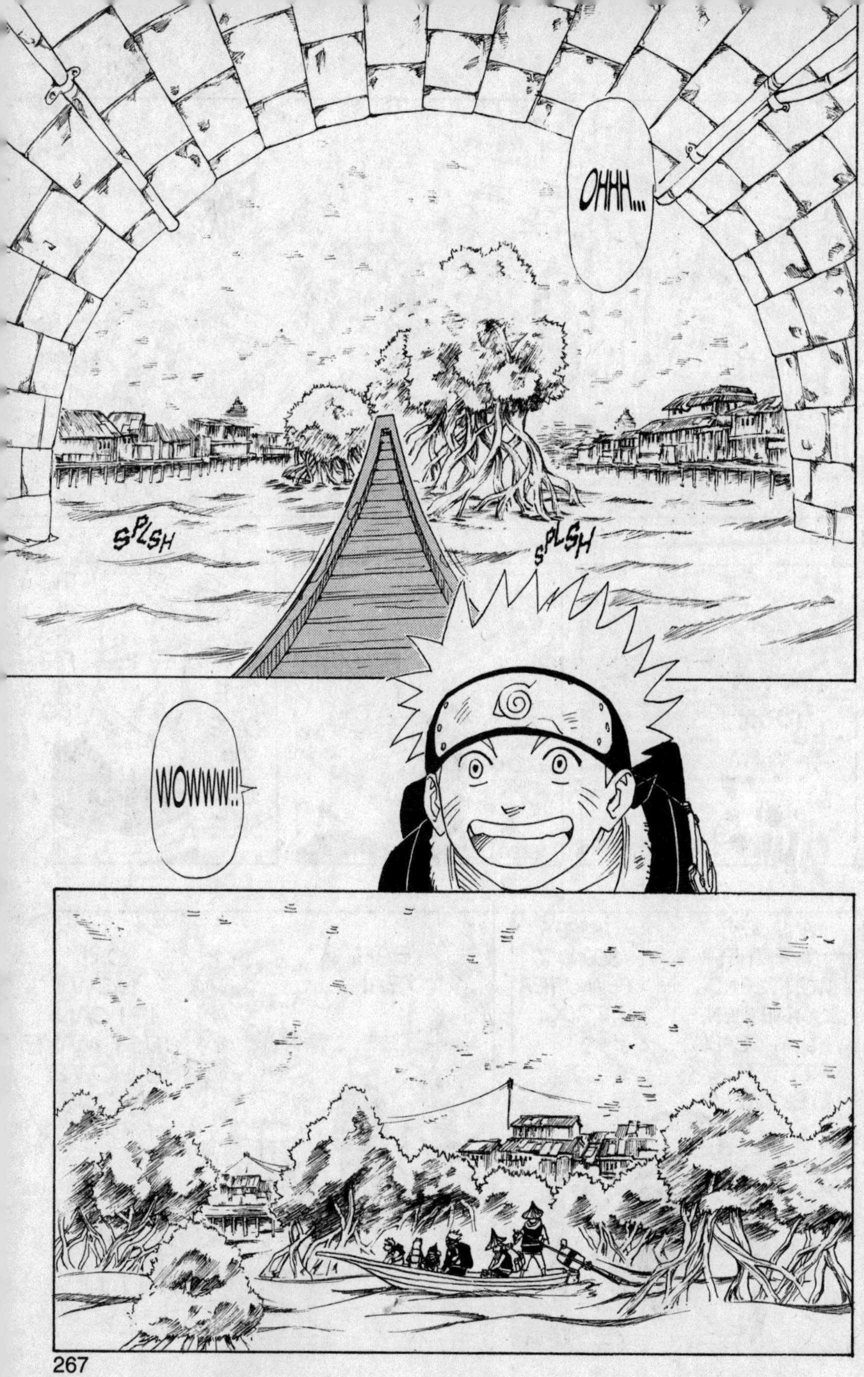
OHHH...
SPLSH
SPLSH
WOWWW!!

READ THIS WAY

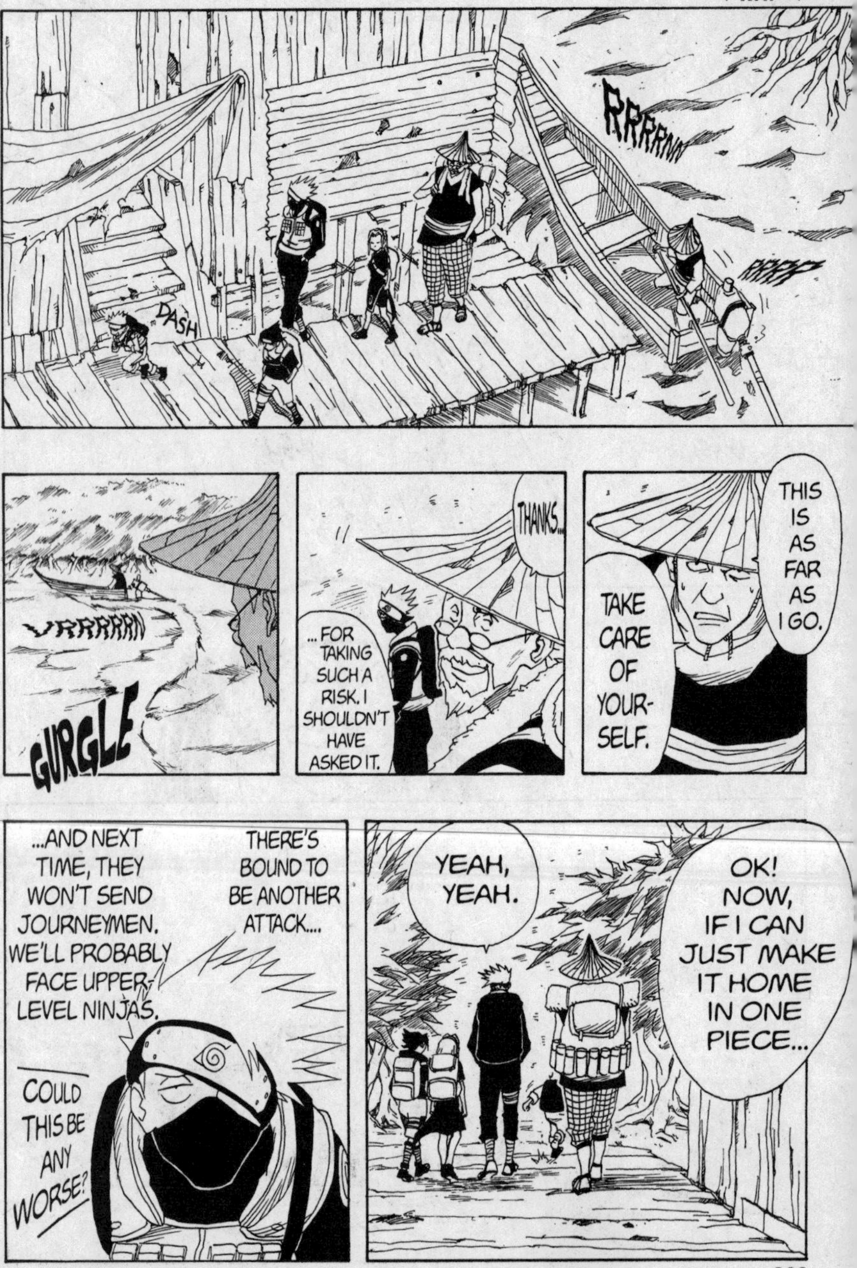
RRRRNN
DASH
THIS IS AS FAR AS I GO.
TAKE CARE OF YOURSELF.
THANKS...
...FOR TAKING SUCH A RISK. I SHOULDN'T HAVE ASKED IT.
VRRRRRN
GURGLE
OK! NOW, IF I CAN JUST MAKE IT HOME IN ONE PIECE...
YEAH, YEAH.
THERE'S BOUND TO BE ANOTHER ATTACK....
...AND NEXT TIME, THEY WON'T SEND JOURNEYMEN. WE'LL PROBABLY FACE UPPER-LEVEL NINJAS.
COULD THIS BE ANY WORSE?

READ THIS WAY

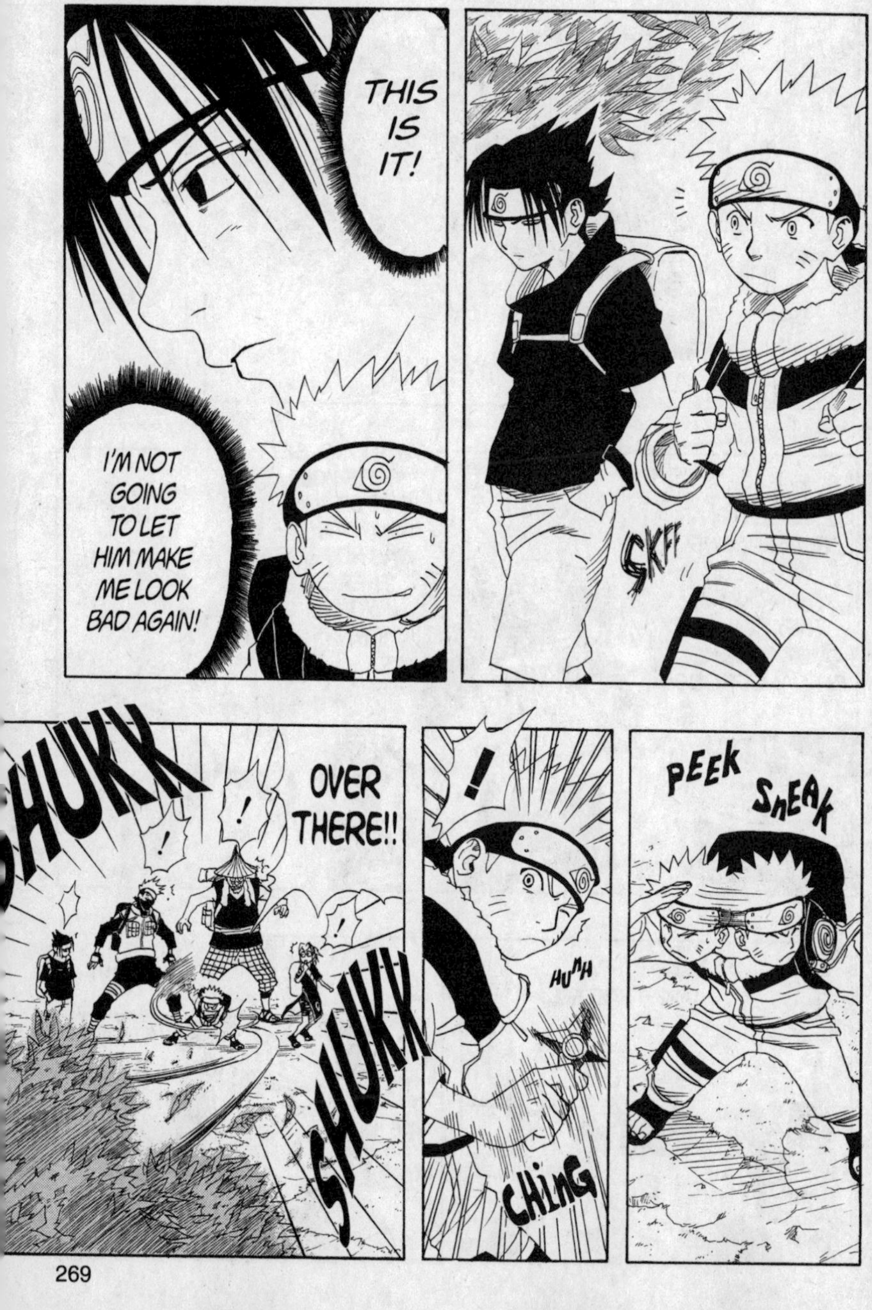
SKFF
THIS IS IT!
I'M NOT GOING TO LET HIM MAKE ME LOOK BAD AGAIN!
PEEK
SNEAK
!
HUNH
SHUKK
CHING
SHUKK
OVER THERE!!
!
!
!
!

READ THIS WAY

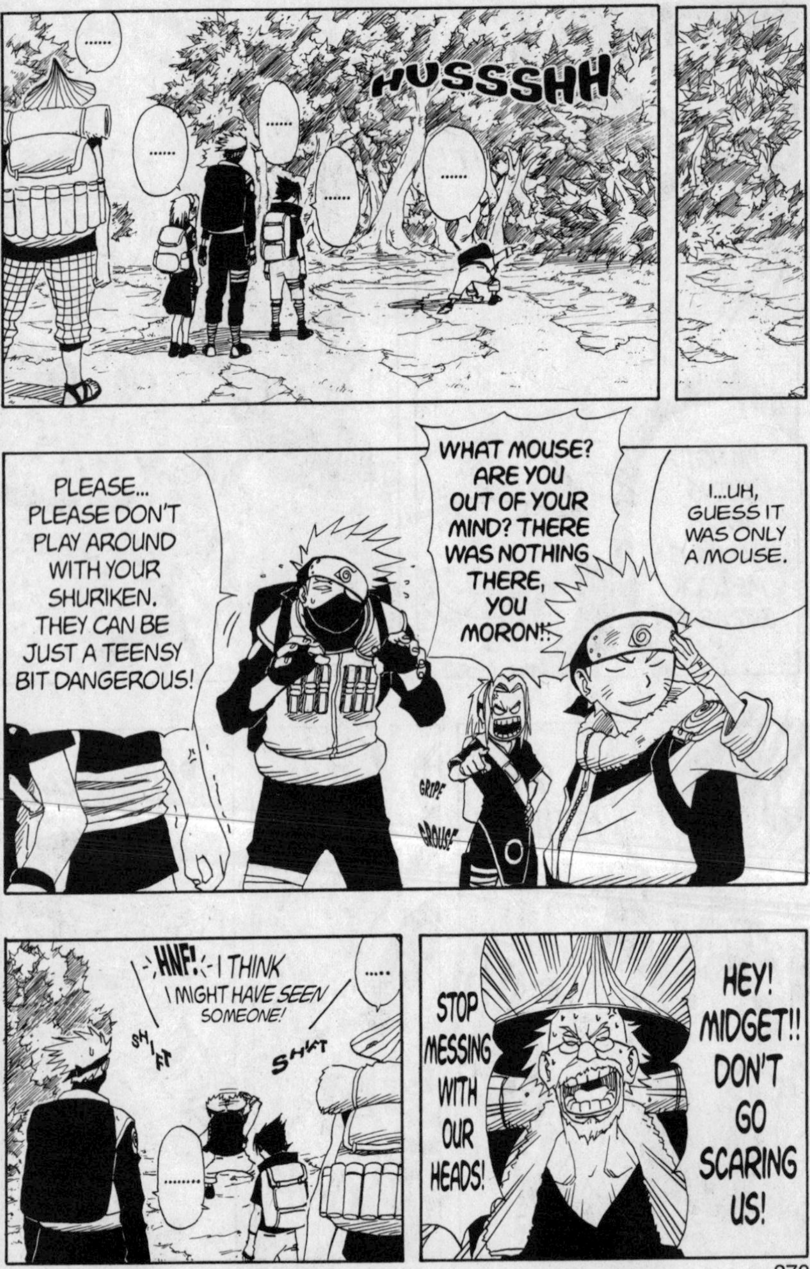
......
HUSSSHH
......
......
......
......
......
I...UH, GUESS IT WAS ONLY A MOUSE.
WHAT MOUSE? ARE YOU OUT OF YOUR MIND? THERE WAS NOTHING THERE, YOU MORON!!
GRIPE
GROUSE
PLEASE... PLEASE DON'T PLAY AROUND WITH YOUR SHURIKEN. THEY CAN BE JUST A TEENSY BIT DANGEROUS!
HEY! MIDGET!! DON'T GO SCARING US!
STOP MESSING WITH OUR HEADS!
.....
HNF! I THINK I MIGHT HAVE SEEN SOMEONE!
SHIFT
SHIFT
....

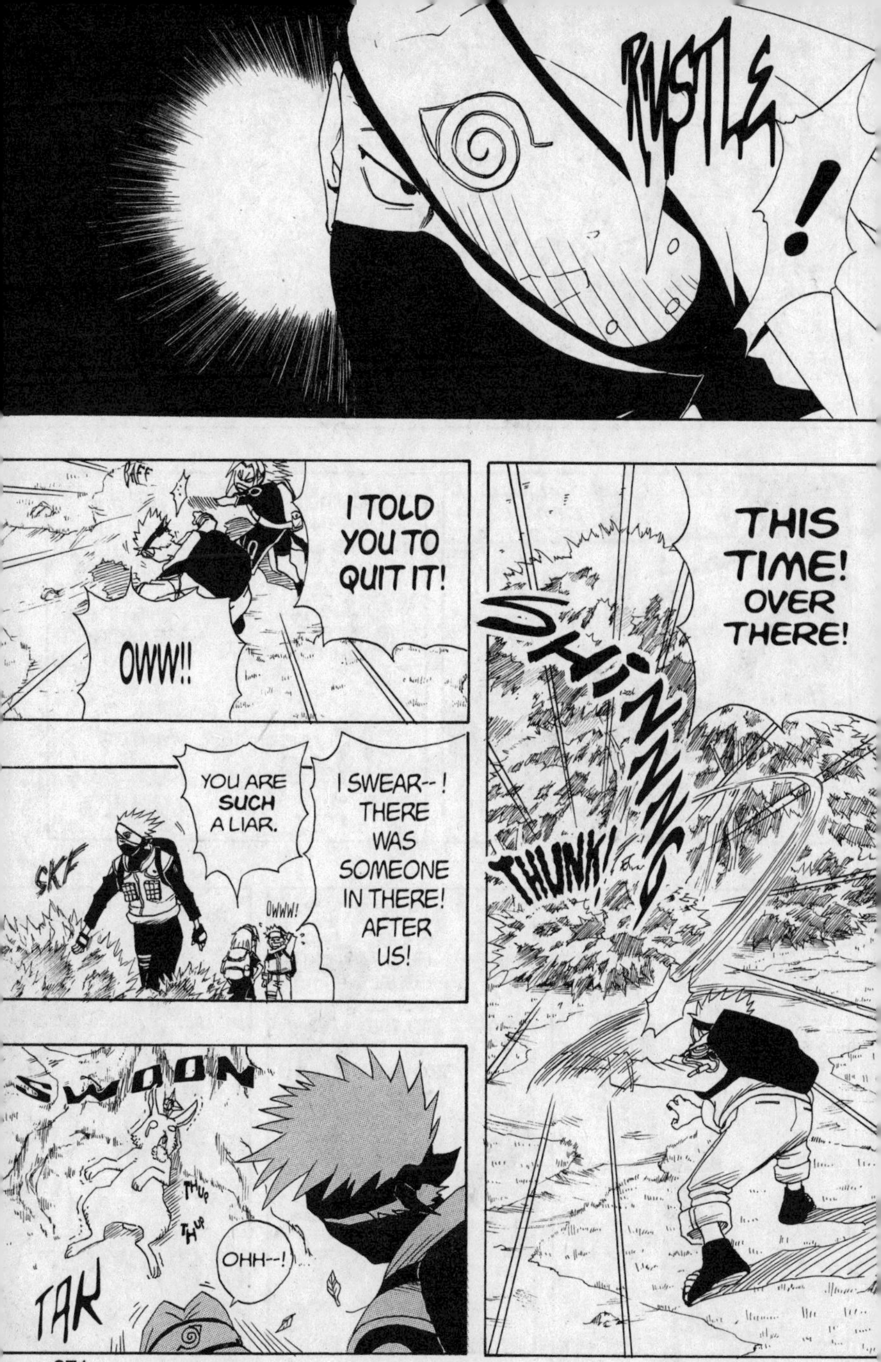
RUSTLE
!
THIS TIME! OVER THERE!
SHINNNG
THUNK!
I TOLD YOU TO QUIT IT!
OWW!!
I SWEAR--! THERE WAS SOMEONE IN THERE! AFTER US!
YOU ARE SUCH A LIAR.
OWWW!
SWOON
THUP
THUP
OHH--!
TAK

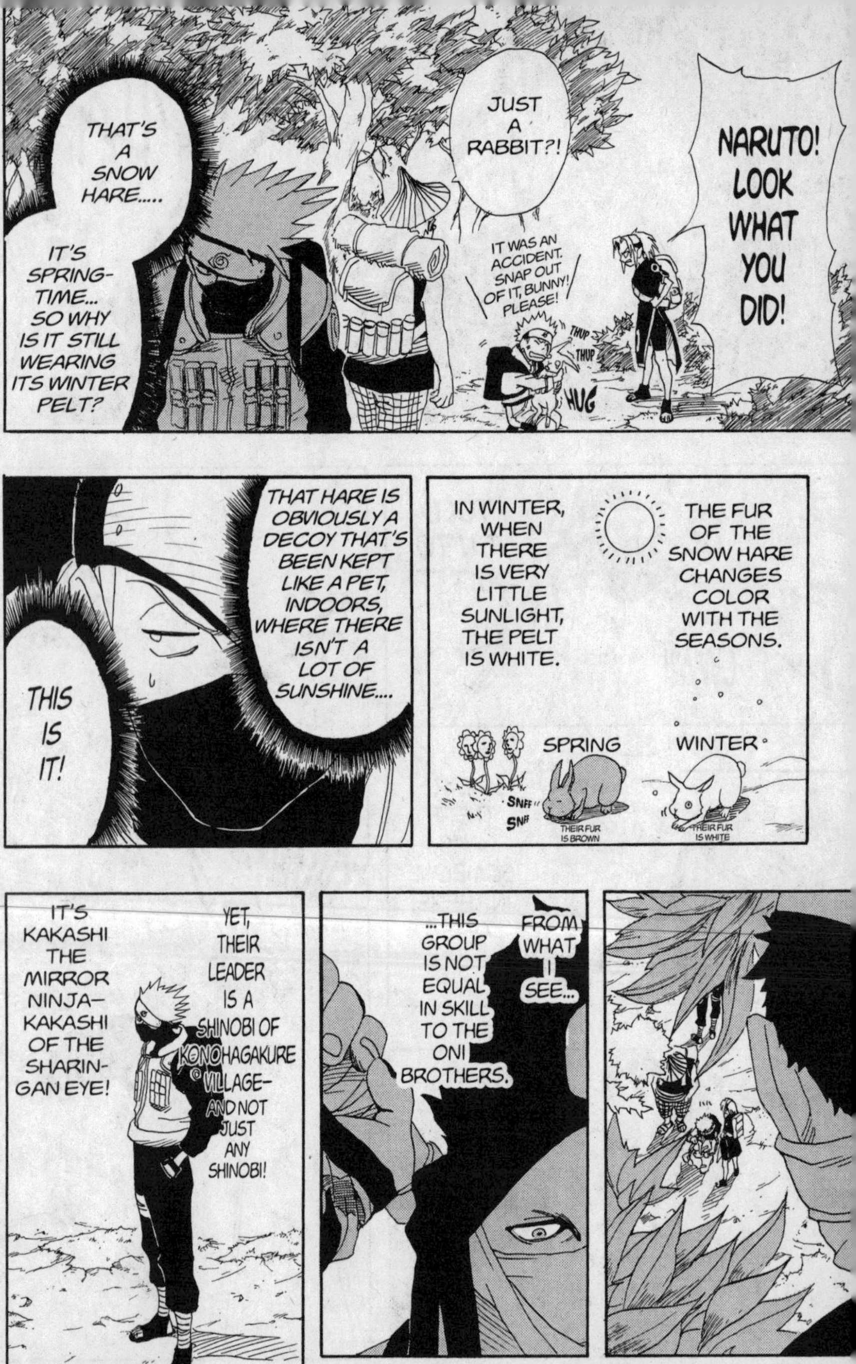
NARUTO! LOOK WHAT YOU DID!
JUST A RABBIT?!
IT WAS AN ACCIDENT. SNAP OUT OF IT, BUNNY! PLEASE!
THUP THUP
HUG
THAT'S A SNOW HARE.....
IT'S SPRING-TIME... SO WHY IS IT STILL WEARING ITS WINTER PELT?
THE FUR OF THE SNOW HARE CHANGES COLOR WITH THE SEASONS.
IN WINTER, WHEN THERE IS VERY LITTLE SUNLIGHT, THE PELT IS WHITE.
WINTER
THEIR FUR IS WHITE
SPRING
SNFF SNFF
THEIR FUR IS BROWN
THAT HARE IS OBVIOUSLY A DECOY THAT'S BEEN KEPT LIKE A PET, INDOORS, WHERE THERE ISN'T A LOT OF SUNSHINE....
THIS IS IT!
FROM WHAT I SEE...
...THIS GROUP IS NOT EQUAL IN SKILL TO THE ONI BROTHERS.
YET, THEIR LEADER IS A SHINOBI OF KONOHAGAKURE VILLAGE— AND NOT JUST ANY SHINOBI!
IT'S KAKASHI THE MIRROR NINJA— KAKASHI OF THE SHARINGAN EYE!

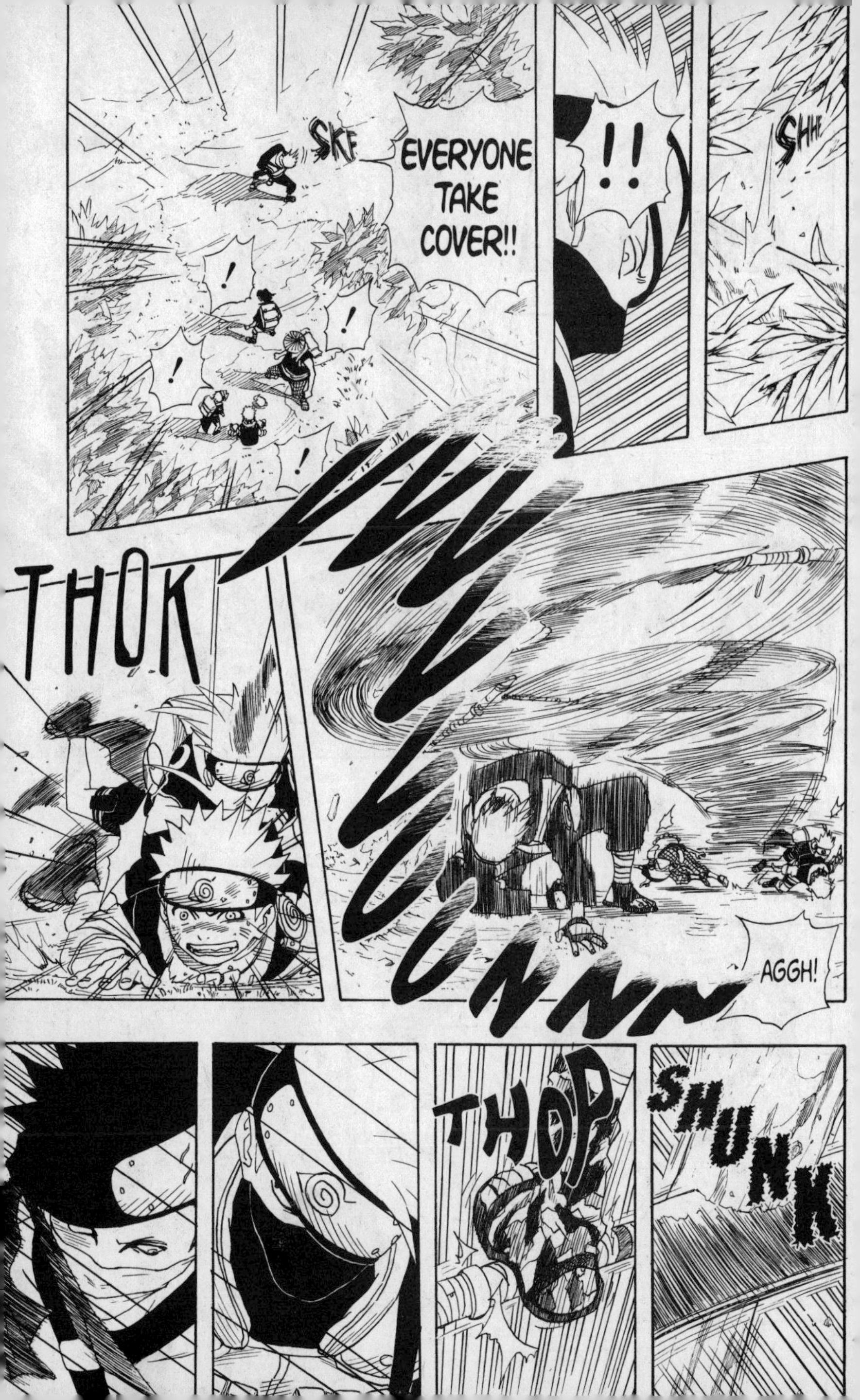
SHH
!!
EVERYONE TAKE COVER!!
SKF
!
!
!
!
AGGH!
THOK
SHUNK
THOP

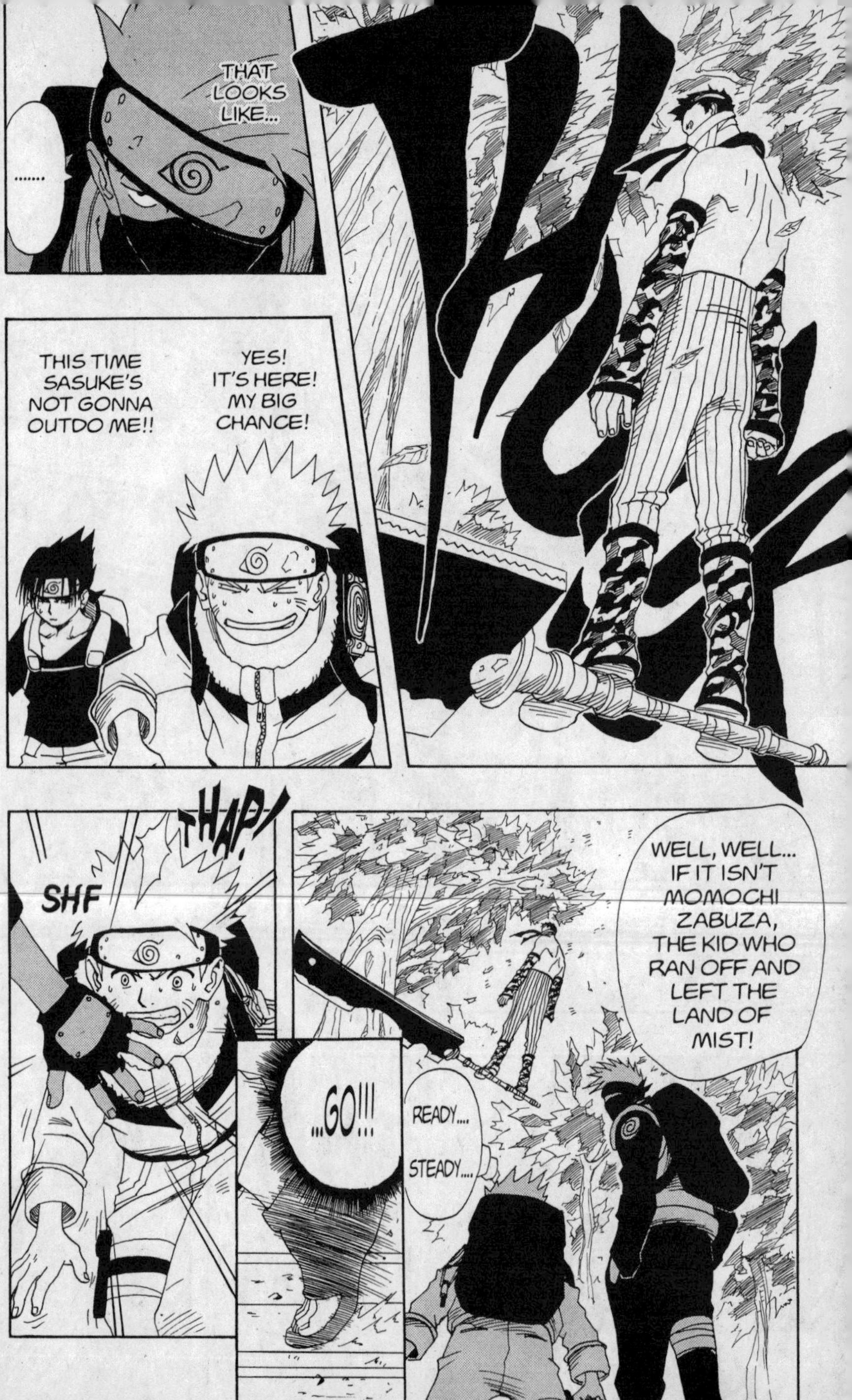
THAT LOOKS LIKE...
....
YES! IT'S HERE! MY BIG CHANCE!
THIS TIME SASUKE'S NOT GONNA OUTDO ME!!
WELL, WELL... IF IT ISN'T MOMOCHI ZABUZA, THE KID WHO RAN OFF AND LEFT THE LAND OF MIST!
READY....
STEADY....
...GO!!!
THAP!
SHF

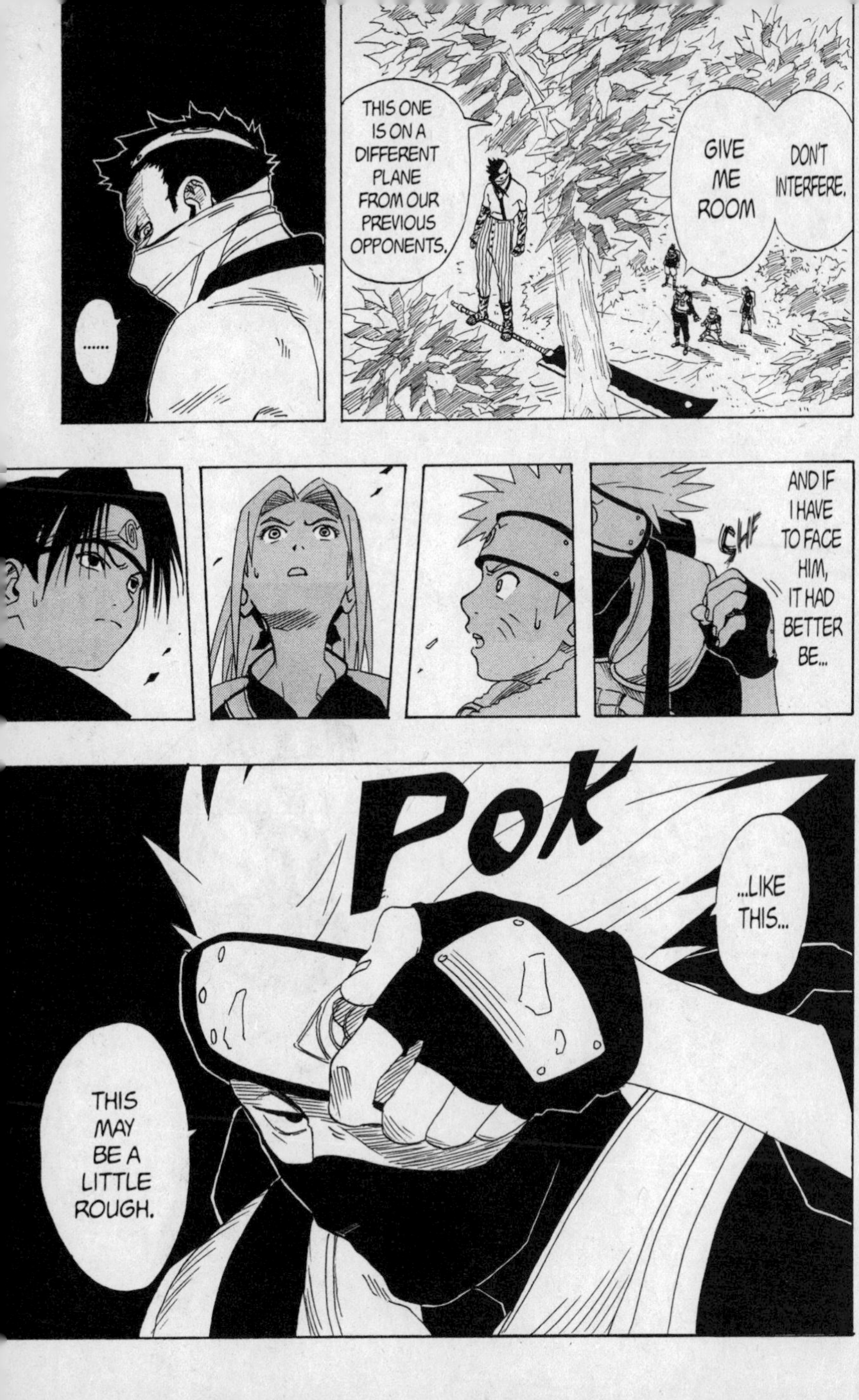
......
THIS ONE IS ON A DIFFERENT PLANE FROM OUR PREVIOUS OPPONENTS.
GIVE ME ROOM
DON'T INTERFERE.
CHF
AND IF I HAVE TO FACE HIM, IT HAD BETTER BE...
POK
...LIKE THIS...
THIS MAY BE A LITTLE ROUGH.

Number 12: Game Over!!!

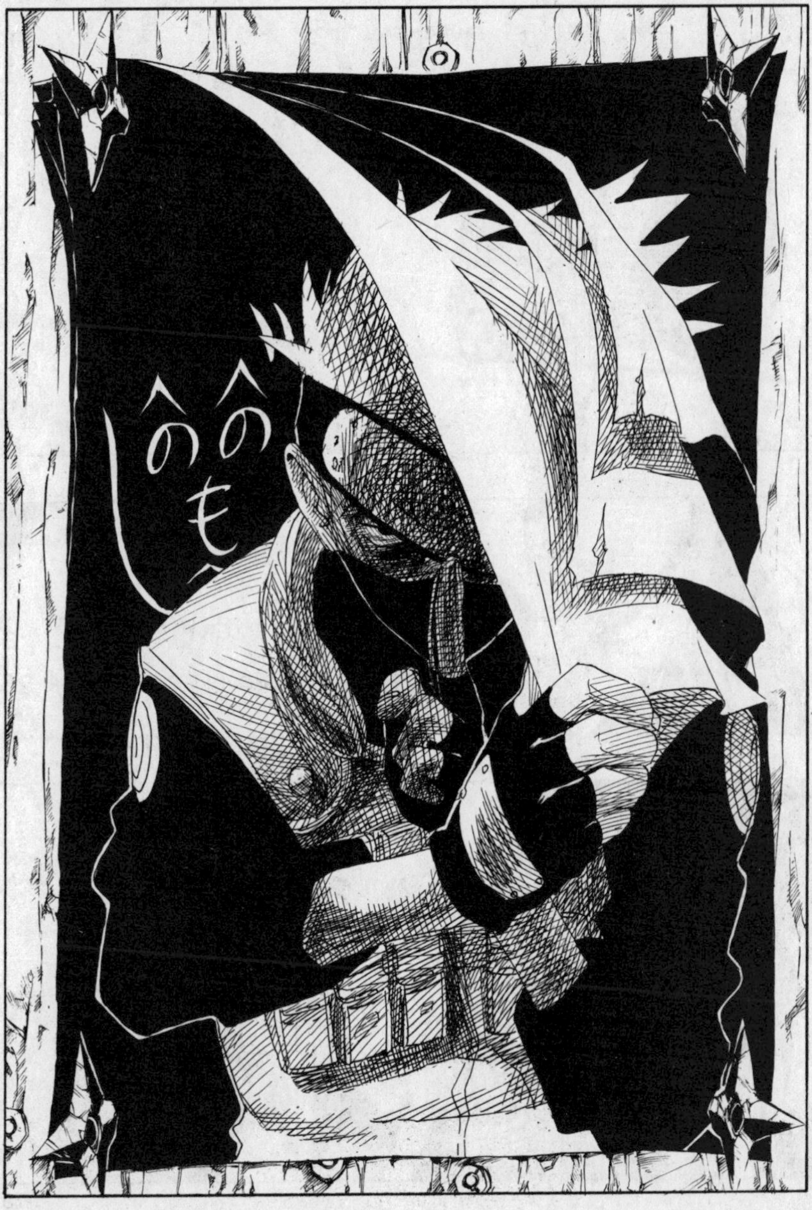

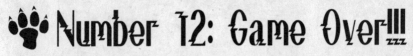

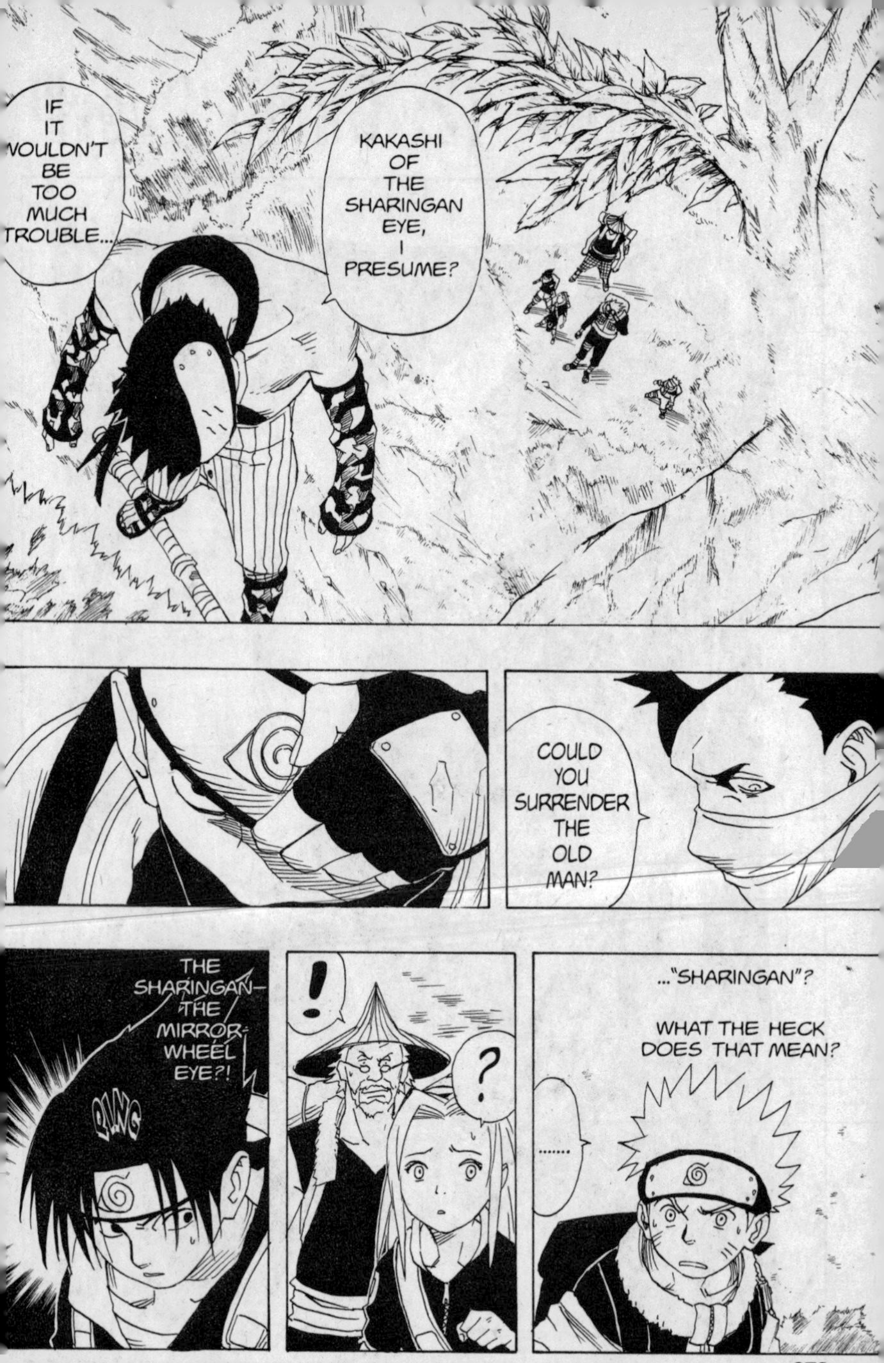
KAKASHI OF THE SHARINGAN EYE, I PRESUME?
IF IT WOULDN'T BE TOO MUCH TROUBLE...
COULD YOU SURRENDER THE OLD MAN?
..."SHARINGAN"?
WHAT THE HECK DOES THAT MEAN?
....
!
?
THE SHARINGAN— THE MIRROR WHEEL EYE?!
QING

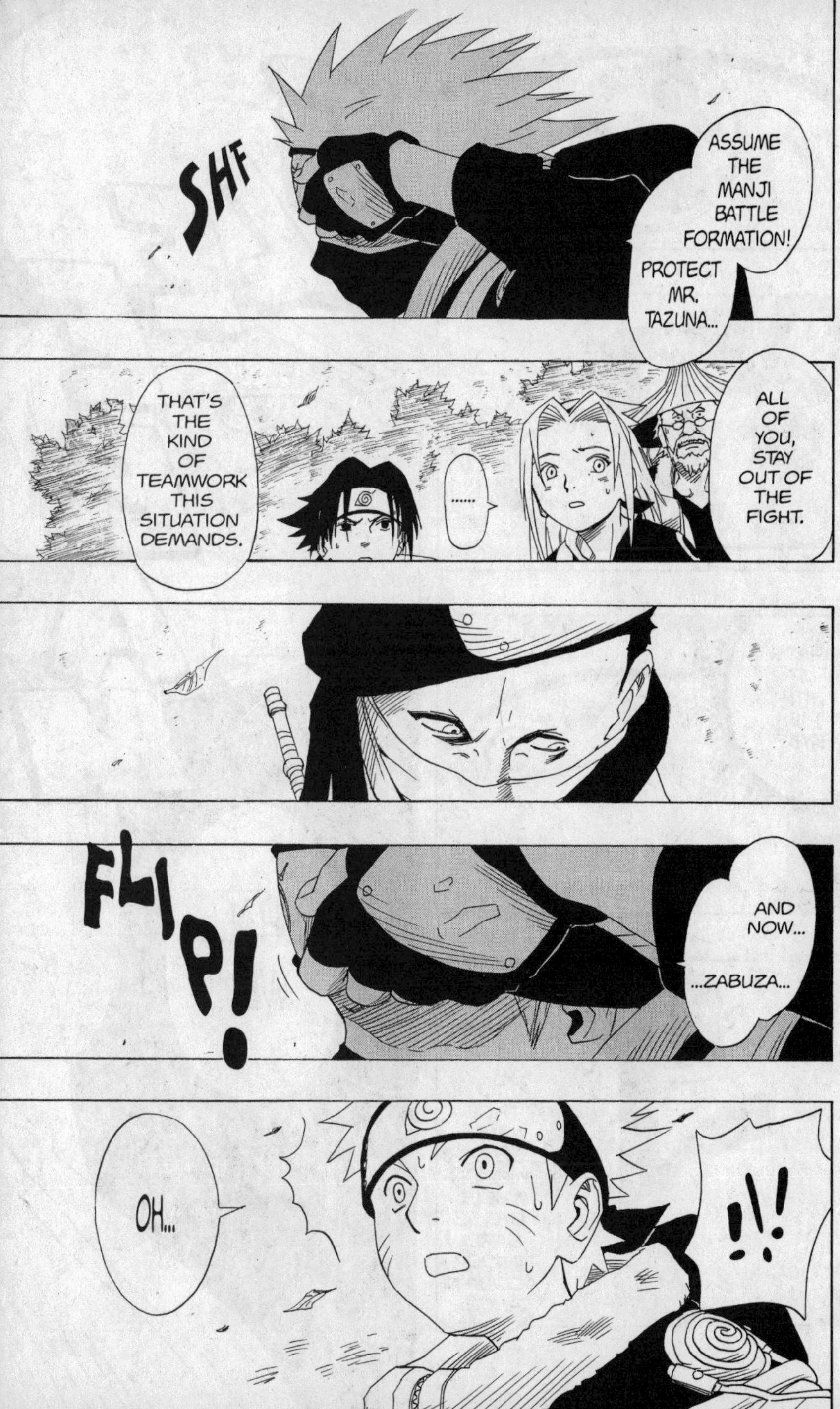
ASSUME THE MANJI BATTLE FORMATION!
SHF
PROTECT MR. TAZUNA...
ALL OF YOU, STAY OUT OF THE FIGHT.
......
THAT'S THE KIND OF TEAMWORK THIS SITUATION DEMANDS.
AND NOW...
...ZABUZA...
FLIP!
!!
OH...

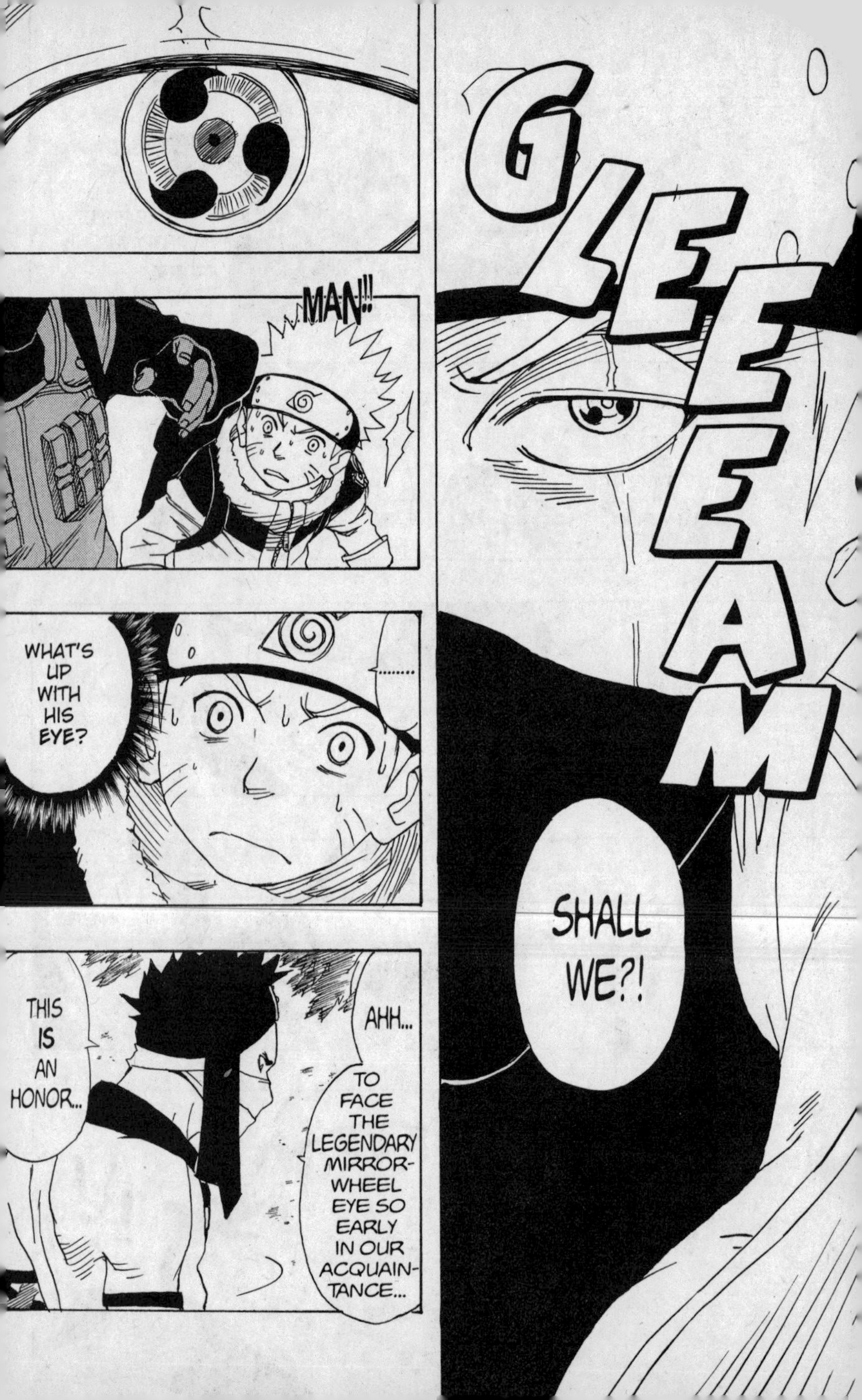
GLEEEAM
SHALL WE?!
MAN!!
......
WHAT'S UP WITH HIS EYE?
AHH...
TO FACE THE LEGENDARY MIRROR-WHEEL EYE SO EARLY IN OUR ACQUAINTANCE...
THIS IS AN HONOR...

READ THIS WAY

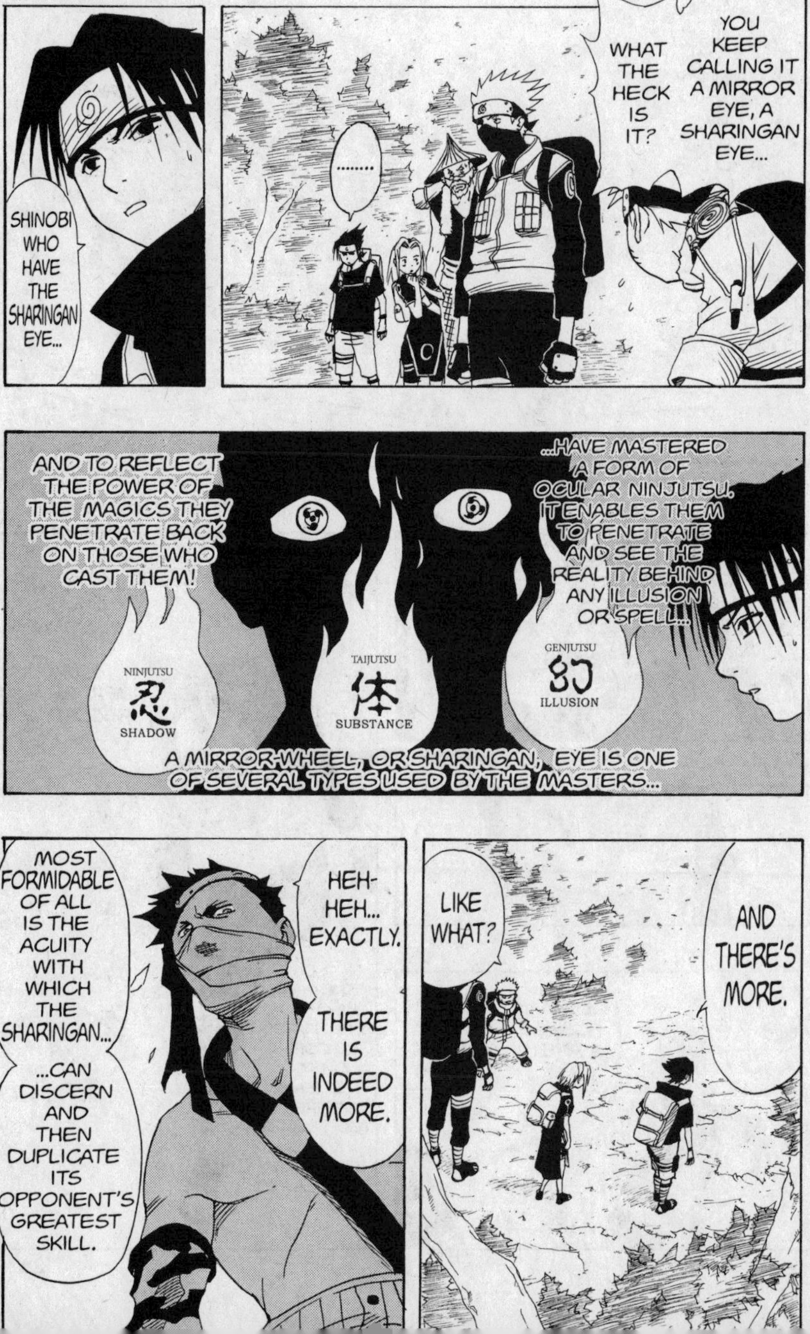
YOU KEEP CALLING IT A MIRROR EYE, A SHARINGAN EYE...
WHAT THE HECK IS IT?
....
SHINOBI WHO HAVE THE SHARINGAN EYE...
...HAVE MASTERED A FORM OF OCULAR NINJUTSU. IT ENABLES THEM TO PENETRATE AND SEE THE REALITY BEHIND ANY ILLUSION OR SPELL...
AND TO REFLECT THE POWER OF THE MAGICS THEY PENETRATE BACK ON THOSE WHO CAST THEM!
GENJUTSU 幻 ILLUSION
TAIJUTSU 体 SUBSTANCE
NINJUTSU 忍 SHADOW
A MIRROR-WHEEL, OR SHARINGAN, EYE IS ONE OF SEVERAL TYPES USED BY THE MASTERS...
AND THERE'S MORE.
LIKE WHAT?
HEH-HEH... EXACTLY.
THERE IS INDEED MORE.
MOST FORMIDABLE OF ALL IS THE ACUITY WITH WHICH THE SHARINGAN...
...CAN DISCERN AND THEN DUPLICATE ITS OPPONENT'S GREATEST SKILL.

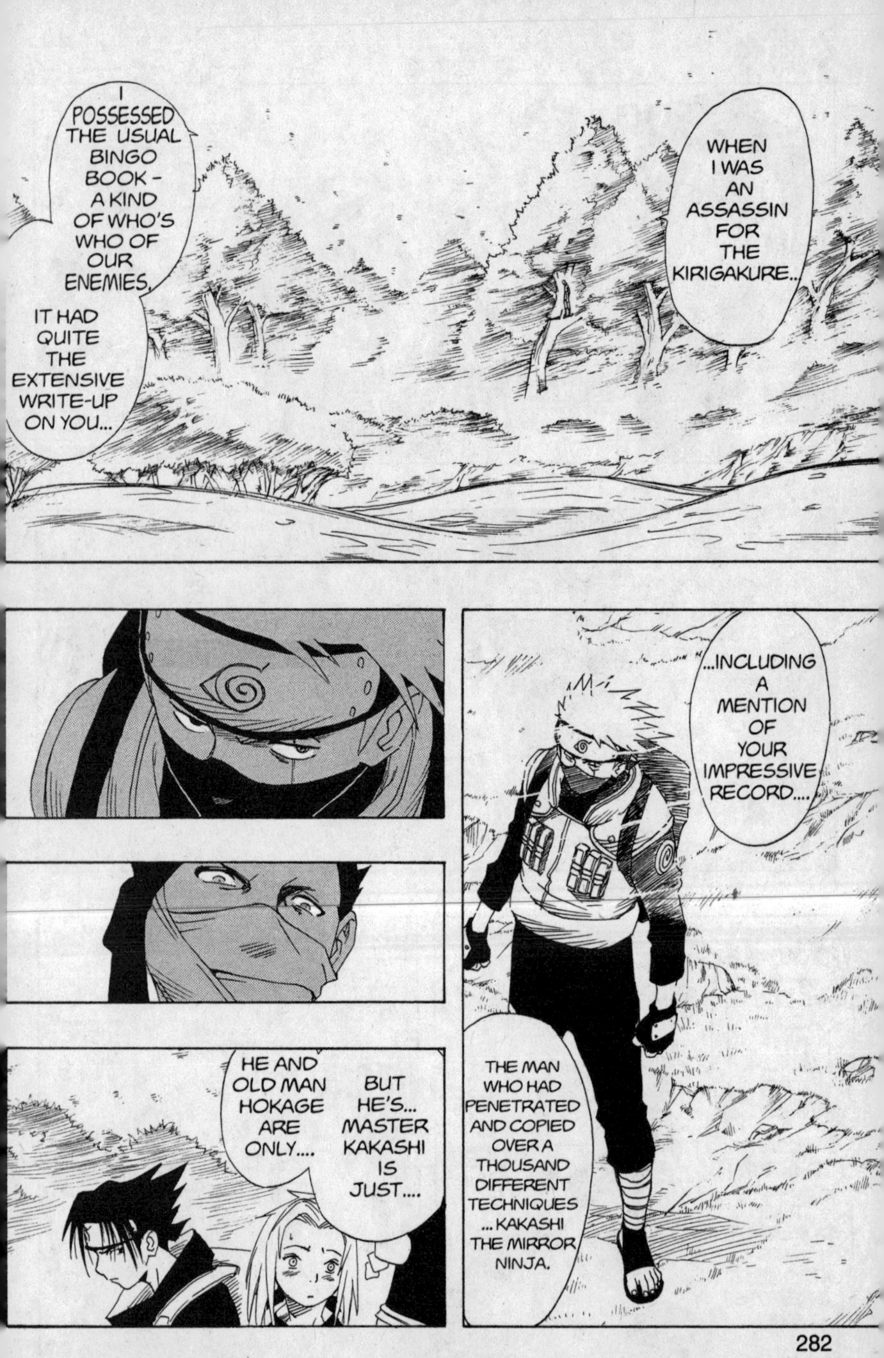
WHEN I WAS AN ASSASSIN FOR THE KIRIGAKURE..
I POSSESSED THE USUAL BINGO BOOK - A KIND OF WHO'S WHO OF OUR ENEMIES,
IT HAD QUITE THE EXTENSIVE WRITE-UP ON YOU...
...INCLUDING A MENTION OF YOUR IMPRESSIVE RECORD....
THE MAN WHO HAD PENETRATED AND COPIED OVER A THOUSAND DIFFERENT TECHNIQUES ...KAKASHI THE MIRROR NINJA.
BUT HE'S... MASTER KAKASHI IS JUST....
HE AND OLD MAN HOKAGE ARE ONLY....

READ THIS WAY

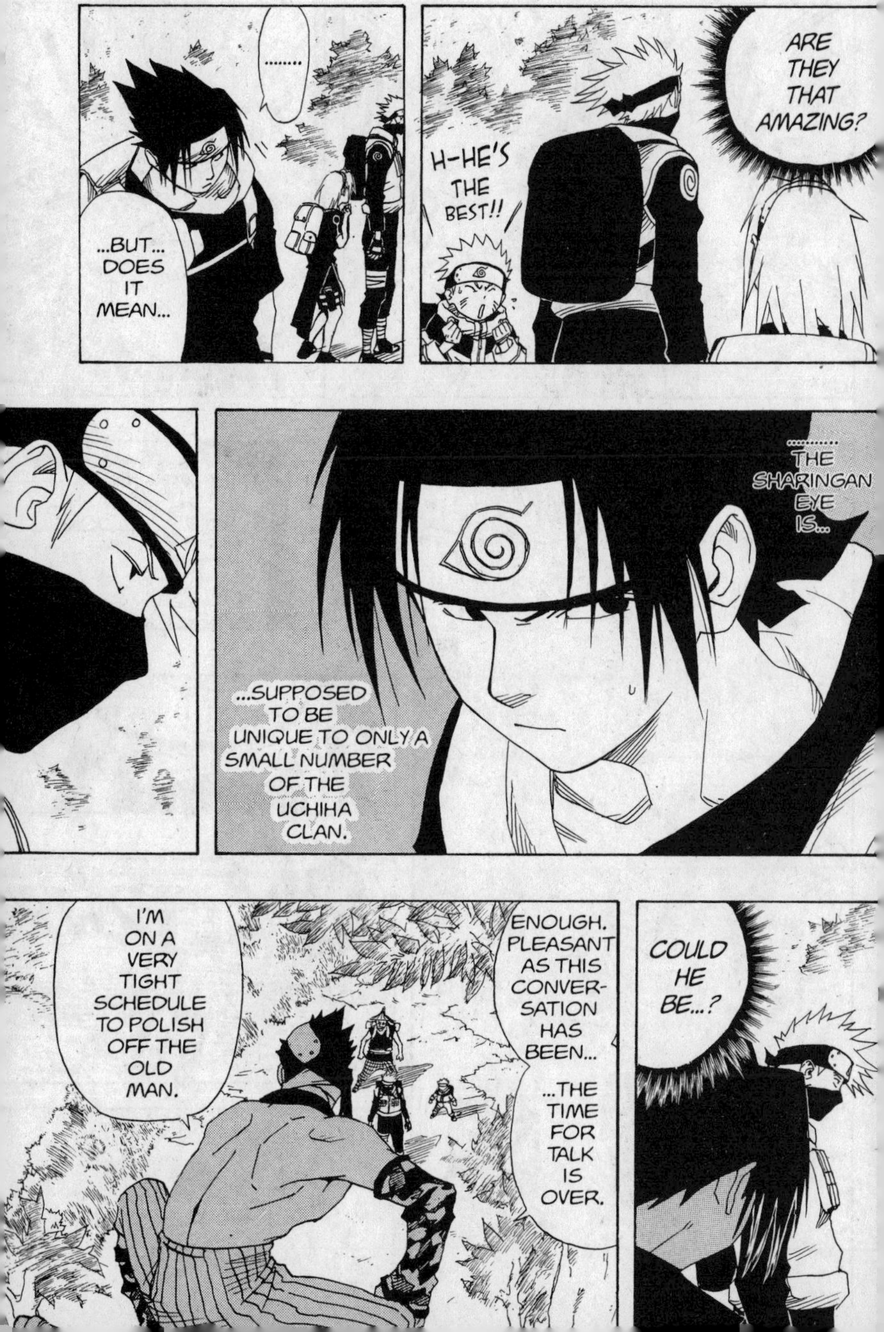
ARE THEY THAT AMAZING?
H-HE'S THE BEST!!
....
...BUT... DOES IT MEAN...
..........THE SHARINGAN EYE IS...
...SUPPOSED TO BE UNIQUE TO ONLY A SMALL NUMBER OF THE UCHIHA CLAN.
COULD HE BE...?
ENOUGH. PLEASANT AS THIS CONVER-SATION HAS BEEN...
...THE TIME FOR TALK IS OVER.
I'M ON A VERY TIGHT SCHEDULE TO POLISH OFF THE OLD MAN.

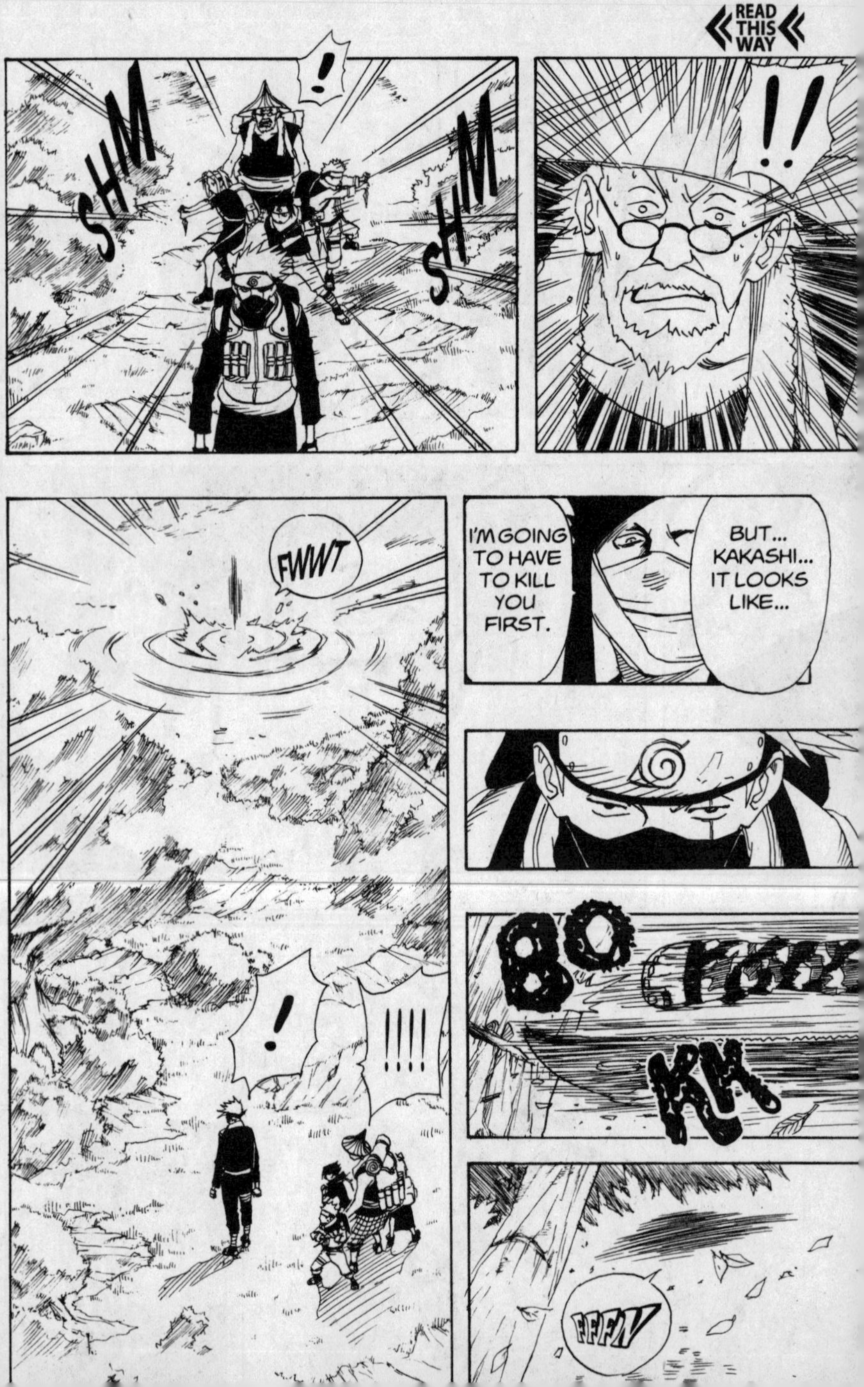
READ THIS WAY
!!
!
SHM
SHM
BUT... KAKASHI... IT LOOKS LIKE...
I'M GOING TO HAVE TO KILL YOU FIRST.
FFFN
FWWT
!
!!!!

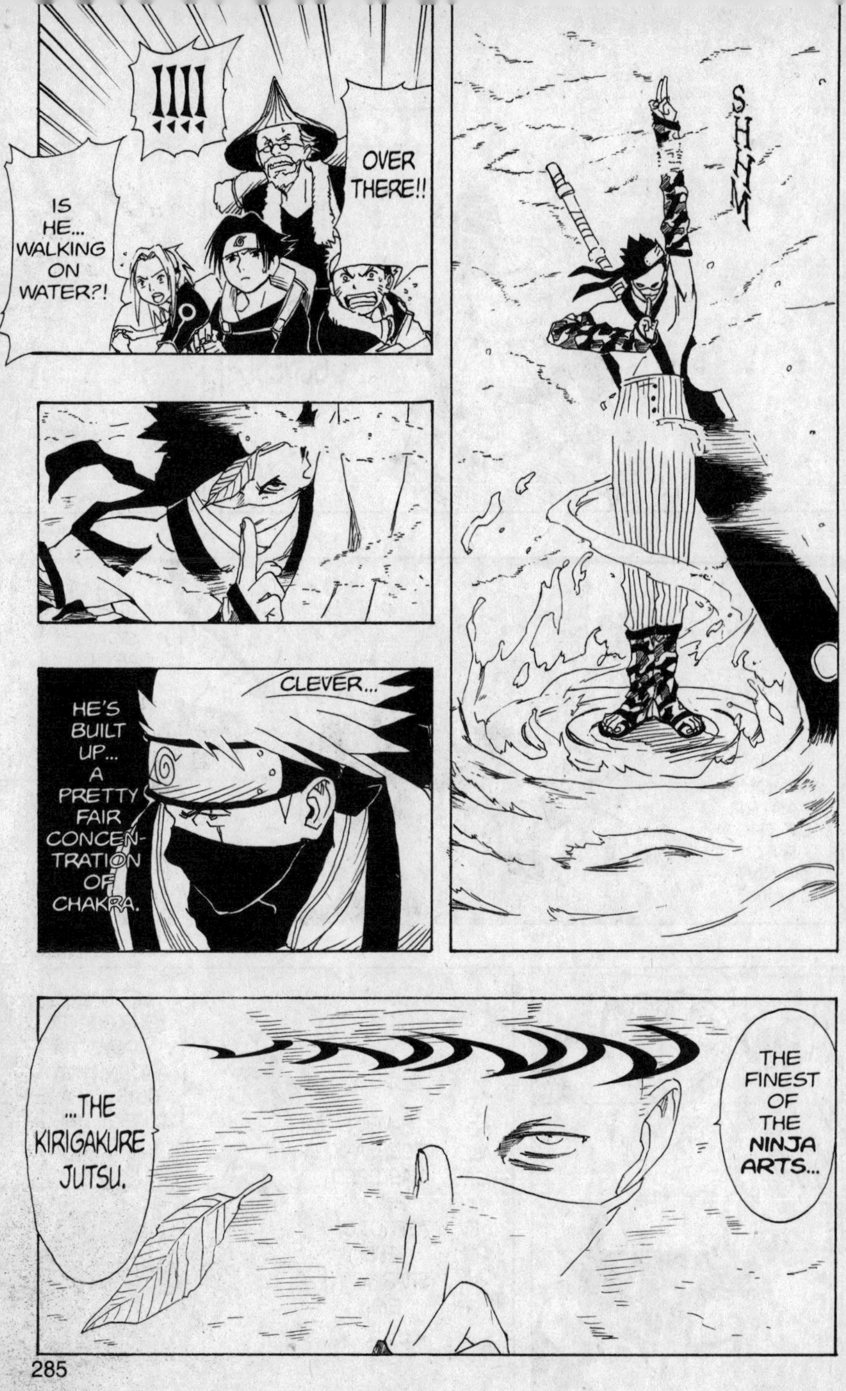
SHHM
!!!!
OVER THERE!!
IS HE... WALKING ON WATER?!
CLEVER...
HE'S BUILT UP... A PRETTY FAIR CONCENTRATION OF CHAKRA.
THE FINEST OF THE NINJA ARTS...
...THE KIRIGAKURE JUTSU.

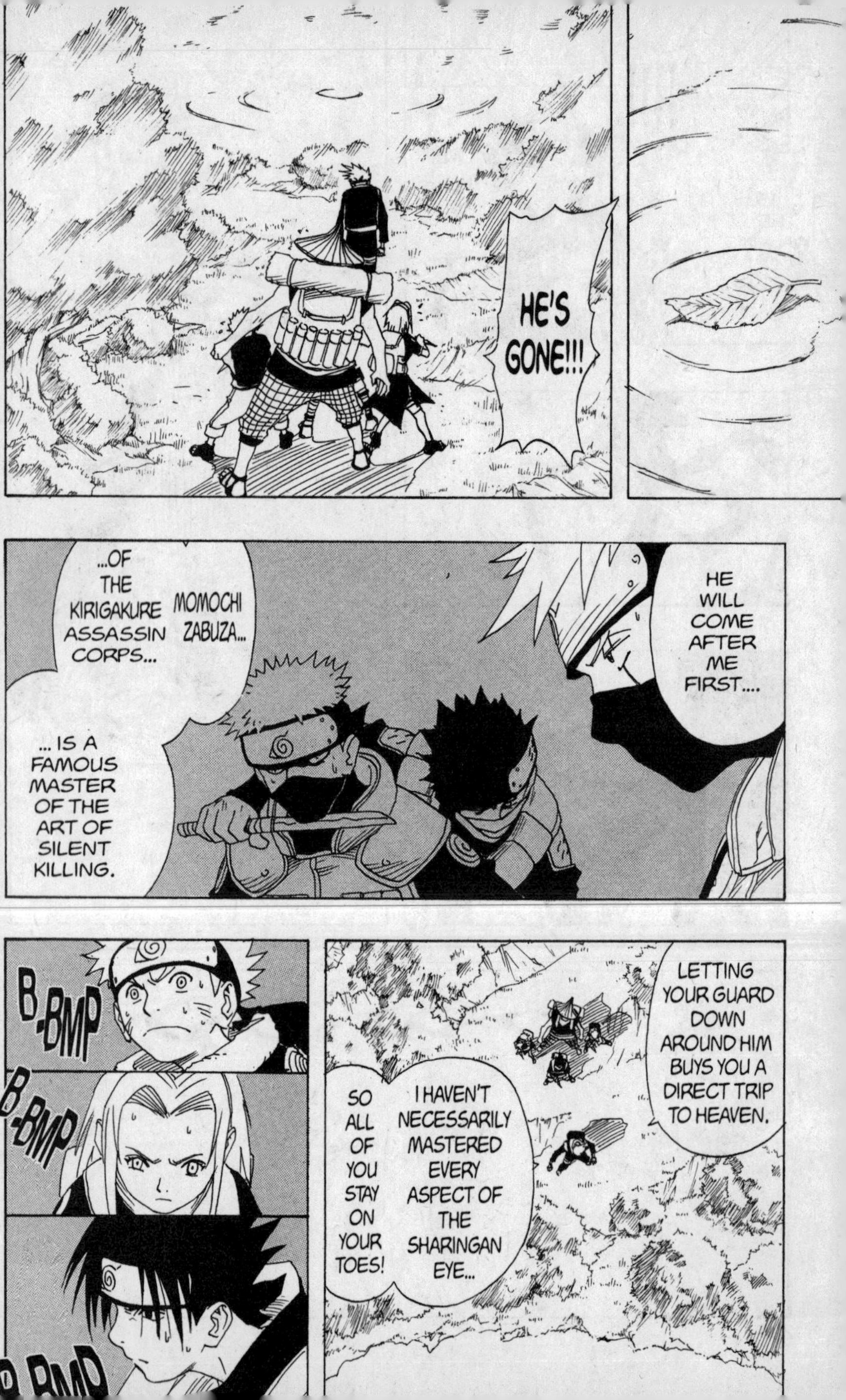
HE'S GONE!!!
HE WILL COME AFTER ME FIRST....
MOMOCHI ZABUZA...
...OF THE KIRIGAKURE ASSASSIN CORPS...
... IS A FAMOUS MASTER OF THE ART OF SILENT KILLING.
LETTING YOUR GUARD DOWN AROUND HIM BUYS YOU A DIRECT TRIP TO HEAVEN.
I HAVEN'T NECESSARILY MASTERED EVERY ASPECT OF THE SHARINGAN EYE...
SO ALL OF YOU STAY ON YOUR TOES!
B-BMP
B-BMP
B-BMP

READ THIS WAY

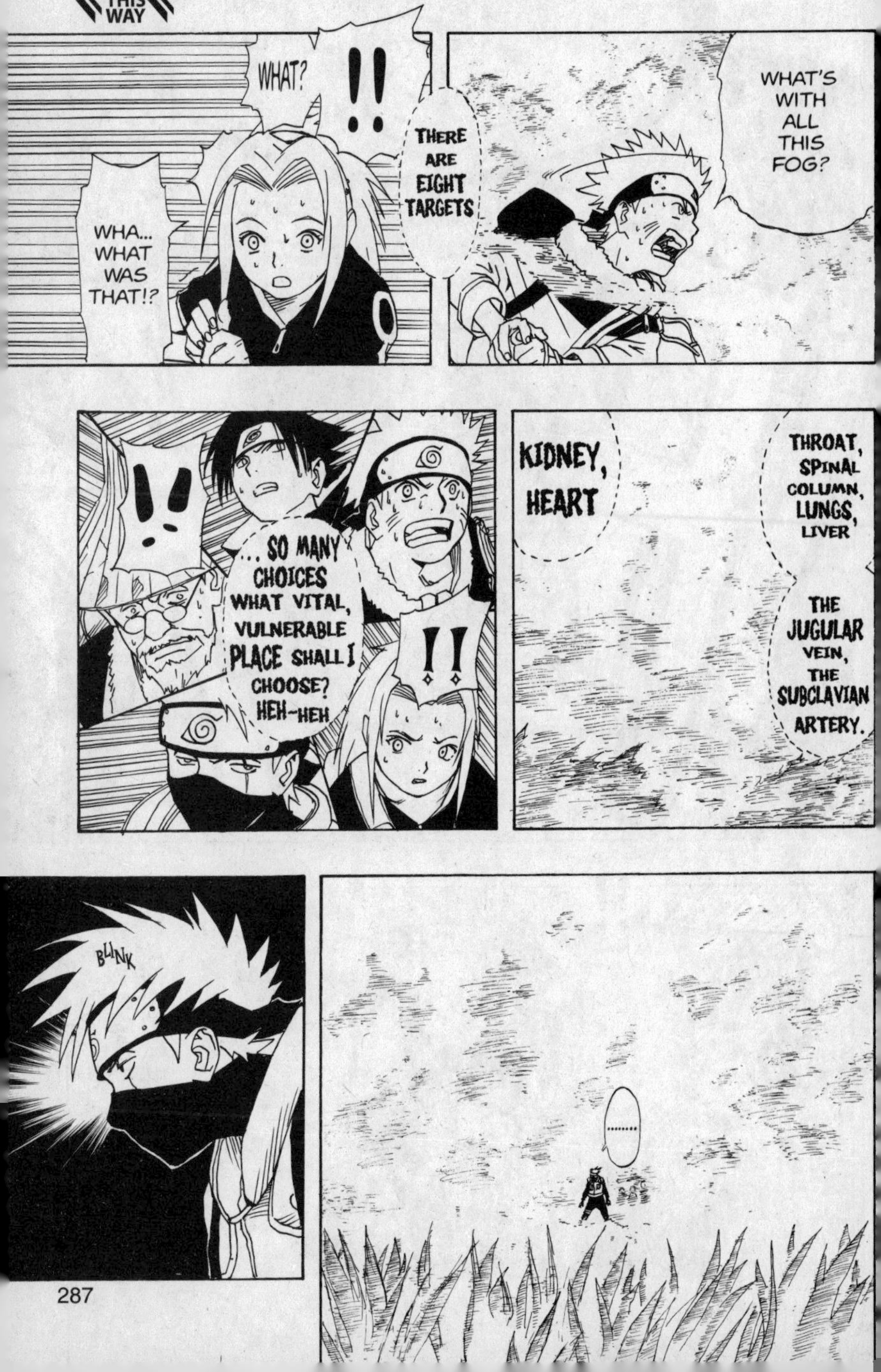
WHAT'S WITH ALL THIS FOG?
THERE ARE EIGHT TARGETS
!!
WHAT?
WHA... WHAT WAS THAT!?
THROAT, SPINAL COLUMN, LUNGS, LIVER
THE JUGULAR VEIN, THE SUBCLAVIAN ARTERY.
KIDNEY, HEART
!!
!
...SO MANY CHOICES WHAT VITAL, VULNERABLE PLACE SHALL I CHOOSE? HEH-HEH
....
BLINK

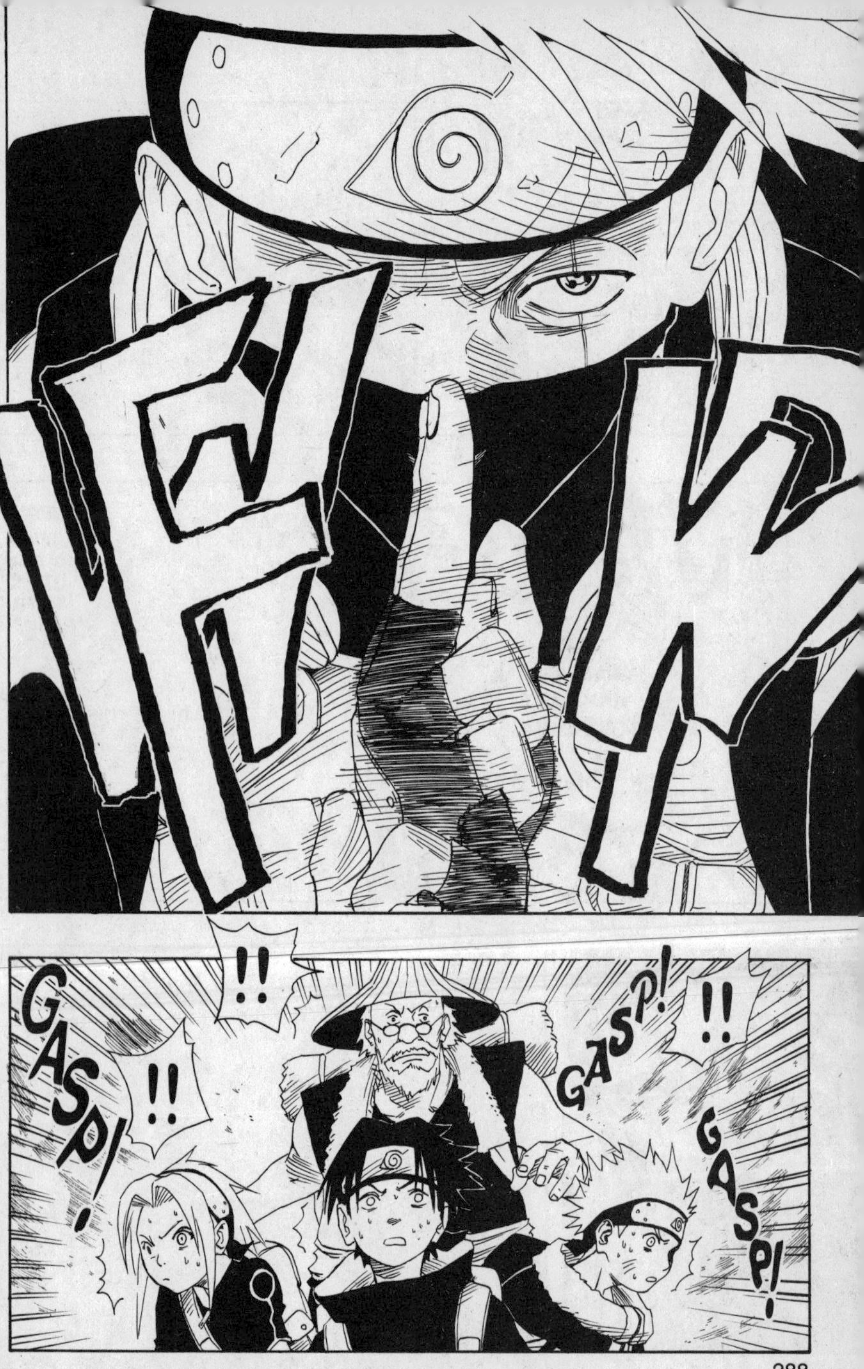
!!
GASP!
GASP!
!!
GASP!
!!

READ THIS WAY

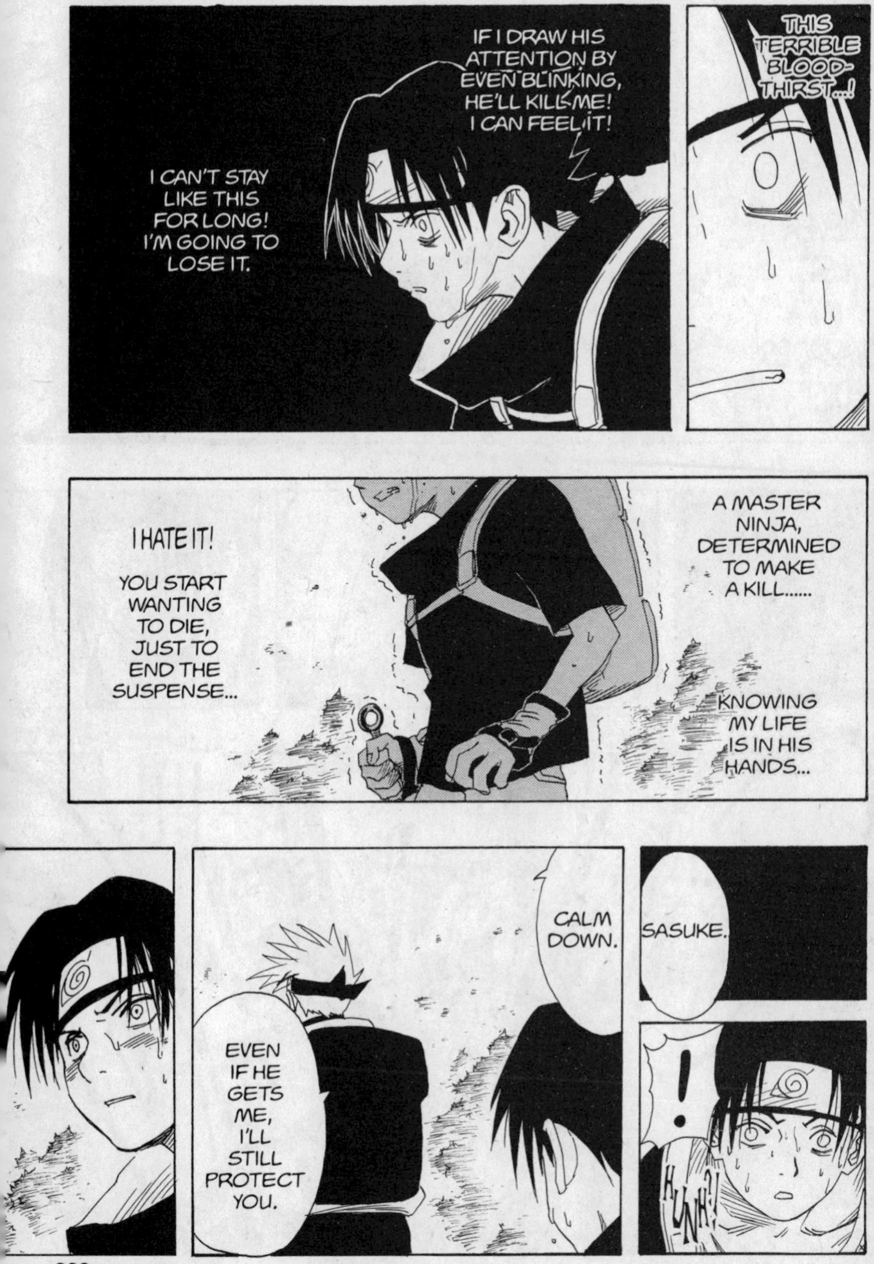
THIS TERRIBLE BLOOD-THIRST...!
IF I DRAW HIS ATTENTION BY EVEN BLINKING, HE'LL KILL ME! I CAN FEEL IT!
I CAN'T STAY LIKE THIS FOR LONG! I'M GOING TO LOSE IT.
A MASTER NINJA, DETERMINED TO MAKE A KILL......
KNOWING MY LIFE IS IN HIS HANDS...
I HATE IT!
YOU START WANTING TO DIE, JUST TO END THE SUSPENSE...
SASUKE.
!
HUNH?!
CALM DOWN.
EVEN IF HE GETS ME, I'LL STILL PROTECT YOU.

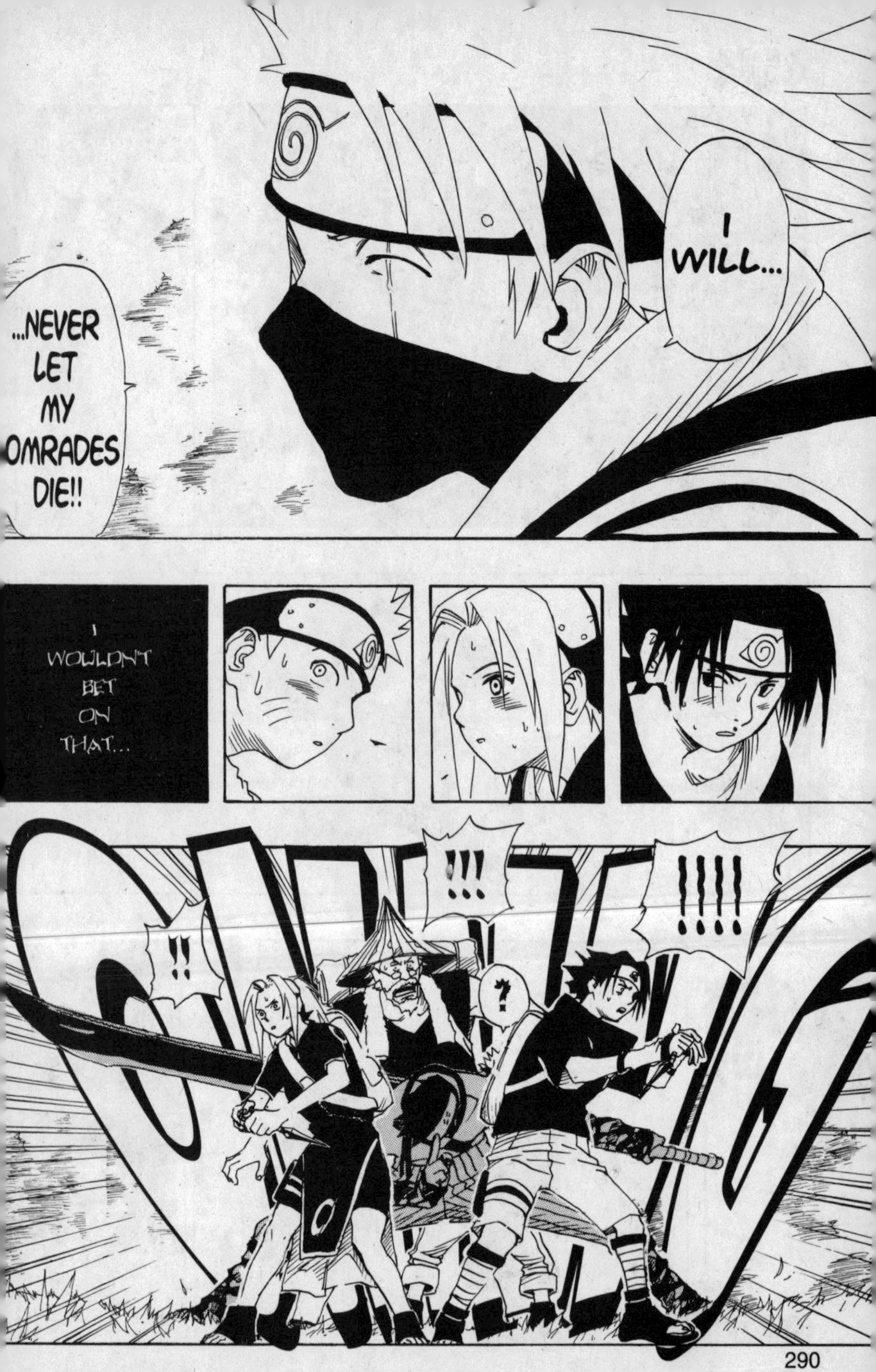
I WILL...
...NEVER LET MY OMRADES DIE!!
I WOULDN'T BET ON THAT...
!!!!
!!!
?
!!

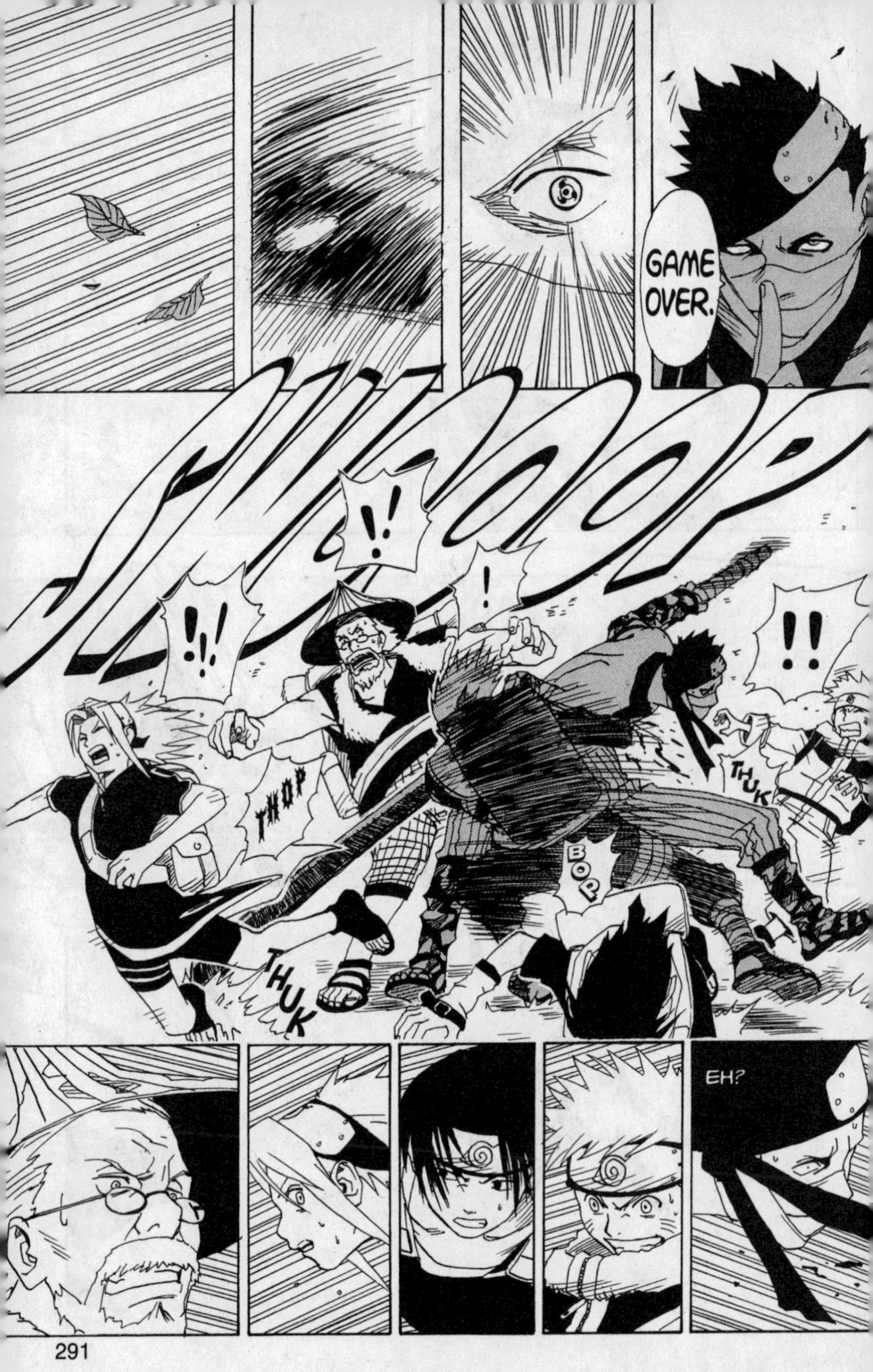
GAME OVER.
THUK
BOP
THOP
THUK
EH?

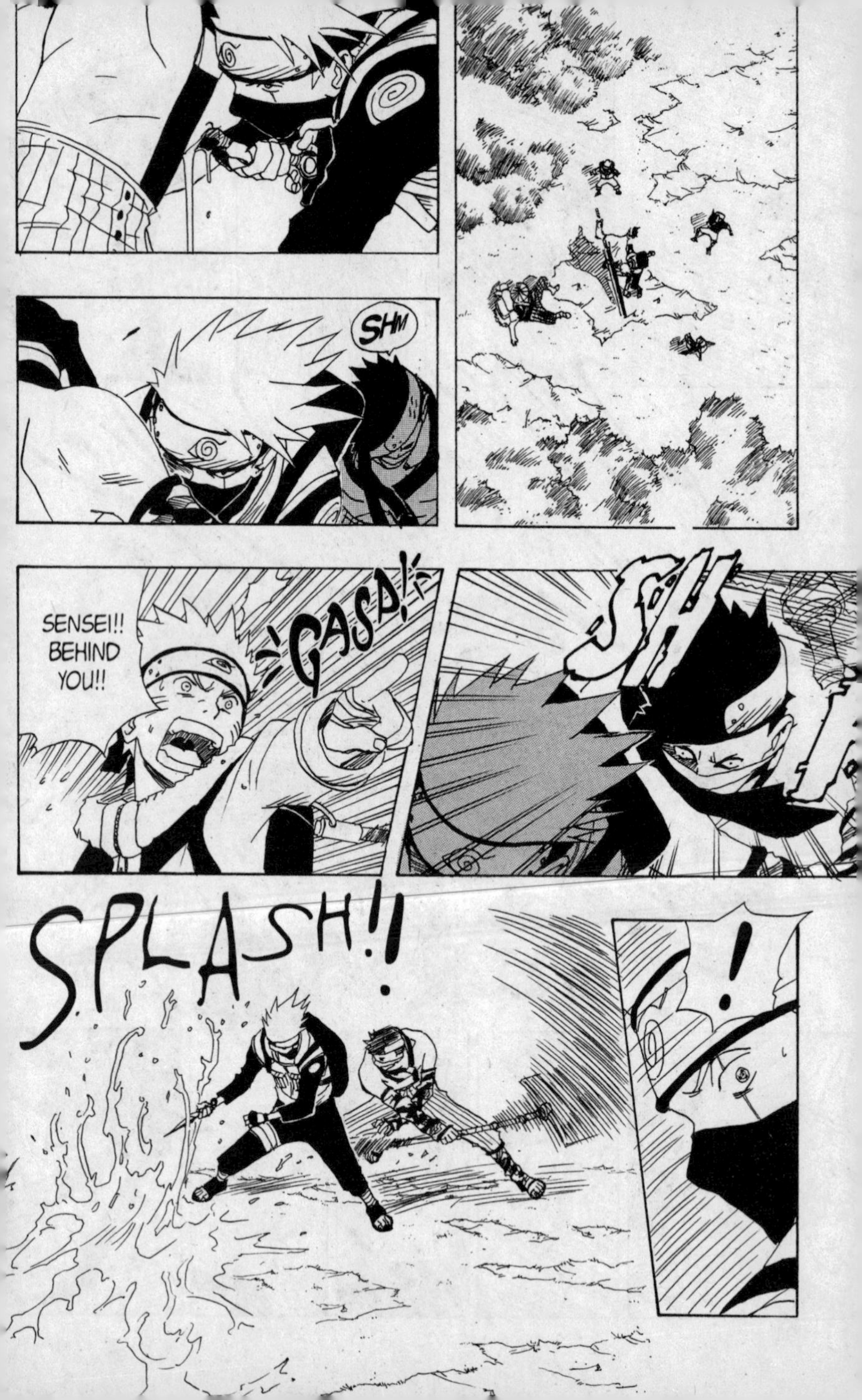
SHM
GASA!
SENSEI!!! BEHIND YOU!!
SH
!
SPLASH!!

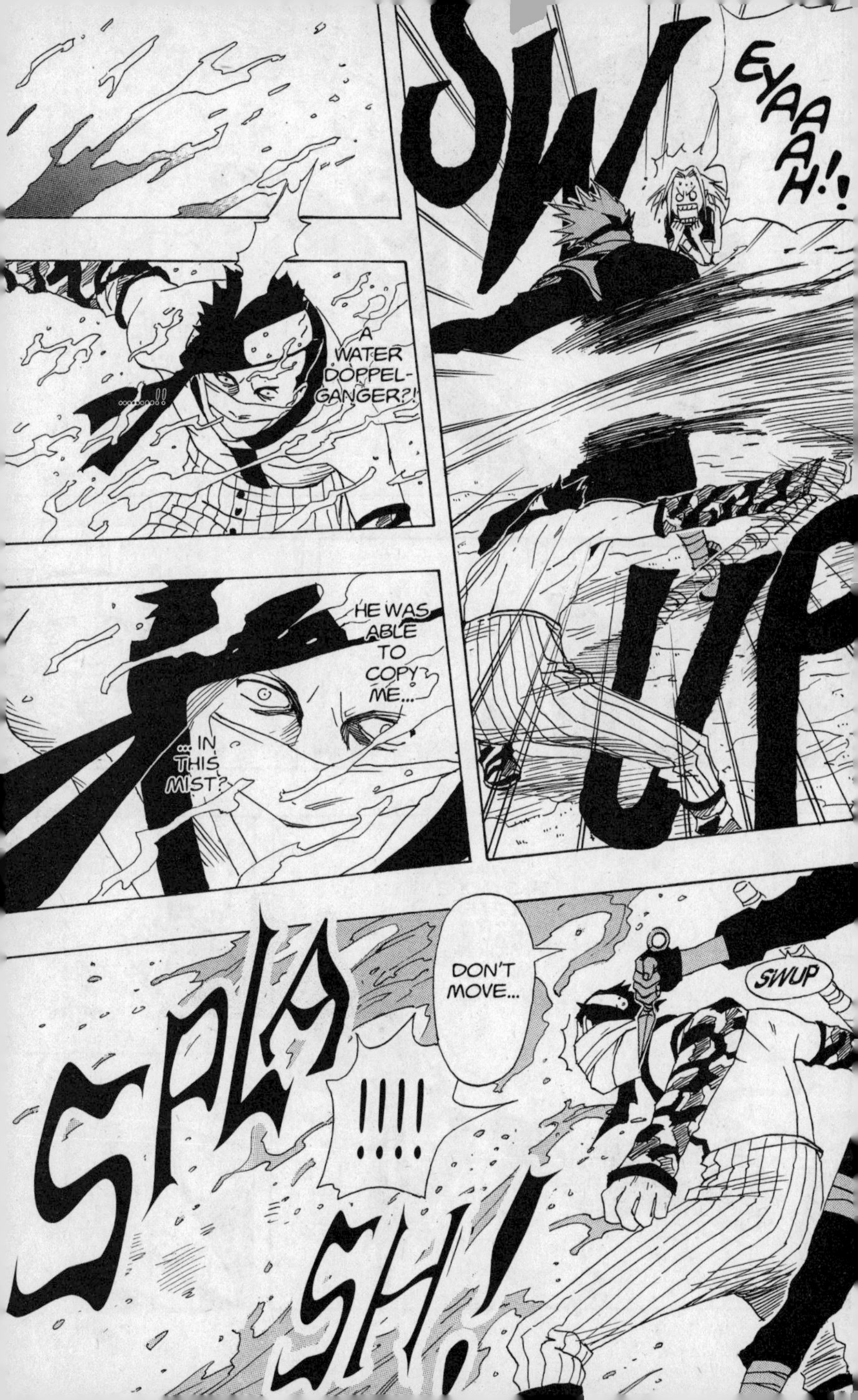

SW
UP
EYAAAH!!
A WATER DOPPEL-GANGER?!
.......!!
HE WAS ABLE TO COPY ME...
...IN THIS MIST?
DON'T MOVE...
SWUP
!!!!
SPLASH!

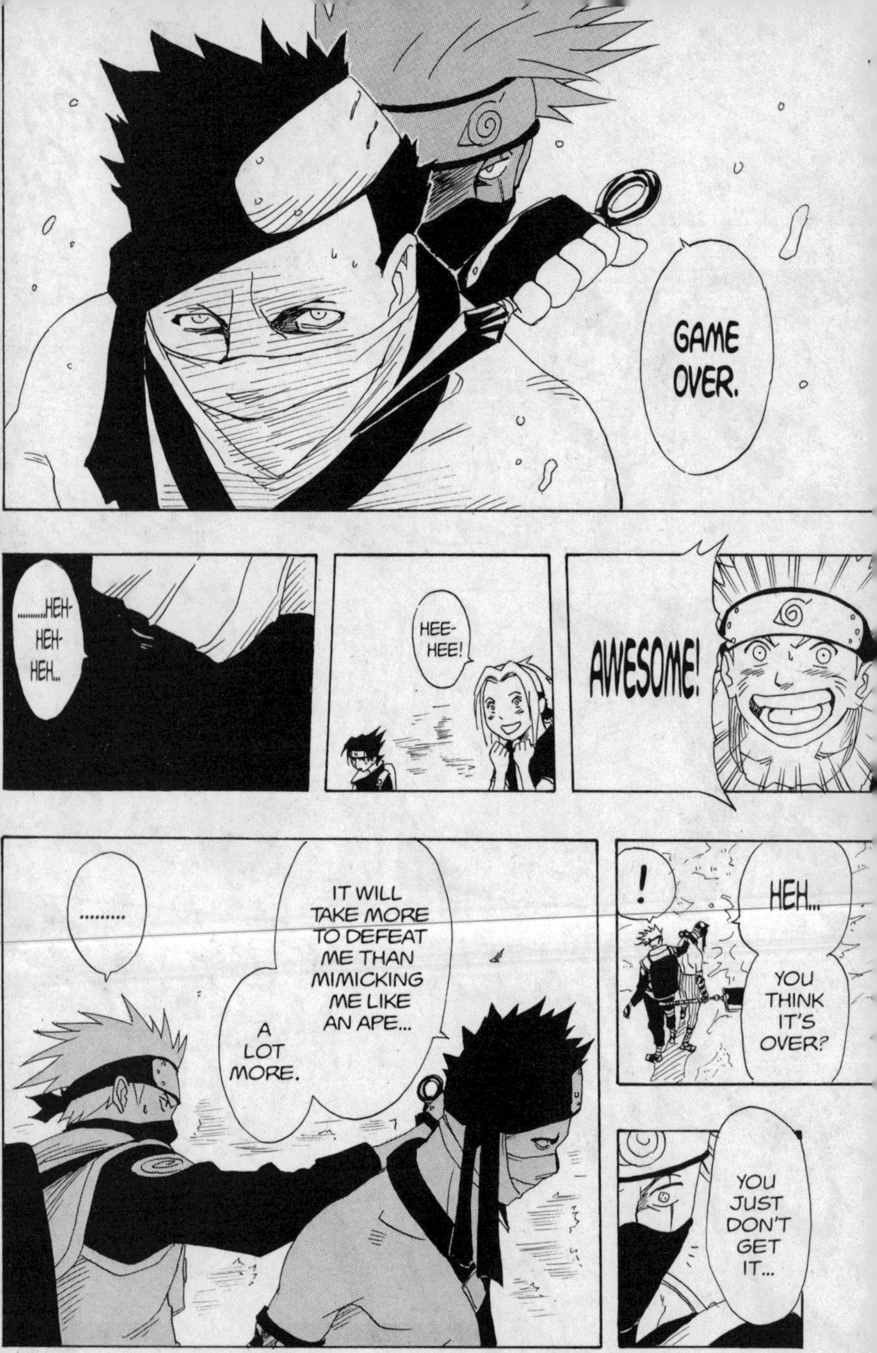
GAME OVER.
AWESOME!
HEE-HEE!
..........HEH-HEH-HEH...
HEH...
YOU THINK IT'S OVER?
!
YOU JUST DON'T GET IT...
IT WILL TAKE MORE TO DEFEAT ME THAN MIMICKING ME LIKE AN APE...
A LOT MORE.
....

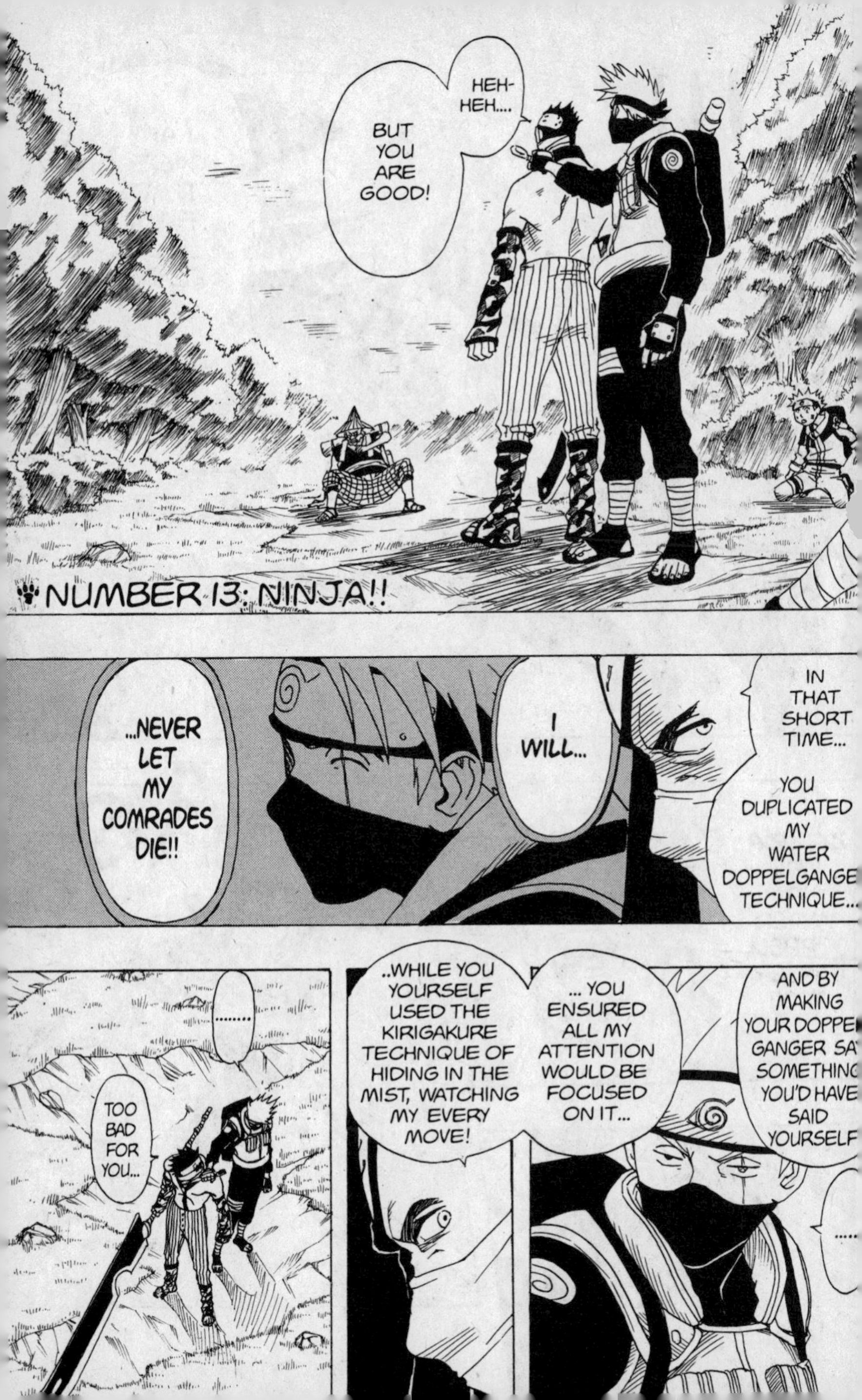
HEH-HEH....
BUT YOU ARE GOOD!
NUMBER 13: NINJA!!
IN THAT SHORT TIME... YOU DUPLICATED MY WATER DOPPELGANGE TECHNIQUE...
I WILL...
...NEVER LET MY COMRADES DIE!!
AND BY MAKING YOUR DOPPE GANGER SA SOMETHING YOU'D HAVE SAID YOURSELF
.....
... YOU ENSURED ALL MY ATTENTION WOULD BE FOCUSED ON IT...
..WHILE YOU YOURSELF USED THE KIRIGAKURE TECHNIQUE OF HIDING IN THE MIST, WATCHING MY EVERY MOVE!
....
TOO BAD FOR YOU...

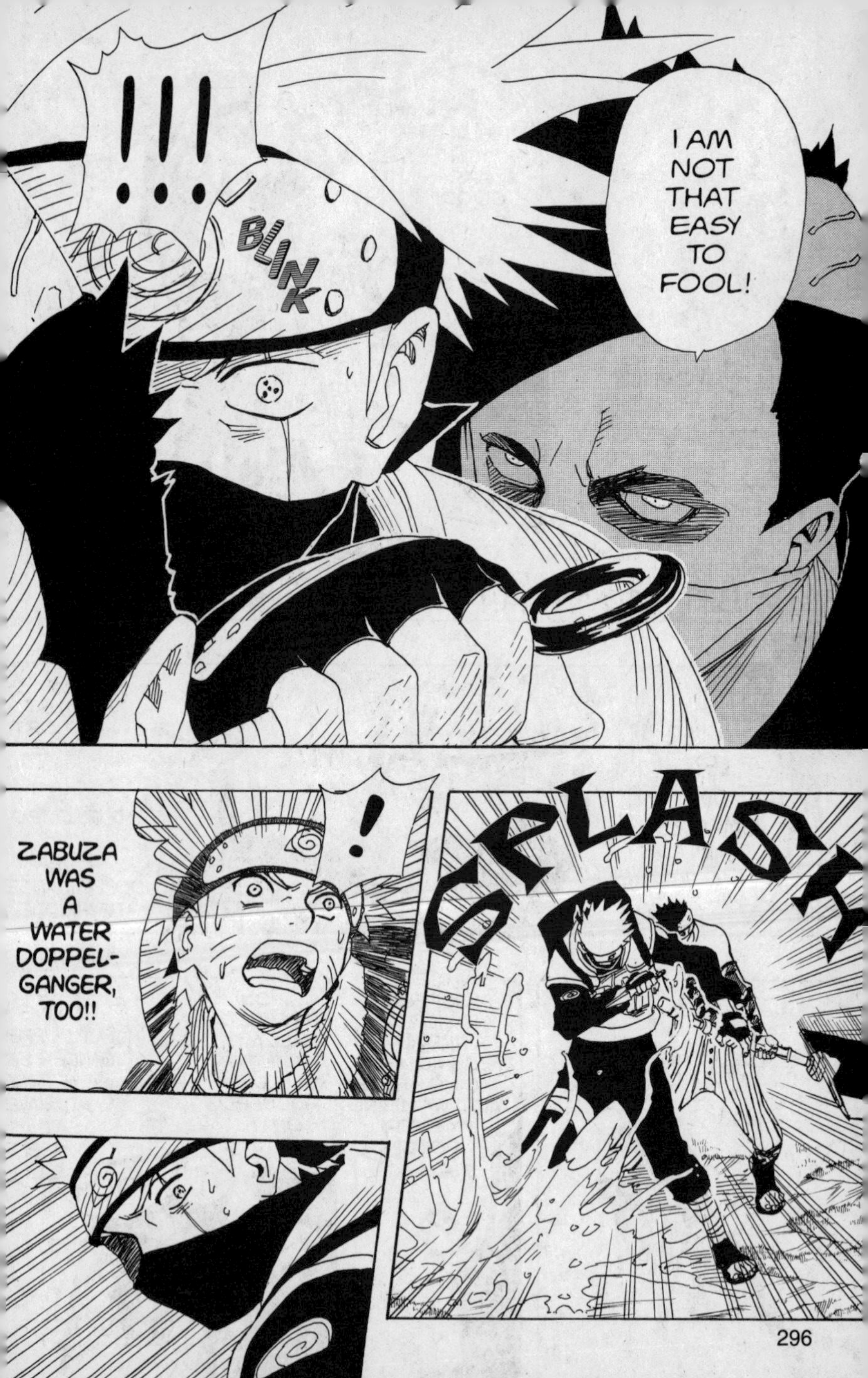
I AM NOT THAT EASY TO FOOL!
!!!...
BLINK
SPLASH
!
ZABUZA WAS A WATER DOPPEL-GANGER, TOO!!

Number 13: Ninja!!!

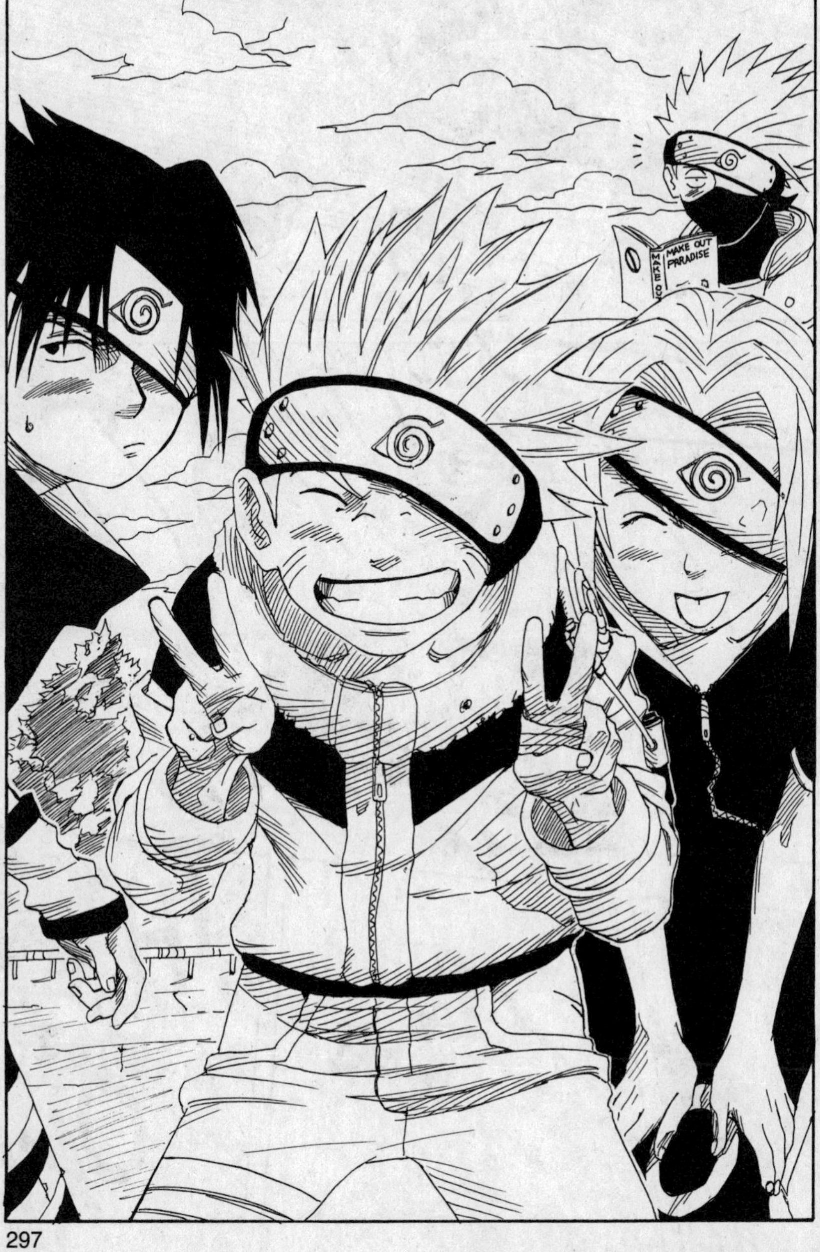
MAKE OUT PARADISE

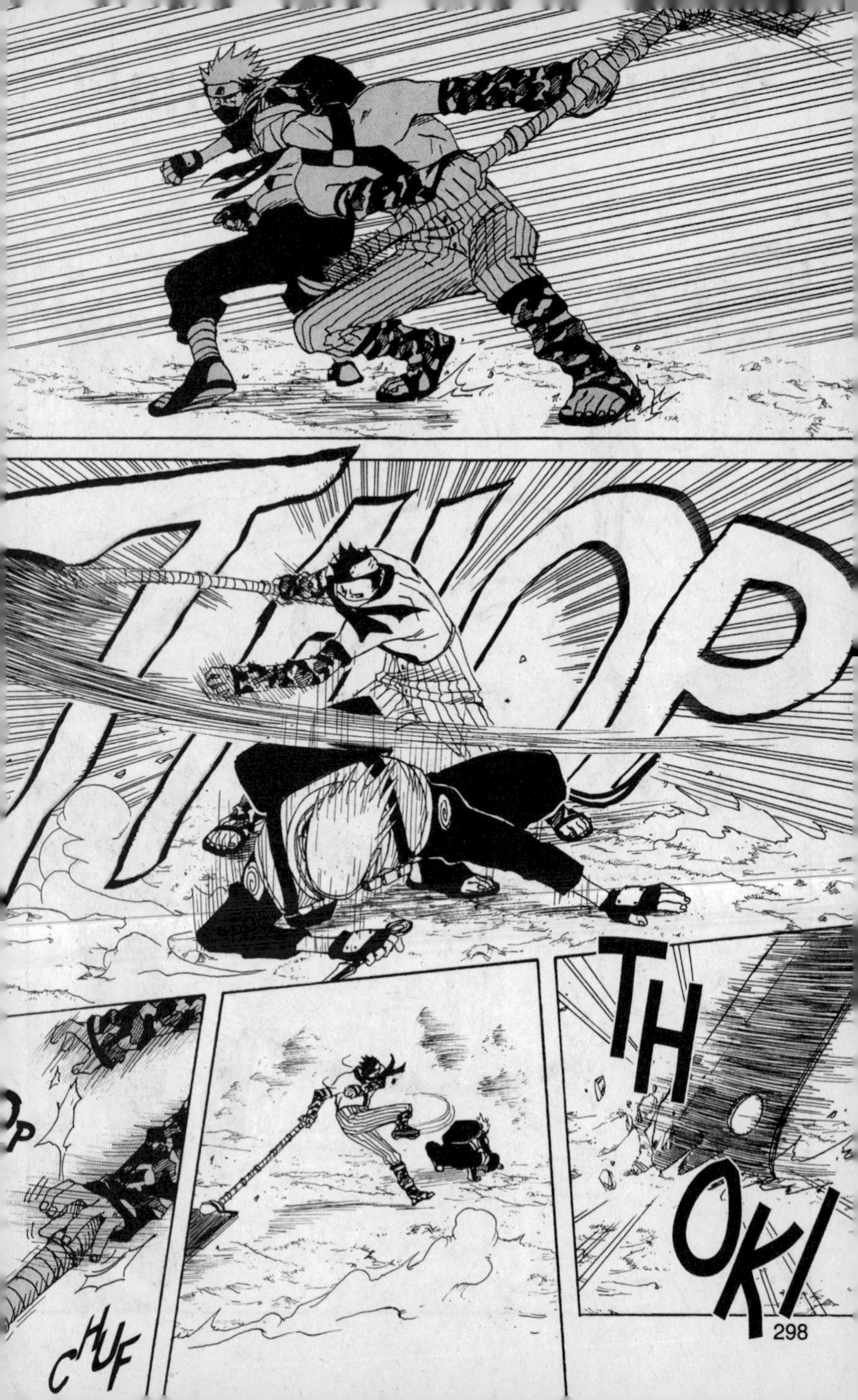
THWOP
THOK!
CHUF

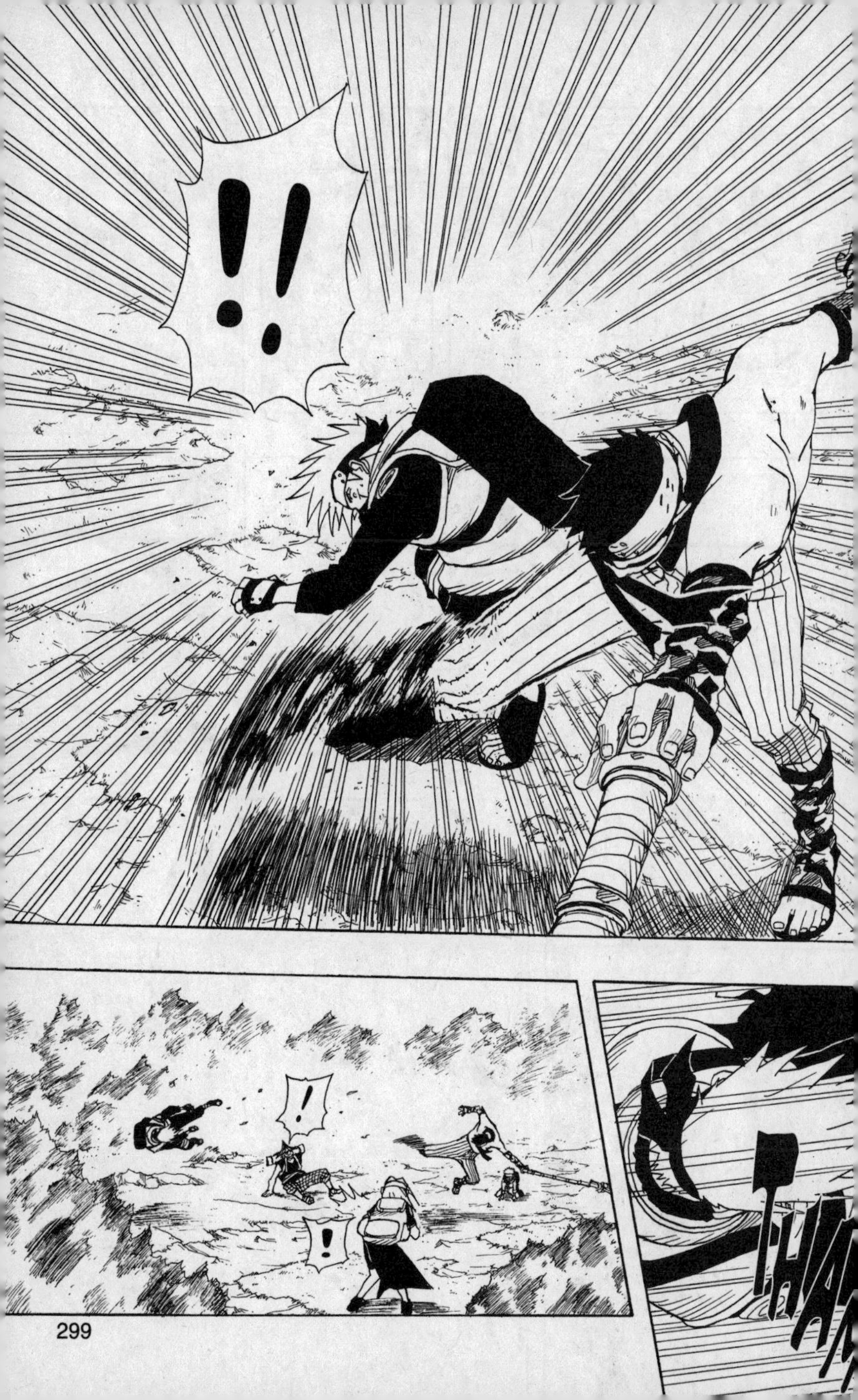
!!
CHA
!
!

READ THIS WAY

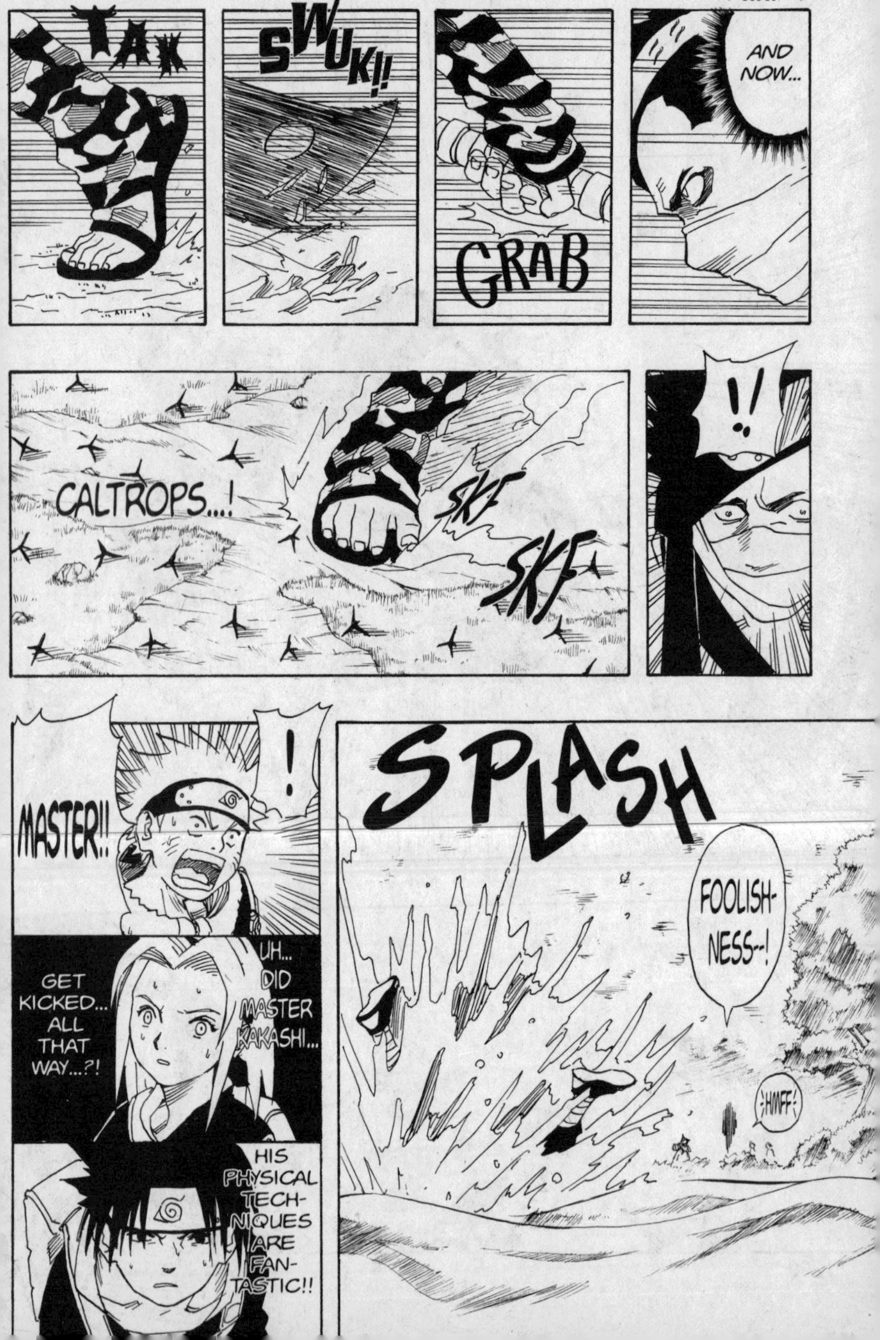
AND NOW...
GRAB
SWUK!!
TAK
!!
CALTROPS...!
SKF
SKF
SPLASH
FOOLISH-NESS--!
HMFF
!
MASTER!!
UH... DID MASTER KAKASHI...
GET KICKED... ALL THAT WAY...?!
HIS PHYSICAL TECH-NIQUES ARE FAN-TASTIC!!

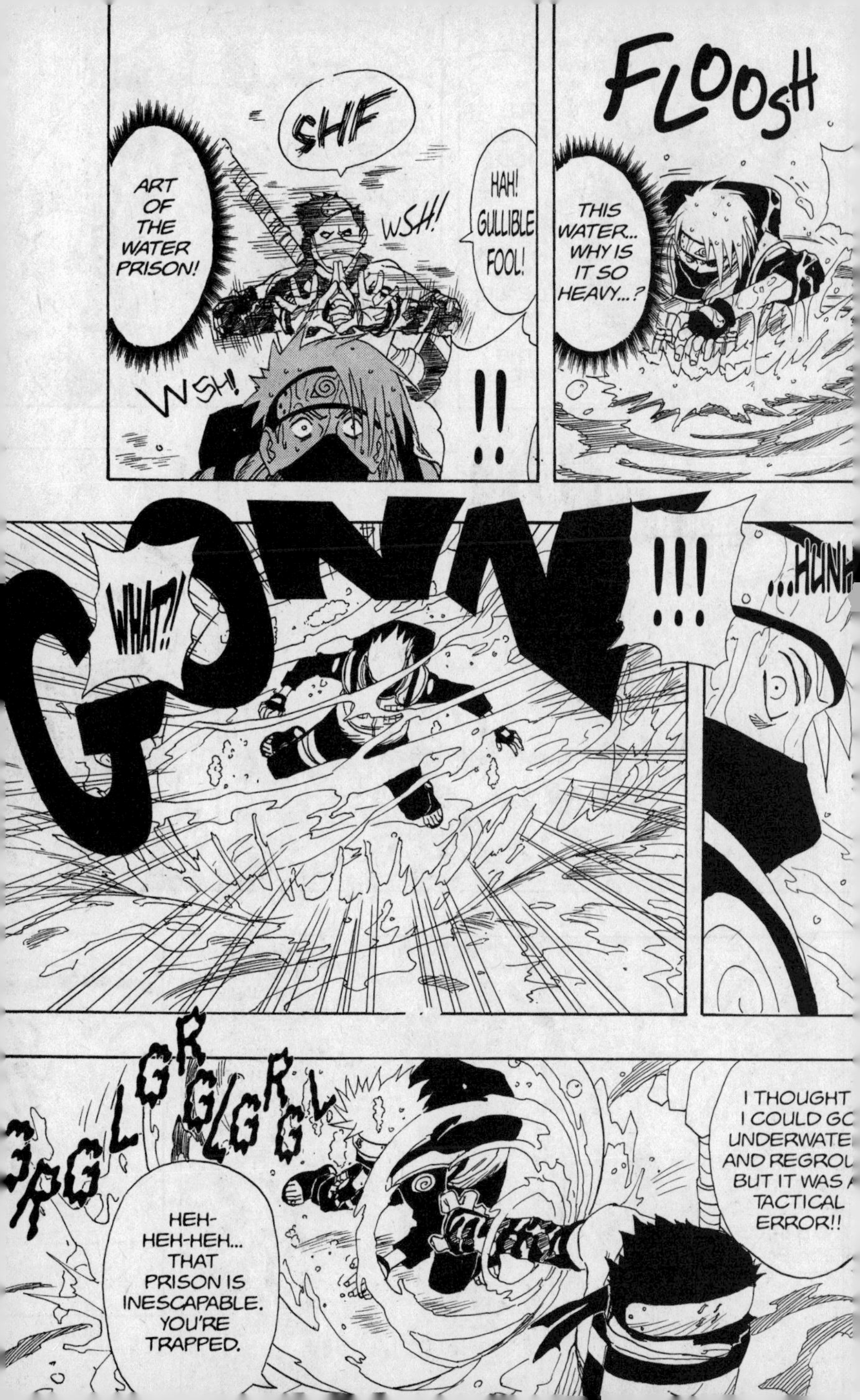
FLOOSH
THIS WATER... WHY IS IT SO HEAVY...?
SHF
HAH! GULLIBLE FOOL!
ART OF THE WATER PRISON!
WSH!
!!
WSH!
...HUNH
GONN!!!
WHAT?!
I THOUGHT I COULD GO UNDERWATE AND REGROU BUT IT WAS A TACTICAL ERROR!!
HEH-HEH-HEH... THAT PRISON IS INESCAPABLE. YOU'RE TRAPPED.

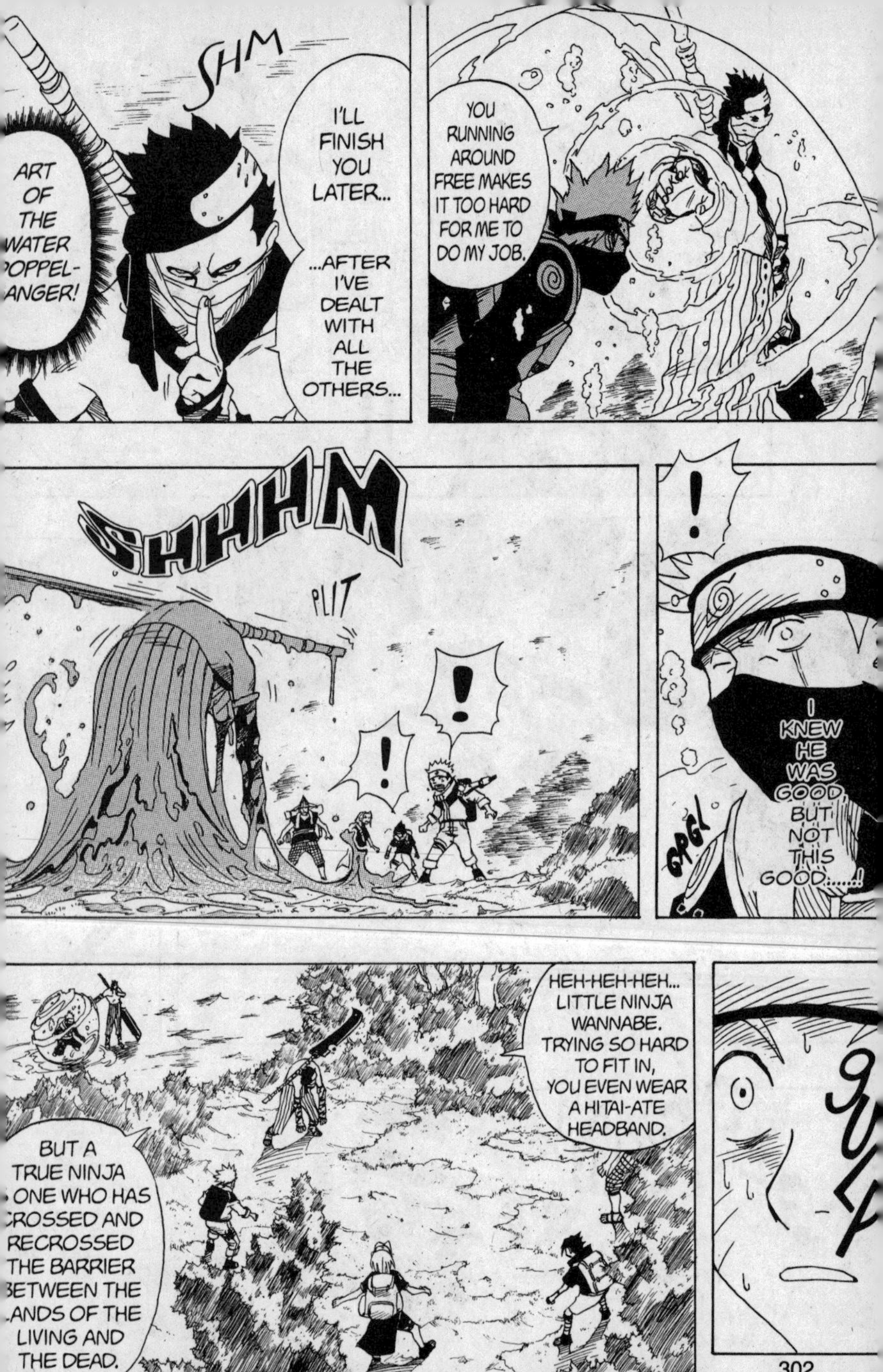
YOU RUNNING AROUND FREE MAKES IT TOO HARD FOR ME TO DO MY JOB.
SHM
I'LL FINISH YOU LATER...
...AFTER I'VE DEALT WITH ALL THE OTHERS...
ART OF THE WATER DOPPEL-GANGER!
!
I KNEW HE WAS GOOD, BUT NOT THIS GOOD......!
GPGL
SHHHM
PLIT
!
!
GULP
HEH-HEH-HEH... LITTLE NINJA WANNABE. TRYING SO HARD TO FIT IN, YOU EVEN WEAR A HITAI-ATE HEADBAND.
BUT A TRUE NINJA S ONE WHO HAS CROSSED AND RECROSSED THE BARRIER BETWEEN THE LANDS OF THE LIVING AND THE DEAD.

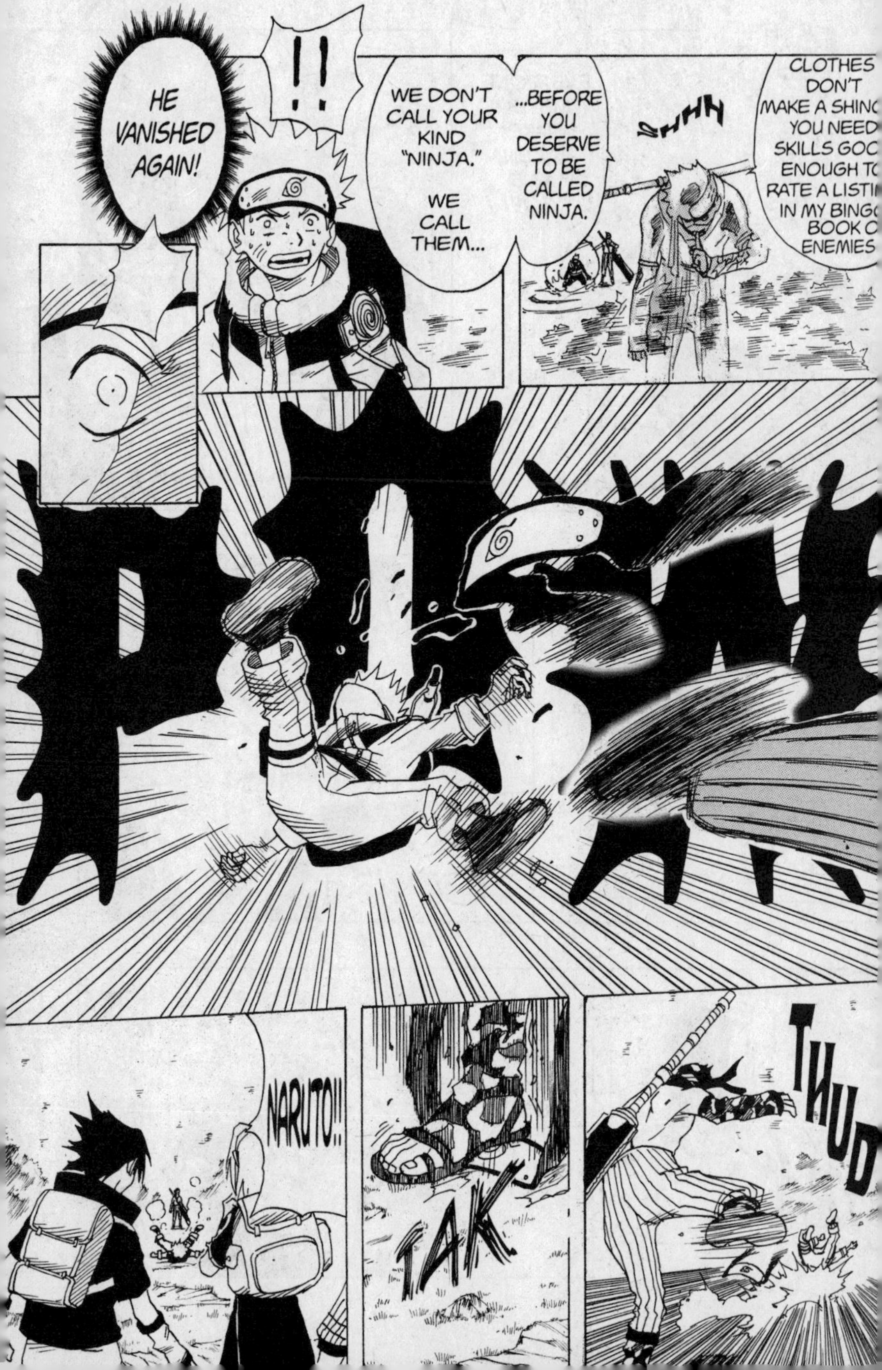
SHHH
CLOTHES DON'T MAKE A SHINC YOU NEED SKILLS GOC ENOUGH TC RATE A LISTI IN MY BINGC BOOK O ENEMIES
...BEFORE YOU DESERVE TO BE CALLED NINJA.
WE DON'T CALL YOUR KIND "NINJA." WE CALL THEM...
!!
HE VANISHED AGAIN!
THUD
TAK
NARUTO!!

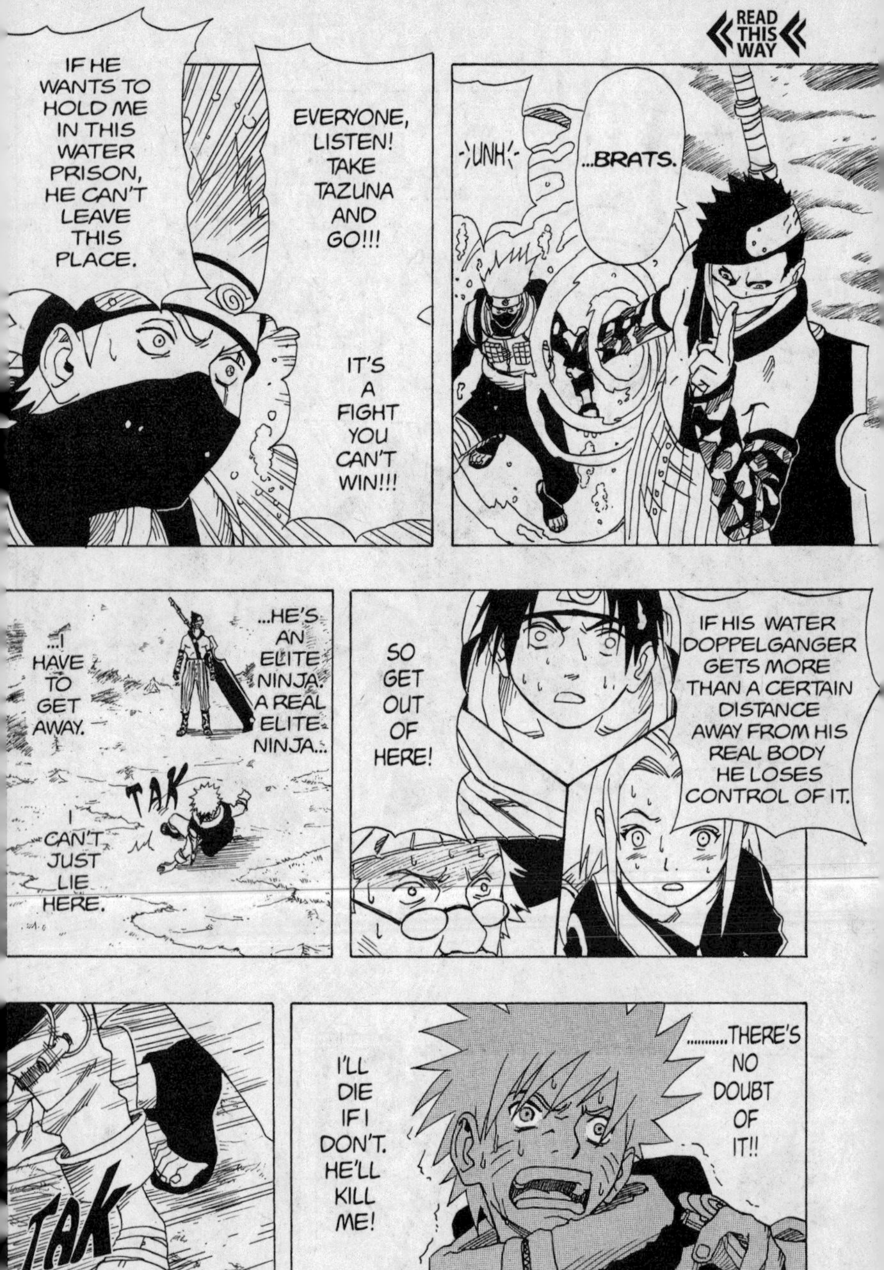
READ THIS WAY
-UNH-
...BRATS.
EVERYONE, LISTEN! TAKE TAZUNA AND GO!!!
IT'S A FIGHT YOU CAN'T WIN!!!
IF HE WANTS TO HOLD ME IN THIS WATER PRISON, HE CAN'T LEAVE THIS PLACE.
IF HIS WATER DOPPELGANGER GETS MORE THAN A CERTAIN DISTANCE AWAY FROM HIS REAL BODY HE LOSES CONTROL OF IT.
SO GET OUT OF HERE!
...HE'S AN ELITE NINJA. A REAL ELITE NINJA...
...I HAVE TO GET AWAY.
TAK
I CAN'T JUST LIE HERE.
..........THERE'S NO DOUBT OF IT!!
I'LL DIE IF I DON'T. HE'LL KILL ME!
TAK

READ THIS WAY

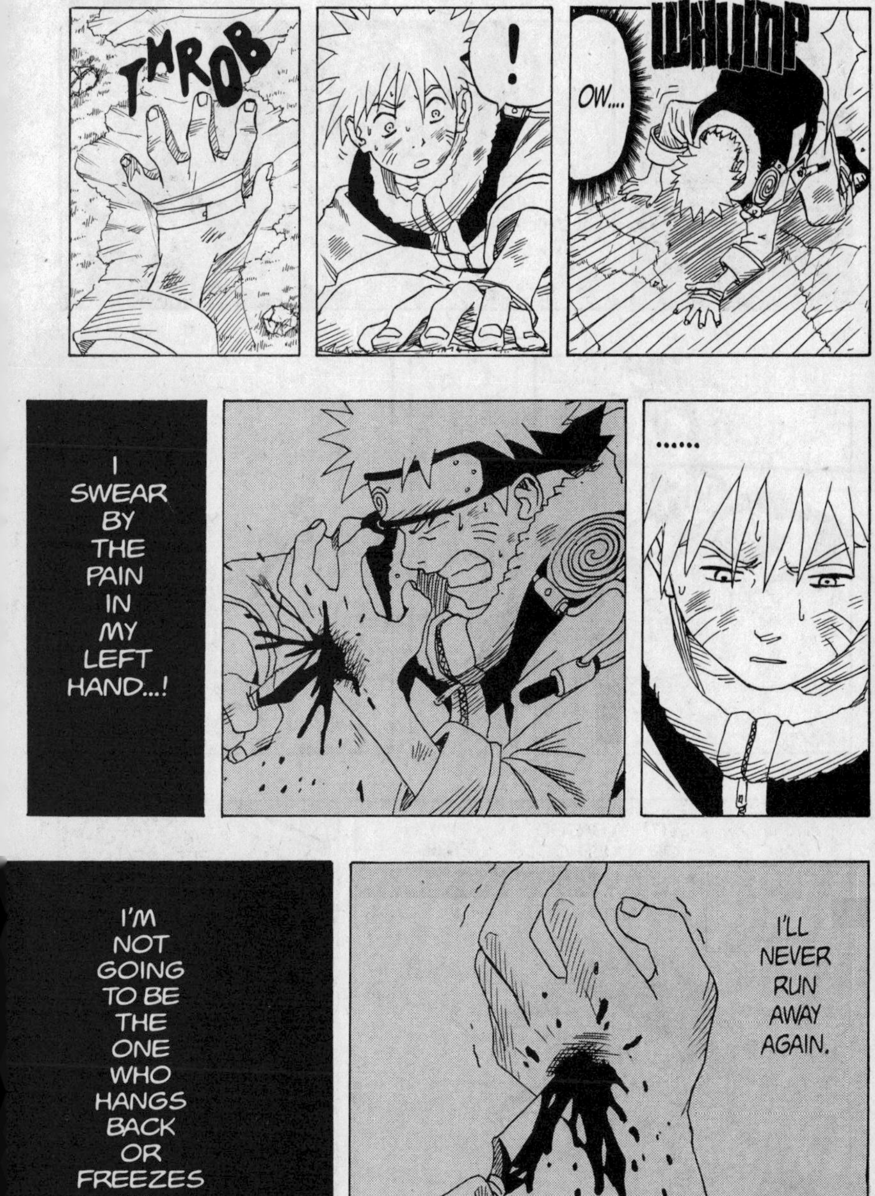
WHUMP
OW....
!
THROB
......
I SWEAR BY THE PAIN IN MY LEFT HAND...!
I'LL NEVER RUN AWAY AGAIN.
I'M NOT GOING TO BE THE ONE WHO HANGS BACK OR FREEZES UP...

READ THIS WAY

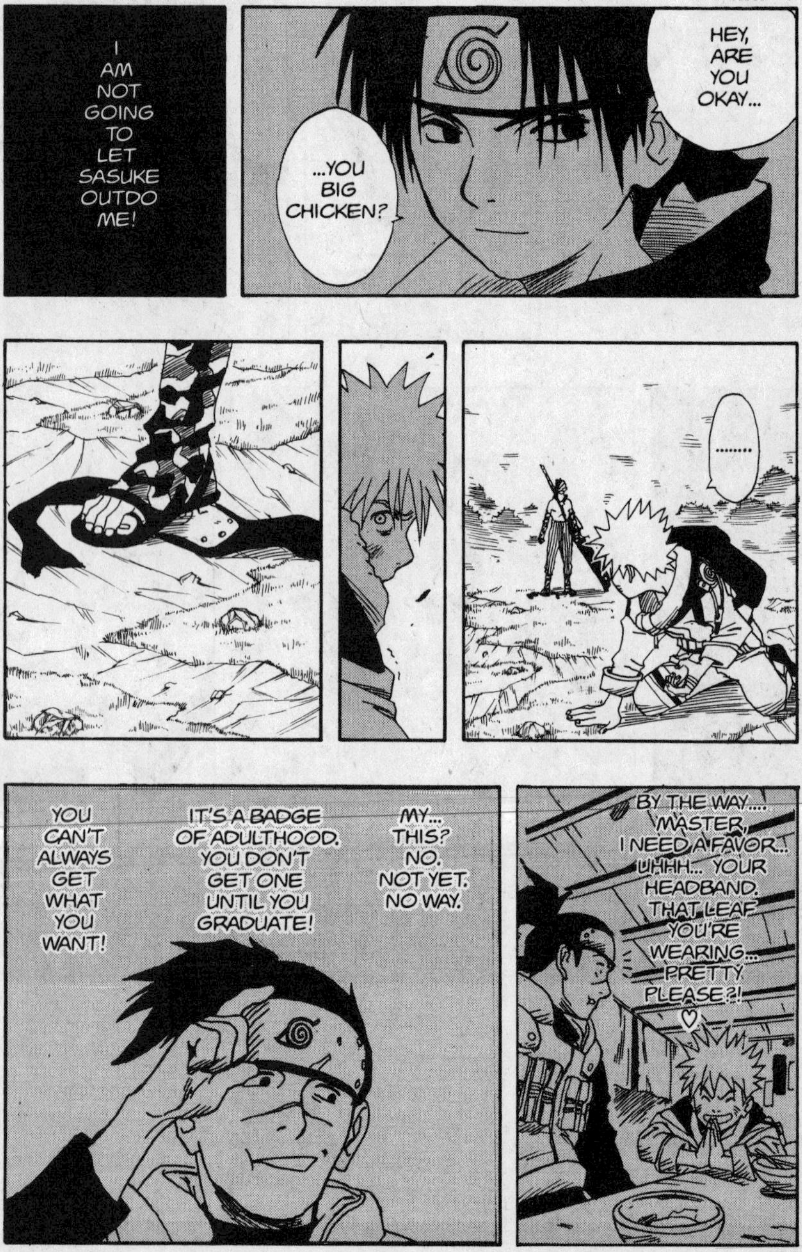
HEY, ARE YOU OKAY...
...YOU BIG CHICKEN?
I AM NOT GOING TO LET SASUKE OUTDO ME!
....
BY THE WAY.... MASTER, I NEED A FAVOR... UHHH... YOUR HEADBAND, THAT LEAF YOU'RE WEARING... PRETTY PLEASE?! ♡
MY... THIS? NO. NOT YET. NO WAY.
IT'S A BADGE OF ADULTHOOD. YOU DON'T GET ONE UNTIL YOU GRADUATE!
YOU CAN'T ALWAYS GET WHAT YOU WANT!

READ THIS WAY

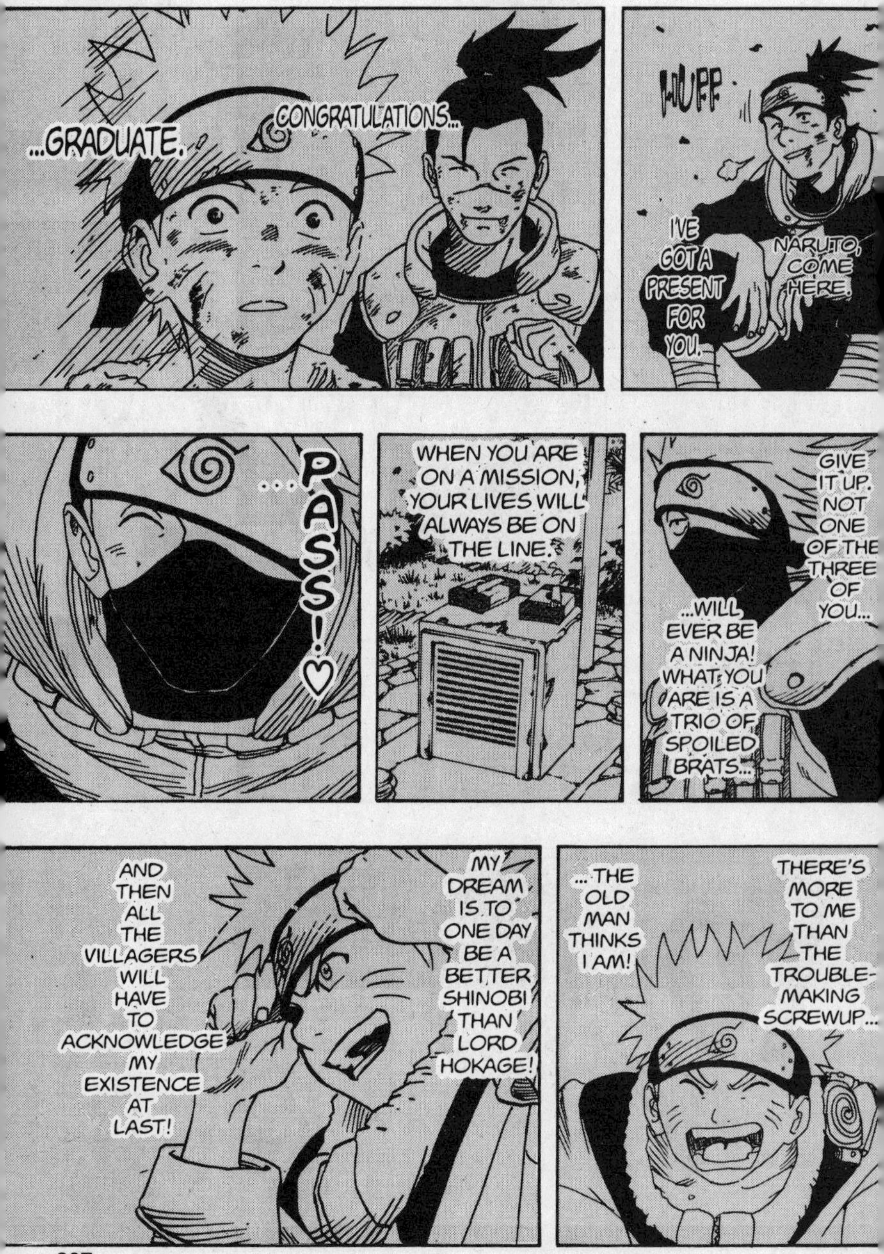
HUFF
NARUTO, COME HERE.
I'VE GOT A PRESENT FOR YOU.
CONGRATULATIONS...
...GRADUATE.
GIVE IT UP. NOT ONE OF THE THREE OF YOU...
...WILL EVER BE A NINJA! WHAT YOU ARE IS A TRIO OF SPOILED BRATS...
WHEN YOU ARE ON A MISSION, YOUR LIVES WILL ALWAYS BE ON THE LINE.
...PASS!♥
THERE'S MORE TO ME THAN THE TROUBLE-MAKING SCREWUP...
...THE OLD MAN THINKS I AM!
MY DREAM IS TO ONE DAY BE A BETTER SHINOBI THAN LORD HOKAGE!
AND THEN ALL THE VILLAGERS WILL HAVE TO ACKNOWLEDGE MY EXISTENCE AT LAST!

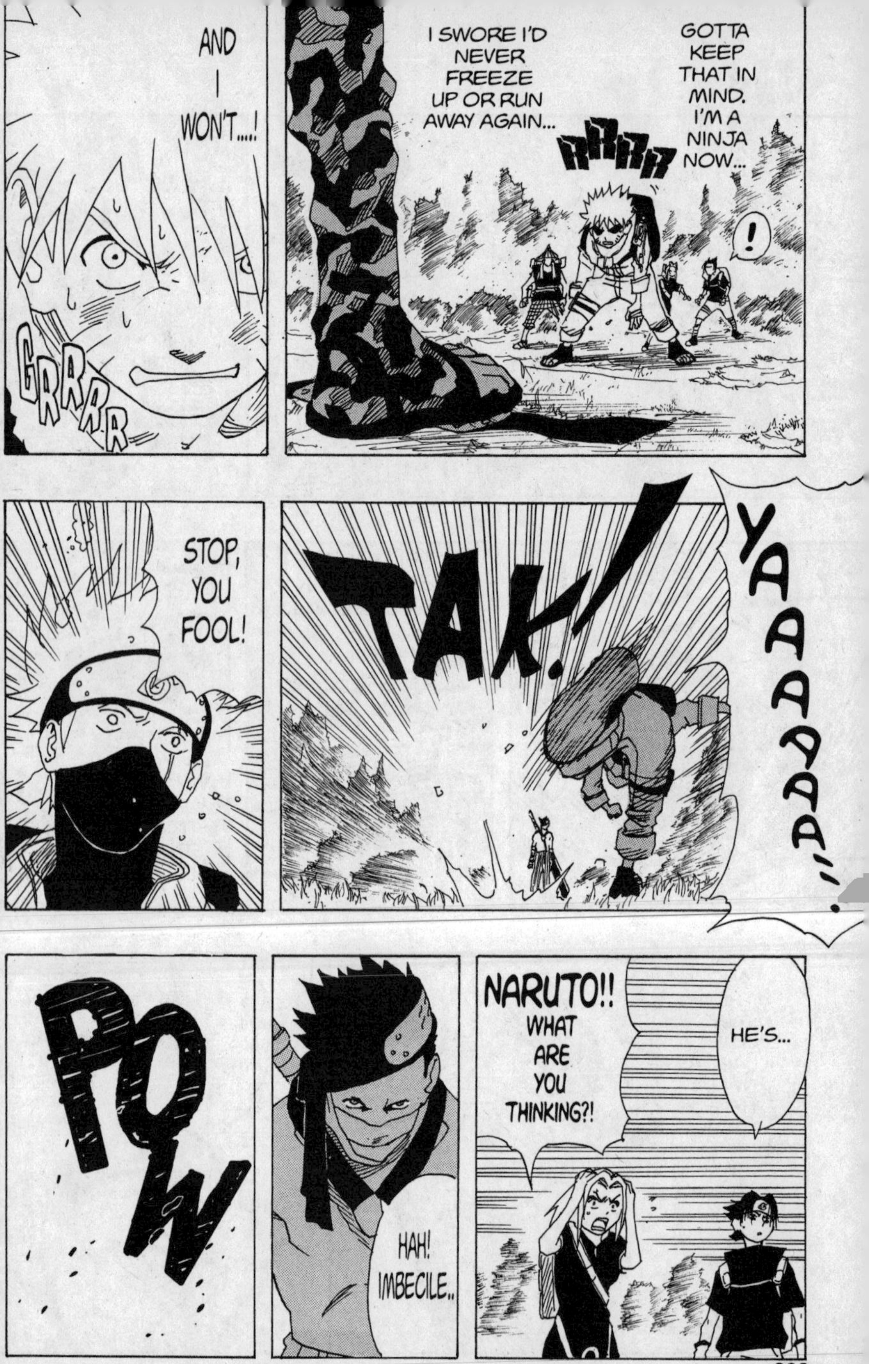
I SWORE I'D NEVER FREEZE UP OR RUN AWAY AGAIN...
RRRR
GOTTA KEEP THAT IN MIND. I'M A NINJA NOW...
!
AND I WON'T...!
GRRRR
YAAAAAA!!
TAK!!
STOP, YOU FOOL!
HE'S...
NARUTO!! WHAT ARE YOU THINKING?!
HAH! IMBECILE..
POW

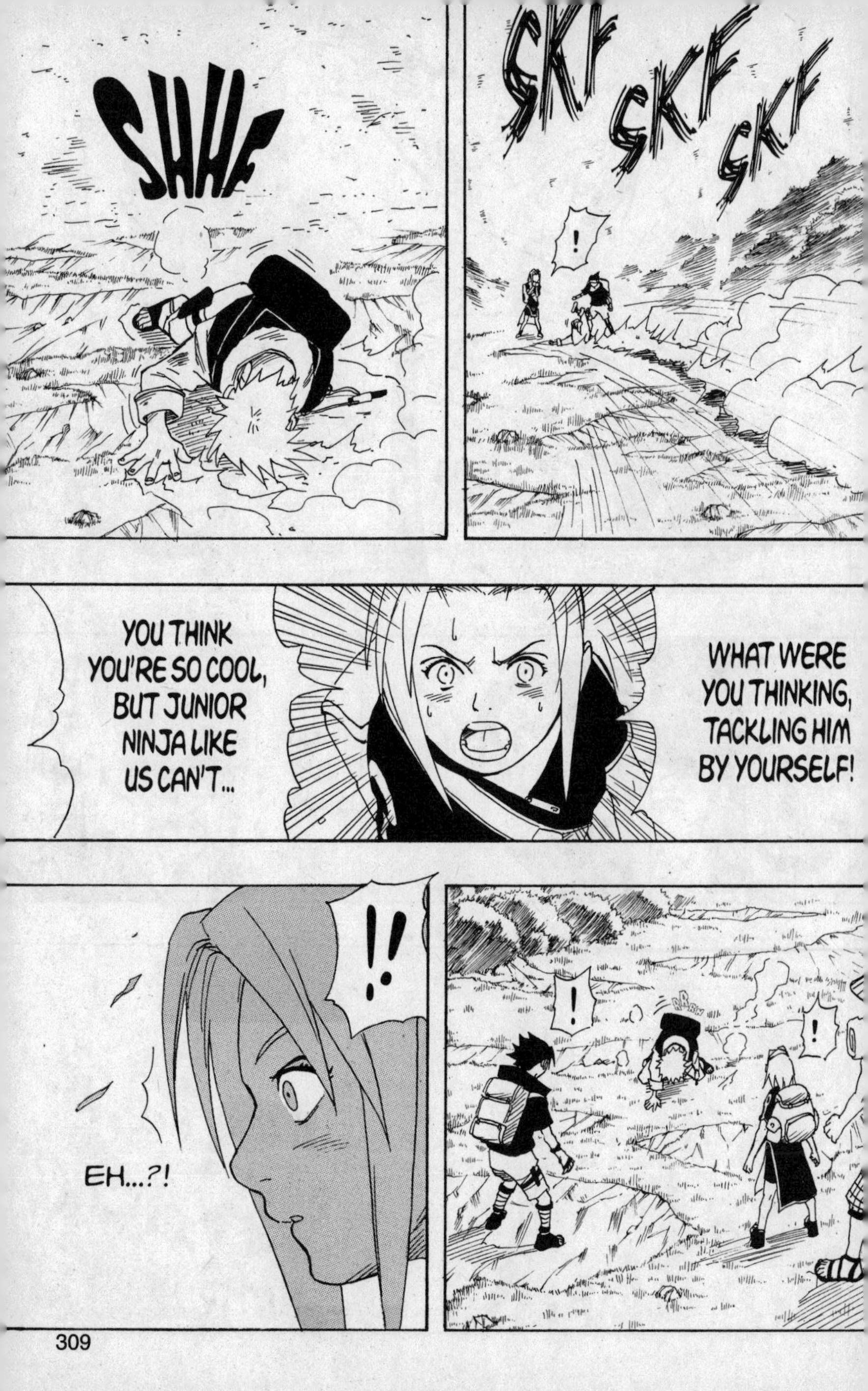
SKF SKF SKF
!
SHHF
WHAT WERE YOU THINKING, TACKLING HIM BY YOURSELF!
YOU THINK YOU'RE SO COOL, BUT JUNIOR NINJA LIKE US CAN'T...
!
!
!!
EH...?!

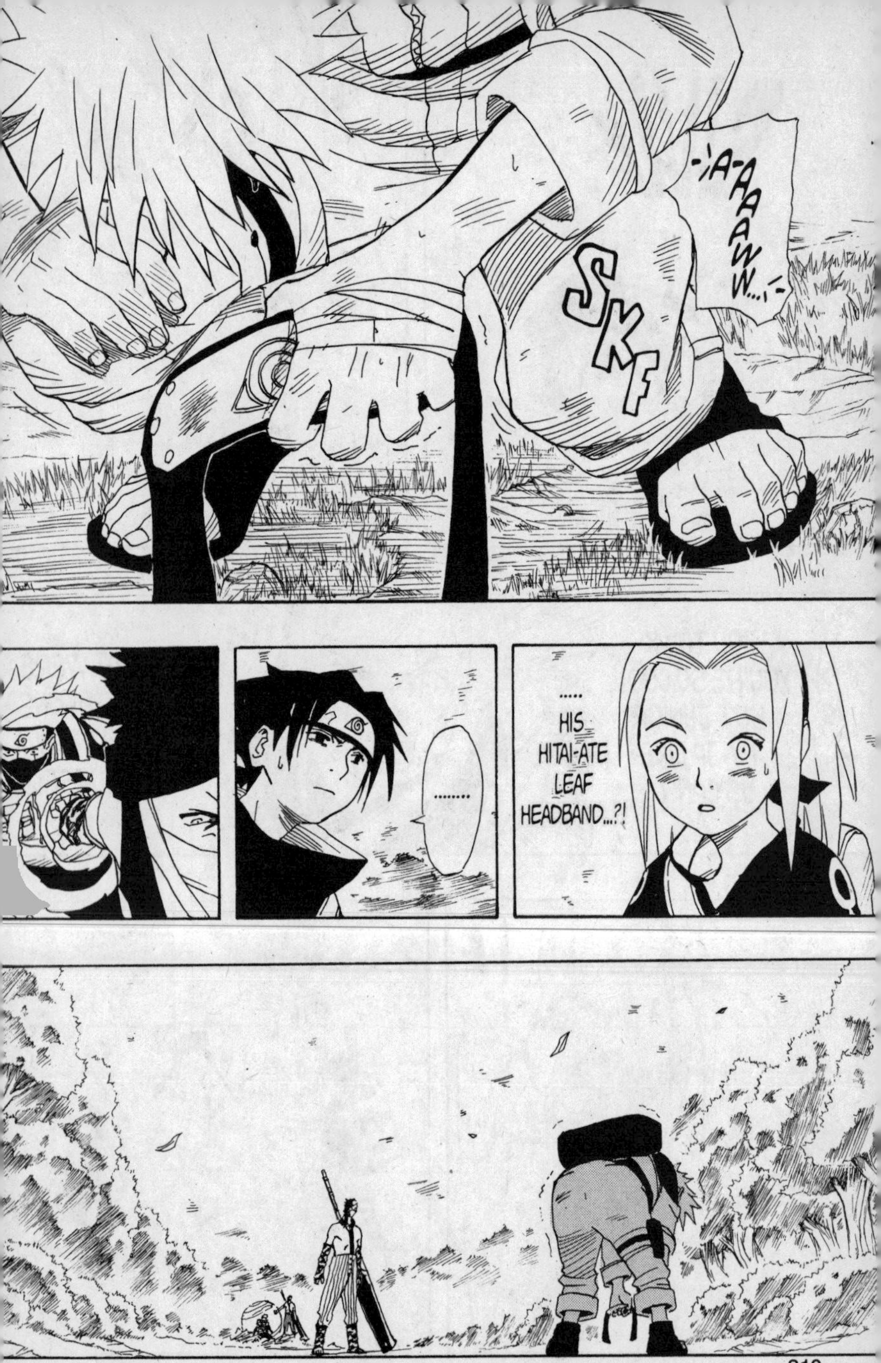
SKF
-¡A-AAAAWW...¡-
.....
HIS HITAI-ATE LEAF HEADBAND...?!
....

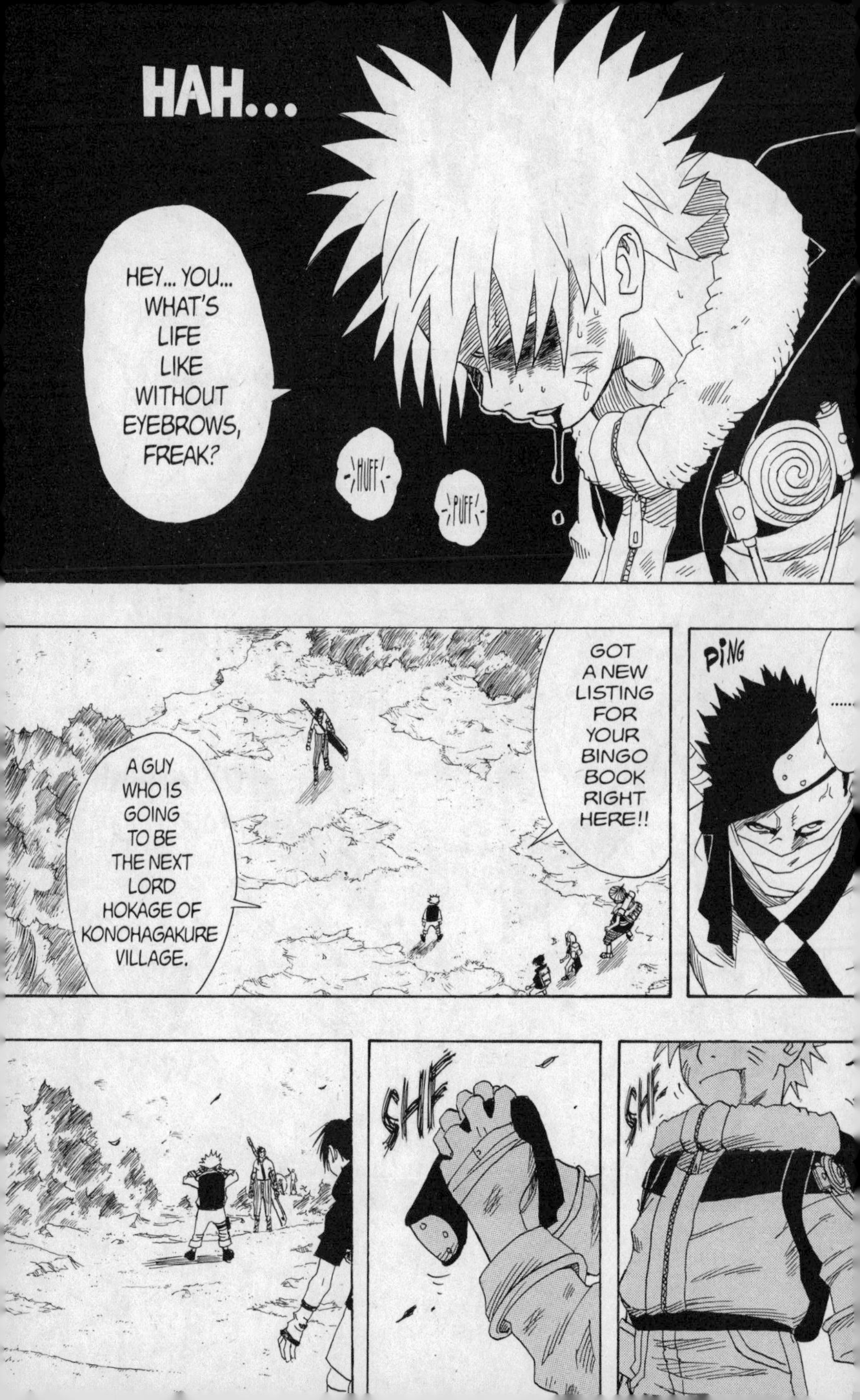
HAH...
HEY... YOU... WHAT'S LIFE LIKE WITHOUT EYEBROWS, FREAK?
HUFF
PUFF
PING
......
GOT A NEW LISTING FOR YOUR BINGO BOOK RIGHT HERE!!
A GUY WHO IS GOING TO BE THE NEXT LORD HOKAGE OF KONOHAGAKURE VILLAGE.
SHF
SHF

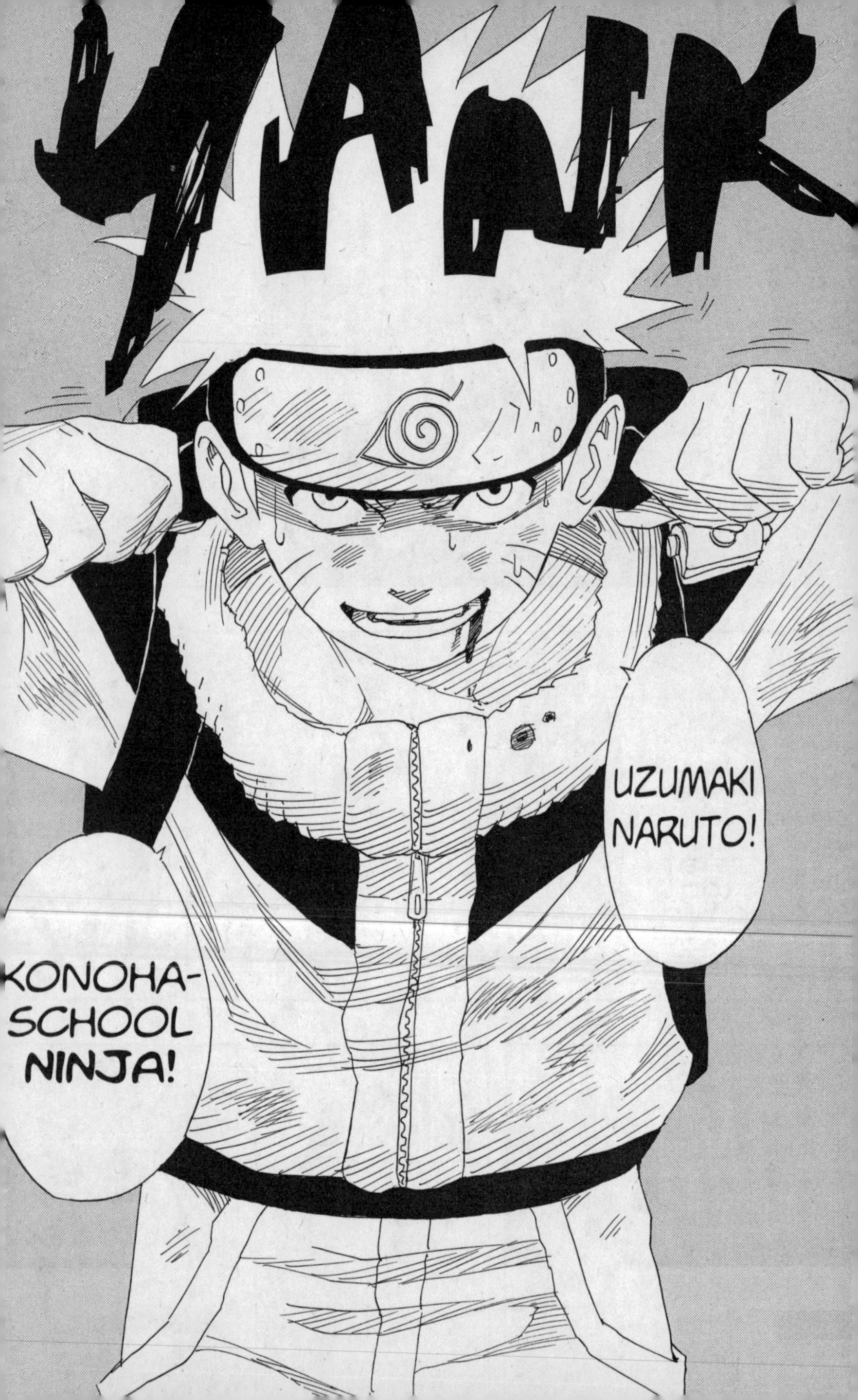
UZUMAKI NARUTO!
KONOHA-SCHOOL NINJA!

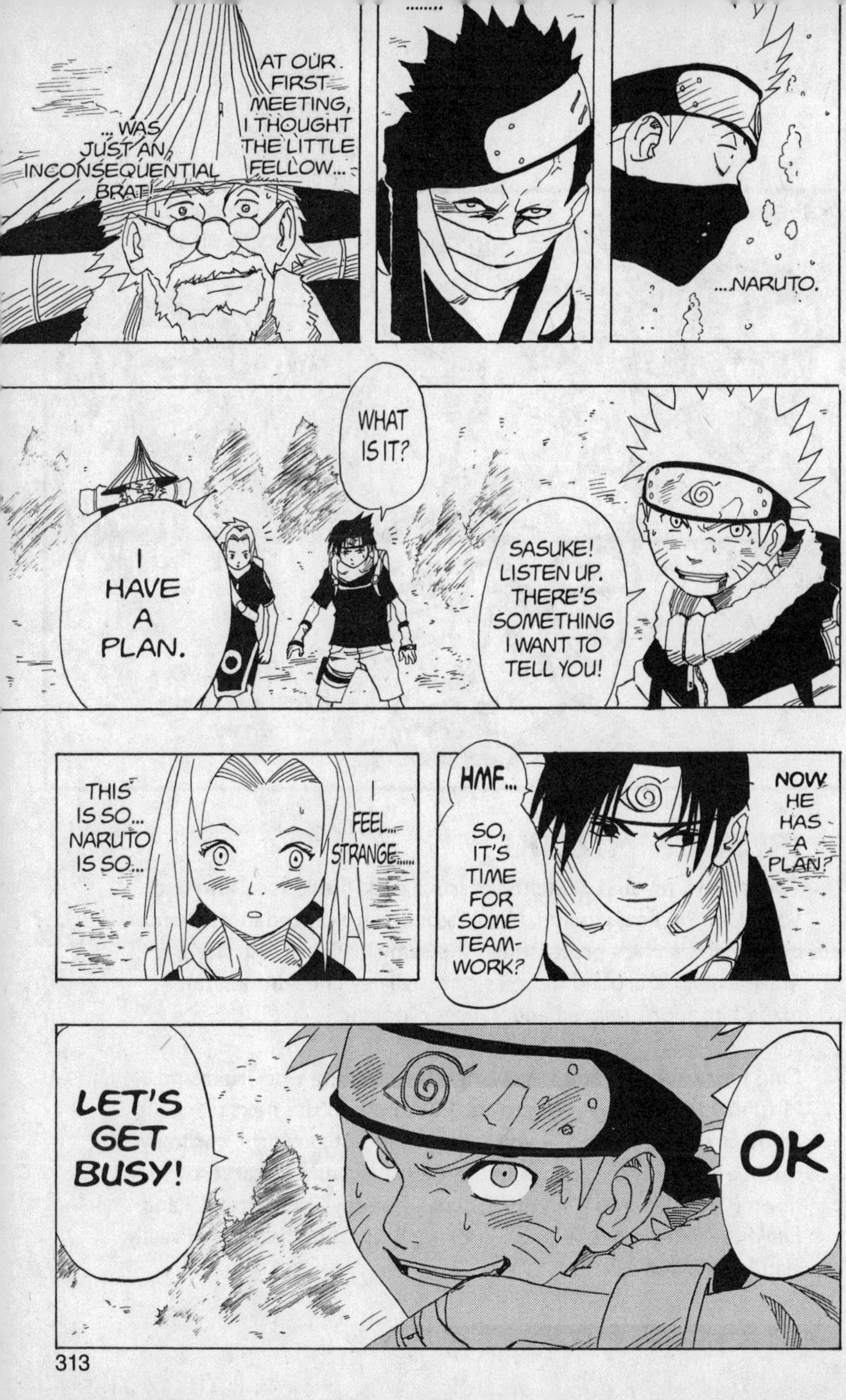

...NARUTO.
....
AT OUR FIRST MEETING, I THOUGHT THE LITTLE FELLOW...
... WAS JUST AN INCONSEQUENTIAL BRAT!
SASUKE! LISTEN UP. THERE'S SOMETHING I WANT TO TELL YOU!
WHAT IS IT?
I HAVE A PLAN.
NOW HE HAS A PLAN?
HMF...
SO, IT'S TIME FOR SOME TEAM-WORK?
THIS IS SO... NARUTO IS SO...
I FEEL... STRANGE......
OK
LET'S GET BUSY!

Iruka-sensei

The evil sensei. Uses Fuma-clan shuriken.

His reaction to the "Ninja Centerfold"

Mizuki

Kakashi · Kuwa · Kama · Botan · Enoki

IRUKA & MIZUKI

These were my first sketches of Iruka and Mizuki (see **Naruto** Vol. 1). In the final version, Mizuki's bangs are parted in the center, but otherwise he's pretty much the same. Iruka used to have a more evil look around his eyes, and sharper cheekbones, but I made him more relaxed and younger-looking.

One more thing. When I was originally planning who Iruka and Mizuki's teacher was going to be, I decided on the next teacher's name at the same time. If you look in the bottom right corner, you can see some of the names I considered: *Kakashi* ("scarecrow"), *Kuwa* ("hoe"), *Kama* ("scythe"), *Botan* ("peony" or "button") and *Enoki* (a Chinese nettle tree). Looking back at it, though, I'm really glad I used "Kakashi."

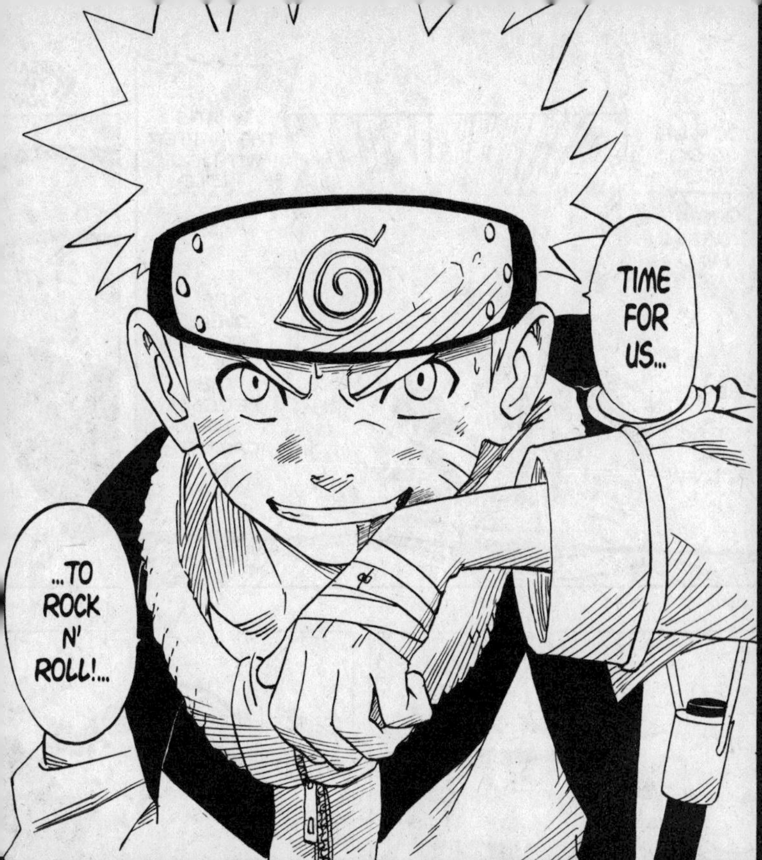
TIME FOR US...
...TO ROCK N' ROLL!...

Number 14: The Secret Plan...!!

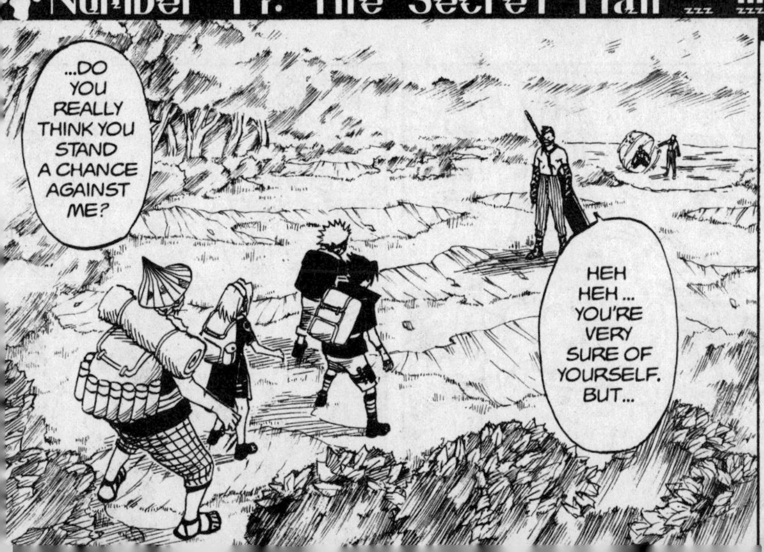
...DO YOU REALLY THINK YOU STAND A CHANCE AGAINST ME?
HEH HEH... YOU'RE VERY SURE OF YOURSELF. BUT...

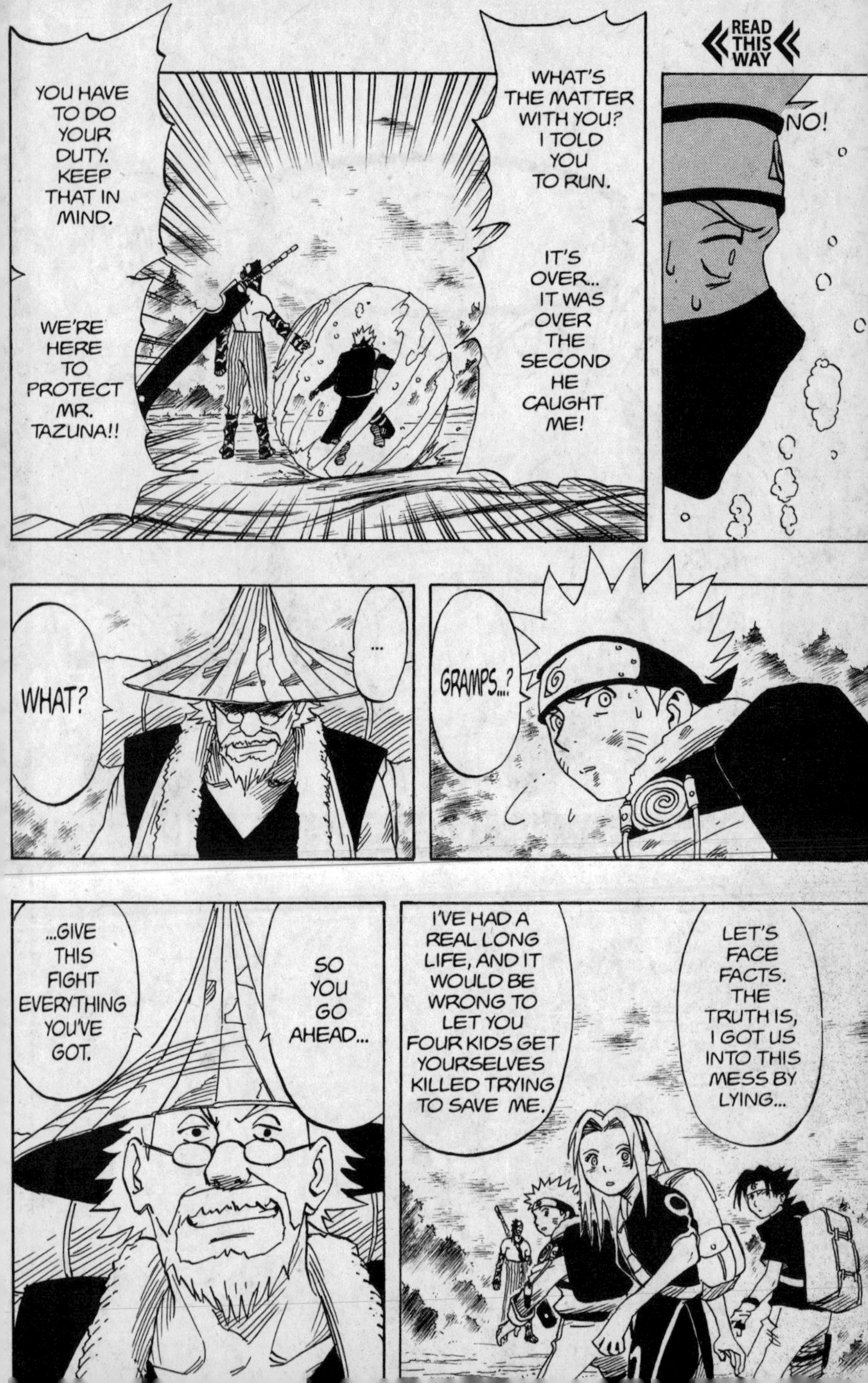
READ THIS WAY
NO!
WHAT'S THE MATTER WITH YOU? I TOLD YOU TO RUN.
IT'S OVER... IT WAS OVER THE SECOND HE CAUGHT ME!
YOU HAVE TO DO YOUR DUTY. KEEP THAT IN MIND.
WE'RE HERE TO PROTECT MR. TAZUNA!!
GRAMPS...?
...
WHAT?
LET'S FACE FACTS. THE TRUTH IS, I GOT US INTO THIS MESS BY LYING...
I'VE HAD A REAL LONG LIFE, AND IT WOULD BE WRONG TO LET YOU FOUR KIDS GET YOURSELVES KILLED TRYING TO SAVE ME.
SO YOU GO AHEAD...
...GIVE THIS FIGHT EVERYTHING YOU'VE GOT.

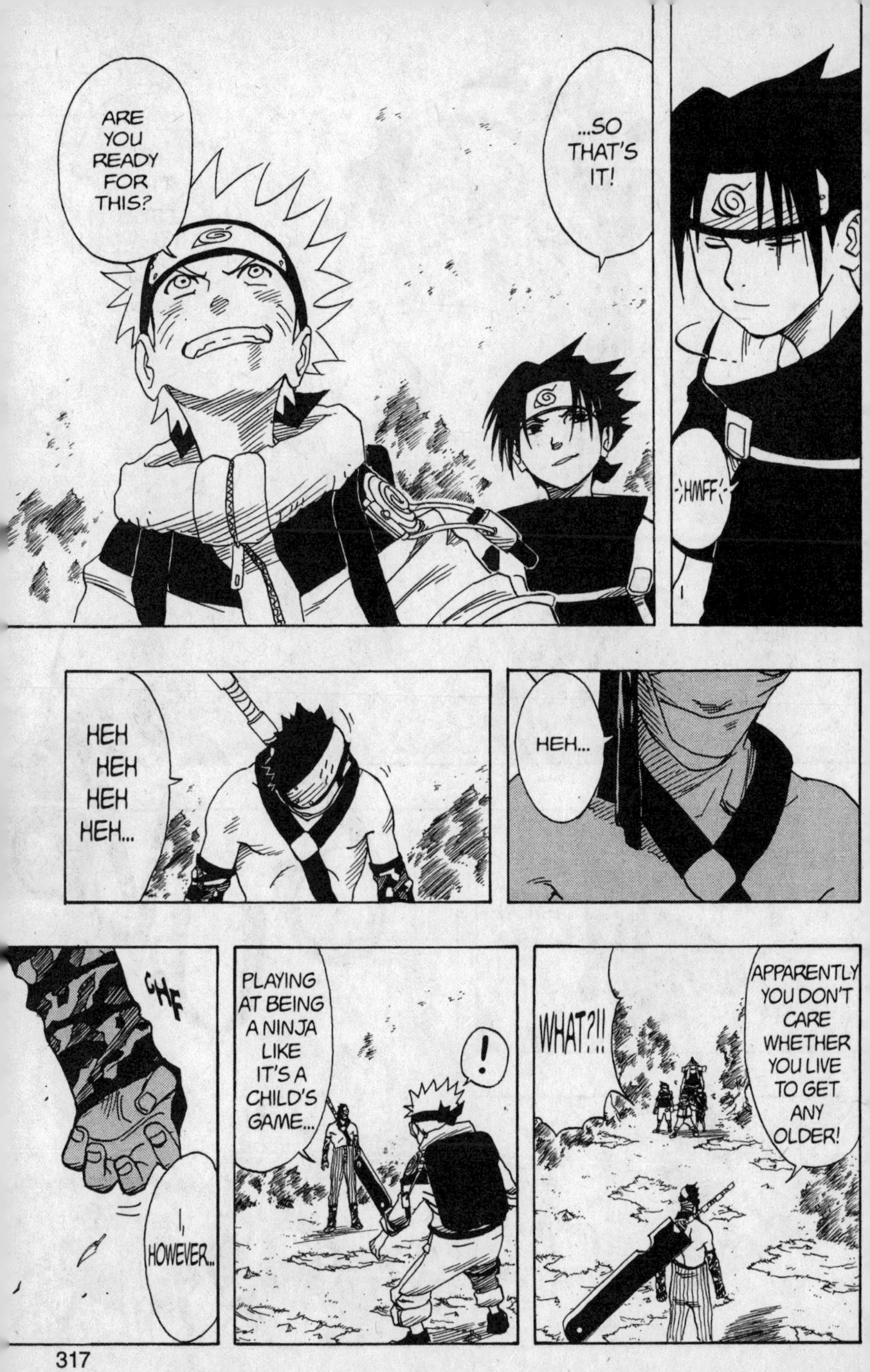
HMFF
...SO THAT'S IT!
ARE YOU READY FOR THIS?
HEH...
HEH HEH HEH HEH...
APPARENTLY YOU DON'T CARE WHETHER YOU LIVE TO GET ANY OLDER!
WHAT?!!
PLAYING AT BEING A NINJA LIKE IT'S A CHILD'S GAME...
!
GHF
I, HOWEVER...

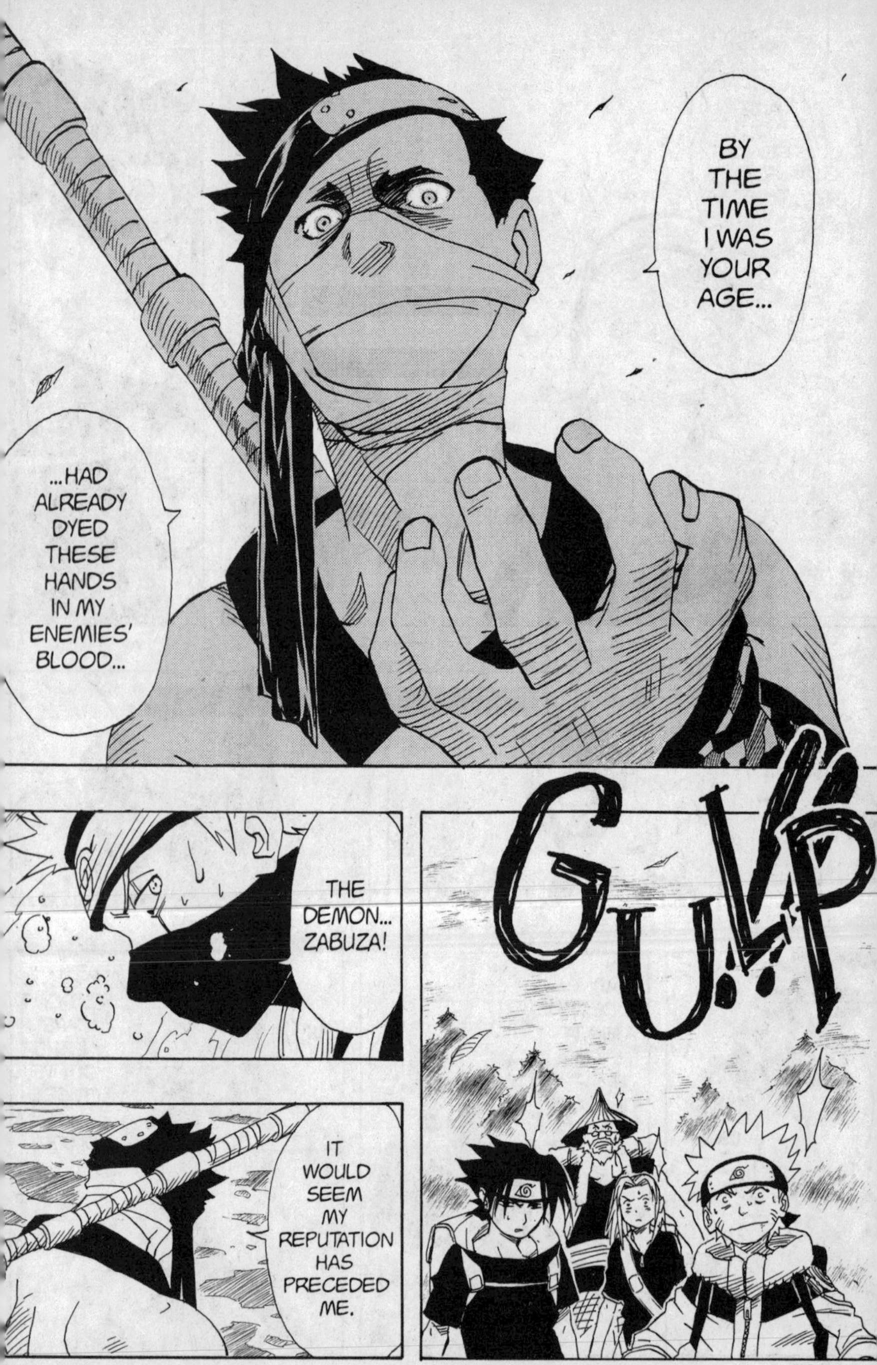
BY THE TIME I WAS YOUR AGE...
...HAD ALREADY DYED THESE HANDS IN MY ENEMIES' BLOOD...
GULP
THE DEMON... ZABUZA!
IT WOULD SEEM MY REPUTATION HAS PRECEDED ME.

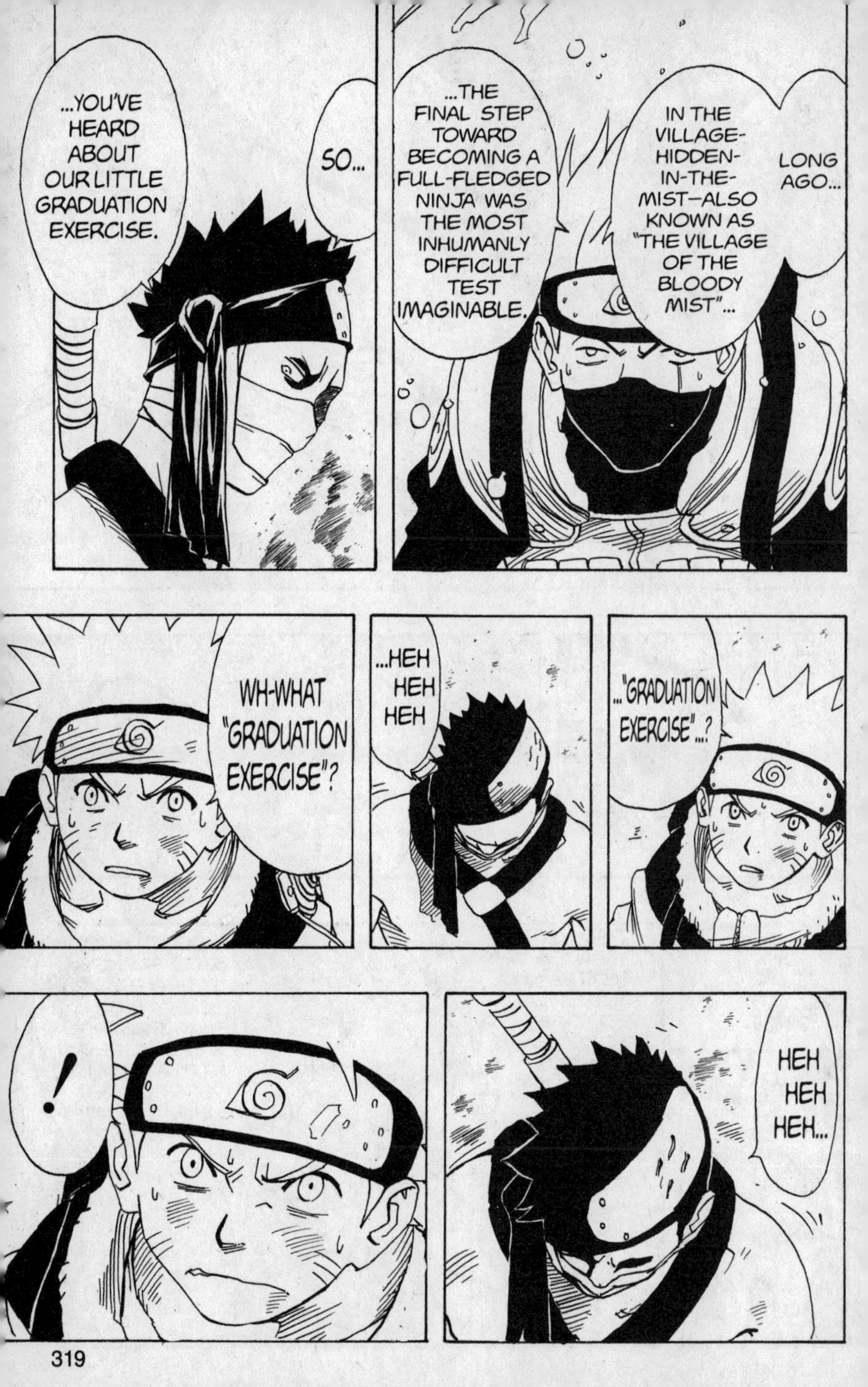
LONG AGO...
IN THE VILLAGE-HIDDEN-IN-THE-MIST—ALSO KNOWN AS "THE VILLAGE OF THE BLOODY MIST"...
...THE FINAL STEP TOWARD BECOMING A FULL-FLEDGED NINJA WAS THE MOST INHUMANLY DIFFICULT TEST IMAGINABLE.
SO...
...YOU'VE HEARD ABOUT OUR LITTLE GRADUATION EXERCISE.
..."GRADUATION EXERCISE"...?
...HEH HEH HEH
WH-WHAT "GRADUATION EXERCISE"?
HEH HEH HEH...
!

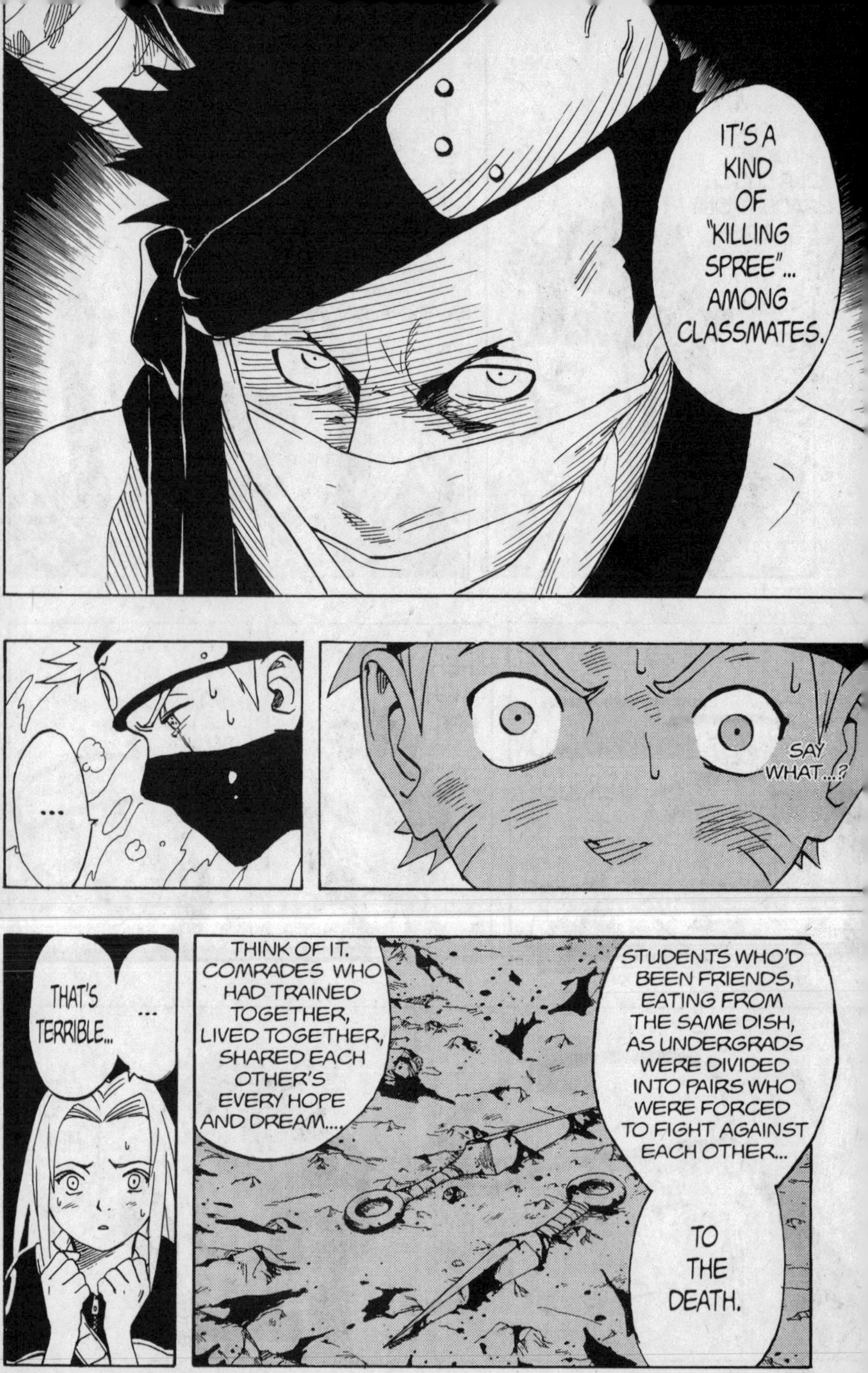
IT'S A KIND OF "KILLING SPREE"... AMONG CLASSMATES.
SAY WHAT...?
...
THINK OF IT. COMRADES WHO HAD TRAINED TOGETHER, LIVED TOGETHER, SHARED EACH OTHER'S EVERY HOPE AND DREAM....
STUDENTS WHO'D BEEN FRIENDS, EATING FROM THE SAME DISH, AS UNDERGRADS WERE DIVIDED INTO PAIRS WHO WERE FORCED TO FIGHT AGAINST EACH OTHER...
TO THE DEATH.
THAT'S TERRIBLE...
...

READ THIS WAY

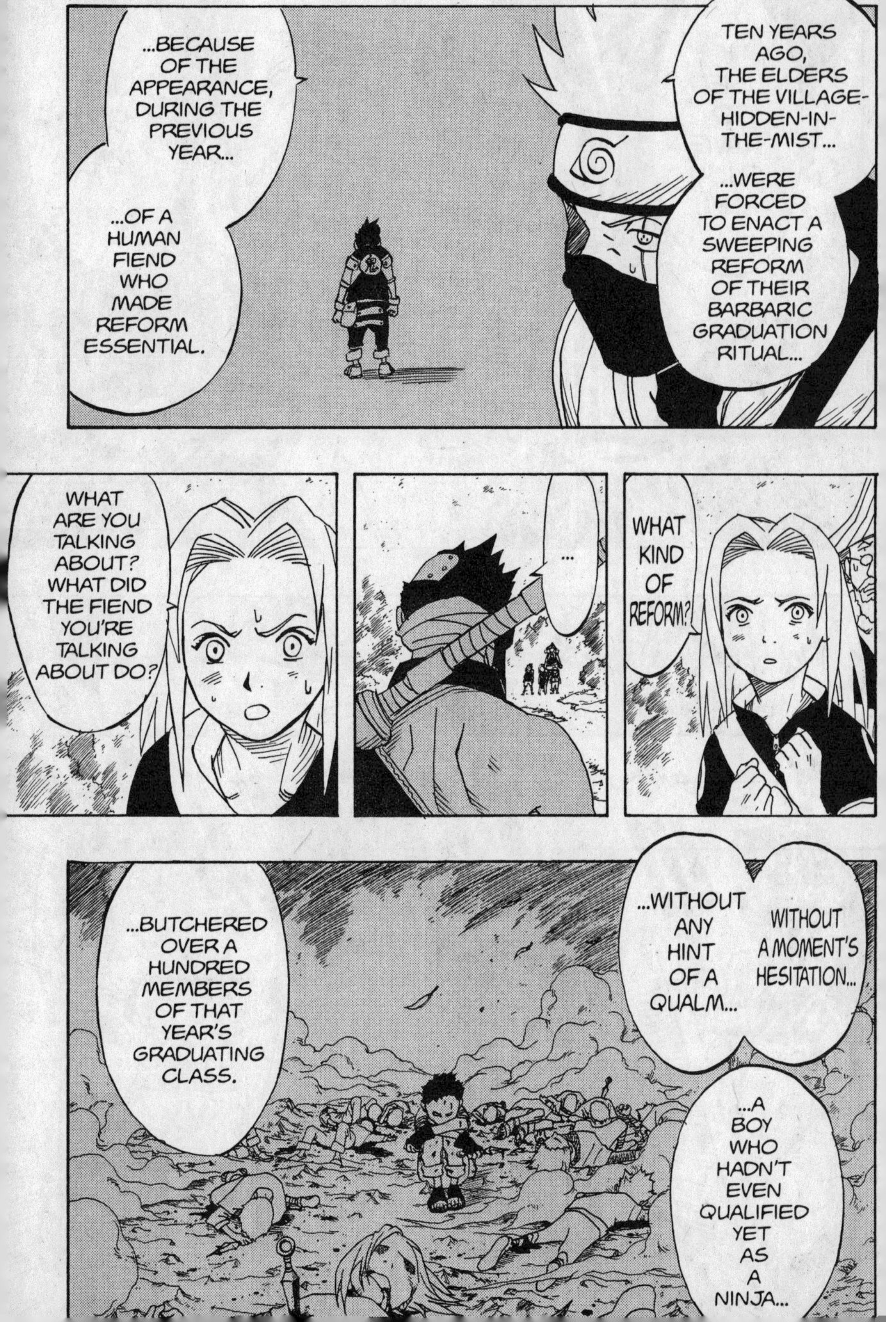
TEN YEARS AGO, THE ELDERS OF THE VILLAGE-HIDDEN-IN-THE-MIST...
...WERE FORCED TO ENACT A SWEEPING REFORM OF THEIR BARBARIC GRADUATION RITUAL...
...BECAUSE OF THE APPEARANCE, DURING THE PREVIOUS YEAR...
...OF A HUMAN FIEND WHO MADE REFORM ESSENTIAL.
WHAT KIND OF REFORM?
...
WHAT ARE YOU TALKING ABOUT? WHAT DID THE FIEND YOU'RE TALKING ABOUT DO?
...A BOY WHO HADN'T EVEN QUALIFIED YET AS A NINJA...
WITHOUT A MOMENT'S HESITATION...
...WITHOUT ANY HINT OF A QUALM...
...BUTCHERED OVER A HUNDRED MEMBERS OF THAT YEAR'S GRADUATING CLASS.

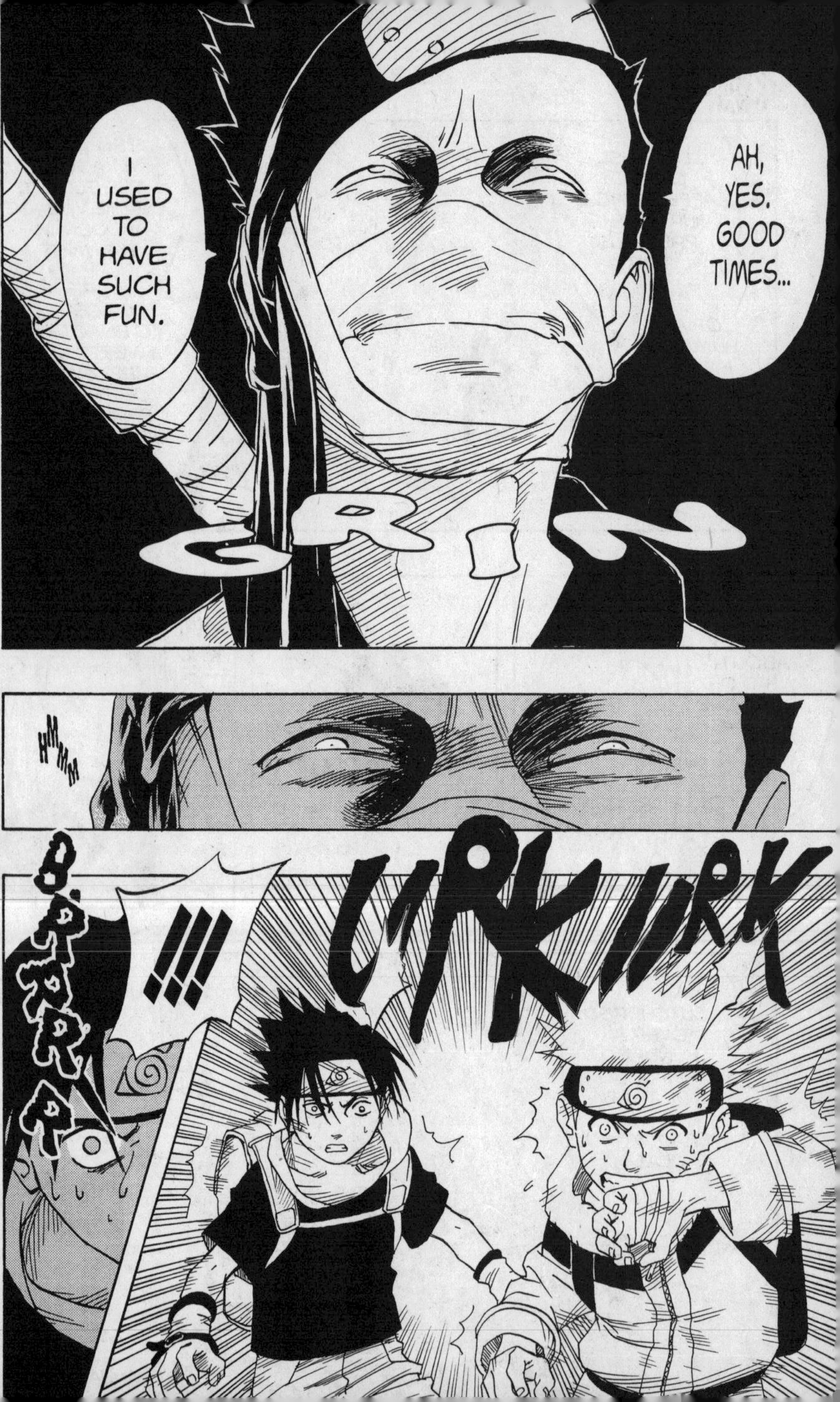
AH, YES. GOOD TIMES...
I USED TO HAVE SUCH FUN.
GRIN
HMMM
URK URK
!!!
B'R'R'R'R

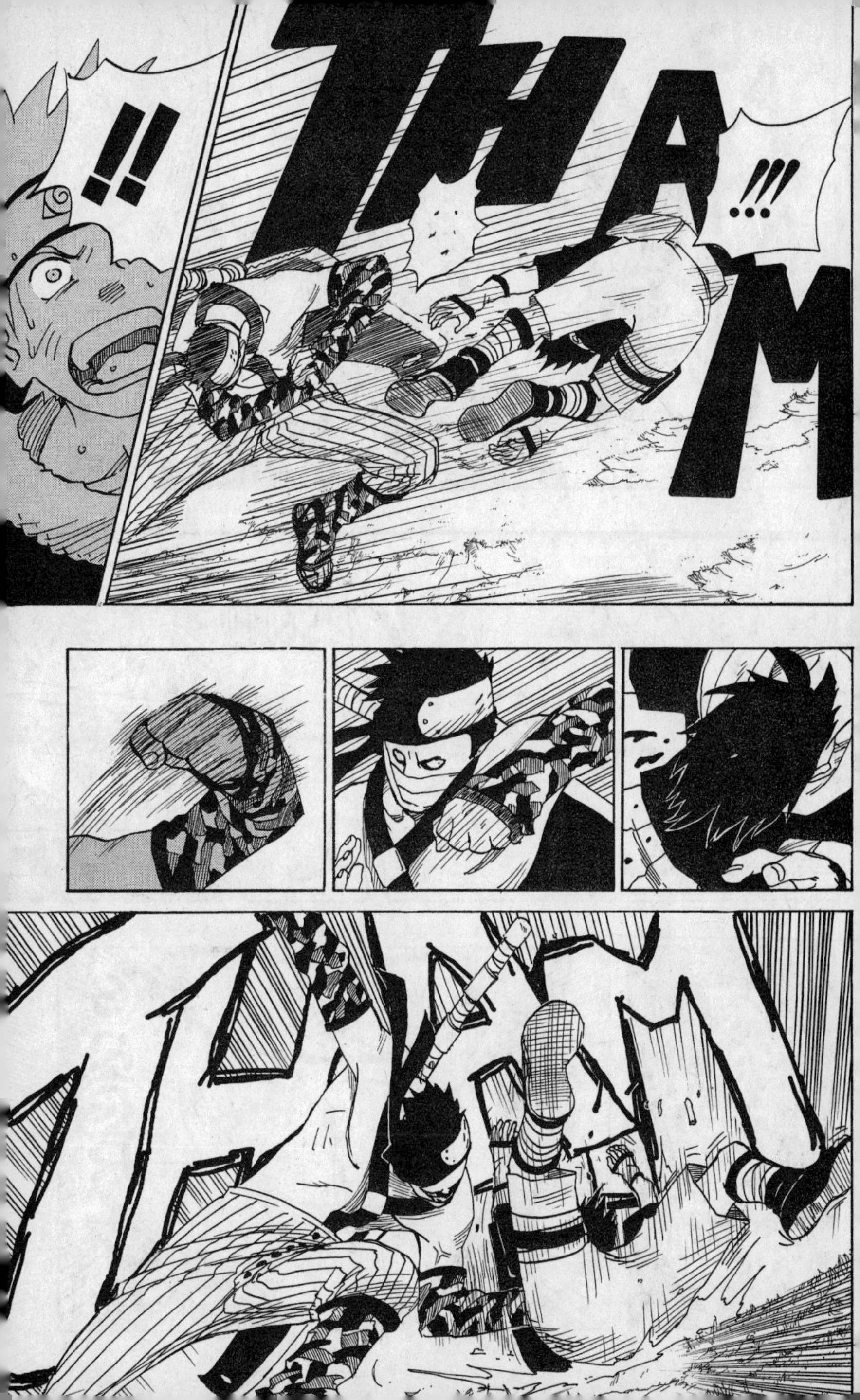
!!!
THAM
!!

TIME TO DIE...

POK

!!

SASUKE!!!

...

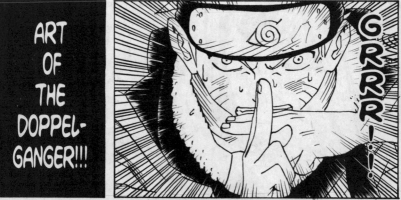

ART OF THE DOPPEL-GANGER!!!

GRRRR!!!

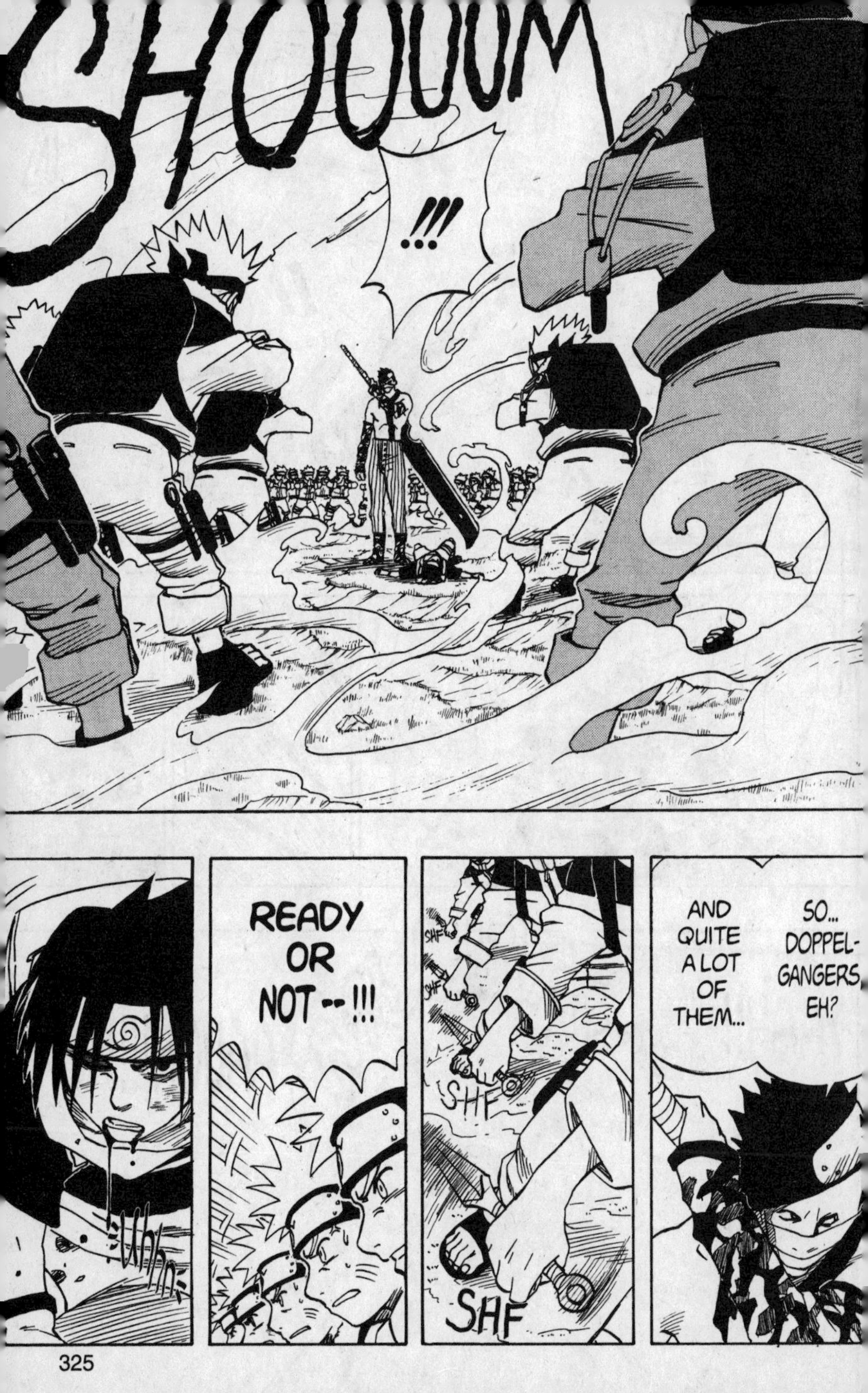
SHOOOOM
!!!
SO... DOPPEL-GANGERS, EH?
AND QUITE A LOT OF THEM...
SHF
SHF
SHF
SHF
READY OR NOT--!!!
Uhn

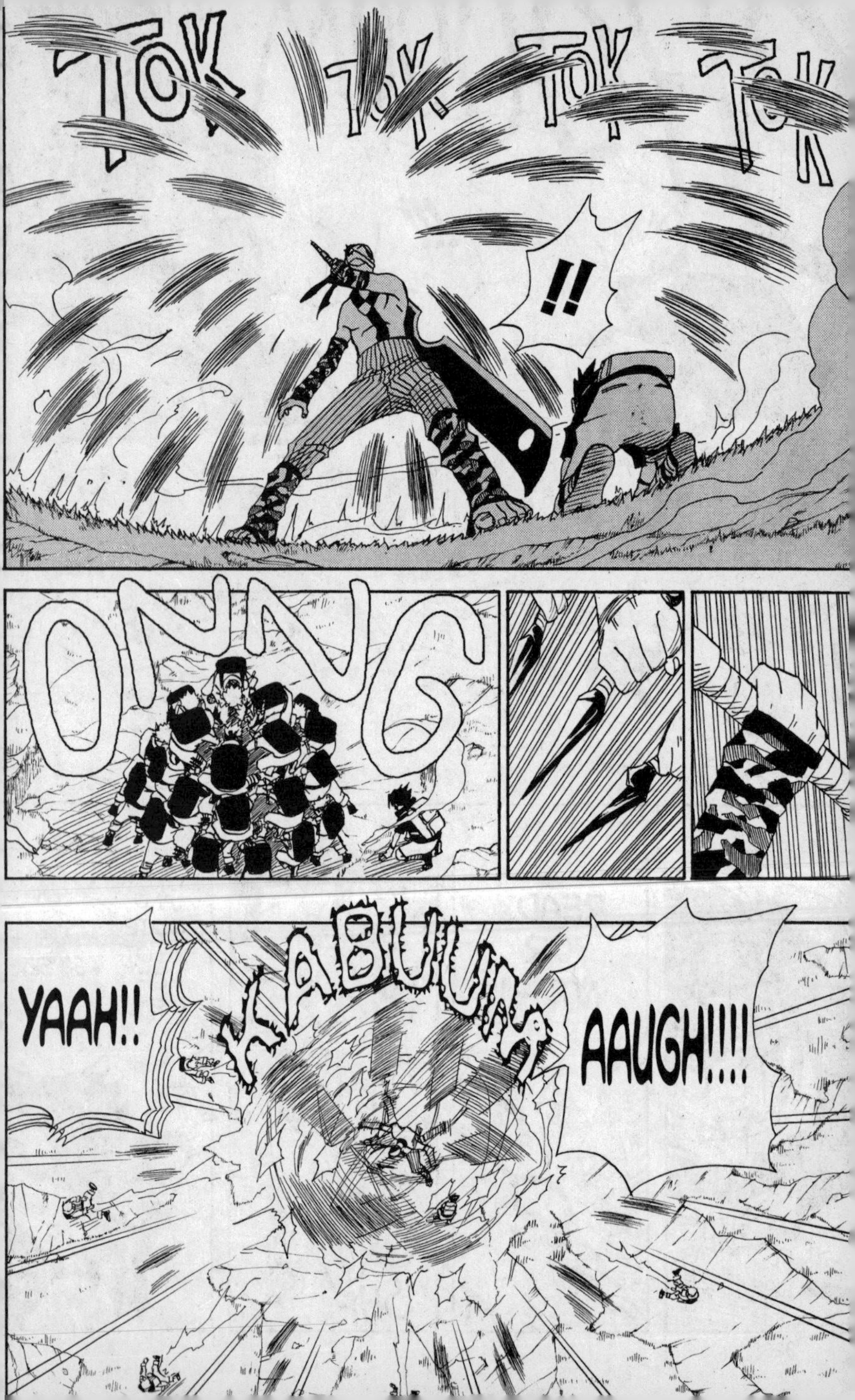
TOK TOK TOK TOK
!!
ONNG
AAUGH!!!!
KABUUM
YAAH!!

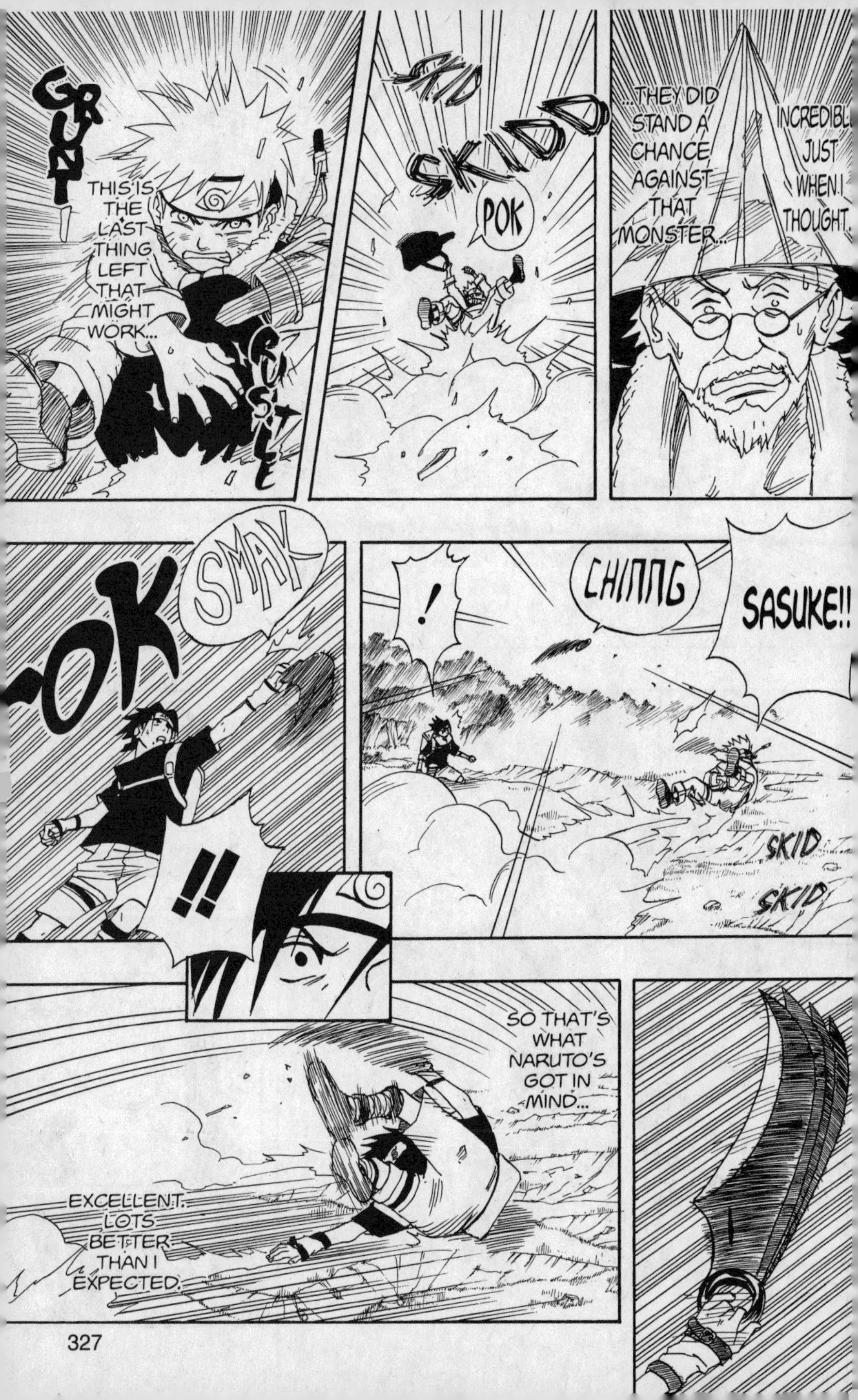
INCREDIBLE! JUST WHEN I THOUGHT...
...THEY DID STAND A CHANCE AGAINST THAT MONSTER...
SKID
SKIDD
POK
GRUNT
THIS IS THE LAST THING LEFT THAT MIGHT WORK...
RUSTLE
SASUKE!!
CHINNG
!
SMAK
POK
!!
SKID
SKID
SO THAT'S WHAT NARUTO'S GOT IN MIND...
EXCELLENT. LOTS BETTER THAN I EXPECTED.

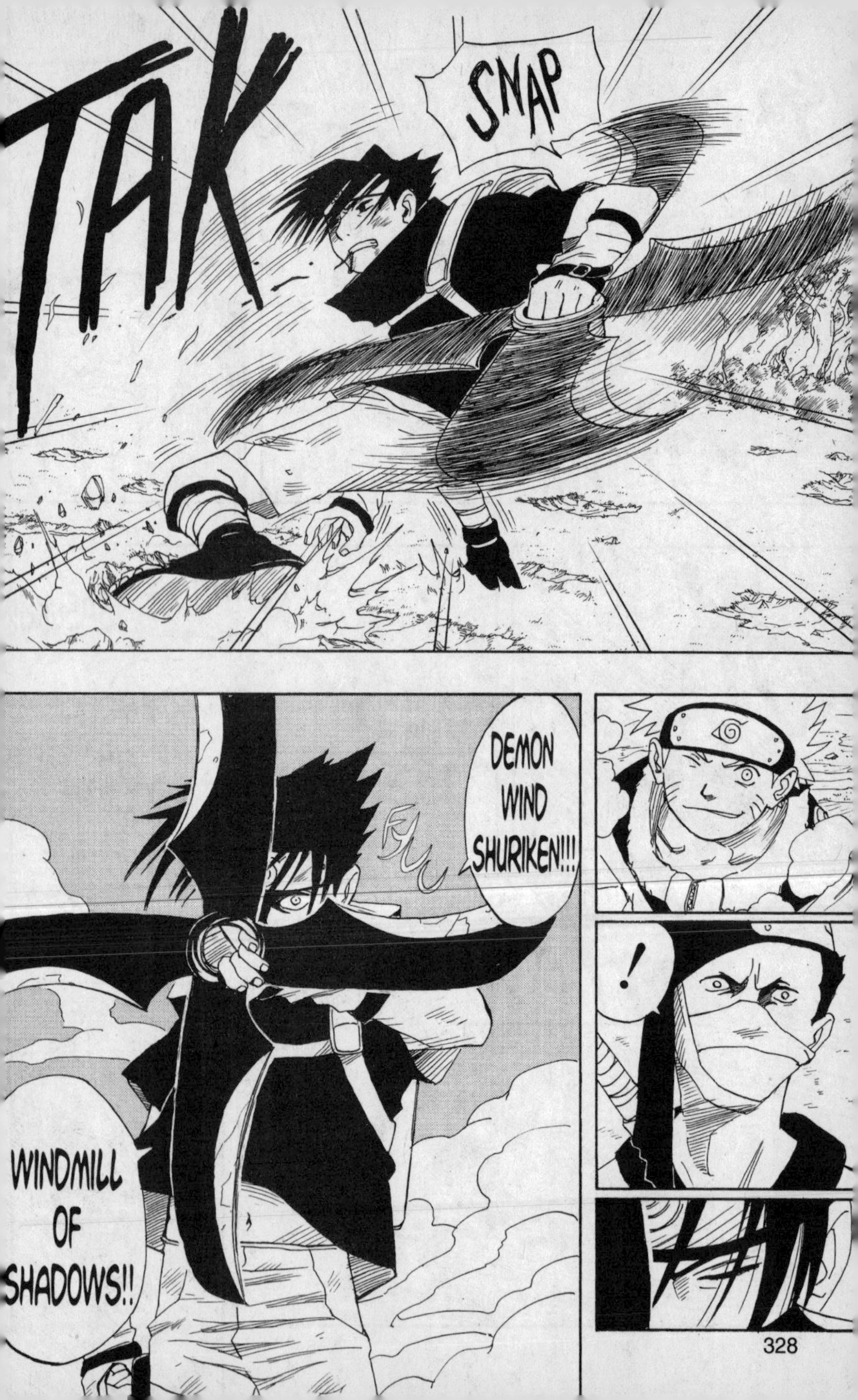
SNAP
TAK
!
FUU
DEMON WIND SHURIKEN!!!
WINDMILL OF SHADOWS!!

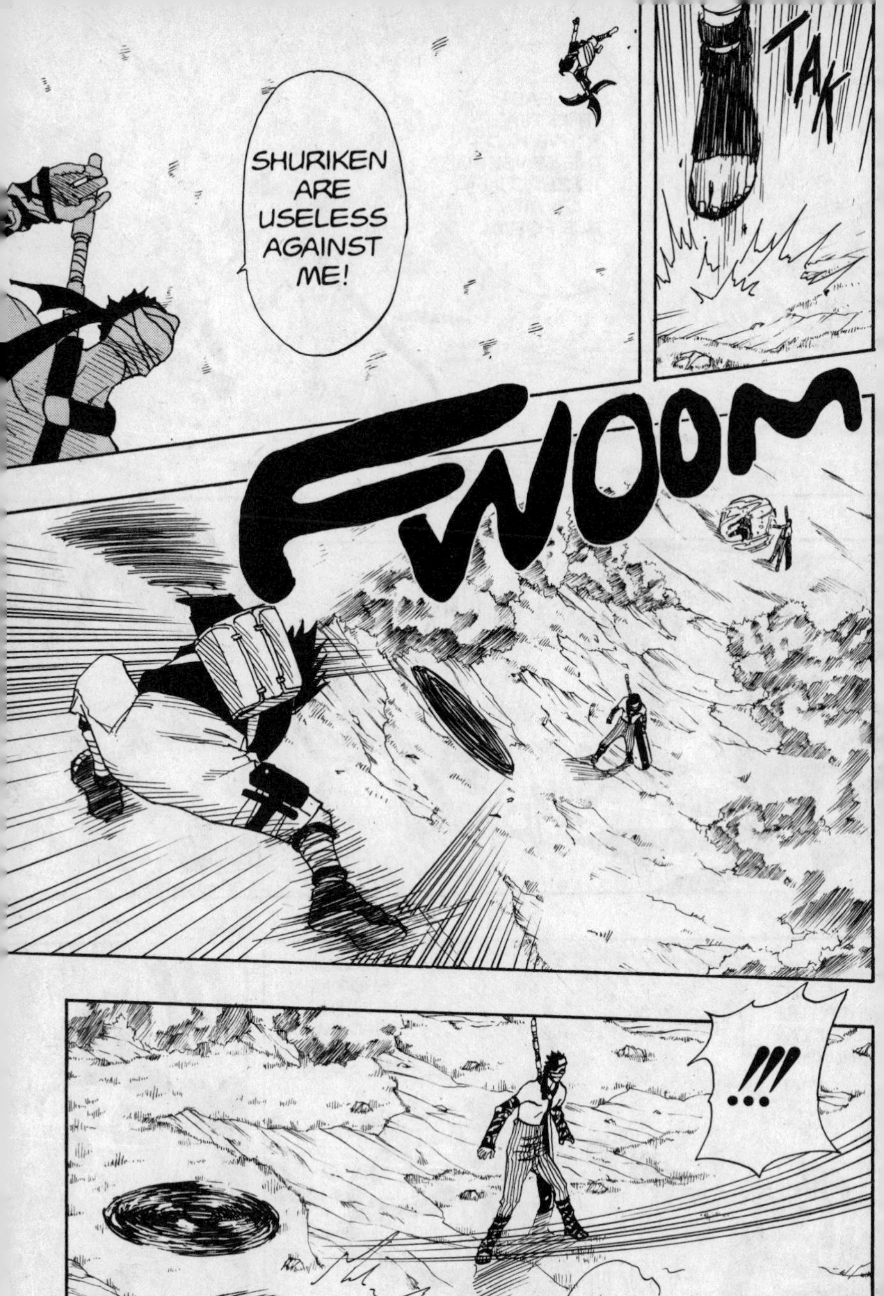
TAK
SHURIKEN ARE USELESS AGAINST ME!
FWOOM
!!!

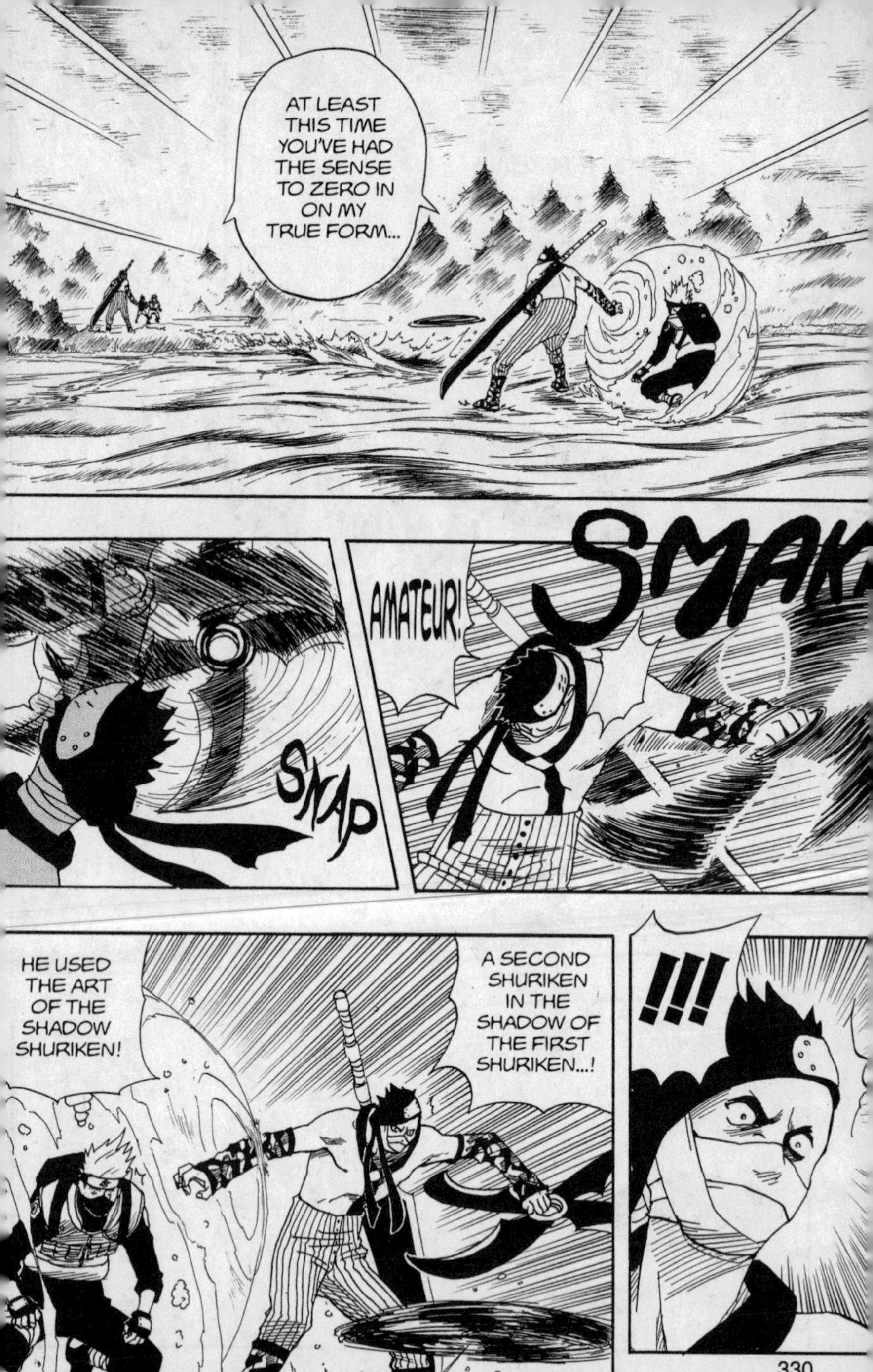
AT LEAST THIS TIME YOU'VE HAD THE SENSE TO ZERO IN ON MY TRUE FORM...
SMAK
AMATEUR!
SNAP
!!!
A SECOND SHURIKEN IN THE SHADOW OF THE FIRST SHURIKEN...!
HE USED THE ART OF THE SHADOW SHURIKEN!

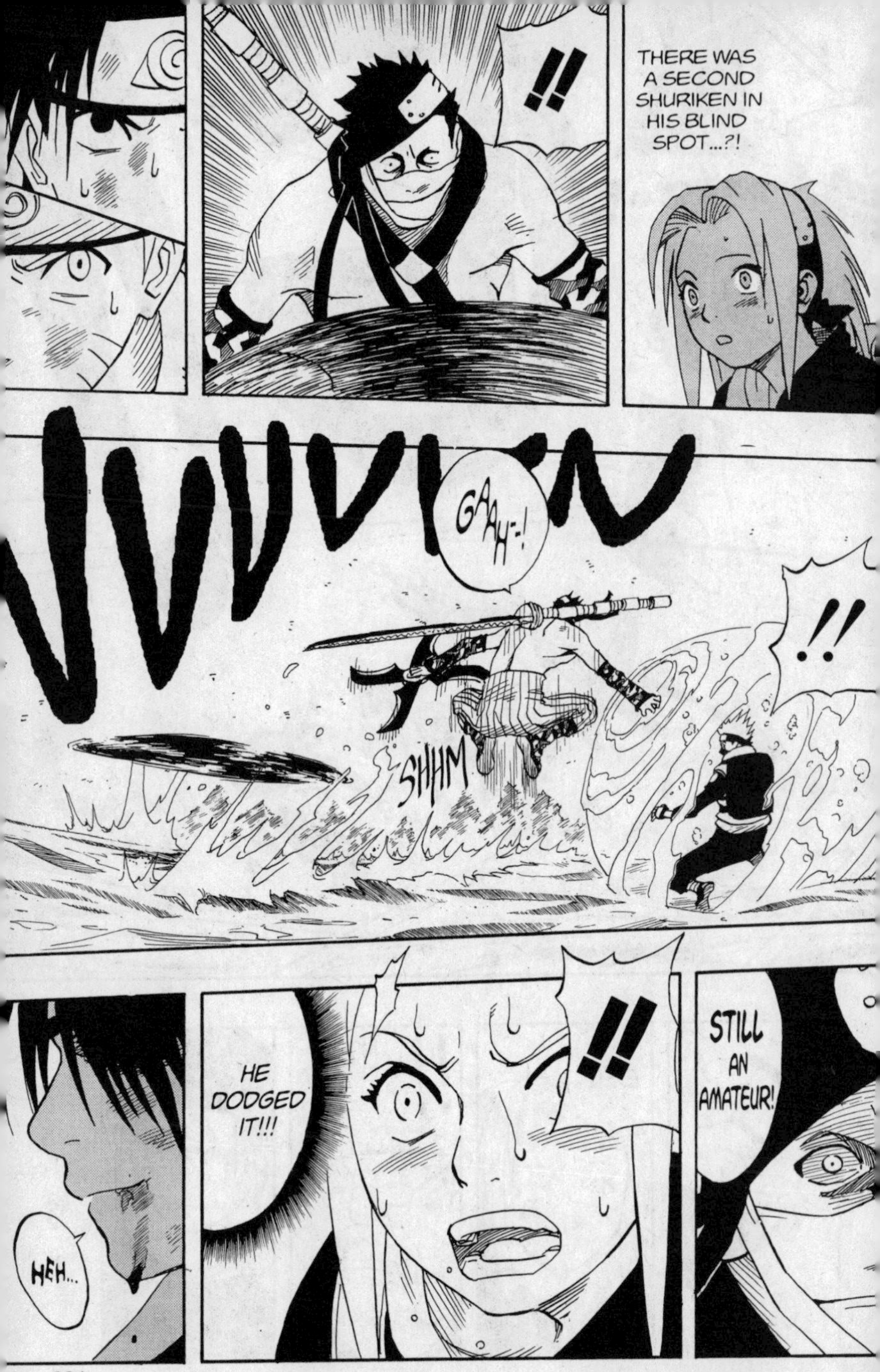
THERE WAS A SECOND SHURIKEN IN HIS BLIND SPOT...?!
!!
GAAH--!
!!
SHHM
STILL AN AMATEUR!
!!
HE DODGED IT!!!
HEH...

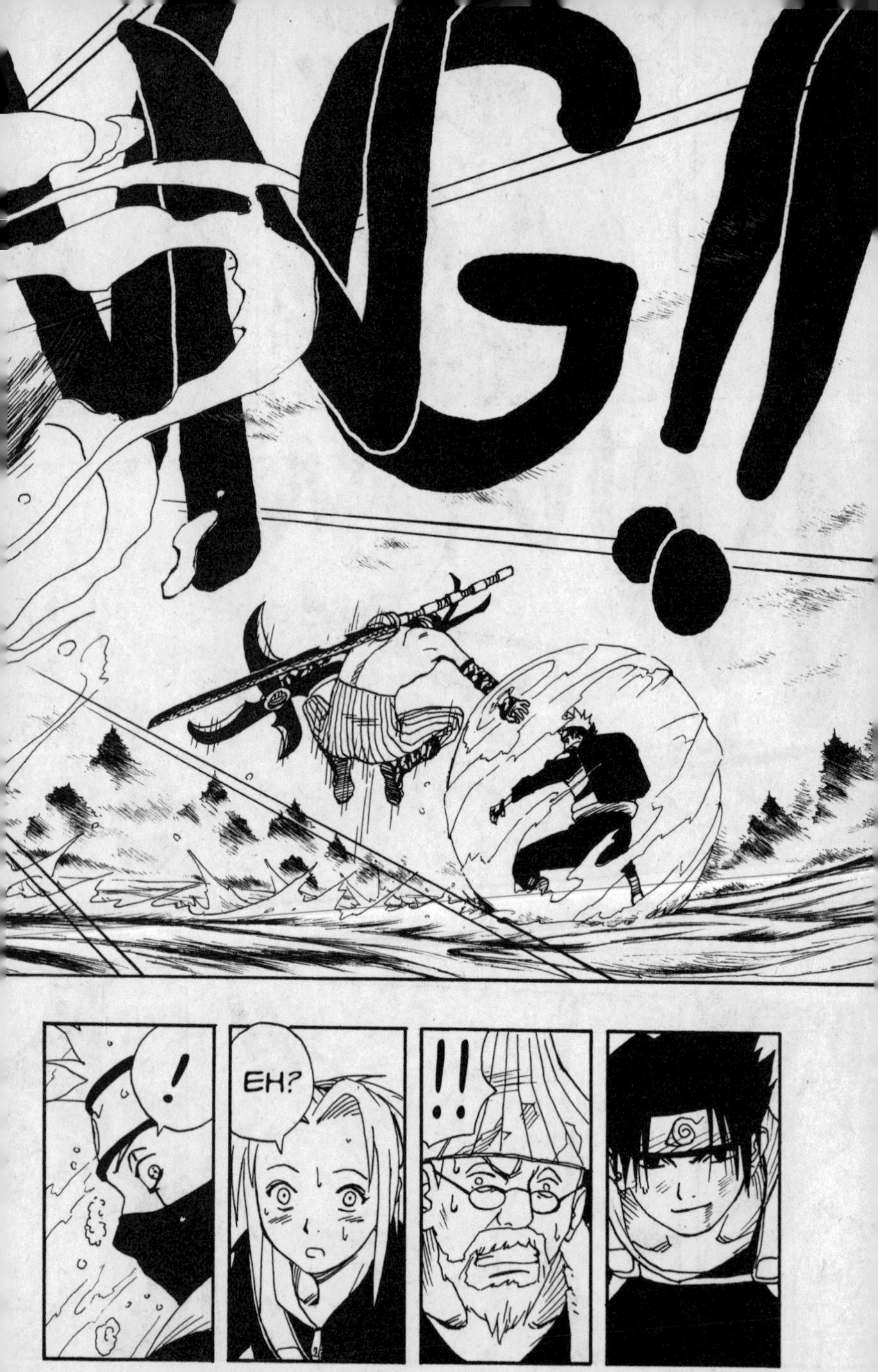
NG!!
!!
EH?
!

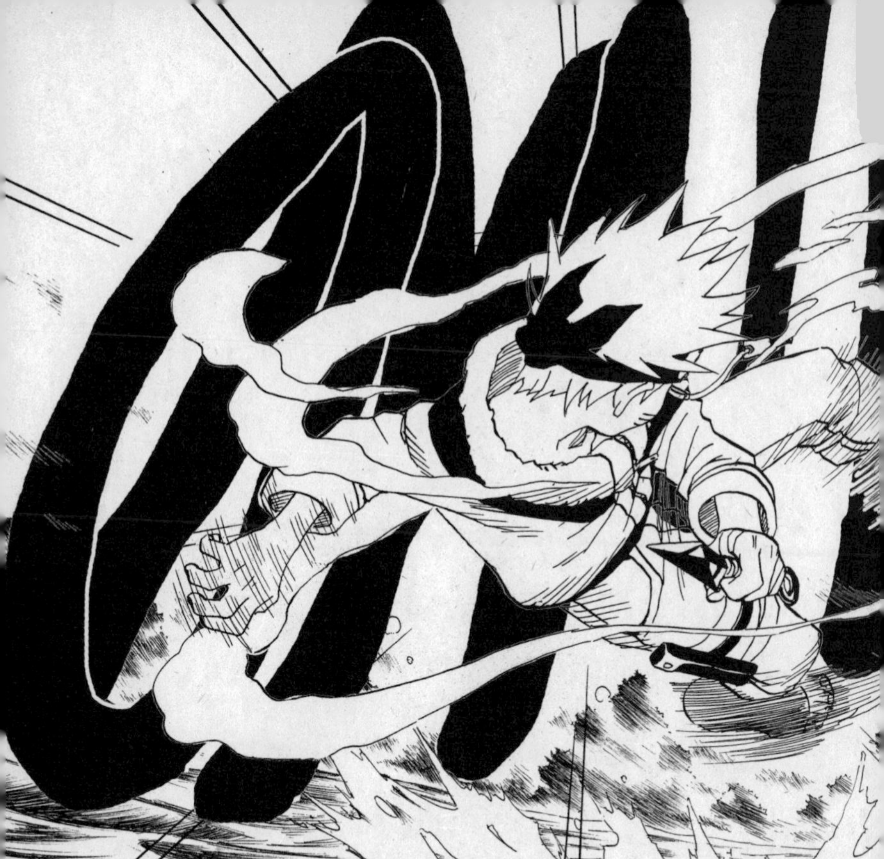

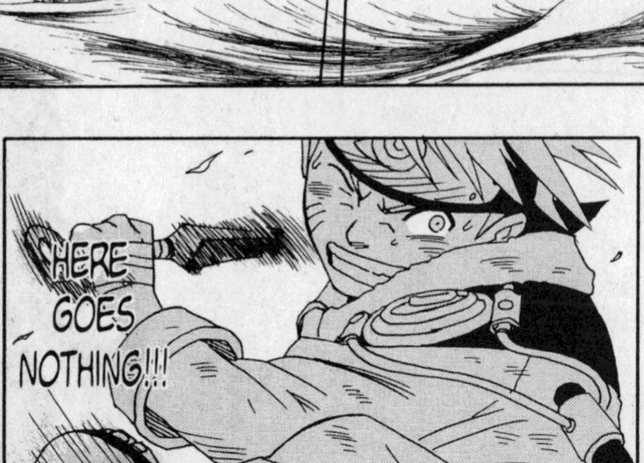
HERE GOES NOTHING!!!

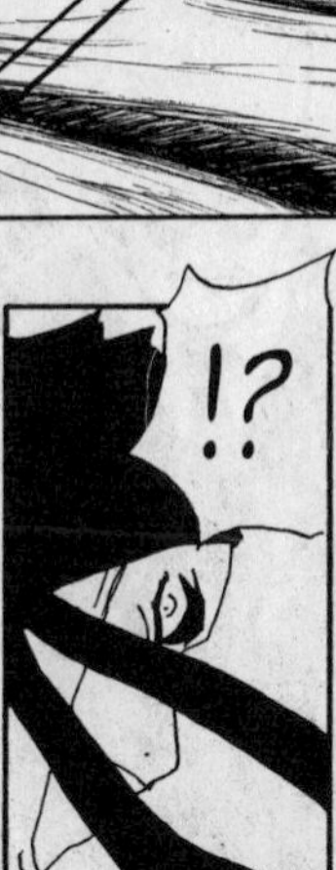
!?

Number 15: Return of the Sharingan

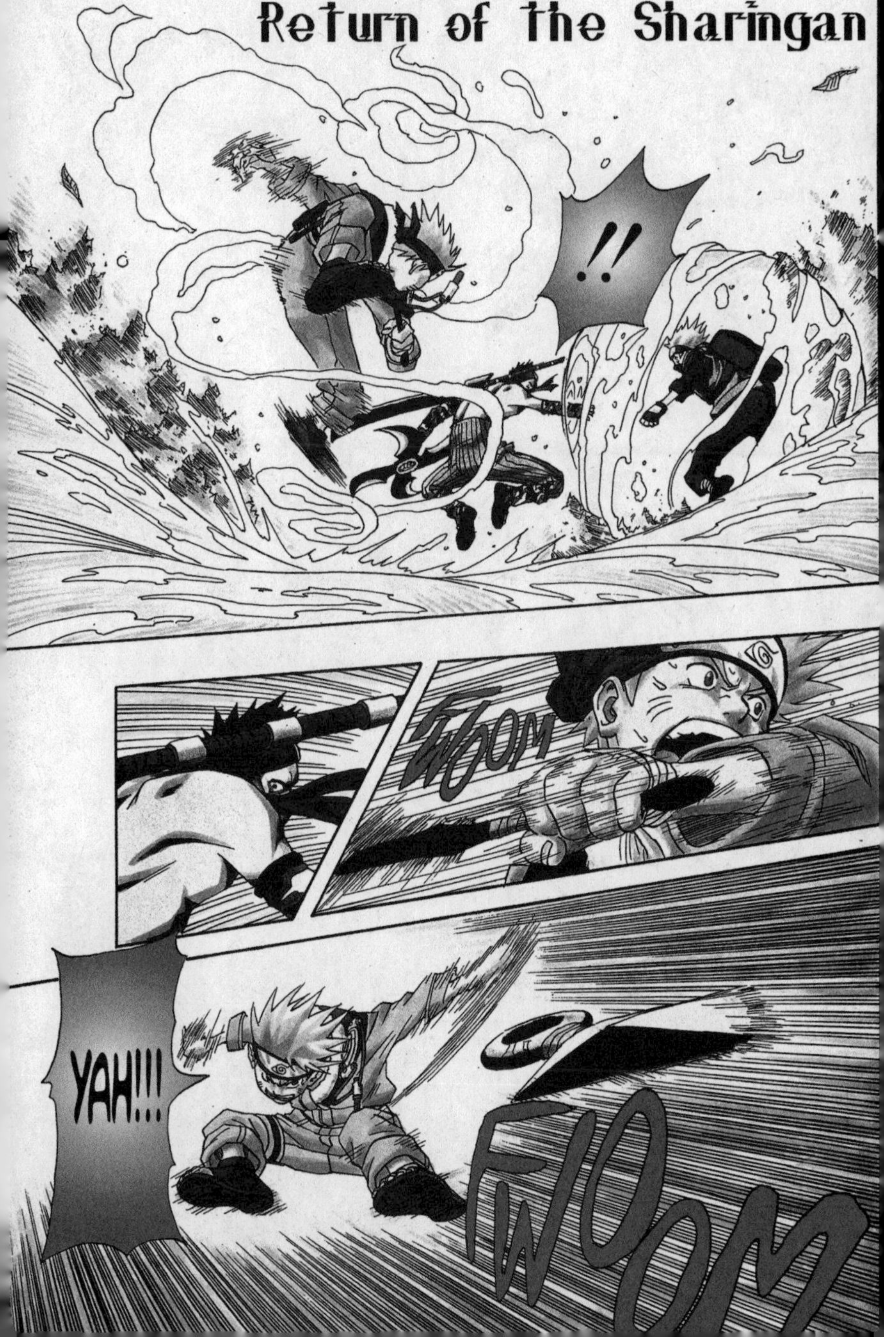
!!
FWOOM
YAH!!!
FWOOM

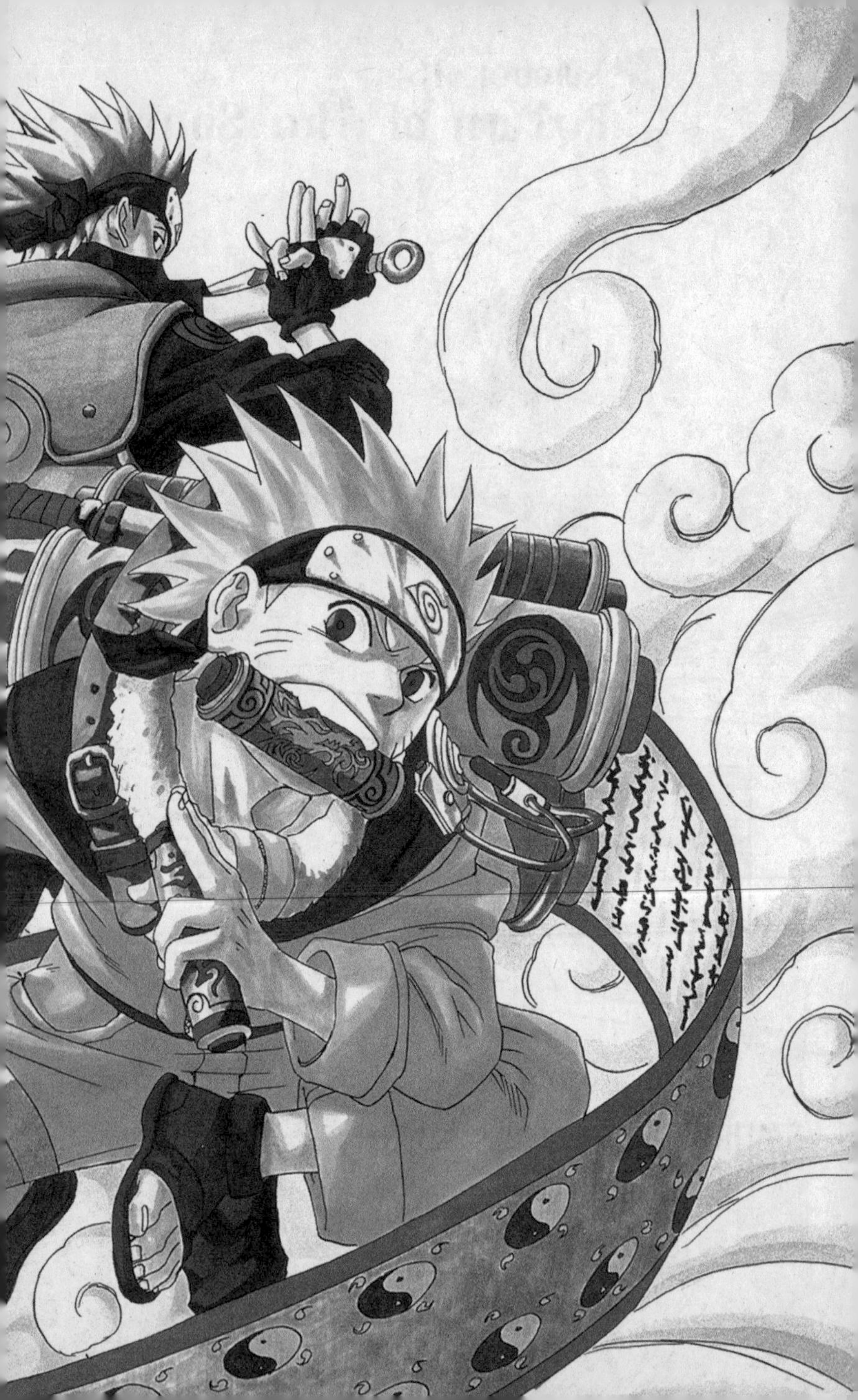

Number 15: Return of the Sharingan

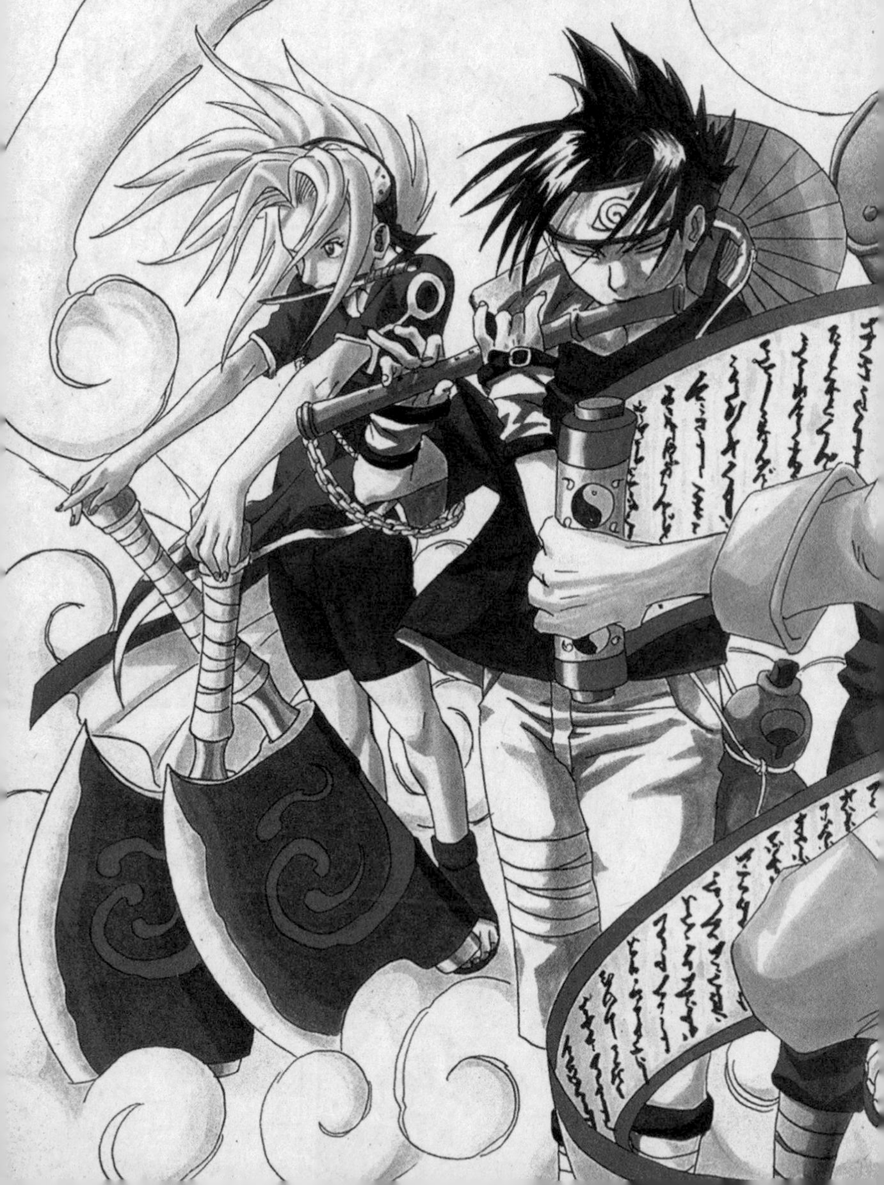

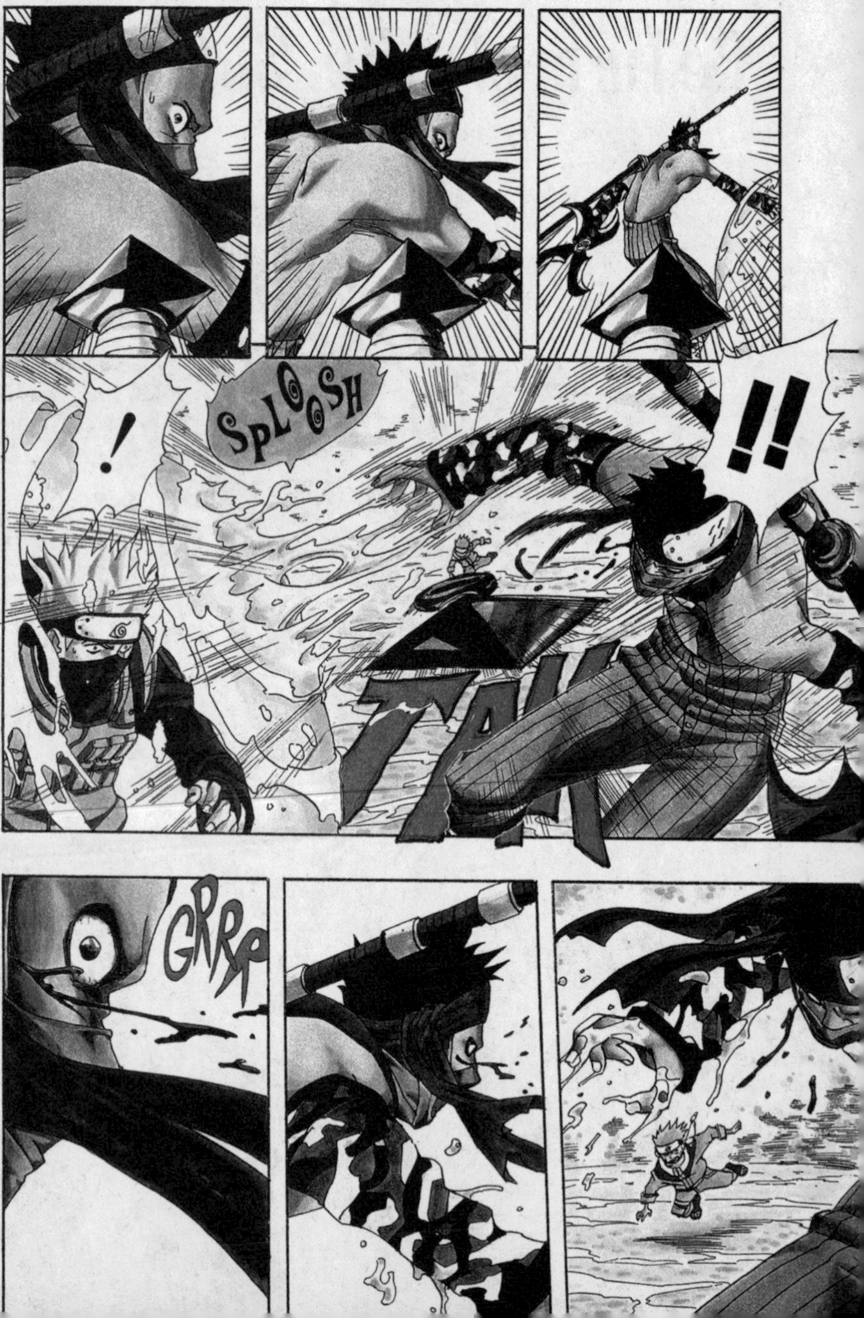

!!
SPLOOSH
!
TAK
GRRR

READ THIS WAY

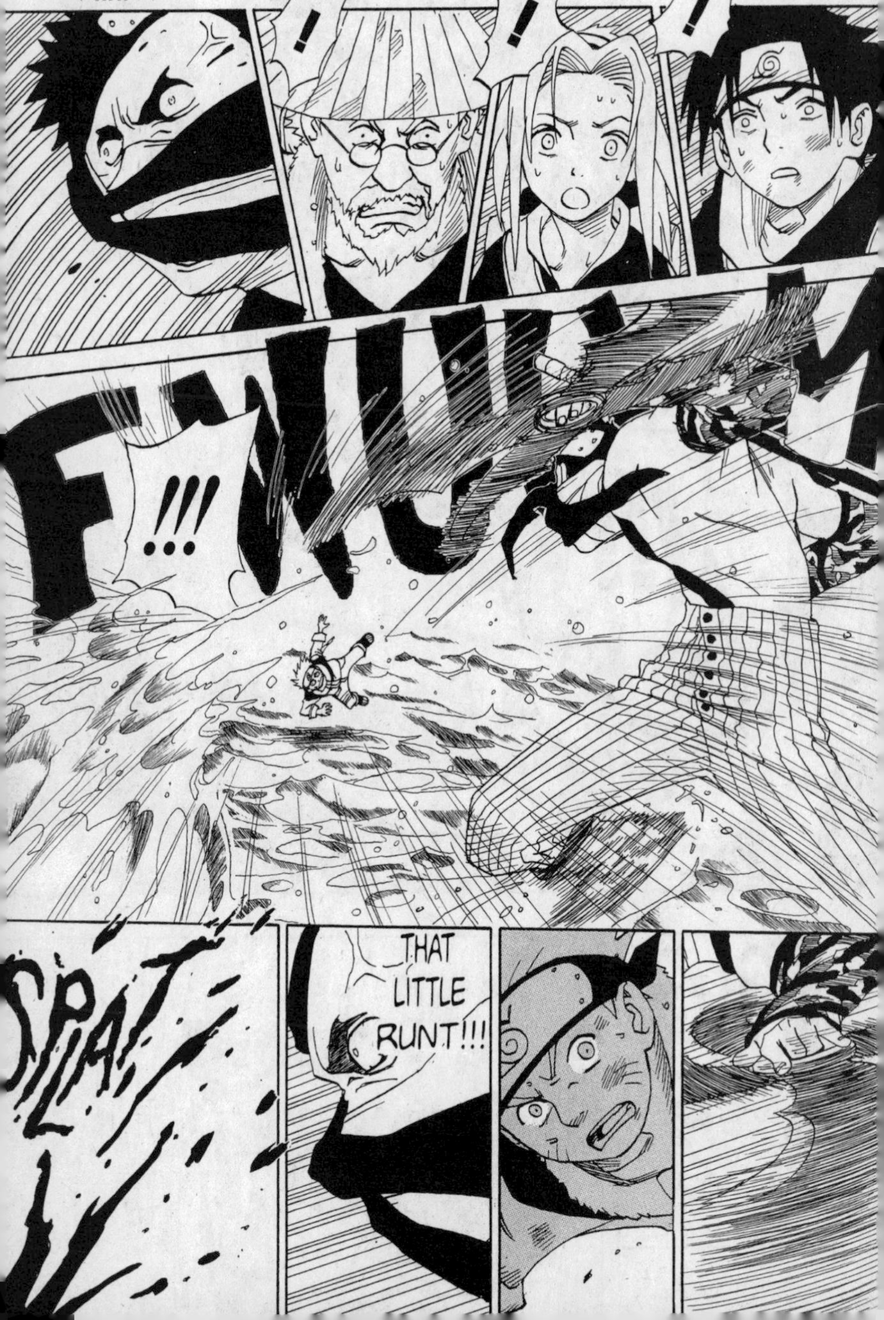
!
!
!
FWUMM
!!!
THAT LITTLE RUNT!!!
SPLAT

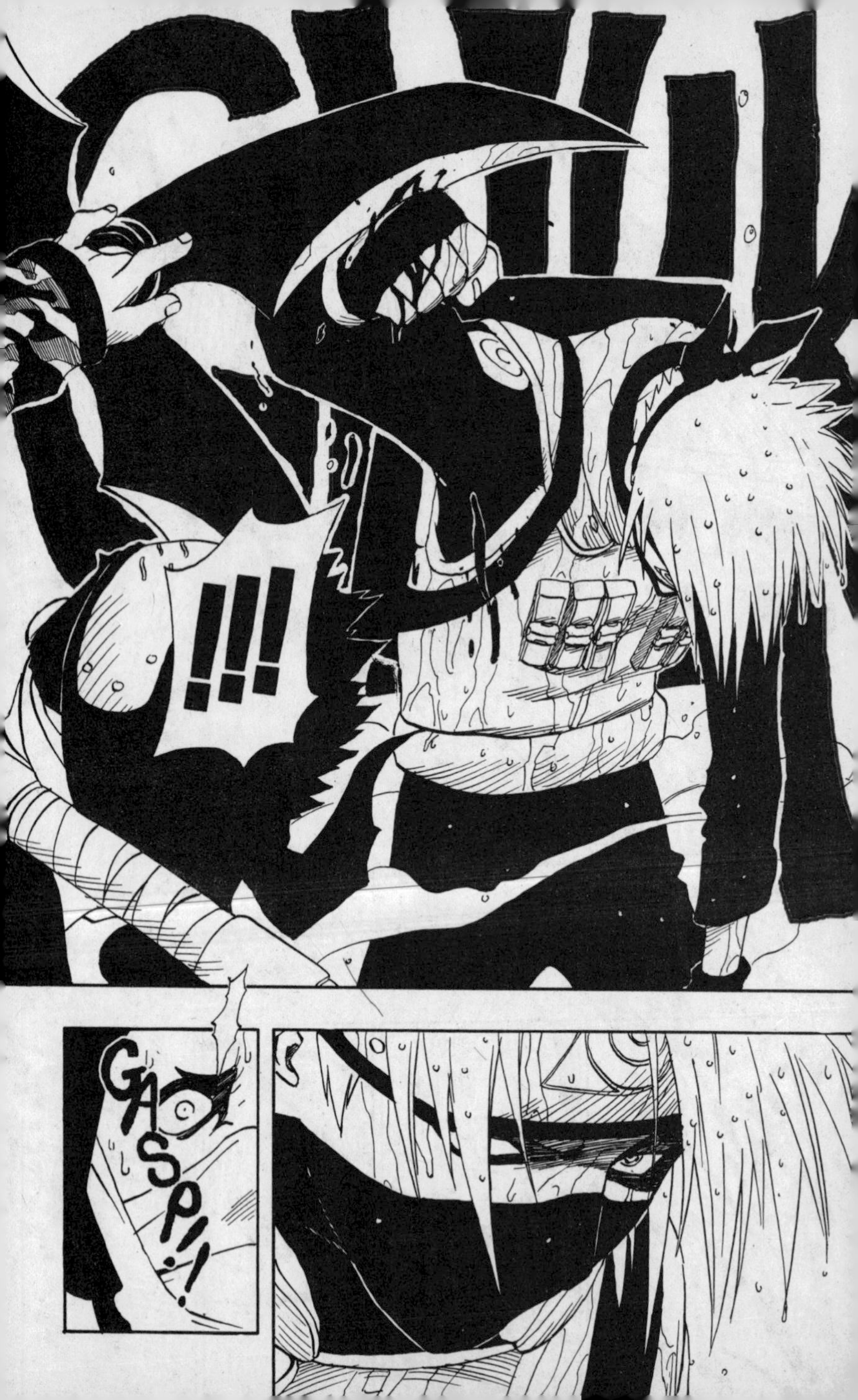
!!!
GASP!!

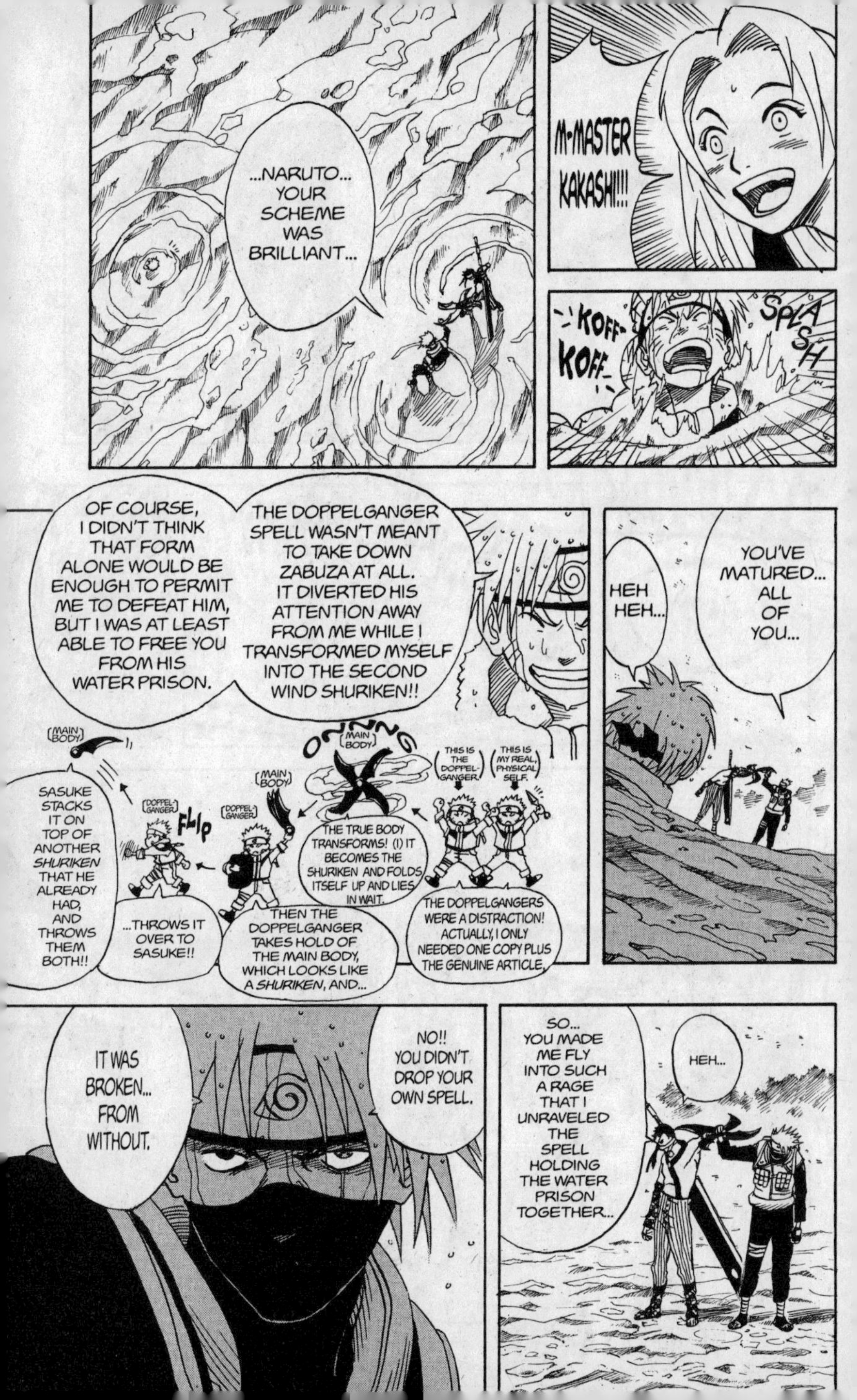
M-MASTER KAKASHI!!!
KOFF KOFF
SPLASH
...NARUTO... YOUR SCHEME WAS BRILLIANT...
YOU'VE MATURED... ALL OF YOU...
HEH HEH...
THE DOPPELGANGER SPELL WASN'T MEANT TO TAKE DOWN ZABUZA AT ALL. IT DIVERTED HIS ATTENTION AWAY FROM ME WHILE I TRANSFORMED MYSELF INTO THE SECOND WIND SHURIKEN!!
OF COURSE, I DIDN'T THINK THAT FORM ALONE WOULD BE ENOUGH TO PERMIT ME TO DEFEAT HIM, BUT I WAS AT LEAST ABLE TO FREE YOU FROM HIS WATER PRISON.
THIS IS MY REAL, PHYSICAL SELF.
THIS IS THE DOPPELGANGER.
THE DOPPELGANGERS WERE A DISTRACTION! ACTUALLY, I ONLY NEEDED ONE COPY PLUS THE GENUINE ARTICLE.
MAIN BODY
ONNNG
THE TRUE BODY TRANSFORMS! (!) IT BECOMES THE SHURIKEN AND FOLDS ITSELF UP AND LIES IN WAIT.
MAIN BODY
DOPPELGANGER
THEN THE DOPPELGANGER TAKES HOLD OF THE MAIN BODY, WHICH LOOKS LIKE A *SHURIKEN*, AND...
DOPPELGANGER
FLIP
...THROWS IT OVER TO SASUKE!!
MAIN BODY
SASUKE STACKS IT ON TOP OF ANOTHER *SHURIKEN* THAT HE ALREADY HAD, AND THROWS THEM BOTH!!
HEH...
SO... YOU MADE ME FLY INTO SUCH A RAGE THAT I UNRAVELED THE SPELL HOLDING THE WATER PRISON TOGETHER...
NO!! YOU DIDN'T DROP YOUR OWN SPELL.
IT WAS BROKEN... FROM WITHOUT.

READ THIS WAY

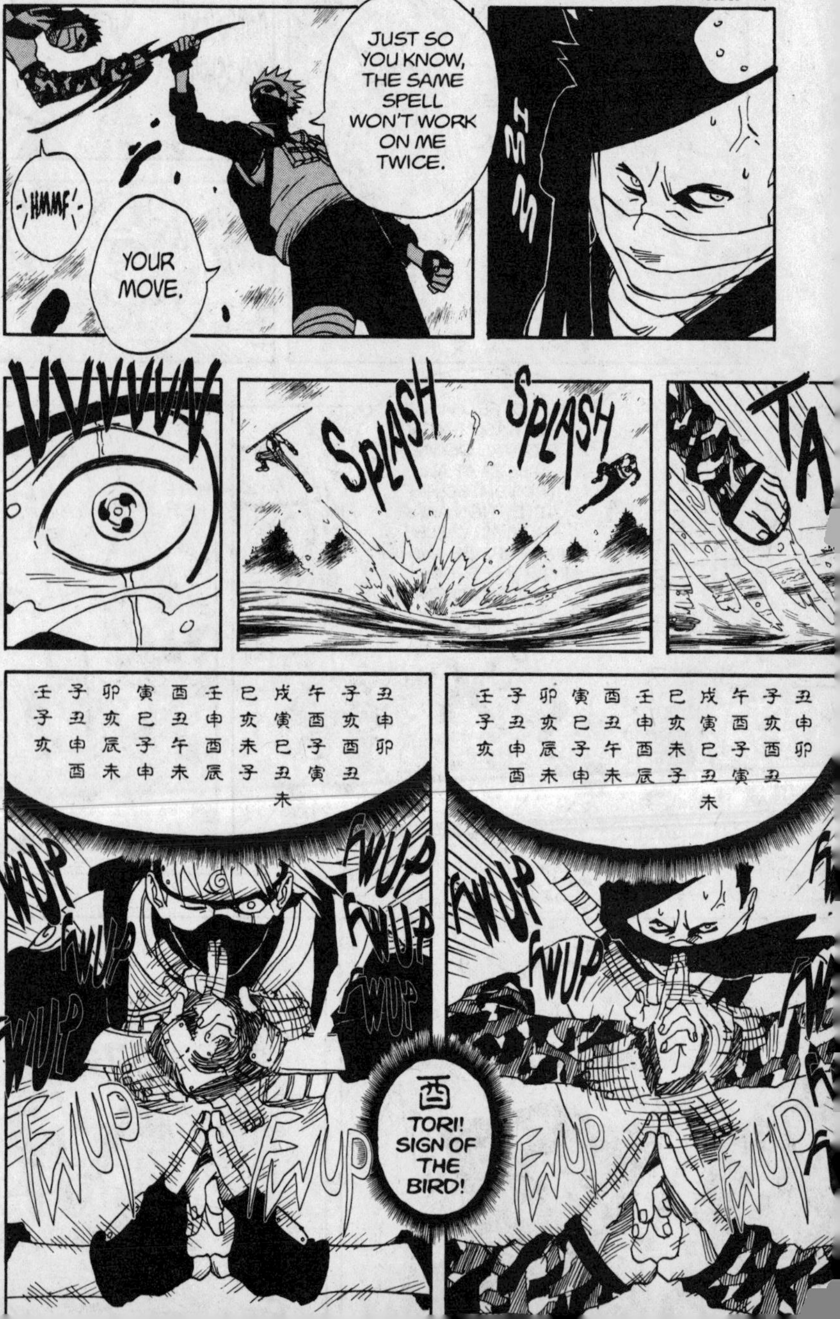
JUST SO YOU KNOW, THE SAME SPELL WON'T WORK ON ME TWICE.
HMMF
YOUR MOVE.
SPLASH
SPLASH
VVVVUN
丑申卯 子亥酉丑 午酉子寅 戌寅巳丑未 巳亥未子 壬申酉辰 酉丑午未 寅巳子申 卯亥辰未 子丑申酉 壬子亥
FWUP
FWUP
FWUP
FWUP
丑申卯 子亥酉丑 午酉子寅 戌寅巳丑未 巳亥未子 壬申酉辰 酉丑午未 寅巳子申 卯亥辰未 子丑申酉 壬子亥
FWUP
FWUP
FWUP
FWUP
FWUP
FWUP
酉 TORI!! SIGN OF THE BIRD!

READ THIS WAY

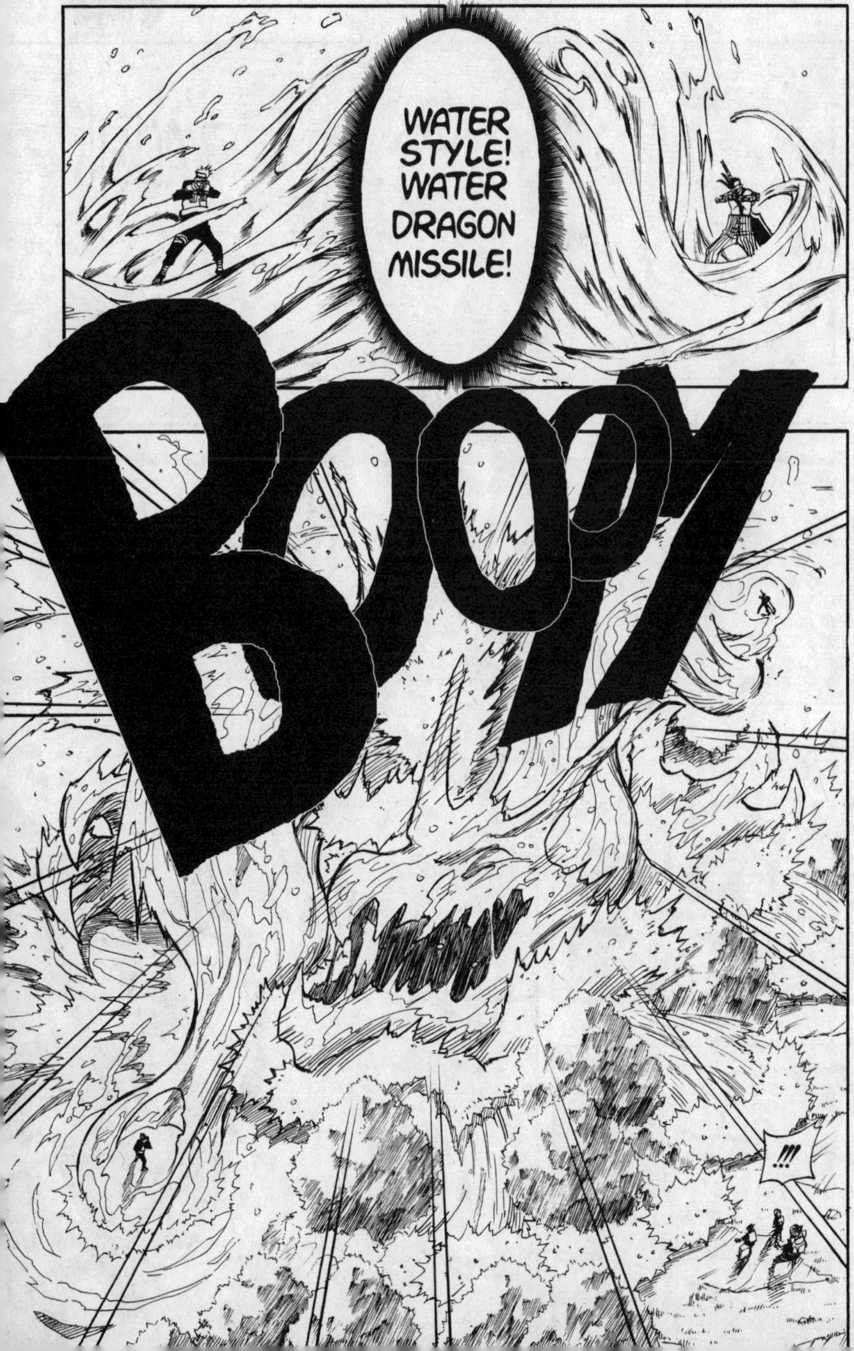
WATER STYLE! WATER DRAGON MISSILE!
BOOOM
!!!

READ THIS WAY

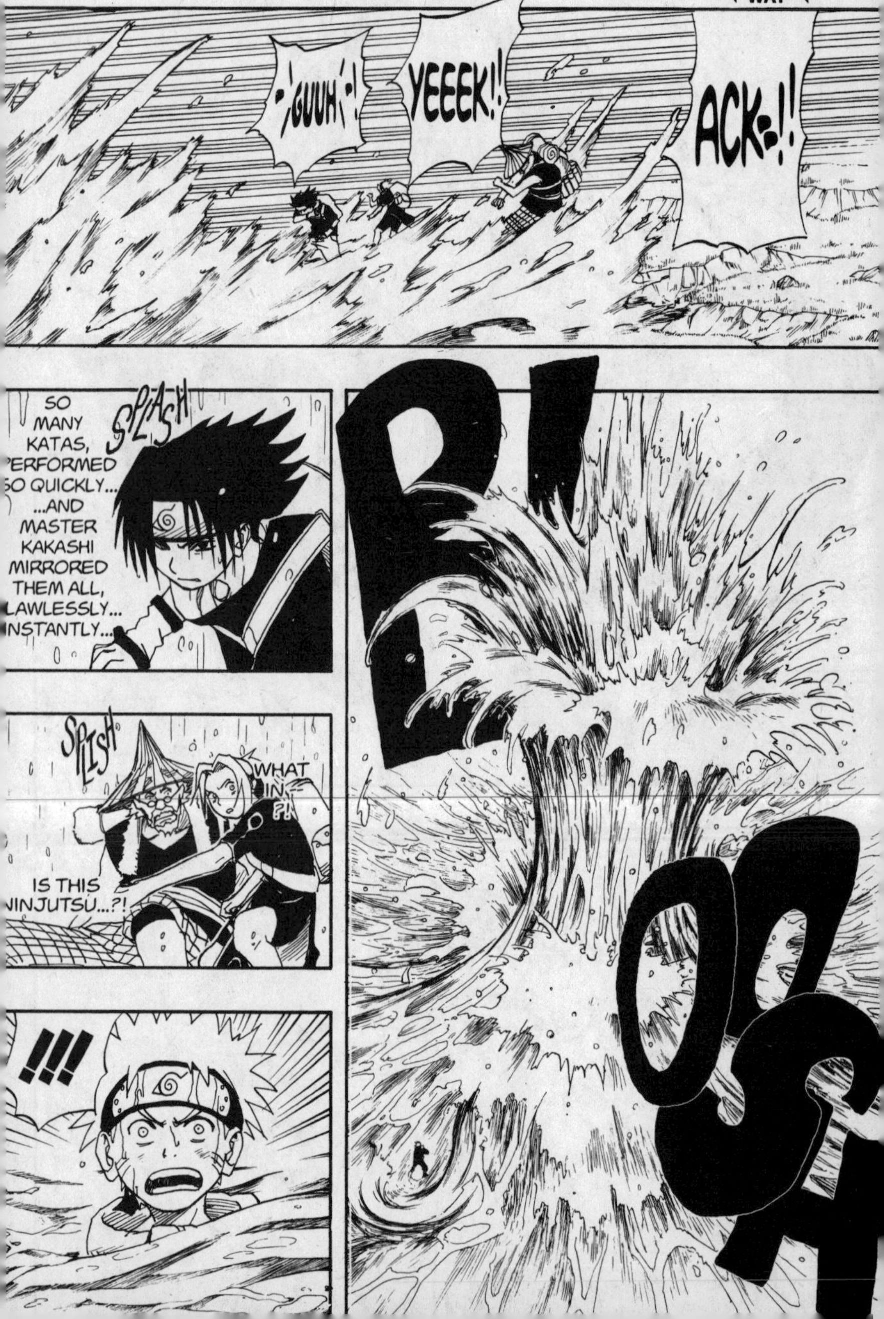
ACK...!!
YEEEK!!
GUUH!
BLOOOSH
SPLASH
SO MANY KATAS, PERFORMED SO QUICKLY...
...AND MASTER KAKASHI MIRRORED THEM ALL, FLAWLESSLY... INSTANTLY...
SPLISH
WHAT IN--?!
IS THIS NINJUTSU...?!
!!!

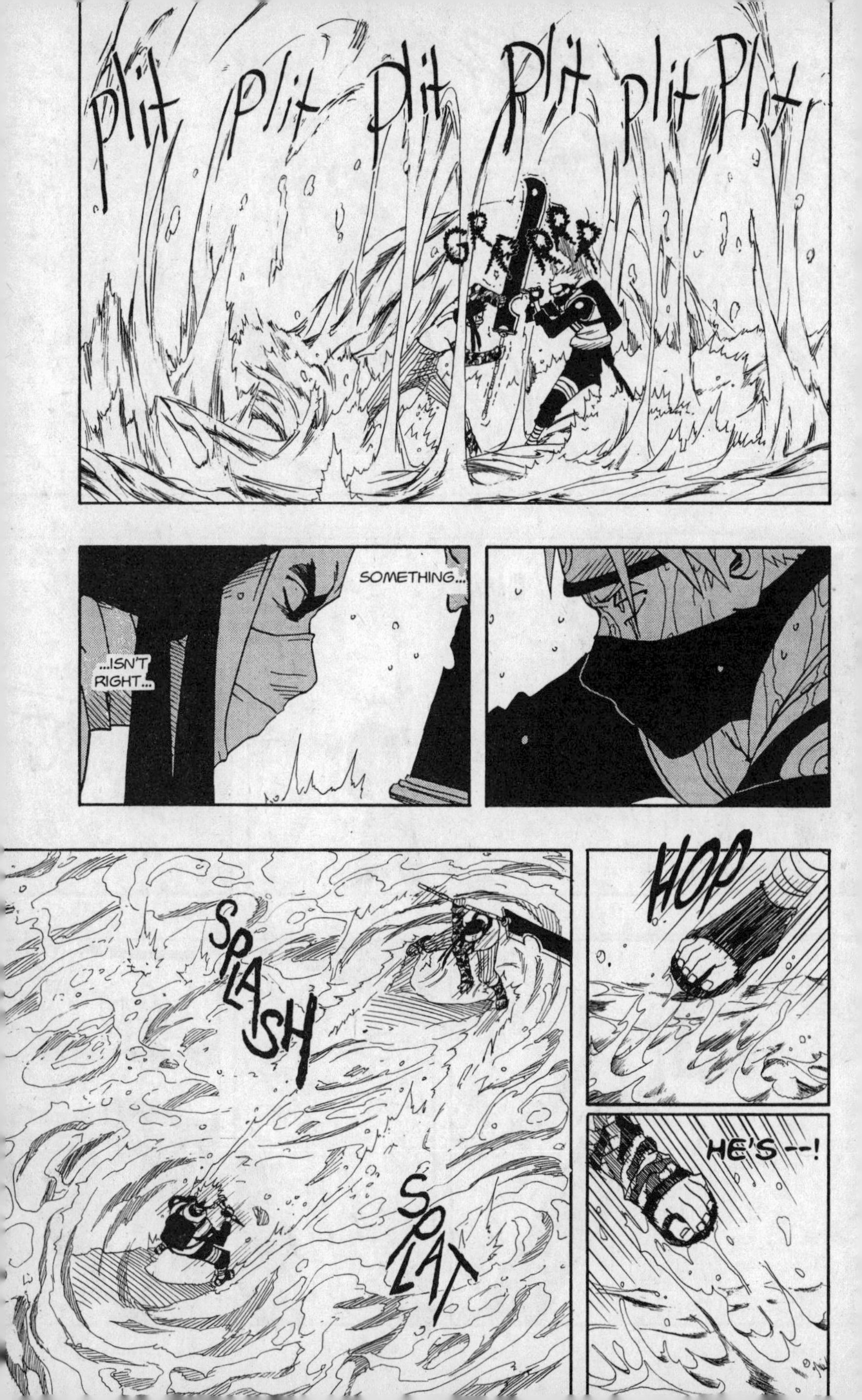
plit plit plit plit plit plit
GRRRRR
SOMETHING...
...ISN'T RIGHT...
HOP
HE'S --!
SPLASH
SPLAT

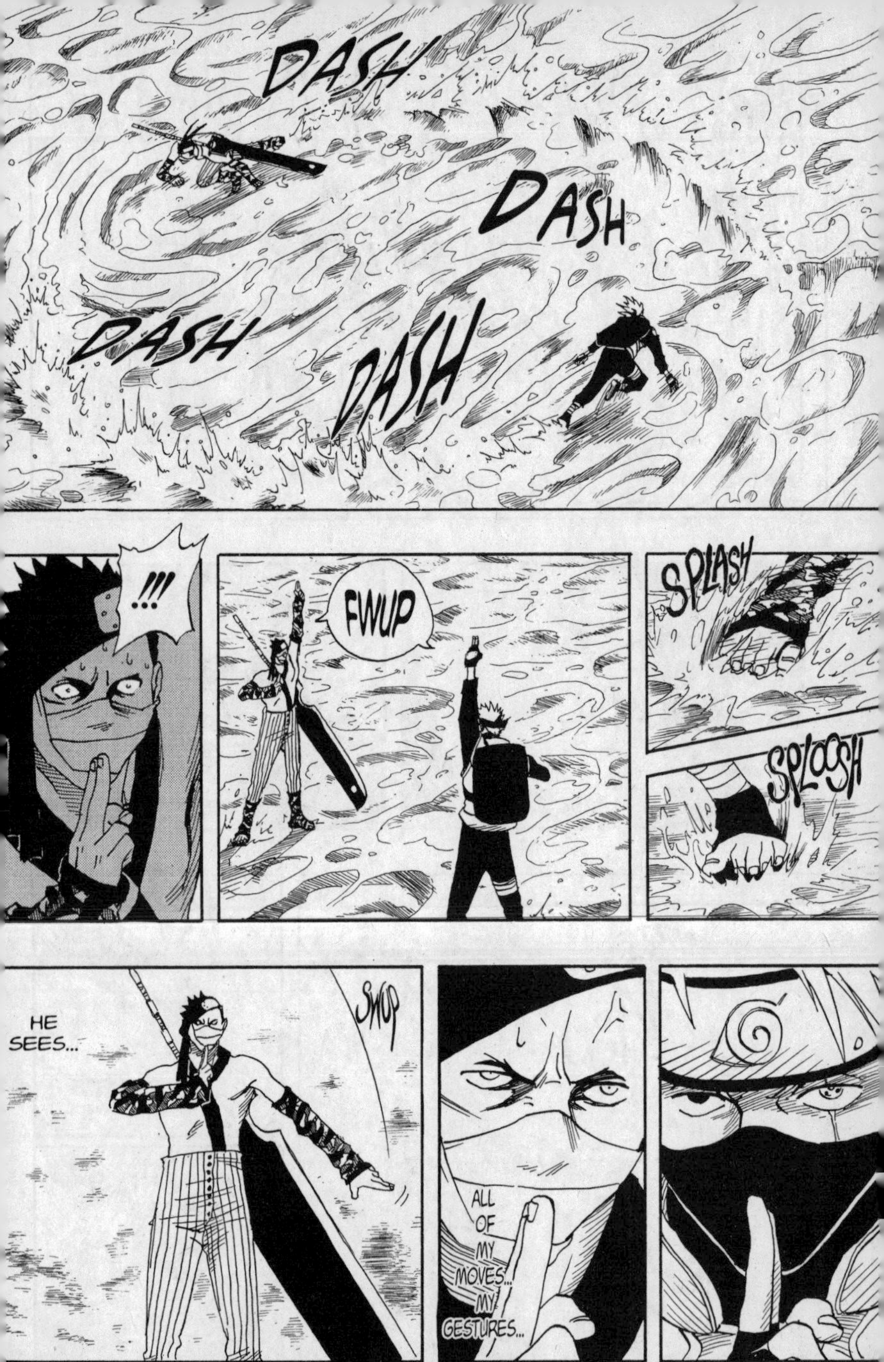
DASH
DASH
DASH
DASH
SPLASH
SPLOOSH
FWUP
!!!
ALL OF MY MOVES... MY GESTURES...
SWOP
HE SEES...

READ THIS WAY

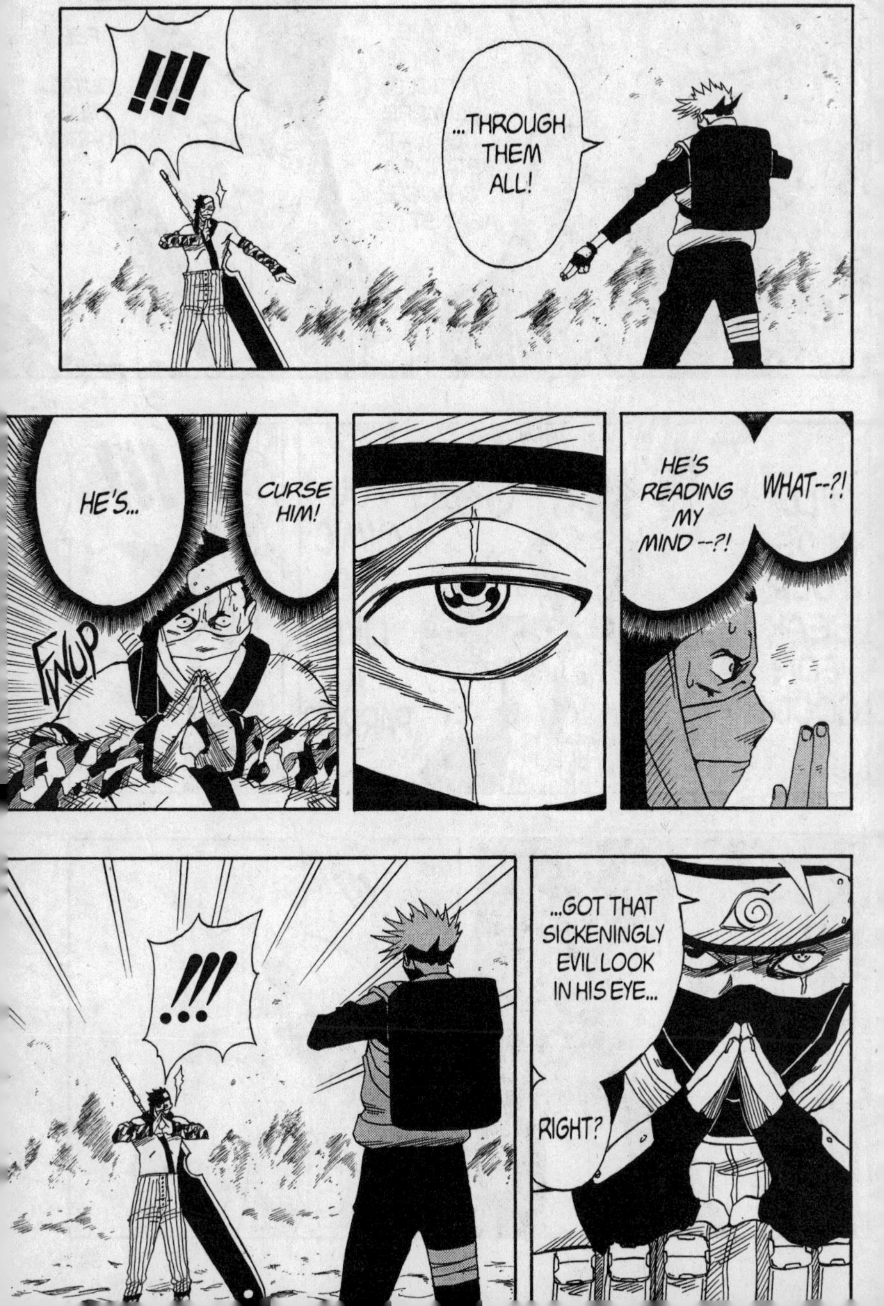
...THROUGH THEM ALL!
!!!
WHAT--?!
HE'S READING MY MIND--?!
CURSE HIM!
HE'S...
FWUP
...GOT THAT SICKENINGLY EVIL LOOK IN HIS EYE...
RIGHT?
!!!

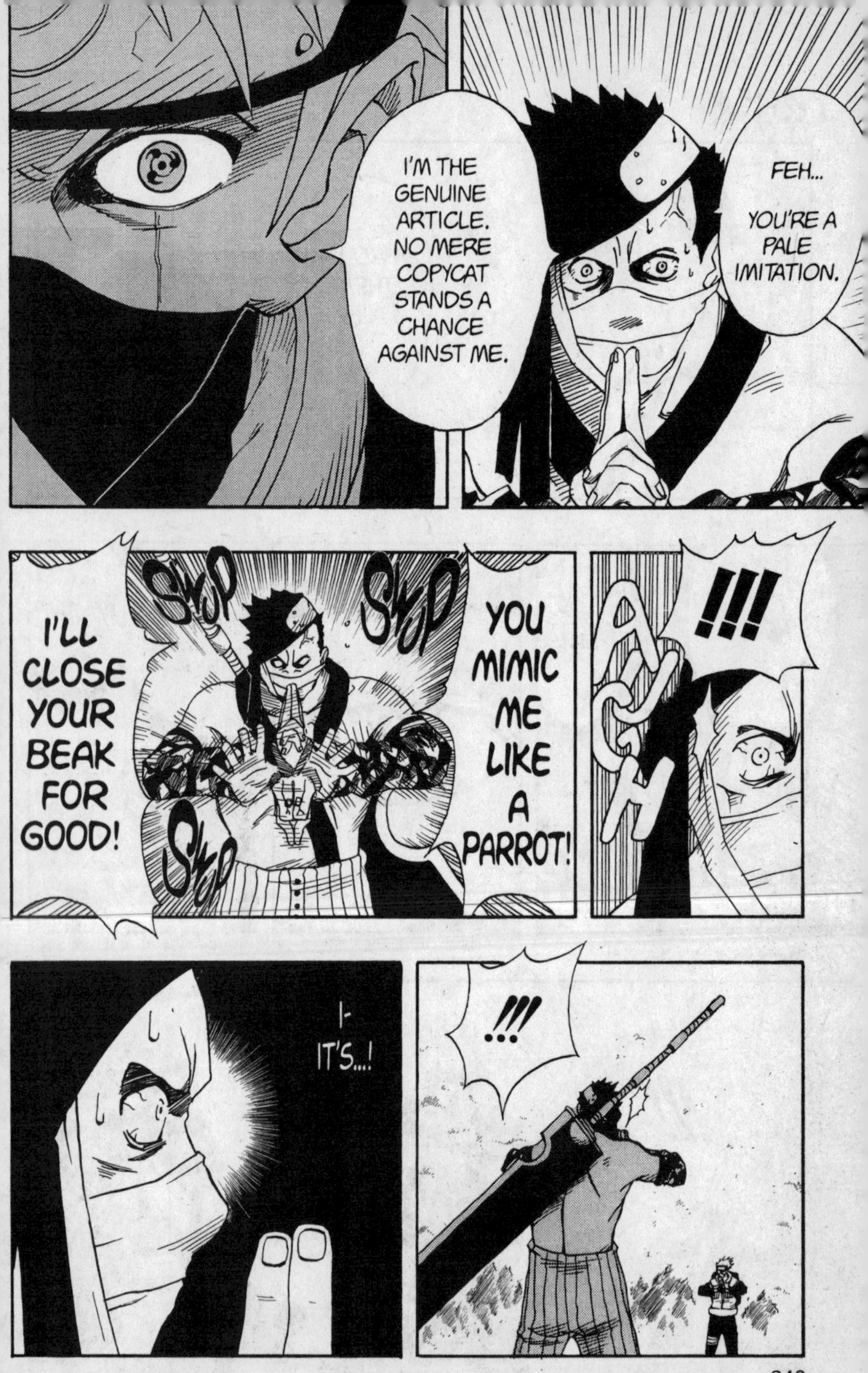
FEH...
YOU'RE A PALE IMITATION.
I'M THE GENUINE ARTICLE. NO MERE COPYCAT STANDS A CHANCE AGAINST ME.
!!!
ACCH
SWOP
SWOP
YOU MIMIC ME LIKE A PARROT!
I'LL CLOSE YOUR BEAK FOR GOOD!
SWOP
!!!
I- IT'S...!

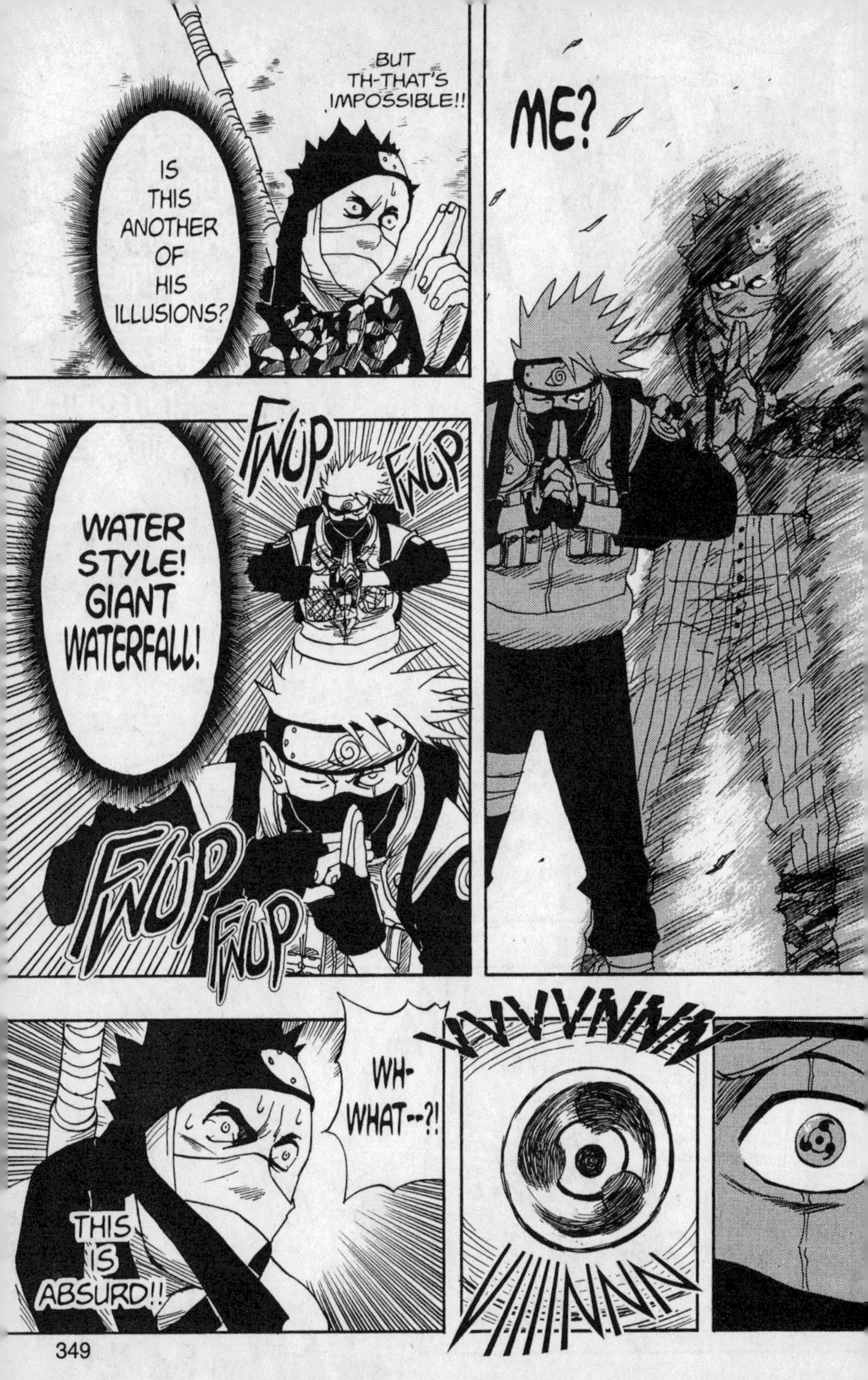
ME?
BUT TH-THAT'S IMPOSSIBLE!!
IS THIS ANOTHER OF HIS ILLUSIONS?
FWUP
FWUP
WATER STYLE! GIANT WATERFALL!
FWUP
FWUP
VVVVNNN
VVVVNNN
WH-WHAT--?!
THIS IS ABSURD!!

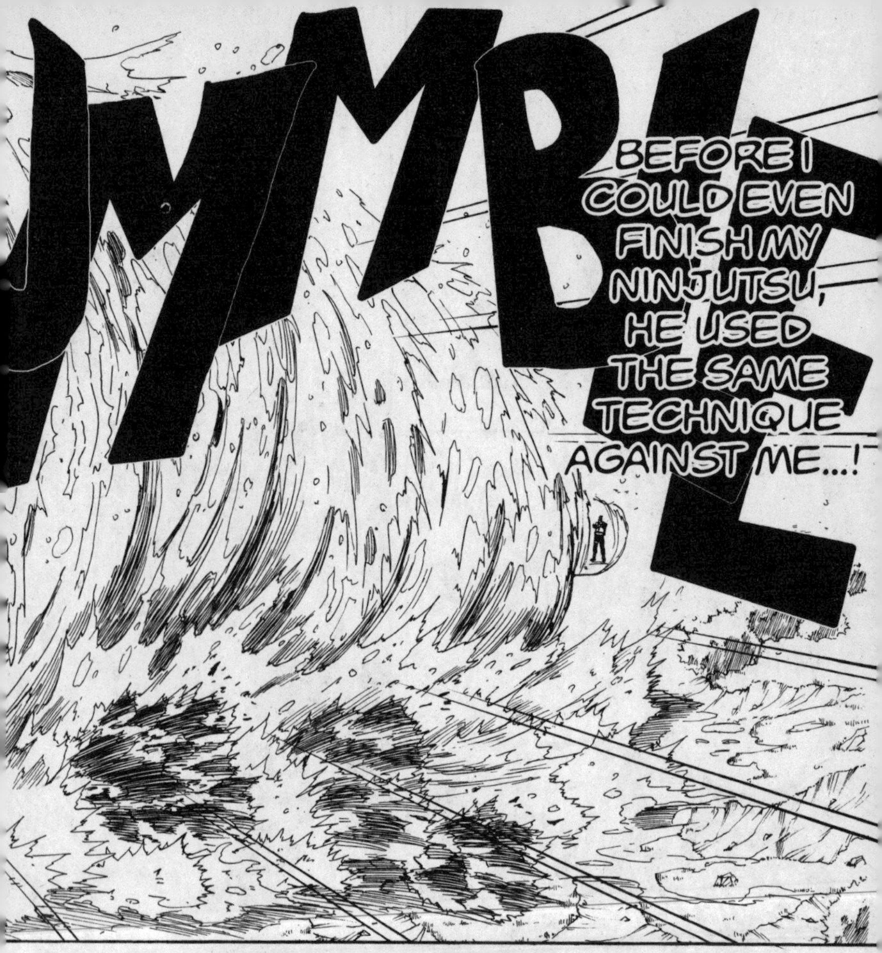
BEFORE I COULD EVEN FINISH MY NINJUTSU, HE USED THE SAME TECHNIQUE AGAINST ME...!
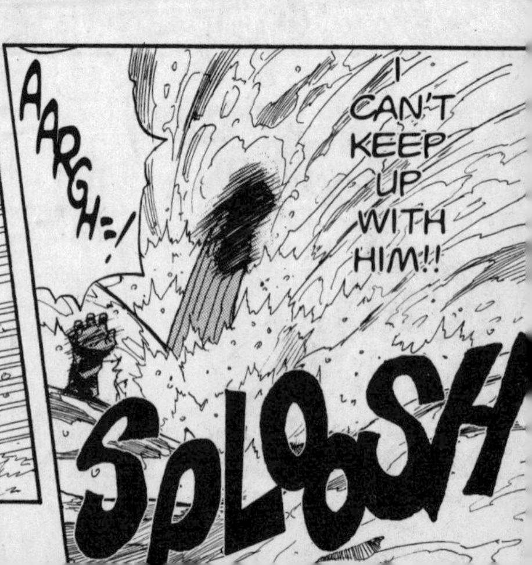
I CAN'T KEEP UP WITH HIM!!
AARGH..!
SPLOOSH
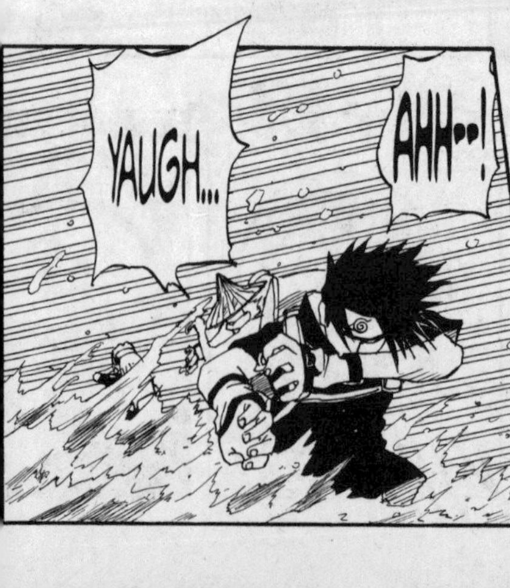
AHH..!
YAUGH...

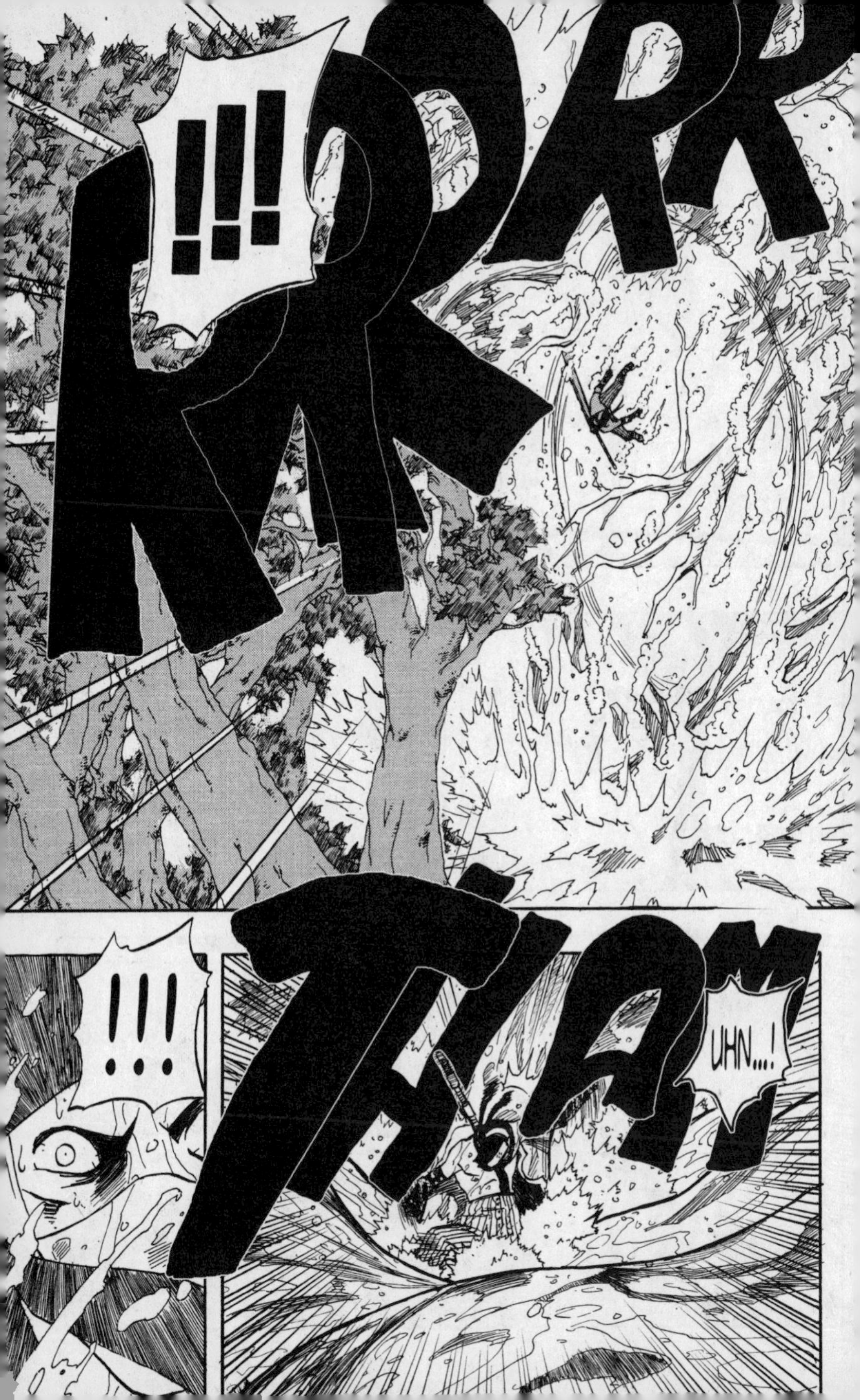
!!!
KRRR
UHN...!
THRM
!!!

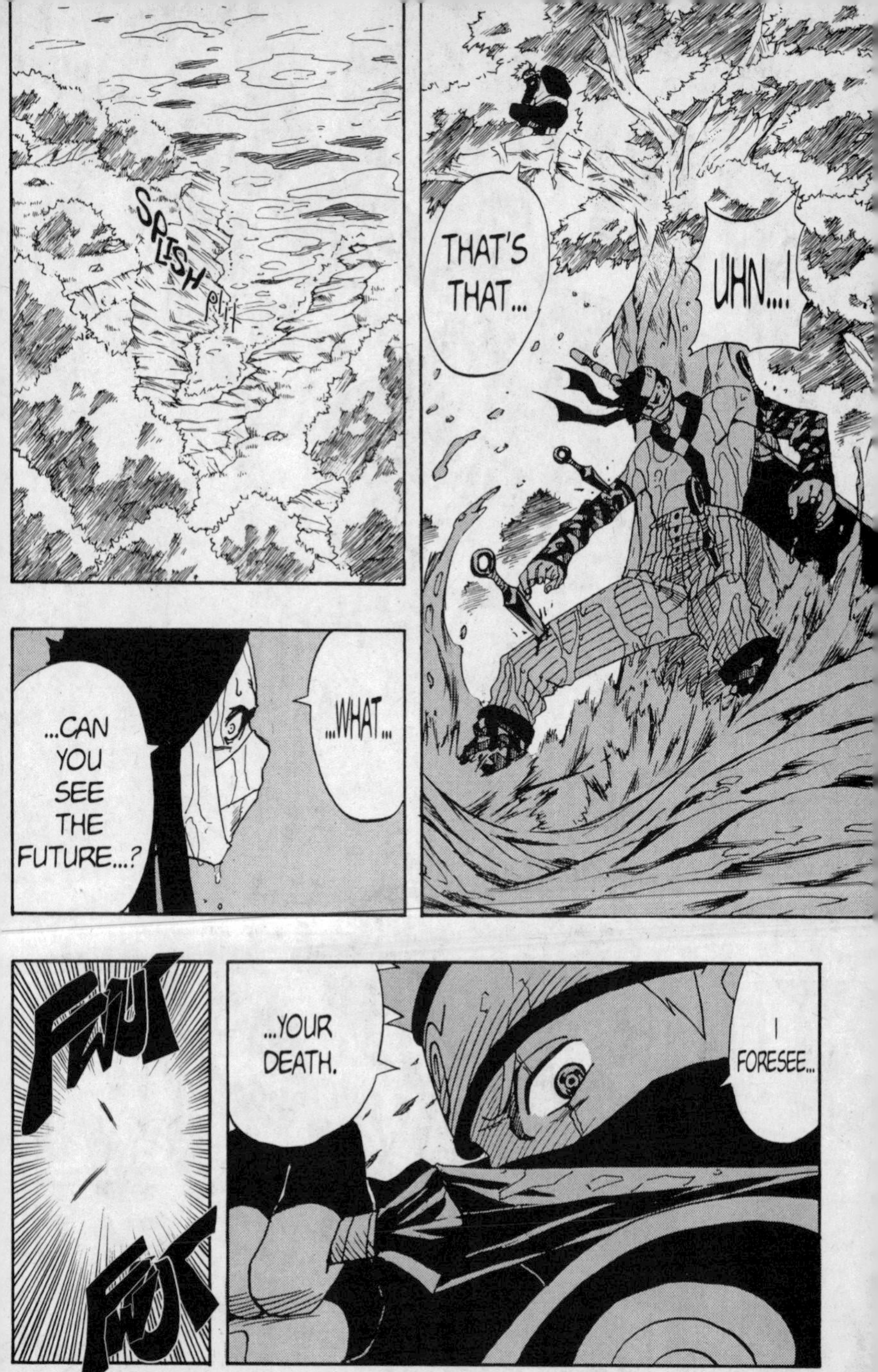
UHN...!
THAT'S THAT...
SPLISH
plit
...WHAT...
...CAN YOU SEE THE FUTURE...?
I FORESEE...
...YOUR DEATH.
FWUT
FWT

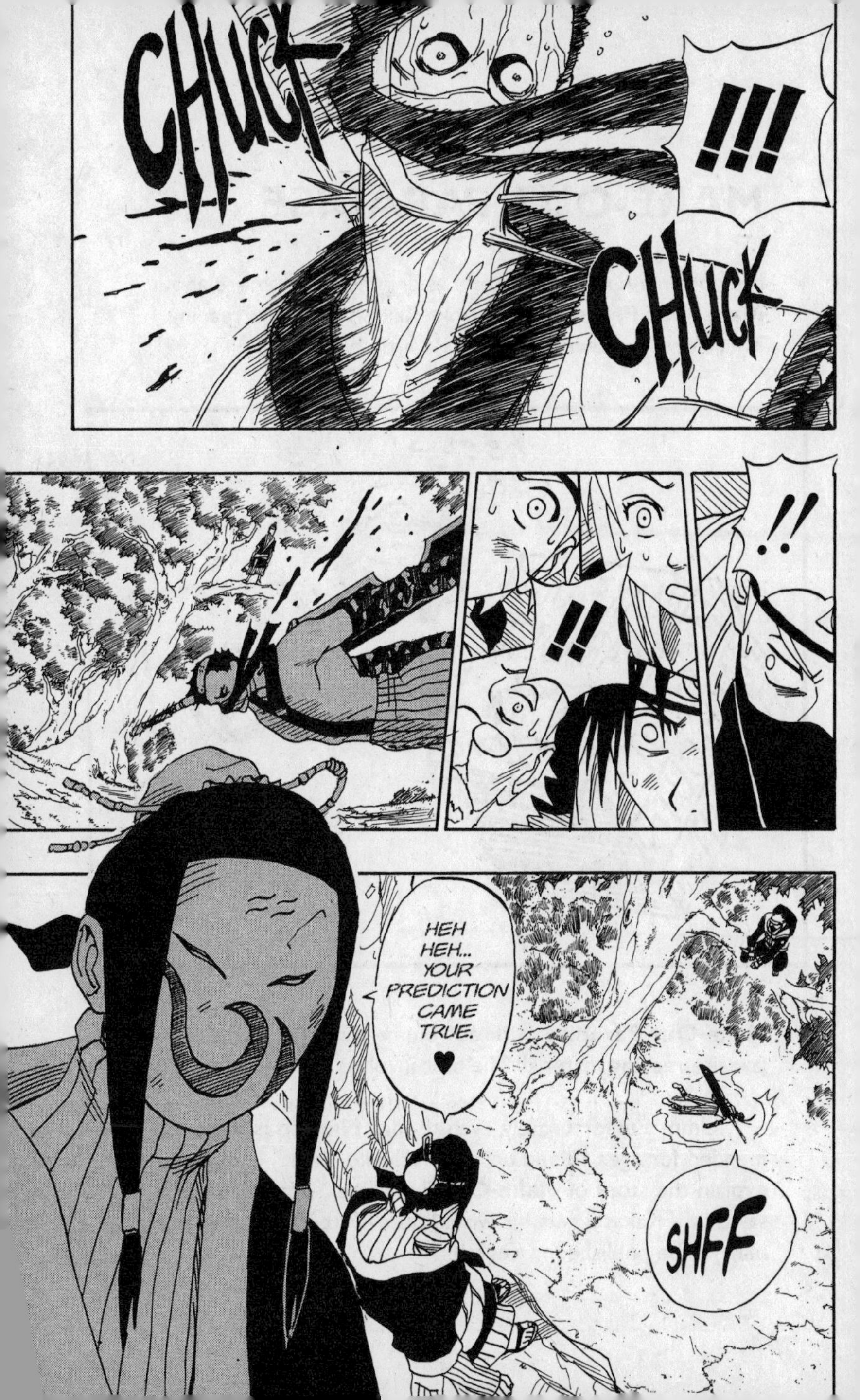
!!!
CHUCK
CHUCK
!!
!!
HEH HEH... YOUR PREDICTION CAME TRUE. ♥
SHFF

MAKE-OUT PARADISE

I've gotten a number of letters asking me to tell more about **Make-Out Paradise**, the books Kakashi is always reading. Therefore, I've decided to write a little bit about it.

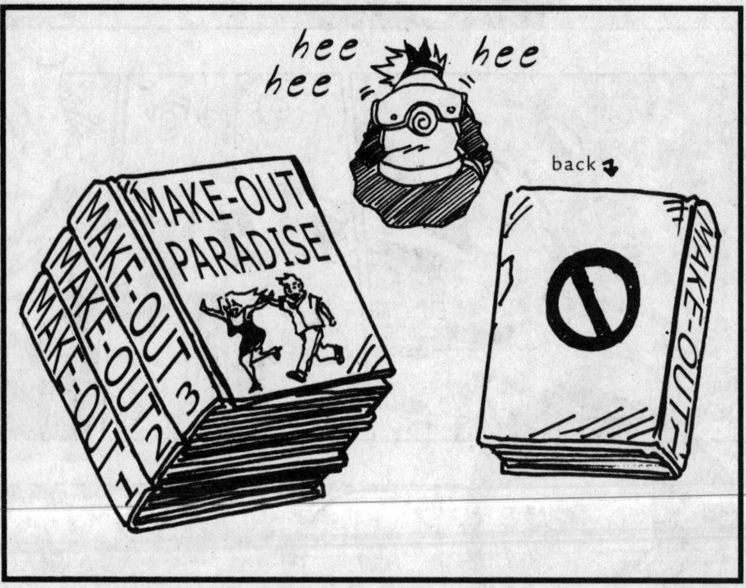
hee
hee
hee
back
MAKE-OUT PARADISE
MAKE-OUT 3
MAKE-OUT 2
MAKE-OUT 1
MAKE-OUT

Make-Out Paradise (a three-volume series) is Kakashi's favorite reading material! The plot involves....................

....

......Umm...unfortunately, even though **Naruto** is "recommended for ages 13 and up," it's not *quite* "adult" enough to explain the story of **Make-Out Paradise**. Sorry! But I will say that if Kakashi gets his wish, **Make-Out Paradise** Vol. 1 may yet be published in English!

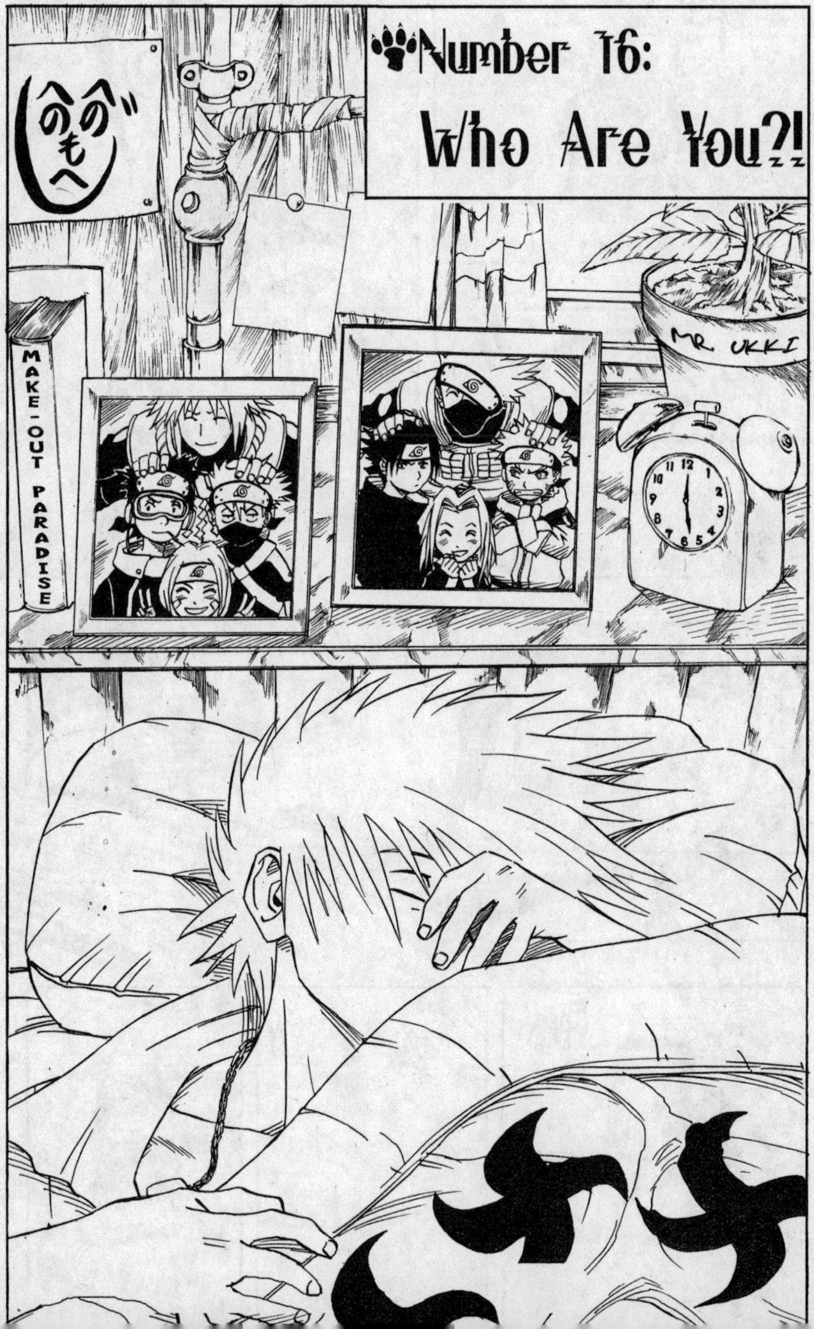

READ THIS WAY
Number 16: Who Are You?!
へのへのもへじ
MAKE-OUT PARADISE
MR. UKKI

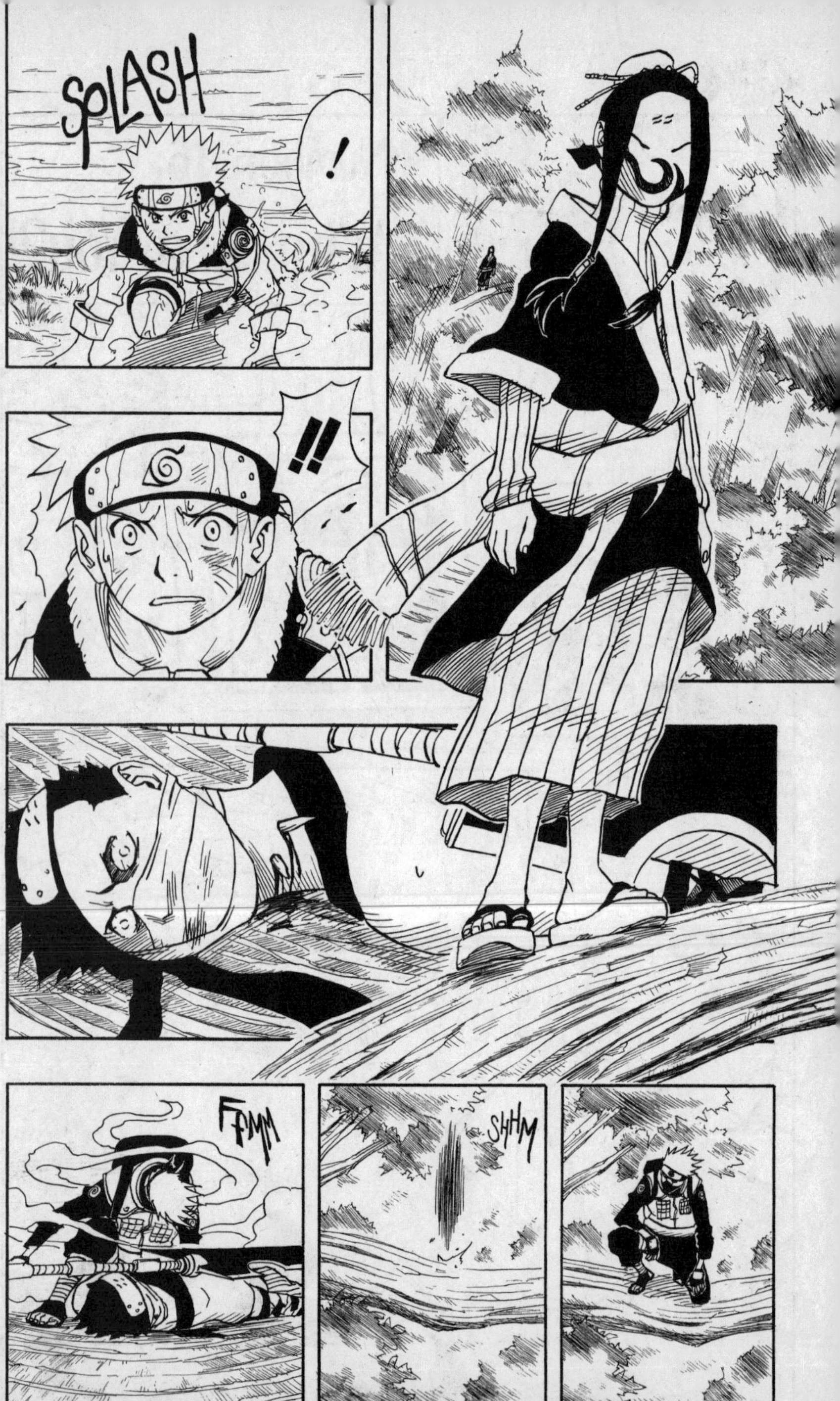
SPLASH
!
!!
SHHM
FFMM

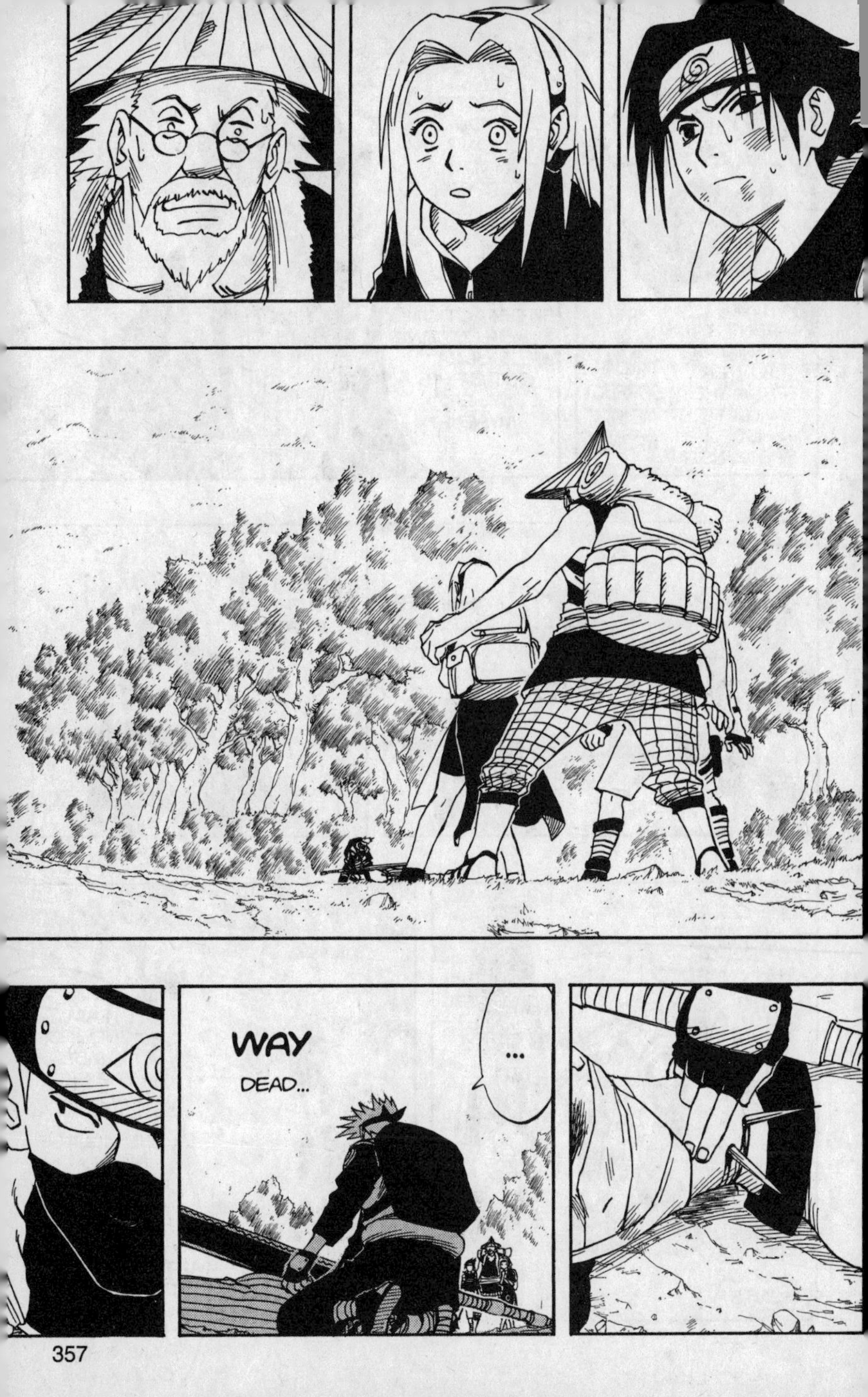
...
WAY
DEAD...

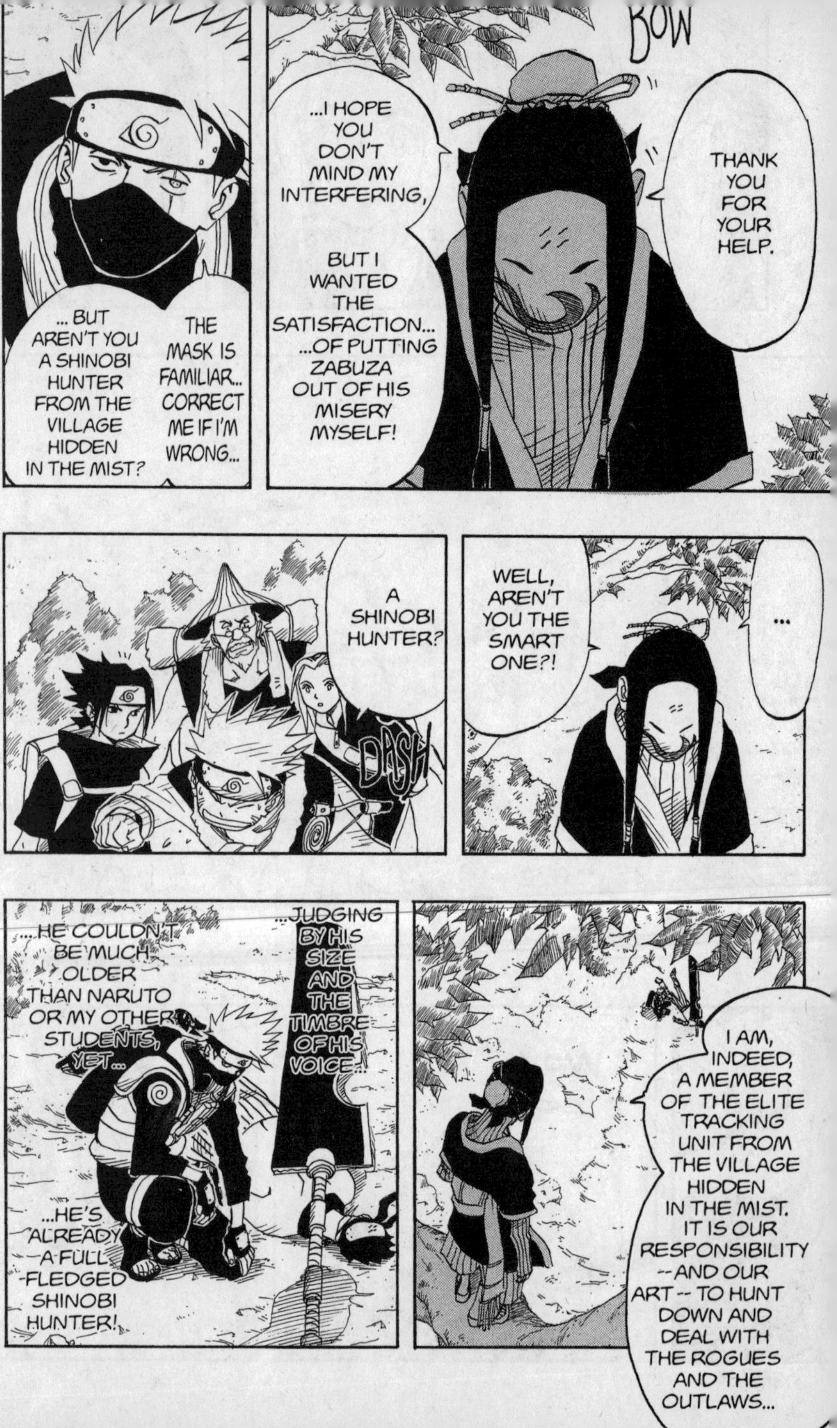
BOW
THANK YOU FOR YOUR HELP.
...I HOPE YOU DON'T MIND MY INTERFERING,
BUT I WANTED THE SATISFACTION... ...OF PUTTING ZABUZA OUT OF HIS MISERY MYSELF!
THE MASK IS FAMILIAR... CORRECT ME IF I'M WRONG...
... BUT AREN'T YOU A SHINOBI HUNTER FROM THE VILLAGE HIDDEN IN THE MIST?
...
WELL, AREN'T YOU THE SMART ONE?!
A SHINOBI HUNTER?
DASH
I AM, INDEED, A MEMBER OF THE ELITE TRACKING UNIT FROM THE VILLAGE HIDDEN IN THE MIST. IT IS OUR RESPONSIBILITY -- AND OUR ART -- TO HUNT DOWN AND DEAL WITH THE ROGUES AND THE OUTLAWS...
...JUDGING BY HIS SIZE AND THE TIMBRE OF HIS VOICE...
...HE COULDN'T BE MUCH OLDER THAN NARUTO OR MY OTHER STUDENTS, YET...
...HE'S ALREADY A FULL-FLEDGED SHINOBI HUNTER!

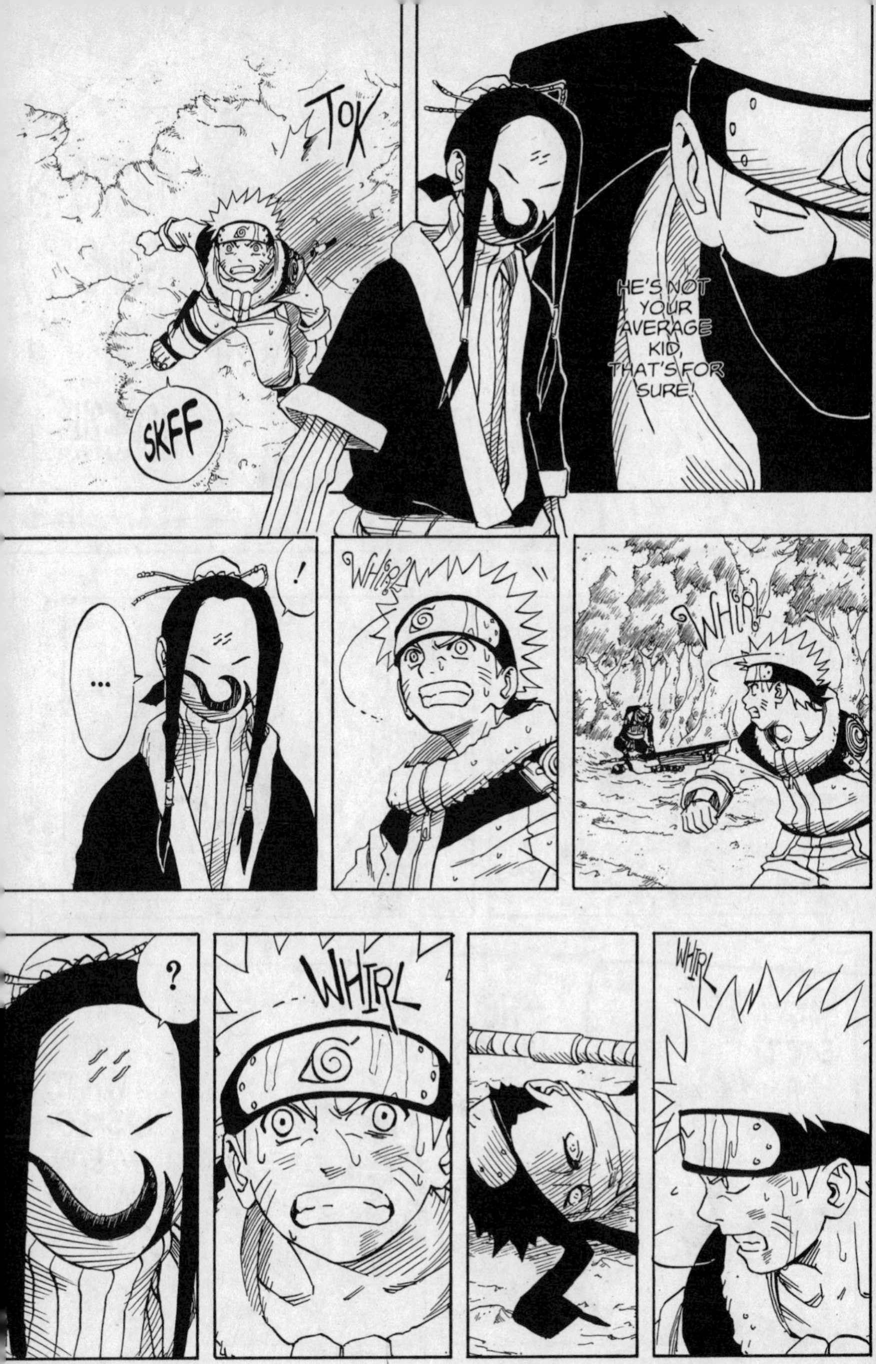
HE'S NOT YOUR AVERAGE KID, THAT'S FOR SURE!
TOK
SKFF
WHIRL
WHIRL
!
...
WHIRL
WHIRL
?

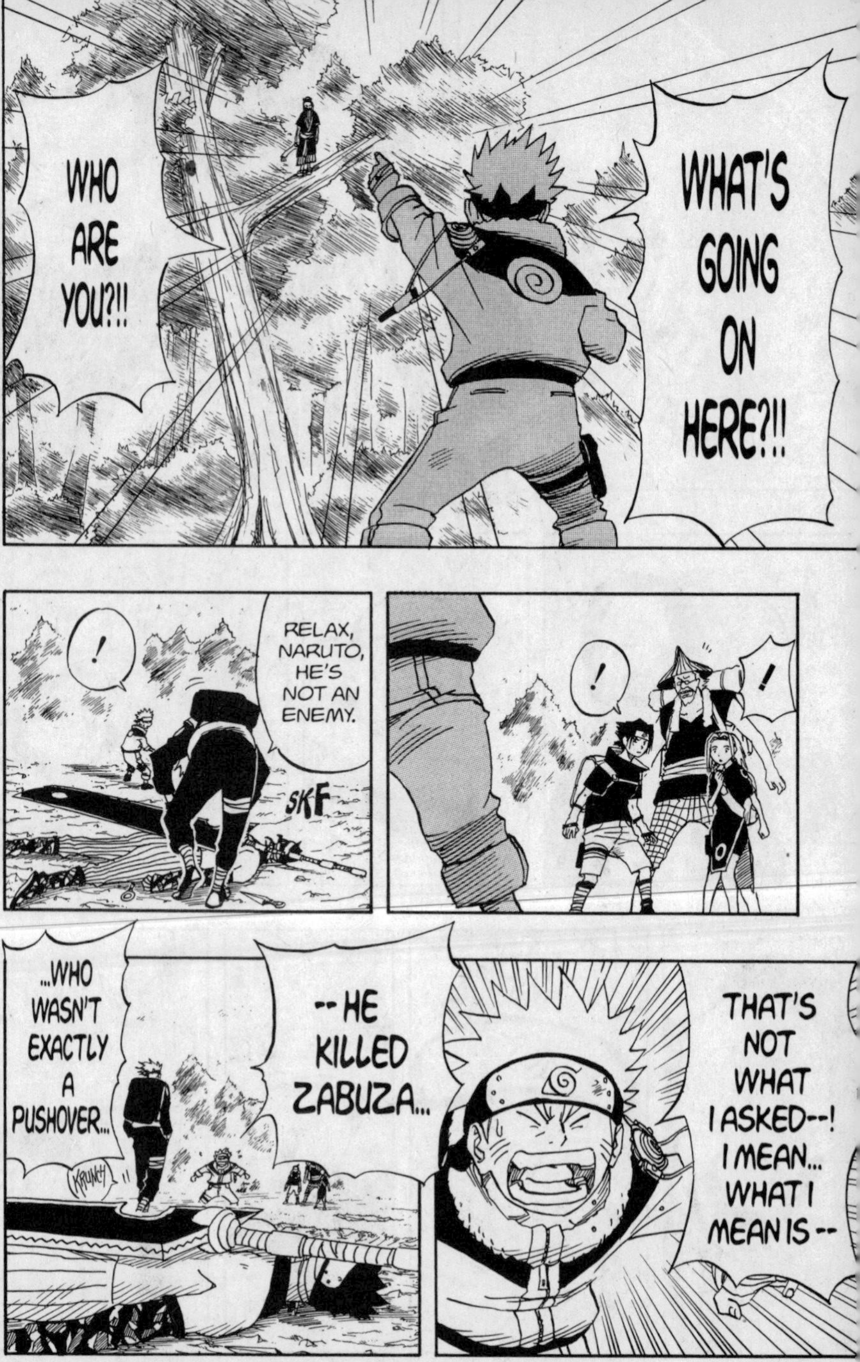
WHAT'S GOING ON HERE?!!
WHO ARE YOU?!!
!
!
RELAX, NARUTO, HE'S NOT AN ENEMY.
!
SKF
THAT'S NOT WHAT I ASKED--! I MEAN... WHAT I MEAN IS --
-- HE KILLED ZABUZA...
...WHO WASN'T EXACTLY A PUSHOVER...
KRUNCH

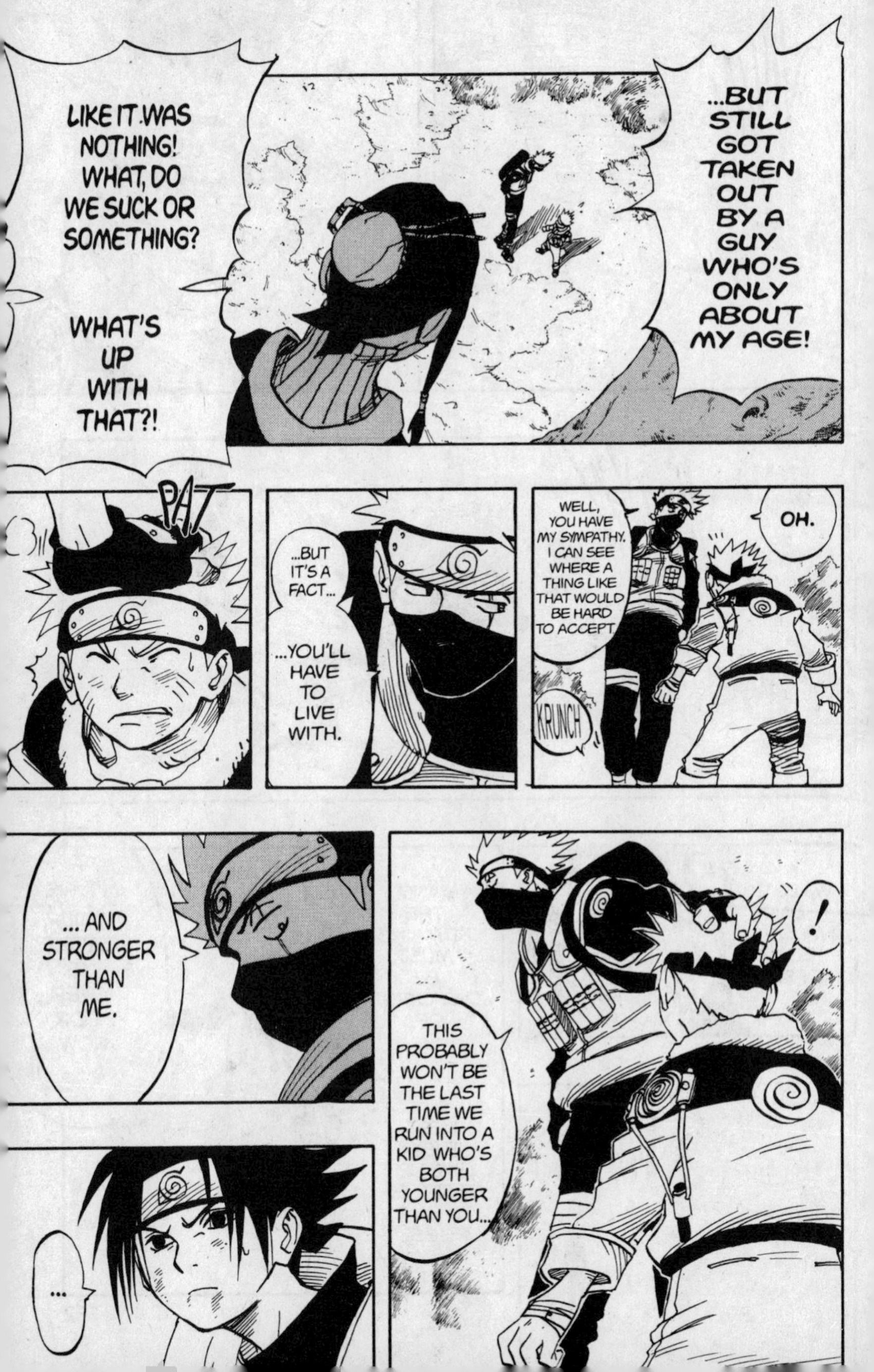
...BUT STILL GOT TAKEN OUT BY A GUY WHO'S ONLY ABOUT MY AGE!
LIKE IT WAS NOTHING! WHAT, DO WE SUCK OR SOMETHING?
WHAT'S UP WITH THAT?!
OH.
WELL, YOU HAVE MY SYMPATHY. I CAN SEE WHERE A THING LIKE THAT WOULD BE HARD TO ACCEPT.
KRUNCH
...BUT IT'S A FACT...
...YOU'LL HAVE TO LIVE WITH.
PAT
!
THIS PROBABLY WON'T BE THE LAST TIME WE RUN INTO A KID WHO'S BOTH YOUNGER THAN YOU...
... AND STRONGER THAN ME.
...

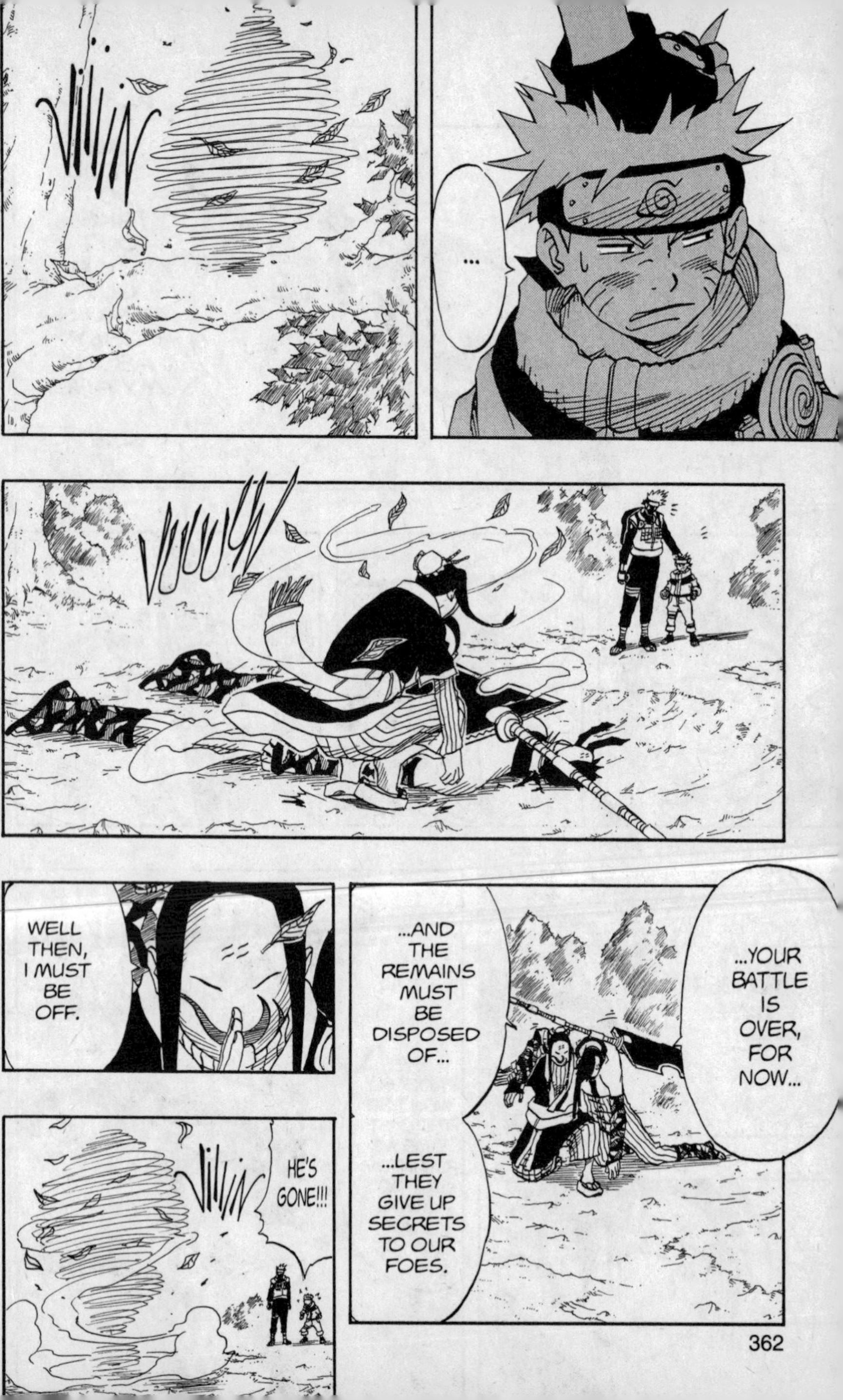
...
...YOUR BATTLE IS OVER, FOR NOW...
...AND THE REMAINS MUST BE DISPOSED OF...
...LEST THEY GIVE UP SECRETS TO OUR FOES.
WELL THEN, I MUST BE OFF.
HE'S GONE!!!

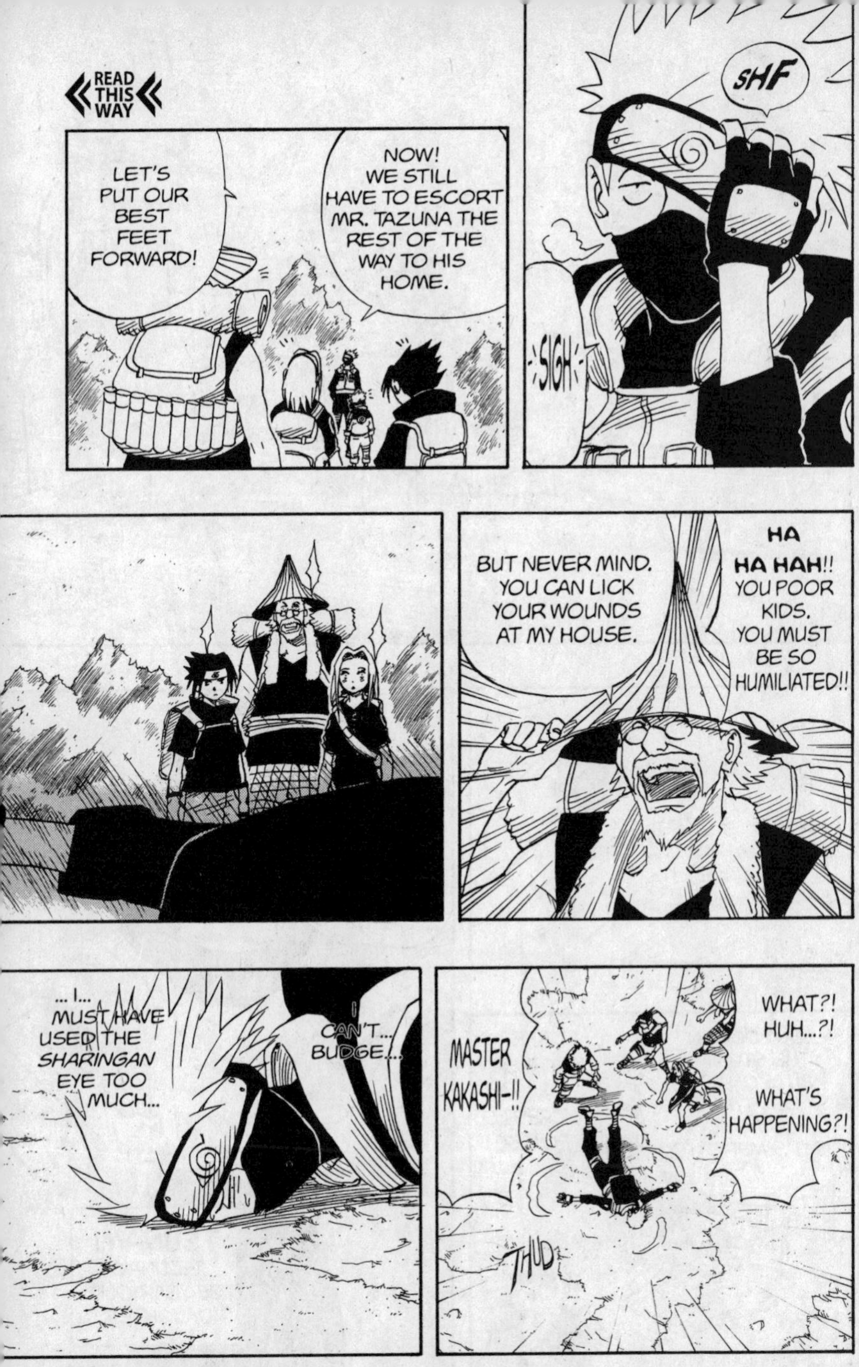
READ THIS WAY
SHF
SIGH
NOW! WE STILL HAVE TO ESCORT MR. TAZUNA THE REST OF THE WAY TO HIS HOME.
LET'S PUT OUR BEST FEET FORWARD!
HA HA HAH!! YOU POOR KIDS. YOU MUST BE SO HUMILIATED!!
BUT NEVER MIND. YOU CAN LICK YOUR WOUNDS AT MY HOUSE.
WHAT?! HUH...?!
WHAT'S HAPPENING?!
MASTER KAKASHI-!!
THUD
I CAN'T... BUDGE...
... I... MUST HAVE USED THE *SHARINGAN* EYE TOO MUCH...

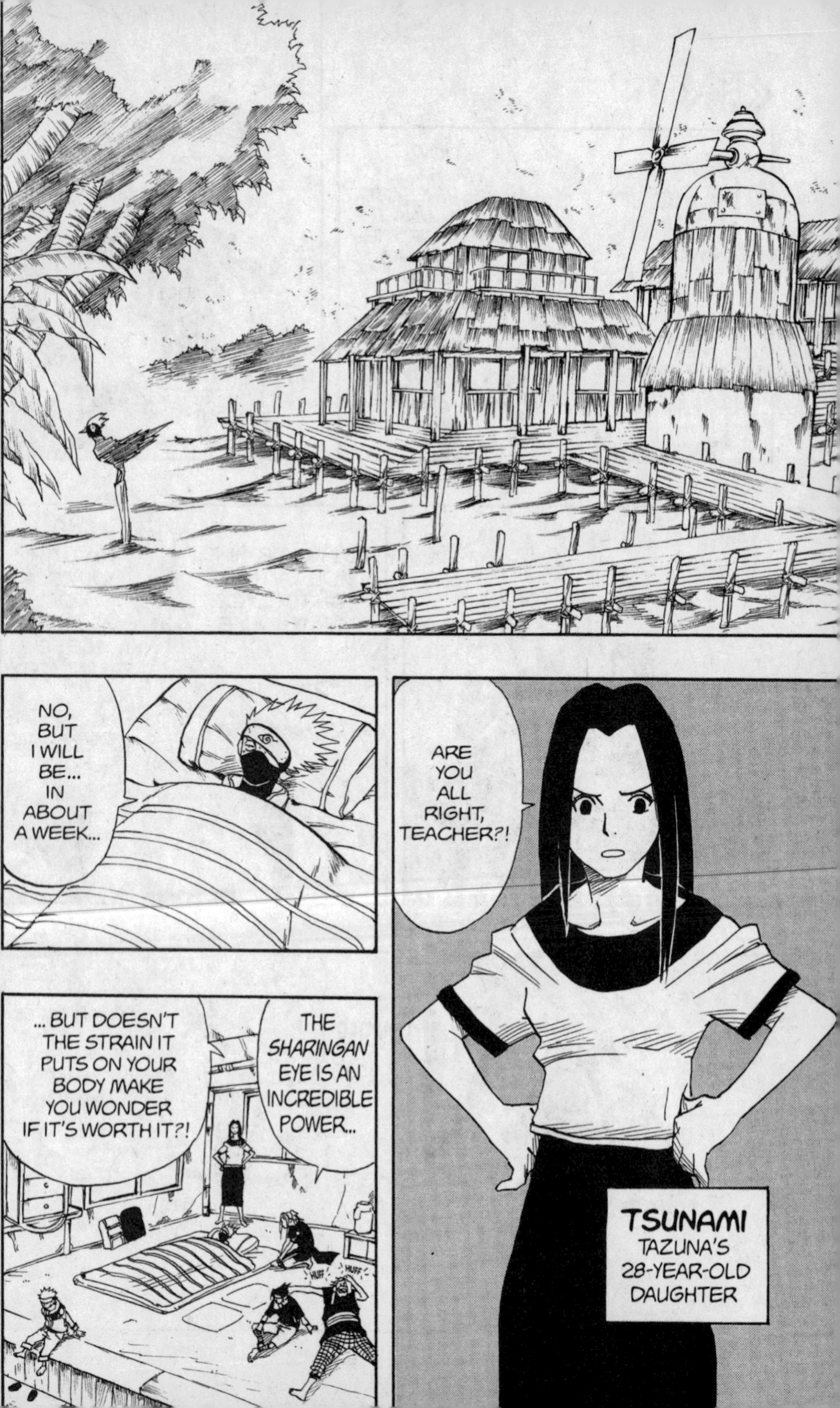
ARE YOU ALL RIGHT, TEACHER?!
TSUNAMI
TAZUNA'S 28-YEAR-OLD DAUGHTER
NO, BUT I WILL BE... IN ABOUT A WEEK...
THE *SHARINGAN* EYE IS AN INCREDIBLE POWER...
... BUT DOESN'T THE STRAIN IT PUTS ON YOUR BODY MAKE YOU WONDER IF IT'S WORTH IT?!
HUFF
HUFF

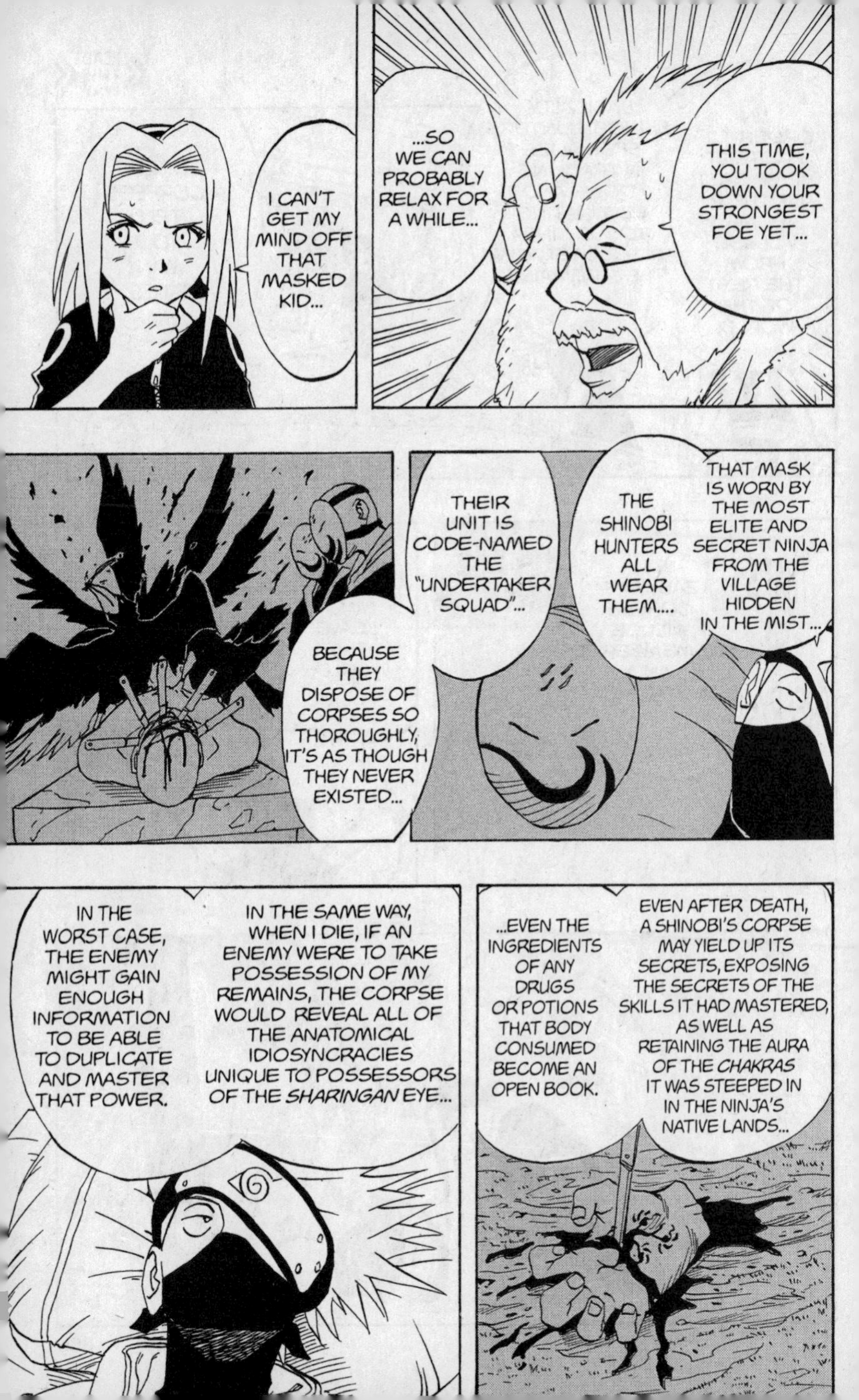
THIS TIME, YOU TOOK DOWN YOUR STRONGEST FOE YET...
...SO WE CAN PROBABLY RELAX FOR A WHILE...
I CAN'T GET MY MIND OFF THAT MASKED KID...
THAT MASK IS WORN BY THE MOST ELITE AND SECRET NINJA FROM THE VILLAGE HIDDEN IN THE MIST...
THE SHINOBI HUNTERS ALL WEAR THEM....
THEIR UNIT IS CODE-NAMED THE "UNDERTAKER SQUAD"...
BECAUSE THEY DISPOSE OF CORPSES SO THOROUGHLY, IT'S AS THOUGH THEY NEVER EXISTED...
EVEN AFTER DEATH, A SHINOBI'S CORPSE MAY YIELD UP ITS SECRETS, EXPOSING THE SECRETS OF THE SKILLS IT HAD MASTERED, AS WELL AS RETAINING THE AURA OF THE *CHAKRAS* IT WAS STEEPED IN IN THE NINJA'S NATIVE LANDS...
...EVEN THE INGREDIENTS OF ANY DRUGS OR POTIONS THAT BODY CONSUMED BECOME AN OPEN BOOK.
IN THE SAME WAY, WHEN I DIE, IF AN ENEMY WERE TO TAKE POSSESSION OF MY REMAINS, THE CORPSE WOULD REVEAL ALL OF THE ANATOMICAL IDIOSYNCRACIES UNIQUE TO POSSESSORS OF THE *SHARINGAN* EYE...
IN THE WORST CASE, THE ENEMY MIGHT GAIN ENOUGH INFORMATION TO BE ABLE TO DUPLICATE AND MASTER THAT POWER.

READ THIS WAY

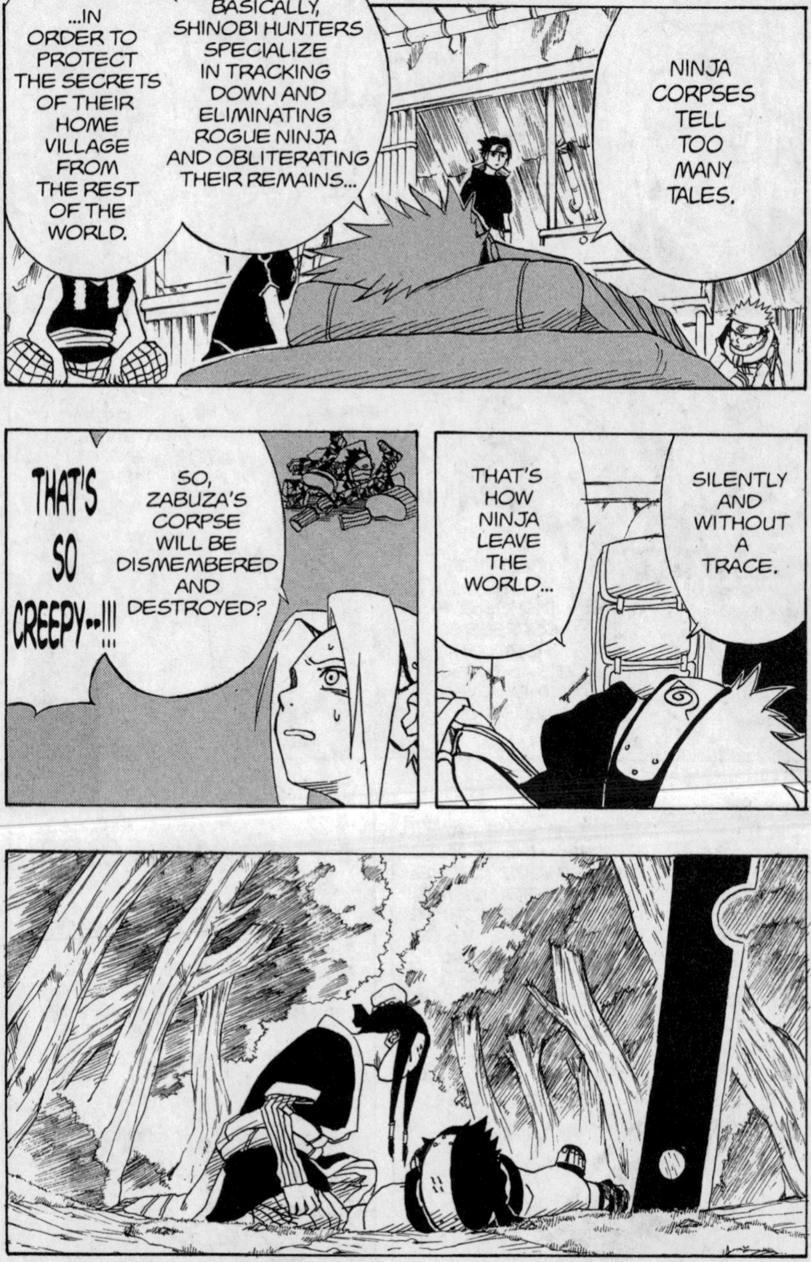

NINJA CORPSES TELL TOO MANY TALES.
BASICALLY, SHINOBI HUNTERS SPECIALIZE IN TRACKING DOWN AND ELIMINATING ROGUE NINJA AND OBLITERATING THEIR REMAINS...
...IN ORDER TO PROTECT THE SECRETS OF THEIR HOME VILLAGE FROM THE REST OF THE WORLD.
SILENTLY AND WITHOUT A TRACE.
THAT'S HOW NINJA LEAVE THE WORLD...
SO, ZABUZA'S CORPSE WILL BE DISMEMBERED AND DESTROYED?
THAT'S SO CREEPY--!!!

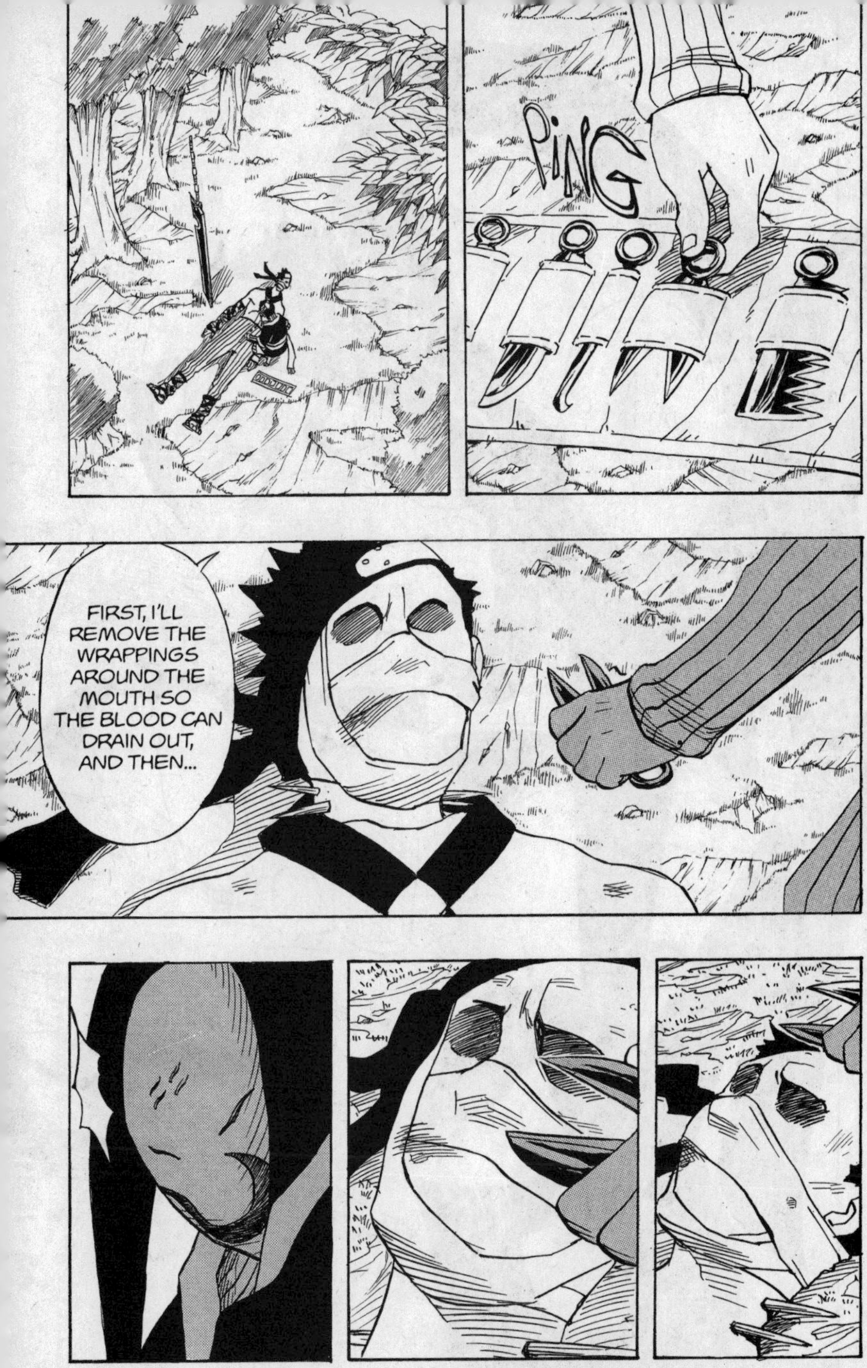
PING
FIRST, I'LL REMOVE THE WRAPPINGS AROUND THE MOUTH SO THE BLOOD CAN DRAIN OUT, AND THEN...

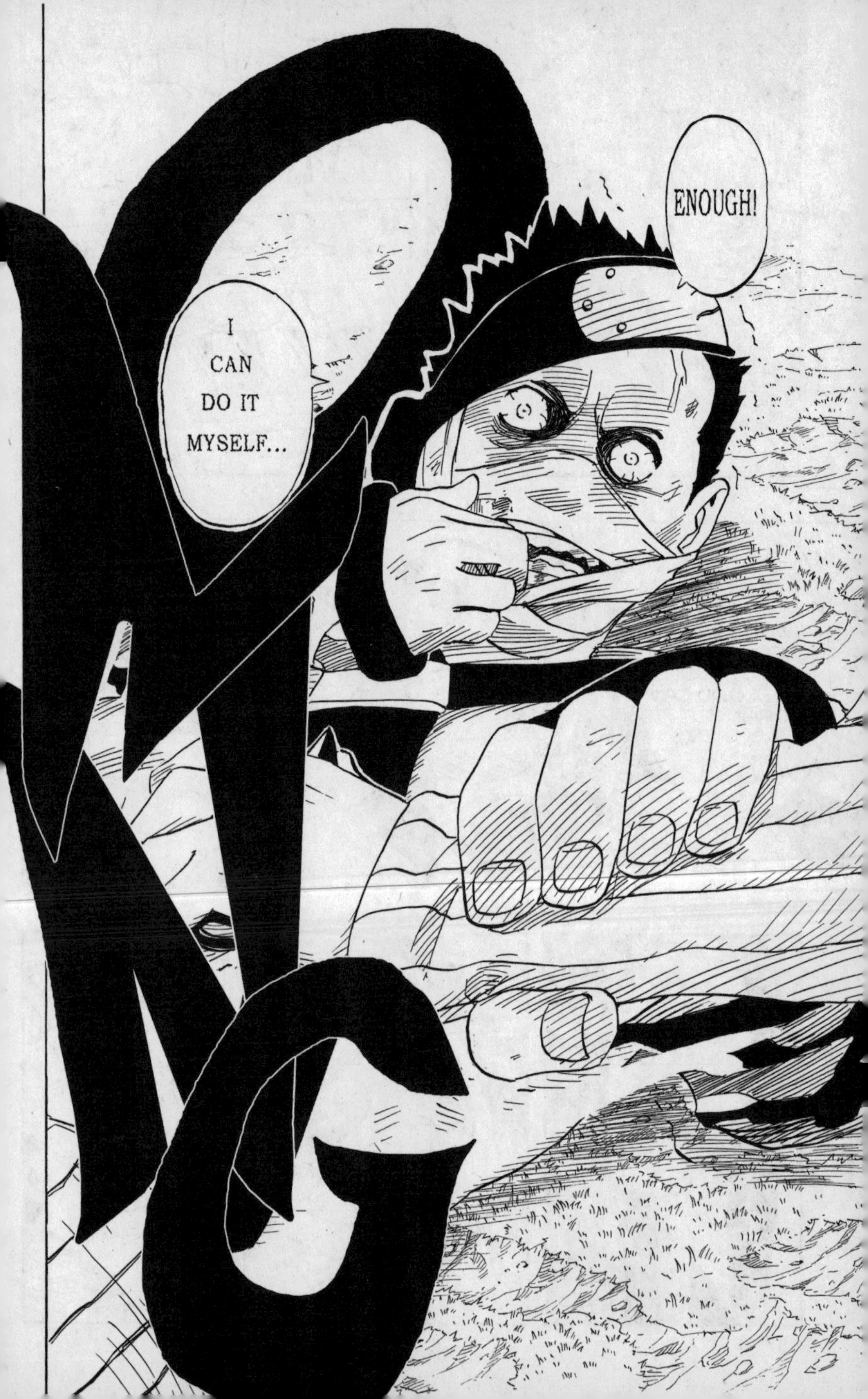
ENOUGH!
I CAN DO IT MYSELF...

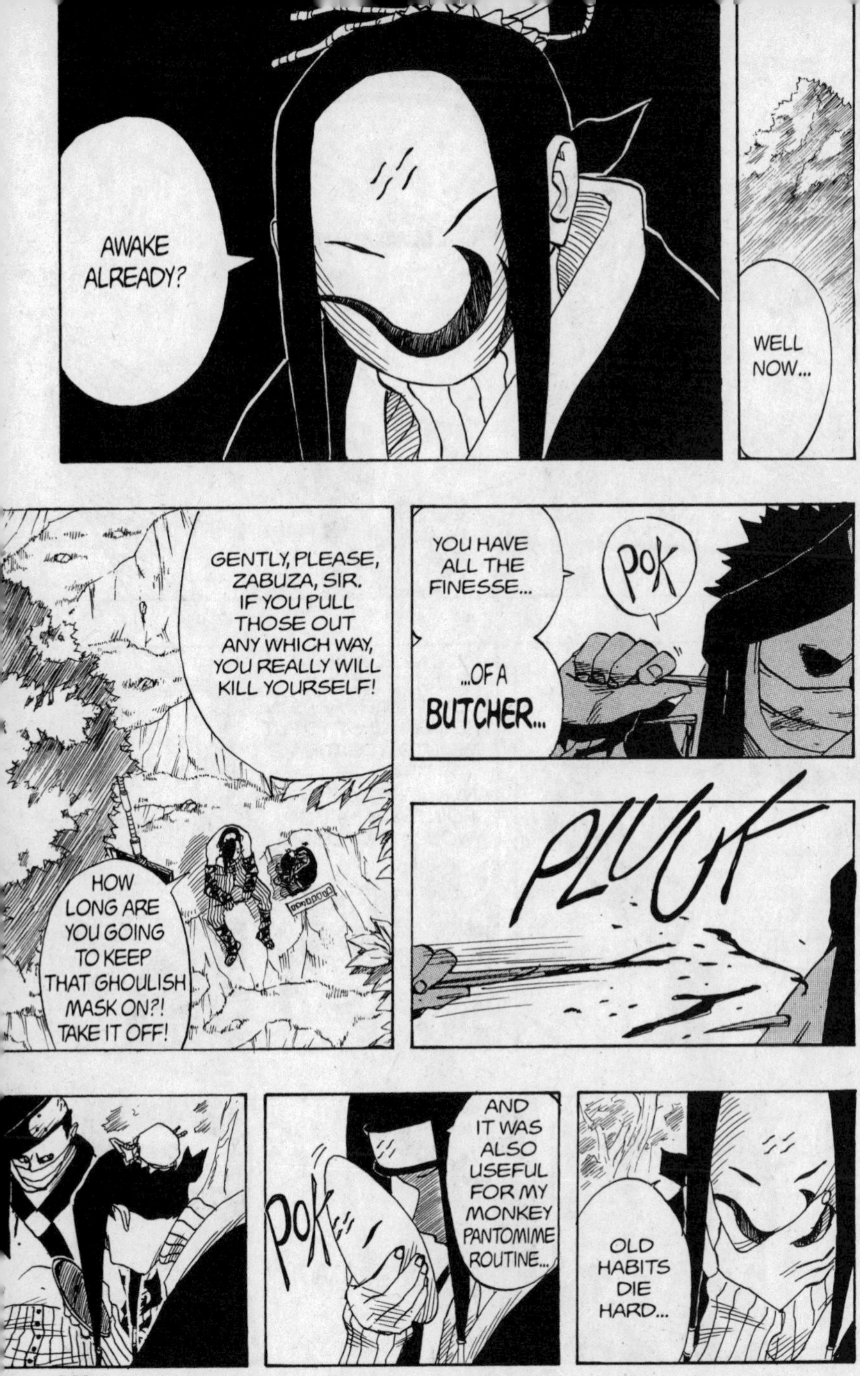
WELL NOW...
AWAKE ALREADY?
YOU HAVE ALL THE FINESSE...
POK
...OF A BUTCHER...
PLUCK
GENTLY, PLEASE, ZABUZA, SIR. IF YOU PULL THOSE OUT ANY WHICH WAY, YOU REALLY WILL KILL YOURSELF!
HOW LONG ARE YOU GOING TO KEEP THAT GHOULISH MASK ON?! TAKE IT OFF!
OLD HABITS DIE HARD...
AND IT WAS ALSO USEFUL FOR MY MONKEY PANTOMIME ROUTINE...
POK

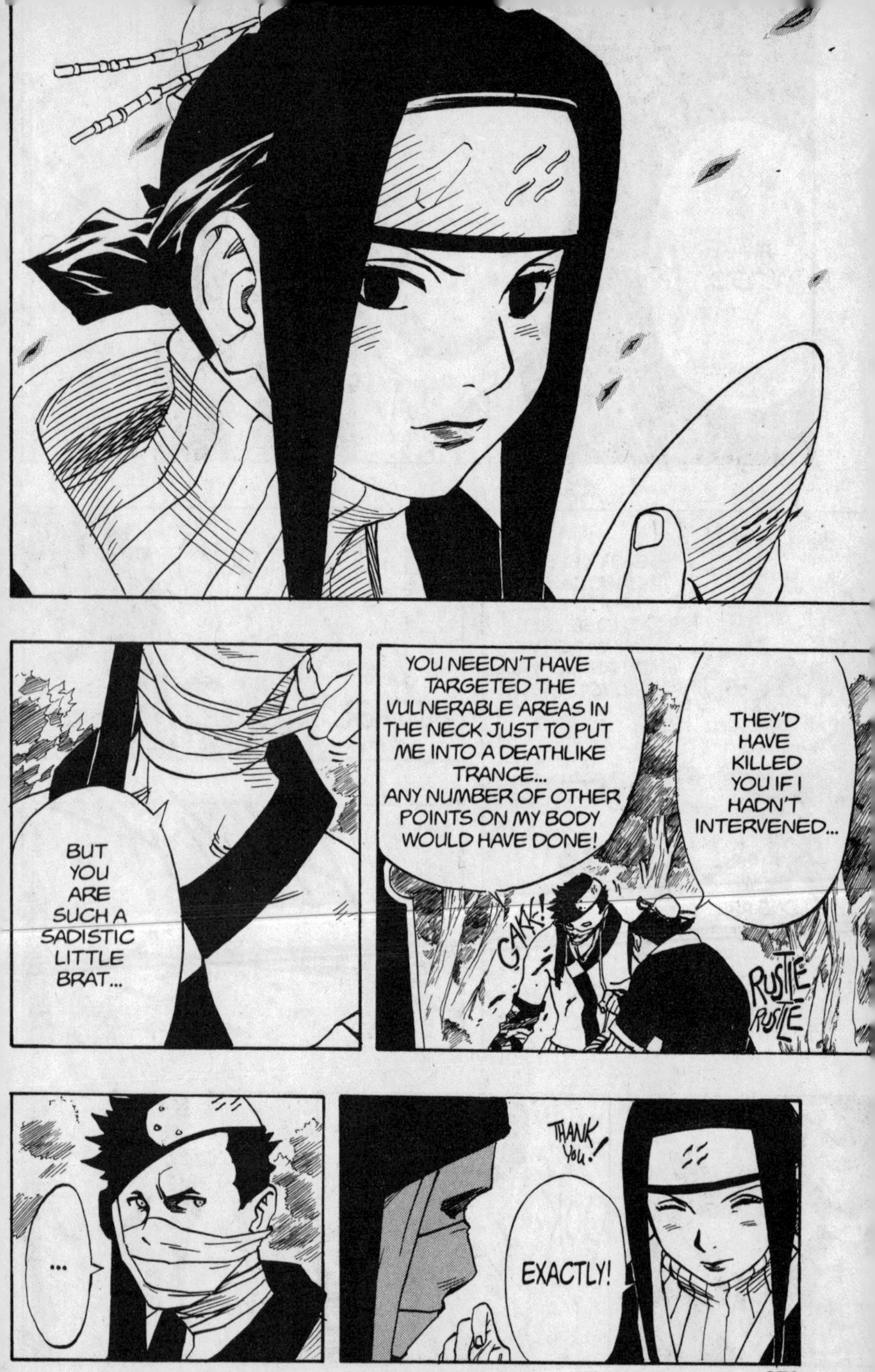
THEY'D HAVE KILLED YOU IF I HADN'T INTERVENED...
YOU NEEDN'T HAVE TARGETED THE VULNERABLE AREAS IN THE NECK JUST TO PUT ME INTO A DEATHLIKE TRANCE... ANY NUMBER OF OTHER POINTS ON MY BODY WOULD HAVE DONE!
GAKK!
RUSTLE RUSTLE
BUT YOU ARE SUCH A SADISTIC LITTLE BRAT...
THANK YOU!
EXACTLY!
...

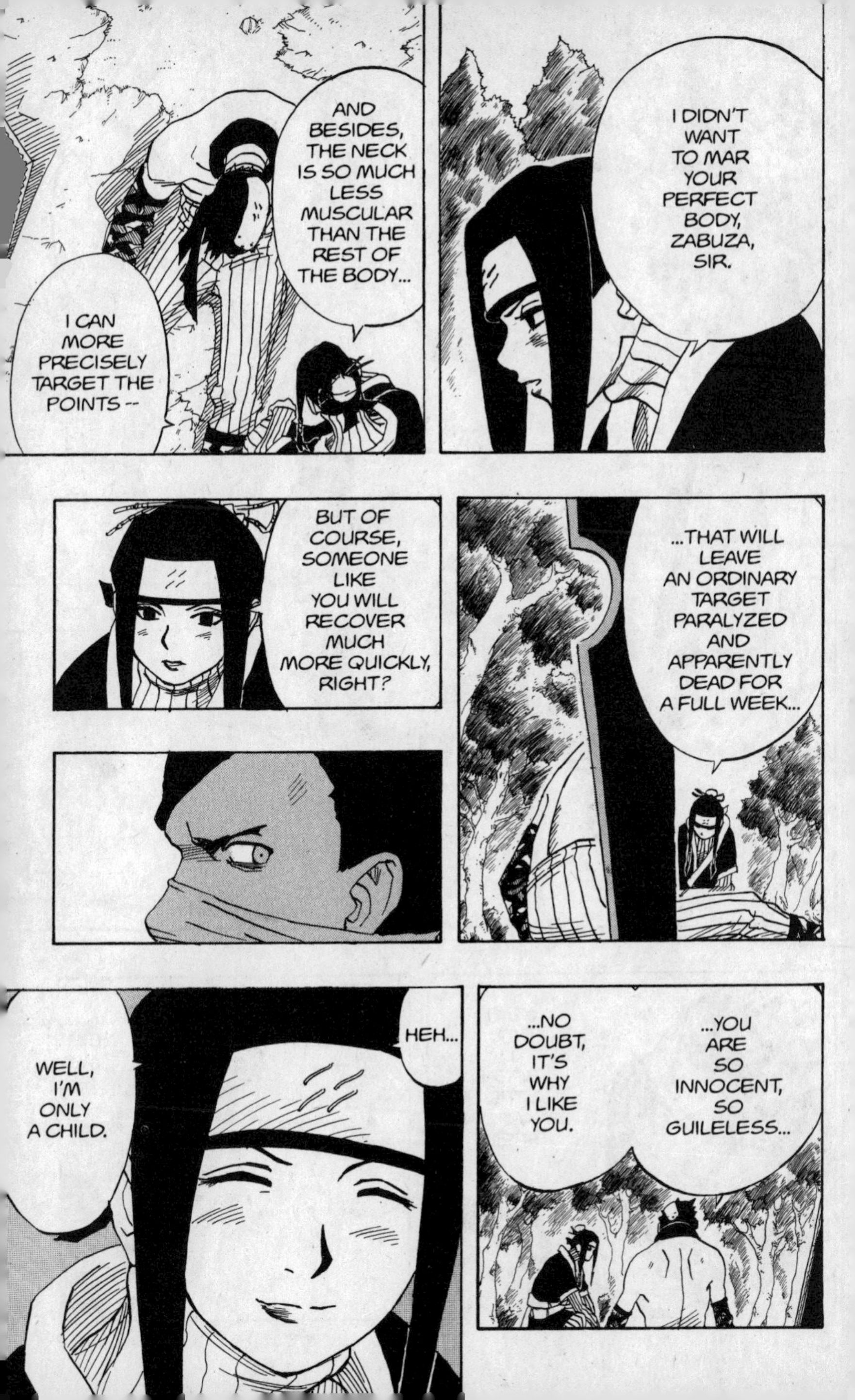
I DIDN'T WANT TO MAR YOUR PERFECT BODY, ZABUZA, SIR.
AND BESIDES, THE NECK IS SO MUCH LESS MUSCULAR THAN THE REST OF THE BODY...
I CAN MORE PRECISELY TARGET THE POINTS --
...THAT WILL LEAVE AN ORDINARY TARGET PARALYZED AND APPARENTLY DEAD FOR A FULL WEEK...
BUT OF COURSE, SOMEONE LIKE YOU WILL RECOVER MUCH MORE QUICKLY, RIGHT?
...YOU ARE SO INNOCENT, SO GUILELESS...
...NO DOUBT, IT'S WHY I LIKE YOU.
HEH...
WELL, I'M ONLY A CHILD.

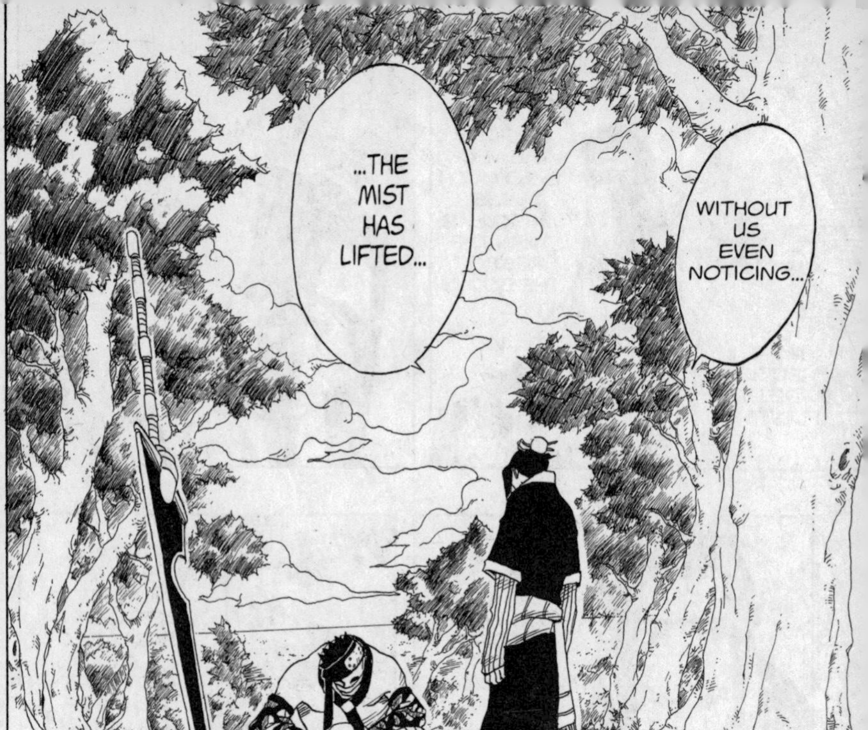
WITHOUT US EVEN NOTICING...
...THE MIST HAS LIFTED...

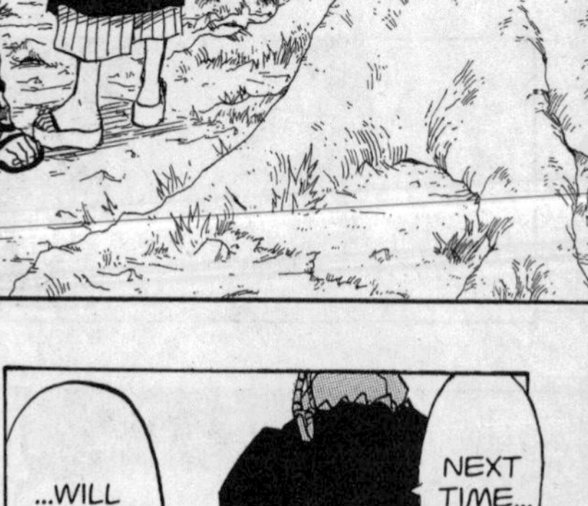
NEXT TIME...
...WILL YOU BE ALL RIGHT?

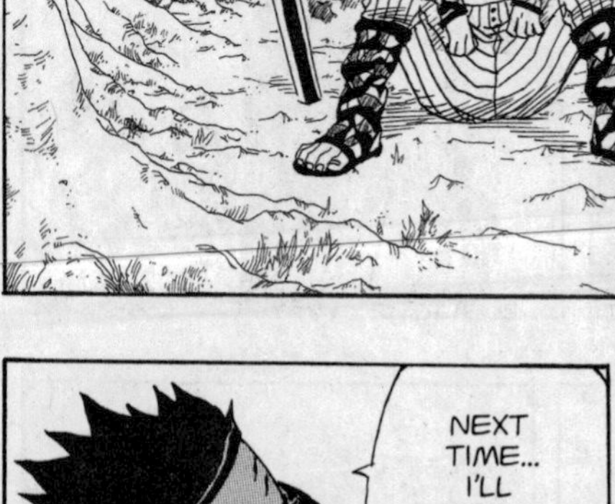
NEXT TIME... I'LL BREAK THE *SHARINGAN* SPELL!

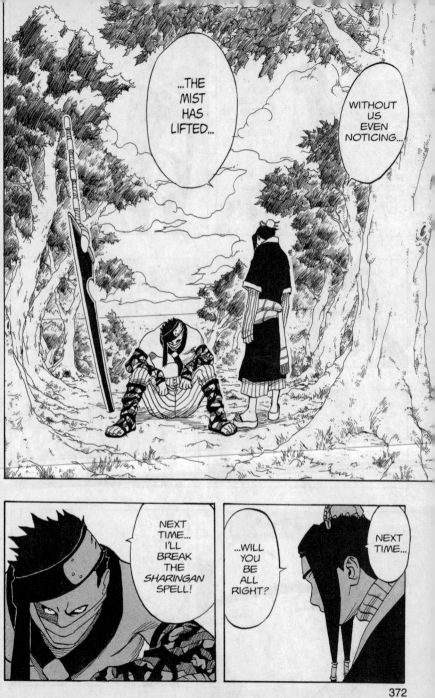

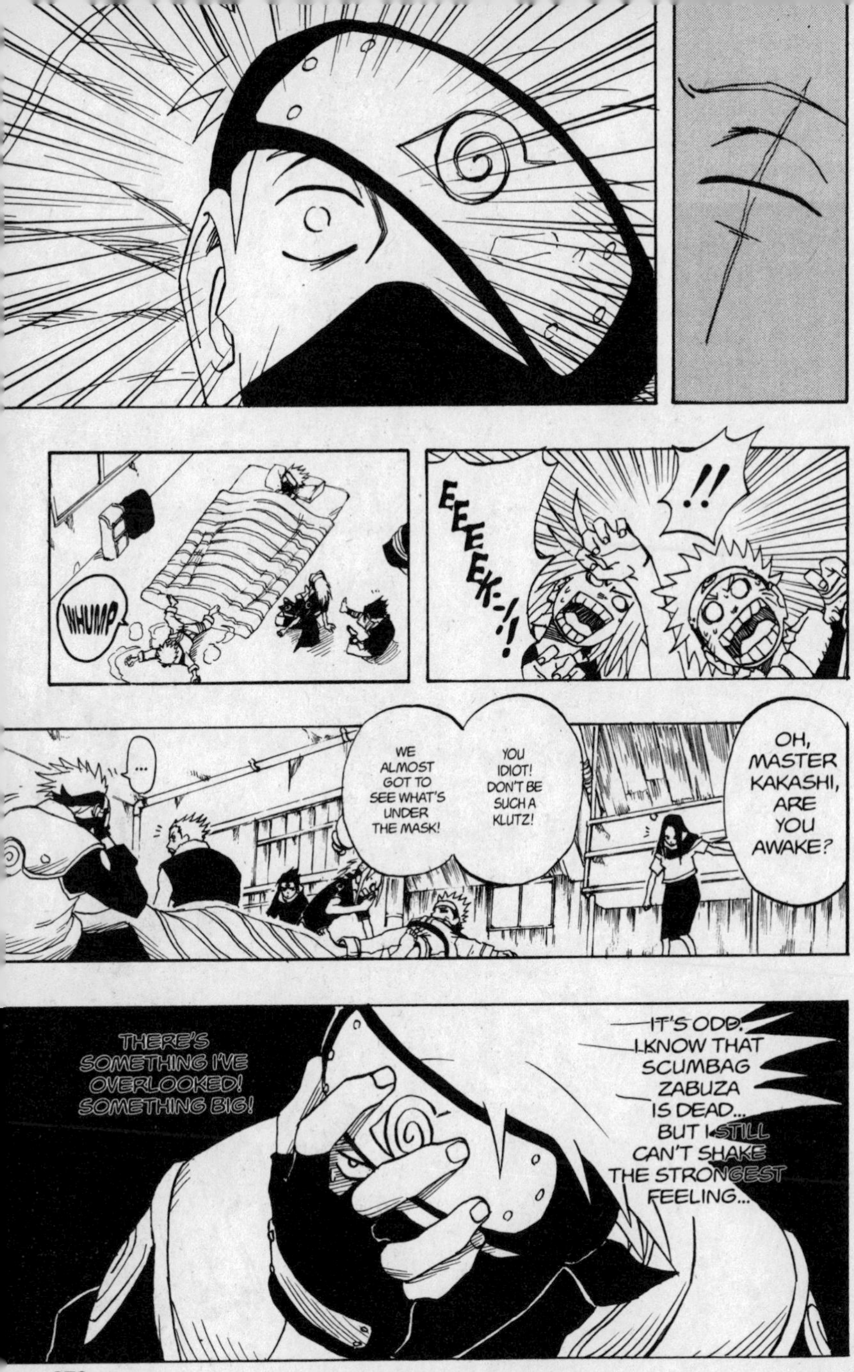
!!
EEEEK-!!
WHUMP
OH, MASTER KAKASHI, ARE YOU AWAKE?
YOU IDIOT! DON'T BE SUCH A KLUTZ!
WE ALMOST GOT TO SEE WHAT'S UNDER THE MASK!
...
IT'S ODD. I KNOW THAT SCUMBAG ZABUZA IS DEAD... BUT I STILL CAN'T SHAKE THE STRONGEST FEELING...
THERE'S SOMETHING I'VE OVERLOOKED! SOMETHING BIG!

Number 17: Preparations for Battle

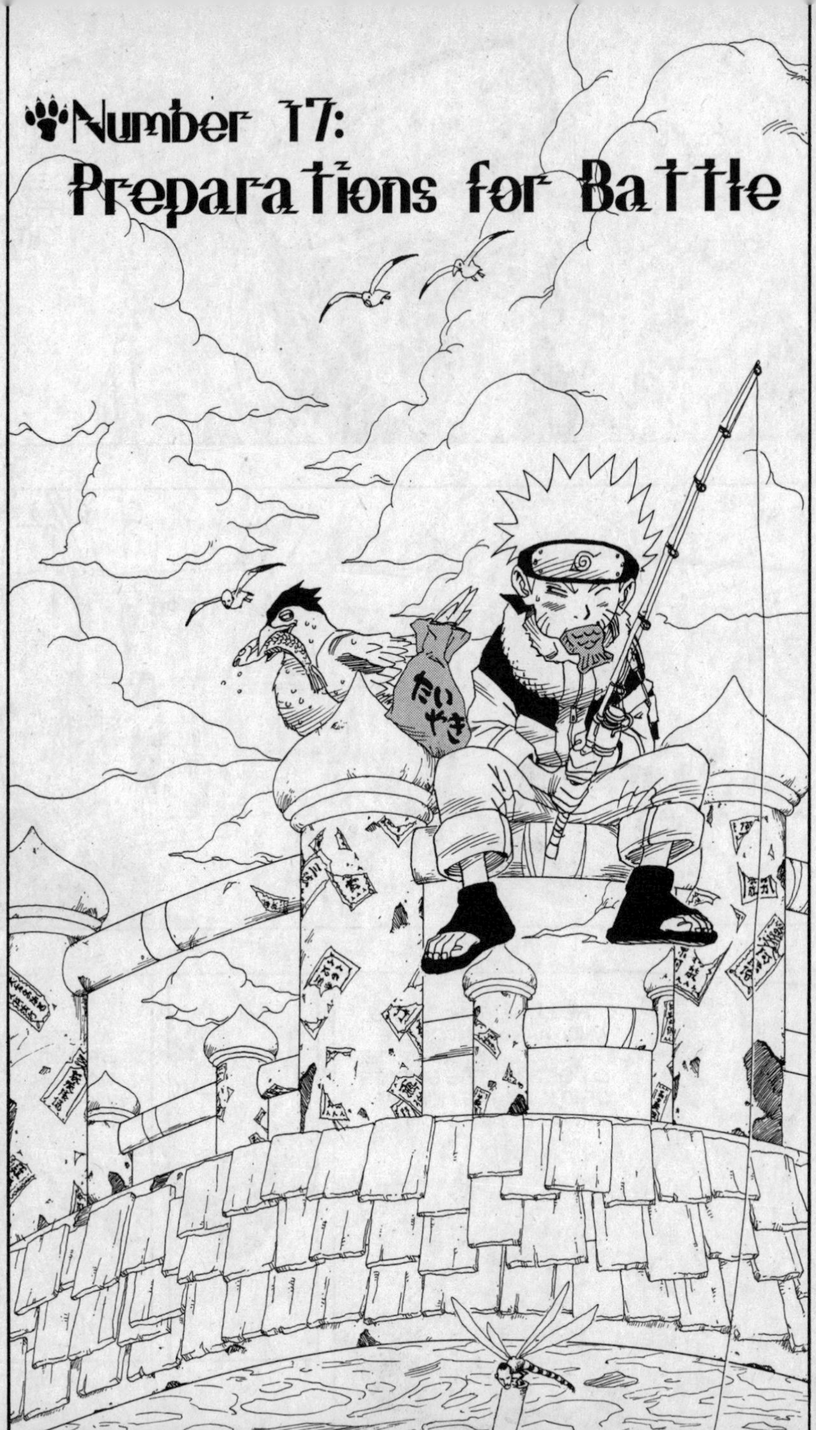
たいやき

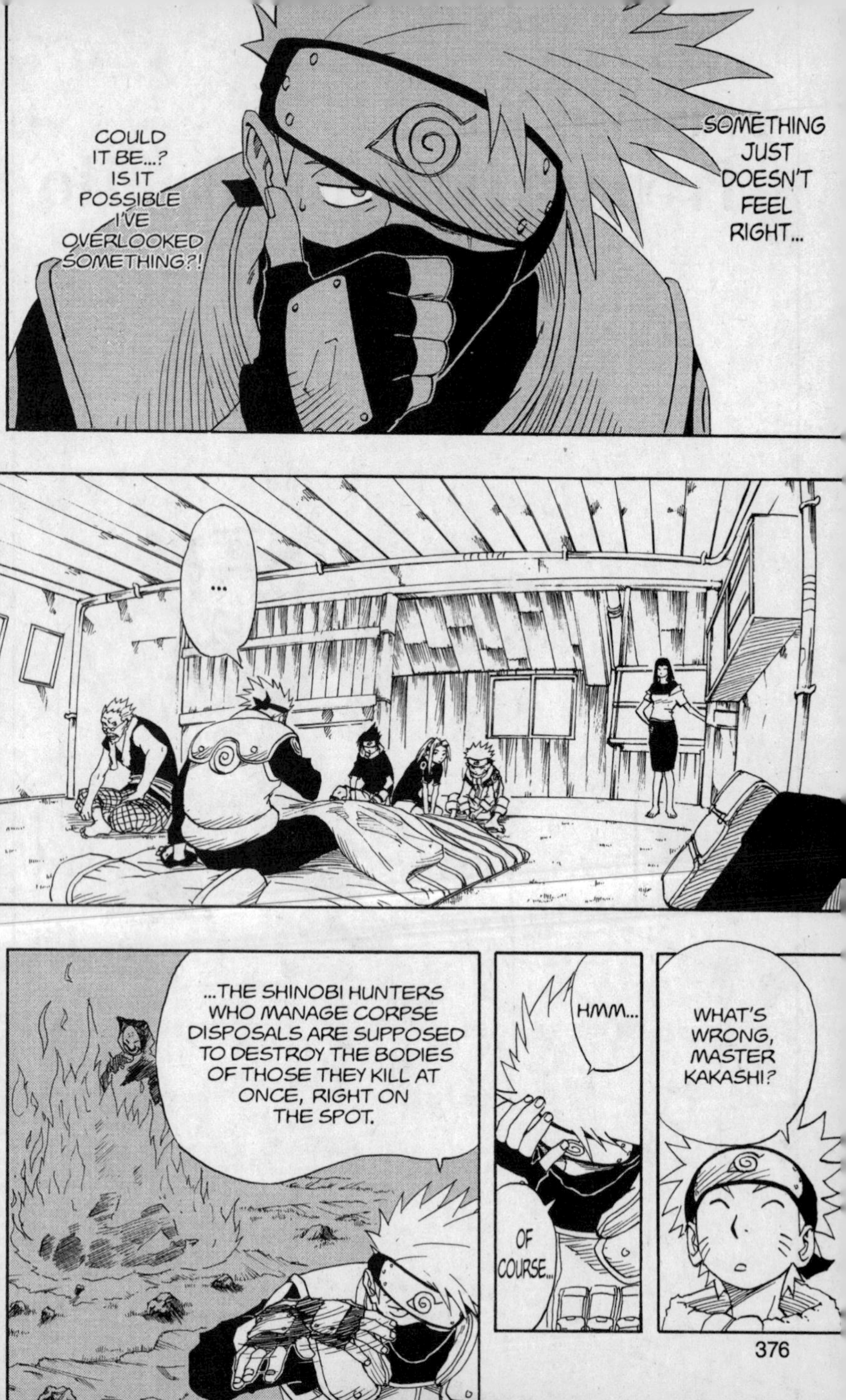
SOMETHING JUST DOESN'T FEEL RIGHT...
COULD IT BE...? IS IT POSSIBLE I'VE OVERLOOKED SOMETHING?!
...
WHAT'S WRONG, MASTER KAKASHI?
HMM...
OF COURSE...
...THE SHINOBI HUNTERS WHO MANAGE CORPSE DISPOSALS ARE SUPPOSED TO DESTROY THE BODIES OF THOSE THEY KILL AT ONCE, RIGHT ON THE SPOT.

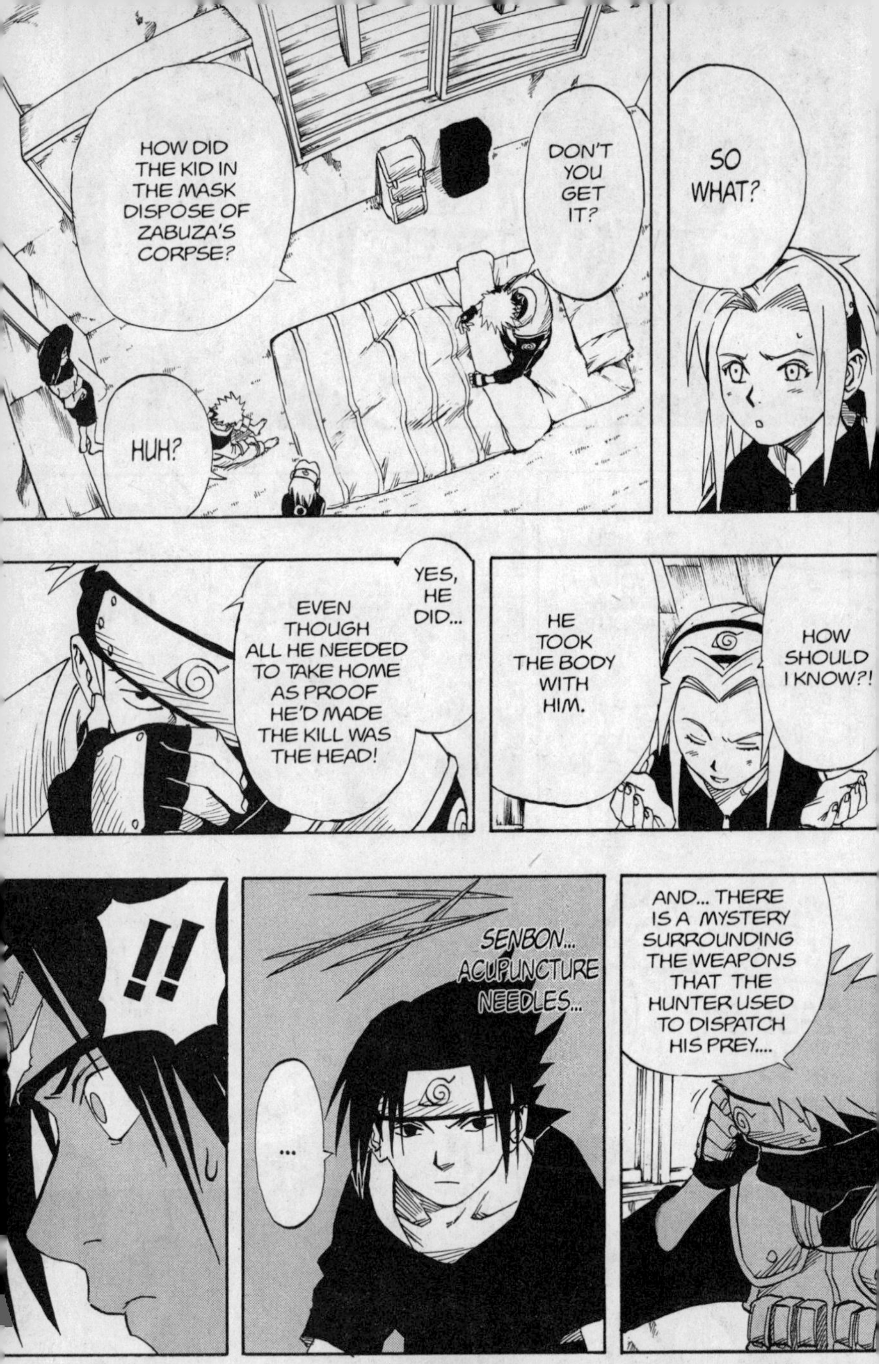
SO WHAT?
DON'T YOU GET IT?
HOW DID THE KID IN THE MASK DISPOSE OF ZABUZA'S CORPSE?
HUH?
HOW SHOULD I KNOW?!
HE TOOK THE BODY WITH HIM.
YES, HE DID...
EVEN THOUGH ALL HE NEEDED TO TAKE HOME AS PROOF HE'D MADE THE KILL WAS THE HEAD!
AND... THERE IS A MYSTERY SURROUNDING THE WEAPONS THAT THE HUNTER USED TO DISPATCH HIS PREY....
SENBON... ACUPUNCTURE NEEDLES...
...
!!

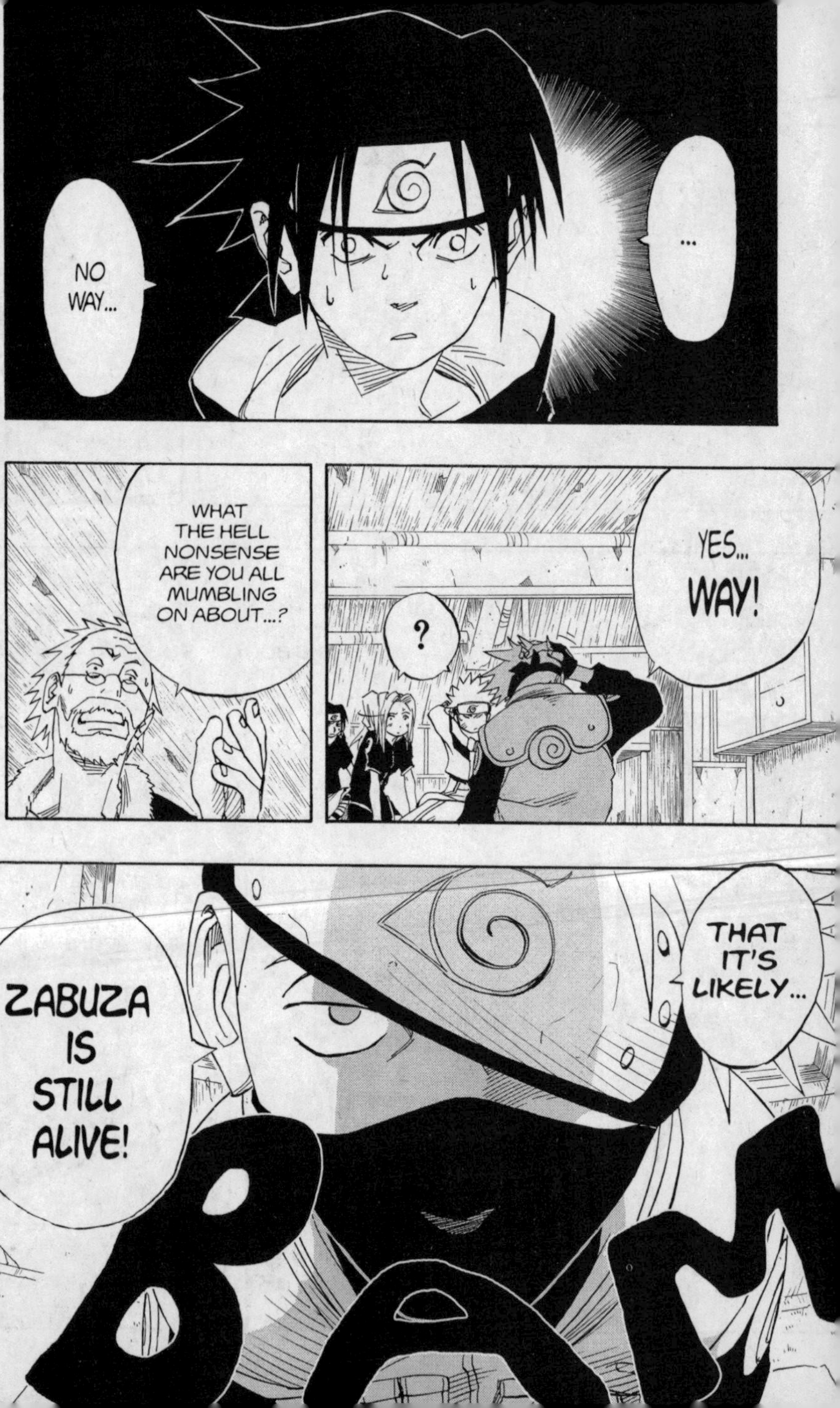
...
NO WAY...
YES... WAY!
?
WHAT THE HELL NONSENSE ARE YOU ALL MUMBLING ON ABOUT...?
THAT IT'S LIKELY...
ZABUZA IS STILL ALIVE!

READ THIS WAY

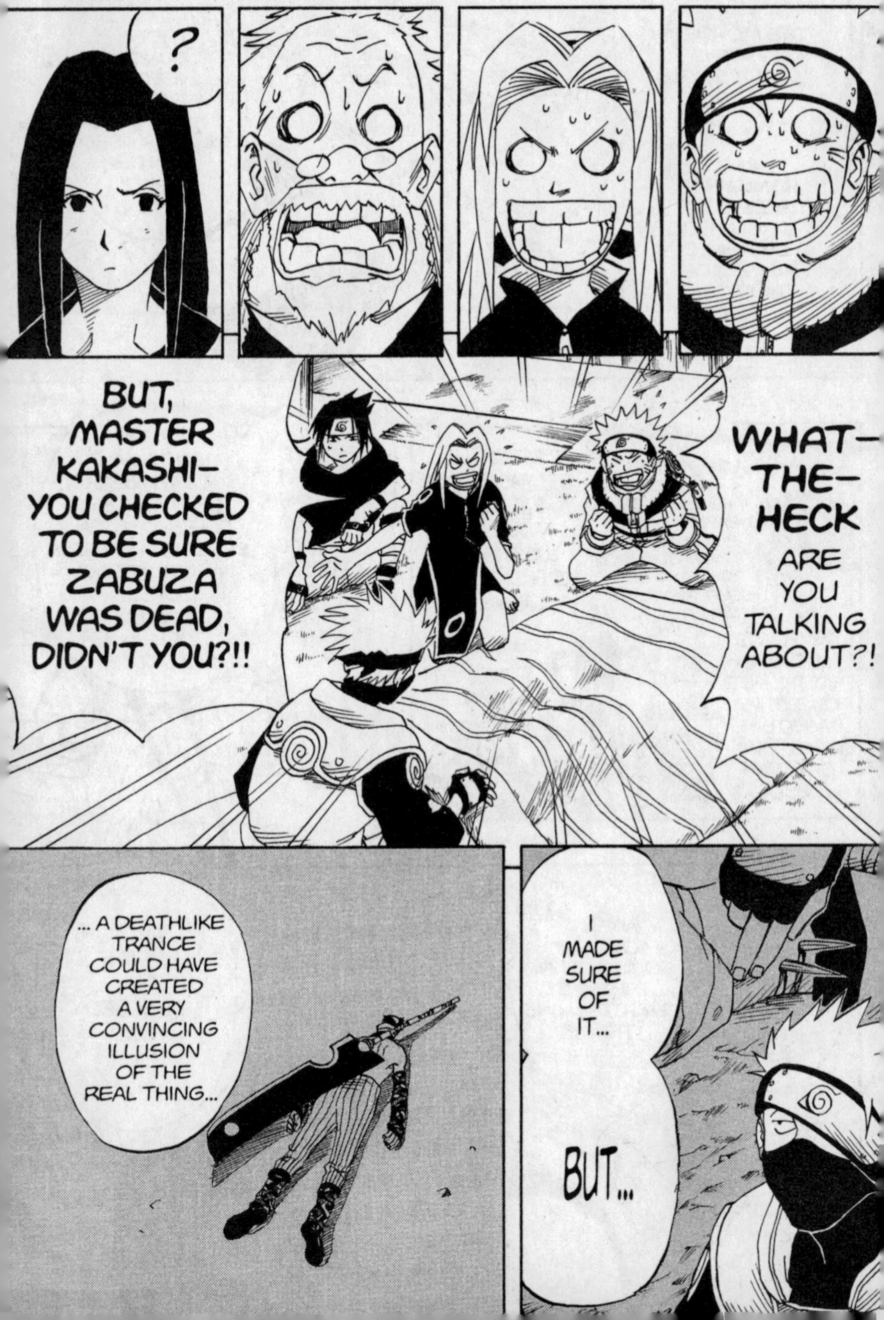
?
WHAT-THE-HECK ARE YOU TALKING ABOUT?!
BUT, MASTER KAKASHI- YOU CHECKED TO BE SURE ZABUZA WAS DEAD, DIDN'T YOU?!!
I MADE SURE OF IT...
BUT...
... A DEATHLIKE TRANCE COULD HAVE CREATED A VERY CONVINCING ILLUSION OF THE REAL THING...

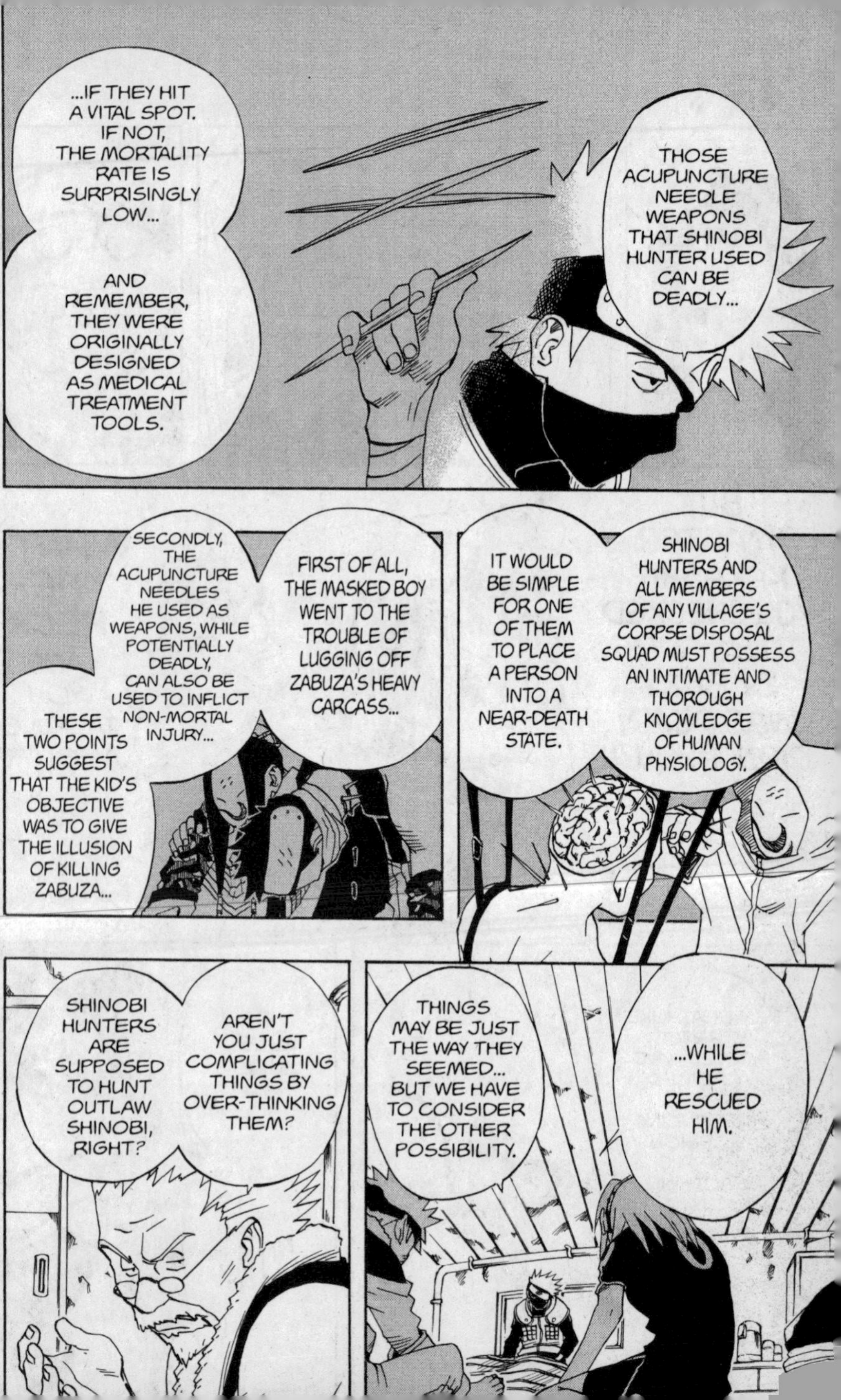
THOSE ACUPUNCTURE NEEDLE WEAPONS THAT SHINOBI HUNTER USED CAN BE DEADLY...
...IF THEY HIT A VITAL SPOT. IF NOT, THE MORTALITY RATE IS SURPRISINGLY LOW...
AND REMEMBER, THEY WERE ORIGINALLY DESIGNED AS MEDICAL TREATMENT TOOLS.
SHINOBI HUNTERS AND ALL MEMBERS OF ANY VILLAGE'S CORPSE DISPOSAL SQUAD MUST POSSESS AN INTIMATE AND THOROUGH KNOWLEDGE OF HUMAN PHYSIOLOGY.
IT WOULD BE SIMPLE FOR ONE OF THEM TO PLACE A PERSON INTO A NEAR-DEATH STATE.
FIRST OF ALL, THE MASKED BOY WENT TO THE TROUBLE OF LUGGING OFF ZABUZA'S HEAVY CARCASS...
SECONDLY, THE ACUPUNCTURE NEEDLES HE USED AS WEAPONS, WHILE POTENTIALLY DEADLY, CAN ALSO BE USED TO INFLICT NON-MORTAL INJURY...
THESE TWO POINTS SUGGEST THAT THE KID'S OBJECTIVE WAS TO GIVE THE ILLUSION OF KILLING ZABUZA...
...WHILE HE RESCUED HIM.
THINGS MAY BE JUST THE WAY THEY SEEMED... BUT WE HAVE TO CONSIDER THE OTHER POSSIBILITY.
AREN'T YOU JUST COMPLICATING THINGS BY OVER-THINKING THEM?
SHINOBI HUNTERS ARE SUPPOSED TO HUNT OUTLAW SHINOBI, RIGHT?

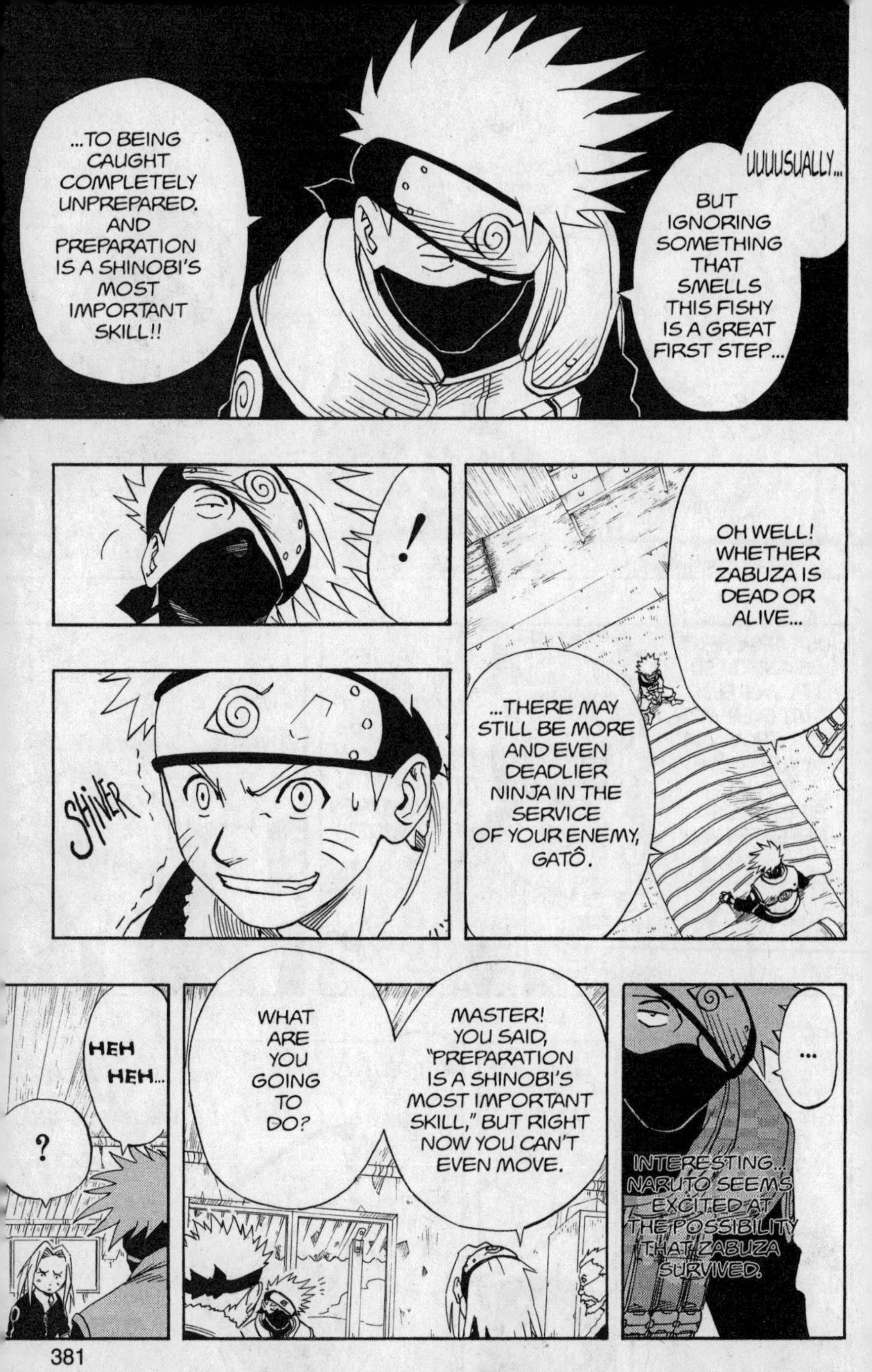
UUUUSUALLY... BUT IGNORING SOMETHING THAT SMELLS THIS FISHY IS A GREAT FIRST STEP...
...TO BEING CAUGHT COMPLETELY UNPREPARED. AND PREPARATION IS A SHINOBI'S MOST IMPORTANT SKILL!!
OH WELL! WHETHER ZABUZA IS DEAD OR ALIVE...
...THERE MAY STILL BE MORE AND EVEN DEADLIER NINJA IN THE SERVICE OF YOUR ENEMY, GATÔ.
!
SHIVER
...
INTERESTING... NARUTO SEEMS EXCITED AT THE POSSIBILITY THAT ZABUZA SURVIVED.
MASTER! YOU SAID, "PREPARATION IS A SHINOBI'S MOST IMPORTANT SKILL," BUT RIGHT NOW YOU CAN'T EVEN MOVE.
WHAT ARE YOU GOING TO DO?
HEH HEH...
?

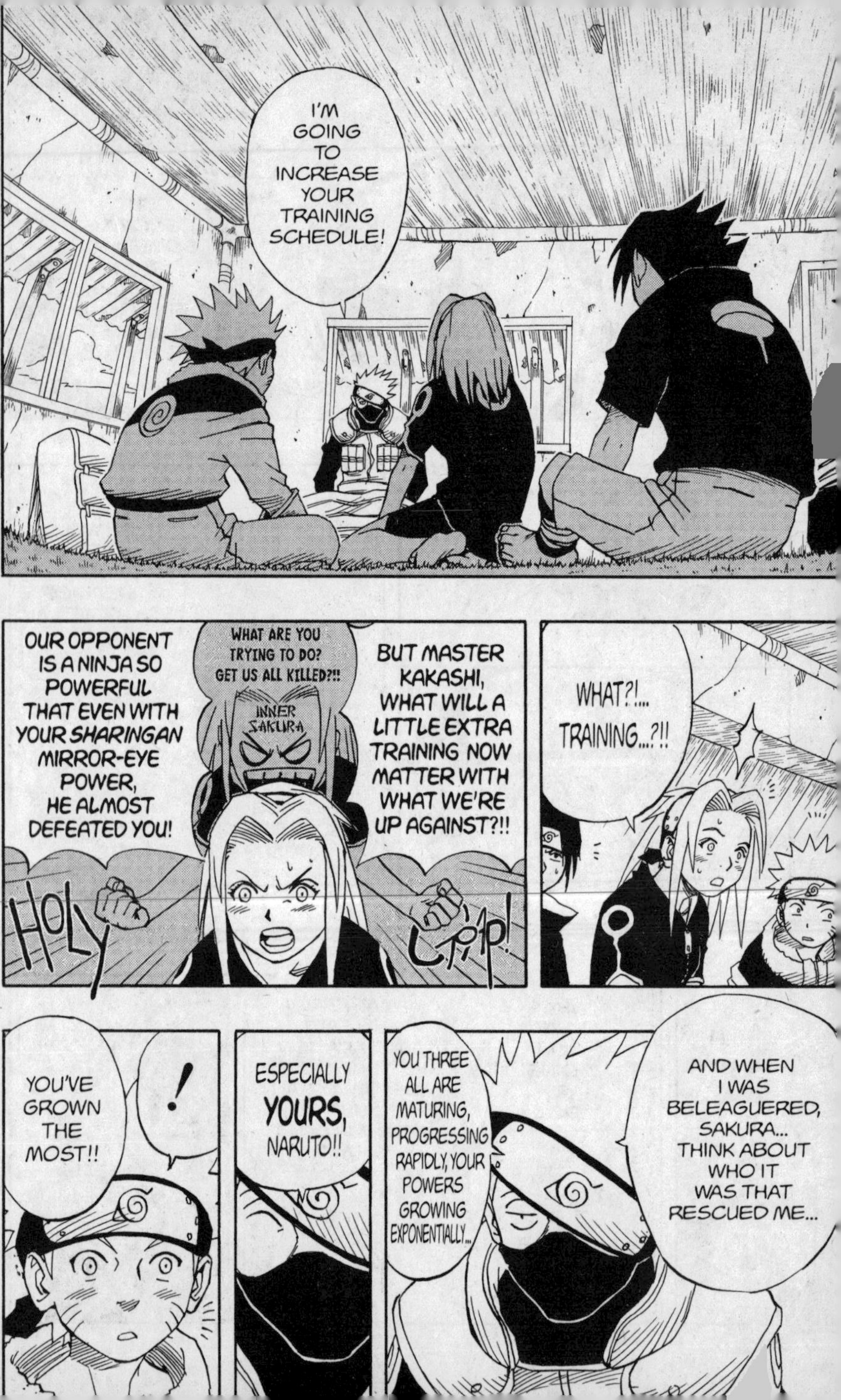
I'M GOING TO INCREASE YOUR TRAINING SCHEDULE!
WHAT?!... TRAINING...?!!
BUT MASTER KAKASHI, WHAT WILL A LITTLE EXTRA TRAINING NOW MATTER WITH WHAT WE'RE UP AGAINST?!!
WHAT ARE YOU TRYING TO DO? GET US ALL KILLED?!!
INNER SAKURA
OUR OPPONENT IS A NINJA SO POWERFUL THAT EVEN WITH YOUR SHARINGAN MIRROR-EYE POWER, HE ALMOST DEFEATED YOU!
HOLY
AND WHEN I WAS BELEAGUERED, SAKURA... THINK ABOUT WHO IT WAS THAT RESCUED ME...
YOU THREE ALL ARE MATURING, PROGRESSING RAPIDLY, YOUR POWERS GROWING EXPONENTIALLY...
ESPECIALLY YOURS, NARUTO!!
!
YOU'VE GROWN THE MOST!!

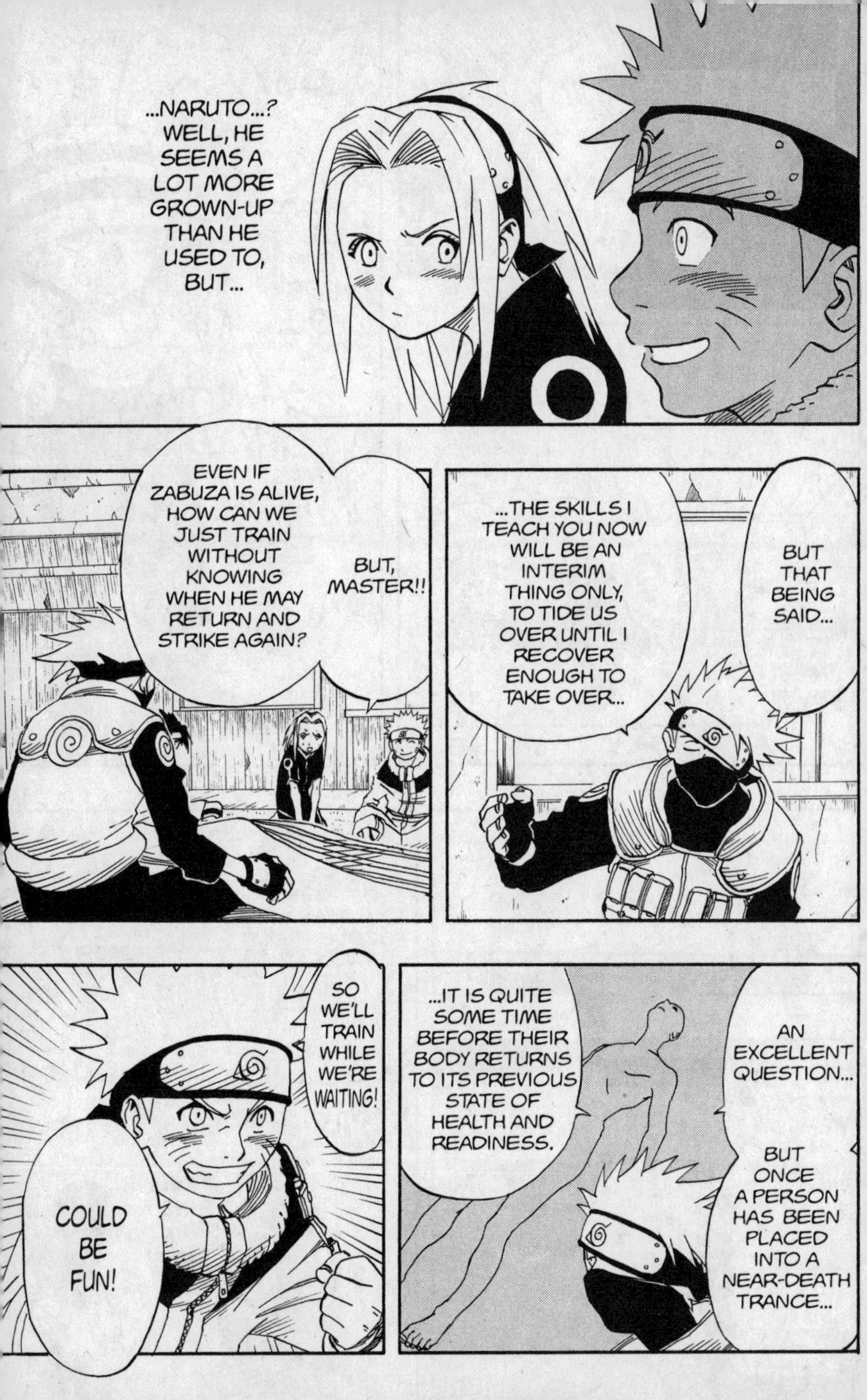
...NARUTO...? WELL, HE SEEMS A LOT MORE GROWN-UP THAN HE USED TO, BUT...
BUT THAT BEING SAID...
...THE SKILLS I TEACH YOU NOW WILL BE AN INTERIM THING ONLY, TO TIDE US OVER UNTIL I RECOVER ENOUGH TO TAKE OVER...
BUT, MASTER!!
EVEN IF ZABUZA IS ALIVE, HOW CAN WE JUST TRAIN WITHOUT KNOWING WHEN HE MAY RETURN AND STRIKE AGAIN?
AN EXCELLENT QUESTION...
BUT ONCE A PERSON HAS BEEN PLACED INTO A NEAR-DEATH TRANCE...
...IT IS QUITE SOME TIME BEFORE THEIR BODY RETURNS TO ITS PREVIOUS STATE OF HEALTH AND READINESS.
SO WE'LL TRAIN WHILE WE'RE WAITING!
COULD BE FUN!

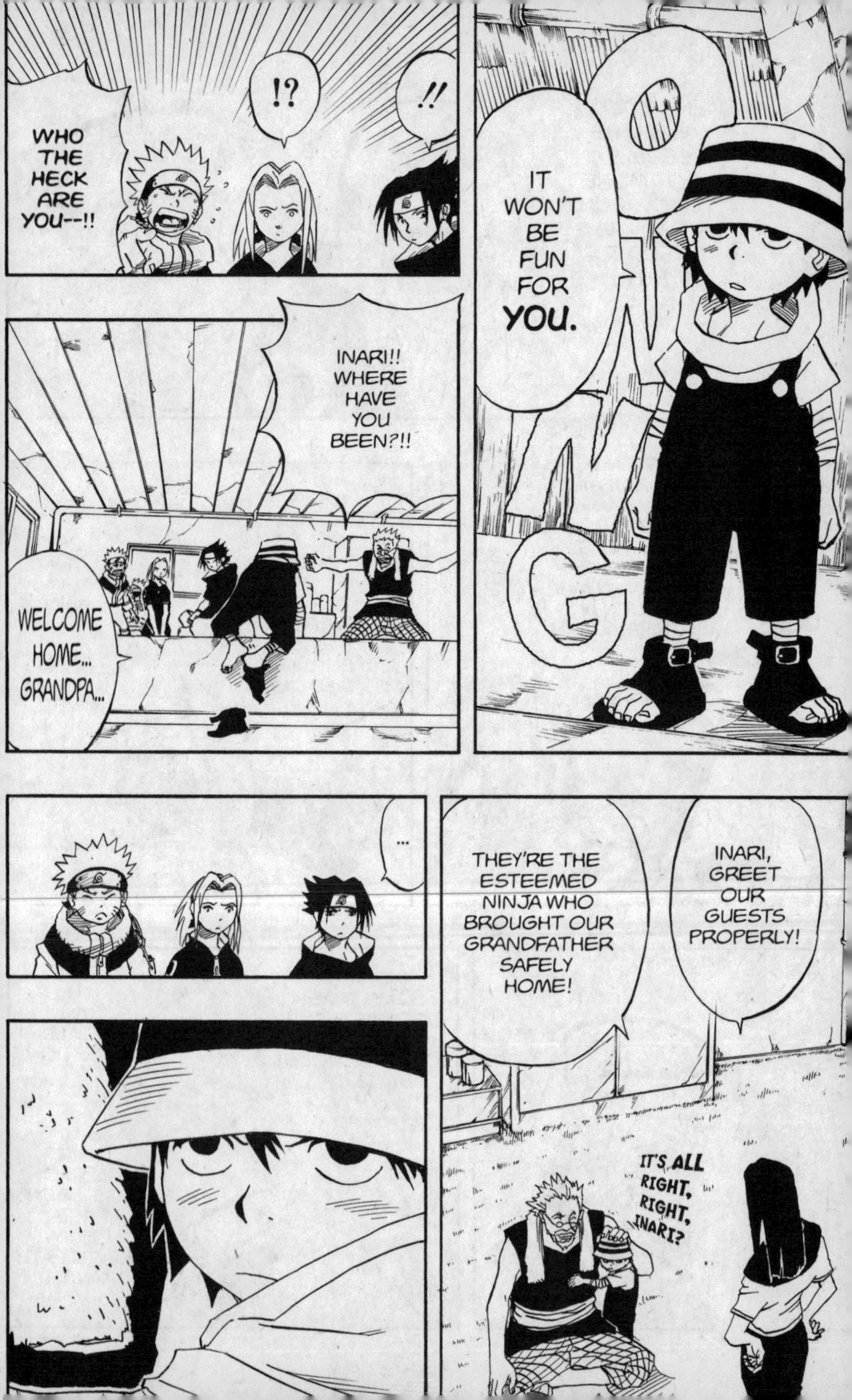
IT WON'T BE FUN FOR YOU.
WHO THE HECK ARE YOU--!!
!?
!!
INARI!! WHERE HAVE YOU BEEN?!!
WELCOME HOME... GRANDPA...
INARI, GREET OUR GUESTS PROPERLY!
THEY'RE THE ESTEEMED NINJA WHO BROUGHT OUR GRANDFATHER SAFELY HOME!
IT'S ALL RIGHT, RIGHT, INARI?
...

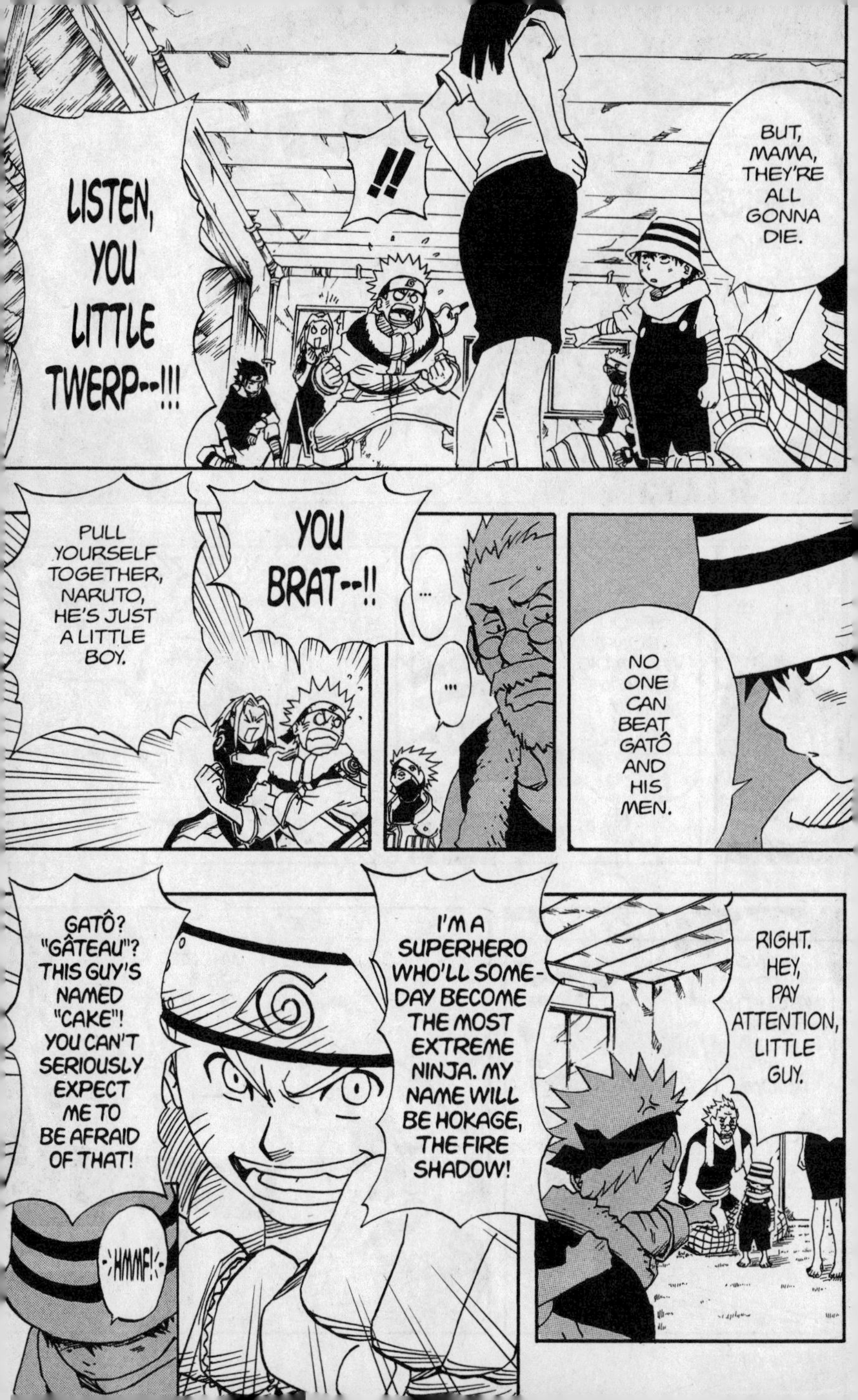
BUT, MAMA, THEY'RE ALL GONNA DIE.
!!
LISTEN, YOU LITTLE TWERP--!!!
NO ONE CAN BEAT GATÔ AND HIS MEN.
...
...
YOU BRAT--!!
PULL YOURSELF TOGETHER, NARUTO, HE'S JUST A LITTLE BOY.
RIGHT. HEY, PAY ATTENTION, LITTLE GUY.
I'M A SUPERHERO WHO'LL SOME-DAY BECOME THE MOST EXTREME NINJA. MY NAME WILL BE HOKAGE, THE FIRE SHADOW!
GATÔ? "GÂTEAU"? THIS GUY'S NAMED "CAKE"! YOU CAN'T SERIOUSLY EXPECT ME TO BE AFRAID OF THAT!
HMMF!

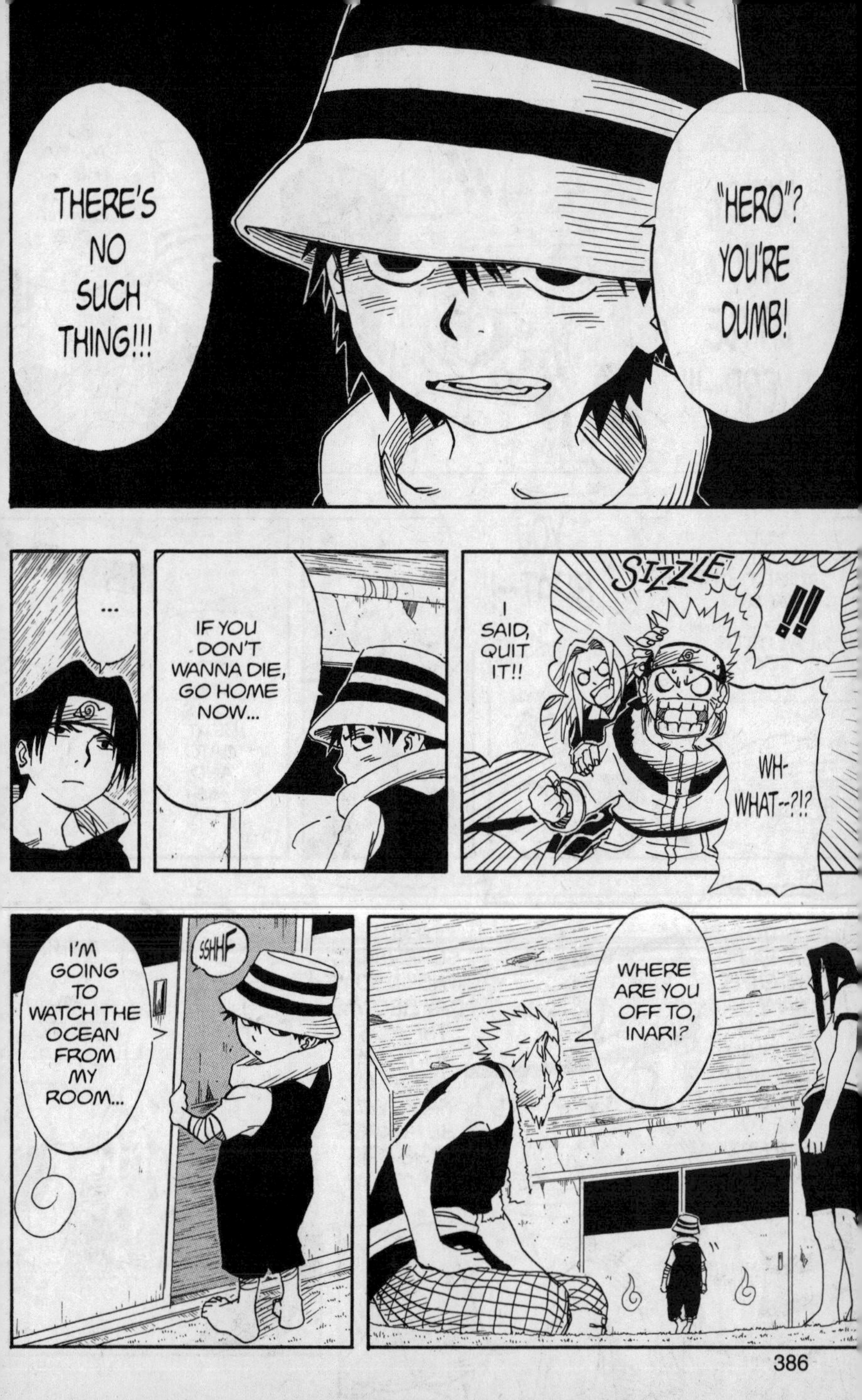
"HERO"? YOU'RE DUMB!
THERE'S NO SUCH THING!!!
!!
SIZZLE
WH-WHAT--?!?
I SAID, QUIT IT!!
IF YOU DON'T WANNA DIE, GO HOME NOW...
...
WHERE ARE YOU OFF TO, INARI?
SSHHF
I'M GOING TO WATCH THE OCEAN FROM MY ROOM...

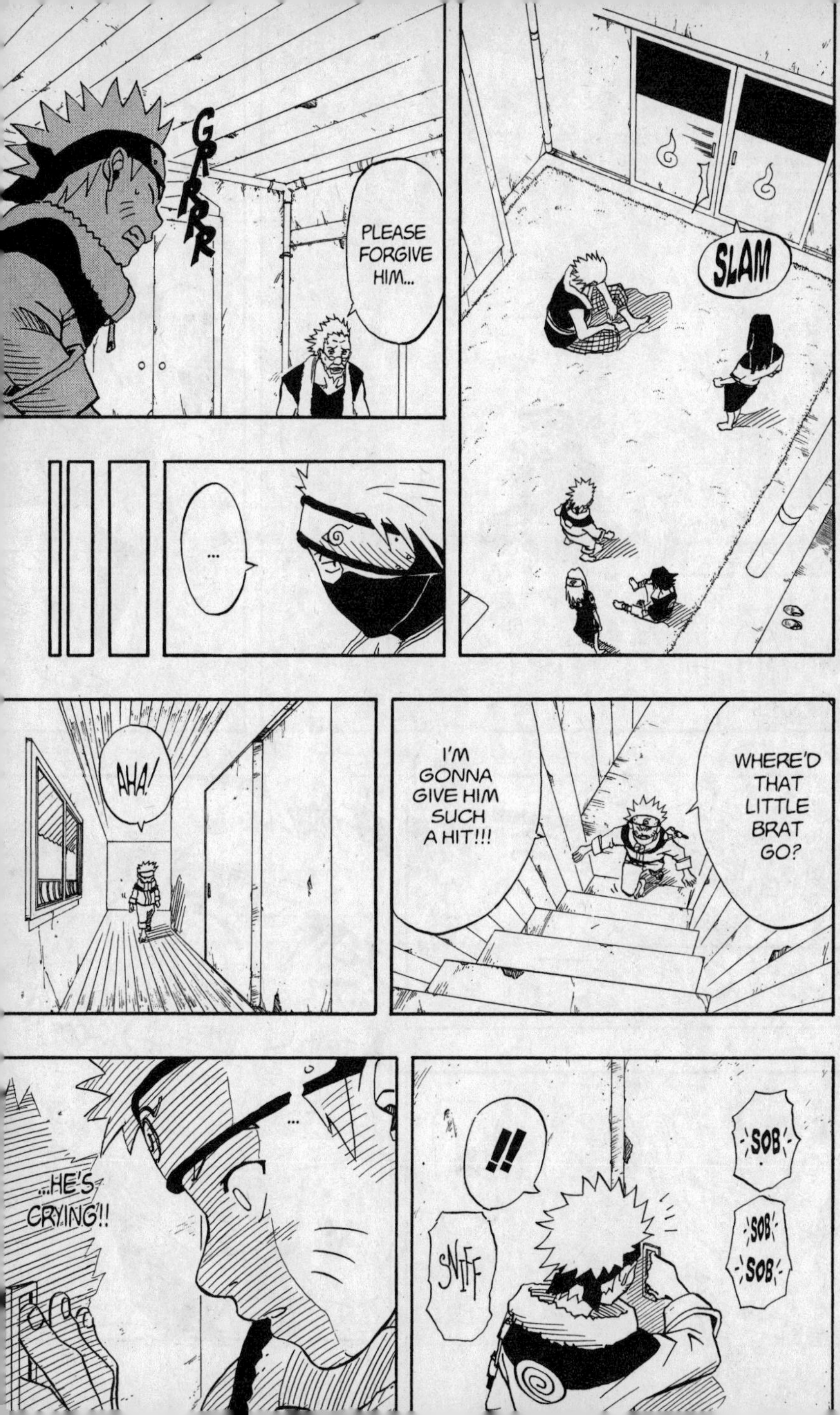
SLAM
PLEASE FORGIVE HIM...
GRRR
...
WHERE'D THAT LITTLE BRAT GO?
I'M GONNA GIVE HIM SUCH A HIT!!!
AHA!
SOB
SOB
SOB
!!
SNIFF
...
...HE'S CRYING!!

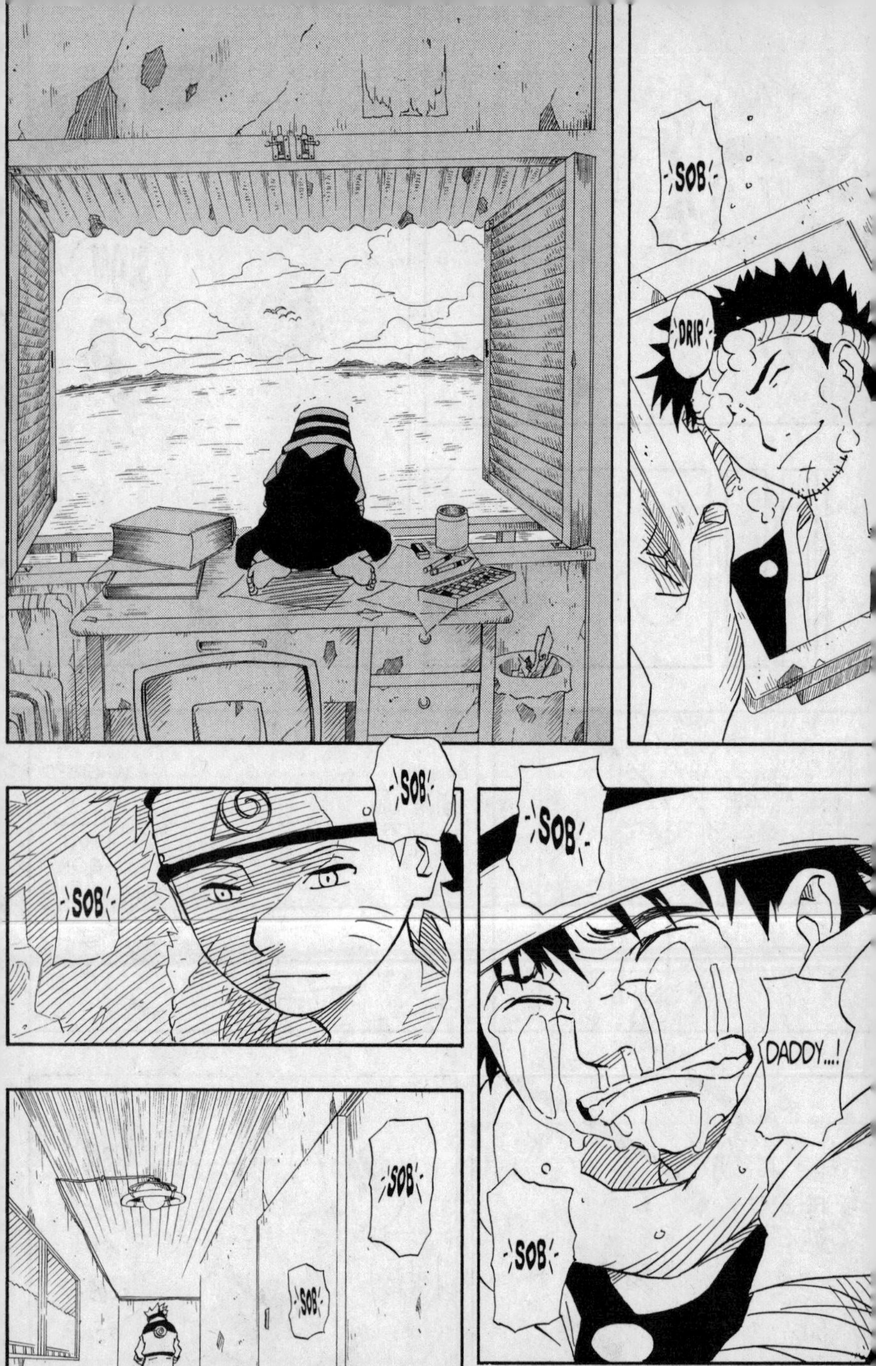
SOB
DRIP
SOB
DADDY...!
SOB
SOB
SOB
SOB
SOB

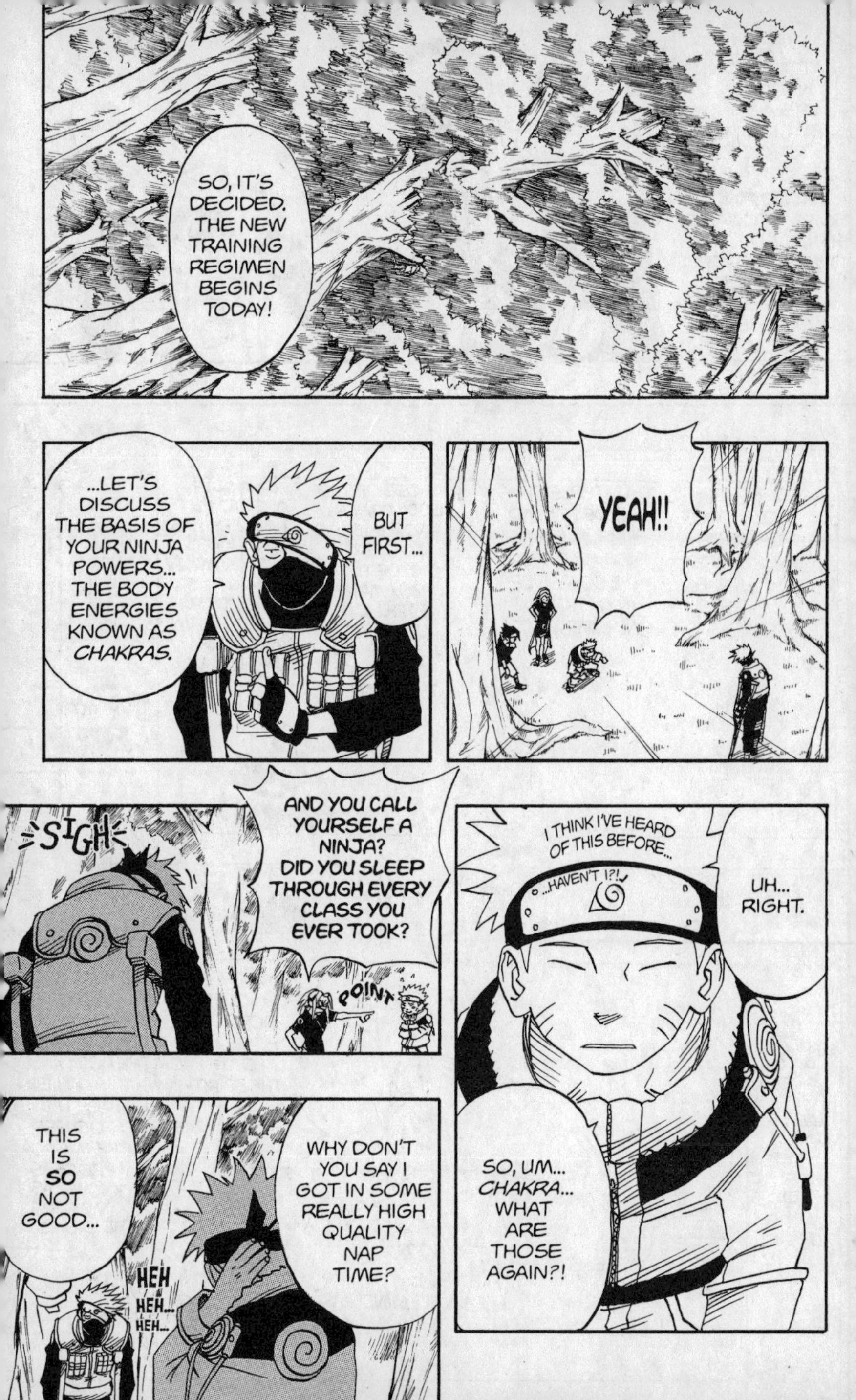
SO, IT'S DECIDED. THE NEW TRAINING REGIMEN BEGINS TODAY!
YEAH!!
BUT FIRST...
...LET'S DISCUSS THE BASIS OF YOUR NINJA POWERS... THE BODY ENERGIES KNOWN AS *CHAKRAS.*
I THINK I'VE HEARD OF THIS BEFORE...
...HAVEN'T I?!
UH... RIGHT.
SO, UM... *CHAKRA*... WHAT ARE THOSE AGAIN?!
SIGH
AND YOU CALL YOURSELF A NINJA? DID YOU SLEEP THROUGH EVERY CLASS YOU EVER TOOK?
POINT
WHY DON'T YOU SAY I GOT IN SOME REALLY HIGH QUALITY NAP TIME?
HEH HEH... HEH...
THIS IS **SO** NOT GOOD...

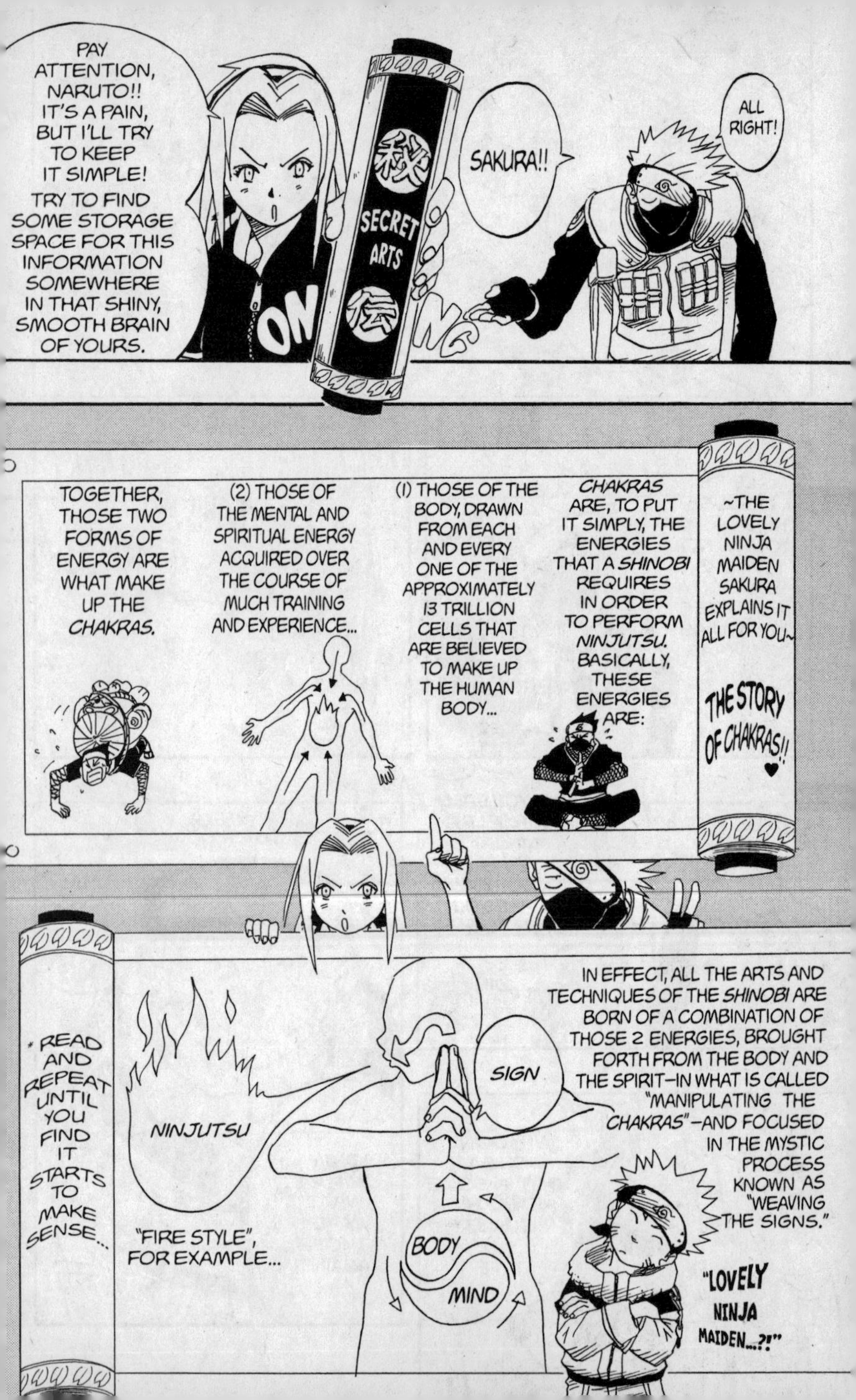
ALL RIGHT!
SAKURA!!
PAY ATTENTION, NARUTO!! IT'S A PAIN, BUT I'LL TRY TO KEEP IT SIMPLE!
TRY TO FIND SOME STORAGE SPACE FOR THIS INFORMATION SOMEWHERE IN THAT SHINY, SMOOTH BRAIN OF YOURS.
秘 SECRET ARTS 伝
~THE LOVELY NINJA MAIDEN SAKURA EXPLAINS IT ALL FOR YOU~
THE STORY OF CHAKRAS!! ♥
CHAKRAS ARE, TO PUT IT SIMPLY, THE ENERGIES THAT A SHINOBI REQUIRES IN ORDER TO PERFORM NINJUTSU. BASICALLY, THESE ENERGIES ARE:
(1) THOSE OF THE BODY, DRAWN FROM EACH AND EVERY ONE OF THE APPROXIMATELY 13 TRILLION CELLS THAT ARE BELIEVED TO MAKE UP THE HUMAN BODY...
(2) THOSE OF THE MENTAL AND SPIRITUAL ENERGY ACQUIRED OVER THE COURSE OF MUCH TRAINING AND EXPERIENCE...
TOGETHER, THOSE TWO FORMS OF ENERGY ARE WHAT MAKE UP THE CHAKRAS.
IN EFFECT, ALL THE ARTS AND TECHNIQUES OF THE SHINOBI ARE BORN OF A COMBINATION OF THOSE 2 ENERGIES, BROUGHT FORTH FROM THE BODY AND THE SPIRIT—IN WHAT IS CALLED "MANIPULATING THE CHAKRAS"—AND FOCUSED IN THE MYSTIC PROCESS KNOWN AS "WEAVING THE SIGNS."
"LOVELY NINJA MAIDEN...?!"
SIGN
NINJUTSU
BODY
MIND
"FIRE STYLE", FOR EXAMPLE...
*READ AND REPEAT UNTIL YOU FIND IT STARTS TO MAKE SENSE...

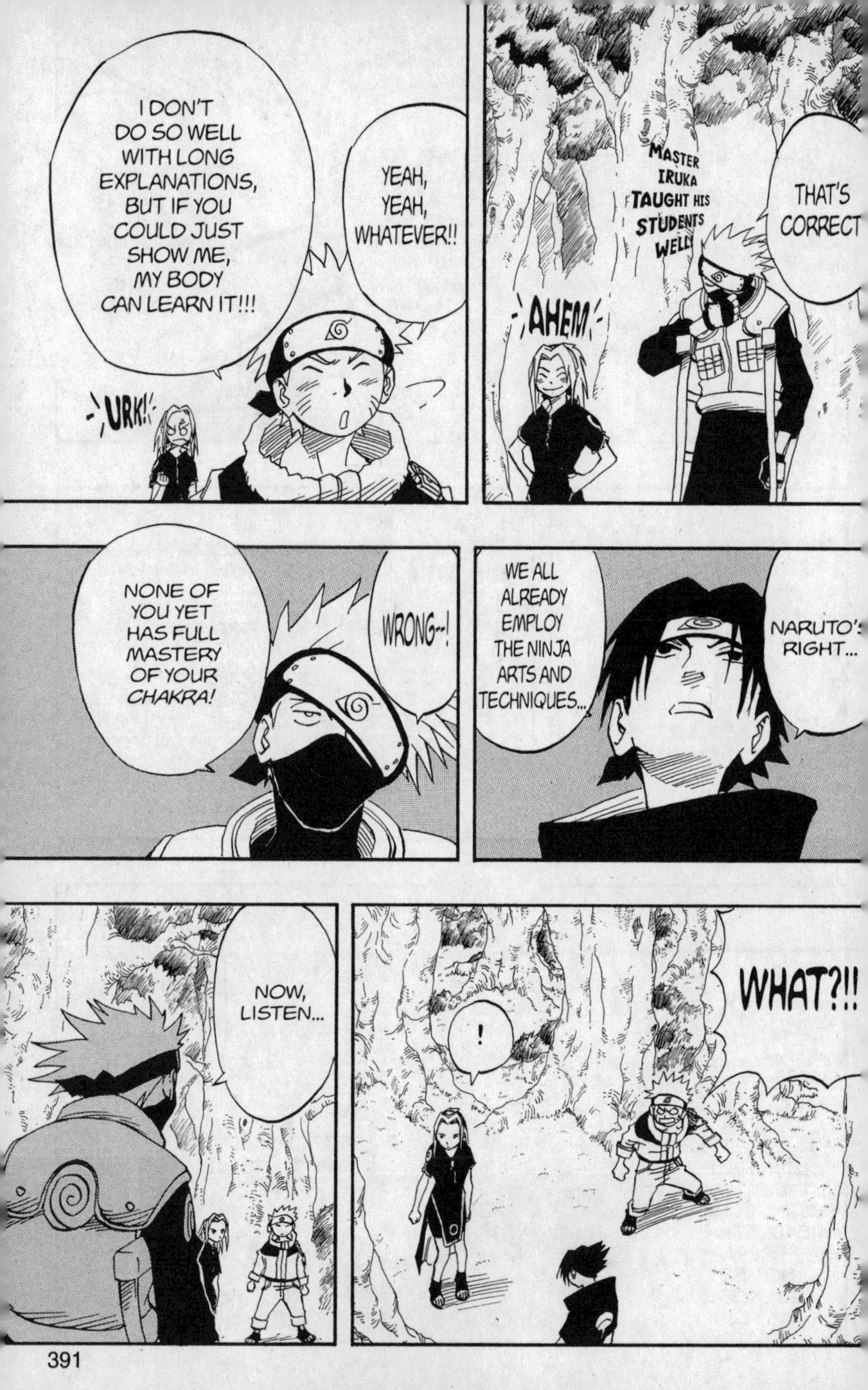

THAT'S CORRECT
MASTER IRUKA TAUGHT HIS STUDENTS WELL
AHEM
YEAH, YEAH, WHATEVER!!
I DON'T DO SO WELL WITH LONG EXPLANATIONS, BUT IF YOU COULD JUST SHOW ME, MY BODY CAN LEARN IT!!!
URK!
NARUTO'S RIGHT...
WE ALL ALREADY EMPLOY THE NINJA ARTS AND TECHNIQUES...
WRONG--!
NONE OF YOU YET HAS FULL MASTERY OF YOUR *CHAKRA!*
WHAT?!!
!
NOW, LISTEN...

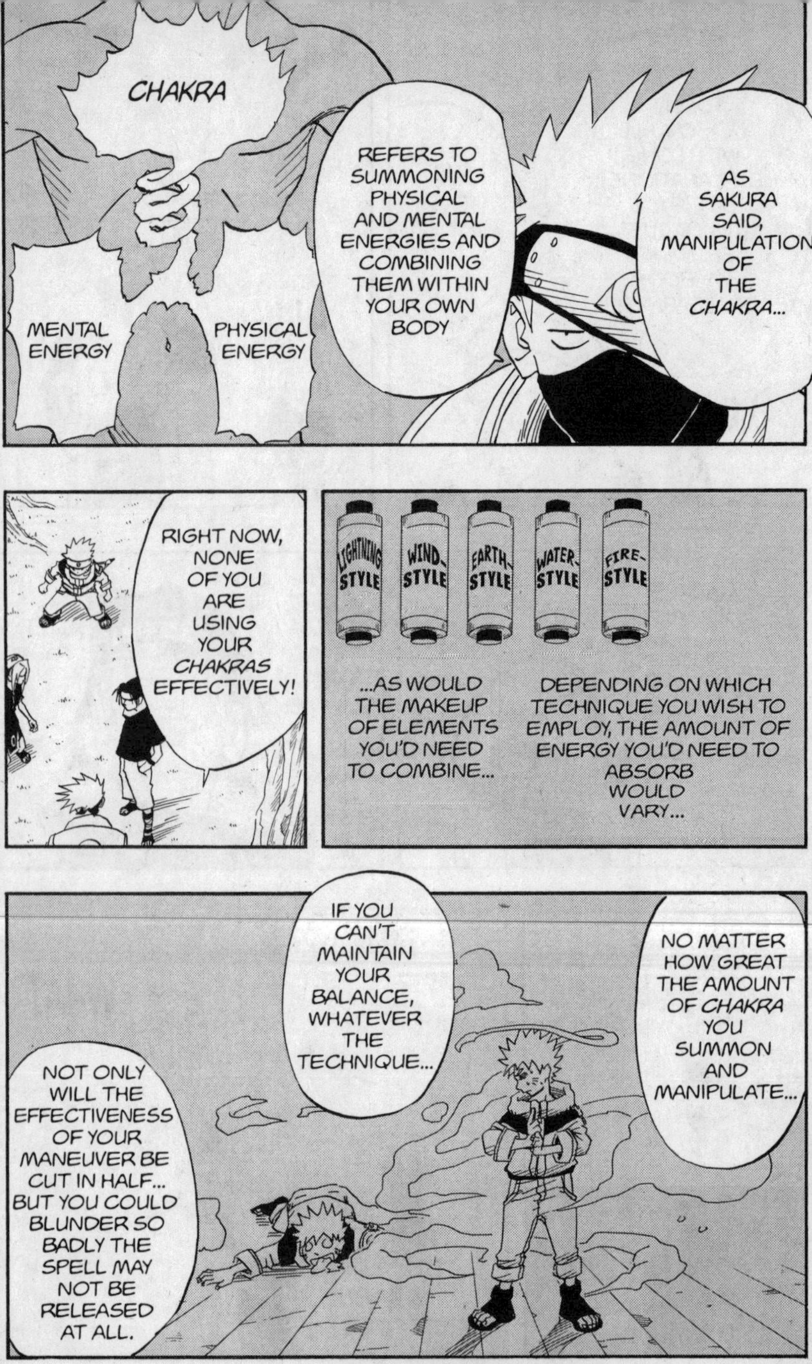
AS SAKURA SAID, MANIPULATION OF THE *CHAKRA*...
REFERS TO SUMMONING PHYSICAL AND MENTAL ENERGIES AND COMBINING THEM WITHIN YOUR OWN BODY
CHAKRA
PHYSICAL ENERGY
MENTAL ENERGY
FIRE-STYLE
WATER-STYLE
EARTH-STYLE
WIND-STYLE
LIGHTNING STYLE
DEPENDING ON WHICH TECHNIQUE YOU WISH TO EMPLOY, THE AMOUNT OF ENERGY YOU'D NEED TO ABSORB WOULD VARY...
...AS WOULD THE MAKEUP OF ELEMENTS YOU'D NEED TO COMBINE...
RIGHT NOW, NONE OF YOU ARE USING YOUR *CHAKRAS* EFFECTIVELY!
NO MATTER HOW GREAT THE AMOUNT OF *CHAKRA* YOU SUMMON AND MANIPULATE...
IF YOU CAN'T MAINTAIN YOUR BALANCE, WHATEVER THE TECHNIQUE...
NOT ONLY WILL THE EFFECTIVENESS OF YOUR MANEUVER BE CUT IN HALF... BUT YOU COULD BLUNDER SO BADLY THE SPELL MAY NOT BE RELEASED AT ALL.

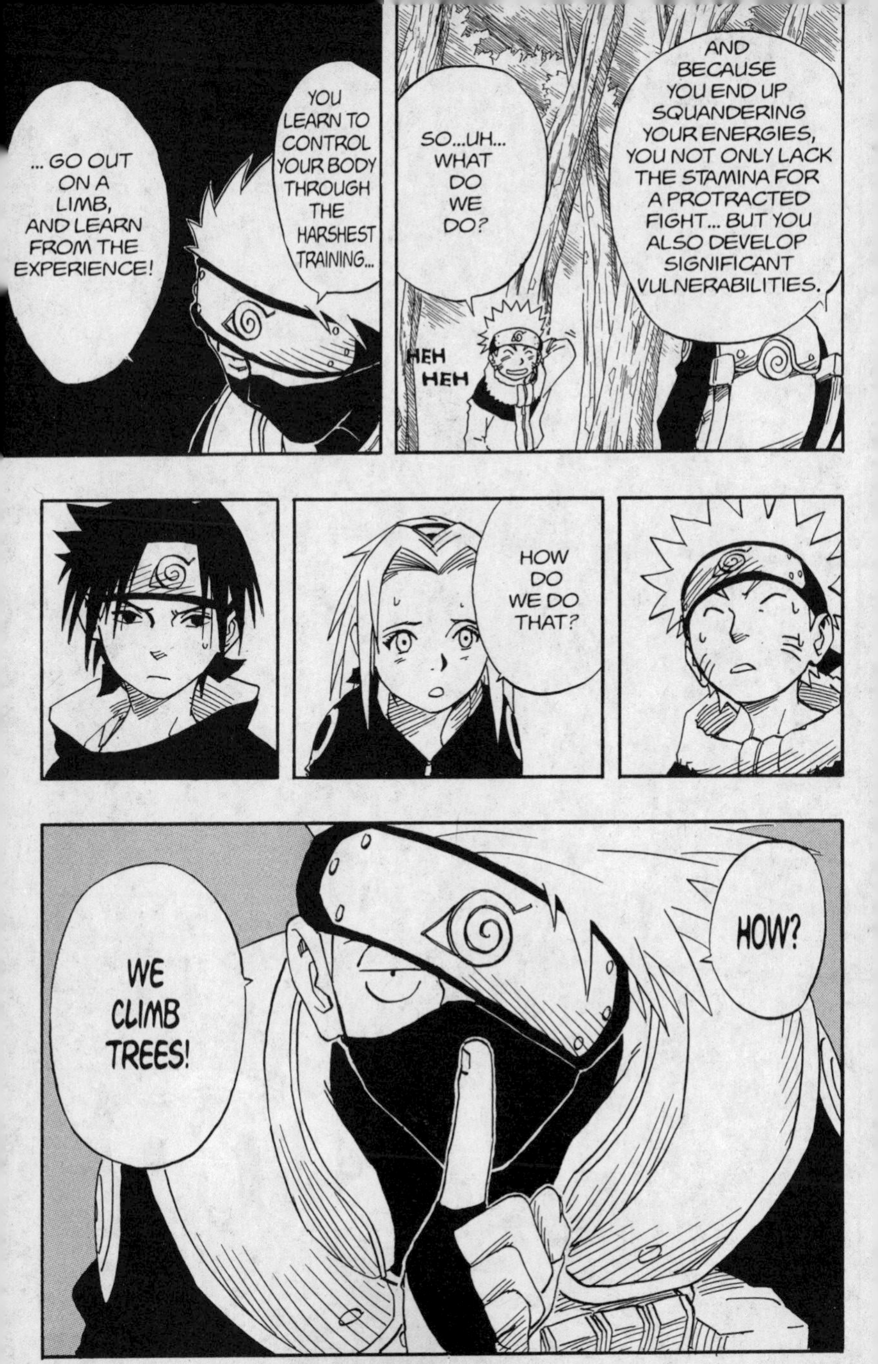
AND BECAUSE YOU END UP SQUANDERING YOUR ENERGIES, YOU NOT ONLY LACK THE STAMINA FOR A PROTRACTED FIGHT... BUT YOU ALSO DEVELOP SIGNIFICANT VULNERABILITIES.
SO...UH... WHAT DO WE DO?
HEH HEH
YOU LEARN TO CONTROL YOUR BODY THROUGH THE HARSHEST TRAINING...
... GO OUT ON A LIMB, AND LEARN FROM THE EXPERIENCE!
HOW DO WE DO THAT?
HOW?
WE CLIMB TREES!

NARUTO

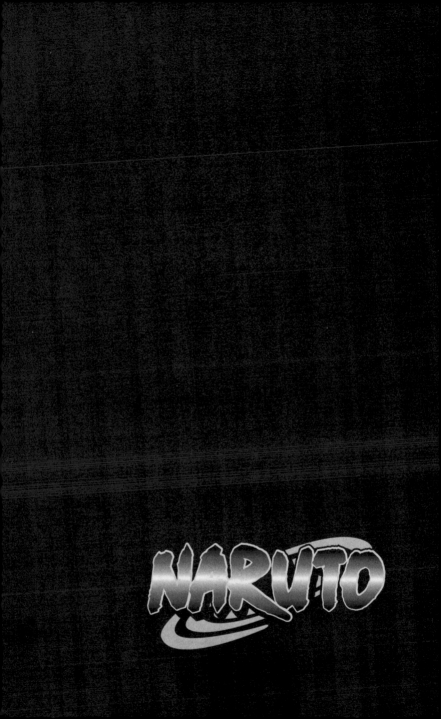

岸本斉史

We're in the third volume of **Naruto**. I feel like I've developed a lot working on this title, but I still have a long way to go. My heart and body are still weak! I must devote a mountain of training to my work on **Naruto**! I want everyone to join me and share in the excitement of **Naruto**!

—*Masashi Kishimoto, 2000*

NARUTO

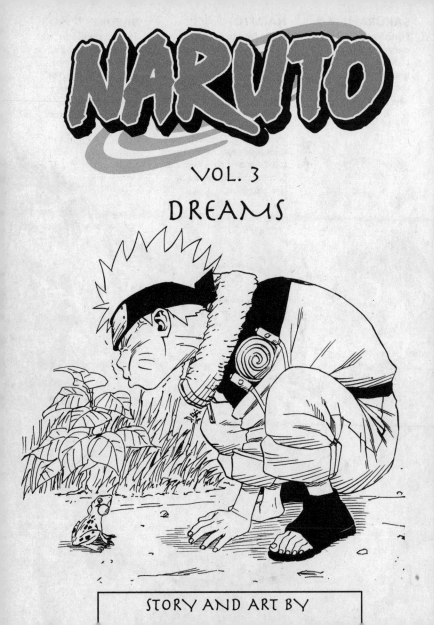

NARUTO

VOL. 3

DREAMS

STORY AND ART BY

SAKURA サクラ
Naruto and Sasuke's classmate. She has a crush on Sasuke, who ignores her. In return, she picks on Naruto, who has a crush on *her.*

NARUTO ナルト
When Naruto was an infant, he was used as a living sacrifice in a magic rite: a demonic fox spirit was sealed inside his body to keep it from wreaking havoc in the outside world. The orphan Naruto grew up to be an attention-seeking troublemaker. Despite the evil spirit inside him, he just wants to be the best ninja ever, and become the *Hokage*, the village champion.

SASUKE サスケ
The top student in Naruto's class, and a member of the prestigious Uchiha clan. His goal is to get revenge against a mysterious person who wronged him in the past.

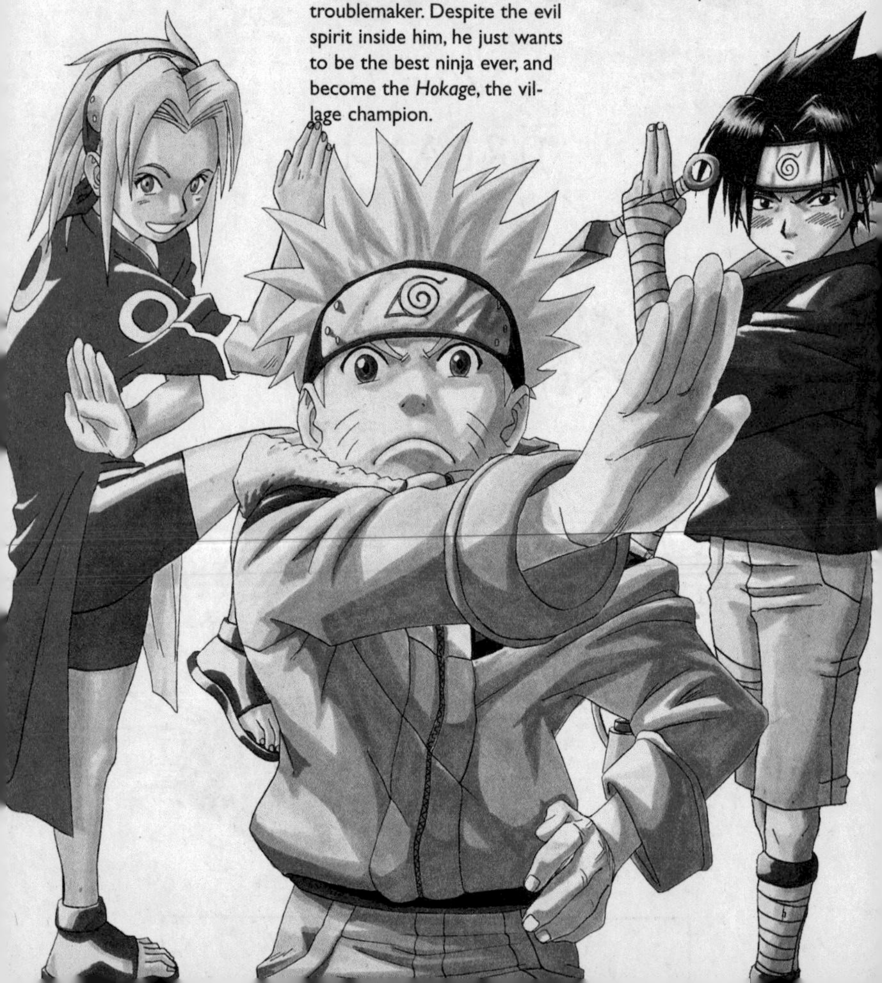

KAKASHI カカシ
An upper-level ninja. His *sharingan* eye can deflect and duplicate enemy *ninjutsu*. Currently injured from his fight with Zabuza.

ZABUZA 再不斬
A sword-wielding assassin-ninja known as "the demon." Currently injured from his fight with Kakashi.

HAKU 白
Zabuza's consort, an agile young ninja of indeterminate gender.

TAZUNA タズナ
A grumpy old bridge-builder. He has a daughter, Tsunami, and a grandson, Inari.

THE STORY SO FAR...

Naruto, Sasuke and Sakura are a team of apprentice ninjas from the ninja village of Konohagakure. On their first big mission, they (and their trainer Kakashi) found themselves bodyguarding the bridgebuilder Tazuna on his way back home to the Land of the Waves. But Tazuna hadn't revealed that he was the target of professional hitmen, hired by the evil millionaire Gatô to keep him from finishing his bridge! In a desperate fight, the four ninja were able to defeat the assassin Zabuza—but a mysterious masked ninja stole Zabuza's body before the heroes realized he wasn't dead. Now, assassins and bodyguards are both preparing for a rematch...

NARUTO

VOL. 3
DREAMS

CONTENTS

Number 18: Training Day

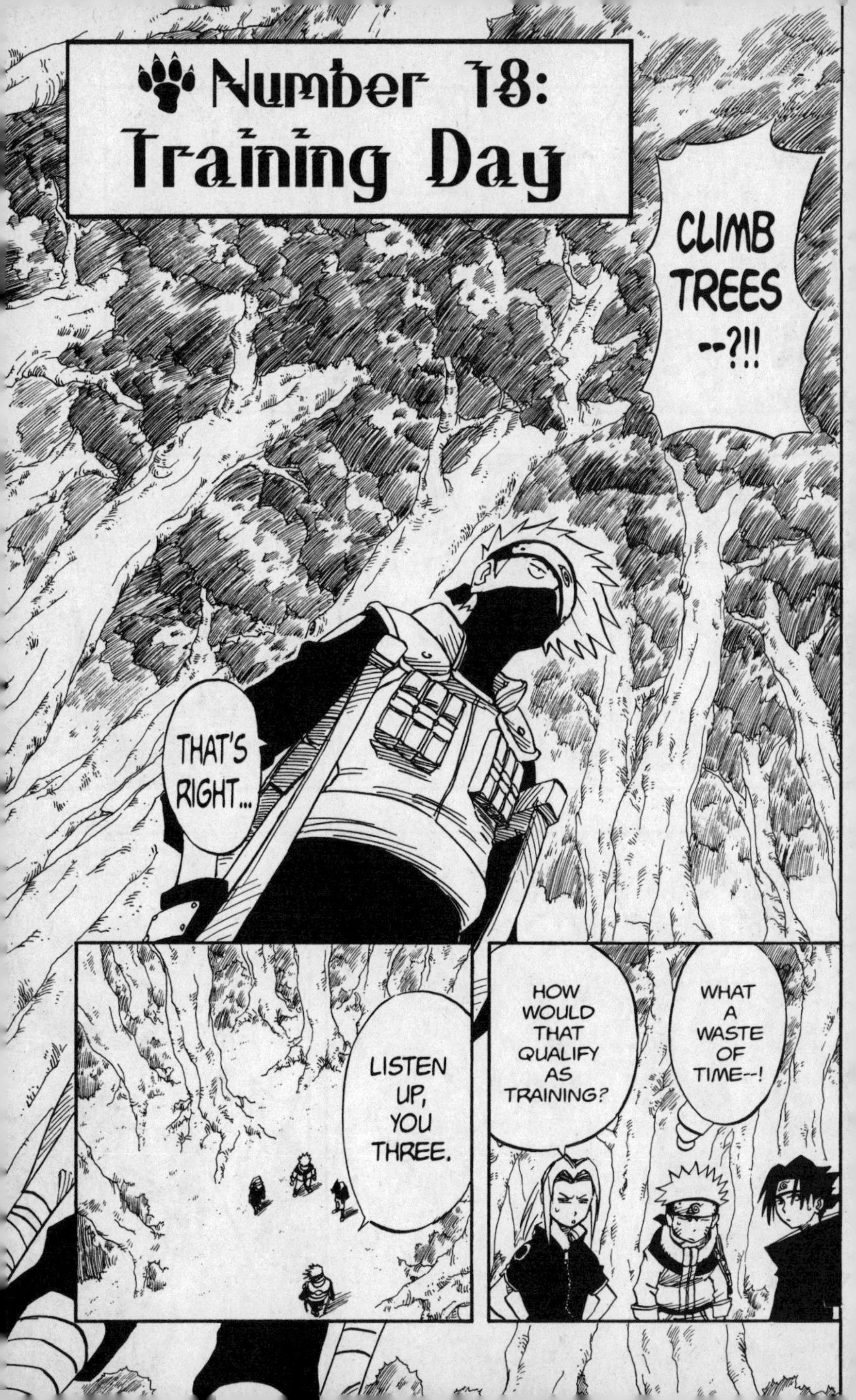
CLIMB TREES --?!!
THAT'S RIGHT...
WHAT A WASTE OF TIME--!
HOW WOULD THAT QUALIFY AS TRAINING?
LISTEN UP, YOU THREE.

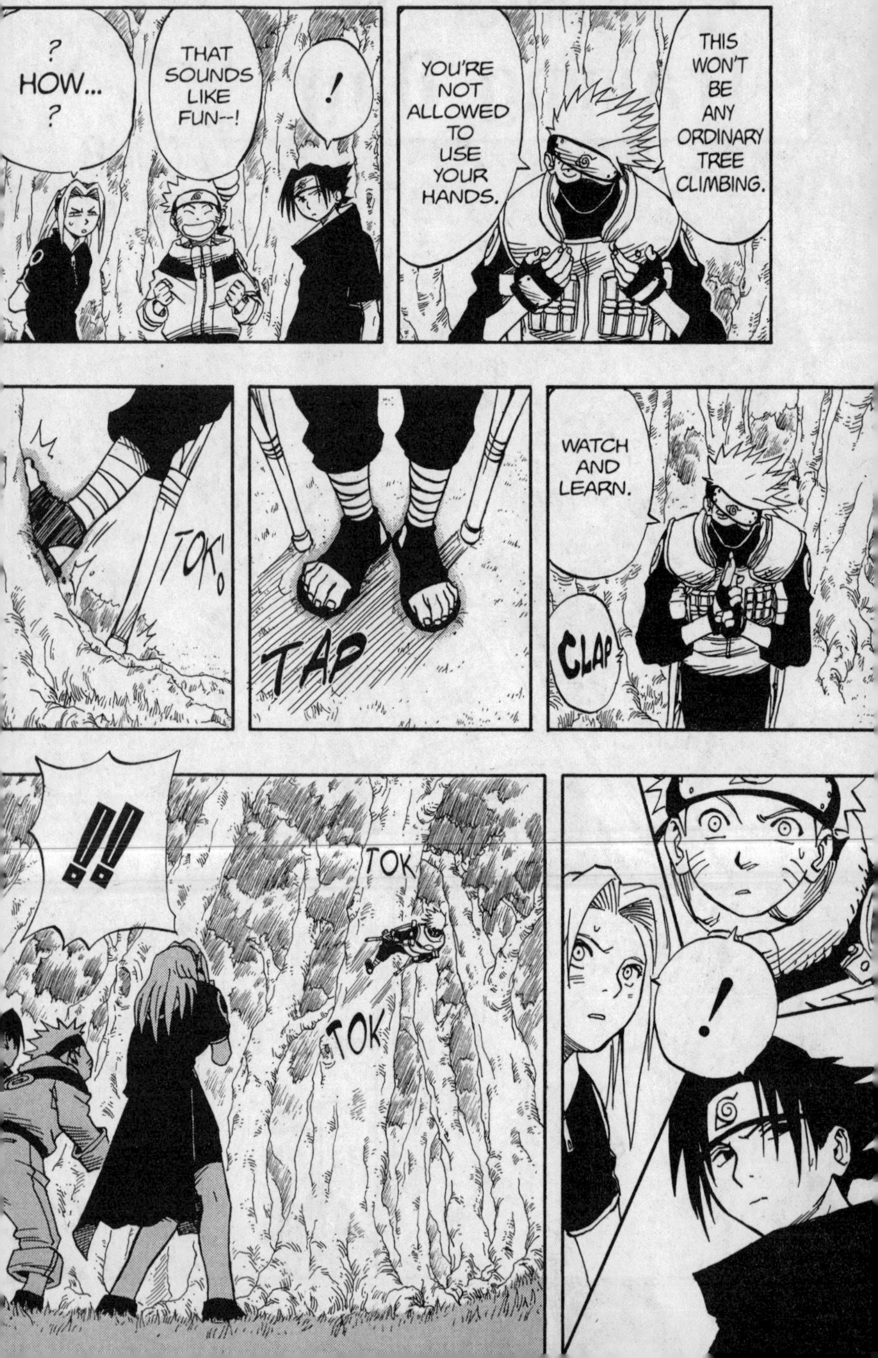
THIS WON'T BE ANY ORDINARY TREE CLIMBING.
YOU'RE NOT ALLOWED TO USE YOUR HANDS.
!
THAT SOUNDS LIKE FUN--!
? HOW... ?
WATCH AND LEARN.
CLAP
TAP
TOK
!
TOK
TOK
!!

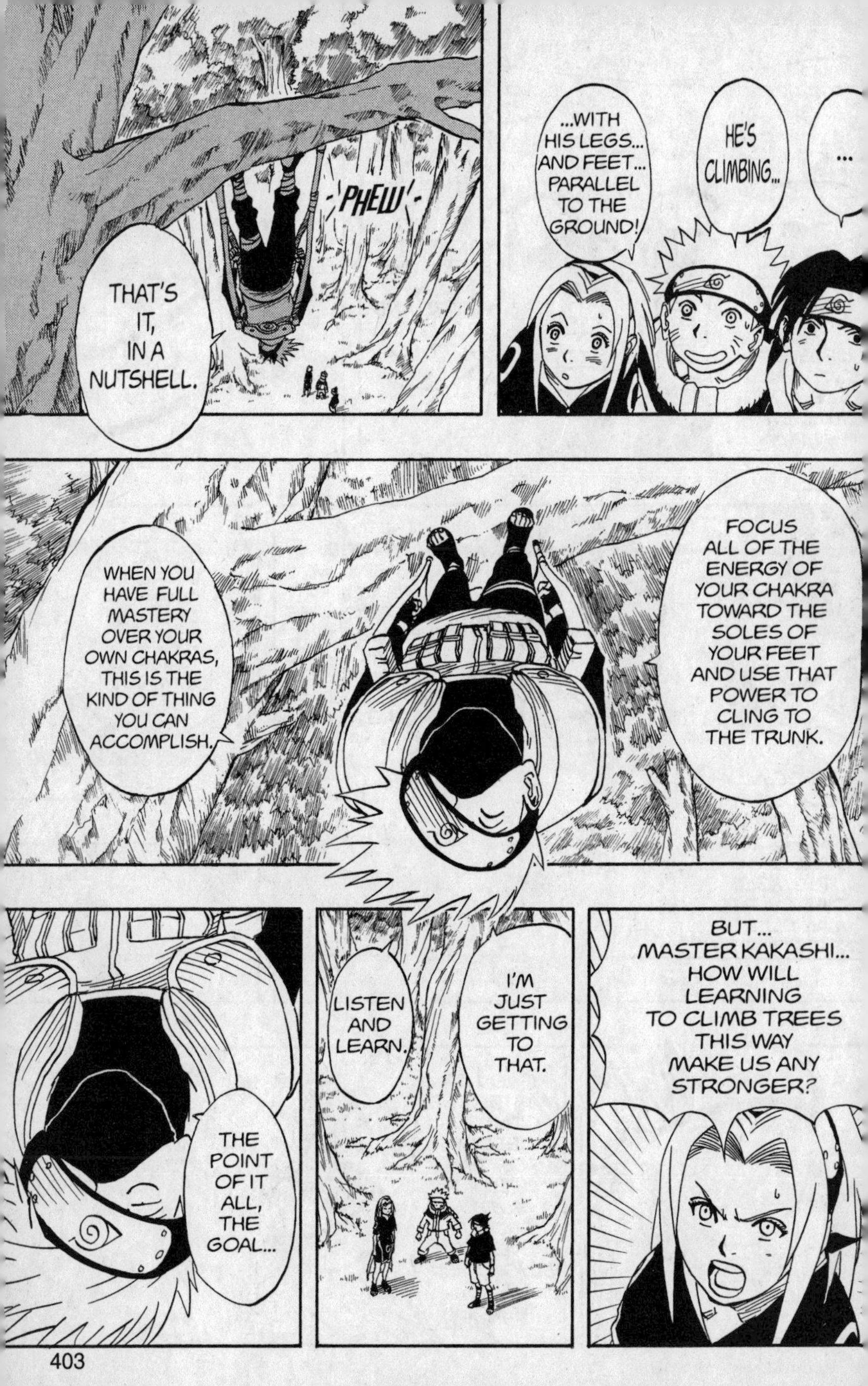
...
HE'S CLIMBING...
...WITH HIS LEGS... AND FEET... PARALLEL TO THE GROUND!
PHEW
THAT'S IT, IN A NUTSHELL.
FOCUS ALL OF THE ENERGY OF YOUR CHAKRA TOWARD THE SOLES OF YOUR FEET AND USE THAT POWER TO CLING TO THE TRUNK.
WHEN YOU HAVE FULL MASTERY OVER YOUR OWN CHAKRAS, THIS IS THE KIND OF THING YOU CAN ACCOMPLISH.
BUT... MASTER KAKASHI... HOW WILL LEARNING TO CLIMB TREES THIS WAY MAKE US ANY STRONGER?
I'M JUST GETTING TO THAT.
LISTEN AND LEARN.
THE POINT OF IT ALL, THE GOAL...

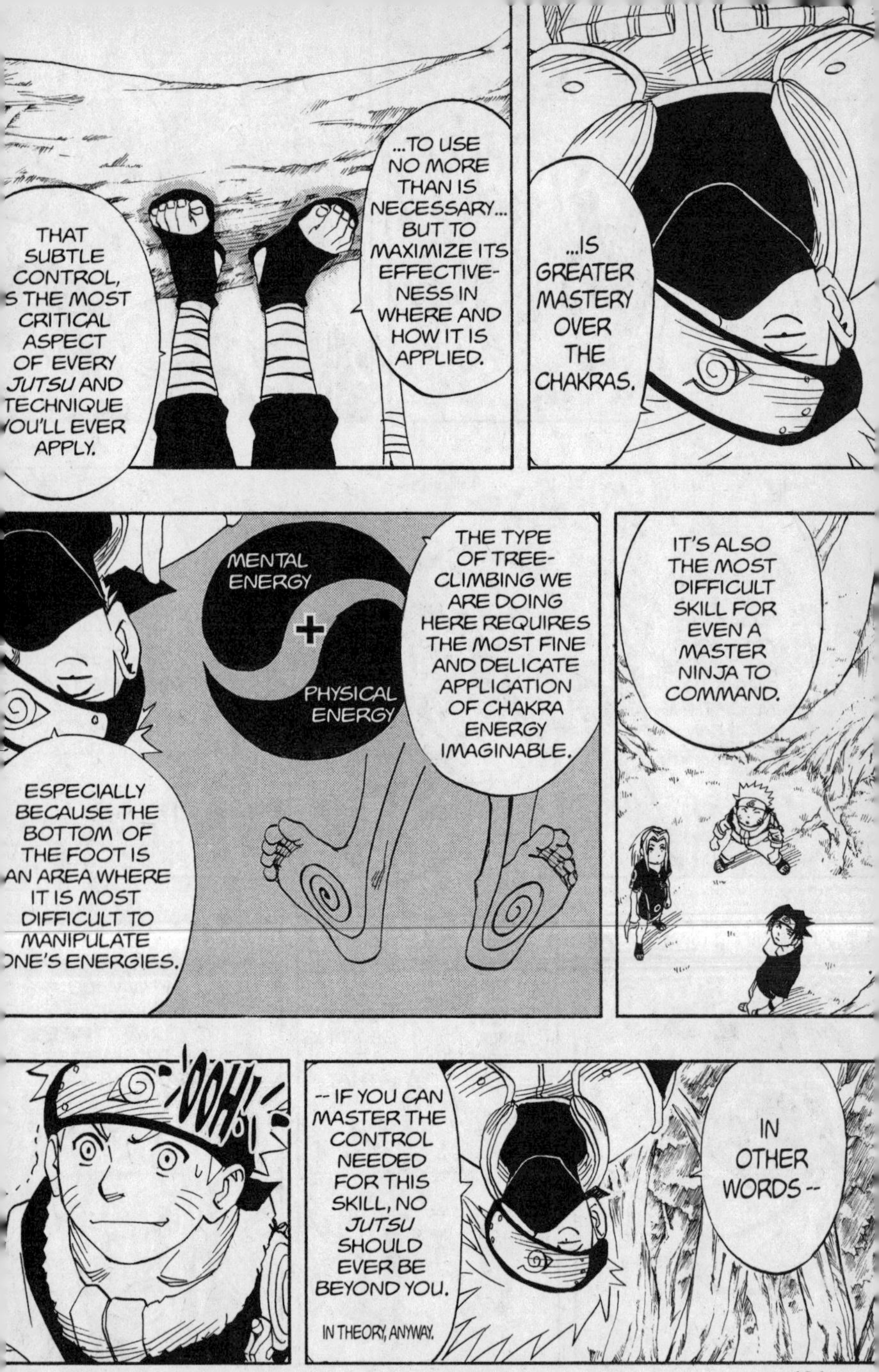
...IS GREATER MASTERY OVER THE CHAKRAS.
...TO USE NO MORE THAN IS NECESSARY... BUT TO MAXIMIZE ITS EFFECTIVENESS IN WHERE AND HOW IT IS APPLIED.
THAT SUBTLE CONTROL, S THE MOST CRITICAL ASPECT OF EVERY *JUTSU* AND TECHNIQUE OU'LL EVER APPLY.
IT'S ALSO THE MOST DIFFICULT SKILL FOR EVEN A MASTER NINJA TO COMMAND.
THE TYPE OF TREE-CLIMBING WE ARE DOING HERE REQUIRES THE MOST FINE AND DELICATE APPLICATION OF CHAKRA ENERGY IMAGINABLE.
MENTAL ENERGY
+
PHYSICAL ENERGY
ESPECIALLY BECAUSE THE BOTTOM OF THE FOOT IS AN AREA WHERE IT IS MOST DIFFICULT TO MANIPULATE NE'S ENERGIES.
IN OTHER WORDS --
-- IF YOU CAN MASTER THE CONTROL NEEDED FOR THIS SKILL, NO *JUTSU* SHOULD EVER BE BEYOND YOU.
IN THEORY, ANYWAY.
OOH!

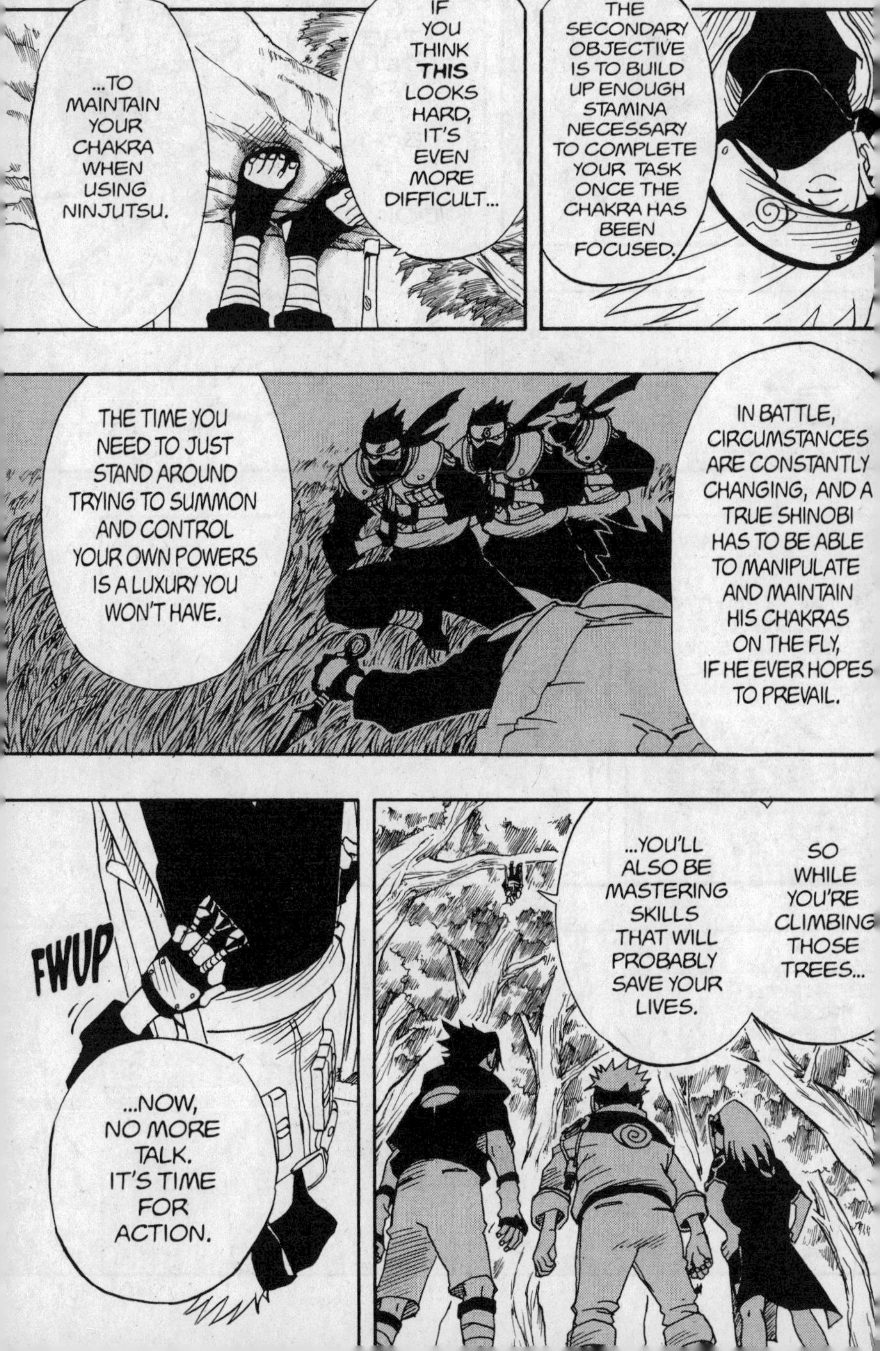
THE SECONDARY OBJECTIVE IS TO BUILD UP ENOUGH STAMINA NECESSARY TO COMPLETE YOUR TASK ONCE THE CHAKRA HAS BEEN FOCUSED.
IF YOU THINK **THIS** LOOKS HARD, IT'S EVEN MORE DIFFICULT...
...TO MAINTAIN YOUR CHAKRA WHEN USING NINJUTSU.
IN BATTLE, CIRCUMSTANCES ARE CONSTANTLY CHANGING, AND A TRUE SHINOBI HAS TO BE ABLE TO MANIPULATE AND MAINTAIN HIS CHAKRAS ON THE FLY, IF HE EVER HOPES TO PREVAIL.
THE TIME YOU NEED TO JUST STAND AROUND TRYING TO SUMMON AND CONTROL YOUR OWN POWERS IS A LUXURY YOU WON'T HAVE.
SO WHILE YOU'RE CLIMBING THOSE TREES...
...YOU'LL ALSO BE MASTERING SKILLS THAT WILL PROBABLY SAVE YOUR LIVES.
FWUP
...NOW, NO MORE TALK. IT'S TIME FOR ACTION.

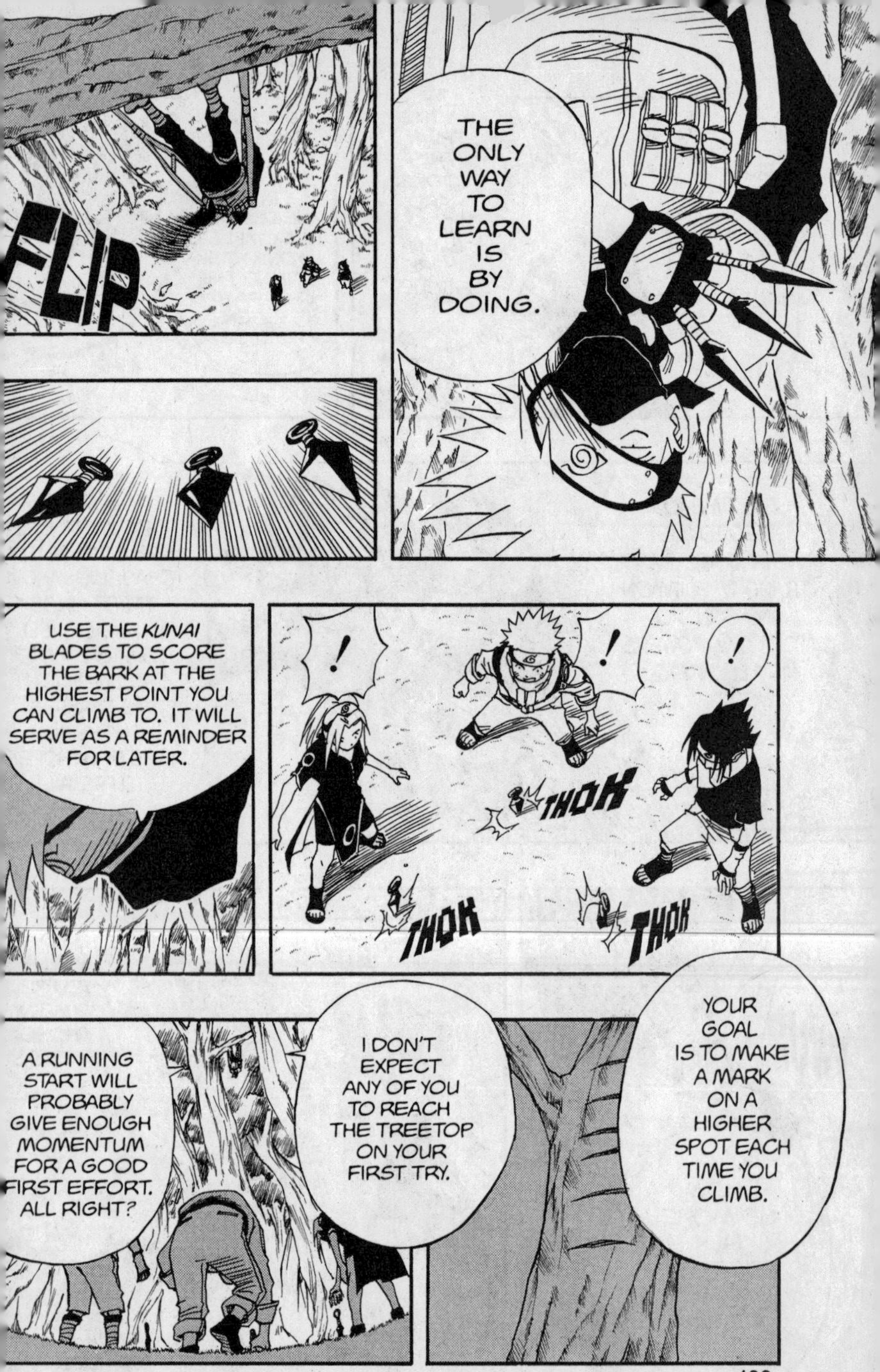
THE ONLY WAY TO LEARN IS BY DOING.
FLIP
!
!
!
THOK
THOK
THOK
USE THE *KUNAI* BLADES TO SCORE THE BARK AT THE HIGHEST POINT YOU CAN CLIMB TO. IT WILL SERVE AS A REMINDER FOR LATER.
YOUR GOAL IS TO MAKE A MARK ON A HIGHER SPOT EACH TIME YOU CLIMB.
I DON'T EXPECT ANY OF YOU TO REACH THE TREETOP ON YOUR FIRST TRY.
A RUNNING START WILL PROBABLY GIVE ENOUGH MOMENTUM FOR A GOOD FIRST EFFORT. ALL RIGHT?

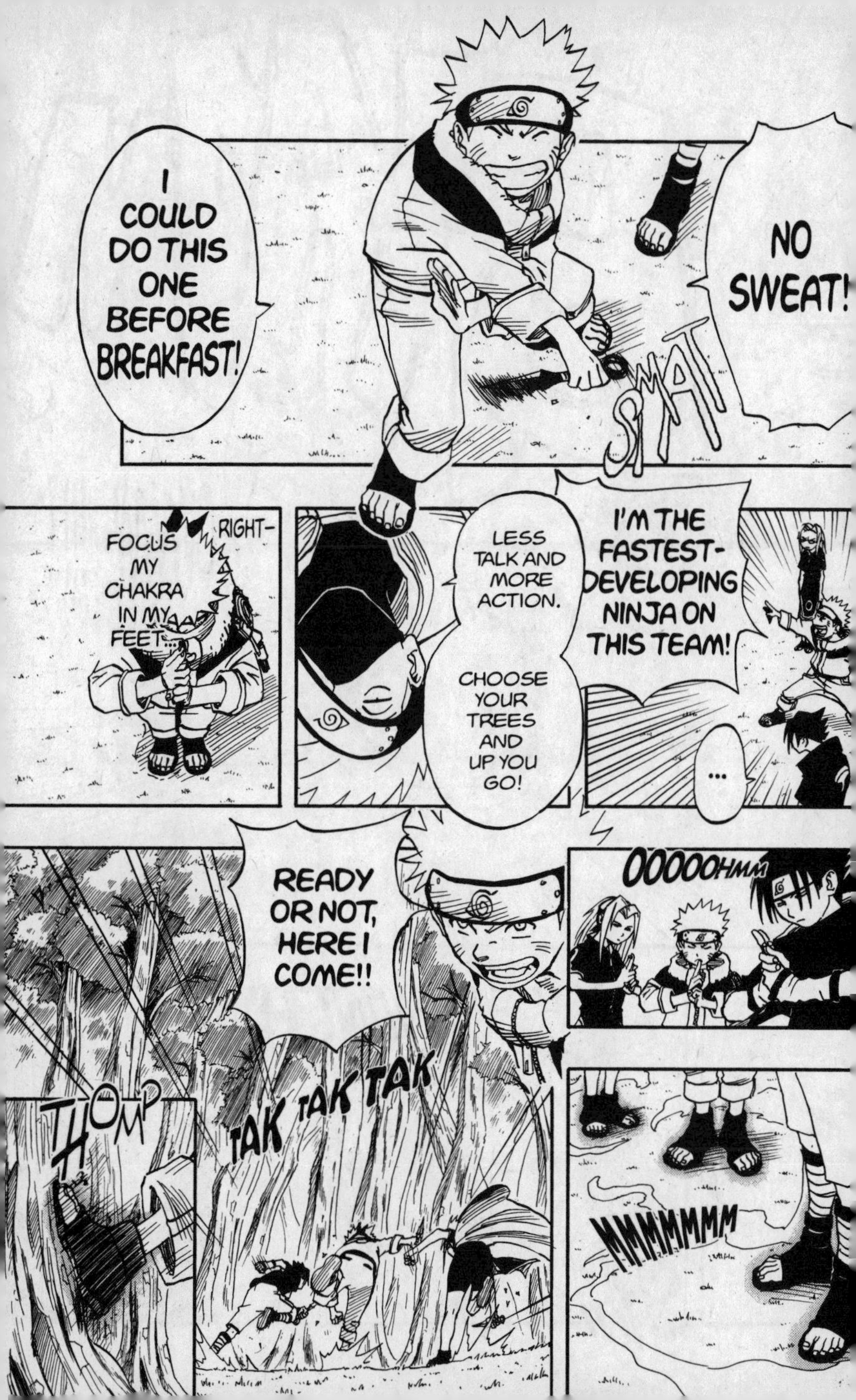
NO SWEAT!
SMAT
I COULD DO THIS ONE BEFORE BREAKFAST!
I'M THE FASTEST-DEVELOPING NINJA ON THIS TEAM!
...
LESS TALK AND MORE ACTION.
CHOOSE YOUR TREES AND UP YOU GO!
RIGHT-
FOCUS MY CHAKRA IN MY FEET...
OOOOOHMM
MMMMMMM
READY OR NOT, HERE I COME!!
TAK TAK TAK
THOMP

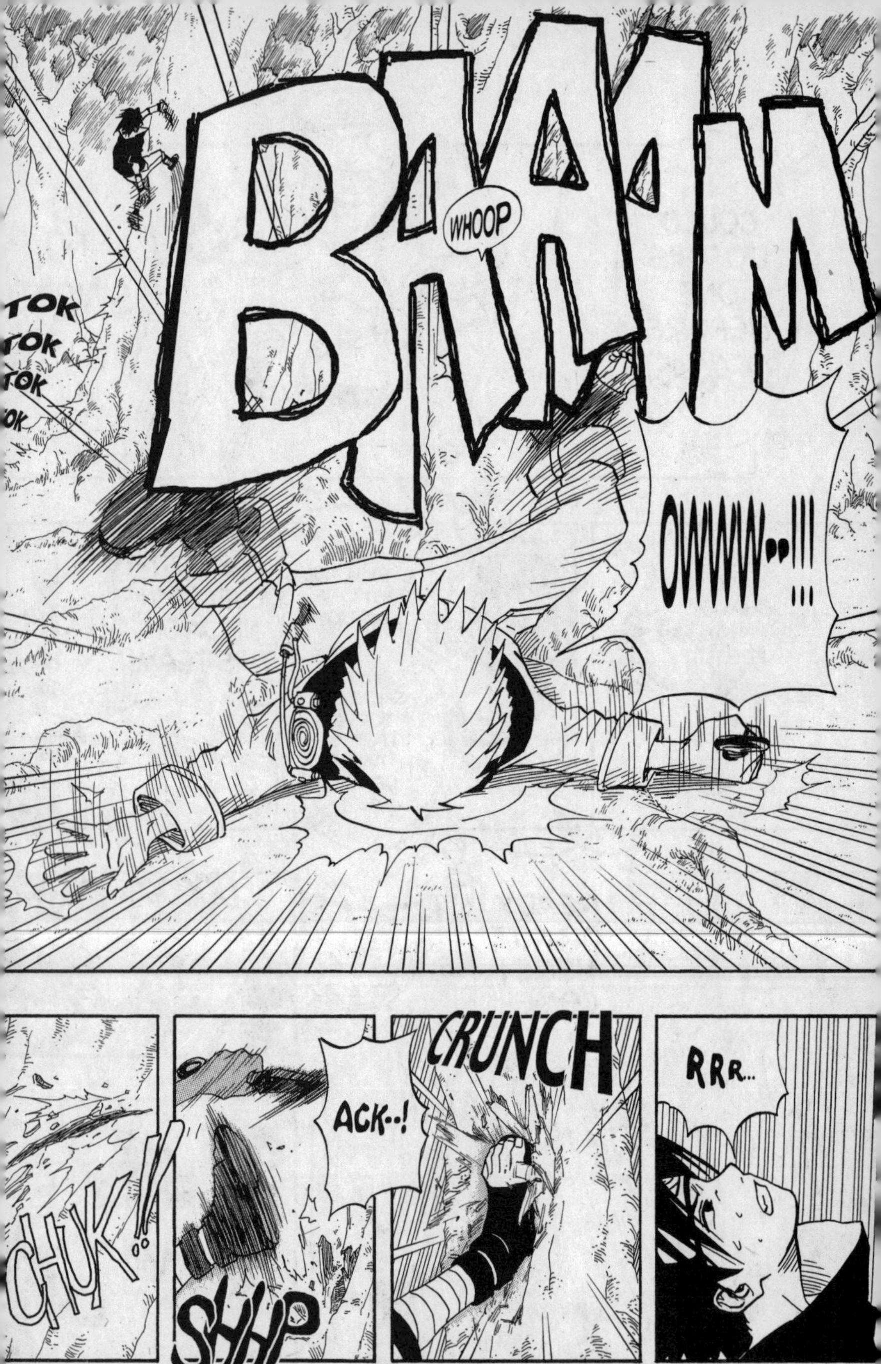
BAAM
WHOOP
OWWWW--!!!
TOK
TOK
TOK
TOK
RRR..
CRUNCH
ACK--!
SHHP
CHUK!!

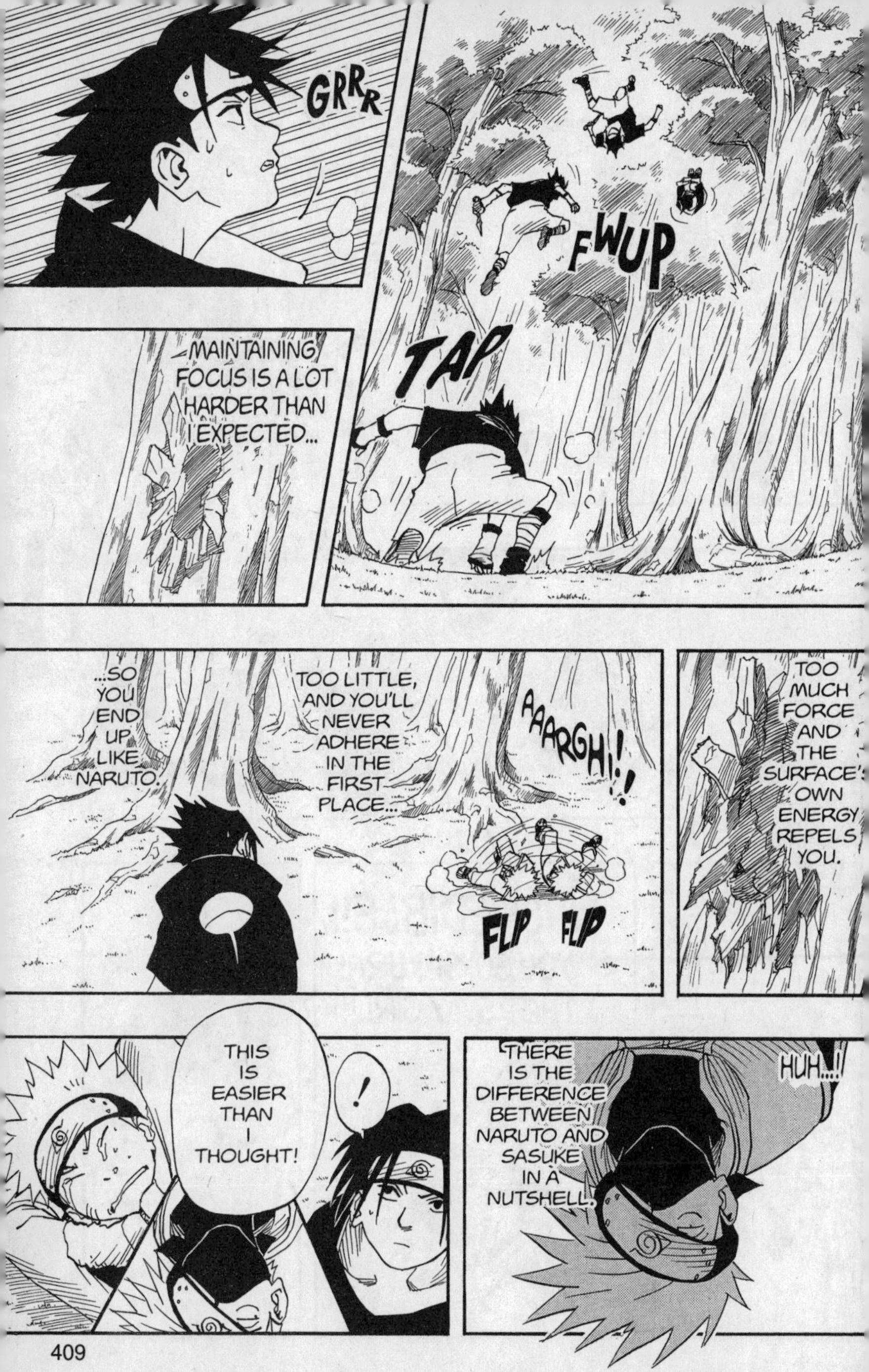
FWUP
TAP
GRRR
MAINTAINING FOCUS IS A LOT HARDER THAN I EXPECTED...
TOO MUCH FORCE AND THE SURFACE'S OWN ENERGY REPELS YOU.
AAARGH!!!
TOO LITTLE, AND YOU'LL NEVER ADHERE IN THE FIRST PLACE...
...SO YOU END UP LIKE NARUTO.
FLIP FLIP
HUH...!
THERE IS THE DIFFERENCE BETWEEN NARUTO AND SASUKE IN A NUTSHELL.
!
THIS IS EASIER THAN I THOUGHT!

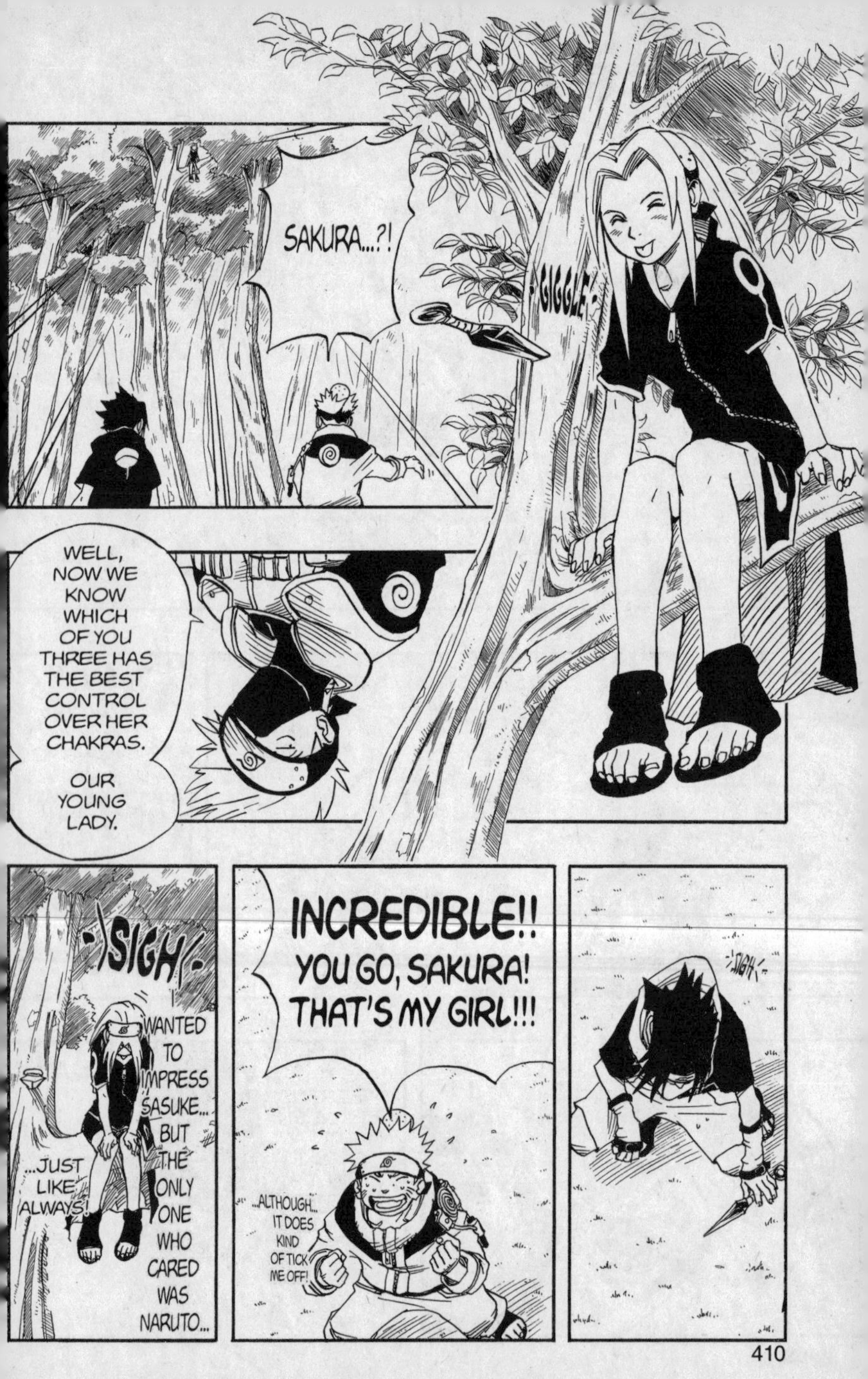
SAKURA...?!
GIGGLE
WELL, NOW WE KNOW WHICH OF YOU THREE HAS THE BEST CONTROL OVER HER CHAKRAS.
OUR YOUNG LADY.
SIGH
INCREDIBLE!! YOU GO, SAKURA! THAT'S MY GIRL!!!
...ALTHOUGH... IT DOES KIND OF TICK ME OFF!
SIGH
WANTED TO IMPRESS SASUKE... BUT THE ONLY ONE WHO CARED WAS NARUTO...
...JUST LIKE ALWAYS!

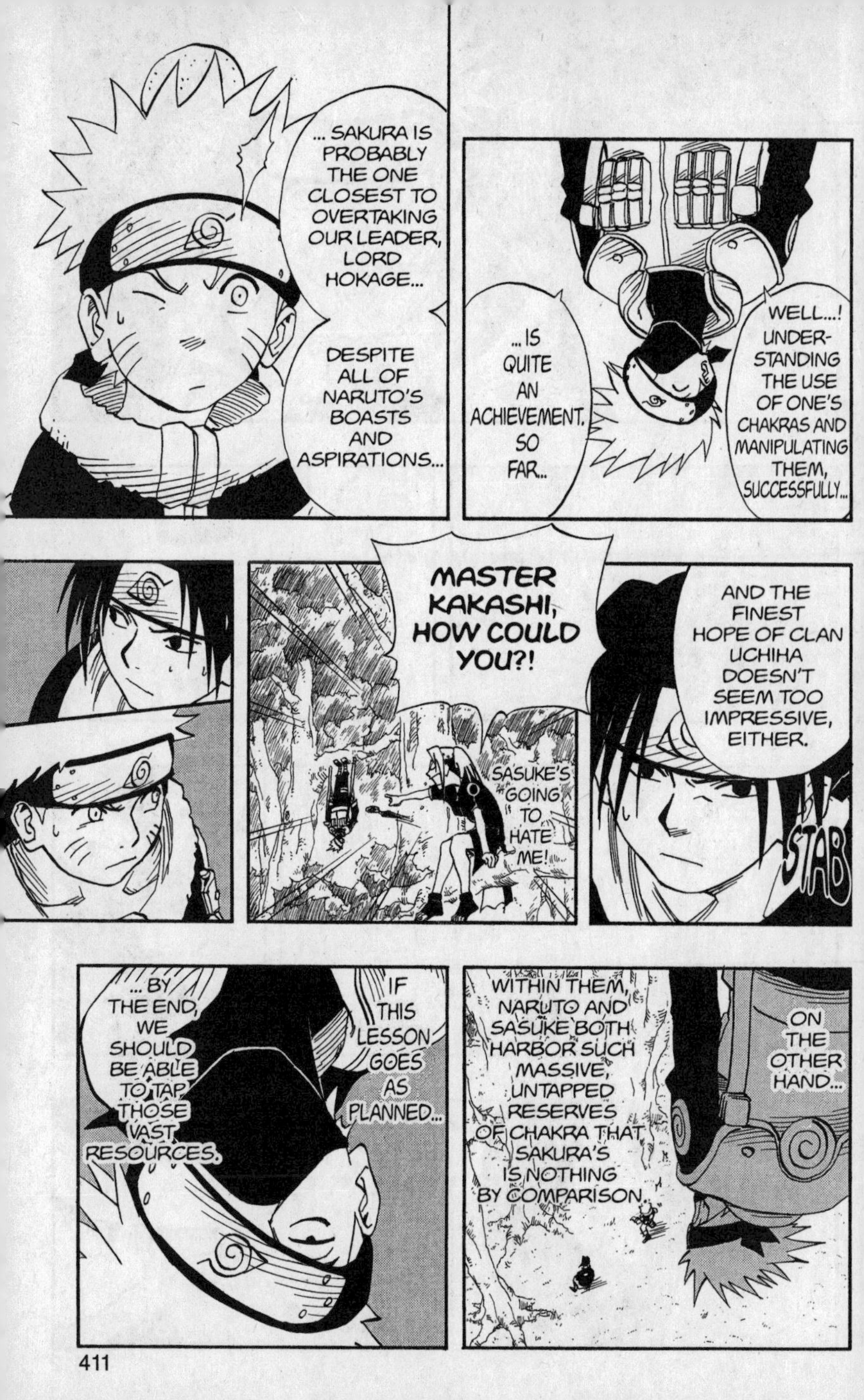
WELL...! UNDERSTANDING THE USE OF ONE'S CHAKRAS AND MANIPULATING THEM, SUCCESSFULLY...
...IS QUITE AN ACHIEVEMENT. SO FAR...
DESPITE ALL OF NARUTO'S BOASTS AND ASPIRATIONS...
...SAKURA IS PROBABLY THE ONE CLOSEST TO OVERTAKING OUR LEADER, LORD HOKAGE...
AND THE FINEST HOPE OF CLAN UCHIHA DOESN'T SEEM TOO IMPRESSIVE, EITHER.
STAB
MASTER KAKASHI, HOW COULD YOU?!
SASUKE'S GOING TO HATE ME!
ON THE OTHER HAND...
WITHIN THEM, NARUTO AND SASUKE BOTH HARBOR SUCH MASSIVE, UNTAPPED RESERVES OF CHAKRA THAT SAKURA'S IS NOTHING BY COMPARISON.
IF THIS LESSON GOES AS PLANNED...
...BY THE END, WE SHOULD BE ABLE TO TAP THOSE VAST RESOURCES.

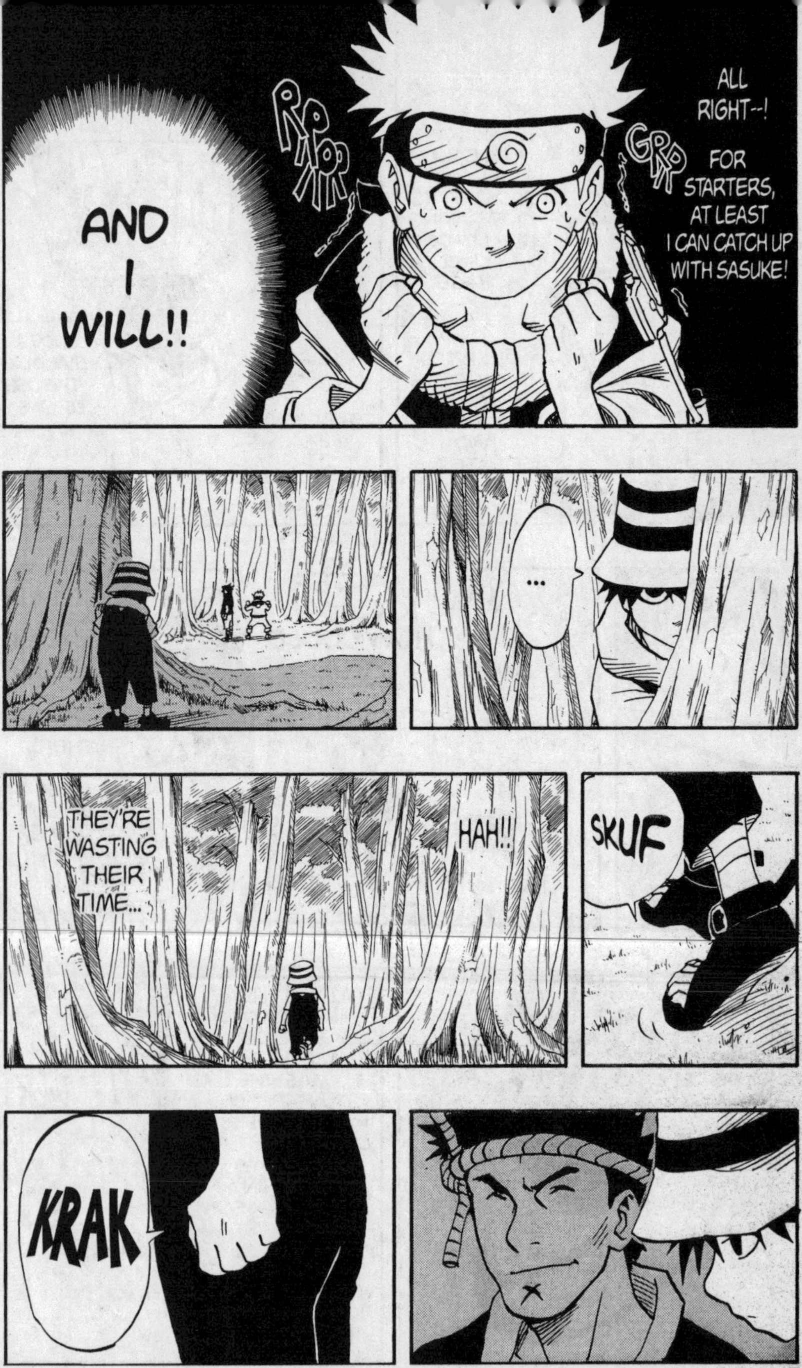
ALL RIGHT--!
FOR STARTERS, AT LEAST I CAN CATCH UP WITH SASUKE!
GRR
RRR
AND I WILL!!
...
SKUF
HAH!!
THEY'RE WASTING THEIR TIME...
KRAK

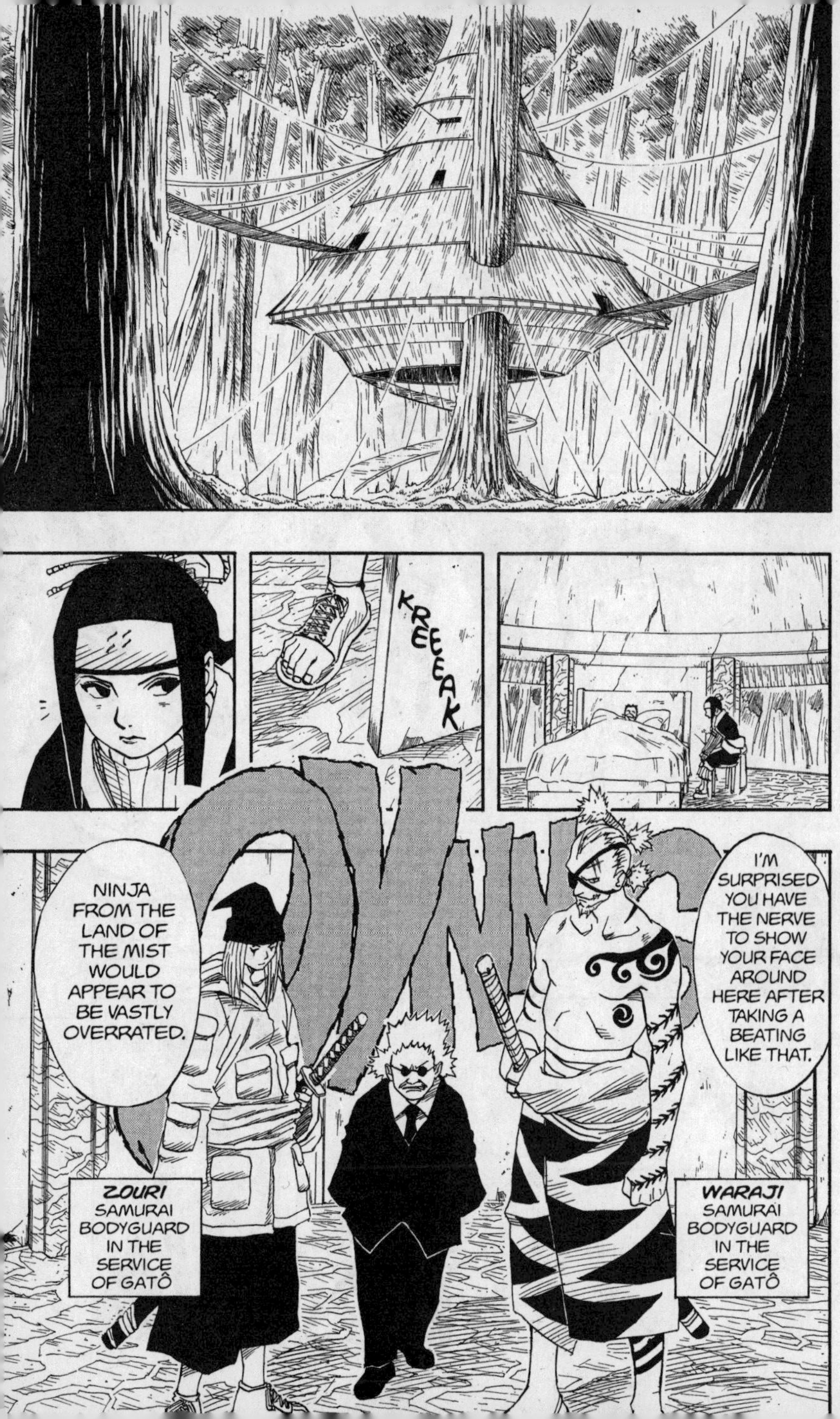
KREEEAK
I'M SURPRISED YOU HAVE THE NERVE TO SHOW YOUR FACE AROUND HERE AFTER TAKING A BEATING LIKE THAT.
NINJA FROM THE LAND OF THE MIST WOULD APPEAR TO BE VASTLY OVERRATED.
WARAJI SAMURAI BODYGUARD IN THE SERVICE OF GATÔ
ZOURI SAMURAI BODYGUARD IN THE SERVICE OF GATÔ

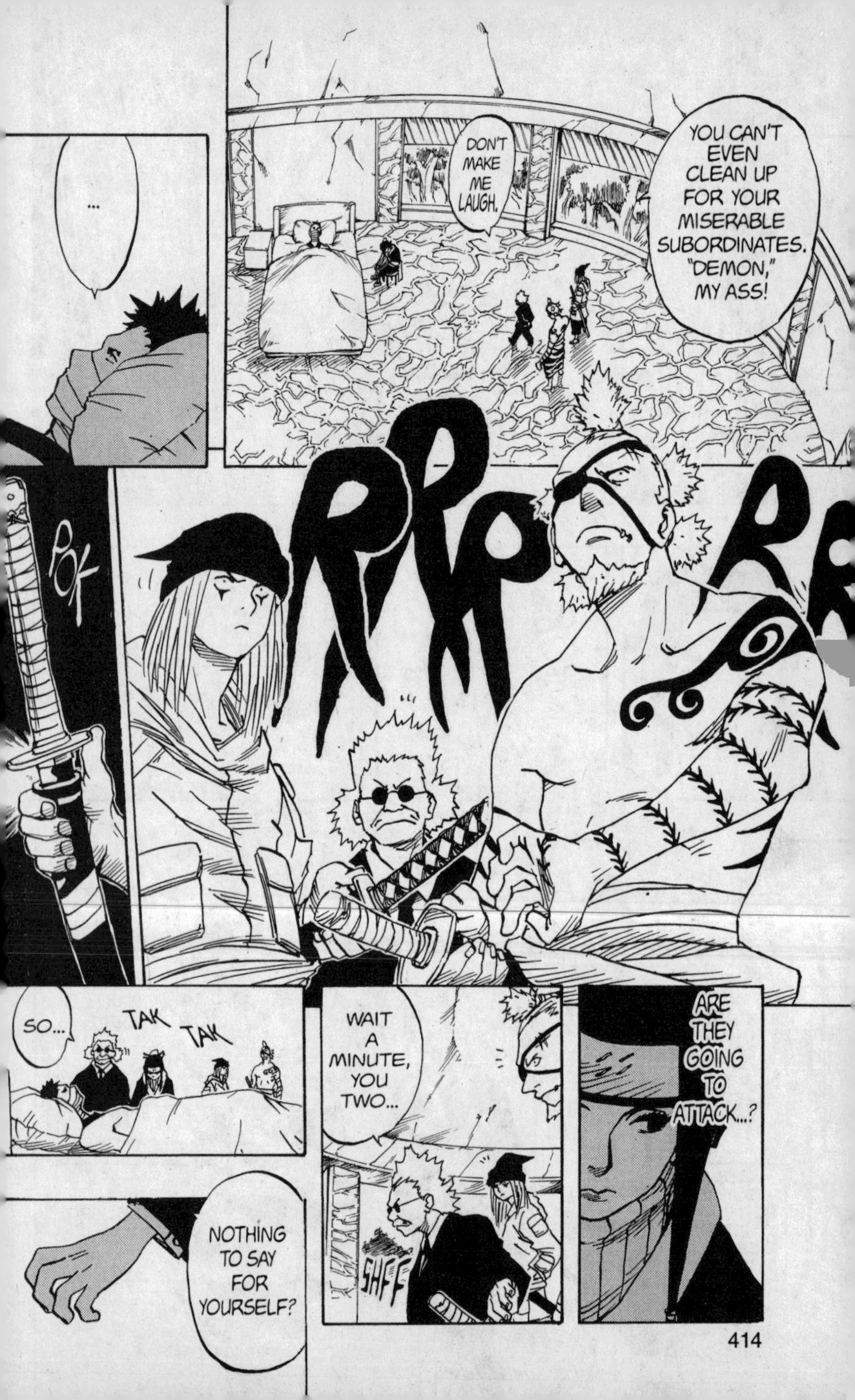
YOU CAN'T EVEN CLEAN UP FOR YOUR MISERABLE SUBORDINATES. "DEMON," MY ASS!
DON'T MAKE ME LAUGH.
...
RRR
POK
ARE THEY GOING TO ATTACK...?
WAIT A MINUTE, YOU TWO...
SHFF
SO...
TAK TAK
NOTHING TO SAY FOR YOURSELF?

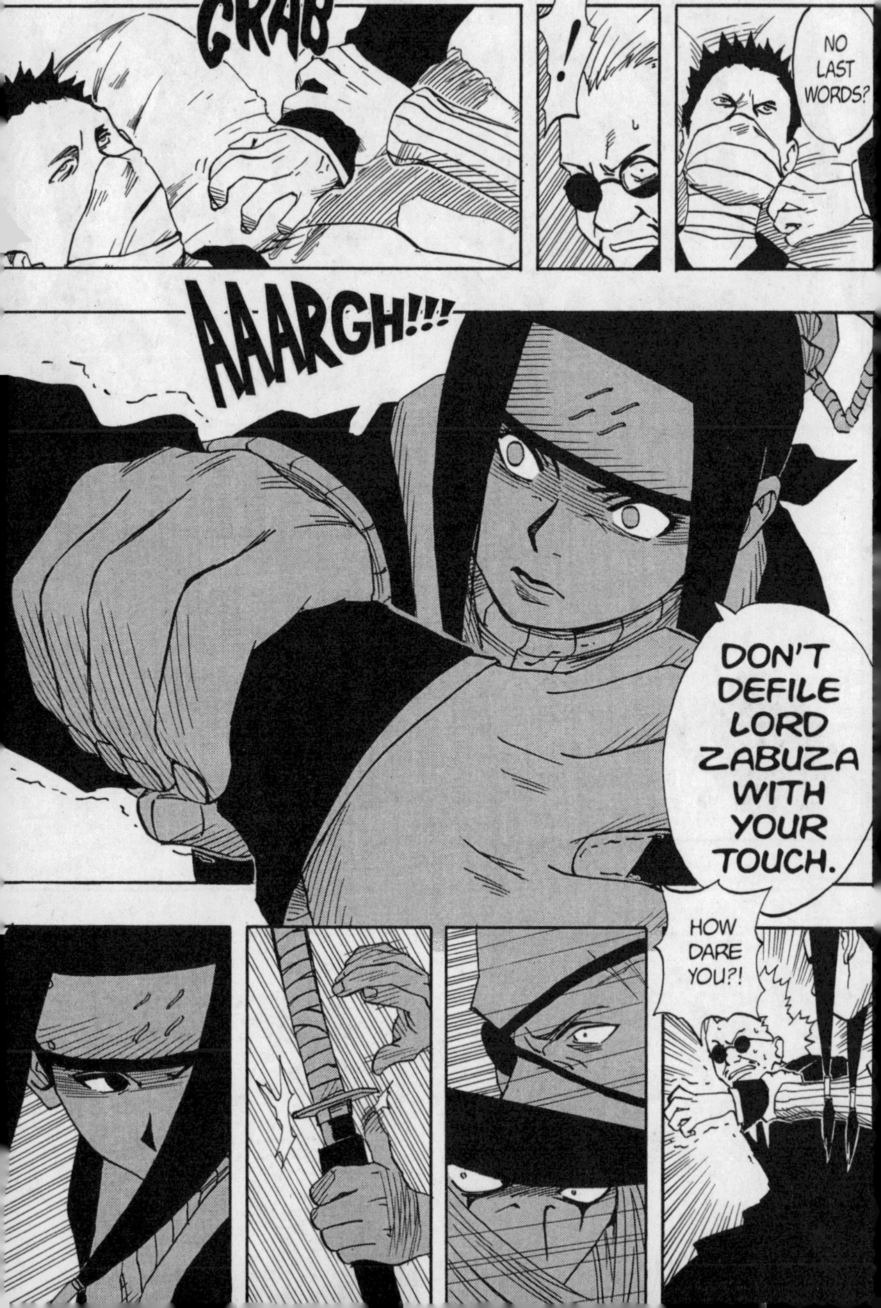
NO LAST WORDS?
!
GRAB
AAARGH!!!!
DON'T DEFILE LORD ZABUZA WITH YOUR TOUCH.
HOW DARE YOU?!

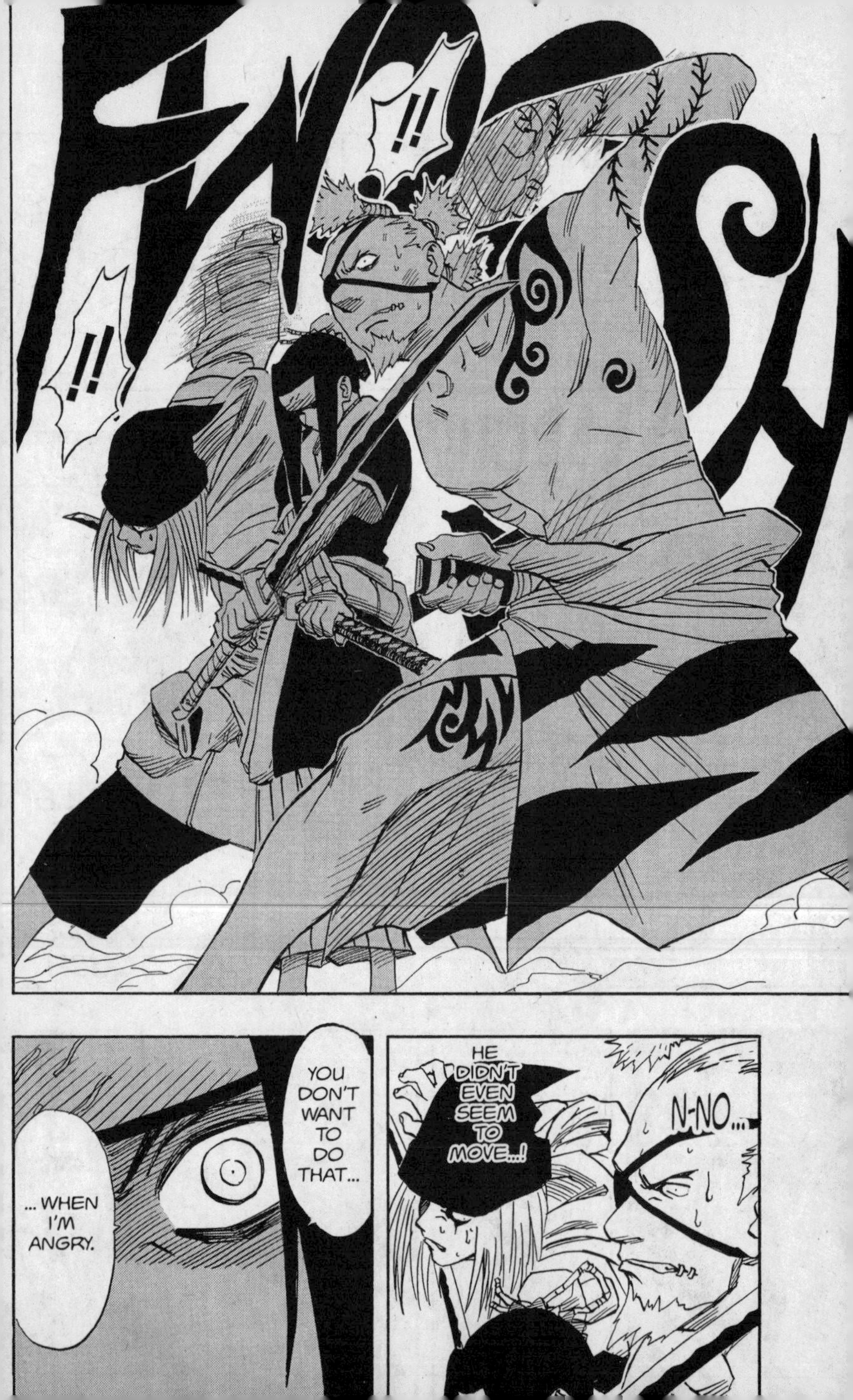
!!
!!
HE DIDN'T EVEN SEEM TO MOVE...!
N-NO...
YOU DON'T WANT TO DO THAT...
... WHEN I'M ANGRY.

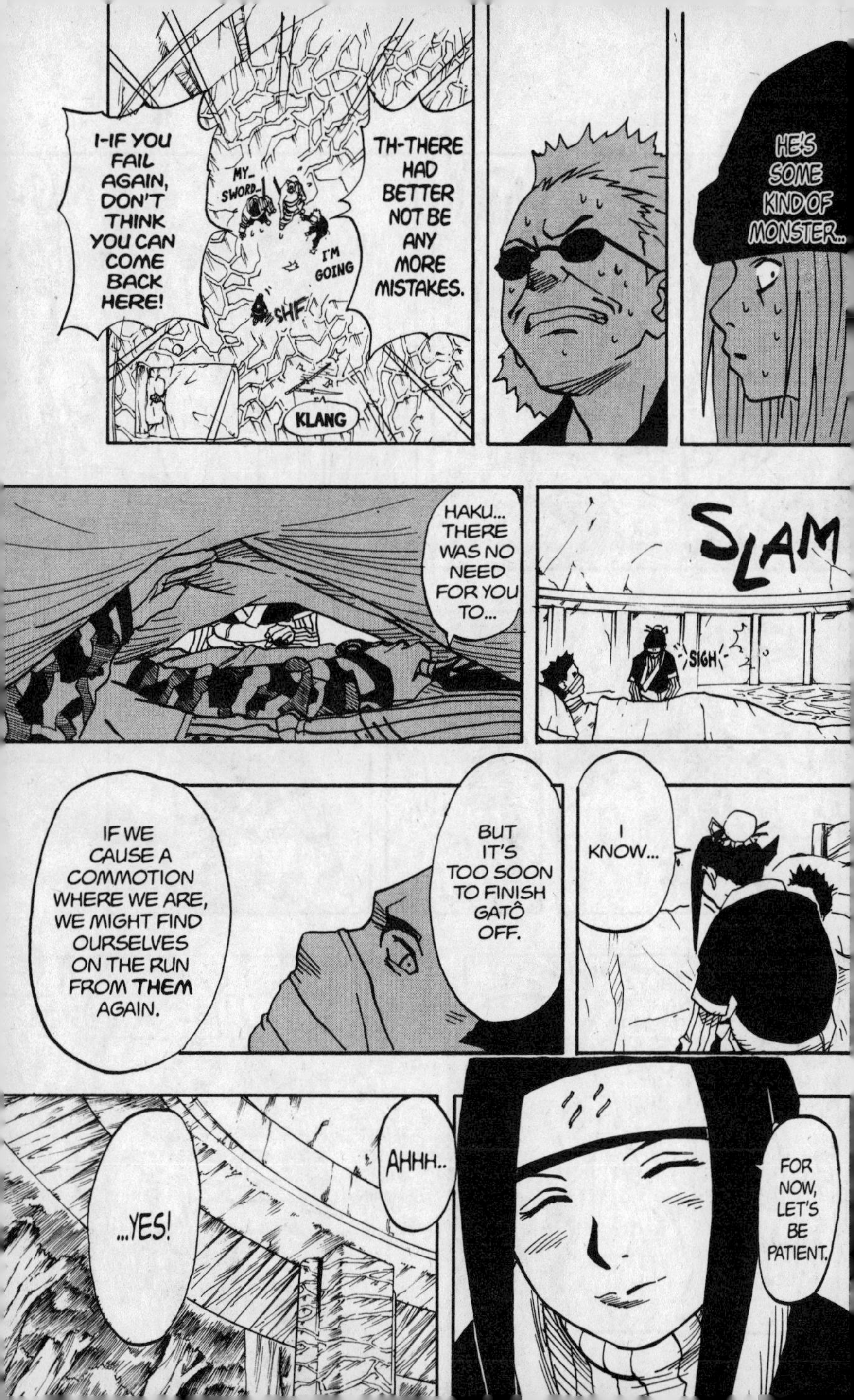
HE'S SOME KIND OF MONSTER...
TH-THERE HAD BETTER NOT BE ANY MORE MISTAKES.
I-IF YOU FAIL AGAIN, DON'T THINK YOU CAN COME BACK HERE!
MY... SWORD...
I'M GOING
SHF
KLANG
SLAM
SIGH
HAKU... THERE WAS NO NEED FOR YOU TO...
I KNOW...
BUT IT'S TOO SOON TO FINISH GATÔ OFF.
IF WE CAUSE A COMMOTION WHERE WE ARE, WE MIGHT FIND OURSELVES ON THE RUN FROM THEM AGAIN.
FOR NOW, LET'S BE PATIENT.
AHHH..
...YES!

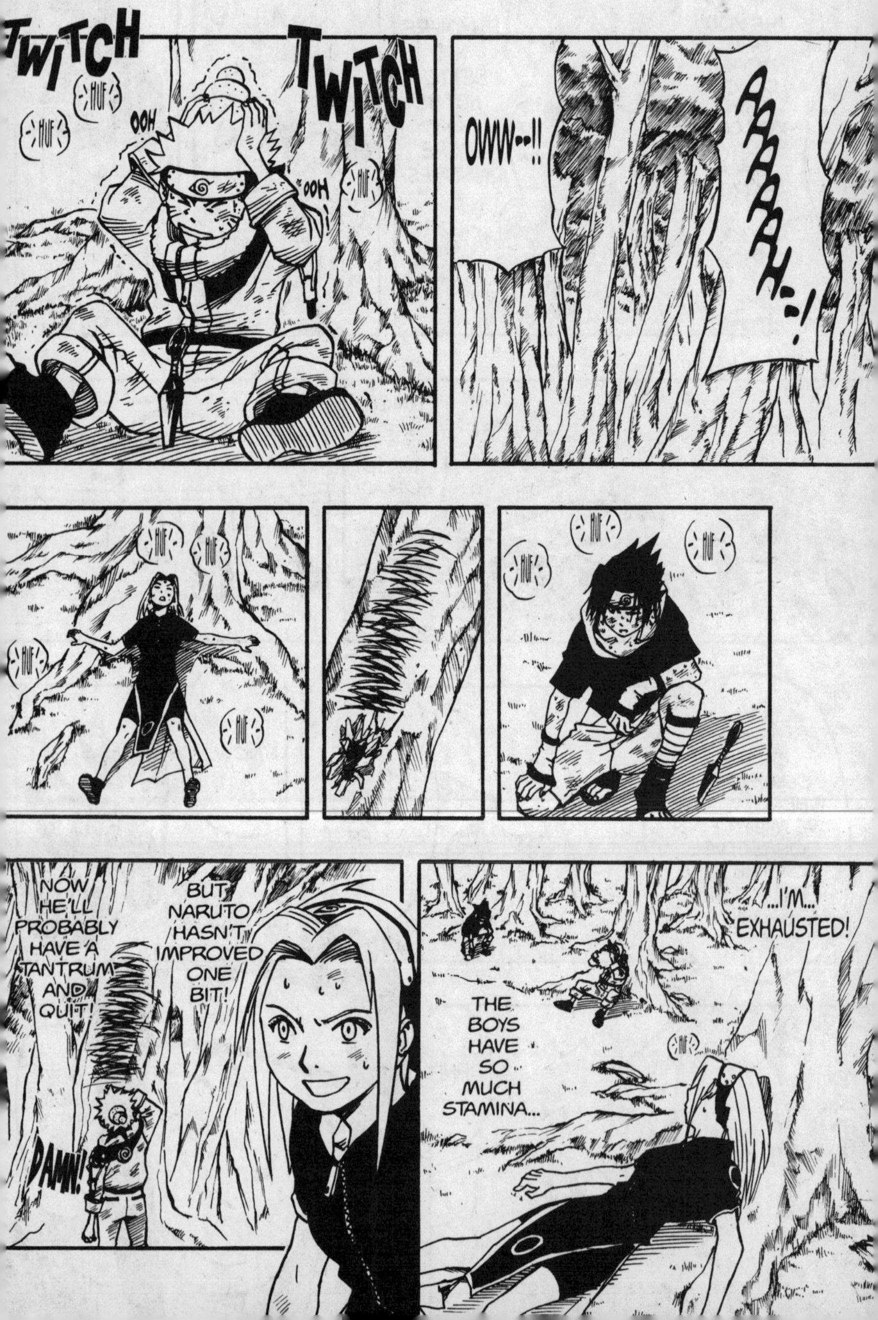
OWWW--!!
AAAAAH--!
TWITCH
TWITCH
HUF
HUF
OOH
OOH
HUF
HUF
HUF
HUF
HUF
HUF
HUF
HUF
...I'M... EXHAUSTED!
THE BOYS HAVE SO MUCH STAMINA...
HUF
BUT NARUTO HASN'T IMPROVED ONE BIT!
NOW HE'LL PROBABLY HAVE A TANTRUM AND QUIT!
DAMN!

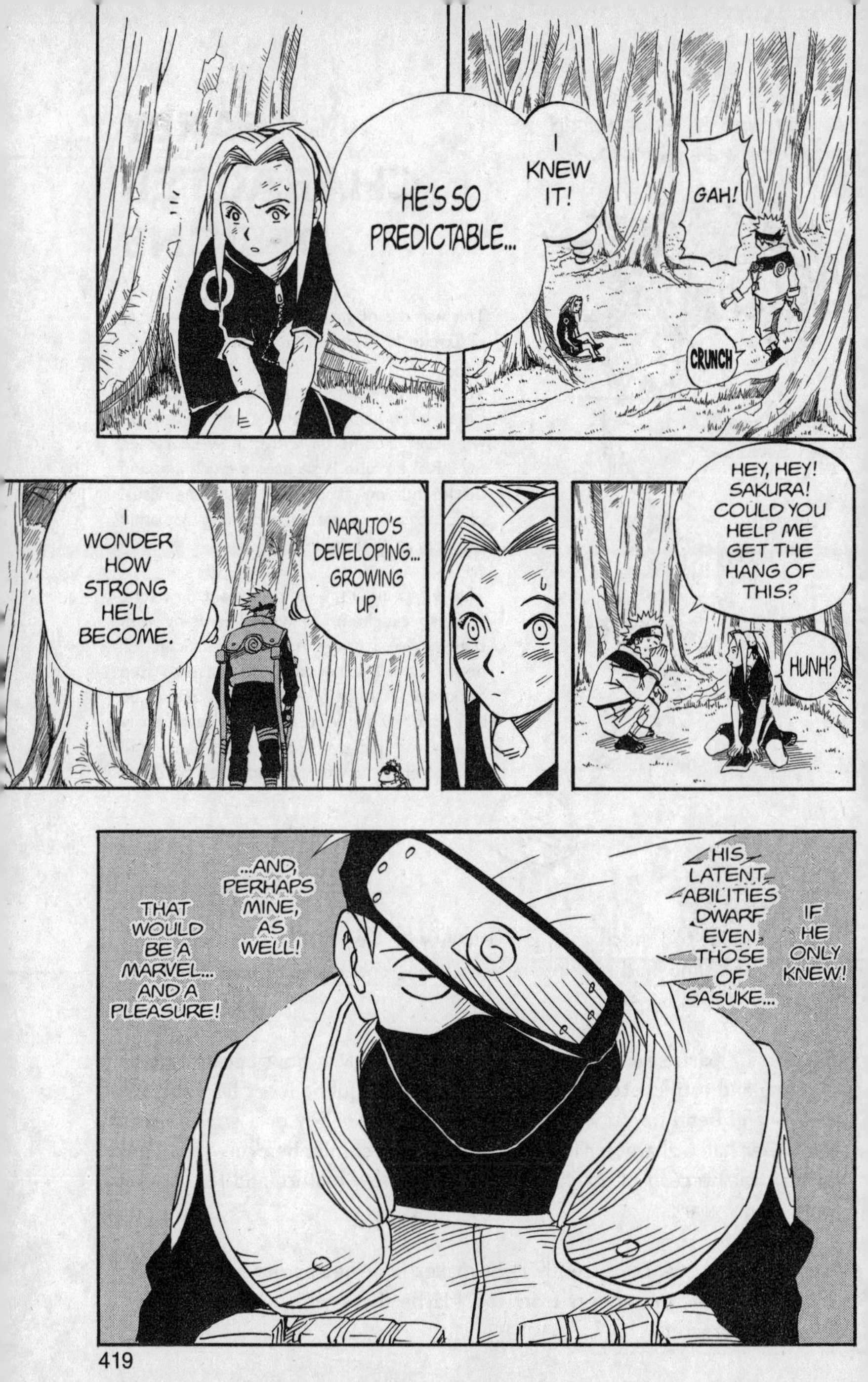
GAH!
CRUNCH
I KNEW IT!
HE'S SO PREDICTABLE...
HEY, HEY! SAKURA! COULD YOU HELP ME GET THE HANG OF THIS?
HUNH?
NARUTO'S DEVELOPING... GROWING UP.
I WONDER HOW STRONG HE'LL BECOME.
IF HE ONLY KNEW!
HIS LATENT ABILITIES DWARF EVEN THOSE OF SASUKE...
...AND, PERHAPS MINE, AS WELL!
THAT WOULD BE A MARVEL... AND A PLEASURE!

A boy who is as isolated and lonely as Naruto.

EARLY CHARACTER DESIGNS

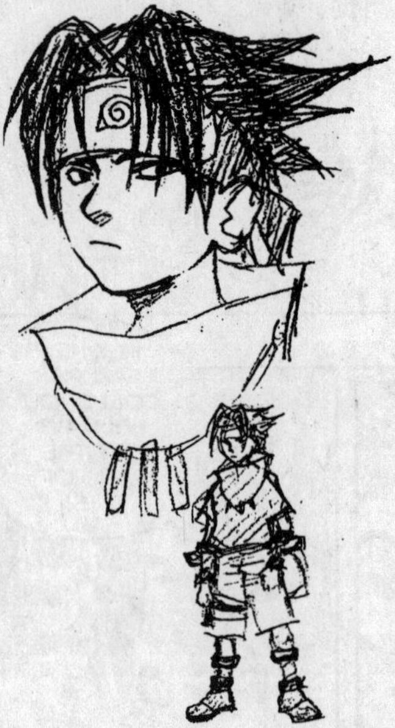

This was the original design for the character of Sasuke. It's hardly changed at all over time.

The main difference is the absence of the talisman he wore around his neck. In general, whenever I come up with a new character, my initial impulse is so use as much line and ornamentation as possible until the visual concept is in danger of becoming lost amid the busy, little details.

This is especially true of principal characters. I get so caught up in what I'm doing with them, I make things much too difficult for myself; until I finally have the sense to step back and ask myself, "Am I really going to be able to draw such a fussy, complicated character over and over, panel after panel, and issue after issue, week in and week out?"

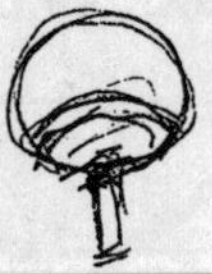

There was far too much going on visually with Sasuke, and too many lines overall, so I simplified him into a good, basic contrast to Naruto's visual image.

Sasuke is a particular challenge for me to draw even now, because he is a young and rather pretty boy, but if I'm not careful he loses his youthful quality and I end up drawing him like a much older boy or a grown man. I've never had a character like him in one of my comics before—that kind of boy on the cusp of manhood, who's somehow mature and handsome beyond his years.

Keeping the visual consistently right makes him the character who takes the most work and energy from me. Maybe that's why he's become my favorite character.

Number 19: The Emblem of Courage

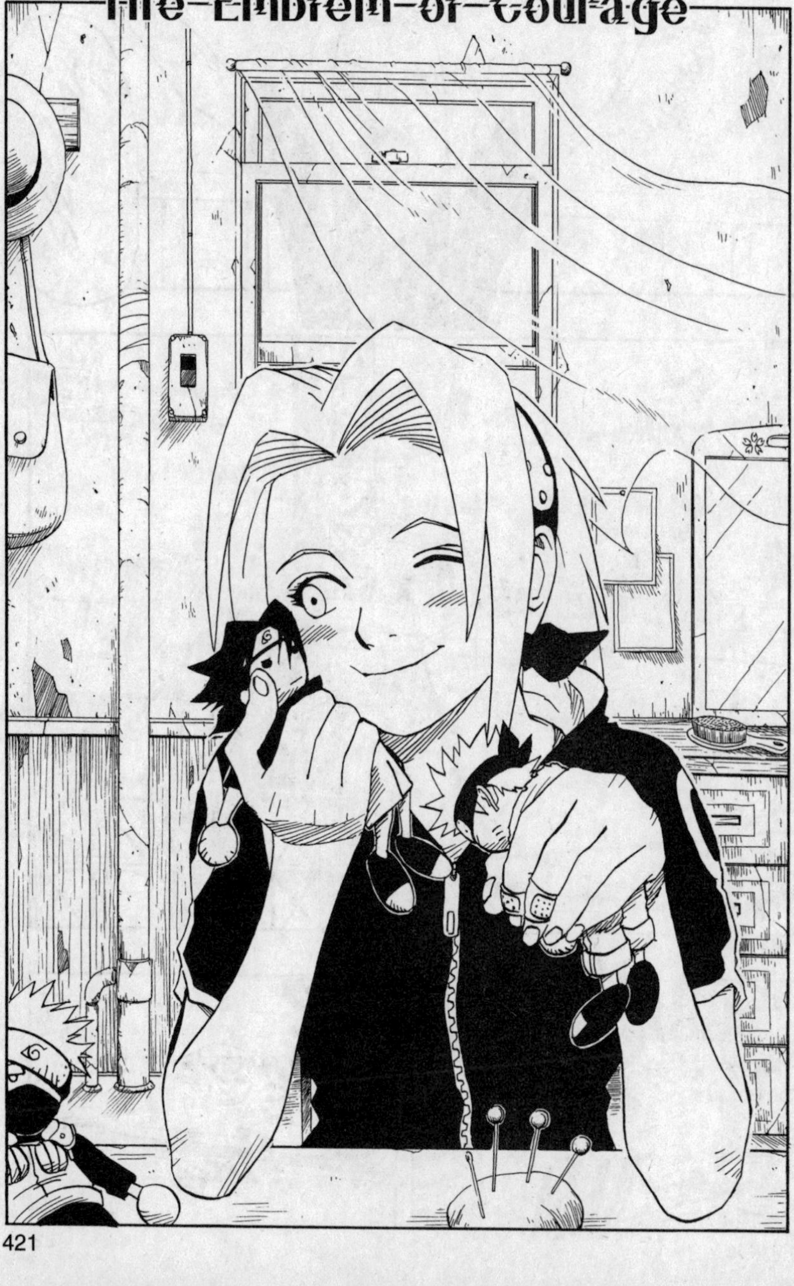

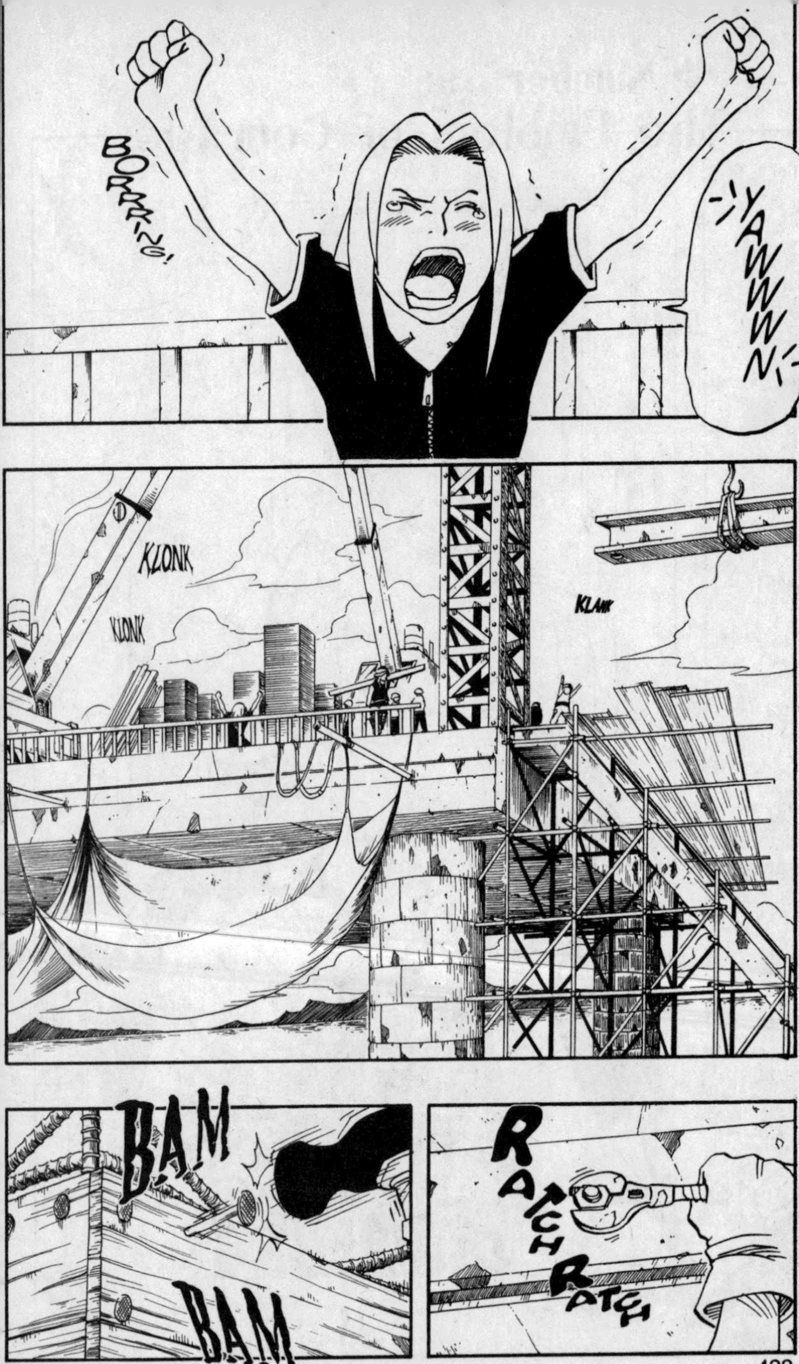
YAWWWN
BORRRING!
KLANK
KLONK
KLONK
RATCH RATCH
BAM
BAM

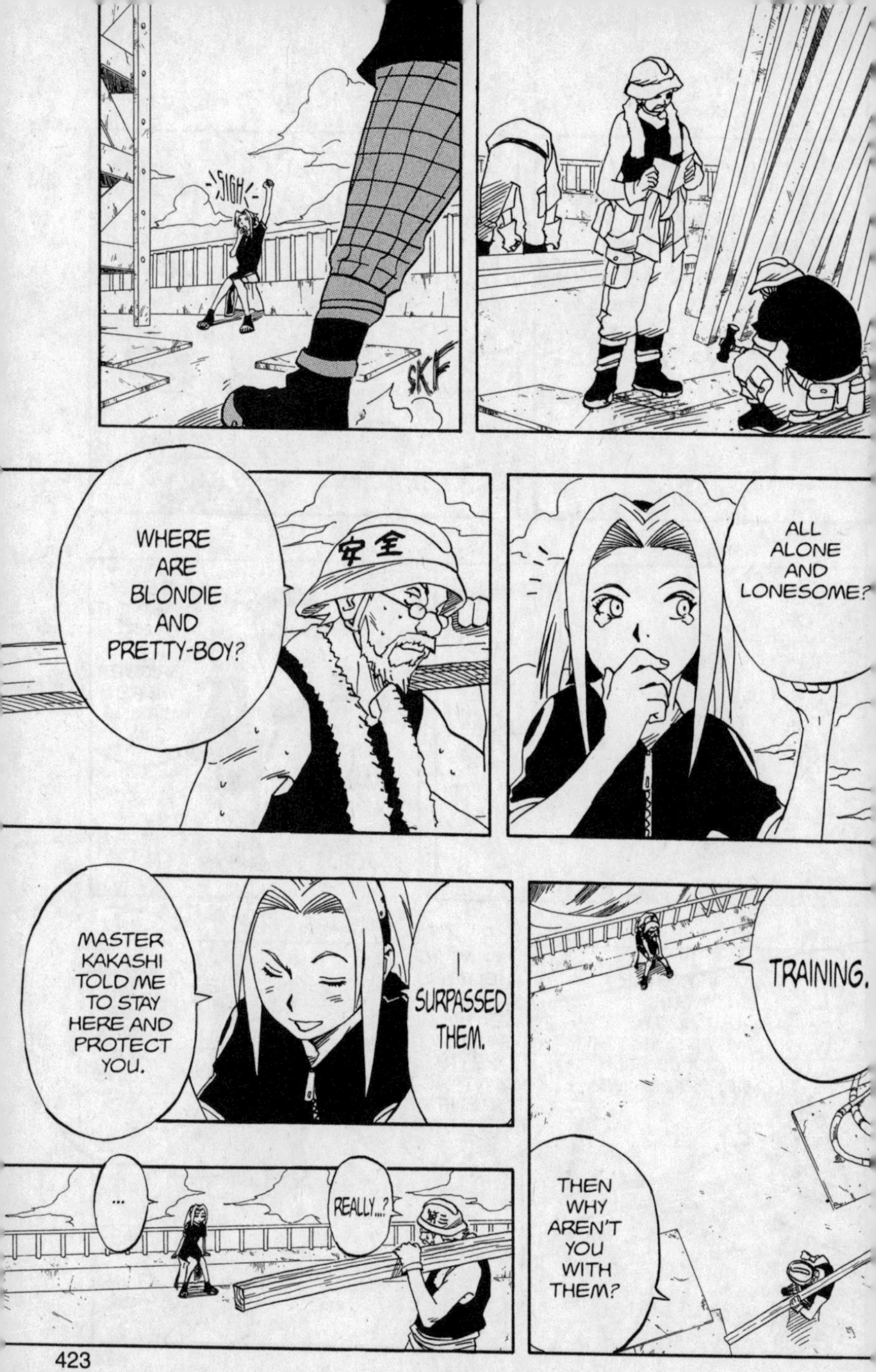
SIGH
SKF
ALL ALONE AND LONESOME?
WHERE ARE BLONDIE AND PRETTY-BOY?
安全
TRAINING.
THEN WHY AREN'T YOU WITH THEM?
I SURPASSED THEM.
MASTER KAKASHI TOLD ME TO STAY HERE AND PROTECT YOU.
REALLY...?
...

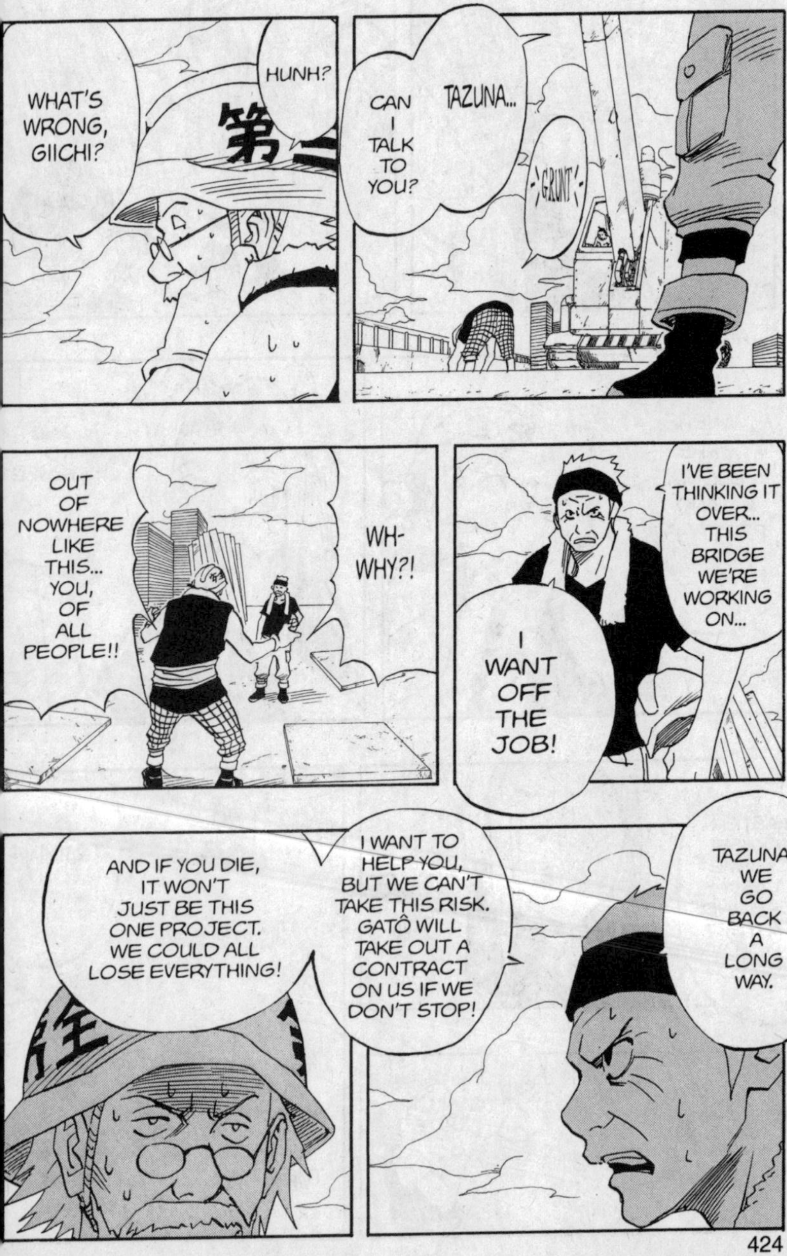
TAZUNA...
CAN I TALK TO YOU?
GRUNT
HUNH?
WHAT'S WRONG, GIICHI?
I'VE BEEN THINKING IT OVER... THIS BRIDGE WE'RE WORKING ON...
I WANT OFF THE JOB!
WH-WHY?!
OUT OF NOWHERE LIKE THIS... YOU, OF ALL PEOPLE!!
TAZUNA! WE GO BACK A LONG WAY.
I WANT TO HELP YOU, BUT WE CAN'T TAKE THIS RISK. GATÔ WILL TAKE OUT A CONTRACT ON US IF WE DON'T STOP!
AND IF YOU DIE, IT WON'T JUST BE THIS ONE PROJECT. WE COULD ALL LOSE EVERYTHING!

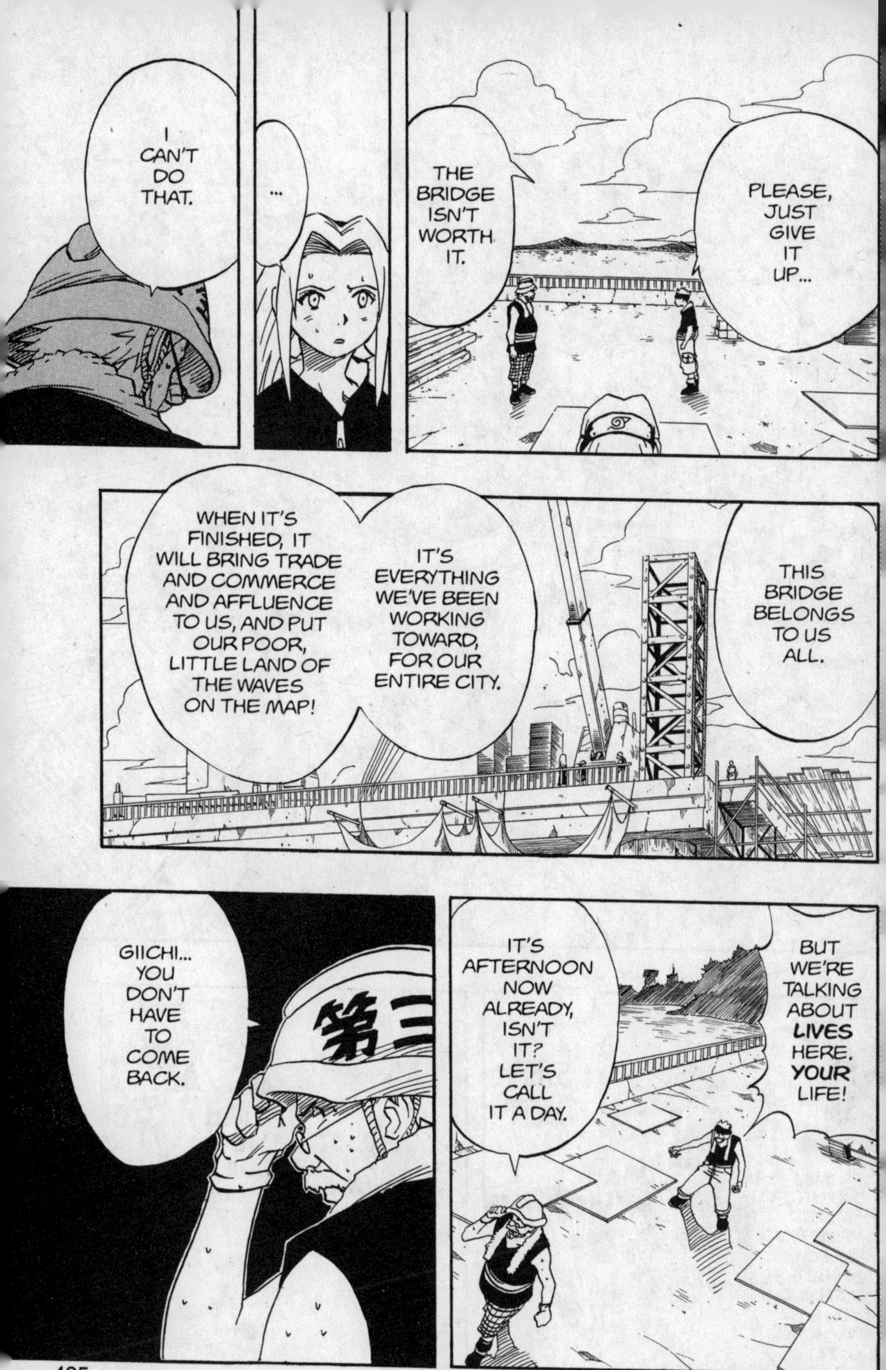
PLEASE, JUST GIVE IT UP...
THE BRIDGE ISN'T WORTH IT.
...
I CAN'T DO THAT.
THIS BRIDGE BELONGS TO US ALL.
IT'S EVERYTHING WE'VE BEEN WORKING TOWARD, FOR OUR ENTIRE CITY.
WHEN IT'S FINISHED, IT WILL BRING TRADE AND COMMERCE AND AFFLUENCE TO US, AND PUT OUR POOR, LITTLE LAND OF THE WAVES ON THE MAP!
BUT WE'RE TALKING ABOUT **LIVES** HERE. **YOUR** LIFE!
IT'S AFTERNOON NOW ALREADY, ISN'T IT? LET'S CALL IT A DAY.
GIICHI... YOU DON'T HAVE TO COME BACK.
第三

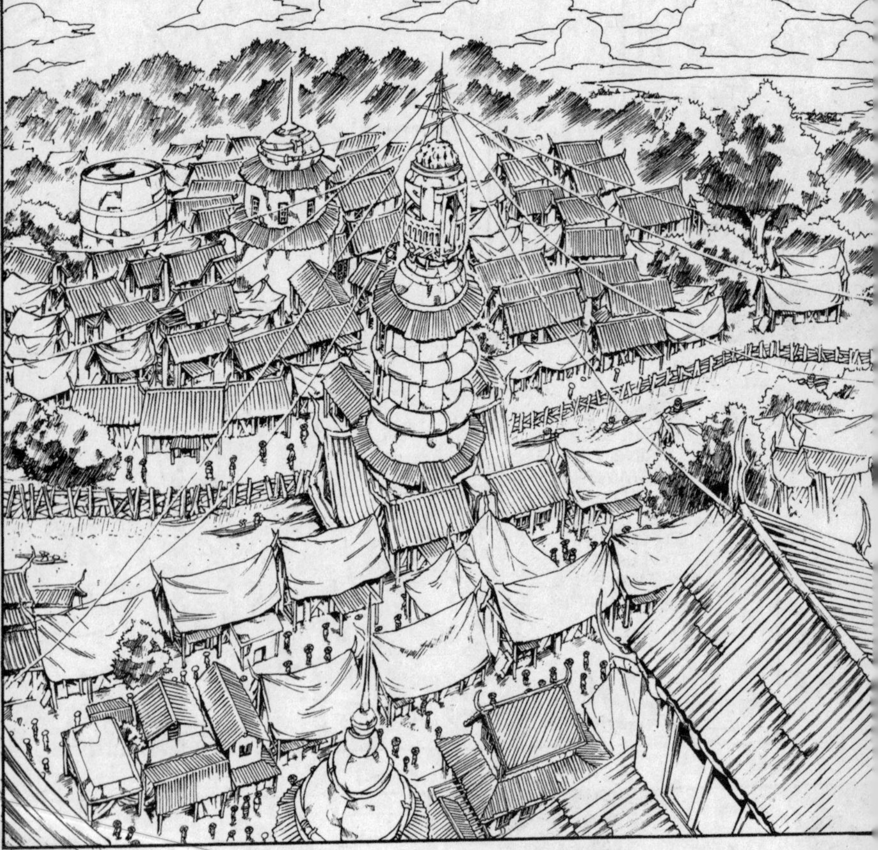

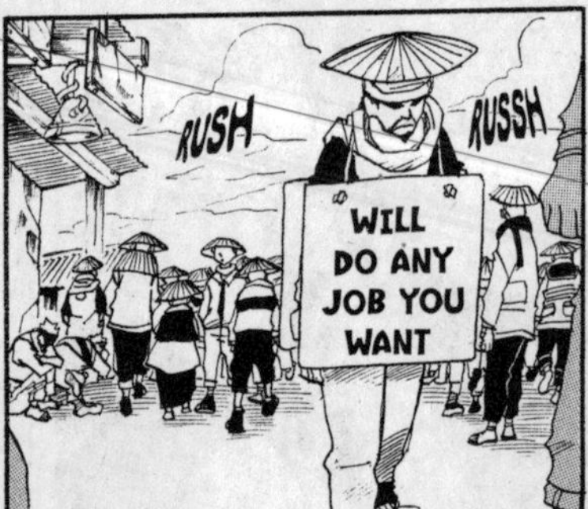
RUSSH
RUSH
WILL DO ANY JOB YOU WANT

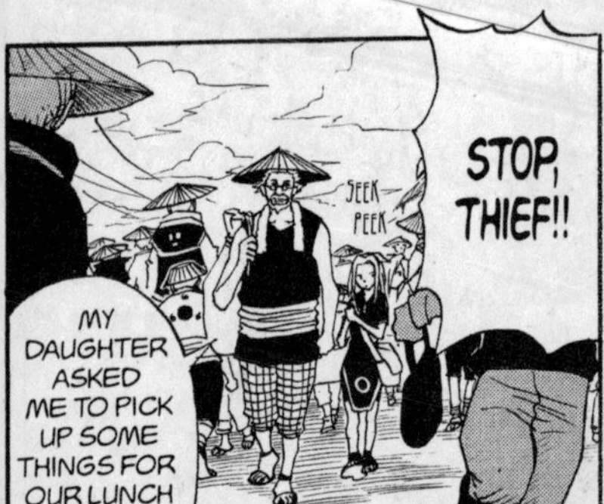
STOP, THIEF!!
SEEK PEEK
MY DAUGHTER ASKED ME TO PICK UP SOME THINGS FOR OUR LUNCH ON THE WAY HOME, SO...

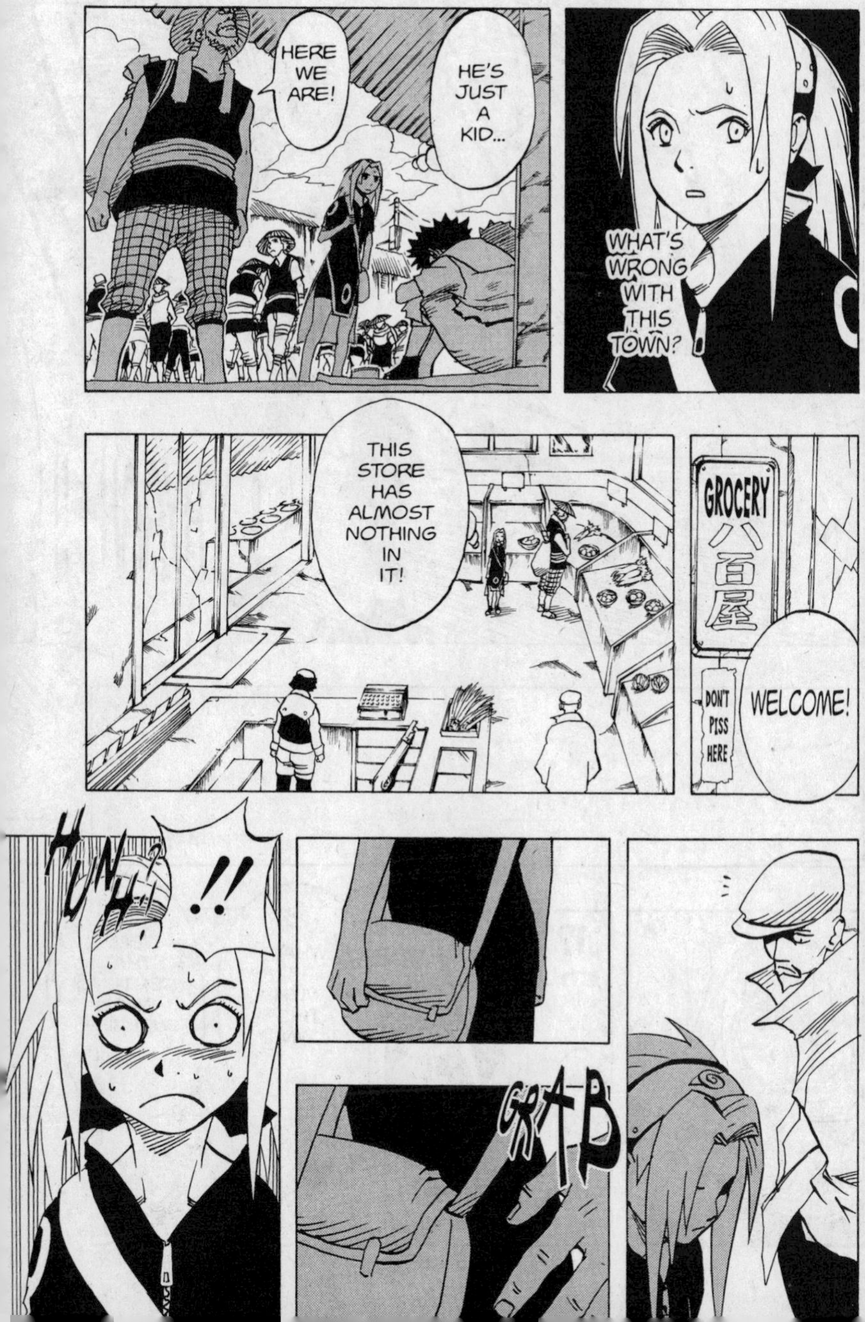
WHAT'S WRONG WITH THIS TOWN?
HE'S JUST A KID...
HERE WE ARE!
GROCERY
八百屋
DON'T PISS HERE
WELCOME!
THIS STORE HAS ALMOST NOTHING IN IT!
GRAB
HUH?!
!!

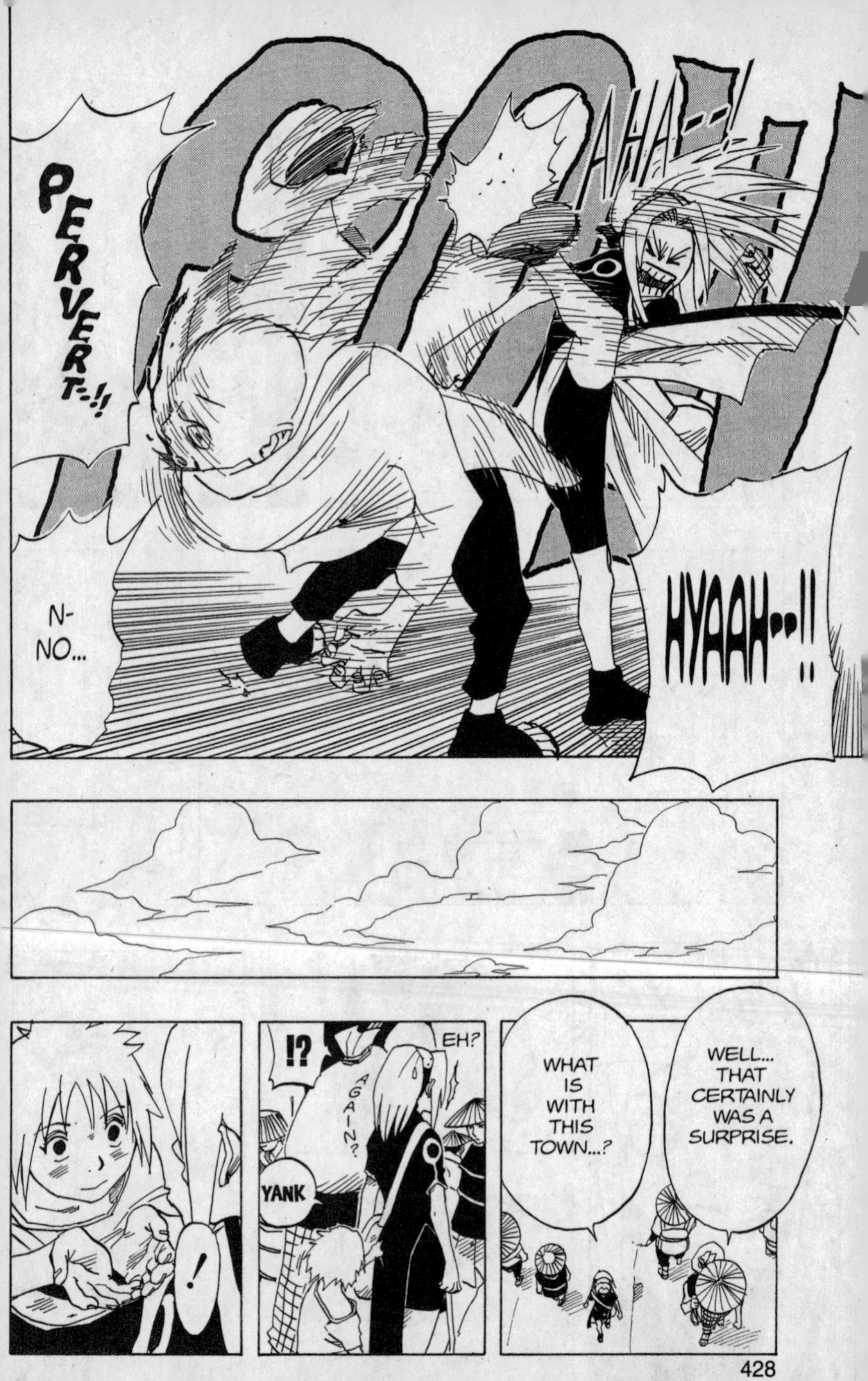
HYAAH--!!
PERVERT--!!
N-NO...
WELL... THAT CERTAINLY WAS A SURPRISE.
WHAT IS WITH THIS TOWN...?
EH?
!?
AGAIN?
YANK
!

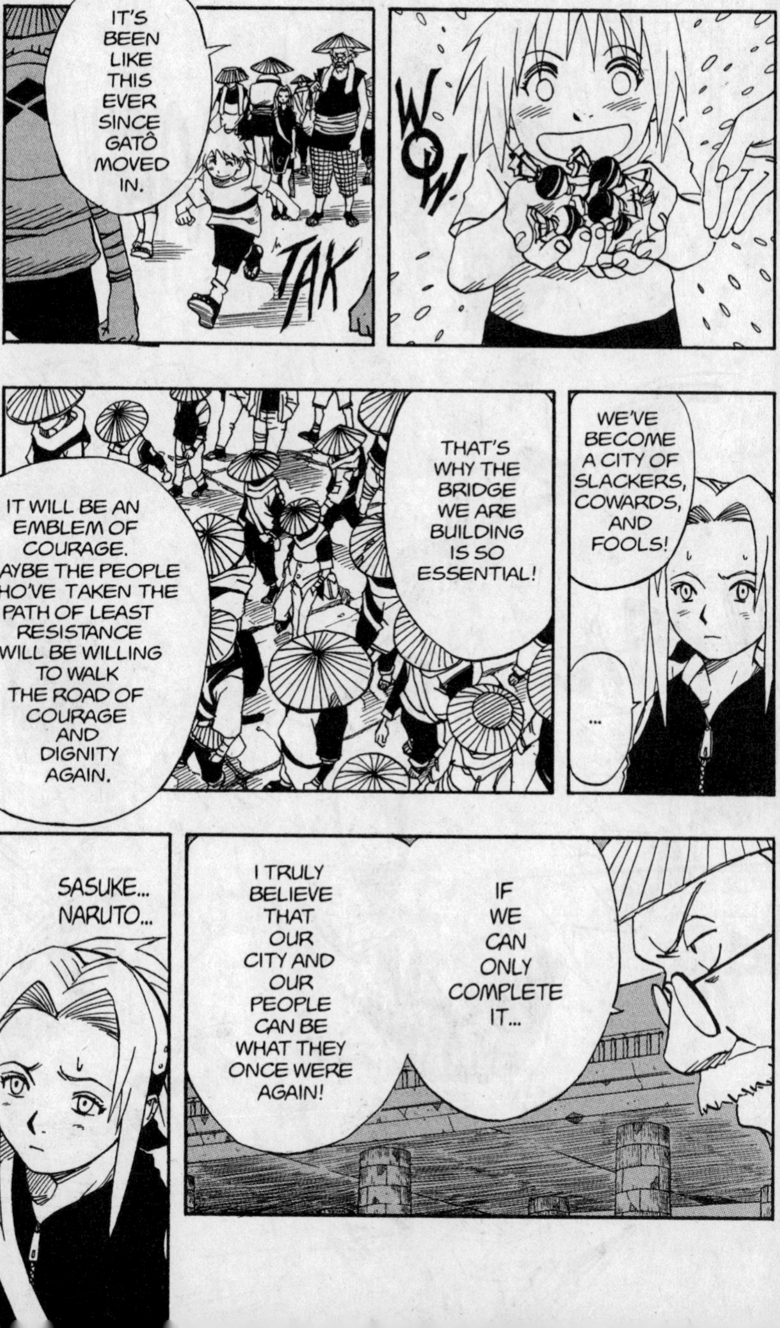
WOW
IT'S BEEN LIKE THIS EVER SINCE GATÔ MOVED IN.
TAK
WE'VE BECOME A CITY OF SLACKERS, COWARDS, AND FOOLS!
...
THAT'S WHY THE BRIDGE WE ARE BUILDING IS SO ESSENTIAL!
IT WILL BE AN EMBLEM OF COURAGE. MAYBE THE PEOPLE WHO'VE TAKEN THE PATH OF LEAST RESISTANCE WILL BE WILLING TO WALK THE ROAD OF COURAGE AND DIGNITY AGAIN.
IF WE CAN ONLY COMPLETE IT...
I TRULY BELIEVE THAT OUR CITY AND OUR PEOPLE CAN BE WHAT THEY ONCE WERE AGAIN!
SASUKE... NARUTO...

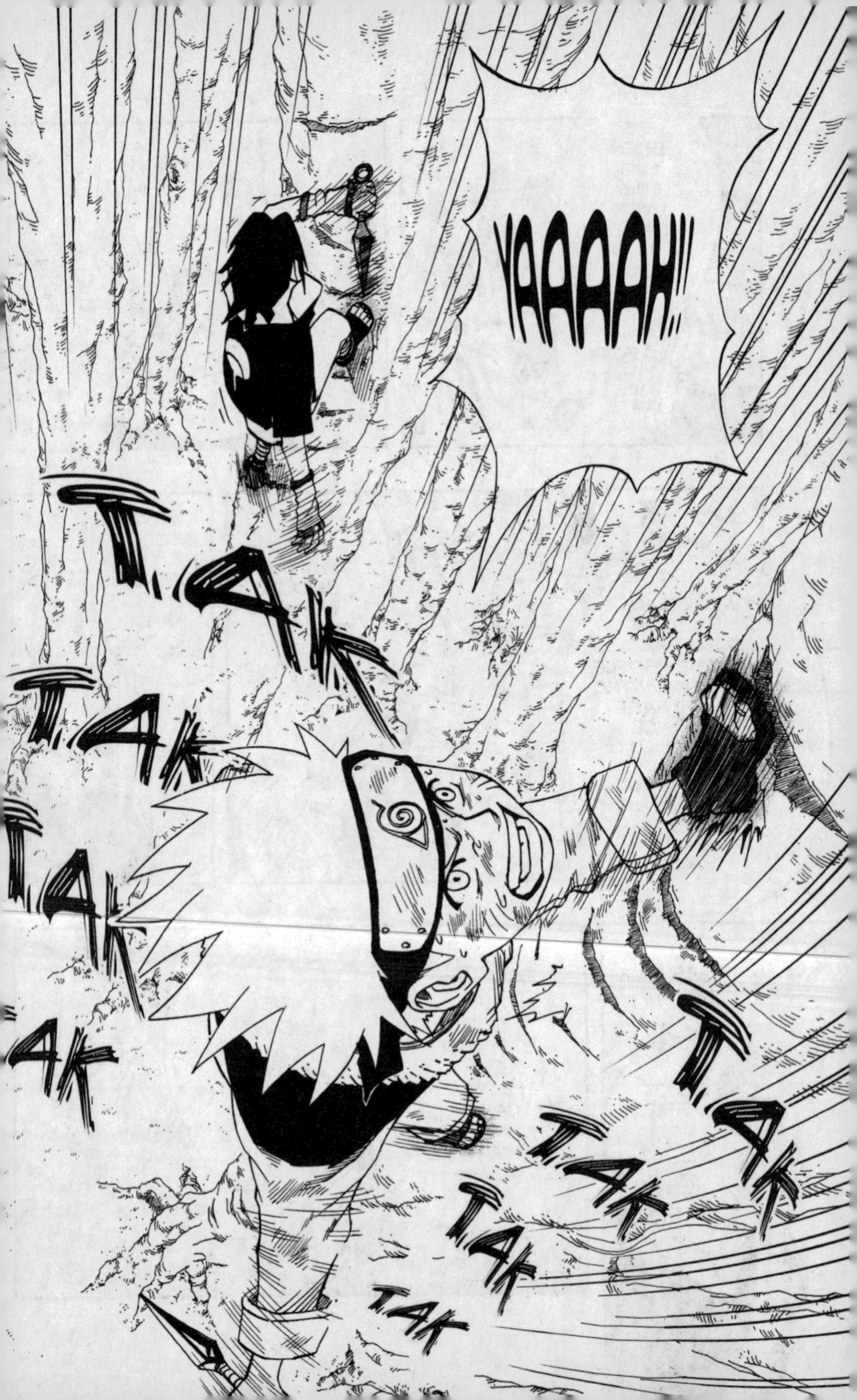
YAAAAH!!
TAK
TAK
TAK
TAK
TAK
AK
TAK
TAK
TAK

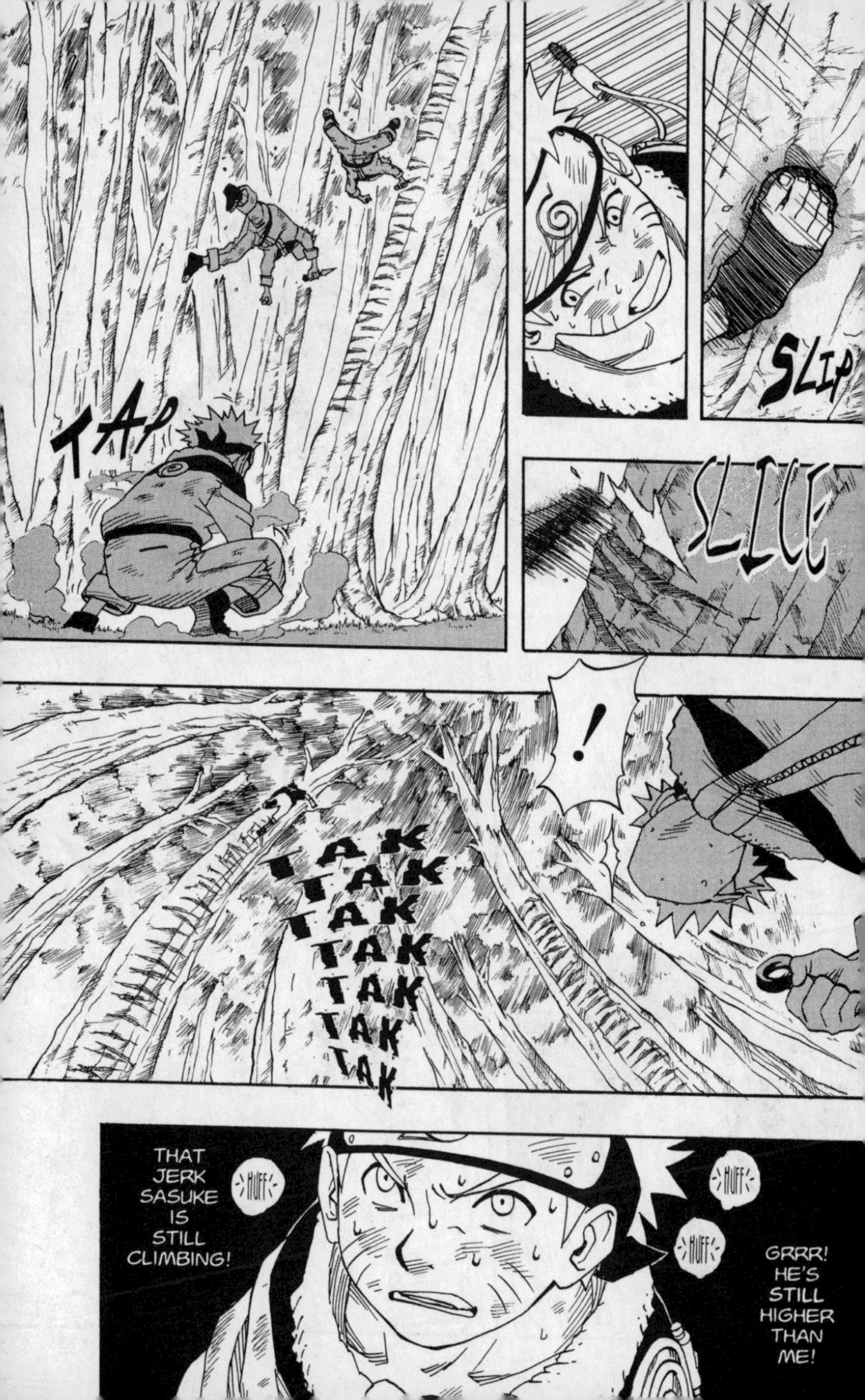

SLIP
TAP
SLICE
!
TAK TAK TAK TAK TAK TAK TAK
HUFF
HUFF
GRRR! HE'S STILL HIGHER THAN ME!
HUFF
THAT JERK SASUKE IS STILL CLIMBING!

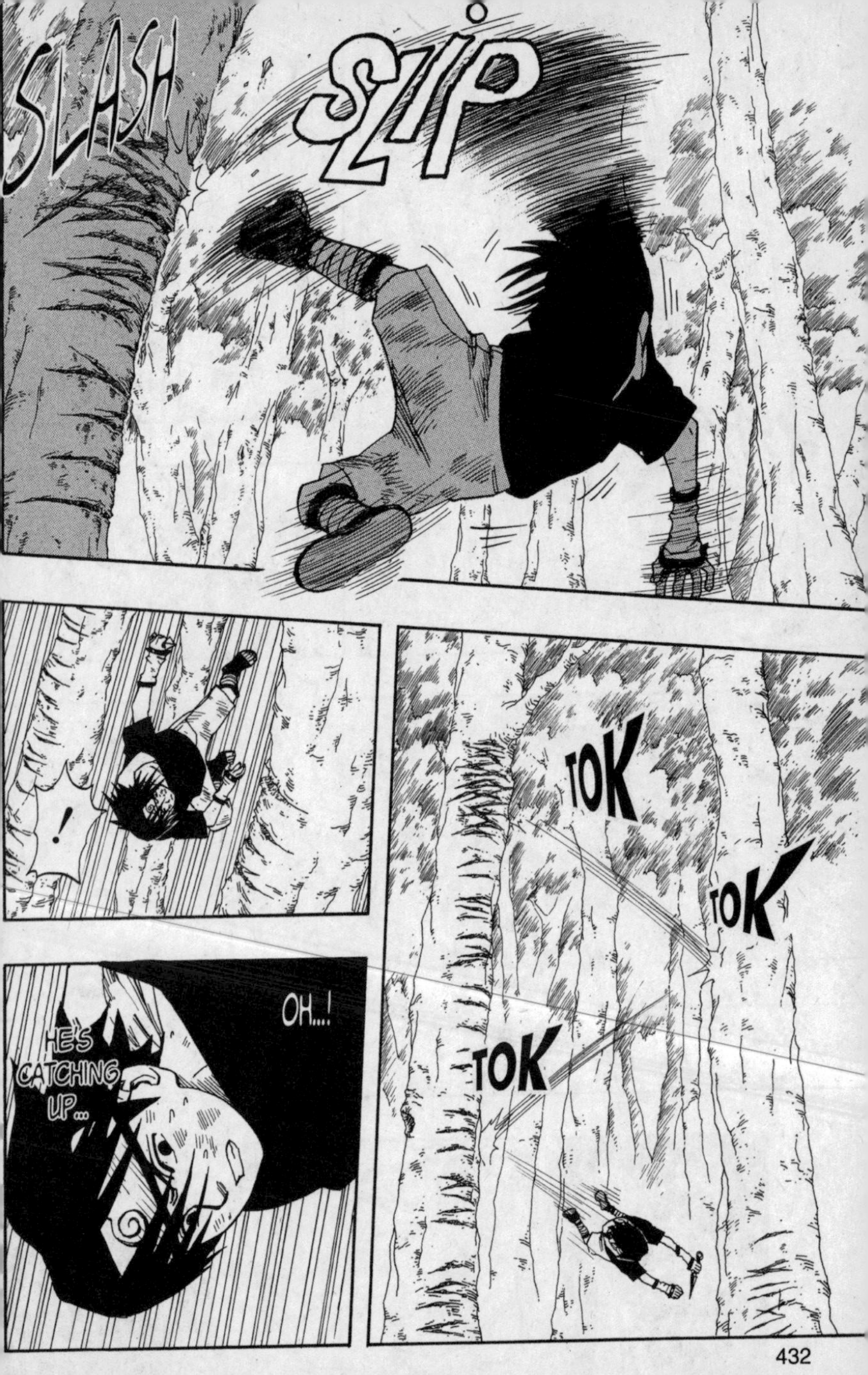
SLIP
SLASH
TOK
TOK
TOK
!
OH...!
HE'S CATCHING UP...

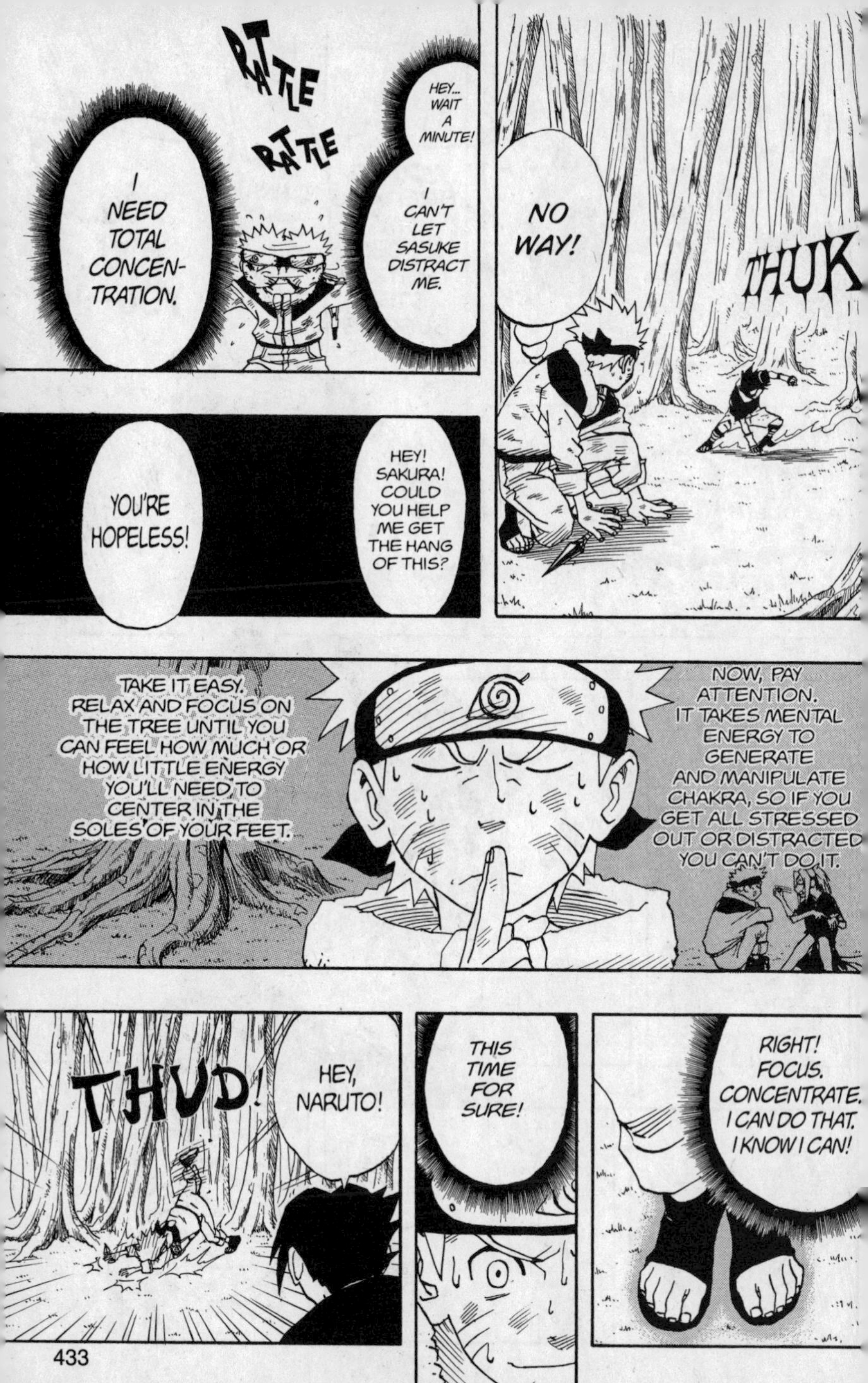
NO WAY!
THUK
HEY... WAIT A MINUTE!
I CAN'T LET SASUKE DISTRACT ME.
RATTLE
RATTLE
I NEED TOTAL CONCENTRATION.
HEY! SAKURA! COULD YOU HELP ME GET THE HANG OF THIS?
YOU'RE HOPELESS!
NOW, PAY ATTENTION. IT TAKES MENTAL ENERGY TO GENERATE AND MANIPULATE CHAKRA, SO IF YOU GET ALL STRESSED OUT OR DISTRACTED YOU CAN'T DO IT.
TAKE IT EASY. RELAX AND FOCUS ON THE TREE UNTIL YOU CAN FEEL HOW MUCH OR HOW LITTLE ENERGY YOU'LL NEED TO CENTER IN THE SOLES OF YOUR FEET.
RIGHT! FOCUS. CONCENTRATE. I CAN DO THAT. I KNOW I CAN!
THIS TIME FOR SURE!
HEY, NARUTO!
THUD!

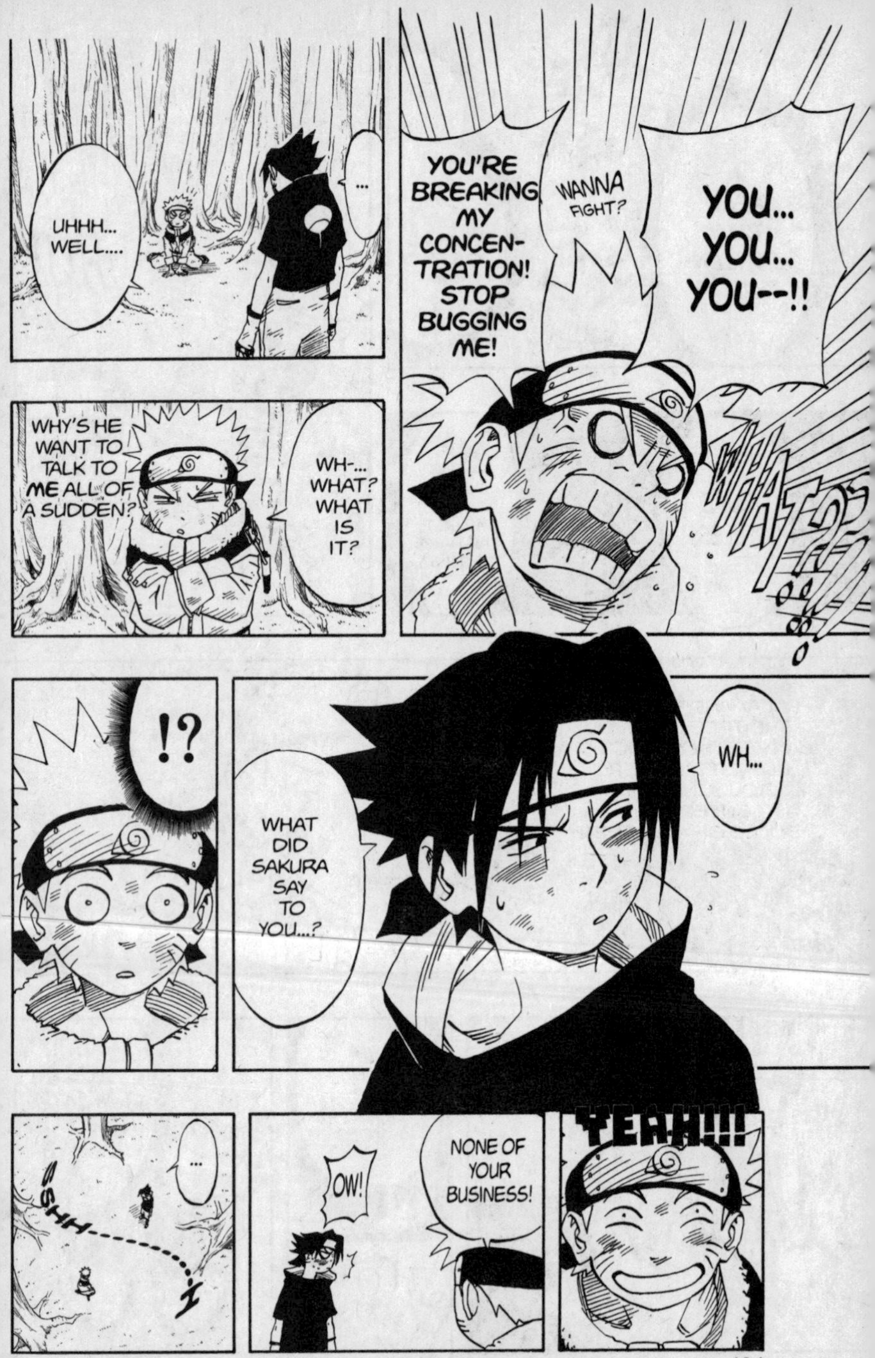
YOU... YOU... YOU--!!
WANNA FIGHT?
YOU'RE BREAKING MY CONCENTRATION! STOP BUGGING ME!
WHAAAT??
...
UHHH... WELL....
WH-... WHAT? WHAT IS IT?
WHY'S HE WANT TO TALK TO ME ALL OF A SUDDEN?
WH...
WHAT DID SAKURA SAY TO YOU...?
!?
YEAH!!!!
NONE OF YOUR BUSINESS!
OW!
...
SSHH

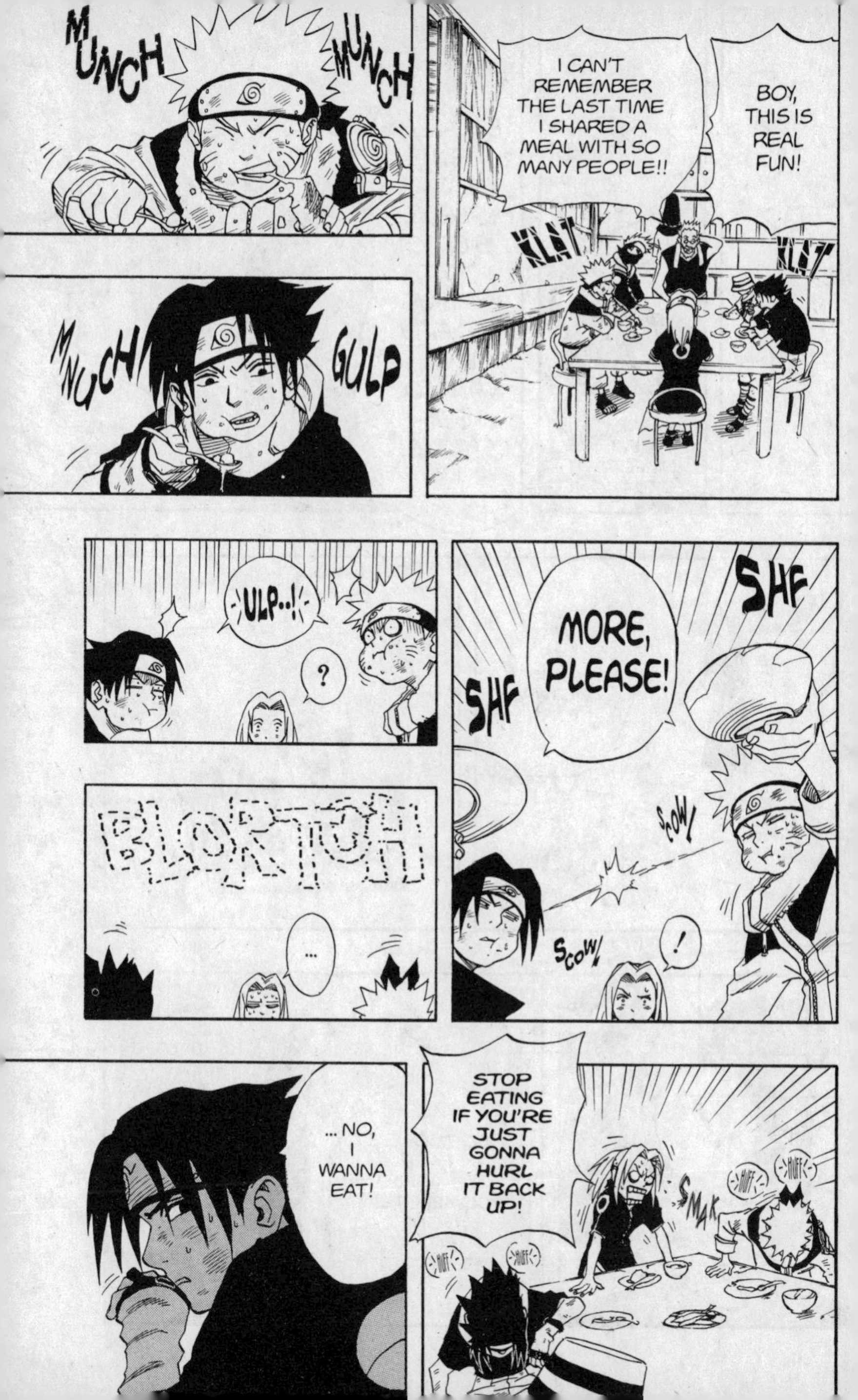
BOY, THIS IS REAL FUN!
I CAN'T REMEMBER THE LAST TIME I SHARED A MEAL WITH SO MANY PEOPLE!!
KLAT
KLAT
MUNCH
MUNCH
MNUCH
GULP
SHF
MORE, PLEASE!
SHF
SCOW!
!
SCOW!
-ULP..!-
?
BLORTCH
...
STOP EATING IF YOU'RE JUST GONNA HURL IT BACK UP!
SMAK
HUFF
HUFF
HUFF
HUFF
... NO, I WANNA EAT!

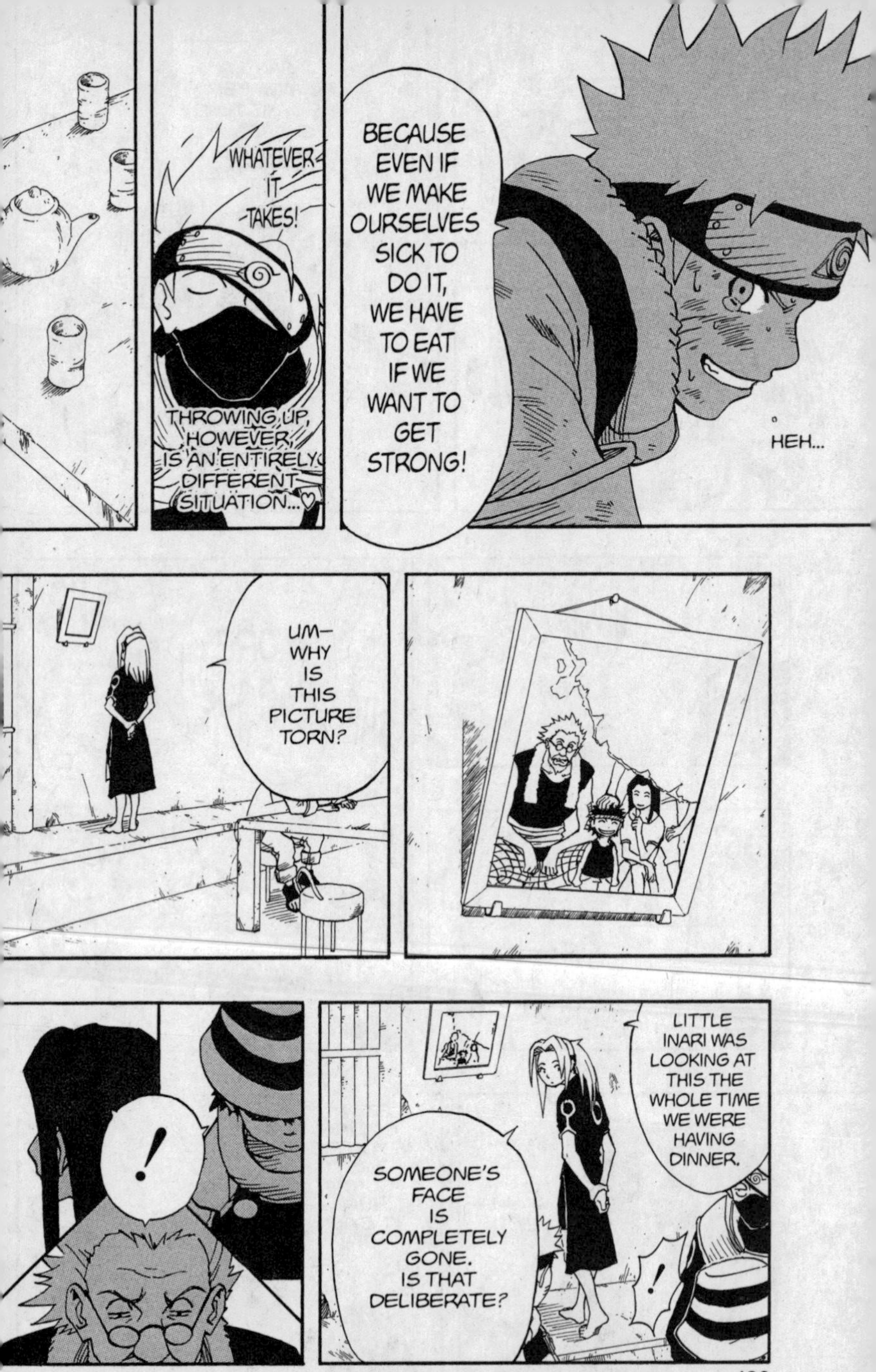
HEH...
BECAUSE EVEN IF WE MAKE OURSELVES SICK TO DO IT, WE HAVE TO EAT IF WE WANT TO GET STRONG!
WHATEVER IT TAKES!
THROWING UP, HOWEVER, IS AN ENTIRELY DIFFERENT SITUATION...♡
UM—WHY IS THIS PICTURE TORN?
LITTLE INARI WAS LOOKING AT THIS THE WHOLE TIME WE WERE HAVING DINNER.
SOMEONE'S FACE IS COMPLETELY GONE. IS THAT DELIBERATE?
!
!

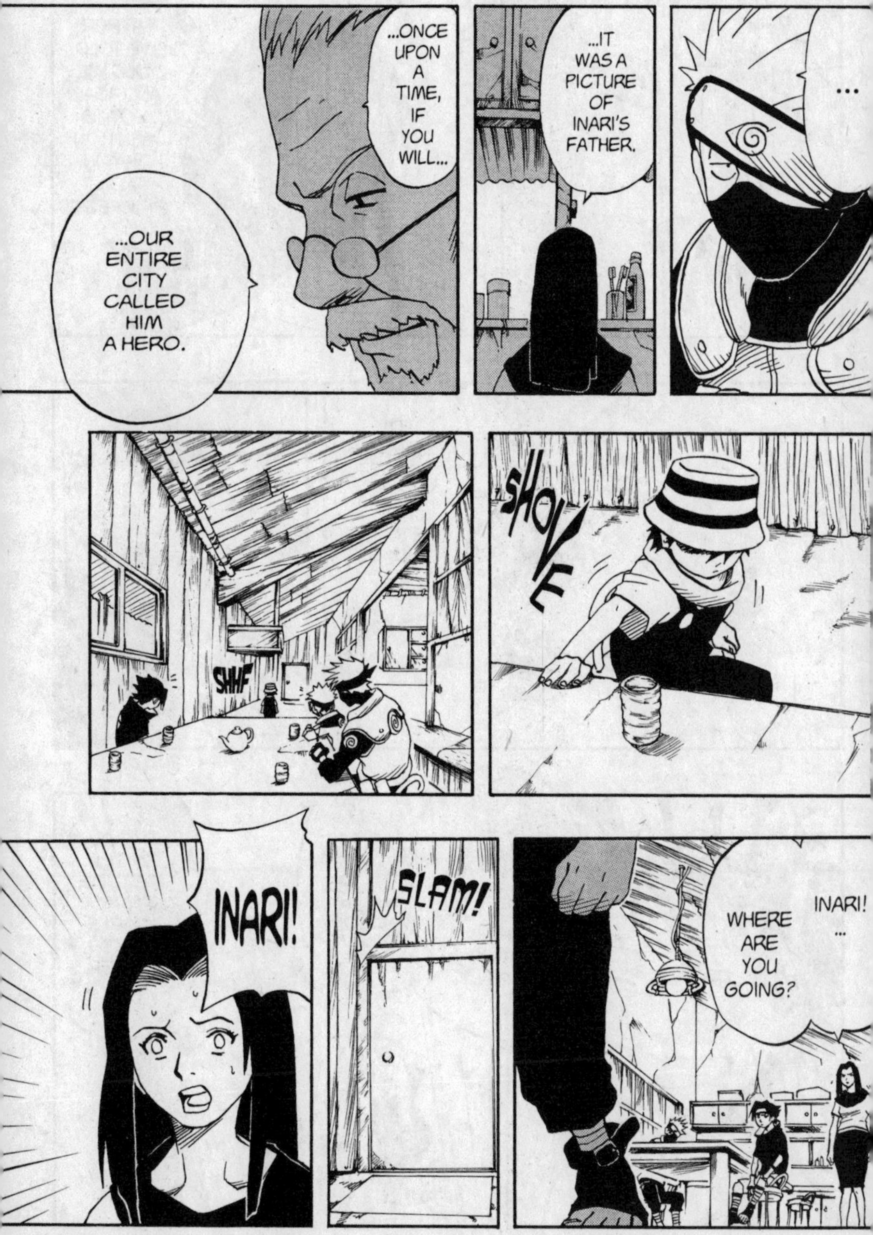
...
...IT WAS A PICTURE OF INARI'S FATHER.
...ONCE UPON A TIME, IF YOU WILL...
...OUR ENTIRE CITY CALLED HIM A HERO.
SHOVE
SHHF
INARI! ...
WHERE ARE YOU GOING?
SLAM!
INARI!

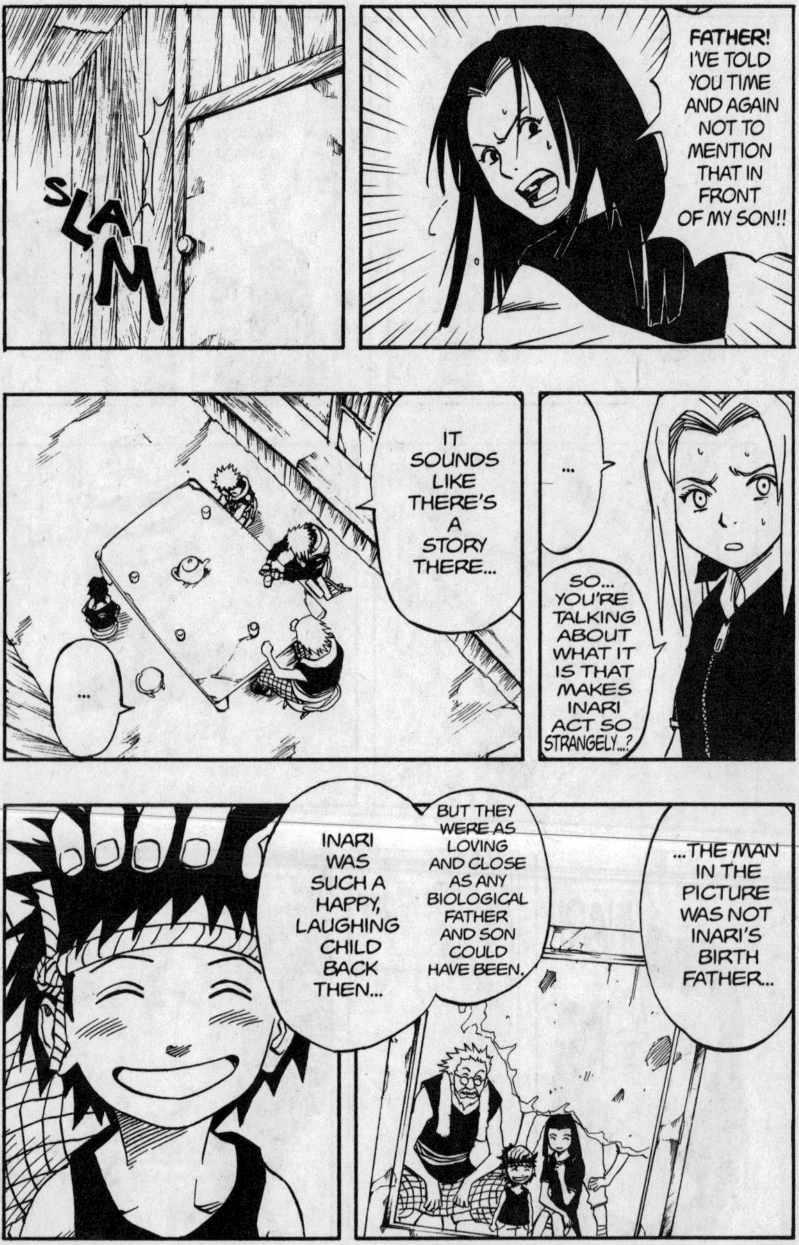
FATHER! I'VE TOLD YOU TIME AND AGAIN NOT TO MENTION THAT IN FRONT OF MY SON!!
SLAM
...
SO... YOU'RE TALKING ABOUT WHAT IT IS THAT MAKES INARI ACT SO STRANGELY...?
IT SOUNDS LIKE THERE'S A STORY THERE...
...
...THE MAN IN THE PICTURE WAS NOT INARI'S BIRTH FATHER...
BUT THEY WERE AS LOVING AND CLOSE AS ANY BIOLOGICAL FATHER AND SON COULD HAVE BEEN.
INARI WAS SUCH A HAPPY, LAUGHING CHILD BACK THEN...

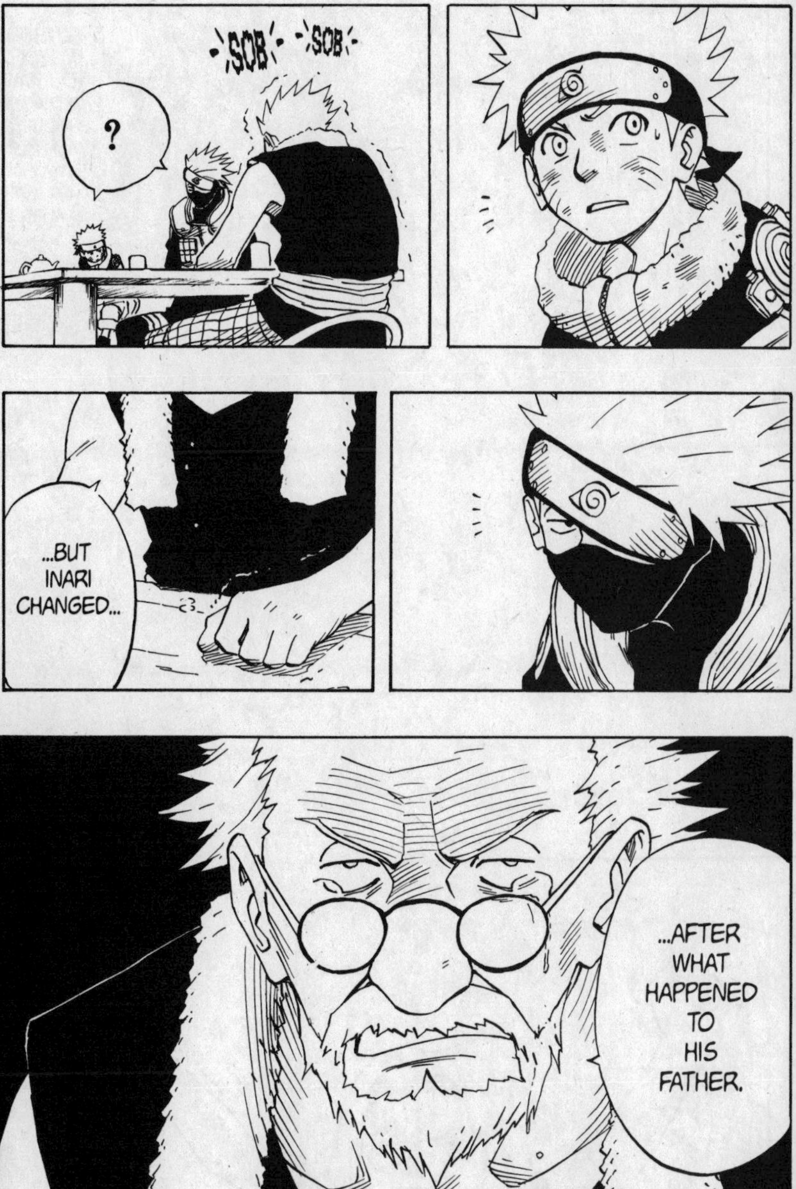
SOB SOB
?
...BUT INARI CHANGED...
...AFTER WHAT HAPPENED TO HIS FATHER.

Number 20: The Land That Had a Hero...!!

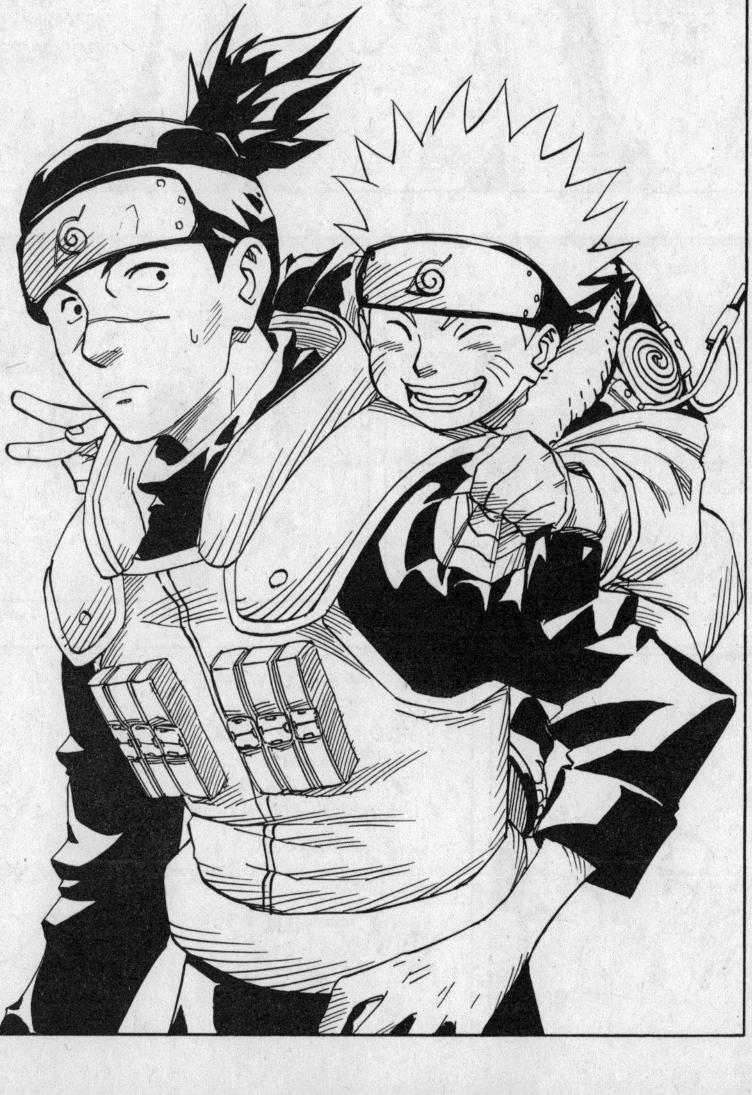

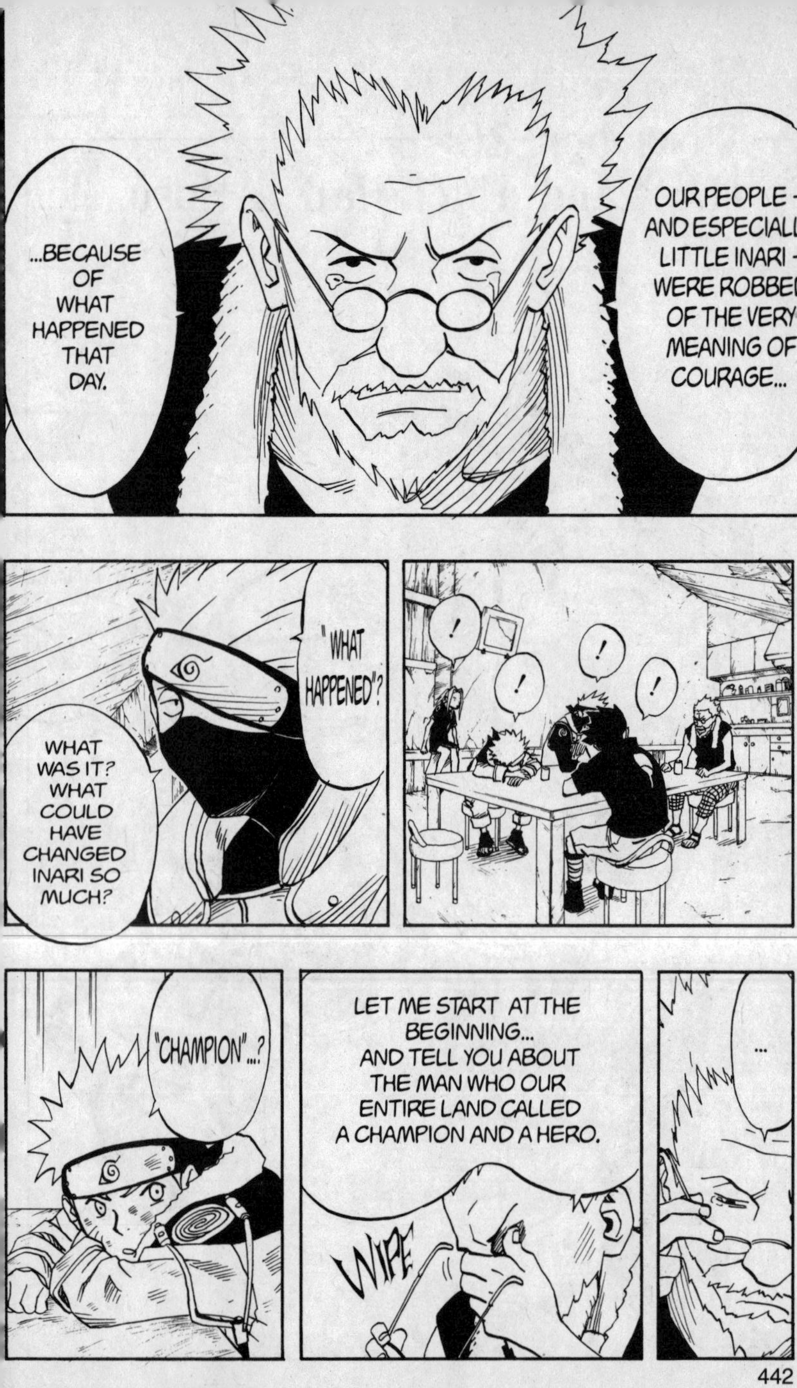
OUR PEOPLE - AND ESPECIALLY LITTLE INARI - WERE ROBBED OF THE VERY MEANING OF COURAGE...
...BECAUSE OF WHAT HAPPENED THAT DAY.
!
!
!
!
"WHAT HAPPENED"?
WHAT WAS IT? WHAT COULD HAVE CHANGED INARI SO MUCH?
...
LET ME START AT THE BEGINNING... AND TELL YOU ABOUT THE MAN WHO OUR ENTIRE LAND CALLED A CHAMPION AND A HERO.
WIPE
"CHAMPION"...?

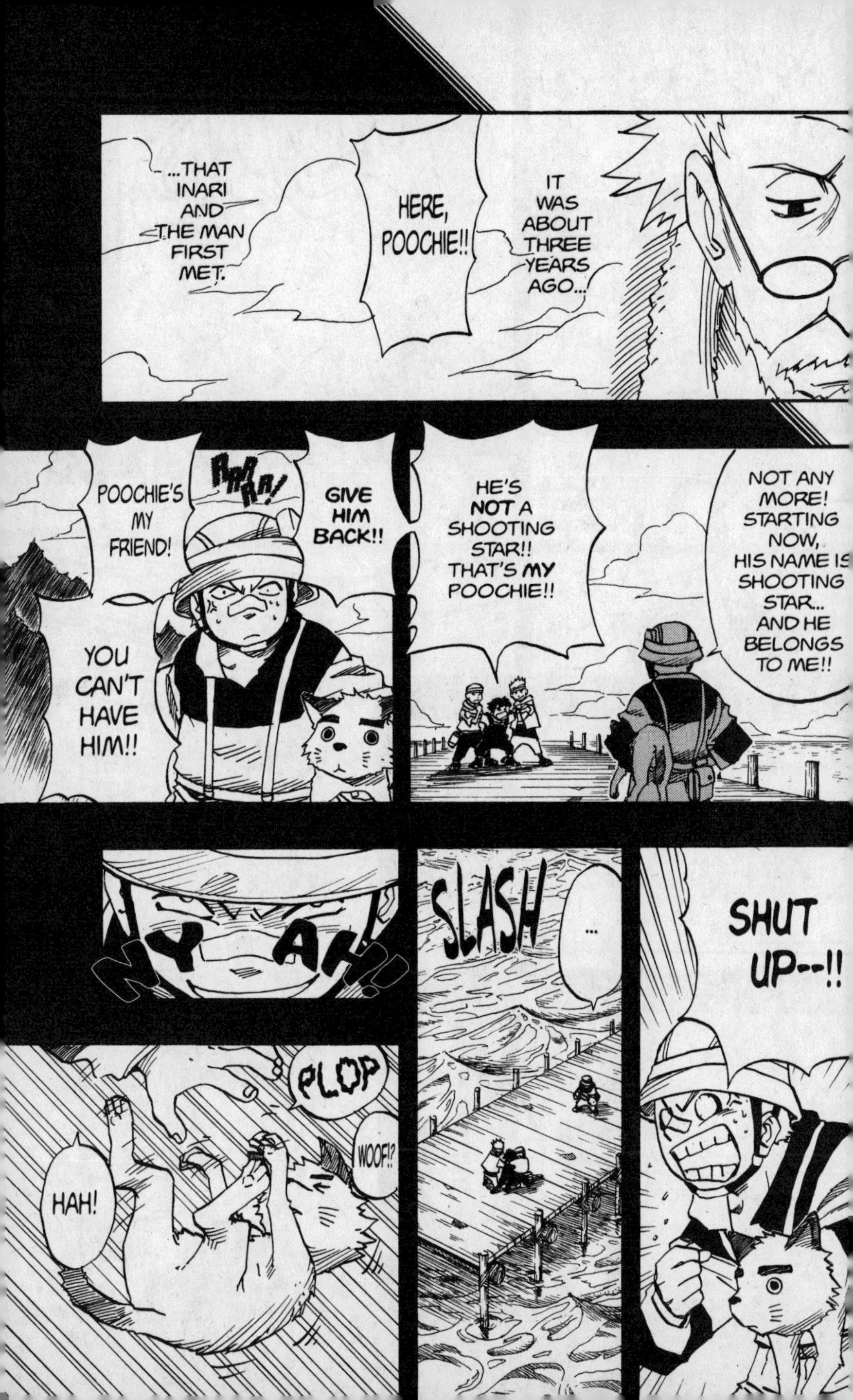
IT WAS ABOUT THREE YEARS AGO...
HERE, POOCHIE!!
...THAT INARI AND THE MAN FIRST MET.
NOT ANY MORE! STARTING NOW, HIS NAME IS SHOOTING STAR... AND HE BELONGS TO ME!!
HE'S NOT A SHOOTING STAR!! THAT'S MY POOCHIE!!
GIVE HIM BACK!!
RARRA!
POOCHIE'S MY FRIEND!
YOU CAN'T HAVE HIM!!
SHUT UP--!!
SLASH
...
NYAH!!
PLOP
WOOF!?
HAH!

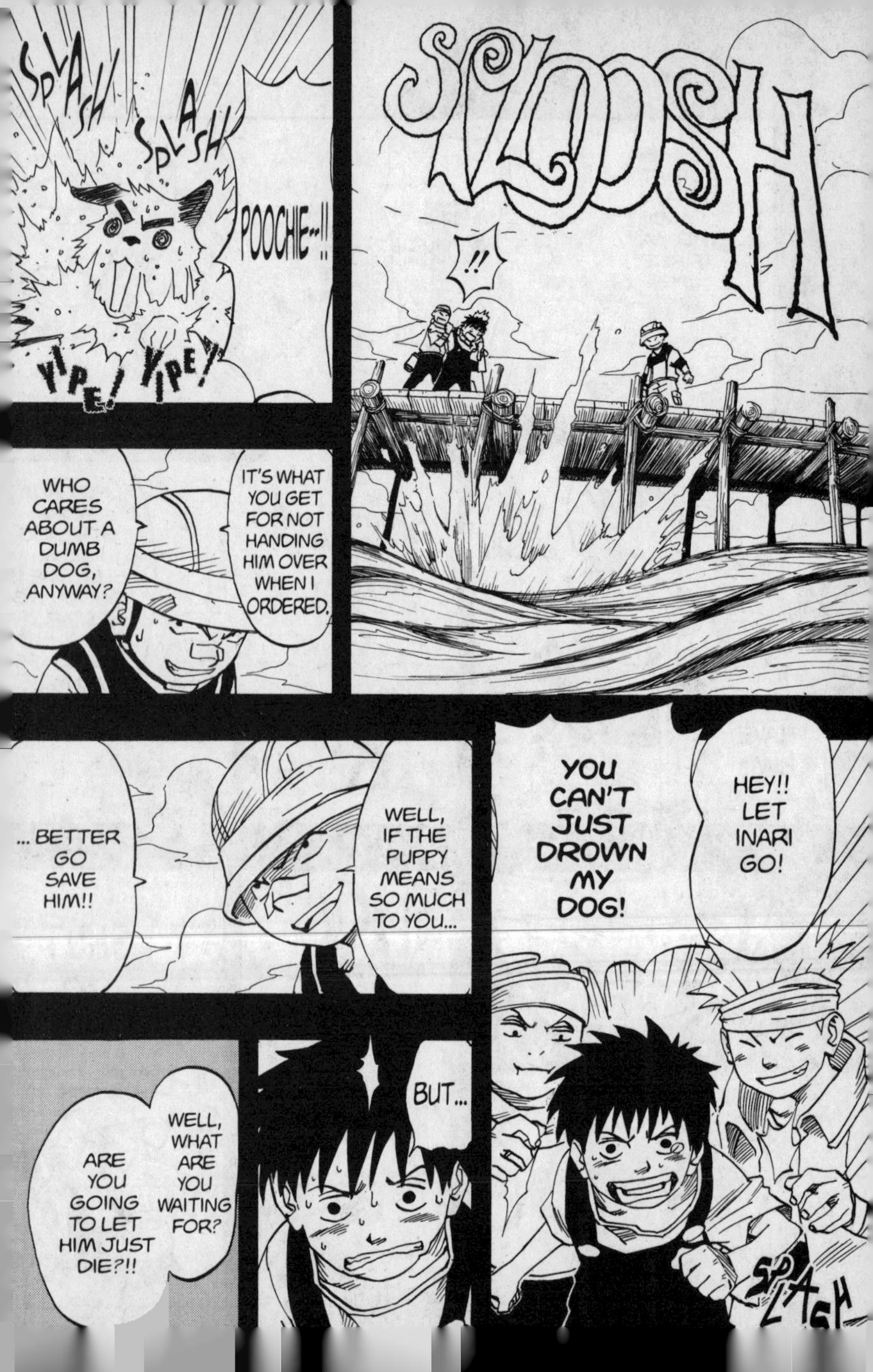
SPLOOSH
!!
POOCHIE--!!
SPLASH
SPLASH
YIPE! YIPE!
IT'S WHAT YOU GET FOR NOT HANDING HIM OVER WHEN I ORDERED.
WHO CARES ABOUT A DUMB DOG, ANYWAY?
HEY!! LET INARI GO!
YOU CAN'T JUST DROWN MY DOG!
SPLASH
WELL, IF THE PUPPY MEANS SO MUCH TO YOU...
... BETTER GO SAVE HIM!!
BUT...
WELL, WHAT ARE YOU WAITING FOR?
ARE YOU GOING TO LET HIM JUST DIE?!!

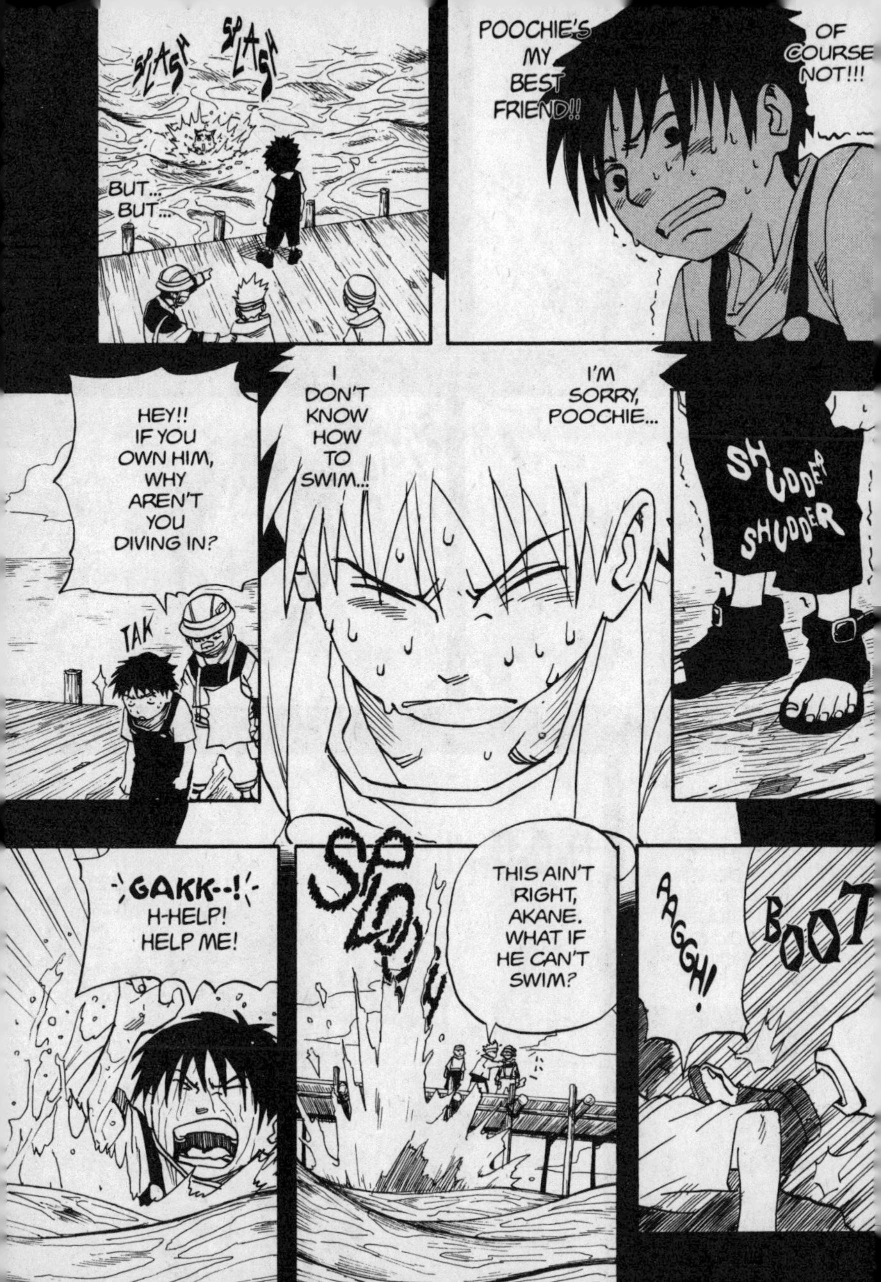

OF COURSE NOT!!!
POOCHIE'S MY BEST FRIEND!!
SPLASH
SPLASH
BUT... BUT...
I'M SORRY, POOCHIE...
SHUDDER SHUDDER
I DON'T KNOW HOW TO SWIM...
HEY!! IF YOU OWN HIM, WHY AREN'T YOU DIVING IN?
TAK
BOOT
AAGGH!
THIS AIN'T RIGHT, AKANE. WHAT IF HE CAN'T SWIM?
SPLOOSH
GAKK--! H-HELP! HELP ME!

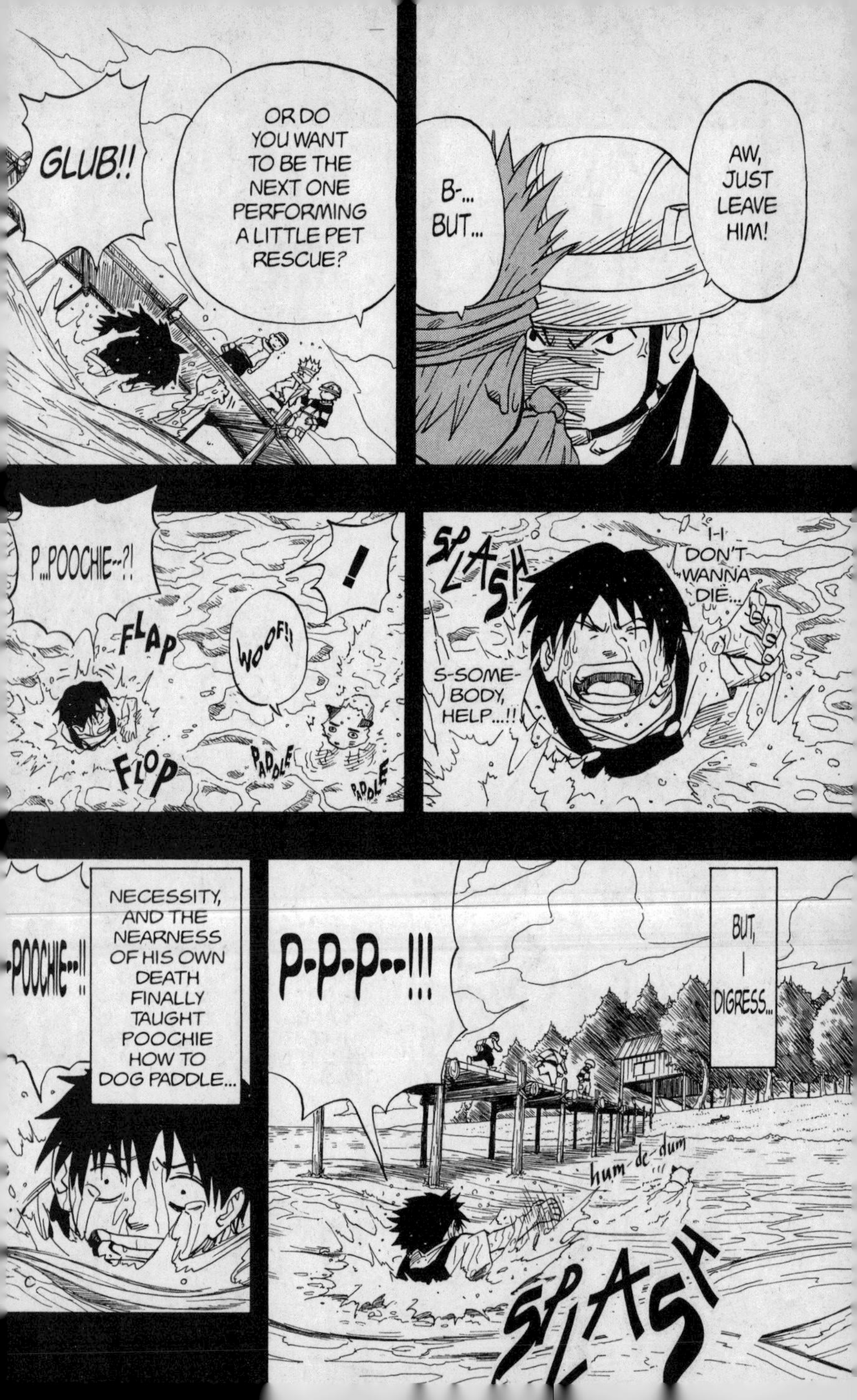
AW, JUST LEAVE HIM!
B-... BUT...
OR DO YOU WANT TO BE THE NEXT ONE PERFORMING A LITTLE PET RESCUE?
GLUB!!
SPLASH
I-I DON'T WANNA DIE...
S-SOMEBODY, HELP...!!
!
WOOF!!
P...POOCHIE--?!
FLAP
FLOP
PADDLE
PADDLE
BUT, I DIGRESS...
P-P-P--!!!
hum-de-dum
SPLASH
NECESSITY, AND THE NEARNESS OF HIS OWN DEATH FINALLY TAUGHT POOCHIE HOW TO DOG PADDLE...
-POOCHIE--!!

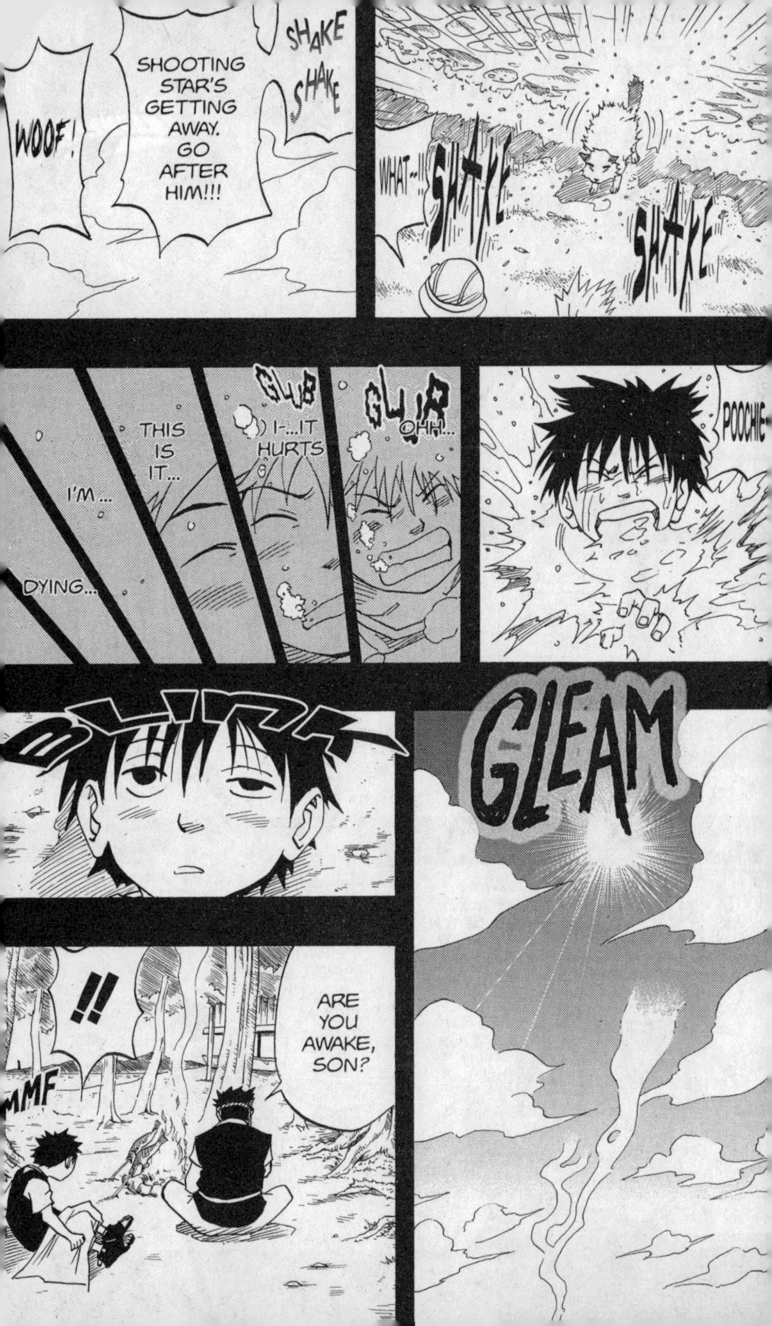
WHAT--!!
SHAKE
SHAKE
SHAKE
SHAKE
SHOOTING STAR'S GETTING AWAY. GO AFTER HIM!!!
WOOF!
POOCHIE--
GLUR
OHH...
GLUB
I-...IT HURTS
THIS IS IT...
I'M...
DYING...
GLEAM
BLINK
ARE YOU AWAKE, SON?
!!
MMF

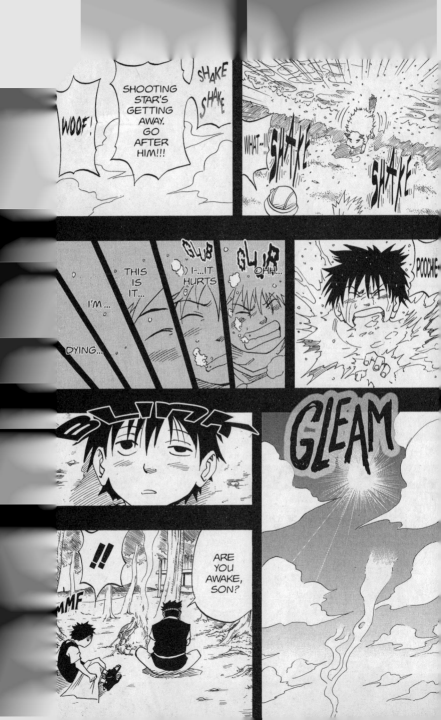

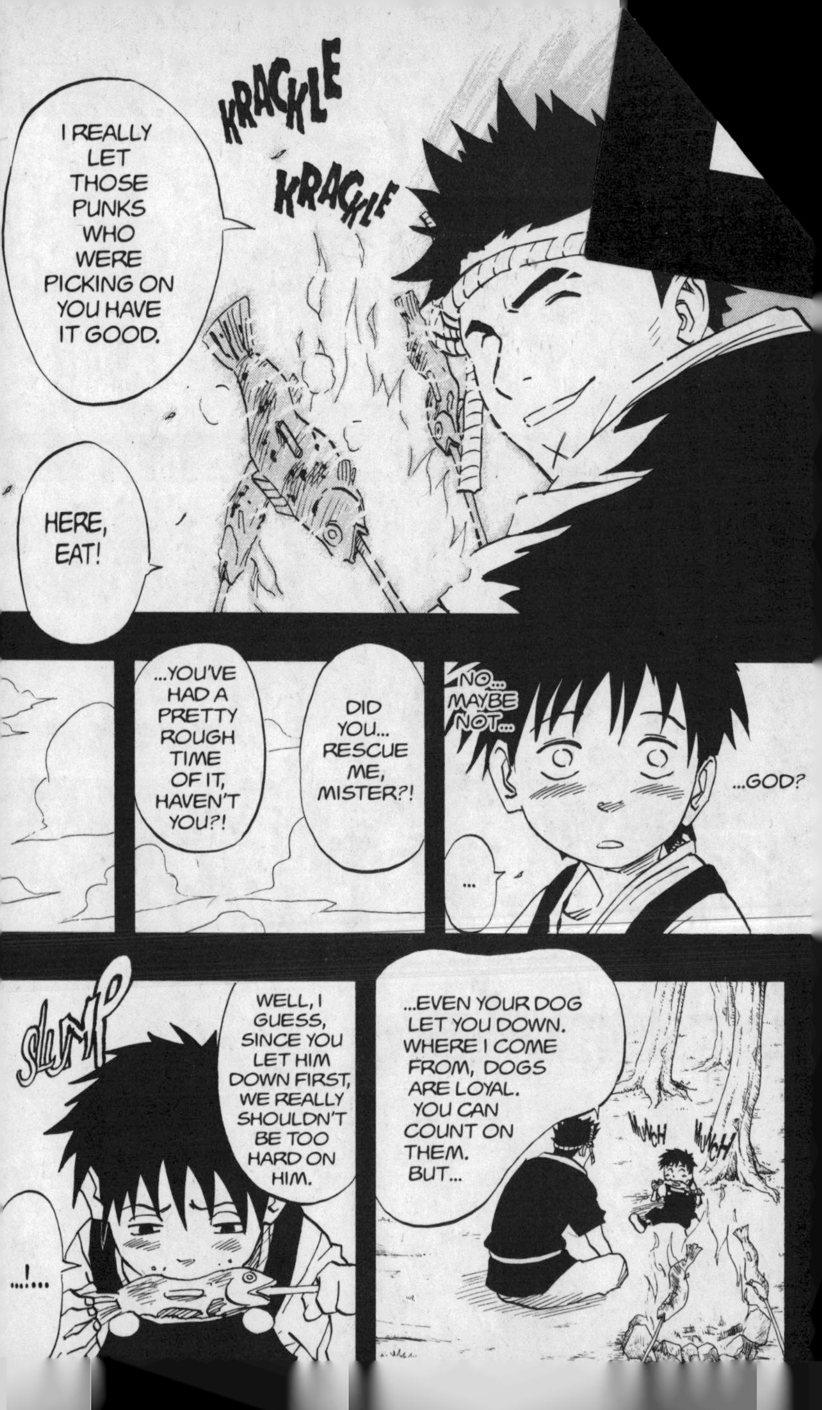
KRACKLE
KRACKLE
I REALLY LET THOSE PUNKS WHO WERE PICKING ON YOU HAVE IT GOOD.
HERE, EAT!
...GOD?
NO... MAYBE NOT...
...
DID YOU... RESCUE ME, MISTER?!
...YOU'VE HAD A PRETTY ROUGH TIME OF IT, HAVEN'T YOU?!
...EVEN YOUR DOG LET YOU DOWN. WHERE I COME FROM, DOGS ARE LOYAL. YOU CAN COUNT ON THEM. BUT...
MUNCH
MUNCH
WELL, I GUESS, SINCE YOU LET HIM DOWN FIRST, WE REALLY SHOULDN'T BE TOO HARD ON HIM.
SLURP
...!...

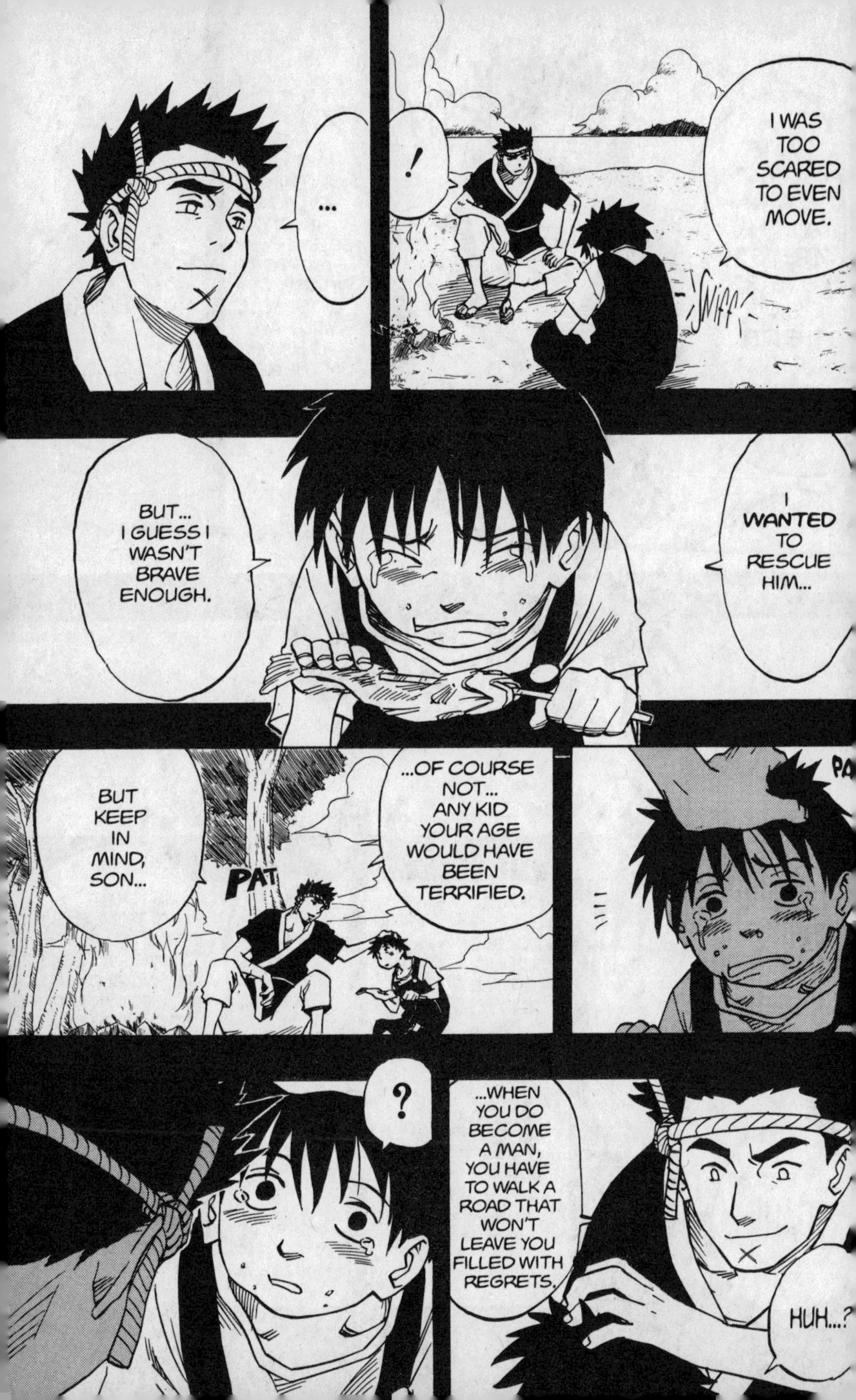
!
I WAS TOO SCARED TO EVEN MOVE.
SNIFF
...
I WANTED TO RESCUE HIM...
BUT... I GUESS I WASN'T BRAVE ENOUGH.
PA
...OF COURSE NOT... ANY KID YOUR AGE WOULD HAVE BEEN TERRIFIED.
PAT
BUT KEEP IN MIND, SON...
...WHEN YOU DO BECOME A MAN, YOU HAVE TO WALK A ROAD THAT WON'T LEAVE YOU FILLED WITH REGRETS.
HUH...?
?

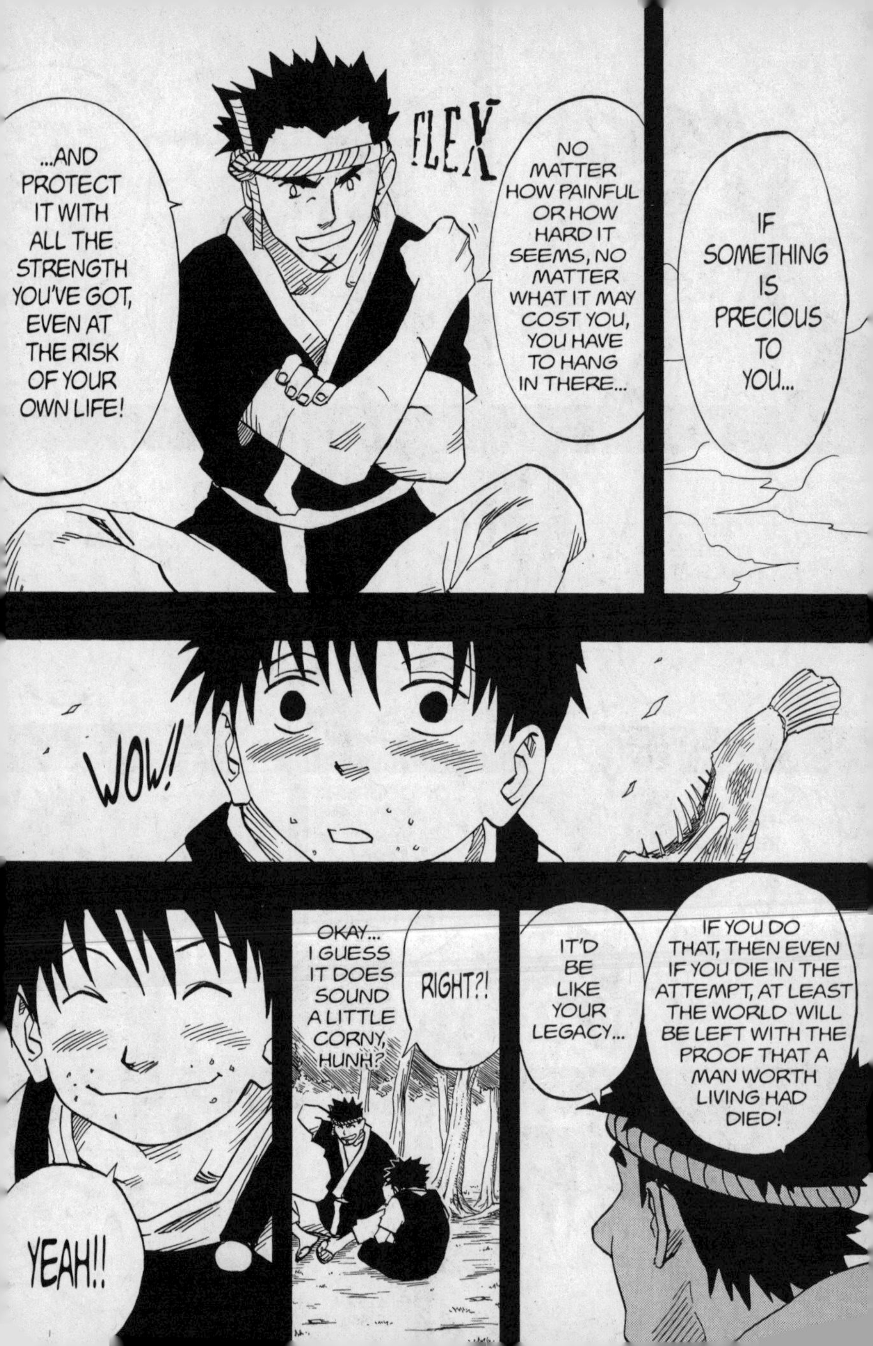
IF SOMETHING IS PRECIOUS TO YOU...
NO MATTER HOW PAINFUL OR HOW HARD IT SEEMS, NO MATTER WHAT IT MAY COST YOU, YOU HAVE TO HANG IN THERE...
FLEX
...AND PROTECT IT WITH ALL THE STRENGTH YOU'VE GOT, EVEN AT THE RISK OF YOUR OWN LIFE!
WOW!
IF YOU DO THAT, THEN EVEN IF YOU DIE IN THE ATTEMPT, AT LEAST THE WORLD WILL BE LEFT WITH THE PROOF THAT A MAN WORTH LIVING HAD DIED!
IT'D BE LIKE YOUR LEGACY...
RIGHT?!
OKAY... I GUESS IT DOES SOUND A LITTLE CORNY, HUNH?
YEAH!!

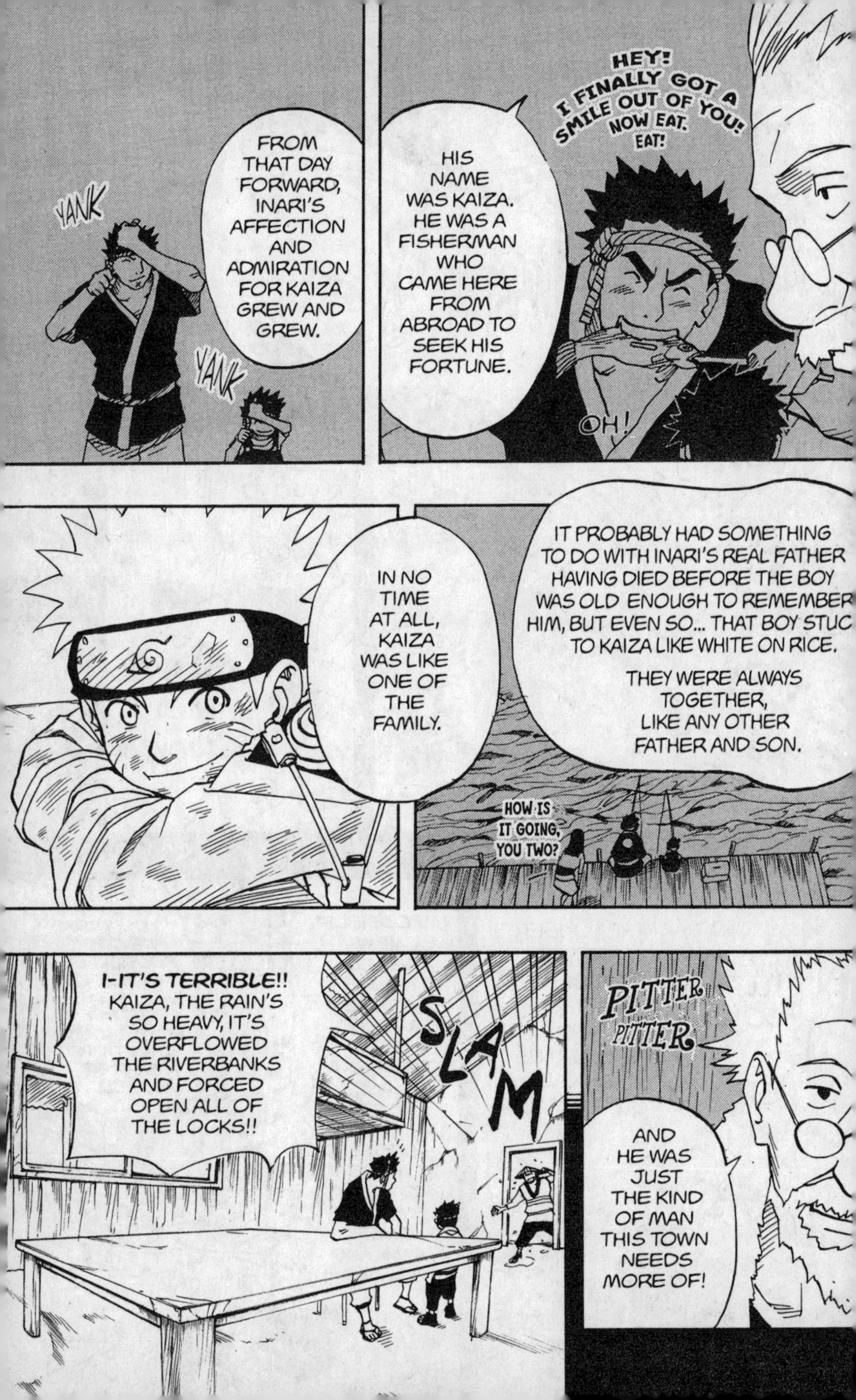
HEY! I FINALLY GOT A SMILE OUT OF YOU! NOW EAT. EAT!
HIS NAME WAS KAIZA. HE WAS A FISHERMAN WHO CAME HERE FROM ABROAD TO SEEK HIS FORTUNE.
OH!
FROM THAT DAY FORWARD, INARI'S AFFECTION AND ADMIRATION FOR KAIZA GREW AND GREW.
YANK
YANK
IT PROBABLY HAD SOMETHING TO DO WITH INARI'S REAL FATHER HAVING DIED BEFORE THE BOY WAS OLD ENOUGH TO REMEMBER HIM, BUT EVEN SO... THAT BOY STUC TO KAIZA LIKE WHITE ON RICE.
THEY WERE ALWAYS TOGETHER, LIKE ANY OTHER FATHER AND SON.
HOW IS IT GOING, YOU TWO?
IN NO TIME AT ALL, KAIZA WAS LIKE ONE OF THE FAMILY.
PITTER PITTER
AND HE WAS JUST THE KIND OF MAN THIS TOWN NEEDS MORE OF!
SLAM
I-IT'S TERRIBLE!! KAIZA, THE RAIN'S SO HEAVY, IT'S OVERFLOWED THE RIVERBANKS AND FORCED OPEN ALL OF THE LOCKS!!

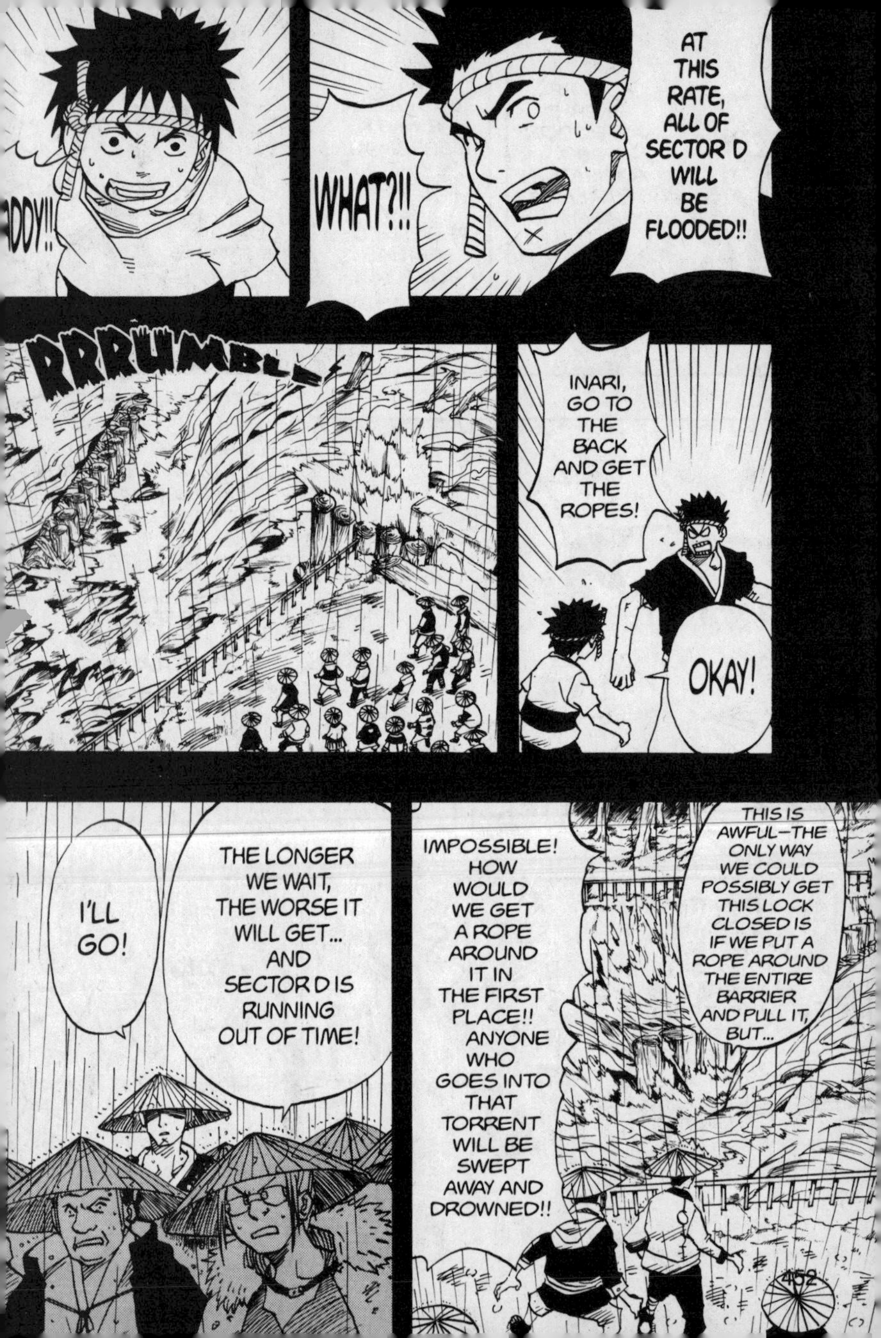
AT THIS RATE, ALL OF SECTOR D WILL BE FLOODED!!
WHAT?!!
DDY!!
INARI, GO TO THE BACK AND GET THE ROPES!
OKAY!
RRRUMBL
THIS IS AWFUL—THE ONLY WAY WE COULD POSSIBLY GET THIS LOCK CLOSED IS IF WE PUT A ROPE AROUND THE ENTIRE BARRIER AND PULL IT, BUT...
IMPOSSIBLE! HOW WOULD WE GET A ROPE AROUND IT IN THE FIRST PLACE!! ANYONE WHO GOES INTO THAT TORRENT WILL BE SWEPT AWAY AND DROWNED!!
THE LONGER WE WAIT, THE WORSE IT WILL GET... AND SECTOR D IS RUNNING OUT OF TIME!
I'LL GO!

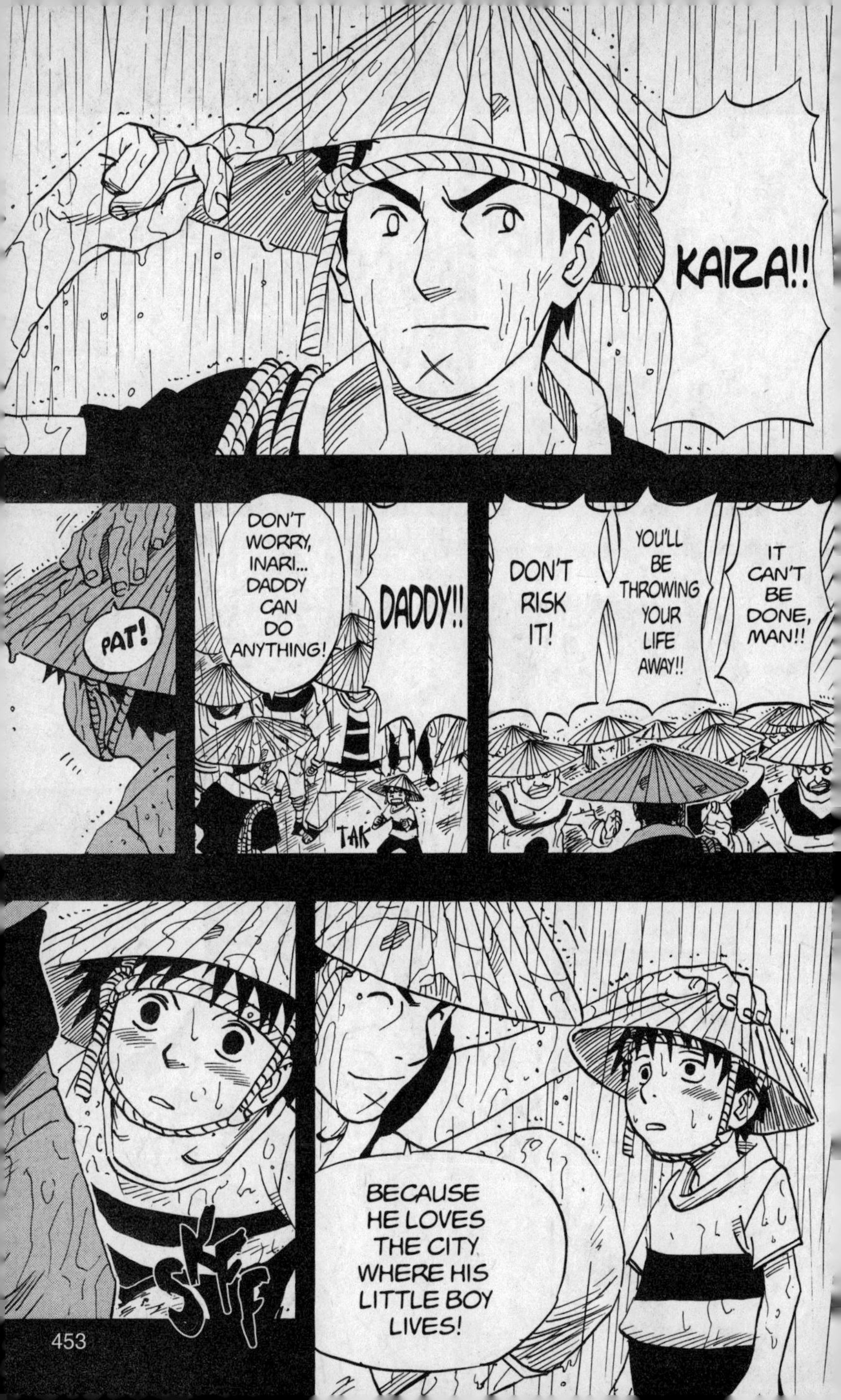
KAIZA!!
IT CAN'T BE DONE, MAN!!
YOU'LL BE THROWING YOUR LIFE AWAY!!
DON'T RISK IT!
DADDY!!
DON'T WORRY, INARI... DADDY CAN DO ANYTHING!
TAK
PAT!
BECAUSE HE LOVES THE CITY WHERE HIS LITTLE BOY LIVES!
SKF

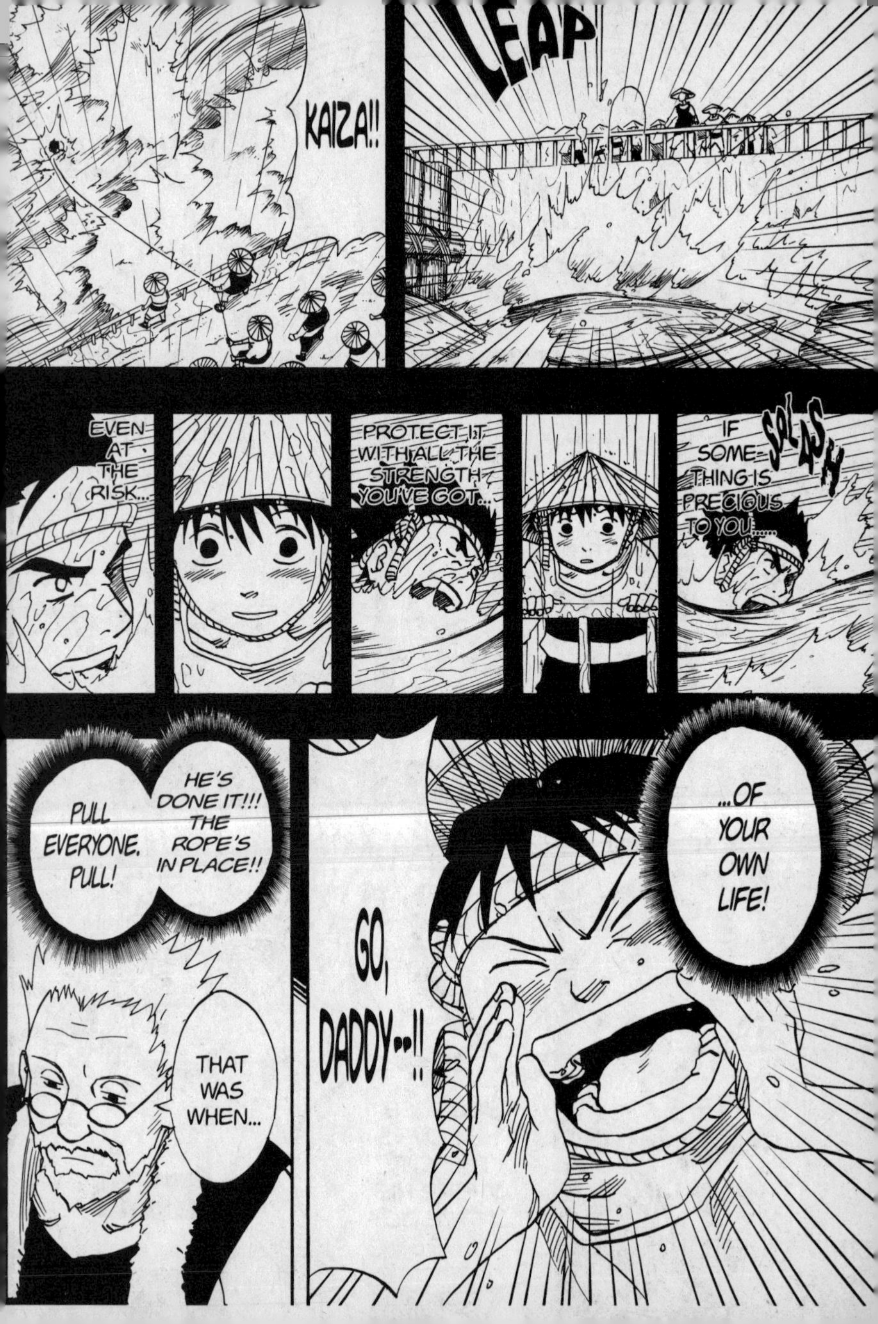
LEAP
KAIZA!!
IF SOMETHING IS PRECIOUS TO YOU......
SPLASH
PROTECT IT WITH ALL THE STRENGTH YOU'VE GOT...
EVEN AT THE RISK...
...OF YOUR OWN LIFE!
GO, DADDY--!!
HE'S DONE IT!!! THE ROPE'S IN PLACE!!
PULL EVERYONE. PULL!
THAT WAS WHEN...

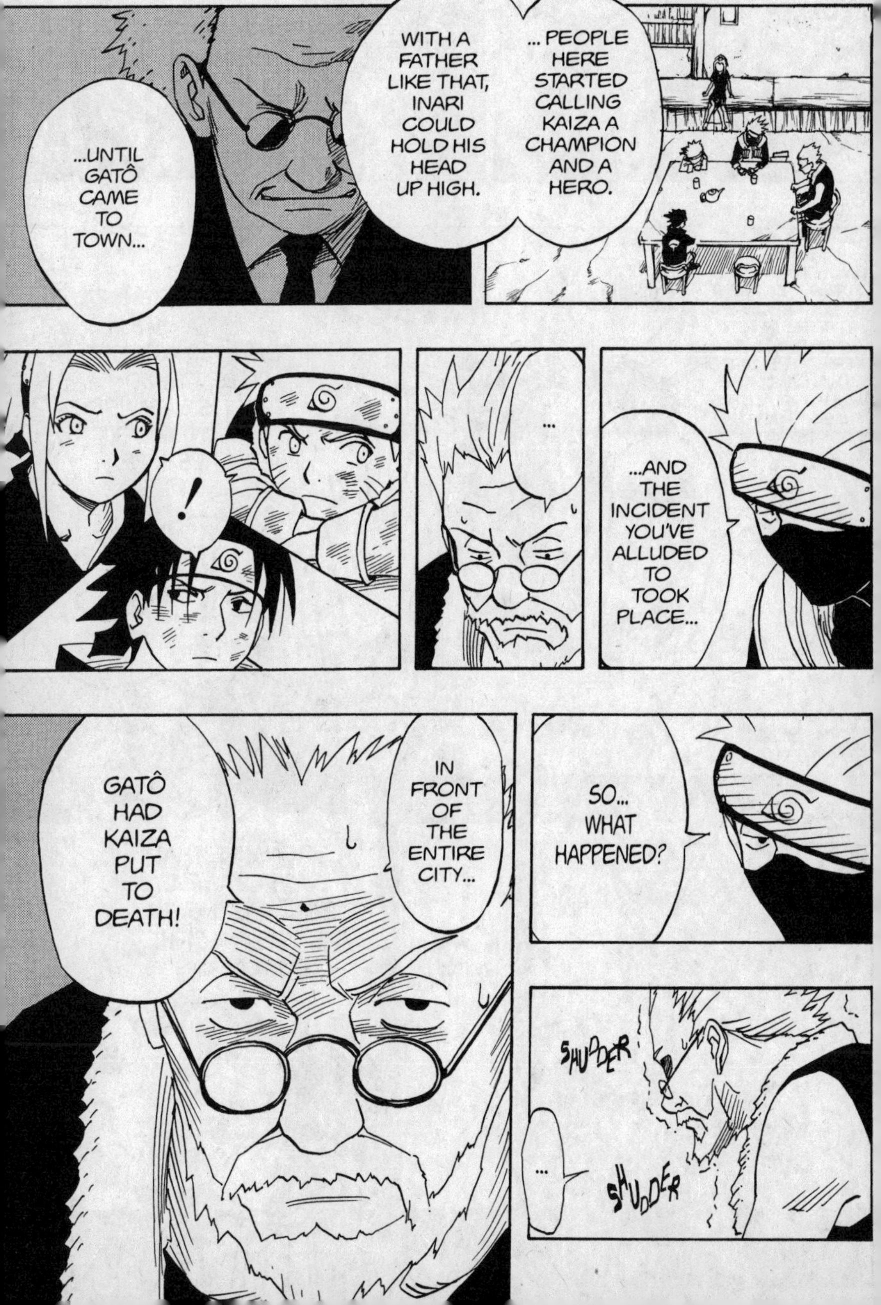
...PEOPLE HERE STARTED CALLING KAIZA A CHAMPION AND A HERO.
WITH A FATHER LIKE THAT, INARI COULD HOLD HIS HEAD UP HIGH.
...UNTIL GATÔ CAME TO TOWN...
...AND THE INCIDENT YOU'VE ALLUDED TO TOOK PLACE...
...
!
SO... WHAT HAPPENED?
SHUDDER
SHUDDER
...
IN FRONT OF THE ENTIRE CITY...
GATÔ HAD KAIZA PUT TO DEATH!

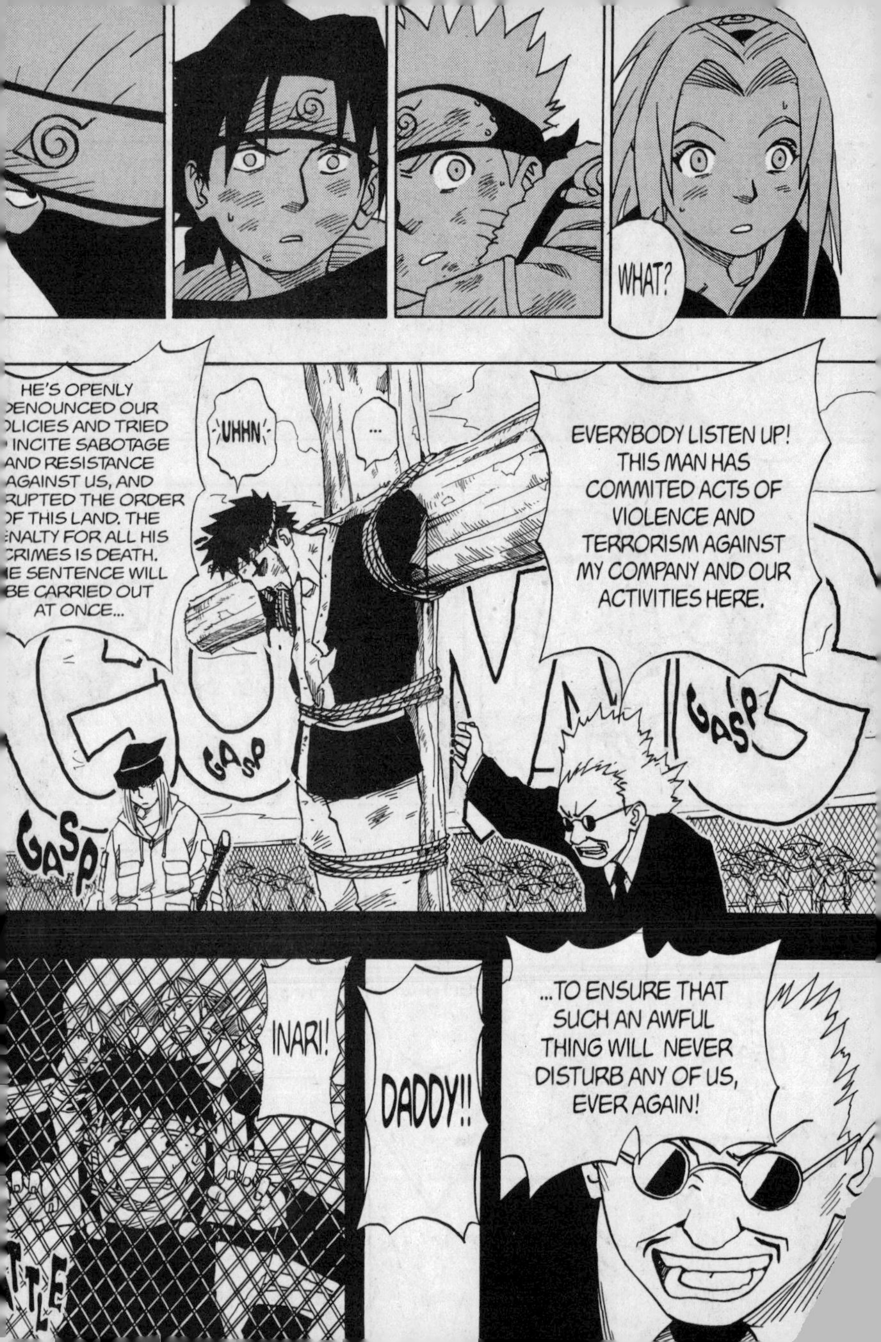
WHAT?
EVERYBODY LISTEN UP! THIS MAN HAS COMMITED ACTS OF VIOLENCE AND TERRORISM AGAINST MY COMPANY AND OUR ACTIVITIES HERE.
GASP
...
UHHN
HE'S OPENLY DENOUNCED OUR OLICIES AND TRIED INCITE SABOTAGE AND RESISTANCE AGAINST US, AND RUPTED THE ORDER OF THIS LAND. THE ENALTY FOR ALL HIS CRIMES IS DEATH. HE SENTENCE WILL BE CARRIED OUT AT ONCE...
GASP
GASP
...TO ENSURE THAT SUCH AN AWFUL THING WILL NEVER DISTURB ANY OF US, EVER AGAIN!
DADDY!!
INARI!

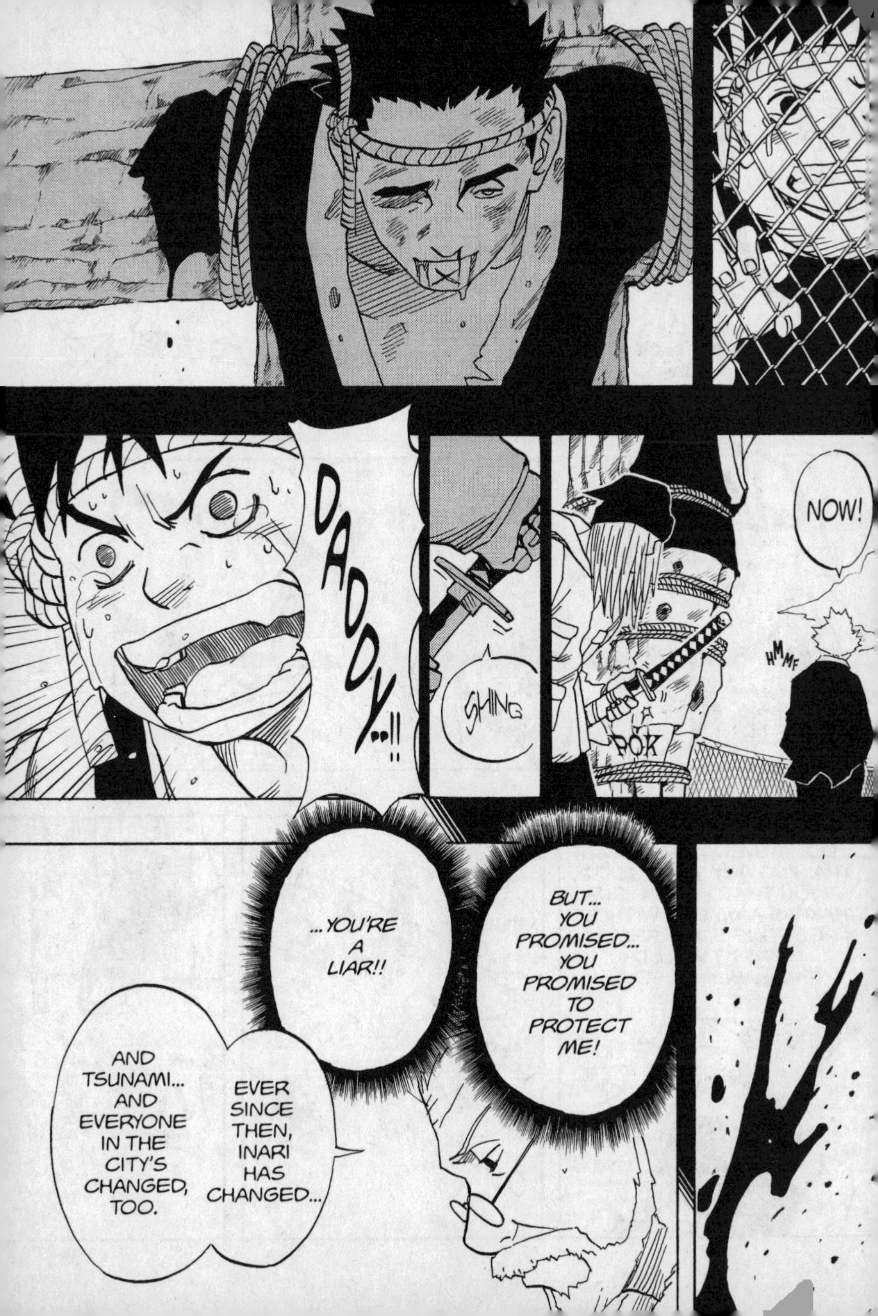
NOW!
HMMF
POK
SHING
DADDY!!
BUT... YOU PROMISED... YOU PROMISED TO PROTECT ME!
...YOU'RE A LIAR!!
EVER SINCE THEN, INARI HAS CHANGED...
AND TSUNAMI... AND EVERYONE IN THE CITY'S CHANGED, TOO.

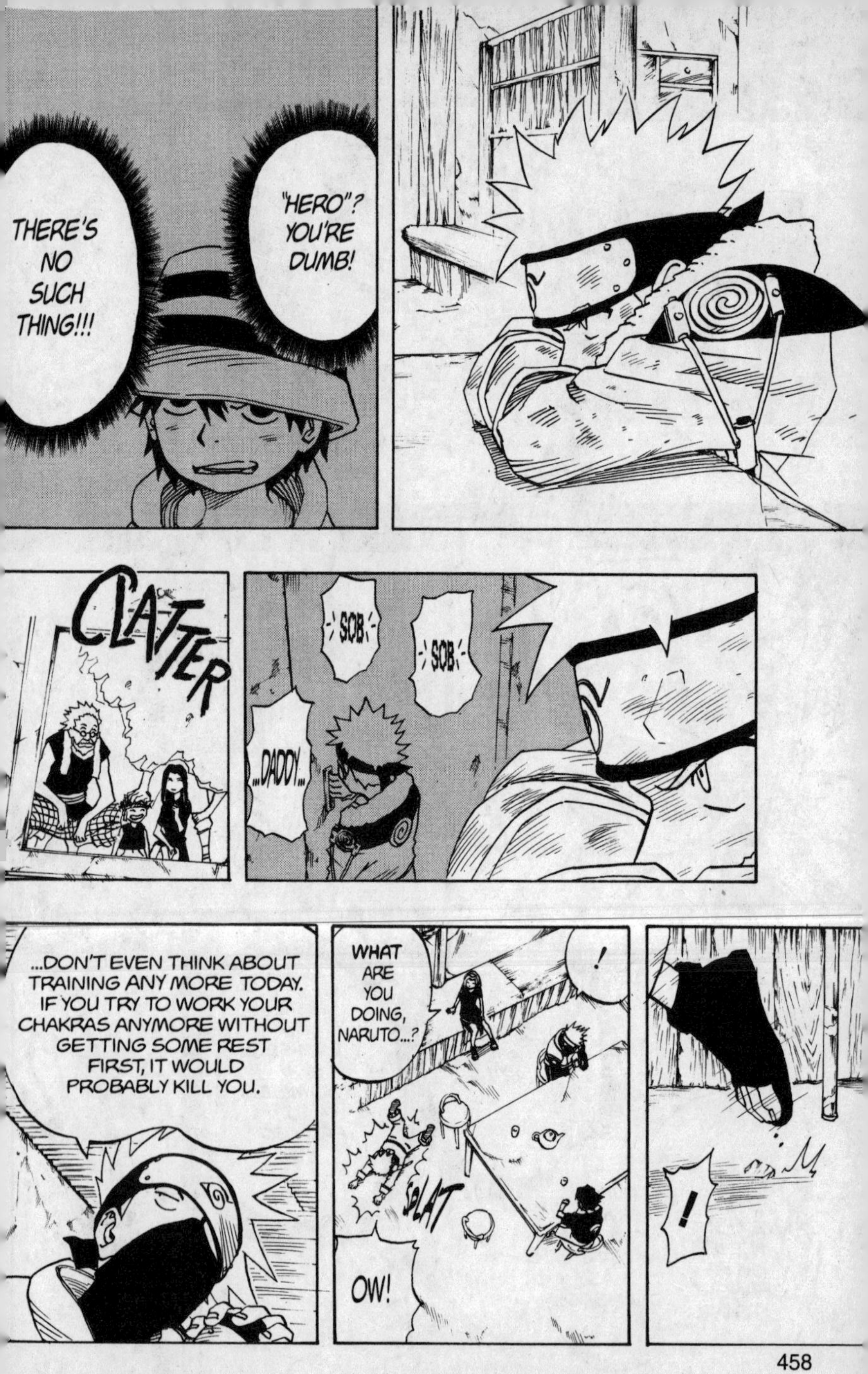
"HERO"? YOU'RE DUMB!
THERE'S NO SUCH THING!!!
SOB
SOB
...DADDY...
CLATTER
!
!
WHAT ARE YOU DOING, NARUTO...?
SPLAT
OW!
...DON'T EVEN THINK ABOUT TRAINING ANY MORE TODAY. IF YOU TRY TO WORK YOUR CHAKRAS ANYMORE WITHOUT GETTING SOME REST FIRST, IT WOULD PROBABLY KILL YOU.

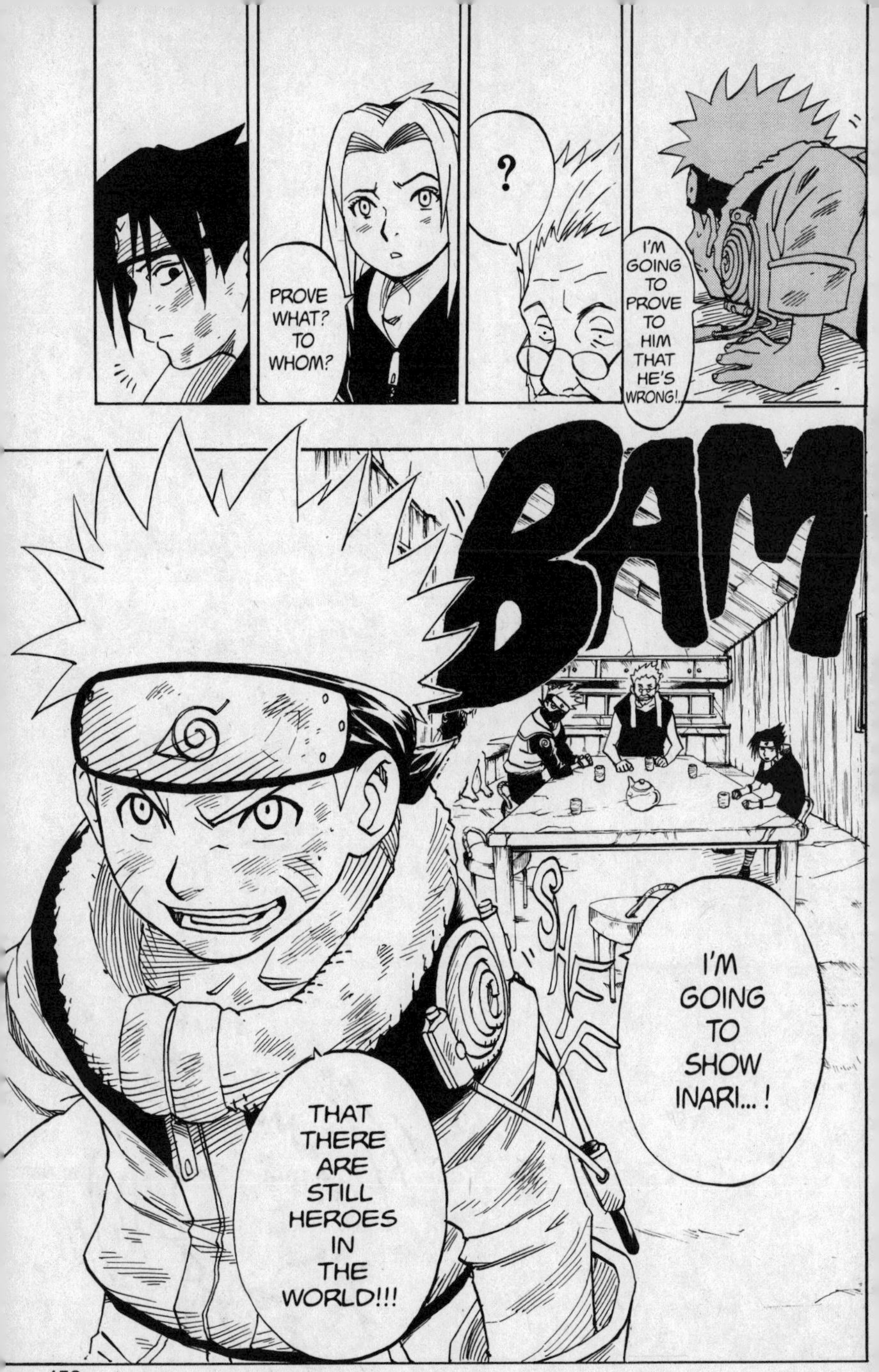
I'M GOING TO PROVE TO HIM THAT HE'S WRONG!
?
PROVE WHAT? TO WHOM?
BAM
I'M GOING TO SHOW INARI...!
THAT THERE ARE STILL HEROES IN THE WORLD!!!

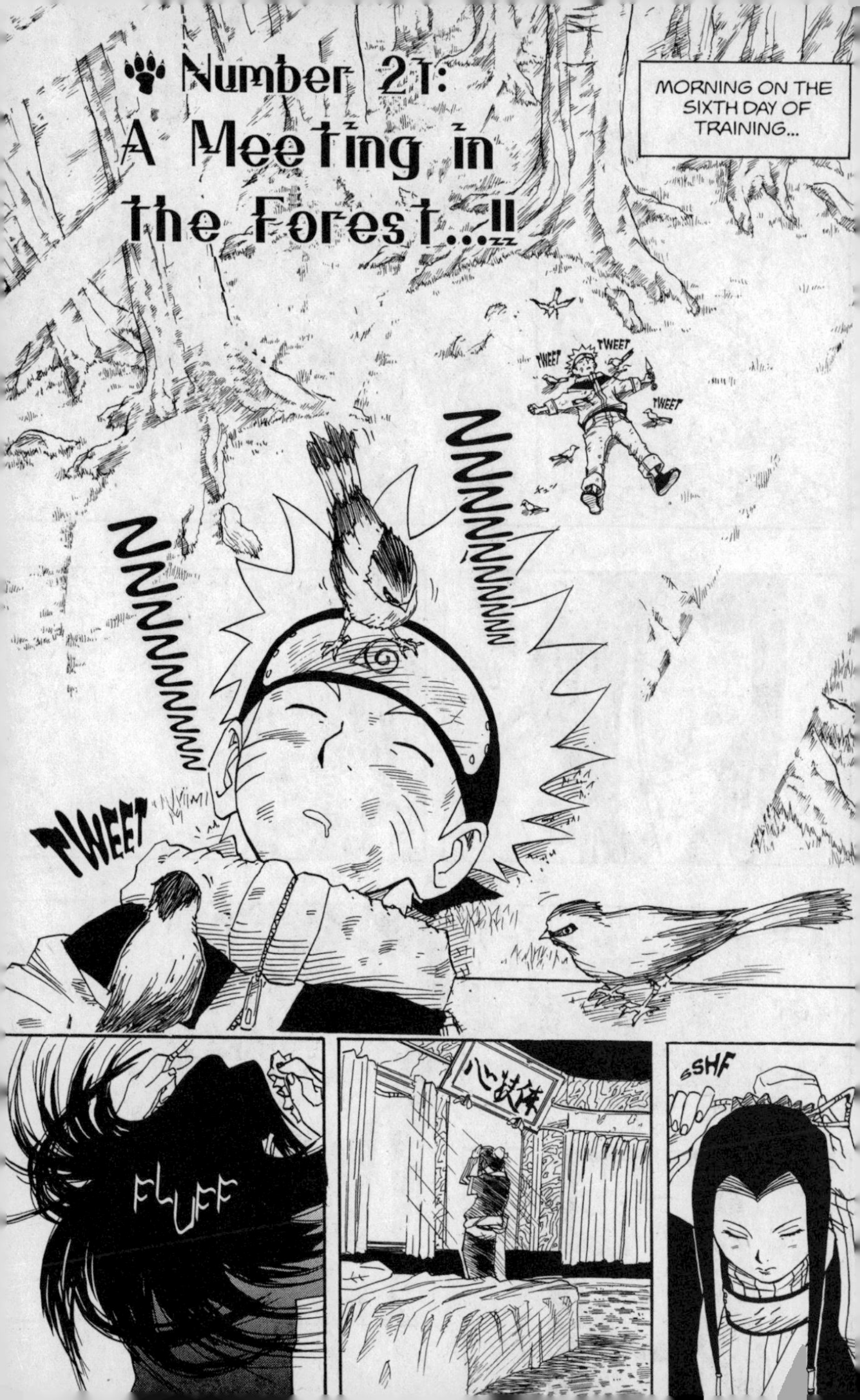
Number 21: A Meeting in the Forest...!!
MORNING ON THE SIXTH DAY OF TRAINING...
TWEET
TWEET
TWEET
TWEET
SSHF
FLUFF

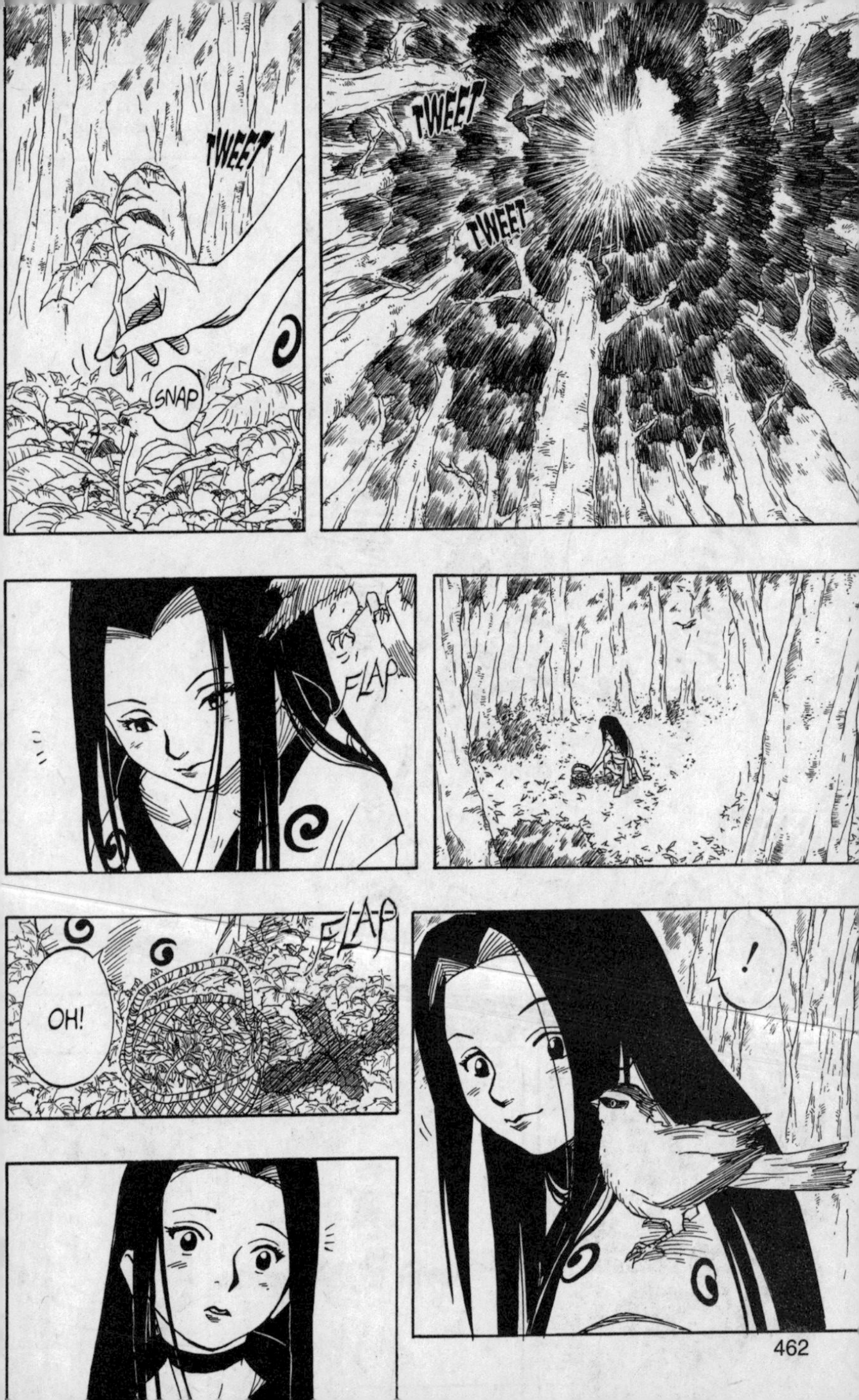
TWEET
TWEET
TWEET
SNAP
FLAP
!
FLAP
OH!

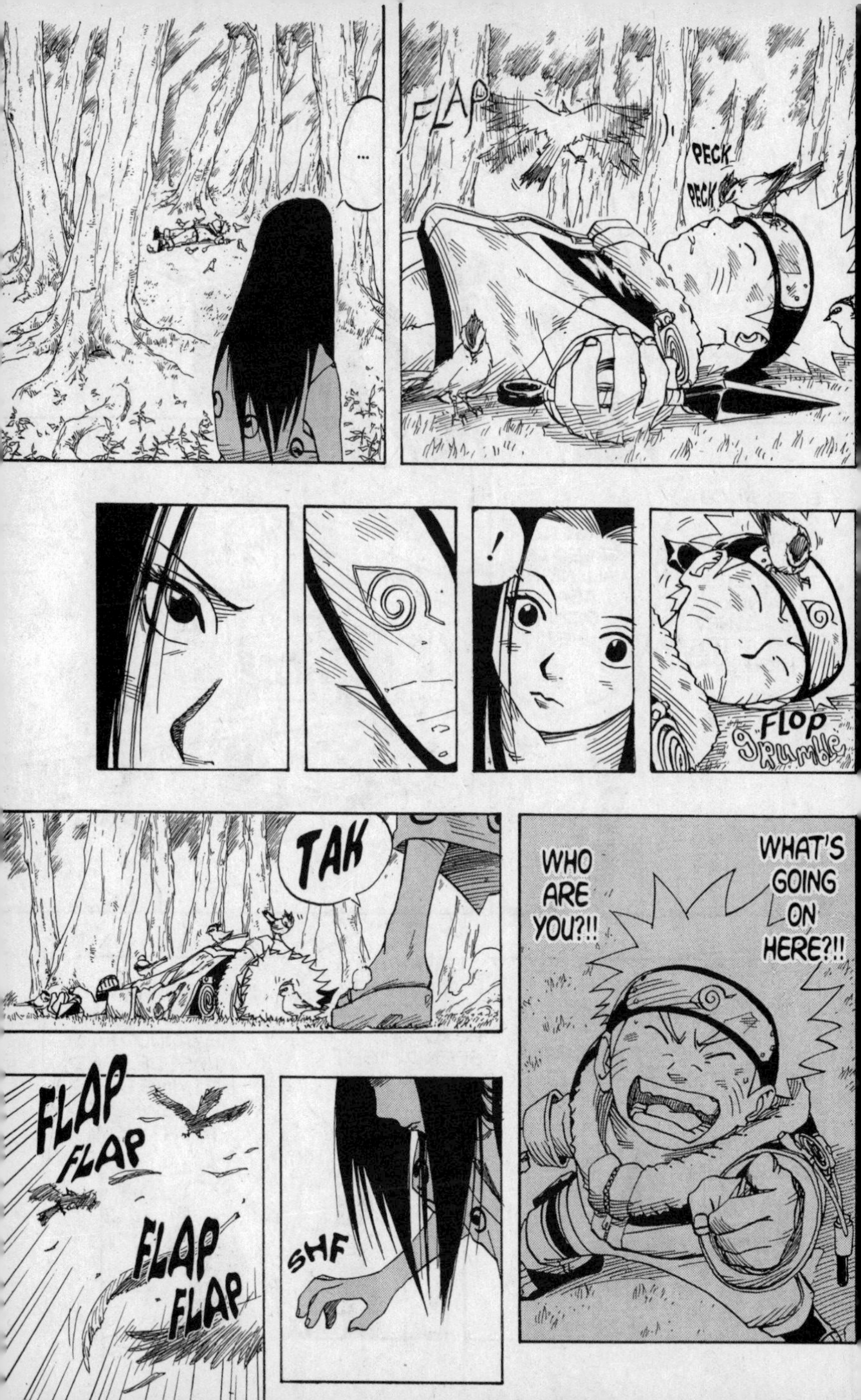
FLAP
PECK
PECK
...
!
FLOP
grumble
WHAT'S GOING ON HERE?!!
WHO ARE YOU?!!
TAK
SHF
FLAP
FLAP
FLAP
FLAP

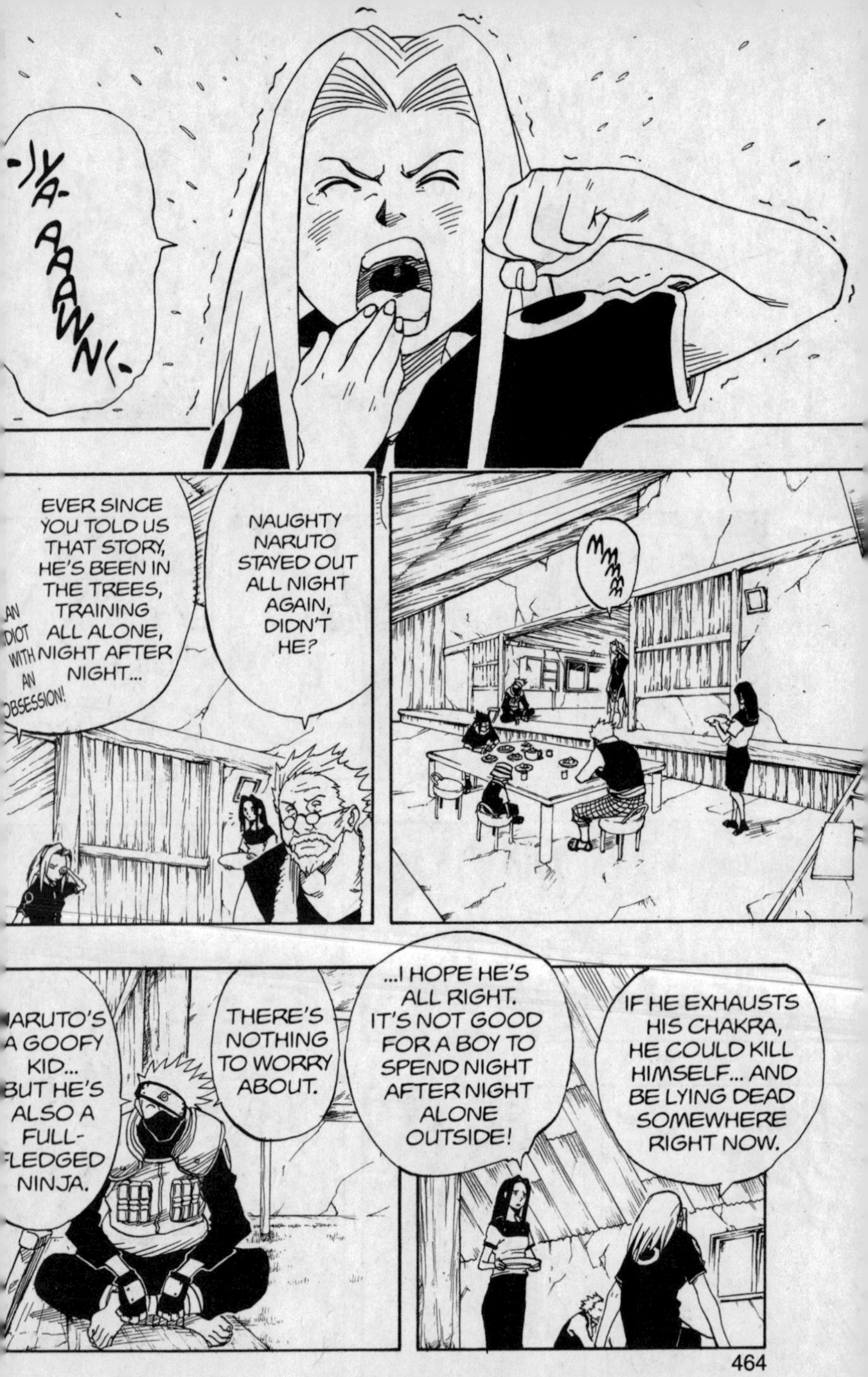

-IYA-AAAWN!-
MMMMM
NAUGHTY NARUTO STAYED OUT ALL NIGHT AGAIN, DIDN'T HE?
EVER SINCE YOU TOLD US THAT STORY, HE'S BEEN IN THE TREES, TRAINING ALL ALONE, NIGHT AFTER NIGHT...
AN IDIOT WITH AN OBSESSION!
...I HOPE HE'S ALL RIGHT. IT'S NOT GOOD FOR A BOY TO SPEND NIGHT AFTER NIGHT ALONE OUTSIDE!
IF HE EXHAUSTS HIS CHAKRA, HE COULD KILL HIMSELF... AND BE LYING DEAD SOMEWHERE RIGHT NOW.
THERE'S NOTHING TO WORRY ABOUT.
NARUTO'S A GOOFY KID... BUT HE'S ALSO A FULL-FLEDGED NINJA.

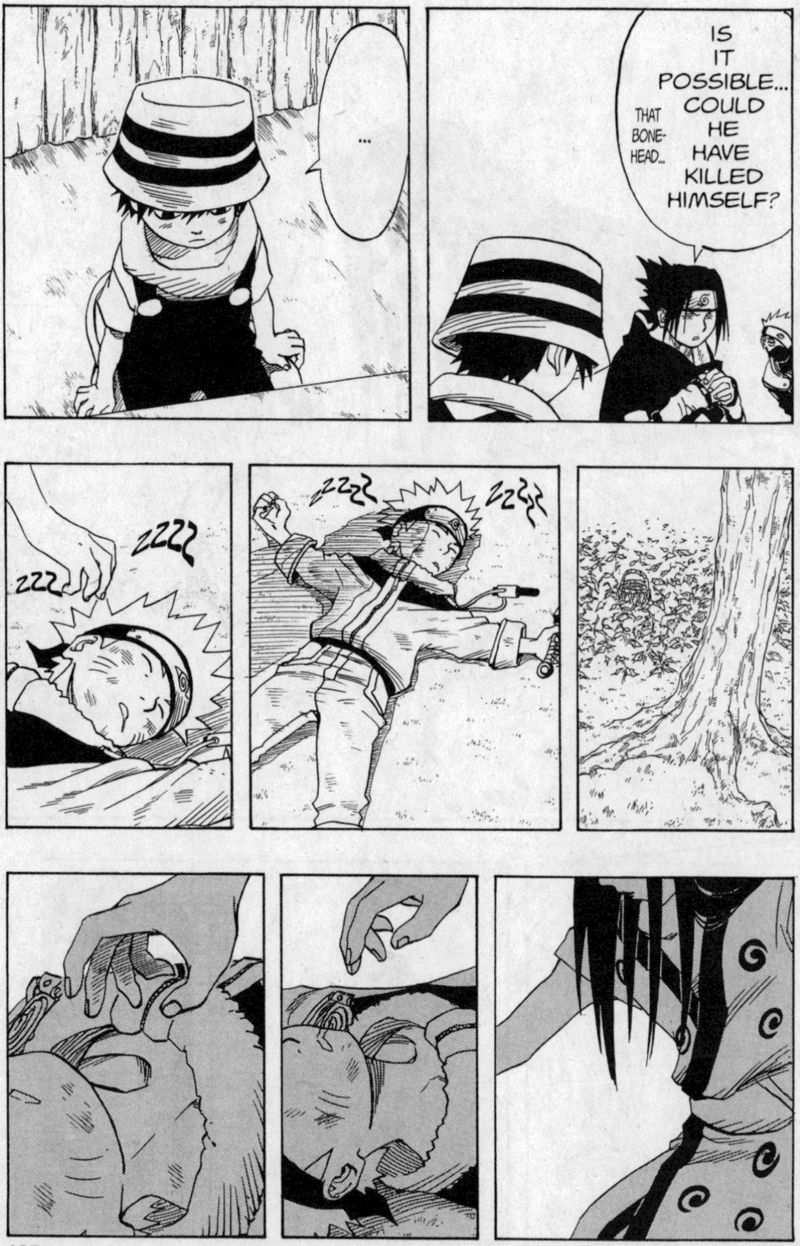
IS IT POSSIBLE... COULD HE HAVE KILLED HIMSELF?
THAT BONE-HEAD...
...
ZZZZ
ZZZZ
ZZZZ
ZZZ

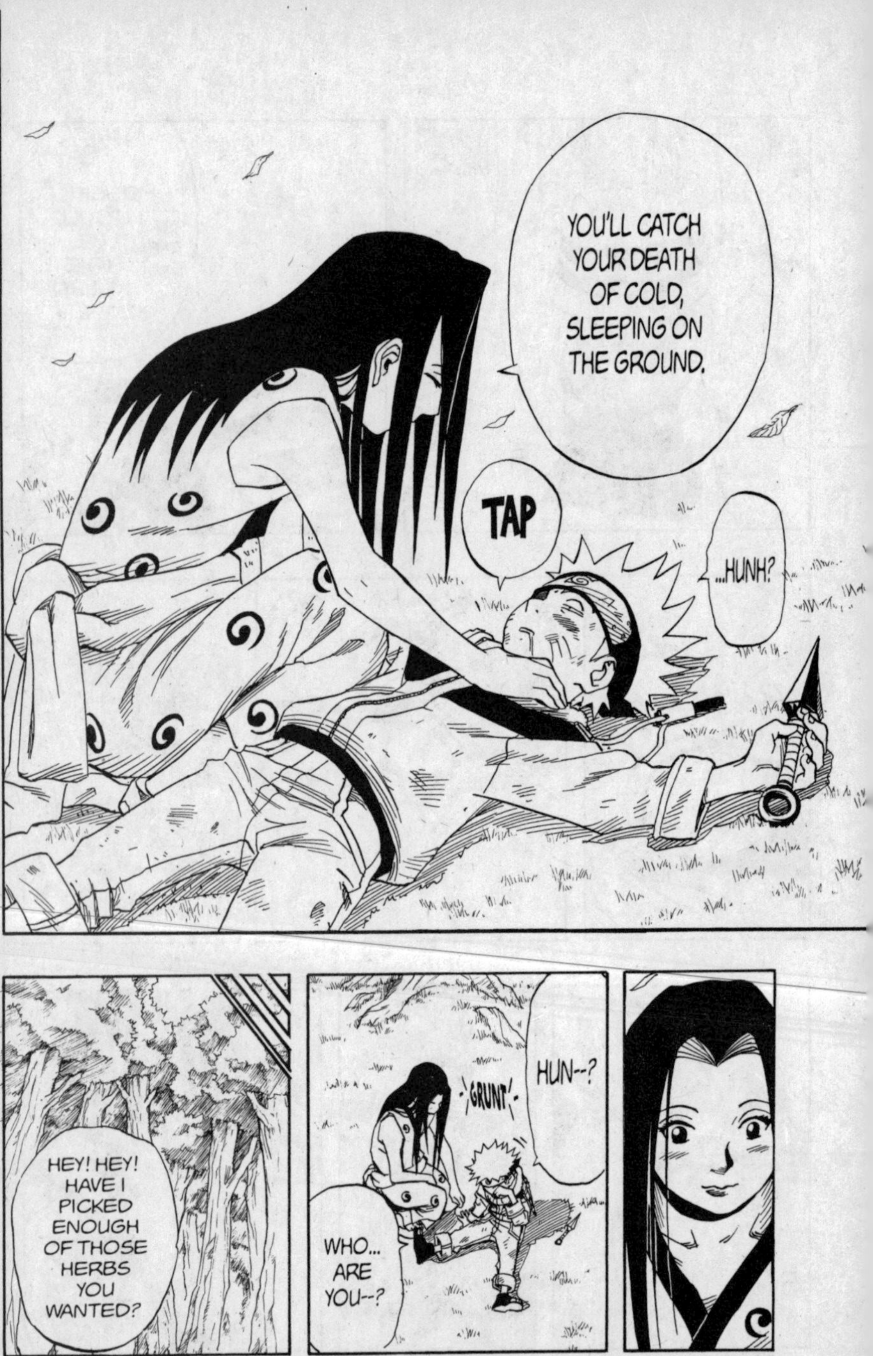
YOU'LL CATCH YOUR DEATH OF COLD, SLEEPING ON THE GROUND.
TAP
...HUNH?
HUN--?
GRUNT
WHO... ARE YOU--?
HEY! HEY! HAVE I PICKED ENOUGH OF THOSE HERBS YOU WANTED?

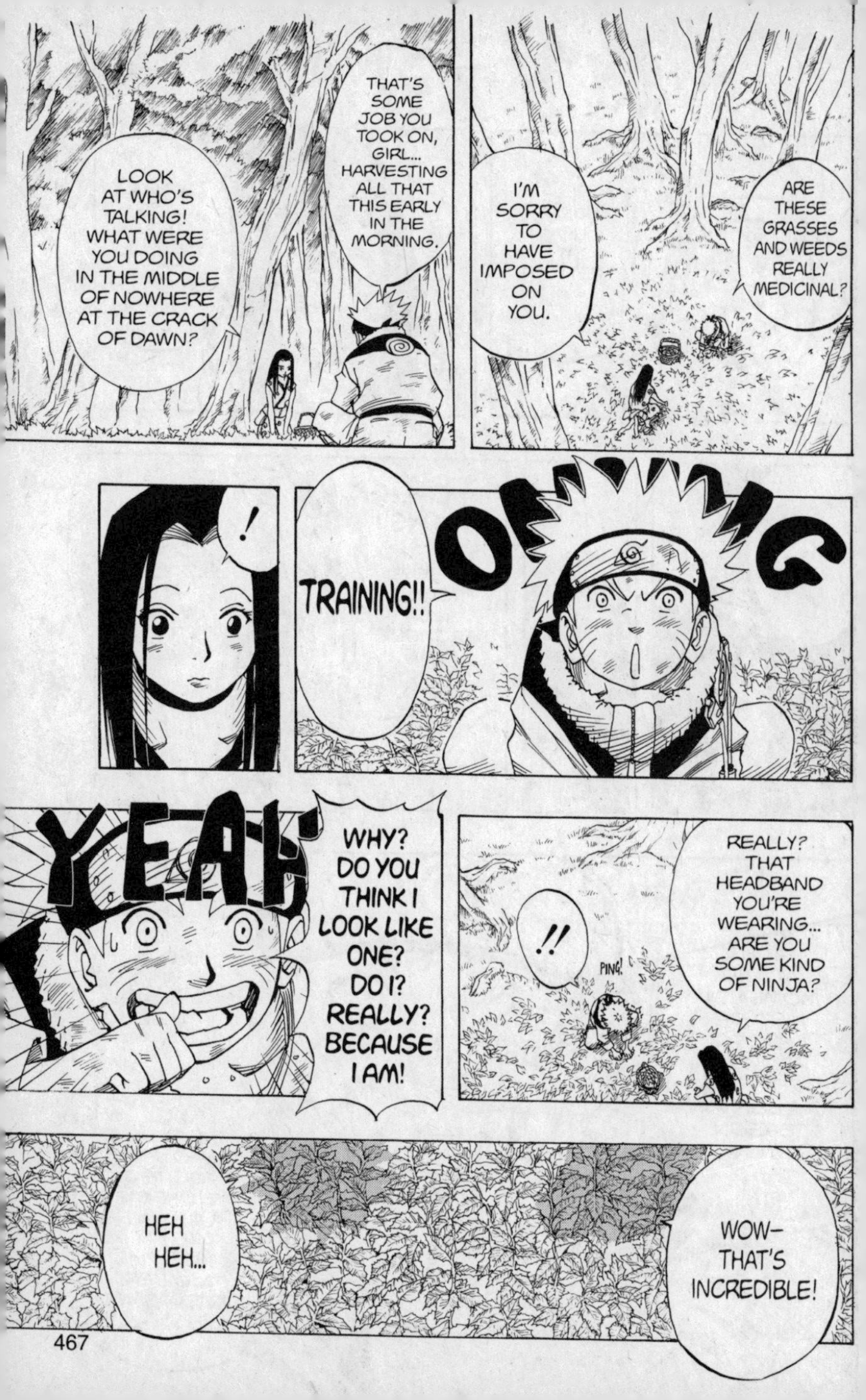
ARE THESE GRASSES AND WEEDS REALLY MEDICINAL?
I'M SORRY TO HAVE IMPOSED ON YOU.
THAT'S SOME JOB YOU TOOK ON, GIRL... HARVESTING ALL THAT THIS EARLY IN THE MORNING.
LOOK AT WHO'S TALKING! WHAT WERE YOU DOING IN THE MIDDLE OF NOWHERE AT THE CRACK OF DAWN?
TRAINING!!
!
REALLY? THAT HEADBAND YOU'RE WEARING... ARE YOU SOME KIND OF NINJA?
!!
PING!
YEAH
WHY? DO YOU THINK I LOOK LIKE ONE? DO I? REALLY? BECAUSE I AM!
WOW— THAT'S INCREDIBLE!
HEH HEH...

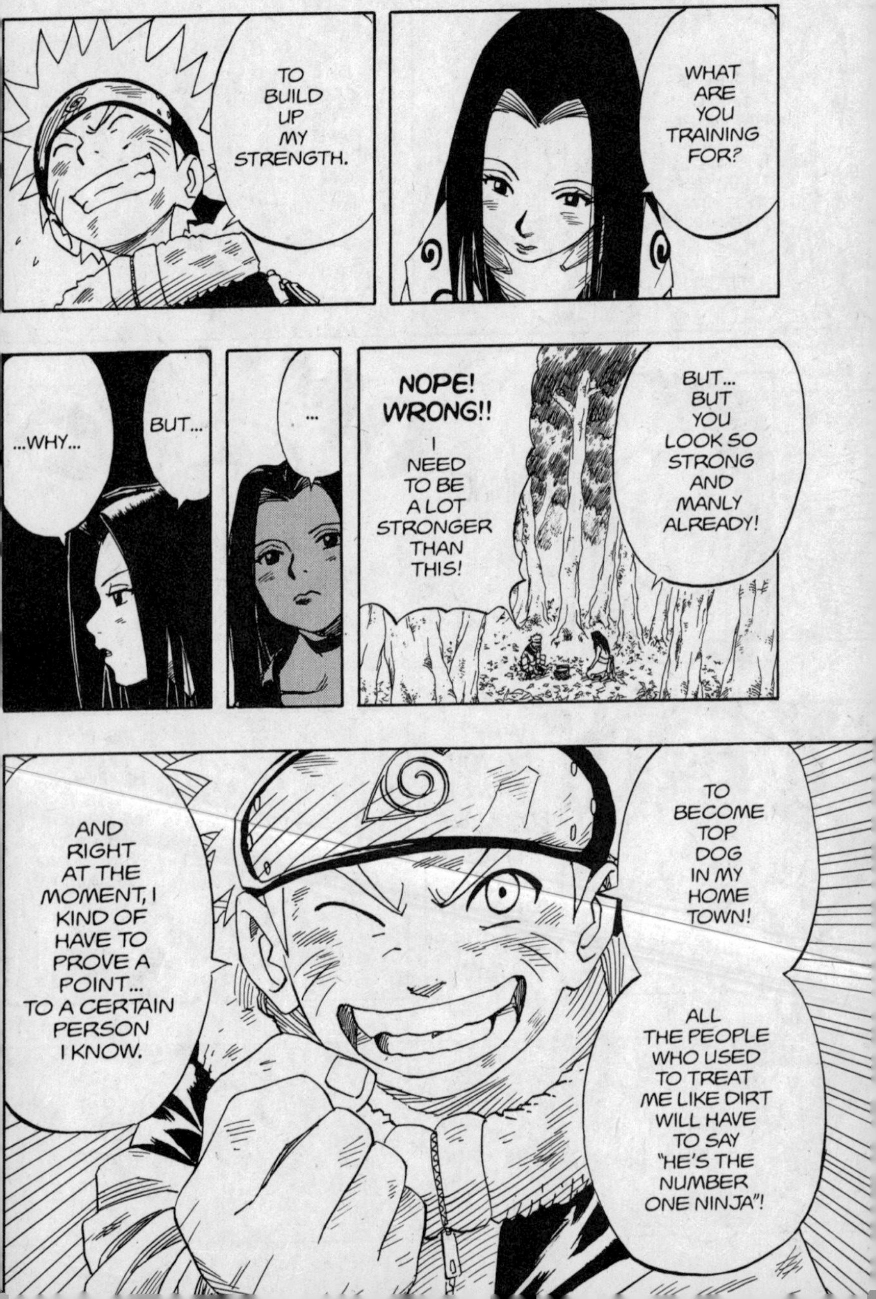
WHAT ARE YOU TRAINING FOR?
TO BUILD UP MY STRENGTH.
BUT... BUT YOU LOOK SO STRONG AND MANLY ALREADY!
NOPE! WRONG!!
I NEED TO BE A LOT STRONGER THAN THIS!
...
BUT...
...WHY...
TO BECOME TOP DOG IN MY HOME TOWN!
ALL THE PEOPLE WHO USED TO TREAT ME LIKE DIRT WILL HAVE TO SAY "HE'S THE NUMBER ONE NINJA"!
AND RIGHT AT THE MOMENT, I KIND OF HAVE TO PROVE A POINT... TO A CERTAIN PERSON I KNOW.

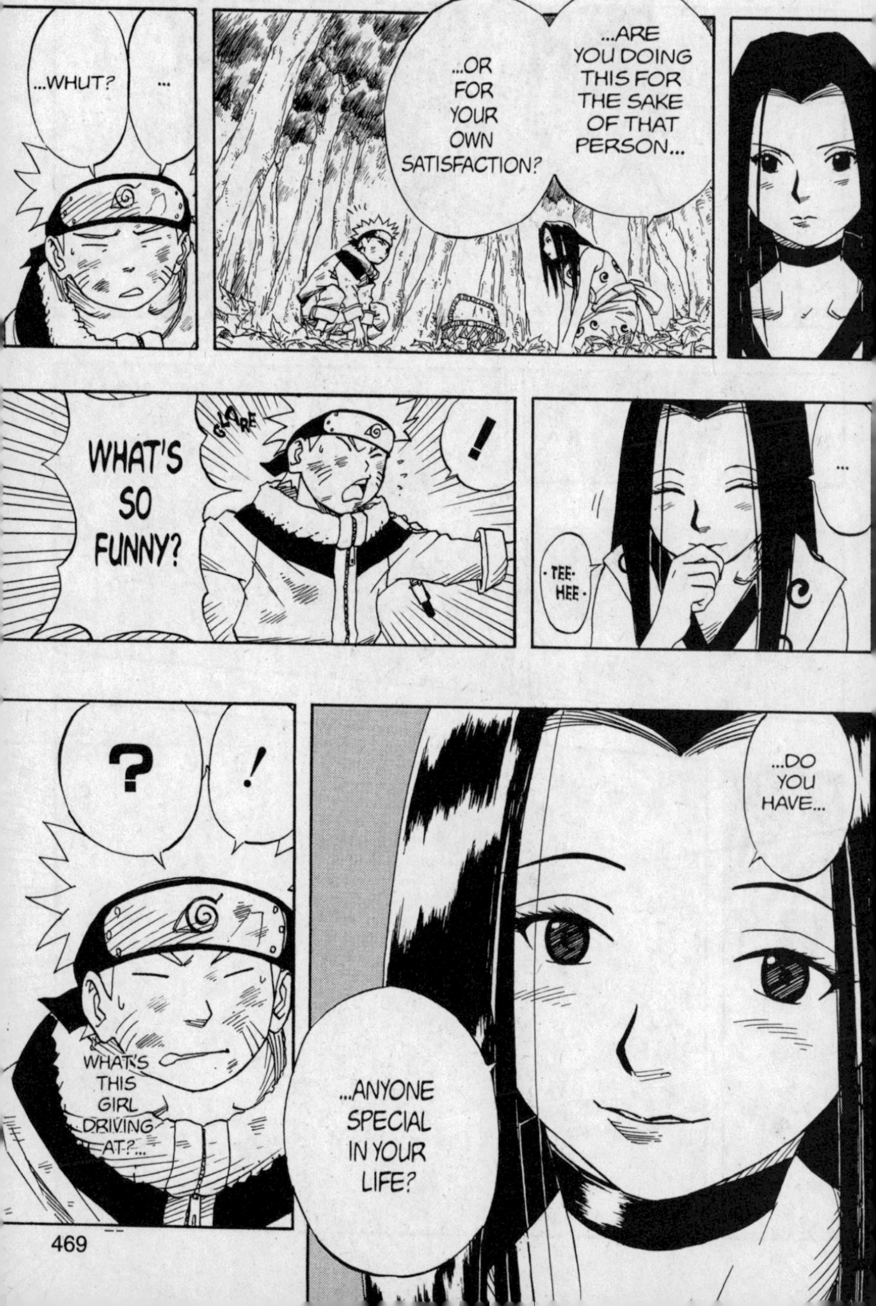
...ARE YOU DOING THIS FOR THE SAKE OF THAT PERSON...
...OR FOR YOUR OWN SATISFACTION?
...
...WHUT?
...
TEE-HEE
!
GLARE
WHAT'S SO FUNNY?
...DO YOU HAVE...
...ANYONE SPECIAL IN YOUR LIFE?
!
?
WHAT'S THIS GIRL DRIVING AT?...

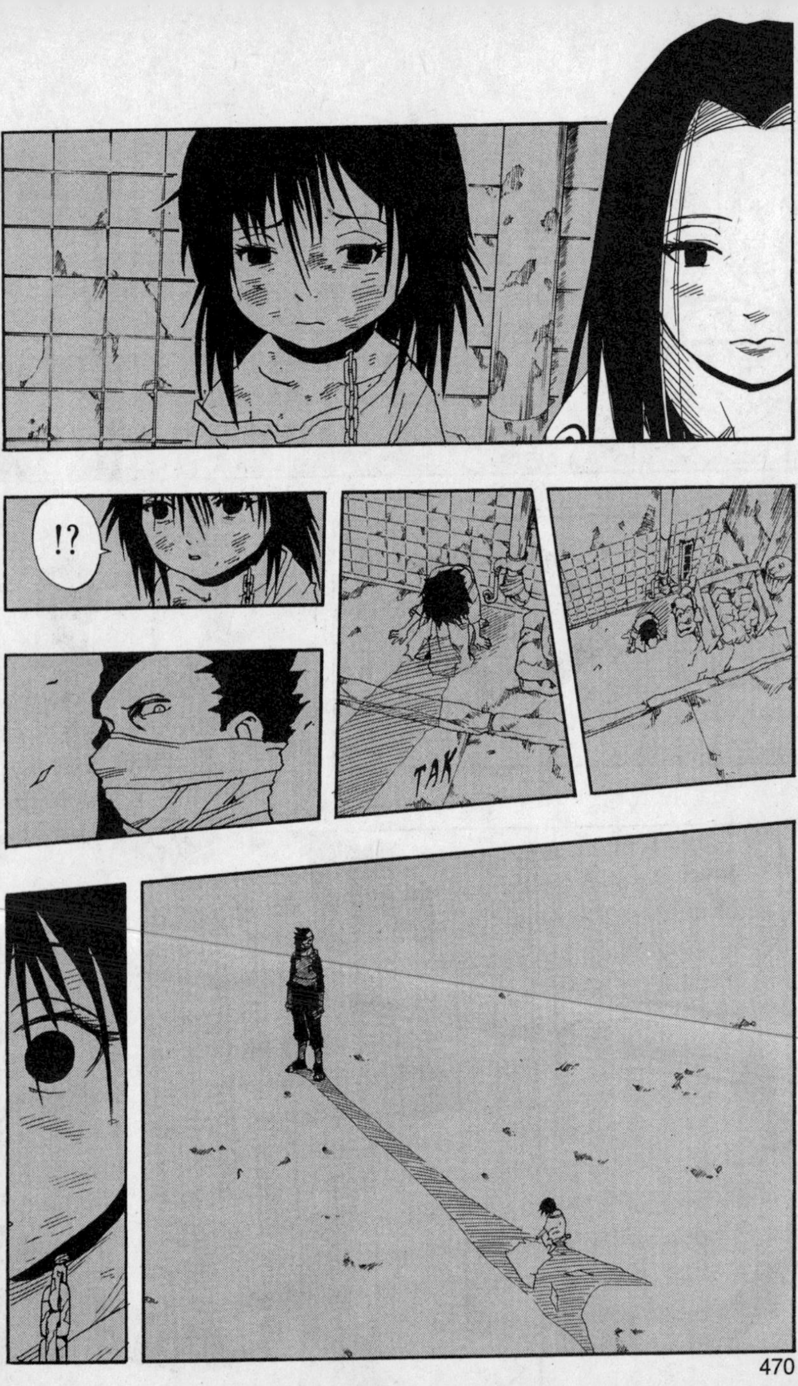
!?
TAK

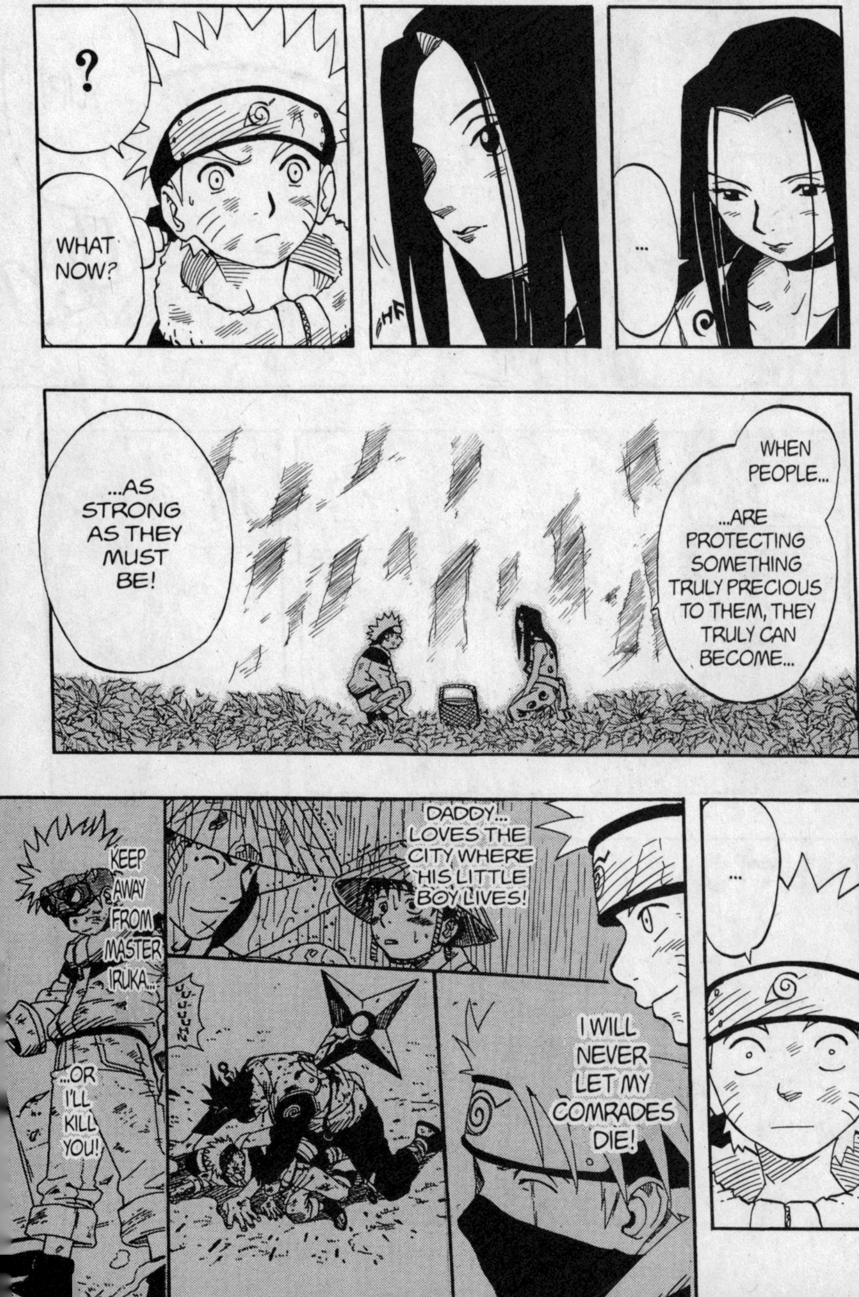
...
GHF
?
WHAT NOW?
WHEN PEOPLE...
...ARE PROTECTING SOMETHING TRULY PRECIOUS TO THEM, THEY TRULY CAN BECOME...
...AS STRONG AS THEY MUST BE!
...
I WILL NEVER LET MY COMRADES DIE!
DADDY... LOVES THE CITY WHERE HIS LITTLE BOY LIVES!
KEEP AWAY FROM MASTER IRUKA...
...OR I'LL KILL YOU!

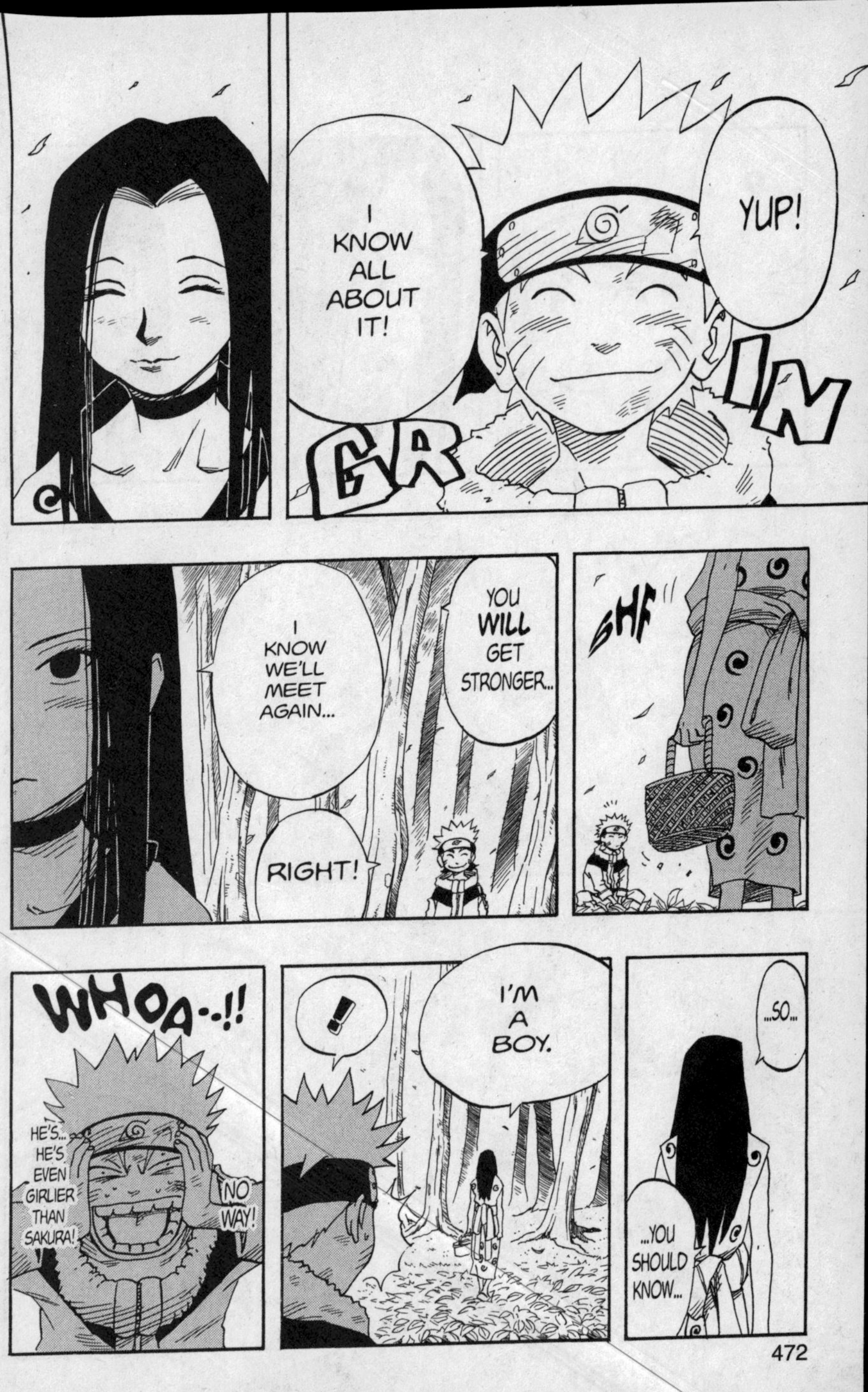
YUP!
I KNOW ALL ABOUT IT!
GR IN
SHF
YOU WILL GET STRONGER...
I KNOW WE'LL MEET AGAIN...
RIGHT!
...SO...
...YOU SHOULD KNOW...
I'M A BOY.
!
WHOA-.!!
NO WAY!
HE'S... HE'S EVEN GIRLIER THAN SAKURA!

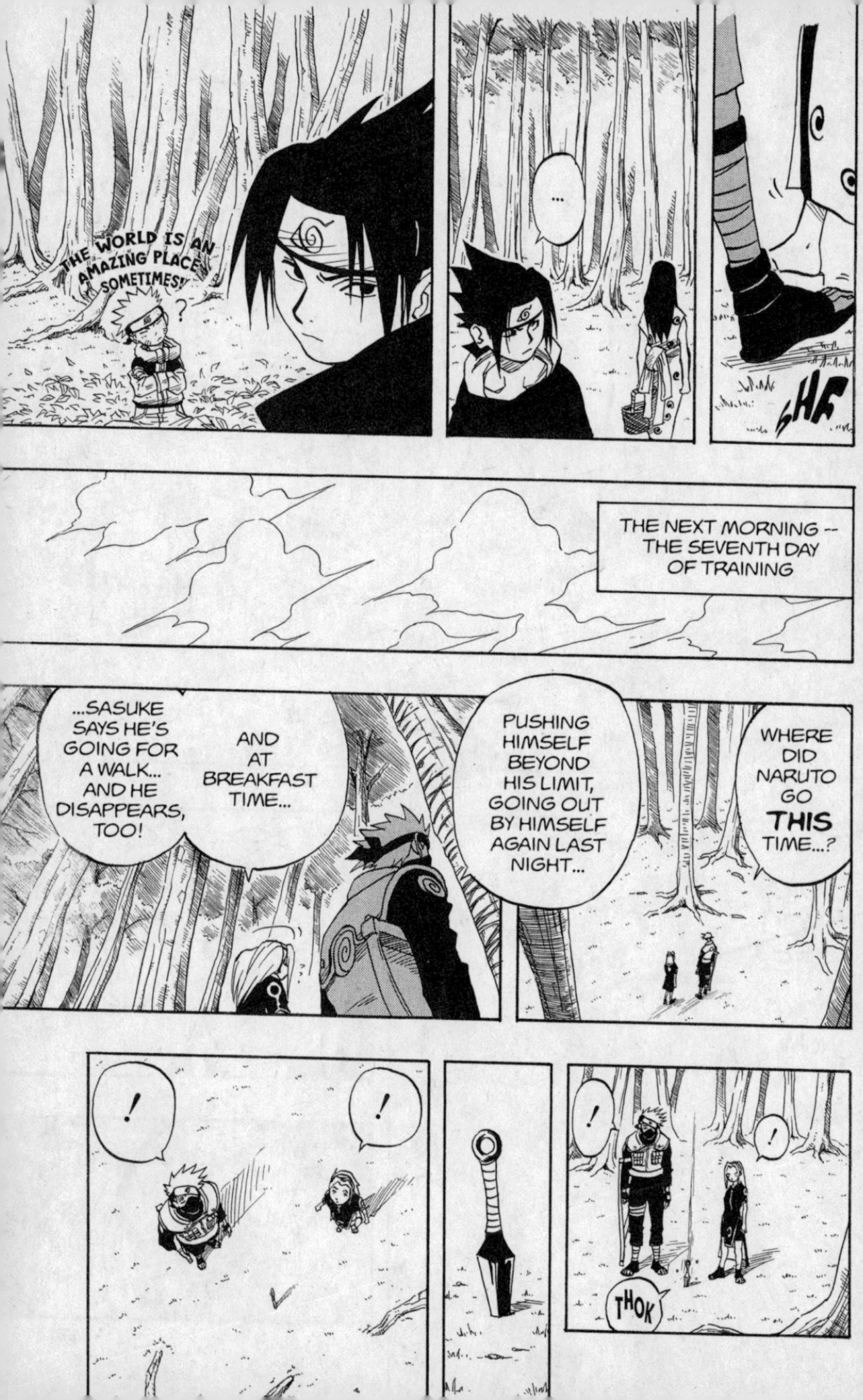
SHF
...
THE WORLD IS AN AMAZING PLACE SOMETIMES!!
?
THE NEXT MORNING -- THE SEVENTH DAY OF TRAINING
WHERE DID NARUTO GO THIS TIME...?
PUSHING HIMSELF BEYOND HIS LIMIT, GOING OUT BY HIMSELF AGAIN LAST NIGHT...
AND AT BREAKFAST TIME...
...SASUKE SAYS HE'S GOING FOR A WALK... AND HE DISAPPEARS, TOO!
!
!
THOK
!
!

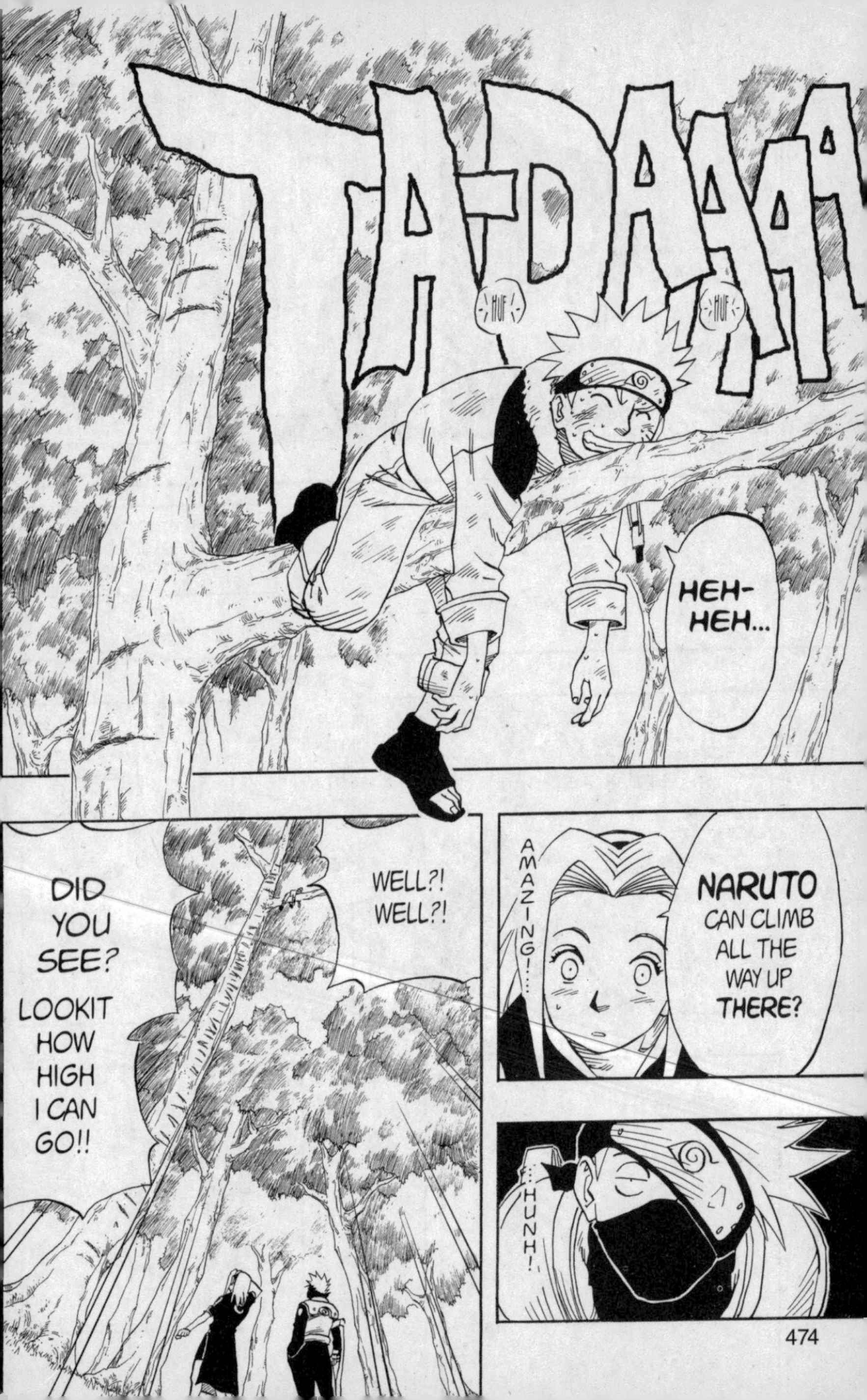
TA-DAAA
HUF
HUF
HEH-HEH...
AMAZING!...
NARUTO CAN CLIMB ALL THE WAY UP THERE?
...HUNH!
WELL?! WELL?!
DID YOU SEE?
LOOKIT HOW HIGH I CAN GO!!

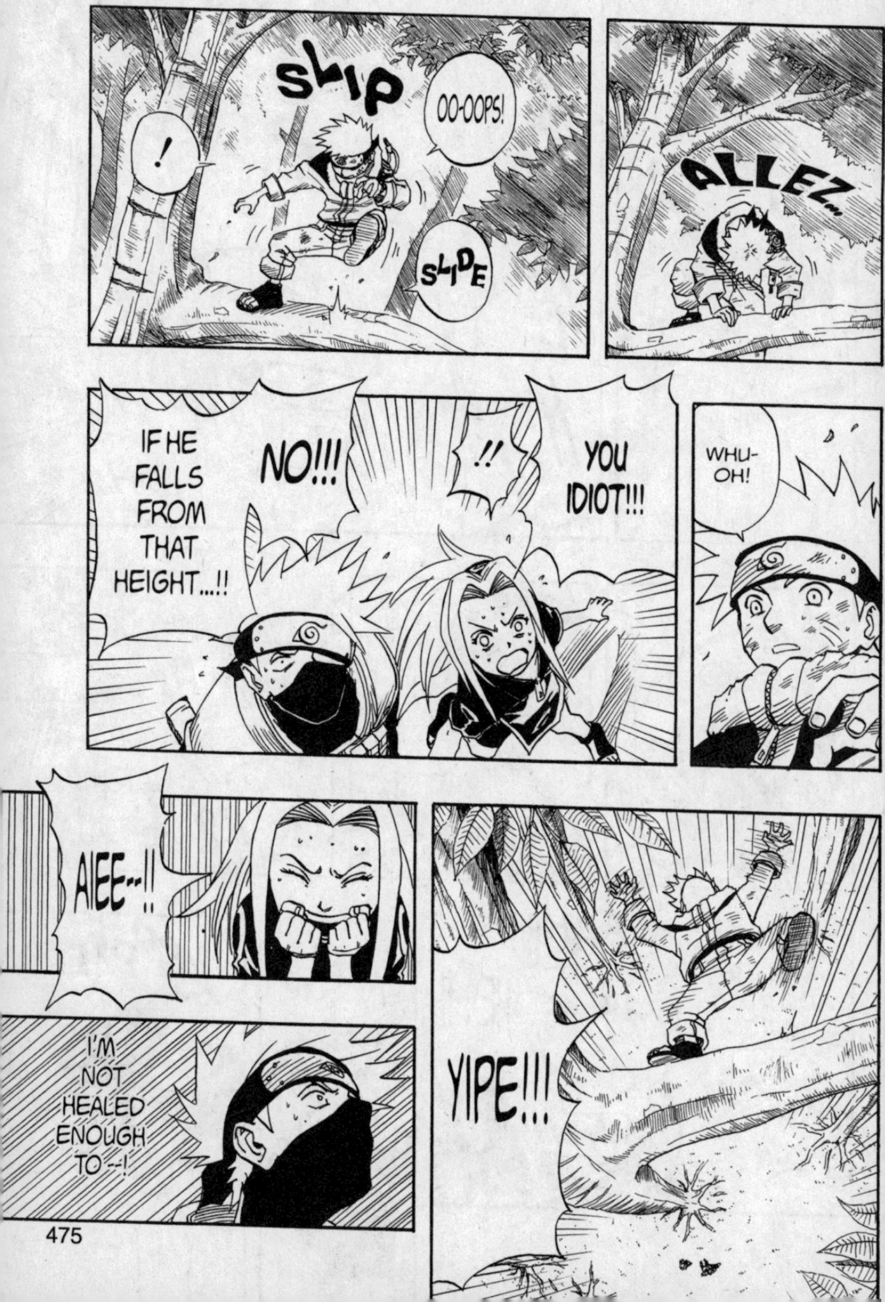
ALLEZ...
OO-OOPS!
SLIP
!
SLIDE
WHU-OH!
YOU IDIOT!!!
!!
NO!!!
IF HE FALLS FROM THAT HEIGHT...!!
YIPE!!!
AIEE--!!
I'M NOT HEALED ENOUGH TO--!

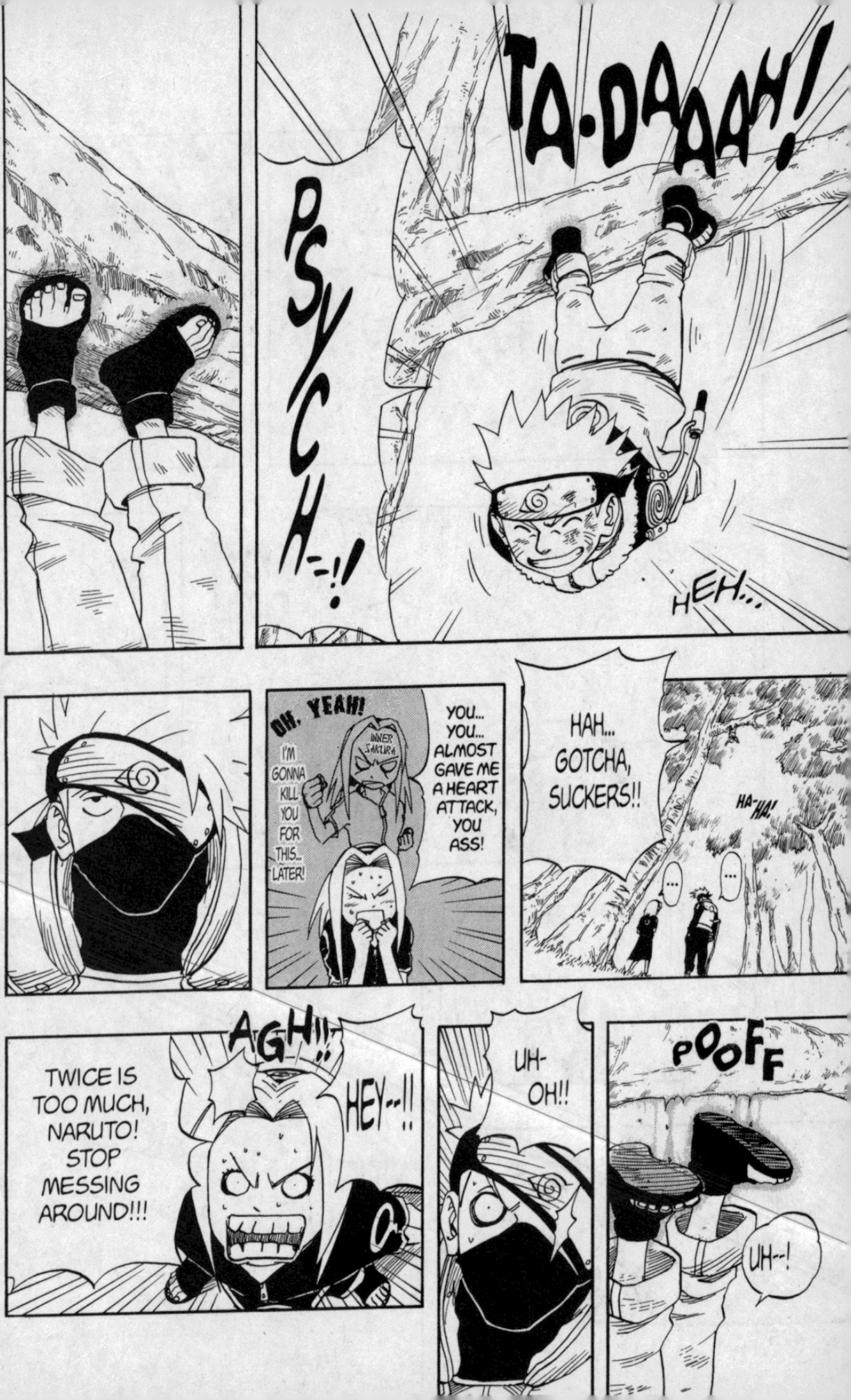
TA-DAAAH!
PSYCH--!!
HEH...
HAH... GOTCHA, SUCKERS!!
HA-HA!
...
...
YOU... YOU... ALMOST GAVE ME A HEART ATTACK, YOU ASS!
OH, YEAH!
INNER SAKURA
I'M GONNA KILL YOU FOR THIS... LATER!
POOFF
UH--!
UH-OH!!
AGH!!
HEY--!!
TWICE IS TOO MUCH, NARUTO! STOP MESSING AROUND!!!

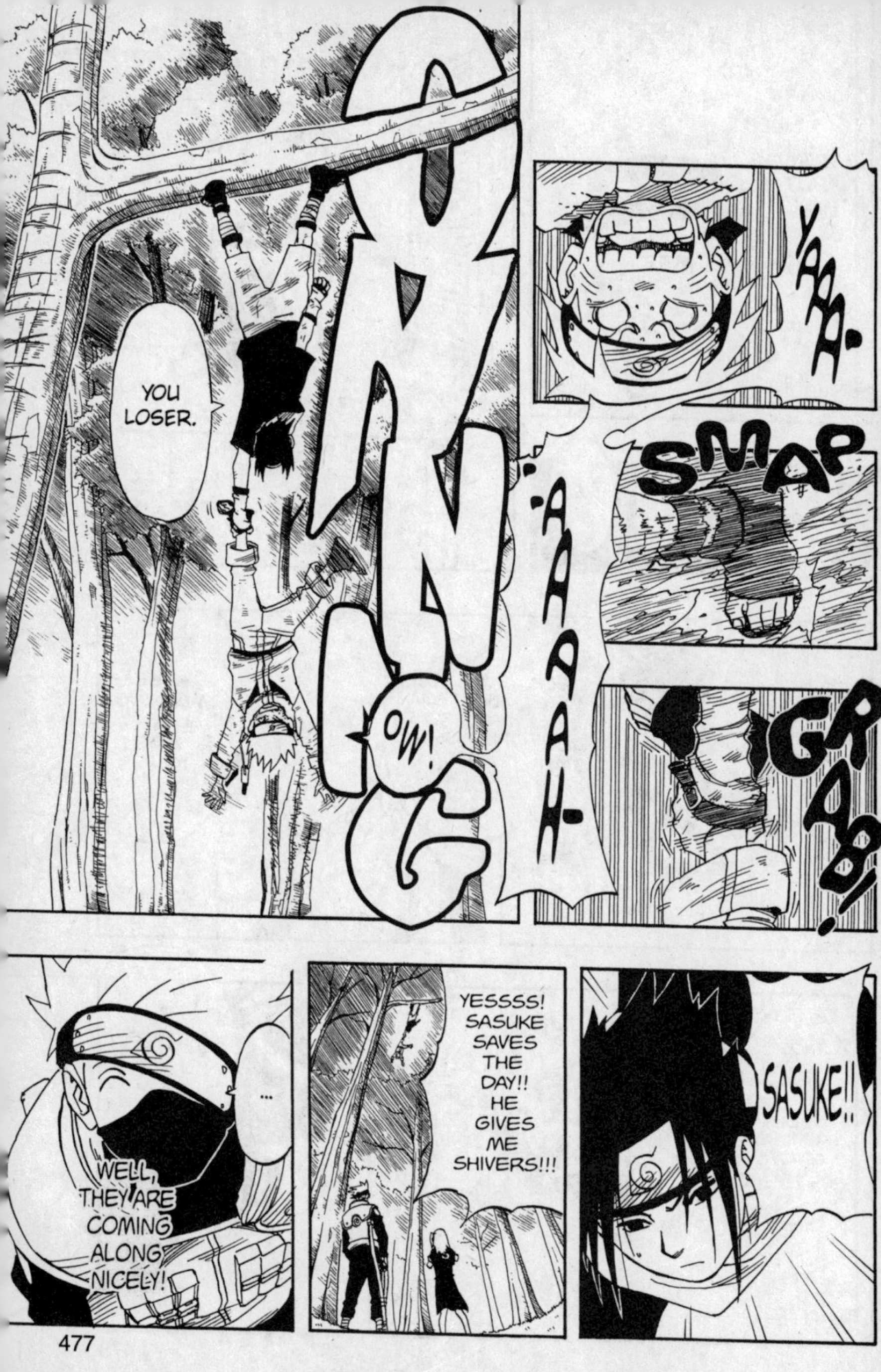
YAAAA-
SMAP
GRAB!
SWING
OW!
YOU LOSER.
-AAAAAH-
SASUKE!!
YESSSS! SASUKE SAVES THE DAY!! HE GIVES ME SHIVERS!!!
...
WELL, THEY ARE COMING ALONG NICELY!

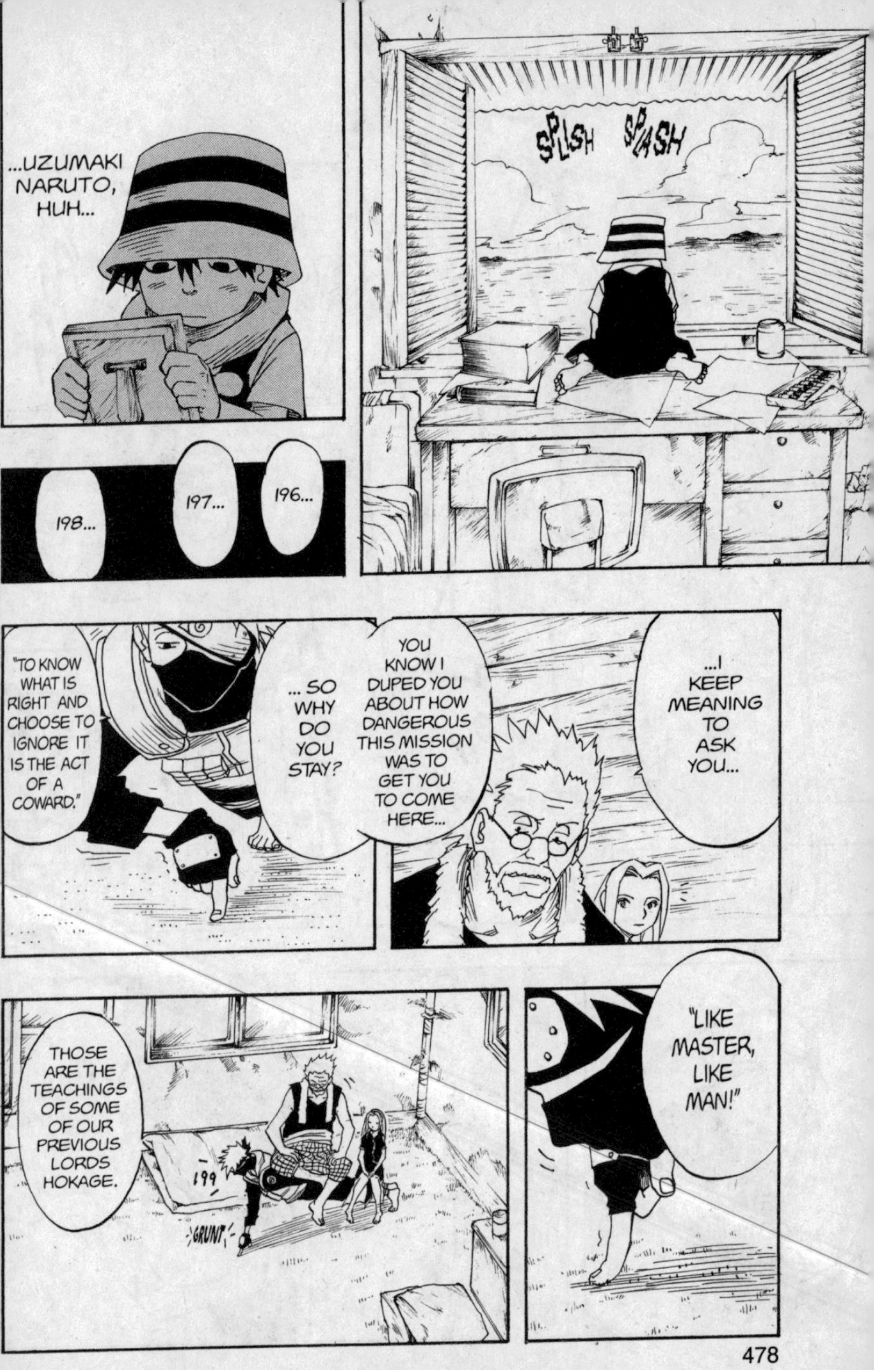
SPLISH SPLASH
...UZUMAKI NARUTO, HUH...
196...
197...
198...
...I KEEP MEANING TO ASK YOU...
YOU KNOW I DUPED YOU ABOUT HOW DANGEROUS THIS MISSION WAS TO GET YOU TO COME HERE...
... SO WHY DO YOU STAY?
"TO KNOW WHAT IS RIGHT AND CHOOSE TO IGNORE IT IS THE ACT OF A COWARD."
"LIKE MASTER, LIKE MAN!"
THOSE ARE THE TEACHINGS OF SOME OF OUR PREVIOUS LORDS HOKAGE.
199
GRUNT

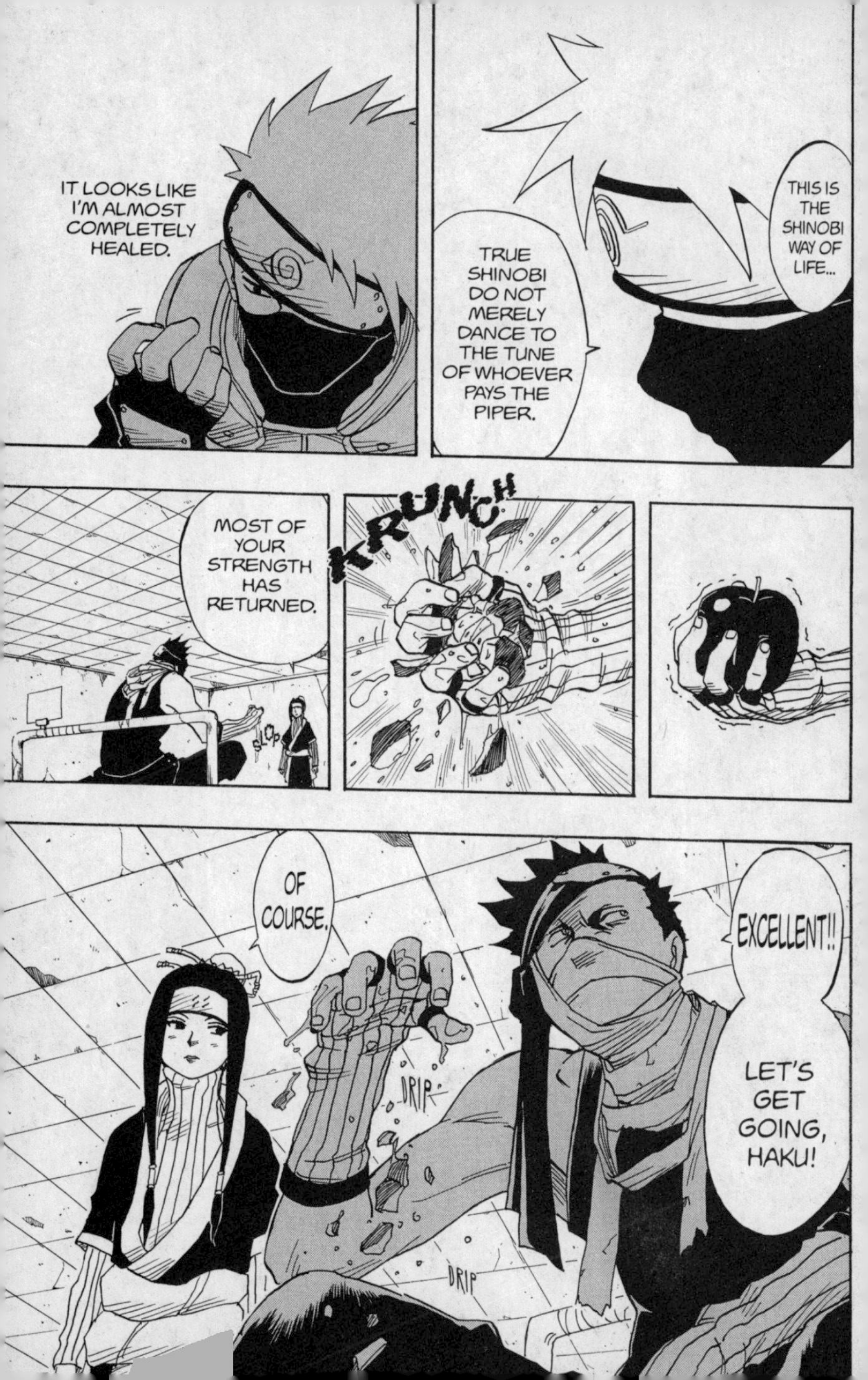
THIS IS THE SHINOBI WAY OF LIFE...
TRUE SHINOBI DO NOT MERELY DANCE TO THE TUNE OF WHOEVER PAYS THE PIPER.
IT LOOKS LIKE I'M ALMOST COMPLETELY HEALED.
KRUNCH
MOST OF YOUR STRENGTH HAS RETURNED.
SLOP
EXCELLENT!!
LET'S GET GOING, HAKU!
OF COURSE.
DRIP
DRIP

NARUTO

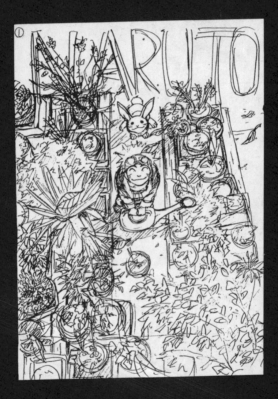

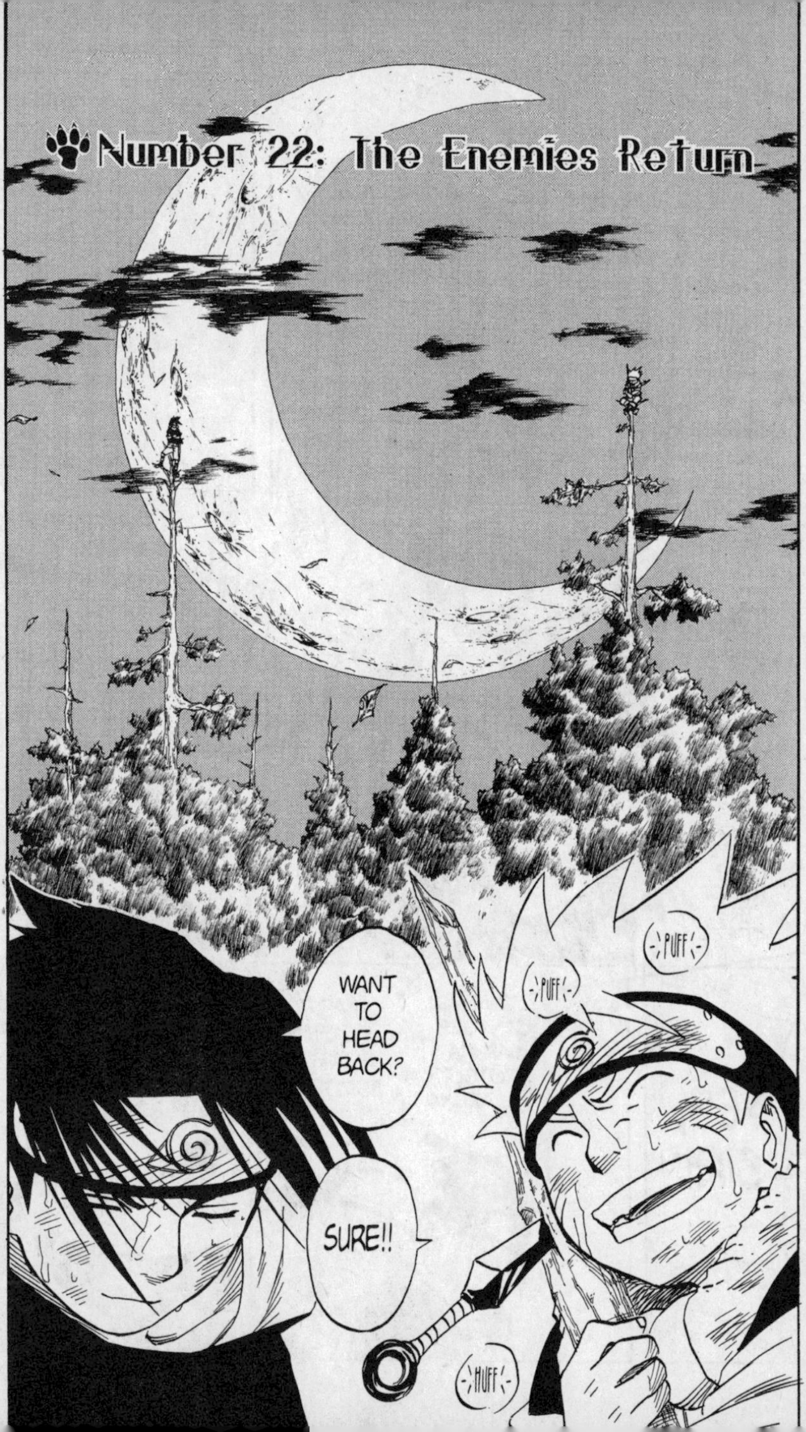
Number 22: The Enemies Return
PUFF
PUFF
WANT TO HEAD BACK?
SURE!!
HUFF

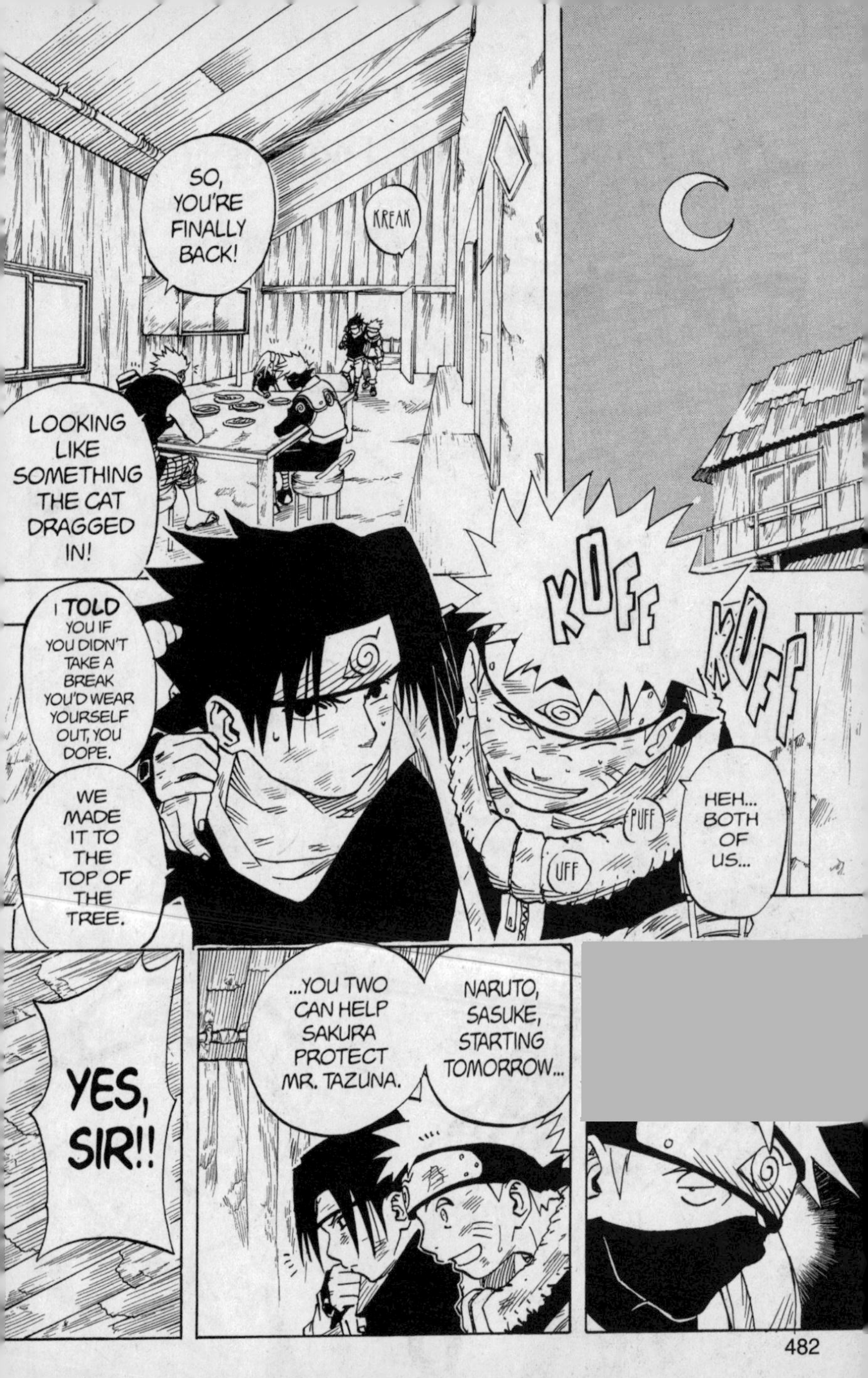
SO, YOU'RE FINALLY BACK!
KREAK
LOOKING LIKE SOMETHING THE CAT DRAGGED IN!
KOFF
KOFF
HEH... BOTH OF US...
PUFF
UFF
I TOLD YOU IF YOU DIDN'T TAKE A BREAK YOU'D WEAR YOURSELF OUT, YOU DOPE.
WE MADE IT TO THE TOP OF THE TREE.
NARUTO, SASUKE, STARTING TOMORROW...
...YOU TWO CAN HELP SAKURA PROTECT MR. TAZUNA.
YES, SIR!!

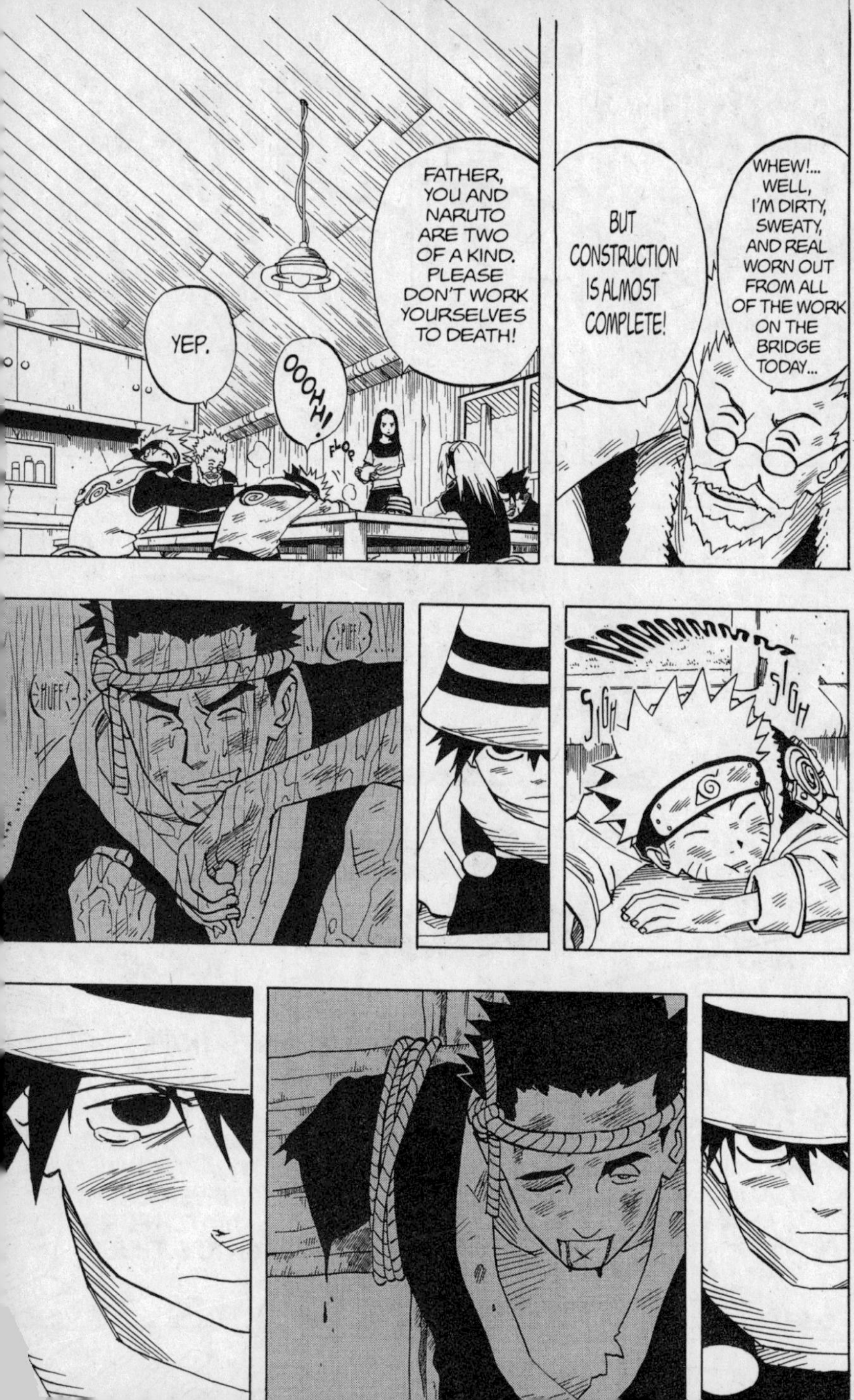
WHEW!... WELL, I'M DIRTY, SWEATY, AND REAL WORN OUT FROM ALL OF THE WORK ON THE BRIDGE TODAY...
BUT CONSTRUCTION IS ALMOST COMPLETE!
FATHER, YOU AND NARUTO ARE TWO OF A KIND. PLEASE DON'T WORK YOURSELVES TO DEATH!
OOOHH!
FLOP
YEP.
SIGH
SIGH
PUFF
HUFF

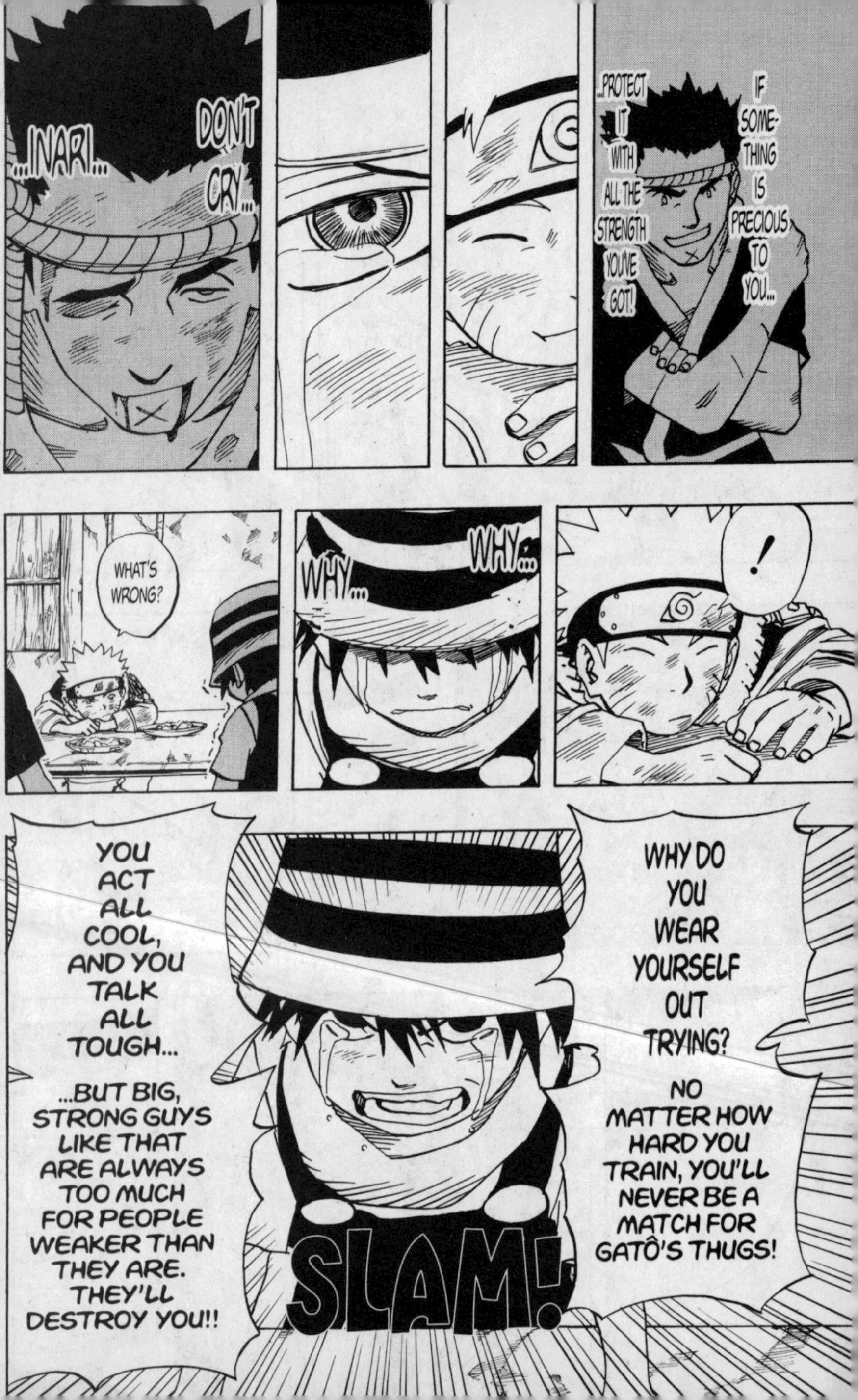
IF SOMETHING IS PRECIOUS TO YOU...
...PROTECT IT WITH ALL THE STRENGTH YOU'VE GOT!
DON'T CRY...
...INARI...
!
WHY...
WHY...
WHAT'S WRONG?
WHY DO YOU WEAR YOURSELF OUT TRYING?
NO MATTER HOW HARD YOU TRAIN, YOU'LL NEVER BE A MATCH FOR GATÔ'S THUGS!
YOU ACT ALL COOL, AND YOU TALK ALL TOUGH...
...BUT BIG, STRONG GUYS LIKE THAT ARE ALWAYS TOO MUCH FOR PEOPLE WEAKER THAN THEY ARE. THEY'LL DESTROY YOU!!
SLAM!

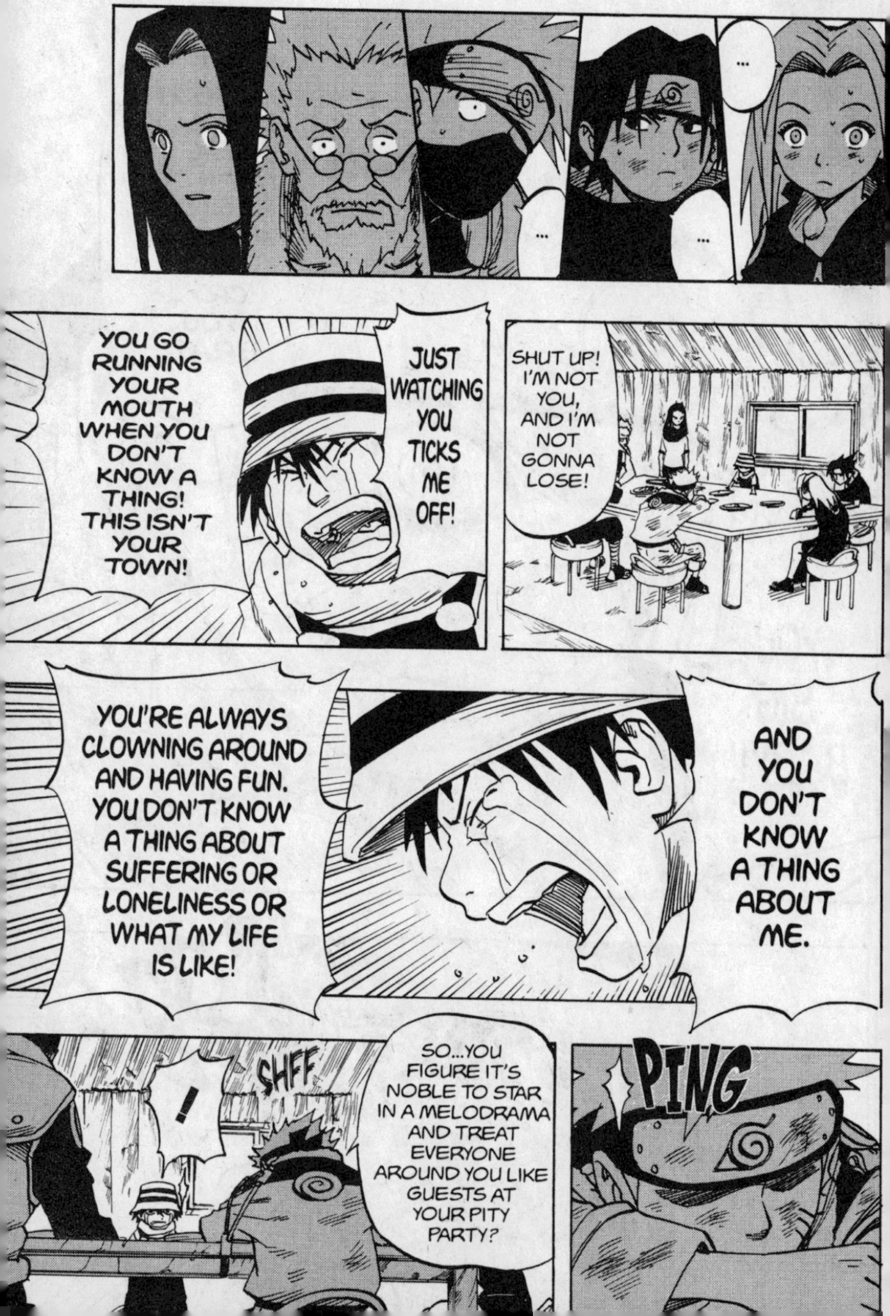
...
...
...
SHUT UP! I'M NOT YOU, AND I'M NOT GONNA LOSE!
JUST WATCHING YOU TICKS ME OFF!
YOU GO RUNNING YOUR MOUTH WHEN YOU DON'T KNOW A THING! THIS ISN'T YOUR TOWN!
AND YOU DON'T KNOW A THING ABOUT ME.
YOU'RE ALWAYS CLOWNING AROUND AND HAVING FUN. YOU DON'T KNOW A THING ABOUT SUFFERING OR LONELINESS OR WHAT MY LIFE IS LIKE!
PING
SO...YOU FIGURE IT'S NOBLE TO STAR IN A MELODRAMA AND TREAT EVERYONE AROUND YOU LIKE GUESTS AT YOUR PITY PARTY?
SHFF
!

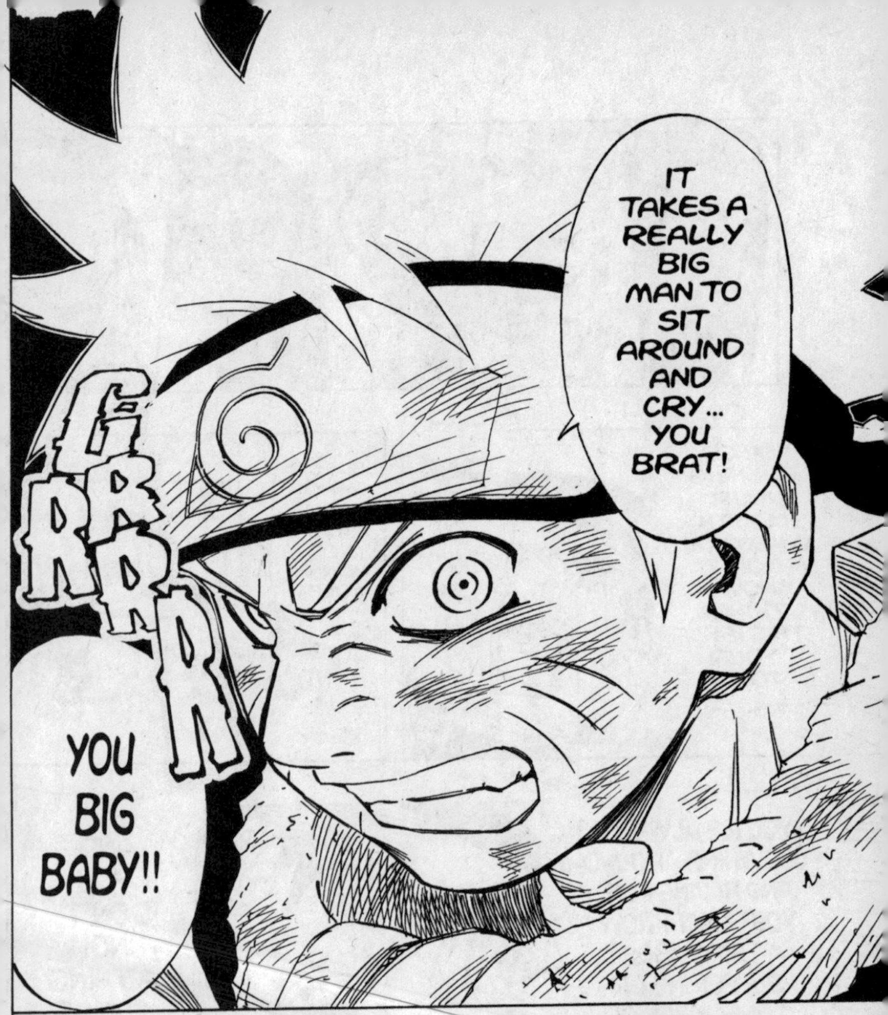
IT TAKES A REALLY BIG MAN TO SIT AROUND AND CRY... YOU BRAT!
GRRRR
YOU BIG BABY!!
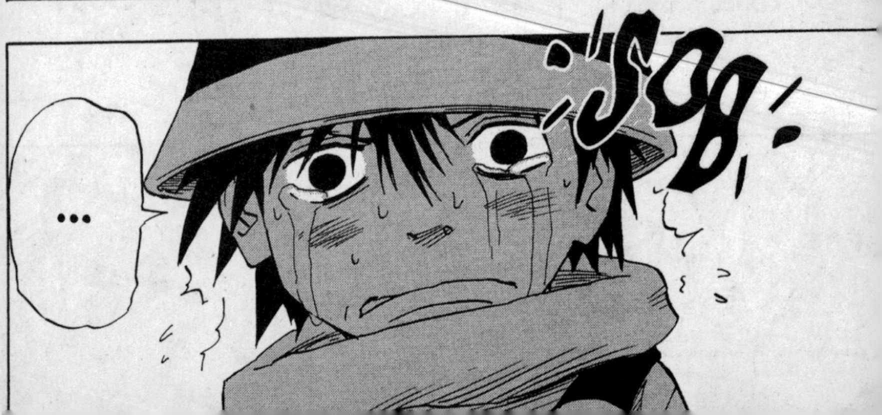
SOB
...

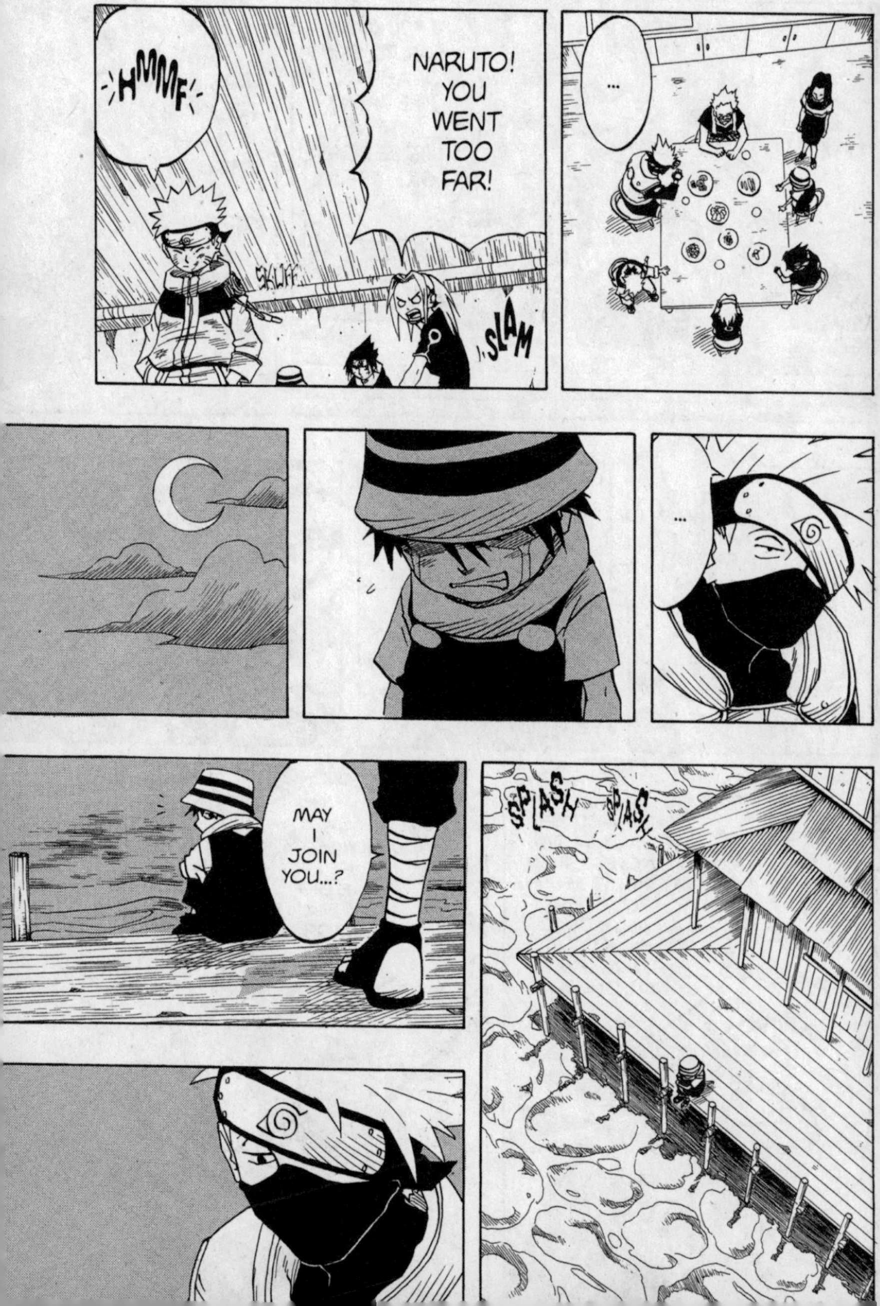
...
NARUTO! YOU WENT TOO FAR!
HMMF
SKUFF
SLAM
...
SPLASH
SPLASH
MAY I JOIN YOU...?

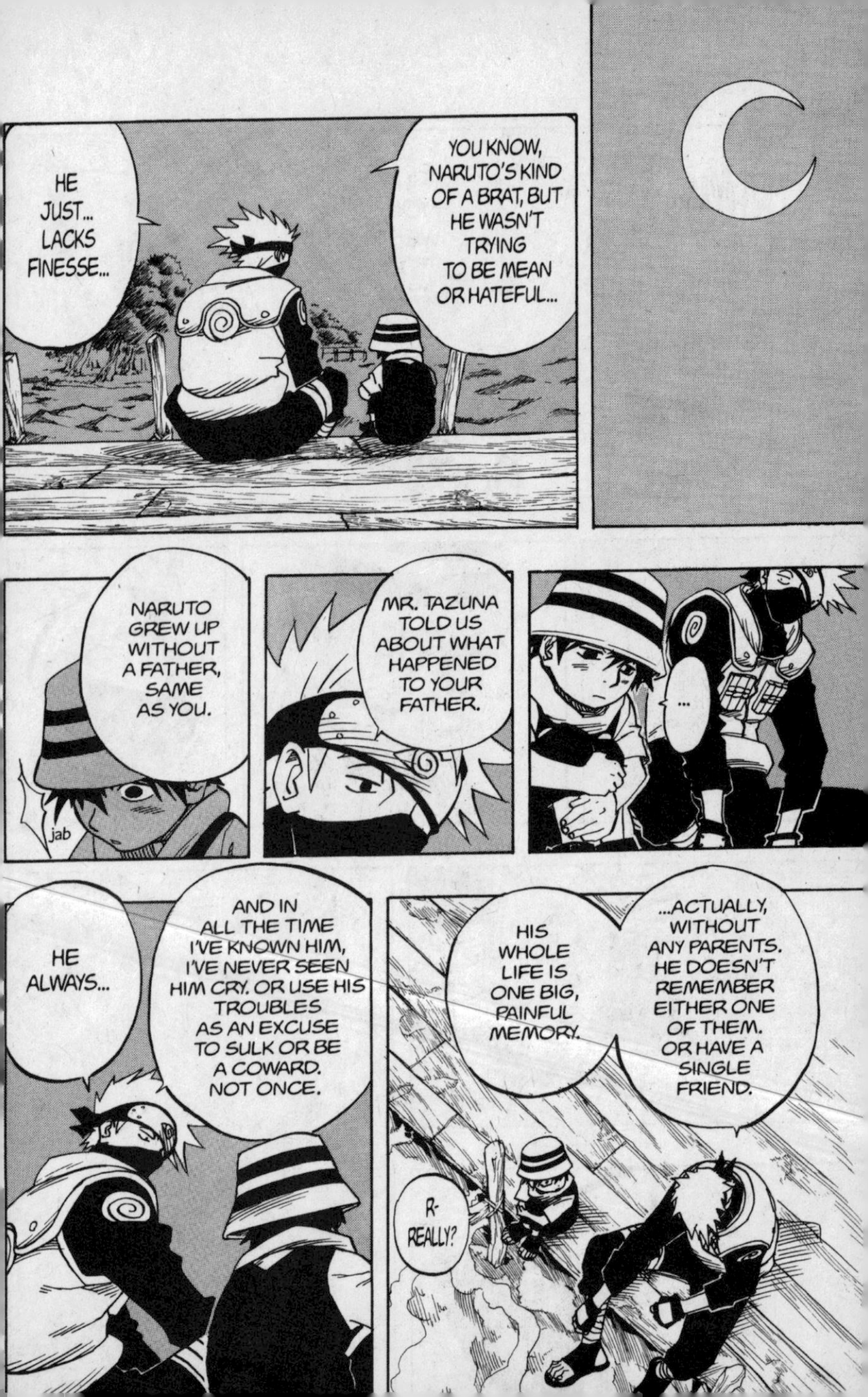
YOU KNOW, NARUTO'S KIND OF A BRAT, BUT HE WASN'T TRYING TO BE MEAN OR HATEFUL...
HE JUST... LACKS FINESSE...
...
MR. TAZUNA TOLD US ABOUT WHAT HAPPENED TO YOUR FATHER.
NARUTO GREW UP WITHOUT A FATHER, SAME AS YOU.
jab
...ACTUALLY, WITHOUT ANY PARENTS. HE DOESN'T REMEMBER EITHER ONE OF THEM. OR HAVE A SINGLE FRIEND.
HIS WHOLE LIFE IS ONE BIG, PAINFUL MEMORY.
R-REALLY?
AND IN ALL THE TIME I'VE KNOWN HIM, I'VE NEVER SEEN HIM CRY. OR USE HIS TROUBLES AS AN EXCUSE TO SULK OR BE A COWARD. NOT ONCE.
HE ALWAYS...

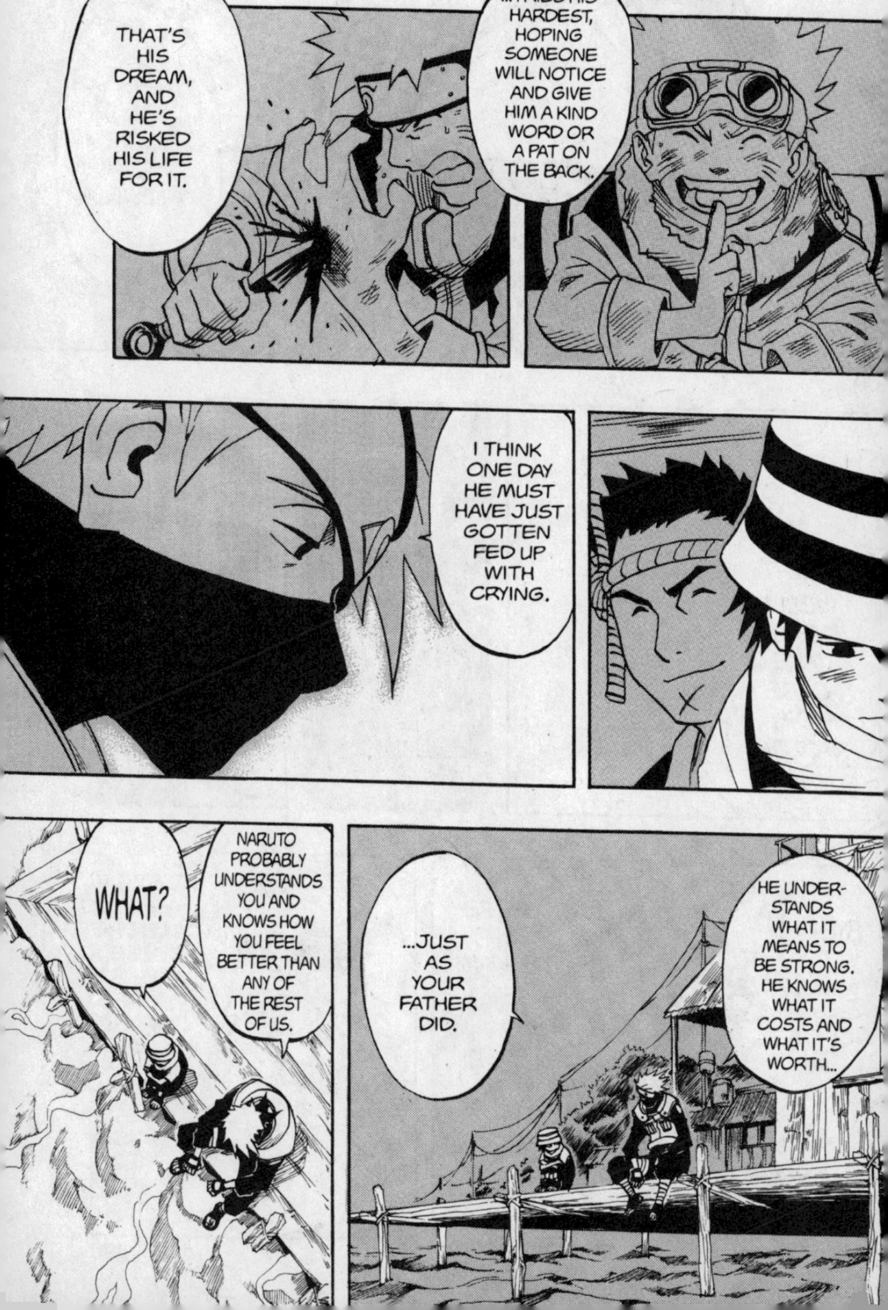
THAT'S HIS DREAM, AND HE'S RISKED HIS LIFE FOR IT.
...TRIES HIS HARDEST, HOPING SOMEONE WILL NOTICE AND GIVE HIM A KIND WORD OR A PAT ON THE BACK.
I THINK ONE DAY HE MUST HAVE JUST GOTTEN FED UP WITH CRYING.
WHAT?
NARUTO PROBABLY UNDERSTANDS YOU AND KNOWS HOW YOU FEEL BETTER THAN ANY OF THE REST OF US.
...JUST AS YOUR FATHER DID.
HE UNDER-STANDS WHAT IT MEANS TO BE STRONG. HE KNOWS WHAT IT COSTS AND WHAT IT'S WORTH...

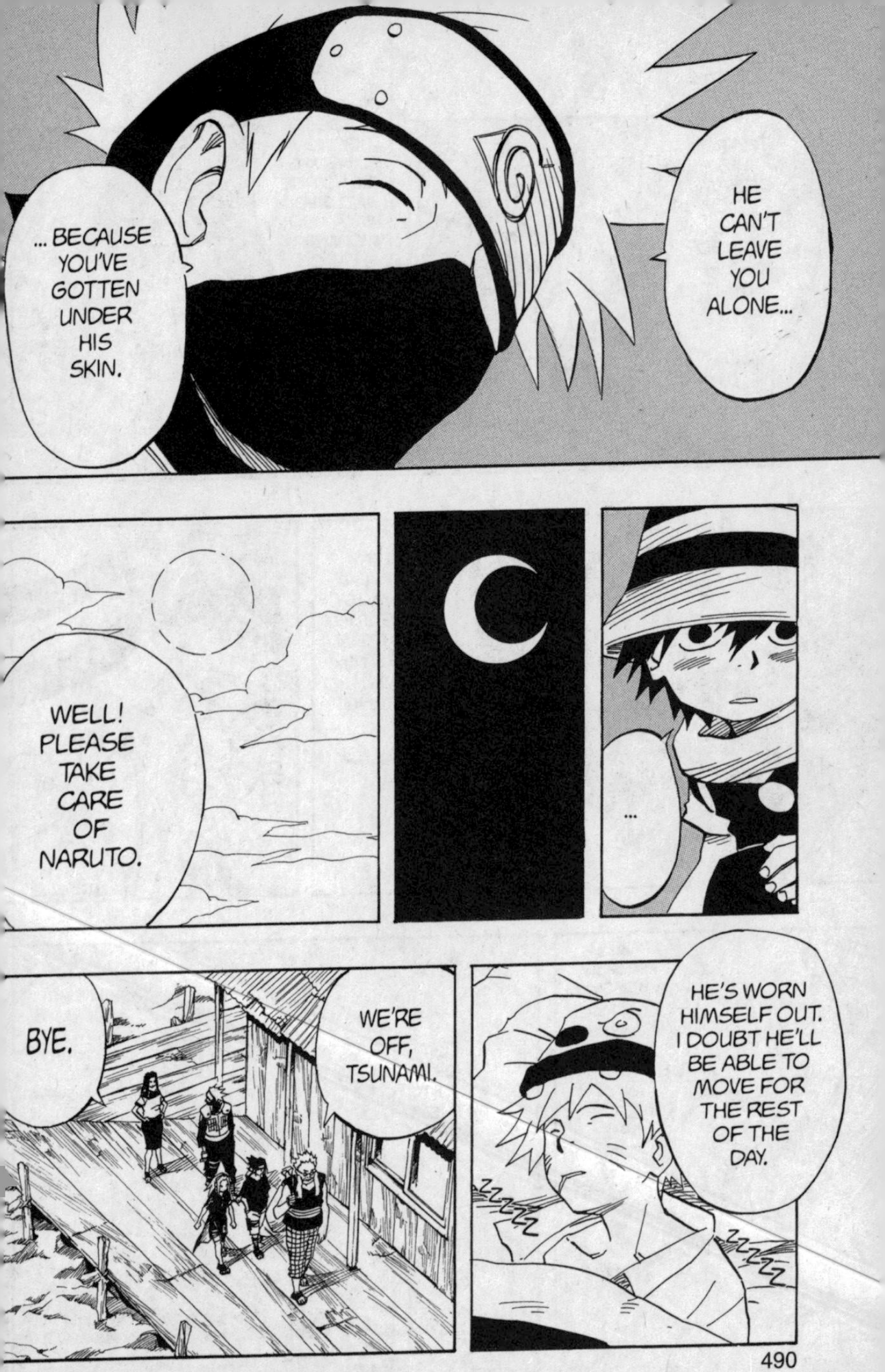
HE CAN'T LEAVE YOU ALONE...
... BECAUSE YOU'VE GOTTEN UNDER HIS SKIN.
...
WELL! PLEASE TAKE CARE OF NARUTO.
HE'S WORN HIMSELF OUT. I DOUBT HE'LL BE ABLE TO MOVE FOR THE REST OF THE DAY.
ZZZZZ
ZZZZZ
WE'RE OFF, TSUNAMI.
BYE.

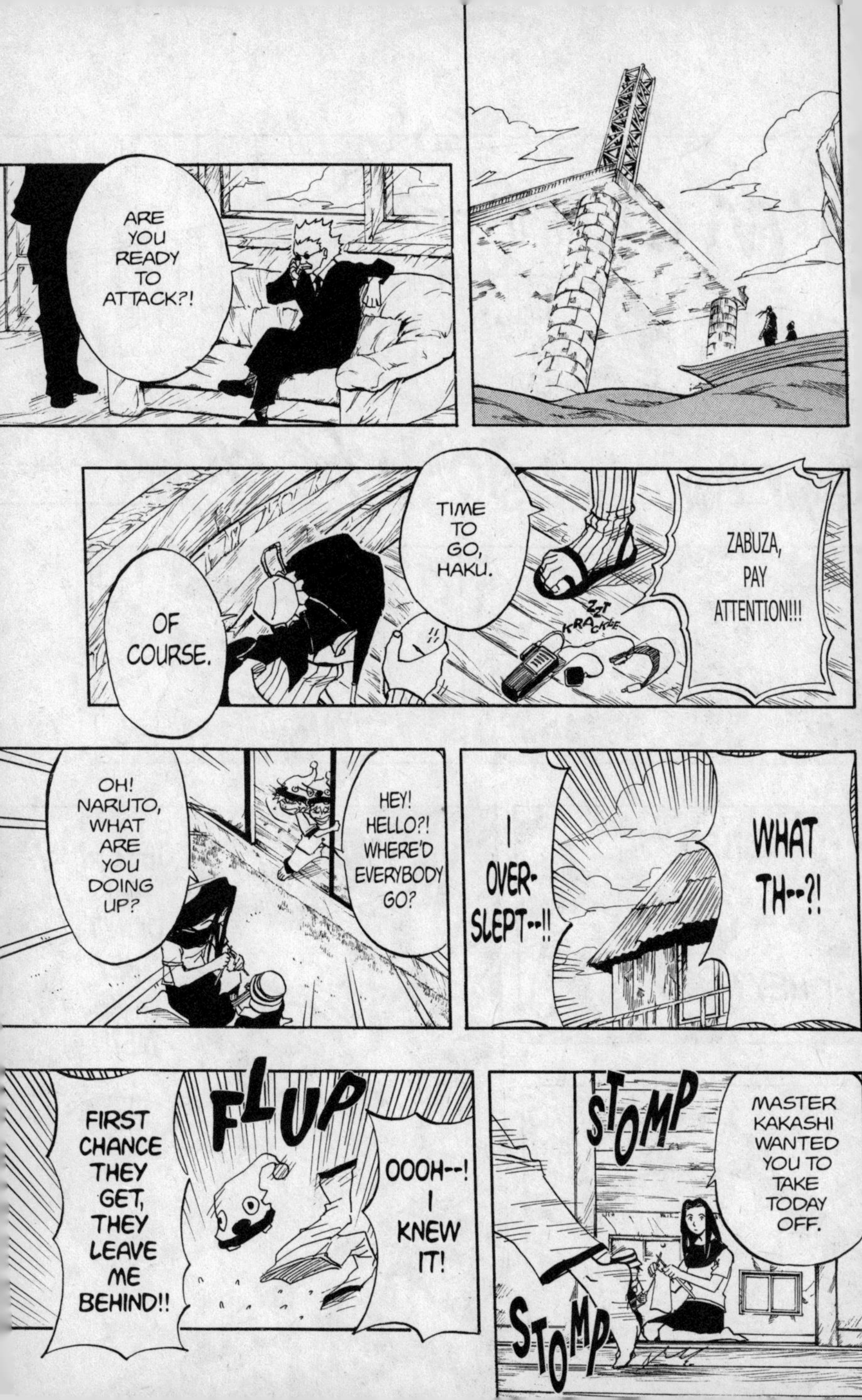
ARE YOU READY TO ATTACK?!
ZABUZA, PAY ATTENTION!!!
ZZT KRACKLE
TIME TO GO, HAKU.
OF COURSE.
WHAT TH--?!
I OVER-SLEPT--!!
HEY! HELLO?! WHERE'D EVERYBODY GO?
OH! NARUTO, WHAT ARE YOU DOING UP?
STOMP
MASTER KAKASHI WANTED YOU TO TAKE TODAY OFF.
STOMP
FLUP
OOOH--! I KNEW IT!
FIRST CHANCE THEY GET, THEY LEAVE ME BEHIND!!

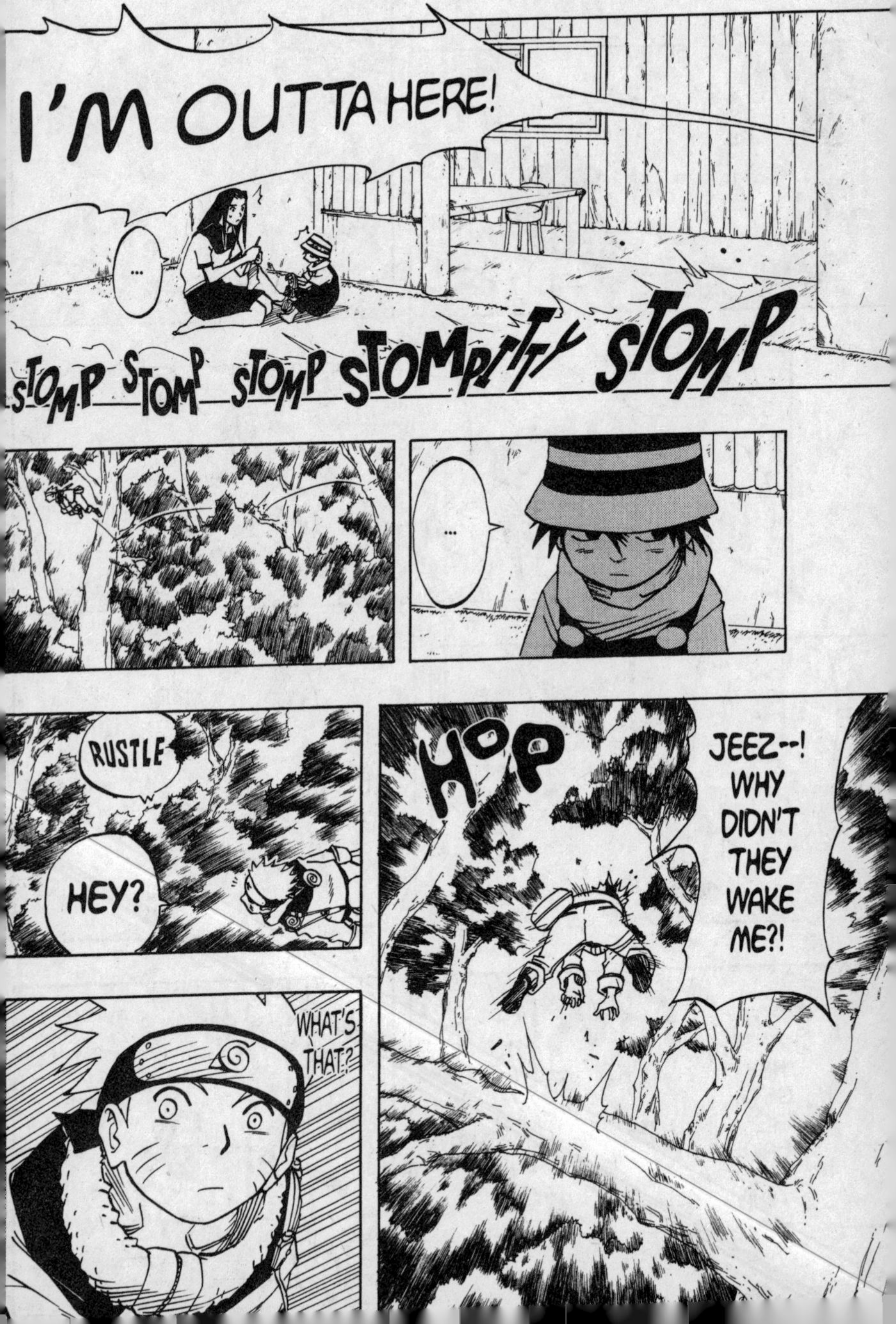
I'M OUTTA HERE!
...
STOMP STOMP STOMP STOMPITTY STOMP
...
HOP
JEEZ--! WHY DIDN'T THEY WAKE ME?!
RUSTLE
HEY?
WHAT'S THAT?

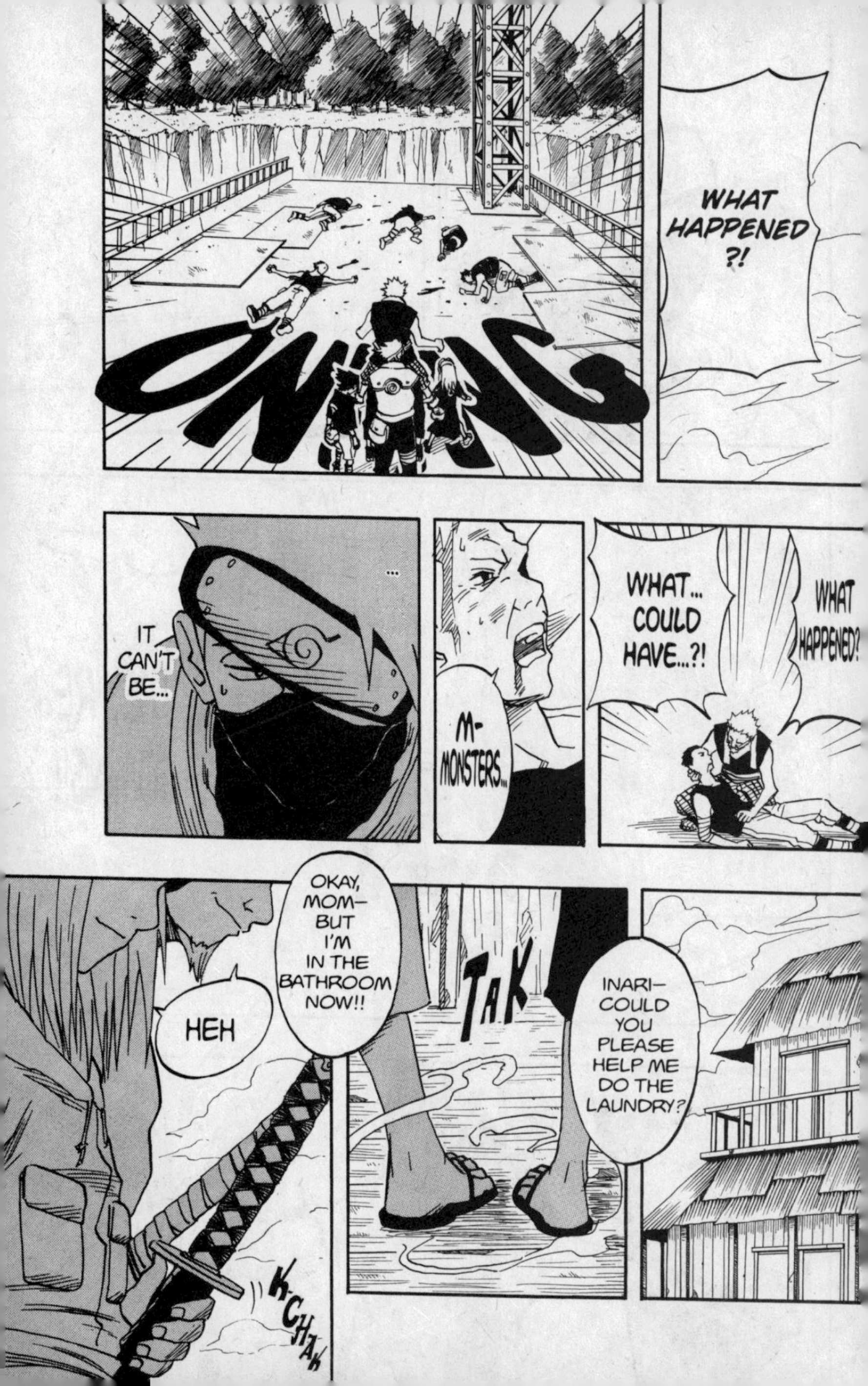
WHAT HAPPENED ?!
WHAT HAPPENED?
WHAT... COULD HAVE...?!
M-MONSTERS...
...
IT CAN'T BE...
INARI— COULD YOU PLEASE HELP ME DO THE LAUNDRY?
OKAY, MOM— BUT I'M IN THE BATHROOM NOW!!
TAK
HEH
K-CHAK

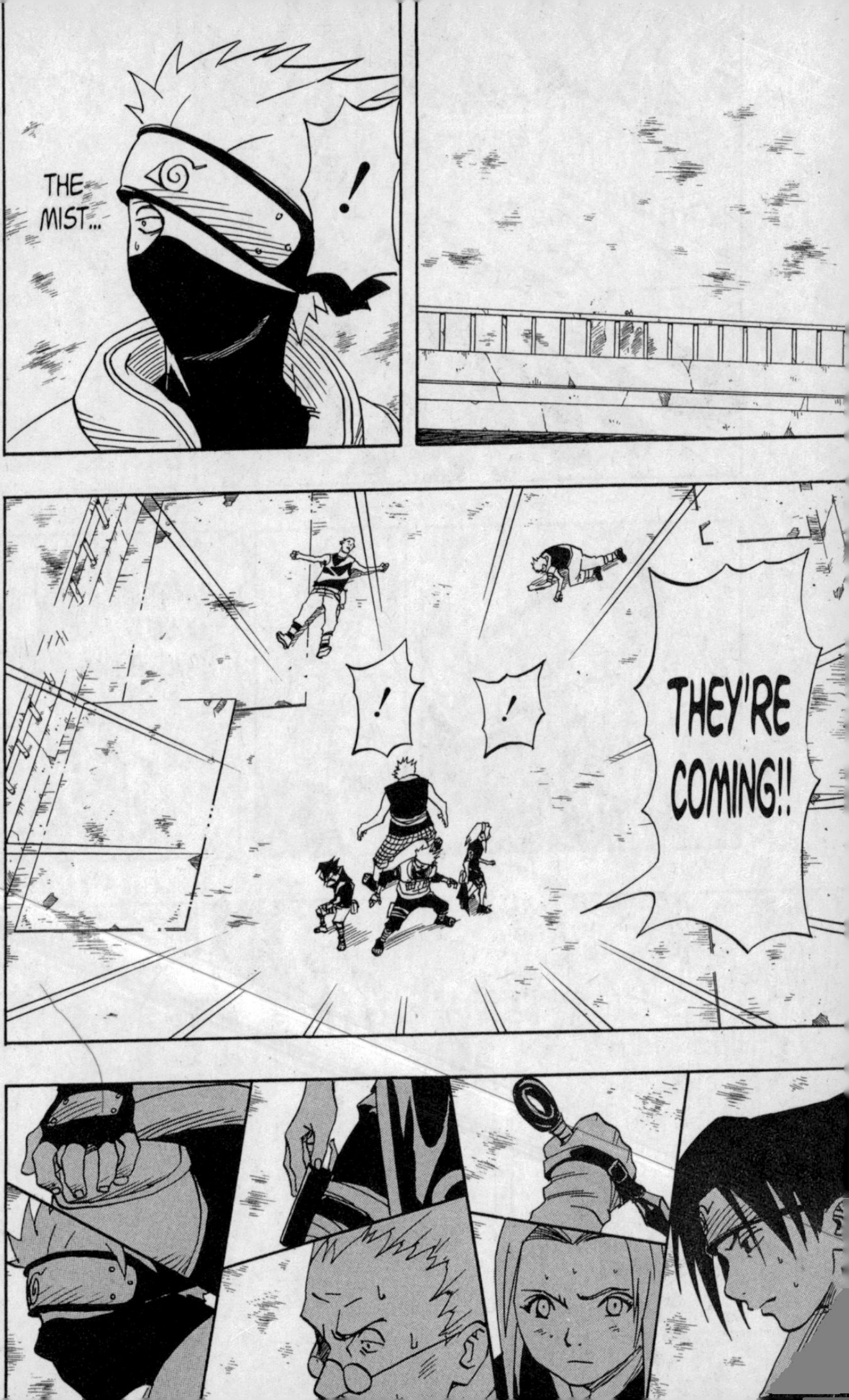
!
THE MIST...
THEY'RE COMING!!
!
!

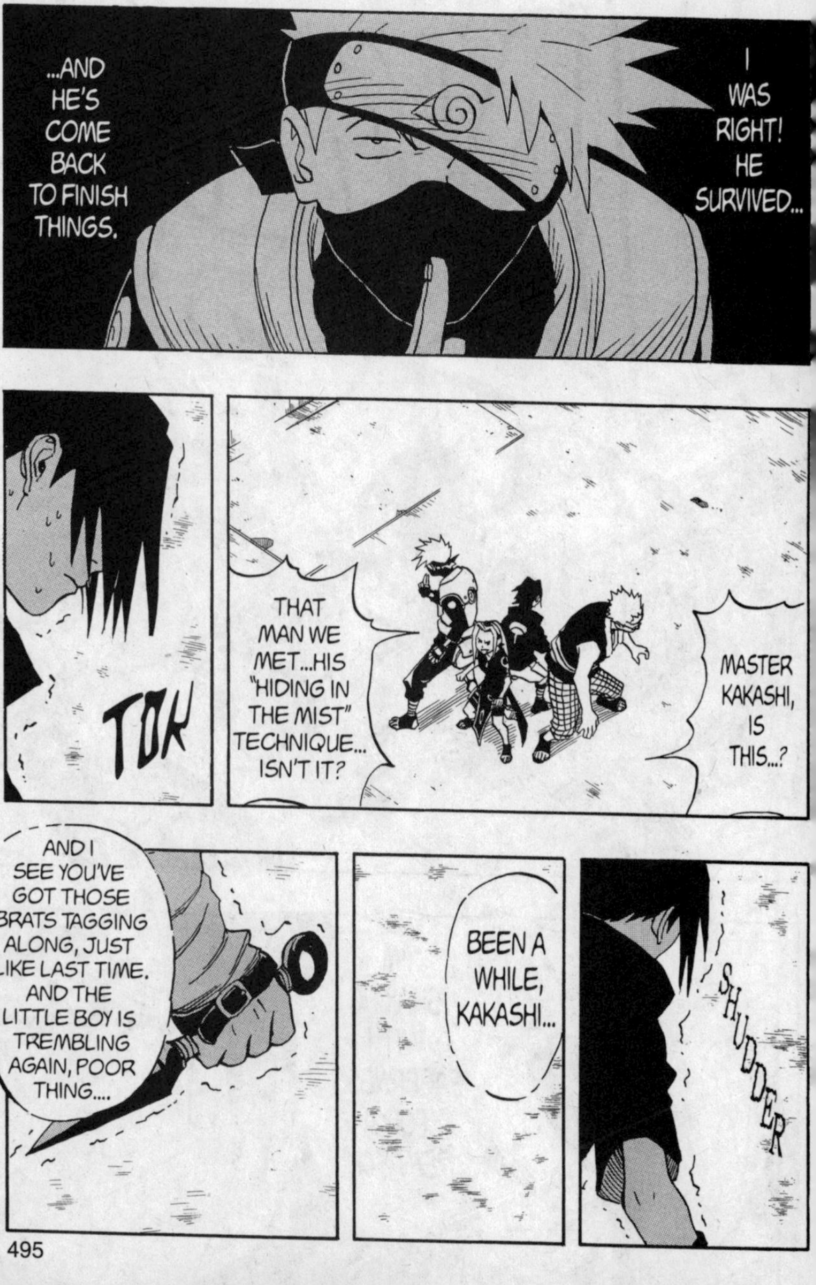
I WAS RIGHT! HE SURVIVED...
...AND HE'S COME BACK TO FINISH THINGS.
MASTER KAKASHI, IS THIS...?
THAT MAN WE MET...HIS "HIDING IN THE MIST" TECHNIQUE... ISN'T IT?
TOK
SHUDDER
BEEN A WHILE, KAKASHI...
AND I SEE YOU'VE GOT THOSE BRATS TAGGING ALONG, JUST LIKE LAST TIME. AND THE LITTLE BOY IS TREMBLING AGAIN, POOR THING....

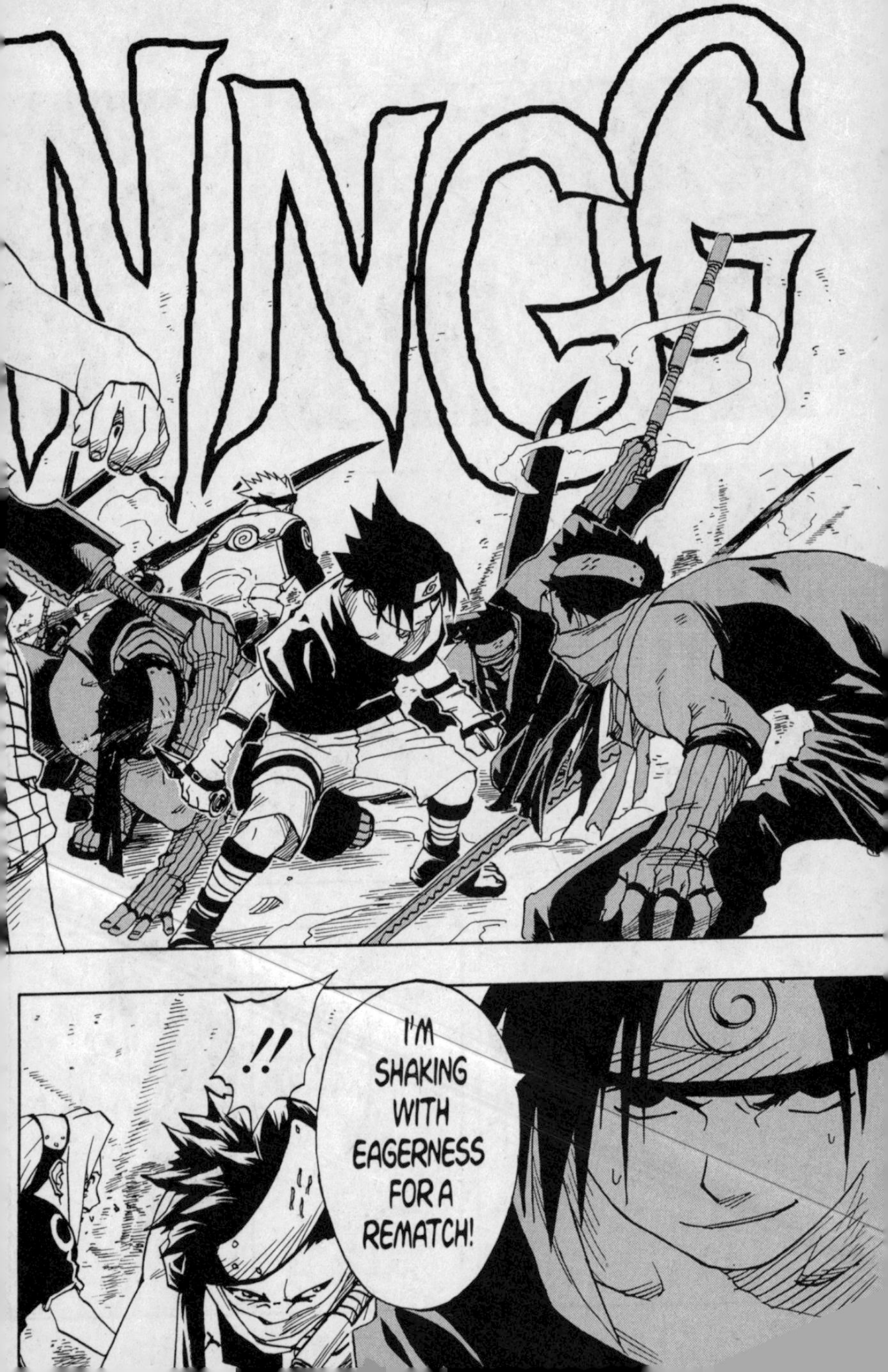
NNGG
!!
I'M SHAKING WITH EAGERNESS FOR A REMATCH!

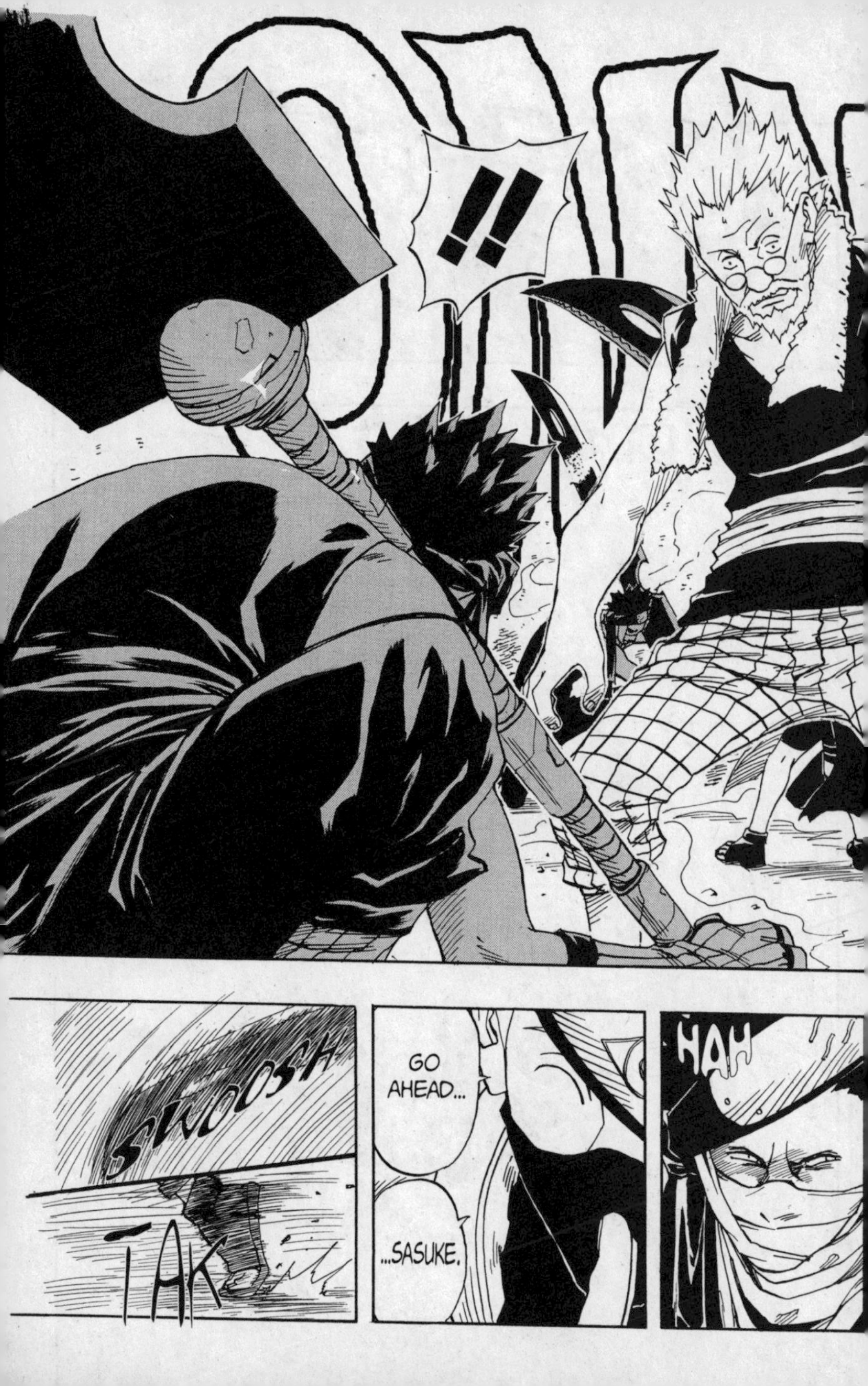
!!
HAH
GO AHEAD...
...SASUKE.
SWOOSH
TAK

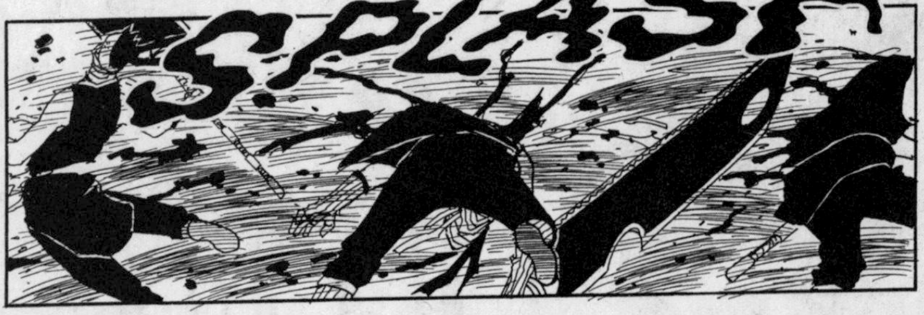
SPLASH
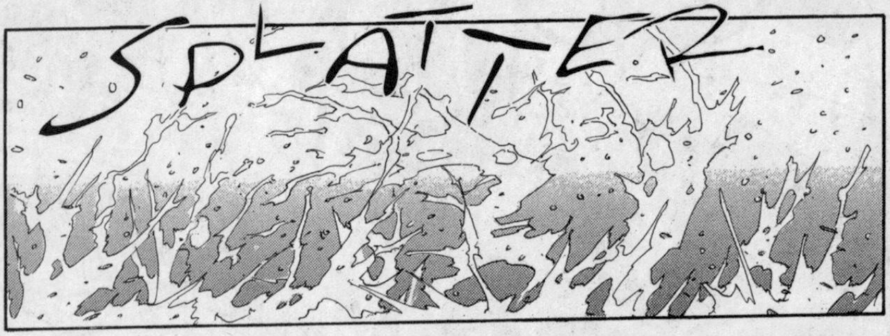
SPLATTER
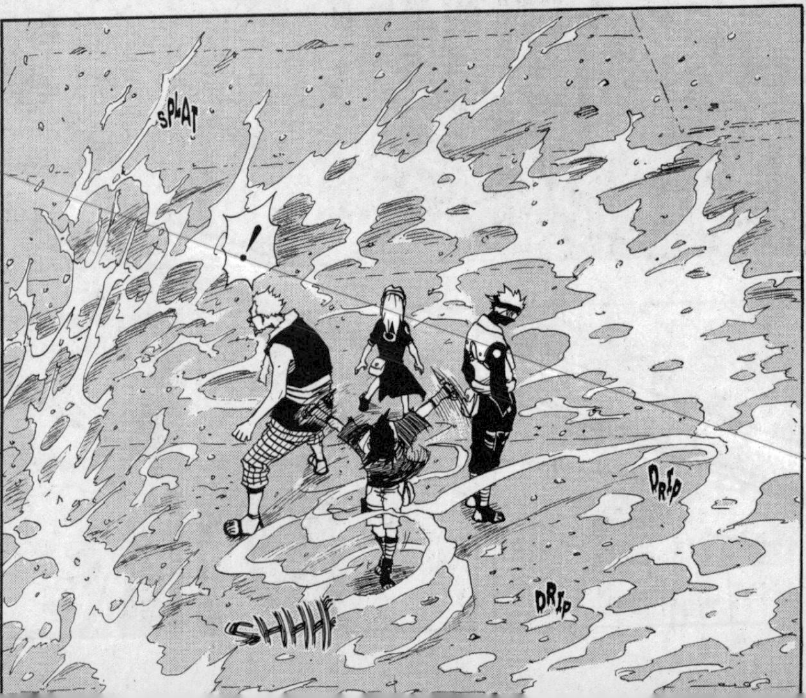
SPLAT
!
DRIP
DRIP
SHHH

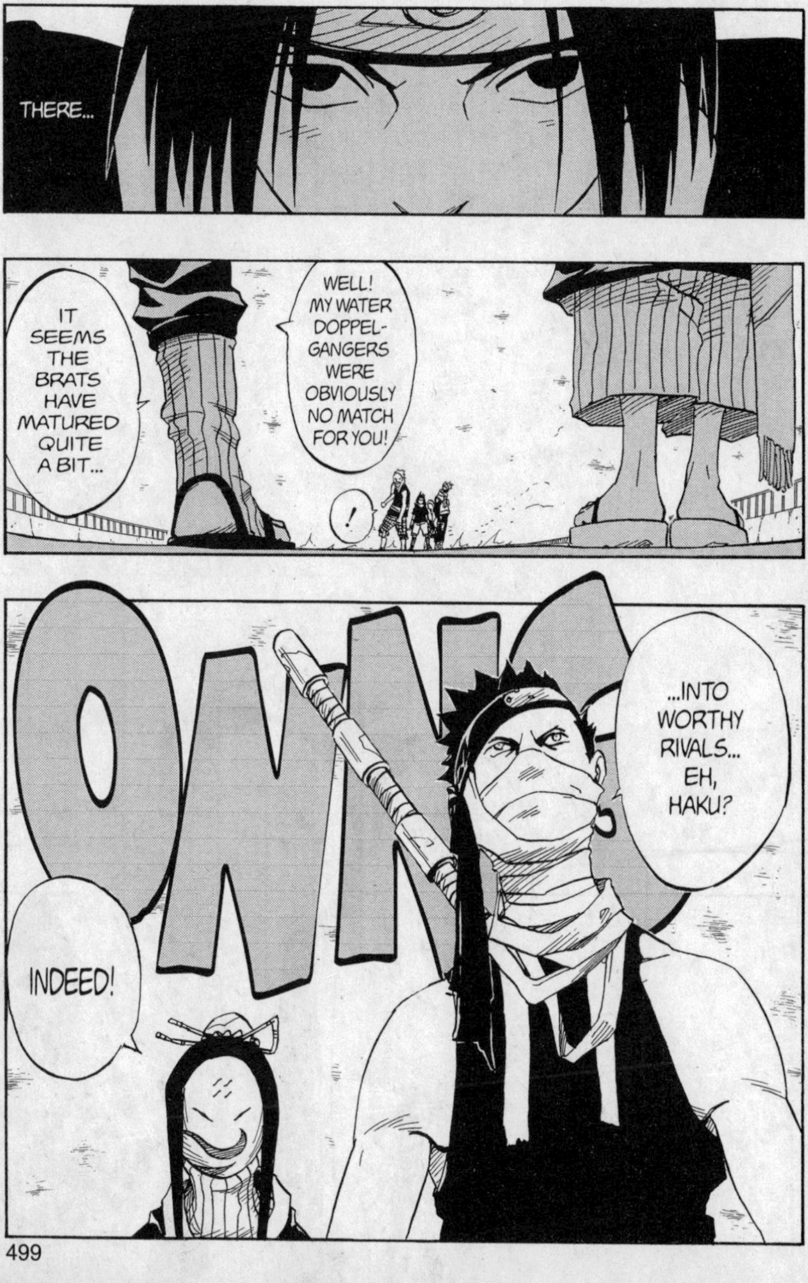
THERE...
WELL! MY WATER DOPPEL-GANGERS WERE OBVIOUSLY NO MATCH FOR YOU!
IT SEEMS THE BRATS HAVE MATURED QUITE A BIT...
!
...INTO WORTHY RIVALS... EH, HAKU?
INDEED!

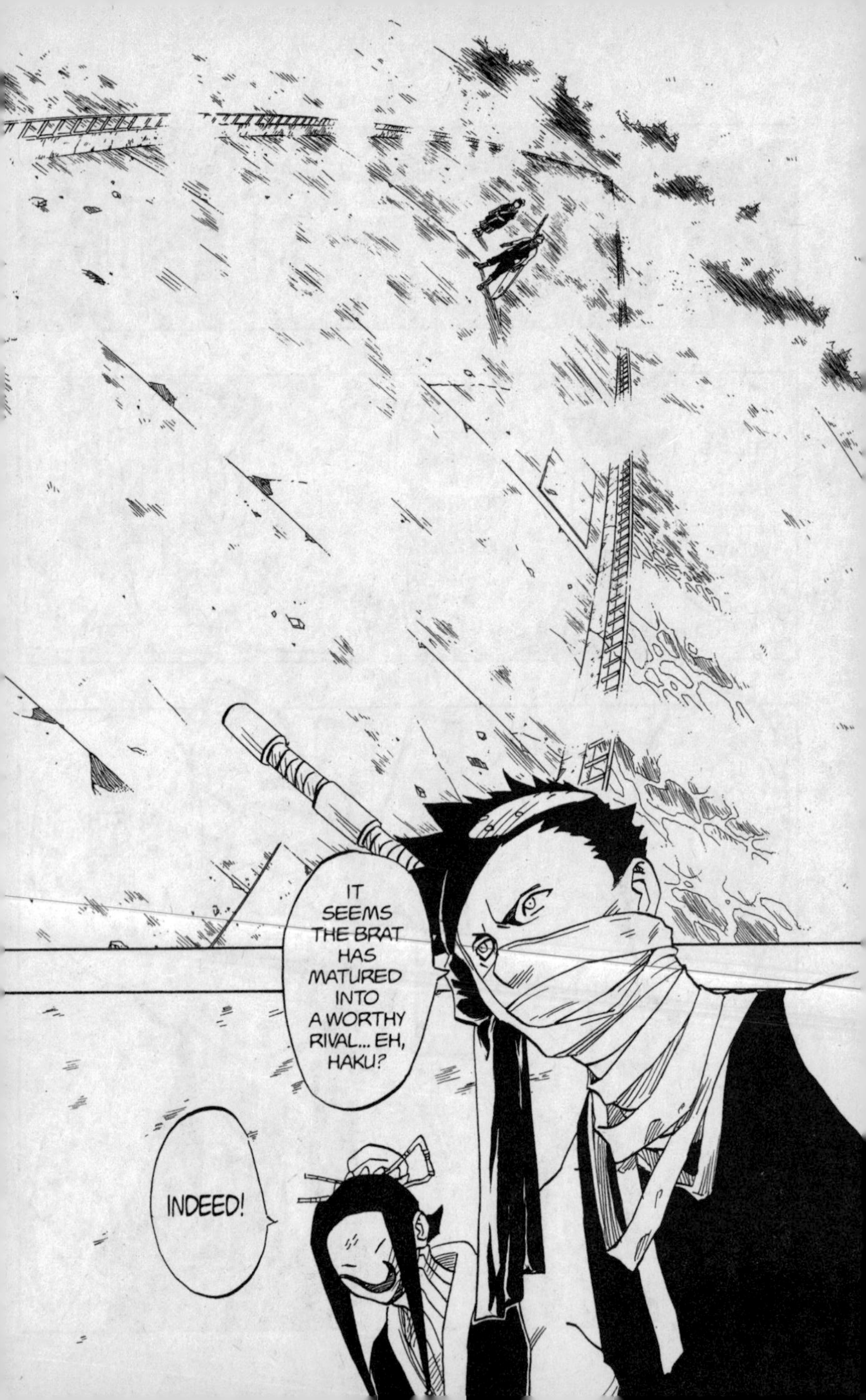
IT SEEMS THE BRAT HAS MATURED INTO A WORTHY RIVAL... EH, HAKU?
INDEED!

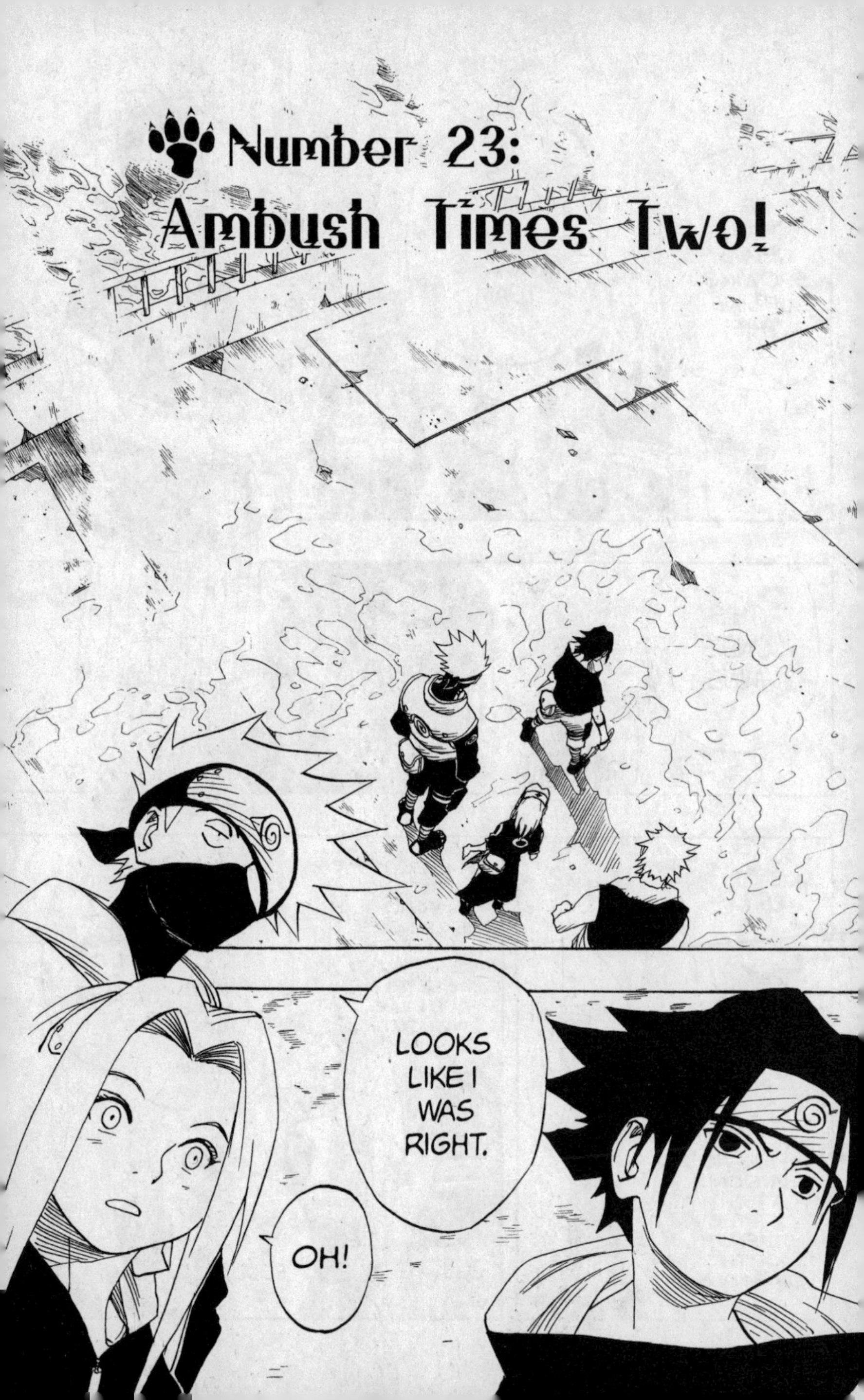
Number 23:
Ambush Times Two!
LOOKS LIKE I WAS RIGHT.
OH!

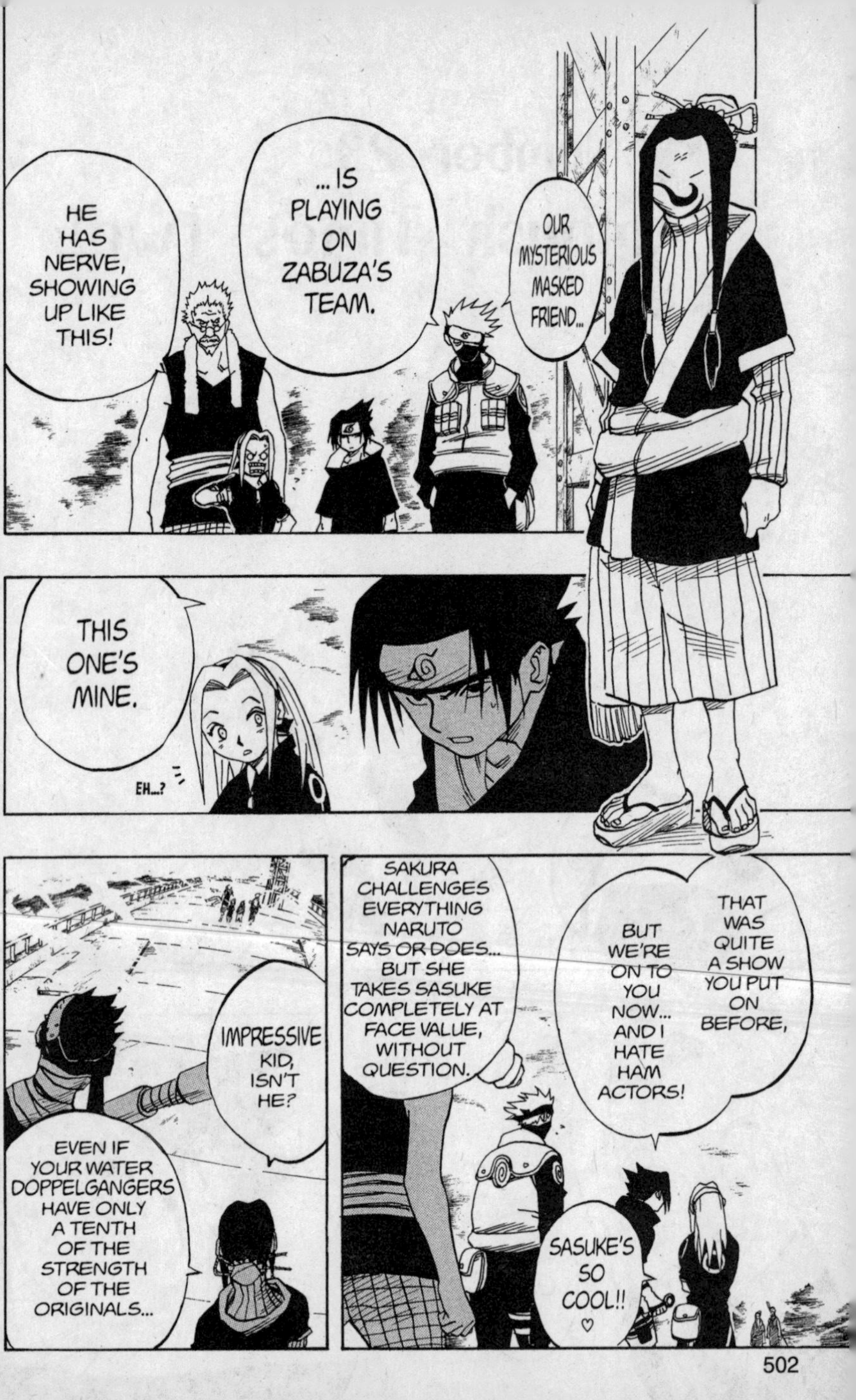
OUR MYSTERIOUS MASKED FRIEND...
...IS PLAYING ON ZABUZA'S TEAM.
HE HAS NERVE, SHOWING UP LIKE THIS!
THIS ONE'S MINE.
EH...?
THAT WAS QUITE A SHOW YOU PUT ON BEFORE,
BUT WE'RE ON TO YOU NOW... AND I HATE HAM ACTORS!
SAKURA CHALLENGES EVERYTHING NARUTO SAYS OR DOES... BUT SHE TAKES SASUKE COMPLETELY AT FACE VALUE, WITHOUT QUESTION.
SASUKE'S SO COOL!! ♡
IMPRESSIVE KID, ISN'T HE?
EVEN IF YOUR WATER DOPPELGANGERS HAVE ONLY A TENTH OF THE STRENGTH OF THE ORIGINALS...

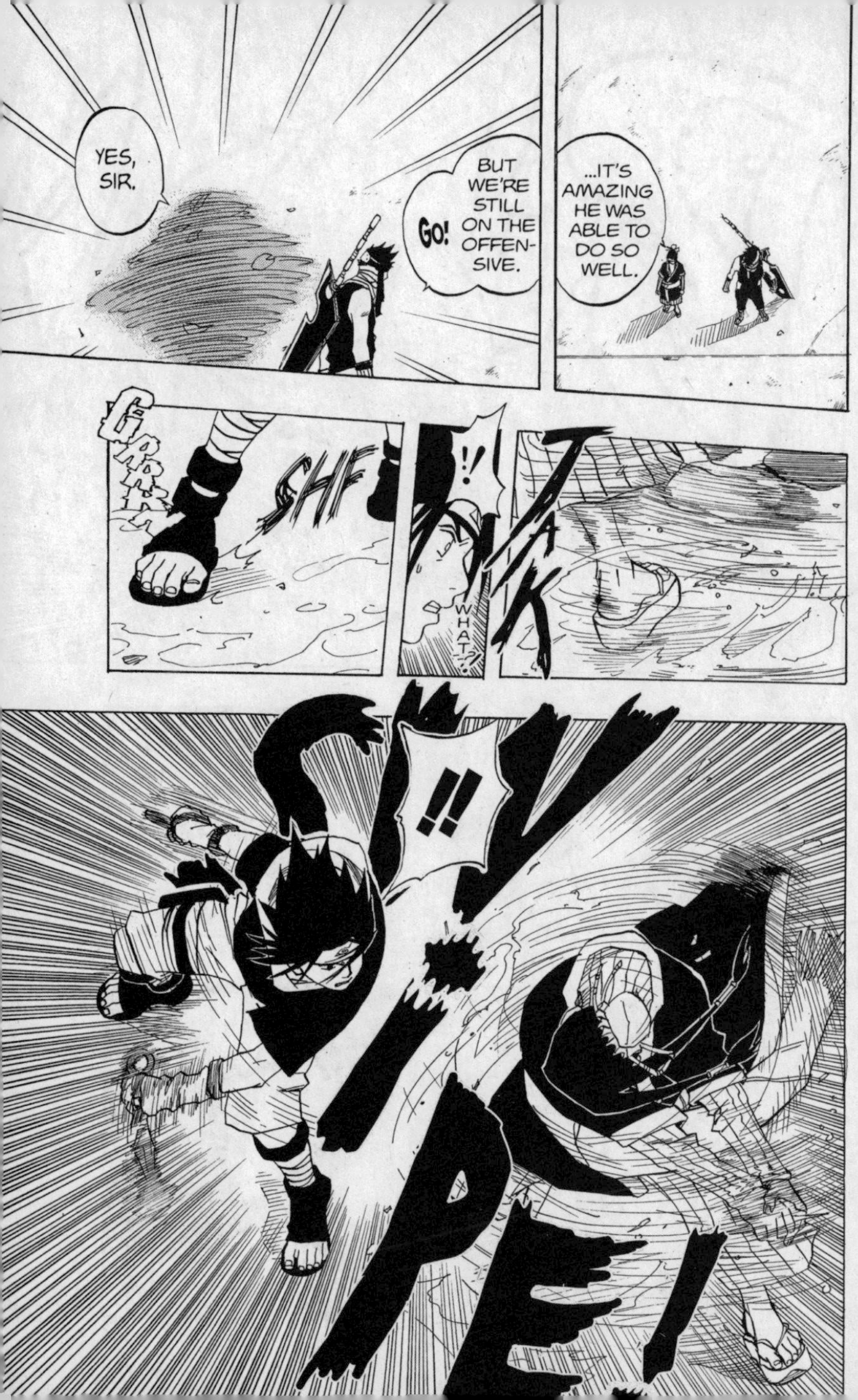
...IT'S AMAZING HE WAS ABLE TO DO SO WELL.
BUT WE'RE STILL ON THE OFFENSIVE.
GO!
YES, SIR.
TAK
!!
WHAT--?!
SHF
!!

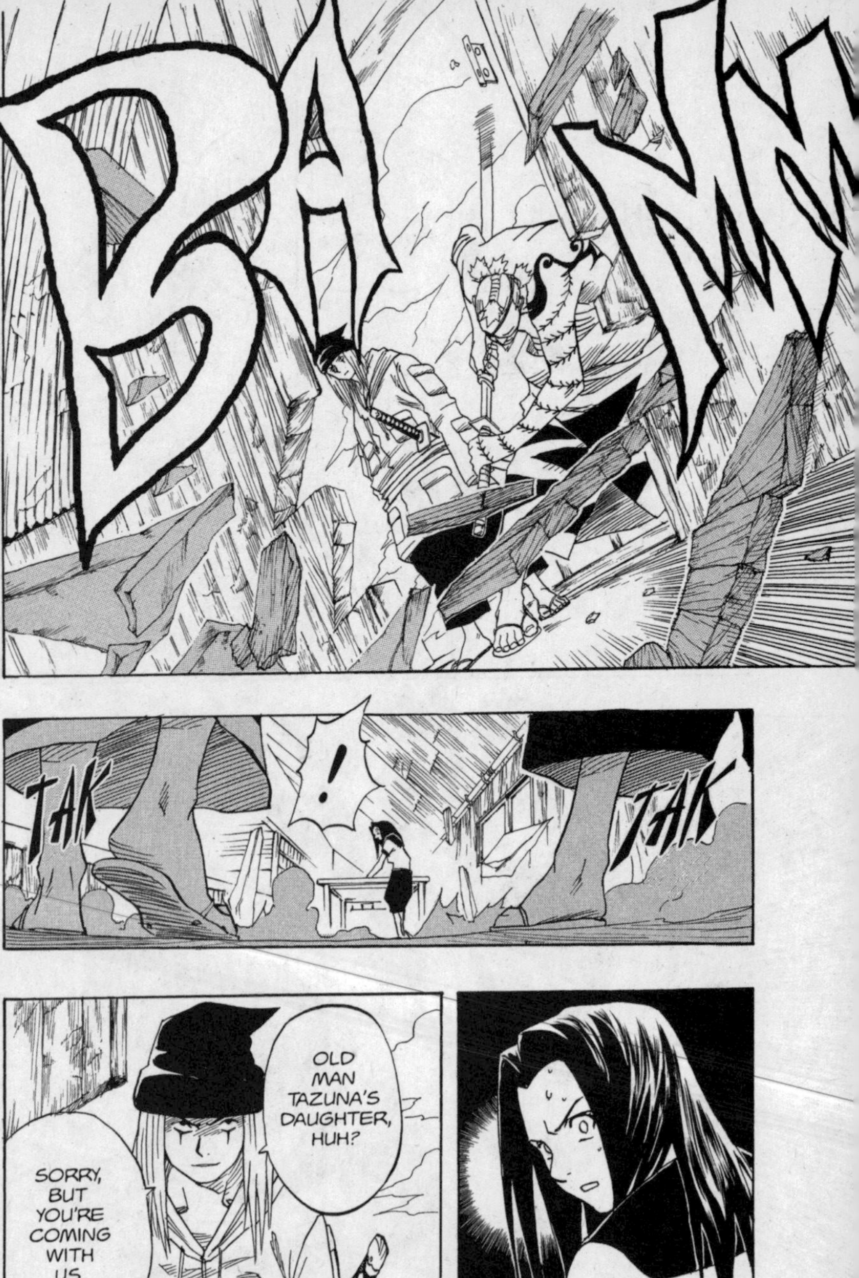
BAM
TAK
!
TAK
OLD MAN TAZUNA'S DAUGHTER, HUH?
SORRY, BUT YOU'RE COMING WITH US.

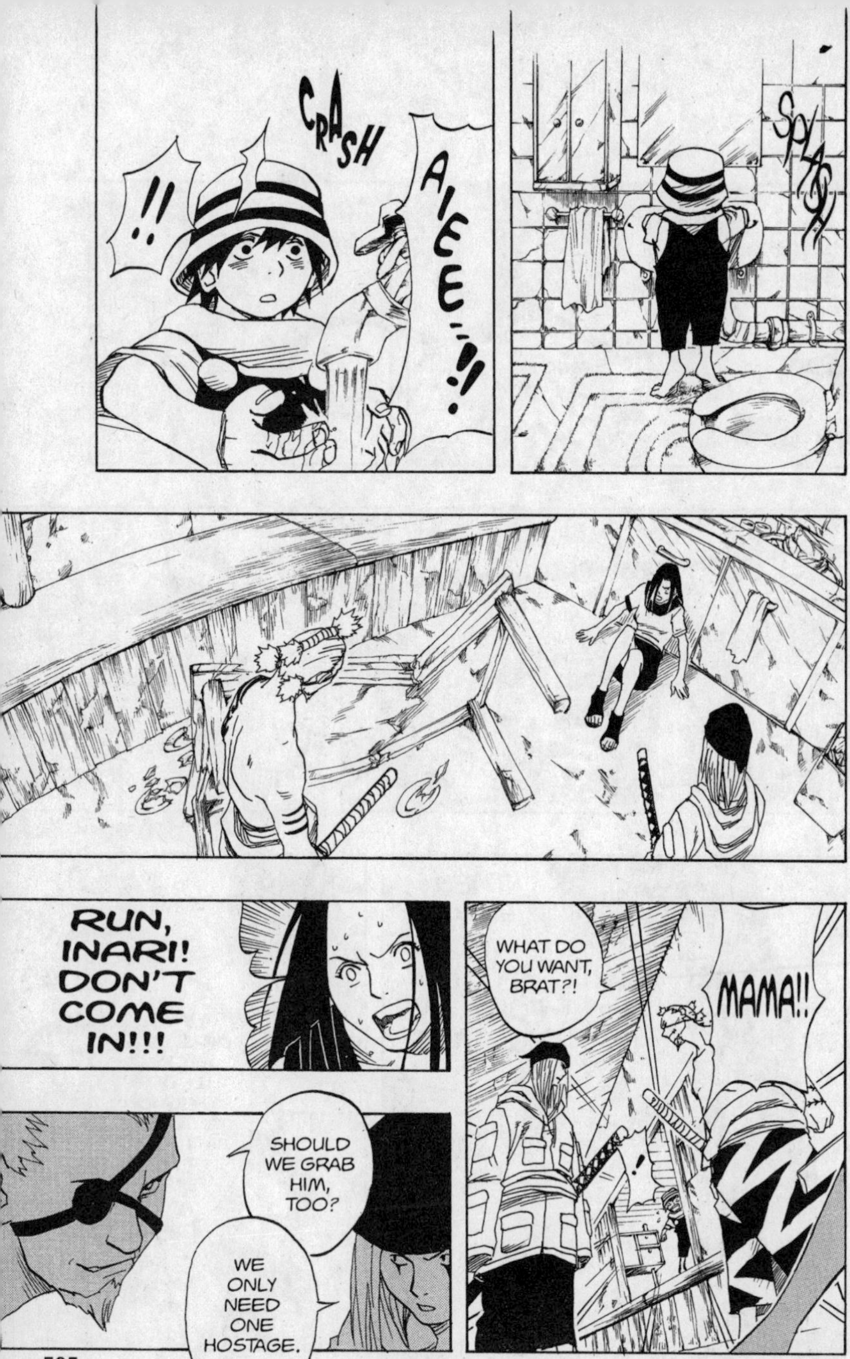
SPLASH
CRASH
!!
AIEE...!!
MAMA!!
WHAT DO YOU WANT, BRAT?!
!
RUN, INARI! DON'T COME IN!!!
SHOULD WE GRAB HIM, TOO?
WE ONLY NEED ONE HOSTAGE.

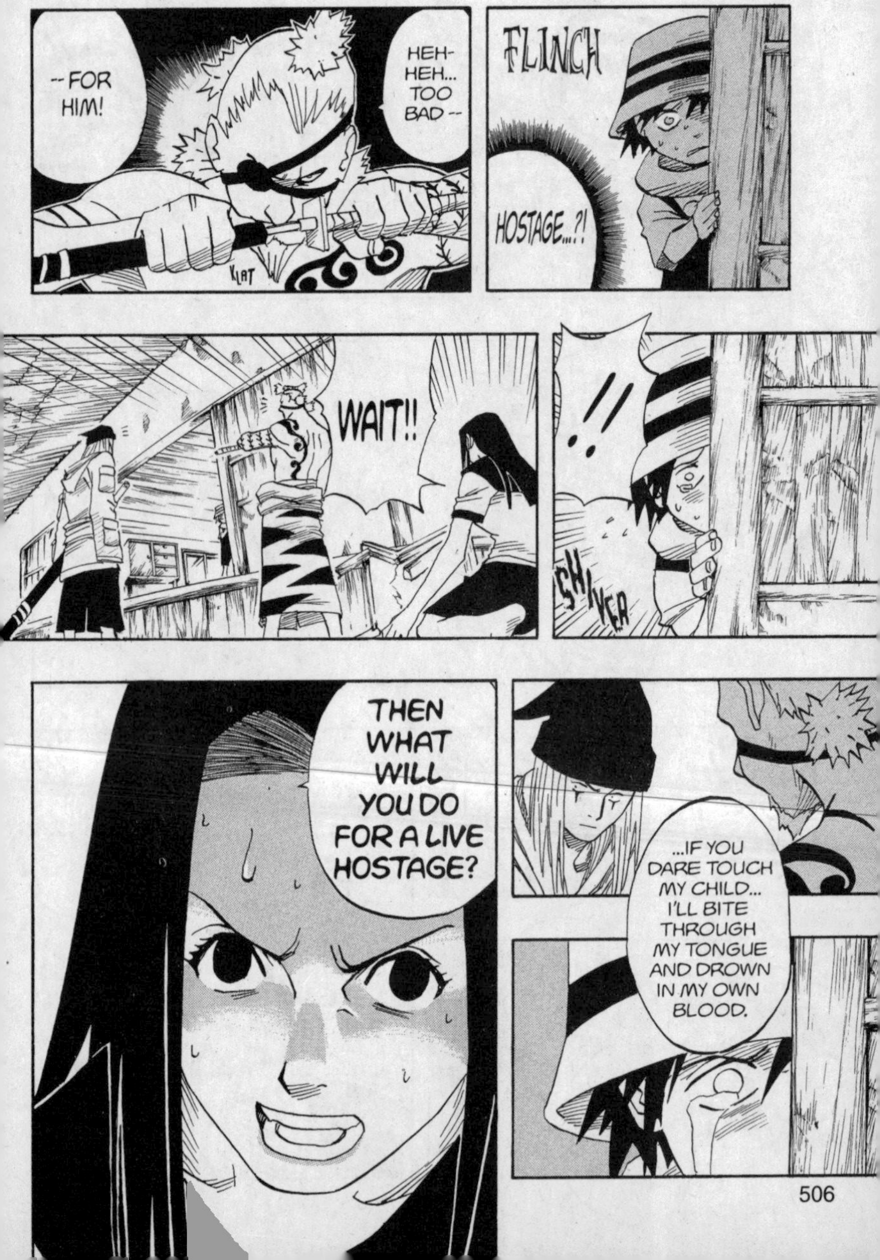
FLINCH
HOSTAGE...?!
HEH-HEH... TOO BAD --
-- FOR HIM!
KLAT
!!
SHIVER
WAIT!!
...IF YOU DARE TOUCH MY CHILD... I'LL BITE THROUGH MY TONGUE AND DROWN IN MY OWN BLOOD.
THEN WHAT WILL YOU DO FOR A LIVE HOSTAGE?

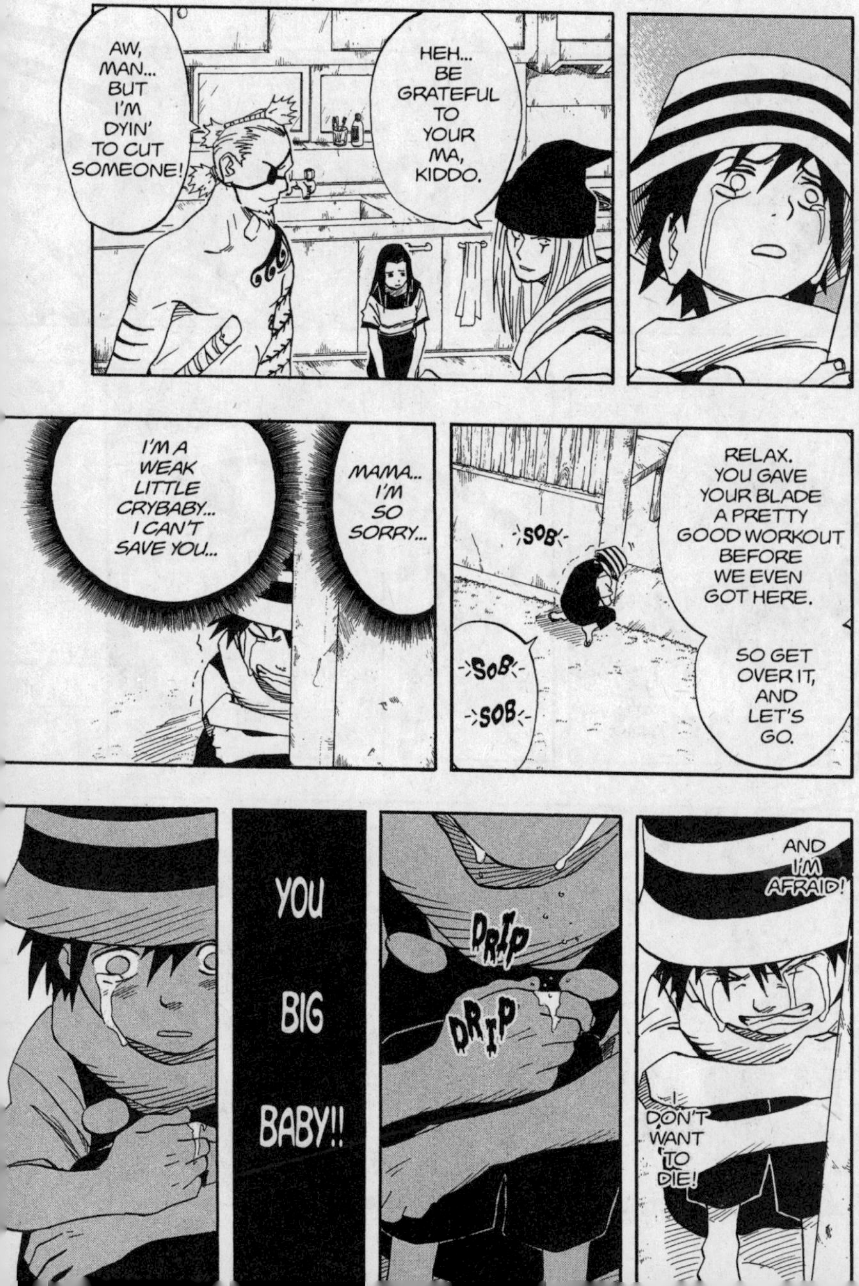
HEH... BE GRATEFUL TO YOUR MA, KIDDO.
AW, MAN... BUT I'M DYIN' TO CUT SOMEONE!
RELAX. YOU GAVE YOUR BLADE A PRETTY GOOD WORKOUT BEFORE WE EVEN GOT HERE.
SO GET OVER IT, AND LET'S GO.
SOB
SOB
SOB
MAMA... I'M SO SORRY...
I'M A WEAK LITTLE CRYBABY... I CAN'T SAVE YOU...
AND I'M AFRAID!
I DON'T WANT TO DIE!
DRIP
DRIP
YOU BIG BABY!!

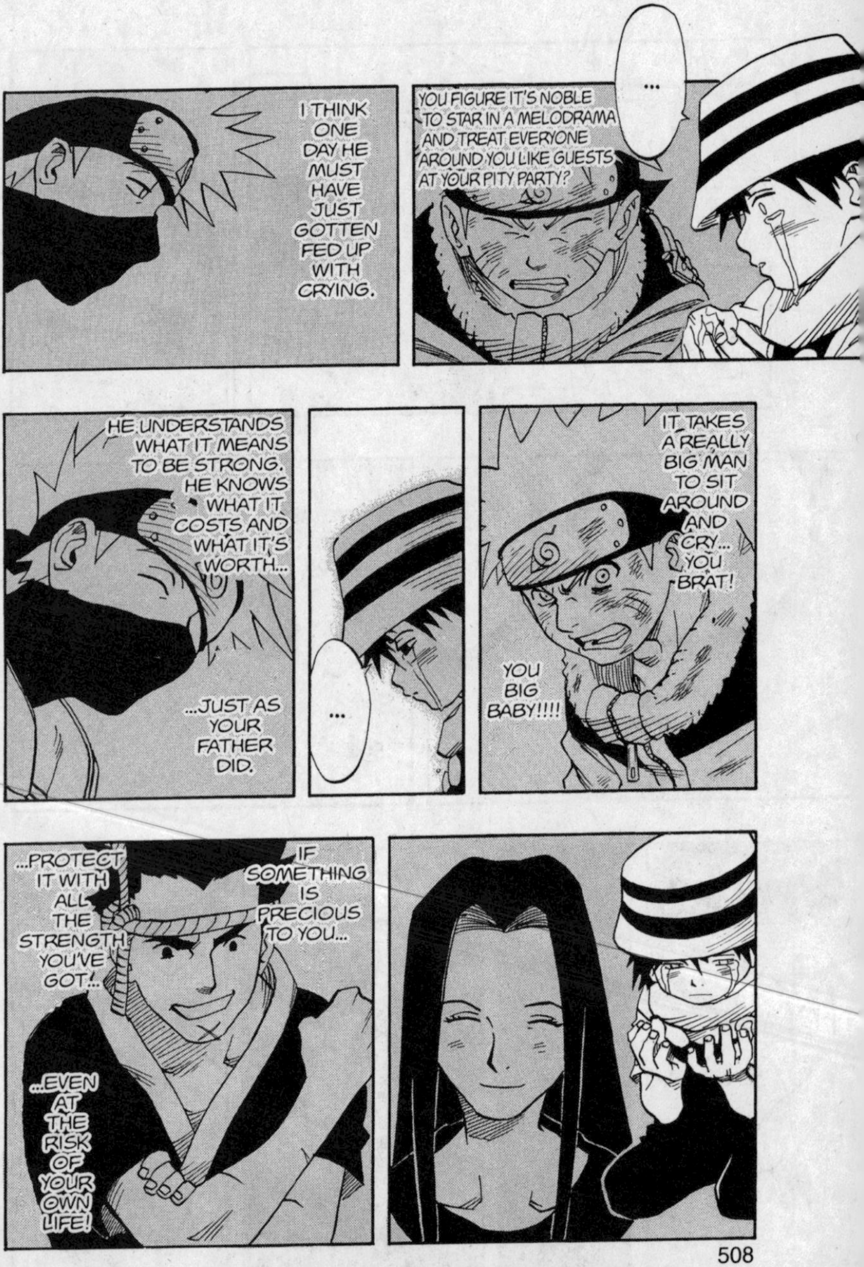
...
YOU FIGURE IT'S NOBLE TO STAR IN A MELODRAMA AND TREAT EVERYONE AROUND YOU LIKE GUESTS AT YOUR PITY PARTY?
I THINK ONE DAY HE MUST HAVE JUST GOTTEN FED UP WITH CRYING.
IT TAKES A REALLY BIG MAN TO SIT AROUND AND CRY... YOU BRAT!
YOU BIG BABY!!!!
...
HE UNDERSTANDS WHAT IT MEANS TO BE STRONG. HE KNOWS WHAT IT COSTS AND WHAT IT'S WORTH...
...JUST AS YOUR FATHER DID.
IF SOMETHING IS PRECIOUS TO YOU...
...PROTECT IT WITH ALL THE STRENGTH YOU'VE GOT!...
...EVEN AT THE RISK OF YOUR OWN LIFE!

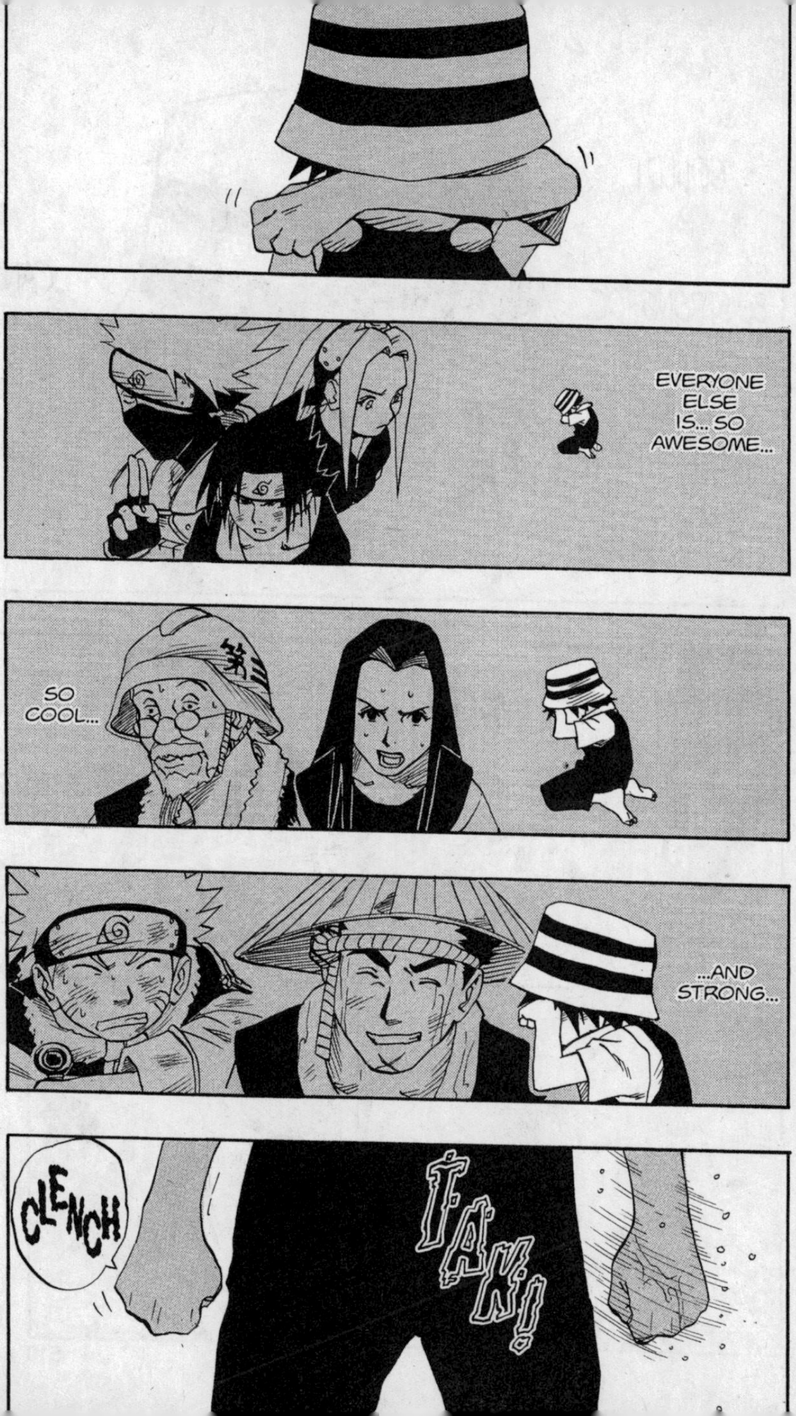
EVERYONE ELSE IS... SO AWESOME...
SO COOL...
...AND STRONG...
CLENCH
TAK!

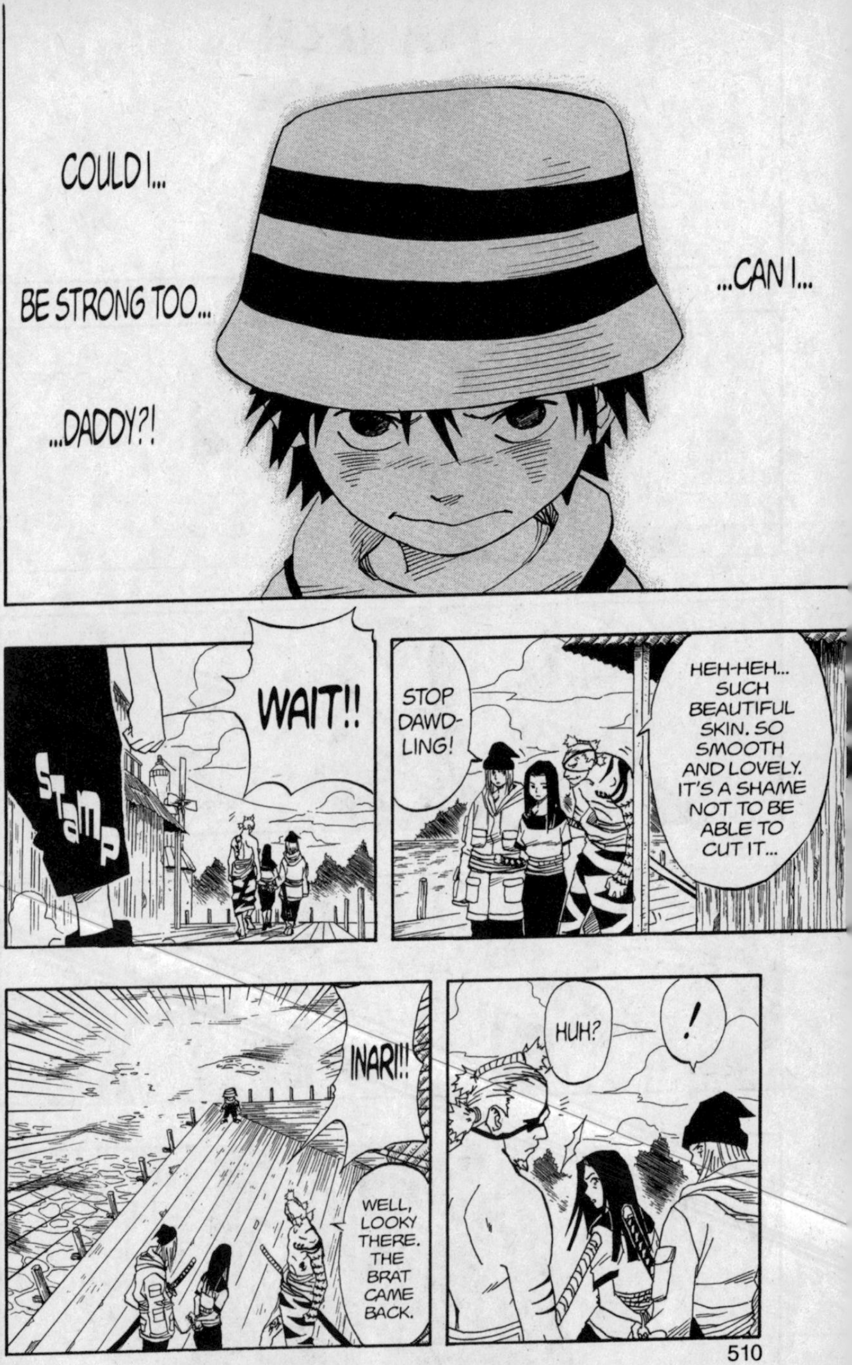
COULD I...
BE STRONG TOO...
...CAN I...
...DADDY?!
HEH-HEH... SUCH BEAUTIFUL SKIN. SO SMOOTH AND LOVELY. IT'S A SHAME NOT TO BE ABLE TO CUT IT...
STOP DAWD-LING!
WAIT!!
STAMP
!
HUH?
INARI!!
WELL, LOOKY THERE. THE BRAT CAME BACK.

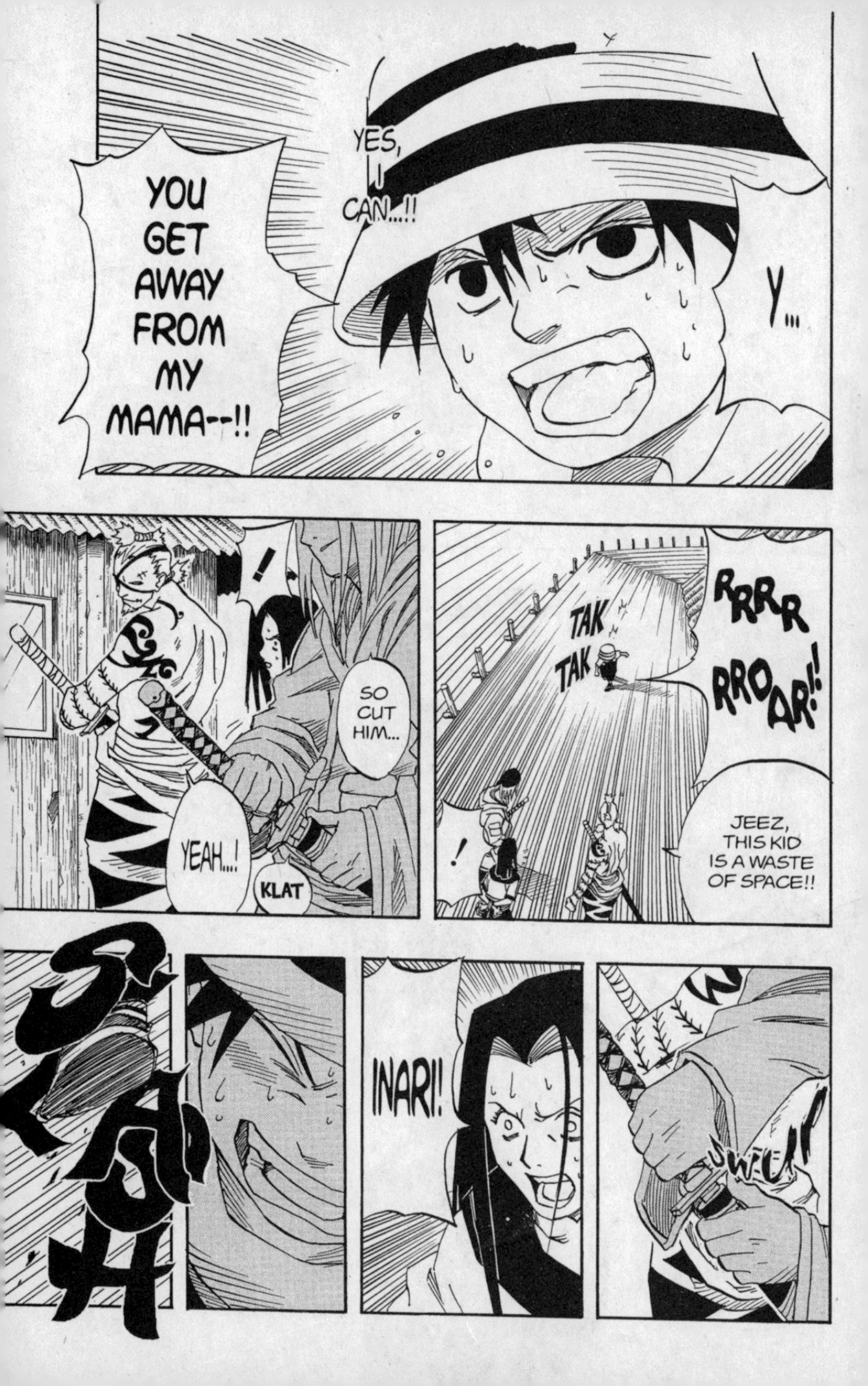
Y...
YES, I CAN...!!
YOU GET AWAY FROM MY MAMA--!!
RRRR RROAR!!
TAK TAK
JEEZ, THIS KID IS A WASTE OF SPACE!!
!
!
SO CUT HIM...
YEAH...!
KLAT
INARI!

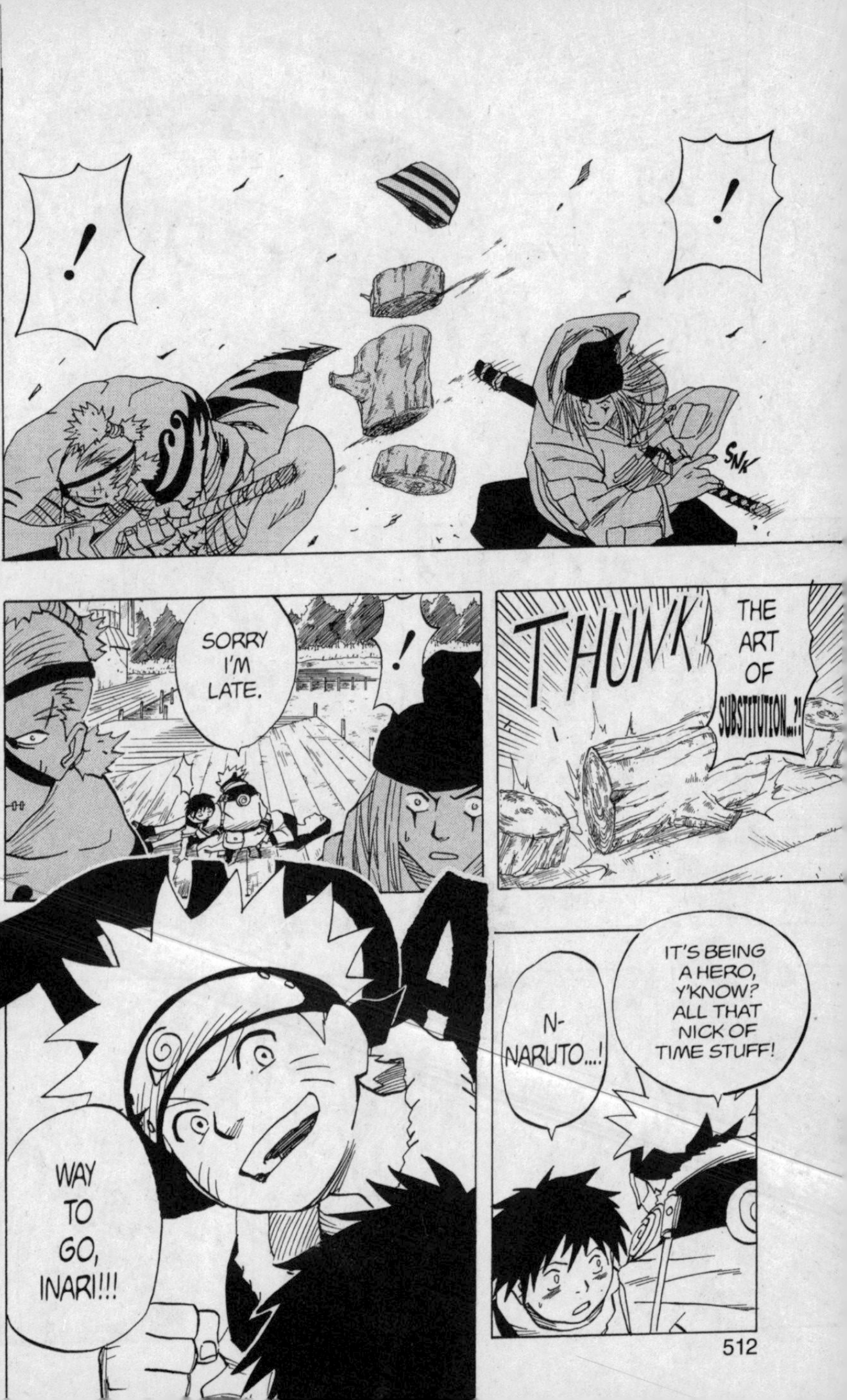
!
!
SNK
THUNK
THE ART OF SUBSTITUTION...?!
!
SORRY I'M LATE.
N-NARUTO...!
IT'S BEING A HERO, Y'KNOW? ALL THAT NICK OF TIME STUFF!
WAY TO GO, INARI!!!

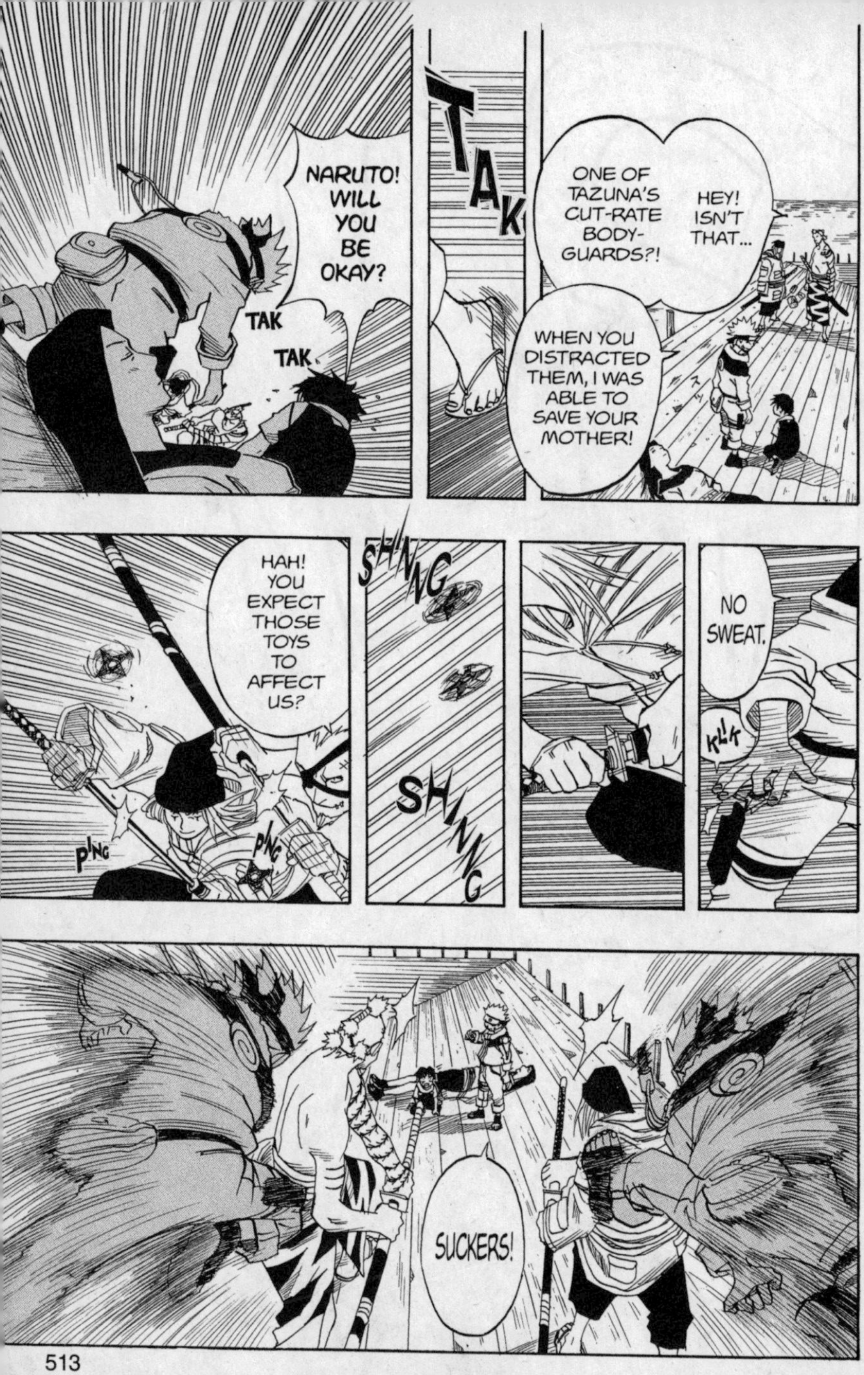
HEY! ISN'T THAT...
ONE OF TAZUNA'S CUT-RATE BODY-GUARDS?!
WHEN YOU DISTRACTED THEM, I WAS ABLE TO SAVE YOUR MOTHER!
TAK
NARUTO! WILL YOU BE OKAY?
TAK
TAK
NO SWEAT.
KLIK
SHINNG
SHINNNG
HAH! YOU EXPECT THOSE TOYS TO AFFECT US?
PING
PING
SUCKERS!

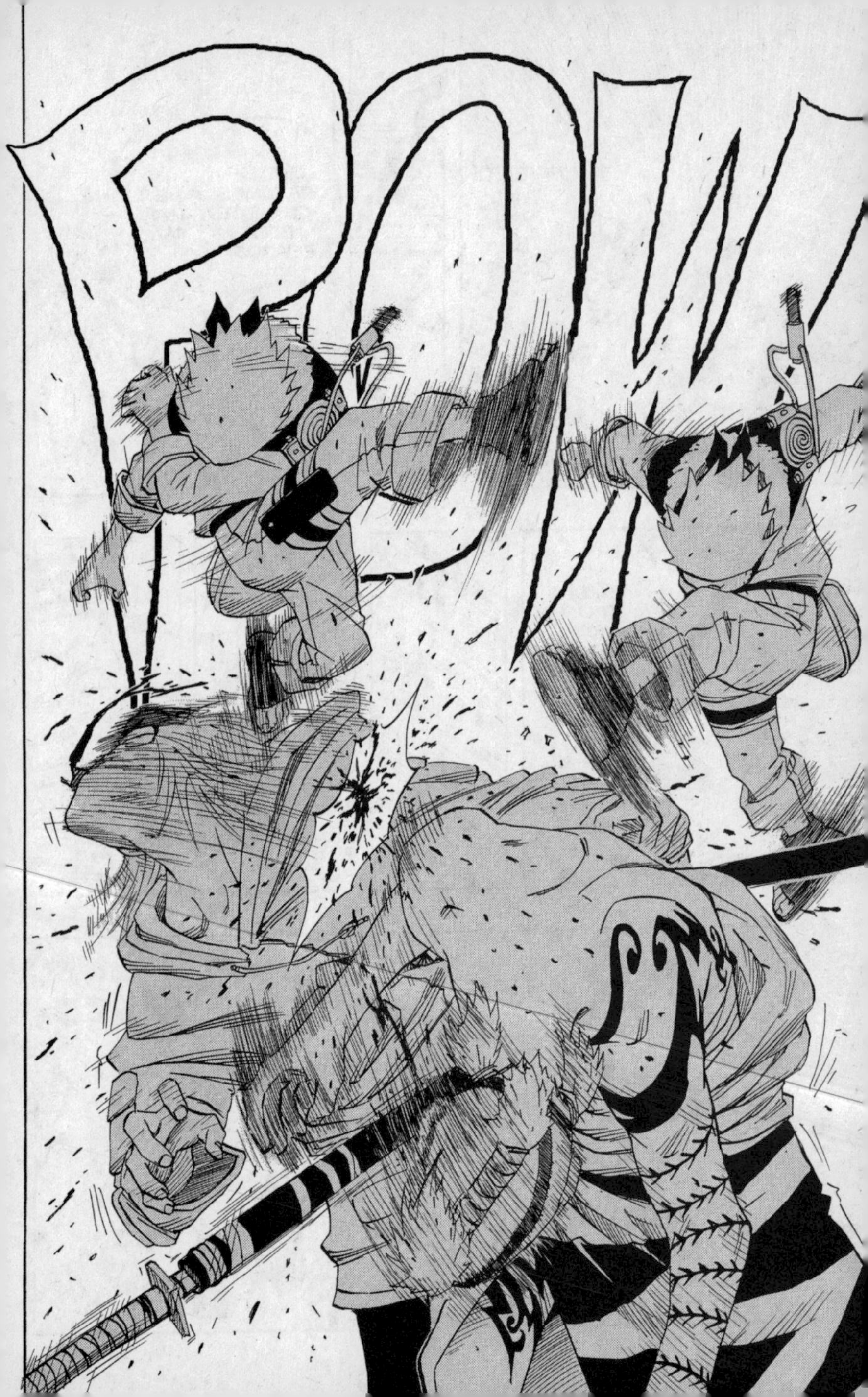
POW

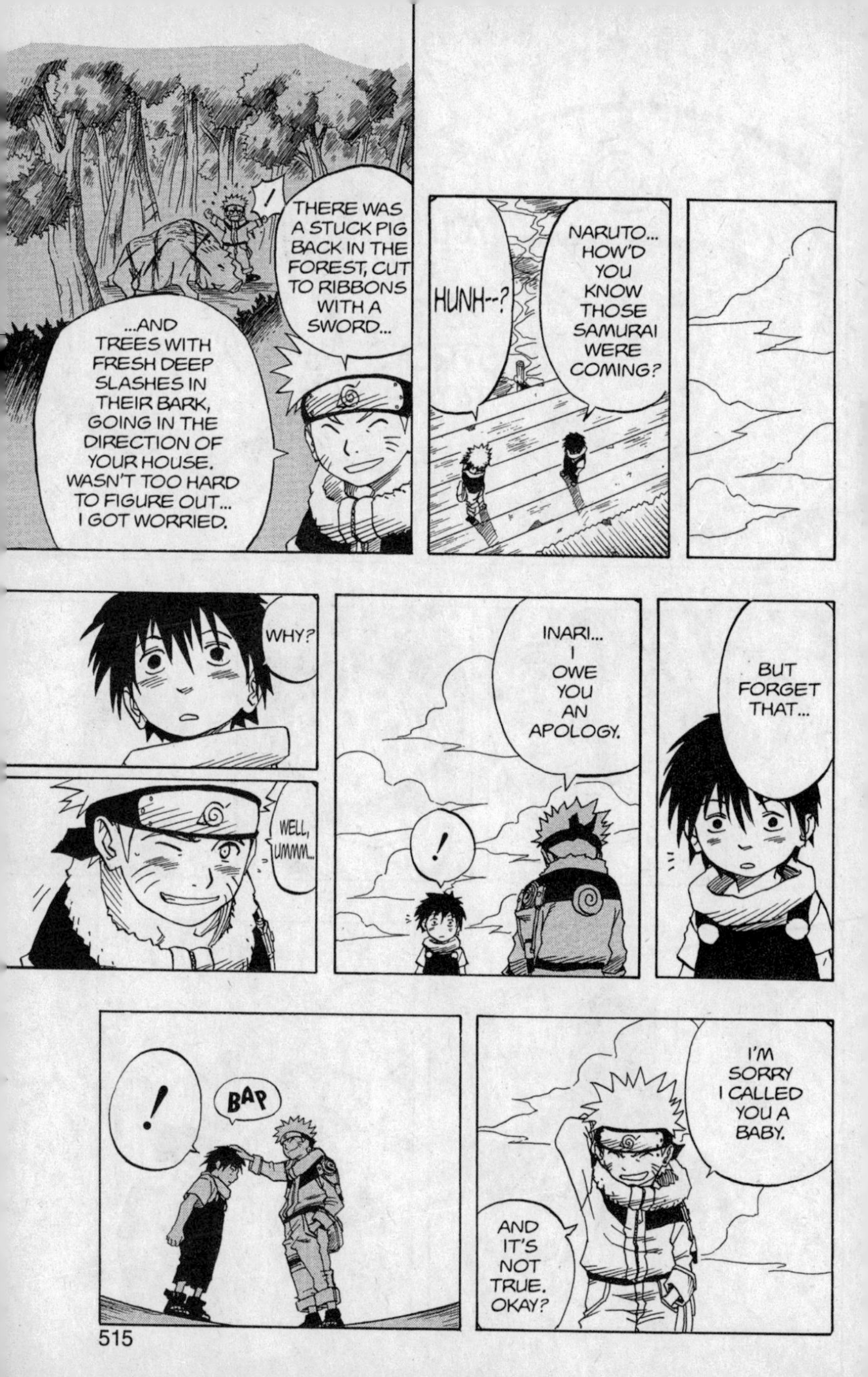
THERE WAS A STUCK PIG BACK IN THE FOREST, CUT TO RIBBONS WITH A SWORD...
!
...AND TREES WITH FRESH DEEP SLASHES IN THEIR BARK, GOING IN THE DIRECTION OF YOUR HOUSE. WASN'T TOO HARD TO FIGURE OUT... I GOT WORRIED.
HUNH--?
NARUTO... HOW'D YOU KNOW THOSE SAMURAI WERE COMING?
WHY?
WELL, UMMM...
INARI... I OWE YOU AN APOLOGY.
!
BUT FORGET THAT...
!
BAP
I'M SORRY I CALLED YOU A BABY.
AND IT'S NOT TRUE. OKAY?

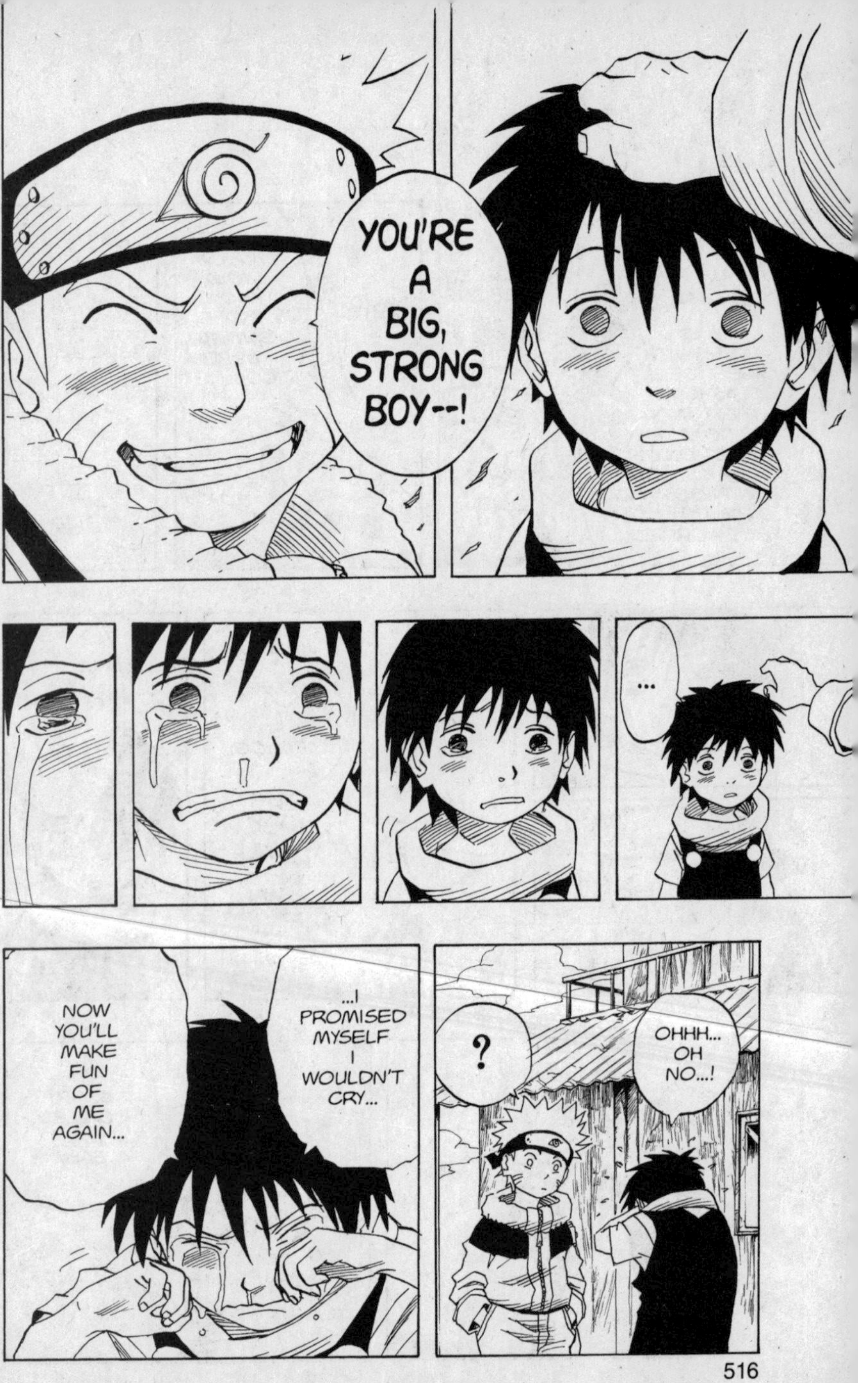
YOU'RE A BIG, STRONG BOY--!
...
OHHH... OH NO...!
?
...I PROMISED MYSELF I WOULDN'T CRY...
NOW YOU'LL MAKE FUN OF ME AGAIN...

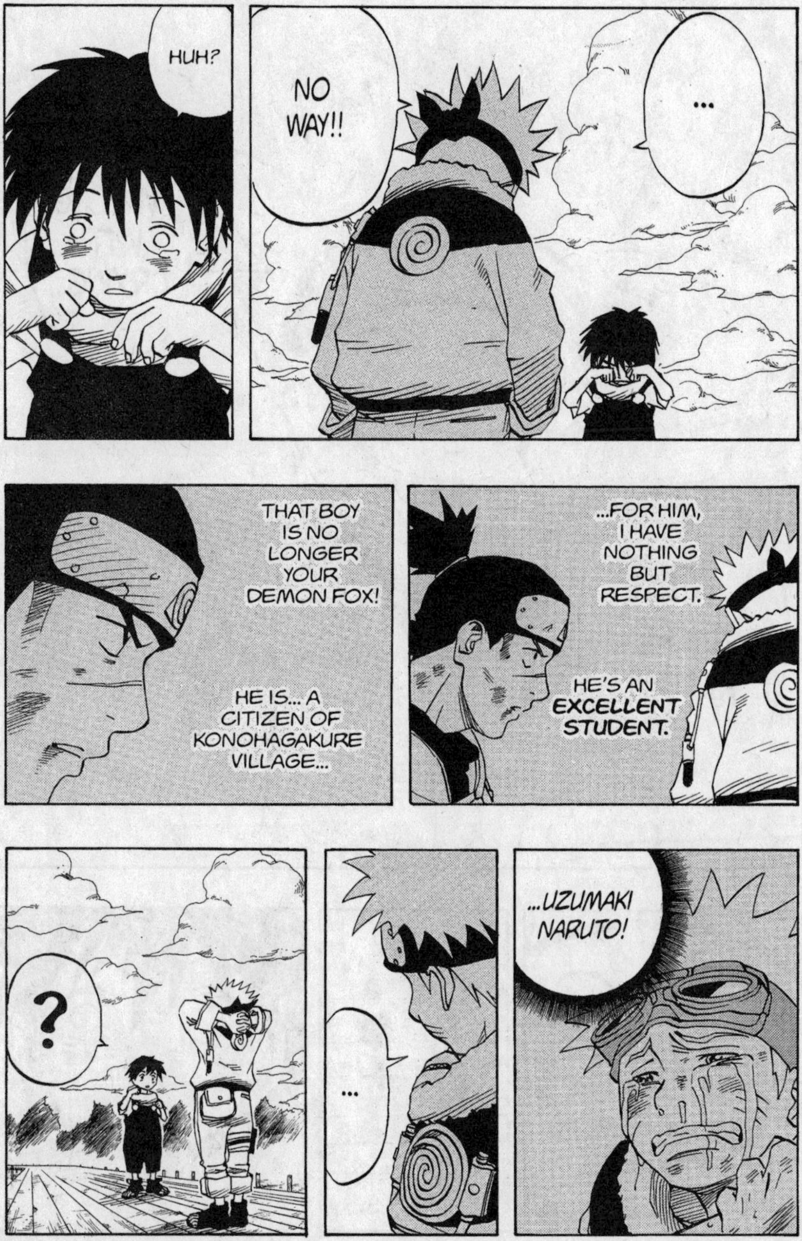
...
NO WAY!!
HUH?
...FOR HIM, I HAVE NOTHING BUT RESPECT.
HE'S AN EXCELLENT STUDENT.
THAT BOY IS NO LONGER YOUR DEMON FOX!
HE IS... A CITIZEN OF KONOHAGAKURE VILLAGE...
...UZUMAKI NARUTO!
...
?

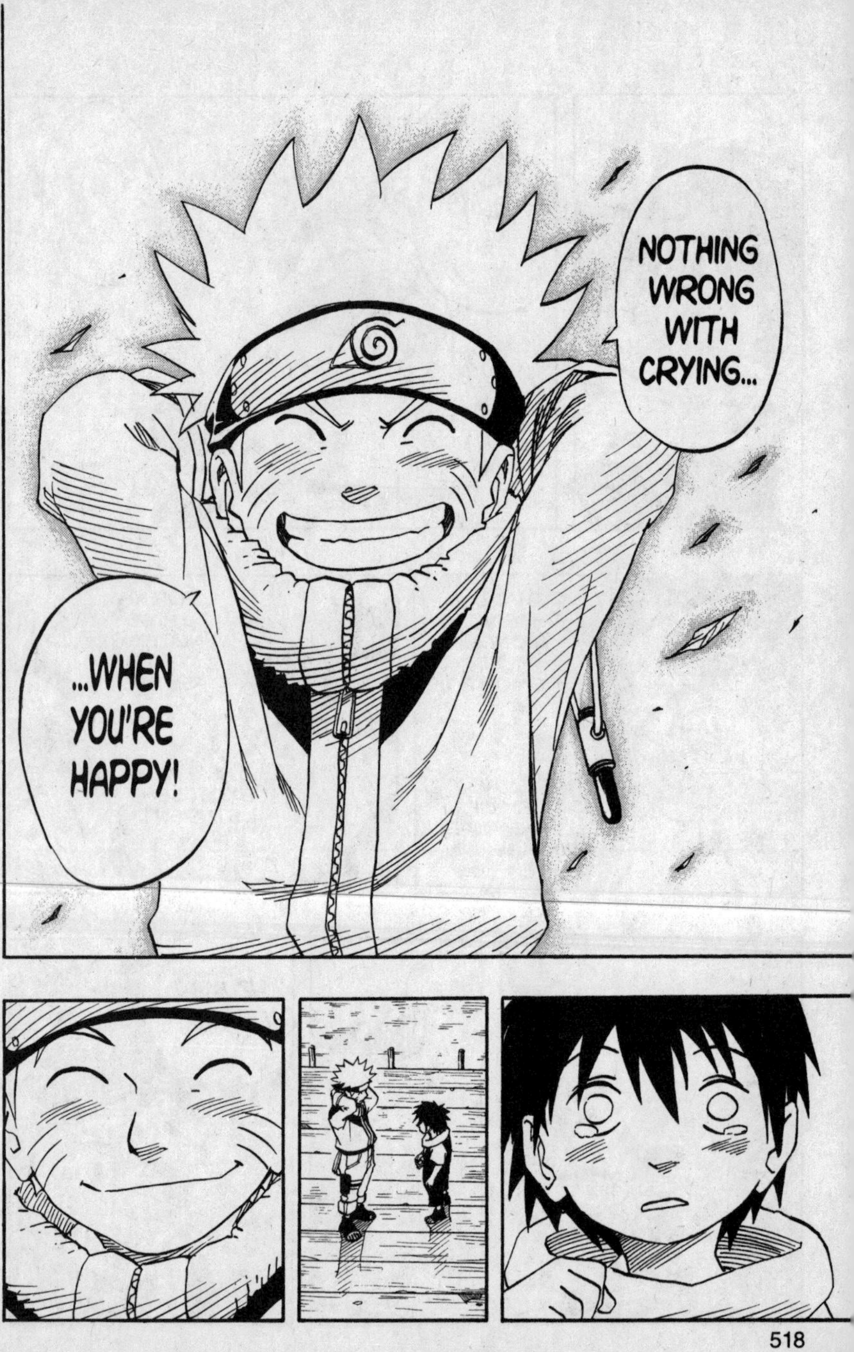
NOTHING WRONG WITH CRYING...
...WHEN YOU'RE HAPPY!

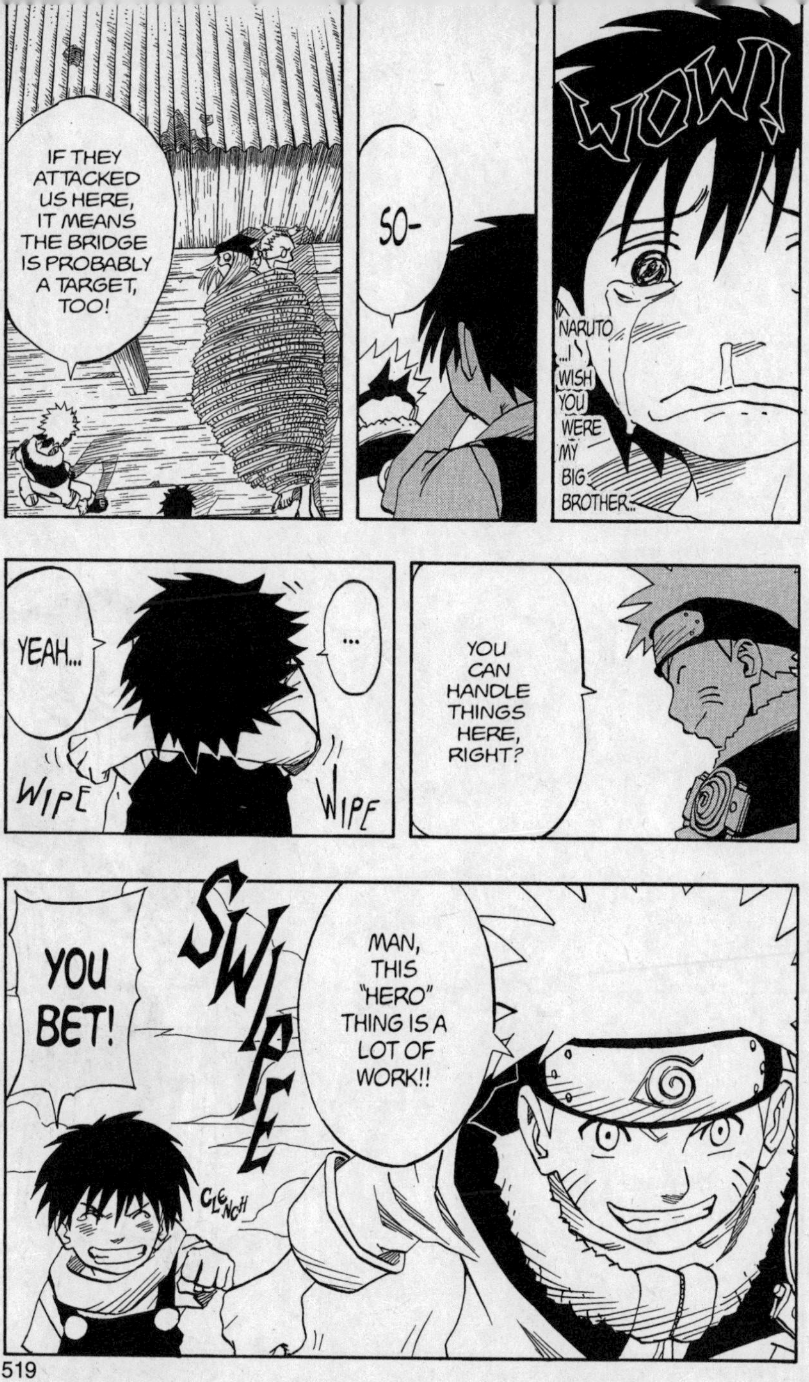
WOW!
NARUTO ...I WISH YOU WERE MY BIG BROTHER...
SO-
IF THEY ATTACKED US HERE, IT MEANS THE BRIDGE IS PROBABLY A TARGET, TOO!
YOU CAN HANDLE THINGS HERE, RIGHT?
...
YEAH...
WIPE
WIPE
MAN, THIS "HERO" THING IS A LOT OF WORK!!
SWIPE
YOU BET!
CLENCH

Number 24: Speed!!

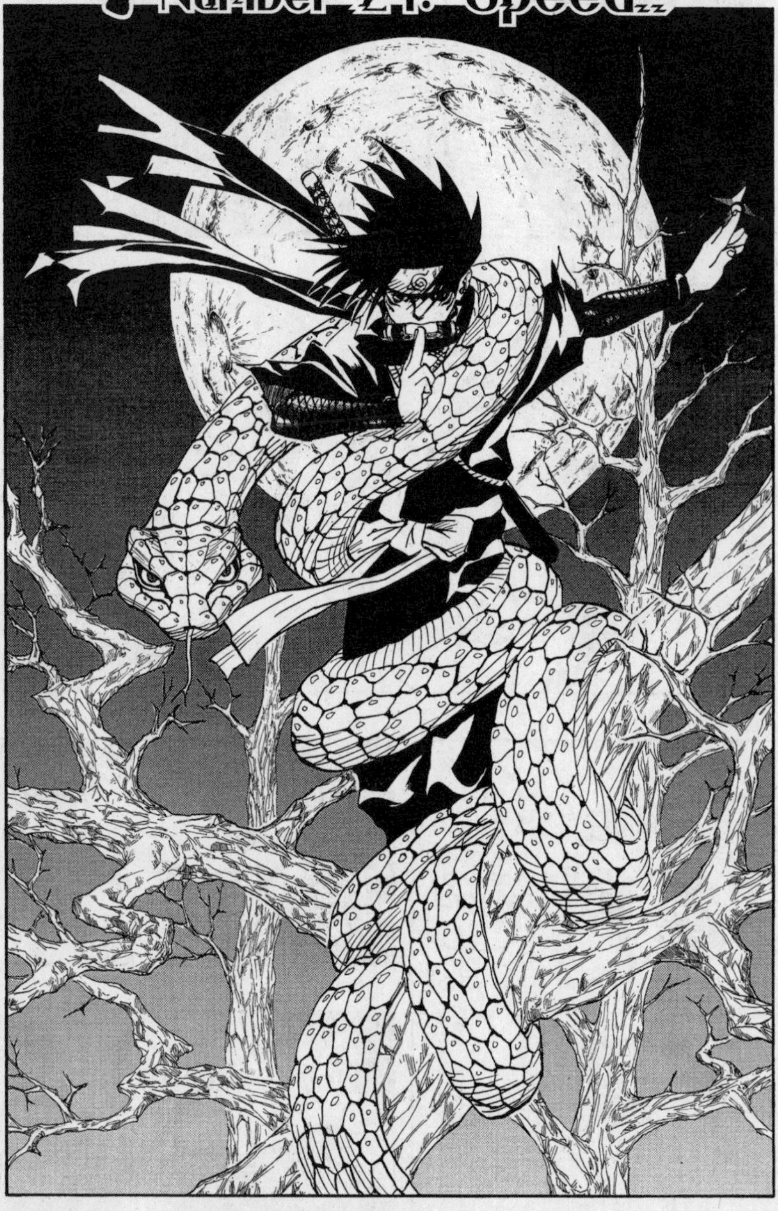

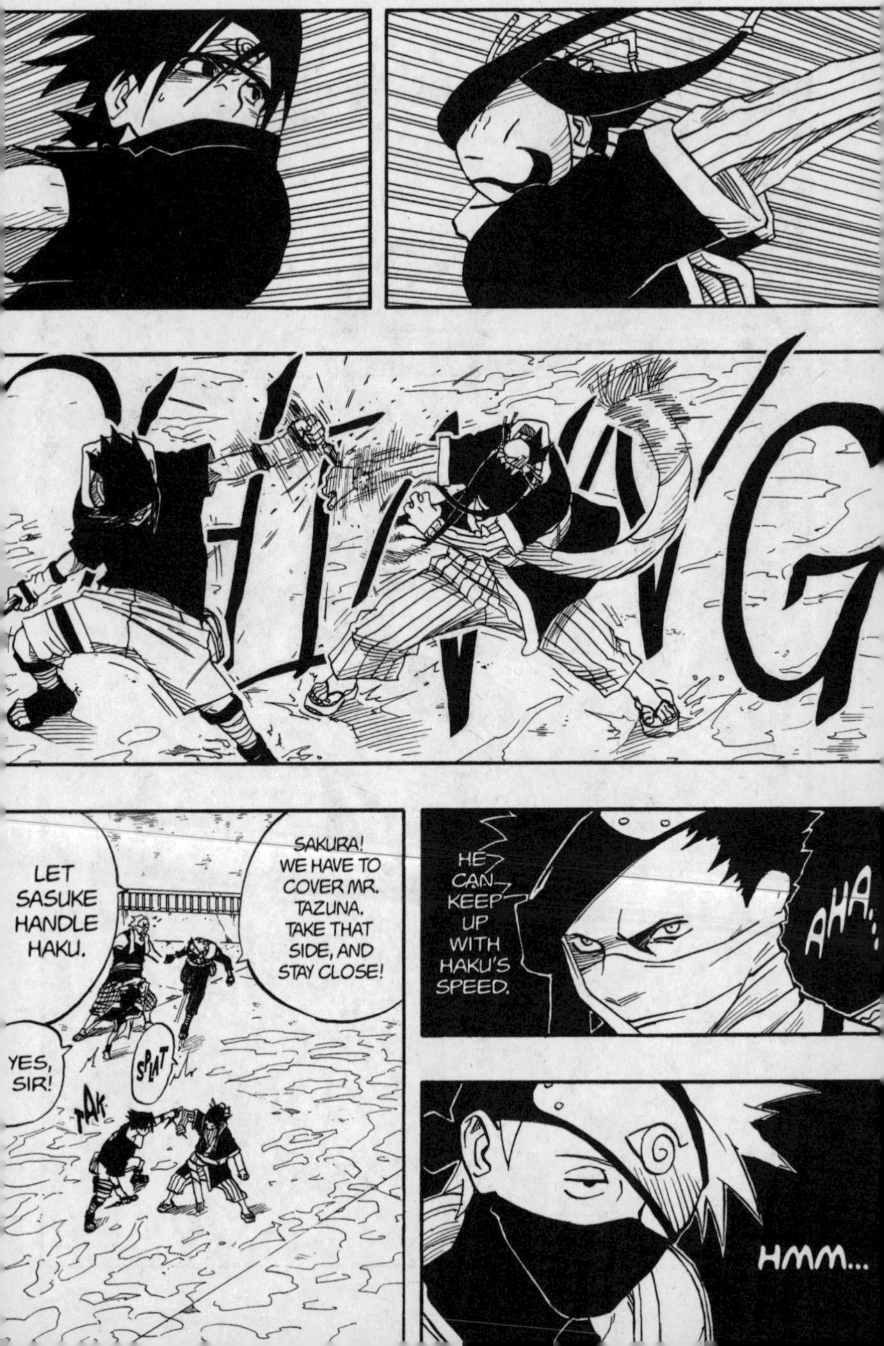
CHING
HE CAN KEEP UP WITH HAKU'S SPEED.
AHA...
HMM...
SAKURA! WE HAVE TO COVER MR. TAZUNA. TAKE THAT SIDE, AND STAY CLOSE!
LET SASUKE HANDLE HAKU.
SPLAT
YES, SIR!
TAK

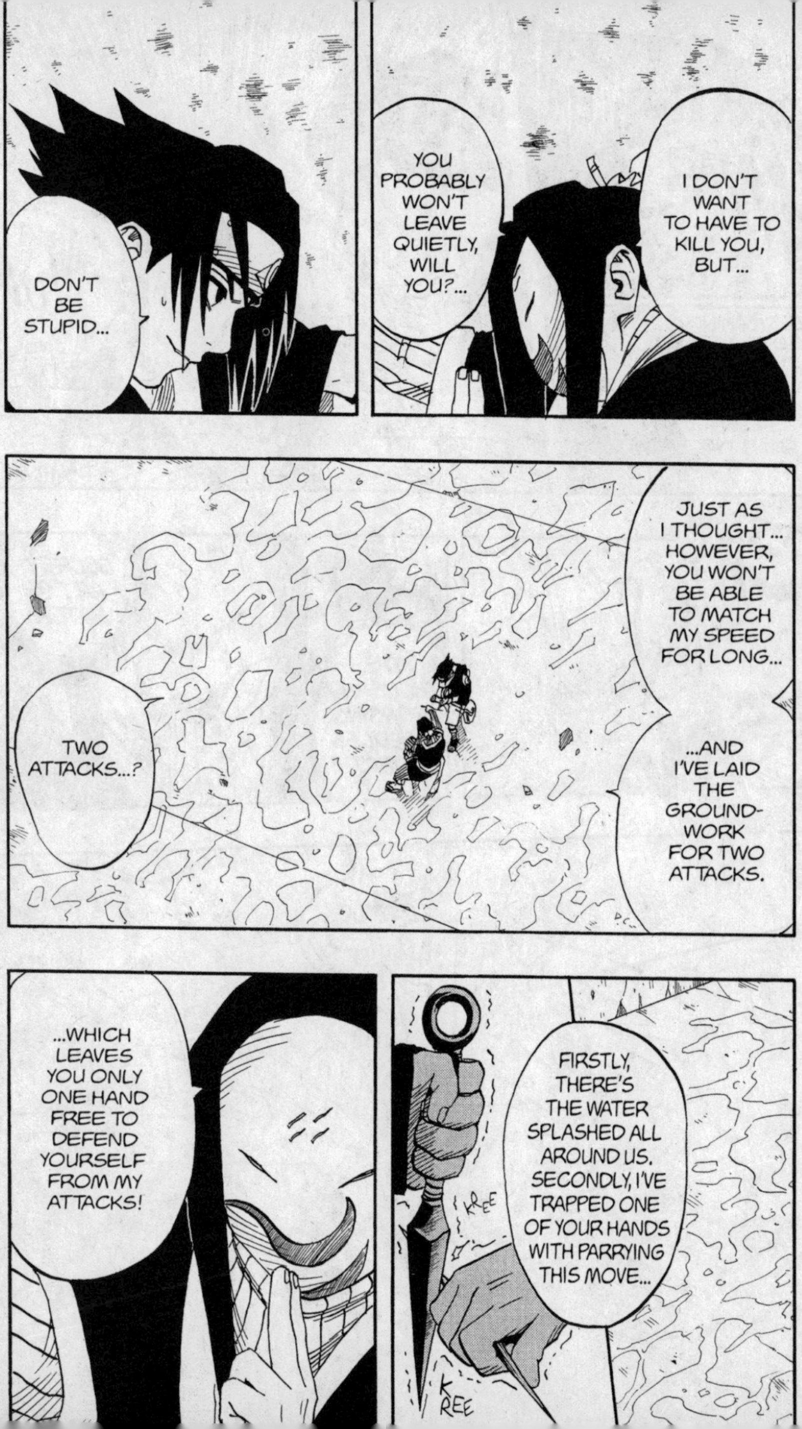
I DON'T WANT TO HAVE TO KILL YOU, BUT...
YOU PROBABLY WON'T LEAVE QUIETLY, WILL YOU?...
DON'T BE STUPID...
JUST AS I THOUGHT... HOWEVER, YOU WON'T BE ABLE TO MATCH MY SPEED FOR LONG...
...AND I'VE LAID THE GROUND-WORK FOR TWO ATTACKS.
TWO ATTACKS...?
FIRSTLY, THERE'S THE WATER SPLASHED ALL AROUND US. SECONDLY, I'VE TRAPPED ONE OF YOUR HANDS WITH PARRYING THIS MOVE...
KREE
KREE
...WHICH LEAVES YOU ONLY ONE HAND FREE TO DEFEND YOURSELF FROM MY ATTACKS!

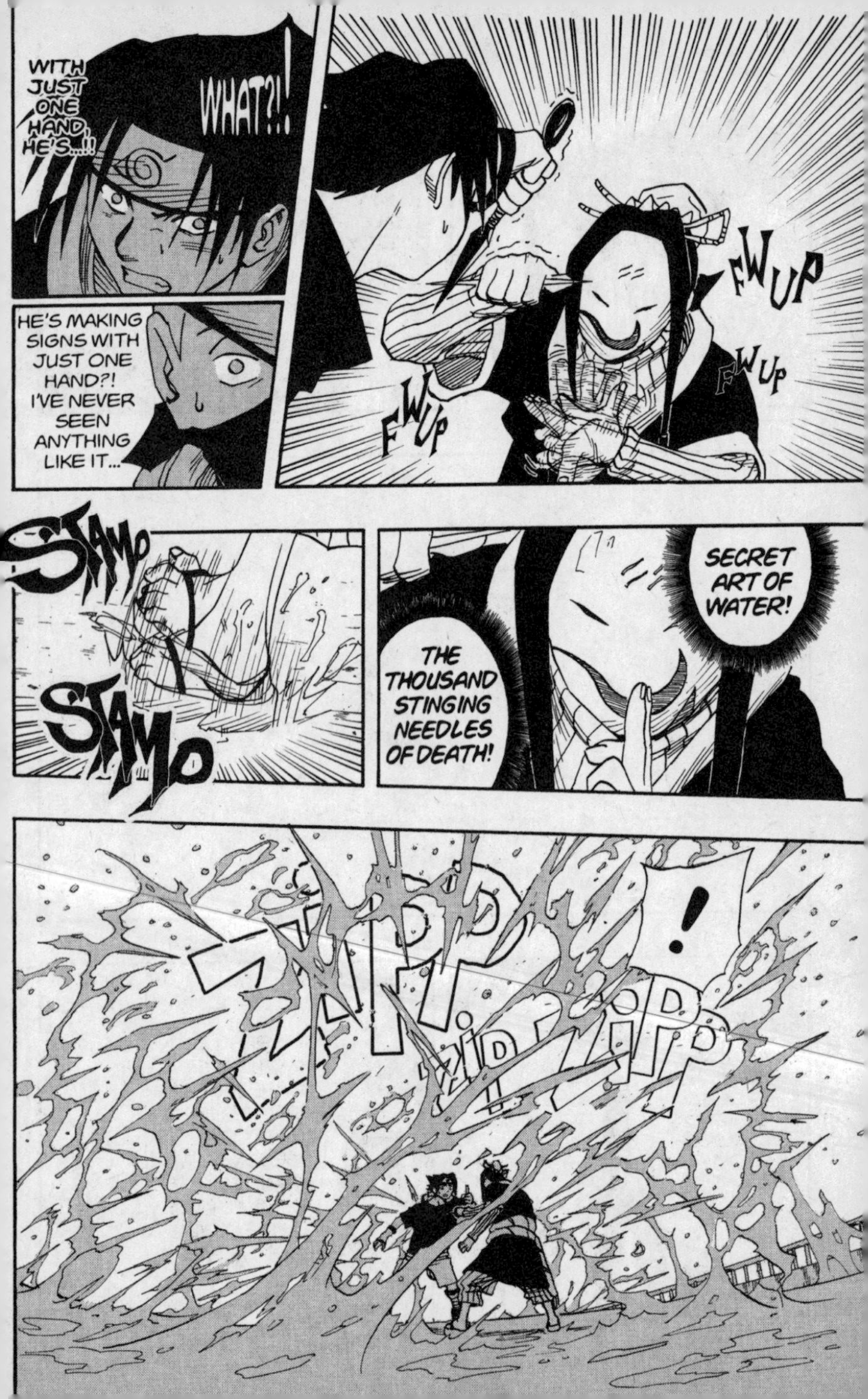
FWUP
FWUP
FWUP
WHAT?!!
WITH JUST ONE HAND, HE'S...!!
HE'S MAKING SIGNS WITH JUST ONE HAND?! I'VE NEVER SEEN ANYTHING LIKE IT...
SECRET ART OF WATER!
THE THOUSAND STINGING NEEDLES OF DEATH!
STAMP
STAMP
!
ZIP
ZIP ZIP

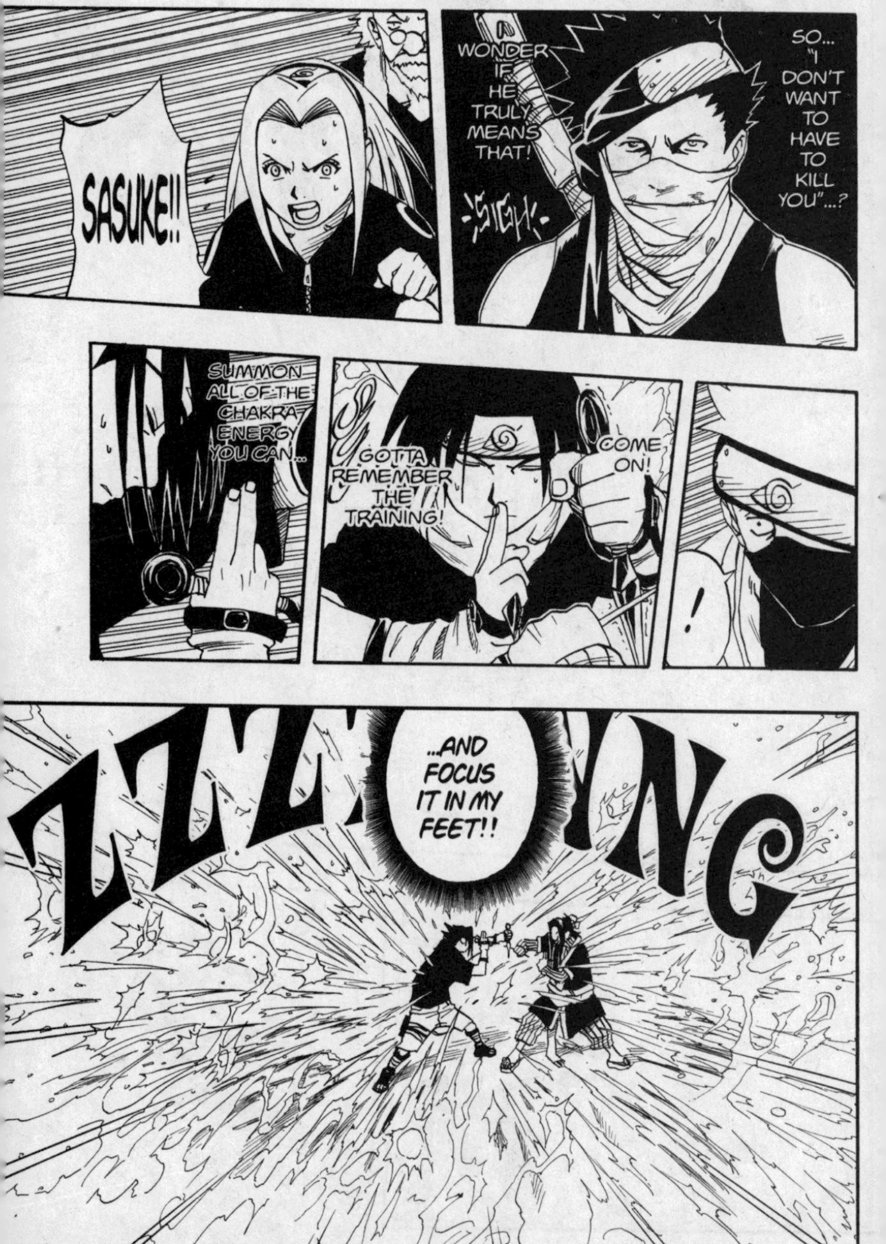

SO... "I DON'T WANT TO HAVE TO KILL YOU"...?
I WONDER IF HE TRULY MEANS THAT!
SIGH
SASUKE!!
COME ON!
GOTTA REMEMBER THE TRAINING!
SUMMON ALL OF THE CHAKRA ENERGY YOU CAN...
ZZZOOONNG
...AND FOCUS IT IN MY FEET!!

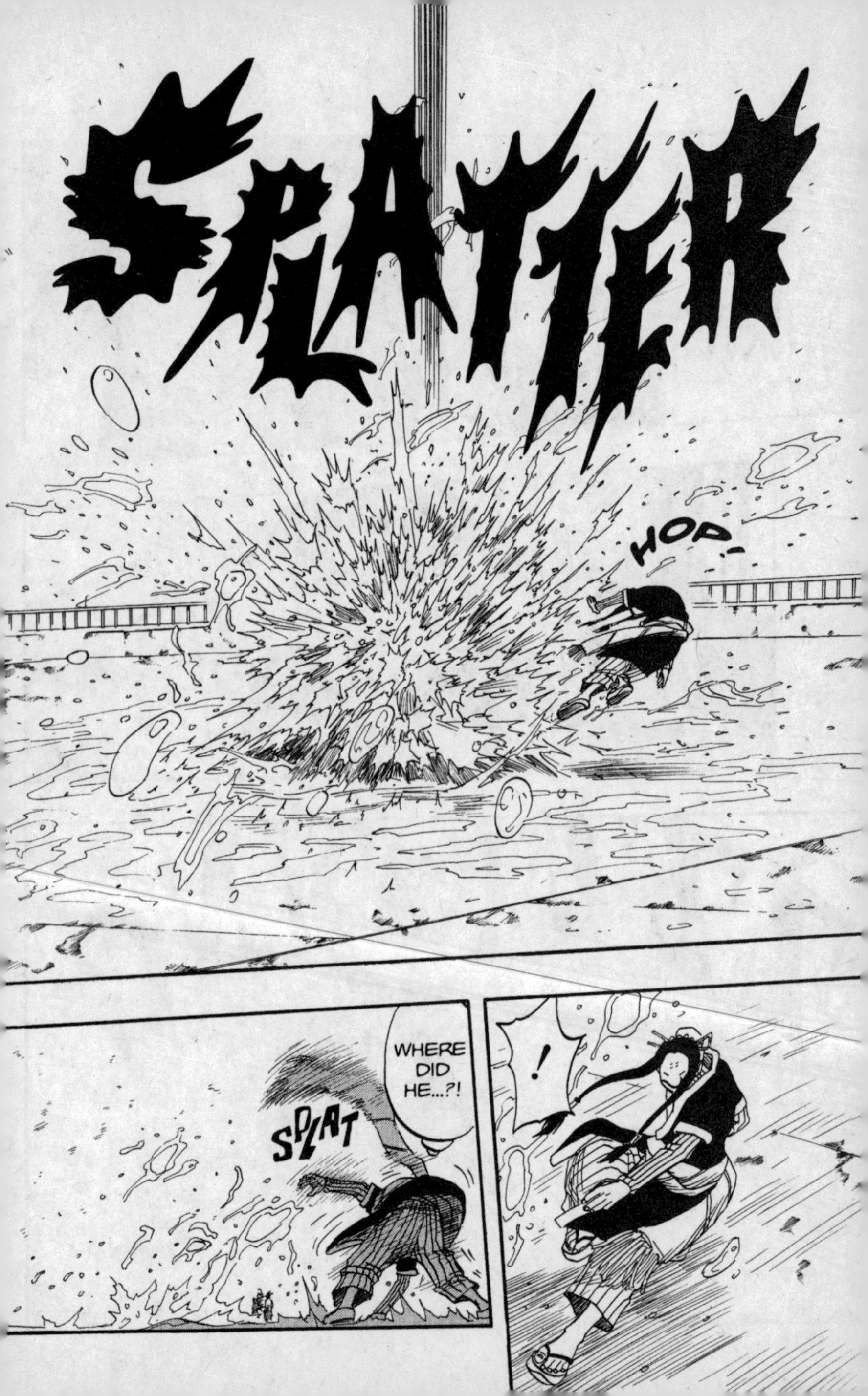
SPLATTER
HOP
!
WHERE DID HE...?!
SPLAT

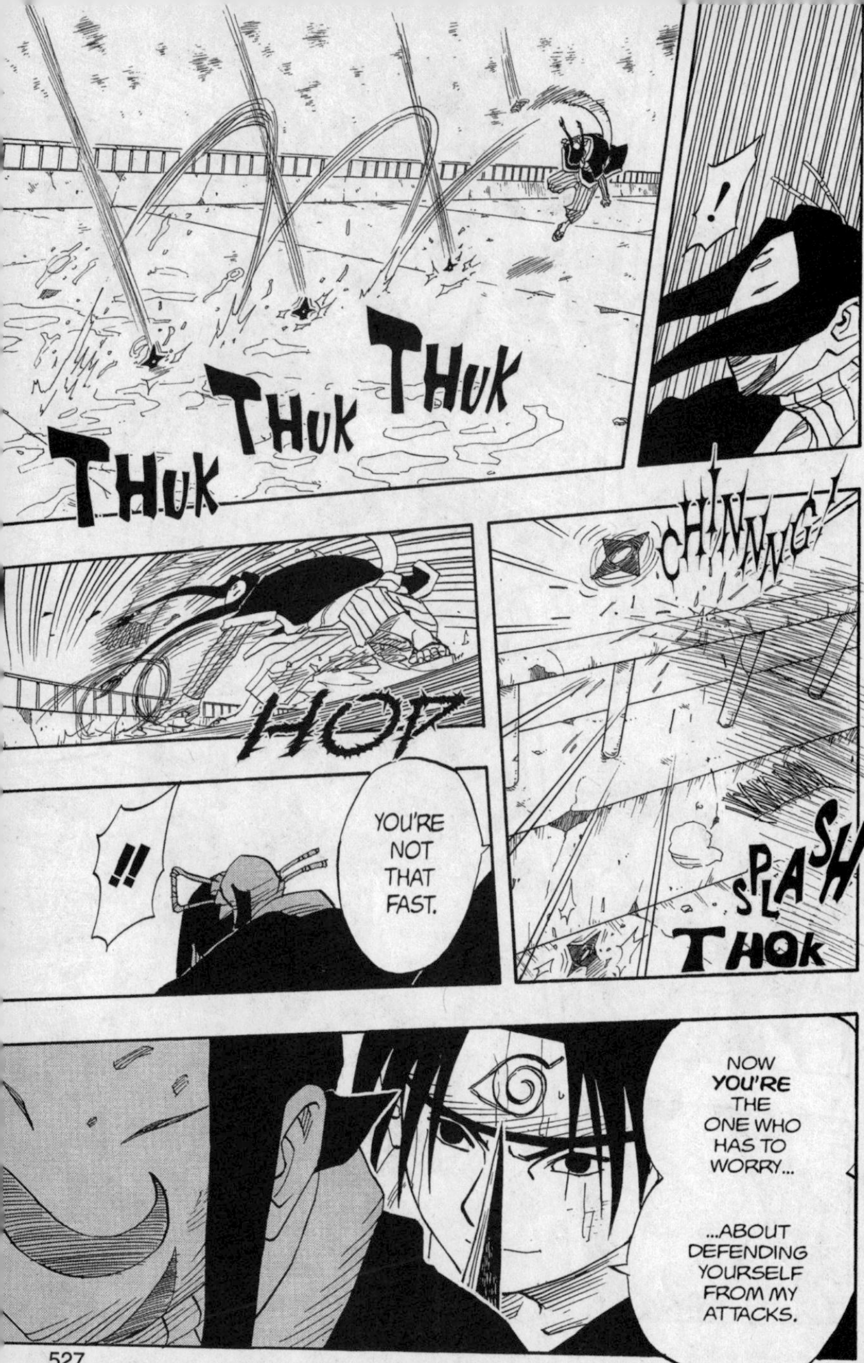
!
THUK
THUK
THUK
CHINNNG!
SPLASH
THOK
HOP
YOU'RE NOT THAT FAST.
!!
NOW **YOU'RE** THE ONE WHO HAS TO WORRY...
...ABOUT DEFENDING YOURSELF FROM MY ATTACKS.

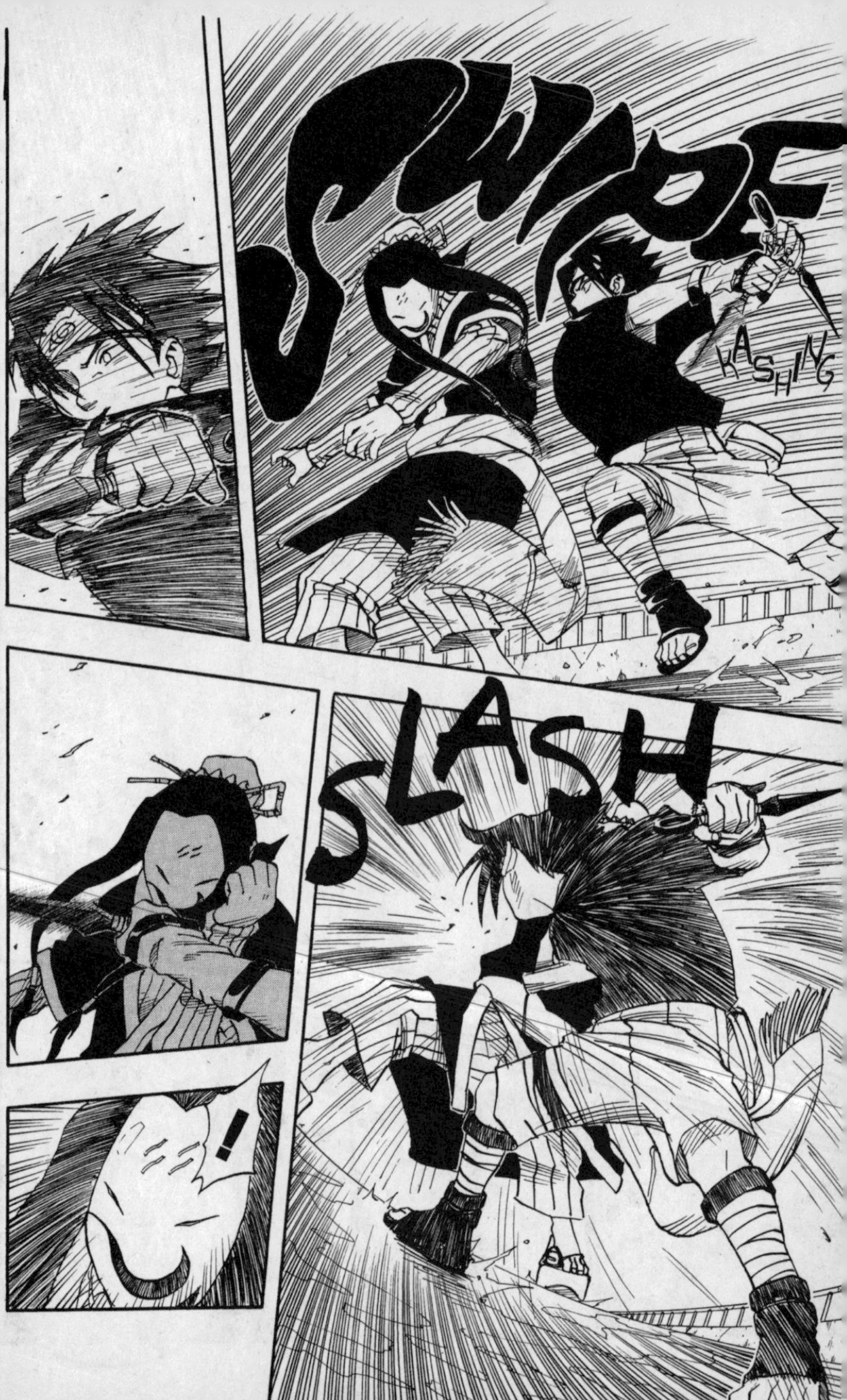
SWIPE
KASHING
SLASH
!

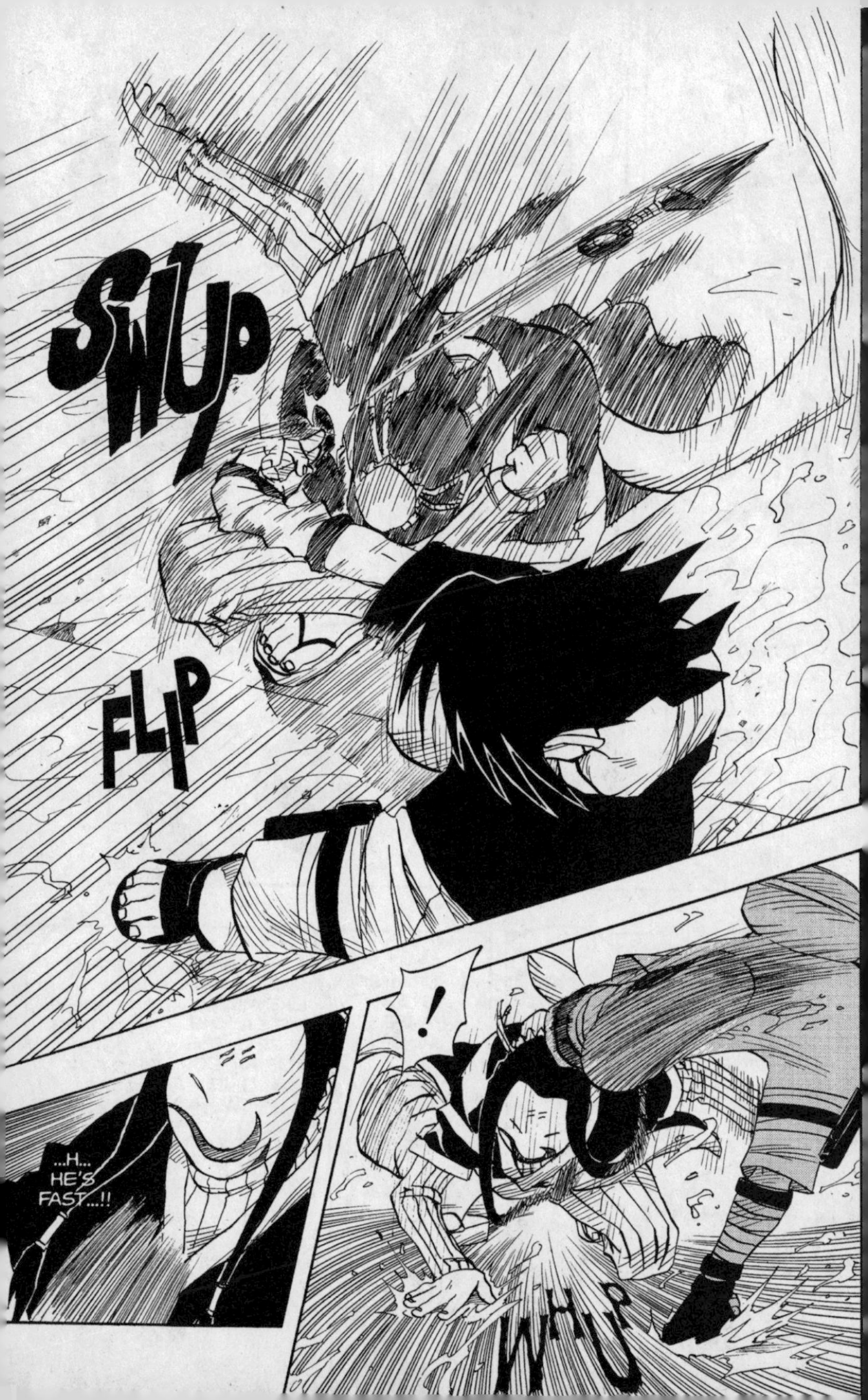
SWUP
FLIP
!
...H... HE'S FAST...!!
WHUP

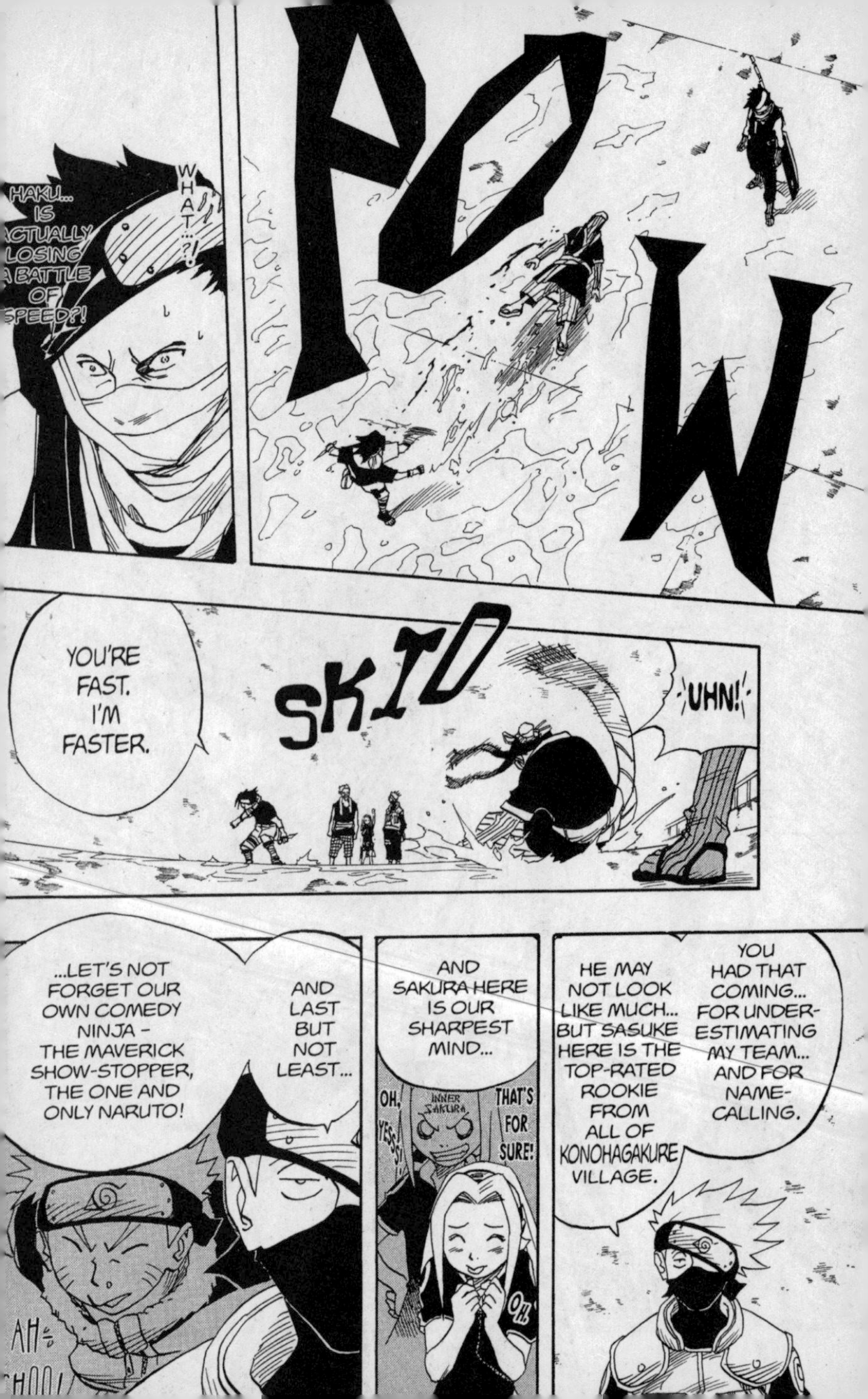
POW
WHAT...?!
HAKU... IS ACTUALLY LOSING A BATTLE OF SPEED?!
UHN!
SKID
YOU'RE FAST. I'M FASTER.
YOU HAD THAT COMING... FOR UNDER-ESTIMATING MY TEAM... AND FOR NAME-CALLING.
HE MAY NOT LOOK LIKE MUCH... BUT SASUKE HERE IS THE TOP-RATED ROOKIE FROM ALL OF KONOHAGAKURE VILLAGE.
AND SAKURA HERE IS OUR SHARPEST MIND...
INNER SAKURA
THAT'S FOR SURE!
OH, YESSS!
OH.
AND LAST BUT NOT LEAST...
...LET'S NOT FORGET OUR OWN COMEDY NINJA - THE MAVERICK SHOW-STOPPER, THE ONE AND ONLY NARUTO!
AH-CHOO!

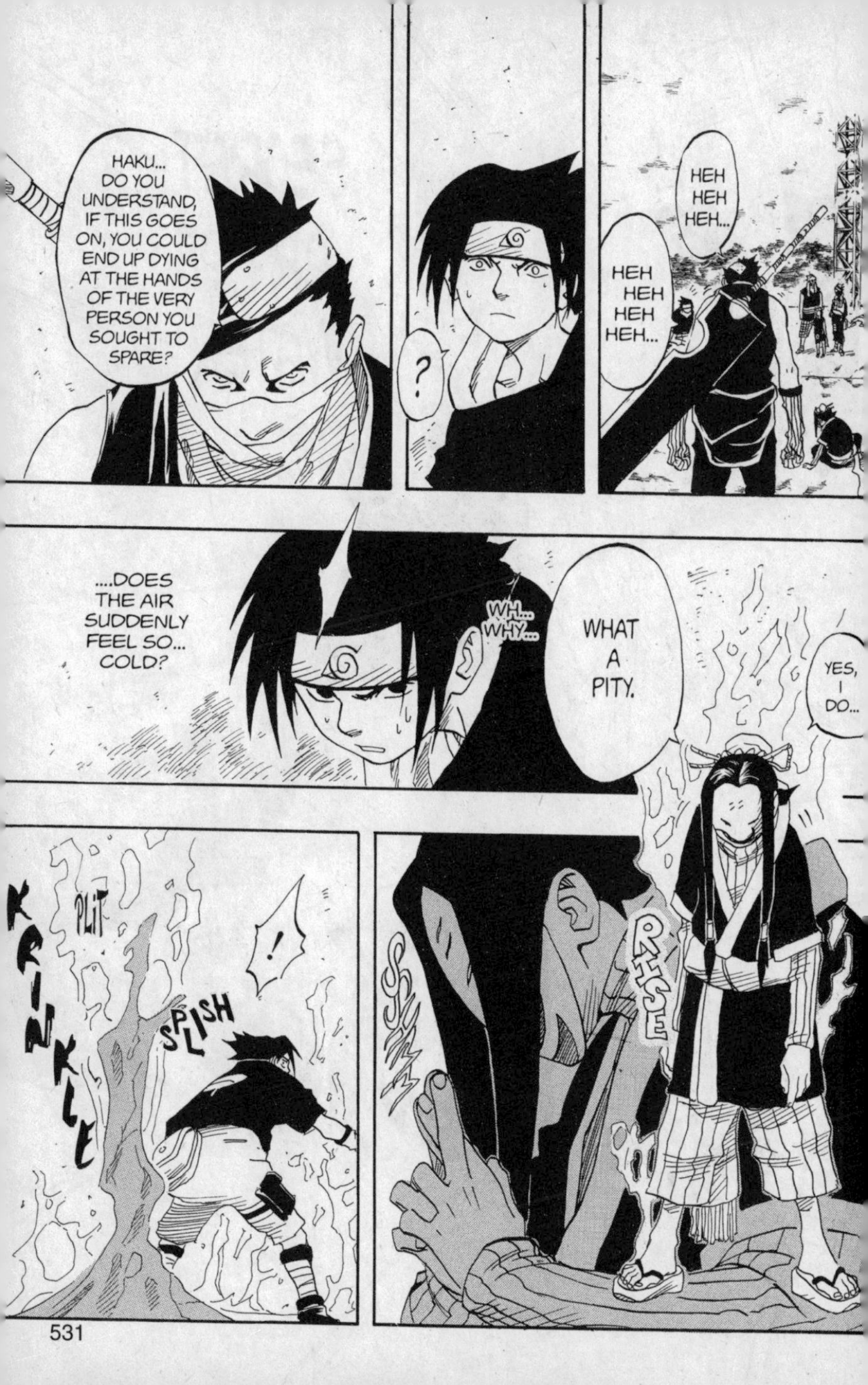

HEH HEH HEH...
HEH HEH HEH HEH...
?
HAKU... DO YOU UNDERSTAND, IF THIS GOES ON, YOU COULD END UP DYING AT THE HANDS OF THE VERY PERSON YOU SOUGHT TO SPARE?
YES, I DO...
WHAT A PITY.
WH... WHY...
...DOES THE AIR SUDDENLY FEEL SO... COLD?
RISE
!
SPLISH
PLIT
KRINKLE

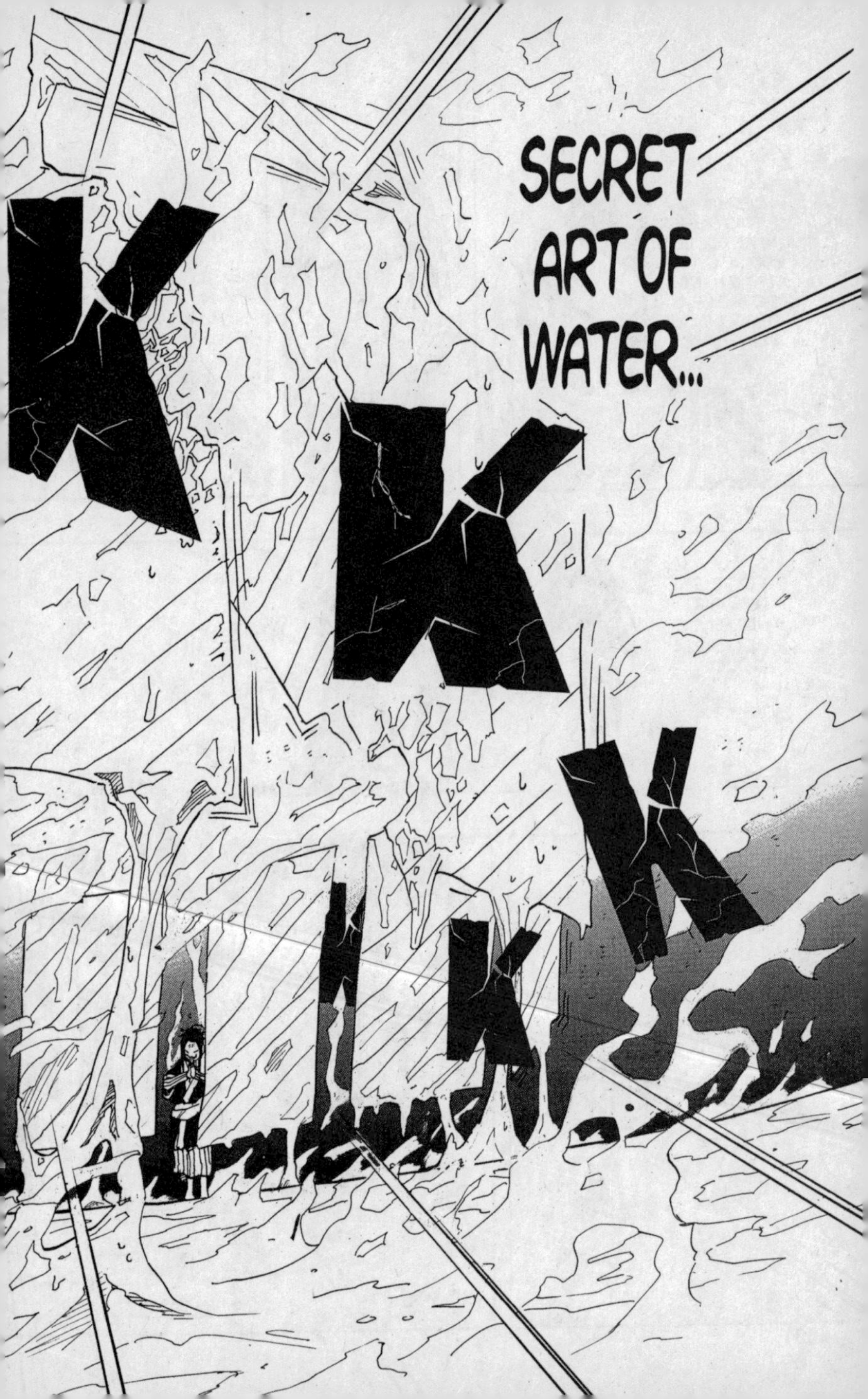
SECRET ART OF WATER...
K
K
K
K
K

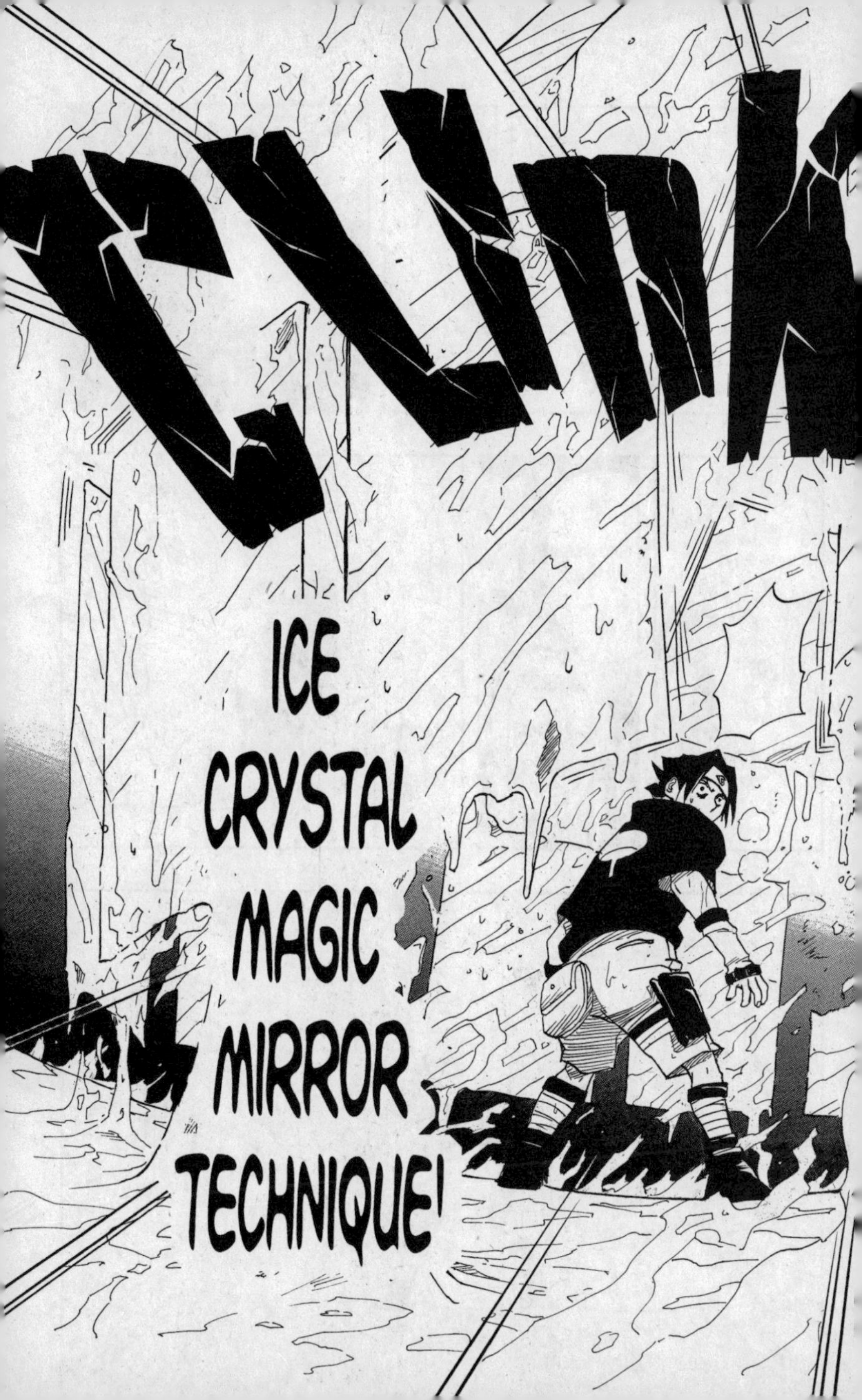
CLINK
ICE CRYSTAL MAGIC MIRROR TECHNIQUE!

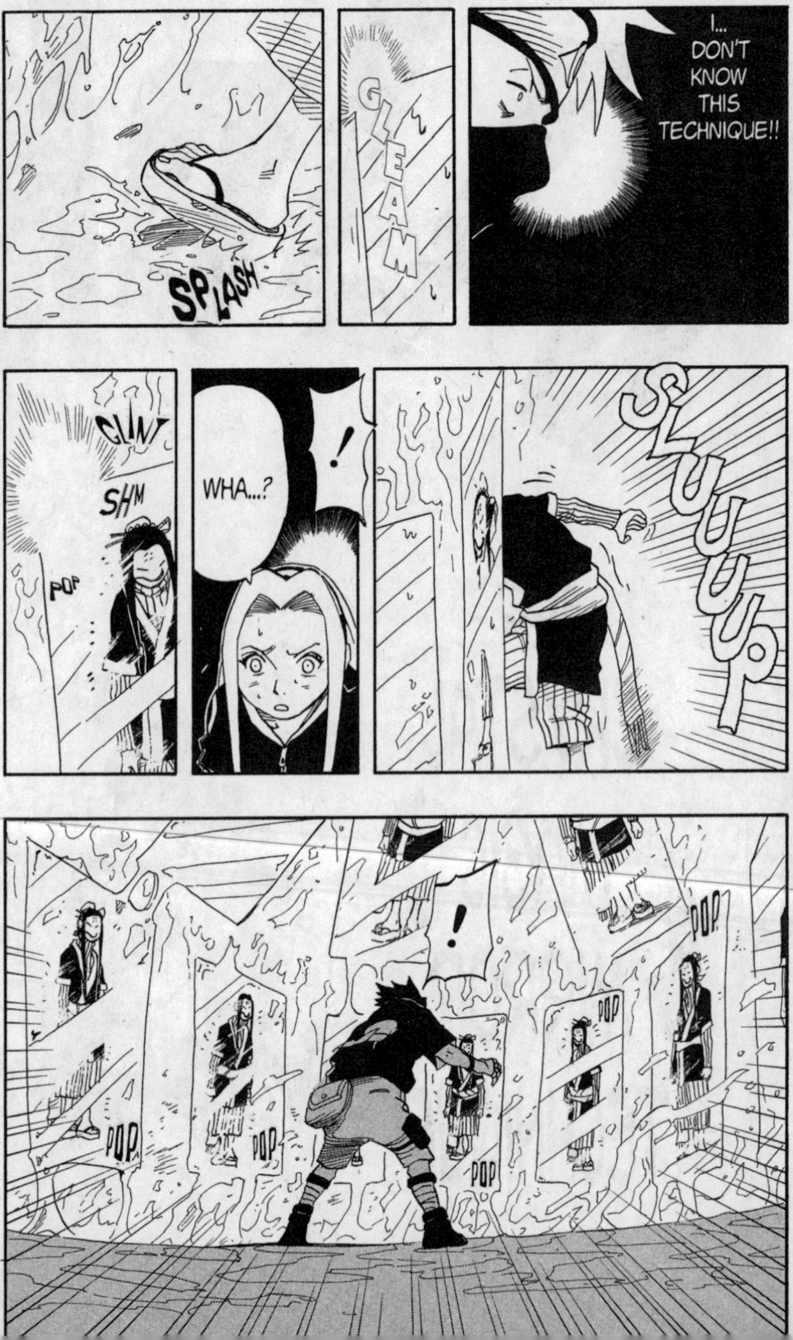
I... DON'T KNOW THIS TECHNIQUE!!
GLEAM
SPLASH
SLUUUUP
!
WHA...?
GLINT
SHM
POP
POP
!
POP
POP
POP
POP

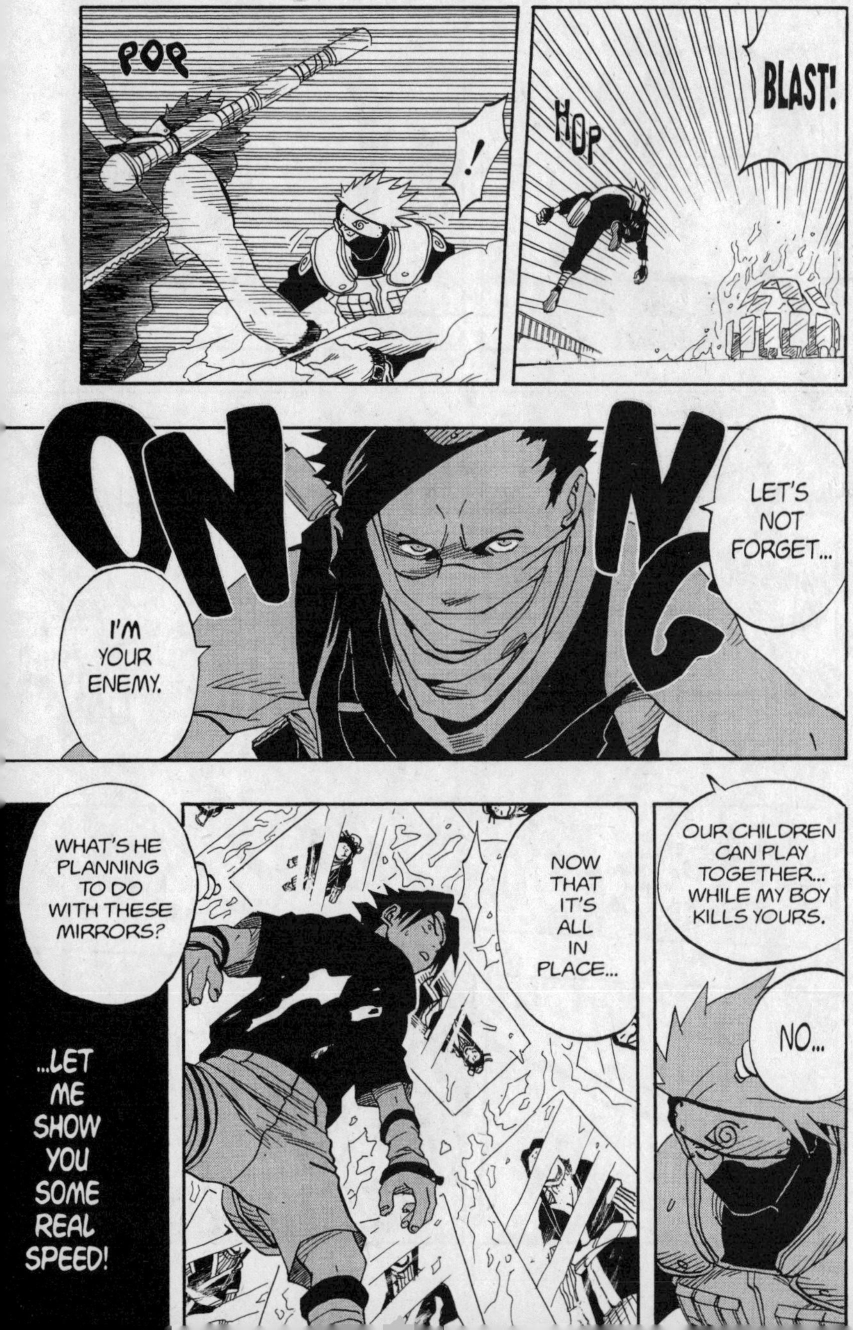
HOP
BLAST!
POP
!
LET'S NOT FORGET...
ONNG
I'M YOUR ENEMY.
OUR CHILDREN CAN PLAY TOGETHER... WHILE MY BOY KILLS YOURS.
NO...
NOW THAT IT'S ALL IN PLACE...
WHAT'S HE PLANNING TO DO WITH THESE MIRRORS?
...LET ME SHOW YOU SOME REAL SPEED!

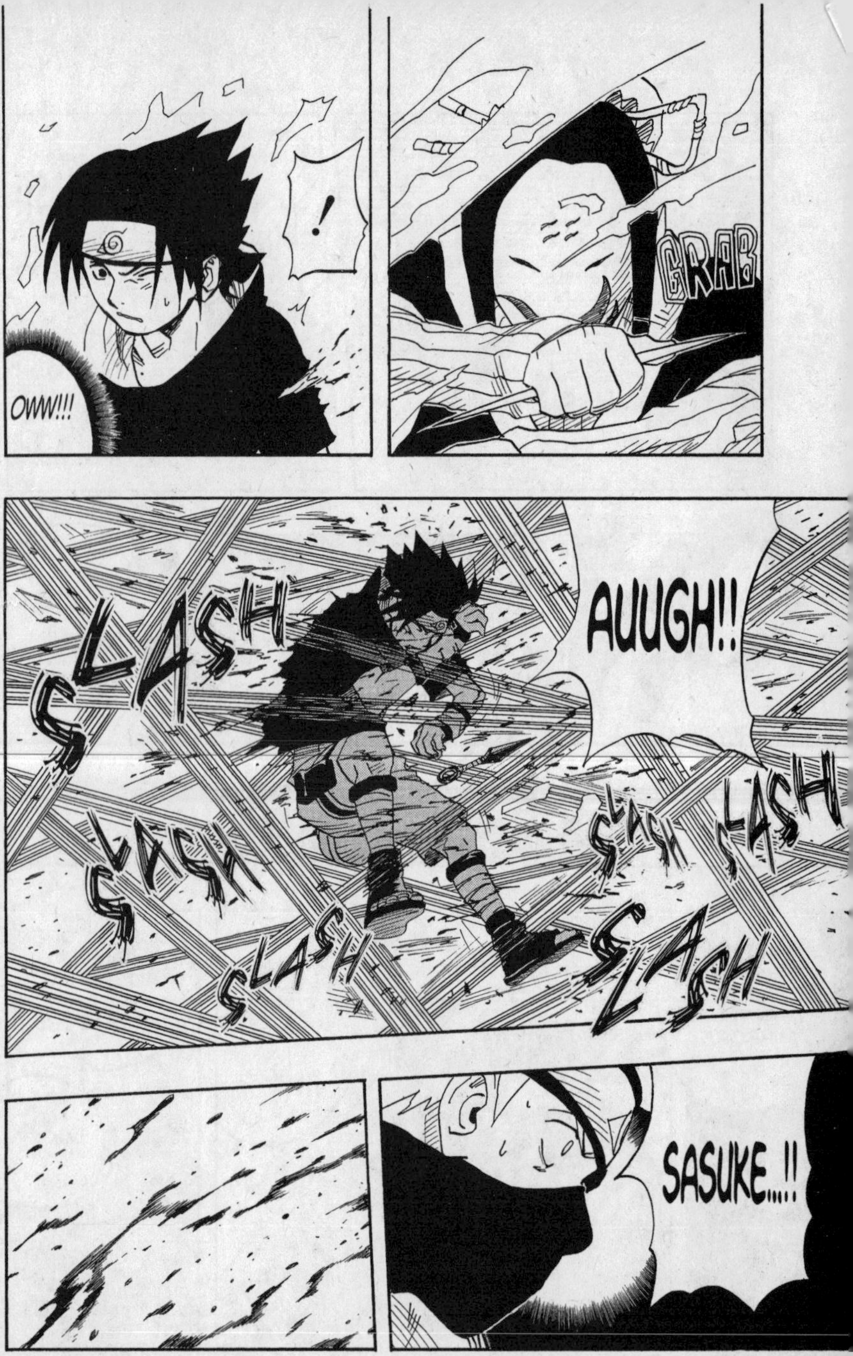
GRAB
!
OWW!!!
AUUGH!!
SLASH
SLASH
SLASH
SLASH
SLASH
SLASH
SLASH
SASUKE...!!

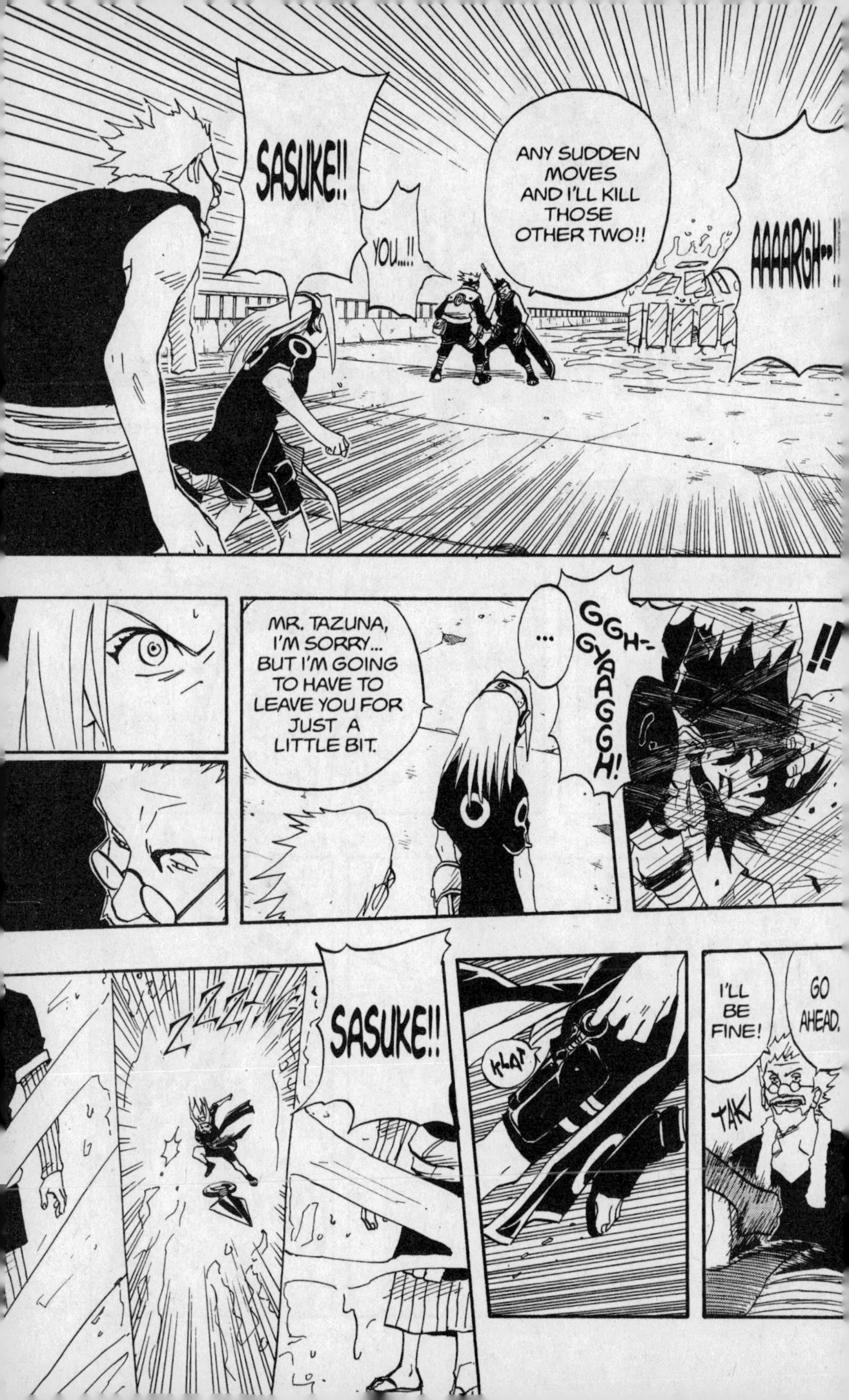
AAAARGH..!!
ANY SUDDEN MOVES AND I'LL KILL THOSE OTHER TWO!!
YOU...!!
SASUKE!!
!!
GGH- GYAAGGH!
...
MR. TAZUNA, I'M SORRY... BUT I'M GOING TO HAVE TO LEAVE YOU FOR JUST A LITTLE BIT.
GO AHEAD.
I'LL BE FINE!
TAK!
KLAK
SASUKE!!

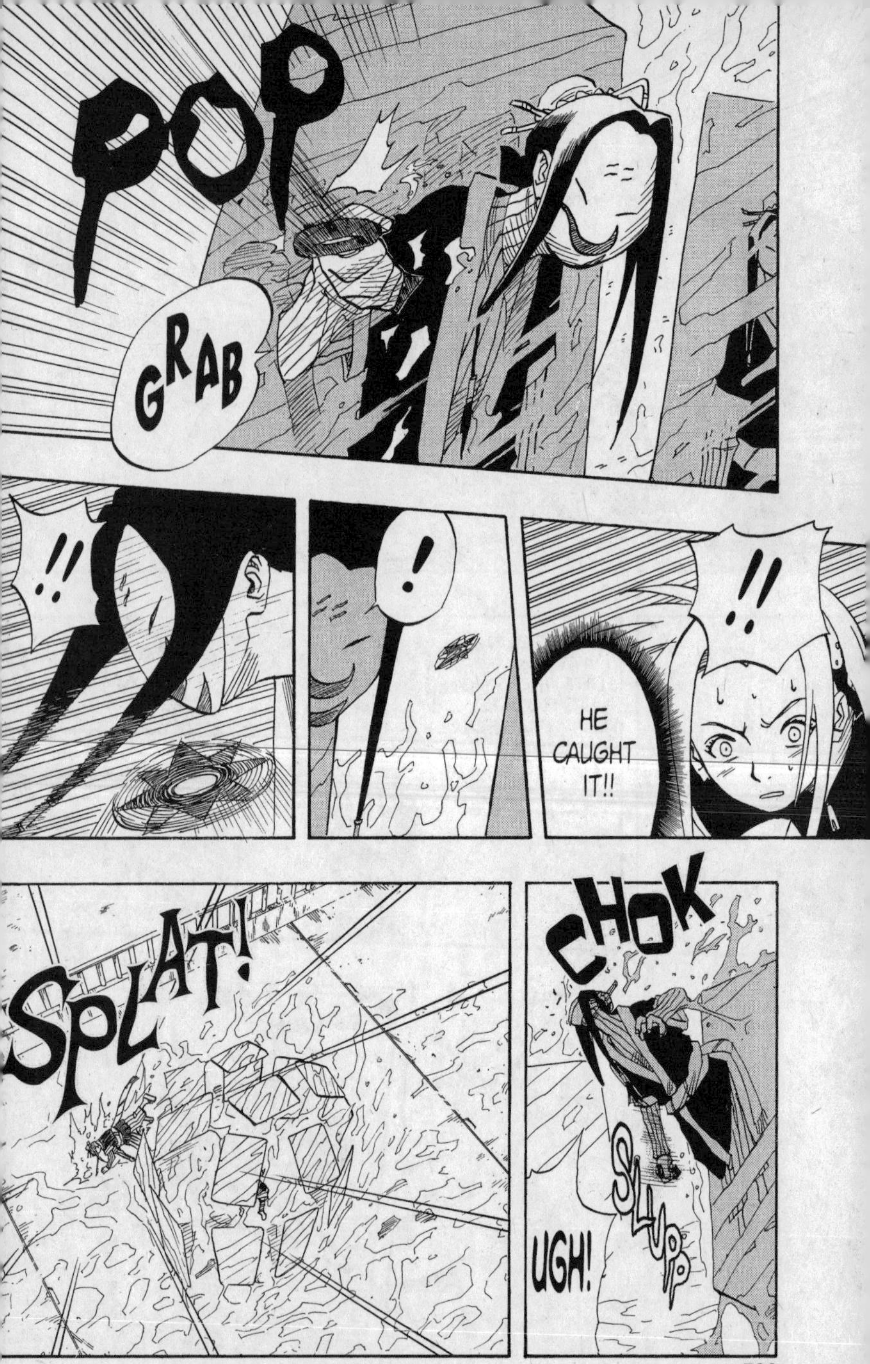
POP
GRAB
!!
HE CAUGHT IT!!
!
!!
CHOK
SLUPP
UGH!
SPLAT!

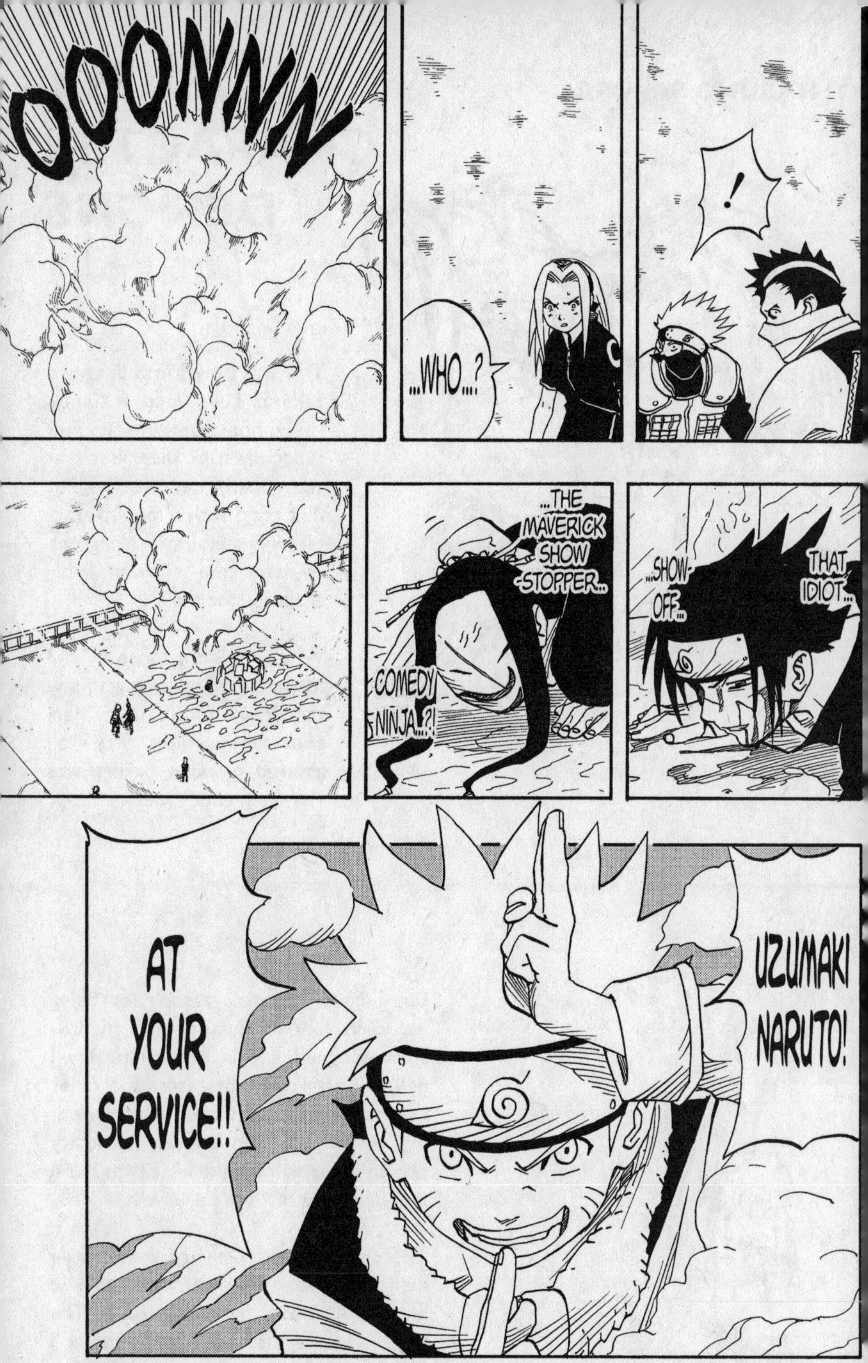
!
...WHO...?
OOONNN
THAT IDIOT...
...SHOW-OFF...
...THE MAVERICK SHOW-STOPPER...
COMEDY NINJA...?!
UZUMAKI NARUTO!
AT YOUR SERVICE!!

HARUNO SAKURA

EARLY CHARACTER DESIGNS

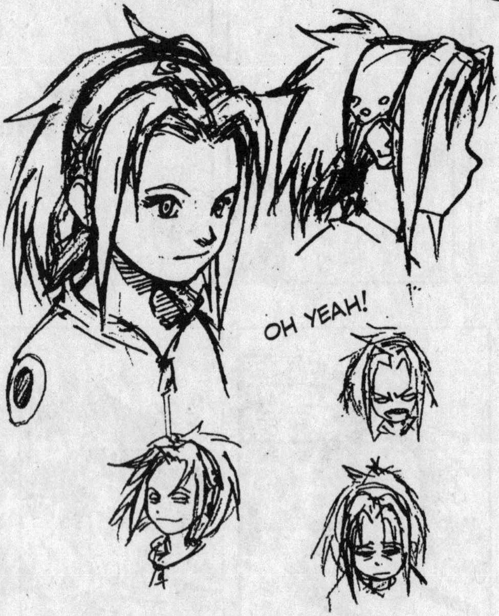
OH YEAH!

This was how I first imagined Sakura. Let's face it...she's really not that cute, is she? Especially back then! But that was mostly because I'm not that good with female characters in general, so making one of them cute is always a big challenge for me.

When my editor, those around me, and even my own staff saw this design and read her personality profile, they all assured me that Sakura was "far from cute"! Heh-heh...

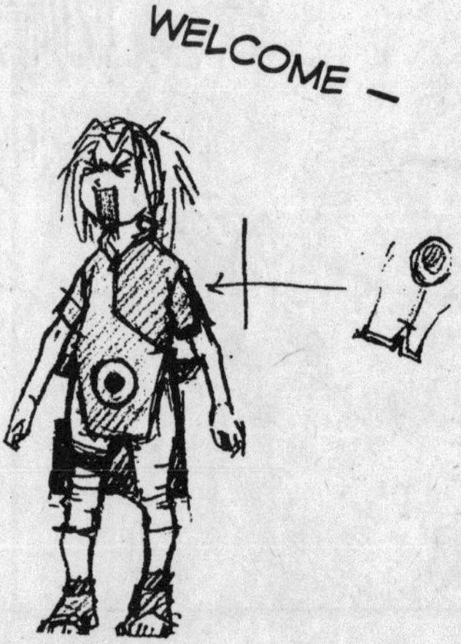
WELCOME –

But I have my own reasons for being especially fond of Sakura, both in how she's designed, and in her personality. I believe everyone possesses an "Inner Sakura" type voice in their heart, including things like her entirely arbitrary choice of love object. I think it gives her a real humanity that's pretty sweet.

There's a lot more to being a good female manga character than just cuteness, you know....At least, that's my excuse. The troublemakers and the curmudgeons I can draw without breaking a sweat... but girls are really hard!

Number 25: Dreams...!!

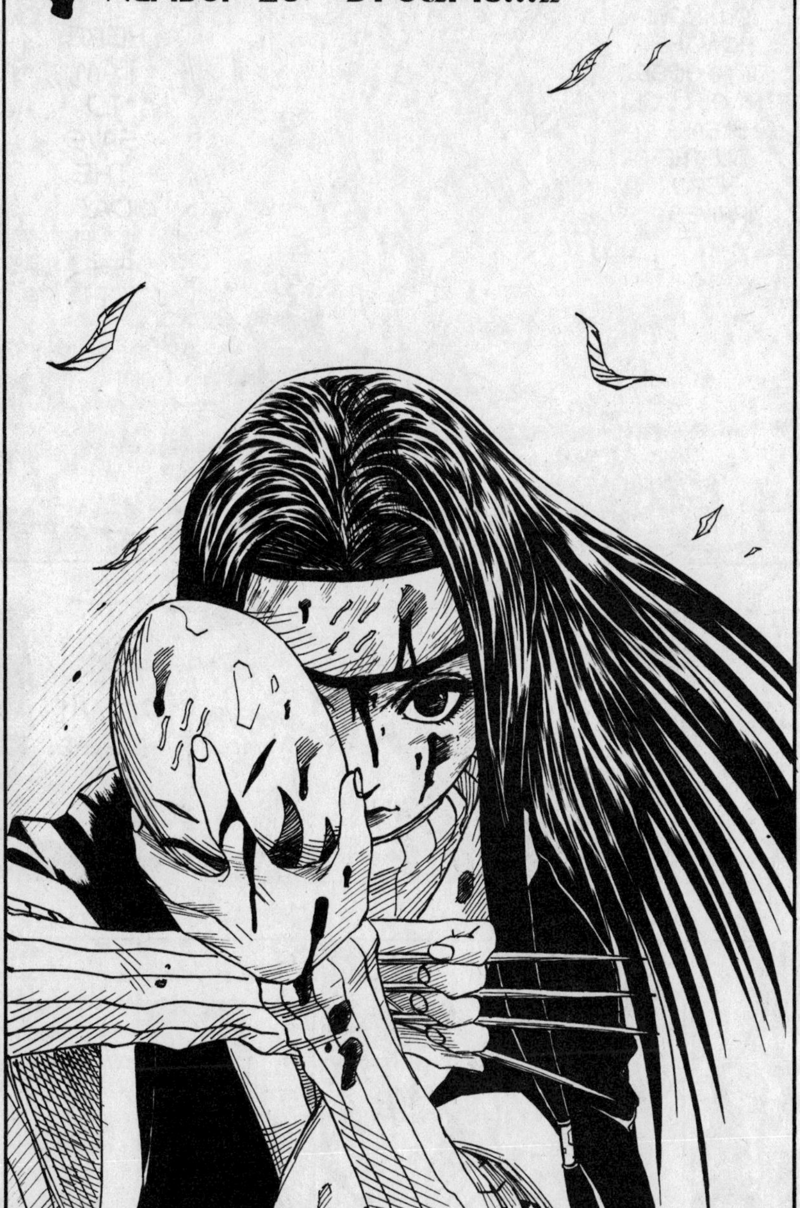

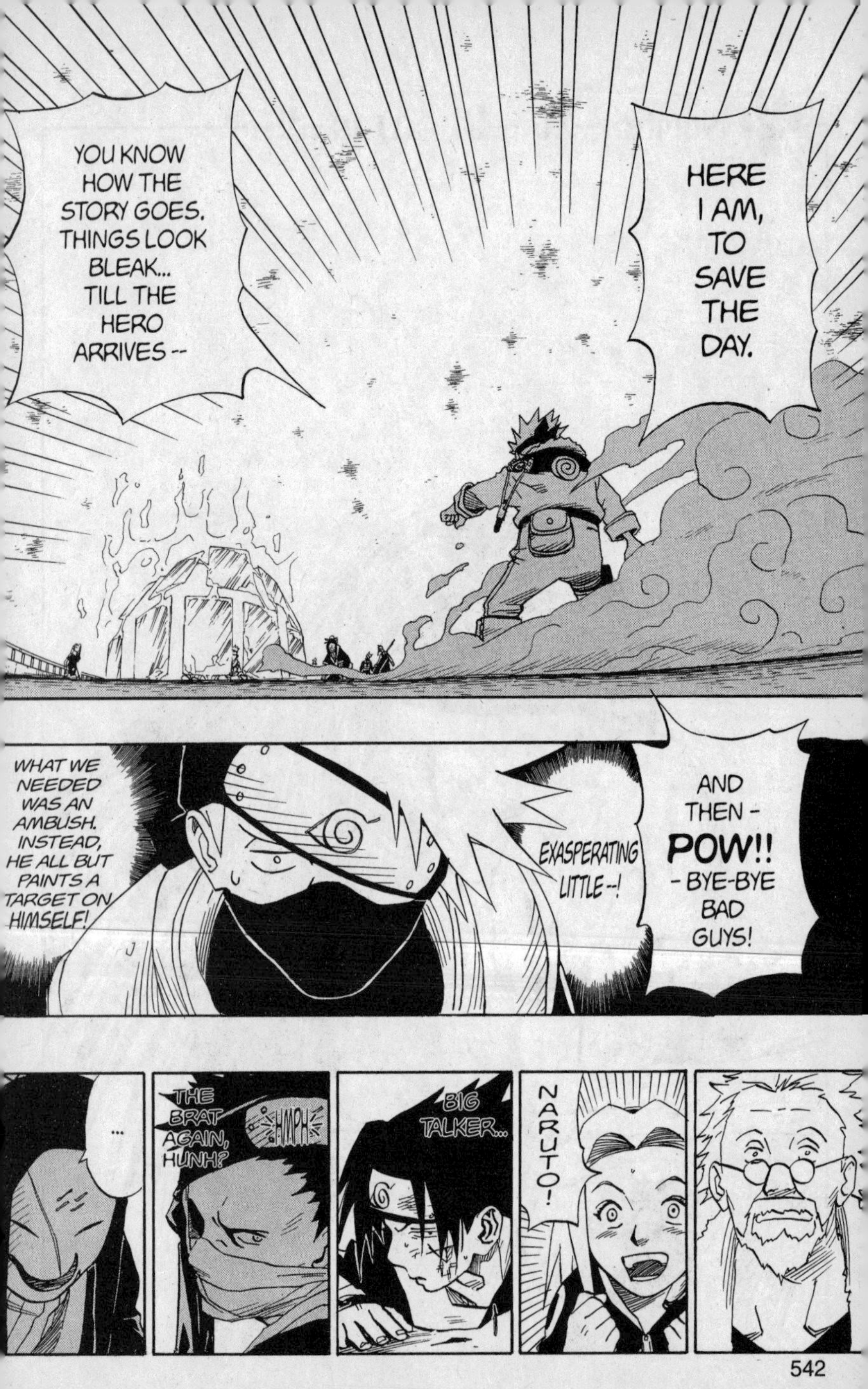
YOU KNOW HOW THE STORY GOES. THINGS LOOK BLEAK... TILL THE HERO ARRIVES --
HERE I AM, TO SAVE THE DAY.
AND THEN - POW!! - BYE-BYE BAD GUYS!
EXASPERATING LITTLE --!
WHAT WE NEEDED WAS AN AMBUSH. INSTEAD, HE ALL BUT PAINTS A TARGET ON HIMSELF!
NARUTO!
BIG TALKER...
HMPH
THE BRAT AGAIN, HUNH?
...

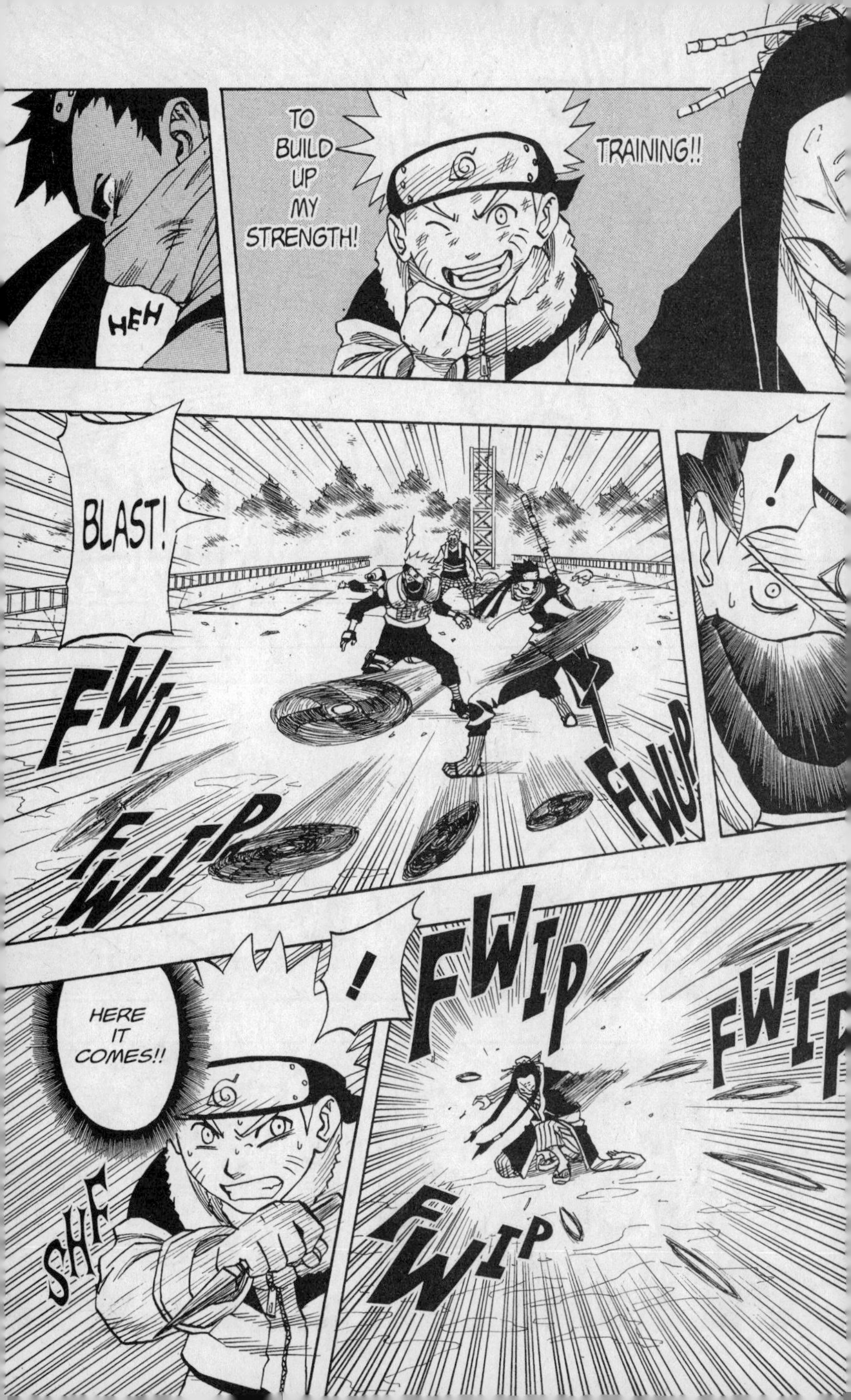
TO BUILD UP MY STRENGTH!
TRAINING!!
HEH
!
BLAST!
FWUP
FWIP
FWIP
FWIP
FWIP
FWIP
!
HERE IT COMES!!
SHF

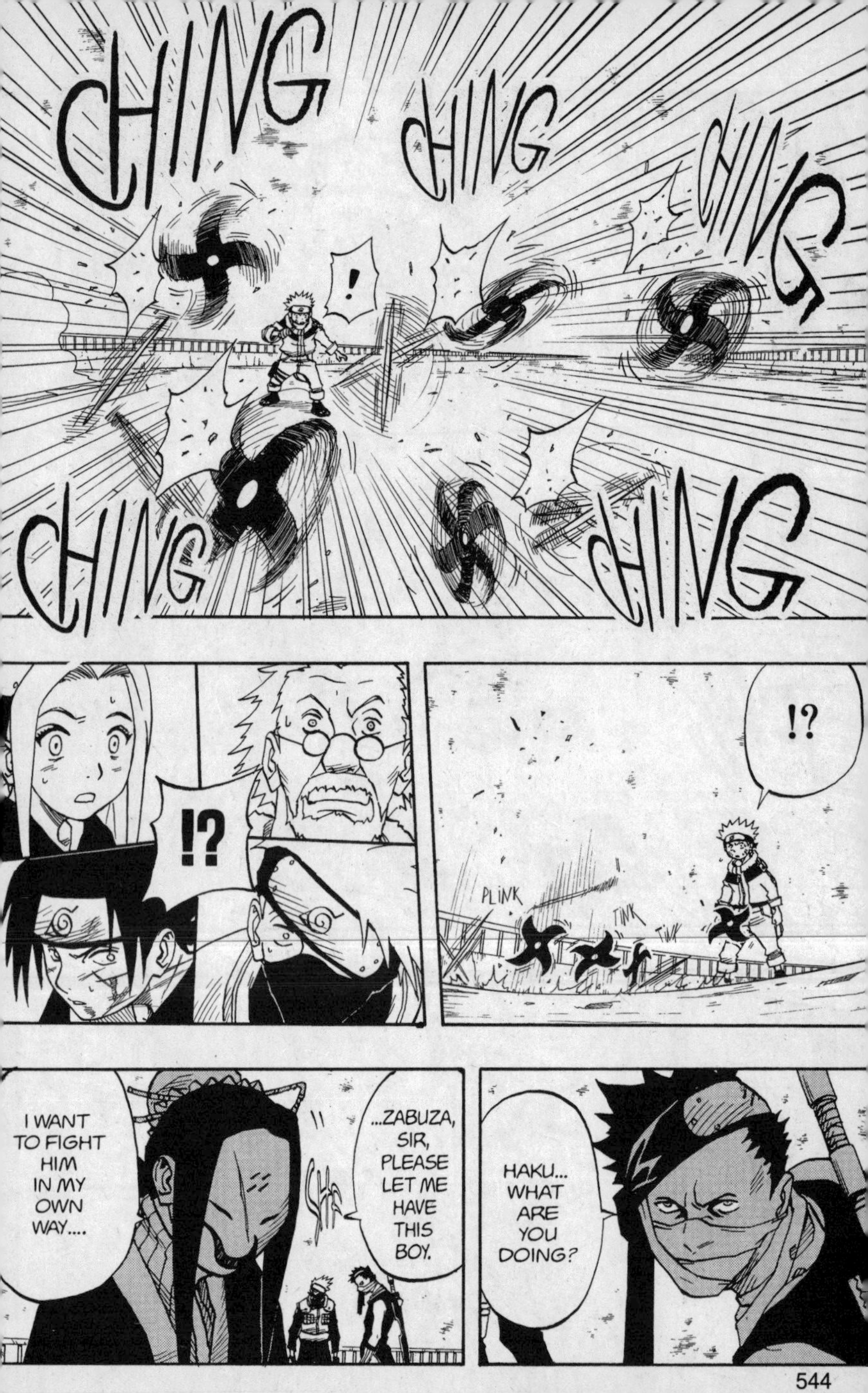
CHING
CHING
CHING
!
CHING
CHING
!?
PLINK
TINK
TINK
!?
HAKU... WHAT ARE YOU DOING?
...ZABUZA, SIR, PLEASE LET ME HAVE THIS BOY.
I WANT TO FIGHT HIM IN MY OWN WAY....

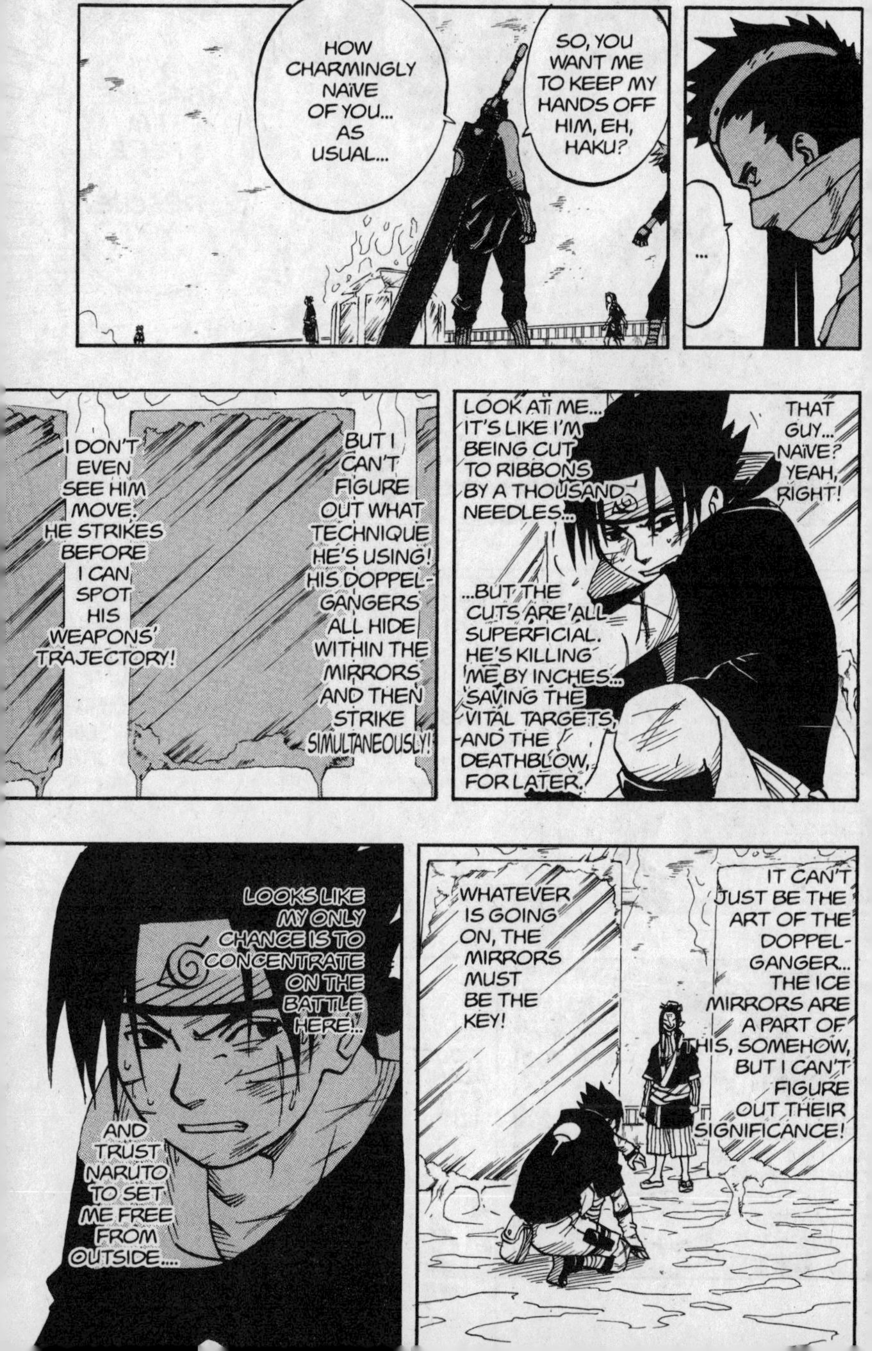
...
SO, YOU WANT ME TO KEEP MY HANDS OFF HIM, EH, HAKU?
HOW CHARMINGLY NAÏVE OF YOU... AS USUAL...
THAT GUY... NAÏVE? YEAH, RIGHT!
LOOK AT ME... IT'S LIKE I'M BEING CUT TO RIBBONS BY A THOUSAND NEEDLES...
...BUT THE CUTS ARE ALL SUPERFICIAL. HE'S KILLING ME BY INCHES... SAVING THE VITAL TARGETS, AND THE DEATHBLOW, FOR LATER.
BUT I CAN'T FIGURE OUT WHAT TECHNIQUE HE'S USING! HIS DOPPEL-GANGERS ALL HIDE WITHIN THE MIRRORS AND THEN STRIKE SIMULTANEOUSLY!
I DON'T EVEN SEE HIM MOVE. HE STRIKES BEFORE I CAN SPOT HIS WEAPONS' TRAJECTORY!
IT CAN'T JUST BE THE ART OF THE DOPPEL-GANGER... THE ICE MIRRORS ARE A PART OF THIS, SOMEHOW, BUT I CAN'T FIGURE OUT THEIR SIGNIFICANCE!
WHATEVER IS GOING ON, THE MIRRORS MUST BE THE KEY!
LOOKS LIKE MY ONLY CHANCE IS TO CONCENTRATE ON THE BATTLE HERE...
AND TRUST NARUTO TO SET ME FREE FROM OUTSIDE...

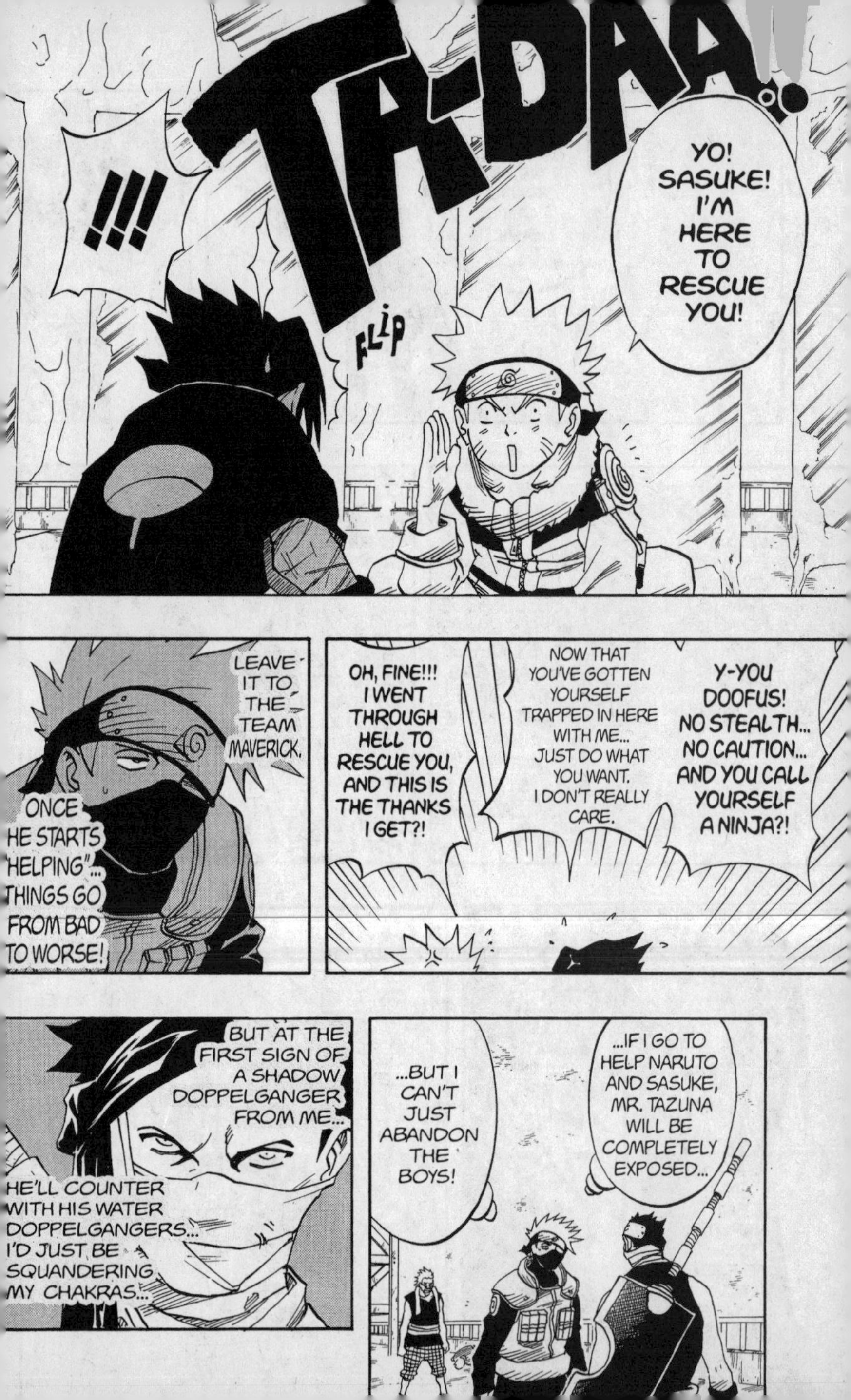
TA-DAA!!
YO! SASUKE! I'M HERE TO RESCUE YOU!
FLIP
!!!
Y-YOU DOOFUS! NO STEALTH... NO CAUTION... AND YOU CALL YOURSELF A NINJA?!
NOW THAT YOU'VE GOTTEN YOURSELF TRAPPED IN HERE WITH ME... JUST DO WHAT YOU WANT. I DON'T REALLY CARE.
OH, FINE!!! I WENT THROUGH HELL TO RESCUE YOU, AND THIS IS THE THANKS I GET?!
LEAVE IT TO THE TEAM MAVERICK.
ONCE HE STARTS "HELPING"... THINGS GO FROM BAD TO WORSE!
...IF I GO TO HELP NARUTO AND SASUKE, MR. TAZUNA WILL BE COMPLETELY EXPOSED...
...BUT I CAN'T JUST ABANDON THE BOYS!
BUT AT THE FIRST SIGN OF A SHADOW DOPPELGANGER FROM ME...
HE'LL COUNTER WITH HIS WATER DOPPELGANGERS... I'D JUST BE SQUANDERING MY CHAKRAS...

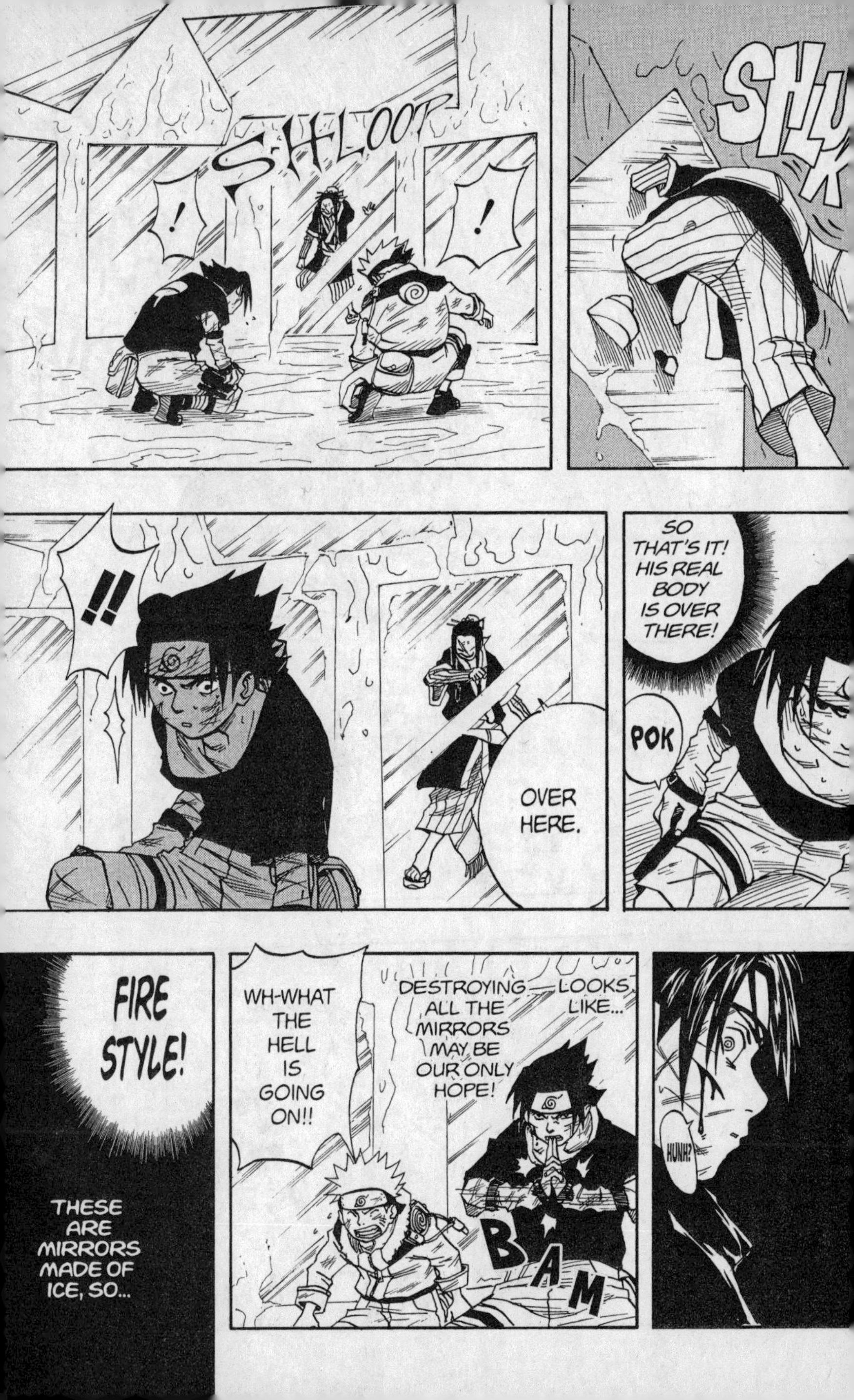
SHLUK
SHLOOP
!
!
SO THAT'S IT! HIS REAL BODY IS OVER THERE!
POK
OVER HERE.
!!
HUNH?
LOOKS LIKE...
DESTROYING ALL THE MIRRORS MAY BE OUR ONLY HOPE!
WH-WHAT THE HELL IS GOING ON!!
BAM
FIRE STYLE!
THESE ARE MIRRORS MADE OF ICE, SO...

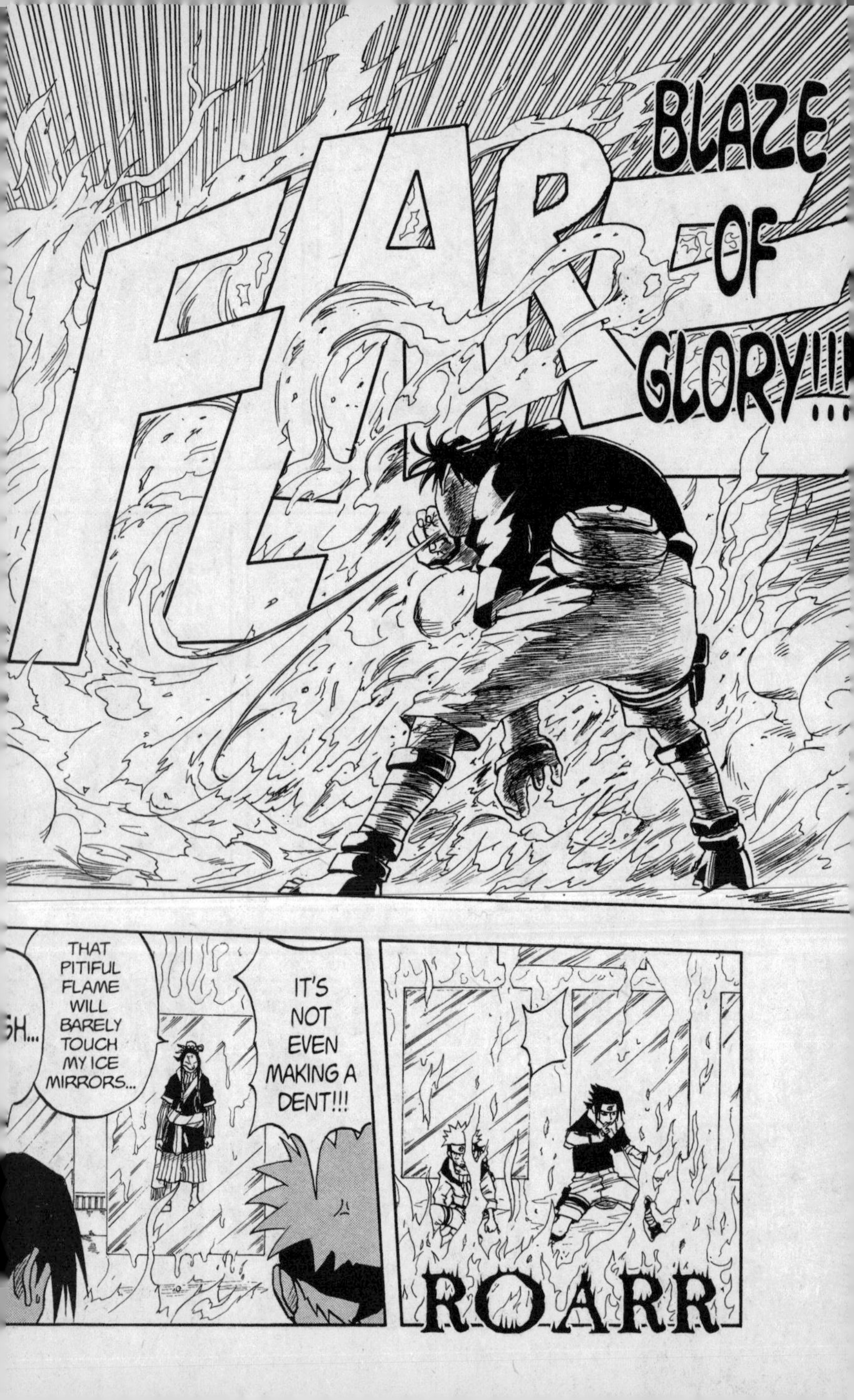
BLAZE OF GLORY!!!...
ROARR
THAT PITIFUL FLAME WILL BARELY TOUCH MY ICE MIRRORS...
IT'S NOT EVEN MAKING A DENT!!!

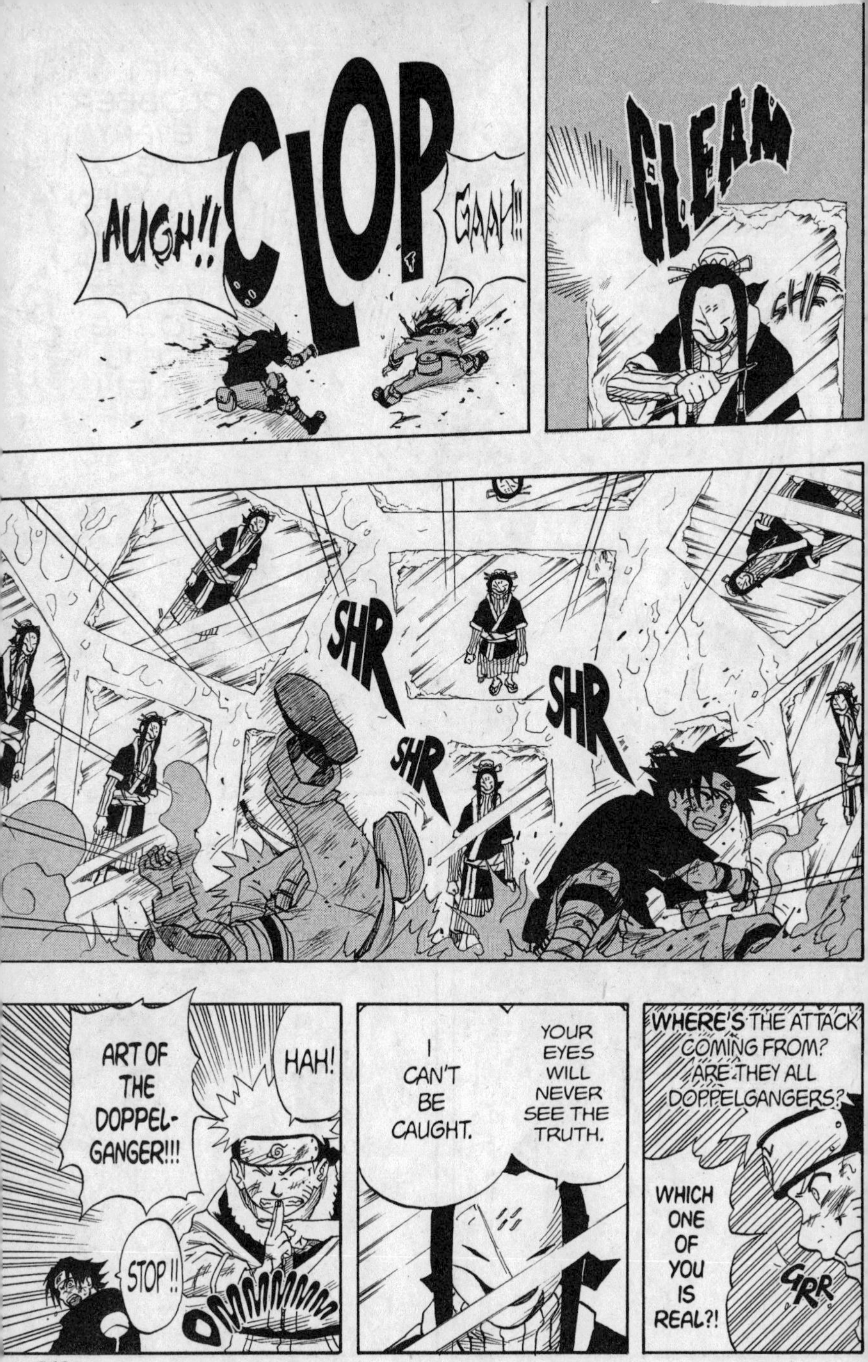
GLEAM
SHF
GAAH!!
CLOP
AUGH!!
SHR
SHR
SHR
WHERE'S THE ATTACK COMING FROM? ARE THEY ALL DOPPELGANGERS?
WHICH ONE OF YOU IS REAL?!
GRR
YOUR EYES WILL NEVER SEE THE TRUTH.
I CAN'T BE CAUGHT.
HAH!
ART OF THE DOPPEL-GANGER!!!
STOP!!

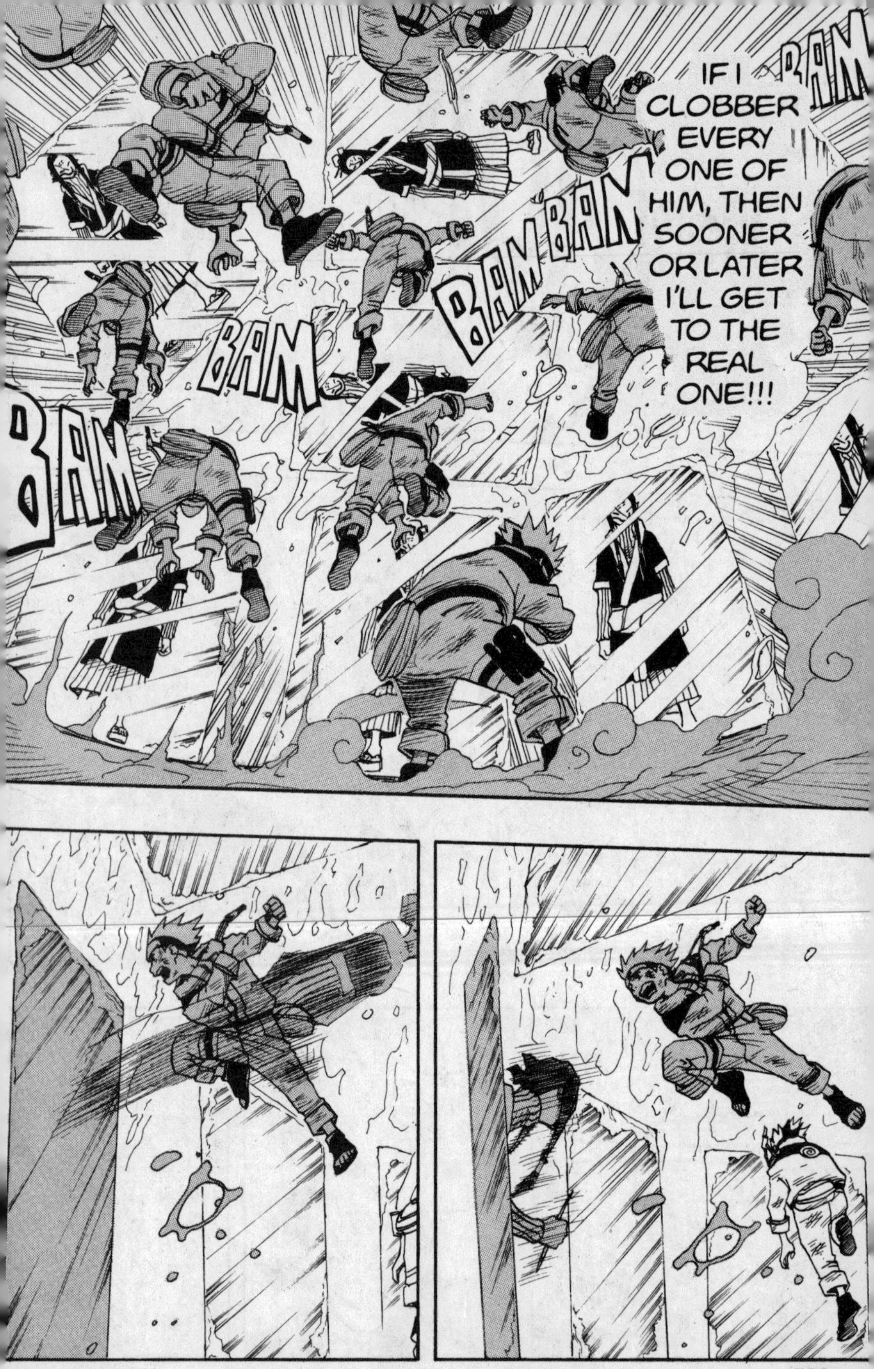
RAM
IF I CLOBBER EVERY ONE OF HIM, THEN SOONER OR LATER I'LL GET TO THE REAL ONE!!!
BAM BAM
BAM
BAM
BAM

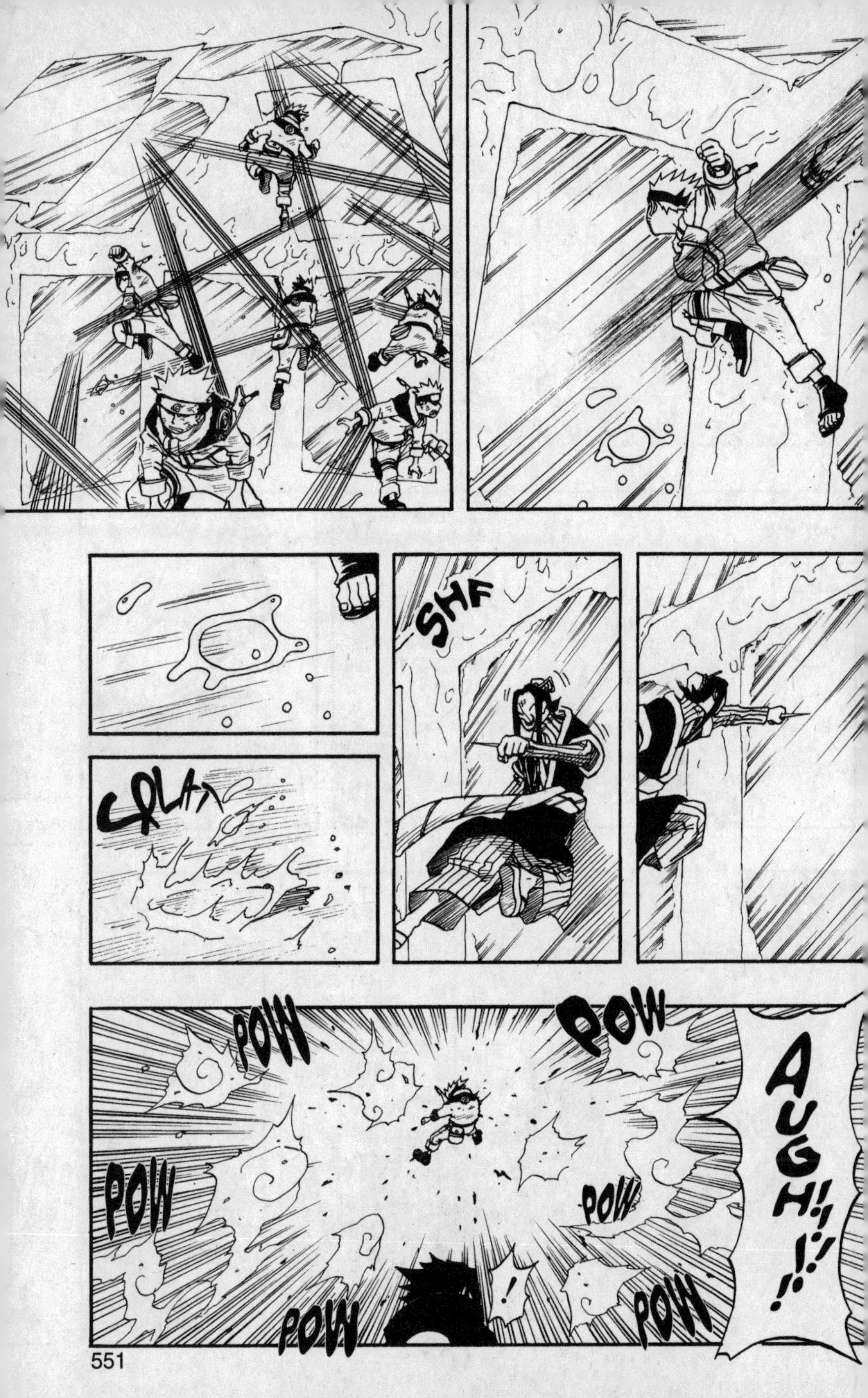
SHF
AUGH!!!!
POW
POW
POW
POW
POW
!
POW

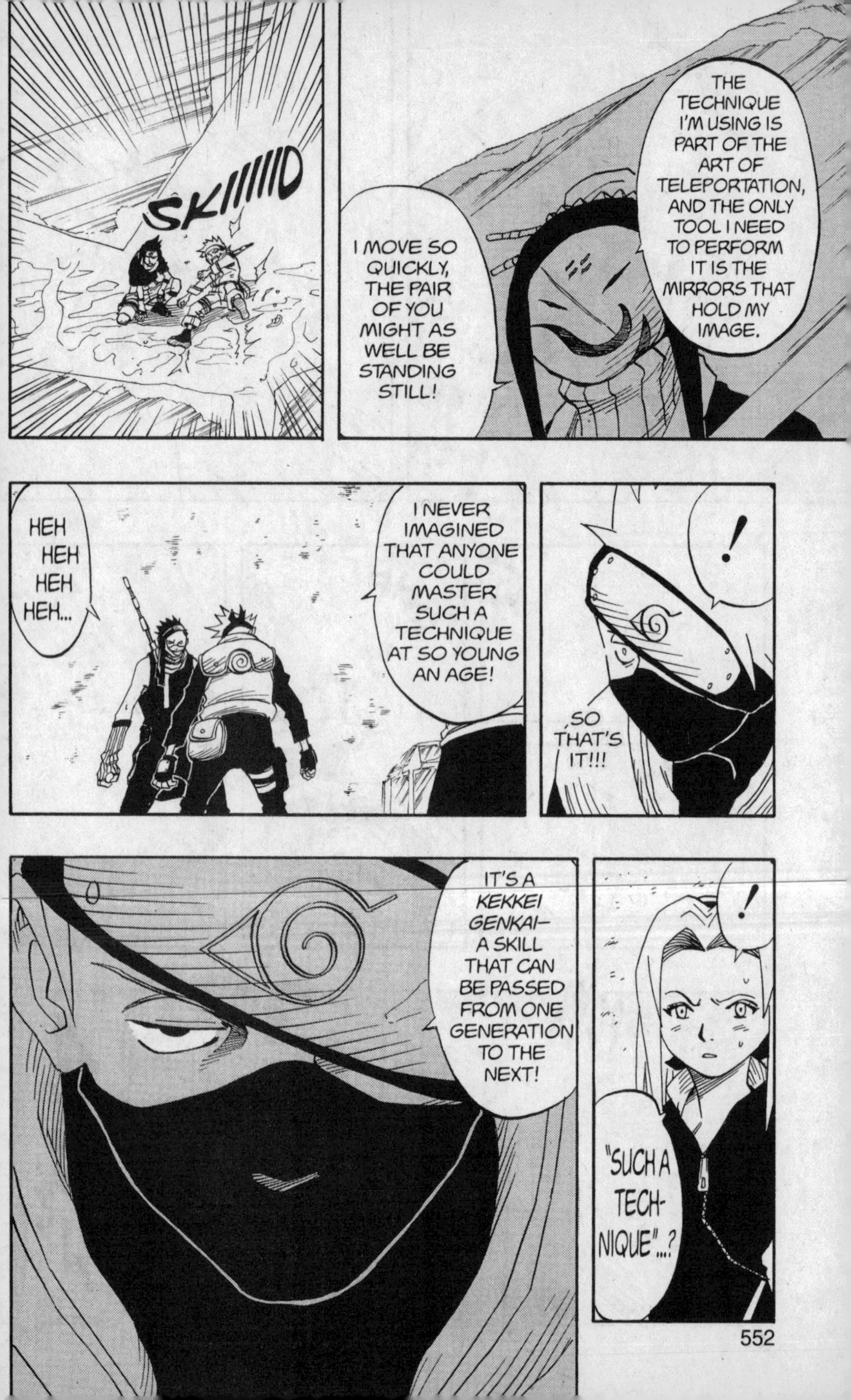
THE TECHNIQUE I'M USING IS PART OF THE ART OF TELEPORTATION, AND THE ONLY TOOL I NEED TO PERFORM IT IS THE MIRRORS THAT HOLD MY IMAGE.
I MOVE SO QUICKLY, THE PAIR OF YOU MIGHT AS WELL BE STANDING STILL!
SKIIIIID
!
SO THAT'S IT!!!
I NEVER IMAGINED THAT ANYONE COULD MASTER SUCH A TECHNIQUE AT SO YOUNG AN AGE!
HEH HEH HEH HEH...
!
"SUCH A TECH-NIQUE"...?
IT'S A *KEKKEI GENKAI*— A SKILL THAT CAN BE PASSED FROM ONE GENERATION TO THE NEXT!

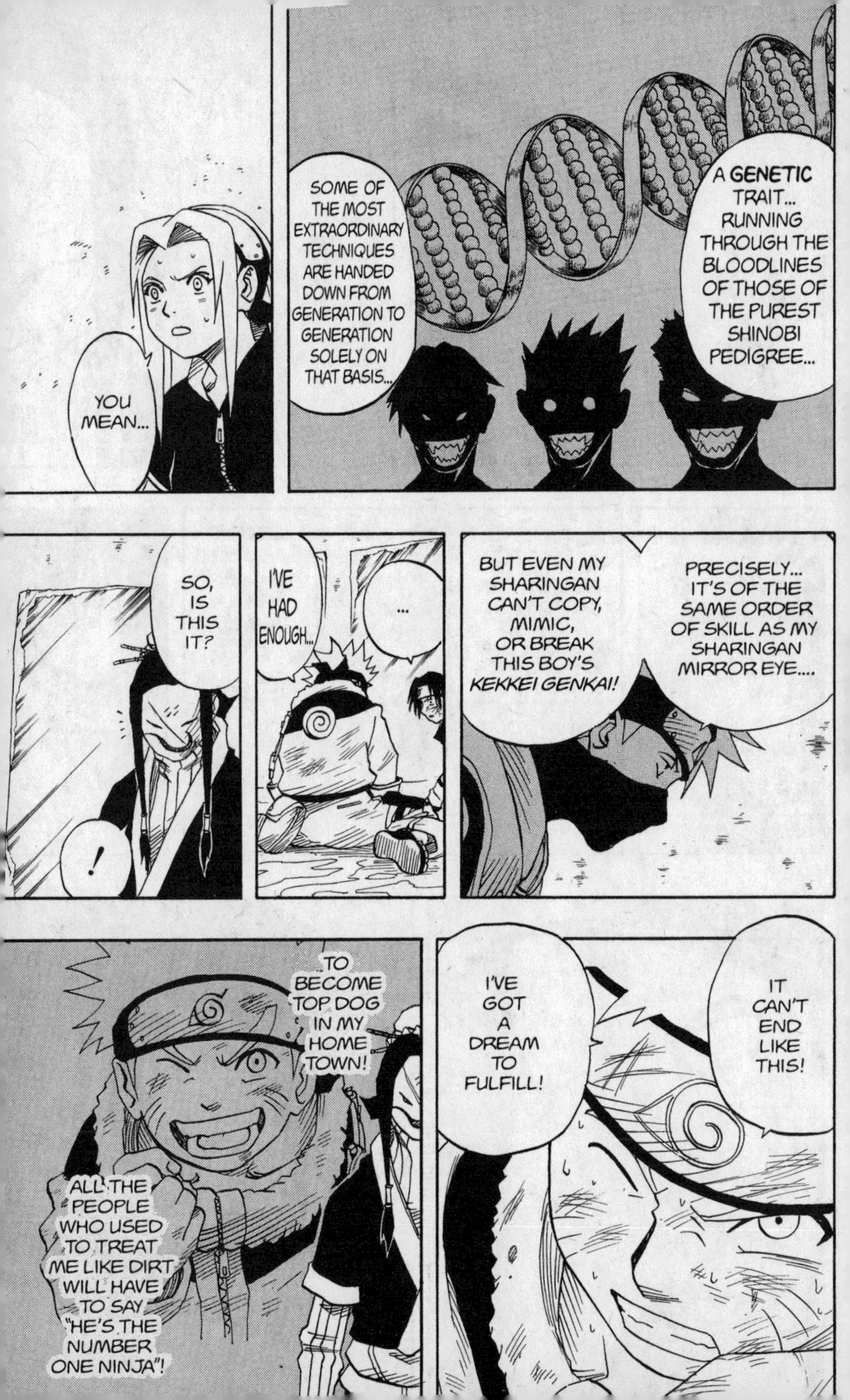
A GENETIC TRAIT... RUNNING THROUGH THE BLOODLINES OF THOSE OF THE PUREST SHINOBI PEDIGREE...
SOME OF THE MOST EXTRAORDINARY TECHNIQUES ARE HANDED DOWN FROM GENERATION TO GENERATION SOLELY ON THAT BASIS...
YOU MEAN...
PRECISELY... IT'S OF THE SAME ORDER OF SKILL AS MY SHARINGAN MIRROR EYE....
BUT EVEN MY SHARINGAN CAN'T COPY, MIMIC, OR BREAK THIS BOY'S KEKKEI GENKAI!
...
I'VE HAD ENOUGH...
SO, IS THIS IT?
!
IT CAN'T END LIKE THIS!
I'VE GOT A DREAM TO FULFILL!
TO BECOME TOP DOG IN MY HOME TOWN!
ALL THE PEOPLE WHO USED TO TREAT ME LIKE DIRT WILL HAVE TO SAY "HE'S THE NUMBER ONE NINJA"!

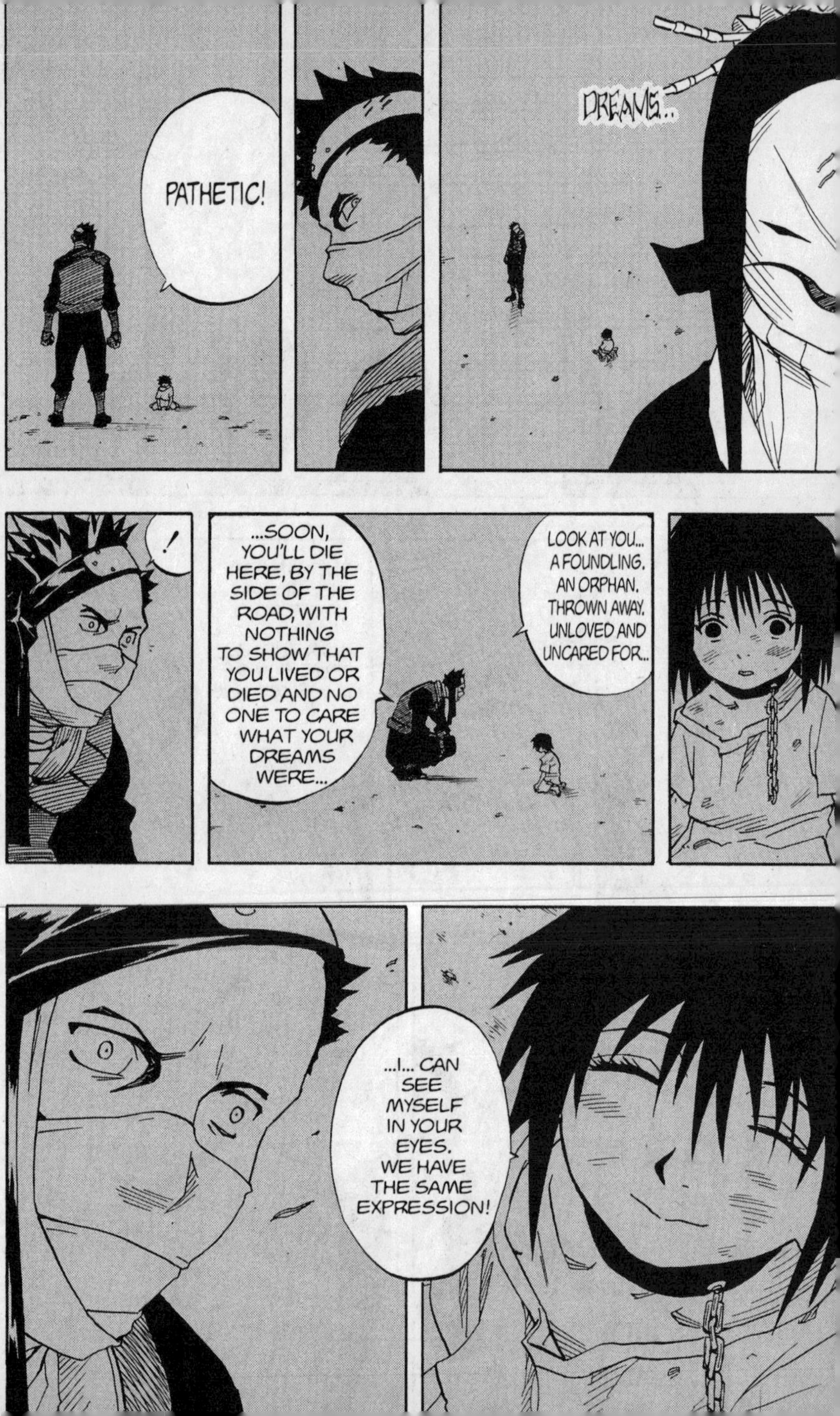
DREAMS...
PATHETIC!
LOOK AT YOU... A FOUNDLING. AN ORPHAN. THROWN AWAY. UNLOVED AND UNCARED FOR...
...SOON, YOU'LL DIE HERE, BY THE SIDE OF THE ROAD, WITH NOTHING TO SHOW THAT YOU LIVED OR DIED AND NO ONE TO CARE WHAT YOUR DREAMS WERE...
!
...I... CAN SEE MYSELF IN YOUR EYES. WE HAVE THE SAME EXPRESSION!

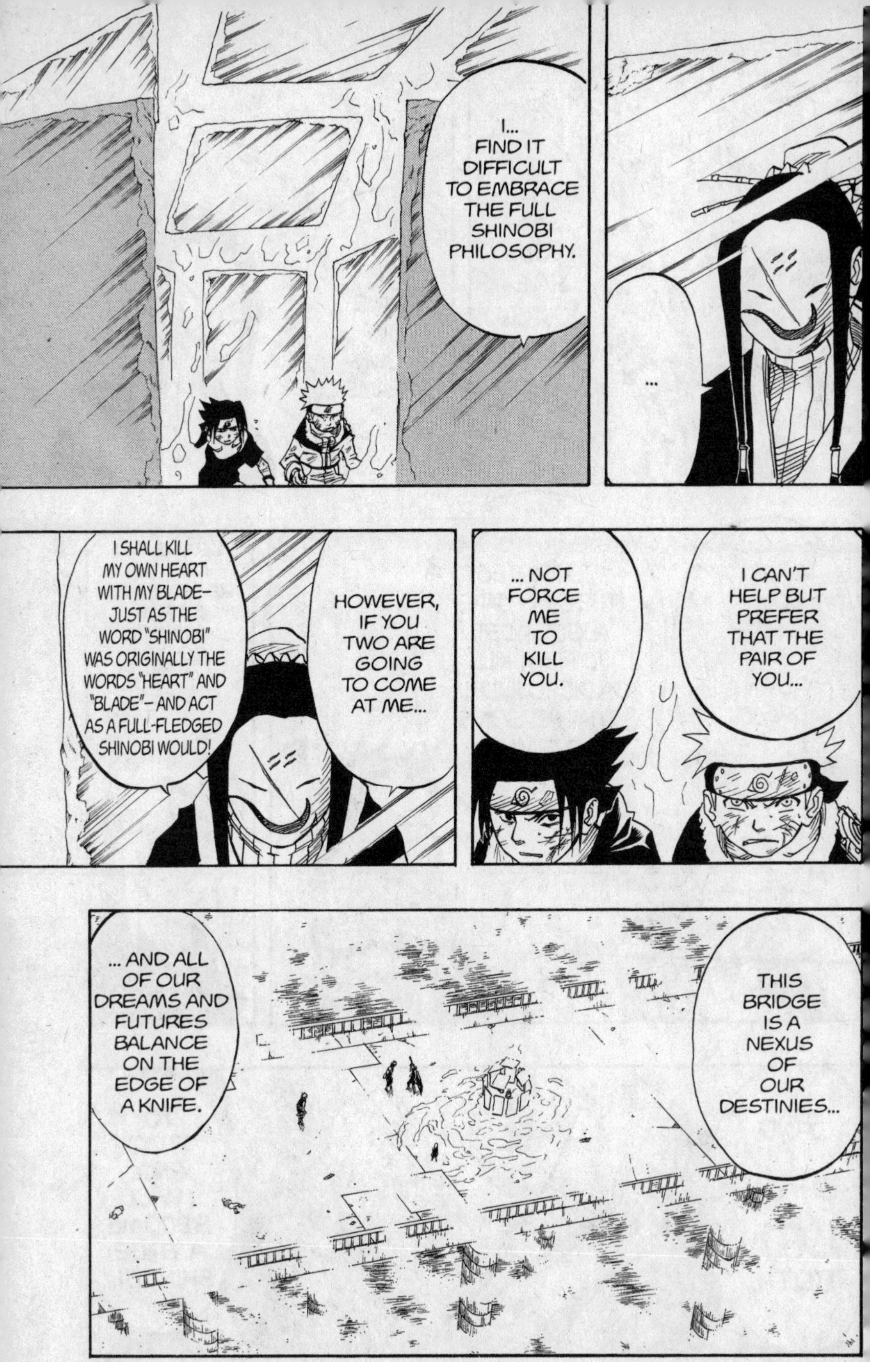
...
I... FIND IT DIFFICULT TO EMBRACE THE FULL SHINOBI PHILOSOPHY.
I CAN'T HELP BUT PREFER THAT THE PAIR OF YOU...
... NOT FORCE ME TO KILL YOU.
HOWEVER, IF YOU TWO ARE GOING TO COME AT ME...
I SHALL KILL MY OWN HEART WITH MY BLADE– JUST AS THE WORD "SHINOBI" WAS ORIGINALLY THE WORDS "HEART" AND "BLADE"– AND ACT AS A FULL-FLEDGED SHINOBI WOULD!
THIS BRIDGE IS A NEXUS OF OUR DESTINIES...
... AND ALL OF OUR DREAMS AND FUTURES BALANCE ON THE EDGE OF A KNIFE.

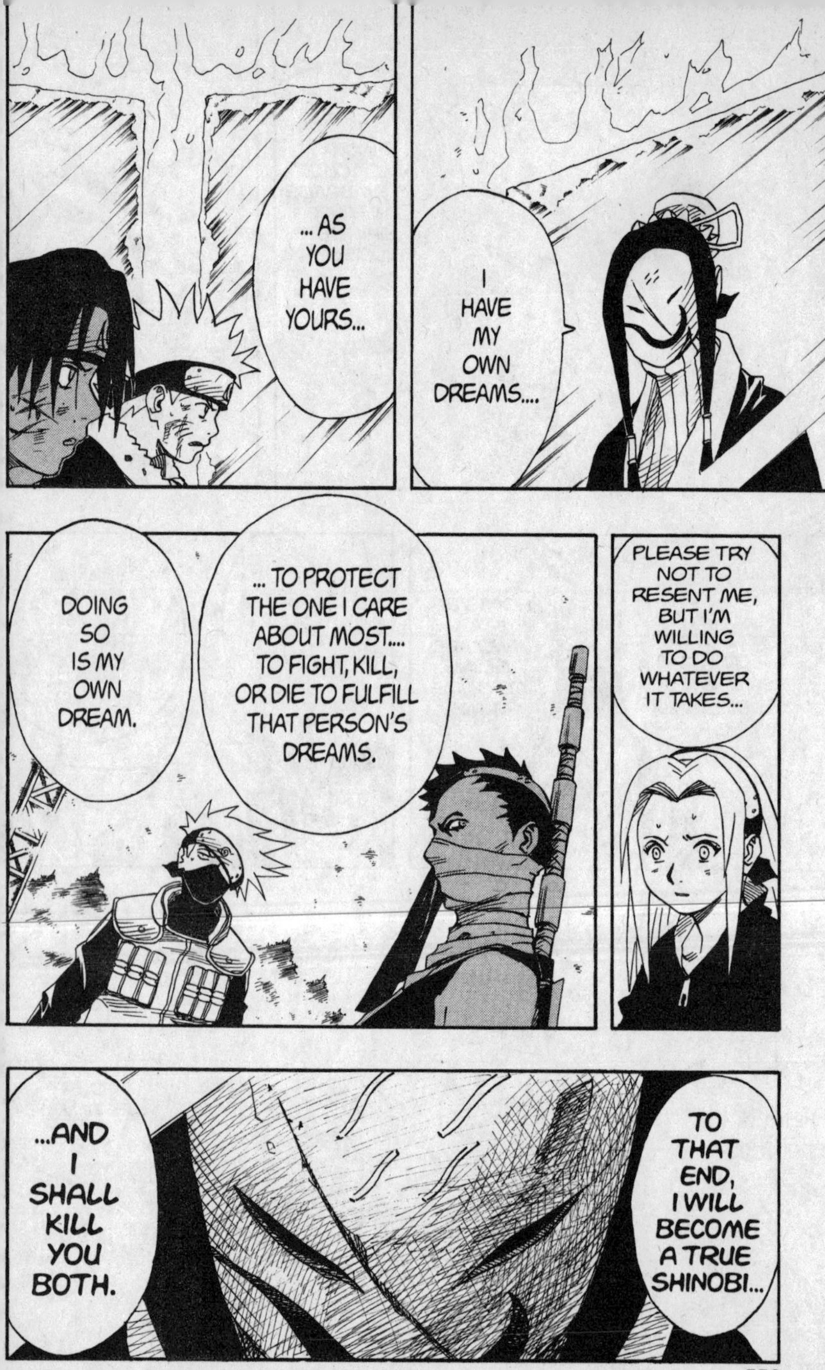
I HAVE MY OWN DREAMS....
... AS YOU HAVE YOURS...
PLEASE TRY NOT TO RESENT ME, BUT I'M WILLING TO DO WHATEVER IT TAKES...
... TO PROTECT THE ONE I CARE ABOUT MOST.... TO FIGHT, KILL, OR DIE TO FULFILL THAT PERSON'S DREAMS.
DOING SO IS MY OWN DREAM.
TO THAT END, I WILL BECOME A TRUE SHINOBI...
...AND I SHALL KILL YOU BOTH.

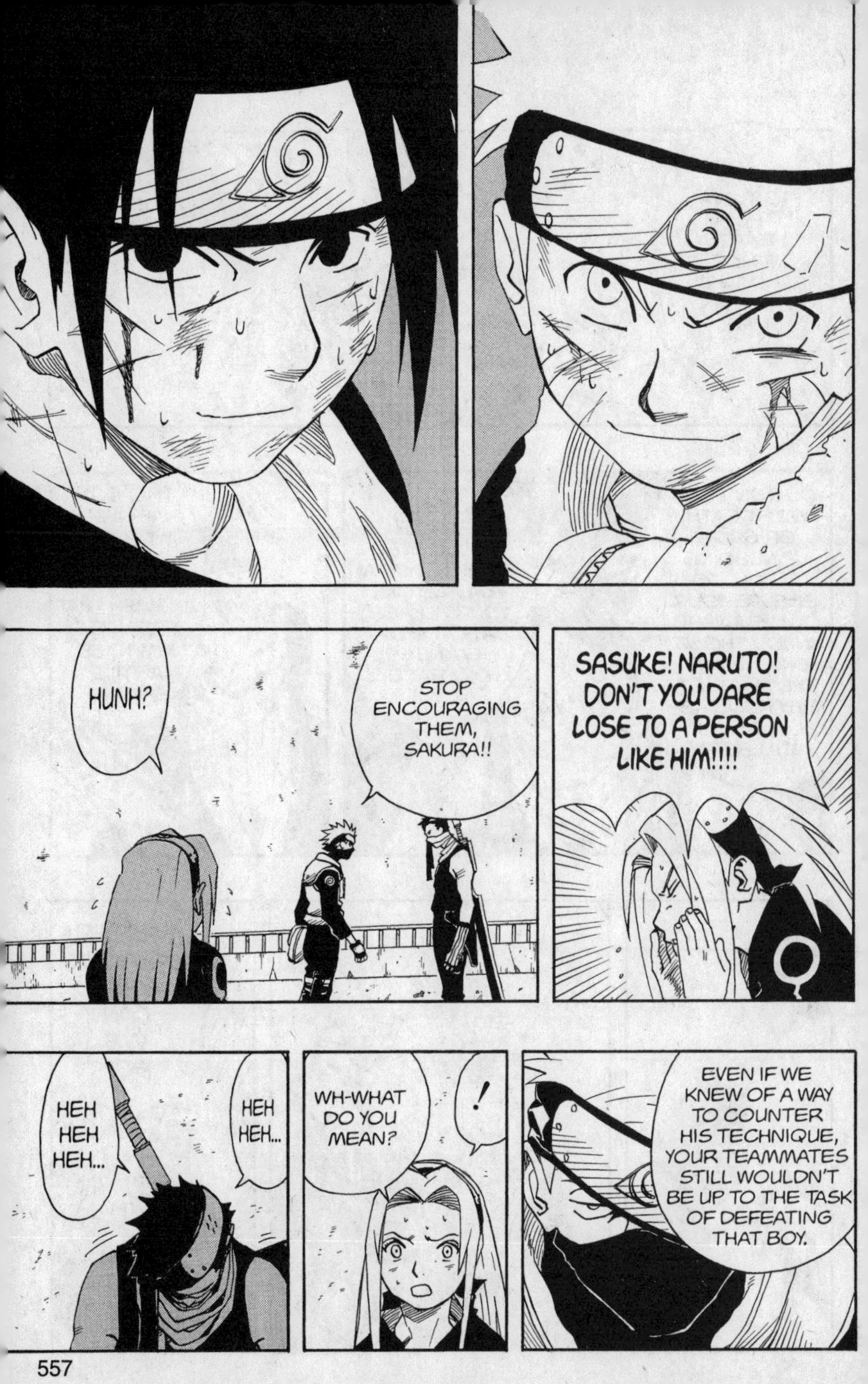
SASUKE! NARUTO! DON'T YOU DARE LOSE TO A PERSON LIKE HIM!!!!
STOP ENCOURAGING THEM, SAKURA!!
HUNH?
EVEN IF WE KNEW OF A WAY TO COUNTER HIS TECHNIQUE, YOUR TEAMMATES STILL WOULDN'T BE UP TO THE TASK OF DEFEATING THAT BOY.
!
WH-WHAT DO YOU MEAN?
HEH HEH...
HEH HEH HEH...

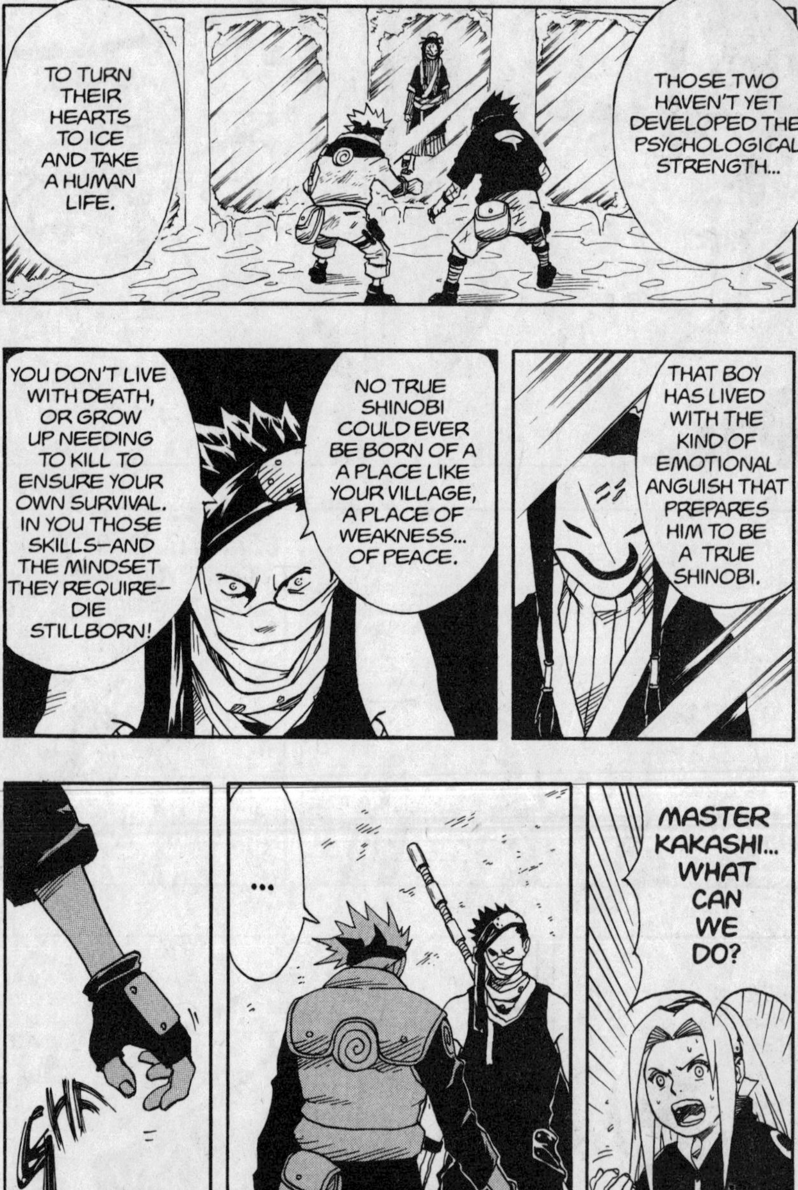
THOSE TWO HAVEN'T YET DEVELOPED THE PSYCHOLOGICAL STRENGTH...
TO TURN THEIR HEARTS TO ICE AND TAKE A HUMAN LIFE.
THAT BOY HAS LIVED WITH THE KIND OF EMOTIONAL ANGUISH THAT PREPARES HIM TO BE A TRUE SHINOBI.
NO TRUE SHINOBI COULD EVER BE BORN OF A A PLACE LIKE YOUR VILLAGE, A PLACE OF WEAKNESS... OF PEACE.
YOU DON'T LIVE WITH DEATH, OR GROW UP NEEDING TO KILL TO ENSURE YOUR OWN SURVIVAL. IN YOU THOSE SKILLS—AND THE MINDSET THEY REQUIRE—DIE STILLBORN!
MASTER KAKASHI... WHAT CAN WE DO?
...
SHF

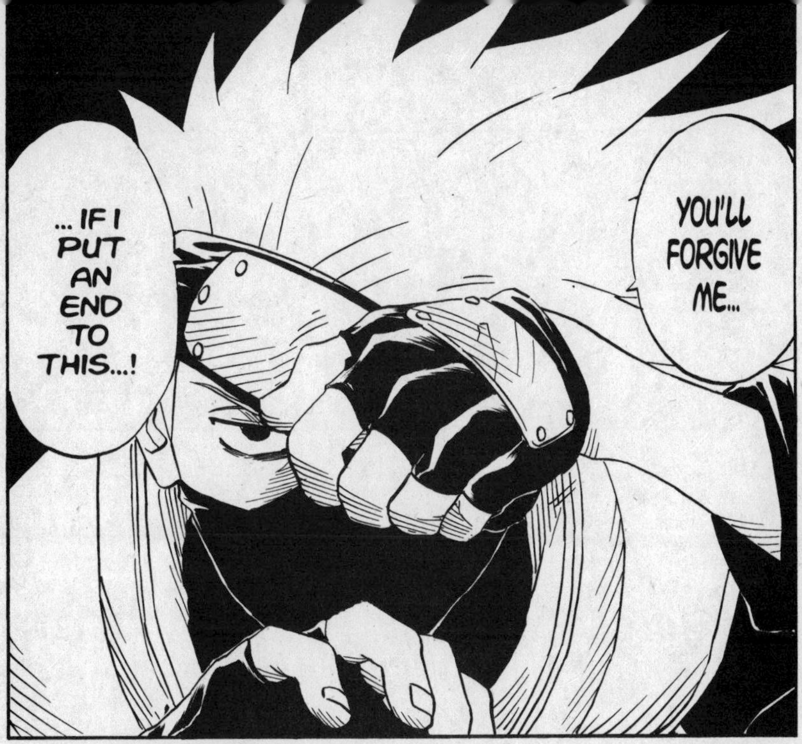
YOU'LL FORGIVE ME...
... IF I PUT AN END TO THIS...!
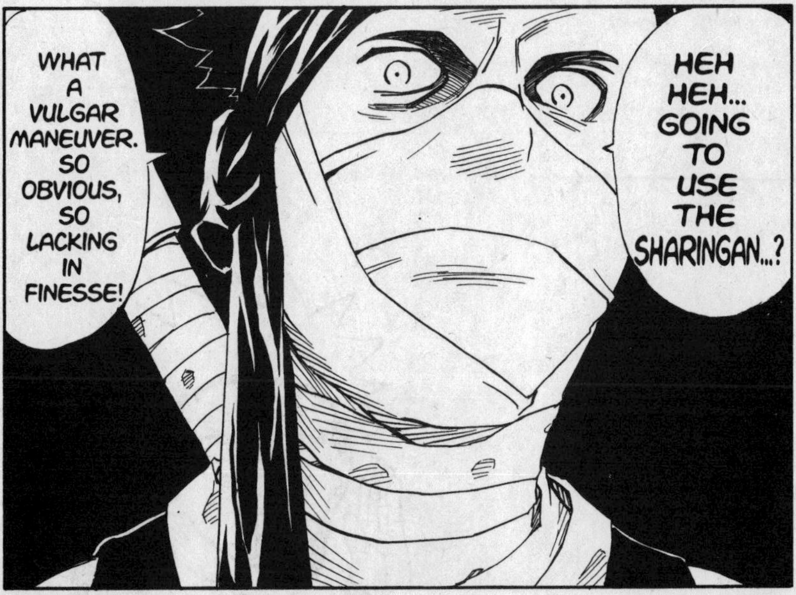
HEH HEH... GOING TO USE THE SHARINGAN...?
WHAT A VULGAR MANEUVER. SO OBVIOUS, SO LACKING IN FINESSE!

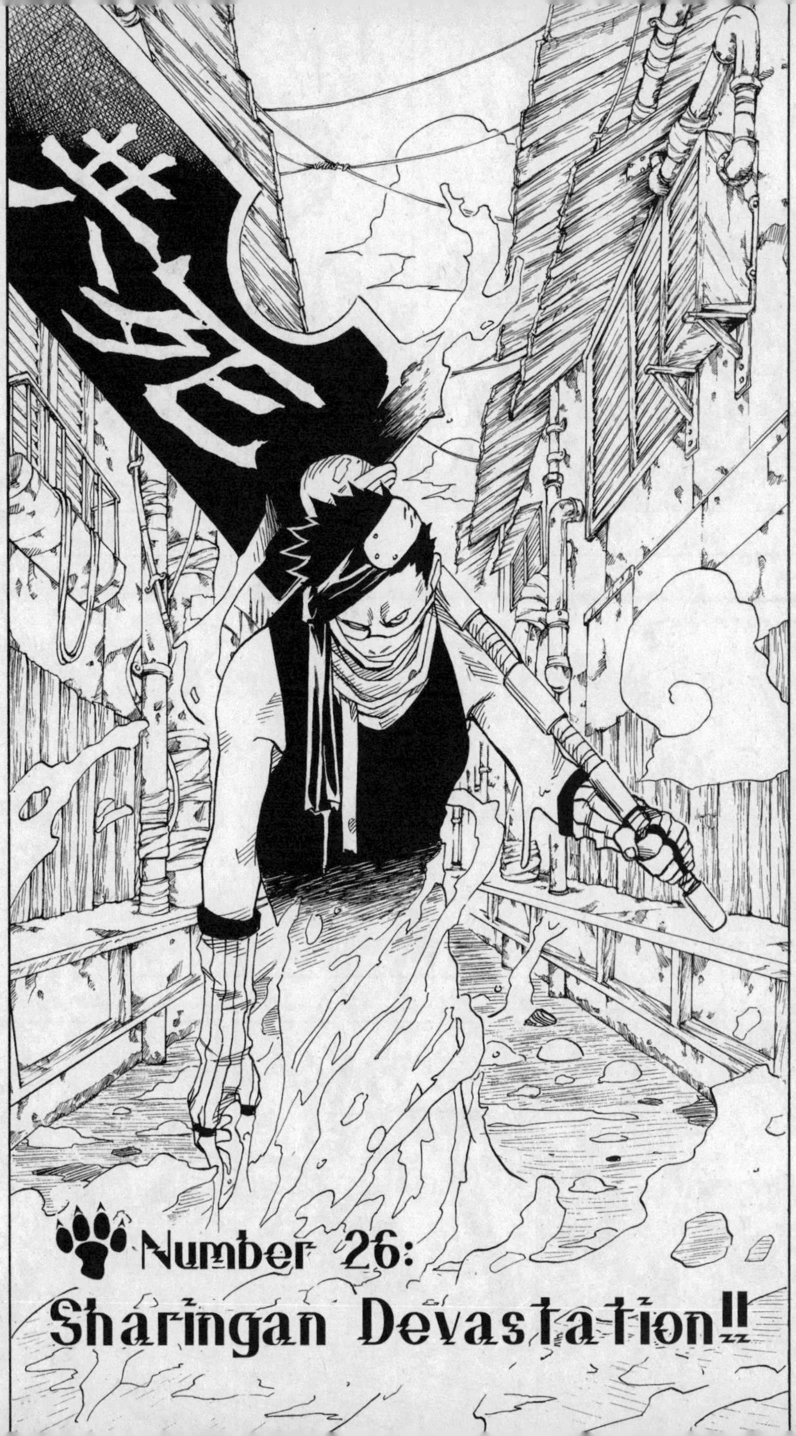
Number 26:
Sharingan Devastation!!

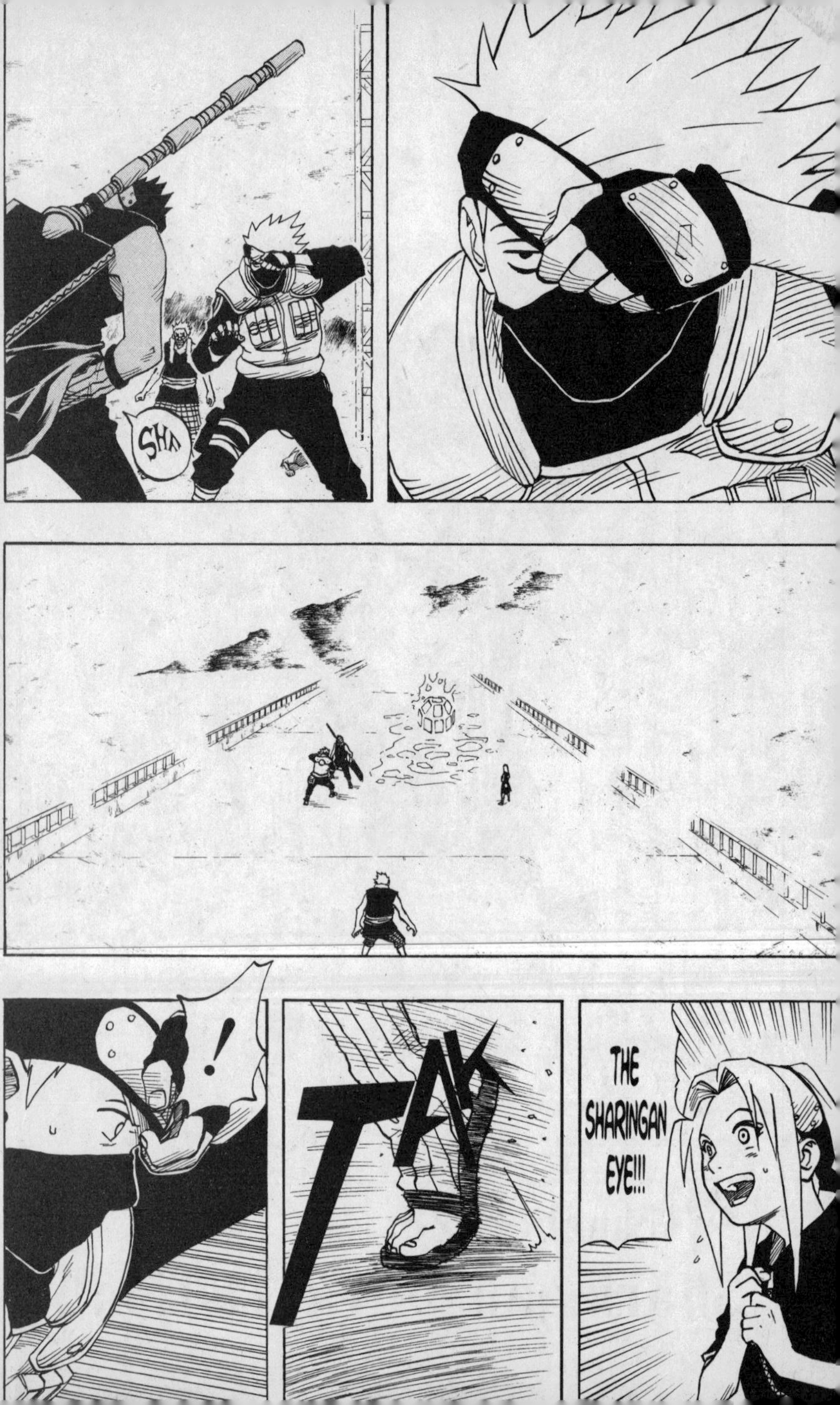
SHA
THE SHARINGAN EYE!!!
TAK
!

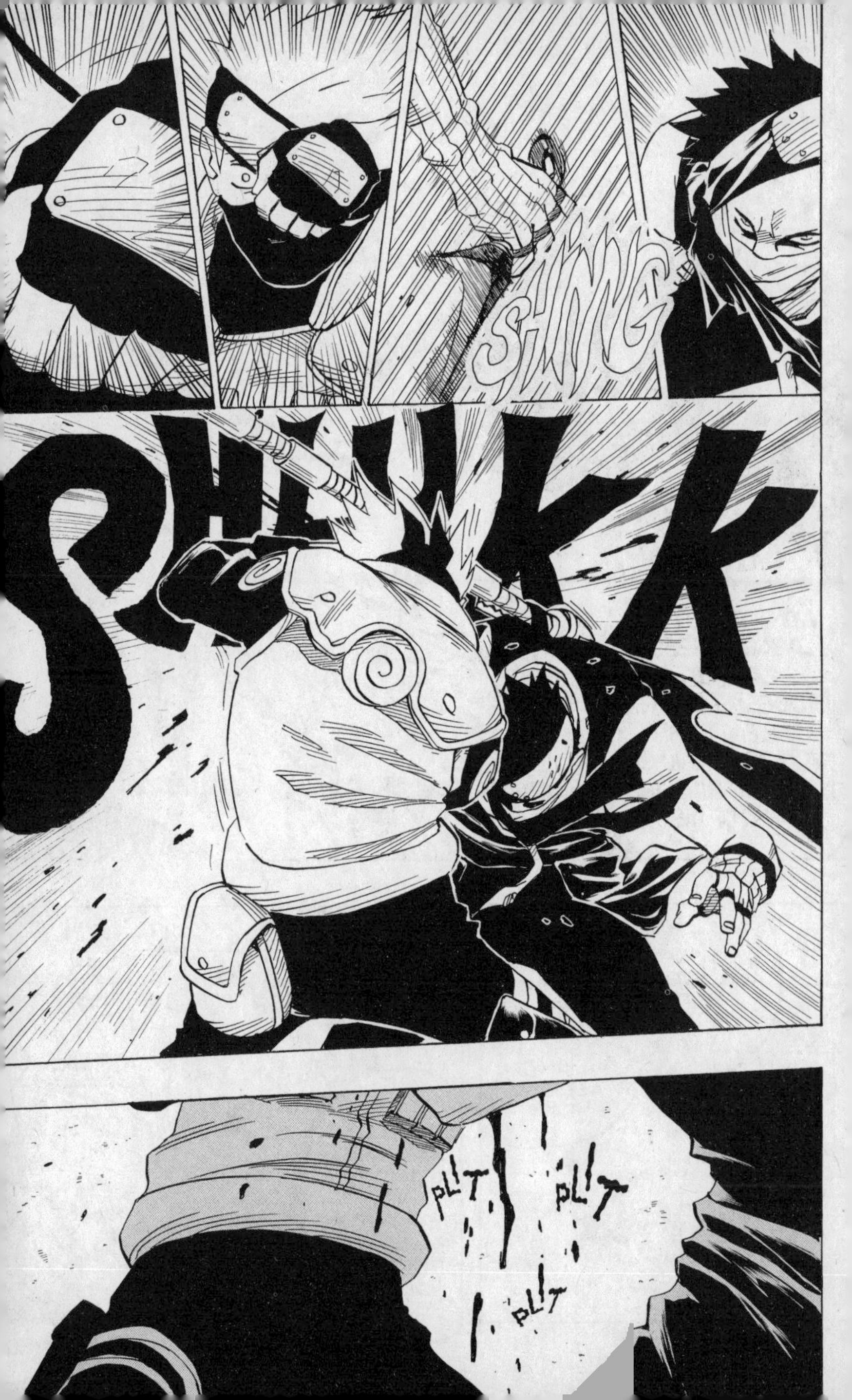
SHING
SHUNK
PLIT
PLIT
PLIT

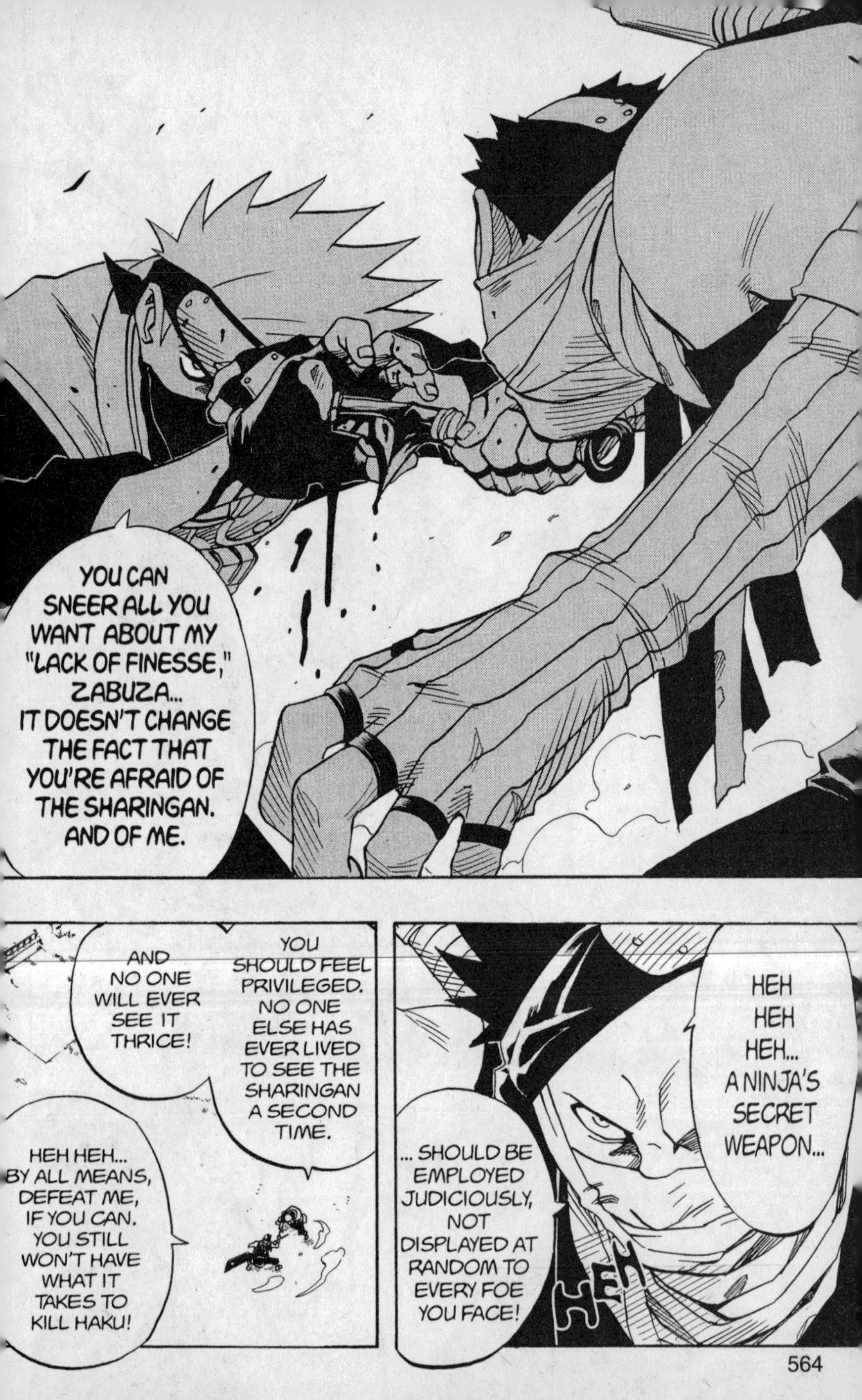
YOU CAN SNEER ALL YOU WANT ABOUT MY "LACK OF FINESSE," ZABUZA... IT DOESN'T CHANGE THE FACT THAT YOU'RE AFRAID OF THE SHARINGAN. AND OF ME.
HEH HEH HEH... A NINJA'S SECRET WEAPON...
... SHOULD BE EMPLOYED JUDICIOUSLY, NOT DISPLAYED AT RANDOM TO EVERY FOE YOU FACE!
HEH
YOU SHOULD FEEL PRIVILEGED. NO ONE ELSE HAS EVER LIVED TO SEE THE SHARINGAN A SECOND TIME.
AND NO ONE WILL EVER SEE IT THRICE!
HEH HEH... BY ALL MEANS, DEFEAT ME, IF YOU CAN. YOU STILL WON'T HAVE WHAT IT TAKES TO KILL HAKU!

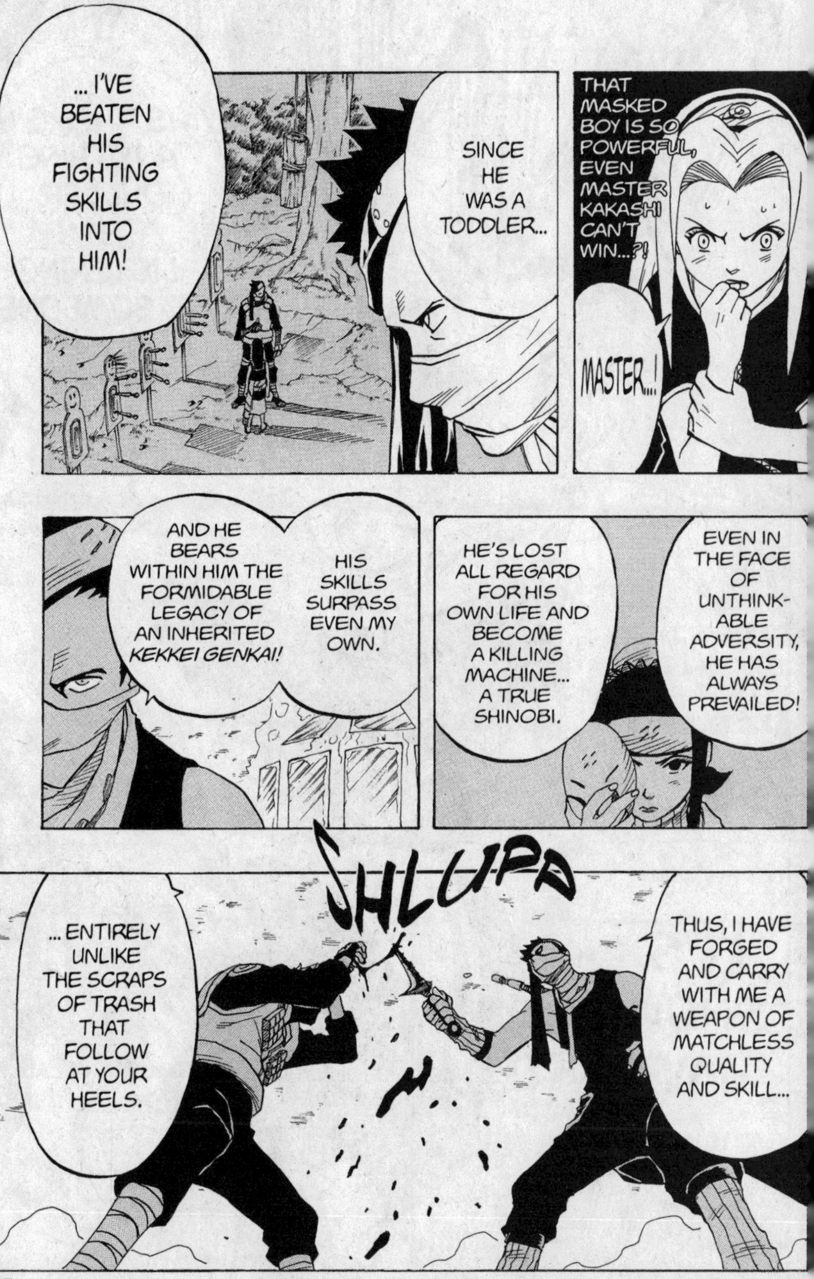
THAT MASKED BOY IS SO POWERFUL, EVEN MASTER KAKASHI CAN'T WIN...?!
MASTER...!
SINCE HE WAS A TODDLER...
... I'VE BEATEN HIS FIGHTING SKILLS INTO HIM!
EVEN IN THE FACE OF UNTHINKABLE ADVERSITY, HE HAS ALWAYS PREVAILED!
HE'S LOST ALL REGARD FOR HIS OWN LIFE AND BECOME A KILLING MACHINE... A TRUE SHINOBI.
HIS SKILLS SURPASS EVEN MY OWN.
AND HE BEARS WITHIN HIM THE FORMIDABLE LEGACY OF AN INHERITED *KEKKEI GENKAI!*
THUS, I HAVE FORGED AND CARRY WITH ME A WEAPON OF MATCHLESS QUALITY AND SKILL...
SHLUPP
... ENTIRELY UNLIKE THE SCRAPS OF TRASH THAT FOLLOW AT YOUR HEELS.

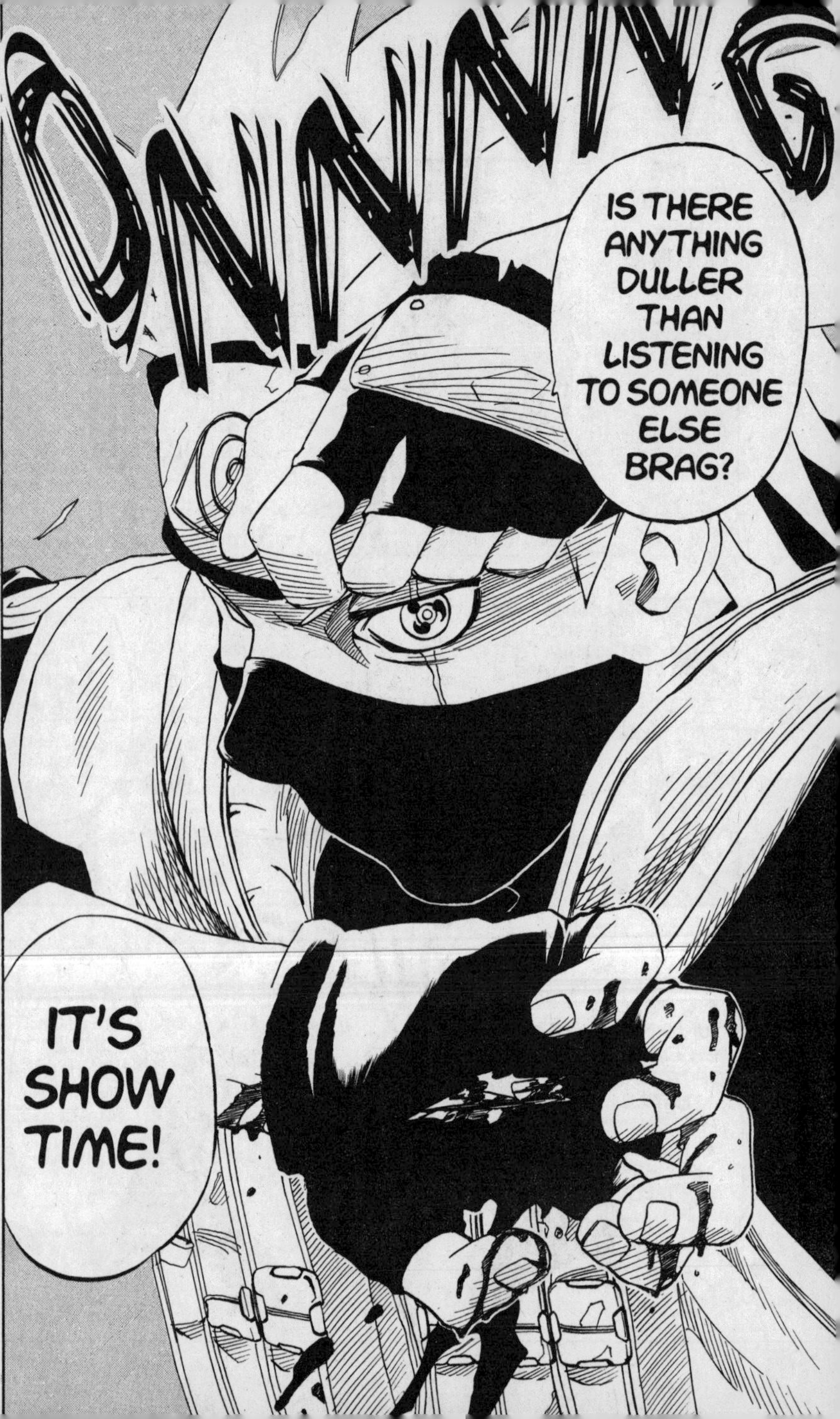
DNNNNG
IS THERE ANYTHING DULLER THAN LISTENING TO SOMEONE ELSE BRAG?
IT'S SHOW TIME!

PERHAPS YOU MIGHT HOLD OFF A MOMENT, NOW THAT I'VE CAUGHT MY BREATH. AND—TO BORROW YOUR OWN IDIOM—PERMIT ME ONE MORE BOAST.
YOU TURNED A VERY PRETTY PHRASE AT OUR LAST ENCOUNTER...
?!
!
FRANKLY, I'VE BEEN DYING TO STEAL IT.
...
?
SOME-THING TO THE EFFECT OF, "JUST SO YOU KNOW"...
..."THE SAME SPELL WON'T WORK ON ME TWICE."
HEH...

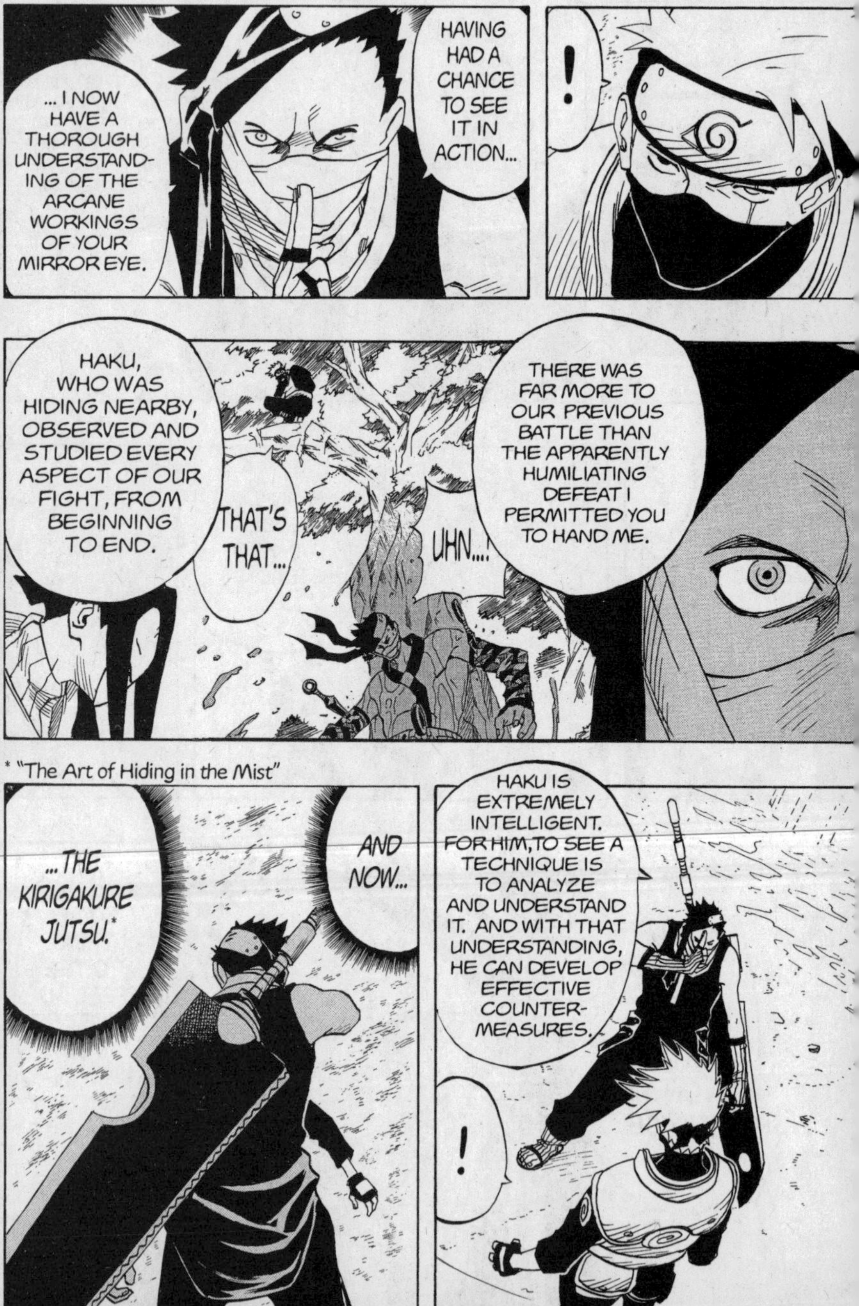
!
HAVING HAD A CHANCE TO SEE IT IN ACTION...
...I NOW HAVE A THOROUGH UNDERSTANDING OF THE ARCANE WORKINGS OF YOUR MIRROR EYE.
THERE WAS FAR MORE TO OUR PREVIOUS BATTLE THAN THE APPARENTLY HUMILIATING DEFEAT I PERMITTED YOU TO HAND ME.
UHN...!
THAT'S THAT...
HAKU, WHO WAS HIDING NEARBY, OBSERVED AND STUDIED EVERY ASPECT OF OUR FIGHT, FROM BEGINNING TO END.
HAKU IS EXTREMELY INTELLIGENT. FOR HIM, TO SEE A TECHNIQUE IS TO ANALYZE AND UNDERSTAND IT. AND WITH THAT UNDERSTANDING, HE CAN DEVELOP EFFECTIVE COUNTER-MEASURES.
!
AND NOW...
...THE KIRIGAKURE JUTSU.*

* "The Art of Hiding in the Mist"

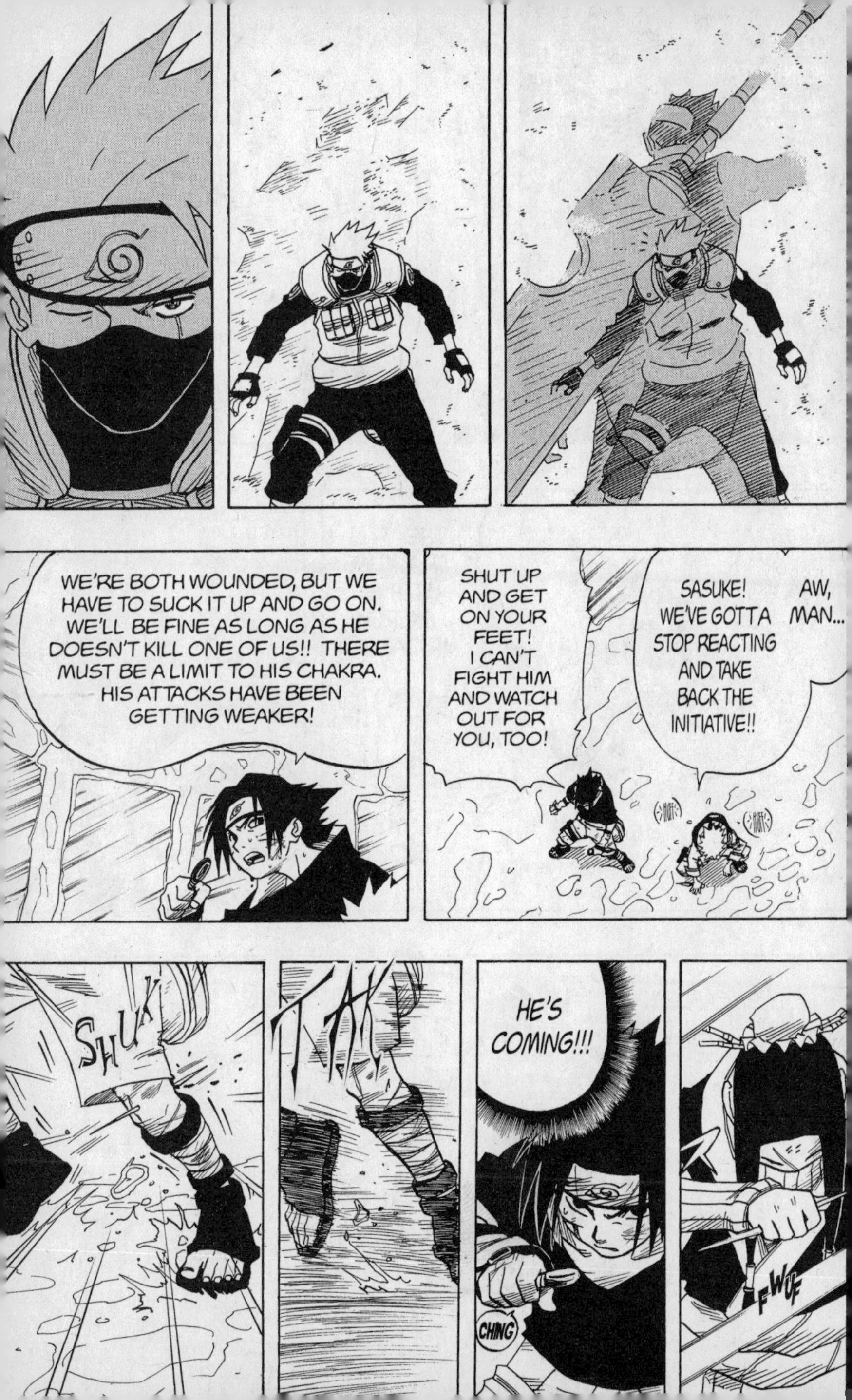
AW, MAN...
SASUKE! WE'VE GOTTA STOP REACTING AND TAKE BACK THE INITIATIVE!!
SHUT UP AND GET ON YOUR FEET! I CAN'T FIGHT HIM AND WATCH OUT FOR YOU, TOO!
HUFF
HUFF
WE'RE BOTH WOUNDED, BUT WE HAVE TO SUCK IT UP AND GO ON. WE'LL BE FINE AS LONG AS HE DOESN'T KILL ONE OF US!! THERE MUST BE A LIMIT TO HIS CHAKRA. HIS ATTACKS HAVE BEEN GETTING WEAKER!
FWUF
HE'S COMING!!!
CHING
TAK
SHUK

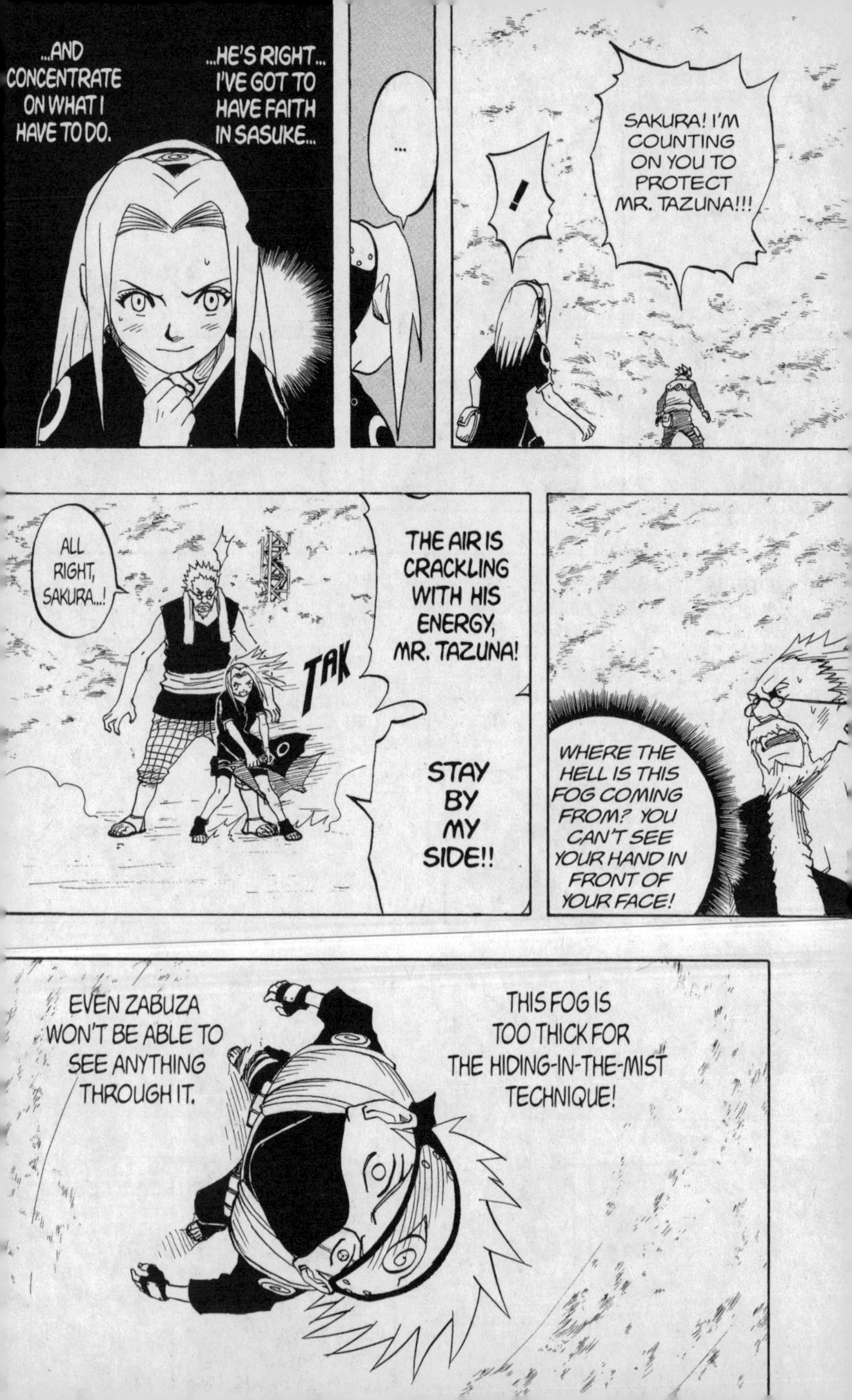
SAKURA! I'M COUNTING ON YOU TO PROTECT MR. TAZUNA!!!
!
...
...HE'S RIGHT... I'VE GOT TO HAVE FAITH IN SASUKE...
...AND CONCENTRATE ON WHAT I HAVE TO DO.
WHERE THE HELL IS THIS FOG COMING FROM? YOU CAN'T SEE YOUR HAND IN FRONT OF YOUR FACE!
THE AIR IS CRACKLING WITH HIS ENERGY, MR. TAZUNA!
STAY BY MY SIDE!!
TAK
ALL RIGHT, SAKURA...!
THIS FOG IS TOO THICK FOR THE HIDING-IN-THE-MIST TECHNIQUE!
EVEN ZABUZA WON'T BE ABLE TO SEE ANYTHING THROUGH IT.

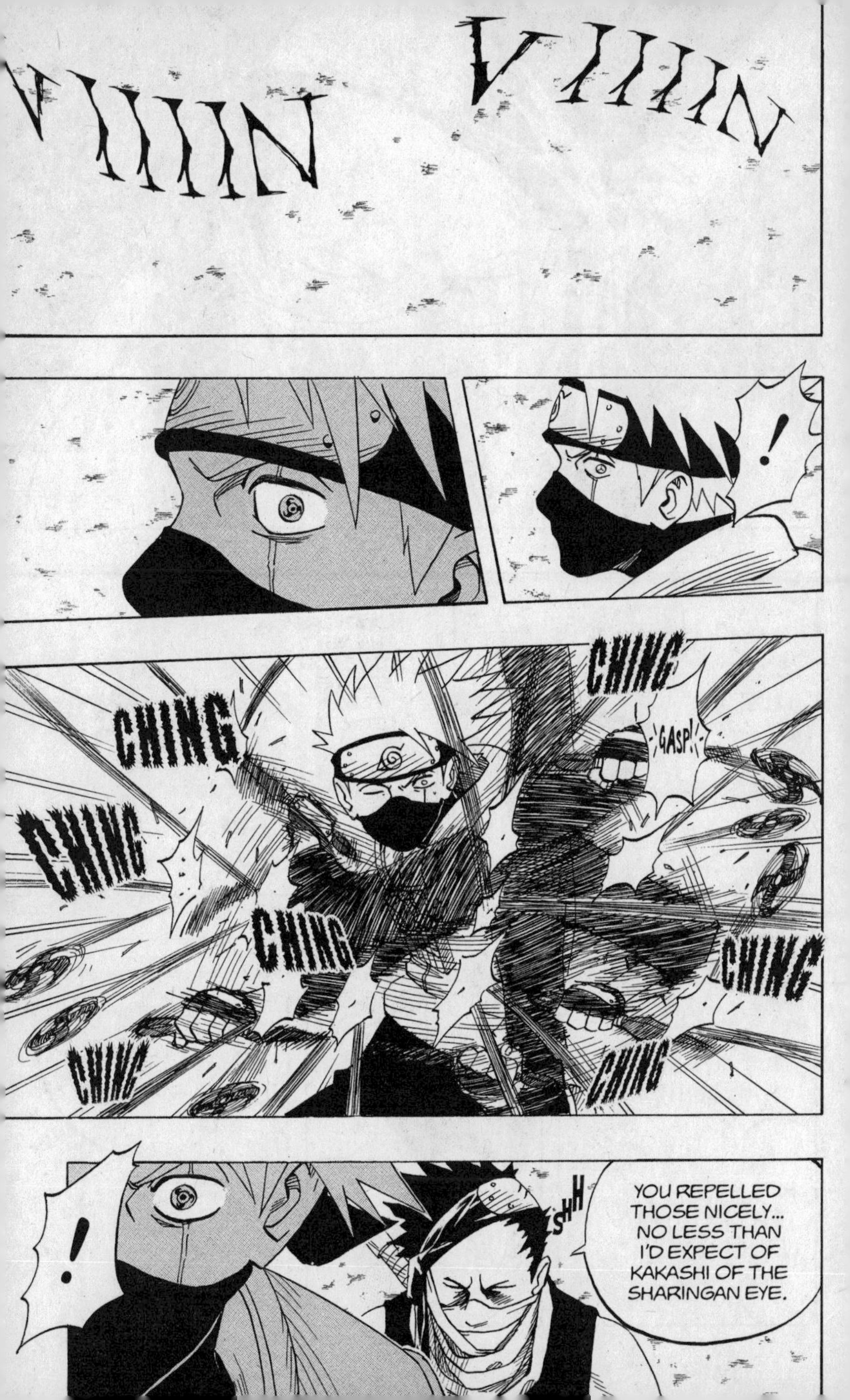
VIIIN
VIIIN
!
CHING
GASP!
CHING
CHING
CHING
CHING
CHING
CHING
SHH
YOU REPELLED THOSE NICELY... NO LESS THAN I'D EXPECT OF KAKASHI OF THE SHARINGAN EYE.
!

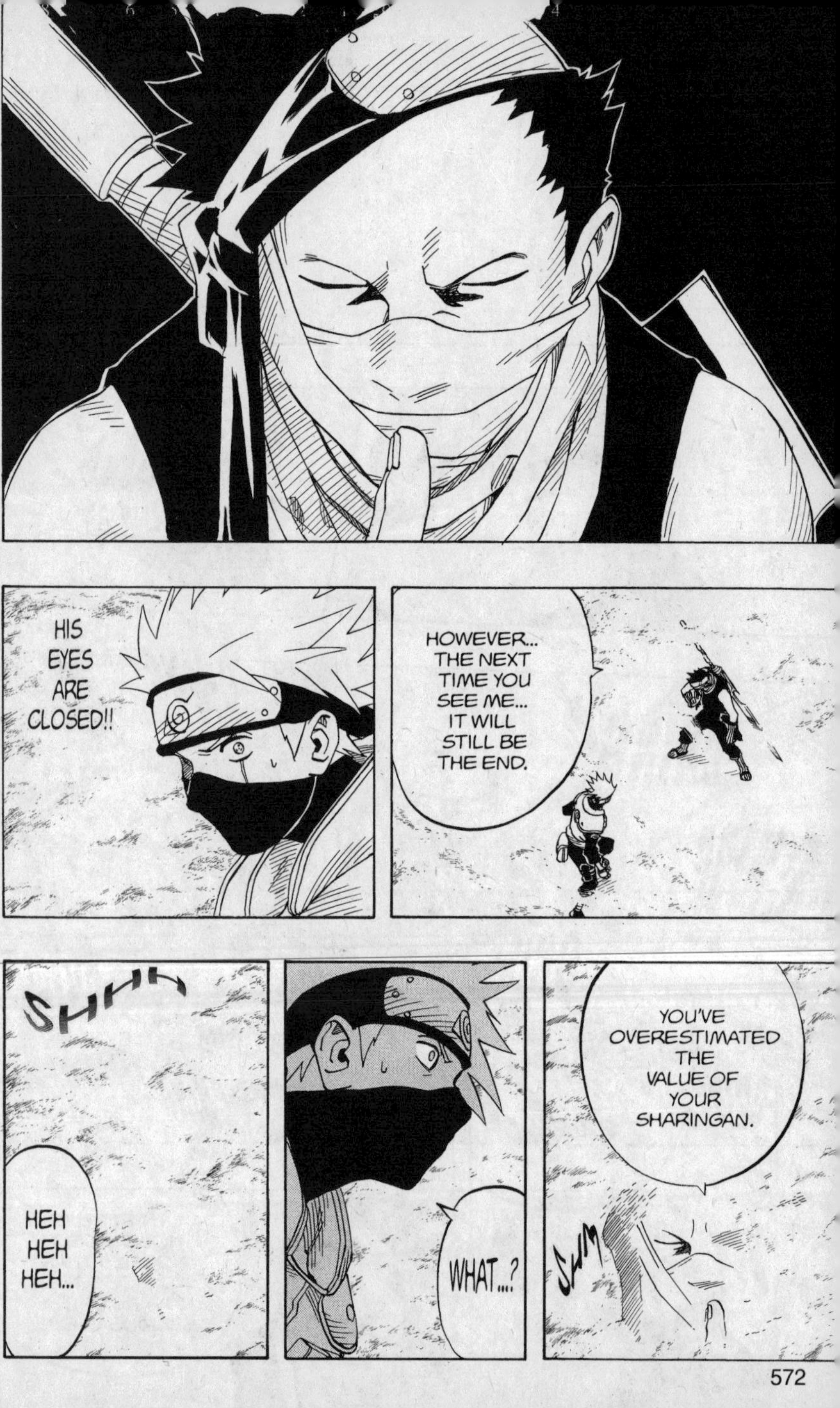
HOWEVER... THE NEXT TIME YOU SEE ME... IT WILL STILL BE THE END.
HIS EYES ARE CLOSED!!
YOU'VE OVERESTIMATED THE VALUE OF YOUR SHARINGAN.
SHM
WHAT...?
SHHH
HEH HEH HEH...

YOU PRETEND IT ENABLES YOU TO PENETRATE ALL... YET...
...CAN YOU SEE THE FUTURE?
I FORESEE... YOUR DEATH.
BUT YOU'VE TURNED OUT TO BE A FALSE PROPHET AFTER ALL, KAKASHI...
YOU CAN NEITHER READ MY MIND NOR THE FUTURE.
IN OTHER WORDS, YOUR PRECIOUS SHARINGAN IS JUST AN ELABORATE HOAX, A CONFIDENCE TRICK YOU PLAY IN ORDER TO PSYCH OUT YOUR OPPONENTS.
MORE PRECISELY, IT COMBINES CLARITY OF PERCEPTION AND INSIGHT ON YOUR OWN PART WITH THE ABILITY TO ALL BUT HYPNOTIZE THOSE AROUND YOU!
USING THOSE SKILLS IN CONCERT, YOU ARE ABLE TO CREATE YOUR ILLUSIONS THROUGH A COMBINATION OF MIMICRY— FROM MOVEMENT, TO THOUGHTS, TO THE SKILLS OF THOSE YOU FIGHT!
PRANCING AROUND ACTING LIKE YOU CAN SEE THE FUTURE!

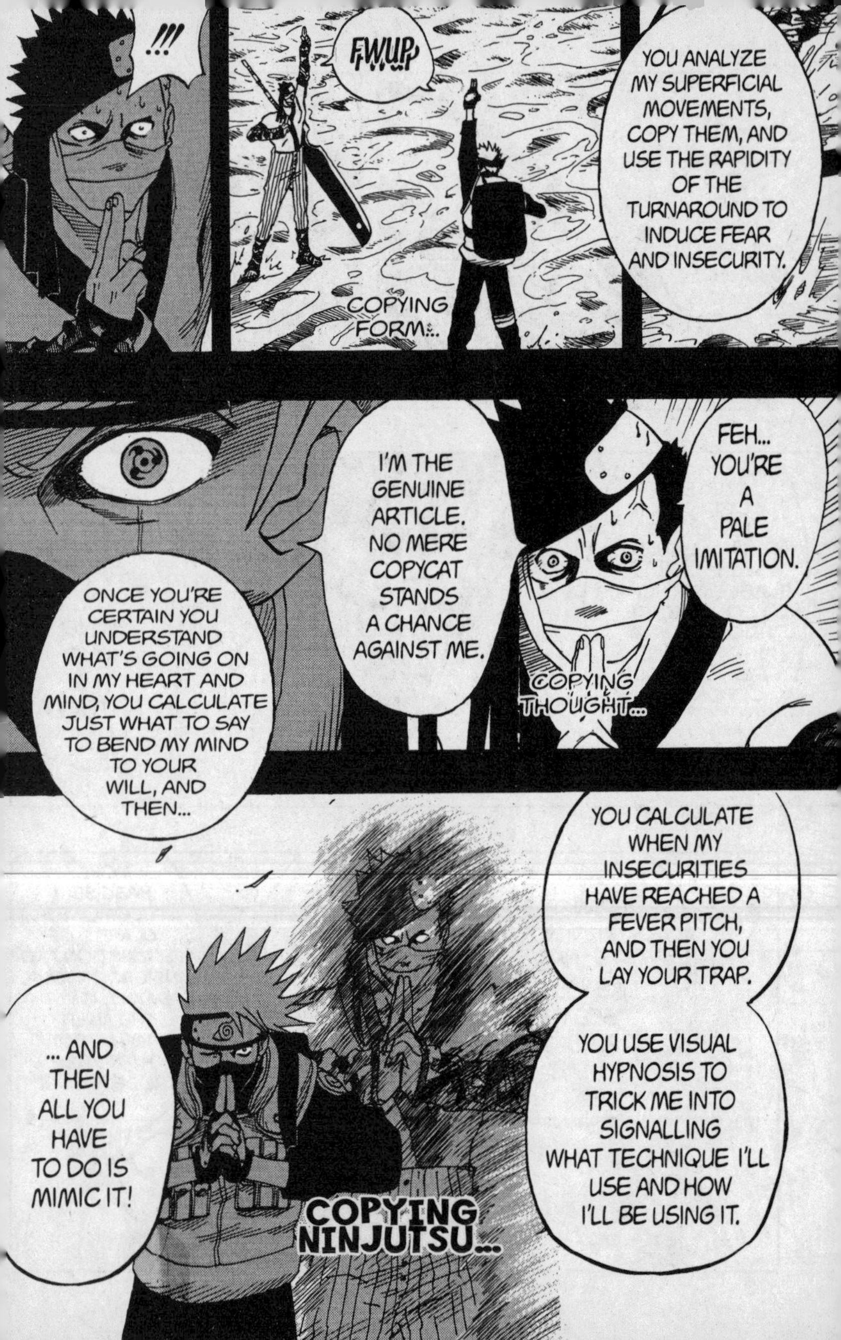
YOU ANALYZE MY SUPERFICIAL MOVEMENTS, COPY THEM, AND USE THE RAPIDITY OF THE TURNAROUND TO INDUCE FEAR AND INSECURITY.
FWUP
COPYING FORM...
!!!
FEH... YOU'RE A PALE IMITATION.
COPYING THOUGHT...
I'M THE GENUINE ARTICLE. NO MERE COPYCAT STANDS A CHANCE AGAINST ME.
ONCE YOU'RE CERTAIN YOU UNDERSTAND WHAT'S GOING ON IN MY HEART AND MIND, YOU CALCULATE JUST WHAT TO SAY TO BEND MY MIND TO YOUR WILL, AND THEN...
YOU CALCULATE WHEN MY INSECURITIES HAVE REACHED A FEVER PITCH, AND THEN YOU LAY YOUR TRAP.
YOU USE VISUAL HYPNOSIS TO TRICK ME INTO SIGNALLING WHAT TECHNIQUE I'LL USE AND HOW I'LL BE USING IT.
COPYING NINJUTSU...
... AND THEN ALL YOU HAVE TO DO IS MIMIC IT!

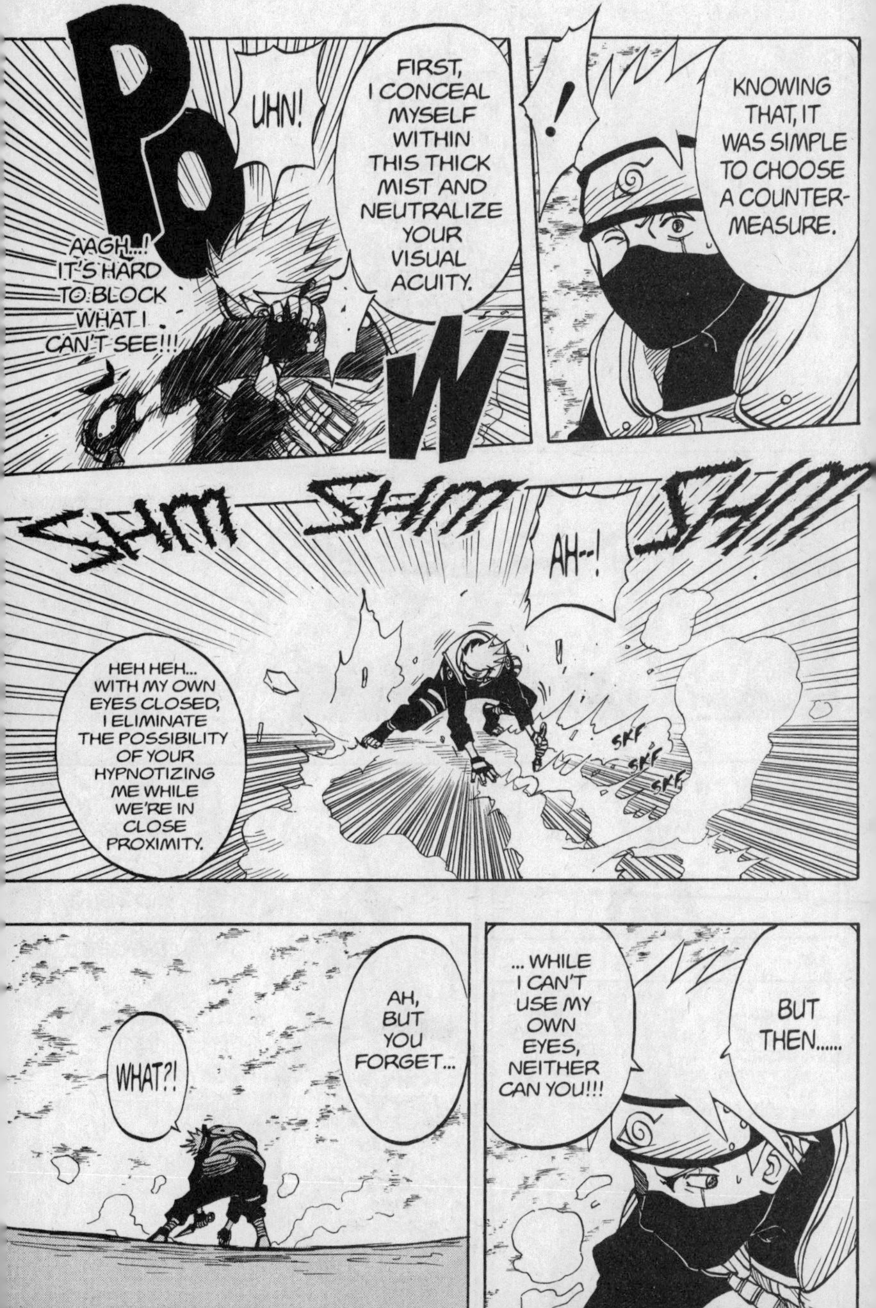
!
KNOWING THAT, IT WAS SIMPLE TO CHOOSE A COUNTER-MEASURE.
FIRST, I CONCEAL MYSELF WITHIN THIS THICK MIST AND NEUTRALIZE YOUR VISUAL ACUITY.
UHN!
POW
AAGH...! IT'S HARD TO BLOCK WHAT I CAN'T SEE!!!
SHM SHM SHM
AH--!
HEH HEH... WITH MY OWN EYES CLOSED, I ELIMINATE THE POSSIBILITY OF YOUR HYPNOTIZING ME WHILE WE'RE IN CLOSE PROXIMITY.
SKF SKF SKF
BUT THEN......
... WHILE I CAN'T USE MY OWN EYES, NEITHER CAN YOU!!!
AH, BUT YOU FORGET...
WHAT?!

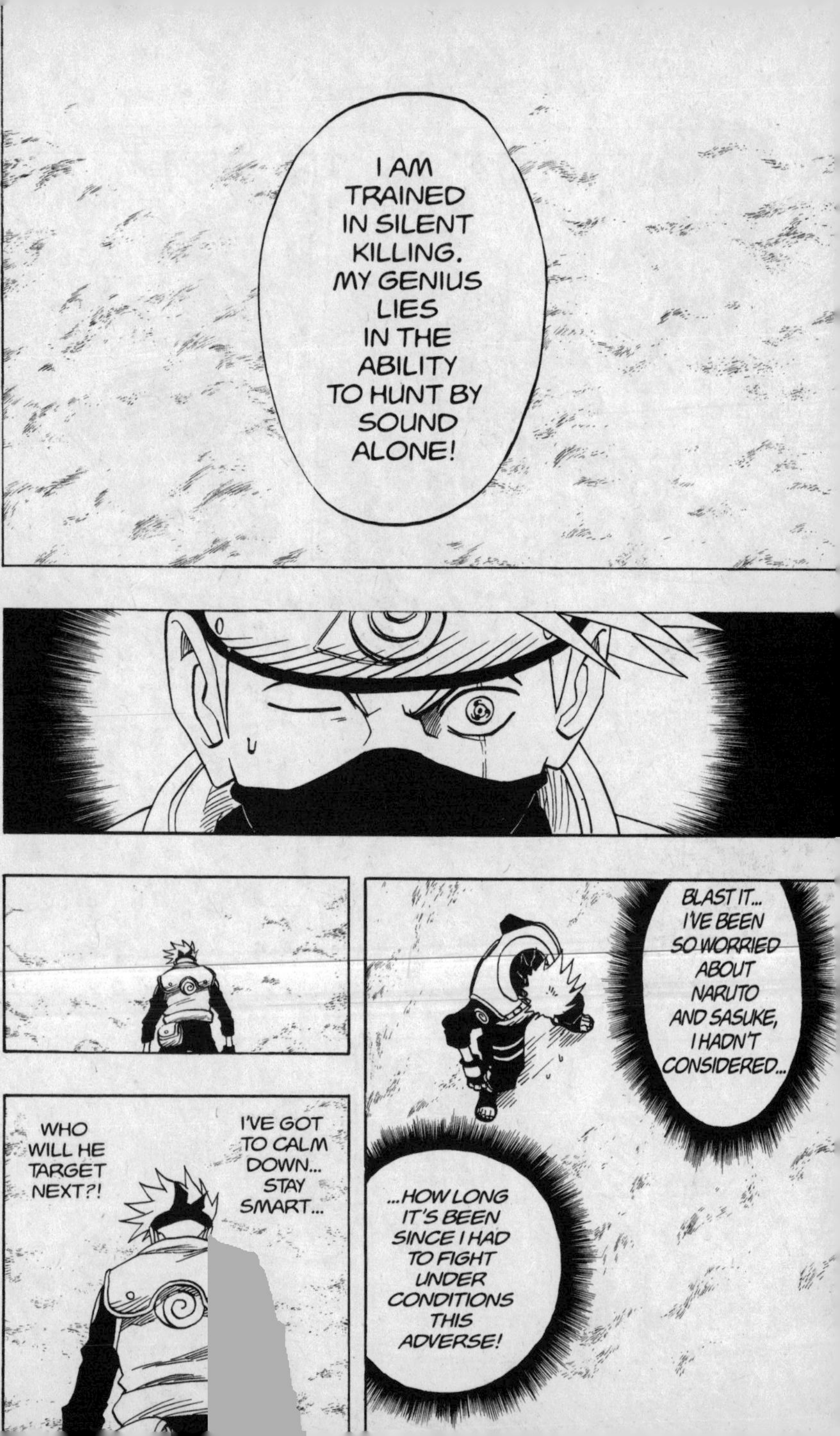
I AM TRAINED IN SILENT KILLING. MY GENIUS LIES IN THE ABILITY TO HUNT BY SOUND ALONE!
BLAST IT... I'VE BEEN SO WORRIED ABOUT NARUTO AND SASUKE, I HADN'T CONSIDERED...
...HOW LONG IT'S BEEN SINCE I HAD TO FIGHT UNDER CONDITIONS THIS ADVERSE!
I'VE GOT TO CALM DOWN... STAY SMART...
WHO WILL HE TARGET NEXT?!

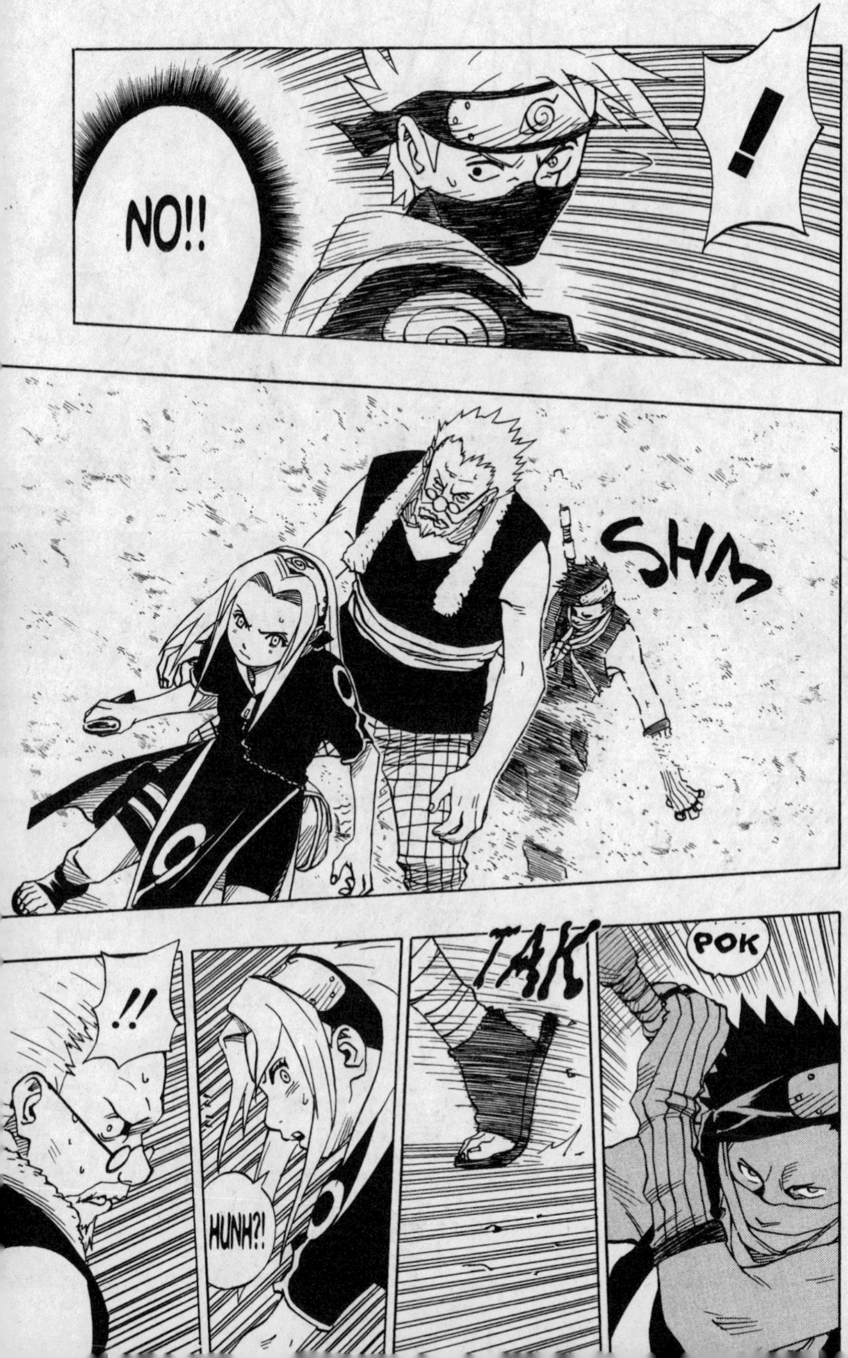
!
NO!!
SHB
POK
TAK
HUNH?!
!!

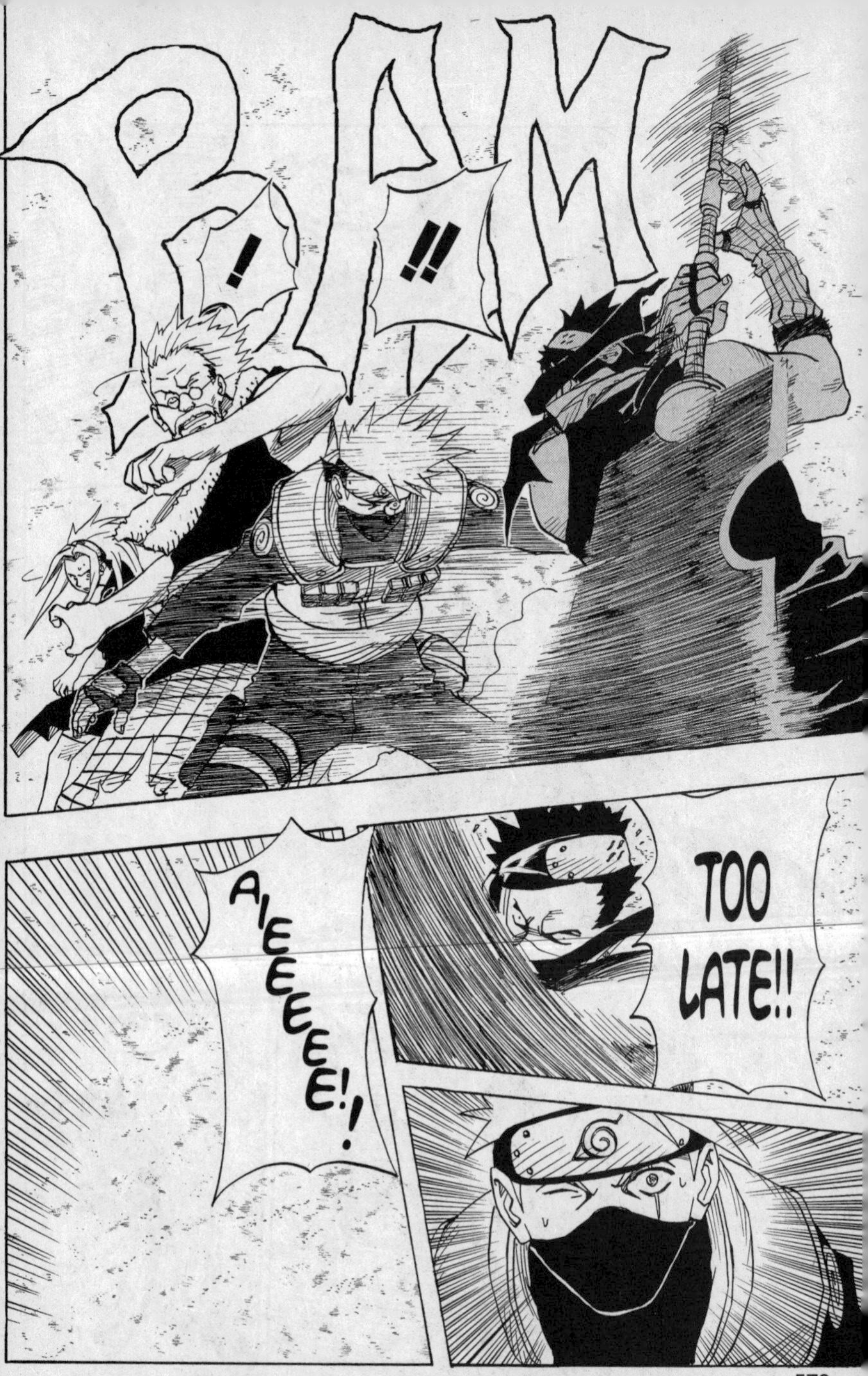
BAM
!!
!
TOO LATE!!
AIEEEEE!!

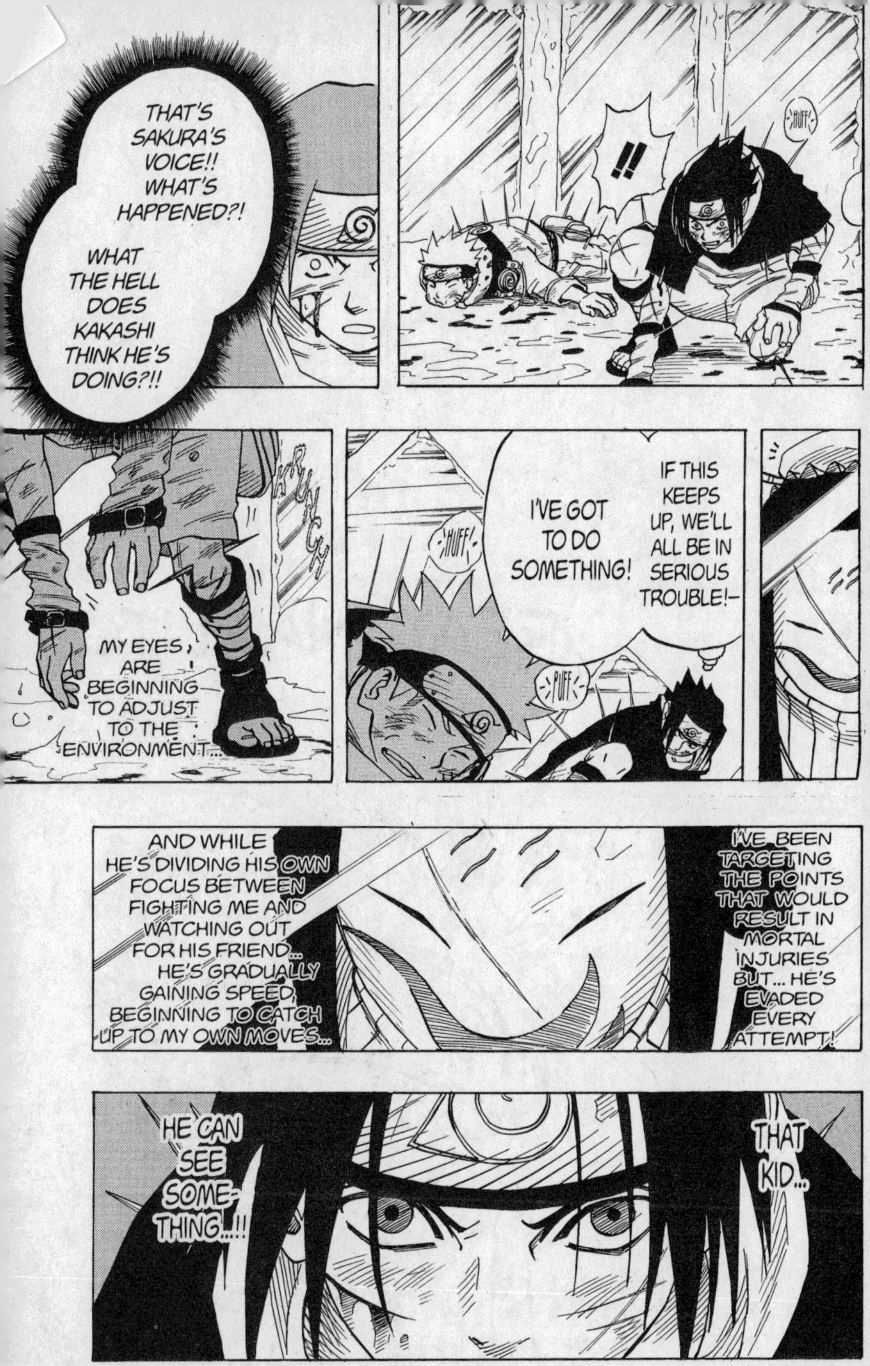

HUFF
!!
THAT'S SAKURA'S VOICE!! WHAT'S HAPPENED?!
WHAT THE HELL DOES KAKASHI THINK HE'S DOING?!!
IF THIS KEEPS UP, WE'LL ALL BE IN SERIOUS TROUBLE!
I'VE GOT TO DO SOMETHING!
HUFF
PUFF
KRUNCH
MY EYES ARE BEGINNING TO ADJUST TO THE ENVIRONMENT...
I'VE BEEN TARGETING THE POINTS THAT WOULD RESULT IN MORTAL INJURIES BUT... HE'S EVADED EVERY ATTEMPT!
AND WHILE HE'S DIVIDING HIS OWN FOCUS BETWEEN FIGHTING ME AND WATCHING OUT FOR HIS FRIEND... HE'S GRADUALLY GAINING SPEED, BEGINNING TO CATCH UP TO MY OWN MOVES...
THAT KID...
HE CAN SEE SOME-THING...!!

REAL NARUTO

Number 27: Awakenings

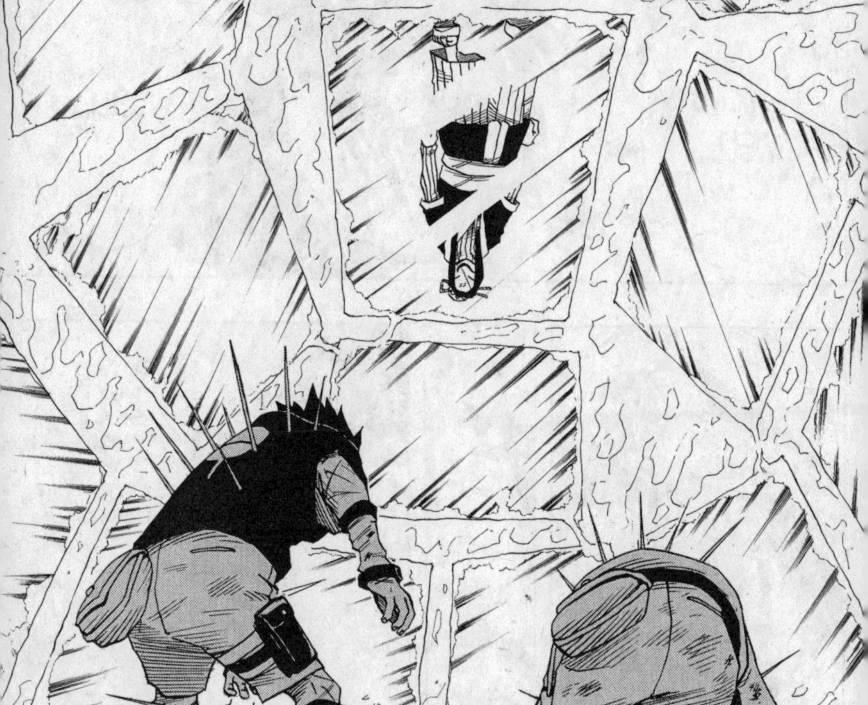

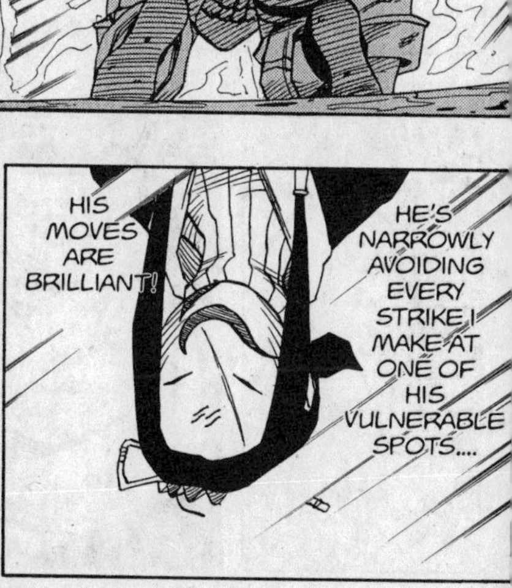
HE'S NARROWLY AVOIDING EVERY STRIKE I MAKE AT ONE OF HIS VULNERABLE SPOTS....
HIS MOVES ARE BRILLIANT!

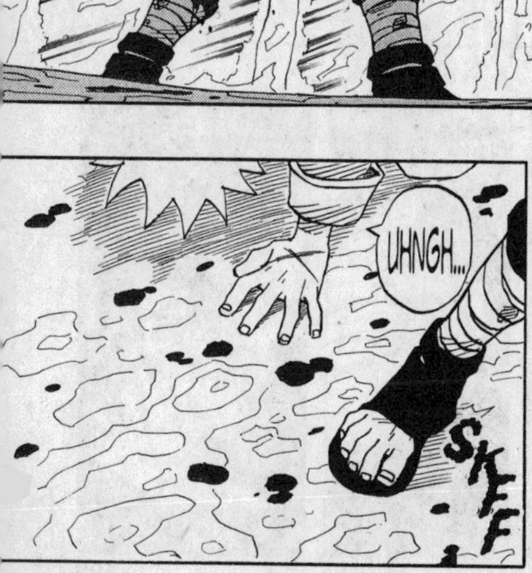
UHNGH...
SKFF

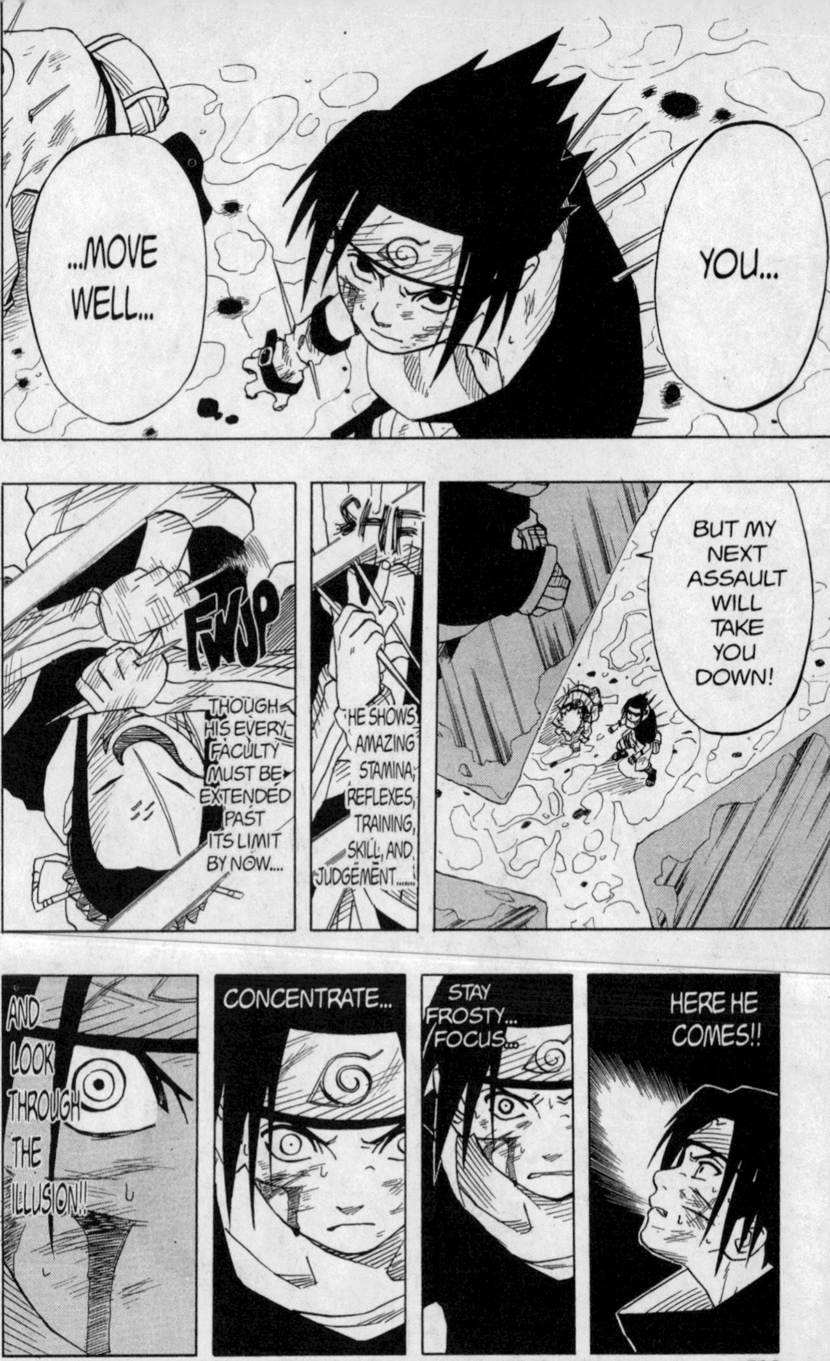
YOU...
...MOVE WELL...
BUT MY NEXT ASSAULT WILL TAKE YOU DOWN!
SHF
HE SHOWS AMAZING STAMINA, REFLEXES, TRAINING, SKILL, AND JUDGEMENT......
FWSP
THOUGH HIS EVERY FACULTY MUST BE EXTENDED PAST ITS LIMIT BY NOW....
HERE HE COMES!!
STAY FROSTY... FOCUS...
CONCENTRATE...
AND LOOK THROUGH THE ILLUSION!!

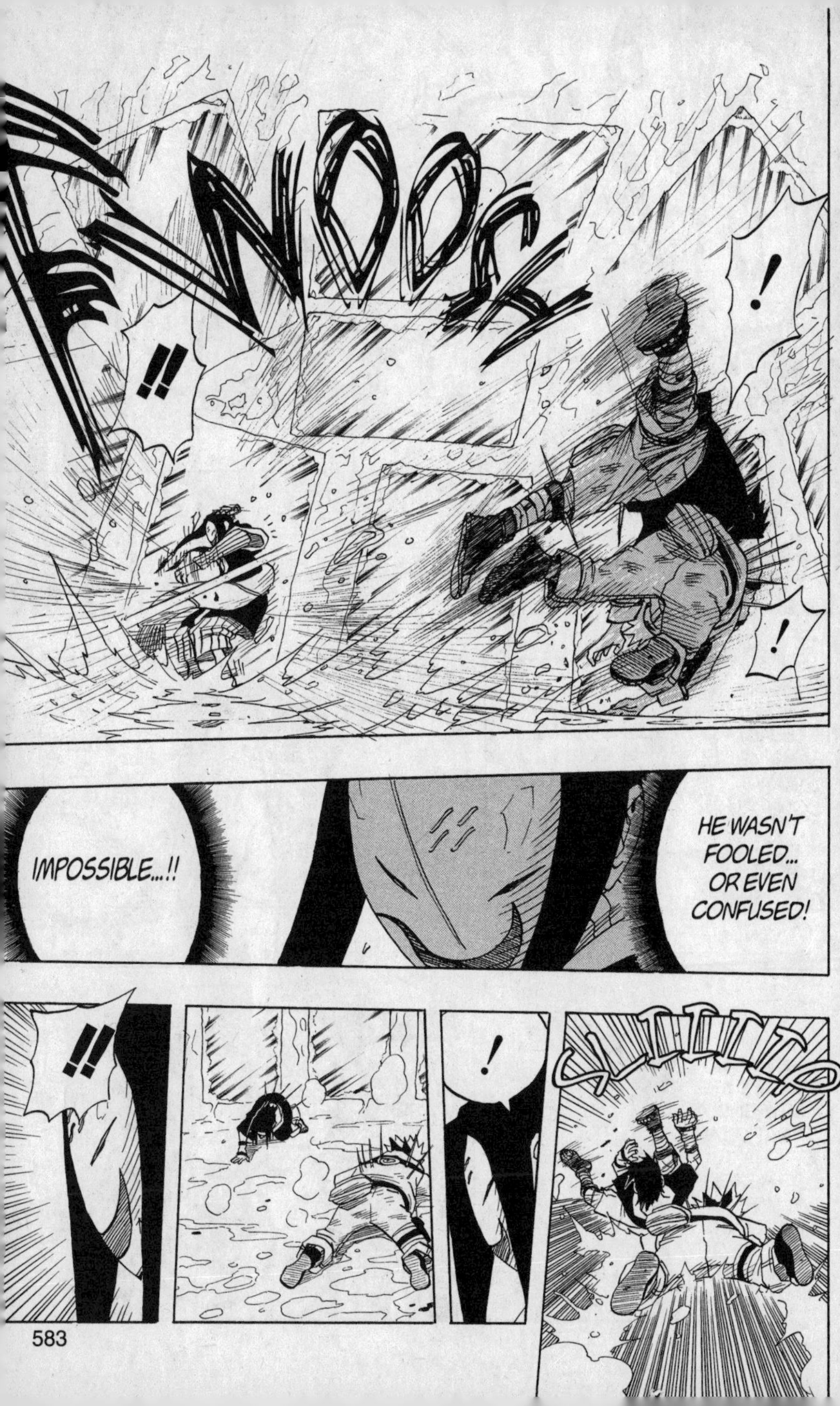
FWOOSH
!
!
!!
HE WASN'T FOOLED... OR EVEN CONFUSED!
IMPOSSIBLE...!!
SLIIIIID
!
!!

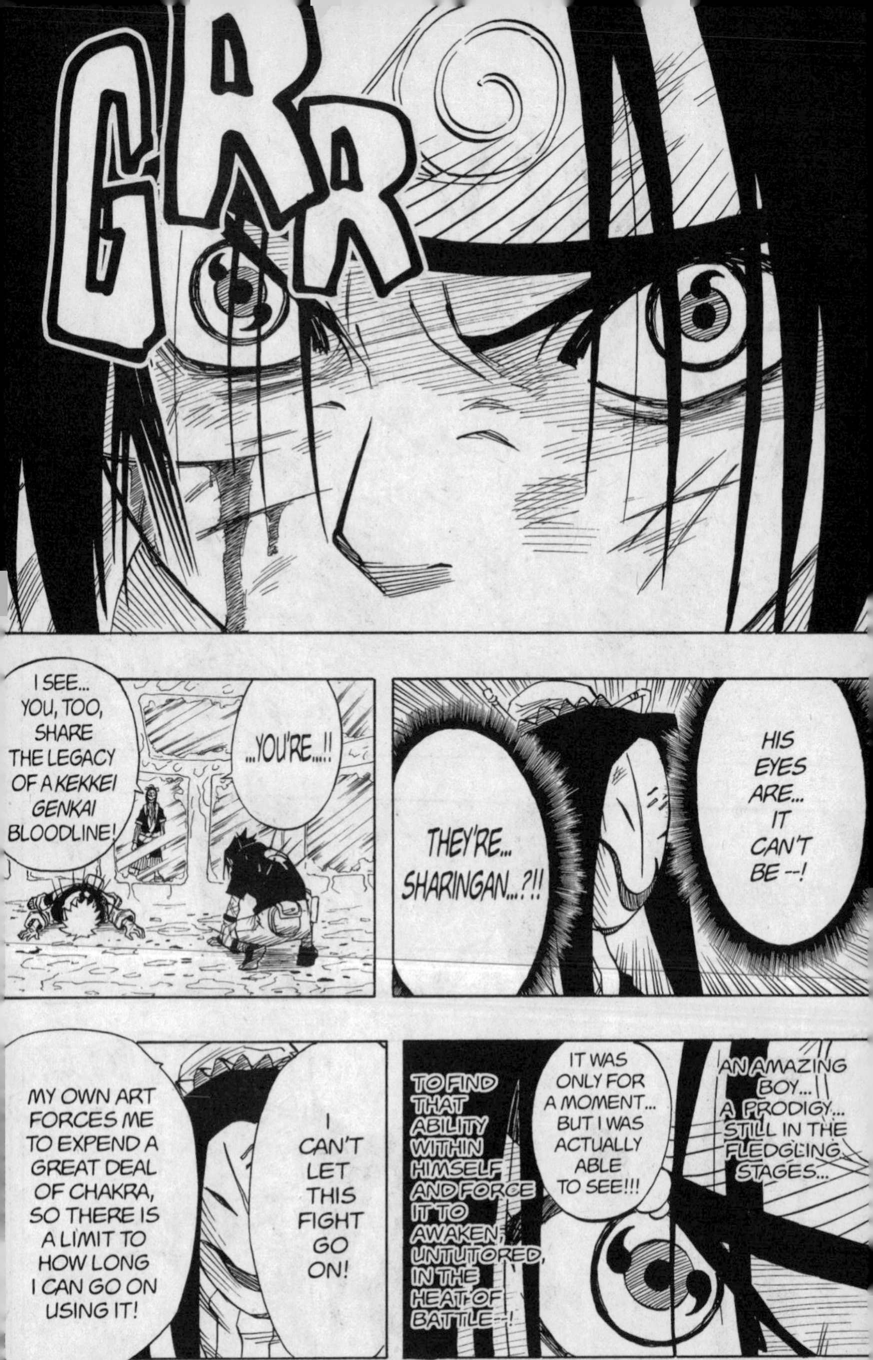
GRR
HIS EYES ARE... IT CAN'T BE --!
THEY'RE... SHARINGAN...?!!
...YOU'RE...!!
I SEE... YOU, TOO, SHARE THE LEGACY OF A KEKKEI GENKAI BLOODLINE!
AN AMAZING BOY... A PRODIGY... STILL IN THE FLEDGLING STAGES...
IT WAS ONLY FOR A MOMENT... BUT I WAS ACTUALLY ABLE TO SEE!!!
TO FIND THAT ABILITY WITHIN HIMSELF AND FORCE IT TO AWAKEN, UNTUTORED, IN THE HEAT OF BATTLE--!
I CAN'T LET THIS FIGHT GO ON!
MY OWN ART FORCES ME TO EXPEND A GREAT DEAL OF CHAKRA, SO THERE IS A LIMIT TO HOW LONG I CAN GO ON USING IT!

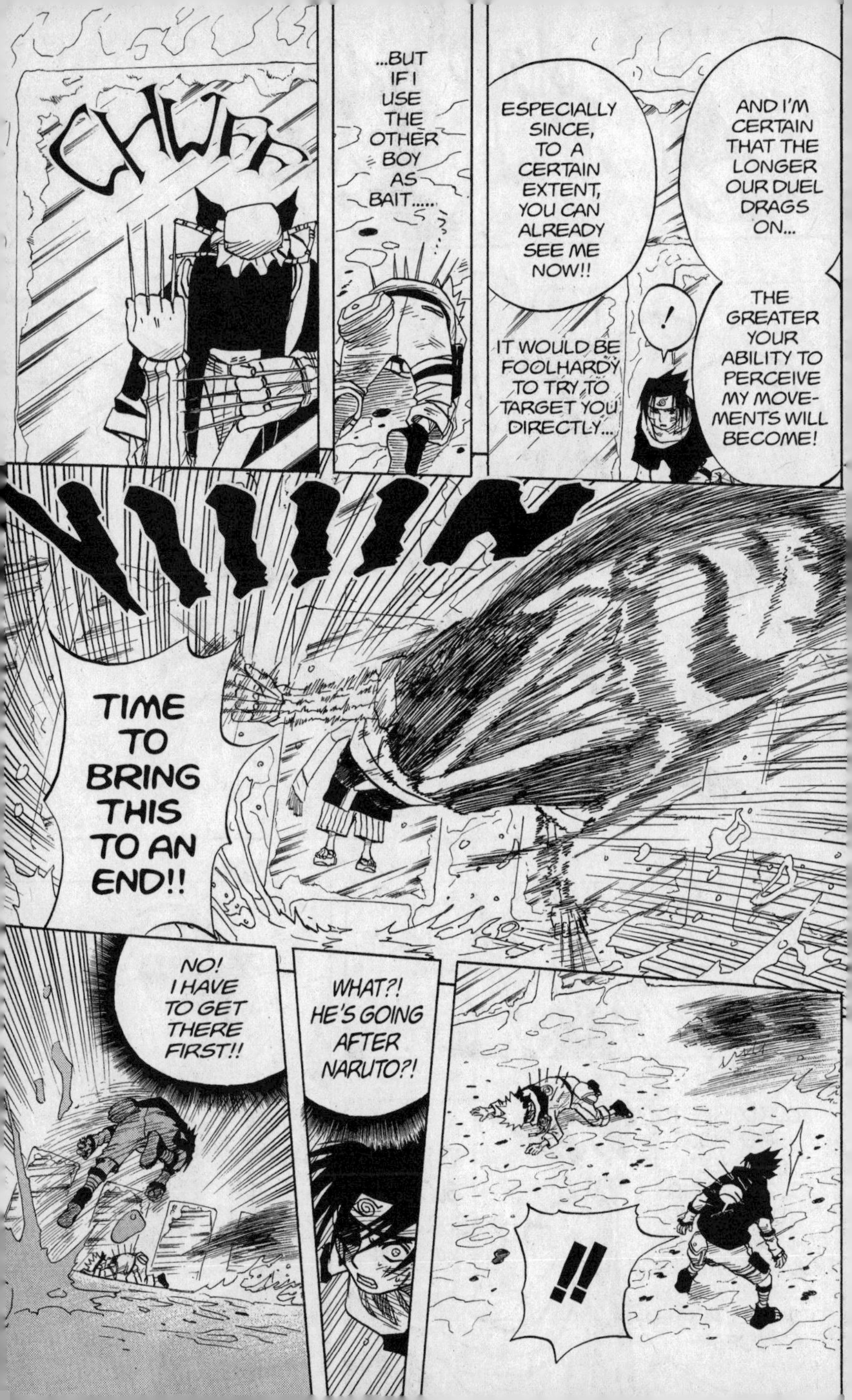
AND I'M CERTAIN THAT THE LONGER OUR DUEL DRAGS ON...
THE GREATER YOUR ABILITY TO PERCEIVE MY MOVEMENTS WILL BECOME!
!
ESPECIALLY SINCE, TO A CERTAIN EXTENT, YOU CAN ALREADY SEE ME NOW!!
IT WOULD BE FOOLHARDY TO TRY TO TARGET YOU DIRECTLY...
...BUT IF I USE THE OTHER BOY AS BAIT......
TIME TO BRING THIS TO AN END!!
!!
WHAT?! HE'S GOING AFTER NARUTO?!
NO! I HAVE TO GET THERE FIRST!!

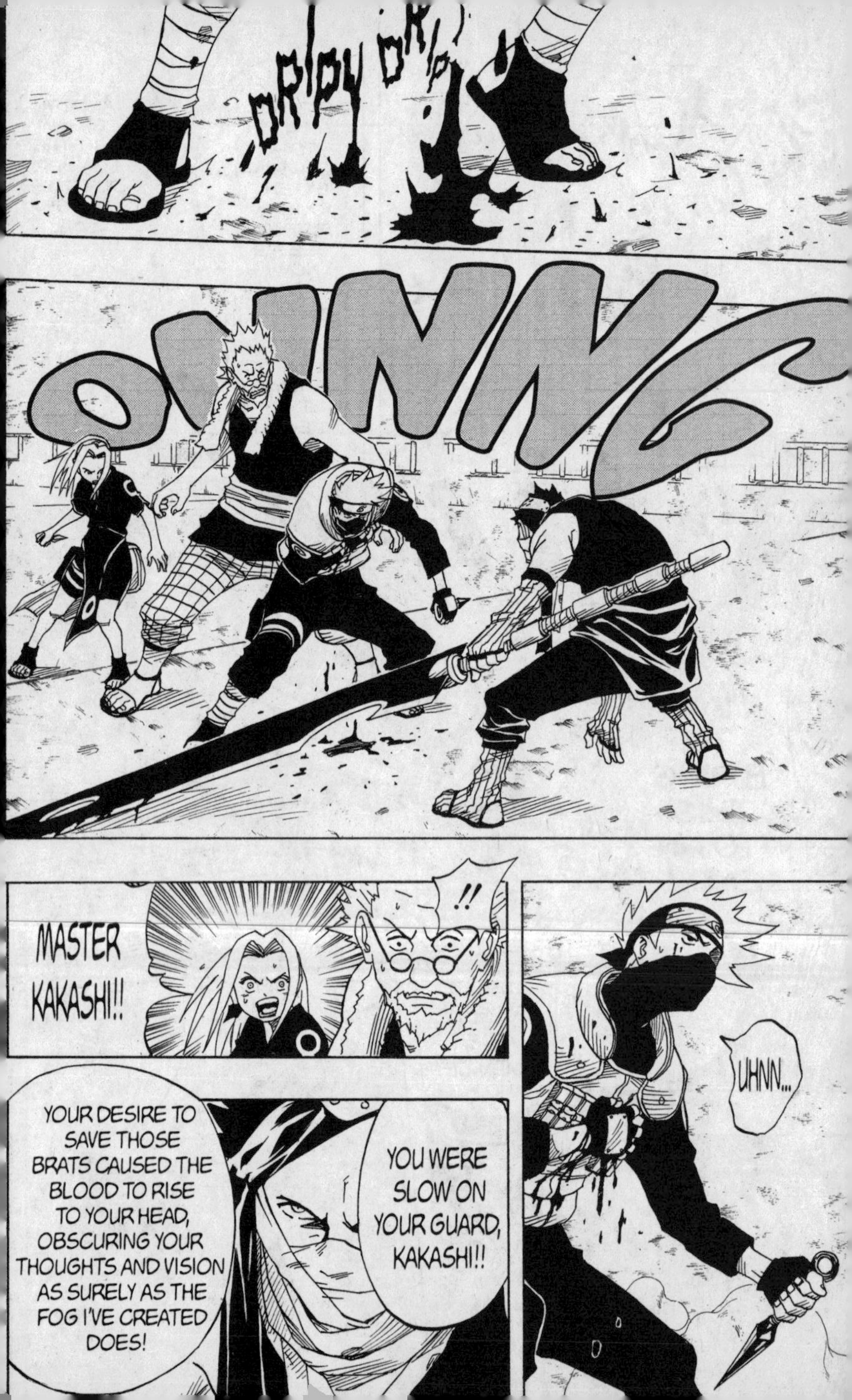
DRIP DRIP
UHNN...
!!
MASTER KAKASHI!!
YOU WERE SLOW ON YOUR GUARD, KAKASHI!!
YOUR DESIRE TO SAVE THOSE BRATS CAUSED THE BLOOD TO RISE TO YOUR HEAD, OBSCURING YOUR THOUGHTS AND VISION AS SURELY AS THE FOG I'VE CREATED DOES!

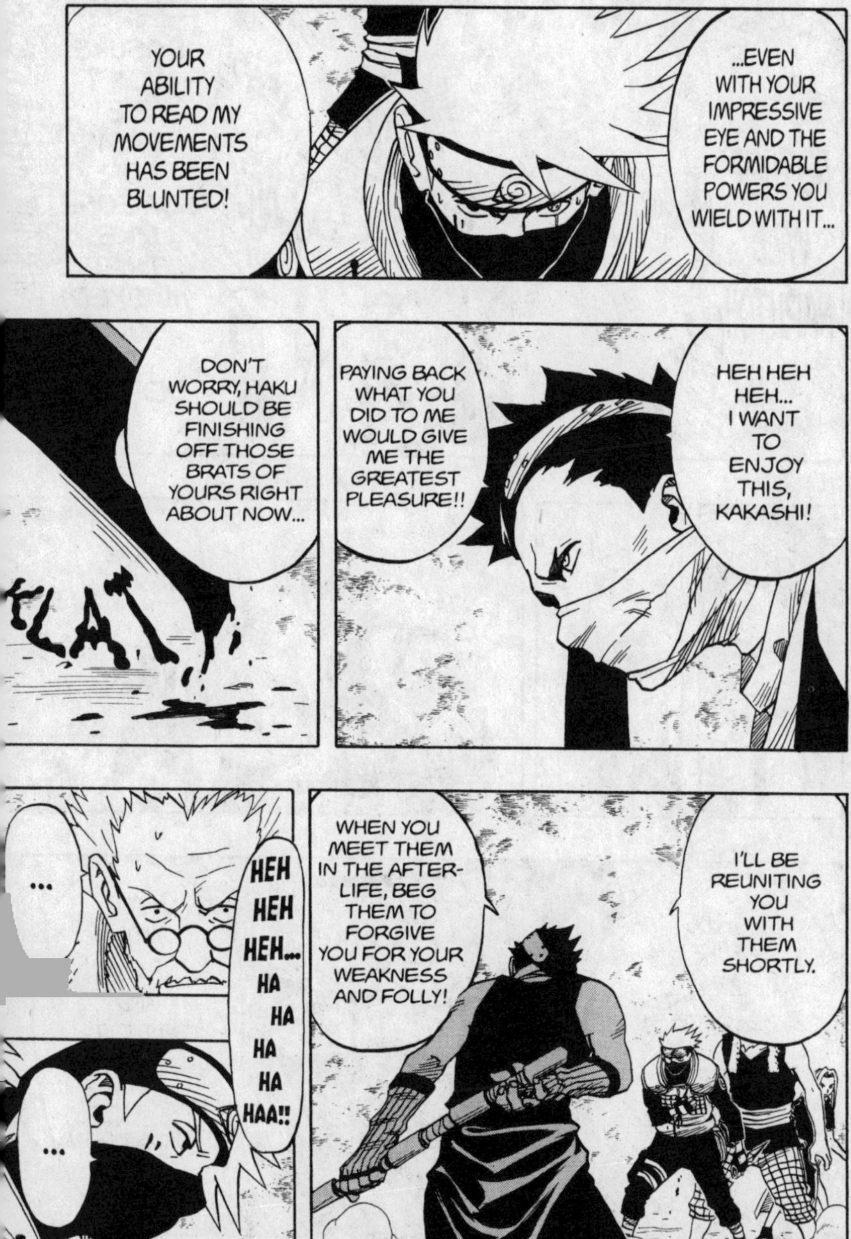
...EVEN WITH YOUR IMPRESSIVE EYE AND THE FORMIDABLE POWERS YOU WIELD WITH IT...
YOUR ABILITY TO READ MY MOVEMENTS HAS BEEN BLUNTED!
HEH HEH HEH... I WANT TO ENJOY THIS, KAKASHI!
PAYING BACK WHAT YOU DID TO ME WOULD GIVE ME THE GREATEST PLEASURE!!
DON'T WORRY, HAKU SHOULD BE FINISHING OFF THOSE BRATS OF YOURS RIGHT ABOUT NOW...
FLAT
I'LL BE REUNITING YOU WITH THEM SHORTLY.
WHEN YOU MEET THEM IN THE AFTER-LIFE, BEG THEM TO FORGIVE YOU FOR YOUR WEAKNESS AND FOLLY!
HEH HEH HEH... HA HA HA HA HAA!!
...
...

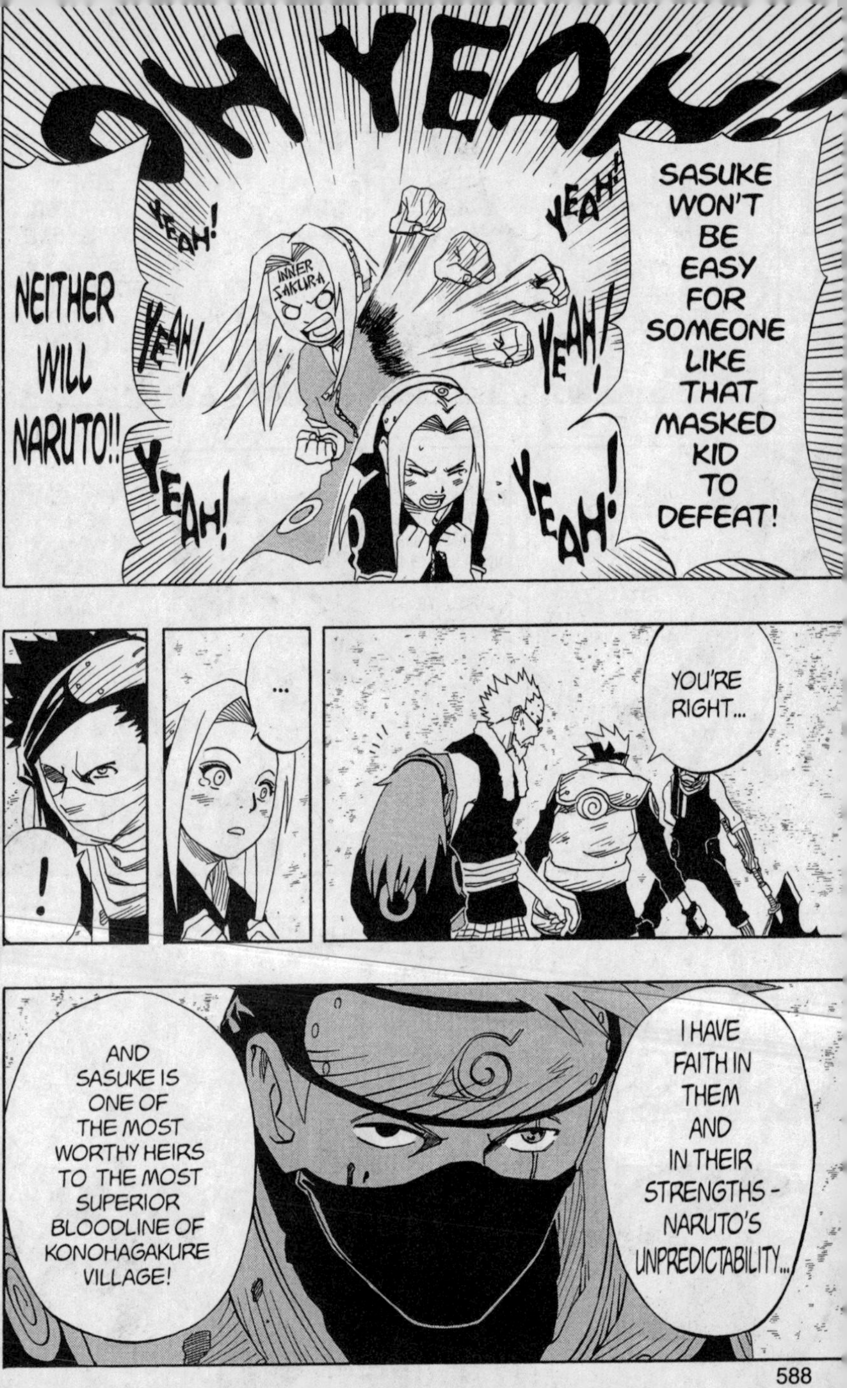
OH YEAH!!
SASUKE WON'T BE EASY FOR SOMEONE LIKE THAT MASKED KID TO DEFEAT!
YEAH!
YEAH!
YEAH!
INNER SAKURA
YEAH!
YEAH!
YEAH!
NEITHER WILL NARUTO!!
YOU'RE RIGHT...
...
!
I HAVE FAITH IN THEM AND IN THEIR STRENGTHS - NARUTO'S UNPREDICTABILITY...
AND SASUKE IS ONE OF THE MOST WORTHY HEIRS TO THE MOST SUPERIOR BLOODLINE OF KONOHAGAKURE VILLAGE!

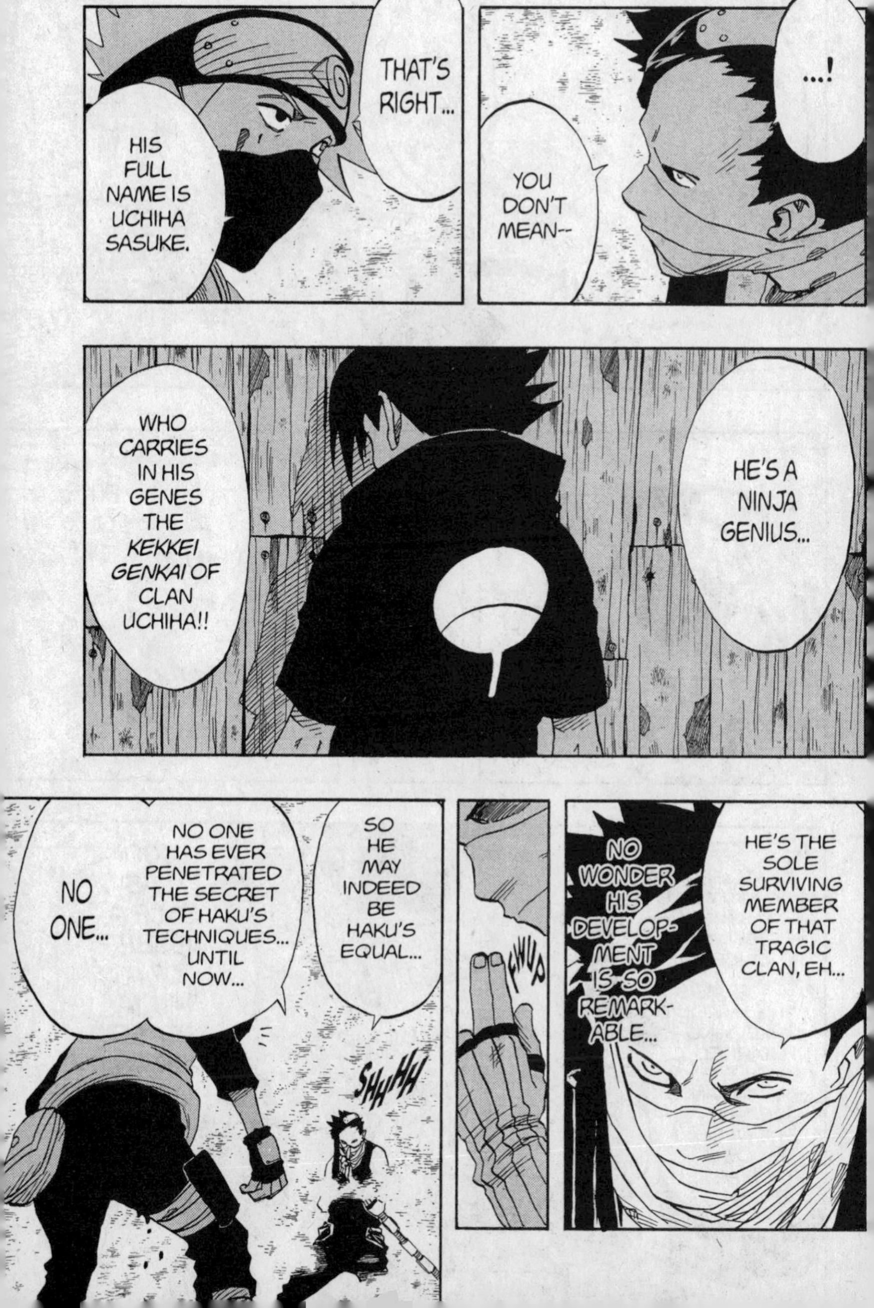
...!
YOU DON'T MEAN--
THAT'S RIGHT...
HIS FULL NAME IS UCHIHA SASUKE.
HE'S A NINJA GENIUS...
WHO CARRIES IN HIS GENES THE *KEKKEI GENKAI* OF CLAN UCHIHA!!
HE'S THE SOLE SURVIVING MEMBER OF THAT TRAGIC CLAN, EH...
NO WONDER HIS DEVELOP-MENT IS SO REMARK-ABLE...
FWUP
SO HE MAY INDEED BE HAKU'S EQUAL...
NO ONE HAS EVER PENETRATED THE SECRET OF HAKU'S TECHNIQUES... UNTIL NOW...
NO ONE...
SHHHH

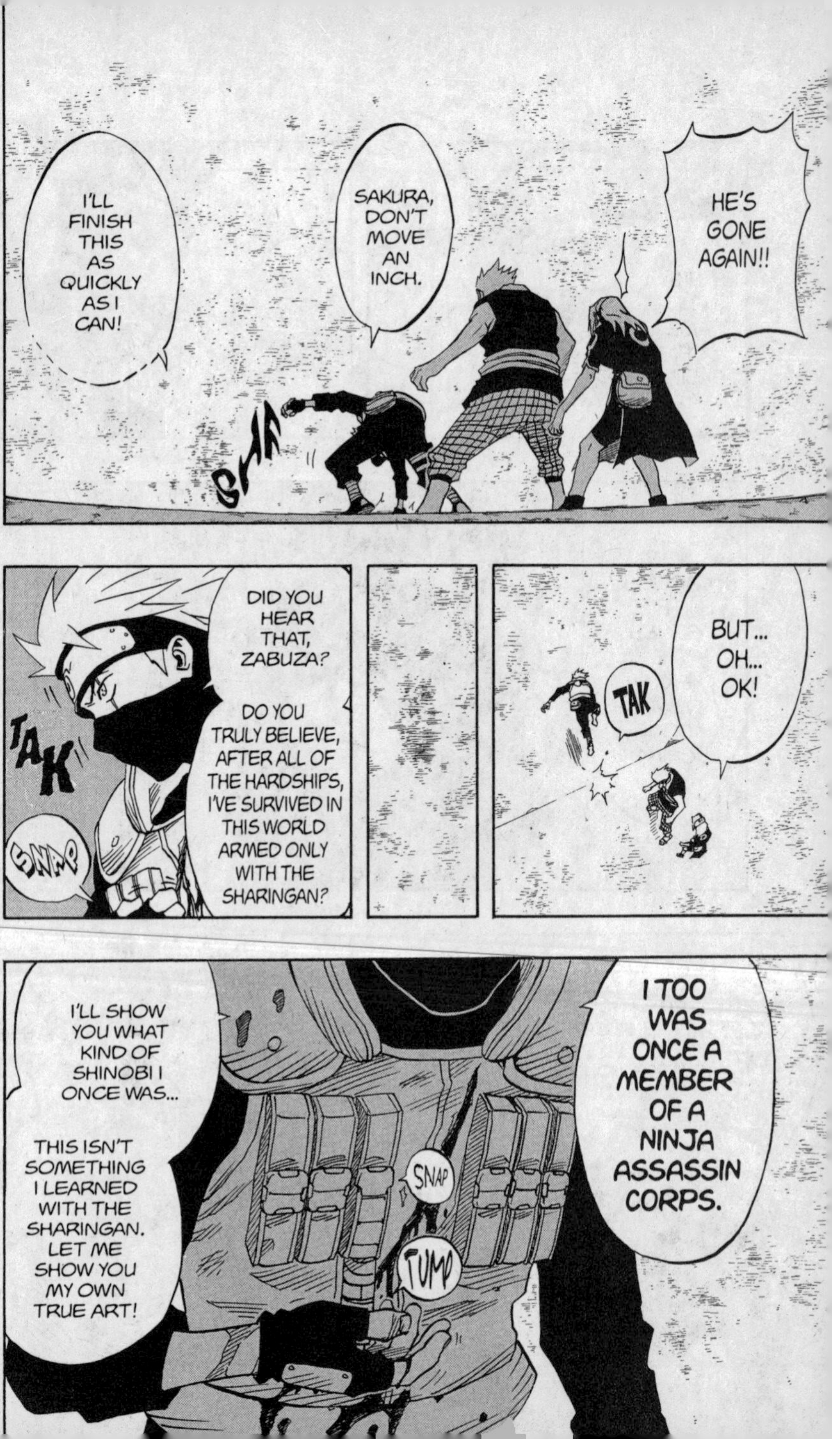
HE'S GONE AGAIN!!
SAKURA, DON'T MOVE AN INCH.
I'LL FINISH THIS AS QUICKLY AS I CAN!
BUT... OH... OK!
TAK
DID YOU HEAR THAT, ZABUZA?
DO YOU TRULY BELIEVE, AFTER ALL OF THE HARDSHIPS, I'VE SURVIVED IN THIS WORLD ARMED ONLY WITH THE SHARINGAN?
TAK
SNAP
I TOO WAS ONCE A MEMBER OF A NINJA ASSASSIN CORPS.
SNAP
TUMP
I'LL SHOW YOU WHAT KIND OF SHINOBI I ONCE WAS...
THIS ISN'T SOMETHING I LEARNED WITH THE SHARINGAN. LET ME SHOW YOU MY OWN TRUE ART!

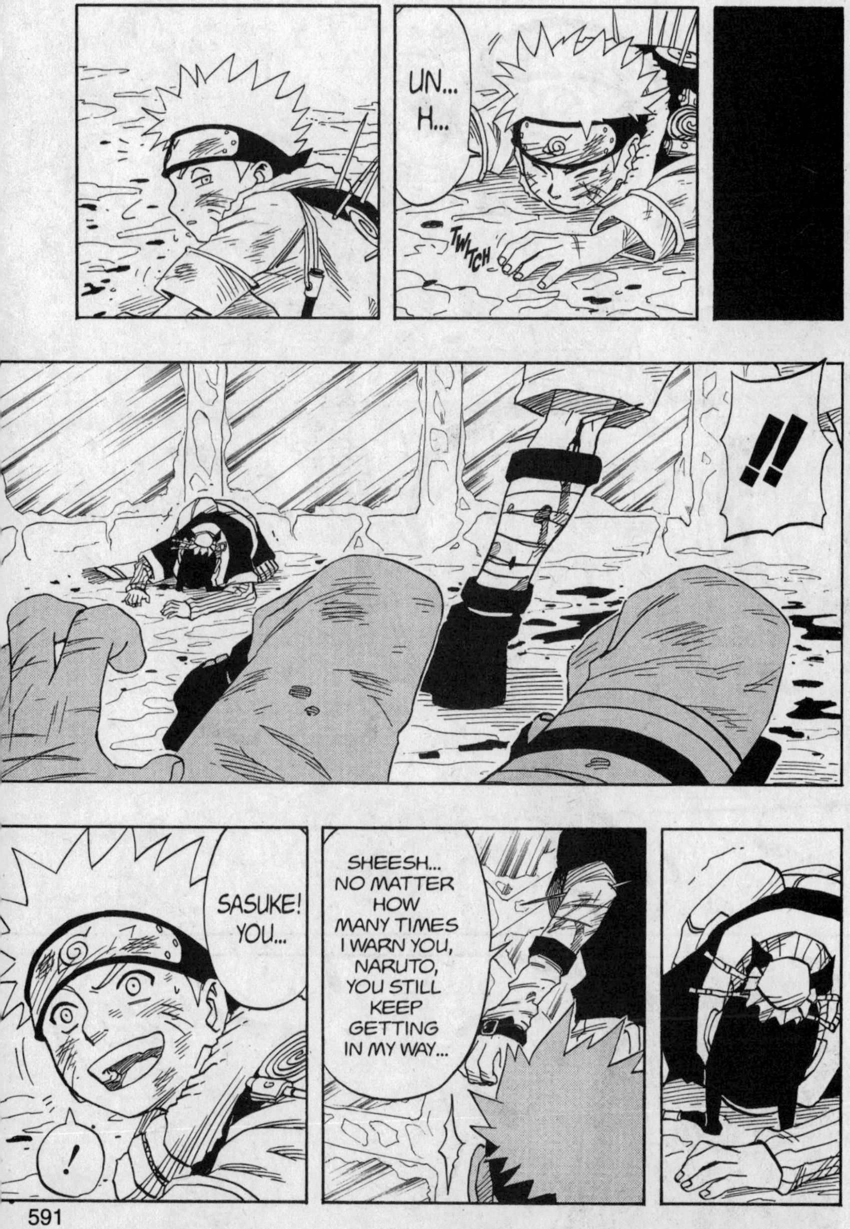
UN... H...
TWITCH
!!
SHEESH... NO MATTER HOW MANY TIMES I WARN YOU, NARUTO, YOU STILL KEEP GETTING IN MY WAY...
SASUKE! YOU...
!

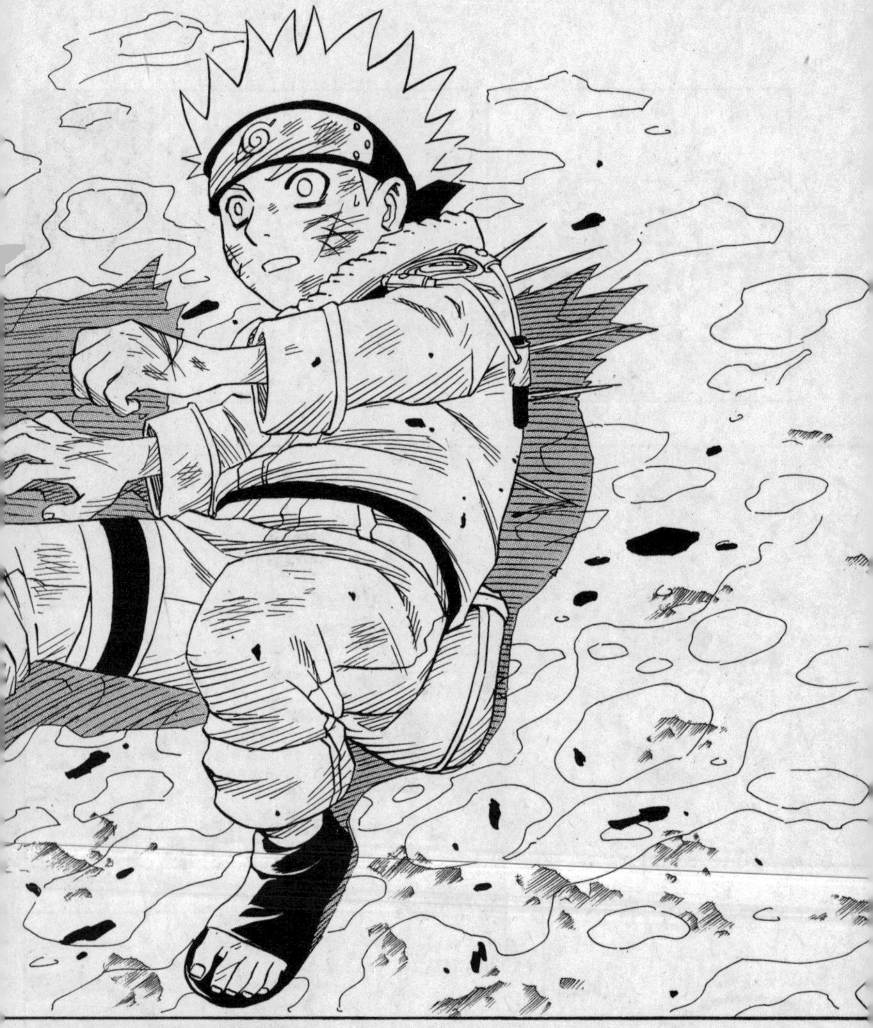
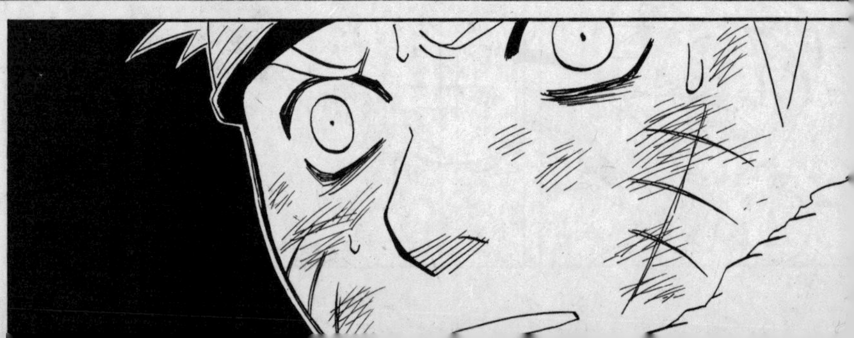

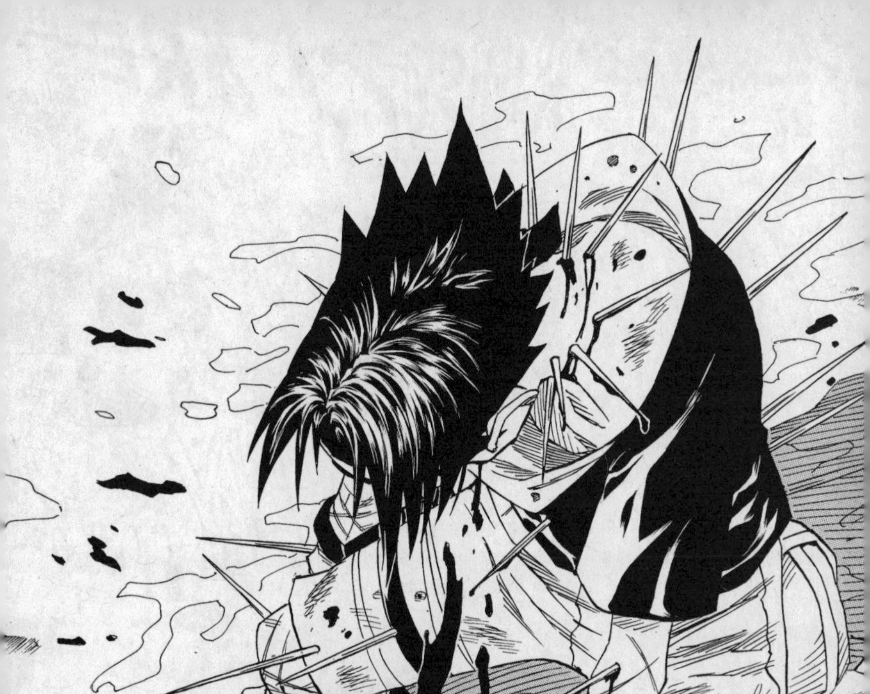

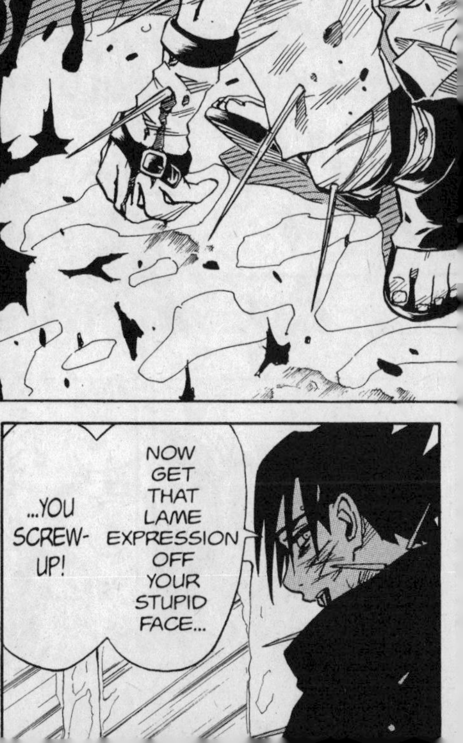
NOW GET THAT LAME EXPRESSION OFF YOUR STUPID FACE...
...YOU SCREW-UP!

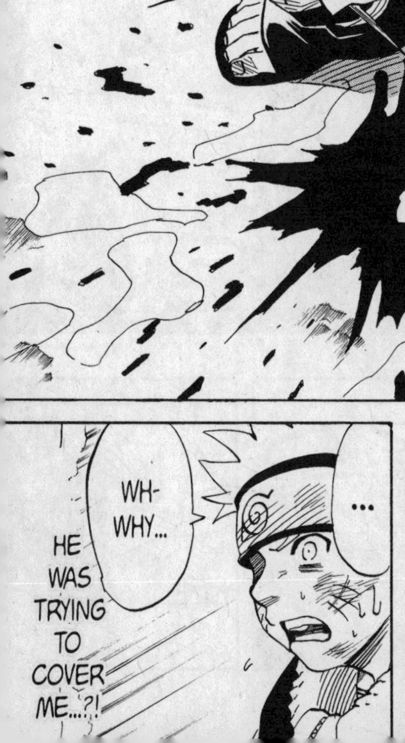
...
WH- WHY...
HE WAS TRYING TO COVER ME...?!

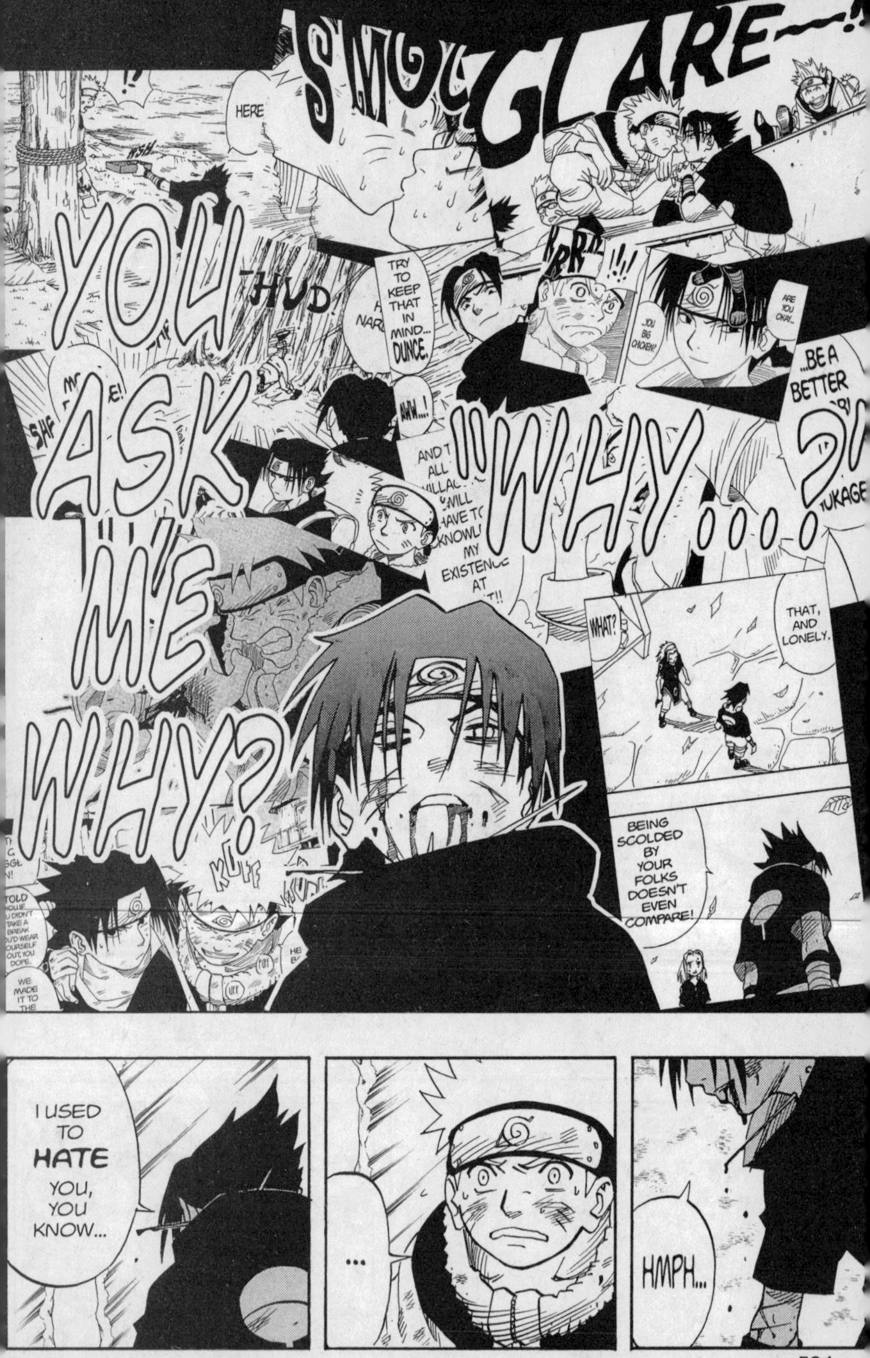
GLARE——!!
ARE YOU OKAY...
...BE A BETTER
...YOU BIG CHICKEN!
TRY TO KEEP THAT IN MIND... DUNCE.
HERE
YOU ASK ME WHY?
WHY...?
AWW...!
THAT, AND LONELY.
WHAT?
BEING SCOLDED BY YOUR FOLKS DOESN'T EVEN COMPARE!
HMPH...
...
I USED TO HATE YOU, YOU KNOW...

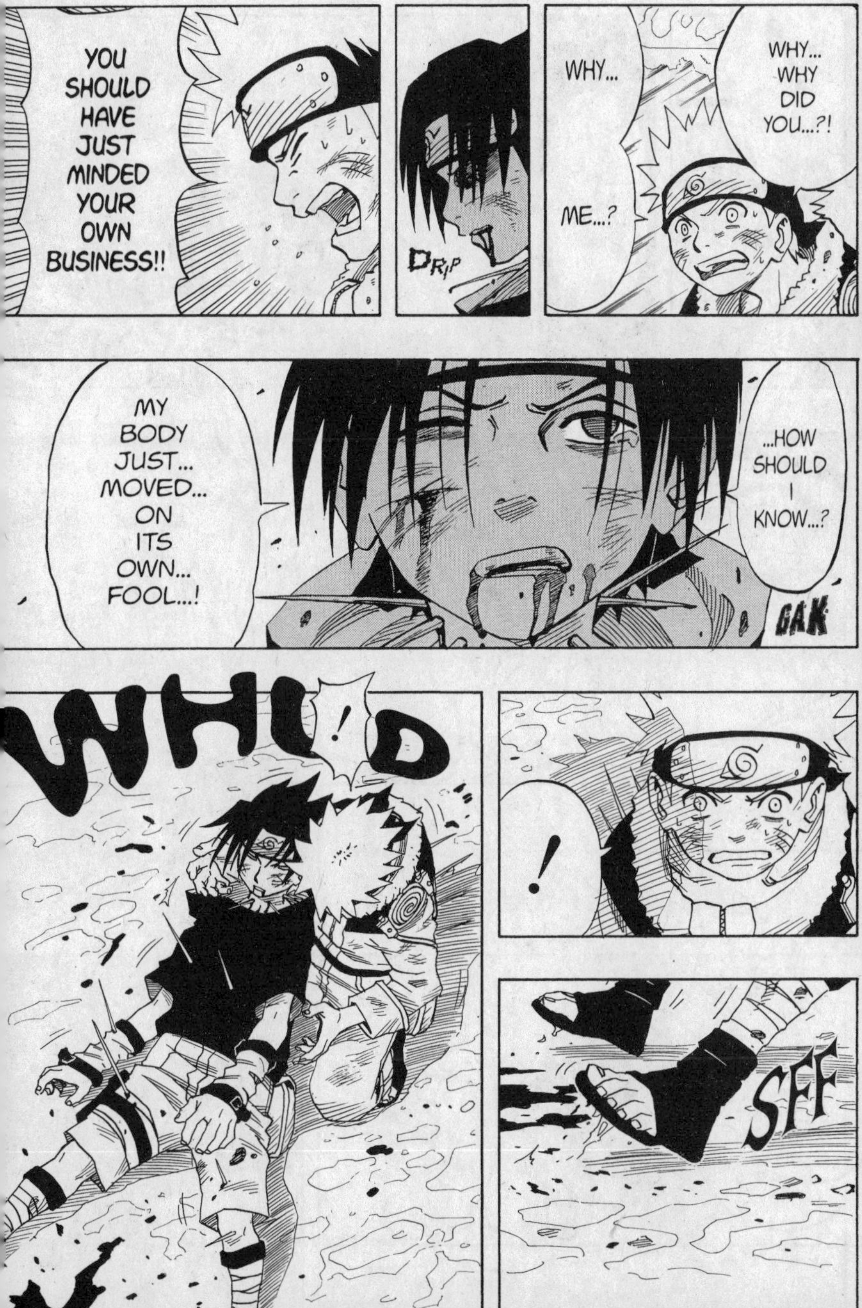
WHY... WHY DID YOU...?!
WHY...
ME...?
DRIP
YOU SHOULD HAVE JUST MINDED YOUR OWN BUSINESS!!
...HOW SHOULD I KNOW...?
GAK
MY BODY JUST... MOVED... ON ITS OWN... FOOL...!
!
SFF
WHUD
!

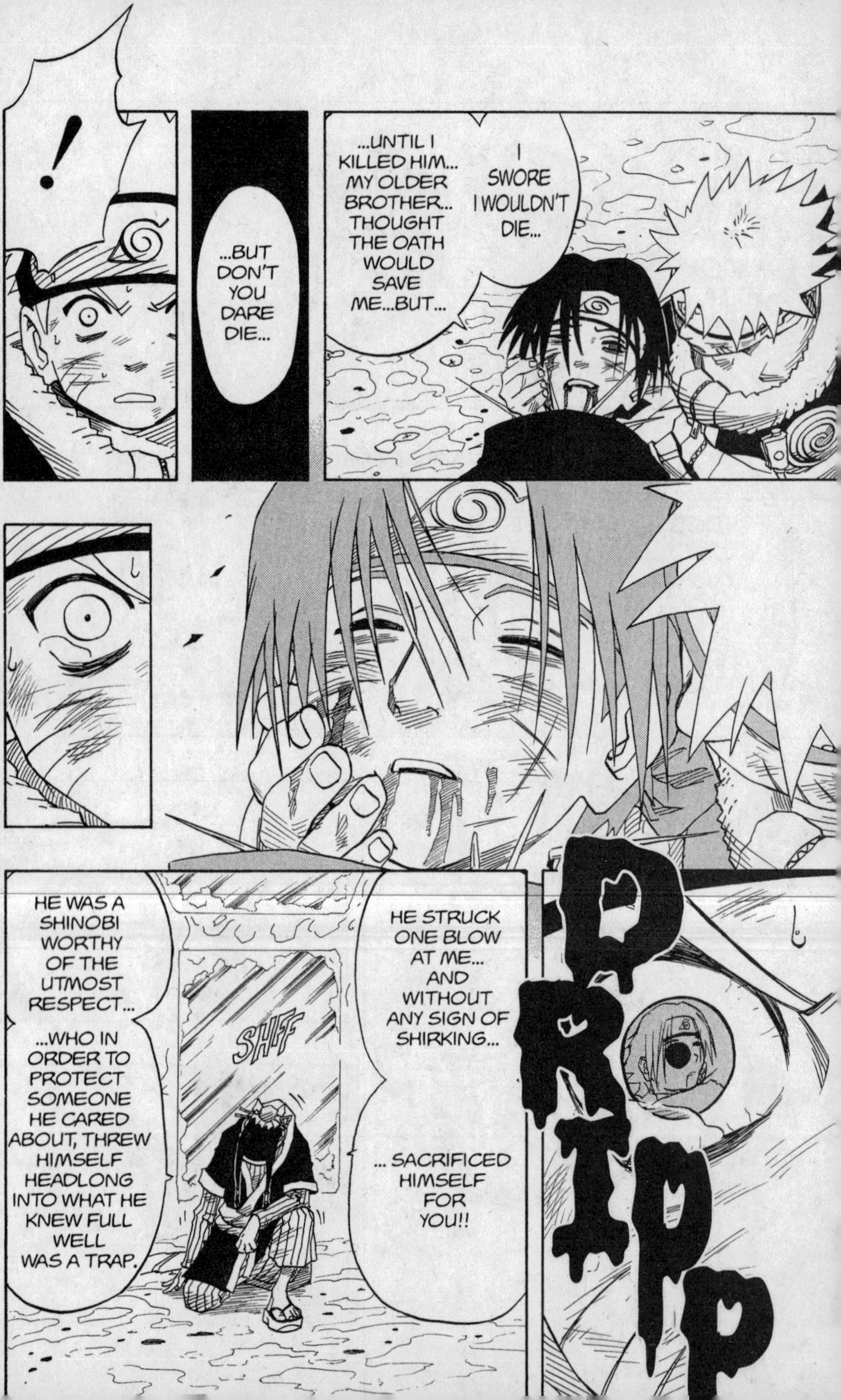
I SWORE I WOULDN'T DIE...
...UNTIL I KILLED HIM... MY OLDER BROTHER... THOUGHT THE OATH WOULD SAVE ME...BUT...
...BUT DON'T YOU DARE DIE...
!
RIPP
HE STRUCK ONE BLOW AT ME... AND WITHOUT ANY SIGN OF SHIRKING...
... SACRIFICED HIMSELF FOR YOU!!
SHFF
HE WAS A SHINOBI WORTHY OF THE UTMOST RESPECT...
...WHO IN ORDER TO PROTECT SOMEONE HE CARED ABOUT, THREW HIMSELF HEADLONG INTO WHAT HE KNEW FULL WELL WAS A TRAP.

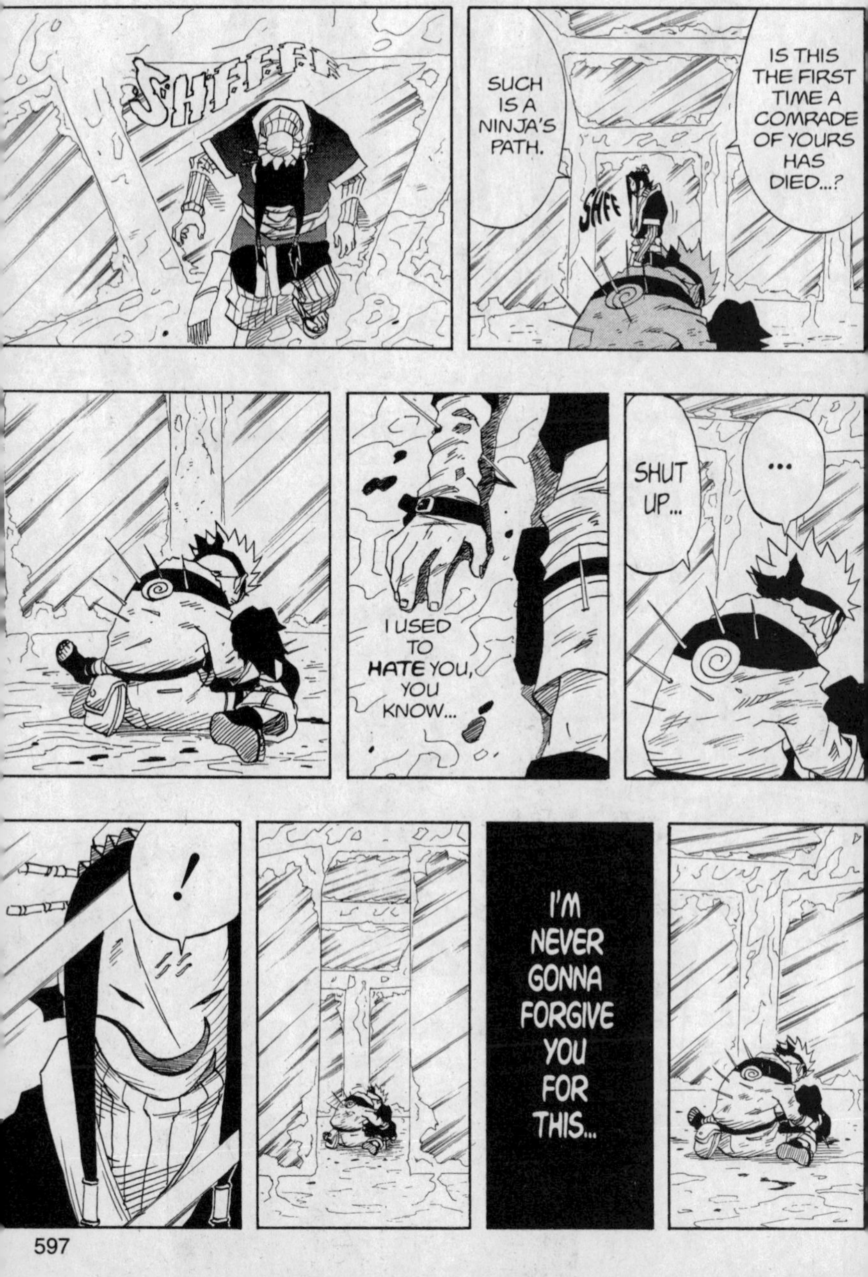
IS THIS THE FIRST TIME A COMRADE OF YOURS HAS DIED...?
SUCH IS A NINJA'S PATH.
SHFF
SHFFFF
...
SHUT UP...
I USED TO **HATE** YOU, YOU KNOW...
I'M NEVER GONNA FORGIVE YOU FOR THIS...
!

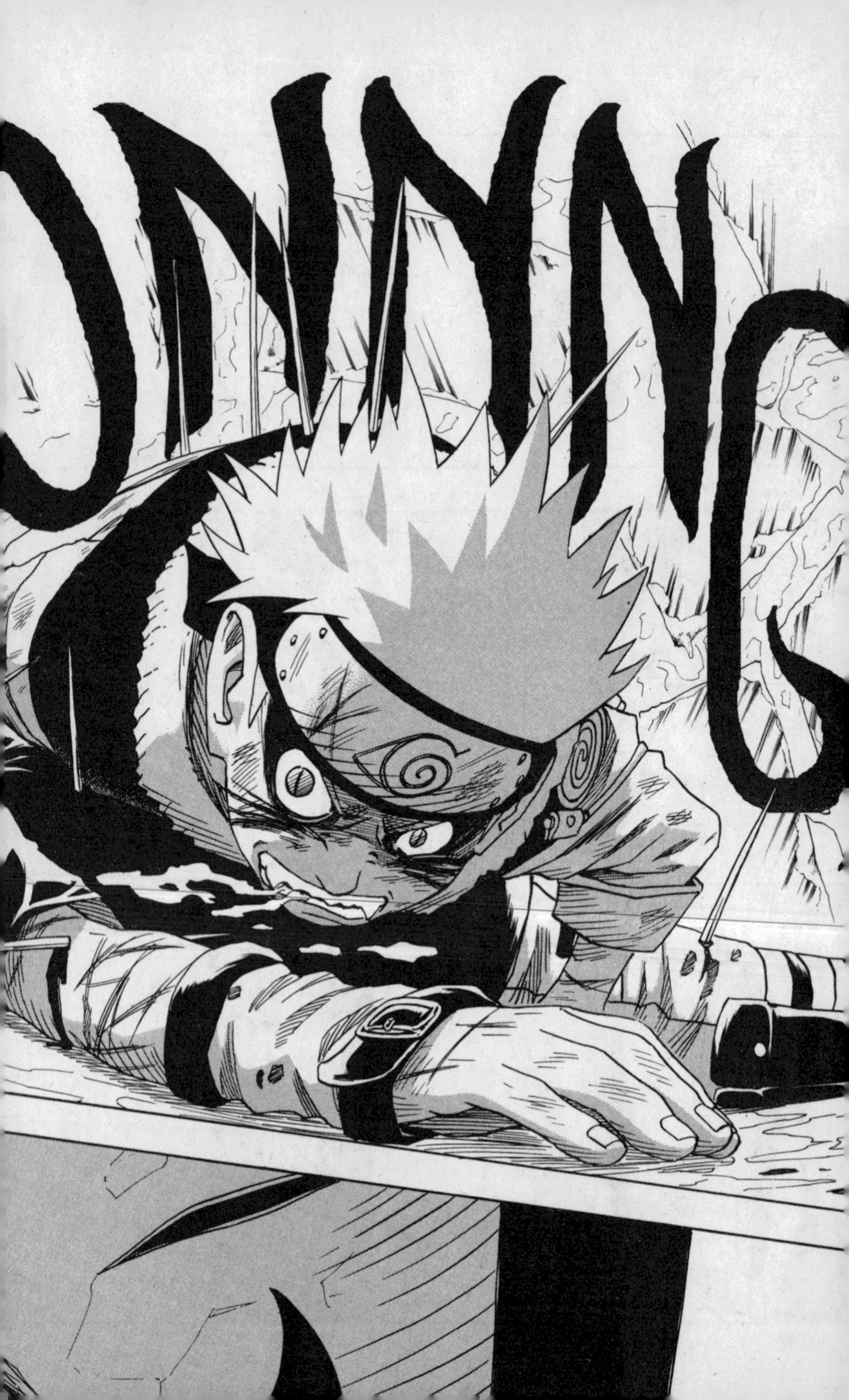